INTRODUCTION TO
PARALEGALISM

INTRODUCTION TO PARALEGALISM

Perspectives, Problems, and Skills

Third Edition

William P. Statsky

Paralegal Series

West Publishing Company

St. Paul/New York/Los Angeles/San Francisco

A STUDENT STUDY GUIDE

A study guide has been developed to assist students in mastering the concepts presented in this text. It reinforces chapter material presenting it in a concise format with review questions. An examination copy is available to instructors by contacting West Publishing Company. Students can purchase the study guide from the local bookstore under the title *Study Guide to Accompany Introduction to Paralegalism, third edition, prepared by William P. Statsky.*

Typesetting by Rolin Graphics

COPYRIGHT © 1974, 1982
COPYRIGHT © 1986 By WEST PUBLISHING CO.
    50 West Kellogg Boulevard
    P.O. Box 64526
    St. Paul, Minnesota 55164-1003

Printed in the United States of America
(H) 96 95 94 93 92 91 90 89   8 7 6 5 4 3
(S) 96 95 94 93 92 91 90 89   8 7 6 5 4 3 2 1

Library of Congress Cataloging in Publication Data
Statsky, William P.
   Introduction to paralegalism

   Bibliography: p.
   Includes index.
   1. Legal assistants—United States.   1. Title.
KF320.L4S73   1986   340′.023′73   85-22731
ISBN 0-314-93516-9
ISBN 0-314-67425-X

Also by William P. Statsky

Case Analysis and Fundamentals of Legal Writing, 2d ed. St. Paul: West Publishing Company, 1984 (with J. Wernet)

Family Law, 2d ed. St. Paul: West Publishing Company, 1984.

Inmate Involvement in Prison Legal Services: Roles and Training Options for the Inmate as Paralegal. American Bar Association, Commission on Correctional Facilities and Services, 1974

Legal Research and Writing: Some Starting Points, 3d ed. St. Paul: West Publishing Company, 1986

Legal Thesaurus / Dictionary: A Resource for the Writer and Computer Researcher. St. Paul: West Publishing Company, 1985

Legislative Analysis and Drafting, 2d ed. St. Paul: West Publishing Company, 1984

Torts: Personal Injury Litigation. St. Paul: West Publishing Company, 1982

Rights of the Imprisoned: Cases, Materials and Directions. Indianapolis: Bobbs-Merrill Company, 1974 (with R. Singer)

The Legal Paraprofessional as Advocate and Assistant: Roles, Training Concepts and Materials. Center on Social Welfare Policy and Law, 1971 (with P. Lang)

What Have Paralegals Done? A Dictionary of Functions. National Paralegal Institute, 1973

For
Patricia Farrell Statsky:
A person whose ability
and love has sustained
more than she knows

The pain and the excitement of paralegalism, and indeed of the law itself, is that the problem we are given will often be smaller than the problem we find.

Preface

This book grows out of a still-developing career whose members may one day outnumber lawyers in the traditional law office. The day has long passed when so many had to ask, "What's a paralegal?" Today, even the United States Supreme Court has taken note of the development and the potential of paralegals. A great deal has happened since the publication of the first edition of this book in 1974 and the second edition in 1982. Yet the dominant themes of the field continue to be challenge, promise, and the opportunity to rethink the major assumptions that have characterized the practice of law.

It is difficult to name all the individuals who have given me guidance in the preparation of this book. I owe a great debt to Jean and Edgar Cahn, founders of the Antioch School of Law; Bill Fry, Director of the National Paralegal Institute and a valued colleague since our days together at Columbia Law School; John Wernet, a collaborator in education; Professor Dan Oran, who helped me plan the first edition and who wrote drafts of some of the early chapters; and MaBel Hill, Willie Nolden, and Linda Saunders, some of my early students who taught me so much.

William P. Statsky

San Diego, California
January 1986

Contents

The *"expanded use of well-trained assistants, sometimes called 'paralegals,' has been an important development. Today there are . . . double the number of . . . schools for training paralegals [than the number of schools for training lawyers]. . . . The advent of the paralegal enables law offices to perform high quality legal services at a lower cost. Possibly we have only scratched the surface on this development."*

Warren E. Burger, Chief Justice
of the United States Supreme Court, February 3, 1980

"Paralegals are an absolutely essential component of quality legal services in the future."

James Fellers, President,
American Bar Association, April 4, 1975

"The number of job openings for legal assistants is expected to increase significantly through the mid-1990s, . . ." Employment in this field will *"grow much faster than the average for all occupations."*

Bureau of Labor Statistics, April 1984

INTRODUCTION TO
PARALEGALISM

Part I

The Paralegal in the Legal System

CONTENTS

1

The Emergence
of a New Career in Law

Section A. THE QUESTIONS, THE FRUSTRATION, AND THE CHALLENGE

Welcome to the field! You probably fall into one or more of the following categories:

- You have never worked in a law office and have many questions about the career of a paralegal.
- You are employed or were once employed in a law office and now want to upgrade your skills.
- You have not made up your mind about whether to become a lawyer and see the paralegal career as a way to learn more about the legal profession.

As Chief Justice Burger points out in the quote at the beginning of this book, the paralegal career is still in a state of "development." By definition, therefore, a number of important questions still exist. The task of the first part of this book is to address these questions:

- What is a paralegal?
- Where do paralegals work?
- What are the functions of a paralegal?
- How do I obtain a job?
- What is the difference between a lawyer and a paralegal?

- What is the difference between a paralegal and the clerical staff of a law office?
- What problems do paralegals encounter on the job and how can these problems be resolved?
- How is the paralegal field regulated? Who does the regulating and for what purposes?
- What is the future of the paralegal field?

Unfortunately *and* fortunately, definitive answers to these questions do not yet exist. As we shall see, considerable controversy surrounds many of them. It would be foolhardy for anyone to enter the field without having a comprehensive understanding of what the controversies are. At times, however, the controversy seems to breed more confusion than constructive dialogue. This confusion can be frustrating to someone new to the field. From another point of view, however, this state of affairs presents you with the ultimate challenge of shaping your own answers to these questions. If Chief Justice Burger is correct that "we have only scratched the surface," the creative opportunities that exist for you are boundless. You will not simply be performing a job—you will be *helping to create a new profession.* This challenge would not exist if all the answers to the fundamental questions had already been written in stone.

Section B. TERMINOLOGY:
THE DEFINITION OF A PARALEGAL

A paralegal is a person with legal skills who works under the supervision of a lawyer or who is otherwise authorized by law to use these skills.

Not everyone, however, agrees on a definition. In fact, not everyone agrees on a name for the career itself.

There are two kinds of names or titles that have been used: (1) *generic* and (2) *specific.* The generic terminology tries to cover broad categories of people and activities, while the specific terminology is usually limited to one particular activity or area of the law.

GENERIC TERMINOLOGY
(examples)

paralegal	freelance paralegal
legal assistant	legal technician
lay assistant	lay advocate
nonlawyer legal assistant	legal service assistant
legal paraprofessional	paralegal associate
lawyer's assistant	legal adjunct
lawyer's aide	legal aide
attorney assistant	certified legal assistant
paralegal specialist	certified attorney assistant

The most commonly used titles today are the first two mentioned above: paralegal and legal assistant. Efforts are occasionally made to distinguish between these terms. For example, one suggestion is to define "legal assistant" as someone who applies specialized knowledge under the supervision of a lawyer, and "paralegal" as anyone else working in the law office, including secretaries. It has also been proposed that the word "paralegal" be used primarily as an adjective and "legal assistant" as a noun (e.g., the legal assistant performs paralegal tasks). *None of these suggestions has been adopted.* Paralegal and legal assistant are synonymous and are as interchangeable as the words lawyer and attorney.

SPECIFIC TERMINOLOGY
(examples)

litigation assistant	probate assistant
welfare advocate	legal research aide
consumer specialist	community worker
title clerk	health advocate
communications paralegal	EEO specialist
international trade paralegal	copyright paralegal
senior citizen paralegal	

There is equal diversity on the definition of a paralegal. The definitions also fall roughly into two groupings: (1) *generic* definitions that give a broad overview of the position and (2) *specific* definitions that try to give (in shopping-list fashion) particular duties in addition to a broad overview of the position.

GENERIC DEFINITION

The definition given at the beginning of Section B of this chapter is an example of a generic definition: A paralegal is a person with legal skills who works under the supervision of a lawyer or who is otherwise authorized by law to use these skills. Another example:

> Legal assistant shall mean a person not admitted to the practice of law who is an employee of or an assistant to an active member of the Bar, and who, under the control and supervision of an active member of the Bar, renders services related to but not constituting the practice of law.[1]

SPECIFIC DEFINITION

For example,

> A paralegal is a person under the supervision and direction of a licensed lawyer, who may apply knowledge of law and legal procedures in rendering direct assistance to lawyers engaged in legal research; design, develop, or plan modifications or new procedures, techniques, services, processes, or applications; prepare or interpret legal documents and write detailed procedures for practicing in certain fields of law; select, compile, and use technical information from such references as digests, encyclopedias, or practice manuals; and analyze and follow procedural problems that involve independent decisions.[2]

[1] New Hampshire Bar Association, *Guidelines for the Utilization by Lawyers of the Services of Legal Assistants* (1977).

[2] Supreme Court of Kentucky, *Paralegal Code,* Rule 3.700, 43 Kentucky Bench and Bar 30 (Oct. 1979). See p. 257.

A number of points need to be made on the definition of a paralegal—or on the absence of a definition about which everyone can agree:

1. To date, there is no official terminology imposed by law. There is nothing to prevent someone from inventing new terminology. There is nothing to prevent a law firm from calling a messenger a paralegal. No legally imposed terminology exists. Bar associations, paralegal associations, and educators have attempted to formulate definitions, but nothing has emerged as universally acceptable. The generic definitions are criticized as being so broad that they tell us very little. The specific definitions are criticized for being incomplete job descriptions rather than definitions. To some, this state of affairs is healthy since the absence of official terminology encourages diversity. To others, it is frustrating:

> Unfortunately, some law firms seem to be using the phrases "legal assistant" and "paralegal" with alarming regularity without regard to the tasks being performed. And firms are hiring these people at a lower pay scale, thus lowering the salary of the average paralegal.[3]

2. Definitions are often phrased in the negative. Some definitions do a better job telling us what a paralegal is *not,* than what one *is.* A paralegal is *not* a lawyer, *not* a secretary, *not* a law clerk, etc. In the law, whenever there is difficulty defining something, there is a tendency to state the definition in the negative.

3. Most of the definitions have four main components.

- The paralegal is not a lawyer.
- The paralegal has legal knowledge and skills.
- The paralegal works under the supervision of a lawyer.
- The paralegal does not practice law.

4. There are problems with each of these four components. First, there *are* some lawyers who are classified as paralegals. There are lawyers working in America, for example, who are licensed in a foreign country. Some states consider such lawyers to be paralegals. The same is true of lawyers working in one state but licensed to practice in another state. Occasionally a disbarred lawyer will try to continue work in the law firm under the title of a paralegal. This, however, is considered unethical in most states.

Second, it is argued that we learn very little when we are told that a paralegal has legal knowledge and skills. So do lawyers, legal secretaries, investigators, many real estate brokers and bankers, etc.

Third, not all paralegals work under the supervision of a lawyer. As we shall see later, many paralegals working for the government are not supervised by lawyers. There are also special laws that permit nonlawyers to engage in legal work independent of lawyers. To be sure, a very large number of paralegals work in private law offices under the supervision of a lawyer. Yet there are some who are otherwise situated.

[3] Hawaii Association of Legal Assistants, Ka L'eo O, Newsletter, vol. VI, no. 1 (Feb. 1983).

Fourth, it is inaccurate to say that paralegals cannot practice law. The more correct statement of the principle is that paralegals cannot engage in the *unauthorized* practice of law. The existence of rules on the *unauthorized* practice of law governing paralegals presupposes the existence of an *authorized* practice of law by paralegals. It is true that the spectrum of authorized practice for paralegals is quite narrow—but it does exist. In our society, the practice of law is not the exclusive domain of the lawyer. This will be explored in greater detail later.

5. The definitions that we have require further definitions.   In law, the presence of a definition usually prompts a search for a definition of the definition! Paralegal definitions often contain words and phrases such as "supervision," the "practice of law," the "unauthorized practice of law," "assistance," etc. We must be concerned about what these words and phrases mean—they must be defined. These definitions will then probably require clarifications that are, in effect, further definitions. This phenomenon is not peculiar to paralegalism. The process of legal analysis itself calls for an extended series of definitions and subdefinitions as we will demonstrate in Part II of this book.

Other disciplines face the same difficulty. In the medical profession, for example, a close counterpart to the paralegal is the *physician assistant.* The following is a proposed definition of this career:

> Physician assistant means an individual who is qualified by academic and clinical training to provide patient care services under the supervision and responsibility of a doctor of medicine or osteopathy.[4]

Among the major phrases in this definition that require further defining are: "qualified," "patient care services," and "supervision."

6. A title and definition should serve three main functions.   In the quest for an acceptable title and definition, there is a danger of losing sight of the reasons that should govern the search. A title and definition should:

- Convey enough information about the field to a prospective student.
- Convey enough information about the field to a prospective employer.
- Convey enough information about the field to the public as prospective clients.

7. Unanimity may be unnecessary, undesirable, and impossible to achieve.   The above three purposes can arguably be served without ever achieving total agreement on terminology. We begin banging our heads against a stone wall when we insist on a title and a definition that:

- Precisely and definitively distinguishes this career from that of other law office personnel.
- Includes everyone who should be included.
- Excludes everyone who should be excluded.

[4] 44 Federal Register 36177 (No. 121, 6/21/79).

This is simply too much to ask because of the great diversity in the field. We do not yet know all the boundary lines. This wiser course at this stage of development is *not* to insist on trying to achieve unanimity.

8. *Terminology and credentialization.*   It does not seem to disturb anyone that we do not have a definitive definition of a lawyer. A lawyer is someone with a license to practice law. The lawyer is defined primarily by the *credential* that s/he holds. Any attempt to provide a functional definition poses substantial difficulties. There has been endless litigation, for example, on trying to define the "practice of law." The same is true of terms such as "legal advice" and "professional judgment." We will explore some of this controversy in the chapter on regulation (p. 205). The point, however, is that a functional definition of a lawyer (in terms of what a lawyer does) is no more easy to identify than a functional definition of a paralegal. We should not ask of paralegalism that it achieve a level of definitional precision that the legal profession has never been able to achieve.

When a career is having difficulty defining itself, it sometimes tries to use credentialization as a way out of the difficulty. The paralegal career may also move in this direction. A paralegal may someday be defined primarily as someone with a license or a certificate to be a paralegal. If this happens, the debate on role will not end. Shifting the question from "what is a paralegal" to "what credentials should a paralegal have" will not stop the controversy. A host of regulation issues must then be confronted.

9. *Point of Departure.*   At the beginning of this section, the following definition was provided: A paralegal is a person with legal skills who works under the supervision of a lawyer or who is otherwise authorized by law to use these skills. Neither the use of the word "paralegal" nor the definition are intended to be the final word. New terminology may eventually emerge. The field is still in a state of development. The terminology is but a point of departure used for discussion purposes in this book.

ASSIGNMENT 1

In this assignment, you will be asked to collect and compare definitions of paralegals or legal assistants in your area. Contact the following individuals and ask the question: "What is a paralegal or legal assistant?"

1. A neighbor or friend who does not work in a law office and who has probably never been in a law office.
2. A neighbor or friend who does not work in a law office but who has hired a lawyer at least once in his/her life.
3. A legal secretary.
4. A lawyer who has never hired a paralegal.
5. A lawyer who has hired a paralegal.
6. A working paralegal who is not now in school.
7. A high school student.
8. A student in a law school studying to be a lawyer.

9. A police officer.
10. A person who runs a small business.
11. A local judge.
12. A clerk in a local court.

Take careful notes on their answers to the question. Compare the answers.

- What common ideas or themes did you find in the definitions?
- What two definitions were the most different, and why?
- Do you think that your survey raises any problems about the perception of paralegals in your area? If so, what are these problems, and how can they be solved?

Section C. HISTORICAL PERSPECTIVE

In the late 1960s, most lawyers would draw a blank if you mentioned the word "paralegal" or "legal assistant." Today the situation has radically changed. There are few law offices that do not employ paralegals or that are not seriously thinking about employing them. It has been estimated that the number of paralegals may eventually exceed the number of lawyers in a law office. What has caused this dramatic change? The following factors have been instrumental in the emergence of paralegalism to its present state of prominence:

1. The pressure of economics.
2. The call for efficiency and delegation.
3. Promotion by the bar associations.
4. The growth of paralegal schools.
5. The organization of paralegals.
6. The restructuring of professions generally.

1. THE PRESSURE OF ECONOMICS

Perhaps the greatest incentive to the development of paralegals has been arithmetic. Law firms simply add up what they earn without paralegals, add up what they would earn with paralegals, compare the two figures and conclude that the employment of paralegals is profitable!

In the best of all worlds, some of this increased profit will result in lower fees to the client. For example, Chief Justice Warren Burger feels that some lawyers charge "excessive fees for closing real-estate transactions for the purchase of a home. A greater part of that work can be handled by trained paralegals, and, in fact, many responsible law firms are doing just that to reduce costs for their clients."[5]

In the following example, a client comes to a lawyer to form a corporation.[6] We will compare (a) the economics of a lawyer and secretary working on

[5] U.S. News & World Rep., Feb. 22, 1982 at 32.

[6] Adapted from Jespersen, *Paralegals: Help or Hindrance?* The Houston Lawyer 111, 114–16 (March/April 1977).

THE PROFITABILITY OF USING PARALEGALS

TASK: TO FORM A CORPORATION

a. Attorney and Secretary

	Time	
Function	Lawyer	Secretary
1. Interviewing	1.0	0.0
2. Advising	1.0	0.0
3. Gathering information	1.0	0.0
4. Preparing papers	2.0	4.0
5. Executing and filing papers	1.0	1.0
	6.0	5.0

Assume that the lawyer hourly rate is $100 per hour. Assume the secretary hourly rate is $10 per hour.

Attorney (6 × $100)	$ 600.00
Secretary (5 × $10)	50.00
Total cost	$ 650.00
Fee	$1000.00
Less cost	650.00
Gross profit	$ 350.00

b. Attorney, Secretary, and Paralegal

	Time		
Function	Lawyer	Paralegal	Secretary
1. Interviewing	0.5	0.5	0.0
2. Advising	1.0	0.0	0.0
3. Gathering information	0.0	1.0	0.0
4. Preparing papers	0.5	1.5	4.0
5. Executing and filing papers	0.5	0.5	1.0
	2.5	3.5	5.0

In addition, assume a paralegal hourly rate of $20 per hour.

Attorney (2.5 × $100)	$250
Paralegal (3.5 × $20)	70
Secretary (5 × $10)	50
Total cost	$370
Fee	$800
Less cost	370
Gross profit	$430

COMPARISON

Fee: a. Attorney and Secretary $1000
      b. Attorney, Secretary, and Paralegal $800
Saving to client $200
Increased profitability to lawyer ($430-$350) $80

The increased profitability of $80 represents an increase of almost 25%. Furthermore, the use of a paralegal on this case has allowed the lawyer to free him/herself for 3.5 hours' work that s/he can bill out on other matters for an additional $350.

the case, assuming a fee of $1,000, and (b) the economics of a lawyer, secretary, *and* paralegal working on the same case, assuming a fee of $800. As you will see, with a paralegal added to the team, the firm's profit is increased almost 25% in spite of the lower fee, and the lawyer has more billable time to spend elsewhere. Some studies have claimed an even higher profit increase because of the use of paralegals.[7]

The example on page 10 assumed that the lawyer billed the client $20 per hour for the paralegal's time. In the following 1984 study by the American Bar Association, the *actual* hourly rate (on average) is reported to be $36. Also note the dramatic comparison between the salary of lawyers not using paralegals ($35,000 or less) and the salary of lawyers employing a designated number of paralegals (above $75,000).

Paralegals [in 1984] Average $14,400 to Start, Bring Profits to Firms

LawPoll by Lauren Rubenstein Reskin
70 American Bar Association Journal 52 (Dec. 1984)

SIXTY-ONE percent of lawyers in private practice say their firms employ paralegals—just fewer than 10 per firm on average. Paralegals' salaries [in 1984] start in the low to mid teens and peak at an average of $20,500. (See table 1.) Their time most often is billed to clients, at an average of $36 per hour. (See table 2.)

TABLE 1. PARALEGAL INCOME

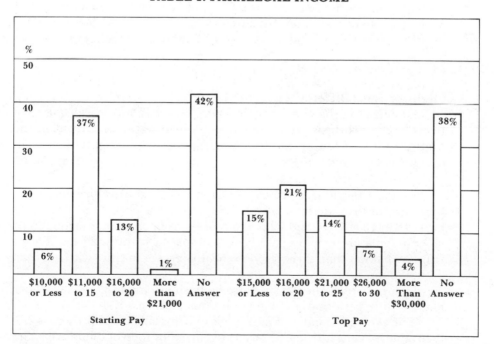

---

[7] See Bethel, *Economics and the Practice of Law: The 1976 Economic Survey of the State Bar of Arizona.* Arizona Bar Journal 57ff (October 1976).

TABLE 2. HOURLY RATE

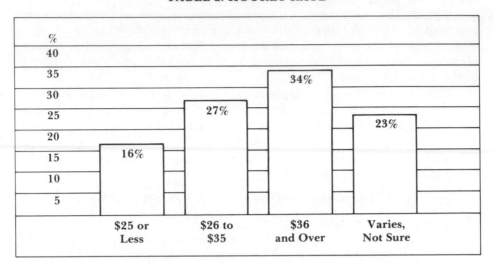

Certain proportions of lawyers to other firm employees correlate with high incomes for lawyers. Lawyers in firms that employ any paralegals, for example, earn more than those in firms without paralegals. The optimum ratio, in terms of high incomes for lawyers, was four to six lawyers per paralegal.

These are some of the findings of the latest LawPoll conducted for the *ABA Journal* by the New York City public opinion research firm of Kane, Parsons & Associates. Interviews were conducted in May [of 1984] by telephone with a random sample of 528 ABA members in private practice.

Slight regional differences

Law firms in the Northeast and West employ more paralegals than firms in the Southeast and Southwest/Prairie states, and firms in the Midwest hire the fewest. But the differences are only slight: 65 percent of northeastern and western firms hire paralegals, and 55 percent of midwestern firms hire them. (See table 3.)

Larger firms in large cities are much more likely to hire paralegals than smaller firms in the small cities. Ninety-three percent of firms with more than 10 lawyers and 72 percent of firms in cities of one million or more population employ paralegals, compared to only 24 percent of firms with fewer than three lawyers and 46 percent in cities with less than 50,000 population

Firms in which lawyers specialize in business and litigation are more likely to hire paralegals than general practice firms.

The average number of paralegals in firms that employ them is 9.6. (See table 3.) Larger firms, those located in major metropolitan areas and firms specializing in business and litigation employ the most paralegals—slightly more than 14 on average.

TABLE 3.

INCIDENCE OF PARALEGALS IN LAW FIRMS		
	PERCENT EMPLOYING PARALEGALS	AVERAGE NUMBER EMPLOYED
TOTAL	61	9.6
REGION		
Northeast	65	13.3
Southeast	59	7.0
Midwest	55	10.0
Southwest/Prairie	61	6.8
West	65	8.5
NUMBER OF LAWYERS IN FIRM		
Fewer than three	24	1.5
Three to 10	48	2.0
More than 10	93	14.2
SIZE OF CITY		
Under 50,000	46	2.5
50,000 to 249,999	52	4.5
250,000 to 999,999	66	9.9
1,000,000 and over	72	14.5
FIELD OF SPECIALIZATION		
General only	44	3.5
Business	70	14.1
Litigation	68	12.6

Hours and pay

Fifty-one percent of paralegals bill more than 20 hours per week, while 15 percent bill less. But 33 percent of lawyers were not sure how many hours they bill. Only 2 percent bill more than 40 hours per week. (See table 4.)

TABLE 4. HOURS BILLED WEEKLY

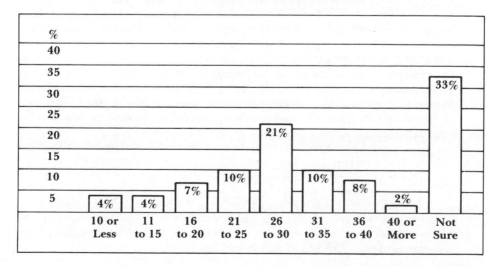

The average starting salary for paralegals [in 1984] is $14,400, and the average top salary is $20,500. Thirteen percent of firms employing paralegals pay $16,000 to $20,000 to start, and 11 percent pay more than $25,000 tops. But 42 percent of lawyers did not know or did not want to report their firms' starting salaries, and 38 percent were silent about top salaries. (See table 1.)

Although job prospects for paralegals are more optimistic in large firms and large cities, their salaries are fairly universal. For example, the average top salary is $17,200 in small firms and $22,700 in large firms.

Staff make-up

How much staff is enough? The survey inquired into the ratio of lawyers to paralegals, and lawyers to total staff, to pinpoint the proportion that translates into high lawyer incomes. Too many nonlawyer employees will bloat a law firm's overhead. Too few will result in the inefficient use of lawyers performing clerical duties.

The largest number of lawyers earning more than $75,000 have four to six lawyers per paralegal, and .5 to .75 lawyers for each staff worker. The largest number of lawyers earning $35,000 or less have no paralegals at all, and .76 to one lawyer per staff person.

Salaries of paralegals generally come out of client fees. There is, however, another source. In special categories of cases, e.g., employment discrimination, antitrust, the *opponent* pays the plaintiff's fees if the latter wins the case. While attorney fees have traditionally been recoverable in such cases, only recently have some courts made it clear that a law firm can *also* recover *paralegal* fees. This, of course, increases the economic value of the paralegal to the firm.

Spray-Rite Service Corp. v. Monsanto Co.
684 F.2d 1126, 1250 (7th Cir. 1982)

Only two circuit courts of appeals have considered whether paralegal fees are recoverable under section 4 of the Clayton Act, 15 U.S.C. § 15. The Second Circuit reversed the district court award of paralegal fees holding that these fees "cannot be considered as input in the fee award determination." *Detroit v. Grinnell Corp.* 495 F.2d 448, 473 (2d Cir. 1974). The Ninth Circuit, however, affirmed the district court's award of paralegal fees. *Pacific Coast Agricultural Export Ass'n v. Sunkist Growers, Inc.,* 526 F.2d 1196, 1210 (9th Cir. 1975). The Ninth Circuit quoted with approval the following language from the district court's opinion:

> As a matter of practice, most attorneys engaged in the antitrust practice use such legal assistants, particularly in digesting and indexing discovery and trial materials, much of the work heretofore performed by relatively inexperienced lawyers. . . . As a matter of policy, the use of paralegal help in this fashion greatly reduces the cost of legal services to the public and thus is a practice to be encouraged.

Id. at 1210 n.19. We think the Ninth Circuit has adopted the better view and, accordingly, we hold that paralegal and law clerk fees are recoverable as a portion of the plaintiff's reasonable attorneys' fees. The court did not abuse its discretion in awarding Spray-Rite $63,370.25 in paralegal fees.

2. THE CALL FOR EFFICIENCY AND DELEGATION

Lawyers are overtrained for a substantial portion of the tasks that they perform in a law office. This is one of the major reasons that traditional law offices are charged with inefficiency. Paralegals have been seen as a major step toward reform. The results have been quite satisfactory as evidenced by the following comments from lawyers who have hired paralegals:[8]

> A competent legal assistant for several years has been effectively doing 25% to 35% of the actual work that I have been doing for many years prior to that time.

> The results of our 3 attorney—3 paralegal system have been excellent. Our office's efficiency has been improved and our clients are receiving better service.

> It has been our experience that clients now ask for the legal assistant. Client calls to the attorneys have been reduced an estimated 75%,...

It has taken a *very* long time for lawyers to realize that something was wrong with the way they practiced law. The following historical perspective presents an overview of how lawyers came to this realization.[9]

Up to the nineteenth century, the lawyer basically worked alone. The lawyer carried "his office in his hat."[10] A very personal attachment to, and devotion to detail was considered to be part of the process of becoming a lawyer and of operating a practice. In the early nineteenth century, George Wythe commented that:

> It is only by drudgery that the exactness, accuracy and closeness of thought so necessary for a good lawyer are engendered.[11]

The same theme came from Abraham Lincoln in his "Notes for a Law Lecture":

> If anyone...shall claim an exemption from the drudgery of the law, his case is a failure in advance.[12]

A lawyer would be somewhat reluctant to delegate such "drudgery" to someone working for him/her according to this theory of legal education.

[8] Oregon State Bar, Legal Assistants Committee, *Legal Assistant Survey* (1977).

[9] The research for part of the section on the historical background of paralegals was conducted by the author and subsequently used with his permission in the following article: Brickman, *Expansion of the Lawyering Process through a New Delivery System: The Emergence and State of Legal Paraprofessionalism,* 71 Columbia Law Review 1153, 1169ff. (1971).

[10] Lee, *Large Law Offices,* 57 American Law Review 788 (1923).

[11] Lewis, editor, "George Wythe," Great American Lawyers: A History of the Legal Profession in America, vol. 1, p. 55 (1907).

[12] Nicolay & Hay, editors, "Notes for a Law Lecture," Complete Works of Abraham Lincoln, p. 142 (1894). See also Frank, Lincoln as a Lawyer, p. 3 (1961).

During the American colonial period, almost anyone could become an attorney without having to meet rigorous admission requirements. Toward the end of the eighteenth century, for example, the Massachusetts legislature authorized litigants to be represented in court by "attorneys-in-fact" who were appointed by the litigants and who were not regularly admitted "attorneys-at-law."[13]

"Pre-lawyers" (for want of a better word) apprenticed themselves to a lawyer in pursuit of a legal career as a lawyer. Periods of apprenticeship varied from state to state. In some states, the distrust of lawyers was strong. This feeling was exported from England where lawyers were an influential part of the system from which the colonists fled. These states tended to have little or no apprenticeship periods. Anyone could practice law immediately. Other states had apprenticeship periods ranging up to ten years.

It is unclear, however, to what extent the apprentice was conceived by the attorney-mentor as a functioning part of the law practice. The attorney often required a substantial fee from the apprentice for the *privilege* of occupying a desk in the law office. In some instances it was understood that the apprentice would be spending some time developing a law business of his/her own, looking to the day when the apprenticeship would end and the apprentice would open a practice. Very often the apprentice was told to undertake a rigorous reading schedule, including such authors as Blackstone, Coke, and Bacon.

The one area in which an apprentice clearly did assist the lawyer's practice was copying. In the eighteenth century, printed forms were not widely used. Documents had to be prepared in longhand. Most apprentices did this kind of work. The lawyer sometimes used special "writing" or "copying" clerks.[14] Beyond this copying function, and excluding any janitorial responsibilities, there is little evidence that the clerk or apprentice had a viable assistantship role with the practicing lawyer. This, in part, was a reflection of the rudimentary state of the practice of law during this period and of the low status that the nonlawyer held.

It took some time before the attorney began making use of office assistants who were not training to become lawyers themselves. When the practice of law was essentially the provision of advocacy services, a high premium was placed on the personal relationship between attorney and client. As late as 1875, Seward and his partners "would have none of the newfangled typewriters" because clients would "resent the lack of personal attention implied in typed letters."[15] The coming of the Industrial Revolution, however, brought the practice of law closer to industry and finance. Some law offices began to specialize. As lawyers assumed new responsibilities, the concern for organization and efficiency grew. To be sure, large numbers of lawyers continued to carry their law offices "in their hats" and to provide an essentially one-to-one service. Many law offices in the 1850s, however, took a different direction.

[13] Reed, Training for the Public Profession of the Law, p. 85 (1921).

[14] Hamlin, Legal Education in Colonial New York, p. 43 (1939).

[15] Swaine, The Cravath Firm and Its Predecessors: 1819–1947, vol. 1, p. 365, p. 449.

Machines created new jobs. The typewriter introduced the typist. Librarians, investigators, bookkeepers, office managers, accountants, tax and fiduciary specialists, and research assistants soon found their way into the large law office. Although nonlawyers were primarily hired to undertake clerical or administrative responsibilities, they soon were delegated more challenging roles. As one study of a law firm noted with respect to several female employees who had been with the firm a number of years:

> In addition, these women were given considerable responsibility in connection with their positions as secretary or head bookkeeper. The head bookkeeper acted as assistant secretary to the partner-secretary of certain charitable corporations the firm represented. In this capacity, she recorded minutes of director's meetings, issued proxy statements, supervised the filing of tax returns for the organization and attended to other significant administrative matters.[16]

During the post-Civil War period, many administrative agencies passed regulations permitting nonlawyers to represent clients before them. Today the number of federal, state, and local agencies that authorize nonlawyer practice is extensive (p. 226, p. 865).

Not until the early 1960s did lawyers begin to think seriously about channeling the energies of nonlawyers and finding a niche for them within the legal profession.[17] In 1963, Prentice-Hall conducted a survey of 311 Missouri attorneys as to "the possibility of utilizing a lay technician (a lay person, but one having special training)." Sixty-three percent of the responding attorneys said that they could *not* use a lay technician. Of the thirty-seven percent indicating they could use one, about two-thirds said the technician would be hired only on a part-time basis.[18]

In 1968, the results of three other significant surveys were published. First, another study of Missouri lawyers was made, this time concentrating on metropolitan St. Louis lawyers. Of the 2,058 lawyers who were sent the survey questionnaire, 443 responded and of the latter, 60.9% stated that there *was* a need in the St. Louis area "for legal technicians possessing general and specialized skills acquired through a college program."[19] The study was conducted in conjunction with Meramec Community College, which was contemplating the establishment of a curriculum in legal technology for the St. Louis area. The survey demonstrated to the College that the area could absorb approximately 400 legal technicians within the next three years.[20] A majority of these lawyers, however, indicated that they saw the legal technician performing predomi-

---

[16] Dodge, *Evolution of a City Law Office,* 1955 Wisconsin Law Review 180, 187.

[17] Statsky, *Paraprofessionals: Expanding the Legal Service Delivery Team,* 24 Journal of Legal Education 397, 399–402 (1972).

[18] Missouri Bar Prentice-Hall survey, p. 140 (1963).

[19] Sample Feasibility Survey Questionnaire: Results of Survey, The Bar Association of Metropolitan St. Louis, p. 2 (1968).

[20] Adams, *New Course to Free Lawyers of Routine,* St. Louis Post Dispatch, p. 7, col. 2 (August 28, 1969).

nantly clerical, bookkeeping, and investigatory functions. They did not view the technician as substantially different from traditional law office personnel. A clearly visible minority of St. Louis lawyers, however, saw a number of more demanding roles for the legal technician. Twenty-four percent, for example, said that a legal technician could be supervised to prepare pleadings—the documents filed in litigation. The lawyers were asked to examine a list of law office functions and to indicate whether they felt a college-trained legal technician could perform any of them under varying degrees of supervision. The results were as follows:

FUNCTIONS	Could assist in this area with considerable independence		Could assist under supervision		Could provide little or no assistance	
Investigations	213	(48%)	167	(38%)	41	(9%)
Research and briefing	15	(3%)	122	(28%)	278	(63%)
Librarian	247	(56%)	90	(20%)	73	(16%)
Office management, administrative work	238	(54%)	119	(27%)	57	(13%)
Serving and filing papers	258	(58%)	121	(27%)	36	(8%)
Bookkeeping and accounting	285	(64%)	82	(19%)	51	(12%)
Income tax work	75	(17%)	208	(47%)	122	(28%)
Preparing pleadings	6	(1%)	108	(24%)	291	(66%)
Preparing deeds and forms	18	(4%)	205	(46%)	190	(43%)
Preparing wills and trusts	9	(2%)	77	(17%)	317	(72%)
Searching and checking public records, court files, etc.	206	(47%)	172	(39%)	43	(10%)
Secretarial and clerical	322	(73%)	69	(16%)	28	(6%)
Detail work pertaining to probate inventories, records, claims settlements, inheritance and Federal Estate Tax Returns	78	(18%)	243	(55%)	88	(20%)

The second 1968 survey was conducted by Kline D. Strong, an attorney from Salt Lake City. He studied 104 small law firms in the United States: 18% were solo practitioners, 22% were two-partner firms, 29% were three-partner, and 31% were four-partner firms. Strong listed the percentage of attorneys that delegated certain responsibilities to their secretaries or other nonlawyer employees: Shepardizing or checking the current validity of opinions (6%); maintaining a tickler (or reminder) system for important dates (74%); handling many of the routine procedures necessary to close a real estate transaction (47%); preparing pleadings of a repetitive nature (68%); briefing and preparing extracts of trial documents (21%); reviewing and condensing factual data (18%).[21]

[21] K. Strong, *Preliminary Results from an In-Depth Study of the Management of Small Firms Conducted in 1968.* American Bar Association, p. 1 (1968). See also, Fuchs, *More Effective Use of Lay Personnel in the Law Office,* 7 Law Notes 7, 10–14 (October, 1970) and K. Strong, *An Analysis of Law Firm Management* (1970).

Interest in the development of new law office personnel was not limited to the private Bar. Publicly funded neighborhood legal service offices were feeling the pressure of an ever-increasing case load that could not be adequately handled by existing personnel. Voices were heard for the creation of new kinds of workers who would serve the legal needs of the poor. The third major 1968 study was undertaken by University Research Corporation—a feasibility study of paraprofessionals in legal service offices.[22] Twenty-four neighborhood legal service attorneys submitted to intensive observation. All their activities on the job were first categorized. These activities were observed in five-minute segments with the observers making one of four judgments as to each five-minute segment:

1. The attorney's action was not delegable to a nonlawyer "because it required the skill, judgment or other attribute which only an attorney would be likely to possess."
2. It could be delegated to an existing nonlawyer staff person.
3. It could be delegated to the hypothetical position of "Superior Secretary," who would maintain the office docket, draft routine documents, gather "inhouse" facts, answer correspondence, retrieve library materials identified by the attorney, and help train other nonprofessional staff.
4. It could be delegated to the hypothetical position of "Legal Technician," who would conduct factual research out of the office, search records out of the office, perform advocacy tasks where the legal rights of the clients are clear, counsel clients on nonlegal or prelegal matters and otherwise maintain contact with office clients.

The observers were able to record 552 five-minute periods of behavior and judged approximately one out of every four segments of behavior to be delegable to existing nonlawyer staff and to the two hypothetical positions listed in 3 and 4 above.

These early studies all had a major theme: lawyers can delegate many tasks to paralegals without sacrificing quality of service. Today this theme has become a dominant principle of law office management. Lawyers no longer ask, "Can I delegate?" Rather they ask, "Why *can't* this be delegated?" Or, "How can the delegation be effectively managed?" It is a given that substantial delegation is a necessity.

This is not to say, however, that all lawyers immediately endorse the paralegal concept with enthusiasm. Many are initially hesitant, as demonstrated by the following report on the adoption of a legal assistant program within the California Department of Health, Education, and Welfare (HEW):

> When the legal assistant program began in early 1977 in HEW, it was met with some skepticism, especially in offices in cities other than Sacramento. There was concern that the quality of the work might be diminished by legal assistants. However, team leaders and deputies are not only no longer skeptical, they are now enthusiastic supporters of the legal assistant program. The attorneys feel that the

---

[22] R. White & J. Stein, *Paraprofessionals in Legal Service Programs: A Feasibility Study,* A Report to the Legal Services Program of the Office of Economic Opportunity (1968).

work product is at least as good, and more thorough, than that provided by attorneys, mainly because the legal assistants have developed an expertise in a narrow area of the law and the work is more stimulating to the legal assistants than it was to the attorneys.

The legal assistants processed 152 cases in fiscal year 1977/78 and 175 cases in 1978/79. It was estimated that legal assistants are as efficient as attorneys in processing the preliminary phase of these cases. As a result, a legal assistant in this instance produces as many pleadings as a deputy attorney general would have produced in the same amount of time. For this reason the section has been able to provide a faster turnaround time for the client agencies.[23]

3. PROMOTION BY THE BAR ASSOCIATIONS

Inevitably, the bar associations assumed a large role in the development of paralegals. This has given great visibility to the field. In 1968, the House of Delegates of the American Bar Association established a Special Committee on Lay Assistants for Lawyers (subsequently renamed the Standing Committee on Legal Assistants) and resolved:

(1) That the legal profession recognize that there are many tasks in serving a client's needs which can be performed by a trained, non-lawyer assistant working under the direction and supervision of a lawyer;
(2) That the profession encourage the training and employment of such assistants. . . .[24]

Most of the state bar associations now have committees that cover the area of paralegal utilization. As we will see in chapter 4, some of these committees have established guidelines for the use of paralegals in a law office. The real impact on the growth of paralegalism, however, has come from those bar association committees that deal with legal economics and law office management. These committees have sponsored numerous conferences for practicing lawyers. These conferences, plus the literature of the bar association journals, have extensively promoted paralegals.

4. THE GROWTH OF PARALEGAL SCHOOLS

Over 300 schools for the training of paralegals exist throughout the country. In some states scores of such programs exist, most within two- and four-year colleges. In addition, there are a number of profit-making proprietary paralegal schools that are not connected with colleges and universities. Less formal training programs exist within large law firms and some governmental agencies. Such programs usually last no longer than a week or two.

[23] *Study of Paralegal Utilization in the California Attorney General's Office,* p. 23, Management Analysis Section, Cal. Dept. of Justice (Dec. 1980).

[24] Proceedings of the House of Delegates of the American Bar Association, 54 American Bar Association Journal 1017, 1021 (1968).

In spite of the large number of paralegal schools, a high percentage of practicing paralegals have received all their legal training *on the job*. Secretaries, for example, are often promoted into paralegal positions. College graduates are sometimes hired by firms without any formal legal training. Both these individuals are then trained on the job.

The in-house training program frequently is created to respond to immediate needs. For example, lawyers in a law firm may decide that a particular secretary should be given increased responsibilities because of the recent arrival of a large and complex client. They quickly compile a package of materials, which includes old forms and files, and call the package his/her "Manual."

Some employers do not know what a paralegal can do until the paralegal does it! This creates the occasion for OJT: on the job training. Once the paralegal demonstrates potential competence in a particular area, the employer rejoices in the discovery and slowly feeds the paralegal more responsibility in that area. At this stage, the OJT may consist of little more than close observation and perhaps written procedural instructions.

In spite of the sometimes haphazard and frustrating nature of OJT, the value of "learning by doing" can be enormous. It will probably continue to be one of the main sources of paralegal education.

5. THE ORGANIZATION OF PARALEGALS

Paralegals have begun to organize. There are over 100 paralegal organizations throughout the country. (See list in appendix B, p. 843.) This has greatly helped raise everyone's consciousness about the potential of paralegalism. There are two major national associations, the National Federation of Paralegal Associations (NFPA) and the National Association of Legal Assistants (NALA). We will examine the work and the impact of these associations in the chapter on regulation (p. 285). It is no longer true that lawyers are the sole organized voice speaking for paralegals and shaping the development of the field.

6. THE RESTRUCTURING OF PROFESSIONS GENERALLY

The creation of new careers within a profession is not unique to the legal profession.

Doctors

There are approximately eleven paramedical personnel for every doctor in the United States. The hospital patient confronts a substantial number of nondoctor personnel: registered nurse, practical nurse, inhalation therapist, laboratory technician, occupational therapist, physical therapist, medical record librarian, medical record technician, medical technologist, cytotechnologist, radiologic technologist, radiation therapy technologist, nuclear medical technician, dietician, etc. It has been estimated that in the field of nursing alone, there are hundreds of different programs. The most recent stratification has been the licensing in some states of the Physician's Assistant whose

ranks were initially filled by many veterans who were medics or medical corps-
men while members of the armed services.

Many types of mental health workers have developed around the psychia-
trist and psychologist. This is most vividly evident in the storefront drug rehabilitation centers that have been established under the inspiration of the original Synanon program in California. Such centers place great emphasis on
confrontation therapy, usually conducted by ex-addict group leaders. The programs have been the subject of considerable controversy, although few dispute
the value of the "paraprofessional therapist" as an instrument of change in the
addict's life. In some instances, programs have experienced open hostility between the professional and paraprofessional staffs as each vied for control of
the program.

Dentists

There are approximately 250 dental assistant training programs, 175 dental
hygiene training programs, and 30 dental laboratory technician training programs. The demand for "dental auxiliary personnel" has been steadily
increasing.

A more radical development is denturism. A denturist is a nondentist who
produces and dispenses removable dentures directly to the public. As might be
expected, denturists are vigorously opposed by organizations such as the
American Dental Association.

Teachers

Studies have shown that teachers spend from 20% to 70% of their time on
nonteaching responsibilities. Teacher aides were initially created to relieve
teachers of some of their clerical tasks so that they could spend more time on
education. A growing number of aides, however, have been participating directly in the instructional process. It has been estimated that we may reach a
ratio of one aide for every two teachers in the various departments of a large
school.

Architects

The American Institute of Architecture reports that the 30,000 American architects need 127,000 supportive personnel in areas such as drafting, estimation, information and data processing, and graphic arts. More than 250 architecture technician programs are currently offered at colleges and institutes.

Social Workers

Although less visible than some of the other paraprofessions, the social work
technician or social work aide has been making an impact in this field. Their
functions have been varied, e.g., tutorial, recreation, door-to-door canvassing,
administrative advocacy, etc. Very often the aides are recruited from the target
population, e.g., welfare recipients, that the social workers serve.

Law Enforcement

Auxiliary police, probation aides, and parole aides are becoming a standard part of law enforcement and correctional administration. In police science, for example, numerous programs have been developed to free the police officer from community relations responsibilities through the hiring of police aides so that the police officer can devote more energies to criminal work. The employment of ex-felons as probation and parole aides has been heralded as one of the most significant innovations in the field in corrections. Such individuals often undertake roles similar to the paraprofessional therapist in drug rehabilitation programs.

ASSIGNMENT 2

In your city, county, or town there are undoubtedly a great variety of paraprofessionals in the fields of medicine, teaching, social work, etc. There are a number of projects that could be undertaken individually or as a class with respect to this diversity of personnel. Several are suggested here:

1. Conduct a "New Professions" or "New Occupations" week at your school. Set up a series of workshops composed of paraprofessionals within defined employment areas, invite speakers, etc. Identify a theme or issue that you want addressed at the conference such as "career ladders" or "collective action through associations or unions."
2. Devise a questionnaire on new careers generally. Include questions such as "How were you trained?" "Are you satisfied with your status?" "Is there a licensing or certification program in your field?" "Why or why not?" "How are you supervised?" "What are the major problem areas in your job?" "How are you evaluated?" "How do others in your office perceive your role?" Class members can be assigned to administer the questionnaire in person to at least five paraprofessionals within a given employment category. Class members then periodically report back to the class on the results of their survey.

Questions such as those listed in part 2 of this assignment have become increasingly important in the paralegal field. As the debate rages on whether paralegals should be licensed (p. 232), a great deal of attention is given to other new careers that are allied to traditional professions. A rich source of relevant data can be found in the experience of these other careers.

The development of a new occupation is due to several different but related factors. One of these factors is *technological*. Just as there would be no such thing as an "airline pilot" without the development of the manned flight, there probably would never be the "secretary" in the modern sense without the development of the typewriter, telephone, etc.

Another basic factor is *economic*. As occupations become more and more complex (or more and more lucrative), the people who perform them begin to delegate their so-called routine tasks to other people who work for them. Nurses "paraprofessionalized" the field of medicine in this way. New specialists and subspecialists then emerged. Occupations not only "routinized down," but "specialized out." One example of the latter is the bank trust manager who is doing work that lawyers previously did. The trust manager's ability to specialize in one small area of the law allowed him/her to take away a share of the trust and estate market from lawyers. This was substantially due to economic forces; the generalist lawyer simply could not compete with the services offered by this particular kind of banker. The public demand for the services of the latter is too acute for the legal profession to regain its full monopoly. The lawyer, of course, saves face by agreeing to refrain from labeling the banker's activities "the practice of law." Underlying such a concession, however, are some elemental laws of economics.

The third major factor influencing the development of occupations is *social*. Society's insistence on universal education, for example, has led to the growth of a large civil-service teacher occupation. Urbanization has launched a variety of occupations, e.g., social workers, criminologists, environmentalists, highway patrol officers, etc.

As occupations proliferate, competition among the occupations develops. This competition has led to some artificial results, the most prominent of which is a tendency to draw rigid jurisdictional lines among workers. Social workers are not psychologists; teachers are not social workers; lawyers are not accountants. We know, however, that such categorizations are misleading. Any one job often requires the individual to function within a wide variety of disciplines. The public school teacher, for example, would be quite surprised if told that s/he need have no skills in psychology, social work, or "police" work to perform in the urban classroom.

There is, however, security in the outward appearance of definitive boundary lines. Twenty years ago, a researcher asked the following question at random: "Who are you?" Most often, the researcher received a geographical answer ("I am a New Yorker"), then an ethnic answer ("I am an Irishman"), and finally an occupational answer ("I am a dentist"). The same question asked today produces an entirely different frequency of responses. An overwhelming majority of the respondents will base their answer on their occupation. We are what we *do*. Hence the tendency to insist on sharp career boundaries.

Within particular occupational categories, however, there is considerable turmoil over who should do what. As indicated, delegation within an occupation has created innumerable suboccupations or cooccupations. The best example of this is, again, the nurse within the medical profession. Doctors defined a series of functions that they were overtrained to perform. They then created the role of the nurse to undertake them. The nurses, in turn, defined a similar set of functions within their own sphere and delegated them to a new entity, the licensed practical nurse.

The legal profession is undergoing a comparable phenomenon. Typical of the progression in the law is the experience of the Paraprofessional Law Clinic at a state prison in Graterford, Pennsylvania. A group of inmates are authorized to set up a paralegal "law firm" to serve the needs of fellow inmates who need help processing their legal papers to challenge the validity of their incarceration (p. 220). No lawyers are involved in the program except for occasional outside attorneys who lend assistance to the paralegals on particular problems encountered in the firm's caseload. The most frustrating aspect of the program to the paralegals is its success. They have been able to win a large number of cases involving a miscalculation of sentence-time by prison administrators who have the responsibility of counting up the day-to-day time owed by the inmates. Apparently the bureaucratic process of identifying the exact release date after deducting time served before trial, time earned for good behavior, etc., is complex. The prison staff often makes mistakes. During the first six months of the firm's existence, the paralegals claim to have had 15,924 days credited to the sentences of 103 inmates. Given the scope of the problem, the paralegals have been deluged with sentence computation cases; they have little time for anything else. While their success rate is a source of satisfaction to them, they are not happy with their caseload because they would prefer to work on cases that involve constitutional law and the so-called test cases. Their plan is to systematize computation cases and train other inmates to undertake them so that they can devote their energies to the more difficult cases. *In effect, these paralegals want to create a class of para-paralegals through delegation.* And so the process continues, leading potentially to an occupational structure of considerable stratification.

NOTE ON THE DELIVERY OF LEGAL SERVICES IN OTHER COUNTRIES

England

The English legal profession has two main branches consisting of solicitors and barristers. The solicitor handles the day-to-day legal problems of the public with only limited rights to represent clients in certain lower courts. The bulk of litigation in the higher courts is provided by the barrister. When representation in such courts is needed, the solicitor arranges for the barrister to enter the case. Solicitors often employ one or more Legal Executives who are delegated many responsibilities under the supervision of the solicitor. Legal Executives undergo extensive training programs and take rigorous examinations of the Institute of Legal Executives. Once qualified, the Legal Executive obtains Fellowship in the Institute and is entitled to use the letters "F.Inst.L.Ex." after his/her name.

Japan

Attorneys are not the only providers of legal services in Japan. A separate category of workers called judicial scriveners have special authority to assist the public in the preparation of legal documents such as contracts and deeds. The granting of this authority is conditioned on the successful completion of an examination.

Cuba

In Cuba, legal assistants work with attorneys in law offices or collectives called bufetes. The assistants draft legal documents, interview clients, conduct legal research, file papers in court, negotiate for trial dates, etc.

Soviet Union

Attorneys-at-law in the Soviet Union are organized in lawyers' colleges. Membership in the colleges is granted to three kinds of individuals: first, graduates from university law schools; second, individuals with legal training of six months or more, with experience in judicial work, or at least one year as a judge, governmental attorney, investigator, or legal counsel; and third, persons without legal training but with at least three years' experience.

Finland

In Finland, only members of the Finnish Bar Association can use the title of advocate. Advocates, however, do not enjoy an exclusive right of audience in the courts. Litigants can plead their own case or retain a representative who does not have to be an advocate.

Germany

In the Federal Republic of Germany, as in many European countries, the notary has a major role in legal matters. As a skilled impartial advisor, the notary (who is not necessarily a lawyer) oversees the contents of documents to ensure that legal transactions will withstand court challenges. S/he often advises parties on the legal implications of commercial affairs.

Section D. STAGES IN THE DEVELOPMENT OF PARALEGALISM

Paralegalism has come a long way since its emergence in the late 1960s. The past and the future can be roughly categorized into five stages or eras. Most have lasted (or are expected to last) about five years.

PARALEGAL DEVELOPMENT	
I.	1967-1971 : : The era of DISCOVERY
II.	1972-1976 : : The era of EDUCATION
III.	1977-1981 : : The era of POLITICS
IV.	1982-1986 : : The era of MANAGEMENT
V.	1987ff. : : The era of CREDENTIALIZATION

A single theme characterizes each era. Of course, there is overlap. The five themes have been discussed throughout the history of paralegalism. Yet, one theme dominates each era.

1. THE ERA OF DISCOVERY

During this time we were finding out what paralegals are and can do. It was a time of discovery. Lawyers experimented with new roles for nonlawyers in the delivery of legal services. Surveys and studies were undertaken. The results were reported at national conferences and within the literature. Since the results were impressive, the news spread quickly. Lawyers were told that there was a new way to practice law. The discovery of paralegals generated considerable enthusiasm, debate, and controversy. There is little doubt that paralegals are now a fixture in the vast majority of settings where law is practiced. The one possible exception is in some rural areas of the country where it is taking a little longer for lawyers to integrate paralegals into the practice of law. To this extent, the discovery of paralegals is still going on.

This is not to say that most lawyers hire paralegals or use them effectively. The expansion and development of paralegalism has by no means reached its peak. The point, however, is that the day has long passed when it was common for the legal profession to ask, "What's a paralegal?"

2. THE ERA OF EDUCATION

Most people thought that the period of the early 1970s would be the era of resolution when the controversies of the late 1960s would be settled. People wanted to know who would *control* this new field. Some within the private Bar feared competition from the paralegal. The time appeared to be ripe for the drawing of boundary lines and the establishment of authority. Regulatory legislation was considered in some states. Yet the period from 1972–1976 did *not* produce the definitive answers. The field consciously or unconsciously came to the realization that the lawyer-paralegal relationship could not be blueprinted in advance. The answers had to await further experience and evolution.

What did happen during this period was an explosion in the creation of paralegal training programs. The American Bar Association introduced its controversial plan to approve paralegal schools (p. 279). Texts for paralegals began to emerge from the law publishers. The American Association of Community and Junior Colleges received a major grant from the U.S. Office of Education to propose a paralegal curriculum.[25] At times, it appeared that few schools were *not* considering whether to institute a paralegal program. More recently the development of new programs has leveled off and some of the early ones have gone out of existence. Today the emphasis is on the creation of *continuing* education for paralegals through vehicles such as weekend conferences similar to those conducted for lawyers. For example, the Certified Legal Assistant program of the National Association of Legal Assistants (p. 288) requires the Certified Legal Assistant to submit evidence of continuing education in order to maintain the certified status. The Indiana State Bar Committee on Legal Assistants now strongly recommends that legal assistants

[25] The Association received its grant in 1974. American Association of Community and Junior Colleges, *Legal Assistant Program: A Suggested Two-Year Post-High School Curriculum* (1978).

maintain professional competence through seminars and other study programs.[26] Yet the pioneer period when institutional training became a permanent part of the scene was roughly during 1972–1976.

3. THE ERA OF POLITICS

Politics, of course, has always been part of paralegal history. For example, during the era of education, paralegals began to organize into local and national associations in part to protect their own interests as well as to pursue their professional development. The time between 1977–1981, however, began a period of intense political debate both among paralegals and between paralegals and lawyers. While the debate continues today, it blossomed between 1977–1981 to such an extent that politics was a dominant theme of this time. For example,

- The lines were sharply drawn between the National Federation of Paralegal Associations and the National Association of Legal Assistants on the issue of whether the certification of paralegals was premature.
- There were intensive lobbying drives by paralegal associations to slow down regulatory efforts of some Bar associations and to ensure that paralegals would be close participants with lawyers in this regulation.
- Strategies were planned within some paralegal associations on how to combat perceived problems of lawyer sexism and exploitation in employment.
- New local paralegal associations were formed with the active encouragement of the older associations. Considerable debate existed within some of these new associations over whether to affiliate with the National Federation of Paralegal Associations or the National Association of Legal Assistants.

4. THE ERA OF MANAGEMENT

Earlier in this chapter, factors such as economics and efficiency were listed as major reasons for the rapid expansion of paralegal use (p. 9). While this enthusiasm has not died down, it is clear that we are in for a period of consolidation. Many law offices hired proportionately large numbers of paralegals within a short time. They were encouraged to expand by the promotional literature of the Bar associations and by the increased income that the employment of the first paralegal generated. Some studies, however, have shown that a law office's increase in income tends to level off when larger numbers of paralegals are hired.[27]

Furthermore, not all offices are equipped to deal with the administrative problems that are found in an office with diverse personnel. Attorneys, for example, "who endorse the paralegal concept and hire recent graduates are often those whose workload is already too heavy. They have little time to provide individualized on-the-job training. The result is that paralegals feel frustrated

---

[26] Newsletter of the Indiana Legal Assistants, 5 *Lex Scripta* 5 (no. 1, June, 1984).

[27] Bower, *Can Paralegals be Profitable?* Michigan Bar Journal 173 (March, 1980).

with their lack of adequate preparation, and employers are disillusioned with their new employees."[28]

Lawyers are not trained as managers, yet management skills are fundamental to the effective use of paralegals. Hiring law office managers and the development of the relatively new career of legal administrator has helped, but they have not eliminated the need for the lawyer to educate him/herself in the principles of management and systemization.

The mentality of the lawyer is to work alone. Lawyers are trained to view each case as unique—every case can eventually be fought to the Supreme Court. This mentality and approach does not always encourage the lawyer to delegate responsibility effectively. It certainly does not necessarily prepare the lawyer to run an office in a "businesslike" and efficient manner. The skills required to have a law declared unconstitutional are radically different from the skills required to manage people. Unfortunately, paralegals can be one of the victims of this defect in lawyer training. It is not enough that the paralegal is competent; s/he must also be *used* competently. The paralegal must be challenged and be secure in his/her relationship with the lawyer and with other law office personnel. This is easier said than done, as we will see in chapter 3 on employment dynamics.

There are, however, some signs of change. Greater attention is given by many law schools to the problems of law office administration. The bar associations are also intensifying their efforts in this direction. Slowly lawyers have come to the realization that the incorporation of paralegals into an office requires careful planning and an understanding of human nature. Management assistance is becoming available. There is now a vast body of experience on which to draw. An important sign that change is on the way is the relatively recent creation of a new position in the larger law office—the *paralegal administrator*. Many firms with four or more paralegals have added a paralegal administrator to oversee the recruitment, training, and management of the office paralegals. Almost always, the paralegal administrator is someone with several years of experience as a paralegal who has an interest in moving into a management position. The number of paralegal administrators is growing every day. Recently they formed a separate organization—the Legal Assistant Managers Association. Lawyers now realize that they need this kind of specialized help to incorporate paralegals into the practice of law. In the old days, many lawyers had the mistaken notion that they could immediately make a lot of money simply by hiring paralegals. Thankfully, we are moving out of this era.

5. THE ERA OF CREDENTIALIZATION

The dust has not yet settled from all the controversies surrounding paralegalism. By the early 1980s none of the credentialing issues had been settled. Most people agreed that it was premature to launch extensive programs of licensing or certification. While some efforts in this direction were taken, as

---

[28] *NFPA/NALA Focus: Two Perspectives,* 3 Legal Assistant Update 90 (American Bar Association, Standing Committee on Legal Assistants, 1983).

we will see in chapter 4, the consensus was that more time was needed to so out all the factors involved in a program of credentialization.

It is anticipated, however, that this will change. A momentum is developing toward some form of official credentialization such as licensing or its equivalent. According to Kay Field, former president of the National Association of Legal Assistants:

> Those of us who have worked hard to become qualified legal assistants resent the law firm who hires a high school girl to do the filing, [and] calls her a legal assistant, . . . We all agree that there needs to be some specific standards, but unfortunately we cannot all agree first of all who is to prepare them, secondly how stringent they will be, and lastly, who will enforce them. I say to you, however, that these matters must be addressed by us before they are done for us.[29]

President Field and her organization do not advocate licensing, but they do advocate action before it is too late. Intense debate rages among paralegals over the issue of credentialization which we will examine in chapter 4. There is a very real danger that while paralegals continue to fight among themselves over the issue, lawyers and legislatures might suddenly step in and impose a scheme of regulation and control that will satisfy no one. Unless paralegals resolve the issue, it will be resolved for them. How could this happen? One possible scenario is as follows: The legislature imposes a license requirement after widespread publicity is given to an incident of negligence committed by an untrained and unqualified paralegal. To prevent such precipitate action by the legislature, it is critical that paralegals collectively decide what they want and how it should be achieved. The next three chapters are designed to provide you with the data that you will need to participate in this still-emerging aspect of paralegalism.

---

[29] K. Field, *Legal Assistants: Where Do We Go from Here?* 10 Facts and Findings 17, 18 (National Association of Legal Assistants, no. 6, May–June 1984).

2

Paralegal Employment

Section A. INTRODUCTION

While considerable competition exists for good paralegal jobs, the future looks promising. In the early 1980s, surveys found that there was one paralegal for every four or five lawyers in the average-sized law firm.[1] During the period of 1982-1995, the Bureau of Labor Statistics projects that the paralegal field will be the fastest growing occupation requiring postsecondary training and education (but less than a bachelor's degree). See figure 1. Paralegal growth will even outstrip the computer field.[2] During this period, paralegal jobs are expected to increase almost 100%. In some areas of practice, we may soon see one paralegal for every lawyer.[4]

This rise in prospects for paralegal employment must be seen in the context of a *decline* in the lawyer market. According to a recent article in *Forbes,* "American lawyers are headed for serious financial trouble. Their golden age is coming to an end. . . . The number of lawyers is growing much faster than the business available to support them."[5] One visible although relatively small

---

[1] *Paralegals Seen Taking Jobs from Associates,* 68 American Bar Association Journal 527 (May, 1982).

[2] Simon, *Paralegals: The Hottest Job Market,* National Law Journal, p. 1 (7/4/83).

[3] U.S. Dept. of Labor, Bureau of Labor Statistics, *Occupational Outlook Handbook, 1984-85 Edition,* Bull. 2205 (April, 1984).

[4] *Fitting Paralegals into the Corporate Legal Department,* 11 Facts and Findings 24 (Nat'l. Ass'n. of Legal Assistants, Issue 2, Sept.–Oct. 1984).

[5] Greene, *Lawyers versus the Marketplace,* p. 73, Forbes (1/16/84).

31

**Figure 1. Employment of legal assistants is expected to
nearly double between 1982 and 1995.**

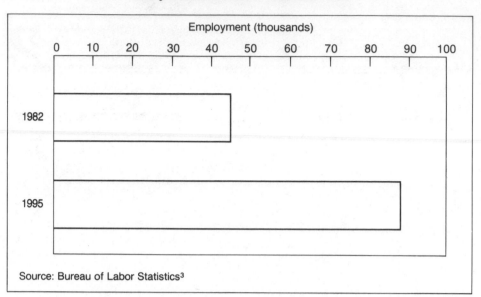

reason for the decline in lawyer jobs is the increased attractiveness of paralegals. Many law firms are finding that a substantial portion of the work formerly
done by newly hired lawyers (i.e., associates) can be more economically performed by paralegals. "As law firms realize the money-saving potential of paralegals, it is logical that more [paralegals] will be hired than associates. . . . This
trend may exacerbate the problem as far as new lawyers are concerned."[6]

Unemployed lawyers have occasionally vented their hostility on paralegals. In an article entitled, "Buddy, Can You Spare a Job," an anonymous lawyer urged

> bar associations [to] push for rules restricting the use of paralegals. It is sad that
> individuals with only two-sevenths of a lawyer's education are allowed to take po-
> sitions which could otherwise be filled by recent admittees to the bar. In the cur-
> rent market, a young attorney might well work for the same salary as a parale-
> gal. . . . Restriction of use of paralegals can be accomplished by requiring
> paralegals to pass an exam the same as lawyers do. . . . Further, various bar associ-
> ations [should] encourage their members to hire attorneys and not paralegals;
> after all, the bar associations represent lawyers, not paralegals. It must be pointed
> out that paralegal steal jobs from lawyers recently admitted to the bar.[7]

Happily, the advice of this sad lawyer is being substantially *ignored* by the bar
associations. Law firms are not social service organizations. They make their
hiring decisions on the basis of economic realities. The question they ask is
"Who can help this firm turn a better profit?" not, "Who needs a job?"

[6] *Paralegals Seen Taking Jobs from Associates,* supra note *1.*

[7] *Buddy, Can You Spare a Job,* by Anonymous, 46 The Shingle 25 (No. 3, Philadelphia Bar Association Quarterly, Fall, 1983).

This is not to say, however, that you will have an easy time finding a job. As you start your search, you are likely to find intense competition from a variety of sources:

- Recent graduates from paralegal training programs;
- Secretaries and clerks in a law office who want to be promoted into paralegal positions;
- Paralegals with a year or more of experience who are seeking a job change;
- People with no legal training or experience who walk into an office "cold" seeking a job (or who walk in with connections, e.g., they are relatives of the senior partner or of a large client of the firm);
- Frustrated attorneys who are applying for paralegal positions!

The frustrated attorneys, however, are seldom successful—except in government. In the federal government, for example, many "legal technician" jobs (p. 43) are filled by recent law school graduates.

When you begin your job search, you will probably find more applicants than available jobs. For some jobs, the ratio of applicants to openings may be as high as 25 to 1.

Hence to the task at hand: How do you find a job in today's market? We will focus on this theme through the following questions:

- Where do paralegals work?
- What are the specific paralegal specialties?
- What are effective job strategies for finding employment?

Section B. THE TEN CATEGORIES OF PARALEGAL EMPLOYMENT

There are ten major categories of paralegal employment. The categories are listed below with the approximate percentages of paralegals working in those categories, e.g., about 45% of paralegals today work in large traditional private law firms.

WHERE DO PARALEGALS WORK TODAY?
WHAT PERCENTAGE OF PARALEGALS WORK IN WHAT
SETTINGS TODAY?

I. Traditional Private Law Firms

    A. Small firm—1-5 lawyers (6%)
    B. Medium firm—6-15 lawyers (8%)
    C. Large firm—over 16 lawyers (45%)

II. New Breed Private Law Firm (3%)

III. Government

    A. Federal government (7%)
    B. State government (2%)
    C. Local government (1%)

IV. Legal Service/Legal Aid Offices (Civil Law) (8%)

V. Law Departments of Corporations, Banks, Insurance Companies, and Other Businesses (10%)

VI. Special Interest Groups or Associations (1%)

VII. Criminal Law Offices

    A. Prosecutor (2%)
    B. Defense (1%)

VIII. Free-Lance Paralegal (1%)

IX. Service Companies/Consulting Firms (2%)

X. Related Fields (3%)

    A. Law librarian
    B. Paralegal teacher
    C. Paralegal supervisor/office administrator
    D. Miscellaneous

As indicated in chapter 1, there is no universal agreement on what workers in this field are called (p. 4). Not everyone in the above categories are called paralegals. Yet they are all people with legal skills that differ from secretaries and other clerical personnel.

I. TRADITIONAL PRIVATE LAW FIRMS

Most paralegals today work for private law firms. While the need for paralegals may be just as great in the other categories, it is the traditional private law firms that have been doing most of the hiring. A "private" law firm is simply one that generates its income primarily from the fees of individual clients. The large law firms (over sixteen lawyers) have the most resources and hence have been the major employers of paralegals to date. It is anticipated, however, that this will change as more and more small- and medim-sized firms increase their paralegal use.

    There are a number of characteristics of paralegals working for traditional private law firms, particularly the larger ones:

- They are the highest paid paralegals.
- They experience more law office management and personnel problems than other paralegals.
- They tend to specialize more and hence have less variety in their work assignments.
- They have been the most politically active paralegals in forming associations and in dealing with the bar associations.
- They are predominantly women.

Strategies for obtaining employment in private law firms will be discussed primarily in Section D of this chapter (p. 116).

The table on page 36 is a survey of the employment of paralegals in the 250 largest law firms in the country.[8] (The addresses of these firms can be obtained through the Martindale-Hubbell Law Directory, p. 123, p. 548, or through other directories, p. 124.)

II. NEW BREED
PRIVATE LAW FIRM

Since the mid-1970s a new kind of private law firm (sometimes called a legal clinic) has come into existence. It also receives its income from fees, but it differs from the traditional law firm in a number of respects:

- it tends to charge lower fees
- it tends to serve the middle class
- it has branch offices that are "store-front" in character (as opposed to a single downtown office in a plush suite on the 11th floor)
- it tends to make a greater proportionate use of paralegals (there are more paralegals per lawyer than in the traditional private law firm)
- it is more likely to advertise in the media and to use devices such as credit-card payment

Such law firms have been controversial in the past. The traditional bar generally does not like these firms. The charge is that they are not dignified enough for the professional image that the bar wishes to project. In fact, during the early days, the bar went to court to try to force such firms out of existence. The bar lost, particularly over the issue of whether lawyers were allowed to advertise (p. 250).

The number of new breed private law firms is relatively small compared to the number of traditional firms. Yet there is a definite trend toward a greater growth of the former. The fear of losing business has caused many small traditional firms to begin imitating some of the characteristics of the new breed firm.

---

[8] From *National Law Journal* (Sept. 24, 1984).

Table 1. **THE EMPLOYMENT OF PARALEGALS IN THE 250 LARGEST LAW FIRMS IN THE COUNTRY.**

LAW FIRM (Number of attorneys listed in parenthesis)	NUMBER OF PARALEGALS IN 1984 (if available)
ARIZONA	
Phoenix	
Lewis & Roca (94)	20
O'Connor, Cavanagh, Anderson, Westover (97)	15
Snell & Wilmer (113)	15
Streich, Lang, Weeks & Cardon (93)	37
CALIFORNIA	
Beverly Hills	
Finley, Kumble, Wagner, Heine, Underberg (198)	—
Century City	
Loeb & Loeb (43)	12
Costa Mesa	
Rutan & Tucker (87)	5
Los Angeles	
Adams, Duque & Hazeltine (105)	11
Buchalter, Nemer, Fields, Chrystie (113)	14
Gibson, Dunn & Crutcher	100
Irell & Manella (108)	26
Kindell & Anderson (92)	9
Latham & Watkins(256)	37
Lillick, McHose & Charles (183)	39
Loeb & Loeb (94)	12
McCutchen Black, Verleger & Shea (85)	10
McKenna, Conner, & Cueno (190)	32
Memel, Jacobs, Pierno & Gersh (104)	15
Mitchell, Silberberg & Knupp (99)	18
Musick, Peeler & Garrett (90)	6
O'Melveny & Myers (392)	61
Paul, Hastings, Janofsky & Walker (194)	60
Sheppard, Mullin, Richer & Hampton (118)	46
Wyman, Bautzer, Rothman, Kuchel & Silbert (111)	14
Oakland	
Crosby, Heafey, Roach & May (108)	20
Palo Alto	
Fenwick, Stone, Davis & West (98)	18
San Diego	
Gray, Cary, Ames & Frye (121)	18
Finley, Kumble, Wagner, Heine, Underberg (14)	—
Luce, Forward, Hamilton & Scripps (91)	13
San Francisco	
Brobeck, Phleger & Harrison (230)	69
Bronson, Bronson & McKinnon (158)	29
Cooley, Godward, Castro, Huddleson & Tatum (101)	22
Graham & James (127)	16
Heller, Ehrman, White & McAuliffe (168)	57
Lillick, McHose & Charles (183)	39
McCutchen, Doyle, Brown & Enersen (146)	43
Morrison & Foerster (234)	58
Orrick, Herrington & Sutcliff (151)	27
Pettit & Martin (135)	20
Pillsbury, Madison & Sutro (373)	82
Sedgwick, Detert, Moran & Arnold (96)	12
Thelen, Marrin, Johnson & Bridges (163)	38
Santa Monica	
Haight, Dickson, Brown & Bonesteel (89)	34

Table 1. THE EMPLOYMENT OF PARALEGALS IN THE 250 LARGEST LAW FIRMS IN THE COUNTRY—Continued.

LAW FIRM (Number of attorneys listed in parenthesis)	NUMBER OF PARALEGALS IN 1984 (if available)
COLORADO	
Denver	
Davis, Graham & Stubbs (130)	24
Holland & Taft (140)	22
Holme, Roberts & Owen (178)	41
Sherman & Howard (141)	19
CONNECTICUT	
Hartford	
Day, Berry & Howard (128)	26
Stamford	
Cummings & Lockwood (125)	29
DISTRICT OF COLUMBIA (See Washington D.C.)	
FLORIDA	
Miami	
Blackwell, Walker, Gray, Powers, Flick (87)	2
Finley, Kumble, Wagner, Heine, Underberg (45)	—
Greenberg, Traurig, Askew, Hoffman, Lipoff (103)	18
Steel, Hector & Davis (90)	16
Tampa	
Carlton, Fields, Ward, Emmanuel, Smith (119)	20
Fowler, White, Gillen, Boggs, Villareal (92)	21
Holland & Knight (210)	25
GEORGIA	
Atlanta	
Alston & Bird (136)	20
Hansell & Post (125)	25
Kilpatrick & Cody (118)	19
King & Spalding (145)	37
Powell, Goldstein, Frazer & Murphy (146)	26
Sutherland, Asbill & Brennan (161)	26
Troutman, Sanders, Lockerman & Ashmore (100)	14
ILLINOIS	
Chicago	
Bell, Boyd & Lloyd (114)	17
Chapman & Cutler (215)	15
Friedman & Koven (104)	19
Gardner, Carlton & Douglas (99)	11
Hinshaw, Culbertson, Moelmann, Hoban (160)	17
Hopkins & Sutter (107)	12
Isham, Lincoln & Beale (116)	13
Jenner & Block (191)	55
Katten, Muchin, Zavis, Pearl & Galler (111)	18
Keck, Mahin & Cate (93)	15
Kirkland & Ellis (267)	40
Lord, Bissell & Brook (215)	42
Mayer, Brown & Platt (307)	53
McDermott, Will & Emery (234)	53
Peterson, Ross, Schloerb & Seidel (119)	24
Rudnick & Wolfe (130)	20
Schiff, Hardin & Waite (130)	19

Table 1. THE EMPLOYMENT OF PARALEGALS IN THE 250 LARGEST LAW FIRMS IN THE COUNTRY—Continued.

LAW FIRM (Number of attorneys listed in parenthesis)	NUMBER OF PARALEGALS IN 1984 (if available)
Seyfarth, Shaw, Fairweather & Geraldson (187)	16
Sidley & Austin (449)	88
Sonnenschein, Carlin, Nath & Rosenthal (148)	20
Vedder, Price, Kaufman & Kammholz (107)	8
Wildman, Harrold, Allen & Dixon (161)	21
Winston & Strawn (216)	41
INDIANA	
Indianapolis	
Baker & Daniels (92)	15
Barnes & Thornburg (126)	16
Ice, Miller, Donadio & Ryan (101)	10
KENTUCKY	
Lexington	
Greenebaum, Doll & McDonald (92)	15
Louisville	
Greenebaum, Doll & McDonald (92)	15
Wyatt, Tarrant & Combs (100)	13
LOUISIANA	
New Orleans	
Jones, Walker, Waechter, Poitevent (128)	23
Phelps, Dunbar, Marks, Claverie & Sims (90)	18
MARYLAND	
Baltimore	
Frank, Bernstein, Conaway & Goldman (92)	16
Miles & Stockbridge (116)	21
Piper & Marbury (143)	39
Semmes, Bowen & Semmes (130)	31
Venable, Baetjer & Howard (143)	25
Weinberg & Green (100)	13
MASSACHUSETTS	
Boston	
Bingham, Dana & Gould (113)	14
Choate, Hall & Stewart (111)	25
Foley, Hoag & Eliot (102)	16
Gaston, Snow & Ely Bartlett (200)	40
Hale & Dore (218)	40
Mintz, Levin, Cohn, Ferris, Glovsky (103)	18
Nutter, McClennan & Fish (115)	18
Palmer & Dodge (119)	25
Ropes & Gray (195)	25
Sullivan & Worcester (123)	16
MICHIGAN	
Detroit	
Dickerson, Wright, Moon, Van Dusen (113)	25
Dykema, Gossett, Spencer, Goodnow & Trigg (188)	55
Honigman, Miller, Schwartz & Cohn (114)	21
Miller, Canfield, Paddock & Stone (141)	30
Plunkett, Cooney, Rutt, Watters, Stanczyk (104)	14

Table 1. THE EMPLOYMENT OF PARALEGALS IN THE 250 LARGEST LAW FIRMS IN THE COUNTRY—Continued.

LAW FIRM (Number of attorneys listed in parenthesis)	NUMBER OF PARALEGALS IN 1984 (if available)
MINNESOTA	
Minneapolis	
Dorsey & Whitney (235)	57
Faegre & Benson (159)	46
Robbins, Zelle, Larson & Kaplan (136)	56
St. Paul	
Oppenheimer, Wolff, Foster, Shepard (108)	15
Robbins, Zelle, Larson & Kaplan (136)	56
MISSOURI	
Kansas City	
Stinson, Mag & Fizzel (102)	15
St. Louis	
Bryan, Cave, McPheeters & McRoberts (181)	42
Thompson & Mitchell (85)	10
NEBRASKA	
Omaha	
Kutak, Rock & Huie (187)	27
NEW JERSEY	
Morristown	
Pitney, Hardin, Kipp & Szuch (86)	14
Newark	
McCarter & English (88)	18
NEW YORK	
Buffalo	
Hodgson, Russ, Andrews, Woods & Goodyear (95)	24
Garden City	
Rivkin, Leff, Sherman & Radler (123)	32
Great Neck	
Hayt, Hayt & Landau (86)	13
New York City	
Breed, Abbott & Morgan (111)	16
Brown, Wood, Ivey, Mitchell & Petty (172)	25
Cadwalader, Wickersham & Taft (206)	43
Cahill, Gordon & Reindel (238)	47
Chadbourne, Parke, Whiteside & Wolff (150)	20
Cleary, Gottlieb, Steen & Hamilton (254)	36
Coudert Brothers (197)	30
Cravath, Swain & Moore (261)	51
Curtis, Mallet-Prevost, Colt & Mosie (115)	16
Davis, Polk & Wardwell (312)	82
Debevoise & Plimpton (240)	31
Dewey, Ballentine, Bushby, Palmer & Wood (216)	41
Donovan, Leisure, Newton & Irvine (127)	13
Epstein, Becker, Borsody & Green (85)	9
Finley, Kumble, Wagner, Heine, Underberg (462)	91
Freid, Frank, Harris, Schriver & Jacobson (243)	53
Haight, Gardner, Poor & Havens (100)	32
Hawkins, Delafield & Wood (109)	23
Hughes, Hubbard & Reed (176)	47

Table 1. THE EMPLOYMENT OF PARALEGALS IN THE 250 LARGEST LAW FIRMS IN THE COUNTRY—Continued.

LAW FIRM (Number of attorneys listed in parenthesis)	NUMBER OF PARALEGALS IN 1984 (if available)
Kaye, Scholer, Fierman, Hays & Handler (250)	46
Kelley, Drye & Warren (210)	45
Kramer, Levin, Nessen, Kamin & Frankel (106)	29
Leboeuf, Lamb, Leiby & MacRae (212)	62
Lord, Day & Lord (121)	16
Milbank, Tweed, Hadley & McCloy (249)	52
Mudge, Rose, Guthrie, Alexander & Ferdon (222)	58
Parker, Chapin, Flattau & Klimpl (96)	16
Patterson, Belknap, Webb & Tyler (124)	27
Paul, Weiss, Rifkind, Wharton & Garrison (276)	57
Phillips, Lytle, Hitchcock, Blaine & Huber (107)	24
Proskauer, Rose, Goetz & Mendelsohn (206)	44
Reavis & McGrath (102)	21
Reid & Priest (124)	20
Rogers & Wells (242)	35
Rosenman, Colin, Freund, Lewis & Cohen (218)	36
Schulte, Roth & Zabel (87)	24
Shay & Gould (180)	47
Shearman & Sterling (397)	59
Simpson, Thacher & Bartlett (305)	51
Skadden, Arps, Slate, Meagher & Flom (416)	110
Stroock, Stroock & Lavan (224)	55
Sullivan & Cromwell (280)	44
Thacher, Proffitt & Wood (85)	14
Webster & Sheffield (94)	13
Weil, Gotshal & Manges (293)	37
Wender, Murase & White (91)	10
White & Case (234)	38
Whitman & Ransom (150)	27
Willkie, Farr & Gallagher (239)	36
Wilson, Elser, Edelman & Dicker (187)	32
Winthrop, Stimpson, Putnam & Roberts (153)	13
Rochester	
Nixon, Hargrave, Devans & Doyle (177)	40
Syracuse	
Bond, Schoeneck & King (99)	13
OHIO	
Cincinnati	
Dinsmore & Shohl (92)	42
Frost & Jacobs (104)	17
Taft, Stettinius & Hollister (111)	33
Cleveland	
Arter & Hadden (144)	17
Baker & Hostetler (272)	40
Benesch, Friedlander, Coplan & Aronoff (85)	16
Calfree, Halter & Griswold (95)	17
Jones, Day, Revis & Pogue (386)	77
Squire, Sanders & Dempsey (308)	43
Thompson, Hine & Flory (145)	22
Columbus	
Porter, Wright, Morris & Arthur (169)	30
Vorys, Sater, Seymour & Pease (151)	27
Dayton	
Smith & Schnacke (120)	27

Table 1. THE EMPLOYMENT OF PARALEGALS IN THE 250 LARGEST LAW FIRMS IN THE COUNTRY—Continued.

LAW FIRM (Number of attorneys listed in parenthesis)	NUMBER OF PARALEGALS IN 1984 (if available)
OKLAHOMA	
Tulsa	
Hall, Estill, Hardwick, Gable, Collingsworth (95)	17
OREGON	
Portland	
Schwabe, Williamson, Wyatt, Moore & Roberts (112)	17
Stoel, Rives, Boley, Fraser & Wyse (144)	22
PENNSYLVANIA	
Philadelphia	
Ballard, Spahr, Andrews & Ingersoll (147)	36
Blank, Rome, Comisky & McCauley (182)	43
Dechert, Price & Rhoads (187)	31
Dilworth, Paxson, Kalish & Kauffman (111)	21
Drinker, Biddle & Reath (154)	31
Duane, Morris & Heckscher (111)	30
Morgan, Lewis & Bockius (370)	47
Pepper, Hamilton & Scheetz (207)	51
Saul, Ewing, Remick & Saul (90)	27
Schnader, Harrison, Segal & Lewis (192)	51
Wolf, Block, Schorr & Solis-Cohen (179)	36
Pittsburg	
Baskin & Steingut (100)	14
Buchanan & Ingersoll (116)	23
Eckert, Seamans, Cherin & Mellott (108)	17
Kirkpatrick, Lockert, Johnson & Hutchison (167)	24
Reed, Smith, Shaw & McClay (213)	24
RHODE ISLAND	
Providence	
Edwards & Angell (88)	20
TEXAS	
Dallas	
Akin, Gump, Strauss, Hauer & Feld (245)	37
Gardere & Wynne (112)	20
Hughes & Hill (90)	8
Jenkens & Gilchrist (138)	20
Johnson & Swanson (170)	26
Locke, Purness, Boren, Laney & Neely (93)	9
Strasburger & Price (123)	34
Thompson & Knight (141)	29
Winstead, McGuire, Sechrest & Minick (105)	17
Houston	
Andrews & Kurth (134)	22
Baker & Botts (259)	41
Bracewell & Patterson (127)	24
Butler & Binion (162)	19
Fulbright & Jaworski (353)	71
Vinson & Elkins (357)	113
Wood, Lucjsinger & Epstein (97)	10

Table 1. THE EMPLOYMENT OF PARALEGALS IN THE 250 LARGEST
LAW FIRMS IN THE COUNTRY—Continued.

LAW FIRM (Number of attorneys listed in parenthesis)	NUMBER OF PARALEGALS IN 1984 (if available)
VIRGINIA	
Richmond	
Hunton & Williams (267)	71
McGuire, Woods & Battle (179)	66
WASHINGTON, D.C.	
Arent, Fox, Kintner, Plotkin & Kahn (146)	25
Arnold & Porter (201)	28
Covington & Burling (214)	47
Crowell & Moring (101)	15
Dickstein, Shapiro & Moran (93)	24
Dow, Lohnes & Albertson (100)	20
Epstein, Becker, Borsody & Green (85)	9
Finley, Kumble, Wagner, Heine, Underberg (75)	—
Hogan & Hartson (192)	36
Howrey & Simon (89)	34
McKenna, Connor & Cuneo (170)	32
Shaw, Pittman, Potts & Trowbridge (140)	21
Steptoe & Johnson (200)	51
Sutherland, Asbill & Brennan (121)	26
Ward, Harkrader & Ross (106)	22
Wilmer, Cutler & Pickering (142)	70
WASHINGTON STATE	
Seattle	
Bogle & Gates (138)	22
Davis, Wright, Todd, Riese & Jones (114)	18
Lane, Powell, Moss & Miller (95)	15
Perkins, Coie, Stone, Olsen & Williams (164)	39
Preston, Thorgrimson, Ellis & Holman (94)	13
WISCONSIN	
Milwaukee	
Foley & Lardner (207)	23
Quarles & Brady (141)	19

III. GOVERNMENT

The civil service departments of federal, state, and local governments have established standards and classifications for many different kinds of government paralegals. These paralegals work in four main areas of the government:

1. In the office of the chief government lawyer, e.g., attorney general, corporation counsel.
2. In the general counsel's office of the individual agencies
3. In other departments of the individual agencies, e.g., enforcement department, civil rights division
4. In the office of individual legislators, of individual legislative committees, of the legislative counsel, or of the legislative drafting office of the legislature

Government paralegals generally have more responsibility and less direct lawyer supervision than the other categories of paralegals.

Federal Government

In 1975 the Civil Service Commission (now the Office of Personnel Management) created a Paralegal Specialist Series (GS-950) to do work that "requires discretion and independent judgment in the application of specialized knowledge of particular laws, regulations, precedents or agency practices based thereon. . . . Work in this series may or may not be performed under the direction of a lawyer."[9] A separate Legal Clerk and Technician Series (GS-986) existed for individuals who did more clerical work calling for less responsibility. Prior to 1975, the U.S. government employed personnel in various legal assistant capacities, but it was not until the establishment of the Paralegal Specialist Series (GS-950) that a wide variety of federal legal positions was grouped within in a single occupation.

To become a Paralegal Specialist, an applicant had to take the Professional Administrative Career Examination (PACE). This exam, however, was abolished following allegations of cultural bias and ineffectiveness in measuring job skills. No entrance exam currently exists.

The official definition of the Paralegal Series as established in 1975 and still in effect today is as follows:

> This series includes positions which involve paralegal work not requiring professional legal competence where such work is of a type not classifiable in some other series. The work requires discretion and independent judgment in the application of specialized knowledge of particular laws, regulations, precedents, or agency practices based thereon. The work includes such activities as (a) legal research, analyzing legal decisions, opinions, rulings, memoranda, and other legal points of law involved; (b) selecting, assembling, summarizing and compiling substantive information on statutes, treaties, contracts, and other legal instruments, and specific legal subjects; (c) case preparation for civil litigation, criminal law proceedings or agency hearings, including the collection, analysis, and evaluation of evidence, e.g., as to fraud and fraudulent, and other irregular activities or violations of laws; (d) analyzing facts and legal questions presented by personnel administering specific Federal laws, answering the questions where they have been settled by interpretations of applicable legal provisions, regulations, precedents, and agency policy, and in some instances preparing information and instructional material for general use; (e) adjudicating applications or cases on the basis of pertinent laws, regulations, policies, and precedent decisions; or (f) performing other paralegal duties. Work in this series may or may not be performed under the direction of a lawyer.[10]

In 1980, the Office of Personnel Management (OPM) began a reevaluation of the Paralegal Specialist Series because of a dissatisfaction with the way in which the above definition was interpreted by the various agencies throughout the federal government. "Many agencies consider all nonprofes-

[9] Civil Service Commission Bulletin No. 930-17 (Aug. 11, 1975).

[10] Ibid.

sional work which requires some legal knowledge to be paralegal work. This includes the work of law clerks, secretarial staff, legal technicians, and, in some cases, research analysts and specialists in various compliance or enforcement programs."[11] To remedy this problem, OPM proposed a *narrower* scope for the Paralegal Specialist Series:

> This series [will cover] a variety of positions that perform quasi-professional legal work ancillary to the work of attorneys or administrative law judges who are engaged in litigation or quasi-judicial functions.[12]

Compare this with the more expansive language in the 1975 definition quoted above: "discretion and independent judgment." OPM received considerable criticism over this proposal from individual paralegals as well as from groups such as the Federal Interagency Attorney Personnel Group. Since the majority of paralegals do not work in the area of litigation, the main fear was that the narrower definition would force over 75% of paralegals out of the Paralegal Specialist role and into other series. The reaction of OPM has been to back away from the proposal. As of 1985, therefore, the broad language of the 1975 definition remains in effect.

In 1983, there were 2,480 Paralegal Specialist positions in the federal government. [13] Of these, 1,330 (54%) were in Washington, D.C. The three largest employers of paralegals in the government were the Department of Health and Human Services (836), the Department of Justice (559), and the Department of Treasury (140).

Here are the figures for other agencies: Department of Transportation (111), Department of Army (92), Department of Interior (67), Small Business Administration (66), Equal Employment Opportunity Commission (63), General Services Administration (63), Interstate Commerce Commission (58), Securities and Exchange Commission (47), Department of Energy (39), Department of State (38), Department of Labor (37), and the Department of the Navy (34).

Paralegal Specialists are classified to the General Schedule (GS), which is the government's largest white-collar pay system. The General Schedule has eighteen grade levels, but most federal positions are found at grades GS-1 through GS-15. The Paralegal Specialist Series is considered a "two-grade interval" administrative occupation that involves the exercise of analytical ability, judgment, discretion, personal responsibility, and the application of a sub-

---

[11] Office of Personnel Management, *Tentative Standards for Paralegal Specialist Standards, GS-950...*, p. 2 (1981?).

[12] Id. at 1.

[13] Most of the numerical data on the Paralegal Statistical Series, GS-950, comes from the series of reports entitled *Federal Civilian Work Force Statistics: Occupations of Federal White Collar Workers*, published by the U.S. Office of Personnel Management (OPM) and its predecessor, the U.S. Civil Service Commission (OPM Pamphlet 56-16). The reports are published every two years, with data in each report as of October 31. Additional data concerning agency populations have been included from the Civilian Personnel Data File as of October 31, 1983, also maintained by OPM.

stantial body of legal principles, concepts, and practices. Administrative occupations are characteristically entered at the GS-5 and GS-7 levels and career promotions are accomplished in two-grade intervals between grades GS-5 and GS-11 (GS-5, GS-7, GS-9, GS-11). Above GS-11, all positions in the General Schedule advance by single interval. While administrative occupations do not require specialized educational majors, they do involve the type of skills (analytical, research, writing, judgment) typically gained through a college-level education , or through progressively responsible experience.

In 1983, the average grade for Paralegal Specialists was 10.42, which was considerably above the average GS grade of 8.38 for federal positions. The median grade for paralegals was GS-11, which was well above the median grade of GS-9 for General Schedule employees. The 1985 salary range for GS-11 is $26,381 to $34,292.[14]

The Paralegal Specialist Series grew more than 25 percent a year in most years between 1976 and 1980. Although the occupation was first defined in the federal service in 1975, the base population was not established until 1976, mainly by a *transfer* of employees and jobs from other legal assistant occupations that were concurrently phased out, rather than by new hiring.[15]

Current information about paralegal jobs in the federal government can be obtained by contacting:

- Office of Personnel Management, Washington, D.C. 20415.
- The Office of Personnel Management in your state. For a list of the Federal Information Centers around the country, see Appendix F, p. 881.
- The personnel office of the particular federal agency in which you are interested (there will usually be a Washington, D.C. office and about eight regional offices throughout the country).

Also consult standard texts such as *The Washington Want Ads: A Guide to Legal Careers in the Federal Government,* published by the American Bar Association. (Former title: *Federal Government Legal Career Opportunities.*)

State Government

There has been considerable growth of paralegal employment in state governments. (See table 2). In California, for example, the 1980-81 Budget Act required the state Department of Justice to "develop a plan to increase its utiliza-

---

[14] In 1983 there were twenty-three positions at GS-15 (.9%), 107 at GS-14 (4%), 304 positions at GS-13 (12%), 372 positions at GS-12 (15%), 688 positions at GS-11 (27%), 565 positions at GS-9 (23%), 293 positions at GS-7 (12%), and 74 positions at GS-5 (3%). The remaining 3% of paralegal positions are found at grades GS-6, GS-8, and GS-10, which are not typical grades for the Paralegal Specialist Series.

[15] Starting with the 1976 population (739), the occupation grew to 1,019 in 1977 (increase of 38%), to 1,291 in 1978 (increase of 27%), to 1,576 in 1979 (increase of 22%), to 2,038 in 1980 (increase of 29%). The largest numerical increase for any single year (462) occurred between 1979 and 1980. Since that time, however, the percentage of increase in the paralegal occupation has slowed even though numerical growth continues. This can be seen in the total numerical increase of 442 for the three years from 1980 to 1983 (increase of 22%).

tion of paralegal personnel."[16] The California Auditor General made a recommendation that eighty attorney positions be converted into 160 paralegal positions![17] While a later study by the California Department of Justice modified this recommendation and called for a less ambitious expansion, the trend continues in the direction of increased paralegal use.

Start your search with the data provided for your state in table 2, page 48. If your state is not listed, check with your state civil service or personnel office to determine whether paralegal positions have been recently created.

Next, locate a directory of agencies, commissions, boards, or departments for your state, county, or city governments. You want to find a list of all (or most of the major) government offices. Many local public libraries will have such a directory. Alternatively, check the office of state and local politicians, e.g., governor, mayor, commissioner, alderman, representative, senator. They will probably have such a directory. Finally, check your local phone book for the section on government offices. In your search, include a list of all the courts in the state. Judges and/or court clerks may have legal positions open for nonlawyers.

Many government offices have their own personnel departments that will list employment openings. Also, whenever possible, talk with lawyers and paralegals who already work in these offices. They may know of opportunities that you can pursue.

Do not limit your search to paralegal or legal assistant positions. Legal jobs for nonlawyers may be listed under other headings, e.g., Research Assistant, Legal Analyst, Administrative Aide, Administrative Officer, Executive Assistant, Examiner, Clerk, Investigator.

IV. LEGAL SERVICE/LEGAL AID OFFICES (CIVIL LAW)

Neighborhood or community legal service offices and legal aid offices receive most of their funds from the government. They receive yearly grants to provide legal services to the poor. The clients do not pay fees. These offices make extensive use of paralegals with the following titles:

Administrative Benefits Representative	Disabled, Specialist in Law of the Domestic Relations Specialist
Administrative Hearing Representative	Employment Law Specialist Food Stamp Specialist
AFDC, Specialist (Aid to Families with Dependent Children)	Generalist Paralegal Health Law Specialist
Bankruptcy Law Specialist	Housing/Tenant Law Specialist
Case Advocate	Immigration Law Specialist
Case Specialist	Information and Referral Specialist
Community Education Specialist	Legal Research Specialist
Consumer Law Specialist	Legislative Advocate

[16] *Study of Paralegal Utilization in the California Attorney General's Office,* 1, Cal. Dept. of Justice (Dec. 1980).

[17] *Need to Expand the Use of Paralegals in the Office of the Attorney General,* Office of Auditor General (1979).

Paralegal

Paralegal Coordinator

Paralegal Supervisor

Public Entitlement Specialist

Senior Citizen Specialist

Social Security Specialist

Tribal Court Representative

Veterans Law Specialist

Wills Procedures Specialist

As we will see in chapter 4 (p. 226), many administrative agencies permit nonlawyers to represent citizens at hearings before those agencies. Legal service and legal aid offices take advantage of this authorization. Their paralegals undertake extensive agency representation. The distinction between lawyers and paralegals in such offices is less pronounced than in any other setting. Unfortunately, however, such paralegals are among the lowest paid because of the limited resources of the offices where they work.

Many placement offices of paralegal schools (and of law schools) have directories of such offices throughout the country. Examples of such directories are those prepared by the Legal Services Corporation (a government agency in Washington, D.C. that funds these programs) and the National Legal Aid and Defender Association (also in Washington, D.C.).

The job announcement in figure 2 on p. 62 will give you some idea of paralegals in one aspect of this area of practice.

There is another important way in which the poor (i.e., the indigent) receive legal services. Judicare is a system of paying *private* attorneys for legal services to the poor on a case-by-case basis. Instead of receiving a government grant to open up an office that will serve only the poor, the attorney maintains a private office and bills the government (through judicare funds) whenever legal services are delivered to the poor. As judicare programs continue to be created, it is anticipated that the participating lawyers will make substantial use of paralegals.

Further variations on methods by which paralegals are used to deliver legal services to the poor include:

- Paralegals who work in special institutions, e.g., mental health hospitals, prisons.
- Paralegals who are senior citizens providing legal services to senior citizens at nursing homes, neighborhood centers, and other similar locations.

V. LAW DEPARTMENTS OF CORPORATIONS, BANKS, INSURANCE COMPANIES, AND OTHER BUSINESSES

Not all businesses use outside law firms to handle their legal problems. Many have their own "in-house" law departments. Such businesses, however, may use outside firms when complex litigation is involved. The client of the in-house law department is the corporation or business itself. These departments are making greater and greater use of paralegals. The latter receive comparatively high salaries because their employer (like the large traditional private law firm) can afford to pay them.

Table 2. SUMMARY CHART—SURVEY OF STATE JOB CLASSIFICATIONS FOR PARALEGALS.

GOVERNMENT	POSITION	RESPONSIBILITIES	QUALIFICATIONS	SALARY
ALABAMA Personnel Dept. Montgomery, AL 36130-2301	Legal Assistant 10/22/82 (11503)	• Legal research • Draft pleadings • Interview witnesses in preparation for trial • Routine investigations • Prepare and interpret legal documents in noncomplex cases • Draft tentative regulations • Office administrative duties	Legal Assistant Certificate from a college or university accredited by a regional accrediting agency.	$15,746 - $23,951 per year
Other positions to check in Alabama: Docket Clerk (11501) Legal Opinions Clerk (11505)				
ALASKA Department of Administration Division of Personnel Pouch C-0201 Juneau, AK 99811	Paralegal Assistant I 4/1/84 (7105-13)	• Interview clients • Obtain statements and affidavits • Investigations • Legal Research • Coordinate witness scheduling • Represent clients at hearings	Certificate from a state paralegal training program <u>OR</u> 3 years' experience as legal secretary, court clerk, etc.	$25,200 - $29,820 per year
Other position to check in Alaska: Associate Attorney I (711-17) (Assists attorneys in the Office of the Attorney General)				
ARIZONA Dept. of Administration Personnel Division 1831 West Jefferson Phoenix, AZ 85007	Legal Assistant 1/11/77 (74510)	• Legal research • Help prepare briefs and pleadings • Take statements and depositions • Interview complainants • Index laws • Serve papers • Help answer court calendars	2 years of college in relevant courses	$14,919 - $20,064 per year

Table 2. SUMMARY CHART—Continued.

GOVERNMENT	POSITION	RESPONSIBILITIES	QUALIFICATIONS	SALARY
ARKANSAS Dept. of Finance and Administration Office of Personnel Management P.O. Box 3278, Little Rock, AR 72203	Legal Assistant 7/1/77 7/1/79-R (R177)	• Receive legal questions from agency attorneys • Collect and evaluate information on the questions • File pleadings and briefs • Maintain law library	The education equivalent of completion of 1 year of law school including a course in legal bibliography	$12,584 - $20,358 per year
CALIFORNIA State Personnel Bd. 801 Capitol Mall Sacramento, CA 95814 ALSO: Dept. of Personnel Administration 1115 11th St. Sacramento, CA 95814	Legal Assistant 3/13/75 9/20/78 (CW55, 1820)	• Assist in reviewing legal documents to determine if they comply with the law • Analyze proposed legislation • Digest and index legal opinions, testimony, depositions, and other trial documents • Undertake research of legislative history • Assist in drafting complaints and other pleadings • Undertake routine legal research	2 years' legal clerical experience in Calif. gov't. OR 3 years' in a law office	$20,016 - $24,024 per year
	Legal Analyst 7/2/81 (LE18, 5237)	• Investigate and analyze facts • Coordinate witnesses • Draft interrogatories • Draft pleadings • Summarize discovery documents • Supervise other staff	1 year as a state Legal Assistant OR 2 years in another paralegal job and 15 semester hours or 22 quarter units in a paralegal curriculum or equivalent to graduation from college	$23,676 - $28,476 per year
COLORADO Dept. of Personnel State Continental Bldg. 1313 Sherman St. Denver, CO 80203	Legal Assistant 6/23/82 ("A" 77500) ("B" 77501)	• Discovery and investigation assistance • Digest and index legal documents • Check legal citations • Take notes during deposition • Prepare simple pleadings and briefs • Maintain case files • Prepare statistical reports • Legal research	Bachelor's degree and approved paralegal studies program (experience can substitute for general education)	$20,004 - $31,008 per year

Table 2. SUMMARY CHART—Continued.

GOVERNMENT	POSITION	RESPONSIBILITIES	QUALIFICATIONS	SALARY
CONNECTICUT Personnel Div. Dept. of Administration Services P.O. Box 806 Hartford, CT 06115	Paralegal Specialist I 6/10/83 (6140)(NL16)	• Act as liaison between legal and clerical staff • Legal research • Assist in drafting legal documents • Maintain tickler systems • Present written and oral argument at administrative hearings • Maintain records	2 years' experience working for a lawyer <u>OR</u> A designated number of college courses in law or paralegal studies	$18,180 - $22,044 per year
Other positions to check in Connecticut: Paralegal Specialist II (6141, NL 20) Legal Office Administrator (5373, 9389c, MP 18)				
DELAWARE State Personnel Office Townsend Bldg. P.O. Box 1401 Dover, DE 19901	Legal Assistant I 8/75 (12845)	• Take dictation • Interview witnesses • Prepare files for court • Conduct directed legal research • Supervise clerical personnel	Associates degree in business or social science and 1 year legal or investigation experience	$11,370 - $19,639 per year
Other position to check in Delaware: Legal Assistant II (12846)				
DISTRICT OF COLUMBIA D.C. Personnel Office 613 G St. NW Wash. D.C. 20001	Paralegal Specialist	Similar to Paralegal Specialist positions in the federal government (p. 43)		
FLORIDA Dept. of Administration Rm. 530, Carlton Bldg. Tallahassee, FL 32301	Paralegal Specialist 1/1/84 (7703)	• Take affidavits from victims and witnesses • Legal research under supervision • Maintain case files and tickler system • Perform notary functions • Prepare case summaries • Draft pleadings	Completion of legal assistant training course <u>OR</u> Bachelor's degree with major in allied legal services <u>OR</u> 4 years' experience as paralegal or legal secretary	Grade 13 $12,089 - $19,564 per year

Table 2. SUMMARY CHART—Continued.

GOVERNMENT	POSITION	RESPONSIBILITIES	QUALIFICATIONS	SALARY
GEORGIA State Merit System of Personnel Administration 200 Piedmont Ave. Atlanta, GA 30334	Legal Assistant 1/1/81 (44330)	• Legal research • Review litigation documents • Summarize law • Develop forms and procedures	2 years' legal experience involving legal research, interpreting laws, or relevant administrative responsibilities	$15,036 - $19,920 per year
Other positions to check in Georgia: Law Clerk (44340)—requires a law degree OR two years' legal assistant experience Para-Legal (non-merit position in State Law Department) Research Assistant (non-merit position in State Law Department)				
GUAM Office of the Attorney General 7th Floor, Pacific News Bldg. 238 O'Hara St. Agana, GU 96910	Paralegal I 12/83 (2.810)	• Legal research • Index public laws • Prepare updates to administrative laws • Draft bills • Compile laws by subject matter	2 years' experience in a law office, agency, or court; AND bachelor's degree in business or related field, OR completion of a paralegal education program OR an equivalent combination of experience and training	Pay Range: 28 $13,930 - $18,610 per year
HAWAII Dept. of Personnel Services 830 Punchbowl St. Honolulu, HI 96813	Legal Assistant II 4/15/83 (2.141)	• Act as conduit between attorneys and client, e.g., provide legal information • Legal research • Summarize laws • Collect and evaluate evidence for trial • Draft legal documents	4 years' legal experience OR Graduation from an accredited legal assistant training program	$16,152 - $23,892 per year

Table 2. SUMMARY CHART—Continued.

GOVERNMENT	POSITION	RESPONSIBILITIES	QUALIFICATIONS	SALARY
IDAHO Personnel Commission 700 West State Boise, ID 83720	Legal Assistant 12/82 (05916)	• Analyze statutes, cases, constitutions, etc. • Prepare and file pleadings • Deliver subpoenas • Monitor proposed legislation • Research files • Maintain official records • Schedule appearances	Education and experience providing a knowledge of legal proceedings, and an ability to use the law library and analyze legal documents	$7.96 - $10.67 per hour
ILLINOIS State Civil Service Commission 425½ South Fourth St. Springfield, IL 62701	Paralegal Assistant 11/17/83 (1887, 30860) [Ill. Dept. of Central Management Services]	• Write legal memoranda and other documents for attorneys • Analyze hearing transcripts • Excerpt data from transcripts • Prepare statistical reports • Edit, index, and proofread decisions • Legal research	Knowledge and skill equivalent to four years of college and knowledge and skills relevant to job responsibilities	$15,888 - $19,944 per year
INDIANA State Personnel Dept. Rm. 513, State Office Bldg. 100 North Senate Ave. Indianapolis, IN 46204-2261	The state has no special classifications for paralegals working in the state government. The Indiana Office of Attorney General has several people with paralegal certificates, but these individuals are not used as paralegals. "We have not needed the position in the past because of a glut of law clerks who are available." Nevertheless, the Office has been working on developing a paralegal position.			
IOWA Merit Employment Dept. Grimes State Office Bldg. East 14th & Grand Des Moines, IA 50319	"We do not have special classifications for para-professional legal work. Agencies have been using the Administrative Assistant I class." 7/1/69; 7/24/81 (00708) $15,433 - $19,240 per year			
KANSAS Dept. of Administration Div. of Personnel Services State Office Bldg. Topeka, KS 66612-1595	Legal Assistant 6/83 (D3 1961)	• Legal research • Draft pleadings • Compile administrative transcript • Investigation	Completion of a Legal Assistant training program of at least 60 semester hours.	$16,812 - $21,204 per year

Table 2. SUMMARY CHART—Continued.

GOVERNMENT	POSITION	RESPONSIBILITIES	QUALIFICATIONS	SALARY
KENTUCKY Dept. of Personnel Capitol Annex Frankfort, KY 40601	Law Clerk 7/16/84 (9801)	• Investigation • Help attorney prepare documents • Legal research • Deliver subpoenas • File pleadings	College degree with a minor in paralegal studies <u>OR</u> Completion of a 2-year paralegal studies program <u>OR</u> 24 law school credits	$13,668 - $21,912 per year
LOUISIANA Dept. of Civil Service P.O. Box 44111 Capitol Station Baton Rouge, LA 70804	Legal Research Assistant 12/12/61 (7049)	• Undertake legal research • Prepare legal summaries and legal memoranda • Prepare cases for court • Draft pleadings • Prepare informational material for the courts and other law enforcement officials on legislation affecting the department operations • Keep the law library current	3 years of college plus 1 year of law school <u>OR</u> Graduation from a curriculum that combines law and arts and sciences, geology, or business	$12,084 - $18,192 per year
MAINE Dept. of Personnel State Office Bldg. State House Station 4 Augusta, ME 04333	Para Legal Assistant (0016, 02025, 119.267-026, 2051, 0979, 20F)	• Assist attorney in title search • Legal research • Assist attorney at hearings	4 years of college and 1 year of paralegal experience <u>OR</u> Graduation from an approved paralegal course	$14,622 - $19,552 per year

Other positions to check in Maine:
Legal Researcher (0018, 02045, 0979, 20E)
Law Clerk (secretarial position with paralegal duties)(0061, 41255, 202.362-014, 0380, 0880, 18R)

Table 2. SUMMARY CHART—Continued.

GOVERNMENT	POSITION	RESPONSIBILITIES	QUALIFICATIONS	SALARY
MARYLAND Dept. of Personnel 301 West Preston St. Baltimore, MD 21201	Legal Assistant I 10/31/47 12/1/81 (0589) Legal Assistant II 6/1/65 12/1/81 (1292)	• Legal research • Investigation • File pleadings • Prepare affidavits of documents • Maintain docket file • Coordinate activities of law office employees	Legal Assistant I: High school diploma or GED <u>AND</u> 4 years' experience as a clerk or secretary in a law office Legal Assistant II: High school diploma or GED <u>AND</u> 1 year of experience in legal research, and document review [college paralegal training can substitute for experience]	Legal Assistant I: $13,482 - $17,637 per year Legal Assistant II: $15,546 - $20,390 per year
Other positions to check in Maryland: Legal Assistant (209, 13); Para-Legal I (e.g., Howard County Office of State's Attorney)				
MICHIGAN Dept. of Civil Service Lewis Cass Bldg. 320 South Walnut St. Box 30002 Lansing MI 48909	Paralegal III 5/81 (8020403, BA, 7)	• Legal research • Investigation • Draft legal documents • Prepare interrogatories • Digest and index laws • Serve and file legal papers	Associates degree in a paralegal program <u>OR</u> Equivalent combination of experience and education to perform the job	Pay range (023): $16,349 - $20,525 per year
Other positions to check in Michigan: Paralegal IV (8020404, BA, 7) Paralegal VB (8020405, BA, 7) Paralegal VI (8031106, BA, 7)				

Table 2. SUMMARY CHART—Continued.

GOVERNMENT	POSITION	RESPONSIBILITIES	QUALIFICATIONS	SALARY
MINNESOTA Dept. of Employee Relations 3rd Floor, Space Center 444 LaFayette Rd. St. Paul, MN 55101	Legal Technician 2/75 3/76 (17526C)	• Legal research • Prepare legal documents • Collect documents for lawyer	Completion of paralegal training program <u>OR</u> 2 years of varied paralegal experience <u>OR</u> 1 year of law school	$17,100 - $21,444 per year
Other position to check in Minnesota: Legal Text Edit Specialist (001936, 206)				
MISSISSIPPI State Personnel Board 800 Robert E. Lee Bldg. Jackson, MS 39201	Paralegal Specialist 7/83 (1848-PR 173-254, D)	• Interpret and explain laws • Assist in preparing legal documents • Review reports • Assist in referring cases for prosecution • Train and supervise staff • Legal research • Supervise cataloging of data	Bachelor's degree in paralegal studies and 1 year of experience <u>OR</u> Certification as a paralegal from an accredited 4-year college and 2 years' experience	$15,006 per year
Other position to check in Mississippi: Legal Clerk I (1962-PR 081-162, B) (clerical position with paralegal duties)				
MONTANA Dept. of Administration Personnel Division Mitchell Bldg. Rm. 130 Helena, MT 59601	Paralegal Assistant I 1/80 (119004)	• Legal research • Compile citations and references; check cites • Assemble exhibits • Explain laws • Arrange interviews and depositions • File pleadings • Supervise clerical staff	Examples of how applicant can qualify: completion of paralegal training program; education and experience equivalent to a bachelor's degree in business, economics, law, etc.	Grade 11 $7.22 - $10.06 per hour
NEBRASKA Dept. of Personnel Box 94905 Lincoln, NB 68509-4905	Legal Aide I 5/1/78 C320131	• Legal research • Proofread legal material • Help draft regulations • Help maintain hearing room, tapes, and films	Each agency sets the qualifications. 1 year of law school is suggested, but someone with paralegal training could fill the position.	$11,045 per year

Table 2. SUMMARY CHART—Continued.

GOVERNMENT	POSITION	RESPONSIBILITIES	QUALIFICATIONS	SALARY
NEW HAMPSHIRE Dept. of Personnel State House Annex Room #1 Concord, NH 03301	Paralegal 2/4/76 2/17/76 (6793-15)	• Legal research and analysis of materials for litigation • Examine contracts, agreements, and related legal documents to ensure they comply with the law • Supervise or advise legal aides and clerical employees • Develop methods for obtaining evidence and developing facts • Develop office procedures	4 years' college plus 9 semester credits in law topics, plus 6 months' experience	Grade 15 $14,527 - $17,569 per year
Other positions to check in New Hampshire: Legal Coordinator and Contracts Monitor (5668-22) Legal Research Assistant (5676-23) Legal Research Aide (5670) Legal Aide (5660-14)				
NEW JERSEY Dept. of Civil Service Div. of Classification East State and Montgomery Streets CN 310 Trenton NJ 08625	Paralegal Technician, Judiciary 8/8/79 (A17-31012)	• Help evaluate appellate briefs • Legal research • Review ethical complaints • Administrative and coordination responsibilities	Bachelor's degree and 1 year of experience with legal documents	$16,081 - $22,794 per year
Other positions to check in New Jersey: Paralegal Technician, Law and Public Safety (A17-30461) Paralegal Technician, Casino Control Commission (X17-98648) Research Analyst (A18-03171) Research Analyst - Civil Service (A18-03171) Supervising Research Analyst - Div. of Youth and Fam. Services (A28-03184B) Senior Research Analyst (A21-03172) Principal Research Analyst (A24-03173)				

Table 2. SUMMARY CHART—Continued.

GOVERNMENT	POSITION	RESPONSIBILITIES	QUALIFICATIONS	SALARY
NEW MEXICO State Personnel Office 130 So. Capitol Santa Fe, NM 87501	Legal Assistant I 8/29/79 (1330)	• Legal research • Help prepare legal documents • Serve legal papers • Prepare and maintain records • Handle routine legal correspondence	Education and legal experience equaling 4 years	$13,236 - $21,576 per year
NEW YORK Dept. of Civil Service State Office Bldg. Campus Albany, NY 12239	Legal Assistant I 2/10/84 (26-182)	• Compile and organize documents • Help prepare legal documents and forms • Respond to inquiries and complaints • Maintain tickler system • Monitor legislation • Legal research	Associates degree in paralegal studies or completion of general practice legal specialty training __AND__ pass a test on law and procedure	$17,563 per year
Other positions to check in New York: Legal Assistant Trainee I (00-107) Legal Assistant II (25-183)				
NORTH CAROLINA Office of State Personnel 116 West Jones St. Raleigh, NC 27611	Paralegal I 6/82 (NC 1422) (1NCAC 8G.0402)	• Draft legal instruments • Prepare routine opinions • Handle complaints and inquiries from the public • Administer the law office • Legal research	Graduation from a certified paralegal school and 1 year of paralegal experience	$15,780 - $23,616 per year
NORTH DAKOTA Personnel Office 1000 East Divide Ave. Box 1537 Bismarck, ND 58502	Legal Assistant I 4/79 (0107)	• Legal research • Maintain case files • Maintain law library • Assist attorneys in litigation • General secretarial duties	2 years of college in business law and office management __AND__ 1 year of office management experience	$12,636 - $18,516 per year

Table 2. SUMMARY CHART—Continued.

GOVERNMENT	POSITION	RESPONSIBILITIES	QUALIFICATIONS	SALARY
OHIO Dept. of Administrative Services Div. of Personnel 30 E. Broad Street Columbus, OH 43215	Legal Aide 8/84 (63810)	• Legal research • Investigation • Draft legal documents • Draft responses to legal questions • Assist attorneys at hearings • File legal papers • Maintain legal records	Courses in legal research, issue recognition, legal analysis, evidence, civil procedure, etc. OR Completion of certified college paralegal program	$6.49 - $7.96 per hour
OREGON Executive Dept. Personnel Div. 155 Cottage St. N.E. Salem, OR 97310	Legal Assistant 6/80 (C0680) (in Public Defender's Office)	• Legal research • Prepare simple briefs • Interview inmates • Type drafts of briefs • May present oral arguments in the Court of Appeals and Supreme Court	Experience and training that demonstrates the knowledge and skills required for the position	
Other positions to check in Oregon: Investigator (C1031) Special Investigator (X1032)				
PENNSYLVANIA Office of Administration Bureau of Personnel 517 Finance Bldg. Harrisburg, PA 17120	Legal Assistant I 4/84 (0701)	• Review work of field personnel for inconsistencies with law • Summarize cases • Prepare reports	1 year of experience as legal assistant trainee OR 4 years' experience in clerical work, investigation, or enforcement	$14,259 - $18,875 per year
Other positions to check in Pennsylvania: Legal Assistant Trainee Legal Assistant II Legal Assistant III Legal Assistant IV				

Table 2. SUMMARY CHART—Continued.

GOVERNMENT	POSITION	RESPONSIBILITIES	QUALIFICATIONS	SALARY
SOUTH CAROLINA Budget and Control Board Division of Human Resource Management 1205 Pendleton St. P.O. Box 12547 Columbia, SC 29211	Paralegal Assistant I 4/84 (2066)	• Obtain and assemble witness statements, reports, and exhibits • Draft and proofread pleadings • Maintain tickler system • Assist in document control	Certification from an ABA-approved paralegal program OR High school diploma and 1 year of experience with a SC attorney	$15,388 - $21,810 per year
TENNESSEE Dept. of Personnel 1st Floor, James K. Polk Bldg. 505 Deaderick St. Nashville, TN 37219-5185	Legal Assistant 7/1/84 (02350)	• Legal research, e.g., cite checking • Draft regulations • Maintain law library • Answer routine inquiries on laws and regulations	Completion of an ABA-approved curriculum in paralegal studies	$13,536 - $20,124 per year
TEXAS Attorney General of Texas Supreme Court Bldg. Austin, TX 78711-2548	Administrative Technician II (Paralegal)	• Responsible and complex legal administrative duties • Interface with client Agency legal departments • Work with attorney in litigation support	High school graduation or GED and paralegal certification or 2 years' paralegal experience	$17,652 per year
VERMONT Agency of Administration Dept. of Personnel 110 State St. Montpelier, VT 05602	Paralegal Technician 9/81 (0801) (P.S.12)	• Assist attorneys in litigation • Investigation • Interview parties • Legal research • Audit records • Interpret laws • Draft briefs and legal documents	30 college credits in paralegal studies and 2 years' legal experience	$12,667 - $22,713 per year

Other position to check in Vermont:
Administrative Legal Assistant (0808, P.S.16)

Table 2. SUMMARY CHART—Continued.

GOVERNMENT	POSITION	RESPONSIBILITIES	QUALIFICATIONS	SALARY
VIRGINIA Office of Compensation Management Dept. of Personnel and Training 101 N. Fourteenth St. Richmond, VA 23219	Legal Assistant 11/1/83 (21521)	• Help supervise clerical staff • Help prepare discovery documents • Attend depositions and trials • Draft briefs and fact narratives • Legal research • Prepare witnesses • Help review agency policies	High school diploma and relevant experience (legal assistant certificate is preferred)	Grade 08 $15,118 - $20,646 per year

WASHINGTON, D.C. (See District of Columbia)

GOVERNMENT	POSITION	RESPONSIBILITIES	QUALIFICATIONS	SALARY
WASHINGTON State Dept. of Personnel P.O. Box 1789 Olympia, WA 98504	Legal Assistant - Transportation 12/11/81 12/11/83 (4669)	• Investigation • Legal research • Help draft pleadings • Help respond to discovery requests	2-year paralegal accredited training, and 2 years' paralegal experience	Pay Range: 33 $16,296 - $20,856 per year

Other position to check in Washington:
Antitrust Legal Examiner I (4661). The Office of the Attorney General is "currently involved in modifying the Antitrust Legal Examiner series to develop a generic class of Legal Assistants."

GOVERNMENT	POSITION	RESPONSIBILITIES	QUALIFICATIONS	SALARY
WEST VIRGINIA Civil Service System 1900 Washington St. East Room B-456 Charleston, WV 25305	Paralegal Assistant 10/7/74 10/21/80 (0550)	• Legal research • Abstract evidence • Supervise clerical staff • Maintain case records • Summarize legal literature • Maintain statistical records • Monitor pending legislation	Completion of approved college paralegal program OR 2 years' relevant legal experience	$12,768 - $21,372 per year
WISCONSIN Dept. of Employment Relations 149 East Wilson St. P.O. Box 7855 Madison, WI 53707-7855	Legal Assistant 1 4/79 (PR2-08)	• Abridge transcripts of testimony • Prepare appendices for appellate briefs • Paginate appeal records • Collect and organize facts for trial preparation • Draft routine pleadings • Conduct elementary research	Qualifications are determined at the time of recruitment. There must be reasonable assurance that the applicant has the skills and knowledge to perform the tasks.	$15,236 - $20,753 per year

Other positions to check in Wisconsin:
Legal Assistant 2 (PR2-09)
Legal Assistant 1 - Confidential (PR1-08) (Dept. of Justice, Attorney General)
Administrative Assistant III

VI. SPECIAL INTEREST GROUPS OR ASSOCIATIONS

Many special interest groups exist in our society: unions, business associations, environmental protection groups, taxpayer associations, consumer protection groups, trade associations, citizen action groups, etc. The larger groups have their own offices, libraries, and legal staff, including paralegals. The legal work often involves monitoring legislation, lobbying, preparing studies, etc. Direct legal services to individual members of the groups usually are not provided. The legal work relates to the needs or a cause of the organization as a whole. Occasionally, however, the legal staff will litigate test cases of individual members that have broad impact on the organization's membership.

A different concept in the use of lawyers and paralegals by such groups is "group legal services." Members of unions or of college students, for example, pay a monthly fee to the organization for which they are entitled to designated legal services, e.g., preparation of a will, divorce representation. The members pay *before* the legal problems arise. Group legal service systems are a form of legal insurance. The group legal service office will usually employ a considerable number of paralegals.

VII. CRIMINAL LAW OFFICES

Surprisingly, criminal law offices for the government (prosecutor) and for the accused (defense counsel or public defender) have *not* made extensive use of paralegals beyond the traditional investigator role. This is slowly changing, particularly due to the interest of a number of criminal law organizations in expanding paralegal use, e.g., the National Association of Attorneys General, the National Legal Aid and Defender Association. For the role of the paralegal in criminal law, see p. 78.

A prosecution paralegal is a government employee. Paralegals who work for defense offices, however, are similar to paralegals who work for legal service offices (p. 46). The offices receive government grants to represent the poor. Fees are not paid. The defense paralegals are not government employees even though their salaries usually come from public funds.

VIII. FREE-LANCE PARALEGAL

A free-lance paralegal is someone who works on his/her own. S/he sells legal services *to lawyers* on a part-time basis. Such paralegals are called independent contractors. The paralegal will usually come to the lawyer's office, although a few free-lancers work out of their own offices. Occasionally, a group of paralegals will form a corporation and advertise its services to law firms through the local legal newspaper. For example:

> Improve the quality and
> ****cost-effectiveness****
> of your practice with the help of:
> **LAWYER'S ASSISTANT, INC.**

Figure 2 Sample job description for paralegal in Legal Service Office
(See p. 46)

GULF COAST LEGAL FOUNDATION
2912 Luell Street, Houston, Texas 77093
March 30, 1978

POSITIONS OPEN FOR PARALEGALS EXPERIENCED IN WELFARE

The Gulf Coast Legal Foundation, formerly the Houston Legal Foundation, has three positions open for paralegals with experience in welfare law. However if experienced persons do not apply, we will seriously consider applicants with no more educational qualifications than a GED. We are discouraging law students and law graduates from applying. Our program has five neighborhood offices in Houston and Galveston and will expand to Fort Bend and Brazoria Counties. Our paralegals are assigned to specialty units. These positions are for the welfare unit whose goals our planner has set at increasing the number of AFDC (Aid to Families with Dependent Children) families by 12,000 in the county and increasing the number of SSI (Supplemental Social Security Income) recipients by 1,500 in the county as well as increasing the level of benefits. The welfare unit represents the local welfare rights organization, which has ten years of history, parent councils of Title XX day care centers, and in cooperation with another unit, groups of handicapped people. The paralegal would maintain a direct service caseload of state welfare appeals and SSI hearings as well as some unemployment, health claims, and other administrative matters. Each paralegal will be expected to handle six pending hearings and perform one research task each month after a training period of half a year. And do their own typing. The paralegal would also maintain a library of state manuals and social security materials. The paralegal would also be expected to participate in saturation leafleting, to attend some group meetings, and to perform minor educational services. The supervising attorney of the welfare unit would supervise the paralegal. The unit will have a total of five lawyers and six paralegals.

Because of inadequate public transportation, the paralegal would be responsible for transporting clients to welfare centers and maintaining a personal automobile.

Applicants should furnish their scores on the SAT or GRE exam, a writing sample, and detailed information concerning any prior legal services experience. We will weigh mathematical skills over writing skills. Our program will give preference to experienced paralegals who intend to continue a career as a paralegal. Our program has also an affirmative action program for the hiring of women and members of minority groups. Our program serves a substantial Mexican-American population and must give an additional preference to applicants who speak Spanish fluently.

The salary range can go up to the equivalent of a moderately experienced attorney.

In addition, the company may send out a mass mailing to local attorneys in which its services are briefly described. The following is an excerpt from such a letter:

> Our staff consists of individuals with undergraduate educations, formal paralegal training, and an average of five years of experience in such areas as estates and trusts, litigation, real estate, tax, and corporate law. Whether you require a real estate paralegal for one day, or four litigation paralegals for one month, we can provide you with reliable qualified paralegals to satisfy your specific needs.

A law firm may be convinced of the value of paralegals but not have enough business to justify taking on a full-time paralegal employee. A free-lance paralegal, or a company of part-time paralegals, is an alternative.

The National Federation of Paralegal Associations (see address, p. 843) recently formed a unit called the Independent Contractors Specialty Section. It publishes its own newsletter.

For an overview of how to start a free-lance business, see Appendix I, p. 901, "How to Start a Free-lance Paralegal Business," by Linda Harrington, one of the pioneers in this area.

IX. SERVICE COMPANIES/CONSULTING FIRMS

Within the last few years, we have seen increased employment of paralegals by numerous service companies and consulting firms that sell services to law firms. Examples of such services include:

- Incorporating a new company in all fifty states;
- Conducting a trademark search;
- Undertaking a UCC (Uniform Commercial Code) search and filing in all fifty states;
- Selecting a computer system for the office;
- Designing and managing a computer-assisted document control system for a large case;
- Helping a law firm establish a branch office;
- Designing a filing or financial system for the office;
- Billing all the clients of the office.

In order to accomplish such tasks, these service companies and consulting firms recruit highly specialized staffs of management experts, accountants, economists, former administrators, etc. More and more paralegals are joining these staffs, particularly paralegals with prior law office experience.

X. RELATED FIELDS

Experienced paralegals have also been using their training and experience in a number of nonpractice legal fields. Many are becoming law librarians at firms. Almost all the paralegal training schools hire paralegals to teach courses and to work in administration, e.g., admissions, internship coordination, placement, etc. Law offices with large numbers of paralegals have hired paralegal administrators or supervisors to help recruit, train, and manage the paralegals (p. 29). Some paralegals have become general legal administrators or office managers with administrative responsibilities throughout the firm.

It is clear that we have not seen the end of the development of new roles for paralegals within the law firm or in related areas of the law.

Section C. PARALEGAL SPECIALITIES: A DICTIONARY OF FUNCTIONS

We now examine forty-seven specialty areas of work throughout the ten categories of paralegal employment discussed above. This listing of the specialties is not meant to suggest that paralegals work in only one of the specialties. There is considerable overlap in the functions performed. The trend, however, is for paralegals to work in specialty areas. This follows the pattern of lawyers, most of whom also tend to specialize.

PARALEGAL SPECIALTIES

(The number in parenthesis is the page where the specialty is treated in the chapter.)

1. Administrative law (64)
2. Admiralty law (65)
3. Antitrust law (65)
4. Banking law (66)
5. Bankruptcy law (67)
6. Change of name law (68)
7. Children, law of (68)
8. Civil rights law (70)
9. Commercial law (collections) (71)
10. Communications law (71)
11. Construction claims (72)
12. Consumer law (72)
13. Contract law (75)
14. Copyright law (75)
15. Corporate law (76)
16. Criminal law (78)
17. Domestic relations law (85)
18. Education law (87)
19. Employee benefits law (88)
20. Employment law (89)
21. Government contract law (90)
22. Health law (91)
23. Immigration law (92)
24. Insurance law (92)
25. International law (93)
26. Labor law (93)
27. Landlord-tenant law (93)
28. Law office administration (96)
29. Legislation (97)
30. Litigation (98)
31. Lobbying (99)
32. Military law (100)
33. Motor vehicle law (101)
34. Oil and gas law (101)
35. Parajudge (102)
36. Partnership law (102)
37. Patent law (103)
38. Post-conviction and corrections (prison) law (103)
39. Real estate law (105)
40. Tax law (107)
41. Tort law (108)
42. Trademark law (108)
43. Tribal law (108)
44. Trusts, estates, and probate law (109)
45. Unemployment compensation law (110)
46. Welfare law (111)
47. Worker's compensation law (114)

Note: Paralegal in the White House (115)

1. ADMINISTRATIVE LAW

I. Government Employee
(See job duties for paralegal in federal government, p. 43, and in state government, p. 48.) Many paralegals work for specific administrative agencies.

A. Handle citizen questions and complaints.
B. Draft proposed regulations and statutes for the agency.
C. Legal research.
D. Litigation assistance.
E. Law office management.
F. Supervise and train other personnel.

II. Representation of Citizens
Paralegals also work for law firms that represent citizens before particular agencies, e.g., U.S. Patent Office (p. 226), welfare departments (p. 111). Some of these agencies permit nonlawyers to represent clients before them (p. 226, p. 865). Paralegals working for legal service and legal aid offices (p. 46) often take advantage of this authorization.

A. Investigation.
B. Legal research.
C. Informal advocacy before agency officials (p. 773).
D. Formal advocacy at agency hearings (p. 787).
E. Drafting "pleadings" for litigation in the agency.
F. Monitoring activities of the agency, e.g., attend rule-making hearings to take notes on matters relevant to particular clients (p. 668).
G. Lobbying, e.g., preparing reports, witnesses, and exhibits designed to influence the writing of regulations (p. 99).

2. ADMIRALTY LAW
This area of the law covers accidents, injuries, or death connected with vessels on navigable waters. Special legislation exists for this area, e.g., the Jones Act, the Longshoremen and Harbor Worker's Compensation Act.

I. Investigation

A. Obtain the facts of the events involved.
B. Arrange to board the vessel to photograph the scene of the accident.
C. Collect facts relevant to the seaworthiness of the vessel.

II. Legal Research

A. Special procedures for seeking compensation.
B. Liability under the statutes.

III. Litigation
(See p. 98.)

3. ANTITRUST LAW

I. Document Control

    A. Pleadings.
    B. Deposition testimony.
    C. Interrogatories.
    D. Special exhibits.

  II. Indexing/Digesting the Above Documents (p. 489)

  III. Draft Pleadings

  IV. Investigation

    A. Statistical data, e.g., market analysis.
    B. Corporate structure.

  V. Legal Research

    A. Price fixing.
    B. Monopolies.
    C. Mergers that restrict or eliminate competition.
    D. Market allocation.
    E. The Federal Trade Commission Act.

4. BANKING LAW

  I. Claims
  Assist legal staff in assessing bank liability for various claims, e.g., negligence, collection abuse.

  II. Compliance Analysis
  Determine whether the bank is complying with the regulations and statutes that regulate the banking industry.

  III. Monitoring
  Keep track of the activities of the various bank regulatory agencies and of the legislative committees with jurisdiction over banks.

  IV. Litigation
  Assist attorneys litigating claims (p. 98).

  V. Miscellaneous

    A. Draft and/or review loan application and accompanying credit documents.
    B. Document analysis
      1. Mortgage.
      2. Assignments.
      3. Security agreements.

C. Conduct UCC (Uniform Commercial Code) searches.
D. Assemble closing documents.
E. Arrange for closing.
F. Prepare notarization of documents.
G. Monitor recordation.

5. BANKRUPTCY LAW

I. Initial Interview
Meet with client to go over extensive questionnaire on assets and liabilities.

II. Investigation

A. Confirm amounts of indebtedness.
B. Identify secured and unsecured claims of creditors.
C. Check UCC (Uniform Commercial Code) filings at the secretary of state's office and at county clerk's office.
D. Check real property records in the clerk's office of the county where the property is located.
E. Verify taxes owed; identify tax liens.
F. Identify exempt property.

III. Asset Control

A. Open bankruptcy file.
B. Prepare inventories of assets and liabilities.
C. Arrange for valuation of assets.

IV. Creditor Contact

A. Answer inquiries of creditors on the status of the case.
B. Request documentation from creditors on claims.

V. Drafting

A. Original bankruptcy petition.
B. Schedule of liabilities.
C. Statement of affairs.
D. Chapter 13 statement.
E. Final account.

VI. Coordination

A. With trustee in bankruptcy.
B. Meeting of creditors.

6. CHANGE OF NAME LAW

I. Preliminary Interview

A. Explain the reasons the state will allow a change of name.
B. Explain the procedures for changing a name.

II. Record Gathering
Assist the client in obtaining necessary documents (e.g., certified birth certificate, criminal record, if any, judgments outstanding against client, consent forms, etc.)

III. Drafting

A. Assist the client in filling out the application form.
B. Make a preliminary draft of the pleadings required in contested and uncontested change-of-name court actions.

IV. Filing/Service

A. File applications and pleadings in court.
B. Serve same on individuals and organizations required.

7. LAW OF CHILDREN (ADOPTION, CHILD ABUSE, CUSTODY, PATERNITY, JUVENILE DELINQUENCY)
(See also domestic relations, p. 85.)

I. Problem Identification

A. Preliminary interview.
1. Identify nonlegal problems for referral to other agencies.
2. Open a case file or update it.
3. Using a basic fact sheet (or form), record the information collected during the interview.
4. Determine next appointment.
5. Instruct client on what to do next, e.g., obtain medical and birth records, etc.
B. Adoption.
1. Adult (nonparent) wants to adopt child of spouse.
2. Parent or relative wants to contest the attempt of another adult to adopt the child.
3. Adult wants to know if a prior "adoption" was legal.
4. Adoptee wishes to determine the identity of his/her natural parents.
C. Custody.
1. Adult wants legal custody of child, but does not want to adopt.
2. Adult wants to contest the custody of child now under the control of another adult or institution.

D. Child abuse/neglect.
   1. Parent/guardian has been served with a child abuse or neglect citation.
   2. Parent/guardian wants to appeal an adjudication of neglect.
   3. Adult wants to initiate a child abuse or neglect petition against the parent/guardian.
E. Termination of parental rights.
   1. Parent is served with a termination petition and wants to defend.
   2. Parent wants to appeal a court-ordered termination of parental rights.
F. Support.
   Custodial parent wants the other parent to contribute more child support due to a modification in financial circumstances.
G. Paternity.
   1. Parent wants to declare paternity.
   2. Parent wants to challenge an adult's denial of paternity.
   3. Adult wants to challenge a claim of paternity against him.
H. Juvenile delinquency.
   1. Parent/guardian wants to institute delinquency petition against child in Juvenile or Family Court.
   2. Parent wants to contest a delinquency petition brought against child in court by someone else, e.g., school, child welfare agency, etc.
   3. Child has been institutionalized under prior delinquency order and parent wants:
      a. Better visitation rights.
      b. Better rehabilitation programs at institution.
      c. Child to come home more often.
      d. Child to be discharged.

II. Problem Resolution

A. Consult with attorney immediately.
   1. Summarize facts for attorney.
   2. Submit the case record to attorney.
   3. Obtain further instructions from attorney.
B. Referral of nonlegal problems to other agencies.
   1. Give name and address of agency to client.
   2. Search for an appropriate agency.
   3. Contact agency for client.
C. Client counseling.
   Help the client identify and consider all factors involved (e.g., support capabilities, welfare options, health of child, health of adults involved, desires of child, consequences of institutionalization, etc.)
D. Time determinations.
   1. Determine whether client has a court date on which to appear.

2. Determine whether client is already in default.
E. Investigation.
Search for and check official records, e.g., birth, death, support, adoption, etc.
F. Informal advocacy/negotiation/mediation.
   1. Call the parties involved into the office to give them the opportunity to "talk it out" in an attempt to reach an informal resolution.
   2. Contact (e.g., call, visit, write letters to, etc.) the administrative agencies involved (e.g., child welfare bureau, probation department) in order to assess the possibilities of resolving the problems without court action.
G. Preliminary drafting.
   1. Adoption pleadings.
   2. Custody petitions, answers to custody petitions.
   3. Paternity petitions.
   4. Child abuse/neglect/delinquency petitions and answers.
H. Placement.
Assist the client in obtaining placement information (e.g., foster care, private home, etc.) and in making a placement decision.
I. Litigation.
   1. Act as court witness.
   2. Act as general litigation assistant during court proceedings (e.g., monitor and index all files).
   3. Prepare interrogatories (or answers thereto).
   4. Digest depositions and write file profiles.
   5. Legal research.

III. Miscellaneous

A. Write community education pamphlets on child law issues.
B. Train other paralegals in the office system of handling child law cases.
C. Provide general assistance (e.g., training) to community groups organized around child law issues.

8. CIVIL RIGHTS LAW

I. Government Paralegal

A. Help identify and resolve discrimination complaints (based on sex, race, age) made by government employees against the government.
B. Help government attorneys litigate discrimination complaints (based on sex, race, age) brought by citizens against the government, against other citizens, or against companies.

II. Representation of Citizens
Assist law firms representing citizens in their discrimination complaints (based on sex, race, age) against the government, other citizens, or companies.

A. In court.
B. In special agencies created to hear discrimination cases, e.g., the Equal Employment Opportunities Commission, Human Rights Commission.

9. COMMERCIAL LAW (COLLECTIONS)[18]
(See also bankruptcy law, p. 67.)

I. Acceptance of Claims

A. Open file.
B. Prepare index of parties.
C. Prepare inventory of debts of debtor.

II. Investigation

A. Conduct asset check.
B. Verify address.
C. Verify filings at secretary of state's office and county clerk's office (e.g., UCC filings).
D. Contact credit bureau.
E. Verify information in probate court, registry of deeds, etc.

III. Litigation Assistant (Civil Court, Small Claims Court)

A. Draft pleadings.
B. Arrange for witnesses.
C. File documents in court.
D. Assist in settlement/negotiation of claim.
E. Enforcement work.
   1. Wage attachment (pre-judgment attachment).
   2. Supplementary process.
   3. Execution.
   4. Seizure of personal property.

10. COMMUNICATIONS LAW

I. Government Paralegal
Assist attorneys in the Federal Communications Commission (FCC) in the work of regulating the communications industry, e.g., rule-making, license applications, hearings.

---

[18] See Commercial Law League of America, Seminar, *A Paralegal Approach to the Practice of Commercial Law* (11/14/75).

II. Representation of Citizens or Companies

A. Draft applications for licenses.
B. Prepare compliance reports.
C. Prepare exemption applications.
D. Prepare statistical analyses.
E. Monitor activities of the FCC.
F. Assist in litigation.
   1. Within the FCC.
   2. In court.

11. CONSTRUCTION CLAIMS

I. Work with engineering consultants in the preparation of claims.

II. Data collection.

A. Daily manpower hours.
B. Amount of concrete poured.
C. Change of orders.
D. Index and digest this data.

III. Graph preparation, e.g., chart with overlay.

IV. Prepare special studies, e.g., compare the planned progress with the actual progress in the construction of the project.

V. Prepare documents for negotiation/settlement.

VI. Assist in arranging for arbitration of claim.

VII. Litigation assistant.

12. CONSUMER LAW

I. Problem Identification

A. Preliminary interview.
   1. Identify nonlegal problems for referral to other agencies.
   2. Open a case file or update it.
   3. Using a basic fact sheet (or form), record the information collected during the interview.
   4. Determine next appointment.
   5. Instruct client on what to do next, e.g., bring in check stubs, copy of contract, etc.
   6. Arrange for client to see office attorney.
B. The identification of crisis problems that require immediate attention.

1. The client's utilities have been shut off (or will be shut off shortly).
2. The client's wages have been garnisheed (or soon will be).
3. The client's furniture (clothing, car, etc.) has been repossessed (or soon will be).
4. The client has just suffered a default judgment (or will do so shortly if the client does not appear in court).
5. A collection agency is causing the client considerable stress.
6. The client lost credit cards.
7. The client's automobile liability insurance has been suspended.
8. The client has been told by a department store (supermarket, etc.) that s/he will no longer be extended credit.

C. The identification of consumer law problems that may not involve immediate crisis.
1. The client disputes a gas/electric/phone bill.
2. Client is dissatisfied with the gas/electric/phone service.
3. The client is told that s/he must make a large deposit before any of the utilities will be turned on.
4. Client has received defective goods.
5. Client bought goods from a merchant on credit; the goods were defective; client complained to the merchant; merchant referred client to collection agency; agency tells client that it has nothing to do with the claimed defect in the goods; agency demands immediate payment.
6. Repair work (auto, TV, washer, etc.) has been unsatisfactory.
7. An insurance company (auto, fire, liability, etc.) refuses to honor a client's claim.
8. The client is inundated with personal (or small business) debts.
9. Client has not received goods ordered and paid for.

II. Problem Resolution

A. Consult with attorney immediately.
1. Summarize facts for attorney.
2. Submit case file to attorney.
3. Obtain further instructions from the attorney.
B. Referral of nonlegal problems to other agencies.
1. Give names and address of agency to client.
2. Search for appropriate agency.
3. Contact agency for client.
C. Time determinations.
1. Determine whether a court appearance has been already scheduled.
2. Determine if any time exists before wages are garnisheed.
3. Determine if any time exists before goods are repossessed.
4. Determine if any time exists in which the client-buyer can rescind a sale.

5. Determine if the client has a certain period in which to complain about defective goods or services.

6. Determine whether the merchant has a time period within which it must take action on a complaint made by a consumer.

D. Investigation.

1. Locate names and addresses of merchants.

2. Make a site visit to examine goods alleged to be defective.

3. Conduct spot verification of merchant advertising.

4. Assist the client in compiling a list of debtors/creditors.

5. Go to government agencies such as insurance bureau, licensing bureau, etc., to collect data on certain merchants.

6. Interview individuals in a neighborhood for an attorney who needs specified information for a possible class action.

E. Informal advocacy/negotiation.

Contact (e.g., call on phone, ask for a meeting, write a letter to, etc.) a wide variety of individuals or organizations (e.g., merchant, bank employer, insurance company, collection agency, credit bureau, utility company, court clerk, repair service, etc.) in order to attempt an informal resolution of the problems outlined above.

F. Contact other consumer advocates for help.

1. Contact the Consumer Fraud Division of the Attorney-General's Office.

2. Contact community consumer groups.

3. Contact Complaint Department of Mayor's Office or of other political office.

4. Contact the Federal Trade Commission or other federal agencies.

G. Drafting.

1. Bankruptcy forms.

2. Complaints to government agencies, e.g., licensing bureaus.

H. Client counseling.

1. Does the client want to declare bankruptcy?

2. Personal budget counseling.

I. Establishing defenses and counterclaims.

Assist the client in the articulation and documentation of defenses to the actions against him/her, (e.g., defective goods as a defense to nonpayment) and of claims that the client may have against the merchant.

J. Litigation.

1. Service of process.

2. Act as court witness.

3. General litigation assistant, e.g., monitor all files.

4. Legal research: shepardizing.

5. Legal research: brief writing.

K. Small Claims Court.

1. Inform the community about the availability and function of Small Claims Court.

2. Assist citizens in the preparation of their cases before the Small Claims Court.
3. Argue the case for the client before the arbitration branch of the Small Claims Court.

L. Miscellaneous.
1. Train other paralegals in the office to handle consumer cases.
2. Train community groups on consumer law.
3. Write community education pamphlets on consumer law.

13. CONTRACT LAW

The law of contracts is involved in a number of different paralegal specialties: antitrust law (p. 65), banking law (p. 66), bankruptcy law (p. 67), commercial law (p. 71), consumer law (p. 72), construction claims (p. 72), corporate law (p. 76), copyright law (p. 75), domestic relations law (p. 85), employee benefits law (p. 88), employment law (p. 89), government contract law (p. 90), insurance law (p. 92), international law (p. 93), landlord-tenant law (p. 93), oil and gas law (p. 101), partnership law (p. 102), real estate law (p. 105), tax law (p. 107), etc. The main activities of paralegals in contract law are as follows:

I. Investigation of facts involving alleged breach of contract.

II. Legal research on the law of contracts in the particular area of the specialty.

III. Litigation assistance in the trial of the breach-of-contract case.

IV. Preparation of form contracts, e.g., separation agreements, contracts for sale.

14. COPYRIGHT LAW

(See also patent law, p. 103, trademark law, p. 108.)

I. Application

A. Assist the client to apply for registration of copyright for a novel, play, or other work with the Copyright Office.
B. Collect data for the application, e.g., nature of the work, date completed, name of creator/author, name of the owner of the work, etc.
C. Help identify the classification for the copyright.
D. Examine the certificate of copyright registration for accuracy.
E. File the application.

II. Marketing

A. Identify potential users/licensees of the copyright.
B. Contract preparation.

III. Infringement

    A. Investigation to determine whether an infringement exists, e.g., compare the copyrighted work with the alleged infringing work.
    B. General litigation assistantship.

15. CORPORATE LAW
(See also Real Estate Law, p. 107.)

    I. Incorporation and General Corporate Work

        A. Preincorporation.
          1. Check availability of proposed corporate name and, if available, reserve it.
          2. Draft preincorporation subscriptions and consent forms for initial board of directors where required by statute.
          3. Record Articles of Incorporation.
          4. Order corporate supplies.
        B. Incorporation.
          1. Draft and file Articles of Incorporation with appropriate state agency:
            a. Sub-chapter S corporation.
            b. Close corporation.
            c. Non-profit corporation
          2. Draft minutes of initial meetings of incorporators and directors.
          3. Draft corporate by-laws.
          4. Obtain corporate seal, minute book, and stock certificate book.
          5. Prepare necessary documents to open a corporate bank account.
        C. Directors' meetings.
          1. Prepare and send out waivers and notices of meetings.
          2. Draft minutes of directors' meetings.
          3. Draft resolutions to be considered by directors.
            a. Sale of stock.
            b. Increase in capitalization.
            c. Stock splits.
            d. Stock option.
            e. Pension plan.
            f. Dividend distribution.
            g. Election of officers.
        D. Shareholders' meetings (annual and special).
          1. Draft sections of annual report relating to business activity, officers, and directors of company.
          2. Draft notice of meeting, proxy materials, and ballots.
          3. Prepare agenda and script of meeting.
          4. Draft oath and report of judge of elections when required.

E. Drafting and general document preparation.
   1. See drafting above in reference to directors' and shareholders' meetings.
   2. Shareholder agreement.
   3. Stock option plan.
   4. Trust agreement.
   5. Tax returns
   6. Closing papers on corporate acquisition.
   7. Employment agreements.

II. Public Sale of Securities

   A. Compile information concerning officers and directors for use in Registration Statement.
   B. Assist in research of Blue Sky requirements.
   C. Closing.
      1. Prepare agenda
      2. Obtain certificates from state agencies with respect to good standing of company and certified corporate documents.
      3. Prepare index and organize closing binders.

III. Research

   A. Legislative reporting: keep track of pending legislation that may affect office clients.
   B. Summarize/digest files; prepare a case profile.
   C. Extract designated information from corporate records and documents.
   D. Assemble financial data from records on file at SEC and state securities regulatory agencies.
   E. Undertake statistical and financial research on companies.
   F. Legal research.

IV. General Assistantship

   A. Maintain "tickler" system (e.g., specifying next corporate meeting, upcoming trial, appellate court dates).
   B. Monitor the daily law journal or newspaper (e.g., specifying certain cases on calendars of courts, current court decisions, articles, etc.) and forward such data in the journal or newspaper to appropriate office attorneys.
   C. Act as file managers of certain clients (index, monitor documents in the file, etc.).
   D. Maintain corporate forms file.

V. Miscellaneous

   A. Prepare documents for qualification to do business in foreign jurisdictions.

B. Prepare filings with regulatory agencies.
C. Assist in processing patent, copyright, and trademark applications.
D. Coordinate escrow transactions.
E. Work on Certificates of Occupancy.
F. Prepare documents needed to amend Bylaws or Articles of Incorporation.
G. Prepare interrogatories.
H. Digest deposition testimony.
I. Check citations.

16. CRIMINAL LAW[19]
   (See also p. 358, p. 466.)

   I. Paralegals Working for Prosecutors

   A. Case review: the paralegal helps the prosecutor screen out inappropriate arrest cases, draw up prosecution charges in others, and identify cases warranting special attention.
      1. Log all incoming cases, noting the officer(s), defendant(s), arrest charge(s), and charges filed, if any.
      2. Check police officer's forms and records to ensure that rap sheet and all necessary papers are assembled.
      3. Check for detainers and outstanding warrants against each arrestee.
      4. Check the disposition of earlier cases indicated on arrestee's rap sheet.
      5. Route the officer and witnesses, if any, to the next available and appropriate DA.
      6. Prepare monthly reports.
   B. Police Liaison: the paralegal works closely with law enforcement officers, reviews their cases as they are submitted to the DA, suggests investigative leads and techniques, and performs troubleshooting between the two agencies.
   C. Diversion: the paralegal helps to identify arrestees that are eligible for informal or formal programs diverting their cases out of the criminal justice system, and monitors their adherence to the conditions of the diversion thereafter.
      1. Perform a daily review of arrestees to identify eligible participants according to written guidelines.
      2. Serve as a point of contact for "outside" referrals, e.g., from police officers or defense counsel.
      3. Assess agencies to which diverted arrestees have been referred; augment these by locating additional appropriate agencies.
      4. Monitor arrestees' progress in the diversion program.

[19] Stein, J. Hoff, B., *Paralegals and Administrative Assistants for Prosecutors* (National District Attorneys Association, 1974). Stein, J., *Paralegals: A Resource for Defenders and Correctional Services* (1976).

5. Formulate recommendations to the DA on whether to prosecute or dismiss cases that have been in diversion status for the specified period of time.

6. Prepare statistical reports on cases considered for diversion.

D. Citizen Complaints: the paralegal interviews citizens seeking the prosecution of alleged wrongdoers, refers their cases to appropriate agencies, or conducts a mediation hearing between the disputants.

1. Interview the complainant and prepare a case file; make a name check against files of prior complainants and respondents; in appropriate cases, examine the respondent's rap sheet.

2. Refer cases seeming to involve serious criminal conduct to a DA and/or the police detective bureau. Refer cases needing civil legal assistance to Legal Aid or the private bar, or to Small Claims Court. Refer purely nonlegal cases to appropriate community agencies.

3. Of the remaining cases, determine which are appropriate for resolution through arbitration or mediation procedures. With the consent of the complainant, schedule hearing date and so notify the respondent.

4. Conduct an arbitration or mediation hearing.

5. Prepare an index of cases, to better monitor the incidence of repeat complainants and respondents; prepare monthly statistical reports on cash flow and case disposition.

E. Consumer Fraud: the paralegal assists in the resolution of minor consumer complaints brought into the office and/or assists the DA in ferreting out, investigating, and prosecuting major white-collar crimes.

1. Citizen-initiated complaints.

   a. Interview the complainant and prepare a case file; make a name check against files of prior complainants and respondents.

   b. Refer cases not covered by the DA's civil or criminal jurisdiction to appropriate agencies (e.g., Legal Aid or the private bar, social service agencies, etc.) under attorney supervision or pursuant to written standards.

   c. In the remaining cases, have the complainant fill out a brief allegation of the facts.

   d. In appropriate cases, under attorney supervision, seek immediate resolution of the problem either by counseling the complainant or calling the business involved.

   e. In more serious cases, draft a letter to the business for the prosecutor's signature, setting out the allegation and requesting a response.

   f. When appropriate, follow the letter with a hearing between the parties to seek a just settlement.

   g. In cases where no resolution is effected, or where, from the outset, a serious incident or pattern of fraud is indicated, order or conduct a field investigation, upon the authorization of the supervising prosecutor.

    h. When appropriate, draft formal civil or criminal complaint and route this, with the case file, to the supervising prosecutor for further proceedings.

    i. Prepare an index of cases; prepare a monthly statistical report on case flow, case disposition, and monetary value of recovery effected in each case.

  2. Fraud case preparation.

    a. Generally perform case preparation functions (see "J" below).

    b. Undertake or coordinate investigations (possibly using volunteers) based on newspaper ads, field inspections, tests as potential buyers of goods and services, etc.

    c. Locate potential witnesses.

    d. Secure documentary evidence.

    e. Prepare statistical reports on case flow.

F. Nonsupport and URESA: the paralegal helps mothers obtain court-ordered child support payments under local statutes or the Uniform Reciprocal Enforcement of Support Act (URESA).

  1. Interview the complainant and fill out the nonsupport or URESA petition if the case falls within the DA's written criteria.

  2. Route the draft petition to a prosecutor for filing or mailing.

  3. Follow up on status of the case, and keep complainant informed.

  4. Monitor defendant payments on incoming URESAs, and check to see if the defendant is actually in noncompliance when a complainant requests a contempt citation.

  5. In appropriate cases, write defendant to direct the payment of arrearages and resumption of regular support; failing voluntary compliance, prepare petition for the prosecutor to file.

  6. Monitor selected defendants' payments, and contact them as soon as they become delinquent.

  7. Prepare case flow, disposition, and monetary impact reports.

G. Bad Checks: the paralegal assists citizens and merchants secure restitution when they have been unlawfully victimized with bad checks.

  1. Advise payees of the pre-conditions of the office's help, e.g., a ten-day or fifteen-day notification by certified mail to the payor, a showing that proper identification has been obtained from the payor, or that the payee can, in fact, identify the defendant, etc.

  2. When pre-conditions are met, prepare a complaint for immediate filing by a prosecutor.

  3. In other cases, prepare and send a directive of compliance to the payor, and, with the remainder, send a follow-up letter; in

the rest of the cases, prepare a formal complaint for the prosecutor to file.

4. When restitution is made, obtain a release from the citizen or merchant.

5. Prepare case flow, disposition, and monetary impact reports.

H. Calendaring: the paralegal serves as an aide to the prosecutor in Calendar Court, to improve the government's case in requesting a delay or adjournment, to record more accurately the results of proceedings in that court, and to better monitor defense requests for adjournments.

1. Examine the files of the next day's cases to ensure that all needed papers, reports, etc., are present; advise the supervising prosecutor of incomplete files.

2. Serve as the contact person with trial attorneys and police officers awaiting a calendar call to inform the Calendar Court attorney if key witnesses are missing; help to locate same; advise the supervising attorney of problems, or the need for a short delay or an adjournment.

3. Serve as a person whom defense counsel may contact if a conflicting appearance in another courtroom is anticipated.

4. Review the history of prior defense-requested adjournments in each case ready for trial; indicate those, and their reasons, to the supervising attorney.

5. Record on the case file and computer-update forms the reasons for adjournments granted in the Calendar Court; review the file and calendar to recommend a date to the supervising attorney for the re-scheduled trial.

6. When the adjournment is requested by the government, perform necessary follow-up to help ensure its readiness next time.

7. Prepare monthly case flow and adjournment reports.

I. Witness Liaison: the paralegal seeks to supply continuing contact with victims and witnesses, to help meet their special needs, and to better ensure their cooperation with the DA's office.

1. Answer inquiries on the status of cases.

2. Contact witnesses as early as possible to identify and offer assistance with problems such as transportation, babysitting, insurance claims, or emergency welfare assistance.

3. Give witnesses an orientation to the criminal justice process and a tour of the courthouse.

4. Seek victims' views, or inform victims of pleas, diversion, or dismissals, and explain the reasons therefor.

5. Telephone witnesses to arrange conferences with the prosecutor or to remind them of the forthcoming trial date.

6. Greet witnesses at trial appearance.

7. Expedite payment of witness fees.

8. Arrange accommodations, travel, and reimbursement for out-of-town witnesses.

9. Prepare periodic statistical reports.

    J. Trial Preparation: the paralegal helps prepare cases for trial.
      1. Following a checklist, ensure that all necessary papers are in the case file, such as the preliminary hearing transcript, police reports, and lab reports.
      2. Handle telephone calls from police officers and lay witnesses, and relay the attorney's response.
      3. Prepare a list of potential witnesses, how they may be contacted, and what they can testify to.
      4. Construct a chain of possession of physical evidence, when needed.
      5. Serve as a contact point for investigators who have been asked to perform further investigation by the prosecutor, contact police officers at the prosecutor's behest.
      6. Contact potential witnesses and report their statements to the prosecutor to determine if s/he wants to interview them.
      7. Assist the prosecutor to identify and have on file defendant and witness statements, exculpatory evidence, or other items that may have to be shown to defense counsel.
      8. Assist the prosecutor at trial.
  II. Paralegals Working for Defense Attorneys
    A. Determination of eligibility.
      1. Interview all defendants recently arrested, whether or not currently detained, to obtain required information as to income, employment status, number of dependants, and anything else that is taken into consideration in deciding eligibility for free legal assistance from the office.
      2. Verify, by telephone calls to family members or by other means, the accuracy of the information given by those who appear eligible for free legal assistance.
      3. Certify the eligibility of those who meet the standards for free legal assistance.
    B. Arranging for bail.
      1. Obtain from eligible clients all relevant information on the question of setting bail. In jurisdictions where a bail agency collects this information, the paralegal obtains a copy of the interview sheet, and, if possible, reviews it for accuracy with the client, and independently seeks to verify the information by telephone calls to family, employers, etc. Where no bail agency exists, the paralegal obtains the same kind of information, using a checklist so that defense counsel may make reasoned arguments for no bail or low bail in the later hearing.
      2. Arrange for family members or others suggested by the client to appear at the bail hearing with cash, evidence of collateral, or a bondsman, in case money bail is set. Their appearance may also convince the judge of the authenticity of the defendant's community ties, thus obviating the need for bail.
      3. Arrange for representatives of narcotic or alcohol addiction treatment agencies in the community to interview appropriate

clients, and, if the client so desires, to appear in court to indicate the client's immediate eligibility for treatment if released.

4. Arrange for ministers, employers, or representatives of community agencies to appear in court to offer to serve as "third-party custodians" of those defendants who would otherwise be ineligible for release without bail.

5. Prepare relevant statements of facts for attorneys who believe a formal appeal of a bail decision is appropriate.

C. Diversion.

Screen all new cases to identify those that are arguably eligible for diversion.

D. Initial client interview.

1. Interview newly assigned clients to obtain all relevant information necessary or useful for preparing a defense. A questionnaire is used to remind the interviewer of points to be covered and to record the answers in a standard format so that they can be easily retrieved later on.

2. Inform, or re-inform, the client of his/her rights, his/her need to be completely cooperative with the defense team, and of the legal steps that will follow.

3. Offer to assist with family or other problems the client may have and indicate other ways in which the defense team can help with nonlegal problems.

4. Collect whatever formal papers are immediately available. Assemble these and the interview form in a new case jacket.

5. Undertake follow-up assignments, such as obtaining "rap sheets" of witnesses, medical reports, requesting an investigation and a community treatment plan, etc.

E. Planning community services for clients.

1. Screen every new defendant coming into the office and select those for whom a plan of obtaining services in the community may prove helpful, i.e., those who, if convicted, would find it difficult but not impossible to obtain a community-based sentence.

2. Interview the client and, when appropriate, his/her attorney, family, etc., and then set out the components of a treatment plan based on this dignosis.

3. Obtain commitments from social and health services agencies and employers in the community to provide placements in accordance with the treatment plan.

4. Monitor the progress of each such client during the pretrial period, and make adjustments as needed, so as to make the best possible record for a sentencing disposition should the case come to that stage.

5. Make similar plans and obtain similar placements, albeit on a contingent basis, for appropriate clients who have been incarcerated pretrial and who cannot make bail. When a community treatment plan is set up, the paralegal works with the lawyer in

seeking a review of the client's bail status before trial. Otherwise, the plan is kept in reserve for use in a sentencing hearing should there be one.

6. To make contact with the person (usually a probation officer) appointed by the court to make an independent background report relevant to sentencing, and to provide as much useful and influential information to this worker as is possible.

F. Liaison with detained defendants.

1. Periodically visit detention centers and meet with clients of the office.
2. Immediately report to the appropriate attorney any emergency situation confronting incarcerated clients.
3. Otherwise serve as a go-between for such clients and their attorneys and perform follow-up assignments given by the attorney.
4. Assist appropriate clients to obtain release on bail, release in the custody of a third party, or release by other means.

G. Fieldwork assistance.

1. Obtain information from records. This may entail tracking down a court jacket, finding needed information (such as the name of a codefendant's attorney), or obtaining a certified copy of a document (e.g., an affidavit in support of a search warrant). Hospital, police, and meteorological records are other examples.
2. Provide transportation and delivery services, such as picking up witnesses.
3. Serve subpoenas in emergency circumstances.
4. Track down elusive witnesses.
5. Provide other, lower-level investigatory services, such as having the value of allegedly stolen articles appraised, or having photographs taken of a crime scene, or checking the defendant's outstanding charges in another jurisdiction.

H. Preparing for trial or plea negotiations.

1. Make sure that every necessary document and report ordered for each case is in the case file (rap sheets, meteorological reports, etc.).
2. Coordinate the investigator's work and keep the attorney informed of its progress. The paralegal participates in thinking through investigative strategy, identifying investigative leads, etc.
3. Serve as liaison with others who are helping clients obtain community services.
4. Maintain weekly contact with clients and answer all calls for the attorney in his/her absence, fielding those that are within his/her competence and otherwise forwarding questions and messages to the attorney.
5. Help organize the attorney's calendar, making appropriate arrangements with the court docket clerk, scheduling client and witness interviews, maintaining a tickler system, etc.

6. Provide the attorney continuous reports and recommendations—including ideas on trial strategy—and obtain instructions on new assignments.

I. Appeals and collateral attacks.

1. Analyze the trial record and any other facts bearing on the propriety of the client's conviction.
2. Identify from these, through legal research and analysis, arguable errors in the manner in which a conviction was arrived at or a sentence was imposed, and support these arguments with appropriate legal authority.
3. Prepare these arguments in the form of a draft brief or petition, for review, correction, and submission by the attorney.
4. Coordinate the total office caseload of appeals so that they are handled in an effective and timely manner. This involves the use of an elaborate "tickler system" and ongoing communication with the appellate staff.

17. DOMESTIC RELATIONS LAW
(See also children, law of, p. 68, change of name law, p. 68.)

I. Problem Identification

A. Preliminary interview.
1. Identify nonlegal problems for referral to other agencies.
2. Open a case file or update it.
3. Using a basic fact sheet (or form), record the information collected during the interview.
4. Determine next appointment.
5. Instruct client on what to do next, e.g., obtain medical and birth records.
6. Arrange for client to see office attorney.

B. Jurisdiction and grounds.
1. Determine present residence (and length thereof) of all parties.
2. Collect data on present marriage (e.g., state married in, number of children by this marriage, by prior marriages, sources of support, etc.)
3. Determine whether the client was validly married to the spouse from whom s/he seeks a divorce (e.g., look at client's documents, inquire about prior marriages and divorces, etc.).
4. Ask questions to determine whether the grounds for divorce exist (e.g., nonsupport, adultery, cruelty, irreconcilability, etc.).
5. Ask questions to determine whether grounds for a separation or annulment exist.
6. Determine whether the client wants to consider less drastic remedies (e.g., seeking a support order).

II. Problem Resolution

   A. Consult with lawyer immediately.
     1. Summarize facts for lawyer.
     2. Submit case file to lawyer.
     3. Obtain further instructions from lawyer.
   B. Time assessments (determined according to office checklists).
     1. Determine when complaint must be served.
     2. Determine when preliminary papers must be filed in court.
     3. Develop a calendar of dates for all subsequent service and filings.
   C. Counseling.
     1. If the state requires an attempt at reconciliation before a divorce can be awarded, the paralegal explains this procedure to the client and assists in initiating the process.
     2. Determine whether the client (and spouse) would like to attempt voluntary marriage counseling and, if so, assist client in initiating this service.
   D. Immediate support needs.
     1. Pending the divorce action, determine whether any support problems exist.
     2. If problems exist, explore options (e.g., pretrial support order).
   E. In forma pauperis status.
     1. Determine whether client is eligible for forgiveness of court costs.
     2. Make a list of all assets of clients (according to office checklist).
   F. Investigation.
     1. Verify that client meets residency requirement.
     2. Trace addresses for purpose of service.
     3. Search for records (marriage records, divorce records, criminal records, e.g., involving assault of one spouse against the other, etc.).
     4. Check for evidence to support any of the possible grounds for divorce.
     5. Uncover assets of other spouse.
   G. Drafting.
     1. Complaint.
     2. Summons.
     3. Judgment.
     4. Separation agreement.
   H. Service and filing.
     1. Serve defendant (respondent).
     2. If defendant is not available, effect service via mailing and/or publication.
     3. Serve attorney for other side.
     4. File papers in court.

I. Court
   1. Act as general litigation assistant.
   2. Act as court witness on service.

III. Miscellaneous

  A. Training other staff in the divorce system of the office.
    1. Secretaries.
    2. Other paralegals.
    3. New attorneys.
  B. Management.
   Assist managing attorney in the design and monitoring of the office divorce system.

18. EDUCATION LAW

I. Problem Identification

  A. Preliminary interview.
    1. Identify nonlegal problems for referral to other agencies.
    2. Open a case file or update it.
    3. Using a basic fact sheet (or form), record the information collected during the interview.
    4. Determine next appointment.
    5. Instruct client on what must be done next, e.g., obtain medical and birth records.
    6. Arrange for client to see office attorney.
  B. Education problems.
    1. Parent has received a notice of suspension concerning his/her child.
    2. Parent/child wants a school transfer.
    3. Parent/child object to the failure of the school to promote the child.
    4. Parent/child object to the failure of the school to give child special programming.

II. Problem Resolution

  A. Consult with attorney immediately.
    1. Summarize facts for attorney.
    2. Submit case file to attorney.
    3. Obtain further instructions from attorney.
  B. Referral of nonlegal problems to other agencies.
    1. Give name and address of agency to client.
    2. Search for appropriate agency.
    3. Contact agency for client.
  C. Investigation.
    1. Interview the parties involved (teachers, other students, etc.) in the alleged disciplinary infraction by the child.

2. Contact admission office(s) of a number of schools to assess transfer options.
3. Interview parents/students in a designated area for an attorney who is contemplating a class action.

D. Informal advocacy.
1. Contact complainant-teacher or complainant-parent to see if the disciplinary charge cannot be resolved without a formal suspension or expulsion hearing.
2. Contact school administrator(s) to see if the school will give special attention to the parent/child's request for a transfer, special programming, extra protection for the child, etc.

E. Lobbying.
1. Appear at School Board hearings to petition for changes in school policy.
2. Appear before legislative committees to petition for changes in the statutory laws governing schools.

F. Formal hearings.
1. Represent the child at school revocation hearing.
2. Represent the child at school suspension hearing.

G. Community work.
1. Help organize segments of the community around school issues.
2. Provide general assistance to parent associations, e.g., speaking to the groups on education law topics.
3. Write community-education pamphlets for students/parents of education law issues.

H. Litigation.
1. Act as court witness.
2. Serve papers.
3. General litigation assistant, e.g., monitor all files.
4. Legal research.

I. Client counseling.
Help the parent/child articulate and decide upon courses of action (e.g., does the parent/child want to fight the administrative action or seek a transfer to another school; does the parent want to consider psychiatric counseling for the child).

19. EMPLOYEE BENEFITS LAW (QUALIFIED PLANS)[20]

I. Work closely with the attorney, the plan sponsor, the plan administrator, and the trustee in the preparation and drafting of qualified employee plans.

A. Stock bonus plan.
B. Profit sharing plan.
C. Money purchase pension.

[20] Rocky Mountain Legal Assistants Association, *The Use of the Legal Assistant* (1975).

D. Other pension plans.

E. Trust agreements.

F. IRA plans (Individual Retirement Account).

G. Annuity plans.

H. HR-10 or Keogh plans.

I. Employee stock ownership plans.

J. Life and health insurance plans.

K. Worker's compensation plans.

L. Social security plans.

II. Prepare accompanying documents and monitor the program.

A. Gather information.

B. Determine eligibility for participation and benefits.

C. Notify of participation.

D. Complete input forms for document assembly.

E. Election to participate.

F. Beneficiary designation.

G. Election to contribute.

H. Allocate annual contributions to individual participant accounts.

I. Prepare annual account statements for participants.

J. Identify potential discrimination problems in the program.

III. Government compliance work.

A. Tax requirements for qualifications, amendment, and termination of plan.

B. Department of Labor reporting and disclosure requirements.

C. Insurance requirements.

D. Welfare and Pension Plans Disclosure Act requirements.

E. ERISA requirements (Employee Retirement Income Security Act).

F. Pension Benefit Guaranty Corporation requirements.

G. Establish and maintain a tickler system to meet reporting and disclosure deadlines.

IV. Draft summary plan descriptions for distribution to employees.

V. Prepare and review annual reports of plans.

VI. Continue education in current law of the field, e.g., become a Certified Employee Benefit Specialist (CEBS).

20. EMPLOYMENT LAW
(See also labor law, p. 93, civil rights law, p. 70.)

I. Problem Identification

A. Individual complains that s/he was not hired because of discrimination.
B. Employee feels that a demotion or failure to promote was due to discrimination.
C. Employee alleges nonpayment of salary.

II. Investigation

A. Gather documents pertaining to the case.
B. Interview employer, other employees, etc.

III. Informal Advocacy/Negotiation/Mediation
Call, write, meet with, or otherwise contact everyone involved in the case in an attempt to determine whether the underlying disputes can be resolved informally.

IV. Hearing

A. Assist the individual in the presentation of his/her claim before Civil Service Board (if government employee).
B. Assist the individual in the presentation of his/her claim before Human Rights Board (if case involves charge of discrimination).

V. Litigation Assistant (p. 98)

21. GOVERNMENT CONTRACT LAW[21]

A. Maintain calendar for Court and Appeals Board appearance dates, for dates briefs are due, etc.
B. Prepare claims.
   1. Gather, review, summarize, and index client files.
   2. Assist in drafting contract claim.
   3. Conduct preliminary research of selected legal issues.
C. Prepare for appeal hearing.
   1. Draft and answer interrogatories and requests for production of documents.
   2. Summarize and index answers to discovery.
   3. Assist in drafting appeal.
   4. Prepare questions for witnesses and summarize prior testimony.
   5. Maintain documents during hearing.
D. Prepare post-hearing briefs.
   1. Summarize and index transcripts.

---

[21] Berg, C. *Annual Survey* (San Francisco Association of Legal Assistants, Dec. 19, 1973).

2. Assist with analysis of government's brief.
3. Conduct preliminary research of particular issues.
4. Assist in drafting the post-hearing brief.

22. HEALTH LAW

I. Problem Identification

   A. Preliminary interview.
      1. Identify nonlegal problems for referral to other agencies.
      2. Open a case file or update it.
      3. Using a basic fact sheet (or form), record the information collected during the interview.
      4. Determine next appointment.
      5. Instruct client on what to do next, e.g., obtain medical and birth records, etc.
      6. Arrange for client to see office attorney.
   B. Health problems.
      1. Client is confused about available hospital services.
      2. Language and communications barriers exist between health-care staff and patients.
      3. Client is told s/he is not eligible for certain health benefits.
      4. Client complains that hospital is not respecting his/her privacy (e.g., physician talks about client in front of other patients).
      5. Client challenges a bill.

II. Problem Resolution

   A. Consult with attorney immediately.
      1. Summarize facts for attorney.
      2. Submit case file to attorney.
      3. Obtain further instructions from attorney.
   B. Referral of nonlegal problems to other agencies.
      1. Give name and address of agency to client.
      2. Search for appropriate agency.
      3. Contact agency for client.
   C. Investigation.
      1. Locate medical records.
      2. Site visits to explore public health issues (e.g., pollution caused by industry).
   D. Interpretation and community education.
      1. Act as interpreter of foreign language between hospital staff and patient.
      2. Explain hospital procedures to clients.
      3. Write pamphlets on health rights.
      4. Speak to community groups about health law issues.
   E. Informal advocacy/negotiation/mediation.
      Contact (call, visit, write a letter to, etc.) individuals involved in

the client's complaint in order to determine whether the problem can be resolved informally.
F. Legislation/regulations.
Appear before legislative committees or health administrative bodies to express views on health-care issues.

23. IMMIGRATION LAW

I. Problem Identification

    A. Difficulty in obtaining visa.
    B. Difficulty in obtaining permanent residency based on occupaion.
    C. Difficulty in obtaining nonimmigrant status.
    D. Difficulty in obtaining citizenship status.
    E. Deportation proceedings against the alien.

II. Providing Information

    A. Visa process.
    B. Permanent residency process.
    C. Nonimmigrant status process.
    D. Registration process.
    E. Citizenship process.
    F. Deportation process.

III. Investigation
Assist the individual in obtaining data and documentation on birth, travel, residency, etc.

IV. Referral
Refer individuals to foreign consulates, nationality organizations, government officials, etc., for assistance concerning their immigration status.

V. Applications/Forms
Assist the individual in filling out visa applications, permanent residency applications, etc.

VI. Monitor Consular Processing Procedure.

24. INSURANCE LAW
(See also employee benefits law, p. 88.)

    A. Compliance with the requirements of insurance regulatory agencies.
    B. Processing disputed benefit claims.
    C. Legal research.

D. Monitoring activities of insurance regulatory agencies and the committees of the legislature with jurisdiction over insurance.
E. Litigation assistance on claims brought to court.

25. INTERNATIONAL LAW
Example: a paralegal working on a "dumping" case in international trade.

A. Investigation.
    1. The normal behavior in the industry/market affected.
    2. Statistical research (cost and price data).
    3. Profiles of domestic competitors.
B. Preparation of documents for presentation before:
    1. Commerce Department.
    2. Court of International Trade.
C. Accounting research.
D. Coordination of data from:
    1. Members of Congress.
    2. Foreign embassies.
    3. State Department.
    4. U.S. Special Trade Representative.

26. LABOR LAW
(See also employee benefits law, p. 88, unemployment compensation law, p. 45, worker's compensation law, p. 114.)

I. Investigation

A. Interview witnesses.
B. Examine documents.

II. Litigation Assistant for Labor Disputes Before the National Labor Relations Board, the State Labor Relations Board, and the Courts.

A. File maintenance.
B. Digest/index data in file.
C. Arrange for depositions.
D. Draft documents:
    1. Petition.
    2. Other pleadings.
E. Maintain "tickler" system of due dates.
F. Prepare exhibits.
G. Prepare statistical data.
H. Prepare appeal.

27. LANDLORD-TENANT LAW
(See also oil and gas law, p. 101, and real estate law, p. 105.)

I. Problem Identification

A. Preliminary interview.
1. Identify non-legal problems for referral to other agencies.
2. Open a case file or update it.
3. Using a basic fact sheet (or form), record the information collected during the interview.
4. Determine next appointment.
5. Instruct client on what to do next (e.g., bring in rent payment receipts, etc.).
6. Arrange for client to see office attorney.
B. Public housing.
1. Application problems (e.g., where to apply, what forms to use, what waiting list to go on, suspicion of discrimination, does client have a priority due to relocation).
2. Maintenance problems (e.g., security dangers, no heat, superintendent is never available, neighbors put garbage in hallway).
3. Termination problems (e.g., client wants to move, client has received notice to evict).
C. Private housing.
1. Application problems (e.g., suspicion of discrimination, does client qualify for FHA buyer loan, does client qualify for rent subsidy).
2. Maintenance problems (e.g., housing code violations on building).
3. Termination problems (e.g., receipt of notice to vacate for nonpayment or for violating other conditions of lease).

II. Problem Resolution

A. Consult with attorney immediately.
1. Summarize facts for attorney.
2. Submit case file to attorney.
3. Obtain further instructions from attorney.
B. Referral of nonlegal problems to other agencies.
1. Give name and address of agency to client.
2. Search for appropriate agency.
3. Contact agency for client.
C. Time determinations.
1. Call sheriff's office to determine if s/he is going to execute an eviction order.
2. Determine time of the next court proceeding.
3. Develop a calendar of dates for all process serving and court filings.
D. Investigation.
1. Visit apartment/house to verify and document (e.g., photograph) code violations.
2. Search city/county records to identify owner of building.
3. Search code records to determine what other violations are on record for the same building.

4. Interview other tenants in building for attorney contemplating a class action or a building receivership action.

E. Document and service of process analysis.
1. Determine whether breach-of-lease notices were properly served and are in proper form.
2. Determine whether a valid lease exists.
3. Examine rent receipts to determine whether any gaps/defaults exist.

F. Establishing defenses and counterclaims.
1. Determine whether the client has a defense (e.g., has paid all rent, does not have a dog, is not unduly noisy).
2. Determine whether client has counterclaim (e.g., improper services or no services).

G. Drafting.
1. Preliminary draft of order to show cause or other pleading to stay further court proceedings or to stay execution of court order.
2. Preliminary draft of answer.
3. Preliminary draft of counterclaim.
4. Preliminary draft of complaint (when client is plaintiff suing landlord).
5. Letter requesting public housing hearing.
6. Assist client fill out forms, e.g., application for reduction of rent (addressed to rent control office).
7. Draft *subpoena duces tecum* order addressed to code-violation agency requesting a listing of code violations on a particular building.
8. Preliminary draft of bill of particulars addressed to attorney of landlord.
9. Preliminary draft of interrogatories addressed to attorney of landlord.
10. Preliminary draft of answers to written interrogatories.

H. Service/filings.
1. Serve pleadings on landlord or his/her attorney.
2. File pleadings in court, at public housing agency, at rent control office, at housing code agency, etc.

I. Formal hearing representation.
1. Represent client at public housing hearing on attempt to evict client.
2. Represent client at welfare fair hearing where client challenges the welfare department's refusal to provide more money for rent.
3. Represent client at rent control hearing where client denies that s/he is in violation of such laws in a proceeding brought by the landlord.

J. Warehouse problems
1. Assist client to obtain personal property from the warehouse that stored the property upon eviction.

2. Assist client to challenge a bill submitted by the warehouse.
3. Assist client to challenge the warehouse for damaging property confiscated after the eviction.

28. LAW OFFICE ADMINISTRATION
(See also p. 737.)

I. Financial Planning

    A. Oversee accounting functions of the firm.
    B. Approve payment of account payables.
    C. Establish procedures for billing verification and approval.
    D. Monitor attorney time reporting procedure.
    E. Prepare analyses of client projects, hours, and costs.
    F. Work on delinquent accounts.
    G. Manage the preparation of the firm's tax returns.
    H. Administer the firm's pension plan.

II. Personnel

    A. Interview and hire office staff positions.
    B. Evaluate performance of office staff.
    C. Take disciplinary action against staff employees when needed.
    D. Train support staff.
    E. Regulate work flow of office and work load of individual staff members.
    F. Schedule vacations of staff.

III. Law Library

    A. Undertake general supervision of the library.
    B. Prepare/approve cost estimates for law books.

IV. Files

    A. Establish and maintain a filing system for active and inactive files.
    B. Maintain a routing system for the files.

V. Physical Facilities/Equipment/Systems

    A. Make recommendations on future physical facility needs of the firm.
    B. Prepare cost projections.
    C. Oversee adaptation of office to construction/installation of new facilities.
    D. Supervise the operation of:
        1. Data processing.
        2. Document production (including dictation and typing).

3. Document reproduction.
4. Document retrieval.
5. Conflict of interest systems.
6. Litigation support.
7. Telephone and mail systems.
8. Use of office supplies and furnishings.
9. Dining and food services.
E. Keep current inventory of all equipment and facilities.

VI. Docket Control
Establish a centralized calendar and document control system.

VII. Insurance
Administer the insurance programs for the firm:

A. Accident and health.
B. Casualty.
C. Professional liability.
D. Bonding.
E. Disability.
F. Life insurance of officers.
G. Accidental death and dismemberment.
H. Worker's compensation.

VIII. Planning

A. Project personnel and space growth for the future.
B. Prepare long-range budget projections.
C. Prepare reports on work/profit productivity of individual attorneys and of departments within the firm.

29. LEGISLATION
(See also p. 655.)

I. Monitoring
Keep track of all events, persons, and organizations involved in the passing of legislation relevant to the client of the firm.

II. Legislative History
Undertake the legislative history of a statute (p. 665).

III. Draft Proposed Legislation

IV. Lobbying (p. 99)

A. Prepare reports/studies on the subject of proposed legislation.
B. Arrange for and help prepare witnesses who will testify at legislative hearings.

30. LITIGATION
(See also p. 465.)

I. Act as File Monitor on Cases in Litigation

A. Index all files.
B. Write case profile based on information in the files.
C. Read attorney briefs to check accuracy of the information in the litigation file.
D. Organize and index documents obtained through discovery.
E. Code documents into the computer.

II. Investigation

A. Document gathering.
1. Medical records.
2. Police records.
3. Birth and death records.
4. Marriage records.
5. Adoption and custody records.
6. Incorporation records.
B. Record research.
1. Prepare a profit history report of a company.
2. Identify corporate structure of parent and its subsidiaries.
3. Trace UCC filings.
4. Find out from court dockets if a particular merchant is being sued, has sued before, etc. Does any pattern exist?
5. Identify the "real owner" of an apartment building.
6. Check housing code agency to find out if a particular landlord has other building code violations against it on record.
C. Fact gathering (other than documents).
In a wide range of cases (e.g., real estate, corporate, criminal, divorce, custody), the investigator substantiates facts, follows leads for possible evidence in connection with litigation, etc.

III. Discovery

A. Draft interrogatories.
B. Draft answers to interrogatories.
C. Draft deposition questions.
D. Prepare witnesses for deposition.
E. Prepare witness books for deposition.
F. Arrange time and place of deposition.
G. Draft requests for admissions.
H. Draft requests for production of documents.
I. Index and digest discovery data.
J. Work with computer programmer in the design of a system to manage discovery documents.

IV. Filings/Serving
In court, at agencies, on parties, on attorneys, etc.

V. General Assistantship

A. Arrange for clients and others to be interviewed.
B. Arrange for expert witnesses to appear in court or at depositions.
C. Reconstruct (from a large collection of disparate records and other evidence) what happened at a particular time and place.
D. Assist clients in completing information questionnaire (e.g., in reference to class-action plaintiffs).
E. Prepare charts/tables to be used as exhibits at trial.
F. Sit at counsel's table at trial to take notes and suggest questions to attorney to be asked of witnesses.
G. Attend (and report on) hearings in related cases.
H. Supervise document encodation on a computer project related to a case in litigation.
I. Prepare and evaluate prospective jurors from jury book.
J. Help prepare trial brief.
K. Help prepare appeal documents, e.g., draft notice of appeal.

VI. Legal Research

A. Shepardizing, cite checking.
B. Preliminary memo and brief writing.
C. Prepare bibliographies of source materials related to litigation.

VII. Pleadings
Preliminary draft of pleadings using standard forms and/or adapting other pleadings written by attorneys on similar cases.

VIII. Expert Analysis
Render expert opinions to attorneys:

A. Taxation.
B. Accounting.
C. Statistics.
D. Economics (e.g., calculation of damages).

IX. Act as Court Witness

A. As to service of process.
B. As to data uncovered or photographed (e.g., the condition of an apartment building).

31. LOBBYING
(See also administrative law, p. 64, and legislation, p. 97.)

I. Monitoring (p. 668)

    A. Keep track of proposed regulations of administrative agencies.
    B. Keep track of proposed legislation of the legislature.

II. Research

    A. Legislative history (p. 655).
    B. Regulatory history.
    C. Statistical and other technical data.

III. Prepare Reports for Submission to Agency or Legislature

32. MILITARY LAW

I. Military Proceedings

    A. Assist in processing the following proceedings:
        1. Special court-martial.
        2. General court-martial.
        3. Courts of inquiry.
        4. Line of duty investigations.
        5. Reclassification board proceedings.
    B. Prepare special orders designating membership of special and general court-martial and courts of inquiry.
    C. Assure that charges are properly prepared and that specifications are complete and accurate.
    D. Make initial determination on jurisdiction of court, status of accused, and subject-matter of offenses.
    E. Examine completed records of investigations, and other records requiring legal review to ensure that they are administratively correct.
    F. Prepare special court-martial orders promulgating sentence.
    G. Assure that records of court-martial are correct and complete before disposing of case.
    H. Transmit bad conduct discharge court-martial cases to appropriate officials.

II. Claims Against the Government

    A. Conduct examinations.
    B. Process claims against the United States, e.g., federal tort claims.
    C. Manage claim funds.
    D. Undertake research on FLITE (Federal Legal Information Through Electronics).
    E. Write briefs.

III. Administrative Duties

    A. Maintain control records of all court-martial and claims cases within command.
    B. Maintain law library.
    C. Examine and distribute incoming correspondence, directives, publications, and other communications.
    D. Supervise cataloging and filing of publications, books, periodicals, journals, etc.
    E. Maintain records of discipline within command.
    F. Administer office budget.
    G. Orient new personnel and monitor their training.

  IV. Court Reporting

    A. Use the steno-mask for recording legal proceedings.
    B. Prepare charges to the jury.
    C. Mark exhibits as they are entered into evidence.
    D. Transcribe and assemble the records of the proceeding.

33. MOTOR VEHICLE LAW

  I. Problem Identification

    A. Client receives a notice of license suspension or revocation.
    B. Client is having difficulty obtaining license or registration certificates.

  II. Investigation

    A. Assist the client in gathering necessary records (e.g., birth certificate).
    B. Interview parties involved (e.g., the officer who gave the client the ticket that led to the suspension proceeding).

  III. Informal Advocacy

    A. Contact department of motor vehicles to determine whether it has any discretion to waive or postpone proceedings against the client.
    B. Ask for a quicker review of the suspension charge than would otherwise occur.
    C. Determine whether the underlying disputes can be resolved informally.

  IV. Formal Advocacy
    Assist the client in the preparation of his/her case before the hearing officer in the suspension/revocation proceeding.

34. OIL AND GAS LAW
  (See also real estate law, p. 105.)

I. Collect and analyze data pertaining to land ownership and activities that may affect the procurement of rights to explore, drill for, and produce oil or gas.

II. Help acquire leases and other operating rights from property owners for exploration, drilling, and producing oil, gas, and related substances.

III. Monitor the execution of the leases and other operating agreements by ensuring that contract obligations are fulfilled (e.g., payment of rent).

IV. Help negotiate agreements with individuals, companies, and government agencies pertaining to the exploration, drilling, and production of oil or gas.

V. Assist in acquiring oil and gas producing properties, royalties, and mineral interests.

VI. Process and monitor the termination of leases and other agreements.

VII. Examine land titles.

35. PARAJUDGE

In many states, the judge presiding in certain lower courts does not have to be a lawyer, e.g., Justice of the Peace Courts, local magistrates courts (p. 213). Some have limited roles such as conducting designated pretrial proceedings and making recommendations to the regular court.

Administrative agencies often hold hearings conducted by hearing officers, referees, or administrative law judges (ALJ). Frequently, these individuals are not lawyers, particularly at state and local agencies.

36. PARTNERSHIP LAW[22]

I. Draft pre-organization agreement.

II. Draft general or limited partnership agreement.

III. Draft and file statements of partnership and certificates of limited partnership.

IV. Prepare, file, and publish fictitious business name statements.

V. Draft minutes of partnership meetings.

---

[22] Supra note *21*.

VI. Draft noncompetition agreements for selling partners, assignments of partnership interests, approval of substituted partner, and appropriate amendments to the partnership agreements, and certificates of limited partnership.

VII. Draft agreements for dissolution of partnership.

VIII. Draft and file termination of fictitious business name statements.

IX. Draft and publish notice of termination of partnership (or continuation of successor business).

37. PATENT LAW
(See also copyright law, p. 75, trademark law, p. 108.)

I. Application

A. Help the inventor apply for a patent with the U.S. Patent and Trademark Office.
B. Help the inventor describe the invention, e.g., assemble designs, diagrams, notebooks.
C. Conduct a patent search. Check technical libraries to determine the current state of the art.
D. Determine filing fees.
E. Help the client apply for protection in foreign countries.
F. Monitor the responses from government offices.
G. Examine certificate of patent for accuracy.

II. Marketing the Invention

A. Help identify licensees, e.g., solicit bids, conduct financial checks, study the market.
B. Prepare contracts.

III. Infringement

A. Investigation, e.g., on products that may have violated the patent.
B. General litigation assistantship.

38. POST-CONVICTION REMEDIES AND CORRECTIONS (PRISON) LAW

I. Problem Identification

A. Inmate wants to appeal conviction directly.
B. Inmate wants to attack conviction collaterally (via coram nobis, habeas corpus, etc.)

C. Inmate wants to challenge a decision of the parole board.
D. Inmate wants to challenge a decision of the prison staff, e.g., denial of the right to subscribe to a particular journal.
E. Inmate wants help in preparing his/her parole board case.
F. Inmate wants help in preparing his/her case before the disciplinary committee.
G. Inmate wants help in preparing his/her administrative appeal of the decision of the disciplinary committee.
H. Inmate feels that the staff has improperly calculated the time s/he must serve because of:
1. A failure to give the inmate credit for time served while waiting trial.
2. A failure to give the inmate credit for good-time earned.
3. A misreading of the court's sentence.
I. Inmate wants help challenging conditions of prison, e.g., cell arrangements, food availability, religious practices, visitation, educational facilities.

II. Writ-Writing, Administrative Complaint Writing (p. 220)

A. Inmate helps another inmate draft a writ after studying other cases and doing research in the prison law library and in the inmate's own personal law "library":
1. To obtain appointment of counsel.
2. To obtain an evidentiary hearing.
3. To obtain a free copy of court records, e.g., trial minutes (via *in forma pauperis* petition).
4. To obtain "good time" credit that the inmate-client claims is due.
B. Inmate helps other inmate draft a written complaint:
1. Addressed to parole board challenging a parole decision.
2. Addressed to prison staff challenging a prison decision, e.g., to discontinue library hours, to transfer an inmate's job assignment.
3. Addressed to prison staff or to court challenging prison conditions.

III. Record Gathering
Assist the inmate in obtaining court papers in the hands of attorneys, DAs, court clerks, etc. (e.g., copy of the judgment, indictment, trial minutes, depositions, correspondence).

IV. Representation

A. One inmate "represents" another at a disciplinary hearing.
B. One inmate "represents" another at a parole board hearing. (Staff members may also "represent" the inmate at both kinds of hearings.)

V. Librarian
Act as clerk-librarian for the prison law library, e.g., keep the texts up to date with new additions.

VI. Mediation
Act as go-between in disputes involving staff and inmate:

A. Inmate as mediator.
B. Staff member as mediator.

39. REAL ESTATE LAW

I. General
Assist law firms, corporations, and development companies in transactions involving land, houses, condominiums, shopping malls, office buildings, redevelopment projects, civic centers, etc.

A. Research zoning regulations.
B. Prepare draft of the contract of sale.
C. Title work.
  1. Done outside: Order title work from the title company; arrange title insurance.
  2. Done in-house.
    a. Examine title abstracts for completeness.
    b. Prepare a map based on a master title plat or the current government survey map.
    c. Construct a chain of title noting defects, encumbrances, liens, easements, breaks in the chain, etc.
    d. Obtain releases of liens, payoff statements for existing loans, etc.
    e. Draft a preliminary title opinion.
D. Mortgages.
  1. Assist in obtaining financing.
  2. Review mortgage application.
  3. Assist in recording mortgage.
E. Closing.
  1. Arrange for a closing time with buyer, seller, brokers, and lender. Obtain letter confirming date of closing.
  2. Collect the data necessary for closing. Prepare checklist of expenses:
    a. Title company fee.
    b. Lender's fee.
    c. Attorney's fee.
    d. Taxes and water bills to be prorated.
    e. Tax escrow, discharge of liens.
  3. Prepare and organize the documents for closing.
    a. Deed.
    b. Settlement Statement.

        c. Note and deed of trust.

        d. Corporate Resolutions.

        e. Performance Bond.

        f. Waivers.

    4. Check compliance with the disclosure requirements of the Real Estate Settlement Act.

    5. Arrange for a rehearsal of the closing.

    6. Attend and assist at the closing, e.g., take minutes, notarize documents.

F. Foreclosure.

    1. Order foreclosure certificate.

    2. Prepare Notice of Election and Demand for Sale.

    3. Compile a list of parties who need to be notified.

    4. Monitor publication of the notice.

    5. Assist with sale documents, e.g., preparation of bid letter.

G. Office management.

    1. Maintain office "tickler" system.

    2. Maintain individual attorney's calendar.

    3. Be in charge of the entire client's file (opening it, keeping it up to date, knowing where parts of it are at all times).

    4. Training other office staff in the office system of handling real estate cases.

II. Tax-exempt Industrial Development Financing.

A. Undertake a preliminary investigation to establish facts relevant to:

    1. Project eligibility.

    2. The local issuer.

    3. Cost estimates of the financing.

B. Prepare a formal application to the issuer.

C. Prepare a timetable of approvals, meetings, and all other requirements necessary for closing.

D. Prepare a preliminary draft of portions of the proposal memorandum (relating to the legal structure of the financing) that is submitted to prospective bond purchasers.

E. Obtain confirmation from the Treasury Department that the company is in compliance with the financing covenants of current external debt instruments.

F. Obtain insurance certificates.

G. Write the first draft of the resolutions of the board of directors.

H. Write the preface and recital of documents for the legal opinion of the company.

I. Contact the bank to confirm the account numbers, amount of money to be transferred, and investment instructions.

J. Prepare a closing memorandum covering the following documents:

1. Secretary's Certificate including resolutions of the board of directors, the certified charter and bylaws of the company, and the incumbency certificate.
2. UCC-1 Financing Statements.
3. Requisition forms.
4. Certificate of Authorized Company Representative.
5. Deed.
6. Legal opinion of the company.
7. Wire transfer instruction letter.
8. Officer's certificate.
K. Confirm that the money has been transferred to the company's account on the day of closing.
L. Order an updated good-standing telegram.
M. Send a copy of the IRS Election Statement.
N. Assemble, monitor, and distribute documents to appropriate departments.

40. TAX LAW

I. Compile all necessary data for the preparation of tax returns:

A. Corporate income tax.
B. Employer quarterly tax.
C. Franchise tax.
D. Partnership tax.
E. Sales tax.
F. Personal property tax.
G. Individual income tax.
H. Estate tax.
I. Gift tax.

II. Communicate with client to obtain missing information.

III. Compile supporting documents for the returns.

IV. Draft extensions-of-time requests.

V. Make corrections in the returns based upon new or clarified data.

VI. Compute the tax liability or transfer client information to computer input sheets for submission to a computer service that will calculate the tax liability.

VII. Organize and maintain client binder.

VIII. Compute cash flow analysis for proposed real estate syndication.

IX. Compile documentation on the valuation of assets.

X. Maintain the tax law library.

XI. Read loose-leaf tax services and other periodic tax data to keep current on tax developments. Bring such developments to the attention of others in the office.

XII. Supervise and train other nonlawyer staff within the tax department of the office.

41. TORT LAW

A tort is a civil wrong that has injured someone. Paralegals who work on PI (personal injury) cases are mainly litigation assistants (see p. 98, p. 341, p. 465). The major torts are negligence, trespass to land, defamation, strict liability, and wrongful death. Paralegals in this area are also often involved in worker's compensation cases for injuries that occur on the job (see p. 114).

42. TRADEMARK LAW

(See also copyright law, p. 75, patent law, p. 103.)

I. Registration

A. Research trademark files or order search of trademark or trade name preliminary to an application before the U.S. Patent and Trademark Office.
B. Examine indexes and directories.
C. Investigation, e.g., to determine when the mark was first used, where, on what products.
D. Prepare foreign trademark application.
E. Respond to official actions taken by government offices.
F. Examine the certificate of trademark for accuracy.
G. Maintain files for renewals.

II. Infringement

A. Investigation, e.g., who else used the mark, when, where, in what market.
B. General litigation assistantship.

43. TRIBAL LAW

Tribal courts exist on Indian reservations and have jurisdiction over many civil and criminal cases in which both parties are Native Americans. Parties are often represented by Tribal Court Advocates who are nonlawyer Native Americans.

I. Trial

A. Civil cases.

    1. Draft and file complaint.
    2. Draft and file answer to complaint.
       a. Raise defenses.
       b. Raise counterclaims.
    3. Conduct the trial.
       a. Jury selection.
       b. Present evidence.
       c. Examine witnesses (direct and cross).
       d. Arguments on damages (e.g., hospital bills).
  B. Criminal cases.
    1. Draft and file complaint.
    2. Draft and file answer to complaint.
    3. Conduct the trial.
       a. Jury selection.
       b. Present evidence.
       c. Examine witnesses (direct and cross).
       d. Arguments on sentencing.

II. Appeal

  A. Present written arguments to tribal court of appeals.
  B. Make oral arguments to tribal court of appeals.

44. TRUSTS, ESTATES, AND PROBATE LAW

I. Estate Planning

  A. Collection of data (birth dates, fair market value of assets, current assets and liabilities, etc.).
  B. Preliminary drafting of wills or trusts from sample forms.
  C. Investment analysis: advise attorney (who is fiduciary of estate) on investments.

II. Office Management

  A. Maintain "tickler" system.
  B. Maintain individual attorney's calendar.
  C. Open, index, monitor, keep current all components of the client's trust and estate office file.
  D. Operate computer in connection with accounting aspects of trusts and estates administered by the office.
  E. Act as office law librarian (keeping loose-leaf texts up to date, etc.).
  F. Train other office staff to handle trusts, estate, and probate cases.
  G. Selectively discard certain mail and underline significant parts of other mail.

III. Estate of Decedent

A. Assets phase.
 1. Collect assets (e.g., bank accounts, custody accounts, insurance proceeds, social security death benefits, safety deposit box openings, apartment openings).
 2. Assist in the valuation of assets.
 3. Maintain records (e.g., recording and filing of will and trust, vault inventory, powers of attorney, property settlements, fee cards, bill payment letter).
 4. Notify beneficiaries.
 5. Prepare profiles of will and trust for attorney review.
B. Accounting phase.
 1. Prepare preliminary draft of federal and state death tax returns.
 2. Apply the income-principal rules to the estate.
 3. Advise attorneys on the tax implications of estates.
 4. Prepare accountings: final, and accounts current (this involves setting up a petition for a first and final accounting).
C. Termination-distribution phase.
 1. Apply for the transfer of securities into the names of the people entitled.
 2. Draw checks for the signature of executors.
 3. Monitor legacies to charitable clients.
 4. File and prepare tax waivers.
 5. Assist in the closing documents.
 6. Calculate distributable net income.
 7. Follow-up action on collection and delivery.

IV. Litigation.

 1. Legal research.
 2. Factual research (investigation), e.g., track down the names and addresses of all possible claimants and contact them.
 3. General litigation assistant.
 4. Prepare sample pleadings.
 5. Digest depositions (review, condense, point out inconsistencies, etc.).
 6. Prepare drafts of interrogatories.
 7. Prepare drafts of answers to interrogatories.
 8. Notarize documents.
 9. Act as court witness (e.g., as to decedent's signature).
 10. Miscellaneous litigation assistantship duties.

45. UNEMPLOYMENT INSURANCE (COMPENSATION) LAW (UI)

I. Problem Identification

 1. Client does not understand UI procedures.
 2. Client disagrees with decision made by UI agency line staff.
 3. Client disagrees with decision made by UI hearing examiner.

II. Problem Resolution

A. Consult with attorney immediately.
   1. Summarize facts for attorney.
   2. Submit case file to attorney.
   3. Obtain further instructions from attorney.
B. Referral of nonlegal problems to other agencies.
   1. Give name and address of agency to client.
   2. Search for appropriate agency.
   3. Contact agency for client.
C. Investigation.
   1. Determine exact employment dates.
   2. Interview witnesses as to the "cause" for the termination from employment.
   3. Solicit affidavits from employers with whom client has tried to obtain employment since the termination.
   4. Determine how long the client has received UI benefits.
D. Time determinations.
   1. Determine whether the client has time to contest the UI action.
   2. Determine how much time the client has left to receive UI benefits.
   3. Determine whether the client has time to appeal a UI action in court, or whether the client has defaulted in an action brought by the UI agency against the client in court.
E. Informal advocacy.
   Contact (call, visit, write a letter to) the parties involved in the dispute (employer, UI representative, etc.) to determine whether the dispute can be resolved without a formal hearing or court action.
F. Formal advocacy.
   Represent the client before a UI hearing examiner.
G. Client counseling.
   Assist client in registering for and pursuing services available at state employment agencies, assist client in obtaining job testing and counseling if s/he desires it, etc.
H. Lobbying.
   Testify and present petitions before legislative and administrative hearings concerning UI policy.
I. Community education.
   1. Write pamphlets on UI law.
   2. Speak to community groups on UI policies and law.

46. WELFARE LAW

I. Problem Identification

A. Preliminary interview.
   1. Identify nonlegal problems for referral to other agencies.
   2. Open a case file or update it.

3. Using a basic fact sheet (or form), record the information collected during the interview.
4. Determine next appointment.
5. Instruct client on what to do next, e.g., obtain medical and birth records, etc.
6. Arrange for client to see office attorney.
B. Welfare problems.
   1. Client does not know what benefits exist in programs such as:
      a. Welfare
      b. Social security
      c. Medicare
   2. Client needs help in filling out application forms.
   3. Client objects to home visits by caseworkers.
   4. Client objects to attempt by welfare department to force him/ her to take a job or enter a training program.
   5. Welfare department wants to reduce the amount of client's welfare check.
   6. Welfare department wants to terminate public assistance altogether.

II. Problem Resolution

A. Consult with attorney immediately.
   1. Summarize facts for the attorney.
   2. Submit the case record to the attorney.
   3. Obtain further instructions from attorney.
B. Referral of nonlegal problems to other agencies.
   1. Give name and address of agency to client.
   2. Search for an appropriate agency.
   3. Contact agency for the client.
C. Investigation.
   1. Verify information (e.g., call caseworker, visit welfare office).
   2. Search for additional information.
   3. Record relevant facts.
   4. Consult with attorney on difficulties encountered.
D. Law analysis.
   1. Check office welfare law manual.
   2. Consult with office attorneys.
   3. Contact legal service attorneys outside office.
   4. Do research in law library.
E. Informal advocacy (to determine if the problem can be resolved without a hearing or court action, p. 773).
   1. Make sure everyone (welfare department, client, etc.) understands the issue.
   2. Provide missing information.
   3. Pressure the welfare department (calls, letters, visits, etc.).
   4. Recordkeeping (e.g., close files).
F. Formal advocacy (p. 787).

1. Prior hearing (administrative review)
    a. Determine if such hearing can be asked for and when request must be made.
    b. Draft letter requesting such hearing.
    c. Prepare for hearing (see "Fair Hearing" below).
    d. Conduct hearing (see "Fair Hearing" below).
    e. Follow-up (see "Fair Hearing" below).
2. Fair hearing
    a. Determine if the hearing can be asked for and when request must be made.
    b. Draft letter requesting the hearing.
    c. Prepare for the hearing:
        i. In advance of hearing, request that welfare department send paralegal the documents they will rely on at the hearing.
        ii. In advance of hearing, make sure that everyone (department representatives, client, etc.) is going to the hearing on the same issues.
        iii. Collect other documents the paralegal will use (e.g., cancelled check stubs).
        iv. Find witnesses (other than client).
        v. Prepare all witnesses (e.g., explain what hearing will be about; conduct a brief role-playing experience to acquaint them with the format and what the paralegal will be seeking from the witnesses).
        vi. Map out a preliminary strategy to use in conducting the hearing.
        vii. Make a final attempt to resolve the issues without a hearing (see above, "Informal Advocacy").
        viii. Make sure client and other witnesses will appear (e.g., give address of the hearing, take them to the hearing on the date of the hearing).
    d. Conduct the hearing (p. 791).
        i. Make sure the name, address, and title of everyone present is identified for the record.
        ii. Make opening statement summarizing client's case.
        iii. Ask for a postponement if the client has not appeared or if an emergency has arisen requiring more time to prepare.
        iv. Clearly state what relief the client is seeking from the hearing.
        v. If confusion exists on the issues, fight for a statement of the issues most favorable to client.
        vi. Take notes on the opening statement of the welfare department representative.
        vii. Complain if welfare department failed to provide sufficient information in advance of the hearing.
        viii. Present the client's case.

                a. submit documents.

                b. conduct direct examination of own witnesses.

                c. conduct re-direct examination of own witnesses (if allowed).

                d. cite the law.

        ix. Rebut case of welfare department.

                a. object to their documents.

                b. object to their use of jargon.

                c. object to their interpretation of the law.

                d. cross-examine their witnesses.

                e. re-cross-examine their witnesses (if allowed).

        x. Make closing statement summarizing the case of the client and repeating the result the client is seeking.

    e. Follow-up.

        i. Pressure the hearing officer to reach a result without undue delay.

        ii. Request a copy of the transcript of the hearing.

        iii. When a result is reached, pressure the welfare department to abide by it.

        iv. Consult with attorney to determine whether the hearing result should be appealed in court.

  3. Court.

    a. Make preliminary draft of the legal argument to be made on appeal.

    b. Assist the attorney in gathering the documents for appeal, interviewing the witnesses for appeal, etc.

    c. Be a general assistant for the attorney at court proceedings.

    d. File papers in court.

    e. Serve the papers.

G. Miscellaneous

  1. Train other paralegals.

  2. Write pamphlets on welfare law for distribution in the community.

  3. Community organization around welfare issues.

47. WORKER'S COMPENSATION LAW

I. Interview

  A. Collect and record details of the claim (e.g., date of injury, nature and dates of prior illness).

  B. Collect or arrange for the collection of documents, e.g., medical records, employment contract.

  C. Schedule physical examination.

II. Drafting

    A. The claim for compensation.

    B. The request for hearing.

    C. The medical authorization.

    D. The demand for medical information in the possession of respondent or insurance carrier.

    E. The proposed summary of issues involved.

III. Advocacy

    A. Informal: Contact (call, visit, write a letter to) the employer and/or the insurance carrier to determine whether the matter can be resolved without a formal hearing or court action.

    B. Formal: representation of claimant at the administrative hearing.

IV. Follow-up

    A. Determine whether the payment is in compliance with the award.

    B. If not, draft and file a statutory demand for proper payment.

    C. If such a statutory demand is filed, a "tickler" system is prepared to monitor the claim.

NOTE
A Paralegal in the White House:
Meg Shields Duke
New Roles in the Law Conference Report, 93 (1982)

[After working as a paralegal on the Reagan-Bush Campaign Committee], I'm a paralegal in the White House Counsel's office. I believe I'm the first paralegal in this office, in the White House. They've had law clerks in the past, but never have they hired a paralegal. There's one paralegal to nine attorneys at the moment. I think that's ridiculous and I hope we'll change that in the next several months to a year. But my responsibilities here are varied. Everybody is still trying to determine what their turf is. But for the first couple of months I've worked on a lot of transition matters, which might be expected. I was the coordinator for our transition audit, congressional transition audit, from the hill, which just ended a few weeks ago. I have engaged in drafting correspondence concerning the use of the president's name; the use of his image; our policy on gifts acceptance by public employees; drafting standards of conduct for public employees in the White House; job freeze litigation; those few controversial things. The last few weeks of my time have been devoted to the Lefever nomination. It's all been fascinating. Anyway, there are a number of areas that we also get involved in, the ethics of government act, for example. It's the first time it's been applied across the board to a new administration. It has been very, very time consuming for all our staff. I've been assisting in that, reviewing each individual file for high level government employees. As I said, I'm in the counsel's office now and intend to stay for a couple of years. But I would like to start my own paralegal firm. I have a close friend who started her own paralegal firm in Florida and we've talked often in the past of expanding it to Washington and a few other cities West where we'd like to spend some time. We're investigating the possibilities of reopening another firm here in Washington at some point, maybe in the next year and a half. But I think there is a place for more paralegals in the public sector, at least in the White House area, and I understand the Department of Justice of course has many, but I'd like to see it expanded and I'd also like to see more people branching out and trying this independent approach because I think it's fun. It's risky, but it's worth it.

Section D. FINDING A JOB: EMPLOYMENT STRATEGIES

The following strategies are primarily for individuals who have never worked with lawyers or held a paralegal job. Many of the strategies are also relevant, however, to people who have worked in law offices as secretaries or who are paralegals and wish to find other employment opportunities in the field.

GENERAL STRATEGIES FOR FINDING EMPLOYMENT

1. Begin now.
2. Start compiling a Job Hunting Notebook.
3. Organize an employment workshop.
4. Locate working paralegals.
5. Locate potential employers.
6. Prepare the resume, cover letter, and writing sample.
7. Prepare for the job interview.

Strategy 1:
Begin Now

You should begin preparing for the job hunt on the first day of your first paralegal class. Never wait until the program is almost over. Whether or not there is a placement office at your school, you should assume that obtaining a job will be your own responsibility. For most students, the job you obtain will be the job *you* find.

As we will see, there are many things that you can begin doing now. It is not too early, for example, to begin collecting the lists called for in your Job Hunting Notebook (p. 141).

It may be that there is still a lot of uncertainty in your mind about the kinds of employment options that exist. How can you begin looking for a job if you don't yet know what kind of job you would like to have? First of all, many of the suggested steps will be helpful regardless of the kind of job you are pursuing. More important, however, the very process of going through these search steps will help you clarify your employment objectives. As you begin seeking information and leads, the insights will come to you.

At this point, keep an open mind, be conscientious, and begin now.

Strategy 2:
Begin Compiling a
Job Hunting Notebook

On p. 141 you will find an outline for a Job Hunting Notebook that you should start preparing now. Following the outline, there are sample pages for the various sections in the Notebook. These sections will be discussed on the following pages.

Strategy 3:
Organize an Employment Workshop

On p. 33, there is a list of ten categories of paralegal employment. Some of these employment settings have subcategories. Begin organizing an employment conference or workshop consisting of a panel of paralegals from as many of the categories and subcategories of paralegals as you can locate in your area. Try to find at least one paralegal to represent each category and subcategory. The guest paralegals could be asked to come to an evening or Saturday session to discuss the following topics:

- How I obtained my job.
- Do's and don'ts in the employment interview.
- My recommendations for finding work.
- What I do (what a typical day consists of).
- What were the most valuable parts of my legal education.
- Etc.

While you might want to ask a teacher or the director of the program at your school to help you organize the workshop, it is recommended that you make it a student-run workshop. It will be good practice for you in taking the kind of initiative that is essential in finding employment. You, of course, will need the help of the school in reserving a room and perhaps in arranging for coffee facilities. If possible, avoid having to charge anything to attend. You might want to consider asking the nearest paralegal association to cosponsor the workshop with your class.

Have a meeting of your class in which a chairperson is selected to help coordinate the event. Then divide up the tasks of contacting participants, arranging for a room, preparing an agenda for the workshop, etc. You may want to consider inviting former graduates of your school to attend as panel members or to be part of the audience.

The ideal time for such a workshop is a month or two after you begin your course work. This means that you need to begin organizing immediately.

Strategy 4:
Locate Working Paralegals

Perhaps the most important step in finding employment is to begin talking with paralegals who are already employed. They are the obvious experts on how to find a job! They are probably also very knowledgeable about employment opportunities in their office and in similar offices in the area. (See Job Hunting Notebook, p. 153.)

Ways to meet paralegals:

1. At an employment workshop (see Strategy 3 above).
2. At a paralegal association meeting. See Appendix B for a list of paralegal associations (p. 843). Contact the one nearest you and ask about joining. There may be a special dues or fee structure for students. Ask if the association has a job bank service. Ask if it has a job-finding manual for paralegals in your area. Begin attending association meetings. Participate in committees. The more active you are as a student member, the more contacts you will make. If there is no paralegal association near you, organize one, beginning with your own student body and past graduates of your school (see *The Formation of Paralegal Associations: An Organizational Manual* by the National Federation of Paralegal Associations, Ben Franklin Station, P.O. Box 14103, Washington, D.C. 20044).
3. Ask the director of your program if s/he has a directory of graduates from your school.
4. Some paralegal associations have directories of paralegals in your area. Check with your program director and/or with the paralegal association nearest you.
5. Members of your own class may be paralegals who are upgrading their skills. Also look for such individuals taking courses that you are not currently taking at the school.
6. Ask your program director if s/he has a copy of the latest newsletter of your local paralegal association and of the two national paralegal associations: the Federation of Paralegal Associations (*Paralegal Reporter*) and the National Association of Legal Assistants (*Facts and Findings*). In these newsletters, look for ads for continuing education conferences in your area of the country. Such conferences are an excellent way for you to meet large numbers of paralegals.
7. Paralegals sometimes attend continuing education conferences conducted by the local bar association.

You should also find out if there is an association of legal secretaries and of legal administrators in your area. If so, they might conduct workshops or meetings that you can attend. Even if no such associations exist in your area, it would be very useful for you to talk with individual legal secretaries and legal administrators about employment opportunities where they work.

Strategy 5:
Locate Potential Employers

There are a number of ways to locate lawyers:

a. Placement office.
b. Personal contacts.
c. Ads.
d. Through other paralegals.
e. Employment agencies.
f. Directories and other lists.
g. Courts and bar association meetings.

h. Miscellaneous.
See Job Hunting Notebook, p. (152.)

For every attorney that you contact, you want to know the following:

- Has the attorney hired paralegals in the past?
- If so, is the attorney interested in hiring more paralegals?
- If the attorney has never hired paralegals, is s/he interested in considering the value of such hiring?
- Does the attorney know of other attorneys who might be interested in hiring paralegals?

The last point is particularly important. Attorneys from different firms often talk with each other about their practice, including their experiences with paralegals or their plans for hiring paralegals. Hence always ask about other firms. If you obtain a lead this way, begin your contact with the other firm by mentioning the name of the attorney who gave you the lead, e.g., "Mary Smith told me that you have hired paralegals in the past and might be interested in hiring another paralegal" or, "John Jones suggested that I contact you concerning possible employment at your firm as a paralegal."

a. Placement office.   Start, of course, with the placement office of your paralegal school. Talk with staff members and/or check the bulletin board regularly. If your school is part of a university that has a law school, you might want to check the placement office of the law school as well. While paralegal jobs are usually not listed there, you may find descriptions of law firms with the number of lawyers and paralegals employed.[23] It would be useful for you to find out what the major resources are for obtaining lawyer jobs, e.g., special directories, lists or ads in bar publications, legal newspapers, etc. Such resources might provide leads on contacting firms about paralegal employment.

b. Personal contacts.   Make a list of attorneys who fall into the following categories:

- Personal friends
- Friends of friends
- Attorneys you have hired
- Attorneys your relatives have hired
- Attorneys your former employers have hired
- Attorneys your friends have hired
- Teachers
- Politicians
- Neighbors
- Etc.

You should consider contacting these attorneys about their own paralegal hiring plans as well as for references to other attorneys. Don't be reluctant to take advantage of any direct or indirect association that you might have with an attorney. (See Job Hunting Notebook, p. 152.)

c. Ads.   You should regularly check the classified pages of your daily newspaper as well as the legal newspaper (p. 546) for your area. If you are seeking em-

[23] See also the chart on paralegals in the largest law firms in the country, p. 36.

ployment in another city, the main branch of your public library and the main library of large universities in your area may have out-of-town newspapers. If you have friends in these other cities, they might be willing to send you clippings from the classified ads of their newspapers. There are several *national* legal newspapers that sometimes have paralegal employment ads, e.g., the *National Law Journal,* the *American Lawyer,* and the *Legal Times of Washington.* Law libraries often subscribe to one or more of these newspapers.

Look for ads under the headings "Paralegal" or "Legal Assistant." For example:

Also look for ads under headings that are law related, e.g., "Research Assistant," "Legislative Aide," "Librarian," etc. For example:

Of course, some of the above jobs may not be what you are looking for. They may not be directly related to your legal training and experience. Nevertheless, you should read such ads carefully. Some might be worth pursuing.

On most classified pages, you will find many ads for legal secretaries. You might want to respond to such ads as follows:

> I saw your ad for a legal secretary. I am a trained paralegal and am wondering whether you have any openings for paralegals. If not, I would greatly appreciate your referring me to any attorneys you know who may be looking for paralegals.

What about applying for a secretarial position in a law office? Many paralegals correctly take the view that this would be a mistake. In a tight employment market, however, some paralegals believe that a secretarial or typing job would be a way to "get a foot in the door," and hope that they will eventually be able to graduate into a position in the office that is commensurate with their paralegal training. Such a course of action is obviously a very personal decision that you must make on your own. It is not uncommon for clerical staff to be promoted to paralegal positions in a firm. It is also not uncommon, however, to get stuck in a clerical position.

d. Through other paralegals.   In Strategy 4 above, we discussed methods of contacting working paralegals. Once you talk with a paralegal, you, of course, can obtain information about contacting the employing attorney of that paralegal.

Most paralegal associations (see Appendix B, p. 843) have newsletters that are published once every two months. Some of the newsletters have employment ads as a regular feature. For example:

> Job Openings
> Municipal Bonding Department of 68 attorney law firm is seeking an experienced legal assistant to begin work in mid-December. Must have excellent organizational, writing and mathematical skills and be detail-minded. Excellent benefits. Salary commensurate with experience. Send resume to . . .

Find out if the paralegal association in your area has job openings listed in its newsletter. If so, ask the association if it has back issues of its newsletters available. Look at some of the ads in these old issues. You might consider contacting firms that once had paralegal job openings. Even though the positions are probably now filled, you might ask the firm if you can send your resume to be kept on file in the event that openings occur in the future. Also ask the firm if it can give you any leads to openings elsewhere. You might even want to try to talk with the paralegal who was hired to fill the opening listed in the old issue of the newsletter. Paralegals who have recently been through an extensive job search may be willing to provide you with valuable suggestions.

e. Employment agencies.   There have always been employment agencies for the placement of lawyers. Many of these agencies also handle paralegal placement.

Recently, a number of agencies have been opened to deal primarily with paralegal placement.

Help Wanted

Paralegal Agency   Fee Paid

PARALEGAL PLACEMENT EXPERTS RECOGNIZED BY OVER 200 LAW FIRMS AND CORPORATIONS

Pensions
Outstanding law firm seeks 1+yrs pension paralegal exper. Major responsibilities, quality clients & liberal benefits. Salary commensurate w/exper.

Real Estate
TWO LAW FIRMS seek real estate paralegals. Your experience will be recognized by these firms. Liberal benefits.

Corporate
TWO LAW FIRMS seek exper'd corporate generalists. Quality client contact, liberal benefits include annual bonus & paid overtime.

Librarian
Number two position at major law firm. MLS & law library exper req'd. Excellent growth opportunity. Liberal benefits incl pension plan & bonus.

Litigation
SEVERAL positions open at LAW FIRMS for litigation paralegals. Major benefits incl bonus

Managing Clerk
Midtown law firm seeks 1+ yrs exper as a managing clerk. Work directly w/top management. Liberal benefits.

These are just a few of the many paralegal positions we have available. Call us for professional career guidance.

Look for such ads in the classified pages of general circulation and legal newspapers. Check your yellow pages under "Employment Agencies." If you are not sure which of the listed agencies cover legal placements, call several at random and ask which agencies in the city handle paralegal placement or legal placement in general. Also, ask your placement office. Caution, however, is needed in using such agencies. Some of them know very little about paralegals in spite of their ads claiming to place paralegals. You may find that the agency views a paralegal as a secretary with a little extra training.

All employment agencies charge a placement fee. You must check whether the fee is paid by the employer or the employee hired through the agency. Read the agency's service contract carefully before signing. Question the agency about the jobs they have available, e.g., whether evening work is expected, typing requirements, if any.

f. Directories and other lists of attorneys. Find out whether there is a directory or list of attorneys in your area. Ask your program director and a librarian at any law library in your area. Your yellow pages may also list attorneys generally and by specialty.

Also check with a librarian about national directories of attorneys. One of the major directories is the Martindale-Hubbell Law Directory (p. 548) which gives descriptions of law firms by state and city or county (see figure 3). For each firm, you are given brief biographies of the attorneys (e.g., colleges at-

Figure 3. Excerpt from a page in Martindale-Hubbell Law Directory.

MASON, KOLEHMAINEN, RATHBURN & WYSS

Patent, Trademark,
Copyright and Unfair
Competition Law
Trials

20 NORTH WACKER DRIVE
CHICAGO, ILLINOIS 60606

Telephone:
(312) 621-1300

Cable Address:
"MAKRAW"
TWX 221-5342

MEMBERS OF FIRM

Richard D. Mason, born Caddo County, Oklahoma, August 2, 1906; admitted to bar, 1935, District of Columbia; 1938, Illinois; 1961, U.S. Supreme Court. Preparatory education, Oklahoma University (B.S., 1929; E.E.; B.A., 1931) and Massachusetts Institute of Technology (M.S., 1931); legal education, George Washington University (LL.B., 1935). *Fraternities:* Sigma Tau; Phi Delta Phi. *Member:* Chicago, 7th Federal Circuit, Illinois State and American Bar Associations; American Patent Law Association; Patent Law Association of Chicago; Legal Club of Chicago.

M. Hudson Rathburn (1908-1973).

Walther E. Wyss, born Medford, Wisconsin, February 17, 1909; admitted to bar, 1938, District of Columbia; 1941, New York; 1942, U.S. Supreme Court; 1946, Illinois. Preparatory education, University of Wisconsin (B.S. in E.E., 1933; M.S., 1934); legal education, George Washington University (J.D., 1939). *Fraternites:* Order of the Coif, Tau Beta Pi; Phi Delta Phi; Phi Eta Sigma; Phi Kappa Phi; Eta Kappa Nu. *Member:* Chicago, 7th Federal Circuit, Illinois State and American (Member, 1968-1973, Special Committee on Complex and Multi-District Litigation; Member of Council, 1968-1972 and Chairman, 1974-1975, Patent, Trademark and Copyright Law Section) Bar Associations; Patent Law Association of Chicago (President, 1971); American Patent Law Association. Fellow, American College of Trial Lawyers.

Reginald K. Bailey, born Lawrence, Kansas, June 13, 1920; admitted to bar, 1949, District of Columbia; 1950, Illinois. Preparatory education, University of Kansas (B.S. in E.E., 1942); legal education, Georgetown University (J.D., 1949). *Fraternity:* Delta Theta Phi. *Member:* Chicago, Illinois State and American Bar Associations; Patent Law Association of Chicago; Legal Club of Chicago.

Robert L. Rohrback, born Washington, D. C., November 17, 1924; admitted to bar, 1953, Illinois; 1973, U.S. Supreme Court. Preparatory education, University of Maryland (B.S.E.E., 1949); legal education, Georgetown University (J.D., 1952). *Fraternities:* Tau Beta Pi; Phi Kappa Phi; Delta Theta Phi. *Member:* American Bar Association; Patent Law Association of Chicago.

Warren D. McPhee, born Belmont, Massachusetts, April 23, 1914; admitted to bar, 1952, Illinois; 1973, U.S. Supreme Court. Preparatory education, Boston University (B.S., 1937); Northwestern University (Ph.D. in Chem., 1940); legal education, Loyola University (J.D., 1952). *Fraternities:* Phi Alpha Delta; Phi Beta Kappa, Sigma Xi. *Member:* Chicago and American Bar Associations; Patent Law Association of Chicago; American Patent Law Association.

James R. Sweeney, born Chicago, Illinois, February 19, 1928; admitted to bar, 1956, Illinois. Preparatory education, University of Notre Dame (B.S., 1950), legal education, Northwestern University (J.D., 1956). *Fraternity:* Phi Delta Phi. *Member:* Chicago (Secretary, 1977—), Seventh Circuit, Illinois State and American (Member, Council, Patent, Trademark and Copyright Law Section, 1976—) Bar Associations; Patent Law Association of Chicago (President, 1974); American Patent Law Association; American Judicature Society.

Clemens Hufmann, born Duisburg-Ruhrort, Germany, December 5, 1927; admitted to bar, 1958, Illinois; 1973, U.S. Supreme Court. Legal education, University of Cologne, University of Bonn, University of Munich, University of Nebraska, Harvard University (LL.M., 1954) and De Paul University (J.D., 1958). *Member:* Chicago, Illinois State and American Bar Associations; Patent Law Association of Chicago.

Philip C. Peterson, born Topeka, Kansas, March 10, 1931; admitted to bar, 1960, Kansas; 1961, Illinois; 1975, U.S. Supreme Court. Preparatory education, Kansas State University, University of Kansas (B.S.M.E., 1953) and Northwestern University (M.B.A., 1974); legal education, Washburn University of Topeka (J.D., 1960). *Fraternities:* Delta Theta Phi; Pi Tau Sigma; Sigma Tau; Tau Beta Pi. *Member:* Chicago and Illinois State Bar Associations; Patent Law Association of Chicago.

Philip M. Kolehmainen, born Evanston, Illinois, October 15, 1938; admitted to bar, 1964, Illinois; 1973, U.S. Supreme Court. Preparatory education, Yale University (B.S., 1960); legal education, Northwestern University (J.D., 1963). *Fraternity:* Phi Delta Phi. *Member:* Chicago Bar Association; Patent Law Association of Chicago; American Patent Law Association.

Joseph Krieger, born Gary, Indiana, June 8, 1944; admitted to bar, 1969, Illinois and Indiana; 1976, U.S. Supreme Court. Preparatory education, University of Michigan (B.S.E. in E.E., 1966); legal education, University of Michigan (J.D., 1969). *Member:* Chicago and American Bar Associations; Patent Law Association of Chicago.

---

tended) as well as the areas of practice for the firm. One strategy might be to select attorneys from a firm who went to the same undergraduate college as you. Mentioning this fact in a cover letter might result in a more sympathetic response.

Also ask a librarian or placement officer about other standard specialty lists of attorneys, e.g., lists of criminal law attorneys, lists of attorney generals, lists of corporate counsel (in-house), lists of women attorneys, lists of black attorneys, lists of Hispanic attorneys, lists of Native American attorneys, etc.

Contact your local bar association to see if it has lists of attorneys available by specialty. Local bar associations, state bar associations, and national bar associations (such as the American Bar Association) all have committees on areas of the law, e.g., family law, corporate law, antitrust law, criminal law. Lists of these committees are usually available from the bar associations. The lists often include names and addresses of the committee members. If names only

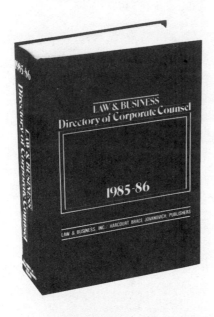

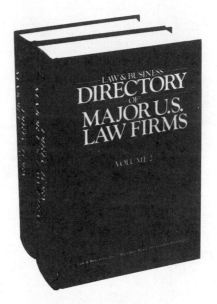

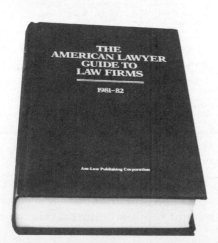

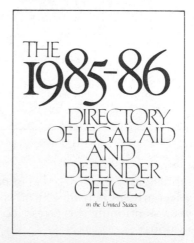

Above photos reprinted with permission of Law & Business, Inc./Harcourt Brace Jovanovich, Inc.

are given, you can obtain the addresses from Martindale-Hubbell Law Directory, from one of the other directories, or from your local phone book.

g. Courts and bar association meetings.   You can also meet attorneys at the courts of your area, e.g., during a recess or at the end of the day. Bar association committee meetings are sometimes open to nonlawyers. When the other strategies for contacting attorneys do not seem to be productive, consider going to places where attorneys congregate. Simply introduce yourself and ask if they know of paralegal employment opportunities at their firms or at other firms. If you meet an attorney who practices in a particular specialty, it would be helpful if you could describe your course work and/or general interest in that kind of law. If you are doing some research in that area of the law, you might begin by asking for some research leads before you ask about employment.

h. Miscellaneous.

- Go to a recent reporter volume (p. 525) or advance sheet (p. 521) of a reporter volume containing court opinions of your state. At the beginning of each opinion, there is a list of the attorneys who represented the parties in that case. You can obtain their addresses from standard directories such as those mentioned above. If the opinion is on an area of law in which you have an interest, call the attorneys after you have read the opinion. Talk about the case. Ask a question or two about the case and that area of the law. Then ask about employment opportunities for paralegals in that area.
- Look for ads in legal newspapers (p. 546) in which an attorney is seeking information about a particular product involved in a suit that is contemplated or underway. Or read feature stories in this newspaper on major litigation that is about to begin. If the area of the law interests you, contact the law firms involved to ask about employment opportunities for paralegals. Many firms hire additional paralegals particularly for large cases.
- Go to the bar journal (p. 546) of your local or state bar associations in the law library. The articles and comments in the journal are often written by attorneys from the state. If the subject of the article interests you, read it and call the author. Ask a question or two about the topic of the article and the area of the law involved. Then ask about employment opportunities for paralegals in that area.

Strategy 6:
Prepare the Resume,
Cover Letter, and Writing Sample

The cardinal principle of resume writing is that the resume must fit the job you are seeking. Hence, you must have more than one resume or you must re-write the resume for each different kind of paralegal job that you are seeking. You should view a resume as an *advocacy* document. You are trying to convince someone (a) to give you an interview and ultimately (b) to offer you a job. You are not simply communicating information about yourself. Advocacy is required for several reasons. First, there are probably more applicants than jobs available. Second, some prospective employers may ignore resumes that are not geared to their particular law firm needs. Third, some prospective employers may not be sure how paralegals can function in a law office. In order to sell yourself, your resume must be responsive to such realities.

Before examining sample resumes, we need to explore some general guidelines that apply to *any* resume.

GUIDELINES ON DRAFTING AN EFFECTIVE RESUME

1. Be concise and to the point. Generally, the resume should not be over two pages. A longer resume is justified only if you have a unique education and experience background that is directly related to law or to the particular law firm or company in which you are interested.
2. Be accurate. Studies show that about 30% of all resumes contain inaccuracies. While you want to present yourself in the best possible light, it is critical that you do not jeopardize your integrity. All the data in the resume should be verifiable if anyone checks.
3. Include personal data, e.g., name, address, zip code, phone number, (with area code) where you can be reached. You do not have to list your marital status, although this is a subject about which prospective employers usually have an interest. Whether you reveal such information is a personal decision. Do *not* include a personal photograph, data on your health, height, religion, etc.
4. Provide a concise statement of your career objective. State the kind of position you are seeking. Be general enough to give yourself flexibility. While the objective is usually phrased in terms of your needs, you must keep in mind that the resume reader's primary interest is the employer's needs. Hence, phrase your career goal or objective in a way that will present obvious benefits to the employer (e.g., you want to work in an environment committed to growth; you want to develop your expertise with coworkers who insist on high standards).
5. State your prior education and training. (See Job Hunting Notebook, p. 147, p. 149.) List each school or training institution and the dates attended. Use a reverse chronological order, i.e., start the list with the most current and work backwards. Do not include your high school unless you attended a prestigious high school, you have not attended college, or you are a very recent high school graduate. When you give your legal education:
   a. List the major courses.
   b. State specific skills/tasks covered in the courses that are relevant to the job you are applying for. Also state major topic areas covered in the courses that demonstrate a knowledge (or at least an exposure) to material that is relevant to the job.
   c. List any special programs in the school, e.g., internship, moot court, special class assignments, term papers, extensive research, semester projects. Give a brief description if any are relevant to the job you are applying for.

   d. State any unusually high grades; give overall grade point average if it is distinctive.

For example, if you are applying for a corporate paralegal job, relevant courses could be stated as follows:

> **Corporate Law** (in this course we studied the formation of a corporation, director and shareholder meetings, corporate mergers, and the dissolution of corporations; we also examined sample shareholder minutes and prepared proxy statements). Grade received: B+.

> **Legal Bibliography** (in this course we covered the basic law books relevant to researching corporate law including the state code, using practice books, finding cases on corporate law through the digests, etc.). Grade received: A−.

List any degrees, certificates, or other recognition that you earned at each school or training institution. Include high aptitude or standard test scores. If the school or institution has any special distinction or recognition, mention this as well.

6. State your work experience. (See Job Hunting Notebook, p. 142, p. 143.) List the jobs you held, your job title, the dates of employment, and the major duties that you performed. (Do not state the reason you left each job, although you should be prepared to discuss this if you are granted an interview.) Again, work backwards. Start with the most current (or your present) employment. The statement of duties is particularly important. Emphasize anything that will be relevant to the position you are seeking. If you have legal experience, then of course you will list specific duties and tasks that demonstrate you have legal skills that are directly relevant to the position you are currently seeking, e.g., drafted pleadings, digested deposition transcripts. Give prominence to such skills and tasks on the resume. Nonlegal experience, however, can also be relevant. Every job that you have had says something about you as an individual. Phrase your duties in such jobs in a manner that will highlight important personality traits. (See p. 147.) In general, all employers are looking for people with the following characteristics:

- Emotionally mature
- Intelligent
- Willing to learn
- Able to get along with others
- Able to work independently (someone with initiative and self-reliance who is not afraid of assuming responsibility)
- A problem-solver
- Able to handle time pressures and frustration
- Loyal
- Stable
- Energetic

As you list duties in prior and current employment settings, you do *not* use any of the language in the above list. But try to state duties that tend to show that these characteristics apply to you. For example, if you had a job as a camp counselor, state that you supervised eighteen children, designed schedules according to predetermined objectives, prepared budgets, took over in the absence of the director of the camp, etc. A listing of such duties will say a lot about you as a person. You are someone who can be trusted, you know how to work with people, you are flexible, etc. These are the kinds of conclusions that you want the reader of your resume to reach as the resume is examined. Finally, try to present the facts to show a growth in your accomplishments, development, and maturity.

7. State other experience and skills that do not fall within the categories of education and employment mentioned above. (See Job Hunting Notebook, p. 146.) Perhaps you have been a homemaker for twenty years, you raised five children, you worked you way through college, you were the church treasurer, a cub scout volunteer, etc. In a separate category on the resume called "Other Experience," list such activities and state your duties in the same manner mentioned above to demonstrate relevant personality traits. Hobbies can be included (without using the work "hobby") when they are distinctive and illustrate special talents or achievement.

8. State any special abilities (e.g., ability to speak a foreign language), awards, credentials, scholarships, membership associations, community service, publications, etc., that have not been mentioned elsewhere on the resume.

9. No one has a perfect resume. There are facts about all of us that we would prefer to downplay or avoid, e.g., sudden change in jobs, school transfer because of personal or family difficulties, low aptitude test scores. There is no need to point out these facts, but in a job interview you must be prepared to discuss any obvious gaps or problems that might be evident from your resume.

10. Give a list of references. State the names and addresses of people who know you and who could be contacted by the prospective employer. When you list paralegal teachers at your current (or most recent school), it is generally a good practice to call these individuals in advance to ask their permission to use their names as a reference on your resume. Seek the advice of your program director on this matter. You may be advised to simply state that "References, letters of recommendation, and writing samples will be provided on request."

11. Do not include salary requirements on the resume. Leave this topic for the interview.

12. The resume should be neatly typed, grammatically correct, and readable. Be sure that there are no spelling errors, or smudge spots from erasures or fingerprints. Avoid abbreviations except for items such as street, state, degrees earned, etc. Do not make any hand-written corrections. Proofread carefully. Ask someone else to proofread the resume for you to see if you missed anything.

You do not have to use complete sentences in the resume. Sentence fragments are adequate so long as you rigorously follow the grammatical rule on parallelism. For example, say, "research<u>ed</u> securities issues, draft<u>ed</u>

complaints, serv<u>ed</u> papers on opposing parties." Do not say, "researched securities, drafting complaints, and I served papers on opposing parties." When you present a series or a list, be consistent in using words ending in "ed" or ending in "ing," etc. Do not suddenly change from an "ed" word to an "ing" word, or add personal pronouns on only some of the items in the series or list.

Leave generous margins. Cluster similar information together and use consistent indentation patterns so that the reader can easily skim or scan the resume and quickly find those categories of information about you in which s/he is most interested.

The resume should have a professional appearance. Consider having your resume typeset on quality paper (with matching envelopes) by a commercial printing company. Such companies are also able to provide multiple copies of your resume. Avoid submitting a resume that was obviously reproduced on a poor-quality Xerox machine at a corner drugstore. The resume is often the first contact that a prospective employer will have with you. You want to convey the impression that you know how to write and organize data. Furthermore, it is a sign of respect to the reader of your resume when it is clear that you took the time and energy to make your resume professionally presentable. Law offices are *conservative* environments. Lawyers like to project an image of propriety, stability, and order. Be sure that your resume also projects this image.

13. Again, the resume concentrates on those facts about you that show that you are particularly qualified *for the specific job you are seeking.* The single most important theme that you want to convey in the resume is that you are a person who can make a contribution to *this* organization. As much as possible, the reader of the resume should have the impression that you prepared the resume for the particular position that is open. In style and content, the resume should emphasize what will be "pleasing" to the reader. A resume is not an autobiography. It is a well-packaged commercial to a specific audience designed to demonstrate what you can contribute to a particular office.

The last guideline is very important. You cannot comply with it unless you have done some background research on the law office where you are applying and, if possible, on the person who will be receiving the resume. How do you do this background research? See strategy #3 on the employment workshop, strategy #4 on contacting working paralegals, and strategy #5 on contacting potential employers. These strategies are calculated to provide you with information about specific job possibilities. This information then becomes the foundation of what to include in the resume, what to emphasize, etc.

THE RESUME AS AN ADVOCACY DOCUMENT

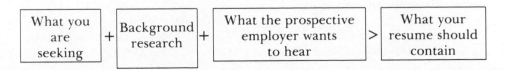

Here is a partial checklist of some of the information you want to obtain through background research on a prospective employer or job (see also p. 139):

- What kind of law is practiced at the office? What are the specialties? Check Martindale-Hubbell as well as some of the other directories mentioned above (p. 124).
- How is the office structured? How is it governed? A management committee?
- How old is the office? Has it expanded recently? If so, in what area?
- What kinds of clients does the office have? A variety of small clients? Several large clients that provide most of the fees?
- If the office is the law department of a corporation, what are the company's main products or services? (Try to obtain copies of recent annual reports of the company. Ask a librarian how to obtain a profile on the company and its chief executive officers. Check a directory of corporate counsel, p. 124.)
- How many lawyers are in the office?
- How many paralegals? What kind of work do they do? Does the office understand the role of paralegals? What kinds of complaints have the paralegals had about the office? What are the advantages and disadvantages of working in the office?
- Has the office had personnel problems? A high turnover?
- Does the office operate through systems? If not, how does it feel about developing such systems?
- Why has the office decided to hire a paralegal now? What problems have prompted this decision? Does everyone in the office agree with the decision?

If you do your homework on a prospective employer, you will have begun collecting answers to such questions so that you can tailor your resume to these answers. You will select those aspects of your prior employment or education, for example, that will suggest or demonstrate that you are able to handle the demands of the particular job.

Of course, for many jobs, you will not be able to obtain answers to such questions in advance no matter how much background research you do. You will simply have to do the best you can to predict what the "correct" answers are and structure your resume, cover letter, and writing sample accordingly.

The main point, however, is that a lot of preparation is needed before you approach a prospective employer. Much time and energy must be expended. A conscientious and organized job search will be good preparation for the career ahead of you. *The same kind of motivation, creativity, and aggressiveness that is needed to find a good job is also needed to perform as an effective paralegal and to advance in this field.* The cornerstone of achievement and success is a heavy dosage of old-fashioned hard work.

Figure 4. Sample Resume I.

John J. Smith
43 Benning Road SE
Salem, Maryland 21455
(301) 456-0427

Professional Objective

Position as a paralegal in the area of probate, trusts, and estates in a firm where my skills will be used and where there are opportunities for growth.

Education

Jan. 1985 - Jan. 1986 Maynard College Paralegal Program. Courses:

Trusts and Estates: (an overview of probate procedure in Maryland; how to conduct a client conference to collect the basic facts; how to prepare the 105 short form)

Tax I: (an introduction to the taxation of estates and general income tax; fundamentals of accounting; valuation of personal and real assets)

Introduction to Law
Family Law
Litigation
Civil Procedure
Legal Research

Internship: part of the curriculum at Maynard involved a six-week internship placement at a law firm; I was placed at Donaldson and Tannance, a general practice firm in Salem.

Tasks undertaken at the internship: drafted answers to interrogatories in a divorce case on the ground of mental cruelty; maintained the office's tickler system; completed cite checking and shepardizing for an appellate brief.

Sept. 1983 - June 1984 Jefferson Junior College Courses:

Business Law
English I, II
Introduction to Psychology
French I

Sociology
Chemistry
Creative Writing

Employment

1981 - 1984 Teller, Salem National Bank
Responsibilities: receiving deposit and withdrawal requests; training trainee tellers, supervising note department in the absence of the assistant manager.

1976 - 1980 Driver, ABC Biscuit Company

Honors

1981 Junior Achievement Award for Outstanding Marketing

Associations

Financial Secretary, Salem Paralegal Association
Regional representative, National Federation of Paralegal Associations
Member, National Association of Legal Assistants

Figure 4. Sample Resume I—Continued.

References	Mary Tannance, Esq. Donaldson and Tennance 65 Market St. Salem, Maryland 21459	Rita Steck Vice President Salem National Bank 1795 South Kendal Ave, Salem, Maryland 21458
	Patricia Farrell Director Maynard College Paralegal Program South Campus Salem, Maryland 21460	Professor Mary Schneider (trusts and estates) Maynard College Paralegal Program South Campus Salem, Maryland 21460
	Writing samples available on request.	

We now examine a sample resume that has a somewhat different emphasis. In the following resume, you will find more attention given to basic skills and achievements than to specific past legal positions or training. This format can be particularly useful when your skills were *not* gained in paralegal employment, training, or life experience. (See Job Hunting Notebook, p. 146.) Careful drafting can indicate to prospective employers that past activities and achievements have prepared you for paralegal work and on-the-job training.

Figure 5. Sample Resume II.[24]

Jane Doe
18 East 7th Avenue
Denver, Colorado 80200
303/555-1198

Job Objective
A position in a legal office requiring skills in communications, research, and organizational ability, leading toward training for and work as a paralegal.

Brief Summary of Background
Bachelor of Arts and Bachelor of Science (Education) with major in English and minor in Library Science. Taught creative writing and communications to high school juniors and seniors; worked several years as research and index assistant in records and research department of large, international organization; worked part-time and on a volunteer basis in schools and libraries as librarian and reading tutor.

Professional Skills Related to Career Objectives

COMMUNICATIONS SKILLS
Taught communications to high school seniors; read extensively in international publications during nonworking years; conducted workshops on library skills and storytelling to children and young adults; participated in workshops with educators on reading skills; served as Circulation Representative for *The Christian Science Monitor,* including promoting and selling subscriptions by telephone and in person. Have considerable writing experience in working toward college degrees in English.

[24] Rocky Mountain Legal Assistants Association, *Employment Handbook for Legal Assistants,* 26-8 (1979).

Figure 5. Sample Resume II—Continued.

CLERICAL SKILLS
    Facility with [a] vocabulary and spelling; [b] rules of diction and usage; [c] typing (80 wpm); [d] filing (helped revise and maintain many files including administrative, subjective, alpha-chrono combinations); [e] systems (maintained and circulated library collections and maintained catalog card files).

RESEARCH SKILLS
    As librarian: helped students and teachers research and retrieve information and materials on various subjects; ordered, received, processed, and shelved library materials.

    As research assistant: indexed correspondence; researched files for information using subject index; collated information on various subjects.

ANALYTICAL AND ORGANIZATIONAL SKILLS
    Handled all phases of management of school library; planned for materials needed, ordering to meet those needs; supervised assistants; set up revised filing systems; helped engineer departmental move to new quarters.

Employment History

9/84 - Present
    Lincoln Elementary School
    100 Oak Street, Denver, Colorado 80000
    John P. Doe, Principal
    Title: Teacher's Aide (Part-time)

6/76 - 6/84
    International Church Center
    Executive Department, Records and Research Section
    465 E. 8th St., Boston, Massachusetts 02127
    Mary Jones, Supervisor
    Title: Research and Index Assistant (12 months full-time; 24 months part-time)

4/84 - 6/84
    Latin Preparatory School
    16 Adams Court, Dorchester, Masschusetts 02139
    Paul Smith, Headmaster
    Title: School Librarian (substitute)

2/83 - 6/84
    James P. O'Reilly Elementary School
    74 Statler Road, Boston, Masschusetts 02140
    George Ryan, Principal
    Title: School Librarian (volunteer)

9/74 - 6/75
    Roosevelt High School
    16 Main St., Minneapolis, Minnesota 55162
    Linda Marshall, Principal
    Title: English Teacher

Education

1983 - 1984
    University of Massachusetts, Boston Campus
    Special courses included:
      Library and the City Child
      Books and the City Child

1979 - 1980
    Harvard Extension, Problems in Urban Education

1969 - 1973
    University of Minnesota, Minneapolis,
      B.S. and B.A., *Major:* English
      Minor: Library Science

School Activities
    National Honor Society; Dramatic Club; Creative Writing Club; YWCA; Member, Minnesota Dance Company, 1969 - 1973.

Figure 6. Sample Cover Letter.

---

43 Benning Road SE
Salem, Maryland 21455
301-456-0427
March 13, 1986

Linda Stenner
Stenner, Skidmore & Smith
438 Bankers Trust Bldg.
Suite 1200
Salem, Maryland 21458

Dear Ms. Stenner:

Michael Diamond, Esq. told me that your firm may have an opening for a trusts and estates paralegal. I am enclosing my resume for your consideration. I am very interested in working in the field of probate, trusts, and estates. The course work that I did at Maynard College and my prior work at the Salem National Bank provided me with an appreciation of the complexity of this area of the law. I find the field fascinating.

I am fully aware of the kind of attention to detail that a paralegal in this field must have. If you decide to check any of my references, I am confident that you will be told of the high level of discipline and responsibility that I bring to the tasks I undertake.

I have two writing samples that may be of interest to you: a draft of a will that I prepared in my course on trusts and estates and a memorandum of law on the valuation of stocks. These writing samples are available on request.

I would appreciate the opportunity to be interviewed for the paralegal position at your firm. I feel confident that my training and experience have prepared me for the kind of challenge that this position would provide.

Sincerely,

John J. Smith

The cover letter should state how you learned of the office. It should also highlight and amplify those portions of the resume that are relevant to the position you are seeking. Explain how you are qualified for the job. Like the resume itself, the cover letter should be well written and give the impression that you are a professional. It is also important that you communicate a sense of enthusiasm about the position.

WRITING SAMPLES. As indicated earlier, you should be constantly thinking about writing samples based upon the course work that you do and any legal employment or internship experiences that you have had. If your writing sample comes from a prior job or internship, be sure that the confidentiality of actual parties is protected by "whiting out" or changing their names. In addition, consider preparing other writing samples on your own. For example:

- a brief memorandum of law (p. 686) on the application of a statute to a set of facts that you make up

- an analysis of a recent court opinion
- an in-take memorandum of law based upon an interview (p. 386) that you role-play with another student
- an annotated bibliography on a particular topic (p. 677)
- a brief article that you write for a paralegal newsletter on an aspect of your legal education or work experience as a paralegal

Prepare a file of all your writing samples. (See Job Hunting Notebook, p. 151.) If possible, try to have a teacher, practicing attorney, or paralegal review each sample. Rewrite it based on their comments. You must take the initiative in preparing writing samples and in soliciting feedback from knowledgeable contacts that you make on your own.

You need to have a large pool of diverse writing samples from which to choose once you begin the actual job hunt. Start preparing these samples now.

Strategy 7:
The Job Interview

Once you have overcome the hurdles of finding a prospective employer who will read your cover letter and resume, the next problem is to arrange for a job interview. For some positions, this may be easy, e.g., if the employer has advertised the position. In other situations you will be approaching the employer cold. You may have to be a bit more assertive in obtaining an interview.

In your cover letter, for example, you may want to add the following sentence at the end:

> Within the next two weeks, I will give you a call to determine whether an interview would be possible.

This strategy does not leave the matter entirely up to the prospective employer as to whether there will be further contact with you. You must be careful, however, not to appear too forward. Some may resent this approach. On the other hand, you may have nothing to lose by trying it several times to see what response you obtain.

Always try to have a paralegal, attorney, administrator, or secretary in the office arrange the interview for you with the person who will be doing the hiring and/or interviewing. Hopefully, your background research into the office will enable you to identify such an in-house person who will put in a word for you.

JOB INTERVIEW GUIDELINES
(See Job Hunting Notebook, p. 155.)

1. Be sure you have the exact address, room number, time of the interview, and the name of the person who will be conducting the interview. Give yourself sufficient time to find the office. If the area is new to you, be sure that you have precise directions. It would be unfortunate to start your contact with the office by having to provide excuses for being late. Arrive at least ten minutes early. You will probably be nervous and will need to compose yourself before the interview. It is important that you are relaxed.

2. Find out in advance whatever you can about the person who will be conducting the interview. If s/he is an attorney, try to obtain his/her professional biography through Martindale-Hubbell or other directories (p. 124). You might be lucky enough to be able to talk with someone who has been interviewed by this person before (e.g., a paralegal now working in the office, a fellow job seeker, someone at the local paralegal association) so that you can obtain a sense of what to expect. (Don't be surprised, however, if the person who greets you tells you that s/he is substituting for the person who was scheduled to conduct the interview.) There are a number of different kinds of people who might do the interviewing: the law office manager, the managing attorney, the supervising attorney for the position, the paralegal supervisor, a staff paralegal, or a combination of the above throughout the day. The style of the interview may be quite different depending on who conducts it, e.g., someone with management responsibility might stress the interpersonal dimensions of the position, whereas a trial attorney might give you the feeling that you are being cross-examined. (Occasionally, you may be confronted by a panel of interviewers who will interview you in a group setting.) Try to determine whether you are being interviewed by the person who has the final authority to hire. In many offices, you will be interviewed by someone whose sole task is to screen out unacceptable applicants. If you make it through this person, the next step will probably be an interview with the ultimate decision-maker.

3. Make sure that you are prepared for the interview. Review the guidelines discussed above on writing your resume (p. 126). In the resume and in the interview you are tyring to sell yourself. Many of the same principles discussed in these guidelines apply to the interview. Know the kind of questions you will probably be asked. Rehearse your responses. Write down a series of questions (tough ones) and ask a friend to role-play an interview with you. Have your friend ask you the questions and help you critique your responses. Also take the role of the interviewer of your friend so that you can gauge both perspectives. (See p. 141.) Be prepared to answer questions such as:
   a. Could you tell me something about yourself?
   b. Why did you leave your prior job?
   c. How have your grown in your prior jobs?
   d. How were you evaluated in these jobs?
   e. What are your strengths and weaknesses as a worker?
   f. Describe an ideal work environment. What factors make a job frustrating? How would you handle these factors? What problems do you think a paralegal might face in a busy law office and how would you handle them?
   g. Can you work under pressure? When have you done so in the past?
   h. How flexible are you in adapting to changing circumstances? Give examples of your flexibility.
   i. How do you feel about routine work?
   j. Do you prefer a large or small firm? Why?

k. What courses did you enjoy the most? Why? Which were the least rewarding? Why?

l. Do you type?

m. Do you smoke?

n. What salary expectations do you have?

o. Why are you interested in this job?

p. What do you hope to be doing in ten years? What are your long-term goals?

q. If you get this position, how long are you prepared to stay? Are you interested in a job or a career? What's the difference?

r. Where else have you interviewed for a job?

s. Why did you become a paralegal? Do you want to become a lawyer?

t. What other questions do you think I should ask in order to learn more about you?

u. What questions would you like to ask me about the office?

Keep in mind, however, that no matter how much preparation you do, you may still be surprised by the course that the interview takes. Be flexible enough to expect the unexpected. If you are relaxed, confident, and generally prepared, you will do fine.

4. If you have done the kind of background research on the office mentioned above (p. 130), you have a fairly good idea what the structure and mission of the office is. Interviewers are usually impressed by applicants who demonstrate this kind of knowledge during the interview. It will be clear to them which applicants have done their homework. A major goal of the interview is to relate your education and experience to the needs of the office. To the extent possible, you want to know what these needs are before the interview so that you can quickly and forcefully demonstrate that you are the person the office is looking for. Most offices decide to hire someone because they have a problem, e.g., they need someone with a particular skill, they need someone to help them expand, they need someone who can get along with a particularly demanding supervising attorney. If you are not sure, ask the interviewer directly why the office has decided to add a paralegal. The success of the interview is directly related to your ability to identify the problem of the office and to demonstrate how you can solve it for them.

5. If the paralegal job is in a certain specialty, e.g., probate, corporate law, you must be prepared to discuss that area of the law if it comes up. You may be asked questions designed to assess your familiarity with the area. Prior to the interview, spend some time reviewing your class notes. Skim through a standard practice book (p. 543) for that area of the law in the state. Be sure that you can back up anything you said in your resume about your prior involvement with the area in your school or work experience. Such discussions are always an excellent opportunity for you to present writing samples in that area of the law. (Be sure to bring extra copies of such writing samples and of your resume).

6. Dress conservatively. A well-groomed appearance is critical. Be sure that you project yourself positively. Take the initiative in greeting the inter-

viewer. A firm handshake is recommended if you are comfortable doing it. Maintain good posture and eye contact. Remember that everything you do will be evaluated. The interviewer will be making mental notes on whether you are shy, articulate, aggressive, prepared, at ease, in control, etc.

7. Try to avoid the topic of salary until the end of the interview when you have completed the discussion of the job itself. Preferably, let the interviewer raise the issue. Think through how you will handle the topic of salary, but try to avoid discussing it until the appropriate time arises.

8. Be an active participant in the interview even though you let the interviewer conduct the interview. Help keep the discussion going.

9. Be enthusiastic, but not overly so. You want to let the office know that you really want the job, not because you are desperate, but because you see it as a challenge for further learning and professional development. You are qualified for the job and you feel that the office is the kind of place that recognizes valuable contributions from its workers.

10. Be yourself. Do not try to overwhelm the interviewer with your cleverness and charm.

11. Be prepared to leave the following documents with the interviewer: extra copies of your resume, a list of references (if not already on your resume), writing samples.

12. You are not required to answer questions on your age or marital status (e.g., who takes care of your children), but you must decide in advance how you will handle such questions if they are asked. You may want to ask why the questions are relevant, or simply steer the interview back to the qualifications that you have and the commitment that you have made to a professional career. Whatever approach you take, be sure to remain courteous.

13. Ask the interviewer if you can be given the opportunity to talk with one or more paralegals currently working at the office. It will be another sign of your seriousness.

14. Ask your own questions of the interviewer. You want to know whether the job is for you. In effect, you are interviewing the office as much as the other way around. Come with a written list and don't be afraid to let the interviewer see that you have a checklist of questions that you want to ask. It is a sign of an organized person. There is a great deal of information about the job that you could inquire about. From your prior background research about the job (p. 130), you should already have some of this information, but you can now verify what you know. You want to ask pertinent and intelligent questions that will communicate to the interviewer that you are serious about the paralegal field, that you are prepared, and that you are grasping what the interviewer has been telling you about the job and the office. In fact, your own questions will take some of the pressure off the interviewer who otherwise may have to do most of the talking.

After you have thoroughly explored the position, if you still want the job, ask for it. Be sure that you make a specific request. Some interviewers go out of their way to stress the difficult aspects of the job in order to gauge your reaction. Don't leave the interviewer with the impression that you may be having second thoughts if in fact you still want the job after you have had all your questions answered.

Here are some of the topics that you could cover in your own questions:

- What are some specific examples of paralegal task responsibilities? Will the paralegal specialize in certain tasks or areas of the law? Ask for a description of a typical workday of a paralegal at the firm.
- What skills will the paralegal need for the job? Digesting? Investigation? Research? Drafting? Interviewing?
- Number of attorneys in the firm? Is the number growing, declining, remaining constant?
- How is the firm managed or governed? Managing partner? Management committees? Legal administrator? Is there a policy manual for the firm?
- Number of paralegals in the firm? Is the number growing, declining, remaining constant? Are all the paralegals at the firm full-time? Does the firm use part-time or free-lance paralegals? Has the firm considered hiring a paralegal coordinator?
- Is there a career ladder for paralegals in the firm?
- How long has the firm used paralegals? What is the average length of time a paralegal stays with the firm? What are the feelings of firm members of the value of paralegals to the firm? How would firm members describe an ideal paralegal employee? Do all members of the firm feel the same about paralegals? What reservations, if any, do some members of the firm have about paralegals? How has the firm dealt with the national problem of high paralegal turnover?
- What other personnel does the firm have? Secretaries, computer staff, library staff, clerks, messengers, part-time law students, etc.? How many of each? What relationship does the paralegal have with each?
- What kind of supervision does a paralegal receive? Close supervision? From one lawyer? Several?
- Will the paralegal work for one attorney? Several? Will the paralegal have his/her own case load? Is there a paralegal pool available to many attorneys?
- What kind of client contact will the paralegal have? Phone? Meetings/interviews? Document inspection at client's office?
- What kind of correspondence will the paralegal be preparing? Letters that the paralegal will sign? Letters for attorney to sign?
- What opportunities does a paralegal have for further learning? Office training programs? (Do paralegals attend new lawyer training sessions?) Does the firm encourage outside training for paralegals, e.g., from paralegal associations, bar associations, area schools?
- Will the paralegals be attending staff meetings? Strategy sessions with attorneys?
- How are paralegals evaluated in the office? Written evaluations? Oral? How often?

- Are paralegals required to produce a set number of billable hours? Per day? Per week? Per month? Annually? What is the hourly rate at which a paralegal's time is billed to a client?
- How often are paralegals required to record their time? Daily, hourly, in ten-minute segments, etc.?
- What secretarial assistance is available to the paralegal? None? A personal secretary? Secretary shared with an attorney? Use of a secretarial pool? Will the paralegal do any typing? Light typing? His/her own typing? Typing for others?
- Does the job require travel?
- What equipment will the paralegal be using? Word processor, typewriter, copier, dictaphone, research computer?
- Office space for the paralegal? Private office? Shared office? Partitioned office?
- Compensation and benefits:

Salary increase policy	Overtime
Bonus policy	Vacation
Fully paid health plan	Fully paid dental plan
Maternity leave	Pension
Life insurance	Disability insurance
Paid parking	Professional dues paid
Travel expenses	Education expenses
Number of sick leave days	Paid holidays

As indicated above, it is probably wise to ask about such conditions of employment last, unless the interviewer raises any of these topics earlier. You want to create the impression that what is most important to you is the work itself. While compensation and benefits are important, your main goal is to find interesting and challenging work.

THE FOLLOW-UP LETTER

After the interview, always send a letter to the person who interviewed you. In a significant number of cases, the follow-up letter is the deciding factor in obtaining the job. In the letter:

- Thank the person for the interview.
- Tell the person that you enjoyed the interview and the opportunity to learn about the office.
- State that you are still very interested in the position.
- Briefly restate why you are qualified for the position.
- Clarify any matters that arose during the interview.
- Submit references or writing samples that may have been asked for during the interview.

Keep a copy of all such letters. In a notebook, maintain accurate records on the dates you sent out resumes, the kinds of resumes you sent, the dates of interviews, the names of people you met, your impressions, the dates when you made follow-up calls, etc. (See p. 155.)

Assignment 3

Role-play an interview in class. The instructor will decide what kind of job the interview will be for, and select students to play the role of interviewer and interviewee. The interviewer should ask a variety of questions such as those presented above in the guidelines for handling the job interview (p. 136). The rest of the class will evaluate the performance of the interviewee. What mistakes did s/he make? How should s/he have dealt with certain questions? Was s/he confident? Overconfident? Did s/he ask the right questions of the interviewer? Were these questions properly timed? What impressions did the interviewee convey of himself or herself? Make a list of do's and don'ts for such interviews.

Section E. THE JOB HUNTING NOTEBOOK

Purchase a large three-ring, loose-leaf notebook. Include the outline of sections listed below in the Job Hunting Notebook. Following the outline, you will find a sample page for each section.

There are a number of purposes for the Notebook:

- To help you identify your strengths based on past legal or nonlegal employment, training, and other life experience.
- To help you organize this data for your resumes.
- To provide you with checklists of contacts that you should start making immediately.
- To help you prepare for job interviews.
- To provide a place to store copies of resumes, cover letters, writing samples, follow-up letters, notes on job leads and strategies, personal impressions, etc.
- To keep your calendar on all aspects of the job search.

The Notebook is your own personal document. No one else will see it unless you choose to share its contents with others.

Outline of Job Hunting Notebook

PART I. Resume & Writing Sample Preparation

1. Prior and Current Nonlegal Employment—Analysis Sheet
2. Prior and Current Legal Employment—Analysis Sheet
3. Volunteer Activity—Analysis Sheet
4. Other Life Experiences—Analysis Sheet
5. Nonlegal Education & Training—Analysis Sheet
6. Legal Education & Training—Analysis Sheet
7. Notes on Resume Writing
8. Draft of General Resume
9. Drafts of Specialized Resumes
10. Writing Samples

PART II. Contacts for Employment

11. Contacts—Attorneys You Already Know or Have Indirect Association with
12. Contacts—Employed Paralegals
13. Contacts—General

PART III. Leg Work in the Field

14. Job Interview Checklist
15. Job Interview—Analysis Sheet
16. Calendar

THE JOB HUNTING NOTEBOOK—SAMPLE PAGE

1. Prior and Current Nonlegal Employment—Analysis Sheet

Fill out a separate Analysis Sheet for *each* prior nonlegal job that you have had and for the present job that you hold if you are currently employed. Attach additional sheets to this page as indicated and where more space is needed.

a. Name, address, and phone number of employer:
b. Exact dates of employment:
c. List the name of every supervisor familiar with your work. (Circle the name of each person who would give you a favorable recommendation.)
d. List the name of every other person (e.g., coworkers, customers) familiar with your work. (Circle the name of each person who would give you a favorable recommendation.)
e. Assume that you are your supervisor. You have been asked to write a recommendation of your work. On a separate sheet of paper (which you will attach to this page), write the recommendation as honestly as you can.
f. On a separate sheet of paper (which you will attach to this page) make a list of *every* task that you had here. Be specific in listing them. If a task involved a number of subtasks, list each subtask separately. Number each task and subtask starting with the number "1." When you make your list, leave about a three-inch *left-hand margin* on the paper. In front of the number for each task and subtask, place as many of the following letters as apply to that task or subtask:

B   It required you to conform to a *budget.*
C   There was (or is) some *competition* in the office on who is the person most qualified to perform it.
E   You were *evaluated* on how well you performed it.
EI To perform it, you occasionally or always had to *exercise initiative;* you did not just wait for detailed instructions.
ET You occasionally or frequently had to put in *extra time* to perform it.
F   It required you to work with *figures,* e.g., calculations.
I   You performed it essentially alone; it was an *independent* task or subtask.
J   It occasionally or always required you to exercise some *judgment.*

M It was essentially a *mechanical* task calling for minimal or no judgment on your part.

MO You performed it *more than once.*

OD *Others depended* on your performing it well.

OO To perform it you had to deal with people *outside the office.*

OT You always or regularly performed it *on time.*

OW To perform it you had to coordinate your work with *other workers.*

P You had some role in *planning* how this task or subtask is performed.

PI You didn't start out performing it; you were *promoted into* it.

PP You are *personally proud* of the way you performed it.

R You made *recommendations* to your supervisor(s) on how the task or subtask could be more efficiently performed.

RR You *received recognition* because of how well you performed it, e.g., praise, salary increase, promotion.

S It required you to *supervise* or help supervise others.

SC It occasionally or often required *some creativity* from you.

SE To perform it you had to operate *special equipment.*

SK It required *special skills* to perform, which the other workers did not have.

SS It was not part of your primary responsibility; you *substituted for someone else.*

T You *taught* or helped teach others to perform it.

TP To perform it you had to work under *time pressures.*

W Some *writing* was involved in performing it which required you to write complete sentences.

WS You could produce a *writing sample* of the kind of writing you did for this task or subtask.

Include other characteristics of the task or subtask that were not covered in the above list.

THE JOB HUNTING NOTEBOOK—SAMPLE PAGE

*2. Prior and Current *Legal* Employment—Analysis Sheet*

Fill out a separate Analysis Sheet for *each* prior *legal* job that you have had and for the present *legal* job that you hold if you are currently employed. Include paralegal, secretarial, or other clerical positions. Attach additional sheets to this page as indicated and where more space is needed.

a. Name, address, and phone number of employer:

b. Exact dates of employment:

c. List the name of every supervisor familiar with your work. (Circle the name of each person who would give you a favorable recommendation.)

d. List the name of every other person (e.g., coworkers, clients) familiar with your work. (Circle the name of each person who would give you a favorable recommendation.)

e. Assume that you are your supervisor. You have been asked to write a recommendation of your work. On a separate sheet of paper (which you will attach to this page), write the recommendation as honestly as you can.

f. On a separate sheet of paper (which you will attach to this page) make a list of *every* task that you had here. Be specific in listing them. If a task involved a number of subtasks, list each subtask separately. Number each task and subtask starting with the number "1." When you make your list, leave about a three-inch *left-hand margin* on the paper. In front of the number for each task and subtask, place as many of the following letters as apply to that task or subtask:

B It required you to conform to a *budget.*
C There was (or is) some *competition* in the office on who is the person most qualified to perform it.
E You were *evaluated* on how well you performed it.
EI To perform it, you occasionally or always had to *exercise initiative;* you didn't just wait for detailed instructions.
ET You occasionally or frequently had to put in *extra time* to perform it.
F It required you to work with *figures,* e.g., calculations.
I You performed it essentially alone; it was an *independent* task or subtask.
J It occasionally or always required you to exercise some *judgment.*
M It was essentially a *mechanical* task calling for minimal or no judgment on your part.
MO You performed it *more than once.*
OD *Others depended* on your performing it well.
OO To perform it you had to deal with people *outside the office.*
OT You always or regularly performed it *on time.*
OW To perform it you had to coordinate your work with *other workers.*
P You had some role in *planning* how this task or subtask is performed.
PI You didn't start out performing it; you were *promoted into* it.
PP You are *personally proud* of the way you performed it.
R You made *recommendations* to your supervisor(s) on how the task or subtask could be more efficiently performed.
RR You *received recognition* because of how well you performed it, e.g., praise, salary increase, promotion.
S It required you to *supervise* or help supervise others.
SC It occasionally or often required *some creativity* from you.
SE To perform it you had to operate *special equipment.*
SK It required *special skills* to perform, which the other workers did not have.
SS It was not part of your primary responsibility; you *substituted for someone else.*
T You *taught* or helped teach others to perform it.
TP To perform it you had to work under *time pressures.*
W Some *writing* was involved in performing it which required you to write complete sentences.
WS You could produce a *writing sample* of the kind of writing you did for this task or subtask.

Include other characteristics of the task or subtask that were not covered in the above list.

THE JOB HUNTING NOTEBOOK—SAMPLE PAGE

3. Volunteer Activity—Analysis Sheet

Fill out a separate Analysis Sheet for *each* volunteer activity in which you participated, e.g., at church, at school, in a political campaign. Attach additional sheets to this page as indicated and where more space is needed.

a. Name, address, and phone number of where you did the volunteer work.

b. Exact dates of your volunteer work.

c. List the name of every supervisor familiar with your work. (Circle the name of each person who would give you a favorable recommendation.)

d. List the name of every other person (e.g., coworkers, customers) familiar with your work. (Circle the name of each person who would give you a favorable recommendation.)

e. Assume that you are your supervisor. You have been asked to write a recommendation of your work. On a separate sheet of paper (which you will attach to this page), write the recommendation as honestly as you can.

f. On a separate sheet of paper (which you will attach to this page) make a list of *every* volunteer task that you performed. Be specific in listing the tasks. If a task involved a number of subtasks, list each subtask separately. Number each task and subtask starting with the number "1." When you make your list, leave about a three-inch *left-hand margin* on the paper. In front of the number for each task and subtask, place as many of the following letters as apply to that task or subtask:

B It required you to conform to a *budget.*

C There was (or is) some *competition* in the office on who is the person most qualified to perform it.

E You were *evaluated* on how well you performed it.

EI To perform it, you occasionally or always had to *exercise initiative;* you didn't just wait for detailed instructions.

ET You occasionally or frequently had to put in *extra time* to perform it.

F It required you to work with *figures,* e.g., calculations.

I You performed it essentially alone; it was an *independent* task or subtask.

J It occasionally or always required you to exercise some *judgment.*

M It was essentially a *mechanical* task calling for minimal or no judgment on your part.

MO You performed it *more than once.*

OD *Others depended* on your performing it well.

OO To perform it you had to deal with people *outside the office.*

OT You always or regularly performed it *on time.*

OW To perform it you had to coordinate your work with *other workers.*

P You had some role in *planning* how this task or subtask is performed.

PI You didn't start out performing it; you were *promoted into* it.

PP You are *personally proud* of the way you performed it.

R You made *recommendations* to your supervisor(s) on how the task or subtask could be more efficiently performed.

RR You *received recognition* because of how well you performed it, e.g., praise, certificate, award.

S It required you to *supervise* or help supervise others.

SC It occasionally or often required *some creativity* from you.

SE To perform it you had to operate *special equipment*.

SK It required *special skills* to perform, which the other workers did not have.

SS It was not part of your primary responsibility; you *substituted for someone else*.

T You *taught* or helped teach others to perform it.

TP To perform it you had to work under *time pressures*.

W Some *writing* was involved in performing it which required you to write complete sentences.

WS You could produce a *writing sample* of the kind of writing you did for this task or subtask.

Include other characteristics of the task or subtask that were not covered in the above list.

THE JOB HUNTING NOTEBOOK—SAMPLE PAGE

4. Other Life Experiences—Analysis Sheet

- Circle *each* of the following experiences that you have had. Do not include experiences that required schooling since these experiences will be covered elsewhere in the Notebook. Do not include experiences that involved volunteer work unless you have not already included them elsewhere in the Notebook. Attach additional sheets as indicated and where more space is needed.

  a. Raised a family alone
  b. Helped raise a family
  c. Traveled extensively
  d. Read extensively in a particular field on your own.
  e. Learned to operate a computer on your own.
  f. Learned a language on your own.
  g. Learned a craft on your own, e.g., fixing cars
  h. Learned an art on your own, e.g., painting, sculpture
  i. Developed a distinctive hobby requiring considerable skill
  j. Other life experiences (list each)

- Attach a separate sheet of paper for *each* of the life experiences or activities that you listed above. Write the activity at the top of the sheet. Answer the following questions for each activity:

  a. How long did you engage in the activity?
  b. Have you ever tried to teach this activity to someone else? If so, describe your efforts.
  c. Do you think you could teach this activity to others? Explain your answer.

d. Which of the following characteristics do you think are necessary or helpful in being able to perform the activity competently. Do not focus at this point on whether you possess these characteristics. Simply compile a list of what would be helpful or necessary.

Intelligence	Compassion	Patience
Creativity	Responsibility	Dependability
Ability to work with others	Punctuality	Determination
Drive	Self-confidence	Stamina
Independence	Poise	Self-control
Talent	Efficiency	Knowledge
Understanding	Skill	Dexterity
Cleverness	Competitiveness	Sophistication
Spirit	Congeniality	Stick-to-itiveness
Conviction	Judgment	Willpower
Fortitude	Strength	Zeal
Ambition	Know-how	Experience
Perserverance	Imagination	Others? (list)

e. Ask *someone else* (whom you trust and who is familiar with you) to look at the above list. Ask this person if s/he would add anything to the list. Then ask this person to identify which of these characteristics apply to *you* for this activity.

f. Now it's your turn. What would *you* add to the list? Which of these characteristics do *you* think apply to you for this activity?

g. If there are any major differences in the answers to (e) and (f) above, how do you explain the discrepancy? Are you too hard on yourself? Do you tend to put yourself down and minimize your strengths?

THE JOB HUNTING NOTEBOOK—SAMPLE PAGE

5. Nonlegal Education and Training—Analysis Sheet

- On a separate sheet of paper, list *every* school or training program not involving law that you have attended or are now attending (whether or not you completed it) starting with the most recent. Include four-year colleges, two-year colleges, vocational training schools, weekend seminars, work-related training programs, internships, church training programs, hobby training programs, self-improvement training, etc. Include your high school only if you have not attended college, you attended a prestigious high school, or you graduated from high school within the last year.

- Devote a separate sheet of paper to each school or training program, writing its name at the top of the sheet and answering the following questions for it. If more than one course was taught, answer these questions for each major course taken.

a. What are the exact or approximate dates of attendance?

b. Did you complete it? What evidence do you have that you completed it? A grade? A certificate? A degree?

c. Were you required to attend? If so, by whom? If not, why did you attend?

d. How did you finance your attendance?

e. What requirements did you meet in order to attend? Was there competition to attend? If so, describe in detail.

f. Describe the subjects taught. What was the curriculum?

g. How were you evaluated?

h. What evidence do you have or could you obtain of these evaluations?

i. Describe in detail any writing that you had to do, e.g., exams, reports. Do you have copies of any of these written items? If not could you obtain copies? Could any of these items be rewritten now for use as a writing sample?

j. What nonwritten skills did you cover, e.g., organization, research, speaking, reading, manual dexterity, machine operation, interpersonal relations?

k. What evidence do you have or could you obtain that you covered these skills and how well you did in them?

l. Did you receive any special award or distinction? If so, describe it and state what evidence you have or could obtain that you received it.

m. Make a list of every favorable comment you can remember that was made about your work. What evidence of these comments do you have or could you obtain?

n. Was the experience meaningful in your life? If so, explain why. How has it affected you today?

o. What, if anything, did you do that called for extra effort or work on your part beyond what everyone else had to do?

p. Have you ever tried to teach someone else what you learned? If so, describe your efforts. If not, could you? Describe what you could teach.

q. List each teacher who knew you individually. Do you think these teachers would write you a letter of recommendation?

r. Would any other teacher or administrator be able to write you a letter of recommendation based on the records of the school or program?

s. Does the school or program have a reputation for excellence? If so, describe its reputation.

THE JOB HUNTING NOTEBOOK—SAMPLE PAGE

6. Legal Education and Training—Analysis Sheet

- On a separate sheet of paper, list *every legal* course or training program that your have ever taken—formal or informal. Include individual classes, seminars, internships, etc., at formal schools, on the job, or at associations.
- Devote a separate sheet of paper to each course or program, writing its name at the top of the sheet and answering the following questions for it.

    a. What are the exact dates of attendance?

    b. Did you complete it? What evidence do you have that you completed it? A grade? A certificate?

    c. What requirements did you meet in order to attend? Was there competition to attend? If so, describe in detail.

    d. What text(s) did you use? Photocopy the table of contents in the text(s) and circle those items that you actually covered.

    e. Attach a copy of the syllabus and circle those items in the syllabus that you actually covered.

    f. Make two lists: a list of the major themes or subject areas that you were required to *know* or understand (content) and a list of the things that you were asked to *do* (skills).

    g. Make a detailed list of everything that you were asked to write for the course or program, e.g., exams, memos, research papers, other reports. For every written work product other than exams, give the specific topic of what you wrote. Describe this topic in at least one sentence.

    h. Which of these written work products could you now rewrite as a writing sample? Whom could you ask to evaluate what you rewrite to ensure that it meets high standards?

    i. Describe in detail everything else you were asked to do other than assignments that called for nothing other than reading. Examples: role-play a hearing, visit a court, verbally analyze a problem, interview a client, evaluate a title abstract, search a title, operate a computer, find something in the library, investigate a fact.

    j. How were you evaluated? What evidence do you have or could you obtain of these evaluations?

    k. Did you receive any special award or distinction? If so, describe it and state what evidence you have or could obtain that you received it.

    l. Make a list of every favorable comment you can remember that was made about your work. What evidence of these comments do you have or could you obtain?

    m. What, if anything, did you do that called for extra work or effort on your part beyond what everyone else had to do?

    n. Describe what was the most valuable aspect of what you learned.

o. Have you ever tried to teach anyone else what you learned? If so, describe your efforts. If not, could you? Describe what you could teach.

p. Describe every individual who evaluated you. Can you obtain a letter of recommendation from these individuals?

THE JOB HUNTING NOTEBOOK—SAMPLE PAGE

7. Notes on Resume Writing

It is important that you have an open mind about resumes. There is no "correct" format. Different people have different views. In the best of all worlds, you are able to do some background research (p. 130) on the particular law office where you are applying for work and you have learned what kind of resume (in form and content) that office prefers. When this kind of research is not possible, you must do the best you can to predict what kind of a resume will be effective.

On this page in the Notebook, you should collect ideas about resumes from a wide variety of peoples such as:

- Teachers
- Working paralegals
- Paralegal supervisors
- Fellow students
- Personnel officers
- Placement officers
- Legal secretaries
- Program administrators
- Unemployed paralegals
- Legal administrators
- Lawyers that you know
- Authors of books and articles on finding employment
- Others?

You want to collect divergent viewpoints on questions such as the following:

- What has been this person's experience with reading or writing resumes?
- What is an "ideal" resume?
- What are the major mistakes that a resume writer can make?
- What is the best way to phrase a career objective?
- How long should the resume be?
- In what order should the data in the resume be presented?
- How detailed should the resume be?
- What kind of personal data should be included?
- How do you phrase educational experiences to make them relevant to the job you are seeking?
- How do you phrase employment experiences to make them relevant to the job you are seeking?
- How do you show that nonlegal experiences (school or work) can be relevant to a legal job?
- How do you handle potentially embarrassing facts, e.g., frequent job changes, low course grades?
- What should the cover letter for the resume say?

THE JOB HUNTING NOTEBOOK—SAMPLE PAGE
8. Draft of General Resume

Prepare a general resume and include it here. We are calling it general because it is not directed at any specific job. It should be comprehensive with no page limitation. Use the guidelines, questions, and checklists on pp. 142–146 of this Notebook to help you identify your strengths. Solicit comments on the general resume from teachers, administrators, fellow students, working paralegals, attorneys, etc. Include these comments in this section of the Notebook. The resumes you write for actual job searches should be specialized and tailored to the job you are seeking. Before you write specialized resumes, however, you should write a general one that will be your main point of reference in preparing these other resumes. The general resume will probably never be submitted anywhere. Take at least one full day to compile and carefully think about the data that will be needed for the general resume.

THE JOB HUNTING NOTEBOOK—SAMPLE PAGE
9. Drafts of Specialized Resumes

Every time you write a resume that is tailored to a specific job, include a copy here. Also include several practice specialized resumes. While taking a course in corporate law, for example, write a resume in which you are seeking an opening at a law office for a corporate paralegal. For each resume that you write (practice or real), solicit the comments of teachers, administrators, fellow students, working paralegals, attorneys, etc. Include these comments in this section of the Notebook.

THE JOB HUNTING NOTEBOOK—SAMPLE PAGE
10. Writing Samples

The importance of collecting a large pool of writing samples cannot be overemphasized. Even if you eventually use only a few of them, the value of preparing them is enormous. The following characteristics should apply to *all* the writing samples:

- It is your own work.
- It is clearly and specifically identified. The heading at the top tells the reader what the writing is.
- It is typed (handwritten work should be typed).
- There are no spelling or grammar errors in it.
- It has a professional appearance.
- Someone whom you respect has evaluated it before you put it in final form.
- You feel that it is a quality product.

- It does not violate anyone's right to privacy or confidentiality. (If the sample pertains to real people or events, you have checked into the propriety of using it and have disguised all names or other identifying features.)

There are two main kinds of writing samples: those that were assigned in school or at work, and those you have generated on your own.

Examples of Required Work that You Could Turn into a Writing Sample

- A memorandum of law (p. 686)
- A legal research report or memo
- An appellate brief (p. 695)
- An answer to a problem in the text book
- An exam answer
- An intake memorandum of law (p. 386)
- A complaint (p. 498)
- An answer to a complaint
- A motion
- A set of interrogatories (p. 494)
- Answers to a set of interrogatories
- An index to discovery documents (p. 489)
- A digest of one or more discovery documents (p. 489)
- Other memos, studies, or reports

Any of the above writing samples could be generated on your own if they are not required in your course work. Ask your teachers or supervisors to help you identify written products that you could do. Also consider writing an article for one of the many newsletters of the paralegal associations (p. 843). The article could cover an aspect of your education or work experience. Or, consider writing a review of a recent paralegal book. Even if what you write is not published in a newsletter, it might still become a writing sample if it meets the criteria listed above.

THE JOB HUNTING NOTEBOOK—SAMPLE PAGE

11. Contacts—Attorneys That You Already Know or Have Indirect Association With

Make a list of attorneys who are:

- Friends of yours
- Friends of relatives
- Friends of friends
- Neighbors or former neighbors
- Ones you have hired
- Ones your friends have hired
- Ones your relatives have hired
- Ones that your present or past employers have hired
- Teachers of yours
- Teachers of your friends
- Teachers of your relatives
- Friends or associates of any of these teachers
- Politicians
- Others?

Not only do you want to know whether any of these attorneys are interested in hiring paralegals, but equally important, you want to know if they can give you any leads to other employers who might be interested in hiring.

THE JOB HUNTING NOTEBOOK—SAMPLE PAGE

12. Contacts—Employed Paralegals

You want to talk with as many employed paralegals as you can in order to obtain leads to possible positions as well as general guidelines for the job search. Make a list of every such paralegal that you contact and what they tell you. If they have nothing useful to say at the present time, ask them if you could check back with them in several months and if you could leave your name and number with them in the event that they come across anything in the future.

How do you locate employed paralegals? Here are some ways:

- Paralegals that you meet at an employment workshop (p. 117)
- Members of the local paralegal association
- Directory of paralegal graduates of your school
- Directories of paralegals in your area compiled by your school or by the local paralegal association
- Fellow classmates who are working paralegals
- Paralegals attending training sessions of paralegal or bar associations
- Paralegal authors of articles in local paralegal newsletters
- Paralegals in law firms that you call at random asking to speak to paralegals in the office.
- Others?

JOB HUNTING NOTEBOOK—SAMPLE PAGE

13. Contacts—General

Here is a general checklist of the wide variety of contacts that you should consider in your job search. Take notes on everyone that you contact, e.g., name, address, phone number; date contacted; comments on contact; notes of follow-up needed. For other leads, see the ten major categories of paralegal employment (p. 33).

- Contacts provided by your placement office.
- Attorneys with whom you already have a direct or indirect association. (p. 119, p. 152).
- Employed paralegals (p. 117).
- Other paralegals searching for work. They may be willing to share leads that were inappropriate for themselves, especially if you do likewise.
- Want ads in general circulation newspapers.

- Want ads in legal newspapers.
- Want ads in paralegal newsletters.
- General directories of attorneys, e.g., Martindale-Hubbell, Directory of Major U.S. Law Firms (p. 124).
- Special directories of attorneys, e.g., Directory of Corporate Counsel (p. 124).
- Check information that might be available at the placement office of local law schools.
- Employment agencies specializing primarily in lawyer placement.
- Employment agencies specializing in paralegal placement.
- Attend bar association meetings open to the public.
- Contact legal secretaries for leads.
- Contact legal administrators for leads.
- Contact local attorneys of record in reporter volumes (p. 125).
- Contact local attorneys who have authored articles in bar journals (p. 125).
- Check the legal newspaper for stories on recent large cases that are in litigation or are about to go into litigation (p. 125).
- Seek the help of local and national politicians that represent your area.
- Service companies/consulting firms (p. 63).

JOB HUNTING NOTEBOOK—SAMPLE PAGE
14. Job Interview Checklist

1. _____ Exact location of interview.
2. _____ Time of arrival.
3. _____ Professional appearance in dress.
4. _____ Extra copies of resume.
5. _____ Extra copies of writing samples.
6. _____ Name of person(s) who will conduct interview.
7. _____ Background research on the firm or company so that you know the kind of law it practices, why it is considering hiring paralegals, etc.
8. _____ Role-play job interview in advance with a friend.
9. _____ Preparation for difficult questions that might be asked, e.g., why you left last job so soon after starting it.
10. Preparation of questions that you will ask, e.g.:
    _____ Responsibilities of position
    _____ Skills needed for the position
    _____ Methods of supervision
    _____ Office's prior experience with paralegals
    _____ Career ladder for paralegals
    _____ Relationship between paralegals and secretaries, and other clerical staff
    _____ Client contact
    _____ Opportunities for growth
    _____ Methods of evaluating paralegals
    _____ Continuing education

_____ Billable hours expected of paralegals
_____ Availability of systems
_____ Working conditions (typing, photocopying, office, etc.)
_____ Travel
_____ Overtime
_____ Equipment use
_____ Compensation and benefits (salary, bonus, health plan, maternity leave, life insurance, parking, sick leave, vacation, etc.)

11. _____ Follow-up letter.

JOB HUNTING NOTEBOOK—SAMPLE PAGE
15. Job Interview—Analysis Sheet

Write out the following information after each job interview that you have.

1. Date of interview.
2. Name, address, and phone number of firm or company you interviewed.
3. Name(s) and phone number(s) of interviewer(s).
4. Kind of position that was open.
5. Date you sent the follow-up letter.
6. What you need to do next (e.g., send list of references, send writing samples, provide missing information that you did not have with you during the interview).
7. Your impressions of the interview (e.g., how you think you did, what surprised you, what you would do differently the next time you have an interview).

JOB HUNTING NOTEBOOK—SAMPLE PAGE
16. Calendar

Obtain a calendar. It should show an entire month on one page, have small boxes for each day (about one inch square), and have removable pages so that you can punch three holes in each page and insert the pages at the end of your Job Hunting Notebook. If you cannot locate such a calendar, draw your own.
Record on this calendar:

• Dates of job interviews
• Dates you sent out follow-up letters
• Dates you sent out writing samples
• Dates on which you must make calls seeking job interviews
• Dates of other contacts you must make
• Dates of meetings you must attend (e.g., paralegal association meeting)
• Etc.

To save space, develop you own abbreviations, e.g., JI (job interview), FL (follow-up letter), and PA (Paralegal Association).

Section F. YOUR SECOND JOB

If you examine want ads for paralegals (p. 120), you will find that many prospective employers want paralegals with experience. The market for such individuals is excellent. If you are new to the field, you are caught in the dilemma of not being able to find a job without experience and not being able to get experience without a job. How do you handle this classic Catch-22 predicament?

- You work even harder compiling an impressive resume. You make sure that you have collected a substantial writing-sample file (p. 152). Such writing samples are often the closest equivalent to prior job experience available to you.
- When you talk to other paralegals, you seek specific advice on how to present yourself for the first job.
- You consider doing some volunteer work as a way to acquire experience for your resume. Legal service offices (p. 46) and public interest law firms (p. 61) often encourage volunteer work. A recent law school graduate struggling to start a practice may be another option.
- You may have to reassess what you will accept for your first job in the hope that you can eventually turn this job into a more acceptable position, or simply use it to gain the necessary experience that will be the foundation for a more acceptable second job.
- You pray for some luck.

Once you have had several years of experience and have demonstrated your competence, you will find considerably more employment options available to you. You will find it substantially easier to negotiate salary and articulate your skills in a job interview. You can also consider other kinds of employment where your legal training, skills, expertise, and experience are valuable. It is not uncommon for a paralegal to be recruited by former or active clients of a first employer. Numerous business contacts are made in the course of a job. These contacts could turn into new careers. Here are some of the kinds of positions that paralegals have taken after they have established their ability and acquired legal experience:

- Paralegal supervisor (p. 29)
- Law office administrator (p. 738)
- Free-lance paralegal (p. 61, p. 901)
- Paralegal teacher and school administrator
- Placement officer
- Lobbyist
- Legislative assistant
- Court administrator
- Paralegal consultant (p. 63)
- Systems analyst; computer analyst.

- Bank research associate
- Assistant loan administrator
- Assistant estate administrator
- Employee-benefit specialist
- Corporate trademark specialist
- Insurance adjustor
- Investigator
- Editor for a legal or business publisher
- Etc.

In short, you face a different market once you have acquired a record of experience and accomplishment. You are in greater demand in law firms. Furthermore, your legal skills are readily transferable to skills needed for numerous law-related positions.

3

On the Job Realities: Assertiveness Training for Paralegals ▬▬▬▬

First, let us begin with the ideal. What is a "perfect" paralegal job? Perhaps it is impossible to describe perfection in its fullest sense, but if we made the attempt, what would the description contain? The following chart is such an attempt; it tries to identify seventy-five factors of an ideal paralegal job environment. The factors are not of equal importance, and there is some overlap among them. Nor would every paralegal agree that all seventy-five are needed. In general, however, these are the factors that must be considered according to most working paralegals:

SEVENTY-FIVE FACTORS THAT AFFECT PARALEGAL JOB SATISFACTION

1. Your pay is satisfactory.
2. You receive overtime and/or regular bonuses.
3. Your fringe benefits are satisfactory (e.g., health plan, life insurance, pension).
4. Your compensation is fair in relation to that of attorneys, other paralegals, and secretaries.
5. You are given "comp" time when you work extra hours.

6. You are given financial support and time off to participate in activities of paralegal associations.
7. You are given financial support and time off to attend training sessions outside the office at paralegal schools, paralegal associations, bar associations, etc.
8. Adequate supplies are readily available.
9. Your hours are satisfactory.

10. You have your own office.

11. You have access to secretarial help.

12. You have access to word processing equipment.

13. You have your own business card.

14. You are challenged by your job.

15. You like your job.

16. Your privacy is respected.

17. No sexism exists.

18. People in the office share the same basic values.

19. The office has high standards of performance; there are many good role models.

20. You are respected.

21. You are not taken advantage of.

22. You are not pressured to fill billable hour quotas.

23. You are not pressured to work evenings or week-ends.

24. You are encouraged to develop new skills.

25. Your paralegal training is being used by the office.

26. You have some client contact.

27. Your name is in the office directory.

28. You do not feel isolated; there are no "attorney only" social events.

29. The office politics are manageable.

30. The secretaries, clerks, and other support personnel understand your job and accept your role in the office.

31. Your supervisors are not afraid of delegating tasks to paralegals.

32. The attorneys in the office understand your job and accept your role.

33. You are not in competition with anyone else in the office.

34. You have good rapport with other paralegals in the office.

35. You respect others in the office.

36. The office functions as a team; everyone does not have a niche or territory that s/he is protecting.

37. People in the office are willing to compromise on personnel methods and procedures.

38. The office has high standards of ethics and moral responsibility.

39. There is a career ladder in the office for paralegals.

40. You are not constantly being relegated to someone else's deadline; it is recognized that you have deadlines of your own that others must respect.

41. You are viewed and treated as a professional.

42. People in the office know how to listen; everyone is not simply talking at everyone else.

43. You feel that you are making a contribution to the office.

44. You have the feeling that your office is offering a social service; it is not "just" a business.

45. There is an adequate flow of communication in the office; you know what is going on because the office makes it known; you don't have to rely on the grapevine.

46. The importance of profit in the office is never emphasized at the expense of people's lives.

47. There is a clear line of authority; you know who your supervisors are.

48. You know what people you can go to for help at all times and you are encouraged to seek this help.

49. You are adequately supervised by attorneys and other senior personnel.

50. You are encouraged to do self evaluations, which are listened to or read.

51. You are regularly evaluated in a constructive manner.

52. You are given credit for the contributions you make.

53. The roof does not cave in if you disagree with your supervisors.

54. The roof does not cave in if you make a mistake.

55. You attend regular staff meetings.

56. You participate in office training programs for new lawyers.

57. You attend strategy meetings on the cases you are assigned.

58. You are not constantly being asked why you don't become an attorney.

59. There is no high turnover in your office; people feel comfortable enough about the office to make a long-term commitment to it.

60. You are not the first paralegal in the office; the office has had experience working with para-legals.

61. You are not constantly interrupted with new assignments, new priorities, new crises; you are not the dumping ground for everyone else's problems.

62. You are kept busy all the time without feeling overburdened; "the time flies by."

63. You are permitted to see the end product of your work, e.g., observe a case from beginning to completion.

64. You are encouraged to make use of the law library in the office or outside.

65. Office manuals or procedure guides are available on many assignments.

66. Personnel policies in the office are clearly spelled out in a manual.

67. Your advocacy of positions on office policy or case strategy is not resented; it is encouraged.

68. You are encouraged to express your opinion about law office management issues.

69. You have some independence; there is opportunity to work alone in the office.

70. You are given authority.

71. You are encouraged to make decisions and there is someone to back you up on these decisions.

72. There is reasonable variety in your assignments.

73. You are given reasonable time to complete your assignments.

74. You are not given assignments beyond your present capacity.

75. You are given reasonable time and training to learn new areas.

ASSIGNMENT 4

(a) Which of the above seventy-five factors do you think are *not* important for job satisfaction? Why?

(b) Select what you feel are the fifteen most important factors. Write out your list and make a copy. Indicate whether you have ever had any law office work experience as a secretary, a paralegal, etc.

(c) Give the copy of your list to a person in the class whom your instructor will designate as the "statistician." The latter will collect all the copies from the students and make the following tabulations: (1) which factors received the most "votes" on the "top fifteen" list by the students who have had prior law office experience; (2) which received the most "votes" from the other students.

In class, discuss the results of these tabulations. Are there significant differences in the opinions of the two groups? How would you explain the differences or similarities?

We move now to the *reality* of paralegal employment. The seventy-five factors obviously do not exist in every paralegal job. To be candid, some paralegals would describe their job as a disaster. As of the late 1970s and early 1980s:

- Paralegal turnover was high; the average length of a paralegal's first job was two to three years.
- Approximately 25% of working paralegals indicated that they did not plan to remain in the paralegal career; in one state survey, almost 50% of the respondents said that they did not intend to continue as paralegals.

In the remainder of this chapter, we will concentrate on what is going wrong and on some of the corrective steps that can be taken.

Of necessity, this chapter will focus on the negative since it is a chapter about *problems* on the job. Do not get the impression, however, that gloom is the order of the day. The fact is that a majority of paralegals express substantial satisfaction with their work and career. While even these paralegals will point to areas in need of improvement, they will tell you that they find their work stimulating and even fascinating at times. Most paralegals are satisfied with the career they have chosen. These are not the paralegals, however, that this chapter is primarily about.

It should also be pointed out that many of the problems we will be discussing are not peculiar to paralegalism. Sexism, for example, and the hassles of worker coexistence are certainly not unique to the law office. It is probably true that this chapter is as much about human nature as it is about this new career in law.

The following themes need to be explored:

1. Economics, the big four employment problems, and the myth of the routine.
2. The problem of underutilization.
3. Expectations.
4. Creating an environment.
5. Office politics.
6. Self-assessment and employer evaluations.
7. Assertive/nonassertive/aggressive behavior.
8. Keeping a diary.
9. The "swoose syndrome."
10. Responsibilities of supervisors.
11. Relationship with secretaries.
12. Sex harassment.
13. Working with systems.
14. Career ladders.

Our discussion of these themes will have a two-part approach: identify the problems and identify techniques of resolving them. While some of the discussion is directed at lawyers and what they must do to solve a problem, it is still important for paralegals to understand the lawyer perspective in order to begin preparing strategies to attack the problem from the perspective of the paralegal. Knowledge of reality is the first step toward changing reality.

Also, while some of the above themes will concentrate on particular employment problems, many of the same problems will also be discussed throughout the themes due to the overlap in the various problems and solutions. All the themes will address the central issue of paralegal fulfillment on the job.

1. ECONOMICS, THE BIG FOUR EMPLOYMENT PROBLEMS, AND THE MYTH OF THE ROUTINE

As we saw in chapter 1, a major reason lawyers are enthusiastic about paralegals is the economic benefit that the latter provide (p. 9). Private law firms are extremely conscious of cost and profit. They would not hire a paralegal unless they felt that the net result would be increased income without sacrifice to the quality of service rendered. This has been the message of the bar associations that have promoted paralegal use.

The time has come for these firms to realize that the same economic arguments require a resolution of the problems that are causing paralegal dissatisfaction and turnover. Paralegals are people. They have strengths as well as insecurities. A paralegal program in a law firm is not self-executing. A firm must use time, money, and effort to incorporate paralegals into a firm effectively. If this is not done, the firm will not achieve the economic benefits that initially prompted it to hire paralegals. An unhappy paralegal is obviously of questionable value to the firm. The best paralegals are not going to stay if their needs are not met. There will be turnover among those paralegals who are most capable of helping a firm. In short, it is in the economic self-interest of lawyers to understand the problems that exist and to solve them.

What are these problems? The big four that are most commonly mentioned by paralegals are:

Inadequate Compensation

Paralegals feel exploited. They generate substantial income for the firm and yet are paid low wages. Some make little more than office secretaries and substantially less than new lawyers. Yet their contribution and skill level exceed that of the secretary and sometimes equal that of the new lawyer.

Underutilization

Paralegals have skills that are not being used. The result is mounting frustration. A paralegal should not be stuck week after week doing the same task over and over again. The paralegal needs to feel challenged and to grow.

Poor Working Conditions

Paralegals need a proper environment within which to work. This means adequate desk space; adequate secretarial, messenger, photocopying, and other clerical help; adequate equipment, etc.

No Opportunity for Advancement

The paralegal career should not be a dead end. Structures within the office must be created for internal advancement. The only way *up* should not be *out*, e.g., to law school. The moment the paralegal begins to feel like a "glorified secretary," it's the beginning of the end.

Later in the chapter we will discuss ways of correcting these problems. *But step one is for lawyers to accept the reality that these problems exist and that they must be addressed at the organizational and planning level.* This will not occur unless lawyers appreciate the economic consequences of *not* doing so.

An unfortunate myth stands in the way of lawyers coming to this realization. The myth is that the paralegal is the technician of the routine. According to some "die-hard traditionalists," paralegals are little more than "secretaries educated beyond their usefulness."[1]

It is frequently stressed that the effective use of paralegals depends on the "systemization" of law office procedures.[2] Practitioners who plan to use paralegals, therefore, must be taught that the practice of law should be a "business"[3] grounded in solid principles of organization.[4] Unfortunately, this emphasis on systemization has led to the conception of the paralegal as the master of the routine. For example, the Association of American Law Schools Committee to Study the Curriculum has stated: "[P]araprofessional training must be primarily concerned with how the mechanical tasks of the law are to be performed, not with why, nor with the judgmental questions of which tasks should be performed."[5]

Other writers have said that the paralegal is involved in tasks that are "highly standardized"[6] and that s/he will free the lawyer from "menial lay

---

[1] Strouse, *On bringing Innovation to the Small Law Office,* 9 Facts and Findings 7, 8 (Nat'l. Ass'n. of Legal Assistants, Jan.–Feb. 1983).

[2] Turner, *Effective Use of Lay Personnel Revisited,* 1970 L. Office Econ. 115 (calls for "the scientific method in the law office").

[3] Strong, "Small Law Firms," in American Bar Association Special Committee on Legal Assistants, *The Utilization of Legal Assistants by Law Firms in the United States: Liberating the Lawyer,* 44 (June 1971) (Preliminary Draft).

[4] See generally, Hourigan, *Today's Lawyer in a Changing Society,* in American Bar Association Third National Conference on Law Office Economics and Management (1969).

[5] Association of American Law Schools Comm. to Study the Curriculum, Individual Training for the Public's Profession 36 (Sept. 1970) Tent. Draft No. 2.

[6] M. Comras & W. Willier, *Consumer Law Training and Practice Materials for Lay Persons* (Jan. 1971).

tasks"[7] that are "essentially repetitive."[8] If this is true, the job of training is simply one of preparing people for relatively low-skilled responsibilities—of fitting the trainees into a law-by-the-numbers approach.

If the result of the systems approach is that paralegals will perform only the routine, mechanical tasks in a law firm, the result is grossly misguided. This is not to say that the paralegal should have nothing to do with the so-called routine functions of a law practice. In fact, paralegals historically have performed the most routine and standardized tasks in law offices. The mechanical tasks, however, are only the paralegal's starting point, from which s/he should eventually move to more difficult tasks that call for considerably more competence and ability. If this move is not made, the paralegal and his/her employer will not tolerate each other for very long.[9] It is a false spectrum that places the lawyer's competence solely in judgmental matters at one end and the paralegal's competence in mechanical tasks at the other end. Rationalizing the practice of law into systems that accommodate the paralegal is fine, as long as the paralegal's needs, deficiencies, and ambitions as a human being are not overlooked.

The potential weak link in the momentum toward systemization is that the program planners may assume that standardization will eliminate the occasions for the paralegal to exercise judgment. These occasions may be minimized, but they can never be eliminated. On paper, it is possible to conceptualize the paralegal as part of a legal service delivery system based on controlled assembly-line principles, in which the paralegal becomes a specialist in the routine and the repetitive. In fact, this system will break down if it downplays the role of the paralegal. In practice the lawyer will find that the most useful paralegal is one who can be trusted to make decisions under general supervision (p. 262). Any attempt at systemization must take account of this fact. Moreover, both the paralegal and the lawyer will insist on it. The paralegal can be trained to handle the so-called routine[10] tasks for which the lawyer is overtrained. The legal profession, however, must be prepared to see the paralegal go beyond the routine. Exactly how far will depend more upon the working relationship that develops between the lawyer and the paralegal than upon any preordained, systemized plan. The most that can be achieved from the system or the plan will be that it will serve as a very useful starting point and frame of reference from which continued development can take place.

The role of the paralegal is similar to that of the new lawyer because both often engage in activities that range from repetitive tasks to those calling for

---

[7] Fuchs, *More Effective Use of Law Personnel in the Law Office,* 7 Law Notes 7 (1970).

[8] *Lawyers: Call for Restructuring,* Time, Mar. 29, 1968 at 76.

[9] At the San Francisco Pilot Project, run by the Special Committee on Legal Assistants for Lawyers, the trainers used a film in the training of legal assistants. "This film with its references to 'transferring the drudgery' was not very popular with the legal assistants." ABA Special Comm. on Lay Assistants for Lawyers, *San Francisco Pilot Project Report: Training for Legal Assistants* 6 (1970) (Preliminary Draft).

[10] One senior partner in a Wall Street firm recently defined a "routine" task as one that someone else in the office performs.

judgment and independent initiative. If this view is not taken, not only will paralegals be poorly motivated in, and indeed hostile to, a structure in which they receive only menial assignments, but also the attorneys will find that the paralegals have added nothing more than the traditional clerical personnel have always provided.

What then is the difference between the lawyer and the paralegal? The conceptual difficulty of determining where the line is drawn is monumental. It is submitted, however, that the profession is overly preoccupied with this question. The only practical answer is that the paralegal is someone who does what a lawyer lets him/her do. A resolution of the boundary question will come in the day-to-day interaction between lawyer, paralegal, and client. It cannot be blueprinted in advance. The real issue is who has final responsibility for what the paralegal does. To whom is s/he accountable? If the problem is approached from this perspective, there is less danger that the paralegal will be undertrained or indeed misused. Paralegal programs, therefore, should not have as their goal the training of an individual to perform only mechanical tasks. The training should be geared to a full development of the paralegal's decision-making faculties.

It has been said of a newly hired attorney that if "he feels that he is just a small cog in a big impersonal machine, he will not be in the most receptive frame of mind" to benefit from all that the firm has to offer, nor to contribute what the firm needs.[11] If this is true of the attorney, it is preeminently true of the paralegal who does not now enjoy the status and recognition of the attorney and who therefore may experience considerably more trouble in changing the situation.

The difficulty, however, is that the myth persists. Too many lawyers continue to perceive and treat paralegals as part of the furniture. The big four problems of low pay, underutilization, poor working conditions, and the lack of advancement continue to exist today because too many employers fail to grasp the fundamental principle that paralegals are people and not machines. They cannot, as some lawyers expect, reach peak efficiency immediately. They will come to resent conditions such as:

- vague job descriptions
- too many masters
- unrewarding piecemeal work
- in-house "caste systems"
- "attorney-only" lunches and parties
- conflicts with secretaries.

Paralegals need mentors. They want to be part of a team. Job rewards and institutional career advancement must become standard procedure.[12]

---

[11] Lowery, W., *Office Training in an American Firm,* Law Office Efficiency, p. 18 (Presentations delivered at the American and Canadian Bar Associations Economics and Management Conference, 1972).

[12] Frank, *Paralegal Burnout,* 70 American Bar Association Journal 30 (ABA, Dec. 1974).

"Miss Jones, you've been at the firm for five years now as a paralegal and I want you to know that we are real pleased with your work. We may be able to give you a $2 raise next year. The other good news is that we're going to get you a new typewriter just as soon as you finish training Mr. Davis to handle corporate filings."

These arguments, of course, are primarily addressed to lawyers. *Their* misconceptions have been largely responsible for the problems that exist. Later, we will discuss some of the things that the *paralegal* can do when confronted with the problems outlined above.

2. THE PROBLEM OF UNDERUTILIZATION

An underutilized paralegal is someone overtrained to do what s/he is doing. It is odd that lawyers begin to use paralegals because lawyers are overtrained to do many of their tasks, and yet hire people who are similarly overtrained for the functions they are assigned. The solution is to broaden the responsibilities of the paralegal. It is proper for a paralegal to perform tasks that a lawyer is overtrained to perform, but it is improper and counterproductive to pigeonhole a paralegal into one area where there is little opportunity for challenge and growth. There must be a variety of tasks and responsibilities for an individual to remain motivated and productive. One enlightened lawyer expressed this theme as follows:

> Is There a Danger of Stagnation or Morale Problems for the Paralegal if They Are Repeatedly Assigned the Same Task?
> Yes, I think that is a potential problem. We think it is good that paralegals receive more exposure to the broad range of legal problems even if that is not the

type of work the paralegal usually performs. This is advantageous to the firm because the broadly trained paralegal is better able to identify problems normally
encountered in an area of law other than the one on which they might be working.

Growth in responsibility is also important. We encourage paralegals to take
all of the responsibility that they both want and feel they can handle.[13]

Unfortunately, not all lawyers are this enlightened.

It is not uncommon for a paralegal to feel underutilized in his/her first
job. "Beginner" positions sometimes do not involve much client contact, meaningful strategy sessions with lawyers, legal research, etc.[14] As indicated in chapter 2, some paralegals do not experience challenge and excitement until their
second job (p. 156).

In fact, there are some law firms that *expect* their paralegals to become
bored in relatively tedious tasks and then move on. This may be so, for example, when a firm is engaged in a large litigated case involving a massive number
of documents. Some of these firms hire bright paralegals to perform the tasks
of digesting, indexing, or computer-coding the documents. The firm knows
that the paralegals will become burned out within a year or so and then leave
for a more challenging position. Since the departure of these paralegals often
coincides with the termination of the case, the firm is not troubled by the departure. If the case is still going on, the employment market is usually large
enough that the firm can hire more full-time, but short-term, paralegals to
complete the tasks.

These realities make it all the more important for the paralegal to know
what s/he is getting into *before* accepting a paralegal position. Review the
guidelines in chapter 2 on doing background research on a law office that is a
prospective employer (p. 130).

What do you do if you have accepted a paralegal position and only later
discover that you are being underutilized? The answer of many successful paralegals is that you must take the initiative in bringing about change. *You do not
necessarily have to accept the pigeon-hole that a law office has consciously or unconsciously established for you.* Before you give up and move on to your second job,
there are many things that you can do to try to bring about change. In the remainder of this chapter, we will examine many of these techniques. The most
important technique, however, is your own self-assertiveness.

According to Laurie Roselle, former president of the National Federation
of Paralegal Associations: "Long gone are the days when paralegals should feel
as though they are second-class legal citizens. If that's the way you feel, that's
the way you will be treated—and that's how you should be treated. However,
if you want respect in this profession, you must command it. To command this
respect, you must be an intelligent professional willing to take on responsibility
without having to be asked. . . . The first step to getting more responsibility is
to show that you deserve it . . . . [F]ind the ways to make yourself even more valuable than you already appear to be. . . . So don't sit and complain about the

[13] McCord, J., *Are You Missing a Good Opportunity?* Kentucky Bench and Bar (April, 1980).

[14] National Capital Area Paralegal Association, *The Paralegal Job-Hunting Handbook,* 3 (1977).

way things are, take charge and change them . . . . [T]he grass *may* be greener on the other side of the fence, but you *can* cross the fence."[15]

While underutilization is a major problem for some paralegals, the opposite problem of *over*utilization also exists. There are paralegals who are given tremendous amounts of responsibility, particularly in the smaller law firms. The constant pressure and tension can be extreme. Some paralegals relish this environment. One paralegal, who loves her job, described her life this way: "I am trusted to the extent that I have nightmares at night about what I may have forgotten to do. I generally work ten to twelve hours a day five days a week and often another five hours on Saturdays or at home. I have children who want to know why I am home so early if I come in the door at seven."[16] Another paralegal, who was once a litigation specialist, commented, "I miss the pressure, the stress. I miss being overworked."[17] For other paralegals, however, this can become overwhelming. As we shall see, President Roselle's "take-charge strategy" is equally relevant to handling this problem.

3. EXPECTATIONS

A fair amount of paralegal frustration on the job is due to unrealistic expectations about the career in general and about a particular job. Frustration is mainly generated by surprise: "I never thought the job would be like this!"

One of the objectives of this chapter is to provide you with the information that is needed to prevent this surprise. You need a candid account of what you might find. In chapter 2, a series of steps was outlined on doing background research on a potential employer *before* you accept a job, e.g., talking with paralegals who have worked or who still work at the office (p. 130). Following these steps, wherever possible, should give you an accurate picture of what is ahead of you if you take the job.

In a seller's market where there are more applicants than jobs, you may be so anxious to obtain a job that you will overlook potential negative aspects of a particular job. This is unfortunate. It is essential that you walk into a job, or any situation, with open eyes. Not only will accurate information help reduce any frustration that may eventually develop, but also the information will be the foundation for corrective steps that you can begin taking as soon as possible.

There is a lot of information that you need. In the best of all possible worlds, you want information relevant to each of the seventy-five factors listed above that affect potential job satisfaction (p. 159). (Alternatively, you would like information on the fifteen factors that you identified as most important in Assignment 4, p. 161.) Of course, it will probably be impossible for you to find out about all seventy-five factors. Furthermore, even the information that you

---

[15] L. Roselle, *I Don't Get No Respect!,* President's Column, 9 National Paralegal Reporter 2 (No. 3, Nov./Dec. 1984).

[16] C. Slate, *Mousebites,* 9 Dallas Association of Legal Assistants Newsletter 3 (March, 1985).

[17] C. Frank, *Paralegal Burnout,* 70 American Bar Association Journal 30 (ABA, Dec. 1984).

receive can at best be a guide to your own prediction of how these factors might apply to you as an individual once you are on the job. This should not, however, deter you from going after whatever information is available. Some investigation is needed on your part.

4. CREATING AN ENVIRONMENT

When you walk into a law office, your first impressions may be as follows:

- The office is very formal and organized.
- The people here know what they are doing and are set in their ways.

These impressions are very misleading. Environments where people interact are *never* static. They are always in the process of development and creation no matter how much tradition and formal procedures appear to dominate.

As you examine a particular law office, the question is not simply, will you fit into the office. More significantly, the question is, how will the office fit into you!

A law office is in a stage of perpetual *becoming*. The environment is always changing. New people are added, new clients come in, old clients are lost, new ways of doing things are developed, personality conflicts arise—numerous factors interact to produce an office that is in constant transition. Furthermore, you go through a process of change along with everyone else as the office continues to grow. On the surface, the office may appear to be a model of stability, but underneath all the layers of order and permanence there is a *live* office that is in motion.

The consequences of this reality for the new paralegal are twofold:

- Do not be deceived by appearances.
- Recognize your own responsibility and *power* to help create the environment in which you are working.

Don't be passive or defeatist. Everyone else in the office is trying to mold the environment to their own needs. Join the club! You may not succeed the first time. You may not succeed the fifth time. You may not even be aware of when your advocacy for yourself is having an impact. *Yet you must assert yourself and do so regularly.* Change usually does *not* occur within the timetable of the person trying to bring about the change. Occasionally you will get the impression that everyone is resisting what you feel is right. You must be prepared to lose on some points. But you must stick with it. The person who wins is often the person who outlasts the others. The losers are those who demand instant success—whether or not there is justice behind their positions.

Three things must happen before change will occur:

- You convince yourself that you have the power to create change.
- Your mind generates ten to fifteen ways or methods of creating the change.
- You have the stamina and perspective to live through the unsuccessful attempts until you finally hit upon the strategy that produces the change.

This is not to say that you must live through misery indefinitely. There are times when you will reach the conclusion that it would be best to leave. But this should occur only after you have stretched your creativity to the point where you have thought of and exhausted a variety of strategies that ultimately prove to be unproductive. Don't view a law office in black and white. View it in changing shades of gray. No environment is static. An environment is simply an opportunity to be molded.

5. OFFICE POLITICS

No one likes office politics. We all want to work where office politics does not exist. If we work where it does exist, we always tend to blame someone else for its presence. We do what is right; others play politics.

These attitudes are illusions and interfere with your chances of bringing about change. Whenever two people work together, politics is involved. When fifty people work together, politics is the order of the day. Since everyone cannot possibly agree about everything, conscious or unconscious *negotiation* is the mechanism by which things get done. Bargaining takes place all the time. More to the point, bargaining in the context of everyone's ego takes place all the time. There is simply no alternative to this process.

If there is harmony in an office, it is because people are engaged in *effective* office politics. People are trading what others want. Disharmony usually results from the fact that people are not responding to each other's needs. A cardinal principle of human relations is that you cannot get anyone to do anything well until you have found a way of making them happy about doing it. Coercion and management by might have within them the seeds of their own defeat. They may work for a while, but at great cost. People generally want to do their jobs well, but this will not happen unless they strive hard to help other people do their jobs well. This is the essence of effective office politics.

The following dimensions of office politics may at first appear to be unpleasant to some paralegals:

- You must make sure that the decision-makers in the firm learn about your work.
- You must make sure that everyone with whom you work has a good opinion of you.

This is distasteful to some because they have the view that good work speaks for itself and is its own reward. Why make a campaign about it?

Unfortunately, there is a danger, particularly in a large firm, of the paralegal and his/her work getting lost in the shuffle. The remedy is to be constantly looking for ways to sell yourself without appearing to be doing so. This goes against the grain of many paralegals. They don't like to sell themselves especially after they have been at an office for a while. They want to settle in and not be obsessed with getting ahead. Yet you can't have it both ways. You can't complain about conditions of employment and refuse to assert your most valuable asset—yourself. This means establishing credibility and making sure that people know your worth. In short, it means selling yourself.

Suppose your immediate supervisor on a case is a junior attorney. By all means, you strive to please by competently carrying out his/her instructions. You want your supervisor to speak well of you. But what about the *senior* partner on the case? Does s/he know about you? Does s/he meet only with your immediate supervisor? Are there inoffensive ways for you to bring yourself to the attention of the senior partner? Can you ask your immediate supervisor if you could sit in on a strategy session that the supervisor will be having with the senior partner? Can you ask about going to court to watch the senior partner argue the case on which you have been working? Several months after the case is over, can you drop in on the senior partner to ask him/her about some aspect of the case? If any of these approaches would be threatening to your immediate supervisor, don't give up; think of some non-threatening approaches. What would happen if you begin your impromptu meeting with the senior partner by praising your immediate supervisor? If you think that this approach is too gimmicky; don't give up; think of a non-gimmicky approach. Office politics? To be sure, but why take the chance that a decision-maker will not know about your hard work and competence? Why take the chance that information about you may become distorted when filtered through others? Your goal is to achieve your objectives in the office. What's wrong with making sure that people who can best help you achieve these objectives know who you are?

It must be admitted, however, that selling yourself can sometimes be risky. You don't want to appear to be pushy, arrogant, or overly aggressive. It will not help you to please one person by making an enemy of someone else. Yet success and risk-taking are not inconsistent. In fact, they are often substantially interdependent.

What do you think of the following advice from a successful paralegal:

> Set your goals and aim for them. Open your mouth and let people know that you're headed up. Search out greater responsibility. Work your tail off—and let everyone know about it.[18]

Too extreme? People really don't get ahead this way? You don't have to advertise talent because it will eventually be discovered? Maybe. Talk with successful and satisfied paralegals around you. Make inquiries. Take a long look at people you respect in a competitive environment. Try to assess whether their abilities might have gone untapped without a healthy, effective, measured dose of self-assertiveness.

6. SELF-ASSESSMENT AND EMPLOYER EVALUATIONS

None of the techniques and strategies discussed in this chapter can ever be a substitute for your own competence as a paralegal. The techniques and strategies are designed mainly to combat unrecognized and unrewarded competence.

---

[18] S. Oder, *Paralegal Upward Mobility,* 6 National Paralegal Reporter 6 (Nat'l. Federation of Paralegal Associations, Fall/Winter, 1981); Los Angeles Paralegal Association, Reporter (Sept. 1981).

CHARACTERISTICS IMPORTANT FOR LEGAL ASSISTANTS AS VIEWED BY EMPLOYING FIRMS (22 firms responding)			
CHARACTERISTICS	VERY IMPORTANT	IMPORTANT	NOT IMPORTANT
a. Training as a legal assistant	10	6	4
b. Ability to understand legal terminology and procedures	17	2	2
c. Interviewing skills	5	6	9
d. Analytical mind	13	8	1
e. At least 4 years of college	6	8	6
f. Get along well with people	11	10	1
g. Willingness to assume responsibility	19	2	0
h. Knowledge of bookkeeping	2	7	11
i. Willingness to follow orders	11	9	1
j. Maturity	17	4	0
k. At least some college or vocational school	7	8	2
l. Intend to make a career as a legal assistant	5	11	5
m. Above-average intelligence	14	6	0
n. Facility in speaking	7	11	3
o. Legal secretary experience	0	4	18
p. Interest in people	4	12	5
q. Writing skills	10	10	0
r. Some law school courses	2	2	17
s. Ambitious	6	15	0
t. Ability to function at a high level under stress conditions	9	10	2
u. Understanding of the legal process	7	9	5
v. Secretarial skills	0	5	0
w. Understand the meaning of "confidentiality"	16	5	0
x. Empathy	3	12	3
y. Desire to eventually become an attorney	0	0	22

You need to take an inventory of your strengths and weaknesses, and the inventory should be reviewed and updated regularly. In chapter 5 we will examine methods of studying law (p. 307). The methods must be applied throughout your paralegal career. A major strength you must have is to be a good learner. A precondition to being a good learner is an awareness of your weaknesses. You must know where to concentrate the learning.

Perhaps an even prior concern is: What does it take to be a paralegal? What are the characteristics of a good paralegal? To be a paralegal, what traits do you need to have? What do you need to be able to do? In the chart above, twenty-two law firms that employed paralegals stated what they felt the important characteristics of a paralegal were. On page 174, there is a chart of what approximately 100 paralegals felt were important.

CHARACTERISTICS IMPORTANT FOR LEGAL ASSISTANTS AS VIEWED BY EMPLOYED LEGAL ASSISTANTS (approximately 100 legal assistants responding)			
CHARACTERISTICS	VERY IMPORTANT	IMPORTANT	NOT IMPORTANT
a. Training as a legal assistant	57	34	5
b. Ability to understand legal terminology and procedures	82	13	1
c. Interviewing skills	22	48	26
d. Analytical mind	59	34	3
e. At least 4 years of college	33	29	34
f. Get along well with people	51	42	3
g. Willingness to assume responsibility	82	13	1
h. Knowledge of bookkeeping	6	34	56
i. Willingness to follow orders	44	44	8
j. Maturity	63	33	0
k. At least some college or vocational school	53	36	7
l. Intend to make a career as a legal assistant	20	39	37
m. Above-average intelligence	56	36	4
n. Facility in speaking	38	47	11
o. Legal secretary experience	17	10	69
p. Interest in people	25	55	16
q. Writing skills	50	43	3
r. Some law school courses	11	33	52
s. Ambitious	34	44	18
t. Ability to function at a high level under stress conditions	63	31	2
u. Understanding of the legal process	63	30	3
v. Secretarial skills	10	11	75
w. Understand the meaning of "confidentiality"	70	25	1
x. Empathy	22	51	23
y. Desire to eventually become an attorney	2	6	88

How would you rate yourself under the categories listed under a–y in each of the charts?[19] Where do you need improvement? Both attorneys and paralegals agree, for example, on the importance of having an "analytical mind" (d) and "writing skills" (q). Few of us could not use improvement in these areas. What steps do you think you can take to achieve this improvement? Chapters 5 on studying law (p. 307) and 7 on legal analysis (p. 371) will provide some guidelines for improvement.

Once you are employed as a paralegal, you may want to try an experiment that will make the charts more relevant to your office. Several options are:

[19] American Bar Association, Special Committee on Legal Assistants, *The Training and Use of Legal Assistants: A Status Report,* Appendix C, D, E, and F (Preliminary Draft, 1973).

OPTION I. Photocopy one of the above charts, leaving out the numbers in the three columns. Ask every lawyer in the office to indicate whether they felt that the characteristics were very important, important, or not important. Leave a space at the end to allow the lawyer to add characteristics to the chart. Tabulate the results to determine how the lawyers rate the characteristics. Do a separate tabulation for the paralegals if there are at least three paralegals in the office.

OPTION II. Photocopy the list of the characteristics in one of the charts, leaving out the three columns. Give this list to your supervisor. There are twenty-five characteristics in the list from a–y. Ask your supervisor to rate the twenty-five characteristics according to what s/he feels as the most important. S/he should place a number from one to twenty-five next to each characteristic with the number "1" indicating that your supervisor feels that this characteristic is the most important one a paralegal should have.

    The results, particularly in OPTION II, should be very revealing. They should prompt an interesting discussion once you ask your supervisor for the reasons s/he scored certain characteristics the way s/he did. This will be an excellent opportunity to open a line of communication between you from perhaps a new perspective for both of you.

    The next logical step (see OPTION III) is for you to ask your supervisor how s/he would rate *you* on the relevant characteristics.

OPTION III. On a separate sheet of paper, write or type the characteristics in b, c, d, f, g, h, i, j, n, p, q, s, t, u, w, and x. Then make three columns with the headings "Above Average," "Average," and "Needs Help." Ask your supervisor to check the appropriate column for each characteristic.

    The final step in the process is for you and your supervisor to discuss improvement strategies for those categories the supervisor checked "Average" or "Needs Help." For this discussion to be honest, you obviously need considerable rapport with your supervisor. You must convey the impression that you want constructive criticism and that you will not take it personally.

    Of course, other evaluation formats are possible. The following is another form that could be used.[20] Read through this form carefully. In the eight categories being evaluated, note the standards used to earn a "Superior" or "Very Good" rating. These standards are your day-to-day employment goals as a paralegal. How well do you think these standards apply to you today as a worker? In your present or prior jobs, in any area of work, what ratings would you give yourself in the eight categories? What ratings do you think your supervisor would give you?

[20] Reprinted with the permission of Heller, Ehrman, White & McAuliffe, San Francisco, California.

Personal and Confidential
LEGAL ASSISTANT EVALUATION FORM

Legal Assistant _____ Hire Date _____
Review Period _____ Department _____
Evaluating Attorney _____

*Note: The information contained in this Evaluation Form may be released to the legal assistant upon request.

A. CONTACT. Indicate the contact you have had with the legal assistant during the review period.

_____ *Substantial.* Regular daily or weekly contact. Included in most attorney briefing/strategy meetings.
_____ *Occasional.* Specific assignments and routine maintenance work requiring occasional personal instruction.
_____ *Infrequent.* Limited contact.

B. WORK PERFORMED. Describe the work performed for you, listing some examples. Specify the degree of difficulty and expertise required.

_____
_____
_____
_____
_____
_____

C. PERFORMANCE EVALUATION. Evaluate the legal assistant in each of the following areas. Check the blank to the left of the rating description that best summarizes the legal assistant's performance. Use the space on the back of the last page for additional comments. Please read all category descriptions before completing the evaluation.

1. *WORK PRODUCT.* (Consider the legal assistant's ability to understand what is required and to provide a work product that is both thorough and complete. Consider the speed and efficiency with which the work product is returned.)

_____ *Superior.* In most cases needs little instruction. Takes initiative in asking questions if aspects of the task are unclear. Is resourceful in developing more efficient ways to complete projects. Demonstrates ability to consider factors not indicated by attorney that make the work product more useful.
_____ *Very Good.* Needs instruction once or twice. Legal assistant completes task thoroughly and keeps attorney informed as to work progress.
_____ *Good.* Sometimes needs to do a task several times before he/she feels comfortable. Substantial attorney supervision is necessary during first attempts at project. Once legal assistant is comfortable with the job requirements, he/she does a thorough and complete work product.
_____ *Marginal.* Has difficulty understanding what kind of work product is required. Sometimes does an incomplete job and takes more time than should be needed.
_____ *Unacceptable.* Seldom masters what is required to the point where he/she cannot provide a thorough and complete work product.
_____ *No Opportunity to Form an Opinion.*

2. *EFFICIENT MANAGEMENT OF WORKLOAD.* (Consider the volume of work produced and the efficient use of time in order to meet deadlines.)

_____ *Superior.* Highly efficient. Completes all assignments successfully, on time, and without prompting.
_____ *Very Good.* Efficient. Most assignments completed successfully. Rarely misses deadlines.

_____ *Good.* Basically efficient. Assignments are generally completed successfully within a reasonable amount of time.

_____ *Marginal.* Needs to improve efficiency. Assignments sometimes go uncompleted. Needs substantial attorney supervision.

_____ *Unacceptable.* Inefficient. Deadlines are rarely met. Assignments often uncompleted.

_____ *No Opportunity to Form an Opinion.*

3. *ABILITY TO WORK WELL UNDER PRESSURE.* (Consider the ability of the legal assistant to make sound judgments and to organize work under pressure.

_____ *Superior.* Nearly always works well under pressure. Maintains organization and control over assignments; continues to make sound judgments.

_____ *Very Good.* In most cases works well under pressure; rarely makes unsound judgments or becomes disorganized.

_____ *Good.* Generally works fairly well under pressure; sometimes makes judgments that are not always carefully considered or becomes slightly disorganized.

_____ *Marginal.* Frequently fails to work well under pressure. Tends to become disorganized and to exercise poor judgment.

_____ *Unacceptable.* Rarely works well under pressure. Allows pressure to interfere with effective management of assignments, and often uses poor judgment.

_____ *No Opportunity to Form an Opinion.*

4. *ANALYTICAL SKILL.* (Consider the legal assistant's ability to digest and analyze the facts of a particular case or assignment and the thoroughness of factual research.)

_____ *Superior.* Is exceptionally thorough in gathering facts and quick to master the facts. Depth of understanding evidenced by the quality of work product.

_____ *Very Good.* Is thorough in gathering information. Masters facts quickly and uses them well in preparation of work product.

_____ *Good.* Generally thorough in gathering information. Masters facts over an acceptable period of time. Sometimes needs attorney direction in developing the information for purposes of work product.

_____ *Marginal.* Sometimes misses essential information during factual investigation. Knowledge of facts is incomplete. Needs substantial attorney direction in order to correctly analyze facts.

_____ *Unacceptable.* Often misses essential information during factual investigation. Knowledge of facts is seriously deficient. Work product needs substantial revision in order to ensure completeness. Sometimes careless in presentation of facts to attorney.

_____ *No Opportunity to Form an Opinion.*

5. *PROFESSIONALISM.* (Consider the extent to which the legal assistant is personally involved in his/her work; the extent to which he/she takes the job requirements seriously; and the extent to which he/she demonstrates responsibility for high quality work in all instances.)

_____ *Superior.* Exhibits exceptionally high level of personal involvement in assignments and is extremely responsible. Takes initiative.

_____ *Very Good.* Highly involved in assignments. Demonstrates strong commitment to his/her work. Very dependable.

_____ *Good.* Generally dependable and involved in assignments. Demonstrates average commitment to his/her work.

_____ *Marginal.* Frequently appears to lack interest in assignments. Needs substantial follow-up by attorney as to both deadlines and quality of work.

_____ *Unacceptable.* Unwilling to assume the necessary responsibility.

_____ *No Opportunity to Form an Opinion.*

6. _ABILITY TO WORK INDEPENDENTLY._ (Consider the legal assistant's ability to exercise good judgment by making well-reasoned choices and then to maintain necessary communication with attorney.)
   _____ _Superior._ Considers all options and makes good decisions. Always keeps attorney well informed.
   _____ _Very Good._ In most cases makes good decisions. Occasionally needs attorney assistance in defining options. Keeps attorney well informed.
   _____ _Good._ Usually considers options before making a decision. May not recognize the need to request attorney assistance in defining options.
   _____ _Marginal._ Has difficulty making well-reasoned choices after options are defined. Neglects to cover necessary material with attorney and does not readily call upon attorney for assistance or explanation.
   _____ _Unacceptable._ Is not able to make reasonable choices after options are defined. Rarely keeps attorney informed and lacks understanding as to appropriate area of legal assistant work as defined by attorney.
   _____ _No Opportunity to Form an Opinion._
7. _QUALITY OF WRITTEN WORK._ (Consider the ability of the legal assistant to express himself/herself in clear, precise language; thoroughness; organization; accuracy and neatness; grammar.)
   _____ _Superior._ Exceptionally clear, precise, and thorough work that is neat and free from errors.
   _____ _Very Good._ In most cases, precise, clear, and thorough. Rarely lacking in one or more respects.
   _____ _Good._ Generally acceptable but occasionally needs improvement.
   _____ _Marginal._ Frequently lacking in one or more respects.
   _____ _Unacceptable._ Work product is almost always lacking in one or more respects.
   _____ _No Opportunity to Form an Opinion._
8. _OUTSIDE CONTACT._ (Consider the extent to which the legal assistant is required to work with persons outside the firm, e.g., co-counsel attorneys, client, state and federal agencies, state and federal court personnel.)
   _____ _Superior._ Consistently demonstrates ability to readily gain the cooperation and confidence the assignment requires. Establishes excellent working relationships.
   _____ _Very Good._ Generally gains cooperation and confidence. Establishes cooperation and confidence.
   _____ _Good._ Needs occasional assistance, but is able to gain the necessary cooperation and confidence.
   _____ _Marginal._ Unable to handle outside assignments without substantial attorney assistance. Has difficulty developing necessary confidence and cooperation.
   _____ _Unacceptable._ No understanding of what is required in order to gain the necessary cooperation and confidence. Complaints received with regard to legal assistant's behavior.
   _____ _No Opportunity to Form an Opinion._

COMMENTS. On the back of this form, space is provided to allow for elaboration of any of the ratings checked under the preceding categories. You are encouraged to comment in general upon the legal assistant's performance: strengths, weaknesses, and suggestions for improvement.

Perhaps the best of all possible worlds is for you and your supervisor to design an evaluation form together. You might want to gear the evaluation more specifically to the tasks that you perform or have performed on a certain case or area of the law. Have a meeting with your supervisor in which you discuss an evaluation format. This should be done even if the office has its own evaluation form. The latter could perhaps be improved and made more relevant to your particular situation. Take notes on what your supervisor thinks should be the evaluation criteria. Describe what you think. Then prepare a draft of an evaluation form that the two of you agree will be used regularly, e.g., every month or every three months. Your own initiative in setting up this structure will be viewed in a very positive light, especially if you make clear that your goal is to use the evaluation to improve communication with your supervisor and to find ways of increasing your skills and productivity.

Unfortunately, most evaluations in law firms are informal and are not communicated until trouble surfaces. This is not a healthy atmosphere. There is a lot you can do to change this.

7. ASSERTIVE/NONASSERTIVE/ AGGRESSIVE BEHAVIOR

Nonassertive behavior is the easiest to define. It is passiveness or undue silence. A nonassertive person rarely, if ever, complains to the person causing a problem. Aggressive behavior is at the other extreme; it is constant complaining. An aggressive person is a negative person who cannot express dissatisfaction without depressing someone else. The aggressive person may be right in many of the things s/he is saying, but s/he is so unpleasant about it that few people listen.

In between these two extremes is *assertive* behavior. An assertive person:

- lets others know what is on his/her mind
- is not offensive
- advocates quietly but with resolve
- is secure enough to be able to say no
- is willing to take risks
- can express an opinion without putting someone down
- has a sense of timing; knows when communication is appropriate as well as when silence is appropriate
- is realistic enough to understand that getting what you want will sometimes take time and a variety of imaginative strategies
- knows the difference between little concerns and major ones—does not view every problem as a crisis
- understands that there are times when one must be prepared to lose and that it must be done gracefully
- does not shy away from the office politics (p. 171)
- recognizes the necessity of compromise
- is confident of his/her competence, but is always willing to learn
- acts like a professional.

An assertive paralegal makes him/herself known. The backbone of assertiveness is competence—you know that you are capable. The trump card of assertiveness is timing—you watch for the right moment to come forward. The foundation of assertiveness is preparation—you have collected all the facts that support your position.

Suppose, for example, that you feel that you are not earning what you are worth. What do you do? A number of approaches can be taken:

NONASSERTIVE.   You hope that things will get better, but you don't want to rock the boat. After all, your salary isn't *that* bad; it could be worse. You talk with fellow paralegals about your salary, and you are very frank with your aunt when the two of you talk on the phone about your work. But there's no sense in trying to get the firm to pay you more. The firm probably doesn't earn that much. And Mr. Smith, the head of the firm, is very pleasant to work with. Money isn't that important. Maybe next year will be better.

AGGRESSIVE.   Three weeks after you begin your job you tell your boss that your salary is ridiculous. "With inflation, how do you expect me to live on this salary?" When your boss is not responsive, you send a memo to all the lawyers in the firm demanding that "something be done about paralegal salaries." When you walk the corridors of the firm, you are always visibly angry.

ASSERTIVE.

- You prepare a fact sheet of paralegal salaries in your area after you talk with paralegals at other firms and examine salary surveys conducted by local and national paralegal associations. You research any other data available, e.g., the annual survey of paralegal salaries in *Compensation of Attorneys* (Abbott, Langer & Associates); the *Altman & Weil Annual Survey of Law Office Economics,* which includes financial data of paralegals.
- You make sure that your supervisors have evaluated you regularly in writing. You summarize these evaluations and add them to the fact sheet.
- You make a list of the various projects on which you have worked. You highlight the special projects, e.g., helping design part of the office manual, training of a new paralegal or attorney.
- You make sure that the decision-makers in the firm know who you are and what you have accomplished.
- You add up your billable hours over a designated period. This is added to the fact sheet.
- You discuss strategies for seeking a raise with other paralegals in the firm, other paralegals in the area, and perhaps with some attorneys in the firm with whom you have developed considerable rapport.
- When others have made a favorable comment about your work, you have asked them if they would put it in writing so that it could go into your personnel file.
- You select the right time to meet with your supervisor. You may want to wait until the supervisor is not hassled with a difficult case.

- You may decide on a two-part strategy: you first ask for a meeting with your supervisor to discuss ways of increasing your contribution and productivity. At a follow-up meeting, you raise the question of a salary increase.
- Months before you ask for a raise, you ask your supervisor to identify those factors s/he will take into consideration in evaluating your overall performance and in recommending a salary level. In the months that follow, you make sure that you organize your efforts and your notes in accordance with the criteria the supervisor initially identified.

8. KEEPING A DIARY

It is recommended that you keep a daily diary or journal in which you record:

- the assignments you are given
- the dates the assignments are given and the due dates for completion
- the dates when the assignments are actually completed
- favorable and unfavorable comments that have been made about your work
- total billable hours per day attributable to your work
- the dates when you work evenings and weekends
- the dates when you work on something at home
- the dates you were late, absent, or had to leave early
- the dates when you came in early or worked through lunch hour
- the names of any clients you referred to the firm
- the amount of time you have spent doing your own typing or photocopying
- the time you spend in courses, seminars, or other ventures to improve your skills.

You need to have the facts of your employment at your command. The diary is your personal record. You keep it to yourself for use as needed. Not only will the facts be valuable when you are making an argument for a raise, they also might be essential when misunderstandings arise about what you have or have not done.

The diary may be burdensome for you at first, and it may take a while before the time comes when you make use of it. It is worth the burden and the wait. A law firm respects someone who has the facts, particularly with dates!

9. THE "SWOOSE SYNDROME"

Is the paralegal part of the clerical staff or part of the professional staff? In most offices the answer is both. It is not uncommon for the paralegal to feel schizophrenic at times. See the chart below. If someone is part swan and part goose, they are experiencing what has been called the "swoose syndrome."[21]

---

[21] Brandom, C., *Comments on Educating the Attorney to Employ, Utilize and Retain Legal Assistants*, 5 Facts & Findings 1, 10 (January–February 1979).

FACTORS AFFECTING PROFESSIONAL vs. CLERICAL STATUS	
PROFESSIONAL STATUS	CLERICAL STATUS
1. Does not do typing for anyone else.	1. Does typing for others.
2. Rarely types his/her own material.	2. Often types his/her own material.
3. Has his/her own office.	3. Does not have own office.
4. Has a dictaphone.	4. Does not have dictaphone (except to listen to someone else).
5. Does not do his/her own photocopying.	5. Photocopies for others.
6. Has access to word processing equipment.	6. Does not have same access to word processing equipment as everyone else.
7. Has secretarial help.	7. Does not have secretarial help.
8. Has a business card.	8. Does not have business card.
9. Has name printed on letterhead of firm.	9. Does not have name printed on letterhead.
10. Is not paid overtime.	10. Is paid overtime.
11. Is paid a salary comparable to attorneys.	11. Is paid a salary comparable to that of secretaries and other clerical staff.
12. Always attends strategy meetings on cases.	12. Never or only occasionally attends strategy meetings on cases.
13. Is given financial support and time off to attend association meetings and training sessions.	13. Is not given financial support and time off to attend association meetings and training sessions.

THERE ARE LONELIER PLACES THAN AT THE TOP
by Margaret Perry
Houston Legal Assistants Association,
Newsletter (Feb. 1983)

The "swoose syndrome" presents some very realistic problems. It is easy to miss out on general office gossip and we often aren't included in the attorneys' strategy sessions. Clients may or may not view you as a professional with valuable

"Good morning Mr. Davis. Here is the research memo I worked on till midnight, plus your coffee and danish."

information to relay to them or to obtain from them. Whom do you give gifts to during the holiday season or on birthdays? With whom do you eat lunch on a daily basis? Unless your organization employs a large number of legal assistants, your choice of lunch partners may be limited. You are likely to be ostrasized by the swans if you steadily lunch with the geese, and vice versa.

Legal assistants, by the very nature of their profession, are often physically isolated from the other legal assistants in their organization. As we specialize into various areas of law and must be near our departments or sections, interaction with legal assistants in other parts of the office is minimized and often restricted to occasional encounters in the restroom. If your office regards you as a swan, you end up with an office with a view, door and four walls that reach the ceiling; geese get unoccupied secretarial stations. Companies have spent considerable time and effort to devise unique office arrangements to accommodate their "swooses." Swooses end up being alone with no privacy. Anyone can walk in anytime and if your walls don't reach the ceiling, you can hear those around you just as well as they can hear you.

If you feel legal assistants in general experience loneliness, imagine being a male legal assistant. You can forget chance encounters in the ladies' restroom and lunches with female legal assistants may raise some eyebrows, unless, of course, everyone knows you're just "good friends." Male legal assistants are never mistaken for geese, even if caught typing, and frequently are mistaken for swans. When the passerby realizes they're swooses, not swans, the inevitable question is raised, why aren't you a swan, is something wrong with you?

10. RESPONSIBILITIES OF SUPERVISORS

What is a good attorney supervisor? The checklist on page 184 lists the factors that constitute effective supervision. You might consider showing this checklist to your supervisor so that s/he might evaluate him/herself as a supervisor.

"I'm headed out for a show tonight, and tomorrow I'll be at the golf tournament. I know the report is due tomorrow. I'll ask Helen, my paralegal, to do the report. She needs something to do."

CHECKLIST FOR EFFECTIVE PARALEGAL SUPERVISION

(Grade each factor on a scale of 1 to 5 with a "1" indicating that the supervisor is excellent in this factor and "5" indicating an unsatisfactory rating.)

FACTOR	RATING (on a scale of 1-5)
a. You give clear instructions to the paralegal on assignments.	a. _____
b. You do not overburden the paralegal with assignments. Before you give a new assignment, you determine what the paralegal already has to do.	b. _____
c. You provide reasonable deadlines on assignments.	c. _____
d. You take affirmative steps to inquire about the paralegal's progress on assignments to determine if help is needed or if deadline extensions are needed. You do not simply wait for the paralegal to come to you with problems.	d. _____
e. You provide adequate training for each assignment given. You take the time that is needed to make sure the paralegal can perform the task.	e. _____
f. You are not afraid to delegate tasks to the paralegal.	f. _____
g. You delegate meaningful tasks, not just the drudgery.	g. _____
h. You are supportive when the paralegal makes a mistake; your corrective suggestions for the future are constructive.	h. _____
i. You make sure that the paralegal has some variety in his/her work.	i. _____
j. You permit the paralegal to experience the end product of cases on which s/he is working.	j. _____
k. You include the paralegal in strategy meetings on cases.	k. _____
l. You encourage the paralegal to use the law library in order to increase his/her knowledge and to appreciate the legal context of a case.	l. _____
m. You use the paralegal's skills and regularly look for ways the paralegal can increase his/her skills.	m. _____
n. You encourage the paralegal to give his/her opinion on cases and on office policy.	n. _____
o. You design systems for the performance of tasks involving paralegals with instructions, checklists, forms, etc.	o. _____
p. You encourage the paralegal to help you write these systems.	p. _____
q. You regularly evaluate the paralegal informally and in writing.	q. _____
r. You encourage the paralegal to help you design a relevant paralegal evaluation form.	r. _____
s. You encourage the paralegal to evaluate you as a supervisor.	s. _____
t. You give credit to the paralegal where credit is due.	t. _____
u. You make sure others in the firm know about the contribution of the paralegal.	u. _____
v. You lobby with other attorneys who do not use paralegals or do not appreciate their value in order to change their attitude.	v. _____
w. You are aware of any conflicts that may exist between paralegal, secretaries, and other staff members in the office in order to help resolve the conflicts.	w. _____

x.	You back the paralegal in his/her reasonable requests on salary and working conditions.	x. _____
y.	You introduce your clients to the paralegal, explain his/her role, and express your confidence in him/her.	y. _____
z.	You do not pressure the paralegal about producing a quota of billable hours.	z. _____
aa.	You make sure the paralegal has suitable office space, supplies, secretarial support, access to word processing, etc.	aa. _____
bb.	When changes must be made that affect the paralegal, you let him/her know in advance so that s/he can make suggestions about the changes.	bb. _____
cc.	You support the paralegal's need for financial help and time off to attend outside training programs.	cc. _____
dd.	You support the paralegal's need for financial help and time off to do some *pro bono* work (e.g., time donated to associations.	dd. _____
ee.	You recognize that the paralegal, like any worker, will need reasonable time off to attend to pressing personal matters.	ee. _____
ff.	You consider letting the paralegal have some reasonable time off to do some *pro bono* work (i.e., time donated to poverty law offices or public interest law firms).	ff. _____
gg.	You don't assume that the paralegal is happy about his/her job simply because you have no complaints and the paralegal hasn't expressed dissatisfaction; you take the initiative to find out what is on his/her mind.	gg. _____
hh.	You treat the paralegal as an individual.	hh. _____
ii.	You treat the paralegal as a professional.	ii. _____

In the following article describing the use of paralegals, note the sensitivity of the supervisors to the role and needs of the paralegal.

THE USE OF LEGAL ASSISTANTS
IN THE SMALL FIRM
by V. Nicholas and J. Kirk,
Arizona Bar Journal, 36 (Oct. 1978)

In what type of environment can the optimum function of a legal assistant be obtained? A legal assistant performs nonsecretarial duties. He or she does not spend time typing, filing, or answering phones. The ideal working situation is a quiet office where he or she can meet with clients, work and concentrate on tasks without a great deal of interruption.

Legal assistants in our firm have access to the use of secretaries, dictating equipment, word processing center, law library, and to the same office equipment as the attorneys they work with.

When possible, office space for legal assistants should be provided for through conscious integration into the architecture for the original construction of the building. . . . Remember that the purpose in providing the legal assistant with a private office is so that you can obtain optimum work results and make the most beneficial and efficient use of the legal assistant's time. Such results are not as easily obtained when working in an environment that is filled with the noise of phones and typewriters.

A relation of trust can be established by the attorney introducing the legal assistant to the client at the initial conference. The client is told that the legal assistant will be working with the attorney on the case and given a general outline of the types of matters the legal assistant will be handling for him. Having the legal assistant present at the initial conference demonstrates to the client that the legal assistant and attorney will be working together as a team. Being present while the attorney explains to the client available options and the direction advised is also helpful to the legal assistant. The role of the legal assistant then can be one of liaison between the attorney and client, helping the client to understand how the case is progressing and the results desired.

Following the initial conference with the attorney, it is beneficial for the legal assistant to have a more lengthy meeting with the client for the purpose of gathering detailed information.

At the conclusion of this initial visit to the law firm, the client knows that the attorney and his staff are fully aware of his needs and problems and have the necessary information to begin working on his behalf. The client knows he can contact the legal assistant at any time to provide him or her with new or additional information or to determine the status of matters. The client knows that when he contacts the legal assistant with questions or problems the attorney will be fully informed, the attorney is overseeing everything being done for the client, and that both the attorney and legal assistant are taking an active part in representing the client. . . .

The responsibility for establishing this "trust relationship" between the client and the legal assistant rests with the attorney. If the attorney has an attitude of confidence and appreciation for the work being done by the legal assistant, the client will learn to do the same.

Unfortunately, not all supervisors are this sensitive to the work environment of the paralegal, particularly in larger law firms.

11. RELATIONSHIP WITH SECRETARIES

There are some secretaries who resent paralegals. Rarely will these secretaries acknowledge this, but the problem is regularly mentioned by paralegals. A number of reasons account for the friction that exists:

- A feeling by secretaries that they should have the paralegal's job since they think that they once performed most of what the paralegal does.
- A resentment at the paralegal's higher status and pay.
- A resentment that the paralegal is coming between them and their attorney supervisors.
- A feeling that paralegals are arrogant in acting as if they are attorneys.
- A resentment at extra workload.
- Resistance to being supervised by a nonlawyer.

The office can become very unpleasant due to these feelings. For example, some secretaries can be hostile to paralegals and give their work low priority on typing and photocopying needs.

In large measure, lawyers are responsible for such problems. They have done a poor job in defining the paralegal role and in inculcating a team spirit among the various members of the office. The following comments from paralegals[22] reveal this sentiment:

"My status is somewhat nebulous. There seems to be a reluctance to give me a clear status apart from other support personnel."

"The law clerks are resentful of our position. The office manager does not understand why we're paid more than clerks or have a secretary do our typing."

"The attorneys still think of me as their secretary and do not utilize me to the fullest."

My boss "is slow to decipher paralegal skills from secretarial skills."

When attorneys are this confused, we should not be surprised when friction arises between paralegals and the clerical staff.

What can be done about this? First of all, the paralegal must be aware of the danger of resentment. The paralegal cannot assume that s/he will be respected by secretaries simply because of the paralegal's authority. Second, the paralegal must be scrupulous in being sure that s/he treats the secretary as an individual with strengths, needs, and legitimate grievances. The paralegal may be condescending without knowing it. Simple courtesy and a respect for the secretary's abilities and contribution can go a long way in avoiding difficulties. The secretary must be treated by the paralegal the way that the paralegal would want to be treated by others. Finally, the paralegal should understand that preventing or correcting paralegal-secretary friction is not the sole responsibility of the paralegal. Management must be aware of and take steps to correct the difficulties. The problems are compounded when secretaries feel that certain attorneys or administrators in the firm condone what is going on. It is perfectly proper for the paralegal to discuss the problems with his/her supervisor and with other managers in the firm. Corrective steps should be suggested that are responsive to the dignity of everyone involved.

"THE ATMOSPHERE AT YOUR OFFICE"
by Yasmin Spiegel, President of the
Sacramento Association of Legal Assistants
7 The Journal 1 (No. 11, Sacramento Association of Legal Assistants)

How is the atmosphere at your office? Do you get along with your co-workers, your secretary, the young associate or the attorney(s) who supervise you? Do you feel welcome, respected for your contributions, one of the team? Or do you find it hard to get anything done, or to get credit for it when things are accomplished?

Paralegals are relatively new members of the law office staff. They take their place in between the legal secretary and the law student, in many cases handling tasks that used to be delegated to them. The time-honored dynamic duo of

---

[22] M. Merzon, *The Status of Legal Assistants in Law Practice: A Cameo Survey* (National Association of Legal Assistants, 1982).

attorney/secretary has been replaced in many offices by the advent of the paralegal. The secretaries who rose through the ranks to become legal assistants may still be fighting to unload their past clerical duties in favor of more challenging paralegal tasks. The other secretaries, who in some cases have spent years working in the law office, may resent any inference that the tasks which they perform are not as valuable or require similar specialized knowledge and skill. They could easily be annoyed at the attitude that a legal assistant is somehow a "professional," whereas they are only "clerk/typists," particularly if they are assigned to work for the paralegal.

The law student, or the young associate could be concerned that the paralegal, being more cost effective to employ, will ultimately compete with them over jobs. Another complaint, which is well taken, is that a paralegal's salary, particularly when the paralegal is a long-time, valued employee earning overtime, can come so close to that of the associate attorney that it narrows that uncomfortable margin between those who have passed the bar and those who are not licensed to perform legal services.

The attorneys who employ us are yet another challenge. Many of them are accustomed to giving their secretaries many of the responsibilities that the paralegals are now assuming. The secretary was a "girl Friday" or a "Jill of all trades," who could type like a freight train, read the boss's mind, find absolutely anything in the office, make coffee with one hand, and do a fair amount of paralegal work as well. Now that the legal assistant is here, there may be some tendency to want the legal assistant to do those secretarial tasks as well—or at least to cater to the boss in the same way that the secretary has done. One friend recently told me (just before she quit her job) that the boss thought it was "so convenient that she knew how to type." The inference, of course, is that because she knows how to type that she will be responsible for her own clerical needs. There is a lack of respect for her worth to the firm in billable time which can go directly to the heart of our own insecurities and lack of job satisfaction.

There is enough uncertainty in our own image of professionals, that we need to thoughtfully consider some of the reasons why we may not have a clearly defined self-image. If we are experiencing negativity, resentment, unclear communication, or lack of respect, perhaps one of the answers is to look at our own attitude toward those we work with. Have we been respectful of their contributions? Have we been courteous of their needs when giving work to the secretarial staff and allowed them sufficient notice to prioritize our task and get it done on time? We can all appreciate how it feels when someone is sensitive and takes the time to thank us when we work for them. Compliments on a job well done are never superfluous, and yet often forgotten. Have we come in with a superior attitude and a demand to be treated as a professional because of our certificate or specialized training? Have we been positively assertive if the attorney has not communicated fully? Are we pleasant to be around, or do we spend most of our time worrying that people do not treat us the way we wish they would? If our needs are not being met, are we willing to make our needs known, rather than blame someone else for not getting our work done?

If the legal assistant is the wave of the future for the provision of legal services, then let us all work together to make this transition a winning transition for all members of the staff. Sometimes we do not have to look any further than our own attitude in order to make the biggest changes.

In the following chart, comparisons are made between paralegal and secretary functions.[23] This data can help counter the argument that secretaries perform the same functions as paralegals. The data is also useful in helping an office conduct an intelligent job function analysis for nonlawyer personnel.

COMPARISONS BETWEEN PARALEGAL AND SECRETARY FUNCTIONS

The following gives a ratio of paralegal use vis-à-vis the legal secretary on each of the forty-nine tasks. If, for example, the ratio is 4, then the paralegal is four times as likely to perform this function as the legal secretary.

Function	Ratio
General	
1. Organize and index files	0.80
2. Interview clients	4.82
3. Discuss fees	2.50
4. Calendar due dates (tickler)	0.81
5. Analyze factual information	3.61
6. Conduct investigation of public or court records	4.06
7. Compose routine correspondence	1.27
8. Draft opinion letters	18.00
9. Schedule meetings and depositions	0.89
10. Set trials and hearings	1.61
11. Participate in administrative hearings	10.00
12. Prepare pleadings	3.05
13. Prepare government reports including tax returns	2.53
14. Conduct client conferences	4.25
15. Legal research	12.75
16. Cite check (p. 585) and/or Shepardize (p. 608)	5.33
Litigation	
17. Draft complaint	5.52
18. Compose discovery documents	3.33
19. Interview witnesses	7.70
20. Digest depositions	5.66
21. Participate in depositions	9.75
22. Conduct depositions	4.00
23. Participate in trials	6.80
24. Obtain, prepare, and evaluate exhibits	4.94
Business	
25. Prepare articles of incorporation and by-laws	2.10
26. Prepare minutes	1.98
27. Prepare tax returns	4.00
28. Prepare documents for corporate mergers	7.00
29. Prepare pension and profit-sharing plans	2.75
30. Prepare SEC documents	4.40
31. Prepare general and limited partnership agreements	4.22
Estates	
32. Draft wills and/or trusts	2.28
33. Analyze investments for estate planning	6.00

[23] Shuey, *CBA Legal Assistants' Committee Survey Report,* 9 The Colorado Lawyer 483, 486–89 (No. 3, March, 1980).

34.	Prepare documents to be filed with Probate Court	2.13
35.	Value and arrange for appraisal of assets	2.18
36.	Prepare Inheritance Tax Statements	2.48
37.	Prepare Federal Estate Tax Returns	3.42
38.	Prepare Fiduciary Income Tax Returns	3.93
39.	Informal estate administration	3.60

Real Estate and Natural Resources

40.	Prepare deeds	1.34
41.	Check legal descriptions	1.18
42.	Create legal descriptions	2.93
43.	Prepare loan documents	1.65
44.	Prepare closing documents	1.70
45.	Conduct closings	4.28
46.	Search titles	7.14
47.	Draft title opinions	4.00
48.	Prepare leases	2.41
49.	Conduct FED actions	4.33

12. SEX HARASSMENT

Sexual harassment is a form of extortion: Someone in a position of power (either real or assumed) makes sexual advances towards another with an explicit or implicit threat of adverse job consequences for a failure to comply.[24] In a 1980 study of the federal workplace, 42% of responding female employees reported being sexually harassed on the job in one form or another.[25] Example:

> Recently a female paralegal began working with an insecure male lawyer who was a first year associate at the firm. He started "making the moves" on her by constantly asking if she was dating anyone. One day he called her in his office, closed the door, dialed a number on the phone, and handed the receiver to the paralegal. "What I heard was an obscene recording. I laughed, opened the door, and left." She did not believe in pursuing office relationships. Resentment developed when they began working on the same case together. He falsely accused the paralegal of lying and of not completing assignments on time. He made derogatory comments to her co-workers. When she confided in a female lawyer at the firm, she was told that the associate acts that way with all the women at the firm, that the paralegal supervisor and the associate are very good friends, and that the partner in charge "sticks to this associate like glue" and does not want to be bothered by "petty personnel problems."[26]

What should a paralegal do in such a predicament? A passive response would be to ignore the problem and hope that it will go away. A similar response would be to blame yourself. Phyllis Schlafly told the Senate Labor and Human Resources Committee that "Men hardly ever ask sexual favors of

---

[24] A. Baca, *Speech to National Capital Area Paralegal Association* (April 29, 1981).

[25] M. Colagiovanni, *Sexual Harassment: An Employment Issue,* 9 On Point 2 (Nat'l. Capital Area Paralegal Ass'n., Oct. 1982).

[26] *Harassment: Personnel Problem or Worse?* 9 National Paralegal Reporter 7 (Nat'l. Fed. of Paralegal Associations, Feb. 1985).

women from whom the certain response is 'no.'"[27] It is highly unlikely, however, that blaming yourself is either correct or productive.

For isolated and less serious problems, all that may be needed is a firm comment to the offender such as:

> Mr. Smith, you know that I respect your ability and authority in the firm. But I want you to know that I do not appreciate the comment that you made at that meeting about women. I did not think it was appropriate.

Unfortunately, this approach may be inadequate when the problem becomes more complicated and persists. Clearly, all internal avenues of trying to resolve the problem should be attempted. Hopefully, *somebody* in a position of responsibility will lend a sympathetic ear. Local paralegal associations should be a source of ideas and support for this problem. Speak with officers of the association. Go to general meetings. Ask for advice. It is highly likely that you will find others who have had similar experiences and who can provide concrete suggestions.

If all else fails, you have a powerful weapon at your disposal: the law. In the above example, the male associate has probably acted illegally. The same may be true for his supervisor who apparently has gone out of his way to ignore the problem. The law that applies to this situation is as follows:

Guidelines on Discrimination Because of Sex
Equal Employment Opportunity Commission
45 Federal Register 74676
(Nov. 10, 1980)

§1604.11 Sexual harassment.

(a) Harassment on the basis of sex is a violation of Sec. 703 of Title VII [of the Civil Rights Act of 1964]. Unwelcome sexual advances, requests for sexual favors, and other verbal or physical conduct of a sexual nature constitute sexual harassment when (1) submission to such conduct is made either explicitly or implicitly a term or condition of an individual's employment, (2) submission to or rejection of such conduct by an individual is used as the basis for employment decisions affecting such individual, or (3) such conduct has the purpose or effect of unreasonably interfering with an individual's work performance or creating an intimidating, hostile, or offensive working environment.

(b) In determining whether alleged conduct constitutes sexual harassment, the [Equal Employment Opportunity] Commission will look at the record as a whole and at the totality of the circumstances, such as the nature of the sexual advances and the context in which the alleged incidents occurred. The determination of the legality of a particular action will be made from the facts, on a case by case basis.

(c) Applying general Title VII principles, an employer, employment agency, joint apprenticeship committee or labor organization (hereinafter collectively referred to as "employer") is responsible for its acts and those of its agents and supervisory employees with respect to sexual harassment regardless or whether the specific acts complained of were authorized or even forbidden by the employer

---

[27] Supra note 24.

and regardless of whether the employer knew or should have known of their occurrence. The Commission will examine the circumstances of the particular employment relationship and the job functions performed by the individual in determining whether an individual acts in either a supervisory or agency capacity.

(d) With respect to conduct between fellow employees, an employer is responsible for acts of sexual harassment in the workplace where the employer (or its agents or supervisory employees) knows or should have known of the conduct, unless it can show that it took immediate and appropriate corrective action.

(e) An employer may also be responsible for the acts of non-employees, with respect to sexual harassment of employees in the workplace, where the employer (or its agents or supervisory employees) knows or should have known of the conduct and fails to take immediate and appropriate corrective action. In reviewing these cases the Commission will consider the extent of the employer's control and any other legal responsibility which the employer may have with respect to the conduct of such non-employees.

(f) Prevention is the best tool for the elimination of sexual harassment. An employer should take all steps necessary to prevent sexual harassment from occurring, such as affirmatively raising the subject, expressing strong disapproval, developing appropriate sanctions, informing employees of their right to raise and how to raise the issue of harassment under Title VII, and developing methods to sensitize all concerned.

(g) Other related practices: Where employment opportunities or benefits are granted because of an individual's submission to the employer's sexual advances or requests for sexual favors, the employer may be held liable for unlawful sex discrimination against other persons who were qualified for but denied that employment opportunity or benefit.

13. WORKING WITH SYSTEMS

Some paralegal employment problems are attributed to the fact that the firm has not carefully thought out how paralegals can be effectively used in the office. Paralegals are supposed to work as part of a lawyer-paralegal-secretary team. The difficulty, however, is that the office may not have done the necessary planning to design the *system* that the team is supposed to execute.

A system is an organized way of accomplishing a task. Each participant is supposed to perform those functions that they are capable of handling and for which they are not overtrained. Someone must create the system:

- Select the task that is to be systematized. It will usually be a task that the office performs regularly, e.g., incorporating a business, probating an estate, filing for divorce, engaging in discovery.
- The task is carefully studied in order to identify the various components of the task. What are the pieces that must always be performed? What facts must always be obtained? What letters must always be sent? What forms must always be prepared?
- A systems or procedural manual is then written containing a description of the task, checklists of things to be done, sample forms, etc.
- The performance of the components of the task are then delegated to various members of the team.

Experienced paralegals are sometimes asked to design systems for tasks with which they are intimately familiar.

It takes considerable sophistication to *design* a system. Even more sophistication is sometimes needed to *implement* the system and make it work. The participants must believe in the system and usually should have had a role in its design if changes in their work habits are required by the system. Many lawyers are notoriously resistant to change, particularly if they believe that the system fails to recognize the role of professional judgment. If you have been doing something the same way for fifteen years, you tend to be suspicious of suggestions that more efficient ways are possible. Furthermore, in the transition from blueprint to operation, there may have to be modifications made in the system in order to work out the bugs. Again, a precondition to this occurring is a willingness of the participants to make it work.

At the time a paralegal walks into an office for the first time, s/he may confront a number of situations:

- There are no systems; everybody practices law in their own individualistic way.
- There may be talk of systemization, but no one has yet done any serious design work.
- An ineffective system may be in place.
- A system may be in place that the participants do not believe in.
- A system may exist on paper, but the time and energy has not been expended by anyone to make the system work.

All these environments can make life difficult for the paralegal. A disorganized office can be very frustrating.

One of the most valuable things a paralegal can do is to observe an effective system in place. One or more may exist in other parts of the firm where you work. It may be possible for you to visit other firms in the area. There are formbooks (p. 543), manuals, and legal periodical literature (p. 625) on law office management that are available, but they are no substitute for seeing the real thing.

Don't be reluctant to try to design your own system. You might want to begin with a system for a portion of one of your tasks. Start out on a small scale with instructions or checklists for functions that you regularly perform. Write the system so that a new paralegal would be able to read it and know what to do. Your supervisor will be very impressed. Your efforts may prompt others to become more active in the design of larger systems. A paralegal with this much initiative and organizational ability will soon become a prized member of the office.

Nancy Siegel, a pioneer in the field, recommends that paralegals design their own systems as part of an overall strategy of self improvement:

> Expand your duties and responsibilities. Develop efficient systems for routine work so that you have time to take non-routine work assignments. Offer to do new, but specific, tasks rather than simply asking for "more responsibility." Ask questions—find out which attorneys in your firm are good teachers. Work with the attorneys and other paralegals to develop a reading list in your specialty . . . ;

such a list would contain statutes, cases, and articles which will give you a broader understanding of the kind of work you are doing.[28]

Substantial benefits result when an office has successfully incorporated systems into its practice of law. The following report describes one such office:

THE USE OF LEGAL ASSISTANTS IN THE SMALL OFFICE
by V. Nicholas and J. Kirk
Arizona Bar Journal 36 (Oct. 1978)

Although our office now consists of six attorneys, seven legal assistants, and 15 support personnel, the change from a "private secretary" for each attorney to a legal assistant was not immediate. It took approximately one year to complete the transition. During that year it became clear that the use of a legal assistant team approach had many advantages over our prior staff organization. Attorneys who initially hesitated to participate in our legal assistant program eventually realized its value and sought its benefits.

Under our team approach, the legal assistant becomes proficient in all steps necessary to accomplish an incorporation, complete a real estate transaction, probate an estate, or conclude a civil lawsuit. Once experienced and trained, the legal assistant will be able to keep all of an attorney's cases progressing without the need for constant instruction from the attorney. While large firms tend to have several attorneys assign specialized tasks of the same nature to one legal assistant, our team approach allows each legal assistant to work on all aspects of a case together with her lawyer teammate. In this way the legal assistant becomes specialized in one area of the law rather than in the performance of one type of task. Moreover, the legal assistant is completely familiar with the team's caseload so that discovery can be initiated or responded to without additional time expenditures. . . .

The team approach has allowed the firm to increase productivity without hiring additional associates. Increased volume is, therefore, smoothly absorbed without substantial rises in overhead. Thus, the use of legal assistants is an effective method by which to expand. . . .

Each system consists of a separate notebook explaining what information our legal assistants (and secretaries) are expected to know [concerning] how and why things are done in the area to which the system pertains. For example, all applicable statutes are set out in a statutory grid which is a reference to the sections of the system where a particular statute is cited; the legal assistant and secretary are instructed on how to meet and communicate with the client; all court procedures and documents are outlined in detail with check-lists; standardized letters are included with instructions as to when they are used; examples are given of documents customarily used in processing a particular matter and every form applicable to that area is set out in its entirety. All standardized letters, documents, forms, pleadings, etc., are cross-referenced to our word processing unit so that

---

[28] N. Siegel, *Out Is Not the Only Way Up,* 6 National Paralegal Reporter 6 (Nat'l. Federation of Paralegal Associations, Fall/Winter, 1981).

legal assistants and secretaries can complete a request form and have the needed document produced by the word processor without awaiting direction from the supervising attorney. Using the system, a legal assistant can produce all types of repetitive documents used. While it is seldom necessary to alter the finished product, when correction is needed the attorney can accomplish it simply through word processing.

By having each system fully recorded in the word processing unit, updating is easily achieved by use of the word processor. Whenever there is a change in a statute or a particular procedure is determined to be ineffective, the appropriate system section is immediately modified in the word processing unit and the revised material inserted in the notebook.

Although a system cannot possibly address every situation which could conceivably arise, an attempt has been made to cover the major procedures which will normally occur in each particular area of the law. The systems are designed for efficient use of both the attorneys' and legal assistants' time. The need to repeat instructions for matters which occur frequently and which can be handled routinely by legal assistants is eliminated; similarly, legal assistants can work independently without searching files for necessary forms or letters, or waiting for instructions from the supervising attorney. By following the systems, the legal assistant is equipped to handle a variety of situations confidently without constant supervision. Moreover, the time available to the attorney to concentrate on the complicated facts, legal theories and issues involved in cases is substantially increased.

While the systems method permits the legal assistant to proceed independently on a file, he or she must understand that use of the system does not obviate the need for the supervising attorney's advice and approval before actions are taken. Whenever any doubts or questions arise, the responsible attorney must be consulted *before* any action is taken. Similarly, the attorney should be cautioned that although the system allows the legal assistant to assume a great deal of responsibility by taking the initiative in various proceedings, he or she should not be lax in the responsibility of overseeing everything that transpires in the case. Although use of the systems enables a legal assistant to assess the status of a file, determine what work needs to be done, and begin compiling necessary information or drafting documents, the responsible attorney must, of course, review, finalize, and/or approve every item coming into or out of his client's file. The attorney must retain the ultimate responsibility for decision-making and "managing" of the caseload. . . .

Our experience has been that the team approach to the practice of law is an economical one. This is true not only because the attorneys are free to develop the practice but because legal assistants produce billable time. When a case is accepted on the basis that a client will pay an hourly charge for the services rendered, that client is informed that there will be an hourly charge for the legal assistants. At the time the fee agreement is entered into, the client has already met the legal assistant and the relationship between the client and the legal assistant has been established. The client does not object to paying the hourly rate of a legal assistant since it is substantially less than that of the attorney. All of us have heard complaints that the legal profession fails to service a large segment of the population for a reasonable fee. There is now some control of that situation in our office. We attempt to meet our responsibility to those people unable to pay the customary attorney fees by using the legal assistant team approach to its maximum.

IS THIS ANY WAY TO RUN
A LAW FIRM?
by Beth Rackley Hesselson, Paralegal
86 *Case & Comment* 27
(No. 4, July-Aug. 1981)

A few years ago at the truly prestigious firm of Herring, Mackerel, & Tuna, the senior partner, Wallace J. Tuna (affectionately known as Wally) issued the following memorandum:

To: All Senior Partners, Junior Partners, and one copy to be shared among the Associates.

It has been brought to my attention by my good friend Harold R. Satterthwaite, III, of Huff, Chuff, Harrumph, & Gargle that they now employ a Paralegal. Please determine what that is and get me one.

One Way

And so it came to pass that one paralegal and then two paralegals and then three, four, five . . . paralegals were added to the staff of Herring, Mackerel, & Tuna until finally there were 27 in all, who had been stuffed into the space of Wally Tuna's former broom closet and told to conduct themselves in a professional manner. No one was quite sure what to do with them.

They were eventually divided up among the various departments of the firm according to a formula scientifically based on the relative power and empire-building ambitions of the various senior partners: that means 26 went to Litigation and one to all the rest. Some who had years of experience were sent to file in the basement. Others, who didn't know a pleading from a correspondence file (and furthermore didn't care), were put in charge. The males, regardless of experience and seniority, were invested with more authority than the females and, naturally, given first dibs on overtime, interesting assignments, and positions on the softball team. No one, but no one, was permitted to set foot in the library, not even to use it as a short-cut to the photocopier, which was where all the paralegals spent most of their time anyway.

Some paralegals became very disgruntled and gave up caring about their work. Others became highly competitive and frustrated. Disagreements and distrust abounded. A few took the easy way out and went to law school.

Another Way

One night at the club, Wally complained that having paralegals wasn't all it was cracked up to be, and he asked Harry Satterthwaite how it was going at good old Huff, Chuff, Harrumph, & Gargle. Harry told him they did things a little differently. . . .

They created a position of Paralegal Coordinator, into which they placed a paralegal of experience and maturity, to keep work assignments flowing evenly and appropriately among all the paralegals. The Paralegal Coordinator also functions as a representative of the paralegals to the administration, presenting their ideas and requests. Experienced paralegals coming into the firm know that their experience will be honored, not only on the salary scale, but also in appropriate job assignments. Novices know they will be given a period of training to orient them to the firm.

Tasks have been identified in a hierarchy from simplest to most complex and paralegals can move from one level to another as they gain experience. Systems have been designed. Paralegals gaining the greatest experience and demonstrating the greatest competence and loyalty to the firm are given special perquisites such as semi-private offices, secretarial assistance, more sophisticated assignments, and merit raises. Morale is terrific.

Conclusion

"All well and good," says Wally, but "Is that really any way to run a law firm?"
"You bet it is," says Harry.

14. CAREER LADDERS

The legal profession must begin to give serious consideration to career ladders for paralegals in law offices. After two or three years of successful work in an office, where is the paralegal to go? Does professional development and advancement necessarily mean *leaving* the paralegal field and becoming a lawyer? The only way up in a law firm is out? Clearly more creative ways are needed to cope with the frustration felt by individuals who have demonstrated their abilities and commitment and who want to continue paralegal work in the law office.

Offices have tried different ways of dealing with this problem such as regular salary increases, larger offices, individual secretarial assistance, greater access to computers and other equipment, opportunities for advance specialization and training, closer working relationships with individual attorneys, etc. While many of these approaches have been successful, they have not solved the problem of high turnover among paralegals who have been on the job for more than two years.

It may be that more public and institutional ways are needed to recognize the contribution of the paralegals in order to be responsive to their need for advancement. Some firms—unfortunately few in number—have moved in this direction by creating career ladders for paralegals. One firm, for example, has established a three-tiered system:

- Case Clerk
- Legal Assistant
- Senior Legal Assistant

Newly hired employees begin work as Case Clerks. These are individuals who are not expected to be in the position for much longer than a year. After this time, they will either leave the office for other pursuits (e.g., go to law school) or seek promotion within the office. Case Clerks perform clerical tasks of a nonsecretarial nature, e.g., index depositions, organize documents, work on closing binders. Legal Assistants, on the other hand, are given broader assignments within an area of practice. The final step up the career ladder is the Senior Legal Assistant who has some management responsibilities over other nonlawyer personnel. This person has been with the office for some time, has demonstrated expertise in one or more aspects of practice, has performed well, and has made a long-term commitment to a paralegal career. While Senior Legal Assistants do not receive overtime pay, they can achieve a salary level comparable to that of a manager with a MBA degree.

Of course, not all law firms are large enough to be able to implement a career ladder of this dimension. As indicated above, other approaches may be taken by offices that have given serious thought to the problem of retaining their most experienced and competent paralegals. Check with paralegal associations to find out what is being done in this regard. Also check the literature. Paralegal newsletters and magazines often have articles on professional development and the issue of burnout. Law office management journals and manuals frequently contain material on personnel policies and employee satisfaction. It is recommended that you do some research into this literature. When you go to your supervisor to discuss the problem, it is always impressive to make a presentation that includes examples of what others have said and done in addressing the problem.

Paralegal associations are extremely valuable institutions. Not only are they a source of excellent information about paralegal practice in your area and in the nation, but they are also potential gold mines of ideas and strategies. It is probably impossible for you to have a problem on the job that has not been experienced by numerous other paralegals within a paralegal association. You must tap this resource. You can suggest that the association conduct regular workshops on employment or working conditions. You can learn a lot simply by listening to the problems of others and how they tried to resolve them. What worked? Why? What didn't work? Why? What is the next thing that should be tried? In addition to these sessions, you should encourage the association to conduct surveys and take positions on issues such as secretarial help for paralegals and compensation. As part of these surveys, the association can collect comments from various attorneys around the city or state on certain practices of their firm that involve paralegals. Such surveys and comments can be very persuasive when you show them to your supervisor.

ASSIGNMENT 5

Examine the following fact situations. For each situation:

- Identify the problem or problems that you see.
- What strategies to you think would be helpful in resolving the problem or problems? Why?
- What strategies do you think would be counterproductive? Why?
- What do you think could have been done to prevent the problem or problems from occurring in the first place? How could they have been avoided?
- In your responses, specify what you think would be assertive, nonassertive, and aggressive behavior.

a. Tom has been a paralegal at a firm for three years. His paralegal training at a school has been in drafting, legal research, investigation, etc. For the entire three years, however, he has been collating and digesting the numerous documents in a big antitrust case. It is a very important case and the firm is reluctant to take him off it due to his familiarity with these documents. The problem, however, is that Tom is becoming thoroughly bored with his job. He is satisfied with his pay, but dreads coming to work each day. He tried to explain this to his supervisor one day, but he was simply told how important he was to the case. The supervisor said, "If you decide to leave the firm, I hope you will give us six months' lead time so that you can train a replacement." This made Tom all the more depressed since he does not want to leave.

b. Ellen is a probate paralegal at a firm. She has worked there two years. At a recent paralegal association meeting, she discovers that other probate paralegals in the city with the same experience are making at least $4,000 more per year than she. She wants to talk with her supervisor about this, but is not sure if this is the right time. The last three months have been difficult for her. She has been out of work a lot due to illness. She also recently began work on a new complex case. She is struggling to keep up with the new work involved in the case. She must constantly ask her supervisor for help. The supervisor appears to be irritated with her progress on the case. Her next scheduled salary review is ten months away.

c. Jim, Janet, Brenda, Helen, and Pat are paralegals at a law firm. They are all unhappy about their job: low pay, long hours, sexism, menial tasks, etc. On a number of occasions they have met with the senior partners in the firm to discuss ways of improving their situation. Minor changes are made, but the problems persist. They are approached by a local union about joining the union.

d. Fran is a paralegal in a firm where she works for the senior partner—the most powerful person in the firm. Fran receives excellent pay and fringe benefits. She loves her work. Other paralegals in the firm, however, resent her because their benefits are much lower and they receive assignments that they hate.

e. Same situation as in (d) above. Fran's boss is currently going through a divorce. The strain on him has been enormous. One consequence of this is that Fran's workload is increasing. More of his work is being shifted to her. The boss is extremely sensitive to any criticism about the way he practices law, so Fran is reluctant to talk with him about the extra work—particularly when he is under so much pressure due to the divorce. Yet Fran is worried about her ability to do her job competently in view of the increased work. She hopes that things will get back to normal when the divorce is over.

f. Tom has been a paralegal at the firm for six years. He works for three attorneys. One day he is told by a memo from the office administrator that an outside consultant has been hired to study Tom's job in order to find ways "to increase productivity." The letter instructs Tom to spend the next two days permitting the consultant to follow Tom around and ask questions about what Tom does. Tom is furious.

g. Mary has been a paralegal at the firm for two years. She works for one attorney, Mr. Getty. One day a client calls Mary and says, "I'm sending you another copy of the form that Mr. Getty said you lost." This is news to Mary. She works with the client's file every day and knows that she has never lost anything. She pauses, trying to think of what to say to this client over the phone before hanging up.

h. Veronica works for a law firm where none of the supervisors give formal evaluations of the paralegals. The supervisors feel that formal evaluations would be too time-consuming and too general to be helpful. Veronica has received yearly raises, and according to her supervisor this is the best indication of what the firm thinks of her. Veronica, however, is not happy with the feedback she has gotten about her work.

i. How would you handle the fact situation presented on p. 190 involving sexual harassment? Assume the paralegal does not want to quit and is afraid that she will lose her job if she institutes legal action.

ASSIGNMENT 6

Karen considers herself a quiet, nonaggressive person. She has two job possibilities: (a) a large law firm (seventy-five lawyers and twenty-two paralegals) and (b) a one-lawyer/one-secretary office. She likes the type of work both offices do. The pay and benefits in both offices are roughly the same. How would you advise Karen on which job to take?

ASSIGNMENT 7

According to Douglas McGregor in *The Human Side of Enterprise* (1960), there are two basic views of human behavior at work. Theory "X" says that a person has a natural dislike of work and will avoid it whenever possible. Theory "Y" says that physical and mental work are as natural to a person as any other activity. Under theory "Y," workers do not naturally shy away from responsibility.

- Describe a law office using paralegals that is managed under theory "X." How would it function? How would the office handle paralegal problems?
- Describe a law office using paralegals that is managed under theory "Y." How would it function? How would the office handle paralegal problems?
- Which theory do you think is correct?
- Which theory describes you?

ASSIGNMENT 8

What needs does a paralegal or any worker have? What is our "hierarchy of needs"? Rearrange the following needs so that you think they reflect the conscious or unconscious priorities of most human beings: the need to be fulfilled; the need to be respected; the need to eat, sleep, and be clothed; the need to be safe; the need to be respected; the need to be admired; the need to belong; the need to have self-worth. See Masloe, A., *Motivation and Personality* (1970).

4

The Regulation
of Paralegals

SUMMARY OF CHAPTER

I. THE PRACTICE OF LAW

Statutes defining the practice of law apply to paralegals. Criminal prosecution can result from a violation of these statutes. In general, the statutes prohibit nonlawyers from appearing for another in a representative capacity, giving legal advice, and drafting legal documents. A common theme in the literature is that if the activity calls for the exercise of professional judgment, a lawyer is required. But clear definitions of such concepts are often difficult to find. Furthermore, there are some major exceptions to the prohibitions on nonlawyer conduct.

In a limited number of circumstances, nonlawyers are authorized to do what would otherwise constitute the unauthorized practice of law. For example:

- In many states, a real estate broker can draft sales contracts.
- Some lower courts, e.g., Justice of the Peace Court, allow a nonlawyer to represent others before such courts in certain kinds of cases.
- A few states allow paralegals to "appear" in court to request a continuance or a new date for the next hearing in a case.
- An inmate can "practice law" in the institution, e.g., by giving legal advice to, and drafting court documents for, another inmate if the institution

does not provide adequate alternative methods of providing legal services.
- Many administrative agencies, particularly at the federal level, allow nonlawyers to represent clients before the agencies.

II. LICENSING OF PARALEGALS

A number of states have considered paralegal licensing statutes. To date, no such statutes have been enacted. There is no license requirement for paralegals in any state. A major objection to licensing is that it will stifle the development of paralegalism and fail to account for the great diversity in the field. The vast majority of paralegals work for lawyers. Since lawyers are licensed and are responsible for what their paralegals do, the argument is that the public does not need the added protection that would come from a separate licensing scheme for paralegals. Yet proposals for mandatory licensing continue to emerge in spite of the fact that organized paralegals (through their associations) and most bar associations feel that licensing is premature.

III. ETHICAL RULES GOVERNING LAWYERS AND PARALEGALS

Lawyers are regulated by their state bar association and state court system. The rules governing their conduct are found in the canons of ethics and in the ethical opinions that interpret these canons.

No lawyer must belong to the American Bar Association. It is a voluntary national organization. The ABA has its own canons of ethics and ethical opinions that individual states are free to adopt, modify, or reject. For years the canons were found in the ABA Model Code of Professional Responsibility. In 1983 the Model Code was revised. The current document is the ABA Model Rules of Professional Conduct.

No canon of ethics at the state or national level can directly apply to paralegals because the latter cannot be members of bar associations. A paralegal, therefore, cannot be disciplined by a bar association for unethical conduct. But a lawyer can be disciplined for the improper use of paralegals, e.g., the failure to supervise them properly.

Over the years, the bar associations have issued guidelines on the permissible scope of paralegal use by lawyers. But the bar associations have not always agreed on what these boundary lines should be. The following are some of the issues that have been addressed:

- What the nonlawyer employees can be called.
- Whether paralegals can sign their name on letters written on law firm stationery.
- Whether the names of paralegals can be printed on law firm stationery.
- Whether paralegals can have their own business card.
- When paralegals should identify themselves as nonlawyers to the public.

- Whether paralegals can be present at real estate closings when their supervising lawyers are not also present.

One ethical responsibility on which there is no disagreement is the obligation of lawyers to ensure that their paralegals preserve the confidences of clients.

IV. BAR ASSOCIATION CONTROL OF PARALEGAL EDUCATION

The American Bar Association "approves" paralegal training schools. The approval is voluntary. No school must be ABA-approved, and most schools have decided not to apply for this approval.

Initially, the entity that conducted the approval program was the ABA Committee on Legal Assistants. The Committee made its recommendations on approval to the governing body of the ABA, which made the final decision. More recently, the ABA has established an Approval Commission to administer the approval process. The Commission reports to the Committee on Legal Assistants, which in turn makes its recommendations to the governing body of the ABA.

The ABA has been ambivalent about the propriety of its role in regulating paralegal schools. While no court or law prohibits the ABA from continuing its approval process, the ABA has decided to withdraw from the process in the expectation that its role will eventually be taken over by an independent accrediting entity. It is unclear, however, whether such an entity is feasible.

V. SELF-REGULATION BY PARALEGALS

There are two national paralegal associations: the National Association of Legal Assistants (NALA) and the National Federation of Paralegal Associations (NFPA). There has been considerable disagreement between the two groups on major issues. For example, NALA favors a proposal to allow paralegals to become associate members of the American Bar Association; NFPA opposes it. More significantly, NALA favors the voluntary certification of paralegals and has launched its own certification program through the Certified Legal Assistant examination. NFPA opposes certification at this time. Both NALA and NFPA agree, however, that mandatory state licensing of paralegals should be discouraged.

VI. FAIR LABOR STANDARDS ACT (FLSA)

The FLSA requires employers to pay overtime compensation to employees unless the employees are employed in an executive, administrative, or professional capacity. Paralegal managers with major responsibility for the supervision of other paralegals would fall within this exception and hence would not be entitled to overtime compensation. The U.S. Department of Labor, which administers the FLSA through its Wage and Hour Division, takes the position that most other paralegals do not fall within the exception and therefore are entitled to overtime compensation.

VII. TORT LIABILITY

If a paralegal commits a tort, e.g., negligence, slander, s/he is personally liable to the defendant. Under the theory of respondeat superior, the supervising attorney is also liable for the wrong committed by the paralegal if it occurred within the scope of employment. Most attorneys have malpractice insurance that covers their employees.

Section A. INTRODUCTION

There are seven ways in which the activities of paralegals are or could be regulated:

1. Laws on the unauthorized practice of law and on the *authorized* practice of law by nonlawyers.
2. State licensing of paralegals.
3. Bar regulation of a lawyer's use of paralegals.
4. Regulation of the education of paralegals.
5. Self-regulation by paralegals.
6. The Fair Labor Standards Act.
7. Tort law, e.g., the negligence of paralegals and of lawyers who use them.

At the outset, there is a need to define the terminology involved in any system of control.

Accreditation is the process by which an organization evaluates and recognizes a program of study (or an institution) as meeting certain predetermined qualifications or standards.

Certification is the process by which a nongovernmental organization grants recognition to an individual who has met certain predetermined qualifications specified by that organization.

Licensure is the process by which an agency of government grants permission to persons meeting predetermined qualifications to engage in a given occupation and/or to use a particular title.

Registration is the process by which qualified individuals are listed on an official roster maintained by a governmental agency or by a nongovernmental organization.[1]

Approval means the recognition that comes from accreditation, certification, licensure, or registration. As we will see, the American Bar Association uses the word "approval" as a substitute for "accreditation" of paralegal education programs.

Code is any set of rules regulating conduct.

Guideline is suggested conduct that will help an applicant obtain accreditation, certification, licensure, registration, or approval.

Regulation is any governmental or nongovernmental method of controlling conduct.

Unfortunately, the distinctions made in the above definitions are often blurred in discussions of the topic.

---

[1] National Commission on Accrediting, *Study of Accrediting of Selected Health Educational Programs*, Part II, Staff Working Papers, p. ii (Feb. 1982).

Section B. THE UNAUTHORIZED AND THE AUTHORIZED PRACTICE OF LAW

(a) DEFINING THE PRACTICE OF LAW

Every state has laws on who can be a lawyer and on the unauthorized practice of law. In most states it is a *crime* to practice law illegally. For example:

> **Alaska Stat. Ann. 08.08.230 (1968).** Any person not an active member of the Alaska Bar who engages in the private practice of law or represents himself as entitled to engage in the private practice of law in the state . . . is guilty of a misdemeanor and upon conviction is punishable by a fine of not more than $1,000, or by imprisonment for not more than one year, or by both.

Normally such rules do not apply when a citizen is acting as his/her own lawyer. The regulation is aimed at people who represent others. It is not a crime to represent yourself in a criminal case or in a civil case such as one growing out of an automobile accident.

What is the practice of law? Most definitions are extremely broad. Examine, for example, the following Louisiana statute:

> **La. Rev. Stat. 37:212 (1964).** "Practice of law" defined.—The practice of law is defined as follows:
> (1) In a representative capacity, the appearance as an advocate, or the drawing of papers, pleadings or documents, or the performance of any act, in connection with proceedings, pending or prospective, before any court of record in this state; or
> (2) For a consideration, reward, or pecuniary benefit, present or anticipated, direct or indirect,
>   (a) the advising or counseling of another as to secular law, or
>   (b) in behalf of another, the drawing or procuring, or the assisting in the drawing or procuring of a paper, document, or instrument affecting or relating to secular rights, or
>   (c) the doing of any act, in behalf of another, tending to obtain or secure for the other the prevention or the redress of a wrong or the enforcement or establishment of a right.

Problems arise, however, in the application of such broad definitions, as you will see in doing the following assignment.

ASSIGNMENT 9

Below you will find excerpts of three opinions from Massachusetts (*Opinion of the Justices*), West Virginia (*Earley*), and New York (*Winder*). Assume that the above Louisiana statute (section 37:212) was in effect in Massachusetts, West Virginia, and New York.

1. Is the *Opinion of the Justices* consistent with section 37:212? Could the "gratuitous furnishing of legal aid to the poor" violate section 37:212? Explain your answer.

2. Is *Earley* consistent with section 37:212? Would *Earley* have reached a different result if the West Virginia court was applying section 37:212? Explain your answer.

3. Is *Winder* consistent with section 37:212? Would *Winder* have reached a different result if the New York court was applying section 37:212? Explain your answer.

Opinion of Justices to the Senate
Supreme Judicial Court of Massachusetts, 1935.
289 Mass. 607, 194 N.E. 313.

The gratuitous furnishing of legal aid to the poor and unfortunate without means in the pursuit of any civil remedy, as a matter of charity, the search of records of real estate to ascertain what may there be disclosed without giving opinion or advice as to the legal effect of what is found, the work of an accountant dissociated from legal advice, do not constitute the practice of law. There may be other kindred pursuits of the same character. All these activities, however, lie close to the border line and may easily become or be accompanied by practice of the law. The giving of advice as to investments in stocks, bonds and other securities in real or personal property, and in making tax returns falls within the same category.

West Virginia State Bar et al. v. Earley
Supreme Court of Appeals of West Virginia, 1959.
144 W. Va. 504, 109 S.E.2d 420.

The courts in numerous decisions in different jurisdictions have undertaken to define and designate what constitutes the practice of law; but it is generally recognized that it is extremely difficult, perhaps impossible, to formulate a precise and completely comprehensive definition of the practice of law or to prescribe limits to the scope of that activity. It is clear, however, that a licensed attorney at law in the practice of his profession generally engages in three principal types of professional activity. These types are legal advice and instructions to clients to inform them of their rights and obligations; preparation for clients of documents requiring knowledge of legal principles which is not possessed by an ordinary layman; and appearance for clients before public tribunals, which possess the power and authority to determine rights of life, liberty and property according to law, in order to assist in the proper interpretation and enforcement of law.

. . .

Section 14, Article 1, Chapter 23, Code, 1931, provides that the State Compensation Commissioner shall prepare and furnish blank forms of applications for benefits, notices to employers, proofs of injury or death, of medical attendance, of employment and wage earnings and other proofs, and that it is the duty of employers to keep on hand a sufficient supply of such blanks at all times. The completion of such blank forms does not require any knowledge and skill beyond that possessed by the ordinarily experienced and intelligent layman, and a layman may properly complete and file such forms in behalf of another person as employer, employee, claimant or beneficiary without engaging in the practice of law. In Shortz v. Farrell, 327 Pa. 81, 193 A. 20, the court said that preparation and filing of pleadings in connection with a workmen's compensation claim do not constitute practice of law for the reason that they are executed on forms prepared by the Workmen's Compensation Board, are elementary in character, and do not rise to the dignity of pleadings as that term is understood in judicial proceedings. A natural person who appears in his own behalf as claimant, litigant, or party in interest in courts or other duly constituted agencies or tribunals does not engage in the unauthorized practice of law. Natural persons may manage, prosecute, or defend their own actions, suits and proceedings and defend prosecutions against themselves except when the public welfare demands otherwise, and such activity does not constitute the practice of law.

The justification for excluding from the practice of law persons who are not admitted to the bar and for limiting and restricting such practice to licensed members of the legal profession is not the protection of the members of the bar from competition or the creation of a monopoly for the members of the legal profession, but is instead the protection of the public from being advised and represented in legal matters by unqualified and undisciplined persons over whom the judicial department of the government could exercise slight or no control.

The admission to membership in the legal profession is a privilege granted in the interest of the public to those who are morally fit and mentally qualified for the sole purpose of protecting the unwary and the ignorant from injury at the hands of persons unskilled or unlearned in the law. The licensing of lawyers is not designed to give rise to a professional monopoly but instead to serve the public right to protection against unlearned and unskilled advice and service in relation to legal matters. The reason for the requirement that the practice of law be engaged in only by duly licensed practitioners of the law is to establish and maintain a legal standard by which the rights of persons may not be jeopardized or sacrificed by counsel and advice of unlicensed and incompetent persons who give or attempt to give legal advice, prepare documents and pleadings, file and prosecute proceedings and examine witnesses in courts or other tribunals. It is essential to the administration of justice and the proper protection of society that unlicensed persons be not permitted to prey upon the public by engaging in the practice of law.

The reason laymen are forbidden to engage in the practice of law is that it is detrimental to the public interest for them to represent themselves to the public that they are qualified to do so when in fact they are not so qualified.

State v. Winder
Supreme Court, Appellate Division, Fourth Dept. of New York, 1973.
348 N.Y.S.2d 270.

MEMORANDUM:

The Divorce Yourself Kit offered for sale by defendant, a layman, purports to offer forms and instructions in law and procedure in certain areas of matrimonial law and the judicial process. In Matter of New York Co. Lawyers' Ass'n v. Dacey, 28 A.D.2d 161, 283 N.Y.S.2d 984, rev'd, on the dissenting opinion in the Appellate Division, 21 N.Y.2d 694, 287 N.Y.S.2d 422, 234 N.E.2d 459, the court dealt with the publishing of a book "How to Avoid Probate!" consisting of 55 pages of text and 310 pages of forms. In the dissenting opinion adopted by the Court of Appeals, Justice Stevens, analyzing the pertinent rules of law, stated at page 173, 283 N.Y.S.2d at page 997: "It cannot be claimed that the publication of a legal text which purports to say what the law is amounts to legal practice. And the mere fact that the principles or rules stated in the text may be accepted by a particular reader as a solution to his problem does not affect this. . . . Apparently it is urged that the conjoining of these two, that is, the text and the forms, with advice as to how the forms should be filled out, constitutes the unlawful practice of law. But that is the situation with many approved and accepted texts. Dacey's book is sold to the public at large. There is no personal contact or relationship with a particular individual. Nor does there exist that relation of confidence and trust so necessary to the status of attorney and client. This is the essential of legal practice—the representation and the advising of a particular person in a particular situation." "At most the book assumes to offer general advice on common problems, and does not purport to give personal advice on a specific problem peculiar to a designated or readily identified person."

Similarly [in the case now before us] the defendant's publication does not purport "to give personal advice on a specific problem peculiar to a designated or readily identified person," and because of the absence of the essential element of "legal practice—the representation and the advising of a particular person in a particular situation" in the publication and sale of the kits, such publication and sale did not constitute the unlawful practice of law in violation of Sec. 478 of the Judiciary Law and was improperly enjoined by the judgment appealed from. There being no legal impediment under the statute to the sale of the kit, there was no proper basis for [1] the injunction against defendant maintaining an office for the purpose of selling to persons seeking a divorce, separation, annulment or separation agreement any printed material or writings relating to matrimonial law or [2] the prohibition . . . against defendant having an interest in any publishing house publishing his manuscript on divorce and against his having any personal contact with any prospective purchaser. The record does fully support, however, the finding of the court that for the charge of $75 or $100 for the kit, the defendant gave legal advice in the course of personal contacts concerning particular problems which might arise in the preparation and presentation of the purchaser's asserted matrimonial cause of action or pursuit of other legal remedies and assistance in the preparation of necessary documents. [The injunction as to] conduct constituting the practice of law, particularly with reference to the giving of advice and counsel by the defendant relating to specific problems of particular individuals in connection with a divorce, separation, . . . should be affirmed.

Judgment unanimously modified. . . .

ASSIGNMENT 10

Rewrite section 37:212 (p. 205) so that it is fully consistent with the *Opinion of the Justices, Earley* and *Winder.* Draft the statute so that it is clear that what these cases authorize is reflected in your new statute. You can add to the statute as now written, take away from it, or change it in any way so that it is in harmony with what the three cases say about what is or is not the practice of law.

ASSIGNMENT 11

Why did the *Earley* case say that there must be regulation of the practice of law? Can you think of an opposing argument? What is a more cynical argument for why lawyers want to control who does or does not practice law? Do you agree with this cynical view?

ASSIGNMENT 12

Prepare an annotated bibliography on the topic of the practice of law by nonlawyers in your state. The instructions for preparing an annotated bibliography are on page 677.

ROSEMARY FURMAN: FOLK HERO

Rosemary Furman, a former legal secretary, believes that you should be able to solve simple legal problems without hiring a lawyer. Hence she established the Northside Secretarial Service in Jacksonville, Florida. She compiled and sold packets of legal forms (for $50) on divorce, name changes, and adoptions. The price included her assistance and advice in filling out and filing the forms. The Florida Bar Association and the Florida courts moved against her with a vengeance for practicing law illegally. She was convicted and sentenced to 30 days in jail.

Widespread support for Ms. Furman developed. Her case soon became a cause célèbre for those seeking increased access to the legal system for the poor and the middle class.[2] Many were outraged at the legal profession and the judiciary for its treatment of Ms. Furman.

---

[2] Peoples & Wertz, *Update: Unauthorized Practice of Law,* 9 National Paralegal Reporter 1 (National Federation of Paralegal Associations, No. 4, Feb. 1985).

The CBS program, "60 Minutes," covered the case. Warner Brothers is considering a docudrama on the story. An editorial in the Gainesville Sun said, "Throw Rosemary Furman in Jail? Surely not after the woman forced the Florida Bar and the judiciary to confront its responsibility to the poor. Anything less than a 'thank you' note would indeed show genuine vindictiveness on the part of the legal profession" (Nov. 4, 1984). There were, however, other views. An editorial in USA Today said, "If she can give legal advice, so can charlatans, frauds, and rip-off artists" (Feb. 2, 1984).

The events in the Rosemary Furman story are as follows:

- 1978 & 1979: the Florida Bar Association takes Rosemary Furman to court, alleging that she is practicing law without a license.
- 1979: the Florida Supreme Court rules against her. She is enjoined from engaging in the unauthorized practice of law.
- 1982: the Florida Bar Association again brings a complaint against her business, alleging that she was continuing the unauthorized practice of law.
- 1983: Duval County Circuit Judge A.C. Soud, Jr. finds her in contempt of court for violating the 1979 order. The judge makes this decision in a nonjury hearing. She is then ordered to serve 30 days in jail.
- 1984: the United States Supreme Court refuses to hear the case. This had the effect of allowing the state jail sentence to stand. The Court was not persuaded by the argument that she should have been granted a jury trial of her peers rather than be judged solely by a legal profession (lawyers and judges) that was biased against her.
- Her attorneys ask the Florida Supreme Court to vacate the jail sentence if she agrees to close her business.
- The Florida Bar Association tells the Florida Supreme Court that the jail term was a fitting punishment and should be served.
- November 13, 1984: the Florida Supreme Court orders her to serve the jail sentence for practicing law without a license. (451 So.2d 808)
- November 27, 1984: Rosemary Furman is granted clemency from the 30 day jail term by Florida Governor Bob Graham and his Clemency Board. She does not have to go to jail.
- Furman and her attorneys announce that they will work on a constitutional amendment that will define the practice of law to make it easier for citizens to avoid a dependency on attorneys in civil cases. Says Ms. Furman, "I have only begun to fight."

NOTE ON "TREATIES" BETWEEN THE BAR AND COMPETITIVE GROUPS

There are a number of occupations that engage in activities that constitute or that border on the practice of law, e.g., the drafting of a sales contract by a real estate broker. Traditionally the legal profession has tried to place restrictions on such activities. Lawyers, however, have not been successful in prohibiting them altogether. Legislatures and the public would not stand for it. The delicate relationship between the legal profession and these occupations has been handled through negotiations where the participants attempt to identify the boundary lines of permitted conduct by these occupations.

YEGGE, R., MOORE, W., HOLME, H., NEW CAREERS IN LAW "Inter-Occupational Treaties" pp. 19, 20 (1969). In some areas, attorneys have attempted to reconcile their differences with ancillary occupations through negotiations. The American Bar Association has negotiated nine "statements of principles" with different groups. In general, each statement provides for a conference committee consisting of lawyers and members of the other group to meet to determine the areas in which attorneys and the other practitioners can cooperate, and to discuss problem areas. The conference committee may also issue additional statements clarifying the statement of principles or discussing certain practices.

Implied in ratification of a statement of principles is bar recognition of the legitimacy of the ancillary occupation and some of its law-related activities. The statements of principles thus recognize the complementarity of the occupations, which include claims adjusters (passed in 1939), banks with trust functions (passed in 1941), publishers (passed in 1941), realtors (passed in 1943), life insurance agents (passed in 1948), accountants (passed in 1951), collection agencies (passed in 1955), social workers (passed in 1965), and architects (passed in 1968). The American Bar Association also instituted a conference with casualty insurers in 1962, . . . Some state and local bar associations have also negotiated agreements with ancillary occupations.

[On the antitrust implications of such agreements or treaties, see p. 281.]

There is a reason to doubt the effectiveness of treaty negotiation:

> Most of the conferences meet at least once a year, but one or two are relatively inactive. In disposing of complaints, the conferences rely on persuasion rather than sanctions. Presumably the various associations of laymen that are parties to the agreements have the power to punish violators by expelling them from association membership, but seemingly there have been no such expulsions. Nor would this be much of a sanction, as association membership is rarely essential to engaging in a trade or profession. And this sanction leaves beyond control those who are not association members, a sizable group in most occupations.[3]

In addition to these negotiated "treaties," some states have enacted legislation that authorizes activities by certain occupations that would otherwise constitute the unauthorized practice of law. For example:

Ga. Code Ann. § 9-401 (Supp. 1970). §9-401 . . . . Provided that, a title insurance company may prepare such papers as it thinks proper, or necessary, in connection with a title which it proposes to insure, in order, in its opinion, for it to be willing to insure such title, where no charge is made by it for such papers.

Utah Code Ann. 1968, 61-2-20. §61-2-20. Rights and privileges of real estate salesmen—brokers.—It is expressly provided that a real estate salesman shall have the right to fill out and complete forms of legal documents necessary to any real estate transaction to which the said broker is a party as principal or agent, and

---

[3] Johnstone, Q., & Hopson, D., Lawyers and their Work: An Analysis of the Legal Profession in the United States and England, 185 (1967).

which forms have been approved by the commission and the attorney general of the state of Utah. Such forms shall include a closing real estate contract, a short-form lease, and a bill of sale of personal property.

Tenn. Code Ann. §62-1325 (1955). §62-1325. Licensed Real Estate Brokers may draw contracts to option, buy, sell, or lease real property.

(b) THE AUTHORIZED PRACTICE OF LAW

Examine the following phrase closely: unauthorized practice of law by nonlawyers. If there is such a thing as the *un*authorized practice of law, then, by implication, there must be an *authorized* practice of law. And indeed there is. The treaties and statutes discussed above are examples of this. Lawyers are not the only members of our society who are permitted to practice law. There are designated areas where nonlawyers are authorized to practice law. Occasionally there are attempts to call what they do something other than the practice of law, but as we will see, these attempts conflict with reality since the nonlawyers are doing what lawyers do within the sphere of the special authorization. All the special authorizations to be discussed below have been vigorously opposed by lawyers at one time or another on the ground that the authorizations conflict with the privileged domain of lawyers. Lawyers are not always this blunt in stating their opposition. Their objections are couched in terms of the "protection of the public," but in large measure, the opposition has its roots in territorial or turf protection. Lawyers are not above engaging in battles for economic self-preservation.

Several reasons account for the fact that lawyers have lost some of the arguments against permitting special authorization to nonlawyers to practice law. First, lawyers are sometimes distrusted. Second, lawyers have failed to meet a demonstrable need for legal services in particular categories of cases.

The public image of a lawyer is sometimes said to be that of a fighter, someone who will pursue an issue to the bitter end. While this trait may place the lawyer in a favorable light in the eyes of the client for whom s/he is doing battle, many feel that the aggressive inclination of the lawyer can be counterproductive. Administrative agencies, for example, are often suspicious of the involvement of lawyers. They are viewed as combatants who want to turn every agency decision into an adversarial proceeding. Courtroom gymnastics and "gimmicks" are often seen as the primary mode of operation of the lawyer. The lawyer is argumentative to a fault. This image of the lawyer as someone who complicates matters is best summed up by an old accountant's joke that taxation becomes more and more complex in direct proportion to attempts by lawyers to *simplify* the tax law. Whether or not this view of the lawyer is correct, it has accounted for some erosion of the legal profession's monopoly over the practice of law.

The unavailability of lawyers has also produced this result. A vast segment of our population has legal complaints that are never touched by lawyers. This, in part, is due to the fact that most of these complaints do not involve enough money to attract lawyers.

We now turn to a fuller exploration of these themes under the following headings:

(i) Court "representation" by nonlawyers.

(ii) Attempted restrictions on the activities of the "jailhouse lawyer" and the broader policy considerations raised by such restrictions.

(iii) Agency representation by nonlawyers.

(i) Court Representation

As we have seen, a paralegal, or anyone else, is usually allowed to represent himself/herself in court (p. 205). In very limited situations, paralegals are also authorized to appear in court on behalf of someone else. This occurs mainly in some Justice of the Peace and Magistrate Courts in a number of states where even the judges often do not have to be lawyers.

> **Idaho Code Ann. §3-104 (Sup. 1969).** . . . any person may appear and act in a magistrate's division of a district court as representative of any party to a proceeding therein so long as the claim does not total more than $300, and so long as . . . he shall do so without making a charge or collecting a fee therefor.

> **Mont. Rev. Code Ann. §93-2008 (1964).** If any person practices law in any court, except a justice's court or a police court without having a license as attorney and counselor, he is guilty of a contempt of court.

The Oregon Small Claims Court specify that there can be an agent representing a party, but does not specify that this agent must be an attorney:

> **Or. Rev. State. 55.020 (1965).** Actions in the small claims departments shall be deemed commenced by the plaintiff appearing in person or by agent. . . .

On Indian Reservations in the Midwest, there are Tribal Courts that have jurisdiction over certain civil and criminal actions where both parties are Indian. Nonlawyer Indian advocates represent the parties at these proceedings, and in some instances, non-Indian lawyers are specifically excluded.

Many Juvenile Courts in the country are very informal in their procedures. Nonlawyer probation officers, for example, often speak of behalf of or against the youngster involved in a juvenile delinquency petition. Their involvement frequently amounts to the assumption of an advocate's role before the judge. In a recent case involving the termination of parental rights in North Carolina, the United States Supreme Court noted the role of nonlawyers in termination hearings:

> In fact, . . . the North Carolina Departments of Social Services are themselves sometimes represented at termination hearings by social workers instead of by lawyers.

Lassiter v. Dept. of Social Services, 452 U.S. 18, 29, 101 S.Ct. 2153, 2161, 68 L.Ed.2d 640, 651 (1981). See also the footnote in Justice Douglas' opinion in the *Hackin* case on the extensive legal advocacy role of social workers (p. 225). Some criminal courts authorize diversion programs for certain types of defendants (p. 78). For example, an employment or drug rehabilitation program may be available in lieu of criminal prosecution. Nonlawyer representatives of these programs interview prospective candidates from among the accused and sometimes go before the judge to argue that the individual should be diverted into their program.

It is well known that lawyers waste a good deal of pre-trial time traveling to court and waiting around simply to give documents to the judge and to set dates for the various stages of pre-trial and trial proceedings. Another problem is that a lawyer may have to be in two different courtrooms at the same time on a particular day. For example, the time spent at an early morning hearing may be unexpectedly extended so that the lawyer cannot appear at a previously scheduled mid-morning proceeding in another courtroom on a different case. In such situations, wouldn't it be helpful if the lawyer's paralegal could "appear" in court for the limited purpose of delivering papers to the judge, asking for a new date, or presenting some other message? *In most states, such activity is strictly prohibited.*

On August 16, 1982, a Kentucky paralegal learned about this prohibition in a dramatic way. Her attorney was involved in a trial at the Jefferson Circuit Court. He asked the paralegal to go to another courtroom during "Motion Hour" where lawyers make motions or schedule future proceedings on a case. He told her to ask for a hearing date on another case that he had pending. She did so. When the case was called during "Motion Hour," she rose, identified herself as the lawyer's paralegal, and gave the message to the judge, asking for the hearing date. Opposing counsel was outraged. He verbally assaulted the paralegal in the courtroom and filed a motion to hold the paralegal and her lawyer in contempt of court for the unauthorized practice of law. When a hearing was later held on this motion, members of a local paralegal association packed the courtroom. Tensions were high. Eventually, when the contempt motion was denied, the audience broke out into loud applause. "Apparently the judge concluded that [the paralegal] had rendered no service involving legal knowledge or advice, but had merely transmitted to the court [the lawyer's] message regarding disposition of the motion, that is, she had been performing a function that was administrative, not legal, in nature." C. Winter, "No Contempt in Kentucky," 7 *National Paralegal Reporter* 8 (No 2, Winter, 1982).

About twenty years earlier, a celebrated Illinois case took a position similar to that of this Kentucky court. *It must be stressed, however, that this position remains a minority view within the courts of the country.* The Illinois case is People v. Alexander, 53 Ill. App. 2d 299, 202 N.E.2d 841 (1964). In this opinion, the defendant was an unlicensed law clerk who appeared before the court to state that his employing attorney could not be present in court at the moment because he was trying a case elsewhere. On behalf of his employer, the law clerk requested a continuance. The defendant's actions were challenged. It was argued that any appearance by a layperson before a court in which s/he gives information as to the availability of counsel or the status of litigation constitutes the unauthorized practice of law. The Illinois court took the unique position that this was not the practice of law. The reasoning of the court was as follows:

In the case of People ex rel. Illinois State Bar Ass'n v. People's Stock Yards State Bank, 344 Ill. 462, at page 476, 176 N.E. 901, at page 907, wherein a bank was prosecuted for the unauthorized practice of law, the following quotation is relied upon:

> *"According to the generally understood definition of the practice of law in this country, it embraces the preparation of pleadings, and other papers incident to actions and special proceedings, and the management of such actions and proceedings on behalf of clients before judges and courts * * *."*

Since this statement relates to the appearance and management of proceedings in court on behalf of a client, we do not believe it can be applied to a situation where a clerk hired by a law firm presents information to the court on behalf of his employer.

We agree with the trial judge that clerks should not be permitted to make motions or participate in other proceedings which can be considered as "managing" the litigation. However, if apprising the court of an employer's engagement or inability to be present constitutes the making of a motion, we must hold that clerks may make such motions for continuances without being guilty of the unauthorized practice of law. Certainly with the large volume of cases appearing on the trial calls these days, it is imperative that this practice be followed.

In Toth v. Samuel Phillipson & Co., 250 Ill. App. 247 (1928) the court said at page 250:

> *"It is well known in this country where numerous trial courts are sitting at the same time the exigencies of such a situation require that trial attorneys be represented by their clerical force to respond to some of the calls, and that the court acts upon their response the same as if the attorneys of record themselves appeared in person."*

After that opinion was handed down, the number of judges was substantially increased in the former Circuit and Superior Courts and the problem of answering court calls has at least doubled. We cannot add to the heavy burden of lawyers who in addition to responding to trial calls must answer pre-trial calls and motion calls—all held in the morning—by insisting that a lawyer must personally appear to present to a court a motion for a continuance on grounds of engagement or inability to appear because of illness or other unexpected circumstances. To reduce the backlog, trial lawyers should be kept busy actually trying lawsuits and not answering court calls. 202 N.E.2d at 843ff.

Again, it must be remembered that most states would *not* agree with Kentucky and Illinois. Most states would prohibit nonlawyers from doing what was authorized in these two states. Fortunately, however, there are at least a few additional states that have begun to move in the direction of the minority view.

The Allen County Bar Association of Indiana has taken the bold move of permitting paralegals to perform what hitherto had been considered lawyer functions in court. A paralegal, under rule 3 of the program (see text of rule below), is authorized:

- To "take" default judgments.
- To set pre-trial conferences, uncontested divorces, and all hearing dates.
- To file motions for dismissal.
- Etc.

The paralegal, however, still cannot communicate directly with judges in performing these tasks.

The vast majority of lawyers in the country would be amazed to learn what is going on in Allen County. Once the shock subsides, however, these lawyers will probably see the wisdom and common sense of what Allen County has done, and begin to think of ways to try it themselves.

The rules of the Allen County program are as follows:

PARALEGAL RULES OF PRACTICE

1. Generally, a legal assistant employee shall be limited to the performance of tasks which do not require the exercising of legal discretion or judgment that affects the legal right of any person.

2. All persons employed as legal assistants shall be registered [see form below] by their employer law firm with the Allen County Circuit and Superior Court Administrator and the Clerk of the Allen Superior and Circuit Courts. Said law firm shall, by affidavit, state that it shall be bound and liable for the actions of its legal assistant employee, and that any and all actions or statements made by such personnel shall be strictly and completely supervised by his employer member of the Bar. All documents the legal assistant presents or files must contain the attorney's signature, either as an attorney for the petitioning party, or a statement affixed indicating that the documents were prepared by said attorney. Each law firm shall certify in writing that the legal assistant employee is qualified in each field in which they will act with the Courts (probate, dissolution of marriage, collection, etc.). A copy of such statement and certification shall be given to such legal assistant and shall be carried by such person whenever activity with the Courts is pursued by such person. There shall be one legal assistant certified by each law office desiring same, but [an] alternate shall be allowed in case of illness, vacation or unavailability. However, in those instances where a single law firm has more than one full time legal assistant, each of whom operate in separate specialized areas, a certification can be had by more than one person, showing that such person's specialization on a full time basis is limited to one specific area. Otherwise, there should be a limit of one person certified as a legal assistant per law firm.

3. Such employee shall be limited to the following acts:
   (a) Such employee may take default judgments upon the filing of an affidavit in each case stating the amount of damages and that proper service was obtained sworn to by affidavit. Caveat: The legal assistant shall not make the affidavits. (Circuit Court will require attorneys to make Default Judgments.)

   (b) Such employee shall have authority to set Pre-Trial Conferences, Uncontested Divorces, and all other hearing dates.

   (c) Such employee shall have authority to obtain trust account deposits at the Allen County Clerk's Office but only in the name of his employer firm.

(d) Such employee shall have authority to file stipulations or motions for dismissal.

(e) Such an employee shall have the authority to do all filing of documents and papers with the Clerk of the Allen Superior Courts and Circuit Court where such documents and papers are not to be given to anyone authorized to affix a judge's signature or issue Court orders.

(f) Notwithstanding the limitations of subparagraph (e) above, such employee shall have the authority to obtain from the law clerk the signature stamp of the judge on non-discretionary standard orders and notices, such as notice of hearing, and orders to appear and to answer interrogatories on the filing of a Verified Motion for Proceedings Supplemental.
Note: Standard orders which depart from the usual format, restraining orders, suit and support orders, bench warrants, and body attachments must be secured by an attorney.

(g) Such employee is not to negotiate with opposing litigants within the Courthouse nor confer with a judge on legal matters. Matters requiring communications with a judge, require an attorney.

(h) Where circumstances permit, attorneys shall take precedence over such employees in dealings with courts and clerks.

STATEMENT OF CERTIFICATION

This is to certify that _____

is employed by the law firm of _____
_____. Said law firm binds itself and takes full responsibility and liability for the actions of its legal assistant employee above-named and that any and all actions or statements made by such personnel shall be strictly and completely supervised by a member of the Bar of the State of Indiana. This is to certify that the above-mentioned legal assistant is qualified to assist an attorney in the _____
area of law.

LAW FIRM OF: _____

BY: _____

STATE OF INDIANA, COUNTY OF ALLEN, SS:

Subscribed and sworn to before me, a Notary Public in and for said County and State, this _____ day _____, 19_____.

_____
Notary Public

Note again that the above program does not allow the paralegal to talk directly with a judge in performing the authorized tasks. ("Matters requiring communications with a judge, require an attorney.") Why such a restriction? Wouldn't it make sense to allow paralegal-judge communication on some procedural matters that are of a routine nature? No, would be the response of most bar associations.

Yes, however, is the refreshing response of several county bar associations in the state of Washington. In these counties, paralegals are allowed to "present" certain orders to judges. Hence the paralegal deals directly with the judge; there is no prohibition against communicating with the judge. The program works as follows:

WHAT THE PARALEGAL IS ALLOWED TO DO:

1. Present agreed and/or ex parte orders (i.e., involving one party only) to Superior Court Judges and to Commissioners based solely on the documents presented and the records in the file.
2. Check out court files from the Clerk of the Court.
3. Use the county law library.

QUALIFICATIONS OF PARALEGAL:

1. The paralegal must be duly registered by the county bar association according to the criteria listed below.
2. The paralegal must be sponsored by a county attorney who is the supervisor of the paralegal. The attorney cannot sponsor more than one paralegal.
3. The paralegal must be currently employed six months or longer by a county law firm, or by a city, county, or state administrative agency or corporation under the direct supervision of an attorney.
4. Seventy-five percent of the paralegal's work time must be devoted to legal assistant (non-clerical) work, consisting of the performance of tasks under the direct supervision of a lawyer, which tasks shall not include the giving of legal advice, the quoting of legal fees, or the appearance in court in contested matters.
5. The paralegal must have obtained (a) a degree or certificate of completion from a legal assistant program of at least two years' duration, or (b) a substantially equivalent college education and/or work experience in the legal field that is deemed adequate by the Legal Assistant Committee of the county bar association.

Among the bar associations participating in this registration program are the Tacoma-Pierce County Bar Association and the Seattle-King County Bar Association. It is anticipated that other counties will adopt a similar program in the state. In Tacoma-Pierce County, the sponsoring attorney must file the following affidavit:

AFFIDAVIT OF SUPERVISING ATTORNEY

STATE OF WASHINGTON   )
　　　　　　　　　　　　　) ss.
County of Pierce　　　　)

_____hereby certifies as follows:

(1)   I am an active member of the Washington State Bar Association. I am with a Pierce County law firm, or a city, county or state administrative agency or corporation.

(2)   I am presently engaged in the active practice of law with

_____

(Name of Firm or Organization)
with office at this address:

_____
_____
_____

(3)   I agree to act as the responsible attorney for

_____

as a legal assistant and will furnish such information and reports regarding his or her practice as a legal assistant as may be prescribed by the Board of Trustees of the Tacoma-Pierce County Bar Association.

(4)   The applicant, if approved, shall be the only legal assistant for whom I am the supervising attorney.

(5)   My legal assistant is trained by experience and/or special education to carry on investigative and information gathering matters, use independent judgment and deal with clients in a professional and ethical manner under my supervision and control and to whom the legal assistant is responsible at all times. I will faithfully supervise and direct his/her work and will be responsible for his/her professional conduct.

(6)   I agree to see that the applicant surrenders his/her registration card upon change of employment of if he/she for any other reason no longer qualifies for registration.

_____

SUBSCRIBED AND SWORN to before me this _____ day of
_____, 19___.

_____
NOTARY PUBLIC in and for the State of Washington, residing at

(ii) The Jailhouse Lawyer

A jailhouse lawyer is a nonlawyer who helps fellow prisoners with their legal problems. Some prisons attempted to prevent the jailhouse lawyer from providing this legal assistance even though no meaningful alternatives for such assistance were provided by the prisons. This prohibition, however, was struck down by the United States Supreme Court in *Johnson v. Avery* in 1969. The basis of the opinion was that without the jailhouse lawyer, prisoners may not have access to the courts. The concurring opinion of Justice Douglas has become one of the most widely quoted and influential statements in the field of paralegalism.

Johnson v. Avery
Supreme Court of the United States, 1969.
393 U.S. 483, 89 S.Ct. 747, 21 L.Ed.2d 718

. . .

Mr. Justice DOUGLAS, concurring.

While I join the opinion of the Court [in striking down the prohibition on the activities of jailhouse lawyers] I add a few words in emphasis of the important thesis of the case.

The increasing complexities of our governmental apparatus at both the local and the federal levels have made it difficult for a person to process a claim or even to make a complaint. Social security is a virtual maze; the hierarchy that governs urban housing is often so intricate that it takes an expert to know what agency has jurisdiction over a particular complaint; the office to call or official to see for noise abatement, for a broken sewer line, or a fallen tree is a mystery to many in our metropolitan areas.

A person who has a claim assertable in faraway Washington, D.C., is even more helpless, as evidenced by the increasing tendency of constituents to rely on their congressional delegation to identify, press, and process their claims.

We think of claims as grist for the mill of the lawyers. But it is becoming abundantly clear that more and more of the effort in ferreting out the basis of claims and the agencies responsible for them and in preparing the almost endless paperwork for their prosecution is work for laymen. There are not enough lawyers to manage or supervise all of these affairs; and much of the basic work done requires no special legal talent. *Yet there is a closed-shop philosophy in the legal profession that cuts down drastically active roles for laymen. That traditional, closed-shop attitude is utterly out of place in the modern world where claims pile high and much of the work of tracing and pursuing them requires the patience and wisdom of a layman rather than the legal skills of a member of the bar.* [Emphasis added.]

> "If poverty lawyers are overwhelmed, some of the work can be delegated to sub-professionals. New York law permits senior law students to practice law under certain supervised conditions. Approval must first be granted by the appellate division. A rung or two lower on the legal profession's ladder are laymen legal technicians, comparable to nurses and lab assistants in the medical profession. Large law firms employ them, and there seems to be no reason why they cannot be used in legal services programs to relieve attorneys for more professional tasks." Samore, Legal Services for the Poor, 32 Albany L.Rev. 509, 515-516 (1968).

The plight of a man in prison may in these respects be even more acute than the plight of a person on the outside. He may need collateral proceedings to test the legality of his detention or relief against management of the parole system or against defective detainers lodged against him which create burdens in the nature of his incarcerated status. He may have grievances of a civil nature against those outside the prison. His imprisonment may give his wife grounds for divorce and be a factor in determining the custody of his children; and he may have pressing social security, workmen's compensation, or veterans' claims.

While the demand for legal counsel in prison is heavy, the supply is light. For private matters of a civil nature, legal counsel for the indigent in prison is almost nonexistent. Even for criminal proceedings, it is sparse. While a few States have post-conviction statutes providing such counsel, most States do not. Some states like California do appoint counsel to represent the indigent prisoner in his collateral hearings, once he succeeds in making out a prima facie case. But as a result, counsel is not on hand for preparation of the papers or for the initial decision that the prisoner's claim has substance.

NOTES

1. The *Johnson* opinion stressed that the prison provided *no* alternative to the jailhouse lawyer. If alternatives had been available, the inmate would not be allowed to practice law. In Williams v. U.S. Dept of Justice, 433 F.2d 958 (5th Cir. 1970), the court held that the presence of law students in the prison could be an alternative, but only if it is demonstrated that the students are meeting the need for inmate legal services. If the inmates had to wait a considerable period of time, for example, before they could be interviewed by the law students, then no alternative existed and the jailhouse lawyer could not be prevented from helping other inmates.
2. In Gilmore v. Lynch, 319 F.Supp. 105 (N.D.Cal.1970), affirmed by the United States Supreme Court in Younger v. Gilmore, 404 U.S. 15 (1971), the court held that California either had to satisfy the legal needs of its prisoners or expand the prison law library to include more comprehensive law books. See also *Bounds v. Smith*, p. 223.
3. How far can the rationale of *Johnson* be extended? Suppose for example, it is demonstrated that many claimants before state administrative agencies are not receiving legal services because attorneys cannot be afforded. Would the *Johnson* opinion permit paralegal representation before such agencies even if the latter prohibited it? What is the difference between an inmate's right to have access to the courts and *anyone's* right to complain to an agency? How do you think Justice Douglas would handle the case if it came before him?

Statsky, W. and Lang, P., The Legal Paraprofessional as Advocate and Assistant: Roles, Training Concepts and Materials, pp. 49-50 (1971): "Although the *Johnson* case is admittedly narrow in scope, it does nevertheless, give aid and comfort to the view that whenever lawyers are unavailable for whatever reason, society will sanction alternative systems for the delivery of legal services. The paramount consideration will not be ethics nor the exclusivity of the right to practice law, but rather it will be the facilitation of access routes to the grievance machinery set up for the resolution of claims. If lawyers are not available to assist the citizenry with these claims, then the question arises as to whether skilled nonlawyers represent a viable alternative. The inevitability of this question becomes clear when we listen to the statistics on the demand for the services of a lawyer. Estimates have been made to the effect that if every lawyer devoted full time to the legal needs of the poor, there would still be significant shortage of lawyers for the poor. If the legal needs of the middle class are added, the legal service manpower shortage becomes overwhelming."

See also, Statsky, W., Inmate Involvement in Prison Legal Services: Roles and Training Options for the Inmate as Paralegal (American Bar Association, Commission on Correctional Facilities and Services, Resource Center on Correctional Law and Legal Services, 1974).

Two other important Supreme Court cases have expanded the role of nonlawyer representation within prisons:

Procunier v. Martinez
Supreme Court of the United States, 1974.
416 U.S. 396, 94 S.Ct. 1800, 1814, 40 L.Ed.2d 244.

. . .

The District Court also enjoined continued enforcement of Administrative Rule MV-IV-02, which provides in pertinent part:

"Investigators for an attorney-of-record will be confined to not more than two. Such investigators must be licensed by the State or must be members of the State Bar. Designation must be made in writing by the Attorney."

By restricting access to prisoners to members of the bar and licensed private investigators, this regulation imposed an absolute ban on the use by attorneys of law students and legal paraprofessionals to interview inmate clients. In fact attorneys could not even delegate to such persons the task of obtaining prisoners' signatures on legal documents. The District Court reasoned that this rule constituted an unjustifiable restriction on the right of access to the courts. We agree.

The constitutional guarantee of due process of law has as a corollary the requirement that prisoners be afforded access to the courts in order to challenge unlawful convictions and to seek redress for violations of their constitutional rights. This means that inmates must have a reasonable opportunity to seek and receive the assistance of attorneys. Regulations and practices that unjustifiably obstruct the availability of professional representation or other aspects of the right of access to the courts are invalid. Ex parte Hull, 312 U.S. 546, 61 S.Ct. 640, 85 L.Ed. 1034 (1941).

The District Court found that the rule restricting attorney-client interviews to members of the bar and licensed private investigators inhibited adequate professional representation of indigent inmates. The remoteness of many California penal institutions makes a personal visit to an inmate client a time-consuming undertaking. The court reasoned that the ban against the use of law students or other paraprofessionals for attorney-client interviews would deter some lawyers from representing prisoners who could not afford to pay for their traveling time or that of licensed private investigators. And those lawyers who agreed to do so would waste time that might be employed more efficaciously in working on the inmates' legal problems. Allowing law students and paraprofessionals to interview inmates might well reduce the cost of legal representation for prisoners. The District Court therefore concluded that the regulation imposed a substantial burden on the right of access to the courts.

Bounds v. Smith
430 U.S. 817, 97 S.Ct. 1491, 52 L.Ed.2d (1977).

[In this opinion the Supreme Court is again concerned with the need of prisoners to have access to the courts and the use of nonlawyers in helping to provide that assistance. The Court held that prisons must assist inmates in the preparation and filing of meaningful legal papers by providing the inmates with adequate law libraries or adequate assistance from persons trained in the law. The Court rejected the claim that nonlawyer inmates were ill-equipped to use the "tools of the trade of the legal profession." In the Court's experience, nonlawyer petitioners are capable of using law books to file cases raising claims that are "serious and legitimate" whether or not such petitioners win the cases. In outlining the options available to a prison, the Court specifically referred to paralegals:]

It should be noted that while adequate law libraries are one constitutionally acceptable method to assure meaningful access to the courts, our decision here, . . . , does not foreclose alternative means to achieve that goal. Nearly half the States and the District of Columbia provide some degree of professional or quasi-professional legal assistance to prisoners . . . . Such programs take many imaginative forms and may have a number of advantages over libraries alone. Among the alternatives are the training of inmates as para-legal assistants to work under lawyers' supervision, the use of paraprofessionals and law students, either as volunteers or in formal clinical programs, the organization of volunteer attorneys through bar associations or other groups, the hiring of lawyers on a part-time consultant basis, and the use of full-time staff attorneys, working either in new prison legal assistance organizations or as part of public defender or legal services offices.

Finally, the right of an inmate to assist a fellow inmate in legal matters does *not* extend to representing the inmate in court. Guajardo v. Luna, 432 F.2d 1324 (5th Cir. 1970.) Nor can a nonlawyer represent an inmate in court even if this nonlawyer is not an inmate him/herself. This latter point was decided by the United States Supreme Court in Hackin v. Arizona, 389 U.S. 143 (1967). Justice Douglas vigorously dissented from the majority opinion in *Hackin.* He made the following telling observations, id. at 144ff:

Rights protected by the First Amendment include advocacy and petition for redress of grievances and the Fourteenth Amendment ensures equal justice for the poor in both criminal and civil actions. But to millions of Americans who are indigent and ignorant—and often members of minority groups—these rights are meaningless. They are helpless to assert their rights under the law without assistance. They suffer discrimination in housing and employment, are victimized by shady consumer sales practices, evicted from their homes at the whim of the landlord, denied welfare payments, and endure domestic strife without hope of the legal remedies of divorce, maintenance, or child custody decrees.

If true equal protection of the laws is to be realized an indigent must be able to obtain assistance when he suffers a denial of his rights. Today, this goal is only a goal. Outside the area of criminal proceedings covered by our decisions in Gideon v. Wainwright, 372 U.S. 335, and Douglas v. California, 372 U.S. 353, counsel is seldom available to the indigent. As this Court has recognized, there is a dearth of lawyers who are willing, voluntarily, to take on unprofitable and unpopular causes.

Some States, aware of the acute shortage of lawyers to help the indigent, have utilized the abilities of qualified law students to advise indigents and even to represent them in court in limited circumstances. But where this practice is not sanctioned by law, the student advocate for the poor may be subjected to criminal penalty under broadly drafted statutes prohibiting unauthorized practice of law.

There is emerging, particularly in the ghetto areas of our cities, a type of organization styled to bring a new brand of legal assistance to the indigent. These groups, funded in part by the federal Office of Economic Opportunity, characteristically establish neighborhood offices where the poor can come for assistance. They attempt to dispense services on a comprehensive integrated scale, using lawyers, social workers, members of health professions, and other nonlawyer aides. These new and flexible approaches to giving legal aid to the poor recognize that the problems of indigents—although of the type for which an attorney has traditionally been consulted—are too immense to be solved solely by members of the bar. The supply of lawyer manpower is not nearly large enough.* But the necessary involvement of lay persons in these programs threatens their success.

The so-called "legal" problem of the poor is often an unidentified strand in a complex of social, economic, psychological and psychiatric problems. Identification of the "legal" problem at times is for the expert. But even a "lay" person can often perform that function and mark the path that leads to the school board, the school principal, the welfare agency, the Veterans Administration, the police review board, or the urban renewal agency.‡ If he neither solicits nor obtains a fee for his services, why should he not be free to act? Full-fledged representation in a battle before a court or agency requires professional skills that laymen lack; and therefore the client suffers, perhaps grievously, if he is not represented by a

---

* See Cahn & Cahn, What Price Justice: The Civilian Perspective Revisited, 41 Notre Dame Law 927 (1966). "Finally, with respect to manpower, we have created an artificial shortage by refusing to learn from the medical and other professions and to develop technicians, nonprofessionals and lawyer-aides—manpower roles to carry out such functions as: "informal advocate, technical, counsellor, sympathetic listener, investigator, researcher, form writer, etc." (P. 934.) "[T]he possibility of advancing the cause of justice through increasing lay involvement in fact finding, adjudication and arbitration, should not be sacrificed a priori out of fear of abuse." (P. 951).

‡ See Frankel, Experiments in Serving the Indigent, in National Conference on Law and Poverty Proceedings 69, 75–76 (1965): "[W]e lawyers must certainly confront constructively the idea that what we have traditionally regarded as legal business cannot permanently be so regarded. The needs of the poor for services in matters that are somehow legal appear pretty clearly to be enormous. Among those needs are many kinds of matters that are narrow, that are specialized, and can be routinized. Matters related to housing, to workmen's compensation, to consumer problems are a few that one could name. . . . [W]e should attempt to create a class of legal technicians who can handle, under lawyers' supervision, some of the problems that have thus far seemed to us to be exclusively the province of the lawyer. I think we have an important creative function to perform in trying to mark out these areas where lawyers are not really needed."

See Paulsen, The Law Schools and the War on Poverty, in National Conference on Law and Poverty Proceedings 77, 81 (1965): "Services to the poor will undoubtedly call for advocacy and advice by lay persons as well as lawyers. A lawyer's time is costly. Not every problem thrown up by legal arrangements requires the skill and costly time of a law-trained person. We can, perhaps, expect the creation of advice centers operated by laymen not unlike Britain's Citizen's Advice Bureaus."

lawyer. But in the intermediate zone where the local pastor, the social worker, or best friend** commonly operates, is there not room for accommodation? Dean Charles E. Ares recently said:

> ". . . [T]he *structure* of the legal profession is middle class in its assumptions. We assume that the lawyer can sit quietly in his office awaiting the knock on the door by a client who has discovered that he has a legal problem and has found the way to the lawyer's office. . . . This assumption is not valid for the great mass of people who live in poverty in the United States. . . . The ways in which this structure can be changed open exciting and interesting prospects." Poverty, Civil Liberties, and Civil Rights: A Symposium, 41 N.Y.U.L.Rev. 328, 346 (1966).

Moreover, what the poor need, as much as our corporate grants, is protection before they get into trouble and confront a crisis. This means "political leadership" for the "minority poor." Id., at 351. Lawyers will play a role in that movement; but so will laymen. The line that marks the area into which the layman may not step except at his peril is not clear.

Legal representation connotes a magic it often does not possess—as for example, the commitment procedure in Texas, where, by one report, 66 seconds are given to a case, the lawyer usually not even knowing his client and earning a nice fee for passive participation. Weihofen, Mental Health Services for the Poor, 54 Calif.L.Rev. 920, 938-939 (1966). If justice is the goal, why need a layman be barred here?

Broadly phrased unauthorized-practice-of-law statutes such as that at issue here could make criminal many of the activities regularly done by social workers who assist the poor in obtaining welfare and attempt to help them solve domestic problems.‡‡ Such statutes would also tend to deter programs in which experienced welfare recipients represent other, less articulate, recipients before local welfare departments.

As this Court's decisions indicate, state provisions regulating the legal profession will not be permitted to act as obstacles to the rights of persons to petition the courts and other legal agencies for redress. . . . Certainly the States have a strong interest in preventing legally untrained shysters who pose as attorneys from milking the public for pecuniary gain. But it is arguable whether this policy should support a prohibition against charitable efforts of nonlawyers to help the poor. It may well be that until the goal of free *legal* assistance to the indigent in all areas of the law is achieved, the poor are not harmed by well-meaning, charitable assistance of laymen. On the contrary, for the majority of indigents, who are not so fortunate to be served by neighborhood legal offices, lay assistance may be the only hope for achieving equal justice at this time.

** In habeaus corpus proceedings, "the practice of a next friend applying for a writ is ancient and fully accepted." United States v. Houston, 273 F. 915, 916 (C.A.2d Cir.).

‡‡ "Social workers in public assistance may already be *required* to practice law as substantially as if they were in a courtroom. In making an initial determination of an applicant's eligibility, the public assistance worker must complete the applicant's financial statement. 'Every question, or nearly every question, on the financial statement, is a legal question. When the social worker advises, or even discusses the questions or answers, he may very likely be giving legal advice.' The private social worker who advises an applicant that he should apply, how to apply, what to answer and how to appeal if the application is rejected is also giving 'legal' advice. When he argues with the public worker on behalf of the applicant, he is giving representation. When and if he goes to a hearing on behalf of the applicant, he is surely engaging in advocacy." [Sparer, Thorkelson & Weiss, "The Lay Advocate," 43 U. of Detroit L.J. 493, 499–500 (1966) Ed.]

(iii) Agency Representation

A considerable number of administrative agencies will permit a paralegal or other nonlawyer to represent clients at the agency. These individuals are usually called agents, practitioners, or representatives. They engage in informal advocacy for their clients at the agency, or formal advocacy including full control of the case in an adversarial administrative hearing. The major issues are often economic, statistical, or scientific, but legal issues are also involved. It is clear that in conducting an agency hearing, the nonlawyer can be practicing law in a manner that is remarkably similar to a lawyer's representation of a client in court.

For federal agencies, Congress has passed a statute, the Administrative Procedure Act, that gives each federal agency the power to decide for itself whether only lawyers can represent clients before it:

> **Administrative Procedure Act 5 U.S.C.A. § 555 (1967).** (b) A person compelled to appear in person before an agency is entitled to be accompanied, represented, and advised by counsel or, if permitted by the agency, by other qualified representative. . . .

See the chart on p. 865 on paralegal representation in federal agencies.

When an agency decides to use this power to permit nonlawyer representation, it can simply allow anyone to act as the agent or representative of another before the agency, or it can establish elaborate qualifications or standards of admission to practice before it. If the agency takes the latter course, its qualification or standards could include a specialized test to demonstrate competency in the subject matter regulated by the agency, minimum educational or experience requirements, registration or enrollment on the agency's approved roster of representatives, and an agreement to abide by designated ethical rules of practice—a violation of which could result in suspension and "disbarment."

The United States Patent Office has established criteria for individuals to practice (as "registered agents") before this agency in drafting and filing applications for patents, searching legal opinions on patentability, etc.[4] In 1982, there were approximately 12,000 registered agents who had met this criteria at the agency. Of this number, about 1,900 (or 15.8%) were nonlawyers. At the Interstate Commerce Commission, close to 10,000 nonlawyer "practitioners" have been authorized to represent clients at ICC proceedings that often involve issues such as rate increases and service extensions for railroads and other transportation carriers.[5] Perhaps the largest use of nonlawyers in federal agencies is at the Internal Revenue Service within the Treasury Department.[6] Any certified public accountant is authorized to practice before the IRS. There are over 190,000 members of the American Institute of Certified Pub-

---

[4] 37 C.F.R. 1.341–1.348 (1983).

[5] 49 C.F.R. 1103.1–1103.5 (1983).

[6] 31 C.F.R. 10.3–10.75 (1983); 20 U.S.C. 1242 (1975).

lic Accountants, most of whom are not lawyers. In addition, thousands of other nonlawyers (called "enrolled agents" or "enrolled actuaries") have acquired the authority to practice.[7]

While these numbers are impressive, it is not true that extensive numbers of nonlawyers actually use the authority that they have. A recent study by the American Bar Association of thirty-three federal administrative agencies reached the following conclusion: "We found that the overwhelming majority of agencies studied permit nonlawyer representation in both adversarial and nonadversarial proceedings. However, most of them seem to encounter lay practice very infrequently (in less than 5% of adjudications), while only a few encounter lay practice as often as lawyer practice. Thus, although universally permitted, lay practice before federal agencies rarely occurs."[8]

One agency where nonlawyer representation is fairly high (about 15%) is the Social Security Administration. Paralegals are frequently appointed by clients (see form on p. 228) to represent them before the agency. In 1983 a study was conducted that compared the success of clients at hearings based upon the kind of representation they received. The results were as follows:

- 59% of clients were successful when they were represented by lawyers.
- 54.5% of clients were successful when they were represented by nonlawyers.
- 43.7% of clients were successful when they were represented by themselves.[9]

Fees can be charged by lawyers or paralegals for these services, but the fee must be specifically approved (see form on p. 229) by the agency. This is not to say, however, that lawyers and paralegals are treated alike. If a lawyer successfully represents a claimant, the agency will deduct up to 25% of the claimant's award, which will be paid directly to the attorney to cover fees. On the other hand, if a paralegal successfully represents a claimant, the paralegal must collect the fee directly from the client since the agency will not deduct anything from the award.[10]

---

[7] Rose, J., *Representation by Non-Lawyers in Federal Administrative Agency Proceedings: An Expanded Role* (Administrative Conference of the United States, 1984); Vom Baur, "The Practice of Non-Lawyers before Administrative Agencies," 15 *Fed. Bar Journal* 99 (1955).

[8] *Report of 1984 Survey of Nonlawyer Practice Before Federal Administrative Agencies* (ABA Standing Committee on Lawyers' Responsibility for Client Protection, Oct. 19, 1984).

[9] *Participant Involvement in Request for Hearing Cases for Fiscal 1983,* Table 6, DSS/OHA (May, 1984).

[10] 42 U.S.C. 406 (1975).

DEPARTMENT OF
HEALTH AND HUMAN SERVICES
SOCIAL SECURITY ADMINISTRATION

APPOINTMENT OF REPRESENTATIVE

I appoint _____

(Print or Type Name and Address of Representative)

to act as my representative in connection with my claim under Titles II, XVI or XVIII of the Social Security Act and/or Title IV of the Federal Coal Mine Health and Safety Act based on the social security record of

NAME	SOCIAL SECURITY NUMBER

I authorize my representative to make or give any request or notice; present or elicit evidence; obtain information; and receive any notice in connection with my claim wholly in my stead.

Date _____ Signature _____

(Claimant)

Address _____

ACCEPTANCE OF APPOINTMENT

I, _____, hereby accept the above appointment. I certify that I have not been suspended or prohibited from practice before the Social Security Administration; that I am not, as an officer or employee of the United States, disqualified from acting as the claimant's representative; and that I will not charge or receive a fee for the representation unless it has been authorized in accordance with the laws and regulations referred to on the reverse side hereof. In the event that I decide not to charge or collect a fee for the representation I will notify the Social Security Administration.

I am _____

(Attorney, union representative, relative, law student, etc.)

Date _____ Signature _____

(Representative)

Address _____

Form SSA-1696-U3 (8-77) (Formerly SSA-1696)

At the *state* level, most states have established a similar system for authorizing nonlawyers to provide representation at many, but by no means all, state agencies. For example:

Cal. Unemployment Insurance Code § 1957 (1956). Any individual claiming benefits in any proceedings before the Appeals Board or its authorized representative may be represented by counsel or agent but no such counsel or agent shall charge or receive for such services more than an amount approved by the Appeals Board. Any person who violates any provision of this section shall for such violation be fined not less than fifty dollars ($50) nor more than five hundred dollars ($500) or be imprisoned not more than six months or both.

DEPARTMENT OF HEALTH, EDUCATION, AND WELFARE
SOCIAL SECURITY ADMINISTRATION

Form Approved
OMB No. 72-R0832

PETITION TO OBTAIN APPROVAL OF A FEE FOR REPRESENTING A CLAIMANT BEFORE THE SOCIAL SECURITY ADMINISTRATION.

No fee may be approved unless the information requested by this form has been received. (20 CFR 404.975 and 976)

I request approval to charge a fee of $ _____ for services

performed as a representative of _____

in a claim before the Social Security Administration.

DO NOT WRITE IN
THIS SPACE

TYPE OF CLAIM

1. Circle claim involved
   (DIB; RIB; B/L; SSI.)

2. Hearings Case:

   Yes _____ No _____

ENTER THE NAME AND ADDRESS OF THE PERSON ON WHOSE SOCIAL SECURITY RECORD CLAIM IS BASED

ENTER THE SOCIAL SECURITY NUMBER OF PERSON ON WHOSE RECORD CLAIM IS BASED

THE INFORMATION BELOW IS FURNISHED IN SUPPORT OF THIS PETITION

1. My services as a representative began *(mo., day, yr.)* _____ and ended *(mo., day, yr.)* _____

2. Itemization of Services Rendered *(Do not include services in connection with court proceedings)*

DATE (Mo., Day Yr.)	*(Itemize each meeting, conference, item of correspondence, telephone call, and each activity engaged in, such as research, preparation of a brief, attendance at a hearing, travel, etc., related to your services as representative in this case.)*	TIME SPENT (To nearest quarter hour)
If more space is needed, attach separate sheet.	TOTAL HOURS	

3. Did you render any services relating to this matter before any State or Federal court? ☐ Yes ☐ No
   If "Yes," what fee did you or will you charge for services in connection with the court proceedings? $

4. Have you and your client tentatively agreend upon a fee for your services? ☐ Yes ☐ No
   If "Yes," please specify the amount (or the agreed-upon formula). $

5. Have you received, or do you expect to receive, any payment for your representa- ☐ Yes ☐ No
   tion other than the fee indicated above, such as reimbursement for expenses you incurred?
   If "Yes," itemize below. (Where funds have been received and held in escrow, e.g., as a retainer, indicate the amount followed by the word "escrow.") $

   $

   $

   TOTAL $

I certify that the above information is true and correct to the best of my knowledge and belief. I further certify that I have furnished a copy of this petition and any attachments to the person(s) for whom the above services were performed.

SIGNATURE OF PETITIONER	DATE	ADDRESS

FIRM WITH WHICH ASSOCIATED, IF ANY   TELEPHONE NO. AND AREA CODE

FORM **SSA-1560-U4** (10-78)

Minn.Stat.Ann. § 290.52 (1962) [State Income Tax Dept. Ed.]. § 290.52 . . . The commissioner may prescribe rules and regulations governing the recognition of agents, attorneys, or other persons representing claimants before the commissioner, and may require of such persons, agents, and attorneys, before being recognized as representatives of claimants, that they shall show that they are of good character and in good repute, possessed of the necessary qualifications to enable them to render such claimants valuable services, and otherwise competent to advise and assist such claimants in the presentation of their case. Such commissioner may, after due notice and opportunity for hearing, suspend and disbar from further practice before him, any such person, agent, or attorney, shown to be incompetent, disreputable, or who refuses to comply with the said rules and regulations, . . .

ASSIGNMENT 13

Make a list of every state and local administrative agency in your state. Have a class discussion in which students identify as many state and local agencies as they can. The total number of agencies will then be divided by the number of students in the class so that each student will be assigned the same number of agencies. For your agencies, find out whether nonlawyers can represent citizens before those agencies. What are the requirements, if any, to provide this representation informally (e.g., calling or writing the agency on behalf of someone else) or formally (e.g., representing someone else at an agency hearing). Check your state statutes (p. 654). Check the regulations (p. 672) of the agency. If possible, call the agency to ask what their policy is and whether they can refer you to any statutes or regulations on the policy.

As indicated earlier, many lawyers have not been happy with the authorization given nonlawyers to practice law such as within administrative agencies. Bitter campaigns have been launched against it by the bar association.

If the agency permitting nonlawyer representation is a *federal* agency, its authorization takes precedence over any *state* laws that would prohibit it. This principle was established by *Sperry v. State of Florida ex rel the Florida Bar,* 373 U.S. 379, 83 S.Ct. 1322, 10 L.Ed.2d 428 (1963). The case involved a nonlawyer who was authorized to represent clients before the United States Patent Office. The Florida Bar claimed that the nonlawyer was violating the state practice-of-law statutes. The United States Supreme Court ruled that the Supremacy Clause of the U.S. Constitution gave federal laws supremacy over conflicting state laws. The Court also said:

> Examination of the development of practice before the Patent Office and its governmental regulation reveals that: (1) nonlawyers have practiced before the Office from its inception, with the express approval of the Patent Office and to the knowledge of Congress; (2) during prolonged congressional study of unethical practices before the Patent Office, the right of nonlawyer agents to practice before the Office went unquestioned, and there was no suggestion that abuses might be curbed by state regulation; (3) despite protests of the bar, Congress in enacting the Administrative Procedure Act refused to limit the right to practice before the administrative agencies to lawyers; and (4) the Patent Office has defended the value of nonlawyer practitioners while taking steps to protect the interests which a State has in prohibiting unauthorized practice of law. We find implicit in this history congressional (and administrative) recognition that registration in the Patent Office confers a right to practice before the Office without regard to whether the State within which the practice is conducted would otherwise prohibit such conduct.

Moreover, the extent to which specialized lay practitioners should be allowed to practice before some 40-odd federal administrative agencies, including the Patent Office, received continuing attention both in and out of Congress during the period prior to 1952. The Attorney General's Committee on Administrative Procedure which, in 1941, studied the need for procedural reform in the administrative agencies, reported that "[e]specially among lawyers' organizations there has been manifest a sentiment in recent years that only members of the bar should be admitted to practice before administrative agencies. The Committee doubts that a sweeping interdiction of nonlawyer practitioners would be wise . . . . "

Suppose, however, that a *state* agency permits nonlawyer representation. Can this be challenged by the bar? The issue may depend on who has the *power* to regulate the practice of law in a particular state. If the state legislature has this power, then the agency authorization of nonlawyer representation is valid since the agency is under the jurisdiction and control of the legislature. So long as the nonlawyer representation is based on a statute of the legislature, it is valid. If, however, the state judiciary has the power to control the practice of law in a state, then the courts may be able to invalidate any nonlawyer representation that is authorized by the agency.

Even though it may be quite legal for a paralegal to represent citizens before administrative agencies, there is a need to distinguish between paralegals who provide this representation on their own, and paralegals who do it within the employ of lawyers. There should be *no* distinction. Some lawyers, however, feel that law firms should not allow their paralegals to engage in any agency representation even if the agency authorizes it. Contrast the following two views within the report of the Pennsylvania Professional Guidance Committee and the Unauthorized Practice of Law Committee on paralegal use:

Majority View

Paralegals may represent claimants not only before federal agencies, but also before state agencies whose federal funding source requires these agencies to meet federal statutory requirements as a condition of federal aid. In AFDC (42 U.S.C. 601 *et. seq.*), Medicaid (42 U.S.C. 1396a *et. seq.*), WIN (42 U.S.C. 602 and 639), Food Stamp (7 U.S.C. 2011 *et. seq.*) and Unemployment Compensation (42 U.S.C. 402) programs, federal law provides that if state programs fail to comply with federal requirements, federal assistance to the state shall be terminated. States that deny paralegals access to due process hearings before such agencies when their presence is requested by claimants, and allowed by federal statute run the risk of forfeiting federal benefits . . . .

[I]f lawyers are prohibited from employing paralegals to represent claimants at administrative hearings, the lawyer in most cases, would find this type of representation economically unfeasible. While an attorney may wish to provide the public with this type of representation, because most claims involve small amounts of money or are concerned with non-monetary benefits, he may find this type of service to represent a loss in income. If the lawyer employs, trains and supervises paralegals who may provide such representation, the public will be assured of competent representation at a price it can afford and which is feasible from the lawyer's perspective. The public, therefore, would be provided with quality representation under the supervision of a lawyer, and would be discouraged from approaching unsupervised, unaffiliated laymen. The result is the provision of more services, more economically, to those persons seeking assistance at administrative agency hearings.

If paralegals are well trained and well supervised, the public should be protected because attorneys have a real stake in ensuring that paralegals provide the best possible representation.

Minority View

By permitting paralegals to appear before administrative agencies of record, [the] principles of control by the attorney [and the restrictions against paralegals holding themselves out to the public] as experts in legal matters, etc., are abandoned. In an administrative hearing of record, the attorney does not have the opportunity to review and correct the error of the non-lawyer. The client can suffer permanent damage to his legal position through errors of omission or commission by the paralegal.

Would any client want to be represented by a paralegal if his lawyer properly described to him the risks of non-lawyer representation in such a hearing? Would the client be adequately protected by relying on the malpractice liability [insurance] of the lawyer for actions of his paralegal in the hearing? I believe the answers to be in the negative.

The only justification for the use of paralegals in administrative hearings is an economic one. There has been no factual presentations beyond the bare conclusion that lawyers are not available at reasonable cost for rendering these services.

ASSIGNMENT 14

Which side is correct, the majority or minority view? Why? Which view do you think Justice Douglas would adopt? Why?

Section C. STATE LICENSING OF PARALEGALS

Many occupations are licensed: electricians, brokers, nurses, etc. What about paralegals? To date, *no* state has required licensing for paralegals. This is not to say, however, that efforts to license paralegals have not been tried, nor that licensing will not eventually come. The proposals of several states will be examined: California, Michigan, Arizona, and Oregon. Read this material carefully since it is highly likely that in the not-too-distant future you will be asked to comment on similar proposals for your state.

The California legislature once considered passing the "Certified Attorney Assistant Statute," which would have permitted the California Bar to set up a certification system for paralegals. It was, in effect, a licensing scheme. The statute did not pass. There was vigorous opposition from many paralegals who objected to lawyer domination in the system of control.

In 1977 the Michigan state legislature considered, but did not enact, the Legal Assistant Act, which would "regulate the practice of legal assistants" and "provide a system to certify legal assistants." This again was a licensure proposal since it would have the sanction of the government. The highlights of the proposed bill were as follows:

- A Commission on Legal Assistants would be established within the state Department of Education.
- Nine members of the Commission would be appointed by the government subject to confirmation by the state Senate. The nine members would be as follows:
  1 from the state bar of Michigan
  1 representing the public
  2 teachers of paralegals (one teacher must be an attorney; the other one must not be an attorney)
  1 practicing attorney in Michigan
  3 legal assistants with not less than one year of experience as a legal assistant
  1 legal assistant student
- Commission members will be paid on a per diem basis and will be expected to meet at least eight times a year.
- The Commission shall establish the requirements for certification of legal assistants; the requirements will deal with the "education, training and experience" of legal assistants.
- The Commission "shall develop and make public guidelines on the appropriate delegation of functions to and supervision of legal assistants according to the level of education, training, or experience of legal assistants. The guidelines shall not be binding, but shall serve to explain how the commission's training criteria coincides with the expectations of attorneys relative to the delegation to and supervision of legal assistants."
- "A person shall not act as a legal assistant, hold himself out as a legal assistant, or use the title or designation indicating he is a legal assistant except as authorized by this act. . . ."
- To be certified, a person must be eighteen years of age or older, be a "graduate of an approved program; or be a licensed, certified, registered, approved, or other legally recognized legal assistant in another state with qualifications substantially equivalent to those established by the commission; or have the education, training, or experience prescribed by this act or the rules of the commission as determined by an examination or evaluation authorized by the commission, . . ."
- "To determine whether an applicant for initial certification has the appropriate level of skill and knowledge as required by this act, the commission shall require the applicant to submit to an examination which shall include those subjects the general knowledge of which is commonly and generally required of a graduate of an accredited legal assistants program in the United States. The commission may waive the examination requirement for graduates of approved programs where such applicants have taken a national examination and achieved a score acceptable to the commission as demonstrating the level of skill and knowledge required by this act. The commission also may waive the examination for applicants who are licensed, certified, registered, approved, or otherwise legally recognized as a legal assistant in another state, when the

commission determines that the other state has qualifications, including completion of a national or state approved examination for legal assistants, that are substantially equivalent to those established by this act. For the purpose of this section, the commission shall not, in any case, preclude applicants from taking an examination because of a lack of specific previous education, training, or experience."

- Someone who fails the examination cannot retake it more than three times.
- Certification, once granted, is not perpetual. The Commission must make "determinations of continuing competence," e.g., by retesting, "not less than once every 4 years."
- A person who has been certified "shall publicly display the current certificate" in that "person's place of practice, if feasible, and shall have available for inspection a pocket card" issued by the state "containing the essential information of the certification."
- A legal assistant "shall not undertake or represent that he is qualified to undertake provision of a legal service which he knows or reasonably should know to be outside his competence or lawfully prohibited."
- A legal assistant "shall perform legal functions only under the supervision of an attorney, and only when those functions are within the scope of practice of the supervising attorney and are delegated by the supervising attorney." "A legal assistant shall perform legal functions only in those settings approved by the supervising attorney."
- A legal assistant "is the agent of the supervising attorney. Communications made to a legal assistant which would be privileged communications if made to the supervising attorney shall be considered privileged communications to the legal assistant and the supervising attorney to the same extent as if the communications were made to the supervising attorney."
- "A person who practices or holds himself out as a legal assistant without approval is guilty of a felony punishable by a fine of not less than $1,000.00 or more than $5,000.00, or imprisonment for not more than 1 year, or both."
- The Commission shall also award "accreditation to qualified institutions offering programs for the training of legal assistants." This shall be done "to determine whether graduates of the programs, who may apply for certification in this state, meet the requirements established for legal assistants pursuant to this act . . . ." The Commission shall consider "and may use where appropriate the criteria established by professional associations, educational accrediting bodies, or government agencies." "The standards for educational and training programs shall be designed to determine that each legal assistant has the necessary knowledge and skill to perform in a competent manner with due regard for the complexity attendant to activities in which a legal assistant engages."

Arizona considered, but did not pass, the following licensing legislation:

State of Arizona
House of Representatives
Thirty-seventh Legislature
First Regular Session
1985

H. B. **2299**

1 Be it enacted by the Legislature of the State of Arizona:
2   Section 1. Purpose
3   The purpose of this act is to protect the paralegal profession
4 and the public by providing for the licensing and regulation of
5 paralegals.
6   Sec. 2. Title 32, Arizona Revised Statutes, is amended by add-
7 ing chapter 31, to read:
8   CHAPTER 31 PARALEGALS
9   ARTICLE 1. GENERAL PROVISIONS
10   32-3101. Definitions
11 IN THIS CHAPTER, UNLESS THE CONTEXT OTHER-
12 WISE REQUIRES:
13   1. "BOARD" MEANS THE BOARD OF PARALEGALS.
14   2. "PARALEGAL" MEANS A PERSON LICENSED PURSUANT
15 TO THIS CHAPTER.
16   3. "PARALEGAL PRACTICE" MEANS ANY OF THE FOLLOW-
17 ING IF DONE ON A REGULAR BASIS FOR A LICENSED
18 ATTORNEY:
19   (a) CONDUCTING INTERVIEWS WITH CLIENTS TO GATH-
20 ER BACKGROUND INFORMATION.
21   (b) CONDUCTING CASE AND STATUTE RESEARCH AND
22 WRITING AN ANALYSIS OR SYNOPSIS OF THE RESEARCH.
23   (c) DRAFTING INTERROGATORIES.
24   (d) PREPARING PLEADINGS.
25   (e) INTERVIEWING AND PREPARING WITNESSES FOR DEPO-
26 SITIONS, CROSS-EXAMINATION AND COURT
27 APPEARANCES.
28   (f) CONDUCTING BUSINESS WITH THE POLICE, ATTOR-
29 NEYS, GOVERNMENT OFFICIALS AND AGENCIES AND ALL
30 LEVELS OF COURTS.
31   (g) PREPARING DRAFTS OF TRIAL MOTIONS, COM-
32 PLAINTS, WILLS, LEASES, CORPORATION FORMATIONS,
33 FICTITIOUS NAME PAPERS, PARTNERSHIP AGREEMENTS,
34 CONTRACTS OR APPELLATE BRIEFS.
35   (h) WORKING CLOSELY WITH ATTORNEYS DURING TRIAL
36 BY KEEPING MATERIAL ORGANIZED AND MAKING NOTES
37 DURING EXAMINATION AND CROSS-EXAMINATION OF
38 WITNESSES.
39   (i) REPRESENTING ATTORNEYS' CLIENTS IN ADMINISTRA-
40 TION PROCEEDINGS SUCH AS SOCIAL SECURITY HEARINGS,
41 UNEMPLOYMENT COMPENSATION HEARINGS OR JUSTICE
42 OF THE PEACE HEARINGS.
43   (j) REVIEWING, ORGANIZING AND DIGESTING DEPOSI-
44 TION AND TRIAL TRANSCRIPTS.
45   32-3102. Board of paralegals; appointment;
46   qualifications; terms
47 A. A BOARD OF PARALEGALS IS ESTABLISHED CONSIST-
48 ING OF THE FOLLOWING FIVE MEMBERS APPOINTED BY
49 THE GOVERNOR:

1   1. ONE PARALEGAL WHO HAS BEEN ACTIVELY PRACTIC-
2   ING IN THIS STATE FOR AT LEAST THREE YEARS.
3   2. TWO PERSONS WHO ARE PARALEGAL EDUCATORS.
4   3. TWO PUBLIC MEMBERS PREFERABLY ONE OF WHOM IS A
5   LICENSED ATTORNEY.
6   B. THE TERMS OF OFFICE OF BOARD MEMBERS ARE FIVE
7   YEARS. MEMBERS SHALL NOT SERVE MORE THAN TWO CON-
8   SECUTIVE TERMS.
9   C. THE GOVERNOR MAY REMOVE A BOARD MEMBER FOR
10   NEGLECT OF DUTY, MALFEASANCE OR MISFEASANCE.
11   32-3103. Organization; meetings; compensation
12   A. THE BOARD SHALL ANNUALLY ELECT A CHAIRMAN,
13   VICE-CHAIRMAN AND SECRETARY-TREASURER FROM ITS
14   MEMBERSHIP.
15   B. THE BOARD MAY HOLD MEETINGS AT TIMES AND PLAC-
16   ES IT DESIGNATES.
17   C. A MAJORITY OF THE MEMBERS OF THE BOARD CONSTI-
18   TUTES A QUORUM.
19   D. MEMBERS OF THE BOARD ARE ELIGIBLE TO RECEIVE
20   COMPENSATION AS DETERMINED PURSUANT TO SECTION
21   38-611 FOR EACH DAY OF ACTUAL SERVICE IN THE BUSINESS
22   OF THE BOARD.
23   32-3104. Powers and duties
24   A. THE BOARD SHALL:
25   1. MAKE AND ADOPT RULES WHICH ARE NECESSARY OR
26   PROPER FOR THE ADMINISTRATION OF THIS CHAPTER, IN-
27   CLUDING REQUIREMENTS FOR PARALEGAL EDUCATION.
28   2. ADMINISTER AND ENFORCE THE PROVISIONS OF THIS
29   CHAPTER AND RULES ADOPTED PURSUANT TO THIS
30   CHAPTER.
31   3. MAINTAIN A RECORD OF ITS ACTS AND PROCEEDINGS,
32   INCLUDING ISSUANCE, REFUSAL, RENEWAL, SUSPENSION
33   AND REVOCATION OF LICENSES, AND A RECORD OF THE
34   NAME, ADDRESS AND LICENSE DATE OF EACH LICENSEE.
35   4. KEEP THE RECORDS OF THE BOARD OPEN TO PUBLIC IN-
36   SPECTION AT ALL REASONABLE TIMES.
37   5. FURNISH A COPY OF ITS RULES TO ANY PERSON ON
38   REQUEST.
39   6. HAVE A SEAL, THE IMPRINT OF WHICH SHALL BE USED
40   TO EVIDENCE ITS OFFICIAL ACTS.
41   B. THE BOARD MAY EMPLOY AN EXECUTIVE DIRECTOR
42   WHO HAS BEEN A PARALEGAL FOR AT LEAST THREE YEARS
43   PRECEDING EMPLOYMENT AND OTHER PERMANENT OR
44   TEMPORARY PERSONNEL IT DEEMS NECESSARY. THE
45   BOARD SHALL COMPENSATE ITS EXECUTIVE DIRECTOR
46   AND OTHER PERMANENT AND TEMPORARY PERSONNEL AS
47   DETERMINED PURSUANT TO SECTION 38-611.
48   32-3105. Board of paralegals fund
49   A. A BOARD OF PARALEGALS FUND IS ESTABLISHED. BE-
50   FORE THE END OF EACH CALENDAR MONTH, ALL MONIES
51   FROM WHATEVER SOURCE WHICH COME INTO THE POSSES-
52   SION OF THE BOARD SHALL BE TRANSMITTED TO THE

1 STATE TREASURER WHO SHALL DEPOSIT TEN PER CENT OF
2 SUCH MONIES IN THE STATE GENERAL FUND AND TRANS-
3 FER THE REMAINING NINETY PER CENT TO THE BOARD OF
4 PARALEGALS FUND.
5   B. MONIES DEPOSITED IN THE BOARD OF PARALEGALS
6 FUND ARE SUBJECT TO SECTION 35-143.01.
7   ARTICLE 2. LICENSURE
8   32-3111. Paralegal license; application; qualifications;
9   reciprocity
10   A. AN APPLICANT FOR A PARALEGAL LICENSE SHALL FILE
11 THE FOLLOWING WITH THE BOARD:
12   1. A WRITTEN APPLICATION ON A FORM PRESCRIBED BY
13 THE BOARD.
14   2. EVIDENCE SATISFACTORY TO THE BOARD THAT THE
15 APPLICANT POSSESSES THE NECESSARY QUALIFICATIONS
16 AND EDUCATION.
17   B. EACH APPLICANT SHALL:
18   1. BE AT LEAST EIGHTEEN YEARS OF AGE.
19   2. HAVE COMPLETED AND RECEIVED APPROPRIATE CRED-
20 ITS FOR HIGH SCHOOL EDUCATION OR ITS EQUIVALENT AS
21 PRESCRIBED BY THE BOARD IN ITS RULES.
22   3. PASS AN EXAMINATION GIVEN UNDER THE DIRECTION
23 OF THE BOARD.
24   4. PAY THE PRESCRIBED FEE.
25   C. AN APPLICANT WHO HOLDS A VALID LICENSE FOR PAR-
26 ALEGAL PRACTICE ISSUED BY ANOTHER STATE WHICH
27 HAS, IN THE OPINION OF THE BOARD, LICENSURE REQUIRE-
28 MENTS THAT ARE SUBSTANTIALLY EQUIVALENT TO THE
29 REQUIREMENTS OF THIS STATE AND WHICH GRANTS SIMI-
30 LAR RECIPROCAL PRIVILEGES TO PARALEGALS LICENSED
31 BY THIS STATE AND WHO HAS AT LEAST ONE YEAR'S EXPE-
32 RIENCE AS A LICENSED PARALEGAL IS EXEMPT FROM SUB-
33 SECTION B, PARAGRAPH 3.
34   32-3112. Examinations
35   A. EXAMINATIONS SHALL BE GIVEN AT LEAST EVERY
36 THREE MONTHS AT TIMES AND PLACES DETERMINED BY
37 THE BOARD.
38   B. EXAMINATIONS SHALL CONTAIN A WRITTEN PART
39 AND MAY INCLUDE ORAL QUESTIONS.
40   C. EXAMINATIONS SHALL TEST THE APPLICANT'S
41 KNOWLEDGE OF PARALEGAL PRACTICE.
42   D. A PASSING GRADE ON AN EXAMINATION IS A SCORE OF
43 SEVENTY-FIVE PER CENT OR BETTER ON BOTH THE WRIT-
44 TEN AND ORAL PARTS OF THE EXAMINATION.
45   E. IF AN APPLICANT WHO IS ELIGIBLE TO TAKE AN EXAMI-
46 NATION FAILS TO DO SO AT EITHER OF THE NEXT TWO
47 SCHEDULED EXAMINATIONS, THE APPLICATION IS DEEM-
48 ED TO BE CANCELLED AND THE APPLICATION FEE IS
49 FORFEITED.
50   F. IF AN APPLICANT FAILS AN EXAMINATION HE IS ENTI-
51 TLED TO A REEXAMINATION.
52   G. IF AN APPLICANT FAILS EITHER PART OF THE EXAMI-

1 NATION HE SHALL ONLY RETAKE THE PART OF THE EXAMI-
2 NATION HE FAILED.
3   H. AN APPLICANT DESIRING TO BE REEXAMINED SHALL
4 APPLY TO THE BOARD ON FORMS IT PRESCRIBES AND FUR-
5 NISHES AND PAY THE PRESCRIBED REEXAMINATION FEE.
6   32-3113. Fees; penalty
7   A. THE BOARD SHALL ESTABLISH AND COLLECT FEES,
8 NOT TO EXCEED THE FOLLOWING AMOUNTS:
9   1. PARALEGAL EXAMINATION, TWO HUNDRED
10 DOLLARS.
11   2. PARALEGAL LICENSE, ONE HUNDRED DOLLARS.
12   3. PARALEGAL LICENSE BY RECIPROCITY, TWO HUNDRED
13 DOLLARS.
14   4. REEXAMINATION, FIFTY DOLLARS.
15   B. A DUPLICATE LICENSE SHALL BE ISSUED TO REPLACE A
16 LOST LICENSE IF A LICENSEE FILES A VERIFIED STATEMENT
17 AS TO ITS LOSS AND PAYS A TWENTY DOLLAR FEE. EACH
18 DUPLICATE LICENSE ISSUED SHALL HAVE THE WORD "DU-
19 PLICATE" STAMPED ACROSS THE FACE.
20   C. IF THE BOARD RECEIVES AN INSUFFICIENT FUND
21 CHECK, IT MAY CHARGE A TEN DOLLAR PENALTY FEE.
22   ARTICLE 3. REGULATION
23   32-3121. Disciplinary action
24   THE BOARD MAY TAKE ANY ONE OR A COMBINATION OF
25 THE FOLLOWING DISCIPLINARY ACTIONS:
26   1. REVOKE A LICENSE.
27   2. SUSPEND A LICENSE.
28   3. IMPOSE A CIVIL PENALTY IN AN AMOUNT NOT TO EX-
29 CEED FIVE HUNDRED DOLLARS.
30   4. IMPOSE PROBATION REQUIREMENTS BEST ADAPTED
31 TO PROTECT THE PUBLIC SAFETY, HEALTH AND WELFARE
32 INCLUDING REQUIREMENTS FOR RESTITUTION
33 PAYMENTS.
34   5. ISSUE A LETTER OF CONCERN.
35   32-3122. Grounds for refusal to issue or renew
36   a license or disciplinary action
37   THE BOARD MAY TAKE DISCIPLINARY ACTION OR REFUSE
38 TO ISSUE OR RENEW A LICENSE FOR ANY OF THE FOLLOW-
39 ING CAUSES:
40   1. MALPRACTICE OR INCOMPETENCY.
41   2. ADVERTISING BY MEANS OF KNOWN FALSE OR DECEP-
42 TIVE STATEMENTS.
43   3. ADVERTISING, PRACTICING OR ATTEMPTING TO PRAC-
44 TICE UNDER A NAME OTHER THAN THE ONE IN WHICH THE
45 LICENSE IS ISSUED.
46   32-3124. Unlawful acts; violation; classification
47   A. A PERSON SHALL NOT:
48   1. PRACTICE OR ATTEMPT PARALEGAL PRACTICE WITH-
49 OUT A CURRENT LICENSE ISSUED PURSUANT TO THIS
50 CHAPTER.
51   2. DISPLAY A SIGN OR IN ANY WAY ADVERTISE OR HOLD
52 ONESELF OUT AS A PARALEGAL OR AS BEING ENGAGED IN

```
1    THE PARALEGAL PRACTICE WITHOUT BEING LICENSED
2    PURSUANT TO THIS CHAPTER.
3      3. KNOWINGLY MAKE A FALSE STATEMENT ON AN APPLI-
4    CATION FOR A LICENSE PURSUANT TO THIS CHAPTER.
5      4. PERMIT AN EMPLOYEE OR ANOTHER PERSON UNDER
6    HIS SUPERVISION OR CONTROL TO ENGAGE IN PARALEGAL
7    PRACTICE WITHOUT A LICENSE ISSUED PURSUANT TO
8    THIS CHAPTER.
9      5. OBTAIN OR ATTEMPT TO OBTAIN A LICENSE BY THE
10   USE OF MONEY OTHER THAN THE PRESCRIBED FEES OR ANY
11   OTHER    THING    OF    VALUE    OR    BY    FRAUDULENT
12   MISREPRESENTATION.
13     6. VIOLATE ANY PROVISION OF THIS CHAPTER OR ANY
14   RULE ADOPTED PURSUANT TO THIS CHAPTER.
15     B. A PERSON WHO VIOLATES THIS SECTION IS GUILTY OF
16   A CLASS 2 MISDEMEANOR.
17     32-3125. Injunctions
18   THE BOARD, THE ATTORNEY GENERAL, A COUNTY AT-
19   TORNEY OR ANY OTHER PERSON MAY APPLY TO THE SUPE-
20   RIOR COURT IN THE COUNTY IN WHICH ACTS OR PRACTIC-
21   ES OF ANY PERSON WHICH CONSTITUTE A VIOLATION OF
22   THIS CHAPTER OR THE RULES ADOPTED PURSUANT TO
23   THIS CHAPTER ARE ALLEGED TO HAVE OCCURRED FOR AN
24   ORDER ENJOINING THOSE ACTS OR PRACTICES.
```

In 1975, the Oregon Bar Association actually launched a certification program that it later abandoned. It administered an examination to candidates who had been graduated from a paralegal school and had some practical experience. Very little interest was generated by the process and it was discontinued in 1980. In 1985 another Oregon proposal surfaced. The Legislative Counsel Committee of the Oregon State Legislature drafted a licensing (referred to as a "registration") program. The future of this proposed legislation is unclear.

Most licensing proposals are primarily restrictive in that they focus on what paralegals *cannot* do. One recent proposal surprisingly goes the other way. The Santa Monica Bar Association has asked the California State Bar Association and the California state legislature to enact a program that would require paralegals in the state to be licensed by a board within the California Department of Consumer Affairs. The board, to be appointed by the Governor, would consist of five legal assistants, one active legal assistant educator, two members of the Bar with experience in the use of legal assistants, and one member of the public at large. An oral or "practical" examination would be a condition of obtaining the license. The board would also approve paralegal schools and set minimal educational requirements for paralegals applying for a license. Among the functions that a licensed paralegal would be able to perform under the supervision of a lawyer are the following:

1. Make court appearances in ex parte matters;
2. Make court appearances for continuances;

3. Make court appearances for status and trial setting conferences;
4. Appear at judgment debtor examinations; and
5. Make court appearances in uncontested probate matters.

As of the present time, the fate of this proposal is uncertain. The chances of passage, however, are slim.

———————————

A number of bar associations have specifically rejected proposals to license or certify paralegals. The following excerpts from bar reports give some of the reasons why:

North Carolina State Bar, *Report of Special Committee on Paralegals,* p. 3 (1980)

Several states have considered the possibility of adopting a licensing statute for paralegals, but none has done so. It is doubtful that the concept of proper lay assistance to lawyers is now well enough or uniformally enough understood for the terms of a licensing statute to find a proper consensus. Licensing itself is subject to great public and legislative concern at present. So long as the work accomplished by non-lawyers for lawyers is properly supervised and reviewed by a licensed and responsible attorney, there would seem to be no need for a further echelon of licensing for the public's protection. Furthermore, licensing might be more dangerous than helpful to the public. The apparent stamp of approval of a license possibly could give the impression to the public that a person having such a license is qualified to deal directly with and give legal advice to the public. Although the Committee would not attempt to close the door on licensing of paralegals in the future if circumstances change and if, for example, the use of independent, non-lawyer employee paralegals were to become widespread, present conditions, at least, do not call for any program of licensing for paralegals.

Illinois State Bar Association, *Report on the Joint Study Committee on Attorney Assistants,* p. 6 (6/21/77)

Our Joint Committee arose because there was a suggestion that attorney assistants be licensed. After due consideration we recommend no program of licensure or certification of attorney assistants or other lay personnel.

We are opposed to licensure because the standards on which licensure are to be based are difficult or impossible to formulate. Furthermore, we have started with a premise that precedes this conclusion; to wit: no delegation of any task to an attorney assistant shall diminish the responsibility of the attorney for the services rendered. We believe that any program which purports to say who is "licensed" and who is "not licensed" creates a standard which will diminish the attorney's responsibility. It furthermore may exclude from useful and desirable employment people who, under the supervision and control of an attorney, may perform useful tasks but who may not meet the standards of licensure involved.

We are further opposed to licensure because of the danger that it poses to the public. If a group of persons appears to be authorized to perform tasks directly for the public, without the intervening control of an attorney, it would be humanly inevitable that many of the licensed persons would try to deal directly with the public. We think these risks would be substantially increased by licensure.

Only one state, Oregon, has experimented with state-certification of paralegals, although several bars have studied the possibility. Oregon's program was started in 1975, but it was discontinued in January, 1980. One of the two national organizations of paralegals (National Association of Legal Assistants) has a program of certification by that organization, but the other (National Federation of Paralegal Associations) does not. The latter's position, as well as the position of the American Bar Association, is that certification programs are premature, and possibly stifling, in a field that is growing and constantly undergoing changes. The Committee agrees and is of the view that such factors as (a) the range of services that can be classified as "paralegal," (b) the numerous methods by which intelligent and responsible persons can attain the skills through which to perform these services, and (c) the possible detriment to efficient and competent (but specialized) employees who could not be pigeonholed into any workable certification program, additionally tend to make a certification program of any sort unwise. We would leave the possible sponsorship of any such program to the future, when the developing occupation of paralegalism has matured.

ASSIGNMENT 15

How would you characterize the opposition to licensure and certification expressed in the above excerpts from the bar reports? Do you think there is a conflict of interest in lawyers making these judgments about paralegal control? Explain.

ASSIGNMENT 16

Evaluate the following observation: "The emerging professions and the more established professions have frequently sought greater regulation of their occupational group. They are often motivated, despite the obligatory language on protection of the public interest, to do so in efforts to establish their 'territorial imperative' or to establish barrier(s) to entry into the profession and thereby enhance their economic self-interest." Sapadin, "A Comparison of the Growth and Development of the Physician Assistant and the Legal Assistant," Journal of the American Association for Paralegal Education: *Retrospective 1983,* p. 142 (1983).

Will paralegals one day be licensed? It is, of course, difficult to predict. While there is considerable opposition from the vast majority of paralegals, paralegal associations, and bar associations to licensing legislation, proposals for such legislation continue to emerge with alarming regularity. It is not uncommon for licensing proposals to be before three or four state legislatures every year.

It is anticipated that one of them will eventually pass in spite of the organized opposition against it. How will this occur? A possible scenario is as follows: One day, while working on a case, a paralegal in some state makes a serious and damaging mistake, e.g., an act of negligence (p. 303). Or the paralegal leads a court to believe that s/he is an attorney in an appearance before the court. The blunder is given a great deal of publicity and is blown out of proportion. Cries are heard for regulation: "There otta be a law!" A licensing statute is quickly drafted and enacted with little opportunity for public comment.

Paralegal associations have a vast array of arguments against licensing. But are they ready for the day when everyone wakes up to discover that licensing legislation squeaked through a particular state legislature?

There are two strategies that can be taken. The first is to continue to oppose all efforts at licensing. Have monitors keep a watchful eye on every legislature in the country. When a proposal emerges, bombard the legislature with reasons why it should be defeated. Thus far, this has been the strategy of the opponents and it has been successful. There is no licensing requirement today in any state. A second strategy is for paralegals to design a licensing proposal of their own, one they can live with. Paralegals can continue their organized opposition to licensing, but when an unacceptable lawyer-written proposal has a serious chance of passage in a given legislature, the paralegals produce their own substitute and lobby for its passage.

There are paralegals who oppose the second strategy since the very existence of a paralegal proposal would lead some to believe that paralegals favor licensing. This indeed is a danger. But a choice must be made. If licensing will eventually come, would paralegals rather have their own program or one forced on them? According to Laurie P. Roselle, former president of the National Federation of Paralegal Associations:

> Where we go from here is an issue we must grapple with now before someone decides for us where we go.[11]

What to do when the Legislature Proposes Legislation to Regulate Paralegals

(In general, see How to Monitor Proposed Legislation, p. 668.)

1. Obtain a copy of the proposed legislation or bill as soon as possible. If you know the name of the legislator sponsoring the bill, write or call him/her directly. Otherwise contact the office of the Speaker of the House, Speaker of the Assembly, President of the Senate, etc. Ask how you can locate the proposed bill.
2. Find out the exact technical status of the bill. Has it been formally introduced? Has it been assigned to a committee? What is the next scheduled formal event on the bill?
3. Immediately inform the sponsoring legislator(s) and the relevant committee(s) that you want an opportunity to comment on the bill. Find out if hearings are going to be scheduled on the bill. Make known your interest in participating in such hearings. Your goal is to slow the process down so that the bill is not rushed into enactment. Be particularly alert to the possi-

---

[11] Roselle, *President's Column,* 9 National Paralegal Reporter 1 (Nat'l. Federation of Paralegal Associations, no. 5, April, 1985).

bility that the paralegal bill may be buried in proposed legislation on a large number of related or unrelated topics. Again, there is a real danger that the bill will get through relatively unnoticed.

4. Determine why the paralegal bill is being proposed. What is the *public* reason given for the proposal of the bill? More important, what is the underlying *real* reason for the proposal? Perhaps some small group or special interest is seeking a special privilege in a law-related field, e.g., real estate agents. Yet the language of the bill they are proposing may be so broad that paralegals will be adversely affected.

5. Alert your local paralegal association. It needs to be mobilized in order to express an organized position on the bill. Contact the major national paralegal associations: NFPA and NALA (p. 285). Do they know about the proposed legislation? Have they taken a position? They need to be activated.

6. If your local bar association has a paralegal committee, seek its support.

7. Launch a letter-writing campaign. Make sure that large numbers of paralegals in the area know about the bill and how to express their opinion to the legislature.

8. Ask local paralegal schools to take a position.

Keep in mind that we are talking about mandatory *licensing* by the state, not voluntary *certification* by entities such as paralegal associations. The certification debate will be covered later (p. 288).

Section D. ETHICAL RULES GOVERNING LAWYERS AND THE LAWYER'S USE OF PARALEGALS

In order to understand how bar associations control a lawyer's use of paralegals, we must understand the controls that the bar associations place on lawyers themselves. The following topics will be covered:

1. Introduction to bar associations and the canons or rules of ethics governing lawyers.
2. The American Bar Association and paralegals.
3. State and local bar associations and paralegals.
4. The attorney-client privilege, confidentiality, and special ethical problems facing the paralegal who switches jobs and the free-lance paralegal.
5. Doing legal research on an ethical issue.

1. INTRODUCTION TO BAR ASSOCIATIONS AND CANONS OR RULES OF ETHICS GOVERNING LAWYERS

Lawyers are regulated by their state bar association under the authority and supervision of the state's highest court. The regulations take the form of canons of ethics, the violation of which can lead to sanctions such as suspension and disbarment. To discipline a lawyer for such violations, a committee of the bar association will usually conduct a hearing on the case and make a preliminary decision. The result can be appealed to a designated state court, which will make the final decision on whether sanctions are to be imposed. The bar associations often write ethical opinions that interpret and apply the canons.

As we will see, one of the canons covers the lawyer's use of paralegals. This canon is the major source of a paralegal's authority to work in a law office. In essence, a lawyer must supervise the paralegal and see to it that the paralegal does not engage in the unauthorized practice of law.

The canons apply to lawyers and not directly to paralegals. Since paralegals cannot be full members of a bar association (p. 283), the canons do not directly control or regulate paralegals. No paralegal can be disciplined by a bar association for unethical conduct. It is the *lawyer* who will be disciplined for what the paralegal (or other nonlawyer) does within the employ of the lawyer. Other kinds of sanctions can be applied to paralegals, e.g., criminal prosecution for the unauthorized practice of law (p. 205) or a negligence claim (p. 303). Bar sanctions govern only lawyers.

The American Bar Association is a *voluntary* association of lawyers. No lawyer is required to be a member of the ABA. One of the major roles of the ABA is to write ethical rules and issue opinions interpreting these rules. The rules and opinions are *not* binding on state and local bar associations. Since, however, the ABA is a respected body, its rules and opinions have been very influential. In fact, most state and local bar associations have adopted all or some of the ABA ethical positions. They are not required to do so, but they seldom ignore what the ABA has said. If you read the ethical rules and opinions of state and local bar associations, you will find that they are often either taken entirely from the ABA positions or adapted from these positions.

Two important sets of ethical rules should be distinguished:

- *ABA Model Code of Professional Responsibility.*
- *ABA Model Rules of Professional Conduct.*

The Model Code is the older of the two documents. It consists of three main parts. First, the nine canons of the Code. The canons are statements of axiomatic norms expressing in general terms the standards of professional conduct expected of lawyers. Second, the disciplinary rules for each of the nine canons. The disciplinary rules (abbreviated "DR") are mandatory statements of the minimum conduct below which no lawyer can fall without being subject to disciplinary action. Third, the ethical considerations for each of the nine canons. The ethical considerations (abbreviated "EC") are aspirational in character and represent the objectives toward which every member of the profession should strive.

The Model Rules, on the other hand, were adopted by the ABA in 1983. They are a revision of the Model Code. Some of the changes are significant while others are minor. The Model Rules consist of eight rules plus commentary on their application.

While the Model Rules represent the current position of the ABA, you must still be aware of the Model Code. As indicated, many states closely examine the ABA ethical positions and decide whether to adopt, modify, or reject them for their own state. All states have been examining the relatively recent Model Rules. An individual state may decide to adopt some of the Model Rules, keep some of the older Model Code, and add items that are in neither ABA document.

Before covering what the ABA and state bar associations have said about the use of paralegals by lawyers, we need to examine the content of the ABA Model Code and Model Rules. You should know what ethical obligations are imposed on lawyers so that you can help your employing lawyers avoid charges of ethical improprieties. Some states strongly urge lawyers to provide their paralegals with training on these ethical obligations. The ABA mandates that lawyers should give their paralegals "appropriate instruction" on the "ethical aspects" of the practice of law (p. 252). In Kentucky, the paralegal has an obligation "to refrain from conduct which would involve the lawyer in a violation" of the canons of ethics (p. 258). Hence paralegals need to understand the ethical standards imposed on the legal profession. Here we will focus on the positions of the ABA. Later we will examine the research steps that you would take to find the specific canons of your state.

THE ETHICAL OBLIGATIONS OF LAWYERS: A SUMMARY OF THE ABA MODEL CODE AND THE ABA MODEL RULES

(At the beginning of each topic you will find summaries of specific canons or standards. All "Rules" are from the ABA Model Rules and all references to "DR" or "EC" are from the Model Code.)

In this summary, we will cover the following topics:
(a) Competence
(b) Criminal Conduct and Fraud by the Client
(c) Candor and Honesty by the Lawyer
(d) Communication with Client
(e) Fees
(f) Confidentiality of Information
(g) Conflict of Interest
(h) Gifts from Clients
(i) Property of the Client
(j) Withdrawal of a Lawyer from a Case
(k) Frivolous Claims
(l) Communication with Opposing Party
(m) Advertising
(n) Solicitation
(o) Reporting Professional Misconduct
(p) The Appearance of Impropriety
(q) Paralegals and Other Nonlawyers

(a) Competence

> *Rule 1.1. A lawyer shall provide competent representation to a client.*
>
> *Rule 1.3. A lawyer shall act with reasonable diligence and promptness in representing a client.*
>
> *Rule 3.2. A lawyer shall make reasonable efforts to expedite litigation.*
>
> *DR 6-101(A)(1). A lawyer should not handle a matter which s/he knows or should know that s/he is not competent to handle without becoming associated with a lawyer who is competent to handle it.*
>
> *DR 6-101(A)(3). A lawyer shall not neglect a legal matter entrusted to him/her.*

A lawyer must have the skills needed to practice law, e.g., analyze precedent, evaluate evidence, draft legal documents. For special legal problems, the lawyer must conduct legal research and, where needed, seek the help of more experienced lawyers. It would be unethical for a lawyer to have a large caseload when each case cannot be handled competently. It would be unethical for a lawyer to proceed with a case without adequate preparation.

Also, unreasonable procrastination is unethical. Undue delay must be avoided.

(b) Criminal Conduct and Fraud by the Client

> *Rule 1.2(d). A lawyer shall not counsel a client to engage, or assist a client, in conduct that the lawyer knows is criminal or fraudulent.*
>
> *DR 7-102(A)(7). A lawyer shall not counsel or assist his/her client in conduct that the lawyer knows to be illegal or fraudulent.*

It is unethical for a lawyer to tell a client how to commit a crime or a fraudulent act, e.g., to cheat on an income tax return, to fabricate evidence, or to destroy evidence that must be preserved.

(c) Candor and Honesty by the Lawyer

> *Rule 3.3. A lawyer shall not knowingly make a false statement of material fact or law to a tribunal, knowingly offer false evidence, or knowingly fail to disclose material facts to a tribunal when disclosure is necessary to avoid assisting the client commit fraud or a crime. If the lawyer knows of legal authority that is against his/her client, the lawyer must disclose this authority to the tribunal if it is not offered by opposing counsel.*
>
> *Rule 3.4. A lawyer shall not unlawfully obstruct another party's access to evidence.*
>
> *DR 7-102, DR 7-109.*

A lawyer can be zealous in the representation of his/her client. But this cannot include deception on the part of the lawyer by making false statements or offering false or perjured testimony. Also, if the lawyer's legal research has uncovered cases, statutes, or other authority in the jurisdiction that go *against* his/her client, the lawyer must tell the tribunal about this authority if it is not raised by the other side.

(d) Communication with Client

> *Rule 1.4. A lawyer shall keep a client reasonably informed about the status of the case and promptly comply with the client's reasonable requests for information.*
> *EC 9-2. A lawyer should fully and promptly inform the client of material developments in the matters being handled for the client.*

Studies have shown that one of the most common client complaints against lawyers is the failure of the lawyer to communicate with the client about the status of the case.

(e) Fees

> *Rule 1.5. A lawyer's fee shall be reasonable. Information about the fee should be communicated to the client, preferably in writing, before or within a reasonable time after commencing the representation. The reasonableness of a fee depends on factors such as the amount of time and skill required, the fees customarily charged in the locality for similar legal services, the experience, reputation, and ability of the lawyer, etc. Contingent fees (i.e., where the existence of a fee or its amount is dependent on the outcome of the case) are prohibited in criminal cases or in domestic relations cases where the fee is contingent upon the securing of a divorce or upon the amount of alimony, support, or property settlement obtained. A lawyer shall not split a fee with a lawyer who is not a member of the same firm unless certain conditions are met, e.g., the client does not object.*
> *DR 2-106(A)(B)(C); DR 107(A); EC 2-17; EC 2-19; EC 2-20.*

(f) Confidentiality of Information

> *Rule 1.6. A lawyer shall not reveal information relating to representation of a client unless the client consents. An exception is made if the lawyer reasonably believes that the revelation is necessary to prevent the client from committing a criminal act that is likely to result in imminent death or substantial bodily harm.*
> *Rule 1.8(b). A lawyer shall not use information relating to representation of a client to the disadvantage of the client unless the client consents.*
> *DR 4-101. A lawyer shall not knowingly reveal a confidence or secret of a client unless the client consents. A confidence is information protected by the attorney-client privilege. A secret is any other information gained in the professional relationship that the client requested to be kept private or that would likely be detrimental to the client if disclosed. A lawyer, however, may reveal the client's intention to commit a crime and the information necessary to prevent the crime.*

Without the principle of confidentiality, clients would be discouraged from communicating fully and frankly with a lawyer, particularly as to embarrassing or legally damaging matters. It would be unethical for a lawyer to disclose client communications even if the lawyer is called as a witness in court, unless the exceptions apply.

For more on confidentiality, see p. 266.

(g) Conflict of Interest

Rule 1.7. A lawyer shall not represent a client if it would be directly adverse to another client unless each client consents and the lawyer reasonably believes that this other client will not be adversely affected.

Rule 1.10. If a lawyer is disqualified from representing a client because of Rule 1.7, all other lawyers in the same firm are also disqualified.

DR 5-105. A lawyer shall decline a case if s/he cannot devote his/her independent professional judgment on behalf of the client, or if accepting the case will likely involve representing differing interests. An exception exists if both clients, whom the lawyer seeks to represent, consent and it is obvious that the lawyer can adequately represent the interests of each.

A client is entitled to a lawyer's undivided loyalty. Assume that a lawyer represents Mary *and* Pat in a fraud case against each other. How can the lawyer be loyal to both? Mary and Pat have adverse interests. For the lawyer to try to represent both would be a conflict of interest. Similarly, a lawyer cannot represent John in a contract case against Bill and *also* represent Fred in a negligence suit against John. Here the subject matter in the two suits is not the same. Yet the lawyer is being asked to use all his/ her professional resources to defeat John in the negligence case and all of his/her professional resources to see that John wins in the contract case. The lawyer's loyalty to John is diminished. For example, in the lawyer's office, the lawyer may find out information that could be used against John in the negligence case. There is a conflict of interest.

In the above case, suppose that the lawyer was a member of a law firm of twenty other lawyers. Could one lawyer in the firm represent John in the contract case, and *another* lawyer in the same firm represent Fred in the negligence case against John? No. A firm of lawyers is essentially *one* lawyer for purposes of the rules governing loyalty to the client. John is entitled to the undivided loyalty of every member of the firm that represents him. If the firm represents John in one case, it is disqualified from representing John's adversary in the other case.

An example of one of the rare instances in which it might be ethical for a lawyer to represent *both* parties would be a divorce case in which both the husband and wife want the divorce, there are no children, no support issues, and no property division involved. If the husband and wife make an informed decision to allow the same lawyer to represent both of them, the multiple representation is allowed in many states. In such a case, there is very little likelihood that the parties will have any adverse interests.

(h) Gifts from Clients

Rule 1.8(c). A lawyer shall not prepare a document for a client, e.g., a will, in which the client gives the lawyer a substantial gift unless the lawyer is related to the client. The prohibition also applies if the gift is given to a close relative or spouse of the lawyer.

> *EC 5-5. If a lawyer accepts a gift from the client, the lawyer is peculiarly susceptible to the charge that s/he unduly influenced the client in making the gift.*

This is another example of a conflict of interest. Whose interest is the lawyer protecting when s/he prepares the legal document that resulted in the gift? The donor or the donee?

(i) Property of the client

> *Rule 1.15. A lawyer shall hold property of clients separate from the lawyer's own property. Funds shall be kept in a separate account in the state where the lawyer's office is situated. Complete records shall be kept. The client shall be promptly notified if other funds are received.*
> *DR 9-102.*

(j) Withdrawal of the Lawyer from a Case

> *Rule 1.16. A lawyer must withdraw from a case (a) if the client demands that the lawyer engage in conduct that is illegal or unethical, (b) if the lawyer's physical or mental condition materially impairs his/her ability to represent the client, or (c) if the client fires the lawyer.*
> *DR 2-110. A lawyer shall withdraw if (a) it is obvious that the client's objective is merely to harass or maliciously injure someone, (b) continuing will result in a violation of the canons of ethics, (c) the lawyer's physical or mental condition makes it unreasonably difficult to represent the client effectively, or (d) the client fires the lawyer.*

A client always has a right to discharge a lawyer with or without giving any reasons, subject to an obligation to pay fees for services already rendered. There are times when a lawyer must have the permission of the court to withdraw, e.g., when the lawyer was initially appointed or assigned by the court to represent the client.

(k) Frivolous Claims

> *Rule 3.1. A lawyer shall not bring frivolous cases.*
> *Rule 3.4. A lawyer shall not make a frivolous discovery request. During a trial, a lawyer shall not allude to matters that the lawyer does not reasonably believe are relevant or supportable by admissible evidence.*
> *Rule 4.4. In representing a client, a lawyer shall not use means that have no substantial purpose other than to embarrass, delay, or burden a third person.*
> *DR 7-102(A)(2). A lawyer shall not knowingly advance a claim or defense that is unwarranted under existing law unless a good faith argument can be made for a change in the existing law.*

If a client asks a lawyer to violate these rules, the lawyer must withdraw from the case.

(l) Communication with Opposing Party

> *Rule 4.2. A lawyer should not communicate with the opposing party on a case unless the latter's lawyer consents. If this party is unrepresented, a lawyer shall not give him / her the impression that the lawyer is disinterested in the case (e.g., neutral). No legal advice should be given other than to obtain separate counsel.*
> *DR 7-104.*

The main concern here is that the lawyer might try to take undue advantage of the unrepresented party.

(m) Advertising

> *Rule 7.1; 7.2. A lawyer shall not make false or misleading statements about his / her services. Advertising is permitted through a telephone directory, legal directory, newspaper, other periodical, radio, TV, and other public media.*
> *DR 2-101. A lawyer may publish or broadcast certain information about his / her legal services in designated areas, e.g., name, address, field of practice, associations, information about fees.*

For more on advertising, see p. 279.

(n) Solicitation

> *Rule 7.3. A lawyer may not solicit legal business from a specific prospective client with whom the lawyer has no family or prior professional relationship when a significant motive for the lawyer's doing so is the lawyer's pecuniary (i.e., monetary or financial) gain. This prohibition does not forbid the use of letters or advertising circulars distributed generally.*
> *DR 2-104(A). A lawyer who has given in-person unsolicited advice to a layperson that s / he should obtain counsel or take legal action, shall not accept employment resulting from that advice. An exception exists when the layperson is a close friend, relative, or former client (if the advice is germane to the former employment).*

(o) Reporting Professional Misconduct

> *Rule 8.3. A lawyer having knowledge that another lawyer has committed a violation of these ethical rules that raises a substantial question as to that lawyer's honesty, trustworthiness, or fitness, shall inform the appropriate professional authority.*
> *DR 1-103.*

(p) The Appearance of Impropriety

> *DR 9-101. A lawyer must avoid even the appearance of professional impropriety.*

Under this provision, a lawyer can be disciplined even if no ethical rules are actually violated. It is unethical for a lawyer to act in such a way that *appears* ethically improper.

(q) Paralegals and Other Nonlawyers

See discussion below.

---

2. THE AMERICAN BAR ASSOCIATION AND PARALEGALS

Both the Model Code and the Model Rules of the ABA (p. 244) have provisions that are relevant to a lawyer's use of paralegals.

The ABA Model Code of Professional Responsibility provides as follows:

DR 3-101(A). A lawyer shall not aid a nonlawyer in the unauthorized practice of law.

EC 3-6. A lawyer often delegates tasks to clerks, secretaries, and other lay persons. Such delegation is proper if the lawyer maintains a direct relationship with his/her client, supervises the delegated work, and has complete professional responsibility for the work product. This delegation enables a lawyer to render legal services more economically and efficiently.

A 1967 opinion elaborates on these standards:

American Bar Association, Formal Opinion 316 (1967). A lawyer can employ lay secretaries, lay investigators, lay detectives, lay researchers, accountants, lay scriveners, non-lawyer draftsmen or non-lawyer researchers. In fact, he may employ non-lawyers to do any task for him except counsel clients about law matters, engage directly in the practice of law, appear in court or appear in formal proceedings a part of the judicial process, so long as it is he who takes the work and vouches for it to the client and becomes responsible for it to the client. In other words, we do not limit the kind of assistance that a lawyer can acquire in any way to persons who are admitted to the Bar, so long as the non-lawyers do not do things that lawyers may not do or do the things that lawyers only may do.

The more recent ABA Model Rules of Professional Conduct provides as follows:

Rule 5.3. Responsibilities Regarding Nonlawyer Assistants

With respect to a nonlawyer employed or retained by or associated with a lawyer:

(a) a partner in a law firm shall make reasonable efforts to ensure that the firm has in effect measures giving reasonable assurance that the person's conduct is compatible with the professional obligations of the lawyer;

(b) a lawyer having direct supervisory authority over the nonlawyer shall make reasonable efforts to ensure that the person's conduct is compatible with the professional obligations of the lawyer; and

(c) a lawyer shall be responsible for conduct of such a person that would be a violation of the Rules of Professional Conduct if engaged in by a lawyer if:

(1) the lawyer orders or ratifies the conduct involved; or

(2) the lawyer is a partner in the law firm in which the person is employed, or has direct supervisory authority over the person, and knows of the conduct at a time when its consequences can be avoided or mitigated but fails to take reasonable remedial action.

COMMENT:

Lawyers generally employ assistants in their practice, including secretaries, investigators, law student interns, and paraprofessionals. Such assistants, whether employees or independent contractors, act for the lawyer in rendition of the lawyer's professional services. A lawyer should give such assistants appropriate instruction and supervision concerning the ethical aspects of their employment, particularly regarding the obligation not to disclose information relating to representation of the client, and should be responsible for their work product. The measures employed in supervising nonlawyers should take account of the fact that they do not have legal training and are not subject to professional discipline.

———————

Both the Model Code and the Model Rules are somewhat general in their coverage of paralegals. The paramount theme appears to be the necessity of supervision of the paralegal. We shall examine this and related themes later (p. 262). For now we turn to the more specific provisions of the state and local bar associations on paralegal use.

3. STATE AND LOCAL BAR ASSOCIATIONS AND PARALEGALS

SUMMARY OF SPECIFIC ETHICAL PROBLEMS
(See also the opinions of bar associations on paralegal use in Appendix G, p. 887.)

1. *Can the titles "paralegal," "legal assistant," "legal technician," etc., be used?*

Yes. Almost all states accept this terminology. Years ago there were several bar associations that were afraid that the terminology might be confusing to members of the public who might think that the person is a lawyer. Given the greater use of paralegals today, this is no longer perceived as a serious danger.

2. *Can a paralegal sign letters using his/her own name on law firm stationery, e.g., to a client, to opposing counsel?*

Most states say yes, so long as the nonlawyer status of the paralegal is clear when s/he signs the letter and the letter does not give legal advice or involve the application of legal knowledge. A minority of states, however, say that paralegals can sign only routine, ministerial letters, e.g., to law firm vendors.

3. Can a paralegal's name be printed at the top of the stationery of a law firm?

The states are split on this question. There was a time when most states prohibited the printing of a nonlawyer's name on law firm stationery. It was felt that this would offend the dignity of the profession and give the impression that the firm was advertising itself. Since *Bates v. State Bar of Arizona*, 433 U.S. 350 (1970), which held that the bar could not prohibit all forms of lawyer advertising, a number of states have allowed a paralegal's name to be printed on law firm stationery. Other states, however, have continued the prohibition.

For an example of the stationery of a well-known lawyer, Melvin Belli—who allows paralegal names to be printed on law firm stationery—see Appendix H, p. 899.

4. Can a paralegal have his/her own business card on which the name of the law firm is also printed?

Yes, in most states. The nonlawyer status of the paralegal must be clear on the card and the law firm must have approved the format and content of the card. The card must not be used to solicit business for the firm.

It is unethical for a lawyer or paralegal to stir up legal business. Lawyers can engage in dignified and truthful advertising, but cannot "ambulance chase," e.g., hand a business card to someone who has just had an automobile accident when the person has not asked for any legal help.

5. In oral communications with those outside the office, must the paralegal make clear early in the conversation that s/he is not an attorney?

Yes, unless the paralegal's nonlawyer status is already known to the outside individual with whom the paralegal is dealing. No one must be misled into thinking the paralegal is an attorney.

6. Can the name and title of a paralegal be printed on the door of the law firm?

The few states that have considered this question have concluded that it is improper for a lawyer to allow this.

7. Can a paralegal's name be listed on any pleading, brief, or other document presented to a court?

The few states that have considered this question have split. Some say no, since only an attorney's name may appear. Others say yes, if the paralegal's name is mentioned in a footnote and his/her nonlawyer status is clear.

It is anticipated that restrictions on the mention of a paralegal's name on such documents will soon disappear. In fact, a paralegal's role in litigation is given formal recognition in some court opinions printed in the reporter volumes (p. 525) that contain the full text of the court opinions. Traditionally, opinions in these volumes list the names of the lawyers who litigated the case. For an example of this, see p. 640. When paralegals have had a major role in the preparation of the briefs submitted to the appellate court (p. 695), the names of these paralegals are sometimes printed along with the names of the lawyers involved. Here is an example of a paralegal listed along with the lawyers who litigated the case found in the opinion of *United States v. Cooke,* 625 F.2d 19 (4th Cir. 1980) written by the United States Court of Appeals for the Fourth Circuit:

> Thomas J. Keith, Winston-Salem, N.C., for appellant.
>
> David B. Smith, Asst. U.S. Atty. (H.M. Michaux, Jr., U.S. Atty., Durham, N.C., Becky M. Strickland, Paralegal Specialist on brief), for appellee.
>
> Before HALL and PHILLIPS, Circuit Judges, and HOFFMAN, Senior District Judge.*

PER CURIAM:

For another example from the Court of Appeals of Oregon, see *Nelson v. Adult and Family Services Division,* 42 Or.App. 865, 601 P.2d 899 (Or.App. 1979).

8. *Can a paralegal and a lawyer form a partnership?*

No, if any part of the partnership involves the practice of law.

9. *Can a paralegal and a lawyer share fees?*

No. This would be the equivalent of the paralegal having a partnership interest in the firm.

10. *Can a paralegal participate in a retirement program of the law firm even though the program is based in whole or in part on a profit sharing arrangement?*

Yes. An exception is made to allow the paralegal to have this kind of financial interest in the firm.

11. *Can a paralegal tell someone outside the firm what s/he learns about a case while working at the firm?*

No. Doing so would be one of the most serious mistakes a paralegal could make. Clients have a right to have information about their cases kept confidential. See also p. 247. Later, we will examine this issue in greater detail when we discuss the free-lance paralegal and the ethical problems involved when a paralegal switches jobs, p. 266.

12. *Can a paralegal communicate with the client of the opposing side?*

No, unless opposing counsel gives permission for such communication.

13. *Can a paralegal communicate with opposing counsel?*

Most states would allow this so long as the paralegal's nonlawyer status is clear and the communication is routine.

14. *Can a paralegal represent clients at administrative hearings?*

Yes, if the agency gives specific authorization for such representation (p. 226, p. 865). This authorization would also cover giving the client legal advice and drafting documents for the client pertaining to the agency matter.

15. *Can an inmate give legal assistance to another inmate?*

Yes, if the prison does not provide any adequate alternatives for inmates to receive legal help. This does not, however, include the right of one inmate to represent another inmate in court (p. 223).

16. *Can a paralegal appear in court?*

In some lower courts, e.g., small claims court, justice of the peace court, paralegals can represent clients (p. 213). A few states authorize paralegals to set dates on cases and perform similar routine or administrative functions (p. 215).

17. *Can a paralegal attend a real estate closing in the absence of a supervising attorney?*

Most states allow this so long as the paralegal does not give legal advice or engage in negotiations. Some states, however, forbid the paralegal's attendance unless the attorney is also present (p. 887).

18. *Can a paralegal prepare and draft legal documents?*

Yes, so long as the supervising attorney approves the documents. The oversight of the attorney must be such that the document loses its separate identity as a document of the paralegal; it must become the document of the attorney.

19. *Can a paralegal ask questions at a deposition?*

No. This would constitute the unauthorized practice of law.

20. *Can a paralegal interview clients without an attorney being present?*

Yes, so long as the attorney has given the paralegal instructions for the interview and is generally supervising the paralegal.

Many states have written ethical opinions specifically on paralegal use. Several of these opinions are printed in Appendix G (p. 887). Some states have also prepared reports that contain guidelines in this area.

Kentucky has adopted comprehensive (and liberal) rules on paralegal use. They are found within the Paralegal Code, which has been officially approved by the Supreme Court of Kentucky and incorporated within Rule 3 of the Court. The Paralegal Code is reprinted below in full. First, however, we need to examine a controversial part of the Code: Sub-Rule 2.

> **Sub-Rule 2**
> *For purposes of this rule, the unauthorized practice of law shall not include any service rendered involving legal knowledge or legal advice, whether representation, counsel or advocacy in or out of court, rendered in respect to the acts, duties, obligation, liabilities or business relations of the one requiring services where:*
> A.   *The client understands that the paralegal is not a lawyer;*
> B.   *The lawyer supervises the paralegal in the performance of his duties; and*

C. *The lawyer remains fully responsible for such representation, including all actions taken or not taken in connection therewith by the paralegal to the same extent as if such representation had been furnished entirely by the lawyer and all such actions had been taken or not taken directly by the lawyer.*

Read this rule slowly three or four times. It is a fascinating statement. By studying it carefully, we not only can gain insight into the paralegal role, but also can learn a great deal about legal analysis (p. 371) and interpretation.

Arguably, there are two possible interpretations of Sub-Rule 2. Do you agree?

Broad Interpretation. Three conditions are laid out in the rule: understanding, supervision, and responsibility. (A) The client must *understand* that the paralegal is a nonlawyer; (B) the lawyer must *supervise* the paralegal; and (C) the lawyer must be fully *responsible* for what the paralegal does. If these three conditions are met, the paralegal can do just about anything. Compliance with the three conditions will prevent the paralegal from being charged with the unauthorized practice of law.

Under this interpretation, the rule constitutes a major *expansion* of paralegal responsibilities.

For example, a paralegal can give legal advice to a client on a divorce case—so long as the client knows that the paralegal is not a lawyer, the lawyer is supervising the client, and the lawyer is responsible for the advice given by the paralegal. Perhaps the main problem here would be the supervision condition. As we will see, however, supervision does not necessarily mean that the lawyer must be standing over the shoulder of the paralegal everytime the latter does something (p. 262). Supervision can mean general supervision, e.g., providing guidelines for the paralegal. The paralegal could be giving the client legal advice within the framework of these guidelines.

Another example: a paralegal under Sub-Rule 2 could conduct a deposition of a witness. A deposition is a pretrial proceeding in which a person is questioned as part of a trial preparation strategy (p. 471). While normally it would be considered the unauthorized practice of law for a paralegal to conduct a deposition, the activity is arguably permitted in Kentucky under this broad interpretation of Sub-Rule 2 if the three conditions can be met. Assume that the client of the office where the paralegal works knows that the paralegal conducting the deposition is not a lawyer; assume also that the lawyer has trained the paralegal to depose witnesses and has provided clear directions on how this particular deposition should be conducted by the paralegal; and finally assume that the lawyer is ultimately responsible for whatever the paralegal does in the deposition. The three conditions, therefore, are met.

Sub-Rule 2 says that paralegals will not be charged with the unauthorized practice of law simply because they render legal advice, engage in representation, counsel, or advocacy in or out of court—so long as the three conditions are met.

Narrow Interpretation. The rule does *not* add any new authorized tasks to the paralegal role. It simply clarifies what we already know.

The critical word is in the second line of the rule: "involving." The word means *connected with* or *pertaining to.* There is a major difference, for example, between (a) giving legal advice and (b) engaging in an activity *involving* legal advice. The rule simply says that the latter is permitted; it does not authorize the former. A paralegal can engage in an activity "involving" legal advice without actually being the person who gives the advice. For example, the paralegal interviews the client to collect facts and does legal research in the library on these facts. The *lawyer* eventually gives legal advice to the client based in part on the interview and research conducted by the paralegal. Sub-Rule 2 is telling us that paralegal activities such as interviewing and research are not prohibited simply because they are part of a process leading to (i.e., "involving") legal advice.

So too, the rule does not authorize paralegals to conduct depositions or to engage in other advocacy and representation roles in or out of court. The lawyer is still the one who is solely authorized to perform these functions. To argue otherwise is to come close to abolishing any meaningful distinction between a paralegal and a lawyer. Again, all Sub-Rule 2 does is make clear that the paralegal is not acting illegally simply because he or she is assigned responsibilities "involving" advocacy and representation *so long as the paralegal is acting in the traditional capacity as assistant to a lawyer.* There is a distinction between being an advocate oneself, and engaging in activities that assist someone else (the lawyer) to act as an advocate. Sub-Rule 2 simply says that the latter is not the unauthorized practice of law; it does not authorize the paralegal to do the former.

Assignment 17

Which interpretation of Sub-Rule 2 is correct? If the narrow interpretation is correct, what does it add? Why was the rule needed?

Here now is the *entire* Kentucky Paralegal Code of which the controversial Sub-Rule 2 is a part.

KENTUCKY PARALEGAL CODE

RULE 3.700 Provisions Relating to Paralegals

Preliminary Statement

The availability of legal services to the public at a price it can afford is a goal to which the Bar is committed, and one which finds support in Canons 2 and 8 of the Code of Professional Responsibility. The employment of paralegals furnishes a means by which lawyers may expand the public's opportunity for utilization of their services at a reduced cost.

For purposes of this Rule, a paralegal is a person under the supervision and direction of a licensed lawyer, who may apply knowledge of law and legal procedures in rendering direct assistance to lawyers engaged in legal research; design, develop or plan modifications or new procedures, techniques, services, processes or applications; prepare or interpret legal documents and write detailed procedures for practicing in certain fields of law; select, compile and use technical information from such references as digests, encyclopedias or practice manuals; and analyze and follow procedural problems that involve independent decisions.

Purpose

Rapid growth in the employment of paralegals increases the desirability and necessity of establishing guidelines for the utilization of paralegals by the legal community. This Rule is not intended to stifle the proper development and expansion of paralegal services, but to provide guidance and ensure growth in accordance with the Code of Professional Responsibility, statutes, court rules and decisions, rules and regulations of administrative agencies, and opinions rendered by Committees on Professional Ethics and Unauthorized Practice of Law.

While the responsibility for compliance with standards of professional conduct rests with members of the Bar, a paralegal should understand those standards. It is, therefore, incumbent upon the lawyer employing a paralegal to inform him of the restraints and responsibilities incident to the job and supervise the manner in which the work is completed. However, the paralegal does have an independent obligation to refrain from illegal conduct. Additionally, and notwithstanding the fact that the Code of Professional Responsibility is not binding upon lay persons, the very nature of a paralegal's employment imposes an obligation to refrain from conduct which would involve the lawyer in a violation of the Code.

Sub-Rule 1
A lawyer shall ensure that a paralegal in his employment does not engage in the unauthorized practice of law.

Commentary

The Kentucky Constitution, Section 109, creates one Court of Justice for the Commonwealth. Section 116 empowers the Kentucky Supreme Court to promulgate rules of practice and procedure for the Court of Justice. In addition, the Supreme Court has statutory authority to govern the conduct and activity of members of the Bar. KRS 21A.160.

Pursuant to constitutional and statutory authority, the Kentucky Supreme Court has adopted rules which govern the unauthorized practice of law. SCR 3.020 defines the practice of law in general and descriptive terms. SCR 3.470 provides that any attorney who aids another in the unauthorized practice of law shall be guilty of unprofessional conduct. SCR 3.460 delineates the procedure to be followed when a person or entity "not having the right to practice law" engages in the practice of law.

As of January 1, 1978, the American Bar Association Code of Professional Responsibility was accepted as a sound statement of professional conduct for members of the Kentucky Bar Association, with the exception of provisions which conflict with *Bates v. St. Bar of Arizona.* [See p. 279.].

Canon 3 of the Code of Professional Responsibility provides that "A lawyer should assist in preventing the unauthorized practice of law." Further, "A lawyer shall not aid a non-lawyer in the unauthorized practice of law." DR 3-101(A). The rationale of this Sub-rule may be found in EC 3-1 through EC 3-6 of the [ABA] Code of Professional Responsibility.

The foregoing authorities demonstrate that paralegals cannot, any more than any other person or entity, engage in the unauthorized practice of law. Members of the Bar who employ paralegals incur a professional responsibility to ensure that their paralegal employees do not transgress the rules governing the practice of law contained in these authorities and thereby involve their employers in violations of their own professional responsibilities. A lawyer may, however, allow a paralegal to perform services involving the practice of law, providing that such services comply with the requirements of Sub-rule 2 and Sub-rule 3.

Sub-Rule 2
For purposes of this rule, the unauthorized practice of law shall not include any service rendered involving legal knowledge or legal advice, whether representation, counsel or advocacy in or out of court, rendered in respect to the acts, duties, obligation, liabilities or business relations of the one requiring services where:
A. *The client understands that the paralegal is not a lawyer;*
B. *The lawyer supervises the paralegal in the performance of his duties; and*
C. *The lawyer remains fully responsible for such representation, including all actions taken or not taken in connection therewith by the paralegal to the same extent as if such representation had been furnished entirely by the lawyer and all such actions had been taken or not taken directly by the lawyer.*

Commentary
The Code of Professional Responsibility, in particular EC 3-6, recognizes the value of utilizing the services of paralegals under certain conditions:

> "A lawyer often delegates tasks to clerks, secretaries, and other lay persons. Such delegation is proper if the lawyer maintains a direct relationship with his client, supervises the delegated work, and has complete professional responsibility for the work product. This delegation enables a lawyer to render legal services more economically and efficiently."

Maintaining a "direct relationship" with the client does not preclude a paralegal from meeting with the client nor does it mandate regular and frequent meetings between the lawyer and client. However, when it appears that consultation between the lawyer and the client is necessary, the lawyer should talk directly to the client.

Sub-Rule 3
For purposes of this rule, the unauthorized practice of law shall not include representation before any administrative tribunal or court where such service or representation is rendered pursuant to a court rule or deci-

sion, statute, or administrative rule or regulation, which authorizes such practice by nonlawyers.

Commentary

Notwithstanding the restrictions imposed upon nonlawyers with respect to engaging in the practice of law, exceptions exist by virtue of statute, administrative rule or regulation, or court rule or decision. Under certain circumstances, lay representation of parties does not constitute the unauthorized practice of law. For example, the Federal Administrative Procedure Act, Title 5, U.S.C. Section 555(b) authorizes federal administrative agencies to permit nonlawyers to represent parties in proceedings before the agencies [p. 226]. Such lay representation is also provided for in statutes and regulations governing administrative proceedings involving the Public Assistance (AFDC), Medicaid, and Food Stamp Programs. See, 42 U.S.C. Section 601, Section 602 (1977); 42 U.S.C. Section 1396 (1977); 7 U.S.C. Section 2019 (1977); and the implementing regulations, 45 C.F.R. Section 205.10(a), and 7 C.F.R. Section 271.1(a)(1) (1977). [See a more complete list in Appendix E, p. 865.]

The Kentucky Department of Human Resources has implemented these federal regulations. Lay representation is specifically provided for in regulations governing hearings and appeals in certain programs. 904 KAR 2:055, Section 1–12.

The United States Supreme Court has held that federal law controls the administration of federal grant-in-aid programs. *See, King v. Smith,* 392 U.S. 309, 332-333 (1968); *Rosado v. Wyman,* U.S. 397, 421–422 (1970). Additionally, the Court has held that in federally regulated areas, federal statutes and regulations prevail over a state's power to define and regulate the practice of law. *See, Sperry v. Florida,* 373 U.S. 379, 385 (1963); and *Keller v. State Bar of Wisconsin,* 374 U.S. 102 (1963), citing *Sperry* [p. 230].

Sub-Rule 4
A lawyer shall instruct a paralegal employee to preserve the confidences and secrets of a client and shall exercise care that the paralegal does so.

Commentary

This Sub-rule reiterates the Code of Professional Responsibility. Canon 4, DR 4-101(D) provides in part that:

"(D) A lawyer shall exercise reasonable care to prevent his employees, associates, and others whose services are utilized by him from disclosing or using confidences or secrets of a client. . . ."

This obligation is emphasized in EC 4-2 under Canon 4:

". . . It is a matter of common knowledge that the normal operation of a law office exposes confidential professional information to nonlawyer employees of the office, particularly secretaries and those having access to the files; and this obligates a lawyer to exercise care in selecting and training his employees so that the sanctity of all confidences and secrets of his clients may be preserved."

Sub-Rule 5
A lawyer shall not form a partnership with a paralegal if any part of the partnership's activities consists of the practice of law, nor shall a lawyer share on a proportionate basis, legal fees with a paralegal.

Commentary

This Sub-rule is based on the express provisions of DR 3-102(A) and DR 3-103(A) of the Code of Professional Responsibility. In accordance with these provisions, the compensation of a paralegal may not include a percentage of the fees received by his employer, or any remuneration, directly or indirectly, for referring matters of a legal nature to the employer.

DR 3-103(A) provides that: "A lawyer shall not form a partnership with a non-lawyer if any of the activities of the partnership consists of the practice of law." The rationale is found in EC 3-8: "Since a lawyer should not aid or encourage a layman to practice law, he should not practice law in association with a layman. . . ." However, "A lawyer or law firm may include non-lawyer employees in a retirement plan, even though the plan is based in whole or in part on a profit-sharing arrangement." CR 3-102(A)(3).

This Disciplinary Rule also reflects the rationale of EC 3-8:

> "Since a layer should not aid or encourage a layman to practice law, he should not . . . share legal fees with a layman."

> "Profit-sharing retirement plans of a lawyer or law firm which include nonlawyer office employees are not improper. These limited exceptions to the rule against sharing legal fees with laymen are permissible since they do not aid or encourage laymen to practice law."

Sub-Rule 6
The letterhead of a lawyer may include the name of a paralegal where the paralegal's status is clearly indicated; A lawyer may permit his name to be included in a paralegal's business card, provided that the paralegal's status is clearly indicated.

Commentary

The Code of Professional Responsibility, in particular DR 2-102(A)(4), provides direction concerning the information which may be provided on a lawyer's letterhead. In keeping with the spirit of DR 2-102(A)(4), paralegals may be listed on the letterhead if there is a clear indication of their status, i.e., they are not lawyers. These names should properly be listed under the separate heading of "Paralegals."

A paralegal may have a business card with the lawyer's name or law firm's name on it, provided the status of the paralegal is clearly indicated. It is not necessary that any lawyer's name appear on such business card. The card is designed to identify the paralegal and to state by whom the paralegal is employed. The business card of a paralegal shall be approved, in form and substance, by the lawyer-employer.

Sub-Rule 7
A lawyer shall require a paralegal, when dealing with a client, to disclose
at the outset that he is not a lawyer. A lawyer shall also require such a dis-
closure when the paralegal is dealing with a court, administrative agen-
cy, attorney or the public, if there is any reason for their believing that the
paralegal is a lawyer or is associated with a lawyer.

Commentary

A lawyer should instruct a paralegal employee to disclose at the beginning of any dealings with a client that he is not an attorney. Whenever
any person dealing with a paralegal has reason to believe that the paralegal is a lawyer or associated with a lawyer, the paralegal shall make clear
that he is not a lawyer. Even if a paralegal appears before an administrative agency or court in which a lay person is entitled to represent a party,
the paralegal should nevertheless disclose his status to the tribunal. Routine early disclosure of non-lawyer status is necessary to ensure that there
will be no misunderstanding as to the responsibilities and role of the paralegal. Disclosure may be made in any way that avoids confusion. Common
sense suggests a routine disclosure at the outset of communication.

If a paralegal is designated as the individual in the office of a lawyer
or law firm who should be contacted, disclosure of his or her non-lawyer
status should be made at the time of such designation.

Paralegal Supervision

The topic of paralegal supervision appears to be an important issue as indicated in the above Code, in the list of specific paralegal issues raised in the states
(p. 252), and in the ABA Model Code and Model Rules (p. 251). We need to
examine this topic more closely.

Attorney Grievance Committee of Md. v. Goldberg
292 Md. 650, 441 A.2d 338, 442 (1982)

[T]he public must be protected. Lawyers must be impressed with the fact that
at all times they have a responsibility to their clients. This responsibility necessarily includes adequate supervision of their employees.

Statsky, W., *Paraprofessionals: Expanding the Legal Service Delivery*
Team, 24 Journal of Legal Education 397, 408 (1972)

A primary requirement of the paralegal-lawyer relationship is the supervision by the lawyer of all delegated work. What is supervision and
how do lawyers exercise it? When a lawyer standardizes and specializes
his/her practice through the utilization of forms and the hiring of paralegals, what kind of supervision is given? Is it the supervision of an overseer
of a system who limits his/her contacts with office personnel to crisis intervention, or is it the supervision of a superintendent who maintains an

event-by-event vigilance? There are no definitive answers to these questions that would satisfy the ethical purist. Consequently the paralegal is given a considerable arena in which to roam depending upon his/her employing attorney's conception of supervision.

ILLINOIS STATE BAR ASSOCIATION,
Report of the Joint Study Committee on
Attorney Assistants, *p. 41 (7/21/77)*

The lawyer must maintain a "direct relationship with his client," he must supervise the *delegated* work and maintain complete professional responsibility for the work product [according to the requirements of EC 3-6, p. 251].

As long as these three standards are maintained no problem arises from the use of lay personnel. The employment of secretaries presents few or no problems in terms of unauthorized practice, or in terms of a misled public, because the employment of a secretary does not interfere with any of the three precepts of EC 3-6.

The employment of lay personnel to prepare material for real estate closings, obtain preliminary data perhaps from the client or from other sources, to abstract depositions, and the like, does present problems under this ethical consideration [EC 3-6], unless the lawyer in the administration of the law office is able to establish the guidelines and job descriptions which prevent a transgression of the three standards.

For example, the maintenance of a direct relationship with the client will be jeopardized frequently unless there are clear directions to the lay person as to what he or she may do or not do. We return again to the importance of the precise job description. Whether this be reduced to writing—which appears to be sound management practice anyway—or is delivered by clear oral instructions, the lay person must know in handling the real estate closing, for example, what is within the job and what lies outside the permitted area of delegation. In the absence of such a clear direction, under the normal tensions of a law office, sooner or later the lay employee will in the pressure of time, transgress the bounds. Prevention thereof lies not in generalized directions of what constitutes unauthorized practice; it lies in precise job descriptions and definitions for all lay personnel.

The second precept of EC 3-6 again calls for a management decision. What constitutes "supervising" the "delegated work"? Obviously, the entire purpose of hiring a lay employee is to avoid the necessity of standing over the assistant's shoulder and saying which blank is to be filled in, what document is to be forwarded, to whom, etc. Supervision must imply some generalization of instructions and follow-through to see if the instructions have been carried out accurately. In short, when it is applied to attorney assistants, EC 3-6 basically means that the lawyer must manage his or her law office. The statement of EC 3-6 is not [merely] a statement that the lawyer signs the payroll and therefore is boss.

New Mexico Proposed Guidelines for the Use of
Legal Assistant Services,
p. 12 (1980)

A lawyer who hires a legal assistant is responsible for carefully evaluating the legal assistant's education and experience to determine if the assistant can competently perform the tasks which it is contemplated will be assigned. Once a legal assistant is in the employ of a lawyer, the lawyer has a continuing obligation to closely supervise the work of the legal assistant. A lawyer may train a legal assistant to perform increasingly complex assignments under the supervision of the lawyer, and a process of gradually escalating the level of difficulty of the type or types of work assigned to the assistant may be used to raise the skill level of a legal assistant. Specialized instruction provided to a legal assistant, whether through the personal efforts of the lawyer who supervises the assistant or through other means such as seminars or classes, may be helpful in maintaining and raising the assistant's level of competence, but it remains the responsibility of the individual lawyer to determine the extent of the assistant's skills and to delegate to the assistant accordingly. In addition, a lawyer should explain to the legal assistant that the legal assistant has a duty to inform the lawyer of any assignment which the assistant regards as being beyond his or her capability.

As a practical matter, it would be impossible for a lawyer to know everything about what a paralegal is doing all the time. The very concept of delegation assumes the exercise of some responsibility by nonlawyers.

It is often pointed out that a lawyer's relationship with his/her client must be direct and personal. A "lawyer's relation to his client should be personal, and the responsibility should be direct to the client." ABA, Formal Opinion No. 303, Nov. 27, 1961. Does this mean that a paralegal working for the lawyer cannot *also* have a direct relationship with the client? A close reading of EC 3-6, p. 251, does not appear to preclude it. According to a former chairperson of the ABA Special Committee on Legal Assistants, lawyers "delude themselves by believing only a lawyer can deal directly with the client."[12] Those members of the private bar who maintain this position apparently do so on the theory that it is possible for a paralegal to have direct dealings with clients that do not amount to giving advice. This position is probably sound, although some might argue that the manner in which a paralegal interviewer or a paralegal investigator asks a client questions may be interpreted by the client as an indication of what the law is in his/her case even though on the surface no such interpretation is intended by the paralegal. This possibility should not change the general rule, however, that the paralegal can directly deal with a client in addition to the direct and controlling relationship that the lawyer has with the same client.

[12] Turner, *Effective Use of Personnel in the Law Office,* Speech before the Section of Legal Education and Admissions to the Bar and the National Conference of Bar Examiners, p. 4 (8/12/69).

Statsky, W., and Lang, P., *The Legal Paraprofessional as Advocate and Assistant: Roles, Training Concepts, and Materials,* **pp. 47–8 (1971).**

The cardinal principle governing the lawyer-lay assistant relationship is that the dynamics of delegation flow primarily from demonstrated ability rather than from ethical codes or statutory practice norms. Given the time and volume pressures of a practicing attorney, it is submitted that there is almost nothing, short of actual court appearances, that a lawyer will not delegate to a competent paralegal, and it is further submitted that in such a setting, supervision is sometimes left on a "handle-it-as-best-you-can" basis. Close supervision, case-by-case, step-by-step, of the paralegal is not only impractical but in contradiction to the economy and efficiency motives that originally led the lawyer to hire the paralegal. Lawyers are oriented to advocacy, client interaction, and legal research; they are not always good personnel managers. Consequently, supervision tends to be loose, even though the lawyer retains full responsibility to the client for the final work product. Once the paralegal has gained the confidence of his/her employing attorney, has acquired substantial experience in the areas delegated to him/her, has learned that the boss places a premium on the exercise of ingenuity, and has sensed that even the boss does not always have immediate answers to the day-to-day problems that arise, the paralegal tends to fall back more and more onto his/her own resources and judgment of what should be done. Take, for example, the case of the corporate paralegal doing blue sky work for a lawyer in the firm. A corporate client decides to go public and wants to register in all fifty states. The paralegal is assigned the task of compiling the necessary documents and exhibits for each state. An employee of the state of Oklahoma calls the law firm in reference to a particular question on a submitted registration application that pertains to the stated valuation of designated assets. The paralegal takes the call. Will s/he refer it to a lawyer or will s/he handle it alone? The answer will *not* totally depend on whether the paralegal decides that the question is "legal" or "non-legal," but rather will depend on very practical considerations such as:

- Would the lawyer want me to bother him/her with this call?
- Can I handle it myself?
- Have I answered calls like this before without difficulty?

A survey conducted by the American Bar Association's Special Committee on Legal Assistants dealt with the issue of the supervision a paralegal should receive once s/he is trained and experienced. Of the twenty-one firms addressing the point, seven firms felt that paralegals should be "closely supervised by attorneys," whereas fourteen of the firms indicated that a paralegal should be allowed to "work independently under the general direction of the attorney with only the completed work reviewed." American Bar Association, Special Committee on Legal Assistants, The Training and Use of Legal Assistants: A Status Report, p. 10 (Preliminary Draft, 1973). In this same survey 103 paralegals were also asked to state their opinion on the issue of supervision. All but two of the respondents thought that "they should be allowed to work independently under the general direction of the attorney," again with only their "completed work" checked by their supervisor. Id. at p. 16.

It is also relevant to note that both attorneys and paralegals responding to the survey indicated that the activities of paralegals "could be broadened considerably." Id. at p. 20.

The California Committee on Economics of Law Practice has taken the following position on the supervision of paralegals:

> A legal assistant should act only under the supervision of an active member of the State Bar. Adequacy of supervision will depend on the type of legal matter, including the degree of standardization and repetitiveness of the matter, and the experience of the legal assistant generally and with regard to a particular legal matter. Supervision is a matter of the attorney's professional responsibility and competence. Determination of adequacy of supervision with regard to particular legal matters is best left to the State Bar disciplinary bodies and the courts. Standards for supervision may have to be promulgated in the future.

"Law Economics Committee Reports on Certified Attorney Assistants," 13 State Bar of California Reports 2 (No. 7, July, 1973).

It's easier to define what supervision cannot mean than to define it affirmatively. A lawyer cannot delegate to a paralegal the task of arguing a case in court or of advising clients as to their legal rights in non-agency cases no matter how closely the paralegal is supervised by the lawyer in such undertakings. Supervision cannot authorize what is clearly the unauthorized practice of law.

ASSIGNMENT 18

Is too much being made about the issue of supervision? Does it make any difference so long as the lawyer is ultimately responsible for what the paralegal does?

4. THE ATTORNEY-CLIENT PRIVILEGE, CONFIDENTIALITY, AND SPECIAL ETHICAL PROBLEMS FACING THE PARALEGAL WHO SWITCHES JOBS AND THE FREE-LANCE PARALEGAL

Dabney v. Investment Corp. of America
82 F.R.D. 464, 465 (E.D. Pa 1979)

> The attorney-client privilege protects from disclosure confidential communications made for the purpose of obtaining a lawyer's professional advice and assistance. *Cohen v. Uniroyal, Inc,* 80 F.R.D. 480, 482 (E.D.Pa.1978). It has long been held that the privilege applies only to members of the bar, of a court, or their subordinates. . . . Examples of such protected subordinates would include any law student, paralegal, investigator or other person acting as the agent of a duly qualified attorney under circumstances that would otherwise be sufficient to invoke the privilege. 8 Wigmore, Evidence § 2301 (McNaughton Rev. 1961).

Communications made in confidence between an attorney and client relating to representation are protected by the attorney-client privilege. If clients knew that what they told their attorney might eventually be revealed to others, the clients would be reluctant to be open with their attorney. As mentioned earlier, the protection of confidential information encourages clients to communicate fully and frankly with the attorney even as to embarrassing or legally damaging topics (p. 247). If a lawyer is called to the witness stand and is questioned or examined concerning such communications, the lawyer can refuse to answer on the ground that the communications are privileged. Paralegals and others employees of the lawyer can also refuse to answer.

Colorado Revised Statutes (1984 Cum. Supp.)
13-90-107. Who may not testify without consent.

(1)(b) An attorney shall not be examined without the consent of his client as to any communication made by the client to him or his advice given thereon in the course of professional employment; nor shall an attorney's secretary, paralegal, legal assistant, stenographer, or clerk be examined without the consent of his employer concerning any fact, the knowledge of which he has acquired in such capacity.

On page 247, we examined the ethical rules on confidentiality in the ABA Model Code (DR 4-101) and in the Model Rules (Rule 1.6). These regulations make it unethical for a lawyer to reveal confidential information. There is also a provision in the Model Code covering nonlawyers:

DR 4-101(D).
A lawyer shall exercise reasonable care to prevent his employees, associates, and others whose services are utilized by him from disclosing or using confidences or secrets of a client, . . .

Similarly, as we have seen, the comments to Rule 5.3 of the Model Rules (p. 252) provide:

A lawyer should give such assistants appropriate instruction and supervision concerning the ethical aspects of their employment, particularly regarding the obligation not to disclose information relating to representation of the client, . . .

The paralegal associations also stress the importance of confidentiality. As we shall see later, the national associations have published ethical standards and rules (p. 285). They include prohibitions against disclosing confidential information. The *Code of Ethics and Professional Responsibility* of the National Associates of Legal Assistants provides:

Canon 7
A legal assistant must protect the confidences of a client, and it shall be unethical for a legal assistant to violate any statute now in effect or hereafter to be enacted controlling privileged communications.

The Affirmation of Professional Responsibility of the National Federation of Paralegal Associations provides:

IV
A paralegal shall preserve client confidences and privileged communications. Confidential information and privileged communications are a vital part of the attorney, paralegal and client relationship. The importance of preserving

confidential and privileged information is understood to be an uncompromising obligation of every paralegal.

An obvious way that a lawyer or paralegal violates such regulations is to tell a stranger something related to a client's case. For example, a paralegal tells his/her spouse that a particular client at the office confessed to a crime during an interview. The spouse has no right to know such information. The paralegal has revealed confidential information. Another example: A lawyer represents Bob Smith on a divorce case and Linda Jackson on an unemployment compensation claim. Bob and Linda happen to know each other. In a conversation with Linda one day, the lawyer tells her that Bob is selling his business at a reduced price in order to try to prevent his wife from interfering with the business in the divorce case. Linda has no right to know such information. The lawyer has revealed confidential information.

Lawyers must be scrupulous in avoiding such breaches of confidentiality. They are under an ethical obligation to avoid even the appearance of impropriety (p. 250).

If there is a danger that a lawyer will breach client confidentiality, the lawyer is *disqualified* from taking or continuing the representation. We will examine this issue from both the lawyer and the paralegal perspective through the following hypothetical:

> Mary is a lawyer in the law firm of Smith & Smith. At the firm, one of her clients is Bill in the negligence case of Bill v. Fred involving an automobile accident. Fred is not represented by counsel.

These facts can give rise to a number of troublesome situations:

> #1: Bill becomes dissatisfied with Mary and dismisses her as his lawyer. *Fred* now tries to hire Mary to represent him in the same negligence case against Bill.

Mary would be disqualified from representing Fred unless Bill consents to such representation. Fred and Bill clearly have adverse interests in the negligence case. If Mary represented Fred, she would surely be using information against Bill that she obtained while she represented Bill. Unless Bill agrees to allow Mary to represent Fred after being fully apprised of the situation, Mary is disqualified from representing Fred.

> #2: Mary decides to leave Smith & Smith in order to become a partner in the firm of Jones & Jones. When she arrives, she discovers that Fred had just retained Jones & Jones in his negligence case against Bill. The firm asks Mary to represent Fred in this case.

To do so would be ethically improper for the same reasons given in situation #1 above. Bill and Fred still have adverse interests. Mary would be using information against Bill that she acquired while representing Bill. This is unethical regardless of the firm for which Mary works—unless Bill consents.

> #3: Bob is a senior attorney at Jones & Jones. The firm asks Bob to represent Fred in the negligence case against Bill.

Again, to do so would be ethically improper. It makes no difference that Bob never represented Bill before. Since Mary is disqualified from representing Bill, *every* member of her new firm is also disqualified if the parties (Bill and

Fred) still have adverse interests, and Mary acquired important or material information while she worked at the other firm on the same or substantially same case.

> #4: Assume that Mary does not change jobs; she remains at the firm of Smith & Smith. Assume also that Bill is *not* dissatisfied with Mary's work in the Bill v. Fred negligence case; he does not fire her as his attorney. George is Mary's paralegal at Smith & Smith. He works extensively with Mary on the Bill v. Fred case. Before the case is over, George decides to leave Smith & Smith in order to take a paralegal position with another law firm, Holmes & Holmes. After he arrives, he discovers that Fred has retained Holmes & Holmes to represent him in the Bill v. Fred negligence case.

The ethical question is whether Holmes & Holmes is disqualified from representing Fred because of George's prior work on the Bill v. Fred case while he worked at Smith & Smith. There are no clear answers to this question. The field of paralegalism is still too new. But the problem is not academic in view of the fact that paralegals frequently change jobs.

If no ethical restrictions existed, Holmes & Holmes would be delighted that George once worked on Bill's behalf while George was a paralegal at Smith & Smith. George could tell the attorneys at Holmes & Holmes everything he learned while he was Mary's paralegal. Such information could be quite useful as the firm prepares its defense of Fred. For example, George might know that Bill was not wearing his contact lenses at the time of the accident. The attorneys at Holmes & Holmes may not know this yet. Clearly Smith & Smith could argue that it would be unfair to Bill if Holmes & Holmes had access to such information.

The courts might handle the problem a number of ways. First, a court could treat the case the same way regardless of whether a lawyer or paralegal is involved. If so, Holmes & Holmes would be disqualified from representing Fred because of the paralegal's prior involvement in the case, in the same manner that it would be disqualified if an attorney had switched firms. The critical tests are the presence of adverse interests between the parties on the same or substantially same case, and the acquisition of material information while working on the case in the first firm. A second and less drastic approach would be to require Holmes & Holmes to remove the paralegal from the case. Smith & Smith may not be happy with such a solution. Its preference would probably be to require Holmes & Holmes to fire the paralegal. But dismissing the paralegal would not be necessary so long as the court is convinced that Holmes & Holmes would completely disassociate the paralegal from the Bill v. Fred litigation. Some overly cautious firms, however, may still dismiss the paralegal even if they are not required to do so. They will probably be less concerned with the paralegal's welfare than the risk of losing the right to represent the party because of potential ethical problems.

> #5: Same situation as in #4 above except that this time George is a free-lance paralegal. He has his own office and sells his services directly to law firms (p. 61, p. 901). For three days in March he worked for Smith & Smith indexing a deposition transcript in the Bill v. Fred negligence case. For six days in May, he undertook some investigation for Holmes & Holmes in the same Bill v. Fred negligence case.

The same problems arise here as in situation #4. It should make no difference whether the paralegal is a salaried employee or an independent free-lancer *if* both kinds of paralegals had the same access to information about the case while they were acting on behalf of Bill at the first firm, Smith & Smith. At one extreme, a court might disqualify Holmes & Holmes from representing Fred, while at the other extreme, it might simply force Holmes & Holmes to stop the paralegal from working on the Bill v. Fred case.

Again, we cannot be sure what a court will do because of the relative newness of the issue and of paralegalism itself.[13]

Finally, a word of advice to the paralegal: keep your own record of case names. Whenever you work on a case, make a note of the names of the parties and of opposing counsel. You do not want to find yourself working on both sides of a case! If you ever change jobs or go into free-lance work, you should refer to this list. Disclose all relevant facts to your supervisors. The most effective way to solve an ethical problem is to avoid it.

5. DOING LEGAL RESEARCH ON AN ETHICAL ISSUE

If you were researching an ethical issue in your state, your strategy would be as follows:

- Find the state bar association's canons of ethics, often called the Canons of Professional Responsibility. The canons will probably have been approved by the state's highest court. They may also be printed in the court rules (p. 534). Check your local bar association and law libraries in your area
- Determine which bar association committee has jurisdiction over the enforcement of these canons. Call or write the state bar association and ask. Find out if this committee writes ethical opinions applying the canons. If the issue you are researching involves paralegals, determine if another bar committee has special jurisdiction over paralegals. If so, find out what this committee has said. Also check the digest covering your state (p. 541) to locate any court opinions on lawyer ethics.
- If the issues you are researching have never been raised in your state bar association and state courts, check the positions of the ABA in its canons and ethical opinions to determine whether they have covered the issue. In particular, read the ABA Model Code of Professional Responsibility, the more recent ABA Model Rules of Professional Conduct, and ethical opinions interpreting both documents (p. 244). Most large law libraries should have these documents.
- If you find that the ABA has covered your issue, examine the ABA position and then make an argument to your state and local bar association on whether it should adopt the ABA position. Remember, however, that the state and local bar association is not required to accept what the ABA

---

[13] For an actual court opinion on a similar issue, see p. 381. See also Marguardt, *Running with the Hares and Chasing with the Hounds: The Emerging Dilemma in Paralegal Mobility,* 2 Journal of Paralegal Education 57 (American Association for Paralegal Education, Oct. 1984).

has said. An ABA position can only be persuasive authority (p. 561).
- You should determine what the bar associations of other states have said about your issue. For example, check the *Code of Professional Responsibility by State* (ABA, National Center for Professional Responsibility, 1980). Also check the *ABA/BNA Lawyer's Manual on Professional Conduct: Current Reports* (BNA, 1984–) and the *National Reporter on Legal Ethics and Professional Responsibility* (University Publications of America, 1983–). Such publications, found in large law libraries, may give you leads to the ethical rules and opinions of other states. Again, your state is not required to adopt what other states have said. They can only be persuasive authority.

ASSIGNMENT 19

Draft your own paralegal code as a class project. First, have a meeting in which you make a list of all the issues that you think should be covered in the code. Divide up the issues by the number of students in the class so that every student has roughly the same number of issues. Each student should draft a proposed rule on each of the issues to which s/he is assigned. Accompany each rule with a brief commentary on why you think the rule should be as stated. Draft alternative versions of the proposed rule if different versions are possible and you want to give the class the chance to examine all of them. The class then meets to vote on each of the proposed rules. Students will make presentations on the proposed rules they have drafted. If the class is not happy with the way in which a particular proposed rule was drafted by a student, the latter will re-draft the rule for later consideration by the class. One member of the class should be designated the "code reporter" who records the rules accepted by the class by majority vote.

After you have completed the code, you should consider inviting lawyers from the local bar association to your class in order to discuss your proposed code. Do the same with officials of the closest paralegal association in your area.

In the following problems, unless otherwise indicated, determine whether any ethical problems exist. If so, state what they are. Use the material on the preceding pages to explain how the problems would be resolved. Also, consult the ethical opinions in Appendix G, p. 887. If there are different ways that have been used to resolve the problems, state the alternative resolutions. Then state what you personally think the resolution of the problems should be.

ASSIGNMENT 20

John Smith is a paralegal who works for the firm of Beard, Butler, and Clark. John's immediate supervisor is Viola Butler, Esq. With the full knowledge and blessing of Viola Butler, John Smith sends a letter to a client of the firm (Mary

Anders). Has Viola Butler acted unethically in permitting John to send out this letter? The letter is as follows:

Law Offices of
Beard, Butler, and Clark
310 High St.
Maincity, Ohio 45238
512-663-9410

Attorneys at Law   *Paralegal*

Ronald Beard   John Smith
Viola Butler
Wilma Clark

                                                                     May 14, 1986

Mary Anders
621 S. Randolph Ave.
Maincity, Ohio 45238

Dear Ms. Anders:

   Viola Butler, the attorney in charge of your case, has asked me to let you know that next month's hearing has been postponed. We will let you know the new date as soon as possible. If you have any questions don't hesitate to call me.

                         Sincerely,

                         John Smith

JS:wps

ASSIGNMENT 21

Same facts as in Assignment 20 except that the word "Paralegal" and John Smith's name are *not* printed at the top of the law firm's stationery letterhead and the closing of the letter is as follows:

                         Sincerely,

                         John Smith
                         Legal Aide

ASSIGNMENT 22

Suppose that as part of your educational program you were placed in a law firm for an internship period in order to gain some practical experience. While there, you are referred to as a "legal intern." Under what circumstances, if any, could you refer to yourself as a "legal intern," e.g., on the phone, in a letter?

ASSIGNMENT 23

Under what circumstances, if any, would it be appropriate for you to refer to a client of the office where you work as "my client"?

ASSIGNMENT 24

John Smith is a paralegal who works for Beard, Butler, and Clark. He sends out the following letter. Any ethical problems?

John Smith
Paralegal
310 High St.
Maincity, Ohio 45238
512-663-9410

June 1, 1985

State Unemployment Board
1216 Southern Ave.
Maincity, Ohio 45238

Dear Gentlepeople:

   I work for Beard, Butler, and Clark, which represents Mary Anders who has a claim before your agency. A hearing originally scheduled for June 8, 1985 has been postponed. We request that the hearing be held at the earliest time possible after the 8th.

Sincerely,

John Smith

JS:wps

ASSIGNMENT 25

John Jones is a paralegal who works for an attorney named Linda Sunders. Linda is away from the office one day and telephones John who is at the office. She dictates a one-line letter to a client of the office. The letter reads, "I advise you to sue." Linda asks John to sign the letter for her. The bottom of the letter reads as follows:

Linda Sunders
by John Jones

Any ethical problems?

ASSIGNMENT 26

John Jones is a paralegal who works for the XYZ law firm that represents hundreds of corporations throughout the United States. John specializes in corporate law at the firm. One of the corporations makes a request of the firm that it send the corporation certain information on filing requirements with the Secretary of State. The attorney supervising John knows that John has handled such matters often in the past and has handled them well. The attorney says to John, "Here, take care of this request on filing requirements." John calls the corporation and provides it with the correct information.

ASSIGNMENT 27

John Jones is a paralegal working for the XYZ law firm. The firm represents a large number of clients in a class action suit against an insurance company. There are a variety of claims that these clients have against the company. Each claim requires the filling out of a different claim form. John has been trained by his supervising attorney to determine which form to send out to which clients. The clients write to the firm. All letters are routed to John who makes the decision on which form to send out.

ASSIGNMENT 28

John Jones is a paralegal working at the XYZ law firm. The firm is handling a large class action involving potentially thousands of plaintiffs. John has been instructed to screen the potential plaintiffs in the class. Those he screens out by the criteria provided by the firm are told by John, in writing or verbally, that "unfortunately, our firm will not be able to represent you."

ASSIGNMENT 29

a. Read the two New Jersey ethical opinions on paralegals found in Appendix G, p. 888. Tom is a paralegal who works for a single-lawyer firm in New Jersey. The lawyer, Jane Frederickson, is out of town for a month. One of the cases Tom is working on will come to trial in six months, the case of Jones v. Smith. Before Jane left town, she told Tom that if the opposing attorneys on the Jones case try to get in touch with her about obtaining a copy of the investigation report, "it's OK to let them have a copy." Examine the following two situations. Has unethical conduct been committed according to New Jersey standards? Why or why not?

- An opposing attorney on the Jones case writes for a copy of the investigation report. Tom sends the attorney the report. Tom's cover letter is signed "Tom Davis, Paralegal."
- An opposing attorney on the Jones case calls the office where Tom works. Tom answers the phone. The attorney asks for Jane Frederickson. Tom explains that she is out of town, and then says, "I'm Tom Davis,

a paralegal working on the case. Can I help you?" The attorney asks for a copy of the investigation report. Tom tells the attorney that he has been instructed to send the report if requested. Tom sends out the report. No cover letter is used.

b. Conduct a debate in class on the merits and demerits of the two New Jersey opinions. One class member will play the role of an attorney who is a member of the New Jersey Advisory Committee on Professional Ethics. Another class member will play the role of the president of the local paralegal association. The setting is a meeting of the paralegal association where the attorney has been invited to speak about the two opinions. The paralegal president begins by explaining what s/he finds objectionable in the two opinions. The attorney then defends the two opinions. Following the two presentations, the rest of the class will be allowed to ask questions of the attorney and the president.

ASSIGNMENT 30

Joan is a paralegal who works for the XYZ law firm that is representing Goff in a suit against Barnard who is represented by the ABC law firm. Joan calls Barnard and says, "Is this the first time that you have ever been sued?" Barnard answers, "Yes it is. Is there anything else that you would like to know?" Joan says "no" and the conversation ends.

ASSIGNMENT 31

John is a paralegal who works for the XYZ law firm that is representing a client against the Today Insurance Company. The Company also employs paralegals who work under the Company's general counsel. One of these paralegals is Mary. In an effort to settle the case, Mary calls John and says, "We offer you $200.00." John says, "We'll let you know."

ASSIGNMENT 32

Viola Butler, Esq., authorizes John Smith (her paralegal) to use the following cards, which John distributes whenever on assignment from Ms. Butler. Has the latter acted unethically in permitting John's use of either of these cards?

Beard, Butler, and Clark Attorneys at Law 310 High Street Maincity, Ohio 45238 John Smith 663-9410 Paralegal X305	John Smith Paralegal Beard, Butler, and Clark Attorneys at Law 310 High Street 663-9410 Maincity, Ohio 45238 X305

ASSIGNMENT 33

Mary Smith is a paralegal who works part time for the ABC law firm. The phone number of the firm is 265-9500. When she is not working for the firm, she represents her own clients before an administrative agency where she is authorized by law to provide this representation. She does not have a business card that mentions the name, address, or phone number of the ABC firm. For her agency work, however, she does have a card that reads as follows:

> Mary Smith
> Paralegal
>
> "The best paralegal in town.
> She'll get results for you."
>
> Call Now
> 265-9500

ASSIGNMENT 34

Paul is a nonlawyer who works at the Quaker Draft Counseling Center. One of the clients of the Center is Michael Diamond. Paul says the following to Mr. Diamond:

> You don't have anything to worry about. The law says that you cannot be inducted until you have had an administrative hearing on your case. I will represent you at that hearing. If you are inducted before that hearing, I will immediately draft a habeas corpus petition that can be filed at the United States District Court.

ASSIGNMENT 35

Mary is a paralegal who is a senior citizen. She works at the XYZ legal service office. One day she goes to a senior citizens center and makes the following statement:

> All of you should know about and take advantage of the XYZ legal service office where I work. Let me give you just one example why. Down at the office there is an attorney named Armanda Morris. She is an expert on insurance company cases. Some of you may have had trouble with insurance companies that say one thing and do another. Our office is available to serve you.

ASSIGNMENT 36

Mary is a paralegal who works at the XYZ law firm. She specializes in real estate matters at the firm. Mary attends a real estate closing in which her role consists of exchanging documents and acknowledging the receipt of documents. Analyze this problem on the basis of the following variations:

- The closing takes place at the XYZ law firm.
- The closing takes place at a bank.
- Mary's supervising attorney is not present at the closing.
- Mary's supervising attorney is present at the closing.
- Mary's supervising attorney is present at the closing except for thirty minutes when he had to leave, during which time Mary continued to exchange documents and acknowledge the receipt of documents.
- During the closing, the attorney for the other party says to Mary, "I don't know why my client should have to pay that charge." Mary responds: "In this state that charge is always paid in this way."

ASSIGNMENT 37

John Jones is a paralegal at the XYZ law firm. The attorney for whom he works is Joseph Troy. The firm represents the Ace Truck Company against Brown. Brown's attorney is Fay Metz. The next scheduled court date is tomorrow. Due to last minute crises on other cases, Troy cannot go to court tomorrow. Troy calls Metz and they both agree to request a one-week continuance. Troy tells John to go down to court tomorrow and when the case of *Ace Truck Co. v. Brown* is called, to request a one-week continuance. John does so.

ASSIGNMENT 38

Alice is a free-lance paralegal with a specialty in probate law. One of the firms she has worked for is Davis, Ritter & Boggs. Her most recent assignment for this firm has been to identify the assets of Mary Stanton who died six months ago. One of Mary's assets is a 75% ownership share in the Domain Corporation. Alice learns a great deal about this company including the fact that four months ago it had difficulty meeting its payroll and expects to have similar difficulties in the coming year.

Alice's free-lance business has continued to grow because of her excellent reputation. She decides to hire an employee with a different specialty so that her office can begin to take different kinds of cases from lawyers. She hires Bob, a paralegal with four years of litigation experience. The firm of Jackson & Jackson hires Alice to digest a series of long deposition documents in the case of Glendale Bank v. Ajax Tire Co. Jackson & Jackson represents Glendale Bank. Peterson, Zuckerman & Morgan represents Ajax Tire Co. Alice assigns Bob to this case. Ajax Tire Co. is a wholly owned subsidiary of the Domain Corporation. Glendale Bank is suing Ajax Tire Co. for fraud in misrepresenting its financial worth when Ajax Tire Co. applied for and obtained a loan from Glendale Bank.

Any ethical problems?

ASSIGNMENT 39

Mary Smith is a paralegal at the XYZ law firm. One of her tasks is to file a document in court. She negligently forgets to do so. As a result, the client has a default judgment entered against her. What options are available to the client? (See p. 303.)

ASSIGNMENT 40

Joe Mookely is an attorney who represents fifty inmates on a consolidated case in the state court. The inmates are in fourteen different institutions throughout the state. Joe asks the Director of the state prison system to allow his paralegal, Mary Smith, to interview all fifty inmates at a central location. The Director responds as follows:

- He refuses to transport the inmates to one location. The inmates would have to be interviewed at the institutions where they are currently living.
- He refuses to let anyone in any institution unless the individual has either a law degree *or* has been through the prison's two-week orientation program totaling twenty hours in the evenings at the state capital.

Mary Smith has not taken the orientation program and it would be very inconvenient for her to do so since she lives 150 miles from the capital.

ASSIGNMENT 41

Mary Smith is a paralegal at the ABC law firm. She has been working on the case of Jessica Randolph, a client of the office. Mary talks with Ms. Randolph often. Mary receives a subpoena from the attorney of the party that is suing Ms. Randolph. On the witness stand, Mary is asked by this attorney what Ms. Randolph told her at the ABC law office about a particular business transaction related to the suit. Randolph's attorney (Mary's boss) objects to the question. What result?

ASSIGNMENT 42

Before Helen became a paralegal for the firm of Harris & Derkson, she was a chemist for a large corporation. Harris & Derkson is a patent law firm where Helen's technical expertise in chemistry is invaluable. Helen's next-door neighbor is an inventor. On a number of occasions he discussed the chemical make-up of his inventions with Helen. On one of these inventions, the neighbor is being charged by the government with stealing official secrets in order to prepare the invention. Harris & Derkson represent the neighbor on this case. Helen also works directly on the case for the firm. In a prosecution of the neighbor, Helen is called as a witness and is asked to reveal the substance of all her conversations with the neighbor concerning the invention in question. Does Helen have to answer? See *United States v. Kovel,* Appendix G, p. 894.

ASSIGNMENT 43

On page 421, the following question is asked: "Has the paralegal given the client legal advice?" Answer this question after reading it in context.

ASSIGNMENT 44

In chapter 2 (pp. 64ff), there is a large list of tasks that paralegals have performed. Identify any three tasks that *might* pose ethical problems or problems of unauthorized practice. Explain why.

ASSIGNMENT 45

- What restrictions exist on advertising by lawyers in your state? Give an example of an ad on TV or in the newspaper that would be unethical. On researching an ethical issue, see p. 270.
- In *Bates v. State Bar of Arizona*, 433 U.S. 350 (1970), the United States Supreme Court held that a state could not prohibit all forms of lawyer advertising. Has *Bates* been cited by state courts in your state on the advertising issue? If so, what impact has the case had in your state? To find out, shepardize *Bates* through Shepard's United States Citations, Case Edition (p. 553). Read the major cases of your state courts that have applied *Bates* to your state. Shepard's will lead you to the citations of such cases. Read them in reporter volumes (p. 525). For a discussion of shepardizing in general, see p. 551 and p. 608. The specific techniques of shepardizing a case are found in Checklist 4a, p. 617.

Section E. BAR ASSOCIATION CONTROL OF PARALEGAL EDUCATION

Since the early 1970s, the American Bar Association has been "approving" paralegal training programs after a recommendation is made by its standing Committee on Legal Assistants. There is no requirement that a school be ABA-approved in order to train paralegals. In fact most training programs are not so approved. The approval process is voluntary and the majority of programs have decided *not* to apply for approval. A program will have to meet state government accreditation standards, but it does not have to seek the approval of the ABA. To date the same is true of state and local bar associations. None of the latter accredit or approve paralegal training programs, although some are moving in this direction.

The ABA approval process has been controversial from its inception. Those who oppose total lawyer control of paralegalism feel that the bar associations are inappropriate mechanisms to regulate training institutions. Nonlawyers cannot be members of bar associations, and even where associate membership status is available for paralegals (p. 283), the ultimate decisions on approval are still left in the hands of the lawyers in the bar associations. Since a major objective of lawyers is to increase their profits by the use of paralegals, critics argue that it is a conflict of interest for lawyers to control the field totally. When regulatory decisions must be made on matters such as the approval of schools, whose interest would the lawyers be protecting in making these decisions? The interest of the paralegals? The interest of the public? Or the profit interest of the lawyer-regulators?

The ABA has been somewhat sensitive to this criticism and, as we will see, at one time considered withdrawing from the approval process. In recent years, challenges have been made to the monopoly that bar associations exercise over the practice of law. In 1975, the United States Supreme Court sent shock waves throughout the legal profession when the Court ruled that lawyers were no longer exempt from the antitrust laws, and that some minimum fee schedules are a violation of these laws. *Goldfarb v. Virginia State Bar*, 421 U.S. 773 (1975). In 1979, an antitrust charge was brought against the ABA on the ground that its paralegal school approval process was designed to eliminate competition from, and restrict entry into, the market for recruitment, training, and placement of paralegals. The ABA won this case. *Paralegal Institute, Inc. v. American Bar Association,* 475 F.Supp. 1123 (E.D.N.Y., 1979). Despite this victory, the ABA remains vulnerable to future challenge.

Note that the ABA uses the word "approval" rather than accreditation in describing its process of exercising control over educational institutions. Yet the process meets the accepted definition of accreditation (p. 204). The use of the more euphemistic word "approval" may be an indication that the ABA is itself not sure whether it should be in the business of regulating paralegal education. Indeed, in 1981, the House of Delegates of the ABA instructed its Committee on Legal Assistants to terminate the ABA involvement in the approval process. Some schools, however, that had already received approval, objected. As a result, the Committee proposed and the House of Delegates accepted an alternative system of approving schools.

The alternative was the creation of an ABA Approval Commission to implement the approval process. The final decision on approval of individual schools is still left in the hands of the ABA. The Commission simply serves the same function that the Committee on Legal Assistants served in making recommendations on approval. The Commission now makes its recommendations to the Committee on Legal Assistants, which in turn makes its recommendations to the House of Delegates of the ABA. The major difference between the Committee and the Commission is that the latter must contain nonlawyer members. There are eleven members of the Commission, all of whom are appointed by the president of the ABA on advice from the Committee:

- Three lawyers (one of whom has taught in a paralegal program).
- One lawyer who represents the ABA Committee on Legal Assistants.
- One paralegal nominated by the National Federation of Paralegal Associations (NFPA).
- One paralegal nominated by the Federation of Paralegal Associations (NFPA).
- Two representatives nominated by the American Association for Paralegal Education (AAfPE).
- One representative nominated by the Association of Legal Administrators (ALA).
- One nonlegal educator.
- One representative of the general public.

The ABA does not view the Commission as a permanent institution. The plan is to phase it out over a period of years and to replace it with an *independent* accrediting body that is equally broad based. It is unclear, however, whether this replacement is feasible. It depends on the willingness of paralegal schools to submit themselves to this still-voluntary approval process. Furthermore, an independent body would be very expensive to run. Its revenues would come from fees paid by the schools that apply for approval and for renewals of approval. If large numbers of schools continue to bypass a national accrediting or approval entity, the process will lose both the political and financial support that is necessary.

ASSIGNMENT 46

Who should control accreditation? Are there too many lawyers on the ABA Approval Commission? Too few paralegals? Could there be too many paralegals on such a body? Do you favor an independent accrediting entity? Who should run it? Should it be voluntary?

———————————

What will the ABA do if an independent accrediting body does not materialize? Will it continue with its Approval Commission? It is unclear what the ABA will do but it is unlikely that it will want to continue in its present role.

Only one thing is sure: Change is on the horizon. The legal profession can no longer feel secure in its privileged position as indicated in the following speech.

J. SIMS, "THE LEGAL PROFESSION: A BOW TO THE PAST— A GLIMPSE OF THE FUTURE"

(Mr. Sims was the Deputy Assistant Attorney General in the Antitrust Division of the United States Department of Justice. The following are excerpts from a speech he delivered on February 11, 1977, before a conference of the Federation of Insurance Counsel in Arizona.)

Today, in Los Angeles, legal services are being advertised on television. That fact alone gives us some idea of how much change has come to the legal profession in the last few years.

That change has not always come easy, but the fact that it has come so far, so fast, tells us quite a bit about what will happen in the future. We lawyers as a group have grumbled and argued, fought and yelled, struggled and been confused—but there are now lawyers advertising on television. Even a casual observer cannot fail to appreciate the significance of this change.

Competition, slowly but surely, is coming to the legal profession. This opening of traditional doors, the breaking of traditional barriers is the result of many forces—the number of new lawyers, the awakening of consumerism, the growing realization that the complexity of our society requires legal assistance in more and more areas. But one contributing factor has been antitrust litigation and the Department of Justice.

. . .

[T]he Supreme Court fired the shot heard 'round the bar [o]n June 16, 1975. [I]n a unanimous decision, [Goldfarb v. Virginia State Bar, 421 U.S. 773 (1975)] the Court held that the minimum fee schedule challenged by the Goldfarbs violated Section 1 of the Sherman Act. This decision broke the dam and released the flood of change that we see engulfing the profession today. For better or worse, the Goldfarbs had set in motion a series of events that were to change the character of the legal profession forever.

The Court decided several things in *Goldfarb,* but the most important was that the legal profession was subject to the antitrust laws—there was no "professional exemption." The response to *Goldfarb* was fascinating. A large number of private suits were filed challenging various aspects of bar regulation.

. . .

[An] area sure to be controversial in the future is unauthorized practice. There is already at least one antitrust challenge, against the Virginia State Bar, seeking to prohibit the bar from promulgating unauthorized practice opinions. This case, which involves title insurance, is a direct challenge to the extraordinary power that the legal profession now has—in most states—to define the limits of its own monopoly. It would be strange indeed for a state to hand over to, say its steel industry, not only the power to regulate entry into the industry and the conduct of those within it, but also the power to define what the industry was. In many states, that is exactly the power the organized bar now has, and that power is being challenged as inconsistent with the antitrust laws.

The heart of this challenge is that lawyers shouldn't be deciding what is the practice of law—defining the scope of the legal monopoly. The papers filed in that case . . . indicate that the objection is not to such a decision being made; the objection is to the State's delegation of that power to the profession.

In fact, of course, the principle behind this lawsuit could be expanded not only to other subject matter areas, but also to arrangements between the organized bar and other professions which have as their basic result the division of commercial responsibilities.

For example, the American Bar Association has entered into "statements of principles" with respect to the practice of law with a variety of other professions and occupations ranging from accountants to claim adjusters, publishers, social workers, and even professional engineers [p. 210]. These documents generally set forth the joint views of the professions as to which activities fall within the practice of law and which activities are proper for members of the other profession. They nearly all provide that each profession will advise its clients to seek out members of the other profession in appropriate circumstances.

As a general rule, two competitors may not agree with each other to allocate markets, or bids, or even functions; if they do, they violate the antitrust laws. At the least, this traditional antitrust principle raises some questions about the legal effect of such "statements of principles."

. . .

[T]he efforts of the bar to limit the scope of paralegal responsibilities and, in some jurisdictions, to seek a certification requirement for paralegals are seen by many as simply another effort to preserve and protect the legal services monopoly. Many believe that non-lawyers could perform many tasks reserved today for people with law degrees. . . .

These latter issues lead right into a somewhat different focus on bar association activities. While the bar has been reeling from a series of legal setbacks on antitrust and Constitutional grounds, there has been a growing movement in a related area that seems sure to impact upon the legal profession. In a way, this movement can also be traced to a Supreme Court case, the case of Gibson v. Berryhill. [411 U.S. 564 (1973)]

There, the Supreme Court applied the federal due process principle to strike down an attempt by a state optometry board, [which] was dominated by privately practicing optometrists, to halt the corporate practice of optometry. The result of this action would have inured to the pecuniary benefit of each board member and his fellow independent optometrists. The Supreme Court affirmed a District Court's finding that the Board was so biased by its pecuniary interests that it could not Constitutionally conduct hearings designed to discipline corporate optometrists.

Consistent with this decision, there has been a growing concern throughout the country about self-regulation. Perhaps nothing illustrates this trend better than the recent swearing-in, by Governor Brown of California, of 60 new members of state regulatory boards. None of the 60 appointees are certified in the occupation they are to help regulate. This concept of lay members on regulatory boards is a growing one, and will inevitably increase. In fact, in California, lay members have been appointed to 39 regulatory boards, and only those boards in the healing arts, law and accountancy, where membership is prescribed by statute, have no lay members. This privileged status, I am reasonably sure, will not last long.

Lay membership makes sense to a lot of people. Indeed, it may be essential if the legal profession and other similar professions are to retain a measure of self-regulatory ability. As long as the regulators are indistinguishable from those they regulate, it is impossible to tell when the public interest stops and self-interest starts.

ASSIGNMENT 47

What are the implications of Mr. Sims's remarks on the role of bar associations in regulating paralegal education?

Section F. SHOULD PARALEGALS BECOME PART OF BAR ASSOCIATIONS?

At present, no paralegals are full members of any bar associations. In 1981, however, the State Bar of Texas created a Legal Assistant Division of the bar. Its unique aspect is that all of its regular members *must* be paralegals. Hence, while paralegals cannot become members of the bar association, they can become members of a Division of the bar association. The Division is not a mere advisory committee of the bar; it is part of the bar association itself, which means that it is under the ultimate control of the Board of Directors of the State Bar of Texas.

The qualifications for membership in the Division are as follows:

- The applicant must *not* be a Texas attorney.
- The applicant must perform "substantial paralegal services in rendering direct assistance to an attorney" (someone who does occasional paralegal work would not qualify).
- The applicant's supervising attorney must certify that the applicant performs substantial paralegal services for that attorney.

Members pay annual dues of $25.

The bylaws of the Division state its purpose as follows: "to enhance legal assistants' participation in the administration of justice, professional responsibility and public service in cooperation with the State Bar of Texas." All the officers of the Division are paralegals elected by the membership. The budget of the Division, however, must be approved by the State Bar of Texas.

The Division has been very popular among paralegals in Texas; large numbers have joined. Other bar associations have adopted similar programs. For example, the Columbus Bar Association of Ohio admits paralegals as associate members, and the North Carolina Academy of Trial Lawyers created a new membership category in 1983 called "Legal Assistant Affiliate Member."

Not every bar association, however, has joined the bandwagon. In fact, considerable controversy surrounds the issue. In 1982 the ABA Committee on Legal Assistants proposed that the ABA create a new category of associate membership for paralegals. To become an associate, the person must be a nonlawyer who is "qualified through education, training or certification," and who assists "in the performance of legal services under the direction and supervision of a lawyer who certifies that the assistance is not primarily secretarial or clerical." The National Association of Legal Assistants (NALA) warmly endorsed the proposal, while the National Federation of Paralegal Associations (NFPA) opposed it. The ABA House of Delegates rejected the proposal on the ground that the addition of this nonlawyer membership category would further "dilute" the primary lawyer membership category.

ASSIGNMENT 48

a. Should paralegals become a formal part of bar associations? What effect do you think associate membership would have on existing paralegal associations? Strengthen them? Destroy them? Is it healthy or unhealthy for paralegals to organize themselves as independent entities? Is it health or unhealthy for them to be able to challenge the organized bar? Do you think there is any validity to the conflict-of-interest argument (p. 279)? What is the relationship between this argument and the issue of whether paralegals should become associate or affiliate members of the bar associations?
b. Should a paralegal association allow *lawyers* to become associate members of the *paralegal* association? Why or why not?
c. If the proposal of the ABA Committee on Legal Assistants to create an associate membership category had been successful, what kinds of paralegals would have been excluded from such membership? Is such exclusion a good idea?

ASSOCIATE MEMBERSHIP v. JOINT EFFORTS
by D. Kuckherman, 10 Update 5
(Cleveland Association of Paralegals, Inc., No. 6, Nov., 1984)

Supporters of associate membership for paralegals in bar associations believe that the added recognition accorded to paralegals by the bar will carry through to working situations and reinforce the role of paralegals; that more communication will take place between the two groups, thus encouraging expanded responsibilities and recognition for the paralegal profession; and that the general public will become more familiar with paralegals and their role in the delivery of legal services.

Supporters of associate membership feel that those who oppose associate categories also oppose any type of cooperative effort between paralegal associations and bar associations. These are separate issues.

Opponents of associate membership are generally in favor of joint efforts between paralegal associations and the bar on common goals. It is not necessary for two associations to share membership (or for two professions to share an association) in order for them to effectively work together to their mutual advantage.

Few would dispute that many worthwhile goals can be accomplished by the joint efforts of paralegal associations and bar associations. However, bar associations do not always agree with paralegal associations on what exactly constitutes a "cooperative effort." The definition of this term must be worked out by the associations if they are to work together effectively. Joint efforts by paralegal and bar associations are almost universally supported and should be encouraged. However, joint efforts do not require associate membership categories.

Section G. SELF-REGULATION BY PARALEGALS

There are two national organizations of paralegals:

- The National Federation of Paralegal Associations (NFPA). This is an organization of organizations; the membership of NFPA consists of paralegal associations across the country.
- The National Association of Legal Assistants (NALA). This organization is a spin-off from the National Association of Legal Secretaries; NALA is an organization of individual legal assistants plus a number of affiliated local paralegal associations.

In Appendix B, p. 843, there is a list of local paralegal associations with a notation as to whether they are part of NFPA or NALA.

NALA is *not* a member of NFPA. In fact, as we have seen, the two national organizations take very different positions on a number of important issues.

Both, for example, have published ethical standards for paralegals. NALA's is called the Code of Ethics and Professional Responsibility. NFPA's is called the Affirmation of Responsibility. The two documents are printed below.

CODE OF ETHICS AND PROFESSIONAL RESPONSIBILITY OF THE NATIONAL ASSOCIATION OF LEGAL ASSISTANTS, INC.

Preamble

It is the responsibility of every legal assistant to adhere strictly to the accepted standards of legal ethics and to live by general principles of proper conduct. The performance of the duties of the legal assistant shall be governed by specific canons as defined herein in order that justice will be served and the goals of the profession attained.

The canons of ethics set forth hereafter are adopted by the National Association of Legal Assistants, Inc., as a general guide, and the enumeration of these rules does not mean there are not others of equal importance although not specifically mentioned.

Canon 1. A legal assistant shall not perform any of the duties that lawyers only may perform nor do things that lawyers themselves may not do.

Canon 2.   A legal assistant may perform any task delegated and supervised by a lawyer so long as the lawyer is responsible to the client, maintains a direct relationship with the client, and assumes full professional responsibility for the work product.

Canon 3.   A legal assistant shall not engage in the practice of law by giving legal advice, appearing in court, setting fees, or accepting cases.

Canon 4.   A legal assistant shall not act in matters involving professional legal judgment as the services of a lawyer are essential in the public interest whenever the exercise of such judgment is required.

Canon 5.   A legal assistant must act prudently in determining the extent to which a client may be assisted without the presence of a lawyer.

Canon 6.   A legal assistant shall not engage in the unauthorized practice of law and shall assist in preventing the unauthorized practice of law.

Canon 7.   A legal assistant must protect the confidences of a client, and it shall be unethical for a legal assistant to violate any statute now in effect or hereafter to be enacted controlling privileged communications.

Canon 8.   It is the obligation of the legal assistant to avoid conduct which would cause the lawyer to be unethical or even appear to be unethical, and loyalty to the employer is incumbent upon the legal assistant.

Canon 9.   A legal assistant shall work continually to maintain integrity and a high degree of competency throughout the legal profession.

Canon 10.   A legal assistant shall strive for perfection through education in order to better assist the legal profession in fulfilling its duty of making legal services available to clients and the public.

Canon 11.   A legal assistant shall do all other things incidental, necessary, or expedient for the attainment of the ethics and responsibilities imposed by statute or rule of court.

Canon 12.   A legal assistant is governed by the American Bar Association Code of Professional Responsibility.

Adopted May 1, 1975

AFFIRMATION OF RESPONSIBILITY OF THE NATIONAL FEDERATION OF PARALEGAL ASSOCIATIONS

Preamble

The National Federation of Paralegal Associations recognizes and accepts its commitment to the realization of the most basic right of a free society, equal justice under the law.

In examining contemporary legal institutions and systems, the members of the paralegal profession recognize that a redefinition of the traditional delivery of legal services is essential in order to meet the needs of the general public. The paralegal profession is committed to increasing the availability and quality of legal services.

The National Federation of Paralegal Associations has adopted this Affirmation of Professional Responsibility to delineate the principals of purpose and conduct toward which paralegals should aspire. Through this Affirmation, the National Federation of Paralegal Associations places upon each paralegal the responsibility to adhere to these standards and encourages dedication to the development of the profession.

I. PROFESSIONAL RESPONSIBILITY

A paralegal shall demonstrate initiative in performing and expanding the paralegal role in the delivery of legal services within the parameters of the unauthorized practice of law statutes.

DISCUSSION: Recognizing the professional and legal responsibility to abide by the unauthorized practice of law statutes, the Federation supports and encourages new interpretations as to what constitutes the practice of law.

II. PROFESSIONAL CONDUCT

A paralegal shall maintain the highest standards of ethical conduct.

DISCUSSION: It is the responsibility of a paralegal to avoid conduct which is unethical or appears to be unethical. Ethical principles are aspirational in character and embody the fundamental rules of conduct by which every paralegal should abide. Observance of these standards is essential to uphold respect for the legal system.

III. COMPETENCE AND INTEGRITY

A paralegal shall maintain a high level of competence and shall contribute to the integrity of the paralegal profession.

DISCUSSION: The integrity of the paralegal profession is predicated upon individual competence. Professional competence is each paralegal's responsibility and is achieved through continuing education, awareness of developments in the field of law and aspiring to the highest standards of personal performance.

IV. CLIENT CONFIDENCES

A paralegal shall preserve client confidences and privileged communications.

DISCUSSION: Confidential information and privileged communications are a vital part of the attorney, paralegal and client relationship. The importance of preserving confidential and privileged information is understood to be an uncompromising obligation of every paralegal.

V. SUPPORT OF PUBLIC INTERESTS

A paralegal shall serve the public interests by contributing to the availability and delivery of quality legal services.

DISCUSSION: It is the responsibility of each paralegal to promote the development and implementation of programs that address the legal needs of the public. A paralegal shall strive to maintain a sensitivity to public needs and to educate the public as to the services that paralegals may render.

VI. PROFESSIONAL DEVELOPMENT

A paralegal shall promote the development of the paralegal profession.

DISCUSSION: This Affirmation of Professional Responsibility promulgates a positive attitude through which a paralegal may recognize the importance, responsibility and potential of the paralegal contribution to the delivery of legal services. Participation in professional associations enhances the ability of the individual paralegal to contribute to the quality and growth of the paralegal profession.

ASSIGNMENT 49

(a) Compare these two documents of NALA and NFPA. What differences in content and emphasis do you see?

(b) Earlier it was pointed out that NALA agreed with and NFPA opposed the proposal of the ABA Committee on Legal Assistants to create an associate category membership in the ABA (p. 284). After reading the above two documents, are you surprised that NALA and NFPA took these opposite positions or could you have predicted the split?

The most intense battle between the two national paralegal associations has been over the question of the paralegal certification. NALA favors certification and has its own certification program. NFPA is opposed to certification as premature.

THE CASE FOR CERTIFICATION[14]
by Jane H. Terhune

(Jane H. Terhune is a past president of the National Association of Legal Assistants, Inc. She is employed as a legal assistant for the firm of Hall, Estill, Hardwick, Gable, Collingsworth & Nelson, Tulsa, Oklahoma.)

Professional competence of an *individual* can be assessed by two recognized mechanisms: licensing or certification. Accreditation or approval, on the other hand, examines educational *programs* to determine whether they meet established standards of quality. Although the ABA has an institutional approval process, this paper is concerned only with the assessment of *individual* competence and therefore will not deal with the issue of institutional accreditation or approval.

Since the early 1970s legal assistants have obtained employment by means of formal training, in-house training, or other law office experience. While each method of training has certain advantages, no one method has proven superior to the others. Thus the dilemma: how can prospective employers or clients assess or legal assistants demonstrate paralegal skills and knowledge when there is no standard for performance?

Is licensing the appropriate mechanism to assure professional competence of legal assistants at this time? Several states have recently considered it, but none have yet adopted it. It is generally agreed that requirements for licensing would either severely limit the growth and development of the still new paralegal field or be so weak as to be meaningless. Licensing, by definition, is a mandatory requirement and is usually administered and controlled by government entities or well-established and strong professional associations. Since the legal assistant concept is still not well understood, it is doubtful that state legislatures can define the profession well enough to regulate it effectively at this time. Therefore, licensing appears to be impractical as well as premature.

Certification, a voluntary professional commitment, appears to be a practical alternative, and the National Association of Legal Assistants believes that one national certification program is preferable to a multitude of possible state programs. Certification is not new or unique. Many professions and paraprofessions

---

[14] American Bar Association, Standing Committee on Legal Assistants, *Legal Assistant Update '80* 5–16 (1980). This article has been updated to reflect current positions of NALA and NFPA.

have developed and supported certification as an alternative to licensing or other forms of regulation. Certification recognizes expertise and proven ability without limiting entrance into or employment in the field, and the same standards are applied regardless of the individual's background or training. Furthermore, a certification program can help guide educational institutions in developing and evaluating their legal assistant curricula. It is argued that certification would limit the development of the paralegal field, but the CPS (Certified Professional Secretary) program has not thus affected the secretarial field, and the PLS (Professional Legal Secretary) certification of legal secretaries has in no way interfered with their employment. To the contrary, secretaries with the CPS or PLS ratings are regarded as professionals in their respective fields.

In 1974, as part of an effort to set high professional standards for legal assistants while the field was in its early development, the NALA Certifying Board for Legal Assistants was created. It was composed of nine members—five legal assistants (working in different areas of the law), two paralegal educators, and two attorneys. The composition of the Board has remained the same to date, and in number is similar to many certification boards or committees in other fields. During the first year of its existence the Certifying Board acted mainly as a feasibility study group. All known national professional associations with certification programs were contacted for advice and guidance. Paralegal educators were contacted for information about their programs as well as entrance and graduation requirements. Legal assistant duties and responsibilities in various areas of the law were surveyed, and correspondence with the Institute of Legal Executives in England began. Our English counterparts were anxious to share their ten years of experience with NALA. After several months of gathering information, replies were tabulated and summarized and the NALA Certifying Board for Legal Assistants was ready to embark on its task.

Although many legal assistants work in special areas of law rather than as generalists, there are general skills and knowledge which apply to all legal fields and, for this reason, general subjects or topics were selected for inclusion in the examination.

The certification program is a two step process, as follows:

First: successful completion of a two day (eleven hour) comprehensive examination covering the following areas:

Communications—Grammar, vocabulary, correspondence, nonverbal communications, concise writing.

Ethics—Unauthorized practice, ethical rules, practice rules, confidentiality.

Interviewing Techniques—General considerations for interviewing situations, initial roadblocks, manner of questions, special handling situations, use of checklists for specific matters.

Human Relations—Delegation of authority, consequences of delegation, working with people.

Judgment and Analytical Ability—Analyzing and categorizing facts and evidence; legal assistant's relationship with the lawyer, legal secretary, and client, other law firms and the courts; reactions to specific situations; data interpretation.

Legal Research—Principles of legal research, sources of the law, finding tools, court reports, Shepardizing, research procedure.

Legal Terminology—Latin phrases, legal phrases or terms in general, utilization and understanding of common legal terms.

Substantive Law—The American legal system: history, branches of the government, constitution. Applicants must also select and complete four sets of general questions from the areas below:

Real Estate	Corporate	Contracts
Bankruptcy	Litigation	Administrative
Criminal	Federal Tax	Probate and Estate Planning

After passing the examination, a legal assistant may use the CLA (Certified Legal Assistant) designation which signifies certification by the National Association of Legal Assistants, Inc. CLA is a service mark duly registered with the U.S. Patent and Trademark Office (No. 1131999). Any unauthorized use is strictly forbidden.

Second: based on the premise that education, a commitment of all professionals, is a never ending process, Certified Legal Assistants are required to submit evidence of continuing education periodically in order to maintain certified status. The CLA designation is for a period of five years and if the CLA submits proof of continuing education in accordance with the stated requirements, the certificate is renewed for another five years. Lifetime certification is not permitted.

Continuing education units are awarded for attending seminars, workshops or conferences in areas of substantive law or a closely related area. The seminars, etc., do not have to be sponsored by NALA, although all NALA seminars and workshops qualify.

The development of the specific test items was a time consuming and difficult project. Rather than employ professional testing companies unfamiliar with the legal assistant field, it was decided that the Certifying Board, composed of legal assistants, attorneys, and educators from the legal assistant field, were best qualified to prepare the exams. Each member was assigned a topic and asked to prepare sample items, including true-false, multiple-choice, matching, and essay questions. Since it was felt that a legal assistant's ability to communicate was vital to success in the profession, essay items were included in each section of the exam. Then followed a series of meetings to review, refine, and evaluate the proposed exams. The exams were pilot-tested, testing times were noted, results were statistically analyzed, and problems were identified. Every question in each section was carefully scrutinized for "national scope" and questions which did not apply to all states were removed from the exam.

Since legal assistants enter the field through a variety of routes including formal education, in-house training, and law office experience, eligibility to take the exam can be established in a variety of ways. Consequently, the following requirements were set up:

1) Graduation from an ABA approved legal assistant course or graduation from a legal assistant training school which is institutionally accredited plus one (1) year's experience as a legal assistant;

2) Graduation from an unapproved training course or from an unaccredited school plus three (3) years' experience as a legal assistant;

3) A bachelor's degree in any field plus three (3) years' experience as a legal assistant;

4) One who successfully completes the PLS (Professional Legal Secretary) examination and has five (5) years' law related experience under the supervision of a member of the bar. (Note: This optional requirement is open until 1986.)

5) Seven (7) years' law related experience under the supervision of a member of the Bar. (Note: this optional requirement is open until 1986.)

Applicants meeting any one of these criteria may take the exam. Furthermore, they need not be members of the National Association of Legal Assistants to apply for or receive the CLA (Certified Legal Assistant) certification.

The CLA examination was first offered in November, 1976, at regional testing centers. Approximately 50 per cent of the first group of applicants passed the entire exam, and the Board was particularly pleased that the passing percentage was uniform throughout the country, a fact which seemed to indicate that the test was free of state or regional bias. Although the passing rate has fluctuated slightly in subsequent testing, the uniformity has been maintained. As of 1980, 300 legal assistants from 35 states successfully completed the CLA examination. As of 1984, the statistics on the examination were as follows:

Number taking the exam: 1,237
Number of times exam was given: 1,722 (includes retakes)
Number who passed: 820
Number who passed on first sitting: 536
Number of states containing legal assistants with CLA status: 44, plus District of Columbia and Virgin Islands
Number of those taking exam who are *not* members of NALA: about 400
Sections of the exam most frequently failed: Substantive Law, Communications, Legal Research
States with the most number of CLAs:

Florida:	202	Michigan:	31
Texas:	130	Alabama:	28
California:	73	Colorado:	26
Arizona:	44	Oklahoma:	25
Kansas:	38	Nebraska:	23

Certification is an ambitious and expensive project for a young professional association. Over $20,000 and thousands of hours were initially invested in the CLA Program, but the National Association of Legal Assistants believes it has been a wise investment. Traditionally, where new professions do not set their own standards, related professions or governments have done so. NALA felt a responsibility to develop a quality national certification program for legal assistants desiring professional recognition. The CLA exam has been in use for a number of years, but work on the project continues. The question bank is continually expanded so that an indefinite number of exam versions can be created, and questions are being reviewed and updated constantly.

Recently, NALA launched a major new component of its CLA program: certification for those who *specialize* in a particular area of the law. In 1983 specialty certification in the areas of Civil Litigation and Probate and Estate Planning was offered for the first time to all CLAs. In 1984, additional specialty examinations were offered in the areas of Corporate and Business Law, and Criminal Law and Procedure. Applicants for the specialty exam sit for a four hour examination to be given during the same time as the regular examination—the third weekend of March and during the July testing session which is held the Friday and Saturday immediately preceding the NALA annual convention.

Legal assistants are becoming more and more specialized—the regular CLA examination tests the broad *general* skills required of *all* legal assistants. Specialty certification is different. It is a goal for those who want to be recognized for achieving significant competence in a *particular* field. Further, a legal assistant may want to take more than one specialty examination if a specialty changes over time.

Conclusion

Although accreditation and/or licensing may become necessary in the future, the National Association of Legal Assistants believes that certification of legal assistants is currently the best device for assessing and assuring professional competence. While no legal assistant must take a test in order to obtain or maintain employment, the NALA certification program offers to legal assistants an opportunity for professional recognition.

THE CASE AGAINST CERTIFICATION
by Judith Current

(Judith Current is a past president of the National Federation of Paralegal Associations. She is employed as a legal assistant in the firm of Holme, Roberts & Owen, Denver, Colorado.)

The National Federation of Paralegal Associations ("the Federation") is a professional organization composed of state and local paralegal associations representing over 7,000 paralegals across the country. The Federation was founded in 1974 and adopted the following purposes in 1975:

- To constitute a unified national voice of the paralegal profession;
- To advance, foster and promote the paralegal concept;
- To monitor and participate in developments in the paralegal profession;
- To maintain a nationwide communications network among paralegal associations and other members of the legal community.

The Federation has continued to foster these goals through its established policies and activities. In 1977 the Federation adopted its Affirmation of Responsibility (p. 286).

The Federation recognizes that certification of paralegals is of national concern, but it feels that there has been insufficient study as to the impact of certification and the means by which certification should be administered. The Federation will only support a certification program which is coordinated by a national, broadly-based, autonomous body in which paralegals have at least equal participation.

The topic of certification of legal assistants has been of concern to the Federation since its inception. It has found every certificate proposal advanced to date to be seriously lacking in the understanding of the true nature of the profession, particularly its diversity, and the proposals have offered a structure that provides little or no representation to the persons most affected, the legal assistants themselves.

Specifically, its reservations fall within the following areas:

NEED/PREMATURITY

The paralegal profession is still a new one and the tremendous diversity in the functions and classifications of its members makes it extremely difficult to create generalized standards that can be fairly applied. This problem may eventually find an acceptable solution; but it will require much study and considerable input from all affected sectors.

No studies have been conducted that have demonstrated a need for certification. A study conducted by the American Bar Association in 1975 concluded that certification was premature. The California State Bar in 1978 rejected a proposal for certification and accreditation after nearly two years of study. Other states have similarly rejected certification. Until a need for certification is clearly demonstrated, certification will be premature.

Premature regulation runs a risk of foreclosing yet unseen avenues of development, as well as creating yet another layer of costly bureaucracy when, in fact, none may be needed. The Federation sees nothing to prevent, and everything to encourage, an extremely cautious approach to the enactment of any program of certification. In the meanwhile, the normal mechanisms of the marketplace, the existing unauthorized practice laws and ethical guidelines, the increasing numbers of legal assistants with demonstrable experience, and the ever growing reputations of various training programs can serve as guidelines for those who seek the sorts of yardsticks that certification might provide.

IMPACT OF CERTIFICATION

No studies have been conducted that satisfactorily assess the potential impact of certification on the delivery of legal services. Some of the possible negative effects include:

1. *The growth, development and diversity of the paralegal profession could be diminished by certification.* The paralegal profession has been developing steadily without a demonstrated need for regulation. Regulating the profession could curtail development into new areas, stifling the potential growth of the field and unnecessarily limiting the role of the paralegals in the delivery of legal services.

2. *Certification could result in a decrease of the availability of legal services to the poor.* Legal aid offices [p. 46] are economically dependent upon paralegals who represent clients at various administrative hearings. Most of these paralegals are in-house trained specialists who are paid lower salaries than private sector paralegals. If certification is implemented, it is conceivable that administrative agencies may initiate a system in which only certified paralegals, or attorneys, would be allowed to represent clients at the hearings. Many paralegals successfully working in this area might not meet the educational or testing requirements imposed by certification, and the legal aid offices would not be able to meet the salary demands that would be made by certified paralegals.

3. *Innovation in paralegal education programs could diminish as a result of certification.* Schools would be forced by necessity to gear their courses to a certification examination rather than to the needs of the legal community and the marketplace. While some standardization of training programs might be desirable in the future, it would be premature at this time because the training programs have not been in existence long enough to determine which types of programs are most effective and because the paralegal profession is still in a dynamic stage of development. Experimentation and variety are currently essential to the field of paralegal education.

4. *Entry into the profession could be curtailed by certification.* At the present time, a paralegal can enter the profession in a variety of ways, including formal education, in-house training, promotion from legal secretary, or a combination thereof. Certification could limit these entry paths by establishing prescribed educational requirements.

5. *Certification could lead to licensing.* Although certification is technically a voluntary program of regulation, certification leads to *de facto* licensing as we have seen

in other fields. Until we truly know whom certification would serve, how it would do so, that its value would equal its cost, and, most of all, that it is needed, those involved should be engaging in study and debate, not regulation.

NO ACCEPTABLE MODEL FOR CERTIFICATION

In the Federation's opinion, no acceptable model or program of certification has yet been devised. Oregon is the only state to have adopted a certification program. This bar-controlled program has not been very successful to date, with most paralegals and most lawyers ignoring the certification process. The Federation questions the propriety of the Oregon State Bar controlling the certification of paralegals, and deplores the fact that the paralegals are denied equitable representation on the certifying board. The Oregon program fails adequately to recognize specialization and fails to make any distinctions between the tasks which may be performed by a certified paralegal and those which may be performed by an uncertified paralegal. Thus, certification does not enhance the position of paralegals in Oregon. [Note: The Oregon program has been discontinued.*]

The Federation holds the opinion that the certification program conducted by the National Association of Legal Assistants (NALA) is unacceptable. The criteria for eligibility to take the certification examination is not based on objective data and appears to be self-serving; for example, a legal secretary with the PLS (Professional Legal Secretary) designation may become a "certified legal assistant" even though he or she has never worked as a legal assistant. The examination, in the Federation's opinion, contains questions irrelevant to a practicing paralegal and is not an effective measure of a person's ability to work successfully as a paralegal. The NALA certification program is not officially recognized by a governmental body, and a person certified under this program is not allowed to perform any tasks other than those which may also be performed by uncertified paralegals.

CONTROL AND REPRESENTATION

No certification program will be acceptable to the Federation unless it is developed, implemented and controlled by an autonomous group which is composed of an equal number of attorneys, paralegals, paralegal educators and members of the public. Self-regulation is unacceptable to the Federation since self-regulation can become self-interest and self-interest can conflict with the public interest. The Federation strongly believes that bar control of paralegals is inappropriate in that such regulation may meet the interests of the organized bar and lawyers, but not necessarily the interests of the public or the paralegal profession. The Federation also questions the propriety of the organized bar attempting to regulate another profession. Control of paralegals by the legislative branch of government could create conflict where the practice of law is controlled by the bar and the judicial branch of the government.

NATIONAL COORDINATION

The Federation believes that any program of certification will be most efficient and equitable if it is developed as a national program rather than on a state-by-

---

* In January, 1980 a representative of the Oregon State Bar telephoned the ABA Standing Committee on Legal Assistants with the information that the Board of Governors of the State Bar had approved the recommendation of the Legal Assistants Committee to discontinue the certification program (p. 239).

state basis. A national program would eliminate duplication of effort on the part of each individual state. It would allow for mobility and would avoid a conflict of standards between states.

The Federation recommends that the need for and possible methods of certification be studied in much greater depth, and that this study be conducted by an autonomous group which provides equitable representation to paralegals, attorneys, paralegal educators and members of the public. The Federation also recommends that bar associations work with paralegals and educators to educate lawyers in the proper and effective utilization of paralegals and that paralegals work to promote the growth and the development of the profession through support of and participation in the local and national paralegal associations.

ASSIGNMENT 50

Which side is correct? Conduct a debate in your class on the advantages and disadvantages of certification.

The most recent friction between NALA and NFPA came in 1984 when NALA promulgated its *Model Standards and Guidelines for the Utilization of Legal Assistants.* The goal of NALA in issuing the *Model Standards* was to present one comprehensive document that would address the critical issues of any profession, namely, identification, qualifications, and the role of the individual within the profession. As mentioned earlier, there is nothing to prevent people from calling themselves paralegals regardless of the type of work they do (p. 6). No one can stop a lawyer, for example, from calling his or her secretary a paralegal even if the duties of this person continue to be 100% clerical. The same is true of the law office messenger and the employee who spends all day photocopying legal documents. The *Model Standards* represent the view of one prestigious organization, NALA, on how to combat such chaos. Little did NALA expect, however, the barrage of criticism that the *Model Standards* received.

Members of the ABA Committee on Legal Assistants charged that the *Standards* "may unjustifiably disqualify many present law office employees and others qualified to begin working as legal assistants immediately, under a lawyer's direct supervision." These Committee members acknowledged that the *Standards* present statements that approximate desired conduct by paralegals. But turning "such statements into ethical prescriptions to lawyers and prohibitions placed upon lawyers is both unnecessary and counterproductive. In particular, the stated qualifications and limitations on legal assistant employment are contrary to a lawyer's own professional responsibility for employing nonlawyer staff. They also discourage employment of legal assistants at a time when increased employment is desirable in enabling lawyers to provide legal services most effectively and at reasonable cost."[15]

---

[15] Littleton & Ulrich, *Comments by the American Bar Association Standing Committee on Legal Assistants Concerning NALA's Model Standards and Guidelines,* 2 Legal Assistant Today 13 (No. 2, Winter, 1985). For NALA's response, see Sanders-West, *The Member Connection,* 11 Facts and Findings 6 (National Association of Legal Assistants, Issue 5, April, 1985).

In order to judge the fairness of this criticism, the *Model Standards* are presented in full below. Following the NALA *Standards,* the reaction of NFPA to them is presented.

MODEL STANDARDS AND GUIDELINES FOR UTILIZATION OF LEGAL ASSISTANTS proposed by the National Association of Legal Assistants, Inc. (1984)

PREAMBLE

Proper utilization of the services of legal assistants affects the efficient delivery of legal services. Legal assistants and the legal profession should be assured that some measures exist for identifying legal assistants and their role in assisting attorneys in the delivery of legal services. Therefore, the National Association of Legal Assistants, Inc., hereby adopts these Model Standards and Guidelines as an educational document for the benefit of legal assistants and the legal profession.

DEFINITION

Legal assistants* are a distinguishable group of persons who assist attorneys in the delivery of legal services. Through formal education, training, and experience, legal assistants have knowledge and expertise regarding the legal system and substantive and procedural law which qualify them to do work of a legal nature under the supervision of an attorney.

STANDARDS

A legal assistant should meet certain minimum qualifications. The following standards may be used to determine an individual's qualifications as a legal assistant:

1. Successful completion of the Certified Legal Assistant (CLA) examination of the National Association of Legal Assistants, Inc.;
2. Graduation from an ABA approved program of study for legal assistants;
3. Graduation from a course of study for legal assistants which is institutionally accredited but not ABA approved, and which requires not less than the equivalent of 60 semester hours of classroom study;
4. Graduation from a course of study for legal assistants, other than those set forth in (2) and (3) above, plus not less than six months of in-house training as a legal assistant;
5. A baccalaureate degree in any field, plus not less than six months' in-house training as a legal assistant;
6. A minimum of three years of law-related experience under the supervision of an attorney, including at least six months of in-house training as a legal assistant; or
7. Two years of in-house training as a legal assistant.

For purposes of these standards, "in-house training as a legal assistant" means attorney education of the employee concerning legal assistant duties and these guidelines. In addition to review and analysis of assignments, the legal assistant should receive a reasonable amount of instruction directly related to the duties and obligations of the legal assistant.

* Within this occupational category some individuals are known as paralegals.

GUIDELINES

These guidelines relating to standards of performance and professional responsibility are intended to aid legal assistants and attorneys. The responsibility rests with an attorney who employs legal assistants to educate them with respect to the duties they are assigned and to supervise the manner in which such duties are accomplished.

Legal assistants should:

1. Disclose their status as legal assistants at the outset of any professional relationship with a client, other attorneys, a court or administrative agency or personnel thereof, or members of the general public;
2. Preserve the confidences and secrets of all clients; and
3. Understand the attorney's Code of Professional Responsibility and these guidelines in order to avoid any action which would involve the attorney in a violation of that Code, or give the appearance of professional impropriety.

Legal assistants should not:

1. Establish attorney-client relationships; set legal fees; give legal opinions or advice; or represent a client before a court; nor
2. Engage in, encourage, or contribute to any act which could constitute the unauthorized practice of law.

Legal assistants may perform services for an attorney in the representation of a client, provided:

1. The services performed by the legal assistant do not require the exercise of independent professional legal judgment;
2. The attorney maintains a direct relationship with the client and maintains control of all client matters;
3. The attorney supervises the legal assistant;
4. The attorney remains professionally responsible for all work on behalf of the client, including any actions taken or not taken by the legal assistant in connection therewith; and
5. The services performed supplement, merge with and become the attorney's work product.

In the supervision of a legal assistant, consideration should be given to:

1. Designating work assignments that correspond to the legal assistants' abilities, knowledge, training and experience.
2. Educating and training the legal assistant with respect to professional responsibility, local rules and practices, and firm policies;
3. Monitoring the work and professional conduct of the legal assistant to ensure that the work is substantively correct and timely performed;
4. Providing continuing education for the legal assistant in substantive matters through courses, institutes, workshops, seminars and in-house training; and
5. Encouraging and supporting membership and active participation in professional organizations.

Except as otherwise provided by statute, court rule or decision, administrative rule or regulation, or the attorney's Code of Professional Responsibility; and within the preceding parameters and proscriptions, a legal assistant may perform any function delegated by an attorney, including, but not limited to the following:

1. Conduct client interviews and maintain general contact with the client after the establishment of the attorney-client relationship, so long as the client is aware of the status and function of the legal assistant, and the client contact is under the supervision of the attorney.
2. Locate and interview witnesses, so long as the witnesses are aware of the status and function of the legal assistant.
3. Conduct investigations and statistical and documentary research for review by the attorney.
4. Conduct legal research for review by the attorney.
5. Draft legal documents for review by the attorney.
6. Draft correspondence and pleadings for review by and signature of the attorney.
7. Summarize depositions, interrogatories, and testimony for review by the attorney.
8. Attend executions of wills, real estate closings, depositions, court or administrative hearings and trials with the attorney.
9. Author and sign letters provided the legal assistant's status is clearly indicated and the correspondence does not contain independent legal opinions or legal advice.

POSITION OF THE NATIONAL FEDERATION OF PARALEGAL ASSOCIATIONS (NFPA) ON NALA's MODEL STANDARDS AND GUIDELINES FOR LEGAL ASSISTANTS

Historically, the NFPA has discouraged implementation of guidelines and standards which serve to restrict and limit the growth of the paralegal profession. The parameters of the profession are already defined by the unauthorized practice of law statutes. Rather than further restrict the profession, the NFPA is committed to expanding the paralegal role within the parameters of the unauthorized practice of law statutes, as well as supporting innovative interpretations as to what constitutes the practice of law.

In examining contemporary legal institutions and systems, the members of the NFPA recognize that a re-definition of the traditional delivery of legal services is essential in order to meet the needs of the general public. We are committed to increasing the availability of affordable, quality legal services, a goal which is served by the constant reevaluation and expansion of the work that paralegals are authorized to perform. Delivery of quality legal services to those portions of our population currently without access to them requires innovation and sensitivity to specific needs of people. Our view is that our future role in the delivery of legal services is almost limitless.

The intent of the guidelines promulgated by the National Association of Legal Assistants ("NALA"), to assure proper utilization of legal assistants to effect efficient delivery of legal services is certainly an admirable goal. However, guidelines should not be adopted without a clear definition of need, a thorough examination of all of the issues involved, and evidence that the program's negative impact would be minimal.

DEFINITION OF NEED

It is unclear who in the legal community needs these guidelines. Is it attorneys, paralegal administrators, educators, paralegals themselves or the public? The guidelines appear to be written to attorneys and therefore perhaps it is assumed that they are the ones that need the guidelines. In any event, it would seem that all of the groups affected by the guidelines should be involved in identifying the need. Once it has been established who needs the guidelines and what their purpose is, we can draft the guidelines to directly correspond to and meet those needs. Guidelines that are too general are ineffective. Since it appears the guidelines are based on already existing ethics opinions again their need becomes a questionable issue.

EXAMINATION OF THE ISSUES INVOLVED

The paralegal profession is still developing. Growth and expansion could be restricted by the requirement that paralegals meet standards and definitions based on current roles rather than allowing paralegals, attorneys and clients the freedom to examine new approaches to the practice of law. The guidelines should recognize the full range of individuals in title companies, corporations, healthcare facilities, governmental agencies, insurance companies, correctional institutions, military service and consumer organizations. Because the profession is evolving at such a rapid pace, definitions, guidelines, or standards should be developed only after a clear need has been established.

Currently employers have the freedom to select paralegals with abilities and backgrounds suited to their individual practice. However, these guidelines may suggest that a single approach will fit the needs of all.

The requirements in the standards portion of the guidelines raise many questions as to what type of education is required to make a paralegal. NFPA has traditionally held the position that accreditation of paralegals should be done by an autonomous group made up of representatives from lawyer, paralegal, paralegal educator, paralegal administration groups and from the public. For that reason, the NFPA would be opposed to a standard which accepted the ABA approval process as the standard.

Additionally, the standards are somewhat vague. What do you call a person who is working to complete the six months of in-house training requirements? Do we create a new position entitled paralegal-in-training?

Use as a criterion for minimum qualifications of the NALA certification exam is another questionable standard. The exam has not been examined in detail by other groups and has not been widely endorsed. The exam fails to recognize the specialized nature of the paralegal profession as it requires in depth knowledge of four specialty areas. For the majority of practicing paralegals, the examination would not be relevant to what their jobs entail. If paralegals are tested on skills that are not applicable to the job they are seeking, firms hiring them would have to train and reeducate them in any event. To impose a test with no relation to improved quality of legal representation is inappropriate and costly. Again NFPA's policy on certification is that if it is determined to be necessary and useful, then it should be done on a nationwide level by an autonomous group representing the various sections within the legal profession so that the public interest and not the self interest of the profession is the prime reason for certifying paralegals.

POSSIBLE NEGATIVE IMPACTS

Employment standards designed to be guidelines only can instead be followed blindly and rigidly and become exclusionary. The NFPA believes the delivery of quality legal services can be better facilitated with the continued expansion of paralegal responsibilities and the development of innovative methods of delivering legal services. The primary reason for the development of the legal assistant concept is to increase the availability of legal services to those who are currently without access to them. Greater access may be hindered by the limitations placed on us by the guidelines.

Educational institutions may design their training to fit into the guidelines, and curriculum could become uniform and rigid. Again, innovation will be hindered by retarding the development both of new roles for paralegals and the diverse types of training that they will need.

How will the guidelines be enforced? In monitoring previously proposed guidelines, the NFPA has noted that guidelines, once adopted, are not usually updated to reflect new developments in the paralegal profession and the practice of law. For example, Guideline VI of the New York State Bar Association's guidelines adopted in 1976 prohibits the inclusion of the name of a non-lawyer on a lawyer's letterhead. However, in light of *Bates v. State Bar of Arizona,* and an informal ABA opinion, the New York State Bar Association Committee Professional Ethics issued Ethical Opinion 500, permitting the inclusion of non-lawyer employees on a firm's letterhead "whenever the inclusion of such name would not be deceptive and might be reasonably expected to supply information relative to the selection of counsel." Years have elapsed since the issuance of Opinion 500, yet, as of this date, Guideline VI has not been revised to reflect the change in the practice of law which is evidenced by this Opinion.

In addition to these more concrete negative impacts, there is a more conceptual problem with the guidelines. Because the guidelines are written for attorneys only and say little to paralegals, the effect is to put paralegals in a very passive position turning control of our profession over to attorneys. The NFPA has always sought to maintain a separate and independent voice that speaks to its members as well as to other groups within the legal community. That independent voice expresses an interest separate from the interests of any other group. The guidelines, by speaking to attorneys and asking that they take control, minimizes the duty of paralegals to take responsibility for their own actions and to take a strong leadership role in educating ourselves in areas such as ethics and unauthorized practice of law. Thus, the guidelines would have the negative effect of weakening the paralegal movement.

CONCLUSION

The need for these guidelines has yet to be determined and should be examined by legal assistants, attorneys, paralegal educators, paralegal administrators and the public. The issues surrounding the guidelines have not been fully discussed and the negative impacts could be prohibitive. All possible ramifications must be thoroughly studied before implementation. If, after study by all affected parties, it is determined that there is sufficient need for guidelines, they must be developed, implemented and controlled by an autonomous group which provokes equitable representation by private and public sector paralegals, attorneys, paralegal educators and consumers of legal services to insure all legitimate interests are represented.

This profession is rooted in the desire to reduce legal fees and demystify the law by creating a pool of lay people who can assist in the delivery of quality legal services. Any guidelines that are adopted should reflect an attempt to meet the needs for legal services of those currently without access to them. The paralegal profession is already restricted by the unauthorized practice of law statutes. Is there a need to further restrict it? We must consider the most important of ramifications; what injury would further restrictions cause in the paralegal fight to assist in the delivery of quality legal services to meet the needs of the general public?

ASSIGNMENT 51

When a new local paralegal association is formed, it is often lobbied by NALA and by NFPA to become a part of one of these national organizations. The local association will usually make one of three decisions: affiliate with NALA; affiliate with NFPA; or remain unaffiliated. In making this decision, the local association will closely examine documents of the two national organizations such as the two ethical codes presented earlier (p. 285), their positions on certification (p. 288), the Model Standards (p. 296), etc. If you were a member of a local association faced with the decision of whether to join NALA or NFPA, what would your vote be? Why?

ASSIGNMENT 52

Is it a good idea to have two national associations? Why or why not?

Throughout this book the importance of paralegal associations has been stressed. They have had a major impact on the development of paralegalism. For example, it was the vigorous opposition of paralegal organizations that helped defeat the California legislation that tried to control the field in that state. Many other state and local bar associations as well as the ABA have felt the effect of organized paralegal advocacy through the associations.

As soon as possible you should join a paralegal association. If one does not exist in your area, you should form one and decide whether you want to become part of the National Federation of Paralegal Associations or the National Association of Legal Assistants. The paralegal association is your main voice in the continued development of the field. Join one now and become an active member. In addition to the educational benefits of association membership and in addition to the job placement services that many provide, you will experience the satisfaction of helping create the shape of the career in the years to come. Lawyers should not be the sole mechanism of control.

Section H. FAIR LABOR STANDARDS ACT

The Fair Labor Standards Act is a federal statute that requires overtime compensation to be paid to employees.[16] There are, however, exceptions to this requirement. An exemption exists for (and hence no overtime need be paid to) those who are employed in a bona fide executive, administrative, or professional capacity.[17] Can an employer avoid paying overtime to a paralegal?

Although there is no universal answer to this question, most authorities agree that paralegal employees are *not* exempt and hence *are* entitled to the protection of the Act. Phrased another way, they are not considered profes-

---

[16] 29 U.S.C. §§201 *et. seq.* (1976).

[17] See 29 C.F.R. (Part 541) (1985).

sionals under the Act and must therefore be paid overtime compensation. If, however, the paralegal is a supervisor with extensive management responsibilities over other employees, the exemption may apply. But this would cover only a small segment of the paralegal population. The following opinion letter explains the position of the government on this issue. As you will see, the criteria used to distinguish exempt from non-exempt employees are the actual job responsibilities of the employee, and not the job title or compensation policy of the office.

Wage and Hour Division
United States Department of Labor
September 27, 1979

This is in further reply to your letter of July 12, 1979, . . . concerning the exempt status under section 13(a)(1) of the Fair Labor Standards Act of paralegal employees employed by your organization, . . .

The specific duties of the paralegal employees (all of which occur under an attorney's supervision) are interviewing clients; identifying and refining problems; opening, maintaining, and closing case files; acting as the liaison person between client and attorney; drafting pleadings and petitions, and answering petitions, and interrogatories; filing pleadings and petitions; acting as general litigation assistant during court proceedings; digesting depositions, and preparing file profiles; conducting formal and informal hearings and negotiations; preparing and editing newsletters and leaflets for community development and public relations purposes; performing outreach services; coordinating general activities with relevant local, State, and Federal agencies; assisting in establishing and implementing community legal education programs; and working as a team with other employees to deliver quality legal services. You state that the job requires at least two years of college and/or equivalent experience.

[The Fair Labor Standards] Act provides a complete minimum wage and overtime pay exemption for any employee employed in a bona fide executive, administrative, or professional capacity, . . . An employee will qualify for exemption if all the pertinent tests relating to duties, responsibilities and salary . . . are met. In response to your first question, the paralegal employees you have in mind would not qualify for exemption as bona fide professional employees as discussed in section 541.3 of the regulations, since it is clear that their primary duty does not consist of work requiring knowledge of an advanced type in a field of science or learning customarily acquired by a prolonged course of specialized intellectual instruction and study, as distinguished from a general academic education and from an apprenticeship and from training in the performance of routine mental, manual, or physical processes.

With regard to the status of the paralegal employees as bona fide administrative employees, it is our opinion that their duties do not involve the exercise of discretion and independent judgment of the type required by section 541.2(b) of the regulations. The outline of their duties which you submit actually describes the use of skills rather than discretion and independent judgment. Under section 541.207 of the regulations, this requirement is interpreted as involving the comparison and evaluation of possible courses of conduct and acting or making a decision after the various possibilities have been considered. Furthermore, the term is interpreted to mean that the person has the authority or power to make an independent choice, free from immediate direction or supervision with respect to matters of significance.

The general facts presented about the employees here tend to indicate that they do not meet these criteria. Rather, as indicated above, they would appear to fit more appropriately into that category of employees who apply particular skills and knowledge in preparing assignments. Employees who merely apply knowledge in following prescribed procedures or determining whether specified standards have been met are not deemed to be exercising independent judgment, even if they have some leeway in reaching a conclusion. In addition, it should be noted that most jurisdictions have strict prohibitions against the unauthorized practice of law by lay persons. Under the American Bar Association's Code of Professional Responsibility, a delegation of legal tasks to a lay person is proper only if the lawyer maintains a direct relationship with the client, supervises the delegated work and has complete professional responsibility for the work produced. The implication of such strictures is that the paralegal employees you describe would probably not have the amount of authority to exercise independent judgment with regard to legal matters necessary to bring them within the administrative exemption. . . .

With regard to your [other] questions, all nonexempt employees, regardless of the amount of their wages, must be paid overtime premium pay of not less than one and one-half times their regular rates of pay for all hours worked in excess of 40 in a workweek. The fact than an employee did not obtain advanced approval to work the overtime does not relieve the employer from complying with the overtime provisions of the Act.

We hope this satisfactorily responds to your inquiry. However, if you have any further questions concerning the application of the Fair Labor Standards Act to the situation you have in mind please do not hesitate to let us know.

Sincerely,

C. Lamar Johnson
Deputy Administrator

Section I. THE TORT LIABILITY OF PARALEGALS

Thus far we have discussed a number of ways that paralegal activities are or could be regulated:

- Criminal liability for violating the statutes on the unauthorized practice of law.
- Special authorization rules on practice, e.g., before administrative agencies.
- The ethical rules governing lawyer delegation to paralegals.
- Licensing.
- Bar rules on paralegal education.
- Self-regulation.
- Labor laws.

Finally, we come to the tort liability of paralegals, e.g., for negligence. Tort law also helps define what is and is not permissible.

The governing principle of liability is *respondeat superior*. According to this concept, the paralegal's *employer* is responsible for the torts of his/her employees so long as they were acting in the scope of their employment at the time they did the acts leading to the torts. Hence, if George Rothwell is a paralegal working for Helen Farrell, Esq., and in the course of George's job he does some work negligently that harms the client, Helen Farrell is liable to the client for the negligence because of the doctrine of *respondeat superior*. Helen is vicariously liable. Assume that she did nothing wrong or negligently herself. She is still liable solely because of what someone else has done—her paralegal employee.

> An attorney may not escape responsibility to his clients by blithely saying that any shortcomings are solely the fault of his employee. He has a duty to supervise the conduct of his office. *Attorney Grievance Committee of Maryland v. Goldberg*, 292 Md.650, 441 A.2d 338, 341 (1982).

It is important to keep in mind, however, that paralegal employees are *also* responsible for their own torts. The client in the above example could elect to bring a direct action against the paralegal, George Rothwell, for negligence. All employees are also responsible for their own torts.

Respondeat superior is simply a basis upon which liability can be imposed on the employer in the event that the client decides not to sue the employee directly, or in the event that the client decides to sue both the employer and the employee. Of course, the client cannot recover from *both* master (employer) and servant (employee). There can be only one recovery. The point is that the injured party (the client) has a choice. The choice selected is usually to pursue "the deep pocket"—the person who has the most money from which a judgment can be collected. Most often, of course, this is the employer.

INTENTIONAL TORTS AND CRIMINAL ACTIVITY

If a paralegal commits an intentional tort, e.g., deceit, battery, malicious prosecution, the paralegal is *personally* liable to the injured party. If the paralegal commits a crime, the criminal act may also be the basis for a *civil* action against the paralegal. What about the employing attorney? Is s/he *also* liable for the employee's intentional torts or for the civil wrong growing out of the paralegal's criminal act?

The answer depends, in part, on whether the paralegal was attempting to further the "business" of his/her employing lawyer at the time the paralegal committed the tort. If so, then the lawyer is liable to the client under the doctrine of *respondeat superior*. The tortious activity in such cases will be considered within the scope of employment. For example, suppose while trying to collect an unpaid law firm bill, the paralegal assaults or slanders the client. Such activity would probably be considered within the scope of employment since the incident centered around a law firm matter—the client's bill. Quite a different result, however, might be reached if the paralegal happens to meet a law firm client at a bar and assaults or falsely imprisons the client following an argument over a football game.

NEGLIGENCE

It is much easier to establish that the paralegal's negligence was within the scope of employment (making the employer vicariously liable under *respondeat superior*) than it is to prove that intentional torts fall within this scope.

One question that might arise concerns the standard of care. When the paralegal makes a negligent mistake, is s/he held to the standard of care of a lawyer or of a paralegal? The basic standard of care is: reasonableness under the circumstances. If the person is engaged in a trade or profession and thereby possesses greater skills than the average citizen, then the standard of care will be the reasonable person possessing such skills. According to the *Restatement of Torts 2d* (p. 550):

> **§ 229 A. Undertaking in Profession or Trade.** Unless he represents that he has greater or less skill or knowledge, one who undertakes to render services in the practice of a profession or trade is required to exercise the skill and knowledge normally possessed by members of that profession or trade in good standing in similar communities.

The implication of section 229A is that if the paralegal "represents" or holds him/herself out as having more skill than most paralegals, s/he will be held to the higher skill standard. Suppose, for example, that the paralegal (or secretary or law clerk) deals directly with a client and does not make clear to the client that s/he is not a lawyer. Assume that by the manner in which the paralegal acts, the client justifiably is under the impression that the paralegal is a lawyer. The paralegal then makes a negligent mistake. If the client brings a negligence action against the paralegal and/or against the paralegal's employing lawyer, the standard of care against which the paralegal's conduct will be measured will be that of a lawyer since the paralegal, in effect, represented him/herself to the client as a lawyer. If, on the other hand, the paralegal makes clear to the client that s/he is not a lawyer and that s/he has less training and skill than a lawyer, then the standard of care, under section 229A, may be "the skill and knowledge normally possessed" by paralegals.

Suppose, however, that the paralegal never deals directly with the client. The entire work product of the paralegal in such situations blends or merges into the work product of the lawyer. Therefore, the legal services are represented to the client as the work product of the lawyer. Hence, even though the negligent act about which the client is complaining was committed by the paralegal, the standard of care will be the reasonable *lawyer* under the circumstances since the client had every right to believe s/he was receiving the services of a lawyer.

ASSIGNMENT 53

Go to the *American Digest System*. For information on this digest and its use, see p. 536 and p. 600. Give citations to and brief summaries of court cases on the topics listed in (a) and (b) below. Start with the Descriptive Word Index volumes of the most recent Decennial (p. 537). After you check the appropriate key numbers (p. 544) in that Decennial, check those key numbers in all the General Digest volumes that follow the most recent Decennial. Then check for case law in at least three other recent Decennials. Once you obtain citations to case law in the digest paragraphs, you do not have to go to the reporters to read the full text of the opinions. Simply give the citations you find and brief summaries of the cases as they are printed in the digest paragraphs.

a. Cases, if any, dealing with the negligence of attorneys in the hiring and supervision of legal secretaries, law clerks, investigators, and paralegals.

b. Cases, if any, dealing with the negligence of doctors and/or hospitals in the hiring and supervision of nurses, paramedics, and other medical technicians.

INSURANCE PROTECTION

Most lawyers have liability or malpractice insurance (sometimes called an error and omissions policy) to protect themselves against suits filed against them for professional negligence or other misconduct growing out of the practice of law. The insurance policy will usually cover paralegals and other employees in the office. An employed paralegal should certainly make inquiries at the firm in order to determine whether the firm has a liability insurance policy, whether it covers paralegals, what exclusions exist in the policy, the maximum coverage, etc. At some point, the paralegal should ask for a copy of the policy and read it carefully.

Free-lance or independent paralegals (p. 61) are in a different situation. They are not full-time, salaried employees of an attorney and hence may not be covered by the firm's insurance policy. Assume that a client sues his/her lawyer for negligence. If the client finds out that the lawyer used a free-lance paralegal on the client's case, the client could join this paralegal as a defendant even though, initially, the client may not be sure what role the paralegal had in the case. A common tactic of angry plaintiffs is to sue *anyone* connected with the case (a) who might be partially responsible for the alleged harm, and (b) who may have assets from which a judgment could be collected. The second criteria is critical. Who has resources or assets? Anyone with a separate office or business, such as a free-lance paralegal, is a tempting target. Even if this paralegal can eventually prove that he or she was not negligent in the case, the costs of presenting this defense can be considerable.

Since the free-lance paralegal concept is relatively new, insurance companies may be initially reluctant to issue separate policies to them except at relatively high rates. As more and more free-lance paralegals go into business on their own, however, it is anticipated that standard insurance policies will be developed to cover them.

5

How To Study Law

Education does not come naturally to most of us. It is a struggle. This is all the more true for someone entering a totally new realm of training such as legal education. Much of the material will seem foreign and difficult. There is a danger of becoming overwhelmed by the vast quantity of laws and legal material that confronts you. How do you study law? How do you learn law? What is the proper perspective that a student of law should have about the educational process? These are our concerns in this chapter. In short our theme is training to be trained—the art of effective learning.

The first step is to begin with a proper frame of mind. Too many students have false expectations of what legal education can accomplish. This substantially interferes with effective studying.

1. Your legal education has two phases. Phase I begins now and ends when you complete this training program. Phase II begins when this training program ends and is not completed until the last day of your employment as a paralegal.

You have entered a career that will require you to be a perpetual student. The learning never ends. This is true not only because the boundary lines of law are vast, but also because the law is changing every day. No one knows all of the law. Phase I of your legal education is designed to provide you with the foundation that will enable you to become a good student in Phase II.

2. Your legal education has two dimensions: the content of the law (the rules) and the practical techniques of using that content in a law office (the skills).

Rules.   There are two basic kinds of law:

SUBSTANTIVE LAW:
those nonprocedural rules that govern rights and obligations, e.g., the requirements for the sale of land;

PROCEDURAL LAW:
those rules that govern the mechanics of resolving a dispute in court or at an administrative agency, e.g., how many days a party has to respond to a claim stated in a complaint.

The law library contains millions of substantive and procedural rules written by courts (in volumes called reporters), by the legislature (in volumes called statutory codes), and by administrative agencies (in volumes called regulations or administrative codes).

A substantial portion of your time in school will involve a study of the substantive and procedural law of your state, and often of the federal government as well.

Skills.   By far the most important dimension of your legal education will be the skills of using rules. Without the skills, the content of the law is close to worthless. Examples of legal skills include:

- How to interview a client (p. 385).
- How to investigate the facts of a case (p. 427).
- How to draft a complaint, the document that initiates a law suit (p. 498).
- How to do legal research in a law library (p. 505).
- How to digest or summarize documents in a case file (p. 489).

The overriding skill that, in one degree or another, is the basis for all the others is the skill of legal analysis (p. 371). There are some who make the mistake of concluding that legal analysis is within the exclusive domain of the lawyer. Without an understanding of legal analysis, however, a paralegal cannot understand the legal system and cannot intelligently carry out many of the more demanding tasks that are assigned.

3. You must force yourself to suspend what you already know about the law in order to be able to absorb (a) that which is new and (b) that which conflicts with your prior knowledge and experience.

Place yourself in the position of training someone to drive a car. Your student undoubtedly already knows something about driving. S/he has watched others drive and maybe has even had a lesson or two from friends. It would be ideal, however, if you could begin your instruction from point zero. There is a very real danger that the student has picked up bad habits from others. This will interfere with his/her capacity to *listen* to what you are saying. The danger is that s/he will block out those things you are saying that do not conform to previously learned habits and knowledge. If the habits or knowledge are defective, your job as a trainer is immensely more difficult.

The same is true in studying law. Everyone knows something about the law from our civics courses as a teenager and from the various treatments of the law in the media. It may be that some of you have been involved in the law as a party or as a witness in court. Others may have worked, or currently work, in law offices. Will this prior knowledge and experience be a help or a hindrance to you in your future legal education? For some it will be a help. For most of us, however, there is a danger of interference.

This is particularly so with respect to the portrayal of the law on TV and in the movies. Millions of Americans still operate under the misconception that the practice of law follows the pattern of TV's "Perry Mason" where most legal problems appear to be solved by dramatically tricking a hostile witness on the stand into finally telling the truth. The law is not a process of forcing confessions out of opponents. While excitement and drama can be a part of the practice of law, they are not everyday occurrences. What is dominant is painstaking and meticulous hard work.

It is strongly recommended that you place yourself in the position of a stranger to the material you will be covering in your courses, regardless of your prior background and exposure to the field. Cautiously treat everything as a new experience. Temporarily, suspend what you already know. Resist the urge to pat yourself on the back by saying, "I already knew that" or "I already know how to do that." For many students, such statements cause a relaxation. They do not work as hard in learning once they have convinced themselves that there is nothing new to learn. No problem exists, of course, if these students are right. The danger, however, is that they are wrong or that they are only partially right. Students are not always the best judge of what they know and of what they can do. Do not become too comfortable. Adopt the following healthy attitude: "I've dealt with that before, but maybe I can learn something new about it." Every new teacher, every new supervisor, every new setting is an opportunity to add a new dimension to your prior knowledge and experience. Be open to these opportunities. No two people practice law exactly the same way. Your own growth as a student and as a paralegal will depend in large part on your capacity to listen for, to explore, and to absorb this diversity.

4. Be sure that you know the goals and context of every assignment.

Throughout your education you may be given a variety of assignments: class exercises, text readings, drafting tasks, field projects, research assignments, examinations, etc. You should ask yourself the following questions about each one:

- What are the goals of this assignment? What am I supposed to learn from it?
- How does this assignment fit into what I have already learned? What is the context of the assignment?

Successfully undertaking the assignment is in part dependent on your understanding of its goals and how these goals relate to the overall context of the course. How do you identify goals and context?

- Carefully listen to and take notes on what your teacher tells the class about the assignment.
- Ask the teacher questions about his/her expectations for the assignment. Demonstrate a polite but probing interest.
- If the teacher has given this assignment before to other classes, ask former students. If they have had any papers returned to them by the teacher, try to read some of them to determine what comments/criticisms the teacher has made on them. These observations will be additional clues to what the teacher is after.
- Take note of what the authors of your texts have expressly or impliedly told you about the importance or purpose of certain tasks.
- Ask fellow classmates about their understanding of purpose and context.

In short, be preoccupied by these concerns. *Do not undertake assignments in isolation or in a vacuum.*

This advice applies on the job as well as in school. A strong indication of one's commitment—an essential ingredient of progress and advancement—is a sincere interest in the broader picture. Avoid the reputation as someone who simply wants to "get the job done and get out as quickly as possible." While speed is sometimes critical, speed is never a substitute for efficiency and professionalism. The latter are directly dependent on the extent of your involvement, interest, and enthusiasm in carrying out a task. Boredom and incompetence often feed on each other.

This is not to say that you must be wildly enthusiastic about everything you do. The goal is to avoid undertaking tasks routinely—even routine tasks! One way to accomplish this goal is to have a constant eye on the broader picture. Why are you being asked to do something in a certain way? Has it always been done this way? Are there more efficient ways? After the pressure of the immediate need has passed, can you think about and eventually propose a more effective *system* of handling the task?

Of course, there is a danger of going to the opposite extreme. You cannot be so preoccupied with purpose, context, and systems that you fail to complete the immediate job before you. Timing is important. Often the office will have no tolerance for suggestions for improvement until immediate deadlines have passed. This simply means that you must always be operating at two levels. First, the *now* level. Mobilize all of your resources to complete the task as efficiently as possible under the present work environment. Second, the *systems* level. Keep your mind open and challenge your creativity to identify steps and procedures that might be taken in the future to achieve greater efficiency in accomplishing the task.

5. Design a study plan.

Make constant and current *lists* of everything that you must do. Divide the list into long-term projects (what is due next week or at the end of the semester) and short-term projects (what is due tomorrow). Have a plan for each day. Establish the following norm for yourself: every day you will focus in some way on *all* of your assignments. Every day you will review your long-term and short-term list. Priority, of course, will be given to the short-term tasks. Yet some time, however small, will also be devoted to the long-term tasks. At a minimum, this time can be used simply to remind yourself that these tasks are hanging over you and that you must make concrete commitments to devote substantial blocks of time to them in the immediate future. Make and renew these commitments every day. If possible, go beyond this. On a day that you will be mainly working on the short-term projects, try to set aside 5% of your time to the long-term projects, e.g., by doing some background reading, by preparing a very rough first draft of an outline. It is critical that you establish *momentum* toward the accomplishment of *all* your tasks. This is done by never letting anything sit on the back burner. Set yourself the goal of making at least *some* progress on everything every day. Without this goal, the momentum will be very difficult to find.

Once you have decided what you will cover on a given study day, the next question is: in what *order* will you cover them. There are a number of ways in which you can classify the things that you must do. For example, (a) easy tasks that will require a relatively short time to complete, (b) complex tasks requiring more time, (c) tasks with time demands that will be unknown until you start them. At the beginning of your study time, spend a few seconds preparing an outline of the order in which you will cover the tasks that day and the approximate amount of time that you will set aside for each task. You may want to start with some of the easier tasks so that relatively soon you can feel a sense of accomplishment. Alternatively, you may want to devote early study time to the third kind of task listed above ("c") so that you can obtain a clearer idea of the scope and difficulty of such assignments. The important point is that you establish a *schedule.* It does not have to be written in stone. Quite the contrary. It is healthy that you have enough flexibility to revise your day's schedule in order to respond to unfolding realities as you study. Adaptation is not a sign of disorganization, but the total absence of an initial plan is.

6. Add 50% to the time you initially think you will need to study a particular subject.

You are kidding yourself if you have not set aside a *substantial* amount of time to study law outside the classroom. The conscientious study of law takes time—lots of it. It is true that some students must work and take care of family responsibilities. You cannot devote time that you do not have. Yet the reality is that limited study time leads to limited education.

Generally, a person will find time for what s/he wants to do. You may *wish* to do many things for which there will never be enough time. You will find the time, however, to do what you really *want* to do. Once you have decided that you want something badly enough, you will find the time to do it.

Most people waste tremendous amounts of time by worrying about all the things that they have to do and in taking rest periods from this worrying through socializing or other casual pursuits. How much *productive* time do you gain out of a single work hour? For most of us the answer is about twenty minutes. The rest of the hour is spent worrying, relaxing, repeating ourselves, socializing, etc. One answer to the problem of limited time availability is to increase the amount of *productive* time that you derive out of each work hour. You may not be able to add any new hours to the clock, but you can add to your net productive time. How about moving up to thirty minutes an hour? Forty? You will be amazed at the time that you can "find" simply by making a conscious effort to remove some of the waste. When asked how a masterpiece was created, a great sculptor once responded that you start with a block of stone and you cut away everything that is not art. In your study habits, start with a small block of time and work to cut away everything that is not productive.

There are no absolute rules on how much time you will need. It depends on the complexity of the subject matter you must master. It is probably accurate to say that most of us need to study more than we do. As a rule of thumb, about 50% more. You should be constantly alert to ways to increase the time you have available, or more accurately, to increase the productive time that you can make available.

Resolving time management problems as a student will be good practice for you when you are confronted with similar (and more severe) time management problems as a working paralegal. Many law offices operate at a hectic pace. One of the hallmarks of a professional is a pronounced reverence for deadlines and the clock in general. Time is money. An ability to find and handle time effectively can also be one of the preconditions for achieving justice in a particular case.

Soon you will be gaining a reputation among your fellow students, teachers, supervisors, and employers, One of the reputations that you should make a concerted effort to acquire is a reputation for hard work, punctuality, and conscientiousness about the time you devote to your work. In large measure, success follows from such a reputation. It is probably more important than raw ability or intelligence. If not more important, it is certainly as important.

7. Create your own study area free from distractions.

It is essential that you find study areas that are quiet and free from distractions. Otherwise, concentration is obviously impossible. It may be that the worst places to study are at home or in your library at school unless you can find a corner that is cut off from noise and people who want to talk. Do not make yourself too available. If you study in the corridor, at the first table at the entrance to the library, or at the kitchen table, you are inviting distraction. You need to be able to close yourself off for two to three hours at a time. It is important for you to interact with other people—but not while you are studying material that requires considerable concentration. You will be tempted to digress and to socialize. You are in the best position to know where these temptations are. You are also the most qualified person to know how to avoid the temptations.

8. Conduct a self-assessment of your prior study habits and establish a program to reform the weaknesses.

If you were to describe the way in which you study, would you be proud of the description? Here is a partial list of some of the main weaknesses of attitude or practice that students have in studying:

- The student has done well in the past with only minimal study effort. Why change now?
- No one else in the class appears to be studying very much. Why be different?
- The student learns best by listening in class. Hence instead of studying on one's own, why not wait until someone explains it in person?
- The student simply does not like to study; there are more important things to do in life.
- The student can't concentrate.
- The student studies with the radio on or with other distractions.
- The student gets bored easily. "I can't stay motivated for long."
- The student does not understand what s/he is supposed to study.
- The student skim reads.
- The student must read something over and over again, but seems to understand it less and less.
- The student does not stop to look up strange words or phrases.
- The student studies only at exam time—crams for exams.
- The student does not study at a consistent pace. It's an hour here and there—no organized, regular study times.
- The student does not like to memorize.
- The student does not take notes on what s/he is reading.

What other interferences with effective studying can you think of? Or more importantly, which of the above items and which additional items apply to you? How do you plead? In law, it is frequently said that you cannot solve a problem until you obtain the facts. What are the facts in the case of your study habits? Make your personal list of attitude problems, study patterns, or environmental interferences. Place the items in the list in some order. Next, establish a plan for yourself. Which item on the list are you going to try to correct tonight? What will the plan be for this week? For next week? For the coming month? What specific steps will you take to try to change some bad habits? Do not be too hard on yourself. Be determined, but realistic. The more serious problems are obviously going to take more time to correct. Improvement will come if you are serious about improvement and regularly think about it. If one corrective method does not work, try another, If the fifth does not work, try a sixth. Discuss techniques of improvement with your fellow students and teachers. Prove to yourself that change is possible.

9. Conduct a self-assessment on grammar/spelling/composition, and design a program to reform the weakness.

The legal profession lives by the written word. Talking is important for some activities, but writing is crucial in almost every area of the practice of law. You cannot function in this environment without a grasp of the basics of spelling, grammar, and composition. A major complaint being made by employers today is that paralegals are consistently violating these basics. The problem is very serious.

Step One. You must take responsibility for your training in grammar/ spelling/composition. Do not wait for someone to teach you these basics. Do not wait until someone points out your weaknesses. You must make a personal commitment to train yourself. If there are English courses available to you, great. It is essential, however, that you understand that a weekly class will not be enough.

Step Two. Raise your consciousness about the writing around you. Your training in writing cannot be compartmentalized. You must be constantly thinking about and worrying about writing. The concern should be a preoccupation. When you are reading a newspaper, for example, you should be conscious of the use of semicolons and paragraph structure in what you are reading. At least occasionally you should ask yourself why a certain punctuation mark was used by a writer. You are surrounded by writing. You read this writing for content. You must begin a conscious effort to focus on the structure of this writing as well.

Step Three. Purchase several grammar books. Do not rely on one grammar book. There are hundreds of texts on the market. They explain things differently. You should consult more than one grammar book on difficult points. It must be admitted that some grammar books are poorly written! They are not always easy to use. They may give examples of grammar rules without clearly defining the rules. Or, they may define the rules without giving clear examples of the application of the rules. A grammar book may be excellent for some areas of writing, but weak on other areas. Hence, have more than one grammar book in your personal library.

You may have saved grammar books you used earlier in your education. In addition, go to second-hand book stores. They often have a section on text books. Some of the best grammar books are old, elementary texts that provide excellent overviews of the basics. Another way to cut down on the expense of purchase is to consider paperback texts. The characteristics to look for in making a purchase are:

- A comprehensive index.
- Clearly defined rules covering the basics.
- Numerous examples of the application of the rules.
- Exercises on the rules *with answers* so that you can check your own progress.

Step Four. Use the grammar books as frequently as you would a dictionary. Have the books at your side every time you write. Force yourself to use these books regularly. The more often you use them now, the less you will need them later as you continue to improve. You will never be able to discard them entirely, however. You will need to consult them when doing any serious writing in the law. How often will they have to be consulted? It depends on the extent of the weaknesses that you have and the frequency with which you begin consulting them now.

Step Five. Improve your spelling. Use a dictionary often. Begin making a list of the words that you are spelling incorrectly. Work on these words. When you have the slightest doubt on the spelling of a word, check the dictionary. Again, the more often you take this approach now, the less often you will have to use the dictionary later.

The following list contains words that are frequently misspelled. It is recommended that you study a designated number of these words every week until you have mastered all of them.

aberration
abridgment
absorb (take in)
   adsorb (adhesion)
abysmal
accede (yield)
   exceed (surpass)
accessory
accommodate
accordion
accouter
ache
acknowledgment
acoustic
adapter
adjuster
ad nauseam
adviser
aegis
affect (influence)
   effect (result)
airplane
allottee
all ready (prepared)
   already (previous)
all right
altogether (completely)
   all together
     (collectively)
aluminum
always
ambidextrous
analog
analogous
anemia
anesthetic
aneurysm
anomalous
anonymous
antibiotics (n.)
  antibiotic (adj.)
appall, -ed, -ing
archeology
artifact
artisan
ascendance, -ant
ascent (rise)
  assent (consent)
assassinate
attester
awhile (for some time)
  a while (a short time)
ax

battalion
bazaar
beginning
believe
beneficent
benefited
bettor (wagerer)

biased
bloc (group)
born (birth)
  borne (carried)
bouillon (soup)
  bullion (metal)
boulder
bourgeoisie
burned
bus, bused, buses, busing
business

caffeine
caliber
calligraphy
callus (n.)
  callous (adj.)
calorie
canceled, -ing
cancellation
candor
canister
canvas (cloth)
  canvass (solicit)
canyon
capital (city)
  capitol (building)
carat (weight)
  caret (omission mark)
cartilage
casual (unimportant)
  causal (cause)
catalog, -ed, -ing
cesarean
chancellor
channeled, -ing
chauvinism
cigarette
clamor
climactic (climax)
  climatic (climate)
cocaine
colloquy
colossal
combated, -ing
commingle
complement (complete)
  compliment (praise)
connoisseur
consensus
consignor
consummate
converter
conveyor
corollary
cough
counseled, -ing
country
county
crystallize

defense
demagog
demarcation
dependent
descendant
desuetude
detractor
device (contrivance)
  devise (convey)
dialog
diaphragm
discreet (prudent)
  discrete (distinct)
dispatch
dissension
distributor
doctrinaire
dossier
dyeing (coloring)
  dying (death)

ecstasy
eleemosynary
elicit (to draw)
  illicit (illegal)
embarrass
embellish
emigrant (go from)
  immigrant (go into)
emigree
enclose
enclosure
encumber
encumbrance
encyclopedia
endorse, -ment
enfeeble
enforce, -ment
enroll, -ed, -ing, -ment
entrepreneur
entrust
envelop (v.)
  envelope (n.)
equaled, -ing
esthetic
evacuee
exhibitor
exhilarate
exonerate
exorbitant
exposé (exposure)
  expose (to lay open)
extant (in existence)
  extent (range)
extoll, -ed, -ing

fantasy
February
fetus
flammable (*not*
  inflammable)

fledgling
fluorescent
focused, -ing
forbade
forbear (endurance, etc.)
  forebear (ancestor)
foresee
foreseeable
forty
fulfill, -ed, -ing, -ment
furor
fuselage
fusillade

gage
germane
glamorous
glamour
gobbledygook
goodby
gram
grammar
grievous
groveled, -ing
gruesome
guerrilla (warfare)
  gorilla (ape)

harass
heinous
hemorrhage
heterogeneous
hijack
homogeneity
hypocrisy

idiosyncrasy
idyl
impaneled, -ing
impasse
imperiled, -ing
impostor
indict
inequity (unfairness)
  iniquity (sin)
inferable
ingenious (skillful)
  ingenuous (simple)
innocuous
innuendo
inoculate
inquire
inquiry
install, -ed, -ing, -ment
installation
instill, -ed, -ing
insure
interment (burial)
  internment (detention)
intern
intransigent (n., adj.)
italic

judgment
kidnaped, -ing
kidnaper
kilogram

labeled, -ing
lengthwise
leukemia
leveled, -ing
liability
liable
liaison
libelant
libeled, -ing
libelee
libeler
license
likable
linage (lines)
  lineage (descent)
liquor
  liqueur
livable
loath (reluctant)
  loathe (detest)
loose
lose

maneuver
manifold
marijuana
marshaled, -ing
marveled, -ing
marvelous
meager
medieval
meter
mil (1/1000 inch)
  mill (1/1000 dollar)
mileage
milieu
misspell
modeled, -ing
moneys
monolog

Moslem
movable

nickel

offense
oneself
ordinance (law)
  ordnance (military)

paralleled, -ing
parceled, -ing
partisan
pastime
patrol, -led, -ling
peddler
percent
peremptory (decisive)
  preemptory (preference)
perennial
perquisite (privilege)
  prerequisite (requirement)
personal (individual)
  personnel (staff)
perspective (view)
  prospective (expected)
plaque
practice (n., v.)
precedence (priority)
  precedents (usage)
pretense
preventive
principal (chief)
  principle (proposition)
privilege
proffer
programed, -er, -ing
promissory
pronunciation
propel, -led, -ling
propellant (n.)
  propellent (adj.)
prophecy (n.)
  prophesy (v.)

protester
pusillanimous

quarreled, -ing
questionnaire

rapprochement
rarity
ratable
reconnaissance
reconnoiter
referable
registrar
renaissance
repellant (n.)
  repellent (adj.)
rescission
rivaled, -ing

sacrilegious
salable
satellite
schizophrenia
scurrilous
separate
seriatim
settler
  settlor (law)
sewage (waste)
  sewerage (drain system)
shriveled, -ing
signaled, -ing
siphon
sizable
skeptic
skillful
spacious (space)
  specious (plausible)
specter
stationary (fixed)
  stationery (paper)
statue (sculpture)
  stature (height)
  statute (law)
staunch

stifling
straight
stratagem
stubbornness
subpoena, -ed
subtlety
surreptitious
surveillance
synonymous

taboo
tactician
technique
theater
therefor (for it)
  therefore (for that reason)
though
threshold
through
tie, tied, tying
tormenter
totaled, -ing
trafficking
tranquilize(r)
tranquillity
transferable
transferor
transferred
traveled, -ing
traveler
typify
tyrannical

vacillate
vicissitude
vilify
villain
vitamin

weather
Wednesday
whether
willful
woeful
worshiped, -er, -ing

Step Six. Enroll in English and writing courses. Check offerings at your school. Also check other area schools, e.g., adult education programs in the public schools or at colleges.

Step Seven. Find out which law courses in your curriculum require the most writing from the students. If possible, take these courses—no matter how painful you find writing to be. In fact, the more painful it is, the more you need to place yourself in an environment where writing is demanded of you on a regular basis.

Step Eight. Simplify your writing. Cut down the length of your sentences. Minimize the use of semicolons that extend the length of sentences. Many have the mistaken idea that legal writing must be "heavy," angust, and flowery; this usually leads to verbosity. The best legal writing, no matter how technical, is evenly paced, clear, and concise.

Step Nine.   Prepare a self-assessment of your weaknesses. Make a list of what you must correct. Then set a schedule of improvement. Set aside a small amount of time each day, e.g., ten minutes, during which you work on your weaknesses. Be consistent about this time. Do not wait for the weekend or for next semester when you will have more time. The reality is that you will probably never have substantially more time than you have now. The problem is not so much the absence of time as it is the unwillingness to dig into the task. Progress will be slow and you will be on your own. Hence, there is a danger that you will be constantly finding excuses to put it off.

10. Consider forming a student study group, but be cautious.

Students sometimes find it useful to form study groups. A healthy exchange with your colleagues can be very productive. One difficulty is finding students with whom you are compatible. Trial and error may be the only way to identify such students. A more serious concern is trying to define the purpose of the study group. It should not be used as a substitute for your own individual study. It would be inappropriate to divide a course into parts, with members of the group having responsibility for preparing notes on and teaching the assigned parts to the remainder of the group.

The group can be very valuable for mutual editing on writing assignments. Suppose, for example, that you are drafting complaints in a course. Photocopy a complaint that one member of the group drafts. The group then collectively comments upon and edits the complaint according to the standards discussed in class and in the materials of the course. Similarly, you could try to obtain copies of old exams in the course and collectively examine answers prepared by individual group members. Ask your teacher for fact situations that could be the basis of legal analysis memos (p. 371) or other drafting assignments. Make up fact situations of your own. The student whose work is being scrutinized must be able to take constructive criticism. The criticism should be intense if it is to be worthwhile. Following a critique session, students should be asked to re-write the draft after incorporating the suggestions made. The re-write should later be subjected to another round of mutual editing. Occasionally, you might want to consider asking your teacher to meet with your group in order to obtain further help in legal writing.

Do not be hesitant to subject your writing to the scrutiny of your fellow students. You can learn a great deal from each other.

11. Use your legal research skills to help you understand components of a course that are giving you difficulty.

The law library is not simply the place to go to find the law that governs the facts of a client's case. A great deal of the material in the law library consists of explanations/summaries/overviews of the same law that you will be covering in your courses. You need to know how to gain access to this material as soon as possible. In chapter 11, a series of techniques are presented on doing background research through texts such as legal dictionaries, legal encyclopedias, treatises, annotations, etc. (p. 595). You should become acquainted with these kinds of law books. They will prove invaluable as outside reading to help resolve conceptual and practical difficulties you are having in class.

12. Organize your learning through definitions or definitional questions.

The most sophisticated question a lawyer or paralegal can ask is: what does that word or phrase mean—what's the definition? To a very large extent, the practice of law is a probing for definitions of key words or phrases in the context of facts that have arisen. Can a five-year-old be liable for negligence? (What is *negligence?*) Can the government tax a church-run bingo game? (What is the *free exercise of religion?*) Can lawyers in a law firm strike and obtain the protection of the National Labor Relations Act? (What is a *covered* employee under the labor statute?) Can a person rape his/her spouse? (What is the definition of *rape?*) Can a citizen slander the President of the United States? (What is a *defamatory statement* and what are the definitions of the defenses to a slander action?) Etc.

For every course that you take, you will come across numerous words and phrases in class and in your readings. Begin compiling a list of these words and phrases for each class. Try to limit yourself to what you think are the major words and phrases. When in doubt about whether to include something on your list, resolve the doubt by including it.

Then pursue definitions. Ask your teacher for definitions. Find definitions in your text and in the law library, e.g., in Words and Phrases (p. 545), legal encyclopedias (p. 629), treatises (p. 630), annotations (p. 605), legal periodical literature (p. 625), statutory codes (p. 557), etc.

For some words, you may have difficulty obtaining definitions. Do not give up your pursuit. Keep searching. Keep probing. Keep questioning. For some words, there may be more than one definition. Others may require definitions of the definitions.

Of course, you cannot master a course simply by knowing the definitions of all the key words and phrases involved. Yet these words and phrases are the *vocabulary* of the course and are the foundation and point of reference for learning the other aspects of the course. Begin with vocabulary.

Consider a system of three-by-five or two-by-three cards to help you learn the definitions. On one side of the card, place a single word or phrase. On the other side, write the definition with a brief page reference or citation to the source of the definition. Using the cards, test yourself periodically. If you are in a study group, ask other members to test you. Ask a relative to test you. Establish a plan of ongoing review.

13. Translate important rules into checklists—developing your own practice manual.

It is important that you learn how to write checklists that could be part of a manual. Every rule that you are told about or that you read about can be "translated" into a checklist. Such checklist formulation should eventually become second nature to you. The sooner you start thinking in terms of do's, don't's, models, etc., the better.

Suppose that you have before you the following statute of your state:

> **§1742.** No marriage shall be solemnized without a license issued by the county clerk of any county of this state not more than thirty days prior to the date of the solemnization of the marriage.

One way to handle this statute is to create a checklist of questions that you would ask a client in order to determine whether the statute applies. (Breaking a statute down into its *elements* will assist you in identifying such questions. See p. 373.) Some of the questions would be:

1. Did you have a marriage license?
2. Where did you get the license? Did you obtain it from a county clerk in this state?
3. On what date did you obtain the license?
4. On what date did you go through the marriage ceremony (solemnization)? Were there thirty days between the date you obtained the license and the date of the ceremony?

These are the questions that must be asked as part of a large number of questions concerning the validity of a particular marriage. If you were creating a manual, the above questions in your checklist for section 1742 could go under the manual topic of "Marriage Formation" or "Marriage License." Whenever you have a class on this topic or whenever you analyze any law on this topic, you translate the lecture into checklists such as the brief one presented above.

To be sure, there are checklists written by others already in existence. They are found, for example, in manuals and practice books. (p. 543). Why create your own? First of all, your checklists are *not* intended as a substitute for those in manuals or practice books. You will undoubtedly make extensive use of the latter. You are encouraged to do so. Your checklists will supplement the others. More significantly, two of the best ways for you to learn how to use manuals are (a) to write checklists of your own and (b) to see the connection between the law (e.g., a statute) and the guidelines and techniques within a checklist. Your understanding of the checklists will be increased if you begin to see how they relate to the law itself. Hence, the emphasis placed on checklists is intended in large measure to increase the effectiveness of your use of manuals and practice books.

14. Develop the skill of note-taking.

Note-taking is essential in the law. You will regularly be told to "write it down" or "put it in a memo." Effective note-taking is often a precondition to being able to do *any* kind of writing in the law.

First, take notes on what you are reading for class preparation and for research assignments. Do not rely exclusively on your memory. After reading hundreds of pages (or more), you will not be able to remember what you have read at the end of semester, or even at the end of the day. Copy what you think are the essential portions of the materials you are reading. Be sure to include definitions of important words and phrases as indicated in guideline 12 above.

To be sure, note-taking will add time to your studying. Yet you will discover that it is time well spent once you begin reviewing for an exam or writing your memorandum.

Second, take notes in class. You must develop the art of taking notes while simultaneously listening to what is being said. On the job, you may have to do this frequently. For example:

- Interviewing a client.
- Interviewing a witness during field investigation.
- Receiving instructions from a supervisor.
- Talking with someone on the phone.
- Taking notes during a deposition.
- Taking notes from a witness giving testimony at trial.

A good place to begin learning how to write and listen at the same time is during your classes.

Most students take poor class notes. This is due to a number of reasons:

- A student may write slowly.
- A student may not like to take notes; it's hard work.
- A student may not know if what is being said is important enough to be noted until after it is said—when it is too late because the lecture has gone on to something else.
- A student does not think it is necessary to take notes on a discussion that the teacher is having with another student.
- A student takes notes only when s/he sees other students taking notes.
- Some teachers ramble.

A student who uses these excuses for not taking comprehensive notes in class will eventually be using similar excuses on the job when the note-taking is required for a case. This is unfortunate. You must overcome whatever resistances you have acquired to the admittedly difficult task of note-taking. Otherwise you will pay the price in your school work and on the job.

Of course, you do not want to write down everything, even if this is physically possible. You ought to make the assumption, however, that if it is important enough for someone to tell you something, it is important enough for you to make note of it.

If you do not know how to take shorthand, develop your own system of abbreviations. Sometimes you will have to begin taking notes at the moment the person starts talking rather than wait until the end of what s/he is saying. Try different approaches to increasing the completeness of your notes.

If you are participating in class by talking with the teacher, it will obviously be difficult for you to take notes at the same time. After class, take a few moments to jot down some notes on what occurred during the discussion.

15. Studying rules—the role of memory.

Memory plays a significant role in the law. Applicants for the bar, for example, are not allowed to take notes into the exam room. An advocate in court or at an administrative hearing may be able to refer to notes, but the notes are

The following are common abbreviations used by students in litigation classes:*

π	plaintiff	CpN	comparative negligence	s/f	statute of frauds
Δ	defendant	LCC	last clear chance	K	contract
θ	third party			T	tort
c.l.	common law	rsb	reasonable	IT	intentional tort
c/a	cause of action	RPP	reasonable prudent person	N	negligence
DV/Δ	directed verdict for defendant	A/R	assumption of risk	SL	strict liability
JV/π	jury verdict for plaintiff	cz	cause	Az	assault
		px cz	proximate cause	Bt	battery
R&R	reversed & remanded	kw/RD	knowledge or reckless regard	A&B	assault & battery
Dem	demurrer	ab dg	abnormally dangerous	FI	false imprisonment
$	suppose	ulhz	ultra-hazardous	cz/f	cause in fact
Q	question	inj	injunction	dp iv cz	dependent intervening cause
O	owner	b.f.p.	bonafide purchaser	ndp cz	independent cause
axn	action	br/wrt	breach of warranty	ss cz	superseding cause
R2T	Restatement (Second) of Torts	dft	defect	RIL	res ipsa loquitur
stat	statute	dsn	design	4cb	foreseeable
L	liable, liability	WD	wrongful death	dfm	defamation
nj	injury	Svv	survival	Dct	deceit
Bx	Blackacre	m-	mal-, mis-	lbl	libel
JD	John Doe Jane Doe	m-fz	misfeasance	sld	slander
ntt	intent	m-pr	malpractice	kct	concert
dmg	damages	m-rep	misrepre- sentation	mut	immunity
dfs	defense	n-	non-	ndp kr	independent contractor
Tp	trespass	n-fz	nonfeasance	impl	implied
pvg	privilege	[	not, un-	impt	imputed
Tfz	tortfeasor	[4cf	unforeseeable	kvn	conversion
JTz	joint tortfeasor	cov[sue	covenant not to sue	jfc	justification
lz	license	jdr	joinder	std	standard
lzc	licensee	b/p	burden of proof	vln	violation
nvt	invitee	s/l	statute of limitations	pun	punitive
tpr	trespasser			nom	nominal
nf k¢	informed consent			nzc	nuisance
ktb	contribution			stfn	satisfaction
ndt	indemnity			rls	release
lr	lessor			pvt	privity
lee	lessee			rem	remedy
CN	contributory negligence			p.f.	prima facie

of little value if the advocate does not have a solid grasp of the case. Most of the courses you will be taking have a memory component. This is true even for open-book exams since you will not have time to go through all the material while responding to the questions.

* From Prosser, Wade & Schwartz, *Cases and Materials on Torts*, p. 1263 (Foundation Press, 1976).

Two mistakes are often made by students with respect to the role of memory:

- They think that memorizing things is beneath their dignity.
- They think that because they understand something they know it sufficiently to be able to give it back in an examination.

Of course, you should not be memorizing what you do not understand. Rote memorization is close to worthless. Not so for important material that you comprehend. Yet, simply because you understand something, you have not necessarily committed it to memory for later use.

We all have our own systems for memorizing material.

- Reading it over and over.
- Copying it.
- Writing questions to yourself about it and trying to answer the questions.
- Having other students ask you questions about it.
- Making summaries or outlines of it.
- Etc.

Those of us who do not have photographic minds must resort to such techniques. Try different systems. Ask fellow students for tips on how they make effective use of their memory.

You will have to find out from your teacher what material you will be expected to know for the course. You can also check with other students who have had this teacher in the past. It may not always be easy to find out how much a teacher expects you to know from memory. Teachers have been known to surprise students on examinations! Some teachers do not like to admit that they are asking their students to memorize a lot of material for their courses and yet still give examinations that call for considerable quantities of material that can only be provided if the students have done a lot of memory preparation.

16. Studying skills—the necessity of feedback.

Memory obviously plays a less significant role in learning the skills of interviewing, investigation, legal analysis, drafting, coordinating, digesting, advocacy, and legal research. These skills have their own vocabulary that you must know, but it is your judgmental rather than your memory faculties that must be developed in order to become competent and excel in the skills.

These skills are developed primarily by *doing*—practice drills or exercises are essential. The learning comes from the feedback that you obtain while engaged in the skill exercises. What are the ways that a student obtains feedback?

- Evaluations on assignments and exams.
- Role-playing exercises that are critiqued in class.
- Comparisons between your work (particularly writing projects) with models provided by the teacher or that you find on your own in the library.
- Critiques that you receive from fellow students in study groups.

You must constantly be looking for feedback. Do not wait to be called on. Do not wait to see what feedback is planned for you at the end of the course. Take the initiative immediately. Seek conferences with your teachers. Find out who is available to read your writing or to observe your performance in any of the other skills. Set up your own role-playing sessions with your fellow students. Seek critiques of your re-writes even if the re-writing was not required. Look for opportunities to critique other students in the various skills. Ask fellow students for permission to read their graded examinations so that you can compare their papers with your own. Create your own fact hypotheticals for analysis in study groups. Do additional reading on the skills. Become actively involved in your own skills development.

17. Studying ambiguity—coping with unanswered questions.

One of the reasons the study of law can be frustrating is the fact that there is so much uncertainty in the law. Legions of unanswered questions exist. Definitive answers to legal questions are not always easy to find no matter how good your legal research techniques are. Every new fact situation presents the potential for a new law. Every law seems to have an exception. Furthermore, advocates frequently argue for exceptions to the exceptions. When terms are defined, the definitions often need definitions. A law office is not always an easy environment in which to work because of this reality.

The study of law is in large measure an examination of ambiguity that is identified, dissected, and manipulated.

The most effective way to handle any frustration that this state of affairs might cause is to be realistic about what the law is and isn't. Do not expect definitive answers to all legal questions. Search for as much clarity as you can, but do not be surprised if the conclusion of your search is further questions. A time-honored answer to many legal questions is: "It depends"! Become familiar with the following equation since you will see it used often:

> If "X" is present, then the conclusion is "A", but if "Y" is so, then the conclusion is "B", but if "Z" is . . . .

The practice of law may sometimes appear to be an endless puzzle. Studying law, therefore, must engage you in similar thinking processes. Again, look for precision and clarity, but do not expect the puzzle to disappear.

18. The value of speed reading courses in the study of law.

Teachers are often asked by students whether they should take speed reading courses in view of the large amounts of reading that must be done in the law. The answer is yes. You should consider taking any reading course that will help you *slow down* the speed of your reading! This advice may be quite distasteful to advocates (and salespersons) of speed reading courses. The reality, however, is that statutes, regulations, and court opinions cannot be speed-read.

They must be carefully picked apart and read word for word almost as if you are translating from one language into another. If you are troubled by how long it takes you to read, do not despair. Do not worry about having to read material over and over again. Keep reading. Keep re-reading. The pace of your reading will pick up as you gain experience. Never strive, however, to be able to fly through the material. Strive for comprehensiveness. Strive for understanding. For most of us, this will come through the slow process of re-reading. It is sometimes argued that comprehension is increased through speed. Be careful of this argument. Reading law calls for careful thinking about what you read, and the taking of notes on these thoughts. There may be no harm in rapidly reading legal material for *the first time*. At your second, third, and fourth reading, however, speed is of little significance.

19. OJT (On the Job Training)—the art of being supervised.

A great deal of learning will occur when you are on the job. Some of it may come through formal in-house office training and by the study of office procedure manuals. Most of the learning, however, will come in the day-to-day interaction with your supervisors as you are given assignments. The learning comes through *being* supervised. Being supervised is not always easy. It will take some effort on your part to maximize the learning potential of the experience. The following guidelines are designed to assist you in increasing this potential:

Don't Play King's Clothes with the Instructions that You Receive

Recall the story of the king's clothes. The king was naked, but everybody kept saying what a beautiful wardrobe he had on. As new people arrived, they saw that he had no clothes, but they heard everyone talking as if he was fully dressed. The new people did not want to appear stupid, so they too began admiring the king's wardrobe. When paralegals are receiving instructions on an assignment, they play king's clothes when they pretend that they understand all the instructions when in fact they do not. They do not want to appear to be uninformed or unintelligent. They do not want to give the impression that they are not sure of themselves. For obvious reasons, this is a serious mistake.

Whenever you are given an assignment in a new area, i.e., an assignment on something that you have not done before, there should be a great deal that you do not understand. This is particularly true during your first few months on the job when everything is new! Do not pretend to be something you are not. Constantly ask questions about new things. Do not be reluctant to ask for explanations. Learn how to ask for help. *It will not be a sign of weakness.* Quite the contrary. People who take steps to make sure that they fully understand all their instructions soon gain a reputation for responsibility and conscientiousness.

Repeat the Instructions to Your Supervisor Before You Leave the Room

Once your supervisor has told you what s/he wants you to do, do not leave the room in silence or with the general observation, "I'll get on that right away."

Repeat the instructions back to the supervisor *as you understand them.* Make sure that you and your supervisor are on the same wave length by explaining back what you think you were told to do. This will be an excellent opportunity for the supervisor to determine what you did or did not understand, and to provide you with clarifications where needed.

Your supervisor will not always be sure of what s/he wants you to do. By trying to obtain clarity on the instructions, you are providing the supervisor with the opportunity to think through what s/he wants done. In the middle of the session with you, the supervisor may change his/her mind on what is to be done.

Write Your Instructions Down

Never go to your supervisor without pen and paper. Preferably, keep an instructions notebook, diary, or journal (p. 181) in which you record the following information:

- Notes on what your are supposed to do.
- The date you are given the assignment.
- The date the supervisor expects you to complete all or part of the assignment.
- The date you actually completed the assignment.
- Comments made by supervisors or others on what you submitted.

The notes will serve as your memory bank. Whenever any questions arise about what you were supposed to do, you have something concrete to which to refer.

**If the Instructions Appear to be
Complicated, Ask Your Supervisor to
Separate and Prioritize the Tasks**

As you receive instructions, you may sometimes feel overwhelmed by all that is being asked of you. Many supervisors do not give instructions in clear logical patterns. They may talk in a rambling, stream-of-consciousness fashion. When confronted with this situation, simply say:

> OK, but can you break that down for me a little more in terms of what you want me to do first? I think I will be able to do the entire assignment, but it would help if I approach it one step at a time. Where do you want me to start?

**As Often as Possible, Write Your
Instructions and What You Do in the
Form of Checklists**

A methodical mind is one that views a project in "do-able" steps and that tackles one step at a time. You need to have a methodical mind in order to function in a busy law office. One of the best ways to develop such a mind is to think in terms of checklists. A checklist is simply a chronological sequencing of tasks that must be done in order to complete a project. Convert the instructions from your supervisor into checklists in a manner similar to translating rules into checklists discussed earlier (p. 318). In the process of actually carrying out instructions, you go through many steps—all of which could become part of a detailed checklist. The steps you went through to complete the task become a checklist of things to do in order to complete such a task in the future. To be sure, it can be time consuming to draft checklists. Keep in mind, however, that:

- The checklists can be invaluable for other employees who are given similar assignments in the future.
- The checklists will be a benefit to you in organizing your own time and in assuring completeness.

You will not be able to draft checklists for everything that you do. Perhaps you will not be able to write more than one checklist a week. Perhaps you will have to use some of your own time to write checklists. Whatever time you can devote to such writing will be profitably spent so long as you are serious about writing and using the checklists. They may have to be re-written or modified later. This should not deter you from the task since most things that are worth doing require testing and reassessment.

Once you have a number of checklists, you have the makings of a how-to-do-it manual that you have written yourself.

Find Out What Manuals and Checklists Already Exist in Your Office

It does not make sense to reinvent the wheel. If manuals and checklists already exist in your office on the topic of your assignment, you should find and use them. The problem is that the how-to-do-it information is usually buried in the heads of the attorneys, paralegals, and secretaries of the office. No one has taken the time to write it all down (p. 193). If this is *not* the case, you should find out where it is written down and try to adapt what you find to the particular assignment on which you are working.

Ask for a Model

One of the best ways of making sure that you know what the supervisor wants is by asking whether s/he knows of any models that you could use as a guide for what you are being asked to do. Such models may be found in closed case files, manuals, form books, practice texts, etc. Care must be applied in using such material. Every new legal problem is potentially unique. What will work in one case may not work in another. A model is a guide, a starting point and nothing more (p. 496).

Do Some Independent Legal Research on Your Own on the Instructions You Are Given

Often you will be told what to do without being given more than a cursory explanation of why it needs to be done that way. All the instructions you are given have some basis in the law. A complaint, for example, is served on an opposing party in a designated way because the law has imposed rules on how such service is to be made. You may be asked to serve a complaint in a certain way without being told what section of the state code (or of your court rules) *requires* it to be served in that way. It would be highly impractical for you to read all the law that is the foundation for the instructions you are given. It is not necessary to do so and you would not have time to do so.

What you can do, however, is to select certain instructions on certain assignments and do some background legal research in order to gain a greater appreciation for why the instructions were necessary to accomplish the task. You will probably have to do such legal research on your own time unless the assignment you are given includes some legal research (p. 505). The research can be time consuming, but you will find it to be enormously educational. It can place a totally new perspective on the assignment and, indeed, on your entire job.

Ask Secretaries and Other Paralegals for Help

Secretaries and paralegals who have worked in the office for a long period of time can be very helpful to you if you approach them properly (p. 186). Everybody wants to feel important. Everybody wants to be respected. When someone asks for something in such a way as to give the impression that s/he is *entitled* to what is being sought, difficulties usually result. Think of how you would like to be approached if you were in the position of the secretary or paralegal. What would turn you off? What would make you want to go out of your way to cooperate with and assist a new employee who needs your help? Your answers (and sensitivity) to questions such as these will go a long way toward enabling you to draw on the experience of others in the office.

Obtain Feedback on an Assignment Before the Date it is Due

Unless the assignment you are given is a very simple one, do not wait until the date that it is due to communicate with your supervisor. Of course, if you are having trouble with the assignment, you will want to check with your supervisor as soon as possible and as often as necessary. It would be a mistake, however, to contact the supervisor only when trouble arises. Of course, you want to avoid wasting anyone's time, including your own. You should limit your contacts with a busy supervisor to essential matters. You could take the following approach with your supervisor:

> Everything seems to be going fine on the project you gave me. I expect to have it in to you on time. I'm wondering, however, if you could give me a few moments of your time so that I can bring you up to date on where I am so that you can let me know if I am on the right track?

Perhaps this contact could take place on the phone or during a brief office visit. Suppose that you have gone astray on the assignment without knowing it? It is obviously better to discover this before the date the assignment is due. The more communication you have with your supervisor, the more likely it is that you will catch such errors before a great deal of time is wasted.

Ask to Participate in Office and Community Training Programs

Sometimes there are training sessions for attorneys conducted in the law firm. You should ask that you be included. Bar associations and paralegal associations often conduct all-day seminars on legal topics relevant to your work. Seek permission to attend them if they are held during work hours.

Ask to be Evaluated Regularly

For a number of reasons, evaluations are not given or are unhelpful when they are given:

- Evaluations can be time consuming.
- Evaluators are reluctant to say anything negative, especially in writing.
- Most people do not like to be evaluated: it's too threatening to our ego.

The major antidote is to let your supervisor know that you want to be evaluated and that you can handle criticism. If you are defensive when you are criticized, you will find that the evaluations of your performance will go on behind your back! Such a work environment is obviously very unhealthy. Consider this approach that a paralegal might take with his/her supervisor:

> I want to know what you think of my work. I want to know where you think I need improvement. That's the only way I'm going to learn. I also want to know when I'm doing things correctly, but I'm mainly interested in your suggestions on what I can do to increase my skills.

If you take this approach *and mean it,* the chances are good that you will receive some very constructive criticism. (See also p. 179.)

One step at a time.

Perhaps the most important advice you can receive in studying law is to concentrate on what is immediately before you. One step at a time. What are your responsibilities in the next fifteen minutes? Block everything else out. Make *the now* as productive as you can. Your biggest enemy is worry about the future: worry about the exams ahead of you, worry about your family, worry about the state of the world, worry about finding employment etc. Leave tomorrow alone! Worrying about it will only interfere with your ability to make the most of what you must do now. Your development in the law will come slowly, in stages. Map out these stages in very small time blocks—beginning with the time that is immediately ahead of you. If you must worry, limit your concern to how to make the next fifteen minutes a more valuable learning experience.

6

Introduction to
Our Legal System

Section A. BASIC TERMINOLOGY

Our legal system is really *three* systems consisting of independent but inter-connected governments: federal government; state government; and city or county government. The interrelationship among these levels of government is what is known as federalism. Each level of government has three *branches:* one that makes laws (legislative branch), one that carries out laws (executive branch), and one that interprets laws (judicial branch).

Federal Government

Legislative Branch: Congress
Executive Branch: The President and the federal administrative agencies (see chart on p. 864).
Judicial Branch: The U.S. Supreme Court, The U.S. Court of Appeal, The U.S. District Courts, and other federal courts (see chart on p. 333).

State Government

Legislative Branch: The state legislature
Executive Branch: The governor and the state administrative agencies
Judicial Branch: The state courts (see chart on p. 332).

Local Government

Legislative Branch: City Council or County Commission
Executive Branch: Mayor or County Commissioner and the local administrative agencies
Judicial Branch: The local courts (see chart on p. 332).

The following is an overview of the basic kinds of law that govern and that are produced by the above institutions:

KINDS OF LAW

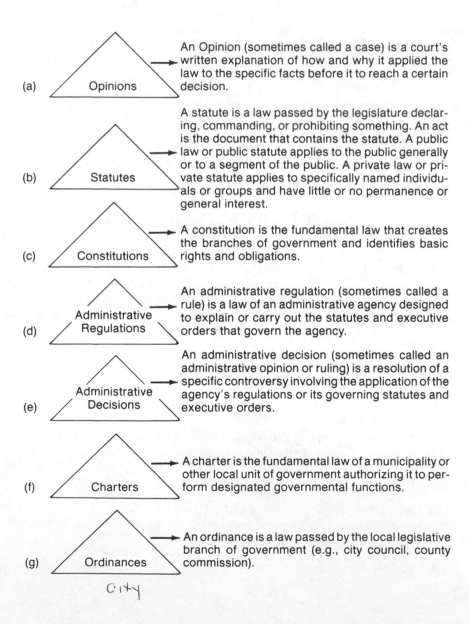

(a) Opinions — An Opinion (sometimes called a case) is a court's written explanation of how and why it applied the law to the specific facts before it to reach a certain decision.

(b) Statutes — A statute is a law passed by the legislature declaring, commanding, or prohibiting something. An act is the document that contains the statute. A public law or public statute applies to the public generally or to a segment of the public. A private law or private statute applies to specifically named individuals or groups and have little or no permanence or general interest.

(c) Constitutions — A constitution is the fundamental law that creates the branches of government and identifies basic rights and obligations.

(d) Administrative Regulations — An administrative regulation (sometimes called a rule) is a law of an administrative agency designed to explain or carry out the statutes and executive orders that govern the agency.

(e) Administrative Decisions — An administrative decision (sometimes called an administrative opinion or ruling) is a resolution of a specific controversy involving the application of the agency's regulations or its governing statutes and executive orders.

(f) Charters — A charter is the fundamental law of a municipality or other local unit of government authorizing it to perform designated governmental functions.

(g) Ordinances — An ordinance is a law passed by the local legislative branch of government (e.g., city council, county commission).

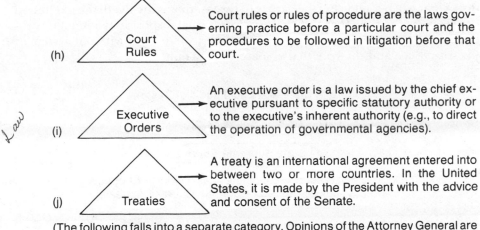

(h) **Court Rules** — Court rules or rules of procedure are the laws governing practice before a particular court and the procedures to be followed in litigation before that court.

(i) **Executive Orders** — An executive order is a law issued by the chief executive pursuant to specific statutory authority or to the executive's inherent authority (e.g., to direct the operation of governmental agencies).

(j) **Treaties** — A treaty is an international agreement entered into between two or more countries. In the United States, it is made by the President with the advice and consent of the Senate.

(The following falls into a separate category. Opinions of the Attorney General are advisory and hence are not considered laws in the same sense as the above ten.)

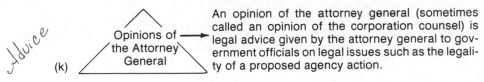

(k) **Opinions of the Attorney General** — An opinion of the attorney general (sometimes called an opinion of the corporation counsel) is legal advice given by the attorney general to government officials on legal issues such as the legality of a proposed agency action.

The judicial systems within the country are outlined in figures 1 and 2. In the remainder of this chapter and in chapter 10, we will cover how the courts function through the litigation process.

Figure 3 illustrates the division of the federal court system into twelve geographic circuits. Each circuit has its own U.S. Court of Appeals. The U.S. District Courts exist within these circuits.

Section B. THE LEGISLATIVE PROCESS

For information on how a bill becomes a law and the steps in the legislative process, see pp. 655 ff.

Section C. INTRODUCTION TO LITIGATION: THE CLIENT PERSPECTIVE[1]

TO THE CLIENT

Introduction

You have suffered a loss, you have placed your claim in the hands of an attorney, and we now begin our joint endeavor to bring about a just and successful disposition of that claim. This is probably the first such experience that you

---

[1] From Jeans, J., *Trial Advocacy,* 62–72 (West, 1975).

have had. There are no doubt a lot of questions in your mind about the procedures that will be followed, the nature of the law that is involved, the likelihood of recovery, the time that will elapse before a final disposition, and many others. We hope to answer these questions and to acquaint you with our system of jurisprudence and the role that you are to play in it.

Figure 1. State and Local Judicial System.

Source: American Bar Association, *Law and the Courts*, 20, (1974).

State Supreme Court

(Court of final resort. Some states call it Court of Appeals, Supreme Judicial Court, or Supreme Court of Appeals.)

Intermediate Appellate Courts

(Only 23 of the 50 states have intermediate appellate courts, which are an intermediate appellate tribunal between the trial court and the court of final resort. A majority of cases are decided finally by these appellate courts.)

Superior Court

(Highest trial court with general jurisdiction. Some states call it Circuit Court, District Court, Court of Common Pleas, and in New York, Supreme Court.)

Probate Court*	County Court*	Municipal Court*

(Some states call it Surrogate Court or Orphan's Court (Pa.). It is a special court which handles wills, administration of estates, guardianship of minors and incompetents.)

(These courts, sometimes called Common Pleas or District Courts, have limited jurisdiction in both civil and criminal cases.)

(In some cities, it is customary to have less important cases tried by municipal justices or municipal magistrates.)

Domestic Relations Court

(Also called Family Court or Juvenile Court.)

Justice of the Peace** and Police Magistrate

(Lowest courts in judicial hierarchy. Limited in jurisdiction in both civil and criminal cases.)

* Courts of special jurisdiction, such as Probate, Family, or Juvenile, and the so-called inferior courts, such as Common Pleas or Municipal courts, may be separate courts or may be part of the trial court of general jurisdiction.

** Justices of the Peace do not exist in all states. Their jurisdictions vary greatly from state to state where they do exist.

Figure 2. The United States (Federal) Court System.

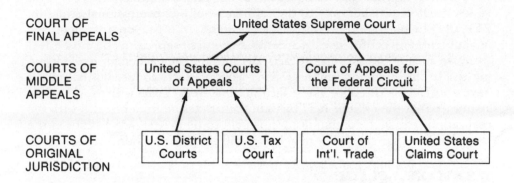

Figure 3. United States Courts of Appeals and District Courts.

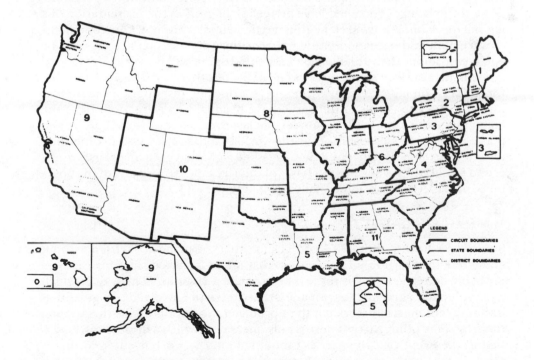

WHAT IS AN ATTORNEY?

The history of the word itself pretty well tells the story. It is derived from an old French word meaning "to recognize one as the person in whose behalf one holds something." You have turned your case over to us. We will handle that case on your behalf. We are your proxy, your alter-ego in the presentation of your claim. This relationship that has been created is a most intimate one and it demands the strictest loyalty from both attorney and client. As your advocate we will advance your case as vigorously as our talent permits.

A greater duty lies only to the fulfillment of our professional ethics (p. 243) and our obligations as officers of the court. In turn, you as a client owe us your trust and confidence. In order that we might represent you most effectively we must know not only the facts surrounding the particular incident giving rise to this litigation, but also many personal facts about you that might have a bearing on this case. These facts must be freely given with the complete assurance that they will be held by us in the strictest confidence and with the realization that such communication is held to be privileged (p. 266) in the same sense as that given to a member of the clergy or to a doctor.

WHY MAKE A CLAIM?

Although you have engaged an attorney, there might still be some reservations in your mind as to whether or not this step should have been taken. You might feel that your act will be misinterpreted by your friends or acquaintances and you will be considered "claim-minded," "greedy," or "wanting to get something for nothing." You need have no feeling of guilt in the presentation of a legitimate claim. We are seeking a just settlement of a dispute. Our courthouses were built and our laws were written for this very reason. No one need be apologetic about that. In all probability this dispute will be settled by mutual agreement. However, if your case is one of the few that has to be presented before a jury, you must remember that there is nothing dishonorable about telling your story to twelve citizens who have been chosen at random from the community and allowing them under the law to reach a verdict. The United States is one of the few countries in the world that has such a system of settling disputes between her citizens. It is a cherished right that each one of us possesses and we should not deprive ourselves of this right merely because of the possibility of criticism from some shallow-thinking persons.

WHY FILE A LAWSUIT?

Statistics show that about 90% of all claims that are made are settled without going to a trial (p. 465). The question that might be asked is "If my case will probably be settled, why is there a need to file a lawsuit?" The way in which most voluntary agreements are made is that the parties involved recognize that if they do not mutually work out their problems, a solution will be thrust upon them by some other party. There is only one way in which a dispute can be settled in the event that the parties cannot voluntarily work it out, and that is through the verdict of a court. Before there can be a court verdict, the suit must be filed and the case processed. This procedure usually takes from six months to a year. Frequently it takes that same length of time before the full extent of your injuries can be determined. If several months elapse before the extent of the claim can be determined and then negotiations are entered into that do not result in a satisfactory settlement, an additional six months or a year will pass before the case can be filed and brought before a court. Rather than face a possibility of this delay, it is best that a lawsuit be filed as soon as practical.

The claim matures as the case is being processed through the court. If for some reason a mutually satisfactory disposition of the claim is not reached, then the parties will be able to present the claim to the court without additional delay.

There are other reasons for the necessity of filing suit. Under the law when a suit is filed there are a number of discovery procedures (p. 471) that are available to both parties. We, as plaintiffs, are entitled to take the deposition (p. 347) or sworn statement of the opposite parties and find out from them under oath their version of the incident. Similarly we may take depositions of witnesses who might otherwise not be willing to disclose the information that they have. A filing of this suit is the only way in which both sides are given the opportunity of finding out full information that will enable both of them to appraise the claim more accurately.

WHAT ARE THE LEGAL PROCEDURES IN THE FILING OF A LAWSUIT?

The filing of a lawsuit is merely a notice to the court and to the persons against whom the claim is made. Generally speaking the place where the lawsuit is filed is determined by the place of the occurrence or the residency of the defendant. However, if more convenient, the claim can be filed in the county where you live if the defendant can be served by the sheriff in that county. A complaint is drafted by the attorney (p. 498). This is merely a formal statement alleging briefly the facts of the accident, the complaints of negligence against the defendant, and the injury or damage that has resulted. This complaint and copies are presented to the court, and the Sheriff then serves a copy to each of the defendants. Upon receipt of the complaint, the defendant then has thirty days in which to file an answer (p. 345). Usually this is in the form of a denial of the allegations of negligence and in some instances a claim is made that the damages suffered were contributed to by your own fault. Frequently, however, there are motions filed by the other side attacking the propriety of the complaint. When this occurs, it necessitates a presentation of these motions before the court and invariably means a delay. When an answer to the complaint is filed, the case then becomes "at issue" and can then be set upon a trial docket. The time that elapses between the filing of the complaint and the setting on the trial docket varies according to many factors, but usually this interim is from nine months to a year. The trial courts are closed during the summer months, but from the middle of September through the middle of June, with the exception of a few weeks for holidays, the courts are open for the trial of civil cases. On the Monday of each of these weeks, a trial docket of about 150 cases is prepared. The order in which these cases appear on the docket is usually determined by the time that they were filed,—that is, the cases that have been pending the longest appear at the top of the docket while those that have been more recently filed appear farther down. Each morning of the week, the docket is called and the attorneys respond as to whether or not they are in a position to try the case. The manner in which the cases are disposed of at the docket occurs at a variable and unpredictable rate. Many of these cases will have been settled, some of them will be continued or delayed to another date, while others will respond that they are ready to try the case. Those cases ready for trial are assigned to trial courts and usually there are about six such courts available. As these cases are disposed of in the trial division, new cases are assigned to trial in the order that they appear on the docket.

WHAT IS EXPECTED OF ME?

Much of the preparation of the lawsuit will depend on you. Of course a full and complete statement must be given to the attorney; all the facts and circumstances surrounding the incident are provided in detail. From this initial interview, we then will be able to follow through with interviews of the witnesses, procurement of the police report and the medical information. Undoubtedly within several weeks the attorney representing the defendant will request that your deposition be taken. Under the law they have the right to take your deposition, that is, a sworn statement as to the facts of the accident and the surrounding circumstances. Although sometimes a witness or a party is subpoenaed in order to appear for the deposition, in most instances your attorneys make arrangements for the voluntary appearance of their clients. Before you are interrogated, it is necessary that adequate time be spent with your attorney in order to acquaint you with the nature of the questions that will be asked. The depositions are usually held in the office of the attorney under informal circumstances. The interrogation is conducted by the attorney representing the opposite party. A court reporter records the interrogation and the transcription of the proceeding is made a part of the court record. Despite the informal setting and the courteousness and friendliness of the opposing party, the deposition is of prime importance and very frequently is a determining factor in the success or failure of your case. It is for that reason that you should have a full understanding of the nature of the proceeding and what will be expected of you.

First, it should be recognized that this is a compulsory proceeding. We are not voluntarily appearing in order to tell "all that we know about the accident." Instead you will be there to answer questions that will be put to you. In this sense you should think of yourself as a reluctant witness answering only those questions that are asked; do not volunteer any information. Frequently a client will ask, "Shall I tell the lawyer such and such?" There need be no worry on your part as to what information you should relay. If a question is asked and it is a proper question, you will be obligated to answer. If no inquiry is made then you should not volunteer any information.

Second, listen to each question and answer it in as brief a fashion as possible. It is surprising how many questions can be answered with a simple "yes" or "no." There will be many questions that will be asked of which you will have no knowledge. In that case, the answer is "I don't know." Remember, regardless of the informality of the proceeding, this is not a conversational exchange. This is part of the legal process and the answers that you give and the manner in which you answer are of extreme importance.

Third, there undoubtedly will be questions concerning estimates of time, speeds, and distances. The answers to such questions should be in terms of approximation. One cannot truthfully say, "I was traveling at 30 miles per hour." It would be much nearer the truth to say that "I was traveling *about* 30 miles per hour" or "*between* 25 and 30 miles per hour." Similarly, in the case of giving the estimation of a distance, it would be much more truthful to say that the street was *about* 40 feet wide rather than to make a flat statement as to its exact width.

Fourth, there will be questions directed not only to the facts of the accident, but to your own personal background, You might think it unnecessary that the opposing party ask you questions about your age, your address, your type of employment, whether or not you have been married before, etc. All this information, however, is considered relevant and must be answered. Remember, your attorney will be present during the taking of this deposition and if there is any improper matter that is sought, an objection will be made.

Fifth, one of the important facets of the questioning will concern the result or the nature of the injuries or damages that you have suffered. Facts of an injury cannot be relayed truthfully with merely "yes" or "no" answers. In order that a fair, full, and complete picture of your injuries and damages can be appreciated by the opposing attorney, it will be necessary to explain not only the nature of the injury but how it has affected you in your daily living. You will be asked about the complaints you have at the present time, as well as those you suffered shortly after the accident. You will also be asked questions as to the number of visits that you have made to the doctor, the type of treatment that s/he gave you, the time that you have lost from work, the expenses that have been incurred, etc. For that reason, it is important that you come to the deposition prepared with information. From the very inception of your case, a record should be kept regarding such information as the time lost from work and financial loss that has resulted, dates of visits to the doctor, expenditures made for drugs, nurses, braces, etc. This information is of primary importance in determining the true value of your loss. Very frequently the information can be known only by yourself.

After the deposition has been taken, and if you have suffered a personal injury, the defendant may request that you be examined by a doctor of his/her own choosing. The law affords this right and we must comply with this request. If you are asked to submit to such an examination, you should remember the following points:

1. The doctor examining you will have but this one opportunity to talk to you and observe you and appraise your injury. Many of the initial effects of the injury such as bruises and swellings will have disappeared and perhaps many of the complaints that you had at one time will have cleared up. For that reason, the doctor will rely most heavily upon your own recollection as to how the injuries were sustained and what their past effects have been.
2. Many of the complaints that persons have following injury are of a subjective nature, those that cannot be found by examination or clinical tests. For instance, a headache is a subjective complaint. No amount of X-rays or observation can indicate to an examining physician that a person is suffering from a headache. Therefore, it is your obligation to recite to the doctor all of the complaints that you have had and are presently suffering from.
3. The examination of the doctor is not meant to be an interrogation as to the details of the accident. It will be important to the doctor to determine how the injuries were suffered, that is, whether or not you were a pedestrian

that was struck by a car or whether you slipped on a defective floor. However, facts concerning the speeds of the automobiles or the nature of the defects of the floor is no concern to the doctor and should not be the subject of his/her examination.

4. Do not be hostile to the doctor. It is true that s/he is examining you on behalf of the opposing party, but generally speaking s/he has been chosen because s/he is a competent doctor whose opinion will be held in high regard by the judge or the jury. Be cooperative in giving as much information as you can concerning your injuries. Remember the difficulty under which the doctor operates. S/he has not seen you before, did not treat you, and in this one short examination must form an opinion as to the nature and extent of your injuries.

During the pendency of your claim, you will no doubt be asked by many persons how your suit is progressing. It is well not to talk about the nature of your claim, the facts of the accident, nor the injuries that you have suffered. It is possible that some of the statements that you make could be misinterpreted by friends or others and such statements would prove detrimental to your claim. It is also true that many persons feel that they have a certain competency in the law and can give you advice concerning your claim. Such advice from "curbstone lawyers" can only lead to uneasiness and worry. You must have confidence in your attorney and that s/he, through experience and special training, will be able to adequately protect your interests.

SETTLEMENT NEGOTIATION

After depositions have been taken and you have been examined by a doctor of the defendant's choosing and the trial date approaches, settlement negotiations will be initiated. These negotiations will be relayed to you, and usually at that time a conference is arranged so that you may become fully aware of the features of the case, the likelihood of recovery, and the factors taken into consideration in evaluating your claim. Usually during the preparation of the case certain expenses will have been incurred. It is desirable that any consideration of settlement be made on the basis of the net settlement after attorney's fees and legal expenses. All this information will be made known to you so that an intelligent decision can be made as to whether the offer should be accepted or rejected. In evaluating a claim, about the only guide that can be used is the anticipation of what a jury might do in the event that the case is tried. Of course, as you must realize, this is at best a guess. Regardless of the facts and the injuries involved, it is impossible to foresee what a jury of twelve persons might do in a particular case. Experience and knowledge of past cases that have been similar in circumstances provide some guidance but no two cases are alike and no two injuries are alike. All the factors concerning the case will be presented to you along with our recommendations, but the final decision will rest with you.

PREPARATION FOR TRIAL

If it appears that the settlement negotiations are not satisfactory, preparations for trial will begin usually a week or two before the case is set. At that time, you will be called in for a conference. The facts of the accident as well as the extent and nature of your injuries will be reviewed with you. Notices will be sent to the doctors and the witnesses alerting them to the possibility of having to testify in the event that the case is tried. Usually it is impossible to determine beforehand when your case might be called for trial. For that reason it is usually acceptable if you go about your regular routine, but that you make yourself available for appearing in court in the event that the case is called. There is usually about an hour or two available for such notice and plenty of time for another brief conference before the case begins. Before testimony is taken, a jury must be chosen and preliminary statements made by the attorneys. This usually takes about an hour or two and allows you to become acclimated to the courtroom.

YOUR ROLE DURING TRIAL

As a party to a lawsuit, you have an important job to do. It is important not only because of the immediate result it will have on you, but also important to our system of justice. For a jury to make a correct and wise decision it must have all the evidence put before it in a truthful manner. Attention should be given not only to what you say, but the manner in which it is said. Testimony given in a stumbling, hesitant manner leaves the jury with a doubt as to whether or not all the facts are being told in a truthful fashion. If, however, the same facts are told in a confident, straightforward manner, the jury has more faith in what you are saying. Here are a few suggestions that must be kept in mind in helping you become a good witness.

1. Your physical appearance is important. Your clothing should be clean and conservative. Some persons are offended by others who wear too stylish clothes, excessive jewelry, severe hairdos, etc. This should be kept in mind.
2. Your whole demeanor should reflect to the jury that you are an intelligent, serious person who has a great deal of concern over the outcome of your case. When the oath is administered to you, you should stand erect, listen to the clerk carefully, and respond in a clear, certain fashion.
3. You should recall that the answers given are not for the benefit of the attorneys asking them nor for the judge, but primarily they are directed for the jury. For that reason, it is well to keep in mind that you are communicating with twelve persons taken from various walks of life and who are under oath to perform their job as jurors. They are conscientiously trying to find out what the truth is and you might turn to them during the course of the questioning and make your answers directly to them in a clear, straightforward, friendly fashion. The acoustics in most of our courtrooms are not very good by reason of the high ceilings. Therefore, it is important not to cover your mouth, but to speak easily and loudly so that the farthest juror can hear you easily.
4. Don't memorize your responses. You will be acquainted with the nature of the questions that will be asked you under direct examination (p. 475), but there should be a certain amount of spontaneity to the way in which they are answered. Listen carefully to the questions asked you. Understand the question before you respond. If you do not understand it, have it repeated.

Do not give a snap answer without thinking. Sometimes an answer cannot be responded to in a simple "yes" or "no" fashion. You have a right to explain the answer and in most cases this will be necessary. You must recall that testifying for a jury is quite different than testimony that is given in a deposition. The purpose of the deposition is for the defendant to ascertain facts that will help him/her in the investigation of a case. As far as the jury trial is concerned, it is your role as plaintiff to place all these facts before the jury and therefore you must be more communicative and detailed in explanation of the facts of the accident and the results therefrom.

5. Don't be a "smart alec" or cocky witness. You are not engaged in some type of a verbal dual with the opposing counsel. Your primary job is to convey truthful, meaningful information to the jury as best you can. It serves no purpose to be argumentative with the opposing counsel. Most jurors do not like persons of this nature. If you respond to an argumentative question in a kind and courteous fashion, it will inure to your benefit.

6. Sometimes during the course of the testimony there are objections. When an objection occurs, stop instantly when you are interrupted until the court can rule on the propriety of the objection. Do not try to "sneak in" an answer.

7. Don't look to your attorney or to the judge for help in answering a question. You are on your own. Frequently if you look to your attorney, the jury might get the idea that you are seeking some kind of a clue as to the proper answer. Remember, you are under oath, you are expected to tell the truth, and you know the answers to the questions that will be asked of you better than anyone else.

8. While you are observing the testimony of others, do not respond in any way. You will be present during the entire case, and it is quite foreseeable that other witnesses will testify to a version of the facts diametrically opposed to your testimony. When this occurs, do not do anything by way of exclamation or gesture that suggests your opposition to such testimony.

WHAT HAPPENS AFTER THE VERDICT?

With the return of the jury verdict, it does not necessarily mean that the case is ended. If any of the parties is disappointed with the result, s/he has the opportunity of filing a motion for a new trial within fifteen days after the verdict. This motion is directed to the trial court and in effect asks the court to correct mistakes in rulings of law that have been made during the trial. The judge must rule upon this within ninety days after its filing. S/he will either sustain the motion for a new trial or overrule it. This action of the court may be appealed by any of the parties. When an appeal is taken, a transcript of the record must be prepared and the party seeking the transcript is given ninety days or in some cases a total of 180 days for the transcript to be prepared. After being prepared, the case can then be set for a hearing before the appropriate appellate court. Appellate briefs (p. 695) must be prepared by both parties and usually there will be an additional three or four months that will pass before the oral argument can be heard. After oral argument, it is usually several months before the written opinion is handed down. This initial opinion by the court can in turn be questioned by either of the parties and motions for a re-hearing filed. However, in most cases, the initial opinion of the appellate court is final. The time usually elapsing between the verdict and the final disposition on appeal is approximately a year or fourteen months. If the verdict was initially in your favor and is sustained on appeal, then you are allowed interest on the amount of the verdict during the pendency of the appeal.

CONCLUSION

We will be working closely together until your case is completed. We hope that you now have a better understanding of the events that will be occurring during these coming months. There might be other questions that you have. Remember, we are your attorneys and you can feel free to call upon us at any time to impart information or seek answers to your questions. However, please consider that our obligations to our clients and frequent commitments before the courts make us unavailable much of the time and may delay our response to you. We are here to serve you and to use all of the proper means available to secure a fair, just and proper disposition of your claim.

Section D. INTRODUCTION TO LITIGATION: THE PARALEGAL PERSPECTIVE

We start with a story—the litigation woes of Michael Brown. The purpose of the story is to provide a more technical overview of the litigation process and to begin building your litigation vocabulary. Following the "Odyssey" of Michael Brown, you will find two charts that summarize the significant litigation steps. Many of the basic concepts in this chapter will also be covered in later chapters.

THE LEGAL ODYSSEY OF MICHAEL BROWN: AN ANATOMY OF THE LITIGATION PROCESS

Michael Brown is a truck driver for the Best Bread Company. Several years ago, as Brown was walking home from work, Harold Clay, an old friend from the past, stopped and offered him a ride. Clay was driving through the state at the time. They had not seen each other since Clay moved out West a number of years ago. They carried on an excited conversation as Clay drove. After driving a few blocks, a car driven by George Miller, a resident of a neighboring state, ran through a red light and struck Clay's car. All three individuals were seriously injured and were taken to a local hospital. Clay died two weeks later from injuries received in the crash.

Several days after the accident, Brown's boss, Frank Best, wrote Brown a letter. In it, Best said that he had learned that the police had found about a one-half ounce of heroin under the front seat of Clay's car and were planning to charge Brown with possession of narcotics with intent to distribute. Best also stated that several thefts had occurred from the company warehouse recently and that he now suspected Brown of having been involved in them. For these reasons, he decided to fire Brown as a company truck driver, effective immediately.

There are at least three different legal disputes involving Brown that could arise out of this fact situation:

1. A dispute among Brown, Miller, and Clay's estate regarding liability for the accident.
2. A dispute between Brown and the government regarding the criminal charges.
3. A dispute among Brown, the Best Bread Company, and the State Unemployment Compensation Board concerning Brown's entitlement to unemployment benefits.

Each of these disputes will be examined in detail.

1. Liability for the Accident

Brown suffered substantial injury as a result of the crash. He wanted to collect *damages* but was not sure who was *liable* for the accident. Was Miller at fault? Clay? Was each of them *jointly and severally* liable?

> Damages: An award of money (paid by the wrongdoer) to compensate the person who has been harmed.

> Liable: Legally responsible.

> Joint and several liability: When two or more persons are jointly and severally liable, they are legally responsible together and individually. Each wrongdoer is individually responsible for the entire judgment. The person who has been wronged can collect from one of them or from all of them together until the judgment has been satisfied.

Brown hired Brenda Davis, Esq. to represent him. Once Brown signed the *retainer,* Davis would later enter an *appearance* and become the *attorney of record.*

> Retainer: A contract between attorney and client stating the nature of the services to be rendered and the cost of the services.

> Appearance: Going to court on behalf of. The attorney usually appears by filing a "notice of appearance" in court, which is often accomplished through a *praecipe.* A praecipe is a formal request to the court that something be done. Here the request is that the attorney become the attorney of record.

> Attorney of record: An attorney who has filed a notice of appearance (e.g., through a praecipe) and who hence is formally mentioned in court records as the official attorney of the party. Once this occurs, the attorney often cannot withdraw from the case without court permission.

The attorney explained that a number of factors had to be considered before deciding on the *forum* in which to sue Miller and Clay's *estate.* Brown might be able to bring the suit in a number of places: (a) in a state court where Brown lives, (b) in a state court where Miller lives, (c) in a state court where Clay's estate is located, (d) in the federal court (United States District Court) sitting in Brown's state, (e) in the federal court sitting in Miller's state, or (f) in the federal court sitting in the state where Clay's estate is located. The reason Brown can sue in a federal court is the existence of *diversity of citizenship:* the parties involved in the litigation came from different states. Davis advised Brown to sue in federal court. The suit would be brought in the U.S. District Court sitting in Brown's own state since this would be the most convenient *venue* for Brown.

> Forum: The court where the case is to be tried.

> Estate: All the property left by a decedent (one who has died) from which any obligations or debts of the decedent must be paid. The word estate also refers to the representative(s) of the decedent.

> Diversity of citizenship: A kind of jurisdiction giving a federal court the power to hear a case based upon the fact that (a) the parties to the litigation are from different states and (b) the amount of money involved exceeds that specified by the federal statute.

> Venue: The place of trial. In most judicial systems, there is more than one trial court, e.g., one for each county or district. The selection of a particular trial court within a judicial system is referred to as a *choice of venue.*

Having decided on a court, Davis was ready to begin the lawsuit. She drafted a *complaint,* naming Brown as the *plaintiff* and *stating a cause of action* in tort for negligence against Miller and Clay's estate as *co-defendants.* The complaint was the first *pleading* of the case. In the complaint, Davis stated the facts that she felt constituted a cause of action for negligence. Some of the factual *allegations* were based upon the personal knowledge of Brown, while others were based upon *informtion and belief.* The *ad damnum* clause of the complaint asked for $100,000. When she finished drafting the complaint, Ms. Davis signed the pleading, attached a written demand for a *jury trial,* and *filed* both documents with the clerk of the court.

> Complaint: The document filed by the plaintiff stating a cause of action and his/her version of the facts concerning the defendant's alleged wrongdoing.

> Plaintiff: The party initiating the lawsuit.

> Cause of action: A legally acceptable reason for suing; a theory of recovery.

> Stating a cause of action: Including in the complaint all the facts that, if proved at trial, would entitle the plaintiff to win (assuming the defendant does not establish any defenses that can defeat the plaintiff's case).

> Co-defendants: More than one defendant being sued in the same litigation.

Pleading: A document filed in court stating the position of one of the parties on the cause(s) of action or on the defenses.

Allegation: A claimed fact; a fact that a party will try to prove at trial.

Information and belief: A standard legal phrase used to indicate that the person making the allegation in good faith believes the allegation to be true.

Ad damnum: A statement in the complaint in which the plaintiff asks for a specified sum of money as damages.

Jury trial: A jury is a group of citizens who will decide the issues or questions of fact at the trial. The judge decides the issues or questions of law. If there is no jury at the trial, then the judge decides both the questions of law and the questions of fact.

Filed: Formally presented to a court (usually to the clerk of the court).

Service of process came next. It was accomplished when a copy of the complaint, along with the *summons,* was served on both Miller and on the legal representative of Clay's estate. Davis did not serve these parties herself. She used a *process server* who served the parties and filed an *affidavit* of service with the court, indicating the circumstances under which service was achieved. Service was made before the *statute of limitations* on the negligence cause of action ran out. Once the defendants were properly served, the court acquired *in personam jurisdiction* over them.

Service of process: The delivery of a formal notice to a defendant ordering him or her to appear in court in order to answer the allegations made by the plaintiff.

Summons: The formal notice from the court ordering the defendant to appear. The summons is *served* on the defendant. The words summons and process are often used interchangeably.

Process server: A person who charges a fee for serving process.

Affidavit: A written statement of fact in which the person (called the *affiant*) swears that the written statement is true.

Statute of limitations: The law establishing the period within which the lawsuit must be commenced; if it is not brought within that time, it can never be brought.

In personam jurisdiction: Personal jurisdiction: the power of the court over the person of the defendant, obtained in part by proper service of process.

Both Miller and Clay's estate filed *motions to dismiss* for *failure to state a cause of action.* The motions were denied by the court.

Motion to dismiss: A request that the court decide that a party may not further litigate a claim, i.e., that the case on that claim be dropped.

Failure to state a cause of action: Failure of the plaintiff to allege enough facts in the complaint. Even if the plaintiff proved all the facts alleged in the complaint, the facts do not establish a cause of action entitling the plaintiff to recover against the defendant. The motion to dismiss for failure to state a cause of action is sometimes referred to as (a) a *demurrer* or (b) a *failure to state a claim upon which relief can be granted.*

Because the case had been filed in a federal court, the *procedural law* governing the case will be the *Federal Rules of Civil Procedure.* (The *substantive law* of the case will be the state law of negligence.) According to the Federal Rules of Civil Procedure, Miller and Clay's estate are each required to file an *answer* to Brown's complaint within twenty days. Miller filed his answer almost immediately. Since Clay was dead and unable to tell his attorney what happened at the accident, the attorney for the estate had some difficulty in *drafting* an answer and was unable to file within the twenty days. In order to avoid a *default judgment* against the estate, the attorney filed a *motion* asking for an extension of thirty days within which to file the answer. The motion was granted by the court, and the answer was filed within the new deadline.

Procedural law: The technical rules setting forth the steps required to conduct a lawsuit.

Federal Rules of Civil Procedure: The technical rules governing the manner in which civil cases are brought in and progress through the federal courts.

Substantive law: The rights and duties imposed by law (e.g., the duty to use reasonable care to avoid injury), other than procedural rights and duties.

Answer: The pleading filed by the defendant responding to or answering allegations of the plaintiff's complaint.

Draft: To write.

Default judgment: An order of the court deciding the case in favor of the plaintiff because the defendant failed to appear or file an answer within the time deadline.

Motion: A request made to the court, e.g., motion to dismiss. The party making the motion is called the *movant.* The verb is *move,* e.g., "I move that the court permit the demonstration."

The answer filed on behalf of Clay's estate denied all allegations of negligence and raised an *affirmative defense* of contributory negligence against Brown on the theory that if Clay had been partially responsible for the collision, it was because Brown had distracted him through his conversation in the car. Finally, the answer of Clay's estate raised a *cross-claim* against the co-defendant, Miller, alleging that the accident had been caused solely by Miller's negligence. The estate asked $250,000 in damages.

> Defense: A response to the claims of the other party setting forth reasons why the claims should not be granted. The defense may be as simple as a flat denial of the other party's factual allegations or may involve entirely new factual allegations. (In the latter situation, the defense is an *affirmative defense.*)

> Affirmative defense: A defense that is based on new factual allegations by the defendant not contained in the plaintiff's allegations.

> Cross-claim: Usually, a claim by one co-defendant against another co-defendant.

Miller's answer also raised the defense of contributory negligence against Brown and stated a cross-claim against Clay's estate, alleging that the accident had been caused solely by the negligence of Clay or of Clay and Brown together. On this same theory, that Brown together with Clay had negligently caused the accident, Miller's answer also stated a *counterclaim* against Brown. Miller sought $20,000 from Brown and $20,000 from Clay's estate as damages.

> Counterclaim: A claim or a cause of action against the plaintiff stated in the defendant's answer.

For a time, Miller and his attorney considered filing a *third-party complaint* against his own insurance company since the company would be liable for any judgment against him. They decided against this strategy since they did not want to let the jury know that Miller was insured. If the jury knew this fact, it might be more inclined to reach a verdict in favor of the plaintiff for a high amount of damages. The strategy was also unnecessary because there was no indication that Miller's insurer would *contest* its obligation to compensate Miller for any damages that he might have to pay Brown or Clay's estate in the event that the trial resulted in an *adverse judgment* against him.

> Third-party complaint: A complaint filed by the defendant against a third-party (i.e., a person not presently a party to the lawsuit). This complaint alleges that the third party is or may be liable for all or part of the damages that the plaintiff may win from the defendant.

> Contest: To challenge.

> Adverse judgment: A judgment or decision against you.

At this point five assorted claims, cross-claims, and counterclaims had been filed by the parties. A sixth, Miller's third-party claim against his insurer, had been considered but ultimately had not been filed. These claims and their relationship to each other are as follows:

1. Brown's original complaint for negligence against Miller and
2. against Clay's Estate, as co-defendants.

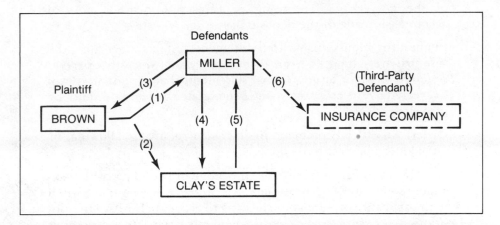

3. Defendant Miller's counterclaim for negligence against plaintiff, Brown.
4. Defendant Miller's cross-claim for negligence against his co-defendant, the Estate.
5. Defendant Estate's cross-claim for negligence against its co-defendant, Miller.
6. Third-party complaint that defendant Miller considered but ultimately decided *not* to file against his insurance company.

Once the pleadings were filed, all three parties started *discovery*. Each attorney first served written *interrogatories* on the opposing parties. These were followed by *depositions* and *requests for admissions*. Miller refused to answer several questions during his deposition in his attorney's office. As a result, Brown's attorney filed a discovery motion, seeking an *order* from the court compelling Miller to answer. A *hearing* was subsequently held on the motion, and after listening to arguments by all the attorneys, the judge granted the motion in full, ordering Miller to answer the questions. Faced with the court's order, Miller answered the remaining questions.

Each party then filed a *motion for summary judgment*. The judge denied these motions, and the case was ready for trial.

> Discovery: The pretrial devices that can be used by one party to obtain facts and information about the case from the other party in order to assist in preparing for trial.

> Interrogatories: A discovery device consisting of written questions about the case submitted by one party to the other party. The answers to the interrogatories are usually given under oath, i.e., the person answering the questions signs a sworn statement that the answers are true.

> Deposition: A discovery device by which one party asks oral questions of the other party or of a witness for the other party. The person who is *deposed* is called the *deponent*. The deposition is conducted under oath outside of the courtroom, usually in the office of one

of the lawyers. (A recording or transcript—word for word account—is made of the deposition.)

Request for admission: Written statements of facts concerning the case that are submitted to an adverse party and which that party is required to admit or deny; those statements that are admitted will be treated by the court as having been established and need not be proven at trial.

Order: An official command by the court requiring, allowing, or forbidding some act to be done.

Hearing: A proceeding in which the judge or presiding officer examines some aspect of the dispute. An *adversary hearing* exists when both parties are present at the hearing to argue their respective positions. An *ex parte hearing* exists when only one party is present at the hearing. Hearings occur in court as well as in administrative agencies.

Summary: Something done quickly without going through an entire adversary hearing or an entire trial.

Motion for a summary judgment: A request by a party that a decision be reached on the basis of the pleadings alone without having to go through with the entire trial. A summary judgment is normally allowed only when there is no dispute between the parties as to any of the material or significant facts of the case.

As the trial date neared, the attorneys received a notice asking them to appear before a *magistrate* for a *pretrial conference.* On the appointed day, the attorneys met with the magistrate to prepare the case for trial. During the conference, the magistrate, with the help of the attorneys, prepared a pretrial statement for the judge on the case. It contained a statement of those facts that had been *stipulated* by the attorneys, the facts that were still *in issue,* and a list describing the *tangible evidence* and witnesses that each attorney intended to *introduce* at the trial.

Magistrate: A judicial officer having some but not all of the powers of a judge. In the federal trial courts (the U.S. District Courts), the magistrate may conduct many of the preliminary or pretrial proceedings in both civil and criminal cases.

Pretrial conference: A conference held between the judge (or magistrate) and the attorneys to prepare the case for trial. At this conference, the presiding officer often encourages the parties to settle the dispute on their own without a trial.

Stipulated: Agreed to. A *stipulation* of fact will not be *contested* or disputed so that no evidence need be presented as to the truth or falsity of that fact at trial.

In issue: In question. A question or issue *of fact* means that the truth or falsity of that fact must be established at the trial. A question or issue *of law* means that the judge must rule on what the law is or how the law applies to the facts.

Tangible evidence: Physical evidence; evidence that can be seen or touched, e.g., letters, photographs, skeletons. *Testimonial evidence* is evidence that can be heard, e.g., the statements made by anyone from the witness box.

Introduce: To place evidence formally before the court so that it will become part of the record for consideration by the judge and jury.

After some delay, the case was finally *set for trial*. All the parties, their attorneys, and the witnesses assembled in the courtroom. The judge entered, took the bench, and ordered the *bailiff* to summon a *jury panel* for the trial. Once the potential or prospective jurors were seated in the courtroom, *voir dire* began. Several jurors were *challenged for cause* and dismissed—one because she worked for the insurance company that issued the policy on Miller's car. The position as to this prospective juror was that she might be *biased*. Several other jurors were dismissed as a result of *peremptory challenges*. A panel of twelve jurors plus two *alternates* was eventually selected and seated in the jury box.

Set for trial: To schedule a date when the trial is to begin.

Bailiff: A court employee who keeps order in the courtroom and renders general assistance to the judge.

Jury panel: A group of citizens who have been called to jury duty. From this group, juries for particular trials will be selected.

Voir dire: The oral examination of prospective jurors by the lawyers, by the judge, or by both.

Challenge for cause: A request from a party to a judge that a prospective juror *not* be allowed to become a member of this jury because of specified causes or reasons.

Bias: The potential for unfairness because of prior knowledge or involvement leading to possible preconceptions and a lack of open-mindedness.

Peremptory challenge: A request from a party to a judge that a prospective juror *not* be allowed to become a member of this jury. No reason or "cause" need be stated for this type of challenge. Both sides are allowed a limited number of peremptory challenges, but they will be granted as many challenges for cause as they can establish.

Alternate: An extra juror who will sit with the regular jurors and who will take the place of a regular juror if one becomes incapacitated during the trial.

When the jury was seated, Brown's attorney rose and told the judge that she wished to invoke the *rule on witnesses.* The judge nodded to the bailiff who then led all the witnesses (except for the parties themselves) out of the courtroom. Brown's attorney then began the trial with her *opening statement* to the jury. When she finished, Miller's attorney also delivered an opening statement. The attorney for Clay's estate, however, decided to reserve his opening statement until the time for him to present the estate's case.

> Rule on witnesses: A rule that may be invoked by any party requiring certain witnesses to be removed from the courtroom until it is time for their individual testimony so that they will not be able to hear each other's testimony.

> Opening statement: A speech or presentation made by each attorney to the jury summarizing the facts the attorney intends to try to prove during the trial.

Brown's attorney, whose client had the *burden of proof,* called her first witness, a ten-year-old boy who had seen the accident. Miller's attorney immediately rose and requested a *bench conference.* When all the attorneys gathered around the bench, he stated that he *objected* to the witness on the basis of *competency.* The judge then *excused the jury* temporarily while he conducted a brief *examination* of the witness. The judge *overruled* the objection upon being satisfied that the boy was old enough to understand the obligation to tell the truth and had the ability to communicate what he knew.

> Burden of proof: The responsibility of proving a fact at the trial. Generally, the party making the factual allegation has the burden of proof as to that allegation.

> Bench conference: A discussion between the judge and the attorneys held at the judge's bench so that the jury cannot hear what is being said.

> Objection: A formal challenge usually directed at the evidence that the other side is trying to pursue or introduce.

> Competency: Legal capacity to testify.

> Excuse the jury: Ask the jury to leave the room.

> Examination: Questioning, putting questions to.

> Overrule: Deny. (The word "overrule" is also used when a court repudiates the ruling of a prior opinion written by the same court.)

The jury was brought back into the courtroom, and Brown's attorney began her *direct-examination.* After a few questions, Miller's attorney again objected, this time on the *ground* that the child's answer was *hearsay.* The judge *sustained* the objection and, after instructing the jury to disregard the boy's answer, ordered it *stricken from the record.* Brown's attorney continued her examination of the witness for a few minutes more before announcing that she had no further questions. The attorney for the estate then rose to conduct a brief *cross-examination* of the boy. He was followed by Miller's attorney, whose cross-examination was also brief. There was no *re-direct examination.*

Direct-examination: Questioning the witness first. Normally the attorney who *calls* the witness to the stand conducts the direct-examination.

Ground: Reason.

Hearsay: Testimony in court on a statement made by someone else out of court when the statement is offered to establish the truth of the statement, and thus its value is based on the credibility of the out-of-court asserter (p. 451).

Sustain: To grant or uphold the objection.

Strike from the record: To remove the testimony or evidence from the written record or *transcript* of the trial.

Cross-examination: Questioning the witness after the other side has completed the direct examination. Generally, the person conducting the cross-examination must limit him/herself to the topics or subject matters raised during the direct examination of this witness by the other side.

Re-direct examination: Questioning the witness after the cross-examination. The attorney who conducted the direct examination conducts the re-direct examination.

Brown's attorney, Davis, called several other witnesses who saw the accident. Each witness was examined and cross-examined in much the same fashion as the boy had been. Davis was about to call her fourth witness, Dr. Hadley, when the judge announced a brief recess for lunch. The judge admonished the jury not to discuss the case with anyone, even among themselves, and ordered everyone to be back in the courtroom by 2:00 P.M.

Dr. Hadley was called to the stand immediately after the luncheon recess. Brown's attorney began her direct examination with a series of questions about the doctor's medical training and experience in order to *qualify* him as an *expert witness.* She then moved that Dr. Hadley be recognized as an expert witness. The *court,* with no objections by either defense counsel, granted the motion.

Qualify: To demonstrate background and experience sufficient to convince the court that the witness has expertise in a particular area.

Expert witness: A witness who has been *qualified* as an expert and who, therefore, will be allowed to give his or her expert opinion in order to assist the jury in understanding those technical subjects not within the understanding of the average layperson.

Court: Here refers to the judge trying the case.

Brown's attorney then asked the doctor to testify as to the nature and extent of the injuries that the plaintiff, Brown, had suffered as a result of the accident. In addition to multiple cuts and bruises, the doctor stated that Brown suffered a broken knee. The knee, in the doctor's opinion, had been permanently injured and Brown would continue to suffer periodic pain and stiffness due to the injury. In order to show the expense that these injuries cost Brown, the attorney produced the original copies of the bills that the doctor sent to Brown. She handed the bills to the *clerk* who marked them as plaintiff's *exhibit* number one. After allowing defense counsel to inspect the bills, Brown's attorney handed them to the doctor who promptly identified them. The attorney then *moved the bills into evidence* and turned the witness over to defense counsel for cross-examination.

> Clerk: The court clerk who assists the judge in recordkeeping at the trial.

> Exhibit: An item of physical/tangible evidence that is to be or has been offered to the court for inspection.

> Move . . . into evidence: To request that the items be formally declared *admissible* (which is not the same as declaring them to be true; they are admitted simply for consideration as to their truth or falsity).

It was late in the afternoon when Brown's attorney finished with her final witness, Brown himself. The judge did not want to recess for the day, however, until the defendants completed their cross-examination of Brown. After about an hour, each of the defense attorneys completed their questioning of Brown, and Brown's attorney *rested his case.* The judge *adjourned* the trial until the following morning.

> Rest one's case: To announce formally that you have concluded the presentation of evidence (e.g., through the introduction of tangible evidence, through direct examination of your own witnesses). While the other side presents its case, however, you will be entitled to cross-examine its witnesses.

> Adjourn: To halt the proceedings temporarily.

On the following morning, the attorney for Clay's estate advised the judge that he had a preliminary matter to bring up before the jury was brought into the courtroom. He then proceeded to make a motion for a *directed verdict* in favor of the estate on Brown's claim of negligence. Miller's attorney made a similar motion on behalf of his client. The judge listened to arguments by the attorneys and then stated his decision. As to defendant Miller, the motion was denied because plaintiff had introduced sufficient evidence to make out a *prima facie case* of negligence that should go to the jury. As to the estate, the judge would neither grant nor deny the motion but would *take it under advisement.*

> Directed verdict: To order the jury to reach a verdict for the party making the motion on the ground that the other side, which has just

rested its case, has failed to produce enough convincing evidence to establish a cause of action.

Prima facie case: The party's evidence, if believed by the jury, would be legally sufficient to support a verdict in favor of that party, i.e., the party has introduced evidence that, if believed, would include all the facts necessary to establish a cause of action. If the plaintiff has failed to establish a prima facie case, the judge will decide the case in favor of the defendant without any further proceedings. If the judge finds that there *is* a prima facie case, the case proceeds and the defendant will be allowed an opportunity to produce contrary evidence. The case will then go to the jury to decide which version of the facts is true.

Take under advisement: To delay ruling on the motion until another time.

The jury was summoned into the courtroom and seated in the jury box for the second day of the trial. The attorney for the estate began his case by making an opening statement to the jury, reserved from the previous day. He then proceeded to call his witnesses. He had only a few witnesses and was able to conclude his case just before noon, at which time he introduced Clay's death certificate into evidence. The judge then declared a recess for lunch.

Miller's attorney began to present his case in the afternoon, and by late afternoon he too had rested his case. The judge dismissed the jury until the following morning and asked the attorneys to be prepared for *closing arguments* at that time. He also requested that they submit any *jury instructions* that they would like to request, so that he could review them. Brown's attorney requested an instruction that the co-defendants had to overcome a *presumption* of negligence against them. The judge denied this request. Finally, he announced that he had decided to deny the estate's earlier motion for a directed verdict.

Closing argument: The final statements by the attorneys summarizing the evidence that they think they have established and the evidence that they think the other side has failed to establish.

Jury instructions: A statement of the guidelines and law given by the judge to the jury that they are to use in deciding the issues of fact. The instructions to the jury are also referred to as the *charge* to the jury. The attorneys are usually allowed to submit proposed instructions for consideration by the judge.

Presumption: An assumption that a certain fact is true. A *rebuttable presumption* is an assumption that can be overcome or changed if the other side introduces enough facts to overcome it. If the other side does not rebut the presumption, then the assumption stands. A *nonrebuttable* presumption cannot be overcome no matter how convincing is the evidence of the other side against the assumption.

Closing arguments began late the following morning. Each attorney carefully reviewed the evidence for the jury and argued for a *verdict* in favor of his or her client. Following a brief recess for lunch, the judge thanked the alternate jurors for their time and dismissed them. He then began to instruct the remaining twelve jurors on the law they were to follow in finding the facts and in reaching a verdict. He explained that they, as jurors, were the finders of fact and were to base their decision solely upon the testimony and exhibits introduced during the trial. He explained the concept of burden of proof and stated which party had to carry this burden as to each of the various *elements* of negligence. He explained that the *standard of proof* as to each of these elements was that each must be proved by a *preponderance of the evidence*. Finally, he described the manner in which they should compute the amount of damages, if any, suffered by the parties. The jury was then led out of the courtroom to deliberate on its verdict. The judge retired to his chambers, and the attorneys settled back with their clients to wait.

> Verdict: The final decision of the jury.

> Elements: Here, the components of a cause of action.

> Standard of proof: A statement of how convincing the evidence must be in order for a party to comply with his or her burden of proof. The main standards of proof are proof *beyond a reasonable doubt* (in criminal cases only), proof *by clear and convincing evidence,* and proof by a *preponderance of evidence.*

> Preponderance of evidence: A standard of proof (used in many civil suits) that is met when a party's evidence on a fact indicates that it is "more likely than not" that the fact is as the party alleges it to be.

After about an hour, the judge received a note from the foreman of the jury, asking that the jury be allowed to view several of the exhibits. The items requested consisted largely of the various medical bills allegedly incurred by Brown and by Clay. The attorneys for Brown and for the estate took this as a good sign—the jury had probably decided the case against Miller and were now trying to compute damages.

A second note arrived in another hour, announcing that the jury had reached a verdict. The bailiff summoned everyone back to the courtroom, and the jury came in a few minutes later. At the clerk's request, the foreman rose to read the verdict. On Brown's original complaint against Miller for negligence, the jury found for Brown and against Miller, awarding Brown $30,000 in damages. However, on Brown's complaint against Clay's estate (the co-defendant), the jury decided in favor of the estate, finding that Clay had not been negligent. The jury found for the estate on its cross-claim against its co-defendant, Miller, awarding $200,000 in damages to the estate. Finally, the jury found against Miller on his own cross-claim against the estate, as well as on his counterclaim against Brown. The judge entered a *judgment* against Miller in the amounts awarded by the jury. After denying a motion by Miller for a *judgment notwithstanding the verdict,* he thanked the jurors and dismissed them.

> Judgment: The final decision of the court resolving the dispute and determining the rights and obligations of the parties. Many judgments order the losing party to do something (e.g., pay damages) or

to refrain from doing something. A *declaratory judgment* establishes the rights and obligations of the parties, but it does not order the parties to do or refrain from doing anything.

Judgment notwithstanding the verdict: A judgment by the court that is the opposite of the verdict reached by the jury, in effect, overruling the jury. (Also referred to as a judgment n.o.v.)

Miller's attorney immediately made a *motion for a new trial,* arguing several possible grounds. When this motion was denied by the trial judge, he moved for a *reduction of the verdict,* arguing that the amounts awarded were excessive. This motion was also denied, and the attorney announced his intention to *appeal.* The judge granted Miller a *stay* of the judgment, conditioned upon his filing a *timely notice of appeal* and posting the appropriate *bond.*

Motion for a new trial: A request that the trial judge set aside the judgment and order a new trial on the basis that the trial was improper or unfair due to specified prejudicial errors that occurred.

Reduction of the verdict: Lowering the amount of the damage award reached by the jury.

Appeal: To ask a court of *appellate jurisdiction* (a higher court within the same judicial system as the trial court) to *review* or examine the decision of the lower court on the basis that the lower court made some errors of law in conducting the trial.

Stay: To delay enforcement or *execution* of the court's judgment.

Timely: On time, according to the time specified by law.

Notice of appeal: A document announcing an intention to appeal, filed with the appellate court and served on the opposing party.

Bond: A sum of money deposited with the court to assure compliance with some requirement.

Miller asked his attorney what the $30,000 verdict against him meant. Since Brown had originally sued for $100,000, could Brown later sue Miller again for the rest of the amount he claimed? The attorney explained that, because of the stay granted by the judge, Miller would not have to pay anything until a decision on appeal had been reached. Furthermore, Brown could not sue Miller again on the same cause of action because Brown had received a *judgment on the merits,* which would be *res judicata* and would *bar* any later suit on the same negligence cause of action. The same would be true of a later negligence action by Clay's estate against Miller.

Judgment on the merits: A decision on the substance of the claims raised. A party who has received a judgment on the merits cannot bring the same suit again. Normally, a judgment of dismissal based solely on some procedural error is *not* a judgment on the merits. The latter kind of judgment is often referred to as a *dismissal without prejudice.* A party whose case has been dismissed without prejudice can bring the same suit again so long as the procedural errors are corrected (i.e., cured) in the later action.

Res judicata: The legal doctrine that a judgment on the merits will prevent the same parties from relitigating the same cause of action on the same facts; the parties have already had their day in court.

Bar: Prevent or stop.

Miller's attorney filed his notice of appeal and posted bond the following week. As attorney for the *appellant,* it was also his duty to see to it that the *record,* including *transcripts* and copies of exhibits, was transmitted to the court of appeals and that the case was *docketed* by the clerk of that court. Miller's attorney then had forty days in which to draft and file his *brief* with the court of appeals. He served copies of the brief on the attorneys for the *appellees,* Brown and Clay's estate, who in turn each file and serve their briefs concerning the *issues on appeal.*

Appellant: The party initiating the appeal; the party who is complaining of error(s) made by the trial court.

Record: The official collection of all the trial pleadings, exhibits, orders, and word-for-word testimony that took place during the trial.

Transcript: Word-for-word typed record of everything that was said "on the record" during the trial. The court reporter types this transcription, which is paid for by the parties requesting it.

Docket: The court's official calendar of pending cases. Once all the necessary papers have been filed, the appeal is "docketed" by the clerk, i.e., placed on the court's official calendar.

Brief: A written argument presented to the appeals court by a party stating the legal issues on appeal and the positions of the party on those issues—all relating to the claimed errors that occurred during the trial. It is called an appellate brief.

Appellee: A party against whom the appeal is brought. (Also called the respondent.) Generally the appellee is satisfied with what the trial court did and wishes the appellate court to approve of or *affirm* the trial court's judgment.

Issues on appeal: The claimed errors of law committed by the trial judge below. The appellate court does not retry every case. No witnesses are called, and no testimony is taken by the appellate court. The court examines the record and determines whether errors of law were committed by the trial judge.

Several months passed before the attorneys finally received a notice from the clerk of the court of appeals that the appeal had been scheduled for *oral argument* before a three-judge *panel* of the court. The arguments were heard a few weeks later. Six months after oral argument, the attorneys received the decision of the court along with its written *opinion.* By a vote of two to one (one judge *dissenting*), the court had *affirmed* the judgments against Miller. The only error that the majority found was the admission of certain of the testimony offered by Brown's expert witness. However, because Miller's attorney had not objected to this testimony at trial, the opinion stated, he had *waived* this defect.

Oral argument: A verbal presentation made by the attorneys before the appellate court during which arguments about the validity or invalidity of what the trial judge did are presented.

Panel: A group of appellate judges, usually three, who preside over the appeal of the case and who vote on the result.

Opinion: A court's written explanation of how and why it applied the law to the specific facts before it to reach a certain decision. Opinions are often collected in official and unofficial *reporters.*

Dissent: Disagree with the decision (the result and the reasons) of the *majority* of the court. If a judge agrees with the result reached by the majority but disagrees with reasons the majority used to support that result, the judge would cast a *concurring* vote and might write a separate concurring opinion.

Affirm: To agree with or uphold the lower court judgment. If the appellate court *remanded* the case, it would send it back to the lower court with instructions to correct the irregularities specified in the appellate opinion. If the appellate court *reversed* the court below, it would have changed the result reached below.

Waive: To make known expressly or impliedly that you will not exercise a right that you have. Here the court is referring to the well-established rule that failure to object during trial is an implied waiver of the right to later complain about the alleged error on appeal.

Miller, undaunted, *petitioned* for a *rehearing* by the court *en banc.* The petition was denied. Miller then discussed the possibility of further appeal with his attorney. The attorney explained that Miller could, if he desired, try to appeal to the United States Supreme Court. He cautioned Miller, however, that he could not *appeal as a matter of right* in this case but would be limited to a petition for a *writ of certiorari.* He advised Miller that it was extremely unlikely that the Supreme Court would grant the petition and that it probably would not be worth the extra expense. Miller agreed, and no further appeal was attempted. Shortly thereafter the court of appeals issued its *mandate,* and the case was returned to the district court where Miller, through his insurance company, *satisfied* the judgment.

Petition: To make a formal request; similar to a motion.

Rehearing: A second hearing by the appellate court to reconsider the decision it made after the first appellate hearing.

En banc: By the entire court. The *panel* of judges that heard the first appeal may have consisted of only three judges, yet the entire number of judges on the court may be much larger.

Appeal as a matter of right: An appeal in which the appellate court has no discretion as to whether to hear the appeal and thus is *required* to review the decision below.

Writ of Certiorari: An order by the appellate court (here the highest court) that is used when the court has discretion on whether to hear an appeal. If the writ is denied, the court refuses to hear the appeal, and, in effect, the judgment below stands unchanged. If the writ is granted, then it has the effect of ordering the lower court to certify the record and send it up to the higher court that has used its discretion to hear the appeal.

Mandate: The order of the court. Here the mandate of the appellate court was to affirm the trial court's judgment.

Satisfy: To comply with a legal obligation, here to pay the judgment award.

2. The Criminal Charges

Brown was involved in a second legal dispute during the same period of time that the negligence suit was in litigation. In addition to suing Clay's estate and Miller, Brown was defending himself in a criminal *prosecution* for possession of narcotics.

Prosecution: The bringing and processing of a criminal charge by the government. (Occasionally the word is also used to mean the processing of a civil claim by a party.)

As Brown was leaving the hospital after having recovered from his injury, he was met at the door by two police officers. The officers produced a *warrant* and advised Brown that he was under arrest. After he was read his rights, he was taken to the police station.

Warrant: An order from a judicial officer authorizing the arrest of an individual, the search of property, etc.

The following morning Brown was taken before a judge for his *initial appearance.* The judge advised Brown that he had been charged with a *felony,* "possession of narcotics with intent to distribute." He then advised Brown of his rights, including his right to be represented by a lawyer. Since Brown was unemployed and without adequate funds to pay an attorney, the judge asked him if he would like the court to appoint a lawyer to handle the case. Brown said yes. An attorney was *assigned* to represent Brown. The judge, at the lawyer's request, then agreed to give Brown a chance to confer with his new attorney before continuing the hearing.

Initial appearance: A court proceeding during which (a) the accused is told of the charges, (b) a decision on bail is made, and (c) arrangements are made for the next judicial proceeding in the case.

Felony: A crime that is punishable by a sentence of one year or more. A *misdemeanor* is a crime punishable by a sentence of less than a year.

Assigned counsel: Attorney appointed to represent an *indigent* (poor) defendant.

When the case was recalled, Brown and his court-appointed attorney again approached the bench and stood before the judge. The attorney handed the clerk a praecipe formally entering his name as attorney of record for Brown and advised the judge that he was prepared to discuss the matter of *bail*. He proceeded to describe for the judge various details about Brown's background—his education, employment record, length of residence in the city, etc. He concluded by asking that he be released on his own *personal recognizance.* The prosecutor was then given an opportunity to speak. He recommended a high *bond,* pointing out that the defendant was unemployed and had no close relatives in the area. These facts, he argued, coupled with the serious nature of a felony charge, indicated a substantial risk that the defendant might try to flee. The judge nevertheless agreed to release Brown on his own personal recognizance and set a date for a *preliminary hearing* the following week.

Bail: Property or a sum of money deposited with the court in order to ensure that defendant will reappear in court at designated times.

Personal recognizance: The defendant's sworn promise that he or she will return to court at the designated times. No bail money is required.

Bond: A written obligation to pay a sum of money to the court in the event that the defendant fails to appear at designated times.

Preliminary hearing: A hearing during which the state is required to produce sufficient evidence to establish that there is *probable cause* (see definition below) to believe that the defendant committed the crimes charged.

The only witness at the preliminary hearing was the police officer who had been at the scene of the accident. The officer said that as he was helping to pull Brown out of the car, he noticed a small paper sack sticking out from under the passenger's side of the front seat. Several glassine envelopes containing a white powdery substance, the officer said, fell out of the sack. The substance, totalling about one-half ounce, was tested and proved to be 80% pure heroin. Brown's attorney cross-examined the officer briefly but little additional information came out. The judge found that there was *probable cause* to hold the defendant and ordered the case *bound over* for *grand jury* action. He continued Brown's release on personal recognizance.

Probable cause: A reasonable basis to believe that the defendant is guilty of the crime charged.

Bound over: Submitted.

Grand jury: A special jury whose duty is to hear evidence of felonies presented by the prosecutor in order to determine whether there is sufficient evidence to return an *indictment* (see definition below) against the defendant and cause him or her to stand trial on the charge(s).

Shortly after the preliminary hearing, Brown's attorney went to the prosecutor to see if he could work out an informal disposition of the charges. He tried to convince the prosecutor to enter a *nolle prosequi* on the charge, explaining that Brown had simply been getting a ride home and was not aware of the fact that the heroin was in the car. The prosecutor was unwilling to drop the charge. However, he was willing to "nolle" the felony charge of possession with intent to distribute if Brown would agree to *plead* guilty to the lesser offense of simple possession of a dangerous drug, a misdemeanor. The attorney said he would speak to his client about it.

> Nolle prosequi: A statement by the prosecutor that he or she is unwilling to prosecute the case. The charges, in effect, are dropped.

> Plead: To formally admit or deny the charges made by the prosecutor.

He spoke to Brown that same afternoon, told him about the *plea bargaining* session, and advised him of the prosecutor's offer. Brown was not interested. He felt he was innocent and was unwilling to plead, even to a misdemeanor.

> Plea bargaining: Negotiation between the prosecution and defense counsel during which an attempt is made to reach a compromise in lieu of a criminal trial. Generally the defendant agrees to plead guilty to a lesser charge in return for the state's willingness to drop a more serious charge.

Several weeks went by before Brown's attorney was notified that the grand jury had returned an *indictment* against his client. The next step would be the *arraignment* on the following Monday. On the appointed date, Brown and his attorney appeared before the judge, and Brown was formally notified of the indictment. He entered a plea of not guilty to the charge. The judge set a trial date about two-and-one-half months away and again agreed to continue Brown's release on personal recognizance.

> Arraignment: A court proceeding in which the defendant is formally charged with the crime and enters a plea. Arrangements are then made for trial.

> Indictment: A formal document issued by a grand jury accusing the defendant of a crime.

The day for the trial arrived, and both sides (Brown's attorney and the prosecutor) announced that they were ready. Voir dire was held, and a jury was *impaneled.* The trial itself was relatively uneventful, lasting less than a day. The prosecutor, following a brief opening statement, presented only two witnesses: the police officer who had been at the scene and an expert from the police lab who identified the substance as heroin. He then rested his case. Brown's attorney then made his opening statement and presented his only witness, Brown himself. The jury listened attentively as Brown, on direct examination, explained the events leading up to the accident and his subsequent arrest. Not only had he been unaware of the heroin, he testified, but he had never even seen it since he had been knocked unconscious by the accident and had not revived until he was in the ambulance. The prosecutor's cross-examination came next. Brown had a previous conviction for shoplifting and the prosecutor attempted to use this conviction to *impeach* Brown's testimony. Brown's attorney successfully objected, arguing that the conviction, which had occurred eight years previously, was too remote to be *relevant*. Its use now would be prejudicial. The judge agreed and prohibited any mention of the prior conviction. After a few more questions, the prosecutor concluded his cross-examination, and the defense rested its case.

> Impaneled: Selected, sworn in, and seated.

> Impeach: To attack or discredit by introducing evidence that the testimony of the witness is not credible (believable).

> Relevant: Tending to prove or disprove a fact in issue. Evidence is relevant if it has a tendency to make the existence of a fact more probable or less probable than it would be without that evidence.

Both sides presented their closing arguments following the lunch recess. The judge then instructed the jury, describing the elements of the offense and explaining that the burden of proof in a criminal case is on the *government*. That burden, he continued, is to show each element of the offense *beyond a reasonable doubt*. The jury took less than forty-five minutes to reach its verdict. All parties quickly reassembled in the courtroom to hear the foreman announce the verdict *acquitting* Brown of the offense. A *poll* of the jury, requested by the prosecutor, confirmed the result, and the judge advised Brown that he was free to go.

> Government: Here, the prosecutor.

> Beyond a reasonable doubt: The standard of proof required for conviction in a criminal case. If any reasonable doubt exists as to any element of the crime, the defendant cannot be convicted.

> Acquit: Find not guilty; absolve of guilt.

> Poll: To question jurors individually in open court as to whether each agrees with the verdict announced by the foreman.

Generally, criminal cases in which the defendant is acquitted may not be appealed by the prosecutor. Hence, in this case, there was no appeal of the trial judgment.

3. The Unemployment Compensation Dispute

The day after his indictment on the felony charge, Brown went down to the State Unemployment Office to apply for benefits. He was interviewed by a clerk and was asked to fill out and sign an application form. The clerk told Brown that he would receive a letter in about a week notifying him of the agency's initial determination on his eligibility. If he was eligible, his benefits would start in about ten days.

Brown received the letter a few days later. It advised him that, although he was otherwise eligible for benefits, a routine check with his former employer had disclosed that he had been fired for "misconduct." For this reason, the letter stated, he would be deemed disqualified for a nine-week period. Moreover, the benefits due for those nine weeks would be deducted from the total amount he would otherwise be entitled to. If he wished to appeal this decision, the letter went on, he would have to request an *administrative hearing* within ten days.

> Administrative hearing: An agency proceeding usually conducted less formally than a court hearing or trial, at which the presiding officer listens to the evidence and makes a preliminary determination on how the controversy should be resolved.

Brown felt that he needed some legal advice, but he was still out of work and broke. (The lawsuit in the civil action had not been filed yet—it would be well over a year before the case would be tried, appealed, and the judgment actually paid.) Brown therefore decided to obtain help from the local legal aid office. He explained his problem to a receptionist and was introduced to the *paralegal* who would be handling his case. The paralegal, an expert in unemployment compensation law, discussed the case with Brown and agreed to represent Brown at the hearing. He helped Brown fill out a form requesting a hearing and promised to let him know as soon as the date was set. Brown left and the paralegal immediately began to research and draft a *memorandum* to submit to the *hearing examiner* on Brown's behalf.

> Paralegal: A person with legal skills who works under the supervision of an attorney or who is otherwise authorized by law to use these skills. (Some state and federal agencies allow nonlawyers to represent clients at administrative hearings.)

> Memorandum: Here, a written presentation of the facts and legal issues in the case and the position of the party on the facts and legal issues.

> Hearing examiner: An employee of the agency (sometimes called a referee or an administrative law judge) who presides over the hearing and either makes findings of fact and law or recommends such findings to someone else in the agency who will make the final decision.

The hearing, held ten days later, lasted about an hour and a half. The only witnesses were Brown and his former boss, Frank Best. Best told the examiner about Brown's arrest and about the thefts from the warehouse. Taken together, he argued, these events made it impossible for him to trust Brown on the job any longer. Brown, in turn, denied any participation in the thefts and maintained his innocence on the drug charge. (As of this time, Brown had not been acquitted of the felony.) The hearing examiner, at the close of the proceedings, thanked the parties and promised a decision within a few days.

The hearing examiner's decision arrived shortly thereafter in a document labeled "*Proposed Findings* of Law and of Fact." The last paragraph contained the examiner's recommended decision. The hearing examiner agreed with Brown that his boss's mere suspicion that Brown was involved in the thefts was not enough to justify a finding of misconduct. However, the decision went on, the pending criminal charges for a drug-related offense did provide the employer with good cause to fire Brown since drug involvement could affect his ability to operate a truck safely. The paragraph concluded by recommending a finding of misconduct and the imposition of a nine-week penalty period.

> Proposed findings: Recommended conclusions presented to someone else in the agency who will make the final decision.

A second letter arrived ten days later giving the *decision* of the agency. The letter, signed by the director of the local agency, adopted the proposed findings and recommended decision of the hearing examiner. This decision, the letter concluded, could be appealed within fifteen days to the State Unemployment Compensation *Board of Appeals.* Brown immediately appealed.

> Decision: Here, the determination by a superior of the hearing examiner adopting, modifying, or rejecting the recommended decision of the hearing examiner.

> Board of Appeals: A nonjudicial, administrative tribunal that reviews the decision made by the hearing officer or by the head of the agency.

Copies of the hearing transcript along with memoranda from both sides were filed with the Board of Appeals. The Board, exercising its *discretion,* refused to allow oral arguments before it and *summarily* reversed the decision reached *below.* It issued a short written decision, which noted that, while Best may have had good cause to fire Brown, that good cause did not rise to the level of misconduct on Brown's part. The Board in this final administrative decision ordered the local office to begin paying benefits immediately, including back benefits to cover the period since he had first applied.

> Discretion: The power to choose among various courses of conduct based solely on one's reasoned judgment or preference.

> Summarily: Quickly, briefly, without formal proceedings such as a hearing.

> Below: The lower tribunal.

Best decided to appeal this administrative decision to a court. He was allowed to do so since he had *exhausted his administrative remedies.* He filed a complaint in a county court seeking review of the Board's decision. He submitted to the court the entire record from the proceedings below and asked for a *trial de novo.* Brown, now represented by an attorney from the legal aid office, filed his answer and immediately made a motion for summary judgment. The court, upon a review of the record and the pleadings, granted the motion and affirmed the judgment of the Board of Appeals. Best, after discussing the case at length with his attorney, decided against a further appeal of the case to the court of appeals.

Exhausting one's administrative remedies: Pursuing *all* available methods of resolving a dispute at the agency level before asking a court to review the administrative decision of the agency. A court generally will not allow a party to appeal an administrative decision until this process has been completed.

Trial de novo: A totally new fact-finding hearing.

CHART 1. CIVIL LITIGATION		
EVENT	**DEFINITIONS**	**RESULT**
I. Agency Stage		
1. Someone protests an action taken by the *administrative agency.* 2. *Agency Hearing.* 3. *Intra-Agency Appeal* to a Commission or Board within the agency or to the Director or Secretary of the agency. If no agency is involved, the litigation begins in court.	*Administrative Agency:* a governmental body whose primary function is to carry out or administer statutes passed by the legislature. *Agency Hearing:* a proceeding, similar to a trial, in which an agency hearing officer or administrative law judge listens to evidence and legal arguments before deciding the case. *Intra-Agency Appeal:* a review within the agency of the earlier decision to determine if that decision was correct.	The hearing officer or administrative law judge writes a *recommended decision.* The Commission, Board, Director, or Secretary issues a final *administrative decision.*
II. Pretrial Stage		
4. Plaintiff files a *complaint.* 5. Clerk issues a *summons.* 6. *Service of process* on defendant. 7. Defendant files an *answer.* 8. *Discovery* by written *interrogatories.* 9. *Discovery* by *deposition.* 10. Other discovery devices, e.g., request for admissions. 11. Pretrial *motions.* 12. *Settlement* efforts.	*Complaint:* Plaintiff states claim(s) against defendant. *Summons:* court notice requiring the defendant to appear and answer the complaint. *Service of process:* the delivery of the summons to the defendant. *Answer:* defendant's response to the plaintiff's complaint. *Discovery:* methods by which one party obtains information from the other party about the litigation prior to trial.	The trial court will often be making rulings concerning these events but rarely will write an opinion on any of these rulings. Occasionally, a party may be allowed to appeal a pretrial ruling to an appeals court that may write an opinion affirming, modifying, or reversing the ruling. Such an appeal is called an *interlocutory* appeal. It takes place before the trial court reaches a final judgment.

CHART 1.—Continued.		
EVENT	**DEFINITIONS**	**RESULT**
	Interrogatories: a method of discovery through written questions submitted by one party to another before trial.	
	Deposition: a method of discovery through a question-and-answer session usually conducted in the offices of one of the attorneys. Parties and prospective witnesses are questioned by the attorneys without a judge present. Their testimony is recorded or transcribed for possible later use.	
	Motions: formal requests to the court, e.g., a motion to dismiss.	
	Settlement: a resolution of the dispute, making the trial unnecessary.	
III. Trial Stage		
13. *Voir dire.* 14. *Opening statement* of plaintiff. 15. *Opening statement* of defendant. 16. Plaintiff presents its case. (a) evidence introduced (b) *direct examination* (c) *cross-examination* 17. *Motions* to dismiss. 18. Defendant presents its case. (a) evidence introduced (b) *direct examination* (c) *cross-examination* 19. Closing arguments to jury by counsel. 20. *Charge* to jury. 21. *Verdict* of jury. 22. *Judgment* of court.	*Voir dire:* selection of the jury. (Not all cases are jury cases.) *Opening statement:* a summary of the facts the attorney will try to prove during the trial. *Direct examination:* questioning by counsel of his/her own witnesses. *Cross-examination:* questioning of witnesses by counsel for the other side. *Charge:* the judge's instructions to the jury on how it should go about reaching its verdict. *Verdict:* the result of the jury's deliberation. *Judgment:* the final statement of the trial court on the rights and responsibilities of the parties.	The trial court will often make rulings concerning these events, but rarely will write an opinion on any of these rulings. After the trial, the trial court will deliver its judgment. Usually an opinion (explaining the judgment) will *not* be written. Several trial courts, however, do sometimes write opinions, e.g., federal trial courts (U.S. District Courts) and New York State trial courts.

CHART 1.—Continued.		
EVENT	**DEFINITIONS**	**RESULT**
IV. Appeal Stage		
23. Filing of *notice of appeal.* 24. Filing of *appellant's brief.* 25. Filing of *appellee's brief.* 26. Filing of reply *brief.* 27. Oral argument by counsel. 28. Decision of court.	*Notice of appeal:* statement by counsel of intention to seek a review of the trial court's judgment. *Appellant:* the party bringing the appeal because of dissatisfaction with the trial court's judgment. *Appellee:* the party against whom the appeal is brought. *Brief:* written arguments by counsel on why the trial court acted correctly or incorrectly.	An opinion of the middle appeals court (i.e., an intermediate appellate court) will often be written. This opinion of the middle appeals court might be further appealed to the highest court, in which event another opinion could be written. [Note that in some states, there is no middle appeals court; the appeal goes directly from the trial court to the highest state court.]

CHART 2. CRIMINAL LITIGATION		
EVENT	**DEFINITIONS**	**RESULT**
I. Pretrial Stage		
1. *Arrest.* 2. *Initial appearance* before a judge or a magistrate. 3. *Preliminary hearing.* 4. *Indictment* by grand jury. 5. *Arraignment.* 6. Limited pretrial discovery. 7. Pretrial motions.	*Arrest:* to take someone into custody in order to bring him/her before the proper authorities. *Initial appearance:* a court proceeding during which the accused is told of the charges, a bail decision is made, and arrangements for the next proceeding are made. *Preliminary hearing:* a court proceeding during which a decision is made as to whether there is probable cause to believe that the accused committed the crime(s) charged. *Indictment:* a formal charge issued by the grand jury accusing the defendant of the crime. (If no grand jury is involved in the case, the accusation is contained in a document called an information.)	The trial court will often be making rulings concerning these events but rarely will write an opinion on any of these rulings. Occasionally, a party may be allowed to appeal a pretrial ruling immediately to an appeals court that may write an opinion affirming, modifying, or reversing the ruling. This interlocutory appeal takes place before the trial court reaches a final judgment.

CHART 2.—Continued.		
EVENT	**DEFINITIONS**	**RESULT**
	Arraignment: a court proceeding in which the defendant is formally charged with the crime and enters a plea. Arrangements are then made for trial.	
II. Trial Stage		
8. *Voir dire.* 9. *Opening statements* of counsel. 10. Government presents its case against the defendant. (a) evidence introduced (b) *direct examination* (c) *cross-examination* 11. Motions to dismiss. 12. Defendant presents its case. (a) evidence introduced (b) *direct examination* (c) *cross-examination* 13. Arguments to jury by counsel. 14. *Charge* to jury. 15. *Verdict* of jury. 16. *Judgment* of court.	*Voir dire:* selection of the jury (not all cases are jury cases). *Opening statements:* a summary of the facts the attorney will try to prove during the trial. *Direct examination:* questioning by counsel of his/her own witnesses. *Cross-examination:* questioning of witnesses by counsel for the other side. *Charge:* the judge's instructions to the jury on how it should go about reaching its verdict. *Verdict:* the result of the jury's deliberation. *Judgment:* the final statement of the trial court on the rights and responsibilities of the parties.	The trial court will often make rulings concerning these events, but rarely will write an opinion on any of these rulings. After the trial, the trial court will deliver its judgment. Usually no opinion (explaining the judgment) will be written. Several trial courts, however, do sometimes write opinions, e.g., federal trial courts (U.S. District Courts) and New York State trial courts.
III. Appeal Stage		
17. Filing of *notice of appeal.* 18. Filing of *appellant's brief.* 19. Filing of *appellee's brief.* 20. Filing of reply *brief.* 21. Oral argument by counsel. 22. Decision of court.	*Notice of appeal:* statement by counsel of intention to seek a review of the trial court's judgment. *Appellant:* the party bringing the appeal because of dissatisfaction with the trial court's judgment. *Appellee:* the party against whom the appeal is brought. *Brief:* written arguments by counsel on why the trial court acted correctly or incorrectly.	An opinion of the middle appeals court (i.e., an intermediate appellate court) will often be written. This opinion of the middle appeals court might then be further appealed to the highest court, in which event another opinion could be written. [Note that in some states, there is no middle appeals court; the appeal goes directly from the trial court to the highest state court.]

Part II

The Skills of a Paralegal

CONTENTS

7

Introduction to
Legal Analysis ==========

Section A. THE STRUCTURE OF LEGAL ANALYSIS

Legal analysis is the application of rules of law to facts. For example:

RULE +	FACTS +	ISSUE +	ANALYSIS= (Summary)	CONCLUSION
§10. "Any business within the city must apply for and obtain a license to do business within the city limits."	Fran owns a grocery store in the city.	Is a grocery store in the city a "business" under §10 requiring a license "to do business"?	A grocery store is a business. Fran runs this business within the city.	§10 requires Fran to have a license.

Legal analysis always has a *legal issue* or question of law. The components of the issue are (a) a brief quote from the language of the rule that is in controversy and (b) a brief reference to the relevant facts that raise this controversy in the language of the rule.

Of course, not all legal analysis is this simple. *Yet the basic structure of a legal argument will always have the above format.* Note the following characteristics of the process.

- You start with a specific rule. You quote the relevant language exactly.
- The major facts are stated.
- The legal issue states the controversy in terms of specific language in the rule and specific facts that raise the controversy.
- You draw the connection between specific language in the rule and specific facts. The analysis *is* this connection.
- You reach a conclusion based upon the above steps. The conclusion is phrased in terms of the rule.

More complicated example:

RULE +	FACTS +	ISSUE +	ANALYSIS = (Summary)	CONCLUSION
§10. "Any business within the city must apply for and obtain a license to do business within the city limits."	Bill and his neighbors in the city have formed a food co-op through which members buy their food collectively from a wholesale company. All funds received by the co-op go for expenses and the purchase of food.	Is a non-profit co-op a "business" within the meaning of §10 requiring a license "to do business"?	The city argues that the co-op is a business in the city. The co-op concedes that it is in the city, but argues that it does not "do business" since the co-op does not earn a profit.	The co-op has the better argument. §10 was not intended to cover non-profit ventures. Hence, the co-op does not have to have a license.

The following is a more detailed statement of the analysis:

§10 provides as follows:

"Any business within the city must apply for and obtain a license to do business within the city limits."

There are two main elements to section 10:
1. There must be a business.
2. The business must do business within the city.

1. A business.

The city claims that the co-op is a business. It does not matter to the city that profits in the traditional sense are not earned by the co-op. According to the city, the co-op members are "selling" goods to each other.

The co-op, on the other hand, argues that section 10 was not intended to cover co-ops. A business is an enterprise that makes a profit over and above expenses. Nothing of this kind occurs in the co-op. Everything taken in by the co-op goes out in the form of food purchases and expenses. Hence, the co-op is not a business and does not have to have a license.

2. Doing business within the city.

There is no dispute between the parties on this element. The city and the co-op agree that the co-op operates within the city limits. The only dispute in this case concerns whether the co-op is a business (see discussion above under the first element).

If you had included legal research data on the meaning of §10, the analysis would *also* have contained:

- A discussion of court opinions, if any, that have interpreted §10 (p. 647, p. 650).
- A discussion of administrative regulations, if any, that implement §10 (p. 672).
- A discussion of the legislative history, if available, of §10 (p. 655).
- A discussion of secondary authority, if any, that has interpreted §10, e.g., legal periodical literature (p. 625), treatises (p. 630).
- A discussion of constitutional provisions, if any, that affect the applicability of §10 (p. 669).
- Etc.

The analysis, the facts, the issues, etc., are often presented in the format of a *memorandum of law*, which will be examined in greater detail in chapter 12 on Legal Writing (p. 686).

In our example, note that the analysis proceeded through a discussion of the *elements* of the rule that is being applied. An element is a portion of a rule that you identify on your own as one of the preconditions of the applicability of the entire rule and that can be conveniently analyzed separately from the other elements of the rule.

Assume that you are analyzing the following rule:

971.22 Change of place of trial. The defendant may move for a change of the place of trial on the ground that an impartial trial cannot be had in the county. The motion shall be made at arraignment.

Step one is to break the rule into its elements. The effect or consequence of the rule is to change the place of the trial. Ask yourself what must happen before this consequence will follow, i.e., ask yourself what are the conditions or preconditions that must exist before the result will occur. The answer will provide you with the elements of the rule:

1. Defendant.
2. Move for a change of the place of trial.
3. An impartial trial cannot be had in the county.
4. The motion must be made at the time of the arraignment.

Hence, there are four elements to section 971.22. All four must exist before the place of the trial will be moved. Let us look at each element more closely. A number of logical questions should come to your mind about each element.

1. Defendant.

Apparently a plaintiff (or the state through the district attorney) *cannot* take advantage of section 971.22. The statute is addressed to a "defendant." What is a "defendant"? Is any accused person a defendant? When does someone become a defendant?

2. Move for a Change of the Place of Trial.

It is not enough that a change is justified; there must be a request for it. There must be a specific motion or request for the change. Does the motion have to be in writing?

3. An Impartial Trial Cannot be Had in the County.

What is an "impartial trial"? Complex definitional problems are likely in analyzing this element.

4. The Motion Must be Made at the Time of the Arraignment.

The motion must be made at a specific time—at the arraignment. The motion will be denied if made at the time of arrest (too early) or at the time of the preliminary hearing or trial (too late).

Once you have broken the rule down into its elements, you have the structure of the analysis in front of you. Each element becomes a separate section of the analysis. You discuss one element at a time, concentrating on those elements that pose the greatest difficulties.

The other benefit of a breakdown of the rule into elements is that you will have begun to identify the legal issues in the case. Each element that is going to pose any dispute will become the basis for a separate issue. There is no need to phrase a separate issue for those elements that both sides will agree on. If both sides will agree that a certain element does apply (or does not apply), there is no need to phrase an issue based on that element.

Some rules are difficult to break into elements because of their length. Tax statutes and regulations, for example, sometimes appear to be endless. Nevertheless, the same process is used. You must take the time to dissect the rule into its component elements.

A rule may also be difficult to subdivide into elements because:

- The rule contains lists.
- The rule is phrased in the alternative.
- the rule has exception or proviso clauses.

Examine the following rule:

> **§5.** While representing a client in connection with contemplated or pending litigation, a lawyer shall not advance or guarantee financial assistance to his client, except that a lawyer may advance or guarantee the expenses of litigation, including court costs, expenses of investigation, expenses of medical examination, and costs of obtaining evidence, provided the client remains ultimately liable for such expenses.

Elements:

1. A lawyer.
2. While representing a client in connection with contemplated litigation *or* in connection with pending litigation.
3. Shall not advance *or* guarantee financial assistance to his client, *except* that the lawyer may advance *or* guarantee the expenses of litigation such as:
   a. court costs *or*
   b. expenses of investigation *or*
   c. expenses of medical examination *or*
   d. costs of obtaining evidence,
   provided the client remains ultimately responsible for such litigation expenses.

When an element is stated in the alternative, list all the alternatives within the same element. The same is true of exception or proviso clauses. State them within the relevant element since they are intimately related to the applicability of that element.

In the above example, the most complicated element is the third—(3). Within it there are lists, alternatives, an exception ("except that . . ."), and a proviso ("provided the . . ."). But they all relate to the same point of the propriety of financial assistance.

Hence, you sometimes must do some unraveling of a rule in order to identify its elements. Do not be afraid to pick the rule apart in order to cluster its thoughts around unified themes that can stand alone as elements. Diagram the rule for yourself as you examine it. If more than one rule is involved in a statute, regulation, constitutional provision, charter, ordinance, etc., treat one rule at a time. Each rule should have its own elements and, when appropriate, each element should be sub-divided into its separate components.

ASSIGNMENT 54

Break the following rules into their elements:

1. A lawyer shall not enter into a business transaction with a client if they have differing interests therein and if the client expects the lawyer to exercise his professional judgment therein for the protection of the client.
2. A person or agency suing or being sued in an official public capacity is not required to execute a bond as a condition for relief under this section unless required by the court in its discretion.
3. A lawyer may not permit his legal assistant to represent a client in litigation or other adversary proceedings or to perform otherwise prohibited functions unless authorized by statute, court rule or decision, administrative rule or regulation or customary practice.
4. If at any time it is determined that application of best available control technology by 1988 will not assure protection of public water supplies, agricultural and industrial uses, and the protection and propagation of fish, shellfish and wildlife, and allow recreational activities in and on the water, additional effluent limitations must be established to assure attainment or maintenance of water quality. In setting such limitations, EPA must consider the relationship of the economic and social costs of their achievement, including any economic or social dislocation in the affected community or communities, the social and economic benefits to be obtained, and determine whether or not such effluent limitations can be implemented with available technology or other alternative control strategies.

ASSIGNMENT 55

Analyze the problem in the following situations. Do not do any legal research. Simply use the facts and rules you are given.

1. Mary is arrested for carrying a dangerous weapon. While in a hardware store, she got into an argument with another customer. She picked up a hammer from the counter and told the other customer to get out of her way. The customer did so and Mary put the hammer back. She was later arrested and charged with violating section 402(b), which provides: "It is unlawful for anyone to carry a dangerous weapon."
2. It is against the law in your state "to practice law without a license" (Section 39). Fred is charged with violating this law because he told a neighbor that a certain parking ticket received by the neighbor could be ignored since the police officer was incorrect in issuing the ticket. In gratitude, the neighbor buys Fred a drink. (Assume that what Fred told the neighbor about the ticket was accurate and that Fred is *not* a lawyer.)
3. Ted and Ann are married. Ted is a carpenter and Ann is a lawyer. They buy an old building that Ted will repair for Ann's use as a law office. Ted asks Ann to handle the legal aspects of the purchase of the building. She does so. Soon after the purchase, they decide to obtain a divorce. Ted asks Ann if she will draw up the divorce papers. She does so. Ted completes the

repair work on the building for which Ann pays him a set amount. Has Ann violated the rule stated in problem 1 in Assignment 54, p. 376, above?

Section B. LEGAL ANALYSIS OF COURT OPINIONS

A court opinion interprets one or more rules of law that are applied to a particular fact situation before the court. There are two main kinds of rules of law that are interpreted and applied in this way:

- Enacted law.
- Common law.

Enacted law consists of: *constitutional provisions* (created by a constitutional convention and by a combination of legislative and voter approval), *statutes* (created by the legislature), *administrative regulations* (created by agencies), *ordinances* (created by city councils and county boards), etc. **Common law** is judge-made law created by the courts when there is no controlling enacted law that governs the controversy before the court. For example, most of the law of negligence was initially created as common law by the courts because the legislature had not provided any statutes in this area. If, however, such statutes did exist, the courts would have to apply them. Since statutes are superior in authority to the common law, new statutes can always change the common law. Statutes that bring about such change are called statutes in derogation of the common law.

The starting point in your analysis is a set of facts presented to you by a client or by your instructor for a school assignment. The goal is to apply the court opinion to this set of facts. The opinion reached a certain result, called a *ruling* or *holding*. The conclusion of your legal analysis of the opinion will be your assessment of whether this holding will apply to the set of facts presented to you. How do you reach this assessment?

- First you *compare* the rule that was interpreted and applied in the opinion with the rule that you have uncovered through legal research as potentially applicable.
- Second you *compare* the facts given to you by the client or by your instructor with the key facts in the opinion.

RULE COMPARISON

Suppose your client is charged with a violation of section 23(b) of the state code on the payment of certain taxes. One of your first steps is to go to the law library and find section 23(b). The legal issue in your case is whether section 23(b) applies to your client. You do an element analysis of the statute in the manner discussed earlier in this chapter (p. 372). In the library you also look for court opinions. Your search is for court opinions that interpreted and applied section 23(b). You would not try to find opinions that interpreted housing or pollution statutes. You focus on opinions that cover the *same* rule involved in the case of the client—here, section 23(b). The same is true of the common law. If the client has a negligence case, for example, you search for opinions that interpret the law of negligence.

Hence rule comparison in the analysis of opinions is fairly simple. The general principle is: you compare the rule involved in your client's case (or school assignment) with the rule interpreted and applied in the opinion, and you proceed only if the rule is exactly the same. While there are some exceptions, this principle will be sufficient to guide you in most cases.

FACT COMPARISON

Here is the heart of the analysis. Before the holding of an opinion can apply, you must demonstrate that the key facts of the opinion are substantially the same as the facts in the client's case (or school assignment). If the facts are exactly the same or almost exactly the same, the opinion is said to be "on all fours" with your facts. If so, then you will have little difficulty convincing someone that the holding of the opinion applies to your facts. It is rare, however, that you will find an opinion "on all fours." Consequently, a careful analysis of factual similarities and differences must be made. If the facts are substantially similar, the ruling applies; if they are substantially different, it does not.

You must make a determination of what the *key* facts are in the opinion since it is these facts alone that are the basis of the comparison. A key fact is a very important fact—a fact that was crucial to the conclusion or holding of the court. In a divorce opinion, for example, it will probably not be key that a plaintiff was thirty-three years old. The court would have reached the same result if the plaintiff was thirty-two or thirty-four. Age may have been irrelevant or of very minor importance to the holding. What *may* have been key is that the plaintiff beat his wife, since without this fact the court may not have reached the ruling that the ground of cruelty existed. You carefully comb the opinion to read what the judge said about the various facts. Which ones were emphasized? Which were constantly repeated? Which did the court label as crucial? These are the kinds of questions you must ask yourself to try to determine which facts in the opinion were key.

Let us assume that you have been able to identify the key facts of an opinion. Your next concern is the comparison between these facts and the facts of your own problem. For example:

YOUR FACTS	THE CASE: Smith v. Apex Co.
Client sees an ad in the paper announcing a sale at a local store. He goes to the back of the store and falls into a pit. There was a little sign that said "danger" near the pit. The client wants to sue the store owner for negligence in failing to use reasonable care in preventing his injury. The law office assigns a paralegal to research the case. The paralegal finds the case of Smith v. Apex Co. and wants to argue that it applies.	Smith is looking for an address. He is walking down the street. He decides to walk into an office building to ask someone for help. While coming down the corridor, he slips and falls on a wet floor. There was a small sign in the corridor that said "wet floors" that Smith saw. Smith sued the owner of the building (Apex Co.) for negligence. The court held that the owner was negligent for failure to exercise reasonable care for the safety of users of the building.

First identify factual similarities:

- The client was in a public place (a store). Smith was also in a public place (an office building).
- Both situations involved some kind of warning (the "danger" sign and the "wet floor" sign).
- The warning in both situations was not conspicuous (the "danger" sign was "little"; the "wet floor" sign was "small").

Next identify the factual differences:

- The client was in a store, whereas Smith was in an office building.
- Your case involved a hole or pit, whereas Smith v. Apex Co. involved a slippery surface.
- The client was there about a possible purchase whereas Smith was not trying to transact any business in the office building.

Next identify any factual gaps:

- Smith saw the "wet floor" sign, but we do not know whether the client saw the "danger" sign.

Ninety percent of your legal analysis is complete if you have been able to make the above identifications. Most students do a sloppy job at this level. They do not carefully pick apart the facts in order to identify similarities, differences, and gaps.

Once you have done this properly, you make your final arguments about the opinion:

- If you want the holding in the opinion to apply, you emphasize the similarities between your facts and the key facts in the opinion. If any of your facts differs from a fact in the opinion, you try to point out that this is not significant since the latter was not a key fact in the opinion.
- If you do not want the holding in the opinion to apply, you emphasize the differences between your facts and the key facts in the opinion. If any of your facts is similar to a fact in the opinion, you try to point out that this is not significant since there is still a dissimilarity with all of the key facts in the opinion.

———————————

Factual gaps sometimes pose a problem. If the factual gap is in the facts of your client's case, you simply go back to the client and ask him/her about the fact. In the above case, for example, the paralegal asks the client whether he saw the "danger" sign. Suppose, however, that the factual gap is in the opinion itself. Assume that your client was running when he fell into the pit, but that the opinion does not tell you whether Smith was running, walking, etc. You obviously cannot go to Smith or to the judge who wrote the opinion and ask. You must make a guess of what the judge would have done in the opinion if Smith was running at the time he slipped on the corridor floor. You may decide that it would have changed the result, or that this additional fact would have made no difference to the ruling reached.

Issue. Did the store use reasonable care for the safety of users of the store when the only warning of a pit in the store was a small "danger" sign near the pit?

Facts. The client saw an ad in the newspaper announcing a sale. He went to the back of the store and fell into a pit. There was a small sign that said "danger" near the pit.

Analysis. An opinion on point is Smith v. Apex Co., 233 Mass. 578, 78 N.E.2d 422 (1980). In this opinion, the court found the owner of an office building liable for negligence when Smith slipped on a corridor floor in the building. There was a small "wet floor" sign in the corridor. This opinion is substantially similar to our own client's case. Both were in a public building where the owner can expect people to be present. In both situations, the warning of the danger was insufficient. The "wet floor" sign in the opinion was "small". The "danger" sign in our situation was "little". Hence it can be argued that the holding in Smith v. Apex Co. applies.

It is true that in the opinion the judge pointed out that Smith saw the sign. Our facts do not state whether the client saw the "danger" sign in the store. This should not make any difference, however, since the judge in the opinion would probably have reached the same result if Smith did not see the "wet floor" sign. In fact, the case would probably have been stronger for Smith if he did *not* see the sign. The building was dangerous in spite of the fact that users of the building such as Smith could see the sign. Obviously, the danger would be considered even greater if such users could not see the sign. We should find out from our client whether he saw the "danger" sign, but I do not think that it will make any difference in the applicability of the holding in Smith v. Apex Co.

The store owner will try to argue that the opinion does not apply. The argument might be that a pit is not as dangerous as a wet floor since a pit is more conspicuous than a wet floor and hence not as hazardous. A user is more likely to notice a hole in the floor than to know whether a floor is slippery enough to fall on. Our client could respond by pointing out that the pit was in the back of the store where it may not have been very noticeable. Furthermore, the wet floor in the opinion was apparently conspicuous due to the fact that Smith saw the "wet floor" sign, but yet the judge still found the defendant in the opinion liable.

ASSIGNMENT 56

In the following situations, point out any factual similarities, differences, and gaps between the client facts and the facts of the opinion.

1. *Client Facts:* Jim is driving his car 30 mph on a dirt road at night. He suddenly sneezes and jerks the steering wheel slightly, causing the car to move to the right and run into Bill's fence. Bill sues Jim for negligence.

   Opinion: A pedestrian brings a negligence action against Mary. Mary was driving her motorcycle on a clear day. A page of a newspaper unexpectedly flies into Mary's face. Since she cannot see where she is going, she runs into the pedestrian who was crossing the street. The court finds for Mary, ruling that she did not act unreasonably in causing the accident.

2. *Client Facts:* Helen is the mother of David, age four. The state is trying to take David away from Helen on the ground that Helen has neglected David. Helen lives alone with David. She works part time and leaves David with a neighbor. Helen's job occasionally requires her to travel. At one time she was away for a month. During this period, David was sometimes left alone since the neighbor had to spend several days at the hospital.

When David was discovered alone, the state began proceedings to terminate Helen's parental rights in David on the ground of neglect.

Opinion: The state has charged Bob Thompson with the neglect of his twins, aged ten. The state wishes to place the twins in a foster home. Bob is partially blind. One day he accidentally tripped and fell on one of the twins causing severe injuries to the child. Bob lives alone with the twins, but refuses to hire anyone to help him run the home. The court ruled that Bob did not neglect his children.

ASSIGNMENT 57

Salem is a factory town of 500 inhabitants in Hawaii. The factory employs 95% of the workers in the town. The town has only two private attorneys: Ann Grote and Timothy Farrell. Forty of the employees have decided to sue the factory over a wage dispute. Ann Grote represents all these employees. She works alone except for her only employee, Bob Davis, a paralegal. In this litigation, the factory is represented by Timothy Farrell who has no employees—no secretaries and no paralegals. Grote and Farrell are young attorneys who have just begun their practices. Their only clients are the forty employees and the factory respectively. The litigation has become quite complicated. Several months before the case is scheduled to go to trial, Farrell offers Davis a job as a paralegal at double the salary he is earning with Grote. He accepts the offer. Grote goes to court seeking a preliminary injunction against Davis and Farrell, which would bar them from entering this employment relationship.

Apply *Quinn v. Lum & Cronin, Fried, Sekiya & Kekina,* printed below, to the facts of the case of Grote v. Davis and Farrell. Do not do any legal research. Limit yourself to the application of this one opinion based on the guidelines of this chapter. (*Quinn* is an actual opinion from a state court in Hawaii.)

QUINN v. LUM & CRONIN, FRIED, SEKIYA & KEKINA
Civ. No. 81284
Hawaii Court of Appeals

On January 25, 1984, Richard K. Quinn, Attorney at Law, a Law Corporation, filed suit against Rogerlene Lum, a member of the Hawaii Association of Legal Assistants (HALA) and formerly legal secretary with the Quinn firm, for injunctive relief based on the allegation that Mrs. Lum possesses confidential client information from her work as Quinn's legal secretary, which information would be transmitted to the co-defendant, Mrs. Lum's new employer, Cronin, Fried, Sekiya & Kekina, Attorneys at Law, if she were to begin her employment with the Cronin firm as a legal assistant.

On or about January 3, 1984 Mrs. Lum notified Quinn that she had accepted a position as a paralegal with the Cronin firm. Quinn subsequently discussed and corresponded with Mr. Cronin regarding the hiring of Mrs. Lum, who was scheduled to begin work with the Cronin firm on January 30, 1984. Mr. Cronin repeatedly refused Quinn's request that she not be hired by the Cronin firm.

On January 26, a hearing on the application for a temporary restraining order was heard by Judge Philip T. Chun of the Circuit Court of the First Circuit, State of Hawaii. The application was denied.

Quinn alleges in the pleadings filed with the Court in Civil No. 81284 that Mrs. Lum's employment with the Quinn firm from December 1, 1982 to January 17, 1984, and as Mr. Quinn's secretary from April 25, 1983 to January 17, 1984, included attendance at the firm's case review committee meetings. Confidential discussions occurred concerning case evaluation, settlement evaluation, strategy and tactics between Quinn, his associates, and their clients.

Cronin et al. are attorneys of record for the plaintiffs in *Firme v. Honolulu Medical Group and Ronald P. Peroff, M.D.* Quinn's firm represents the defendants. The case was set for trial on March 19, 1984. According to exhibits attached to the records filed in the instant case, Mr. Cronin recognized the *Firme* situation and agreed that Mrs. Lum would not be involved in the *Firme* case in her new employment, nor would his firm "[ever] seek to obtain any information from her concerning cases with which she was involved while in [Quinn's] office, nor would we have her work on any while here." Mr. Cronin goes on to say in his January 24 letter to Quinn that Quinn should consult with his clients in the *Firme* case as to whether Quinn's "attempt . . . to stop Mrs. Lum from working for [the Cronin firm] is with their approval."

Quinn also alleges that while his firm is known in the Honolulu legal community as one which represents hospitals, doctors and other health care providers, the Cronin firm is known as a plaintiff medical malpractice firm. Quinn lists in several pleadings that on more than one occasion, these firms found themselves adversaries in the same cases.

[Quinn contends] that this action was brought not to "bar Lum from working as a legal secretary or even as a paralegal, since that would be ludicrous given the size of Hawaii's legal community." In fact, Quinn states he would have "no objection to Lum's working for any other law firm in Hawaii other than one which specializes in medical malpractice plaintiffs' work, like [Cronin's]."

A subsequent hearing on the original compliant for injunctive relief was then held in Judge Ronald Moon's court on February 6. Plaintiff's motion for a preliminary injunction that would bar such employment "for at least two years" was denied, with the judge noting *Quinn v. Lum* as a case of first impression.

The Court explained its decision in light of the standards to be met before a preliminary injunction could be issued, as dealt with in depth by Mrs. Lum's attorney, David L. Fairbanks, who is also the current President of the Hawaii State Bar Association.

The standards which must be met in order to obtain a preliminary injunction, as listed by Judge Moon, follow:

1. The Court did not feel there was a substantial likelihood that plaintiff would prevail on the merits. If an injunction were to be issued, it would:

"[E]ssentially prevent a paralegal or legal secretary, [or] attorney from joining any law firm that may have had some case in the past, . . . cases pending at the present time, or potential cases which may be worked on in the future" (Transcript of the Hearing, page 82).

2. The evidence is lacking regarding irreparable damage to Richard Quinn's clients.

3. The public interest would not be served by issuing such an injunction.

When an attorney enters practice in the State of Hawaii, he or she agrees to abide and be governed by the Hawaii Code of Professional Responsibility. This code does not attempt to govern the ethical actions of the non-attorneys. While Canon 37 of the American Bar Association's Code of Professional Responsibility, adopted pre-1971, states that a lawyer's employees have the same duty to preserve client confidences as the lawyer, this Canon is not included in the Hawaii code.

Compliance, therefore, with the same rules of ethics guiding the Hawaii attorney is currently left to the discretion—and conscience—of the non-attorney.

If an attorney in Hawaii breaches the Code of Professional Responsibility, the office of Disciplinary Counsel may choose to investigate the matter and may pass the matter on to the Disciplinary Board and possibly, to the Hawaii Supreme Court for adjudication.

If an employee of a law office becomes suspect of some breach of ethics or acts of omission, the employing attorney becomes responsible for the employee's deeds. For example, if a legal secretary fails to file the compliant the day the Statute of Limitations expires thinking the next day would suffice, it is the attorney who is responsible to the client. The attorney can fire the secretary "for cause" but the attorney, nevertheless, stands responsible. It appears the only way for an attorney to further censor the employee directly is via a civil suit for tortious damages.

Whether a permanent injunction can or will be granted has yet to be seen in this case. What is clear is that neither the office of Disciplinary Counsel nor the Hawaii Supreme Court would or could become involved; they have no jurisdiction over the non-attorney working in a law office.

8

Legal Interviewing

Section A. INTRODUCTION

There are at least three kinds of legal interviews:

1. The initial client interview.
2. The follow-up client interview.
3. The field interview involving someone other than the client.

In the initial client interview, the client is introduced to the kind of legal services offered by the office, legal problems are identified, and the way in which the office will handle the case is explained. Follow-up interviews occur subsequent to the initial interview. The client is asked about additional facts and is consulted about a variety of matters that require the client's attention, consent, and participation. Finally, there is the field interview conducted during investigation in which the interviewer encounters a great diversity of people for a wide range of purposes. Investigation will be examined in the next chapter. Here our focus will be the *initial client interview*.

Interviewing is among the most important skills used in a law office. Since it appears to be relatively easy to engage in interviewing (all you need is a person to interview and some time), it is commonly assumed that legal interviewing, like good conversation, requires little more than intelligence and a pleasing personality. This misconception often leads to incomplete and sloppy interviewing. Legal interviewing is much more than conversation. They are similar in that both frequently involve building a relationship and exchanging information. In legal interviewing, however, the goal is to help solve a client's problem. In order to do this, a relationship must be established between the interviewer and client that is both warm/trusting and professional/goal-oriented.

Paralegals in different settings have different duties and authority. In a private law office, an attorney will usually conduct the initial interview and assign the paralegal the task of gathering detailed information from the client on a specific topic. For example, a paralegal may be asked to help a bankruptcy client detail all debts and financial entanglements by listing them all on a worksheet. On the other hand, in a government agency or in a government-funded legal service office (p. 46), the interviewing responsibilities for the paralegal can be extensive. For example, a paralegal may conduct the initial interview with a client and could remain the primary office contact for the client throughout the resolution of the case.

The initial client interview is critical because it sets the foundation for the entire litigation process: the facts obtained from this interview are further pursued through field *investigation;* the law governing these facts are *researched* in the law library; the facts and the governing law are informally argued between counsel for the parties in an effort to *settle* the case through *negotiation;* if there is no settlement, a *trial* is held in which the facts are formally established; finally, the process ends with an *appeal.* Everything begins with the facts obtained from the initial client interview.

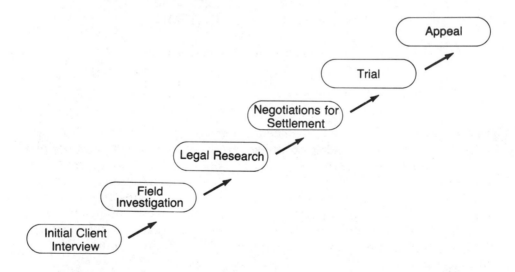

Section B. THE FORMAT OF AN INTAKE MEMO

Before analyzing the interviewing process, we should look briefly at one of the end products of the interview—the *intake memo.* This is the document that the paralegal writes on the basis of notes taken at the interview. The intake memo goes first to the supervisor and then into a newly opened case file on the client. The memo often has five parts:

1. Heading

   The heading provides the following information at the top of the first page:

   a. Who wrote the memo.
   b. The supervisor in charge of the case.
   c. The date the memo was written.
   d. The date the interview was conducted.
   e. The name of the case.
   f. The office file number of the case.
   g. The kind of case (general area of the law).
   h. The subject matter of the memo following the notation "RE."

2. Personal Data

   a. Name of the client.
   b. Home address.
   c. Phone numbers where client can be reached.
   d. Age of client.
   e. Marital status.
   f. Place of employment of client.
   g. Etc.

3. Statement of the Assignment

   The first paragraph of the memo should state the precise objective the paralegal was given in conducting the interview.

4. Body of the Memo

   Here the facts are presented in a coherent, readable manner according to a number of possible organizational principles:

   a. A chronological listing of the facts so that the events are unfolded as a story with a beginning, middle, and end.
   b. A categorizing of the facts according to the major topics or issues of the case, each with its own subject heading under which the relevant facts are placed.
   c. Any other format called for by the supervisor.

5. Conclusion

   Here a number of things could be included:

   a. A brief summary of the major facts listed in the body of the memo.
   b. The impressions of the paralegal of the client, e.g.,

—how knowledgeable the client appeared to be,

—how believable the client appeared to be.

  c. A list of the next steps, e.g.,

—what further facts should be sought through investigation,

—what legal research needs to be undertaken,

—any other recommendations on what should be done on the case based on what was learned during the interview.

  d. A list of anything the paralegal told the client to do, e.g.,

—bring in specified documents relevant to the case,

—check on further facts and call back,

—return for another interview.

The following is a sample of the introductory parts of an intake memo:

INTER-OFFICE MEMO

TO: Ann Fuller, Supervisor   CASE: John Myers vs. Betsy Myers
FROM: Jim Smith, Paralegal   FILE NUMBER: 87-102
DATE OF MEMO: KIND OF CASE: Child Custody
  March 13, 1987   RE: Intake Interview of John Myers
DATE OF INTERVIEW:
  March 12, 1987

PERSONAL DATA:

NAME OF CLIENT: John Myers
ADDRESS: 34 Main Street, Salem, Massachusetts 01970
PHONE: 966-3954 (H) 297-9700 (x 301) (W)
AGE: 37
MARITAL STATUS: Married but separated from his wife, Betsy Myers
EMPLOYMENT: ABC Construction Co., 2064 South Street, Salem, Massachusetts 02127

    You asked me to conduct a comprehensive intake interview of John Myers, our client, in order to obtain a listing of his assets and the facts surrounding his relationship with his children.

    A. ASSETS
       John Myers owns. . .

Section C. WHAT FACTS DO YOU SEEK? GUIDES TO THE FORMULATION OF QUESTIONS

Unless the paralegal knows what to accomplish in the interview, valuable time will be wasted. For example, suppose what a client is being interviewed concerning the grounds (legally sufficient reasons) for a divorce. The paralegal does not simply write down *all* the facts about the marriage and the client's problems in it. The facts must be clustered or arranged in categories that are relevant to the grounds for divorce. Unless paralegals have this objective in mind before and during the interview, they may end up with such a confusing collection of facts that they will have to conduct a second interview to go over matters that should have been covered initially. This does not mean that the paralegal cannot talk about anything other than what is directly related to the objective, but it does mean that each interview must have a definite *focus*.

There are six major ways that a paralegal can achieve a focus in the formulation of the questions to be asked of the client:

1. The instructions of the supervisor for the interview
2. Checklists
3. Legal analysis
4. Fact particularization
5. Common sense
6. Flexibility

The above methods are designed to avoid all the following examples of an *ineffective* interview:

- You fail to seek the information that the supervisor wanted you to obtain.
- You miss major relevant facts.
- You fail to obtain sufficient detail on the major relevant facts.
- You fail to ask questions about (and record) the extent to which the client was sure or unsure about the facts given to you.
- You fail to pursue leads provided by the client to other relevant themes or topics that may not have been part of the supervisor's explicit original instructions.

THE INSTRUCTIONS OF THE SUPERVISOR FOR THE INTERVIEW

These instructions, of course, control what you do in the interview. As indicated above, you may be asked to do a limited interview or a comprehensive one. Be sure to write down the instructions on what the supervisor wants from the interview. One concern that frequently arises is the amount of detail that is desired. Lawyers like facts. During three years of law school, they were constantly asked by their law professors, "What are the facts?" The likelihood is that the lawyer for whom you work will want considerable detail from the interview. Even if you are told to limit yourself to obtaining the basic facts from the client, you may find that the supervisor wants a lot of detail about those basic facts. When in doubt, the safest course is to be detailed in your questioning. If possible, try to sit in on an interview conducted by your supervisor in order to observe his/her method of questioning and the amount of detail sought. Also, examine some closed case files that contain intake memos. Ask the supervisor if s/he considers any of these memos to be exemplary and if so why. Once you have a "model," it can be very useful as a guide.

CHECKLISTS

The office where you work may have checklists that are used in conducting an interview. For some kinds of cases, such as probate or estate matters, the checklists may be extensive. If such checklists are not available, you should consider writing your own for the kinds of cases in which you do a good deal of interviewing (p. 325).

Caution, however, is needed in using checklists:

• You should find out why individual questions were inserted in the checklist.
• You should be flexible enough to ask questions not on the checklist when the situation calls for such adaptation.

A checklist must be viewed as a guide that should be adjusted to adapt to the case and client in front of you, rather than as a rigid formula from which there can never be deviation.

LEGAL ANALYSIS

Extensive legal analysis does not take place while the interview is being conducted. Yet *some* legal analysis (p. 371) must occur in order to conduct an intelligent interview.

Most of the questions you ask in the interview must be *legally relevant,* which means that the answer is needed in order to determine whether a particular legal principle governs. It takes some understanding of legal analysis to apply the concept of legal relevance intelligently. It would be dangerous for the paralegal to be asking questions by rote, even if checklists are used. The question-and-answer process is a little like a tennis match—you go where the ball is hit or it passes you by.

Suppose that you are interviewing a client on an unemployment compensation claim. The claim has been denied by the state because the client is allegedly not "available for work." You cannot conduct a competent interview unless you know the legal meaning of this phrase. From this understanding you can formulate questions that are legally relevant to the issue of whether the client has been and is "available for work." You will ask obvious questions such as:

> What is your present health?
> Where have you applied for work?
> Were you turned down, and if so, why?
> Did you turn down any work, and if so, why?

Suppose that during the interview, the client tells you the following:

> There were some ads in the paper for jobs in the next town, but I didn't want to travel that far.

At this point the interviewer must decide whether to pursue this matter such as by inquiring about the distance to the town, whether public transportation is available to the town, the cost of such transportation, whether the client owns a car, etc. Again, legal analysis can be helpful. Does "available for work" mean available in the same area? Is one *un*available for work because of a refusal to make unreasonable efforts to travel to an otherwise available job in another area? What does unreasonable mean? Questions such as these must go through the paralegal's mind in order to decide whether to seek more details about the ads for work in the other town. These are questions of legal analysis.

The paralegal must be thinking while questioning. Some instant mental analysis should be going on all the time. This does not mean that the paralegal must know the answer to every legal question that comes to mind while interviewing the client. But the paralegal must know something about the law and must be flexible enough to think about legal questions that should be generated by unexpected facts provided by the client.

When in doubt about whether to pursue a line of questions, the safest course is to pursue it. As you gain more experience in interviewing and in the area of law of the interview, you will be better equipped to know what to do. Yet you will never know everything. There will always be fact situations that you have never encountered before. Legal analysis will help you handle such situations.

FACT PARTICULARIZATION (FP)

Fact particularization is perhaps one of the most important concepts in this book. Fact assessment is critical to the practice of the law; fact particularization is critical to the identification of the facts that must be assessed. FP is a fact-collection technique. It is the process of viewing every person, thing, or event as unique—different from every other person, thing, or event. To *particularize a fact* means to ask an extensive series of questions about that fact in order to explore its uniqueness. Every important fact a client tells a paralegal in an interview should be particularized. This is done by a large number of follow-up questions once you have targeted the fact that you want explored.

FP can be a guide to the formulation of questions in a number of situations:

- in a client interview (our focus in this chapter)
- in investigations (p. 427)
- in drafting interrogatories (p. 494)
- in preparing for a deposition (p. 471)
- in examining witnesses on the stand at trial (p. 474).

In legal interviewing, the starting point for the FP process is an important fact that the client has told you during the interview, for example, "I tried to find work"; "the car hit me from the rear"; "the pain was unbearable"; "the company was falling apart"; "he told me I would get the ranch when he died"; "he fired me because I am a woman"; etc. Then eight categories of questions are asked the client about the fact that is being particularized:

FACT PARTICULARIZATION

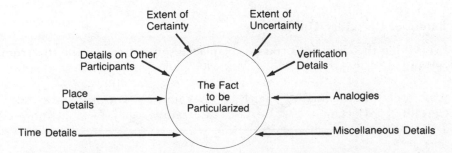

The eight categories are not mutually exclusive and all eight categories will not necessarily be applicable to every fact that you will be particularizing. There is no definite order in which the questions must be asked so long as you are comprehensive in your search for factual detail. The point of FP is simply to get the wheels of your mind rolling so that you will think of a large number of questions and avoid conducting an interview that is superficial.

Time Details

When did the fact occur or happen? Find out the precise date and time. The interviewer should be scrupulous about all dates and times. If more than one event is involved, ask questions about the dates and times of each. If the client is not sure, ask questions to help jog the memory and ask the client to check his/her records or to contact other individuals who might know. Do not be satisfied with an answer such as, "It happened about two months ago." If this is what the client says, record it in your notes, but then probe further. Show the client a calendar and ask about other events going on at the same time in an effort to help the client be more precise.

Place Details

Be equally scrupulous about geography. Where did the event occur? Where was the thing or object in question? Where were you at the time? Ask the client to describe the surroundings. Ask questions with such care that you obtain a verbal photograph of the scene. If relevant, ask the client to approximate distances between important objects or persons. You might want to have the client draw a diagram, or you draw a diagram on the basis of what you are told and ask the client if the drawing is accurate. Ask questions about the weather or about lighting conditions. You want to know as much as you can about the environment or whatever the client could observe about the environment from the senses of touch, sight, hearing, and smell.

Details on Other Participants

Who else was involved? Ask questions about who they were, their role, their age, appearance, etc., if relevant. Where were they at the time? When did they act? Why did they act? Why did they fail to act? Could you have anticipated what they did or failed to do? Why or why not? Have they ever acted or failed to act in this way before? Ask questions designed to obtain a detailed picture of who these other participants were and their precise relationship to the fact being particularized.

Extent of Certainty/Uncertainty

Everything the client tells you can be placed somewhere on the spectrum of certainty:

Absolutely Certain	Substantially Certain	Fairly Certain	A Vague Certainty	Unsure	Do Not Know

Where on the spectrum does a fact the client tells you fall? One of the major pitfalls of the interviewer would be, for example, to record that the client said a letter was received two weeks ago when in fact the client said, "I think it came two weeks ago." Do not turn uncertainty into certainty by sloppy listening and sloppy recording in your intake memo of what the client said. Of course, it may be possible for a client to be uncertain about a fact initially and then become more certain of it with the help of your questioning. If so, record this transition by saying, "the client was first unsure of who else was present, but then said she was fairly certain that Fred was there."

Explain to the client right at the beginning how critical it is for you to obtain accurate information. Encourage the client to say "I'm not sure" when it is so. It is important that the client be relaxed and unthreatened. It would not be wise for you to keep asking "Are you sure?" following every fact the client tells you. Yet you must find out where on the spectrum of certainty a fact falls. Temper your probe with tact and sensitivity.

Verification Details

The fact that the client tells you something happened is *some* evidence that it happened. Verification data is evidence that supports what the client has said. Verification data is *additional* evidence to support the client. Always pursue such verification details. Ask yourself how you would establish the truth of what the client has said if the client suddenly disappeared so that you had to rely exclusively on other sources. Inquire about documents (e.g., letters, check stubs) that support the client's statements. Inquire about other people who might be available to testify to the same subject. Ask the client questions that will lead you to such verification details. This approach, of course, does not mean that you do not trust the client, nor that you think the client is lying. It simply means that it is always a good practice to view a fact from many perspectives. You are seeking the strongest case possible. This calls for questioning leading to verification details.

Analogies

Some facts that you are particularizing are difficult to pin down, e.g., "the pain was unbearable"; "I was careful"; "it looked awful"; "I was scared"; etc. In the interview, you should ask the client to explain such statements. Sometimes it is helpful to ask the client to use some analogies to describe what is meant. An analogy is simply an explanation of something by comparing it to something else. For example, you ask the client:

> What would you compare it to?
> Was it similar to anything you have ever seen before?
> Have you observed anyone else do the same thing?
> Have you ever been in a similar situation?
> Did it feel like a dentist's drill?

You ask the client to compare the fact to something else. Then you ask about the similarities and differences. Through a series of directed questions you are encouraging the client to analogize the fact s/he is describing to some other fact. This is done in a further attempt to obtain as comprehensive a picture as possible of what the client is saying.

Miscellaneous Details

Here you simply ask about any details that were not covered in the above categories of questions. Include questions on anything else that might help in particularizing the fact under examination.

ASSIGNMENT 58

In this assignment, FP will be role-played in class. One student will be selected to play the role of the client and another student the role of the paralegal interviewer. The rest of the class will observe and fill out the FP Score Card on the interview.

Instructions to Interviewer. You will not be conducting a complete interview from beginning to end. You will be trying to particularize a certain fact that will be given to you. Go through the eight categories of FP described above. Use any order of questioning that you want so that you probe for comprehensiveness in the facts from the client. Your instructor will select one of the following facts which will be used as the basis of the interview:

1. "I was hit in the jaw by Mary."
2. "The neighbor's tree fell on my land."
3. "I have not been promoted because I am a woman."

Your opening question to the client will be, "What happened?" The client will make one of the three statements above. You then use the process of FP to particularize this statement.

Instructions to Client. The interviewer will ask you what happened. Simply make one of the three statements above as selected by the instructor. Then the interviewer will ask you a large number of questions about the statements. Make up the answers—ad lib your responses. Do not, however, volunteer any information. Answer only the questions asked.

Instructions to Class. Observe the interview. Use the following score card to assess how well you think the interviewer particularized the fact.

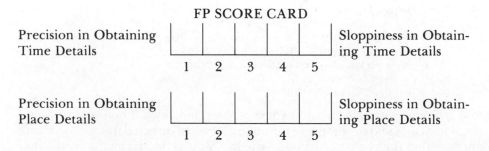

FP SCORE CARD

| Precision in Obtaining Time Details | 1 2 3 4 5 | Sloppiness in Obtaining Time Details |

| Precision in Obtaining Place Details | 1 2 3 4 5 | Sloppiness in Obtaining Place Details |

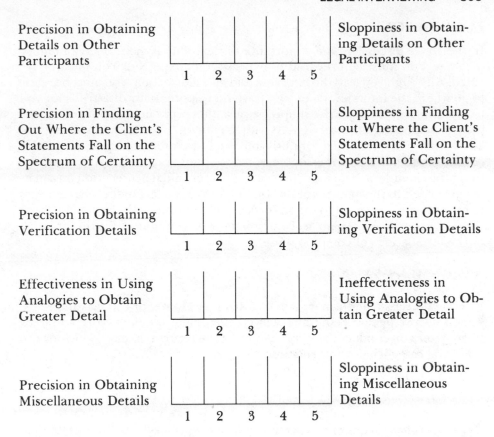

| Precision in Obtaining Details on Other Participants | | | | | | Sloppiness in Obtaining Details on Other Participants |

1 2 3 4 5

| Precision in Finding Out Where the Client's Statements Fall on the Spectrum of Certainty | | | | | | Sloppiness in Finding out Where the Client's Statements Fall on the Spectrum of Certainty |

1 2 3 4 5

| Precision in Obtaining Verification Details | | | | | | Sloppiness in Obtaining Verification Details |

1 2 3 4 5

| Effectiveness in Using Analogies to Obtain Greater Detail | | | | | | Ineffectiveness in Using Analogies to Obtain Greater Detail |

1 2 3 4 5

| Precision in Obtaining Miscellaneous Details | | | | | | Sloppiness in Obtaining Miscellaneous Details |

1 2 3 4 5

Following the interview, put a check on the appropriate number for each of the above categories of assessment. A "1" score means you thought the interview was very precise or effective in fulfilling the goal of FP. A "5" score means the opposite. Also, make mental notes of questions that you think the interviewer should have asked. These questions as well as your scores will be discussed in class after the interview.

COMMON SENSE

Common sense is another major guide on what questions to ask in an interview in order to achieve comprehensiveness and give the interview a focus. Law is full of legalisms and technicalities. Yet good judgment and common sense are still at the core of the practice of law. It is common sense, for example, to organize an interview by having the client tell the relevant events chronologically in the form of a story with a beginning, middle, and end. It is common sense to follow up on topics mentioned by the client by further questioning even though you had not initially anticipated the topic. If the client says something you do not understand, common sense would require that you ask what the client means before continuing with the interview. At times, it may be common sense to stop the interview for a moment in order to obtain further guidance from the supervisor.

FLEXIBILITY

In the above discussion, the importance of flexibility is mentioned a number of times. You must be prepared to expect the unexpected. You must be relaxed. Although you lead the interview and give it direction, you must be ready to go where the interview takes you. It would be potentially disastrous for you to block out topics that arise simply because they were not part of your game plan in conducting the interview. As with so many areas of the law, you may not know what you are looking for until you find it. In interviewing a client on incorporating a business, for example, you may stumble across a lead from something the client says that could involve fraud or criminal prosecution on a matter unrelated to the incorporation. Don't block this out. Pursue what appears to be reasonably relevant to the law office's relationship with the client. Check with your supervisor. Again, let common sense be your guide. Flexibility is one of the foundations of common sense.

ASSIGNMENT 59

Interview a classmate for purposes of writing a resume for this classmate. Assume that the person being interviewed eventually wants to work for a law firm. After you conduct the interview, write the resume. It should include the following categories of information:

- *Basic data* (name, address, phone, marital status, etc.).
- *Career objective* (what does the person hope to be doing—hope to be accomplishing—in the immediate future? five years from now?).
- *Education* (begin with current school and work back, including names of schools, dates of attendance, degrees or certificates awarded, etc.).
- *Prior employment* (begin with most recent and work back, including name of employers, addresses, dates of employment, title, responsibilities, etc.).
- *Community activities* (volunteer work, etc.).

The trouble with most resumes is that they focus only on *events* and rarely spend enough space listing specific *skills* and *accomplishments:*

- Have you ever supervised other people? How many? To do what tasks?
- Have you had responsibility for handling someone else's money?
- Have you ever had to write a budget?
- Have you ever had the responsibility of evaluating someone else?
- Have you ever written a proposal?
- What kind of reports have you written?
- What work products have resulted from your prior employment and schooling, e.g., have you ever drafted a complaint (in what area of the law and under what circumstances), have you done any legal research (on what specific issues and under what circumstances), etc.?
- Have you ever written a speech and delivered it?
- Have you ever run for any elective office (politics or club, etc.)?
- Etc.

When someone reads the resume, what impression would they get of the individual? A self starter? Someone who can act without constant supervision? An unstable person who moves from job to job to job? A doer? A person with enthusiasm? A "live" person or a collection of statistics? When you are conducting the interview, be sure to bring out facts that will enable you to place the person in a positive light in the resume.

Try to keep the resume under two pages. This will mean, of course, that you cannot be long-winded in your description. Obtain extensive detail from the interview. Particularize the person you are interviewing. Be highly selective and succinct, however, in writing the resume.

Type the resume and make at least one carbon copy. Give the carbon copy to the person you interviewed who is the subject of the resume. Ask that person to read the resume and give it *as many* of the following RATINGS as s/he feels are applicable:

RATING I: The resume describes me to a "T."
RATING II: I would definitely hire me on the basis of this resume!
RATING III: The resume is substantially accurate, but there are some factual errors in it.
RATING IV: I would use this resume in looking for a job.
RATING V: The facts in the resume are fairly accurate, but it's rather flat; it doesn't describe me as a live person.
RATING VI: I hardly recognized myself.
RATING VII: The person described in this resume is impersonating me!
RATING VIII: Nice try, but . . . .

On the resume that you hand in to the teacher (the original) indicate on the top of the front page the rating(s) your resume was given by the subject of the resume.

Section D. WHAT DOES THE CLIENT WANT?

There are a number of assumptions that can be made about many clients:

- The client is not sure what s/he wants.
- The client is not aware of what legal and nonlegal options are available to help solve the problem that exists.
- The problem probably involves other legal problems about which the client is unaware and about which even you may be unaware at the outset.

Suppose that a client walks into the office and says "I want to get a divorce." The following observations *might* be possible about this client:

- The client has an incorrect understanding of what a divorce is.
- The client says she wants a divorce because she thinks that this is the only legal remedy available to solve her problem.
- If the client knew that other remedies existed (e.g., annulment, legal separation), she would consider these options.

- What the client is really troubled about is the fact that her husband beats the kids and a divorce is the only way she thinks can stop it.
- The client consciously or unconsciously wants and needs an opportunity to tell someone how bad the world is treating her and, if given this opportunity, she may not want to terminate her marriage.
- If the client knew that marriage counseling was available in the community, she would consider using it before taking the drastic step of going to a law office for a divorce.

If any or all of these observations are correct, think of how damaging it would be for someone in the law office to take out the standard divorce forms and quickly fill them out immediately after the client says, "I want a divorce." This response would not be appropriate because there was no probing beneath the statement to determine what in fact was on the client's mind. It may be, after all factors are examined, that the client *does* want a divorce. The danger, however, is that the client wants something else, but is steered in the direction of a divorce because no other options are presented to her, because no one has taken the time to listen to her and to help her express ideas, intentions, and desires that are lurking beneath the otherwise clear statement, "I want a divorce."

This is not to say that you must psychoanalyze every client, nor that you must always distrust what the client tells you. Rather it is a recognition of the fact that *most people are confused about the law and make requests based upon misinformation as to what courses of action are available to solve problems.* Common sense tells us to avoid taking all statements at face value. People under emotional distress, particularly in situations of conflict, need to be treated with sensitivity. We should not expect them to be able to express their intentions with clarity all the time.

ASSIGNMENT 60

A client walks into the office where you work and makes the statements below. What areas do you think it would be reasonable to probe in order to determine if the statement is an accurate reflection of what the client wants? What misunderstandings do you think the client might have? What further questions would you want to ask in order to be sure that you have identified what the client wants?

A. "I want to commit my husband to a mental institution."
B. "I can't control my teenage son anymore. I want him placed in a juvenile home."
C. "I want to put my baby daughter up for adoption."
D. "I want to dissolve my business."
E. "I want to sell my house."
F. "I'm fed up with that department store. I want to sue the store so that it goes out of business."

Section E. HUMAN RELATIONS AND COMMUNICATION SKILLS IN INTERVIEWING
ASSIGNMENT 61

Write down your answers to the following questions. When you have finished this chapter, come back to what you have written and ask yourself whether your perspective has changed.

1. List some of the times you have interviewed someone. List some of the times you have been interviewed by someone.
2. Describe what you feel are the central ingredients of a good interview in any setting.
3. Describe a bad interview. From your experience, what are some of the worst mistakes an interviewer can make?
4. Describe what you think are some of your own strong and weak points as an interviewer.

———————

Thus far our main emphasis has been on obtaining the facts. We now pursue this theme in the broader context of human relations and communications skills. On the following pages, we will explore interviewing from the perspective of handling people. This will raise some basic questions about who you are, how you view other people, how you are perceived by others, how you handle sensitive problems in the lives of others, etc.

Interviewing is a reflection of your personality. There are no absolute answers to interviewing problems; there is no such thing as the "perfect interview." There is such a thing, however, as an interview that "works," that achieves its purpose. We need to find out what works in a legal interview.

In the following class assignment, you will observe an interview role-played in class. After watching this interview, you will be asked to deduce some principles of communication in interviewing.

ASSIGNMENT 62

In this assignment two students will be asked to role-play a legal interview in front of the class. The rest of the class will be observing the interview for purposes of making comments later.

Instructions to Client.   You will be role-playing the part of a client. A month ago you sprained your back while lifting a typewriter and carrying it from one room to another. You are an accountant. When you came into work that day you found the typewriter on your desk. It did not belong there and you did not know how it got there. You decided to move the typewriter to another desk. That was when you sprained your back.

You have come to the law office for legal advice. You have already seen an attorney in this office who has agreed to take your case. An interviewer has been assigned to conduct an interview with you in order to obtain a complete picture of what happened. This interview will now be role-played in front of the class.

The basic facts involve the typewriter as indicated above. You can make up all other facts needed to answer the questions that will be put to you by the interviewer, e.g., make up the name of the company for which you work, make up the details surrounding the accident, etc. You can create *any* set of facts so long as your answers are reasonably consistent with the basic facts given to you above.

Instructions to Interviewer.   You will play the role of the interviewer in the case involving the sprained back. All you know about the case thus far is that the office has agreed to represent the client and you have been assigned to interview the client to get detailed information about the client and about the accident. Start off by introducing yourself and stating the purpose of the interview. Then proceed to the questions that you need to ask. You are a paralegal in the office.

You do not need to know any law in order to conduct the interview. Let common sense be your guide. In order to obtain a comprehensive picture of the facts as this client is able to convey them, what questions would you ask? The material on fact particularization (FP) on page 391 should be consulted in order to help you prepare and formulate questions.

As you will see below in the instructions to the class, you will be observed in order to assess the manner and content of the interview. A good deal of constructive criticism may develop from the class discussion. As you listen to the criticism, try to be as objective as you can. It is difficult to conduct a comprehensive interview and probably impossible to conduct one flawlessly. For every question that you ask, there may be twenty observations on how you could have asked it differently. Hence, try not to take the comments personally.

Instructions to Class.   You will be watching the interview involving the sprained back. You have two tasks:

1. Fill out a LICS (Legal Interview Communications Score) form on the interview. After the interview, take a moment to score the interview according to the LICS form below. The teacher will ask you to state the total score you gave the interview and/or you will submit this score to someone who will calculate the average score from all scores submitted by individual students.
2. Identify as many "do's" and "don'ts" of interviewing as you can. If you were writing a law office manual on How to Interview, what would you include? What guidance would you give an interviewer, e.g., on taking notes during the interview, on asking follow-up questions, on keeping eye contact with the client, etc. After you observe the interview involving the sprained back, be prepared to discuss specific suggestions on what an interviewer should or should

not do. Ideas will come to your mind while you are filling out the LICS form. Following the class discussion on the "do's" and "don'ts" of interviewing, your teacher may ask you to make a written list of these "do's" and "don'ts" to be handed in later. Thoughts may come to you after class that you will also want to include.

A class project might be for someone to collect all the written "do's" and "don'ts" and consolidate them into a manual of legal interviewing principles that reflects the best thinking of your class after having observed an interview, discussed it in class, and thought about it.

LICS
LEGAL INTERVIEWING COMMUNICATION SCORE

HOW TO SCORE: You will be observing the role-playing of a legal interview and evaluating the interviewer on a 35-point scale. These 35 points will be earned in the four categories listed below. The score is not based on scientific data. It is a rough approximation of someone's oral communication skills in a legal interview. The interpretation of a score is as follows:

33–35 Points: Outstanding Interviewer
29–32 Points: Good Interviewer
25–28 Points: Fair Interviewer
00–24 Points: A Lot More Work Needs to Be Done

(Of course, the LICS does *not* assess the interviewer's ability to *write* an intake memorandum of law in which s/he writes out his/her notes in a coherent format for the file. See pp. 386 ff.)

CATEGORY I: FACTUAL DETAIL
On a scale of 0–20 how would you score the interviewer's performance in asking enough questions to obtain factual comprehensiveness? How well was FP performed?

(A 20 score means the interviewer was extremely sensitive to detail in his/her questions. A 0 score means that the interviewer stayed with the surface facts with little or no probing for the who-what-where-why-when-how details. The more facts you think the interviewer did *not* obtain, the lower the score will be.)

CATEGORY I SCORE: [   ]

CATEGORY II: CONTROL
On a scale of 0–10 how would you score the interviewer's performance in controlling the interview and in giving it direction?

(A 10 score means the interviewer demonstrated an excellent sense of control and direction in terms of knowing what his/her objectives were in asking the questions and in seeing to it that the time spent in the interview fully carried out those objectives. A 0 score means the interviewer rambled from question to question or let the client ramble from topic to topic without giving coherence to the interview.)

CATEGORY II SCORE: [   ]

CATEGORY III: EARNING THE CONFIDENCE OF THE CLIENT

On a scale of 0–3 how would you score the interviewer's performance in gaining the trust of the client and in setting him/her at ease?

(A 3 score means the interviewer appeared to do an excellent job in gaining the trust and confidence of the client. A 0 score means the client seemed to be suspicious of the interviewer and probably doubted his/her professional competence. The more the interviewer made the client feel that the interviewer was genuinely concerned about the client, the higher the score. The more the client obtained the impression that the interviewer was "just doing a job" in a kind of ritual fashion, the lower the score.)

CATEGORY III SCORE: ☐

CATEGORY IV: ROLE IDENTIFICATION

On a scale of 0–2 how well did the interviewer explain his/her role and the purpose of the interview?

(A 2 score means the interviewer took the time to explain clearly what his/her job was in the office and what s/he hoped to accomplish in the interview. A 0 score means either that the interviewer gave no explanation at all or mumbled through an explanation without being sensitive to whether the client understood.)

CATEGORY IV SCORE: ☐

TOTAL SCORE: ☐

ASSIGNMENT 63

In your area there are probably many television programs in which some form of interviewing takes place, e.g., news programs, talk shows, etc. The instructor will select a program that will be aired within the next few days. It should be a program that everyone in the class will be able to watch. Take notes on the communication skills of the interviewer for the program that you will watch. Make comments on the following topics:

- The setting of the interview. How did it facilitate or detract from communication?
- Focus. What techniques or mannerisms of the interviewer facilitated or detracted from the interview's focus or direction?
- Listening. Was the interviewer a good listener? Explain.
- Style of questioning. How would you characterize the interviewer's style?
- Self-image. What image of him/herself was the interviewer trying to project? Why? Did it work? Why or why not?
- Achieving the purpose of the interview. What purpose do you think the

interviewer had in conducting the interview? Was it achieved? Why or why not?

- Handling resistance. Did the person being interviewed appear to resist any of the questions? If so, how was this handled by the interviewer? How should it have been handled?
- Make a list of "do's" and "don'ts" of interviewing that you would deduce from watching the interview.

Make a copy of your comments and send it to the person who conducted the television program along with an explanation of this class assignment interview. If you receive a reply, share it with the class.

Communications Checklist for Legal Interviewing

PURPOSE: There are no absolute rules on how to interview. There are, however, a number of considerations that you should have in mind while interviewing. The following questions are designed to increase your sensitivity about the manner in which an interview is conducted. *The more aware an interviewer is of the factors that might affect communication, the greater the likelihood that an effective interview will result.* These factors are posed below as questions or as communication checklists to ponder as you prepare for an interview and think back over ones just conducted in terms of how it could have been improved. The checklist items are not mutually exclusive. Nor will there be anything approaching universal agreement on how some of the questions should be answered.

_____ Do I fully understand the purpose of this interview? Do I know what my supervisor wants me to accomplish?

_____ How do I prepare for this interview? From an office manual checklist? By talking with others who have conducted similar interviews in the past? Trial and error?

_____ Do I want to conduct this interview? Do I view this interview as my 1,000th? Do I wish someone else would do this interview? Do I feel that I am doing the office a favor in conducting the interview? Do I feel that I am doing the client a favor? Has the day long passed when I view each interview as a potential learning experience? What parts of my day are performed as ritual?

_____ Where should the interview be conducted? In my office? At the client's home or place of work? Would it make any difference?

_____ How am I dressed? Do I dress to suit *my* personal taste? Have I thought about the impact my clothes and appearance may have on the client and on the effectiveness of the interview? Am I secure enough to ask the opinion of a colleague? How could I encourage such a colleague to give me an honest opinion on "how I come across to people?"

_____ Do I have enough time to conduct this interview? If not, on whom will I take out my frustration?

_____ How should I introduce myself to the client? I understand my title and everyone else in the law office understands my title. Does this automatically mean that the client will understand my title? Should I assume that the client won't care? Does the client think I am a lawyer? Does the client think that I am experienced and competent in the kind of case that is the subject of the interview? After the interview, if the client were asked by a friend or relative who I was, what would the client say other than "someone who works in the office"? To what extent does the client need to know my job description and background?

_____ How is my office arranged? Professionally? Casually? Can anyone overhear my conversation with the client? How private is the interview?

_____ Do I know what client confidentiality means? Do I have a clear understanding of when confidentiality is violated? Do I appreciate the gray areas? Does the client understand his/her confidentiality rights? Should I make specific assurances to the client about confidentiality?

_____ Do I know what legal advice is? Do I know how to answer questions that might require me to give legal advice?

_____ Do I use a questionnaire in the interview? If so, do I know the reason why each question is on the questionnaire? How closely do I follow the questionnaire? Do I know when I can deviate from it? Is it only a guide or is it something that I must follow rigorously?

_____ What should I say, if anything, to the client about the questionnaire I am using?

_____ Do I take notes on what the client says? If so, what do I say to the client, if anything, about the fact that I am taking notes?

_____ How extensive are my notes? What am I doing to increase the speed of my note-taking?

_____ Answers of clients can fall into two categories: those that express answers about which the client is sure and those about which the client is confused or unclear. Do I know how to take notes about _both_ kinds of answers? Do I fall into the trap of taking notes on only concrete answers of the client? Do I understand the importance of articulating on paper (in my client intake memo) when the client _"thinks"_ something happened, or _probably_ did something on a given date?

_____ How do I help the client recall factual details?

_____ How do I help the client unravel complicated facts so that the "story" of the case can be told coherently, e.g., chronologically?

_____ Have I been scrupulous about dates? About places? About verification details?

_____ Do I know how to *particularize* a fact by asking all the appropriate who-what-where-why-when-how questions concerning that fact?

_____ Do I ask follow-up questions to help the client give more specific factual detail? Or do I let the interview wander from topic to topic, question to question, answer to answer?

_____ When the client answers a question by saying, "I'm not sure," or "maybe," do I ask questions designed to help the client remember with greater specificity? (If no greater specificity is possible, see the standard above on the importance of stating when the client was ambiguous or unsure about a fact.)

_____ Do I make the distinction between facts that establish what happened and facts that help verify someone's version of what happened? Do I ask questions that elicit both kinds of facts?

_____ Is the client answering my questions? If not, is it due the manner in which I am asking the questions?

_____ Am I condescending to the client? Do I know when I am condescending?

_____ Do I talk distinctly?

_____ Do I use words the client cannot understand, e.g., legal jargon, terms of art? Since most people do not want to admit that they don't understand a word or phrase, how do I know whether the client understands everything I am saying?

_____ Interviewers have a mental picture or at least a general idea of the topic of the interview, e.g., a car accident. What do I do when something comes up during the interview that does not fall into the pigeonhole of this mental picture or general idea? Do I block it out of my mind? How do I know that I *don't* block it out?

_____ Have I made the client feel welcome?

_____ Am I aware of the impact and importance of attentive listening? Am I one of the few attentive listeners around?

_____ Do I build the client's ego? Do I understand that ego-building is not achieved merely by praising someone?

_____ Am I offended if the client does not build my ego? Am I aware of my ego needs in an interview situation?

_____ Do I know how to say to the client, "I don't know"?

_____ How do I handle the client's embarrassment over one of my questions?

_____ How do I handle my own embarrassment over one of my questions or over one of the client's answers? Am I aware of the embarrassment?

_____ How do I handle the client's irritation over one of my questions?

_____ How do I handle my own irritation over an answer to one of my questions? Am I aware of the irritation?

_____ How do I handle a client who is telling me something I do not believe?

_____ When I have personal knowledge of some aspect of what the client is saying, do I record the client's perspective or my own? Do I know the difference?

_____ When, if ever, should I role-play with the client? (For example, if I am trying to help the client recall a conversation, I take the role of the other party of the conversation to see if it helps recollection.)

_____ Have I determined what the client wants? Do I know what his/her expectations are?

_____ At the conclusion of the interview, have I made it clear to the client what I will do, what the office will do, and what the client is to do as the next step?

_____ Am I a good interviewer? How do I know? Who has evaluated me? How can I obtain feedback on the quality of my interviewing skill? Who is around whom I respect enough to give me this feedback? How can I approach this person? For 99% of us, intensive criticism is unsettling and threatening to us—even if it is constructive. What makes me think that I fall into the 1% category?

Section F. ANALYSIS OF A LEGAL INTERVIEW

What follows is an analysis of a particular hypothetical interview involving Sam Donnelly, a senior citizen who walks into a law office seeking legal assistance. He will be interviewed by Miss Collins, a paralegal. We will assume that her attorney-supervisor has instructed her to find out as much as possible about his problem. Since the office is government funded, the question of fees will not be involved. In analyzing this interview, our central concern will be the techniques or principles of communication that can be effective in interviewing.

[Setting: There is a knock at Miss Collins' door. She gets up from her chair, goes over to the door, opens it, and says to the man facing her as she extends her hand for a handshake:]

Paralegal: _Hello, my name is Miss Collins. Won't you come in?_

Suppose that the paralegal did not go to the door to greet the client, and instead merely called from her chair, "Come in," in a loud voice. Do you think that it makes any difference whether the interviewer walks over to the client or not? When an individual walks with someone into a room, is the individual saying "come share my room with me"? If, on the other hand, the individual is seated at his/her desk and calls the visitor in, is the message to the visitor likely to be: "This is my room; I am in control of it; you may enter"? Consciously or unconsciously, the interviewer may want to project him/herself as a figure of authority to the client.

The interviewer cannot assume that the client will approve of and be receptive to everything the interviewer does simply because the interviewer is trying to help the client. It may be more appropriate to assume that the client is confused about who the interviewer is, and therefore will be somewhat suspicious of what the interviewer does until some trust has been established.

Principle: The interviewer has the responsibility of building a relationship of trust with the client.

Why this great concern for the feelings and state of mind of the client? There are two answers to this important question. First, the provision of legal aid is a *human* service that in and of itself demands the treatment of clients with dignity. Second, providing legal services requires a close, cooperative relationship between client and legal service personnel. The danger of the client giving misinformation because of a lack of understanding of what information s/he is being asked for or the danger of a client being a poor witness on his/her own behalf or in doing an inadequate job in helping the office locate other witnesses or documents is increased if the client is mistrustful, confused, or otherwise uncomfortable about what the interviewer says or does, or just as importantly, about what the interviewer doesn't say or doesn't do. Studies have shown that clients rate "evidence of concern" as being even more significant than the results that they obtain from a law office.[1]

> Paralegal: *Let me take your coat for you. Won't you have a seat? [The paralegal points the client toward a chair that is at the opposite end of the desk where the paralegal sits. They are facing each other.]*

Note the seating arrangement selected by the paralegal as illustrated in diagram A. "I" stands for "interviewer" and "C" stands for "client."

Diagram A

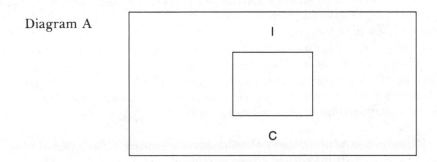

A number of other seating arrangements could have been used.

---

[1] Freeman, H., & Weihofen, H., *Clinical Law Training, Interviewing and Counseling: Text and Cases,* p. 13 (1972).

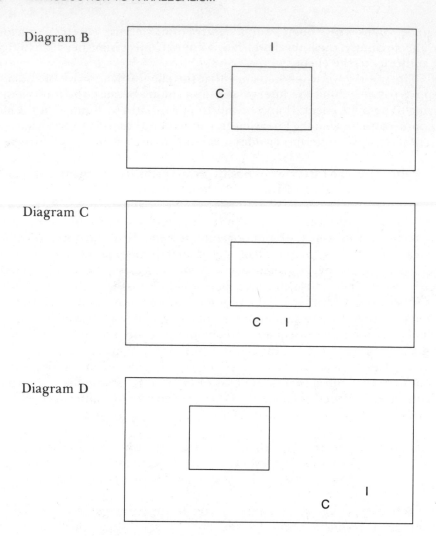

Diagram B

Diagram C

Diagram D

The chairs can be arranged so that the interviewer and the client sit at opposite ends of a desk (diagram A), diagonally across a desk (diagram B), at the same end of a desk (diagram C), or at another end of the room away from the desk altogether (diagram D). Seating arrangements are usually made at the convenience of the "owner" of the office. Rarely is enough thought given to how a particular arrangement may help or hurt the flow of communication. Sometimes the seating arrangement will create an austere and official atmosphere; other settings may be close and warm.

Principle: An interviewer should select a seating arrangement that will maximize communication.

Of the four seating arrangements diagrammed above, which do you think would be most effective? Which would you feel more comfortable with? Which do you think the client would be more comfortable with? There are a number of factors that can be considered in helping you answer these questions. First, there is probably no single seating arrangement that will be perfect for all situations. The interviewer must be flexible enough to experiment with different arrangements. Will you be taking notes while interviewing? If so, do you want the client to be able to see what you are writing? Would this make him/her more at ease? If so, which arrangements would facilitate this? Do you want to project yourself as an authority figure? Do you, on the other hand, want the client to feel closer to you and not have the impression that you are hiding behind a desk? Do you think it would ever be wise to change a seating arrangement in the middle of an interview? If a particular arrangement is used for the initial interview, do you think a different arrangement might ever be appropriate for follow-up interviews with the same client? When a client lifts his/her head, do you want him/her to be always looking straight at you (diagram A), or do you think that it might be more comfortable for the client to be able to face his/her head in other directions (diagram B) without appearing to have his/her attention roaming about the office?[2]

Of course, an office is much more than an arrangement of desks and chairs. What are your reactions to the potential benefits or disadvantages of the following:

1. On the wall there are numerous posters containing politically liberal or conservative slogans.
2. On the wall there are a half-dozen citations, certificates, and degrees.
3. The interviewer's desk is cluttered with papers and books.
4. The room is completely bare except for two chairs and a desk.
5. The interviewer is dressed very casually.
6. The interviewer is wearing a formal three-piece suit.
7. The interviewer is smoking, eating lunch, or drinking coffee.
8. The interviewer has no ashtray visible in the room.
9. On the wall there is a "Please Don't Smoke" sign.
10. On the interviewer's desk is an open case file of another client.
11. The secretary keeps knocking on the door or calling the paralegal on the phone for "emergencies" that require immediate attention.
12. The paralegal does not have his/her own office and talks to the client with secretaries or other personnel around.

Generally speaking, room settings that are extreme should always be avoided. Furthermore, the paralegal must be scrupulous in preserving the confidentiality of a client's case. Item 10 above, therefore is totally inappropriate. What about item 12?

Principle: Paralegals should always preserve the client's right to have his/her case remain confidential.

Client: *It's a little hard getting around lately.*
Paralegal: *What do you mean?*

---

[2] See also White, *Architectural Suggestions for a Law Office Building,* 9 Practical Lawyer 66 (No. 8, 1956).

Client: *Oh, I just ache all over, you know, and on a hot day like this . . . my asthma gets up and, you know, I can hardly breathe sometimes. I'm sorry. I'm just a little out of breath coming up the stairs and all.*

Paralegal: *Well, just take your time and relax a bit.*

Client: *It's these bus drivers . . . I don't have a car, I lost it. It's not easy to get around . . . [Pause] Well, I feel a little better now.*

Paralegal: *Uh-huh.*

Client: *My wife is sick, and me, I'm not feeling too good. I've been sick about two or three years. It goes back about eight or nine years. The last two or three years, I honestly haven't been able to do anything.*

Paralegal: *Sir, I didn't get your name.*

Client: *Donnelly, Sam Donnelly, the wife's name is Sarah.*

In this sequence, it's perhaps more significant to note what the paralegal did *not* do than what she did do. It may have been very tempting for the paralegal to have begun by asking the client, "What's the problem?" as soon as he sat down. Instead, the paralegal allowed the client to talk about what was on *his* mind. The interview did not begin by the paralegal directing the course of the interview through questions or comments. There are a number of benefits to this approach. First, the client is given an opportunity to relax; he is not immediately pressured by questions. Second, the message that comes across is that the paralegal is interested in the client as a person. The client obviously wants someone to listen to his story of how the world is mistreating him. He's sick; he can't get around, etc. Avoid dismissing such talk as either irrelevant to the interview or as typically senile. Much more sensitivity is required. Apparently this client is old and without substantial means. Perhaps to him the most significant information about his life is that he is old and sick. It is an extremely important event to him to be able to share this with others and to have it listened to with concern. Third, by letting the client talk, indeed, by letting him ramble on a bit, the paralegal may be able to collect information not as easily obtainable by pointed questioning at the outset.

There are, of course, limitations in this approach. The paralegal does not have all day to interview this client. There may be other clients outside waiting to be interviewed as well. In the interview under analysis, however, the exchange was not burdensome; it took a matter of seconds before the paralegal began to direct the attention of the client to such basic data as his name. It is not always easy to break off the conversation in this way. The interruption needs to be handled with tact.

> **Principle: The interviewer should consider the advantages of permitting the client to say what is on his/her mind at the outset in place of beginning with a series of questions.**

If the client has nothing to say at the outset, then of course the paralegal will have to take the initiative with questions such as, "How are you today?" "Is there anything I can help you with?" or "I understand you've come to this office about a legal matter."

Soon after the interview begins, the paralegal should be taking notes on what the client is saying. The notes should be extensive. The paralegal should say something about the notes to the client such as, "I hope you don't mind if I make a few notes on what you say so that I don't forget them." This should set the client's mind at ease about the writing. The client will probably respect the paralegal for this thoroughness and consideration in explaining the writing to him. In addition to aiding the paralegal's memory, the notes serve another important function: recordkeeping. In a law office, every case must be adequately documented. Personnel other than the paralegal will probably be working on the case at any number of stages. A well-kept case record can save a great deal of time and ensure accuracy. After the initial interview, the paralegal should take the time necessary to compose a coherent report (intake memo) on the interview from his/her notes (p. 386).

> **Principle: The interviewer should take notes and explain to the client why s/he is doing so.**

The paralegal is always looking for clues (or "flags") of potential legal problems. From the brief exchange between the paralegal and Mr. Donnelly, a number of such problems may have surfaced. At some point in the interview, the paralegal must ask questions about them if further information is not volunteered by the client. Note that the client may not know which of his problems are legal and which are not. He may have come in with one problem on his mind but reveal a number of problems as he speaks. Here again we see the value of letting the client talk. This approach is much more beneficial than saying to the client, "Tell me all your legal problems." It is the job of the interviewer to assist the client in identifying such problems. What are some of the potential legal problems that he has that will require further inquiry?

1. He lost his car. Was it stolen or repossessed?
2. He is sick. Is he getting proper medical attention? Is he receiving all the public medical services to which he is entitled?
3. His wife is sick; same questions as to her.
4. Is there an emergency that requires immediate attention?

The fourth question is essential. Very early in the interview, the paralegal must determine whether a crisis exists with respect to such matters as health or housing. If so, then the office must immediately act either through legal proceedings or through helping the client obtain government emergency social services.

> **Principle: The interviewer is always alert to the flags indicating potential legal problems.**

Paralegal: *Mr. Donnelly, I am a paralegal...*
Client: *A what?*
Paralegal: *A paralegal. I am not an attorney. My job is to get some preliminary information so that when you do see a lawyer, he'll be able to help you a lot more quickly.*

Do you think that the client understands who Miss Collins is? If he were asked what a paralegal is, what do you think he would answer? What obligation does the interviewer have, if any, to be sure that the client knows whom s/he is talking to before asking the client for personal information?

Principle: It should be made absolutely clear to the client that the paralegal is not a lawyer.

The client probably came into the office expecting to see a lawyer. The paralegal may describe who s/he is so quickly that the client does not understand, and doesn't have time to collect his/her thoughts about whether s/he wants to talk to a nonlawyer. The danger is that the interviewer will be so preoccupied with doing his/her job that s/he won't be sensitive to the reactions of the client.

A paralegal is a person skilled in the tasks of providing legal services. S/he derives authority to act from two sources: (1) the supervision of his/her work by a lawyer and (2) the authorization granted by specific laws, e.g., to permit nonlawyers to represent clients before agencies (p. 226).

Unfortunately, too many paralegals describe their role in the negative; they start off by stating that they are nonlawyers. A more positive approach should be taken. In consultation with the paralegal's supervisor, terminology and role description should be agreed upon that will positively reflect the value and skills of the paralegal.

Client: *I don't have any money and I went to these welfare people and they won't put me on the program. They say I'm not sick enough. And I haven't been able to do a solid day's work in, oh, two and a half years now. Every once and a while I do a little bit and I have to lay down for two or three weeks. Go to the doctor a couple times a month. I've been to the hospital two or three times. So, you know, I don't really know how or what you can do about this. I really don't. I don't know what to do. My wife has been sick too. I'm not being treated right by those government people.*

Paralegal: *Everything's been hitting you at once, it seems.*

Note again how the client's story is beginning to unfold. The paralegal learns for the first time that Mr. Donnelly has been to a welfare department and has been told that he does not qualify for a "program" because he is not sick enough. Most assuredly, this information should go into the paralegal's notes for further questioning. Clients tend to tell their stories piecemeal rather than in a coherent fashion that would be readily understandable by everyone. The job of the interviewer is to put these pieces together.

How would you characterize the paralegal's statement that, "Everything's been hitting you at once, it seems"? Patronizing? Sympathetic? Unprofessional? What effect do you think it had on the client? Do you think that the paralegal is taking sides with this statement? Suppose the paralegal said, "It sounds like the government is really trying to do you in," or "Well, of course, you know, Mr. Donnelly, the government is made up of a large group of people and it's almost impossible for them to please everyone." Would these be appropriate opinions for the paralegal to express, if she believes either of them? Shouldn't she be honest about her feelings?

Generally speaking, it is more appropriate for the paralegal to be *neutral* in the expression of personal opinions. It is not the paralegal's job to comment upon the evils of government nor to be apologetic about government. This does not mean, however, that s/he should always refrain from expressing personal feelings about subjects. If the client is telling a "horror story" about his/her life, it would be only natural for the paralegal to react with surprise or dismay. This is fine so long as the paralegal does not lose perspective and a measure of objectivity in trying to gather all the facts.

> **Principle: The interviewer should exercise self-restraint in the expression of personal opinions or feelings. Remain neutral unless it would be awkward and unnatural not to express oneself in the context of the interview.**

It is too tempting and easy for the paralegal to become overly involved in the emotional aspects of assisting people with legal problems. The paralegal must retain composure in a milieu where tempers can run high and where facts can change rapidly. The best legal service can be provided by someone with a cool head. Again, this does not necessarily mean that the paralegal cannot identify with the very real frustrations and problems of the client. Objectivity is not inconsistent with empathy.

Paralegal: *Mr. Donnelly, before we get down to the specifics of your case, I need to ask you a few questions. As you may know, this office does not charge clients for its services so long as the client lives within the area served by this office and you do not have income above a certain level. We only provide free service to low-income clients.*

Client: *Well, I'll tell you, I think I could pass the test, yes, ma'am! The welfare people don't think I'm poor, I have a little nest egg, but I haven't been able to work over the years . . .*

Paralegal: *How much do you have left?*

Client: *I have about $200, $300 in the bank.*

Paralegal: *Uh-huh.*

Client: *But I'll tell you, that's about to be eaten up. I don't have a car. It's really hard to get around on public transportation. Other than that, the wife's got a little bit of jewelry, a wedding ring, stuff like that. And that's about it.*

Paralegal: *Do you rent an apartment?*

Client: *Yes, we do.*

Paralegal: *What about Social Security. Do you receive any income there?*

Client: *Well, we get a little bit of Social Security.*

Paralegal: *How much is that?*

Client: *$305 a month. I can't live on that. My wife is taking work into the house like . . . She's been sick lately. We don't have the money coming in.*

Paralegal: *Do you have any children?*

Client: *We have no children.*

Paralegal: *Okay, Let me ask you a couple of other questions. I want to make sure that I have the street right. You want to give that to me?*

Client: *Delores, 1429 Delores Street, Apartment 7-B.*

Paralegal: *What about a phone? Still have it?*

Client: *Well, we keep the phone because I have to have it. I fall down, get dizzy, need medication for my head, my back, and I have to have it, so we do have a phone. The number is 824-8027.*

Paralegal: *824-8027. Fine. Well, it's pretty clear that you're eligible for our services.*

Client: *Very good, I sure do need it.*

Paralegal: *Okay, I've got some other questions that I want to ask you, and if there are things that you want to say, just stop me. If you have any questions, just stop me and ask.*

Client: *Okay.*

Government-funded legal service offices do not charge clients for their services so long as they live within a designated geographical area and meet an income test. Regulations exist on how much income and assets a family can have in order to be eligible. The paralegal (or sometimes the receptionist) has the job of determining eligibility based upon office charts.

Matters of income and wealth are intensely personal and must be approached with great delicacy. A rapid-fire series of questions such as, "Do you work?" "How much to you make?" "How much do you have in the bank?" "Do your relatives give you money?" etc. can be very demoralizing. The common complaint against bureaucracy is the distance and impersonality with which it deals with the public. There is absolutely no reason why a law office must act in the same manner, no matter how busy it is.

Note that the client was somewhat hesitant about answering some of the questions and took every opportunity to demonstrate how poor he was. This is understandable. Perhaps he was not aware of the fact that the office was *not* actively looking for ways to disqualify people, and that he will normally be taken at his word on eligibility. The dignity of the client requires that the interviewer not assume that everything said is a lie until proven otherwise.

> **Principle: Whenever an interviewer is asking a client for any personal information, the client should clearly know why the information is needed and it should be taken with great sensitivity.**

Paralegal: *Mr. Donnelly, do you have any papers with you . . . anything that was sent to you concerning the problem that you want some help with?*

Client: *Yes, I brought it along here. There's stuff on there—numbers and everything—I didn't understand it all.*

Paralegal: *Okay, let's take a look at it.*

Now the paralegal has gotten through the preliminaries and the central core of the interview is about to begin. There are a number of options available to the paralegal. Here the paralegal began concretely by asking a directed or close-ended question, one that required the attention of the client to narrow into a very specific area—the legal papers. This is usually a good way to begin. The event that convinces clients that they should receive legal help is often the receipt of papers, either through the mail, or delivered (served) to them in person. The papers may be confusing and upsetting. It is comforting for the client to have someone focus on them soon.

Principle: The interviewer should always try as soon as possible to focus upon concrete matters that are bothering the client.

There are other ways that the paralegal could have proceeded. The paralegal could have asked, "What's the problem?" or "What's on your mind?" These are open-ended questions. They invite the client to respond in a wide variety of ways within the general confines of the question. Unlike the directed or close-ended question, the client is given "control" of the situation when asked an open-ended question. The danger of such a question is that the client will ramble on at great length, providing relevant and irrelevant data. It may be difficult for the paralegal to follow the answer. On the other hand, the client may have a need to vent his/her frustrations in this way. It is often important to "get it off one's chest" and have someone listen to the complete story. Once the client has been allowed to experience this catharsis, s/he may be better able to relate to the more specific questions of the interviewer.

Principle: Interviewers must be prepared to know when clients are ready to answer directed questions.

Another approach would be to refer back to something the client said earlier in the interview. For example, the paralegal could have said, "Mr. Donnelly, you said earlier that you applied for a program. Could you tell me a little bit more about that?" It can be reassuring for the client to know that the interviewer has been listening to what s/he has been saying and wants to know more.

One of the most effective ways to assist a client is to help him/her give the facts in sequence. "When did you become ill?" "How was the illness treated?" "When did you apply at the welfare department?" "What happened next?" The client has one large story to tell and perhaps a series of sub-stories. Each story can be conceived of as a unit with a beginning, middle, and end. Assisting the client to reconstruct the stories chronologically will aid him/her to recall details and will assist the paralegal in later organizing notes for the records.

Paralegal: *This is a letter from the welfare department denying your application for disability payments. When did you get this, Mr. Donnelly?*

Client: *Oh, just a couple of weeks ago. They are liars, Miss, I want you to know. They are not treating me right. I should stay away from there; they don't treat me with respect.*

Clients are very much inclined to think in terms of opinions, conclusions, and characterizations, as opposed to facts. A primary objective of the interviewer to identify the *facts*. The client's interpretations of the facts may be important. However, the discussion must go beyond or behind the interpretations in order to cover the basic factual questions: *who, when, where,* and *how?* When a client gives an opinion or a characterization of a fact or series of facts, the interviewer must ask the client to talk about what happened that led to the interpretation. When and if a client becomes involved in an agency proceeding or a court hearing, the referee or judge will focus primarily on the facts that are alleged. Hence it is the job of the interviewer, as early as possible, to uncover as many underlying facts as are relevant.

> **Principle: An interviewer should always encourage a client to spell out all the facts that led him/her to a particular conclusion or interpretation of what happened or is happening.**

The paralegal asked the client when he had received the letter. From the paralegal's study of welfare law, she knows that there are certain requirements that must be met whenever the welfare department makes decisions that affect the case of applicants or recipients. One such requirement relates to the time span between the date of the decision and the date the client is notified of the decision. Another problem is the length of time the client has to appeal after receiving written notice of a decision.

Paralegal: *Why did you wait two weeks to come in?*
Client: [Mr. Donnelly slumps a little in his chair and looks around the room].
Paralegal: *Well, it's not that important.*

Here the paralegal has asked a "why" question, potentially calling into question either the client's motives or his competence. Luckily, the paralegal picked up on the inappropriateness of the question right away from the nonverbal cues that the client was giving through the change in his seating posture and in the apparent loss of his attention. If the "why" information is important, it may be better to wait until later to try to obtain it. The paralegal must always be alert to nonverbal communication: mannerisms, gestures, silence, etc.

> **Principle: The interviewer must be able to interpret nonverbal forms of communication.**

Paralegal: *Well, Mr. Donnelly, what I'd like to do is find out a little bit more about what happened. When did you first apply?*

Client: [A long silence].
Paralegal: *Mr. Donnelly, when did . . .*
Client: *I'm not sure.*

This particular client is very opinionated and may have taken offense at the interviewer's sudden shift from his (the client's) opinions (e.g., "liars") to the "why" inquiry, and to the cold facts ("When did you first apply?") A client who is silent or who uses comments such as "I'm not sure" or "I don't know" may be on a different wavelength from the interviewer. The client often has his/her own agenda and expectations from the interview that, if not respected, may lead to a noncooperation or even hostility. Of course, the statement "I don't know" may mean nothing more than the absence of knowledge, just as silence may simply mean that the client needs more time or guidance to remember the facts. On the other hand, they could be a signal to the interviewer that communication is breaking down. There are a number of ways to deal with this. The interviewer could change the topic for the moment. She could ask the client if anything is troubling him. Or, she could simply proceed and try to "play it by ear." In Mr. Donnelly's case, all that may be required is the opportunity to express his opinions as often as possible. This is fine so long as they do not interfere with the fact-gathering function of the interview.

Principle: Interviewers must be able to recognize client discomfort or noncooperation and to deal with it flexibly.

Paralegal: *Could I ask you what you mean when you say that they are not treating you with respect?*
Client: *I am disabled and they tell me I'm not. It's plain for anyone to see.*
Paralegal: *What we would have to do then, Mr. Donnelly, is to try to show that they are wrong.*
Client: *Yes, very wrong.*
Paralegal: *And to do it, what we need to do is get a complete picture of all the facts so that when we challenge them, we will be able to do it right. So, I'd like to start by your giving me an estimate (in days, weeks, or even months) of how long ago you first applied.*
Client: *I think it was a month ago. I have it written down at home.*

How would you analyze this exchange? What do you think the paralegal did that was or was not effective? Note the sensitivity with which the paralegal is questioning the client. The client was initially asked when he first applied. The paralegal got no response. Then the same question is asked less directly, in terms of estimates, with greater success.

Principle: The style or manner of questioning should flexibly fit the unfolding and often shifting context of the interview.

Paralegal: *Looking at your letter here, I see that it was signed by Ralph Smith of the welfare department. After you leave, I will call him and ask*

> *him about things such as the date you applied. In addition, I'd appreciate it if you would call me when you get home and have had time to look at your own notes of when you applied. Could you do that?*
>
> Client: *Yes, I will.*

Whenever practical, it is wise to have the client take some steps on his/her own behalf. This tends to ensure a sense of involvement and cooperation between office staff and client. It also is a step in the direction of accuracy since the client is often in the best position to collect certain facts or perform certain tasks. The client should not be asked to undertake anything beyond his capacity, however. In this case, checking the client's own records to obtain a date is sufficiently definite and realizable to warrant his undertaking it.

> **Principle: Whenever practical, the interviewer should ask the client to perform tasks on his/her own to aid the office in handling the case.**

Exactly how much you can ask a client to do depends on the circumstances. Some clients may be willing and able to do a good deal, e.g., locate a lost relative, make a written list of all known debts. Again, however, this aspect of legal services must be handled with care. The client cannot be asked to do the job of the paralegal or the attorney.

The paralegal told the client that she was going to call the welfare department. The client should be told what steps the office proposes on his/her behalf. A client needs to know what action will be taken.

> **Principle: As often as possible, the concrete steps the office proposes to take on behalf of the client should be explained to the client.**

A primary reason for explaining the steps to the client is that it is his/her case. S/he is the one who will suffer if inappropriate steps are taken. Normally, the client will defer totally to the judgment of the office, but s/he deserves the opportunity to hear what your plan of action is and reject it if s/he wishes. Ultimately, of course, the client always has the right to "fire" the law office and seek other assistance.

> **Principle: The interviewer must alway remember that it is the client who makes the final decision on whether s/he wants the office to represent him/her. S/he always has the option of calling it all off.**

> Paralegal: *Time and again here in the office we have clients who are unsure about such basic things as dates, amounts, what was signed, and so on. Of course, you can't be expected to have a record of everything. We have to be practical. All I'm saying is that it's a good idea for a person to keep a record of as many basic things as possible.*

Here we have the paralegal stepping out of her role as interviewer and becoming a teacher. This can be upsetting to some clients; others will appreciate it very much. The lecture was on what is called preventive law or "community" legal education. Preventive law is the taking of steps to avoid problems *before* they occur, or of dealing with them effectively when they arise so that matters do not become worse. Here, the lecture on the client keeping his own records is fundamental since documentation is fundamental in the law.

Paralegal: *Okay, fine. Just as soon as you can call me, please do it. Now, I want to ask you some questions about your medical history. First, let's get back to this letter. It says that your application for Aid for the Totally Disabled was denied because they say you are not disabled. It also says that they examined the medical records that you brought with you. Is that right?*

Client: *Yes, I brought my papers there.*

Paralegal: *Do you have these papers with you now?*

Client: *No, they are at home. Do you want me to bring them to you?*

Paralegal: *Yes, would you? Why don't you take this piece of paper and make a note of the things you should do. First, you are going to call me to let me know the date you first applied. Then you are going to bring me the medical records that the welfare department looked at when they were deciding on your application. Do you have all that?*

Client: *Yes, I think so.*

Paralegal: *Could you give me the name and address of the doctor who most recently examined you?*

Client: *Dr. Edward Zuder of 7th Avenue; I don't know the exact address.*

Paralegal: *What other doctors have examined you?*

Client: *Well, I'm not sure. There was one that I saw a few months ago in Mason County.*

Paralegal: *Do you remember the doctor's name?*

Client: *Johnson, or Thompson, I don't recall fully. I think my wife would know. I'll ask her. She's better at names than me.*

Paralegal: *That would be fine. Have her do that. In fact, Mr. Donnelly, what I am going to need is a list of every doctor that you have seen within the last five years. When you bring me your medical records, a lot of the names and addresses will be there. Some may not be. Just try to remember—you and your wife—as many as you can. Why don't you add that to the list of things you are going to do? With your permission I will call some of them for some basic information.*

Client: *For five years? Why do you need all that?*

Paralegal: *I know it's a lot of information, but from experience we know that old medical records are often very important. We should be prepared.*

Client: *Well, I'll get what I can.*

The paralegal is probing for information. Probing is important, but sometimes difficult to do. The client should never feel that he is being interrogated or cross-examined. It is obvious that Mr. Donnelly cannot be pushed much further. He cannot be expected to recall all the information the paralegal is seeking. When he was surprised at being asked for information dating back five years, he may have been reacting not simply to the difficulty of obtaining such data, but also to the possible implication that the paralegal doubted his claim that he has been very sick. Do you think that the client felt that he had to prove something *to the paralegal?*

> **Principle: Probing is a valid technique of data-gathering, but it must be employed with care in order to avoid making the client uncomfortable.**

The paralegal did not simply rely on probing the client to obtain information. Miss Collins has a talent for organizing approaches to data-gathering. She asked the client to check his records and call her, and she also asked him to bring records to her. Finally, *she* will take some *initiative* in making some calls herself. These are a series of comprehensive steps calculated to obtain facts and to cross-check the validity of facts.

> **Principle: Probing is one technique used by the interviewer in conjunction with other techniques to obtain the facts.**

The steps used by the paralegal demonstrate the intimate relationship between interviewing and investigation. The interviewer is laying the groundwork for the investigative function (which in this office may or may not be performed by the same paralegal). Both the interviewer and the investigator seek relevant facts that can be verified or documented. If names, dates, and witnesses must be tracked down in the field by the investigator, the process is begun by a thorough interview.

The same is true of the informal and formal advocacy function. At some later point, the office may try to negotiate the case with the welfare department through informal advocacy (p. 773) in order for Mr. Donnelly to obtain what he wants without resorting to a formal agency hearing or a court proceeding. If informal advocacy does not work, formal advocacy at agency hearings (p. 787) or in court may be tried. All these steps begin with and are dependent upon a competent initial client interview. The groundwork is established at this level with fact and problem identification, on the one hand, and a trustful, cooperative client on the other.

> **Principle: Interviewing is intimately connected with and is the foundation for investigation, negotiation, and formal advocacy.**

Client: *Do you think I have a chance of winning?*
Paralegal: *Well, we're going to study your case carefully. I can tell you definitely that you do have a right to fight the department for denying your application. This could mean forcing them into a fair hearing. Before any final decision on strategy is made, however, I and one of the attorneys here in the office will be checking with you.*
Client: *I see.*

Has the paralegal given the client legal advice? The paralegal is interpreting administrative regulations on challenging welfare decisions in reference to a particular client's case.

Generally, if an administrative agency authorizes a lay person to represent clients before it, this authorization should include the giving of legal advice in preparation for such representation. The welfare department provides such an authorization. Hence, the paralegal can give legal advice to Mr. Donnelly in this case. If there is no specific authorization for lay representation at agency hearings, then the paralegal cannot give legal advice. Normally, no such authorization exists when the case involves traditional court cases of divorce, landlord-tenant, consumer fraud, etc. In such cases, the role of the paralegal is limited to fact-gathering in interviewing and investigation, preliminary drafting of legal documents for lawyers, legal research, etc. Of course, in every case, a paralegal can give clients legal advice when the advice is specifically dictated by a lawyer. In such situations, the paralegal is merely relaying a message from the lawyer to the client.

Principle: The paralegal must know what legal advice is and when s/he can and cannot give it to clients.

The paralegal properly instructed the client on how the office functions in handling cases: paralegals work closely with attorneys and both are in regular communication with the client.

The paralegal used the phrase "fair hearing" without explaining that this is the technical procedure used by the welfare department to permit clients to challenge its actions. The client, on the surface, appeared to understand when he said, "I see." It is more probable, however, that the client was simply covering up his confusion by being polite.

Principle: Technical terms (legal or otherwise) should either be rejected in favor of understandable English or explained clearly to clients.

Paralegal: *Well, I think that we have gone about as far as we can today. Is there anything else that you want to tell me, anything that I should know? Are you sure you've told me everything?*

Client: *What do you mean?*

Here again it is possible that the client could take offense to this last question of the paralegal. The client might be thinking, "Doesn't she trust me? I've tried to tell her everything." On the other hand, experienced interviewers know that clients have a natural inclination to overstate their case, to highlight what they feel are the good points of their case, and to minimize anything negative about their case. They do this perhaps out of fear that the office would not take their case if it knew the whole story. Furthermore it may take more than one interview for the client to place his/her full trust in the paralegal or in the office as a whole. Nevertheless, the interviewer must pursue every aspect of the case, even that which may be damaging. Better to learn everything now so that the office can be prepared for potentially negative factors than to be caught surprised at a hearing with information that is damaging.

While it is true that the paralegal must try to uncover everything, there are effective and ineffective ways of going about it. The approach taken by the paralegal here does *not* appear to be effective. The blanket question she asked is not likely to communicate the message that she needs to know everything. She was indirect, vague, and potentially condescending. If the paralegal suspected that there were aspects of the case that the client was concealing, she should have asked specific questions designed to determine whether her suspicions were valid. Furthermore, she should have explained to the client why it is important to provide all the facts. Perhaps this would necessitate some explanation to the client of how our adversarial system of justice works. When advocates for clients go before referees, judges, or juries, it is their duty to present the best case possible for the client. It is the job of the advocate for the other side to point up the negative aspects of the case. The advocate for the client, however, must be ready in advance to respond to what the other side will say. Hence, the necessity of knowing everything as soon as possible. The key point that must be made to the client is that the office will not refuse to serve a client simply because s/he doesn't have a perfect case.

> **Principle: Interviewers must uncover both the positive and damaging aspects of a case.**

> Paralegal: *I have a few forms here that I would like you to sign. They simply give this office your authority to represent you and to look at your welfare and medical records. You'll sign these here, won't you?*
> Client: *You want me to sign this here?*
> Paralegal: *Yes, would you?*
> Client: *Okay, should my wife sign?*
> Paralegal: *No, that won't be necessary.* [Client signs.] *Fine.*

Asking the client to sign papers is always a delicate matter. Very often, the client does not know what s/he is signing. The interviewer should assume that the client is confused about the signing. The client should be given the chance to read over what s/he is being asked to sign and encouraged to ask questions about what s/he doesn't understand. Not only is this good practice as a matter of courtesy, but it is also good training for the client to read carefully and ask questions about *any* papers s/he is asked to sign *before* s/he signs.

> **Principle: Before a client is asked to sign anything, the interviewer should be sure that the client knows what s/he is signing, why s/he is being asked to sign, and that it is up to the client to decide whether s/he wants to sign.**

Whenever a question is asked and the answer is strongly stated or implied in the question, we have a *leading question* (p. 435). Leading questions are potentially dangerous because of the manipulative way in which words are put into the mouth of the person being asked the question. Here are some examples: "Mr. Jones, you knew that it was past midnight when you called, isn't that right?" "Wasn't it past midnight when you called?" Leading questions attempt to pressure the individual to answer in a certain way. This is not to say that a person asking leading questions is always devious. People can ask leading questions without even realizing it. They may feel that they are helping out by asking the question in this manner.

Now, look again at the statement "You'll sign these here, won't you?" Is this a leading question? Should the question have been asked in this way?

> **Principle: Interviewers must be able to recognize their own leading questions and to understand the dangers of such questions.**

Paralegal: *Just a couple of points before we conclude, Mr. Donnelly. You said something earlier about having lost your car. What did you mean?*

Client: *Well, I had to give it to my nephew. It wasn't safe for me to drive, you know. I've been very ill lately.*

Paralegal: *I see. What about your wife? You said that she was sick. Has she applied to the welfare department for the same benefits that you applied for?*

Client: *Why, no. I never thought of her going ahead. Do you think I should?*

Paralegal: *You certainly can't lose anything. It's up to you if you want to give it a try.*

Here the paralegal is going back to her notes to ask about some matters that she picked up earlier. This is the sign of a thorough interview. The office is interested in all legal aspects of the client's needs. The paralegal may have suspected creditor or car repair problems. It was totally appropriate to check this out. The law, however, is critical of lawyers who try to stir up legal problems and who go on so-called "fishing expeditions" to discover legal problems of citizens in order to generate business for themselves. Such stirring up of litigation is frowned upon. This was not the case here, however. The paralegal properly inquired about issues suggested by what the client told her.

The suggestion to the client that his wife apply for benefits raises another question about the role of the paralegal and the office. Clients should not be pressured, persuaded, or urged to take courses of action. The task of the office is to lay out *options* for the client, explain the merits and demerits of each option, and leave it for the client to decide what he wants to do. If the client asks for a recommendation on what option to choose, an answer should be given, but it should always be made clear to the client that he has the final responsibility to decide what he wants to do. The paralegal in this case acted properly. She did not urge Mr. Donnelly to do anything. She made the client aware of the option concerning his wife and responded to the client's specific request for her opinion about whether he should take the option.

> **Principle: The interviewer should not pressure the client to take any course of action.**

Paralegal: *Okay, Mr. Donnelly, let's leave it at that. If you don't have any more questions, we can conclude now. I will be talking to an attorney about your case shortly. You will call me concerning the date we spoke about, bring me your medical records, and put together a list of the doctors who treated you in the last five years. I will call Mr. Smith at the welfare department to find out what I can from him. If your wife wants to talk to me about applying, have her come by or call me. We'll be glad to help her in any way we can.*

Client: *Okay, and I thank you.*

Paralegal: *Thank you for coming by. I hope we can help you. Good-by.*

Client: *Good-by.*

The final comment of the paralegal is very significant. It is important not to leave the client with the impression that the office is definitely going to win the case. It would be easy to raise this expectation in the mind of the client, since undoubtedly this is what s/he wants to believe. More realistically, all the office can say is that it will do the best it can for the client, and that no guarantees of success can be given. The comment "I hope we can help you" is appropriate to convey this message.

> **Principle: The interviewer must not raise false expectations in the mind of the client about what the office will be able to do.**

ASSIGNMENT 64

Form a circle of chairs centered around a single chair in the middle. The student sitting in the middle will play the role of the client. The students in the circle (numbering about ten) will be the interviewers in rotation. The instructor will ask one of the students to begin the interview. As this student runs into difficulty during the interview, the student to his/her right picks up the interview, tries to resolve the difficulty in his/her own way, and then proceeds with the interview. If *this* student cannot resolve the difficulty, the student to his/her right tries, and so on. The objective is to identify as many diverse ways of handling difficulties as possible in a relatively short period of time. No one interviewer should have the floor for more than two or three minutes at any one time. The student playing the role of the client is given specific instructions about how to play the role, e.g., sometimes s/he is asked to be shy, other times s/he is asked to be demanding. The client should not overdo the role, however. S/he should respond naturally within the role assigned. Here are four sets of instructions to attempt this "interview in rotation."

1. The interviewer greets the client and says, "I am a paralegal." The client is confused about what a paralegal is. The interviewer explains. The client is insistent upon a comprehensive definition that s/he can understand.

2. The client comes to the law office because s/he is being sued for negligent driving. The interviewer asks the client if s/he must wear eyeglasses to drive. The answer is yes. The interviewer then asks if s/he was wearing eyeglasses during the accident. The client is very reluctant to answer. (In fact, s/he was not wearing glasses at the time.) The client does not appear to want to talk about this subject. The interviewer persists.

3. The client is being sued by a supermarket for $750.00 in grocery bills. The client has a poor memory and the interviewer must think of ways to help him/her remember. The client wants to cooperate but is having trouble remembering.

4. The client wants to sue an auto mechanic. The client gives many opinions, conclusions, and judgments (e.g., "The mechanic is a crook," "I was their best customer," "The work done was awful.") The interviewer is having difficulty in encouraging the client to state the facts underlying the opinions. The client insists on stating conclusions.

After each exercise, the class should discuss principles, guidelines, and techniques of interviewing.

ASSIGNMENT 65

Below are two additional role-playing exercises to be conducted in class.

1. The instructor asks the class if anyone was involved, in any way, in a recent automobile accident. This individual is interviewed by another class member whose job is to obtain as complete a picture as possible of what happened. The interviewer at the outset knows nothing other than that some kind of an automobile accident occurred.

2. The instructor asks the class if anyone has recently had trouble with any government agency (e.g., post office, sanitation department). This individual is interviewed by another class member whose job is to obtain as complete a picture as possible of what happened. The interviewer at the outset knows nothing other than the fact that the person being interviewed has had some difficulty with a government agency.

REFERENCES

Allen, *Dynamics of Interpersonal Communication,* 3 Washburn Law Journal 135 (1964).

Barbara, D., *The Art of Listening* (1958).

Benjamin, A., *The Helping Interview* (1969).

Binder, D., & Price, S., *Legal Interviewing and Counseling: A Client Centered Approach* (1977).

Bingham, W., *How to Interview,* 4th ed. (1959).

Blenker, Hunt, & Kogan, *A Study of Interrelated Factors in the Initial Interview with New Clients,* 32 Social Casework 23 (1951).

Burtt, H., & Gaskill, H., *Suggestibility and the Form of the Question,* 16 Journal of Applied Psychology 315 (1932).

Dominick, B., *The Art of Listening* (1958).

Freeman, H., & Weihofen, H., *Clinical Law Training, Interviewing and Counseling: Text and Cases* (1972).

Garrett, A., *Interviewing: Its Principles and Methods* (1972).

Gordon, R., *Interviewing: Theory, Strategy, Techniques and Tactics* (1963).

Hunt, *Problems and Processes in the Legal Interview,* 50 Illinois Bar Journal 726 (1962).

Kahn, R., & Connell, C., *The Dynamics of Interviewing* (1957).

Karcher, *What Does a Client Expect of a Lawyer: "Effect" or "Results"?* 14 New Jersey State Bar Journal 26 (1970).

Merton, R., Fiske, M., & Kendall, P., *The Focused Interview* (1956).

Payne, S., *The Art of Asking Questions* (1951).

Shaffer, T., *Legal Interviewing and Counseling in a Nutshell* (1976).

Statsky, W., & Lang, P., *Interviewing* in The Legal Paraprofessional as Advocate and Assistant: Roles, Training Concepts and Materials, pp. 135ff (1971).

Wiseman, *Lawyer-Client Interviews: Some Lessons from Psychiatry,* 39 Boston University Law Review 181 (1959).

9

Investigation
in a Law Office

Section A. COLLECTING YOUR THOUGHTS ABOUT INVESTIGATION AT THE OUTSET

Investigation is fact gathering. Before examining investigation in detail, you should take the opportunity to reflect upon what you already know about fact gathering. What follows are ten hypotheticals involving Tom. Some of them deal with his home life while others stem from his employment as a paralegal. *Before studying the remaining sections of this chapter,* proceed as follows:

- Read each hypothetical carefully.
- If you were Tom in each hypothetical, what specific things would you do to deal with the situation? What would you *not* do?
- From all the lists that you have made in response to these hypotheticals, organize a four-to-ten page manual on investigation. In your lists, you have written down concrete things that Tom should or should not do. Now generalize it all into principles or guidelines of investigation, e.g., be suspicious of your first impressions until you have sought verification. These general statements, in effect, constitute your own manual on investigation.
- When you have completed studying this chapter, come back to the manual that you have written. Has your perspective changed? If you had to write the manual over again, would you change any of it?

- When you are on the job as a paralegal and have had some investigation assignments, go back again to the manual that you wrote. Has your perspective changed? If you had to write the manual over again, would you change any of it?

1. On September 1st, Tom decides that he wants to enter a community college. School opens in five days. There are only two colleges that still allow time for registration. Both are about the same distance from his home and he can afford both. Tom's problem is that he doesn't know enough about either college to make a decision. He works fulltime from 9–6 and *must* continue to work right up to the first day of school in order to be able to finance his education.

2. Tom teaches a second-grade class. It is the end of the school day on Friday and the bus is in front of the school ready to take about half his class home. If the students are not out in time for the bus, it will leave without them. It is 2:50 P.M. and the bus is scheduled to leave at 3:05 P.M. Tom discovers that his briefcase is missing from the top of his desk.

3. Tom is the father of two children, Ed and Bill. He comes home one day and finds a small package of marijuana in the front hall. He immediately suspects one of his two sons. He turns around and goes out to look for them.

4. Tom's son Bill has been accused of using abusive language in front of his teacher. Tom calls the teacher who refuses to talk about it. The teacher refers Tom to the principal. The principal refuses to talk about it and refers Tom to the Assistant Superintendent at the central office.

5. Tom's sister is ill. She received a letter from a local supermarket where she often buys goods on credit. The letter informs her that she owes $22.00 and that unless she pays within a week "legal proceedings will be instituted" against her. She calls Tom and tells him that she paid the bill by sending $22.00 in cash last week. She asks Tom to help her.

6. Tom works for a local legal service office. The office has a client who wants to sue her landlord because the kitchen roof is falling down. Tom is assigned to the case.

7. A welfare department has told a client that it is going to terminate public assistance because the client's boyfriend is supporting her and her family. The client denies this. Tom is assigned to the case.

8. A client has been to the office seeking help in obtaining a divorce. She claimed that her husband beat her. Tom is assigned to the case.

9. Sam owes Tom $1,000.00. When Tom asks for his money, Sam tells him that he is broke. Tom suspects differently.

10. Tom's uncle once lived in Boston. After spending two years in the Army, he started traveling across the country. He has not been heard from for five years. Tom wants to locate his uncle.

Section B. FACT PARTICULARIZATION AND OTHER INVESTIGATION GUIDES

In chapter 8 on Legal Interviewing, we examined the six major guides to fact gathering (p. 389):

1. Instructions of the supervisor.
2. Checklists.
3. Legal analysis.
4. Fact Particularization (FP).
5. Common sense.
6. Flexibility.

You should review these guides now since they are equally applicable to investigation. Fact Particularization (FP) is especially important (p. 391). FP helps provide direction in the search for factual detail.

Section C. INTRODUCTION TO INVESTIGATION

1. *Investigative techniques are often very individualistic.*

Styles, mannerisms and approaches to investigation are often highly personal. An investigator usually works alone. Through a sometimes arduous process of trial and error, s/he develops techniques that are effective. While some of these techniques come from the suggestions of fellow investigators, most are acquired from on-the-job experience.

2. *It is impossible to substitute principle for hustle, imagination, and flexibility.*

If there is one characteristic that singles out the effective investigator, it is the willingness to dig. While many investigation assignments may be relatively easy (e.g., photograph the ceiling of a bathroom that a tenant claims is falling down), most assignments are open-ended in that the range of options and possible conclusions to a problem are extensive. The answer is not always there for the asking. As to such assignments, the investigator must be prepared to identify and pursue leads, to be unorthodox, to let his/her feelings, hunches, and intuition lead where they will. In short, the formal principles of investigation must give way to hustle, imagination, and flexibility.

Good investigators are always in pursuit. They are on the offensive and don't wait for the facts to come to them. They know that legwork is required. They know that 50% of their leads will become dead ends. They are not frightened by roadblocks and therefore do not freeze at the first hurdle. They know that there are no perfect ways of obtaining information. They know that they must take a stab at possibilities and that it takes persistent thinking and imagination to come up with the possibilities. At the same time, good investigators are not fools. The do not pursue blind alleys. After being on the job for a while, they have developed "a feel" for what is or is not a reasonable possibility or lead. They have been able to develop this "feel," however, only because when they first started investigating, they had an open mind and were not afraid to try things out. It is almost always true that when an investigator comes back from the field and says, "I couldn't find anything," s/he has probably not done a thorough job.

3. *An investigator may not know what s/he is looking for until s/he finds it.*

As with legal interviewing and legal research, good investigation may sometimes live a life of its own in terms of what it uncovers. There are two kinds of investigation assignments. First, the closed-ended assignment where the end product is carefully defined in advance, e.g., the photograph assignment mentioned above in the tenant case. Second, the open-ended assignment where the investigator begins with only the general contours of a problem and is asked to fill in the facts, e.g., a client has been charged with a burglary and the investigator is assigned to find out as much as s/he can about the case. In the open-ended assignment (and in some closed-ended ones), the investigator, by definition, is walking into the unknown. S/he may have no idea of what s/he will uncover or fail to uncover. Suppose in the burglary assignment the investigator sets out to focus on whatever is relevant to the burglary charge and in the process discovers that a homicide was involved but is as yet unknown to the police. The investigator had no idea that s/he would find this until s/he found it. Suppose that the law firm has a client who is charging his employer with racial discrimination, and in the process of working on the case the investigator discovers that this employee had a managerial job at the company and that several of the workers under this employee have complained that *he* practiced sex discrimination against them. The investigator had no idea that s/he would uncover this until s/he uncovered it. In short, the key frame of mind in undertaking an assignment is an open mind.

4. *Investigation and interviewing are closely related.*

The interviewer conducting the initial client interview (p. 385) has two responsibilities: help identify legal problems and obtain from the client as many relevant facts on those problems as possible. The starting point for the investigator is the report or intake memo (p. 386) prepared by the interviewer on what the client said. It is either clear from this report what the investigation needs are, or they become clear only after the investigator and his/her supervisor have defined them more precisely.

The investigator should approach the interview report with a healthy skepticism. Thus far, all the office may know is what the client has said, or what the interviewer thinks the client said. The perspective of the office is therefore narrow. Without necessarily distrusting the client's word, the investigator's job is to verify the facts given during the interview and to determine whether new facts exist that were unknown or improperly identified during the interview. S/he cannot accept the interview report at face value. New facts may be revealed or "old" facts may for the first time be seen in a context that give them an unexpected meaning. The investigator must be willing to approach a case almost as if the office knows nothing about it or as if what the office knows is invalid. By adopting this attitude, the investigator will be able to give the case an entirely different direction when the product of the investigation warrants it.

5. *The investigator must be guided by goals and priorities.*

It is one thing to say that the investigator must be open-minded enough to be receptive to the unexpected. It is quite another to say that the investigator should start in a void. The starting point is the set of instructions from the supervisor. How clear a supervisor is about an investigation may vary with each assignment. For example:

- The supervisor may have a very definite idea of what s/he wants.
- The supervisor thinks s/he knows what s/he wants, but is not sure.
- Whatever conception the supervisor has about what s/he wants, s/he is not effective in explaining it to the investigator.
- The supervisor has no idea what s/he wants other than a desire to obtain as many facts about the case as possible.

The first responsibility of the investigator is to establish communication with the supervisor. With as much clarity as possible, determine what the supervisor wants accomplished through the investigation.

6. *There is a close relationship among investigation, negotiation, and trial.*

There are two ultimate questions that should guide the investigator's inquiry into every fact being investigated:

- How will this fact assist or hurt the office in attempting to settle or negotiate the case without a trial?
- How will this fact assist or hurt the office in presenting the client's case at trial?

A large percentage of legal claims never go to a full trial; they are negotiated in advance. Opposing counsel have a number of bargaining sessions in which attempts will be made to hammer out a settlement that will be acceptable to their clients. Very often they discuss the law that they think will be applicable if the case goes to trial. Even more often they present each other with the facts that they think they will be able to establish at trial. Here the investigator's report (p. 458) becomes invaluable. As a result of this report, the attorney should be able to suggest a wide range of facts that could be used at trial (e.g., "we have reason to believe . . ." or "we are now pursuing leads that would tend to establish that . . ."). The attorney's bargaining leverage is immeasurably increased by a thorough investigation report.

For the cases that may go to trial, the significance of the investigation report cannot be overstated. Some of the ways in which it can help the attorney are as follows:

- Deciding whether or not to go to trial at all.
- Deciding what witnesses to call.
- Deciding what questions to ask of witnesses.
- Deciding how to impeach (i.e., contradict or attack the credibility of) opposing witnesses.
- Deciding what tangible or physical evidence to introduce.
- Deciding how to attack the tangible or physical evidence the other side will introduce.

The investigator should be familiar with the standard, formal fact-finding devices of depositions (p. 471), interrogatories (p. 471), requests for admissions (p. 348), medical examination reports (p. 471), etc. These devices are called discovery procedures. A deposition is a pretrial question-and-answer session conducted outside of court, usually in the office of one of the attorneys. The attorney asks questions of the other party (or of a witness of the other party) in order to obtain facts that will assist in preparing for trial. Depositions are often transcribed so that typed copies of the session are available. The same objective exists with the use of interrogatories, except that the questions and answers are usually submitted in writing rather than in person. An interrogatory is simply a question. A request for admission is a statement of fact submitted by one party to another. The latter is asked to admit or deny the statement. Those that are admitted do not have to be proven at trial. A medical examination is ordered by the judge when medical issues will be relevant to the trial.

If the investigator has done some preliminary field work before the pretrial discovery devices are used, what s/he uncovers can be of great help to the attorney in preparing to use these devices, e.g., in deciding what questions to ask in a deposition or in an interrogatory, in deciding what admissions to request, and in determining whether to ask for a medical examination.

After the discovery devices have been used, the investigator carefully studies all the facts obtained through these devices in order to:

- Cross-check or verify these facts.
- Look for new leads (names, addresses, incidents) that should be the subject of future investigation.

7. *It is important to distinguish between "absolute proof of a fact" and "some evidence of a fact."*

The investigator must not confuse his/her role with that of a judge or jury in deciding truth or falsity. The investigator's function is to identify reasonable options or fact possibilities. To be sure, s/he can speculate as to whether a judge or jury would ever believe a fact to be true. The danger of such speculation, however, is that it will be engaged in regularly at the expense of coming up with options. The tests that an investigator should apply in determining whether to pursue a fact possibility are:

- Am I reasonable in assuming that a particular fact will help establish the case of the client? Am I reasonable in assuming that if I gather enough evidence on such a fact that a judge, jury, or hearing officer *might* accept it as true?
- Am I reasonable in assuming that a particular fact will help to challenge or discredit the case of the opposing party? Am I reasonable in assuming that if I gather enough evidence on such a fact (i.e., that will challenge or discredit the case of the other side) that a judge, jury, or hearing officer *might* accept it as true?

The investigator should also approach the case from the perspective of the opponent, even to the point of assuming that s/he works for the other side! What facts will the opponent go after to establish its case? What is the likelihood that such facts will be accepted? Again, do not confuse proof with evidence.

8. *The investigator must know some law.*

The investigator does not have to be an expert in every area of the law or in any particular area of the law in order to perform his/her job. For field work to have a focus, however, the investigator must have at least a general understanding of evidence (p. 448), civil procedure (p. 364), and the areas of the law governing the facts of the client's case. S/he must know, for example, what "hearsay" and "relevance" mean; s/he must understand the basic steps in litigation (p. 465) in order to see where fact gathering can be used and how it is often used in different ways at different steps in the litigation process. If the action, for example, is a divorce proceeding, the investigator must know what the grounds for divorce are in the particular jurisdiction. The same kind of basic information is needed for every area of the law involved or potentially involved in the client's case. Such knowledge can be obtained:

- In paralegal course work or seminars.
- Through brief explanations from the supervisor.
- By talking to experienced lawyers and paralegals whenever they have time to provide their perspective on the law.
- By reading a chapter in a hornbook (p. 544) or a legal encyclopedia (p. 629) that provides an overview in a relevant area of the law.

9. *The investigator must know the territory.*

When the investigator is on the job, it will be important to begin acquiring a detailed knowledge on the makeup of the city, town, or state where s/he will be working. Such knowledge should include:

- The political structure of the area: Who is in power? Who is the opposition? In what direction is the political structure headed?
- The social and cultural structure of the area: Are there racial problems? Are there ethnic groupings that are diffuse or unified? Are there different value systems at play?
- Miscellaneous specific information: If you want something done at city hall, whom do you see? Does the director of a particular agency have any control over the staff? What agencies have "real" services available? What court clerk is most helpful?

It is usually very difficult for the investigator to acquire this knowledge in any way other than going out into the field and obtaining it by experience. Others can provide guidance, and often will. In the final analysis, however, you will probably discover that what others say is biased or incomplete. You must establish your own network of contacts and sources of information. First and foremost, you must establish your credibility in the community. People must get to know and trust you. Simply by announcing yourself as an investigator (or by presenting a printed card indicating title and affiliation), you will not find instant cooperation from the community. You must *earn* this cooperation. If you gain a reputation as arrogant, dishonest, opportunistic or insensitive, you will quickly find that few people will want to deal with you. An investigator could be in no worse predicament.

Often the best way to learn about an area and to begin establishing contacts is by being casual and unassuming. Have you ever noticed that insurance agents often spend three fourths of their time talking about the weather, sports, politics, the high cost of meat, etc., *before* coming to their sales pitch? Their approach is to relax you, to find out what interests you, to show you that they are human, and then they hit you with the benefits of buying their insurance. The investigator can learn from this approach not only in establishing contacts at agencies and in the community generally, but also in dealing with prospective witnesses on specific cases.

Section D. FACT ANALYSIS: ORGANIZING THE OPTIONS

The process of structuring or organizing the fact options may initially appear to be complex and cumbersome. The point to be remembered is that the process, once learned (and modified to suit particular needs), can become second nature to you once you understand it, try it out, evaluate it, and find it helpful. It is, of course, perfectly proper to adopt any other process that you find to be more effective. Whatever method is used, there is a great need to develop the *discipline* of fact analysis as soon as possible.

There are a number of fundamental characteristics of facts that should be understood:

- Events take place.
- Events mean different things to different people.
- Different people, therefore, have different versions of events.
- Inconsistent versions of the same event do not necessarily indicate fraud or lying.
- Although someone's version may claim to be the total picture, it may contain only a piece of the picture.
- When someone is giving a version of an event, s/he usually mixes statements of *why* the event occurred with statements of *what* occurred.
- Whenever it is claimed that an event has occurred in a certain way, one can logically expect that certain signs, indications, or traces (i.e., evidence) of the event can be found.

Given these truisms, the investigator should analyze the facts along the lines indicated in the chart on page 435.

It is not inconceivable for a single client's case to have hundreds of individual facts that are in dispute. Nor is it unlikely that facts will change, or that people's versions of facts will change in the middle of a case. As to each new or modified fact, the same comprehensive process of fact analysis must be applied.

Obtaining the different versions of a fact may be difficult. The differences may not be clear on the surface. Of course, every fact will not necessarily have different versions. It is recommended, however, that you assume there will be more than one version until you have demonstrated otherwise to yourself. Undoubtedly, you must do some probing in order to uncover the versions that exist. Better to do so now than to be confronted with a surprise version at trial or at an agency hearing.

FACT ANALYSIS IN INVESTIGATION

STARTING POINT:
All the facts you presently have on the case.
PROCEDURE:
• Arrange the facts chronologically. • Place a number before each individual fact that must be established in a legal proceeding, that might be in dispute.
STATE THE FOLLOWING VERSIONS OF EACH FACT:
VERSION I: The client's. VERSION II: The opponent's (as revealed or as assumed). VERSION III: A witness's. VERSION IV: A witness's. VERSION V: From your own deductions. VERSION VI: Any other reasonable version.
AS TO EACH VERSION:
• State precisely (with quotes if possible) what the version is. • State the evidence or indications that tend to support the version according to the person presenting the version. • State the evidence or indications that tend to contradict this version. • Determine how you will check out or verify whether the evidence or indications exist.

People will not always be willing to share their accounts or versions of facts with you. If you are not successful in convincing them (or in "manipulating" them) to tell their story, you may have to make some assumptions of what their story is *likely* to be and to check out these assumptions.

Section E. REAL vs. MANIPULATED VERSIONS OF FACTS: PUTTING WORDS INTO SOMEONE ELSE'S MOUTH

An investigator is not a mere newspaper reporter or a photographer who simply reports what s/he sees, hears, or otherwise experiences. You have a much more dynamic role. In a very significant sense, you sometimes have the power of "controlling" what someone else says about the facts. This can have negative and positive consequences.

At its worst, this can mean that you are not listening to the person or that you are asking questions in such a manner that you are putting words into the person's mouth. The primary technique that can bring about this result is the leading question (p. 422). A leading question is a pressure question, one that contains (or suggests) the answer in the statement of the question. For example, "You were in Baltimore at the time, isn't that correct?" "You earn over $200 a week?" "Would it be correct for me to say that when you drove up to the curb you didn't see the light?"

Questions can manipulate someone's answer by including a premise in the question that has yet to be established. It takes an astute person to say to such questions, "I can't answer your question (or it is invalid) because it assumes another fact that I haven't agreed to." In the following examples of questions and answers, the person responding to the question refuses to be trapped by the form of the question:

Q: *How much did it cost you to have your car repaired after the accident?*
A: *It's not my car and it wasn't an accident; your client deliberately ran into the car that I borrowed.*

Q: *Have you stopped beating your wife?*
A: *I never beat my wife!*

Q: *Can you tell me what you saw?*
A: *I didn't see anything; my brother was there and he told me what happened.*

The last leading question containing the unestablished premise can be highly detrimental. Suppose the question and answer went as follows:

Q: *Can you tell me what you saw?*
A: *The car was going about 70 mph.*

In fact, the person answering the question did not see this himself; his brother told him that a car was traveling at this speed. There are a number of reasons why this person may have failed to tell the investigator that he didn't see anything first-hand:

- Perhaps he didn't hear the word "saw" in the investigator's question.
- He may have wanted the investigator to think that he saw something himself; he may want to feel important by conveying the impression that he is special because he has special information.
- He may have felt that it was not significant enough to correct the investigator's false assumption; he may have thought that the investigator was more interested in *what* happened than in *who* saw what happened.

Whatever the reason, the investigator has carelessly put him/herself in the position of missing a potentially critical fact, namely that the person is only talking from hearsay (p. 451).

Another way to blur communication is by completely avoiding certain topics and concentrating on only selected ones. If you do not ask questions about certain matters, intentionally or otherwise, you are likely to end up with a distorted picture of what the person's version of the facts is. Suppose there was an automobile collision involving Smith and Jones. The investigator's office is representing Jones. The investigator finds a witness who says that she saw the accident. The investigator asks her to describe what she saw. The investigator fails, however, to ask her where she was at the time she saw the collision. In fact, she was sitting in a park over two blocks away and could see the collision only through some shrubbery. The investigator didn't ask questions to uncover this; it wasn't volunteered and, therefore, the investigator walks away with a potentially distorted picture of what light this individual can shed on what took place. This is the same damage that can occur by the use of questions that contain an unestablished premise.

In some instances, these techniques can have beneficial results. First of all, a leading question can help jar someone's memory so that they are better able to recall the facts. If, however, this individual is constantly in need of leading questions in order to remember, you have strong reason to suspect that the person knows little or nothing as opposed to being merely shy or inarticulate and in need of a push now and then.

Suppose that the witness being questioned is not cooperative or has a version of the facts that is damaging to the client of the investigator's office. It may be that the techniques described in this section as normally improper can be used to challenge a version of the facts. A leading question with an unestablished premise, for example, may catch an individual off guard and give the investigator reasonable cause to believe that the person is not telling the truth.

Suppose that the person being questioned is not hostile, but is neutral, or seemingly so. The way in which this individual is questioned may help him/her emphasize certain facts as opposed to others. Once the witness has committed him/herself to a version of the facts either completely on his/her own, or with some subtle help from the questioner, there is a chance that s/he will stick by this version because s/he does not want to appear to be vague, uncertain, or inconsistent later. An investigator who takes such a course of action, however, must be extremely careful. You are taking certain risks, not because your conduct is illegal or unethical, but because a witness who needs subtle pressuring in order to state a version of the facts in a certain way is probably going to be a weak witness at trial or at an agency hearing. On cross-examination, the witness may fall apart.

Section F. SOURCES OF EVIDENCE/SOURCES OF LEADS

Evidence is whatever tends to establish the existence or nonexistence of a fact. Evidence can be testimonial (what someone says) or physical (what can be seen or touched). Simply because something is evidence does not mean that it is *admissible* in court or in an agency proceeding. The confession of a defendant, for example, is clearly evidence, but it is inadmissible in criminal court if the police obtained it in such a way that it violated the defendant's privilege against self-incrimination (p. 454). A "lead" is simply a path to potentially admissible evidence. Of course, evidence is often its own lead to other evidence.

Here is a partial checklist containing some of the standard sources of evidence and leads at the disposal of the investigator. (The list is not presented in order of any priority.)

CHECKLIST ON THE STANDARD SOURCES OF EVIDENCE AND LEADS

1. Statements of the client.
2. Documents the client brings or can obtain.
3. Information that may be voluntarily or involuntarily provided by the attorney for the other side.

4. Information from attorneys involved with the case in the past.
5. Interrogatories, depositions, other discovery devices (p. 471); letters requesting information.
6. Pleadings (e.g., complaint) filed thus far in the case (p. 470).
7. Newspaper accounts, notices in the media requesting information.
8. General records of municipal, state and federal administrative agencies.
9. Business records (e.g., cancelled receipts).
10. Employment records.
11. Photographs.
12. Hospital records.
13. Informers or the "town gossip."
14. Surveillance of the scene.
15. Reports from the police and other law enforcement agencies.
16. Fingerprints.
17. School records.
18. Military records.
19. Use of alias.
20. Bureau of vital statistics and missing persons.
21. Court records.
22. Office of politicians.
23. Records of Better Business Bureaus and other consumer groups.
24. Telephone book.
25. Accounts of eyewitnesses.
26. Hearsay accounts.
27. Automobile registrar.
28. Object to be traced (e.g., auto).
29. Credit bureaus.
30. Reports of investigative agencies written in the past.
31. Resources of public library.
32. Associations (trade or otherwise).
33. Who's Who directories.
34. Insurance Company Clearing House.
35. Standard and Poor's Register of Directors and Executives.
36. Telling your problem to a more experienced investigator and asking for other leads.
37. "Shots in the dark."

Section G. GAINING ACCESS TO RECORDS

It is one thing to say that the investigator should check records for evidence and leads; it may be quite another to gain access to these records. There are four categories of records:

1. Those already in the possession of the client or of an individual willing to turn them over to you on request.
2. Those in the possession of a governmental agency or of a private organization and available to anyone in the public.
3. Those in the possession of a governmental agency or of a private organization and available only to the client or to the individual who is the subject of the records.
4. Those in the possession of a governmental agency or of a private organization and claimed to be confidential for everyone except in-house staff.

There should obviously be no difficulty in gaining access to the first category of records unless they have been misplaced or lost, in which event the person who once had possession would ask the source of the records to provide another copy. As to records in the latter three categories, the checklist below should provide some guidelines on gaining access.

GUIDELINES TO GAINING ACCESS TO RECORDS

1. Write, phone, or visit the organization and ask for the record directly.
2. Have the client write, phone, or visit and ask for it directly.
3. Draft a letter for the client to sign asking for it directly.
4. Have the client sign a form that states that s/he gives you authority to see any records that pertain to him/her and that s/he specifically waives any right to confidentiality that s/he has with respect to such records.
5. Find out if one of the opposing parties has it, and if so, ask them to send you a copy.
6. Find out if others have it (e.g., a relative of the client, a co-defendant in this or in a prior court case) and ask them if they will provide you with a copy.
7. For records available generally to the public, find out where these records are and go use them.
8. If you meet resistance (fourth category of records) make a basic fairness pitch to the organization as to why you need the records.
9. Find out (via legal research, p. 505) if there are any statutes, regulations, or cases that arguably provide the client with the right to access to the records, e.g., the Freedom of Information Act.
10. If the legal research looks even slightly promising, let the organization know that you are (or that your office is) in the process of establishing a legal basis to gain access to the records, and that the office is contemplating the initiation of litigation to finalize the right.
11. Solicit the intervention of a politician or of some other respectable and independent person in trying to gain access.
12. If the person who initially turns down the request for access is a line officer, appeal the decision formally or informally to his/her supervisor and on up the "chain of command" to the person with final authority (p. 776).

Section H. EVALUATING TESTIMONIAL AND PHYSICAL EVIDENCE

At all times, you must be making value judgments on the usefulness of the evidence that you come across. Again, the test is not whether the evidence would be absolute proof of the truth or falsity of a fact. As indicated earlier, there are a number of tests that should be applied:

- Is it relevant (p. 449); does it tend to prove or disprove any fact involved in the case?
- Is it worth pursuing either because it might be used in court or because it might be a lead to other evidence?
- Will it involve an inordinate amount of time and energy to pursue and, if so, is its potential worth minimal or substantial?

Generally speaking, the primary tests are *imagination* in coming up with options and *reasonableness* in carrying them out. There are a number of specific criteria that can be used to assist you in assessing the worth of what you have. The checklists below may be helpful in determining this worth.

CHECKLIST ON THE VALIDITY OF TESTIMONIAL EVIDENCE

CHECKLIST TO USE IF THE WITNESS IS SPEAKING FROM FIRST-HAND (EYEWITNESS) INFORMATION	CHECKLIST TO USE IF THE WITNESS IS SPEAKING FROM SECOND-HAND (HEARSAY) INFORMATION
• How long ago did it happen? • How good is the memory of this witness? • How far from the event was the witness at the time? • How good is the sight of the witness? • What time of day was it and would this affect vision? • What was the weather at the time and would this affect vision? • Was there a lot of commotion at the time and would this affect vision or ability to remember? • What was the witness doing immediately before the incident? • How old is the witness? • What was the last grade of school completed? • Employment background? • What is the reputation of the witness in the community for truthfulness? • Was the witness ever convicted of a crime or are any criminal charges now pending against him/her? • Is the witness an expert in anything? • What are the qualifications of the witness? • Is the witness related to, an employee of, or friendly with the other side in the litigation? Would it be to this person's benefit, in any way, to see the other side win? • Does any direct evidence exist to corroborate what this witness is saying? • Does any hearsay evidence exist to corroborate it? • Is the witness willing to sign a statement covering what s/he tells the investigator? Is s/he willing to say it in court? • Is the witness defensive when asked about what s/he knows?	• How well does the witness remember what was told to him/her by the other person (i.e., the declarant) or what the witness heard him/her say to someone else? • How is the witness sure that it is exact? • Is the declarant now available to confirm or deny this hearsay account of the witness? If not, why not? • Under what conditions did the declarant allegedly make the statement (e.g., was declarant ill)? • Is there other hearsay testimony that will help corroborate this hearsay? • Does any direct evidence exist to corroborate this hearsay? • How old is the witness? How old is the declarant? • What are the educational and employment backgrounds of both? • Is either of them related to, an employee of, or friendly with the other side in the litigation? Would it be to the benefit of either of them to see the other side win? • Is the witness willing to sign a statement covering what s/he tells the investigator? Is s/he willing to say it in court? • Is the witness defensive when asked about what s/he was told by the declarant or what s/he heard the declarant say to someone else? • Are there any inconsistencies in what the witness is saying? • How does the witness react when confronted with the inconsistencies? Defensively? • Are there any gaps in what the witness is saying? • Does the witness appear to exaggerate?

CHECKLIST ON THE VALIDITY OF
TESTIMONIAL EVIDENCE — Continued

CHECKLIST TO USE IF THE WITNESS IS SPEAKING FROM FIRST-HAND (EYEWITNESS) INFORMATION	CHECKLIST TO USE IF THE WITNESS IS SPEAKING FROM SECOND-HAND (HEARSAY) INFORMATION
• Are there any inconsistencies in what the witness is saying? • How does the witness react when confronted with the inconsistencies? Defensively? • Are there any gaps in what the witness is saying? • Does the witness appear to exaggerate? • Does the witness appear to be hiding or holding anything back?	• Does the witness appear to be hiding or holding anything back? • What is the reputation of the witness in the community for truthfulness?

CHECKLIST ON THE VALIDITY OF PHYSICAL (TANGIBLE) EVIDENCE

CHECKLIST FOR WRITTEN MATERIAL	CHECKLIST FOR NONWRITTEN MATERIAL
• Who wrote it? • Under what circumstances was it written? • Is the original available? If not, why not? • Is a copy available? • Who is available to testify that the copy is in fact an accurate copy of the original? • Is the author available to testify on what s/he wrote? If not, why not? • Is there any hearsay testimony available to corroborate the authenticity of the writing? • Is there any other physical evidence available to corroborate the authenticity of the writing? • What hearsay, direct evidence, or physical evidence is available to corroborate or contradict what is said in the writing (as opposed to who wrote it)? • Can you obtain sample handwriting specimens of the alleged author?	• Who found it and under what circumstances? • Where was it found? • Why would it be where it was found? Was it unusual to find it there? • Who is available to identify it? • What identifying characteristics does it have? • Who owns it? Who used it? • Who owned it in the past? Who used it in the past? • Who made it? • What is its purpose? • Does it require laboratory analysis? • Can you take it with you? • Can you photograph it? • Is it stolen? • Is there any public record available to trace its history? • What facts does it tend to establish? • Was it planted where it was found as a decoy?

Section I. INTERVIEWING WITNESSES

1. *Know what image you are projecting of yourself.*

In the minds of many people, an investigator is often involved in serious and dangerous undertakings. What reaction would you have if a stranger introduced him/herself to you as an "investigator"? Would you be guarded and suspicious? You may not want to call yourself an investigator at all. You may want to say "My name is _____, I work for (name of law office) and we are trying to get some information on _____." On the other hand, you may find that you are most effective when you are direct and straightforward. Can you think of different people who would respond more readily to certain images of investigators? The following is a partial list of some of the images that an investigator could be projecting by dress, mannerisms, approach, and language:

- A professional.
- Someone who is just doing a job.
- Someone who is emotionally involved in what s/he is doing.
- A neutral bystander.
- A friend.
- A manipulator or opportunist.
- A salesperson.
- A wise person.
- An innocent and shy person.

You must be aware of (a) your own need to project yourself in a certain way, (b) the way in which you think you are projecting yourself, (c) the way in which the person to whom you are talking perceives you, and (d) the effect that all this is having on what you are trying to accomplish.

2. *There are five kinds of witnesses: hostile, skeptical, friendly, disinterested or neutral, and a combination of the above.*

The hostile witness wants your client to lose; s/he will try to set up roadblocks in your way. The skeptical witness is not sure who you are or what you want in spite of your explanation of your role. S/he is guarded and unsure of whether s/he wants to become involved. The friendly witness wants your client to win and will cooperate fully. The disinterested or neutral witness doesn't care who wins. S/he has information that s/he will tell to anyone who asks.

If the hostile witness is the opposing party who has retained counsel, it is improper for the investigator to talk directly with this person without going through his/her counsel (p. 254). If the hostile witness is not a party but is closely associated with a party, you should check with your supervisor on how, if at all, to approach such a witness.

The fifth category of witnesses is probably the most common. Witnesses are seldom totally hostile, skeptical, friendly, or neutral. At different times during the investigation interview, and at different times throughout the various stages of the case, they may shift from one attitude to another. While it may be helpful to determine what general category a witness fits into, it would be more realistic to view any witness as an individual in a state of flux in terms of what s/he wants to say and what s/he is capable of saying.

3. *The investigator must have the trust of the witness.*

You have the sometimes difficult threshold problem of "sizing up" the witness from whom you are trying to obtain information. What are some of the states of mind that such a person could have:

- The witness may want to feel important.
- The witness may want to be "congratulated" for knowing anything, however insignificant, about the case.
- The witness may want absolute assurance from you that s/he won't get into trouble by talking to you. S/he shies away from talk of courts, lawyers, and law.
- The witness may be willing to talk only after you have given full assurance that you will never reveal the source of the information s/he will give you.
- The witness may be willing to talk to you only in the presence of his/her friends.
- If the witness knows your client, s/he may want to be told that you are trying to keep the client out of trouble.
- The witness may want the chance to meet you first and then have you go away in order to decide whether s/he wants to talk to you again.
- The witness may not be willing to talk to you until you fulfill some of his/her needs, e.g., listen to his/her troubles; act in a fatherly or motherly manner; play subtle, seductive games, etc.

In short, the investigator must gain the trust of the individual by assessing his/her needs and by knowing when s/he is ready to tell you what s/he knows. If you take out your notebook immediately upon introducing yourself, you are probably too insensitive to establish the communication that is needed.

4. *The investigator must assess how well the witness would do under direct and cross-examination.*

As the witness talks, you must be asking yourself a number of questions:

- Would the witness be willing to testify in court? Whatever the answer to this question is now, is this witness likely to change his/her mind later?
- Would the witness be effective on the witness stand?
- Does the witness know what s/he is talking about?
- Does the witness have a reputation for integrity, credibility, or truthfulness in the community?
- Is the witness defensive?
- Would the witness know how to say "I'm not sure" or "I don't understand the question," as opposed to giving an answer for the sake of giving an answer to avoid being embarrassed?

- When the witness talks, is s/he internally consistent?
- Does the witness know how to listen as well as talk?
- Does the witness understand the distinction between right and wrong, truth and lying?

Section J. SPECIAL INVESTIGATIVE PROBLEMS: SOME STARTING POINTS

JUDGMENT COLLECTION

A lawyer could win a money judgment in court, but have great difficulty collecting it later on. An investigator may be asked to assist the law firm in ascertaining the financial assets of a particular individual or corporation against whom the judgment was obtained.

One of the best starting points for such an investigation is government records. The following is a partial list of records available from the county clerk's or court office:

- Real property tax assessments.
- Personal property tax assessments.
- Filings made under the Uniform Commercial Code.
- Federal tax liens.
- Whether the individual or corporation has been plaintiff or defendant in prior litigation (p. 603).
- Whether the subject has inherited any property or money (determined by checking records of Surrogate's Court or whatever court in the jurisdiction handles inheritance and trust cases).

Such records could reveal a good deal of information on the financial status of the party under investigation.

For corporations, you should check the records of state and federal government agencies (e.g., Securities and Exchange Commission) with whom the corporation must file periodic reports or disclosures on its activities and finances. You should also check with people who have done business with the corporation (e.g., customers or other creditors) as well as with its competitors in the field. These records and contacts could provide good leads.

MISSING PERSONS

An investigator may be asked to locate a missing heir, a relative of a client, a person who needs to be served with process (p. 470) in connection with current litigation, etc. A missing person is generally not difficult to locate—unless this person does not want to be found. The first step is to send a registered letter to the person's last-known address, "return receipt requested," which requests the post office to send you back a notice of who accepted the letter. Other possible sources for leads:

- Former landlord, neighbors, mail carrier, local merchants in area of last-known address.

- Local credit bureau.
- Police department, hospitals.
- Relatives.
- References listed on employment applications.
- Naturalization certificate, marriage record, drivers license, car registration.
- Ad in the newspaper.

BACKGROUND INVESTIGATIONS

Below is a form used by a large investigative firm for its general background investigations on individuals. The first part of the form seeks information that goes to the identification of the subject. The antecedent data covers prior history.

BACKGROUND INVESTIGATIONS
IDENTIFICATION OF SUBJECT

1. Complete Name _____ Age _____ SS# _____ Marital Status _____

Wife's Name; Pertinent Info _____

_____

Children's Names and Ages _____

_____

_____

2. Current Residence Address and Type of Neighborhood _____

_____

_____

Own or Rent _____ Local Informants _____

_____

_____

_____

How Long at Present Address—Prior Residence Info _____

_____

_____

3. Business Affiliation and Address, Position, Type of Bus. _____

_____

_____

_____

ANTECEDENT HISTORY

1. Place & Date of Birth _____

Parents' Names & Occupations _____

_____

Where Did They Spend Their Youth? _____

_____

2. Education—Where, Which Schools, Dates of Attendance _____

_____

_____

Degree? What Kind? _____ Any Other Info Pertaining to Scholastic
Achievement, Extra Curric. Activities _____

_____

_____

_____

3. First Employer, to Present—F/T or P/T, Position or Title, Job Description, Exact Dates of Employment. Type of Company _____

_____

_____

_____

_____

_____

4. Relationship with Peers, Supervisors, Subordinates—Where Do His/Her
Abilities Lie? Any Outside Activities? Honesty, Trustworthiness, Integrity?
Does S/he Work Well Under Pressure? Anything Derogatory? If So, What Are
Details? Reasons for Leaving? Would They Rehire? Salaries? Health? Reputation? Reliability? Job Understanding? Willingness to Accept Responsibility? _____

_____

_____

_____

_____

_____

_____

_____

_____

If Self-Employed—What Was the Nature of the Business? With Whom Did
S/he Deal? Corp. Name? _____

Date & Place of Incorporation _____

Who Were Partners, If Any? _____

What % of Stock Did Subj. Own? _____ Was Business Successful? _____ What

Happened to it? _____

If Sold, to Whom?_____ Any Subsid.

or Affiliates? _____

_____

_____

5.   What Is His/Her Character or Personality Like? Did Informer Know

Him/Her Personally? _____

Hobbies? _____

Family Life? _____

Even Tempered? _____ Loner or Joiner? _____

Introverted, Extroverted? _____ Written or Oral Abilities? _____

Does Informer Know Anyone Else Who Knows Subj? _____

_____

6.   Credit _____

_____

7.   Litigation_____ Civil_____ Criminal_____ Bankruptcy_____

State _____ Federal _____ Local _____

_____

_____

8.   Banking-Financial: Bank _____

Types of Accounts—Average Bal. _____

How Long Did Subj. Have Accounts?_____ Any Company Accounts?

_____

Is S/he Personally Known to Officers of the Bank?___ Any Borrowing?___

Secured or Unsecured?_____ If Secured, by

What? Do They Have Financial Statement on the Subj.? _____

What Is His/Her Net Worth? _____ Other Assets? Real Estate _____

Stocks_____

Equity in His/Her Co., etc. _____

_____

ASSIGNMENT 66

Which of the following statements do you agree or disagree with? Why? For those statements that you are unsatisfied with, how would you modify them to reflect your own view?

1. Investigation is a separate profession.
2. There is a great difference between investigation conducted by the police and that conducted by a paralegal working for a law office.
3. An investigator is an advocate.

4. It is impossible for the investigator to keep from showing his/her own personal biases while in the field investigating.

5. There is often a need for a separate investigation to verify the work of another investigation.

6. A good investigator will probably be unable to describe why s/he is effective. There are too many intangibles involved.

7. It is a good idea for an investigator to specialize in one area of the law, e.g., automobile negligence cases.

8. If someone is willing to talk to and cooperate with an investigator, there is reason to suspect that this person is trying to manipulate the investigator.

Section K. EVIDENCE AND INVESTIGATION

There is a close relationship between investigation and the law of evidence. One of the aims of investigation is to uncover and verify facts that will eventually be *admissible* in court (p. 352). Admissibility is determined by the law of evidence. When attorneys are negotiating a case to reach a settlement in order to avoid a trial, they frequently talk (and argue) about the admissibility of the facts in the event that a trial does occur.

EVIDENCE IN GENERAL

- *Evidence* is that which tends to prove or disprove a fact.
- *Admissible evidence* is evidence that the judge will permit the jury to consider. Admissible evidence does not mean that the evidence is true. It simply means that there are no valid objections to keep the evidence out. The jury is free to conclude that it does not believe the evidence that the judge ruled admissible.
- *Direct evidence* is evidence (usually from personal observation or knowledge) that tends to establish a fact without the need for an inference.
- *Circumstantial evidence* is evidence of one fact from which another fact can be inferred.

Example: The police officer says, "I saw skid marks at the scene of the accident."
Direct evidence—that the police officer spoke these words
          —that skid marks were at the scene of the accident
Circumstantial evidence—that the driver of the car was speeding (this is the inference that can be drawn form the officer's statement)

Direct evidence that someone was speeding would include (1) an admission by that person that s/he was speeding, (2) radar results, (3) testimony of people who saw the car being driven, etc.

INVESTIGATION GUIDELINE

Direct evidence is preferred over circumstantial, although both kinds of evidence can be admissible. It is important that you identify the inference in the circumstantial evidence. Then try, if possible, to find direct evidence of what was inferred.

RELEVANCE

Relevant evidence is evidence that reasonably tends to make the existence of a fact more probable or less probable than it would be without that evidence. Relevancy is a very broad concept. It simply means that the evidence may be helpful in determining the truth or falsity of a fact involved in a trial. The test of relevancy is common sense and logic. If, for example, you want to know whether a walkway is dangerous, it is relevant that people have slipped on this walkway in the immediate past. Prior accidents under the same conditions make it more reasonable for someone to conclude that there is danger.

All relevant evidence is not necessarily admissible evidence. It would be highly relevant, for example, to know that the defendant told his/her attorney that s/he was driving 80 mph at the time of the accident, yet the attorney-client privilege (to be considered below) would make such a statement inadmissible. Also, relevant evidence is not necessarily conclusive evidence. The jury will usually be free to reject certain relevant evidence and accept other relevant evidence that is more believable. Relevancy is a *tendency* of evidence to establish or disestablish a fact. It may be a very weak tendency. Prior accidents may be relevant to show danger, but the jury may still conclude, in the light of all the evidence, that there was no danger.

INVESTIGATION GUIDELINE

Let common sense be your main guide in conducting investigations. Take a broad view of what you go after. So long as there is some logical connection between the fact you are pursuing and a fact that must be established at trial, you are on the right track.

ASSIGNMENT 67

Examine the following four situations. Discuss the relevance of each item of evidence being introduced.

1. Mrs. Phillips is being sued by a department store for the cost of a gas refrigerator. Mrs. Phillips claims that she never ordered and never received a refrigerator from the store. The attorney for Mrs. Phillips wants to introduce two letters: (a) a letter from Mrs. Phillips's landlord stating that her kitchen is not equipped to handle gas appliances and (b) a letter from another merchant stating that Mrs. Phillips bought an electric refrigerator from him a year ago.

2. Phil Smith has been charged with burglary in Detroit on December 16, 1986. His attorney tries to introduce testimony into evidence that on December 7, 8, 11, 15, and 22 the defendant was in Florida.
3. Al Neuman is suing Sam Snow for negligence in operating his motor vehicle. Al's attorney tries to introduce into evidence the fact that Snow currently has pending against him four other automobile negligence cases in other courts.
4. Jim is on trial for the rape of Sandra. Jim's attorney wants to introduce into evidence (a) the fact that Sandra subscribes to *Cosmopolitan* magazine, (b) the fact that Sandra is a member of AA, and (c) the fact that Sandra is the mother of Jim's child who was born three years ago when they were dating. They separated in bitterness five months after the birth and never married.

COMPETENCE OF WITNESSES

A witness is competent to testify if the witness:

- Understands the obligation to tell the truth.
- Has the ability to communicate.
- Has knowledge of the topic of his/her testimony.

A child or mentally ill person is not automatically disqualified. They are competent to testify if the judge is satisfied that the above criteria are met.

The competence of a witness must be carefully distinguished from the *credibility* of the witness. Credibility goes to the *weight* of the evidence. This weight is assessed by the trier of fact—usually the jury. Competence goes to whether that witness will be allowed to testify at all. The jury may decide that everything said by a competent witness is unworthy of belief.

OPINION EVIDENCE

An opinion is an inference from a fact. For example, after you watch George stagger down the street and smell alcohol on his breath, you come to the conclusion that he is drunk. The conclusion is the inference. The facts are the observation of staggering and the smelling of alcohol on his breath. Technically, a lay witness is not supposed to give opinion evidence. S/he must state the facts and let the trier of fact form the opinions. (Under certain circumstances, *expert* witnesses *are* allowed to give opinions, p. 351.) The difficulty with the lay opinion rule, however, is that it is sometimes difficult to express oneself without using opinions, e.g., it was a sunny day, the noise was loud. Courts, therefore, are lenient in permitting opinion testimony by lay witnesses when the witness is talking from his/her own observations and it would be awkward for the witness not to express the opinion. If people regularly use opinions when discussing the topic in question, it will be permitted.

> *INVESTIGATION GUIDELINE*
>
> Know when a person is stating an opinion. Even though an opinion may be admissible, you should assume that it will *not* be admissible. Pursue all the underlying facts that support or disprove the inference in the opinion. In the event that the person is not allowed to testify to the conclusion, be prepared with a list of the underlying facts upon which the person relied for the conclusion or inference.

ASSIGNMENT 68

Make a list of the questions that you would ask in order to uncover the underlying facts that formed the basis of the following opinions.

1. He was insane.
2. She couldn't see.
3. It was cold out.
4. He was traveling very fast.

HEARSAY

Hearsay evidence is oral or written testimony presented in court on a statement made by someone else out of court when the statement is being offered to show the truth of matters asserted therein, and thus its value is based on the credibility of the out-of-court asserter.[1] If evidence is hearsay, it is inadmissible unless one of the exceptions to the hearsay rule applies.

Example: A witness on the stand says, "Fred told me on the street that he was speeding." The attorney questioning this witness wants to prove that Fred was traveling 50 mph in a 30 mph zone.

Note the conditions for the presence of hearsay:

- Testimony in court: the witness is on the stand.
- Statement made out of court by someone else: the statement is by Fred and was made on the street, not in court; Fred is not on the stand.
- Assertion of the truth of the matter in the statement: the purpose of the attorney questioning this witness is to show that Fred was speeding, i.e., that the statement is true.
- The value of the statement depends on the credibility of the out-of-court asserter. Fred is the out-of-court asserter. The value of the statement depends upon how believable or credible *Fred* is.

If the statement is not offered to prove the truth of the matters asserted in the statement, it is not hearsay. Suppose, for example, that the attorney wants to prove that Fred was *alive* immediately after the accident—that death was not

---

[1] *McCormick's Handbook of the Law of Evidence,* 584 (Cleary, E., Editor, 1972).

instantaneous. The above statement would be admitted to prove that Fred actually said something, i.e., that Fred was alive long enough to make a statement. If the testimony of the witness is offered to prove simply that the words were spoken by Fred rather than to prove that Fred was speeding, then the statement is not hearsay. The testimony that "Fred told me on the street that he was speeding" would therefore be admissible. The jury would have to be cautioned to examine the testimony for the limited purpose for which it is offered and not to consider it evidence that Fred was speeding.

Conduct intended as a substitute for words can also be hearsay. For example, the witness is asked, "What did Fred say when you asked him if he was speeding?" The witness answers, "He nodded his head yes." This testimony is hearsay if it is offered to prove that Fred was speeding. Conduct—nodding the head—was intended as a substitute for words.

INVESTIGATION GUIDELINE

Know when hearsay exists so that you can try to find alternative, nonhearsay testimony to prove the truth of the assertations made in the hearsay.

ASSIGNMENT 69

Is hearsay evidence involved in the following situations? Examine the four conditions of hearsay in each.

1. Tom is suing Jim for negligence. On the witness stand, Tom says, "Jim was speeding at the time he hit me."
2. Tom is suing Jim for negligence. While Tom is on the stand, his lawyer introduces into evidence a mechanic's bill showing that the repair of the car cost $178.
3. Mary and George were passengers in Tom's car at the time of the collision with Jim. George testifies that just before the collision, Mary shouted, "Look out for that car going through the red light!"
4. He told me he was God.

ASSIGNMENT 70

Smith is being prosecuted for criminally assaulting Jones who later died. The following exchange occurs. How would you rule on the objection?

> Counsel for Smith: *Did you strike the decedent, Jones?*
> Smith: *Yes.*
> Counsel for Smith: *Did Jones say anything to you before you struck him?*
> Smith: *Yes, he told me that he was going to kill me.*

Prosecutor: *Objection, your honor, on the grounds of hearsay. Smith cannot give testimony on what the decedent said since the decedent is obviously not subject to cross-examination.*

There are a limited number of exceptions to the hearsay rule that have the effect of making evidence admissible even if it fulfills all the conditions of hearsay.

1. *Admissions*

An out-of-court statement made by a party to the litigation that is inconsistent with a position the party is taking in the litigation. Example: Tom is being sued for negligence in driving a car that resulted in a collision. After the accident, Tom told the victim that he was driving. (Before the trial, Tom died of unrelated causes.) At the trial, the attorney for Tom's estate is claiming that Tom was only a passenger in the car. The victim's testimony that Tom said he was driving is admissible hearsay since it is an admission by a party—Tom.

2. *Declaration Against Interest*

An out-of-court statement made by a nonparty (who is now unavailable) when the statement is against the interest of the nonparty. Example: Fred sues Bob for conversion of a car. Bob introduces a statement of Kevin, who is now dead, that he (Kevin) stole the car. The testimony is admissible hearsay since it is a declaration by Kevin, who is unavailable, that is against the interest of Kevin.

3. *Dying Declarations*

An out-of-court statement concerning the causes or circumstances of death when made by a person whose death is imminent. Example: Tom dies two minutes after he was hit over the head. Seconds before he died, he says, "Linda did it." Tom's statement is admissible hearsay since it is a dying declaration. Some courts limit this exception to the hearsay rule to criminal cases. Other states would allow it to be used in a civil case such as in a civil battery or wrongful death case against Linda.

4. *Business Entries*

An out-of-court statement found in business records made in the regular course of business by someone whose duty is to make such entries. (Applies also to records of non-businesses such as universities, government agencies, or associations.) Example: a party seeks to introduce into evidence a hospital report containing a description of the plaintiff's condition upon admission to the emergency room. The records were made by the supervising nurse who is not in court. The record containing the description of the plaintiff's condition is admissible hearsay as a business entry made in the regular course of business by someone whose duty is to make such a report (assuming that the supervising nurse has this duty).

5. *Spontaneous Declarations*

An out-of-court statement or utterance made spontaneously during or immediately after an exciting event by an observer of the event. Example: On the witness stand, Fred says, "I heard John say 'Oh my God, the truck just hit the child.'" This testimony is admissible hearsay as a spontaneous declaration.

6. *Declaration of Bodily Feelings, Symptoms, and Conditions*

An out-of-court statement or utterance made spontaneously about the person's present bodily condition. Example: On the witness stand, Carol says, "My husband told me he had a sharp pain in his stomach." This testimony is admissible hearsay as a declaration of present bodily condition.

7. *Declaration of Mental State of Mind*

An out-of-court statement made about the person's present state of mind. Example: On the witness stand, Len says, "The manager said she knew about the broken railing and would try to fix it." This testimony is admissible hearsay as a declaration of mental state of mind.

8. *Declaration of Present Sense Impression*

An out-of-court statement that describes an event while it is being observed by the person making the statement. Example: On the witness stand, Bill says, "As the car turned the corner, a bystander turned to me and said, 'she'll never make it.'" This testimony is admissible hearsay as a declaration of present sense impression.

NOTE: Exceptions 5–8 are referred to as the *res gestae* exceptions; the statements or utterances are closely connected or concurrent with an occurrence.

PRIVILEGE

A privilege in the law of evidence is the right to refuse to testify or the right to prevent someone else from testifying on a matter.

1. *Privilege Against Self-Incrimination*

An accused cannot be compelled to testify in a criminal proceeding nor to answer incriminating questions that directly or indirectly connect the accused to the commission of a crime.

2. *Attorney-Client Privilege*

A client can refuse to disclose any confidential communication with his/ her attorney that relates to legal services (p. 496). The client can also prevent the attorney from making such disclosures. Confidential simply means that the communication was made in private. The attorney cannot disclose the communication without the permission of the client.

3. *Doctor-Patient Privilege*

A patient can refuse to disclose any confidential (private) communication with his/her doctor that relates to the medical care. The patient can also prevent the doctor from making such disclosures. The doctor cannot disclose the communication without the permission of the patient.

4. *Clergy-Penitent Privilege*

A penitent can refuse to disclose any confidential (private) communication with his/her priest, minister, rabbi, or other member of the clergy that relates to spiritual counseling or consultation. The penitent can also prevent the member of the clergy from making such disclosure. The member of the clergy cannot disclose the communication without the permission of the penitent.

5. *Marital Communications*

One spouse can refuse to disclose confidential (private) communications made to the other spouse during the marriage. The spouse can also prevent the other spouse from making such disclosures. Both spouses must agree to the disclosure. This privilege does not apply to litigation between the spouses such as a divorce case.

6. *Government Information*

Some information collected by the government about citizens is confidential and privileged, e.g., adoption records, tax records. The privilege would not prevent use of the information to prosecute the citizen in connection with the citizen's duty to provide accurate information. It would, however, prevent third parties from gaining access to information that is meant to be kept confidential.

INVESTIGATION GUIDELINE

You must know what the privileges are in your state. When a privilege applies, look for alternative, nonprivileged sources of obtaining the information protected by the privilege.

BEST EVIDENCE RULE

To prove the contents of a private (nonofficial) writing, the original writing should be produced unless it is unavailable, e.g., because it was destroyed, through no fault of the person now seeking to introduce a copy of the original.

AUTHENTICATION

Authentication is evidence that a writing (or other physical item) is genuine and that it is what it purports to be, e.g., the testimony of witnesses who saw the document being prepared.

PAROL EVIDENCE RULE

Oral evidence cannot be introduced to alter or contradict the contents of a written document if the parties intended the written document to be a complete statement of the agreement.

Section L. TAKING A WITNESS STATEMENT

There are four major kinds of witness statements:

1. Handwritten statement.
2. Recorded statement in question-and-answer format, e.g., tape recorded.
3. A questionnaire that is mailed to the witness to answer.
4. A statement taken in question-and-answer format with a court reporter.

The most common kind of statement is the first, which we shall consider here.

In a handwritten statement, the investigator writes down what the witness says, or the witness writes out the statement him/herself. There is no formal structure to which all written statements should conform. The major requirements for the statement are clarity and accuracy.

The statement should begin by identifying (1) the witness (name, address, place of work, names of relatives, and other identifying data that may be helpful in locating the witness later), (2) the date and place of the taking of the statement, and (3) the name of the person to whom the statement is being made. For example:

Statement of John Wood

> I am John Wood. I am 42 years old and live at 3416 34th Street, N.W., Nashua, New Hampshire 03060. I work at the Deming Chemical Plant at region circle, Nashua. My home phone is 966-3954. My work phone is 297-9700 x301. I am married to Patricia Wood. We have two children, Jessica (fourteen years old) and Gabriel (eleven years old). I am making this statement to Rose Thompson, a paralegal at Fields, Smith & Farrell. This statement is being given on March 13, 1986 at my home, 3416 34th street NW.
>
> On February 15, 1986, I was standing on the corner of . . . .

Then comes the body of the statement in which the witness provides information about the event or circumstance in question, e.g., an accident that was observed, what the witness did and saw just before a fire, where the witness was on a certain date, etc. It is often useful to have the witness present the facts in a chronological order, particularly when many facts are involved in the statement. It is important that the witness give detailed facts in order to lend credibility to the statement, e.g., those facts demonstrating that the witness was in a good position to observe.

At the end of the statement, the witness should say that s/he is making the statement of his/her own free will without any pressure or coercion from anyone. The witness then signs the statement. The signature goes on the last page. Each of the other pages is also signed or initialed. If others have watched the witness make and sign the statement, they should also sign an attestation clause, which simply states that they observed the witness sign the statement.

Before the witness signs, s/he should read the entire statement and make any corrections that need to be made. Each correction should be initialed by the witness. Each page should be numbered with the total number of pages indicated each time. For example, if there are four pages, the page numbers would be "1 of 4," "2 of 4," "3 of 4," and "4 of 4." The investigator should not try to correct any spelling or grammatical mistakes made by the witness. The statement should exist exactly as the witness spoke or wrote it. Just before the signature of the witness at the end of the statement, the witness should say (in writing), "I have read all ____ pages of this statement and the facts within it are accurate to the best of my knowledge."

Investigators sometimes use various tricks of the trade to achieve a desired effect. For example:

- If the investigator is writing out the statement as the witness speaks, the investigator may *intentionally* make an error of fact. When the witness reads over the statement, the investigator makes sure that the witness catches the error and initials the correction. This becomes added evidence that the witness carefully read the statement. The witness might later try to claim that s/he did not read the statement. The initialed correction helps rebut this position.
- The investigator sees to it that some of the minor things the witness says in the statement are *un*favorable to the client of the investigator. This is to reinforce the point that the investigator acted impartially and without pressure on the witness.

Not all witness statements are eventually admitted into evidence at the trial. They may be admitted to help the attorney demonstrate that the witness is being inconsistent in his/her trial testimony and what s/he said before the trial. The main value of witness statements is thoroughness and accuracy in case preparation. Trials sometimes occur years after the events that led to the litigation. Witnesses may disappear or forget. Witness statements taken soon after the event can sometimes be helpful in tracking down witnesses and in helping them recall the details of the event.

ASSIGNMENT 71

Select any member of the class and take a witness statement from him/her. The statement should concern some accident in which the witness was a participant and/or an observer. The witness, however, should not be a party to any litigation growing out of the accident. You write out the statement from what the witness says in response to your questions. Do not submit a statement handwritten by the witness except for his/her signature, initials, etc. Assume that you (the investigator-paralegal) work for the law firm of Davis and Davis, which represents someone else involved in the accident.

Section M. THE SETTLEMENT WORK-UP

One of the end products of investigation is the "settlement work-up," which is a summary of the major facts in the case obtained through investigation, client interviewing, answers to interrogatories, deposition testimony, etc. The work-up, in one form or another, is used in negotiation with the other side or with the other side's liability insurance company in an effort to obtain a favorable settlement in lieu of trial.

The following is a sample settlement work-up involving the kind and extent of injury.[2] Note its precision and attention to detail. Excellent FP (Fact Particularization, p. 391) had to be used as the basis of this report.

INTEROFFICE MEMORANDUM

TO: Mary Jones, Esq.
FROM: Katherine Webb, Paralegal
DATE: June 12, 1975
RE: Joseph Smith vs. Dan Lamb et al.
    Case Summary—Settlement Work-up

I. FACTS OF ACCIDENT:

The accident occurred on September 6, 1973, in Orange, California. Joseph Smith was driving westbound on Chapman Avenue, stopped to make a left turn into a parking lot, and was rear-ended by the one-half ton panel truck driven by Dan Lamb.

The defendant driver, Mr. Lamb, was cited for violation of Vehicle Code Sections 21703 and 22350, following too close and unsafe speed for conditions.

II. INJURIES:

Severe cervical and lumbar sprain, superimposed over pre-existing albeit asymptomatic spondylolisthesis of pars interarticulus at L5-S1, with possi-

---

[2] Prepared by Katherine Webb, Legal Assistant at Cartwright, Sucherman, Slobodin & Fowler, Inc., San Francisco, California.

ble herniated nucleus pulposus either at or about the level of the spondylolisthesis; and contusion of right knee.

Please see attached medical reports for further details.

III. MEDICAL TREATMENT:

Mr. Smith felt an almost immediate onset of pain in his head, neck, back, and right knee after the accident, and believes that he may have lost consciousness momentarily. He was assisted from his car and taken by ambulance to the St. Joseph Hospital emergency room, where he was initially seen by his regular internist, Raymond Ross, M.D.

Dr. Ross obtained orthopedic consultation with Brian A. Ewald, M.D., who reviewed the multiple X-rays taken in the emergency room and found them negative for fracture. Lumbar spine X-rays did reveal evidence of a spondylolisthesis defect at the pars interarticulus of L5, but this was not felt to represent acute injury. Dr. Ewald had Mr. Smith admitted to St. Joseph Hospital on the same day for further evaluation and observation.

Upon admission to the hospital, Mr. Smith was placed on complete bed rest, with a cervical collar and medication for pain. On September 10, neurological consultation was obtained with Michael H. Sukoff, M.D., who, although he did not find any significant objective neurological abnormality, felt that there might be a herniated disc at L4-L5, with possible contusion of the nerve roots.

Drs. Ewald and Sukoff followed Mr. Smith's progress throughout the remainder of his hospitalization. He was continued on bed rest, physiotherapy, and medication, and fitted with a lumbosacral support. He was ultimately ambulated with crutches, and was discharged from the hospital on September 25, 1973, with instructions to continue to rest and wear his cervical collar and back brace.

Upon discharge from the hospital, Mr. Smith was taken by ambulance to the Sky Palm Motel in Orange, where his wife and children had been staying during his hospitalization. Arrangements were made for home physiotherapy and rental of a hospital bed, and Mr. Smith was taken by ambulance on the following day to his residence at the Riviera Country Club in Pacific Palisades.

After returning home, Mr. Smith continued to suffer from headaches, neck pain, and severe pain in his lower back, with some radiation into both legs, especially the right. He was totally confined to bed for at least two months following the accident, where he was cared for by his wife. Daily physical therapy was administered by Beatrice Tasker, R.P.T.

Mr. Smith continued to receive periodic outpatient care with Dr. Ewald. By the end of December, 1973, Mr. Smith was able to discontinue the use of his cervical collar and was able to walk, with difficulty, without crutches. At the time of his office visit with Dr. Ewald on December 21, he was noted to be having moderate neck discomfort, with increasingly severe low back pain. At the time, Dr. Ewald placed Mr. Smith on a gradually increasing set of Williams exercises, and advised him to begin swimming as much as possible.

Mr. Smith continued to be followed periodically by Dr. Ewald through March, 1974, with gradual improvement noted. However, Mr. Smith continued to spend the majority of his time confined to his home, and often to bed, using a cane whenever he went out. In addition, he suffered periodic severe flareups of low back pain, which would render him totally disabled, and would necessitate total bed rest for several days at a time.

During this period of time, Mr. Smith also experienced headaches and blurred vision, for which Dr. Ewald referred him to Robert N. Dunphy, M.D. Dr. Dunphy advised that the symptoms were probably secondary to his other injuries, and would most likely subside with time.

On April 1, 1974, Mr. Smith consulted Dr. Ewald with complaints of increased back pain following an automobile ride to San Diego. Dr. Ewald's examination at that time revealed bilateral lumbar muscle spasm, with markedly decreased range of motion. Due to his concern about the extremely prolonged lumbar symptoms, and suspecting a possible central herniated nucleus pulposus, Dr. Ewald recommended that Mr. Smith undergo lumbar myelography. This was performed on an inpatient basis at St. Joseph Hospital on April 4, 1974, and reported to be within normal limits.

Mr. Smith continued conservative treatment with Dr. Ewald through February, 1974, following the prescribed program of rest, medication, exercise, and daily physiotherapy administered by his wife. He was able to graduate out of his lumbosacral support by approximately October, 1974, resuming use of the garment when he experienced severe flareups of low back pain.

In his medical report dated January 2, 1975, Dr. Ewald stated that he expected a gradual resolution of lumbar symptomatology with time. However, in his subsequent report dated January 10, 1975, Dr. Ewald noted that since his original report, Mr. Smith had suffered multiple repetitive episodes of low back pain, secondary to almost any increase of activity. At an office visit on February 25, Mr. Smith was reported to have localized his discomfort extremely well to the L5-S1 level, and range of motion was found to have decreased to approximately 75%. Since his examination in February, Dr. Ewald has discussed at length with both Mr. Smith and his wife the possibility of surgical intervention, consisting of lumbar stabilization (fusion) at the L5-S1 level, secondary to the spondylolisthesis present at that level. Dr. Ewald has advised them of the risks, complications, and alternatives with regard to consideration of surgical stabilization, noting that surgery would be followed by a 6 to 9 month period of rehabilitation, and further warning that even if the surgical procedure is carried out, there is no guarantee that Mr. Smith will be alleviated of all of his symptomatology.

As stated in Dr. Ewald's medical report dated March 10, 1975, Mr. Smith is himself beginning to lean toward definite consideration with regard to surgery, although he is presently continuing with conservative management.

Dr. Ewald recommends that in the event Mr. Smith does choose to undergo surgery, a repeat myelogram should be performed in order to rule out, as much as possible, the presence of a herniated nucleus pulposus either above or at the level of the spondylolisthesis.

IV. RESIDUAL COMPLAINTS:

Mr. Smith states that his neck injury has now largely resolved, although he does experience occasional neck pain and headaches. However, he continues to suffer from constant, severe pain in his low back, with some radiation of pain and numbness in the right leg.

Mr. Smith notes that his low back pain is worse with cold weather, and aggravated by prolonged sitting, walking, driving, or nearly any form of activity. He finds that he must rest frequently, and continues to follow a daily regime of swimming, Williams exercises, pain medication, and physiotherapy administered by his wife. He has also resumed the use of his lumbosacral brace.

Mr. Smith was an extremely active person prior to the accident, accustomed to working 12 to 16 hours per day and engaging in active sports such as tennis. Since the accident, he has had to sell his business and restrict all activities to a minimum, since he has found that any increase in activity will trigger a flareup of low back pain so severe that he is totally incapacitated for several days at a time.

As stated by Dr. Ewald, Mr. Smith is now seriously considering the possibility of surgical stabilization, despite the risks and complications involved. He has always viewed surgery as a last resort, but is now beginning to realize that it may be his only alternative in view of his prolonged pain and disability. However, he currently intends to delay any definite decision until after the summer, during which time he intends to increase his swimming activity and see if he can gain any relief from his symptomatology.

V. SPECIALS

(Copies of supporting documentation attached hereto.)
A. MEDICAL:
1. Southland Ambulance Service
   (9/6/73) ....$ 37.00
2. St. Joseph Hospital
   (9/6–9/25/73) 2,046.29
3. Raymond R. Ross, M.D.
   (Emergency Room, 9/6/73)...................   25.00
4. Brian A. Ewald, M.D.
   (9/6/73–4/28/75) 604.00
5. Michael H. Sukoff, M.D.
   (9/10–9/22/75) 140.00
6. Wind Ambulance Service
   (9/25/73) 39.50
7. Wind Ambulance Service
   (9/26/73) 89.00

   8. Beatrice Tasker, R.P.T.
     (9/21–10/22/73) 825.00
   9. Abbey Rents (Rental of hospital bed and trapeze bar,
     9/25–11/25/73) 222.00
  10. Allied Medical & Surgical Co.
     (Purchase of cane, 1/10/73) 10.45
  11. Rice Clinical Laboratories
     (2/1/74) 4.00
  12. Robert N. Dunphy, M.D.
     (2/1–4/15/74) 95.00
  13. St. Joseph Hospital
     (X-rays and lab tests, 2/9/74) 156.00
  14. St. Joseph Hospital
     (Inpatient myelography, 4/23–4/24/74) 251.60
  15. Medication 357.70
     TOTAL MEDICAL EXPENSES .... $ 4,902.54

B. MISCELLANEOUS FAMILY EXPENSES
(During plaintiff's hospitalization, 9/6–9/25/75.)
   1. Sky Palm Motel
     (Lodging for wife and children) .... $ 1,050.50
   2. Taxicab (9/6/73) 2.45
     TOTAL MISCELLANEOUS EXPENSES......... $ 1,052.95

C. WAGE LOSS:

At the time of the accident, Mr. Smith was employed as president and co-owner, with Mr. George Frost, of the Inter Science Institute, Inc., a medical laboratory in Los Angeles. As stated in the attached verification from Mr. Mamikunian, Mr. Smith was earning an annual salary of $48,000.00, plus automobile, expenses, and fringe benefits.

In a telephone conversation with Mr. Frost on May 6, 1975, he advised me that the Inter Science Institute had grossed $512,000.00 in 1973, and $700,000.00 in 1974. He further confirmed that prior to the accident of September 6, 1973, both he and Mr. Frost had been approached on at least two to three different occasions by companies, including Revlon and a Canadian firm, offering substantial sums of money for purchase of the business. On the basis of the foregoing, both Mr. Smith and Mr. Frost place a conservative estimate of the value of the business at $2,000,000.00.

Due to injuries sustained in the subject accident, Mr. Smith was unable to return to work or perform the necessary executive and managerial functions required in his position as president and part owner of the business. As a result, on or about October 26, 1973, while still totally incapacitated by his injuries, Mr. Smith was forced to sell his 50% stock interest in the Inter Science Institute for a total sum of $300,000.00.

On the basis of the prior estimated value of the business at $2,000,000.00, *Mr. Smith sustained a loss of $700,000.00 in the sale* *of his one-half interest in Inter Science Institute, Inc., in addition to the loss of an annual salary of $48,000.00, plus automobile, expenses, and fringe benefits.*

Even if one were to assume that the sale of his interest in the business was reasonable value, Mr. Smith has sustained a loss in salary only in the sum of *$84,000.00* to date, based on an annual salary of $48,000.00 for one year and 9 months up to today's date, June 12, 1975.

References

A *Citizen's Guide on How to Use the Freedom of Information Act.* Superintendent of Documents, U.S. Government Printing Office, Washington, D.C. 20402.

W. Batko, *How to Research Your Local Bank (or Savings and Loan).* Institute for Local Self-Reliance, Washington, D.C., 1976.

Burtt & Gaskill, *Suggestibility and the Form of the Question,* 16 Journal of Applied Psychology 315 (1932).

H. Freeman, & H. Weihofen, "Interrogating," in *Clinical Law Training, Interviewing and Counseling:* Text and Cases, pp. 30ff. (1972).

Gardner, *The Perception and Memory of Witnesses,* 18 Cornell Law Quarterly 391 (1933).

Kittredge, *Guideposts for the Investigation of a Negligence Case,* 19 Practical Lawyer 55 (No. 5, May 1973).

Kubie, *Implications for Legal Procedure of the Fallibility of Human Memory,* 108 University of Penn. Law Review 59 (1959).

Marshall, Marquis & Oskamp, *Effects of Kinds of Questions and Atmosphere of Interrogation on Accuracy and Completeness of Testimony,* 89 Harvard Law Review 1620 (1971).

Open the Books: How to Research a Corporation, Urban Planning Aid, 1974. Distributed by the Midwest Academy, 600 W. Fullerton, Chicago, IL 60614.

S. Payne, *The Art of Asking Questions* (1951).

People Before Property: Guide to Real Estate Research, Urban Planning Aid, 1972. Distributed by the Midwest Academy.

Rokes, *Psychological Factors Governing the Credibility of Witnesses,* 1968 Insurance Law Journal 84.

W. Statsky, "Advocacy and Investigation," in *Teaching Advocacy: Learner-Focused Training for Paralegals,* pp. 59–66 (National Paralegal Institute, 1973).

10

Litigation Assistantship

Section A. STAGES OF LITIGATION

Litigation is the process of resolving controversy through the courts and/or through the quasi-judicial proceedings of administrative agencies. *Civil* litigation involves conflict between one person and another or between the government and a person when a crime is not at issue. *Criminal* litigation involves a government's attempt to prove that a person is guilty of a crime.

"Quasi" means "like" or "similar to." The word "judicial" refers to the operation of the courts. An agency proceeding that is "quasi-judicial" is one in which the agency is acting like or similar to a court such as through its administrative hearings. While the word litigation is sometimes meant to refer only to court proceedings, the interplay between courts and agencies is often so strong that the word is used here to include the quasi-judicial dispute settlement mechanisms of agencies.

Litigation is activated only when a conflict is brought to the attention of a government official or agency. Many, if not most, of these conflicts are never brought into the open in this way. For example, take the case of a neighbor chopping down her tree which falls onto someone else's property. A civil suit (e.g., trespass) would certainly be possible on these facts. The neighbors, however, may decide between themselves to settle the matter, e.g., the neighbor who did the tree cutting may remove the tree from her neighbor's yard and repair any damage. The courts never become involved. An employee is caught stealing a small amount of money. The employer may decide to "let him go" without calling in the police. He may be reprimanded or discharged after making restitution (e.g., returning the money taken). The prosecutor or district attorney never hears about the case. A vast number of civil cases and a good number of criminal cases are resolved in this fashion; they are never litigated.

Litigation can have five stages: agency, pretrial, trial, appeal, and enforcement. After an examination of these stages, we will cover the role of the paralegal at each stage.

1. AGENCY STAGE (see Chart 1)

a. Criminal Cases

Before the criminal courts become involved in a case, the police department or the district attorney's office has usually taken some action. (The police department and the district attorney's office are administrative agencies.) Unless a citizen is making the arrest, the decision to arrest is made by the police. The initial decision on whether to prosecute (i.e., to proceed with the litigation) is made by the district attorney. The police do not arrest everyone whom they suspect of committing a crime, nor does the district attorney prosecute everyone arrested. Both have considerable discretion with respect to the arrest and prosecution decisions. The suspect (alone or through counsel) may sometimes try to bring certain facts to the attention of the police or district attorney in order to influence their decisions on whether to arrest or prosecute.

b. Civil Cases

There may be no agency in existence, with authority or jurisdiction over the dispute. An automobile accident or a divorce case, for example, normally does not involve an administrative agency; such cases go directly to the courts if the parties have not resolved the conflict among themselves informally.

Other civil cases *do* involve agencies, e.g., suspension of drivers license (Department of Motor Vehicles), tax claim (Internal Revenue Service), stock

CHART 1
STAGES OF LITIGATION: AGENCY

CIVIL	CRIMINAL
a) The client or his/her representative may try to contact agency officials to resolve the conflict informally.	a) The individual or his/her attorney may try to influence the exercise of the police's discretion on whether to arrest.
b) Recourse may be made to upper echelon officials at the agency to resolve the conflict informally.	b) The individual or his/her attorney may try to influence the exercise of the district attorney's discretion on whether to prosecute.
c) A formal agency hearing may be held in which witnesses are sworn, testimony taken on direct and cross-examination, documents submitted into evidence, etc.	
d) If possible, a re-hearing may be requested.	
e) An appeal may be available within the agency to the person or entity with the power to make the final decision.	

issue (Securities and Exchange Commission), welfare claim (Department of Social Services). Disputes involving such matters may eventually find their way into the courts, but under the doctrine of the *exhaustion of administrative remedies,* the parties normally must go through the procedures set up by the agency to try to resolve the dispute within the agency *before* taking it to the courts. After exhausting (going through all) administrative remedies (procedures designed to resolve conflict), if a party is still dissatisfied with the decision of the agency, it can take the case to the courts.

Of course, the dispute might be resolved informally at the agency. An agency employee, for example, may be available on the phone, through the mail, or in person to listen to the side of the client. Many disputes are resolved at this level. Misunderstandings are cleared up, missing facts are provided, etc. Many times the client is representing him/herself at this stage. If still dissatisfied with the agency decision, the client may seek the assistance of counsel or other representative. The client or representative may go back to the individual who made the initial decision and try to have it changed. If unsuccessful, the client or representative may go up the "chain of command" (p. 776) to the supervisor in a further effort to resolve the matter informally.

If the informal channels prove unfruitful, recourse may be made to the quasi-judicial hearing procedures of the agency. The agency may have a hearing process in which evidence is presented, witnesses sworn, etc. in a fashion similar to a court hearing or trial. A hearing officer, referee, or administrative law judge will then make a decision. If the party is dissatisfied with the decision, s/he may be able to petition for a re-hearing before the same official. Finally, an appeal process may be available within the agency to another body or to the director of the agency who may have the power to overrule any decision made. Once all these routes have been exhausted, the individual will be able to take the case to court if still dissatisfied.

Some agencies do not have formal quasi-judicial tribunals in this manner. To exhaust administrative remedies in such agencies simply means to go through whatever informal routes are available in order to give the agency a chance to resolve the matter.

2. PRETRIAL (see Chart 2)

a. Criminal Cases

Different jurisdictions often have different pretrial criminal procedures. The process described here is typical of many states. Once an individual is arrested, the prosecutor must act quickly in deciding whether to prosecute since the individual has a right to be brought before a magistrate[1] soon after the arrest. Delay sometimes occurs, however, in bringing the accused before the magistrate due to the time taken by the police to complete its investigation. At the *initial appearance,* the magistrate notifies the accused of the charge or complaint. A decision is then made on what to do with the accused until the next court proceeding. Two options are available:

1. The accused can be released on his/her "personal recognizance" without having to post bail.
2. The accused can be released only if bail is posted. Bail is a sum of money paid into court that is forfeited if the accused fails to appear at scheduled court proceedings. Normally, the accused will have a bondsman post bail for which the accused pays the bondsman a nonreturnable fee. In some states, the court will allow the accused to pay into court only a designated percentage of the total bail imposed.

The accused is also notified of his/her right to remain silent, to hire an attorney, or, in serious cases, to have an attorney assigned free of charge if s/he is indigent.

Many cases never go beyond this stage. A majority of defendants plead guilty immediately.

At the initial appearance in misdemeanor[2] or felony[3] cases, the magistrate sets a date for the preliminary examination. The purpose of this *preliminary hearing* is to permit the court to decide whether there is sufficient evidence of guilt to justify a trial. Careful analysis of the evidence is a rarity, however, at this hearing. Its primary value to the accused is the opportunity to discover or learn more about the evidence that the prosecutor might later attempt to establish at trial. This can be invaluable to defense counsel in preparing for trial.

A common occurrence during the preliminary hearing (although not limited to this stage) is *plea bargaining.* Suppose that the accused has been charged with burglary and assault. In a bargaining session, s/he may "agree" to plead

[1] The word magistrate can have a number of different meanings. Here, it refers to a lower court official who may or may not be a lawyer. His/her primary function is to conduct the initial court proceedings.

[2] A crime punishable by a sentence of less than a year.

[3] A crime punishable by a sentence of a year or more.

guilty to one of the charges if the other is dropped. A great number of criminal cases never go to trial because of the bargained convictions that are obtained in this way.

In about half the states (mainly in the West) the preliminary hearing is the last screening stage before trial. In the other states and in the federal system, the *grand jury* can enter the picture before trial, usually in felony cases. The grand jury process is similar to the preliminary hearing in that a decision is made on whether sufficient evidence exists to hold the accused over for trial. Its decision to prosecute comes in the form of an *indictment*.

The next step is the *arraignment*. The accused is formally given the opportunity to plead to the charges at the arraignment. The usual pleas are guilty, not guilty, or "nolo contendere" ("no contest"). The latter is not an admission of guilt but a statement that the accused will not dispute the charge. It has the same effect, however, as a conviction. If the defendant pleads not guilty, a date for trial is set. During this stage, there again is often considerable discussion of plea-bargaining deals.

Throughout this process, but particularly toward the end as the trial date approaches, the defendant's attorney often makes motions or petitions that are requests to the court that certain things be done. For example, a motion for discovery is a request that the court order the prosecutor to provide the defendant with certain information concerning the case. A motion to suppress is a request that the court refuse to permit the prosecutor to use certain evidence.

If the accused has requested a jury trial, a "voir dire" proceeding is held before the judge in which the prospective jurors are interviewed by the attorneys, by the judge, or by both, for selection to the jury on that case.

b. Civil Cases

The procedures governing civil litigation can vary extensively from state to state—usually much more so than with criminal litigation. What is presented here are the procedures that generally are followed.

The first concern in bringing civil litigation is jurisdiction. The court must have *subject-matter jurisdiction* or the power to hear the kind of case being brought. A tax court, for example, has no subject-matter jurisdiction over granting divorces. So, too, federal courts have limited subject-matter jurisdiction. For example, a federal court can take the case if (1) the dispute arises under the U.S. Constitution or a statute of Congress or (2) the dispute is between citizens of different states—called diversity of citizenship—and the amount in controversy exceeds a certain amount.

In most cases, there must also be *personal jurisdiction* over the defendant, referred to as *in personam jurisdiction*. Such jurisdiction enables the court to require the defendant personally to satisfy a judgment out of any reachable assets of the defendant whether or not they are directly involved in the dispute. For example, a defendant who has been found liable for negligence in a car accident must pay the judgment out of personal assets s/he may have, e.g., wages, savings account, land.

There are statutory and constitutional requirements that must be met before a court can acquire personal jurisdiction over a defendant. The statutory requirements include service of the summons and complaint (explained below) on the defendant in a designated manner. The constitutional requirements include giving adequate notice of the litigation to the defendant and ensuring that the defendant has sufficient minimum contacts with the state where the suit is brought.

Sometimes a court that cannot obtain personal jurisdiction over a defendant can still hear the case. *In rem jurisdiction* is the power of the court to resolve a controversy involving a specific property or status, e.g., a dispute involving the ownership of land that is physically in the state. *Quasi in rem jurisdiction* is the power of the court to resolve a claim against the defendant, with the judgment being satisfied only out of property or assets that the defendant has in the state. The court's power is over the defendant's interest in the property or assets.

Venue is a separate topic from jurisdiction. Venue is the place of the trial. More than one court within the same judicial system (p. 563) may have the right kind of jurisdiction to hear a case. Choice of venue refers to the selection of one among several courts that have jurisdiction. There are different requirements for venue selection, e.g., the residence of the parties to the dispute.

To commence civil litigation, the plaintiff files a *complaint* that presents the main facts that s/he alleges against the defendant. Pleadings are the formal papers filed by plaintiffs and defendants containing their positions on the disputes in litigation. The complaint is the plaintiff's first pleading. It is filed with the clerk of the court who then issues a *summons* (p. 471), which is a notice to the defendant that a civil suit (called an action) has been filed and that unless the defendant answers the complaint within a designated time, s/he will lose the case by default. The plaintiff has this summons plus a copy of the complaint "served" on the defendant. To be served means to be handed something in person, although in special circumstances service may be made in other ways, e.g., through the mail or a notice in a newspaper. The person who completes this service on the defendant then files with the clerk of the court an "affidavit of service" (p. 472) in which s/he swears that service has been made.

The defendant must then file an answer in order to avoid a default judgment. S/he may take a number of positions in the answer. For example:

1. *Demurrer:* A statement that even if all of the facts alleged in the plaintiff's complaint are true, the law governing those facts would not permit the plaintiff to win anything. In other words, the defendant is saying that the plaintiff has not stated a "cause of action," or has failed to state a claim upon which relief can be granted (p. 345).
2. *Admissions and Denials:* When the defendant reads the facts alleged to be true by the plaintiff in the complaint, the defendant may decide to admit the truth of some of the facts and deny the truth of others.
3. *Counterclaim:* The defendant may feel that s/he has his/her own cause of action against the plaintiff. If so, the counterclaim alleges the facts that state a cause of action against the plaintiff.

If there is more than one defendant in the case, a *cross-claim* might be filed, which is a claim made by one co-defendant against another. If the defendant wishes to bring in someone who is not currently a party in the litigation, the defendant will file a *third-party complaint* alleging that this third party may be liable for all or part of the damages that the plaintiff might win from the defendant.

Once the plaintiff receives the answer of the defendant, s/he usually files a *reply* stating his/her position with respect to what the defendant said in the answer.

The next major stage is discovery. Discovery procedures are used to permit the parties to obtain more facts from each other in order to prepare more effectively for trial. *Interrogatories* are written questions addressed to a party in which information pertaining to the claims in litigation is sought. A more formal way in which greater factual detail is obtained is through a *bill of particulars.* A *deposition* is a question-and-answer session before trial and outside the courtroom (usually in the office of one of the attorneys). A party or witness (called the deponent) is questioned during this session by counsel with the objective of discovering facts for purposes of preparation. Other discovery devices include a *request for admissions* (asking the other side to admit certain facts as true so that they do not have to be proven at trial), a *request for production and inspection of documents and things,* and a request that the plaintiff undergo a *physical or mental examination.* The only discovery device requiring court approval is the physical or mental examination.

Figure 1. Summons.

Name of Court

A.B.,
                    Plaintiff,
          —vs—   NO. _____
C.D.,
                    Defendant.
                              SUMMONS

THE STATE OF _____
To All and Singular the Sheriffs of the State:
    YOU ARE COMMANDED to serve this summons and a copy of the complaint or petition in this action on defendant _____.
    Each defendant is required to serve written defenses to the complaint or petition on _____, plaintiff's attorney, whose address is _____, within 20 days after service of this summons on that defendant, exclusive of the day of service, and to file the original of the defenses with the clerk of this court either before service on plaintiff's attorney or immediately thereafter. If a defendant fails to do so, a default will be entered against that defendant for the relief demanded in the complaint or petition.
    WITNESS my hand and the seal of this court on _____, 19___.

                                                    (Name of Clerk)
                                                    As Clerk of Court
                                    By _____
                                                    As Deputy Clerk

Figure 2. Affidavit of Service.

AFFIDAVIT OF SERVICE

STATE OF _____
COUNTY OF _____

_____, being first duly sworn, upon oath deposes and says that in said County and State on the _____ day of _____, 19___, he served the complaint and summons upon the within named _____ by then and there _____.

Subscribed and Sworn to before me this _____ day of _____, 19___.

_____

_____
Notary Public, _____ County,
State of _____
My Commission Expires: _____
* * * * * * * * * *

Filed in the Clerk of Courts office:

_____
(date)

_____
Clerk of Court
by _____,
Deputy

While discovery is going on, a number of motions may be made by the parties to the court (before the trial begins). As indicated above, a motion is a written or oral application by a party addressed to the court requesting a particular order or ruling. For example, a *motion for summary judgment* is a request to end the case without a full trial. A party is saying to the court that if it looks at every document and pleading that has been submitted thus far, the other side could not possibly win; there is no need for a trial.

Throughout this pretrial period, the parties may be attempting to negotiate a settlement. A bargaining process takes place privately between the attorneys during which each side tells the other what it thinks it would be able to prove at trial, why the other side should settle, and what it is prepared to settle for.

A *pretrial conference* is held before the judge (usually in the latter's office or private chambers) with the attorneys present. They talk about the general outline of the pending trial. The judge often urges the attorneys to be more precise in the identification of the issues that will be the subject of the trial. The judge may also use the opportunity to encourage the parties to settle the case or to attempt some form of arbitration.

In certain situations, there are arbitration procedures available to the parties. In arbitration, the parties agree to submit their dispute to a nonjudicial third person or body and to abide by its decision on the dispute. This is a separate proceeding from the court process.

If the case will go to trial and a jury has been requested, there must be a jury selection process—the "voir dire."

CHART 2
STAGES OF LITIGATION: PRETRIAL

CIVIL	CRIMINAL
a) Plaintiff files complaint with the clerk of court.	a) Arrest.
b) Clerk issues a summons.	b) Investigation.

c) Summons and copy of complaint are served on the defendant.	c) Initial appearance before magistrate:
	  1. accused notified of charge(s)
	  2. bail
	  3. right to be silent
	  4. attorney representation.

d) Whoever serves the summons and complaint files an affidavit of service with the clerk of court.	d) Preliminary hearing.

e) Defendant then files an answer with the clerk of court with a copy served on the plaintiff. The answer could contain a number of positions:
  1. demurrer
  2. some admissions of fact and some denials
  3. counterclaim.
	e) Grand jury—indictment.
	f) Plea bargaining.
	g) Arraignment.
	h) Pretrial motions, e.g., motion for discovery, motion to suppress.
	i) Jury selection—voir dire.

f) Third parties may be joined.	
g) The plaintiff may file a reply to the defendant's answer.	

h) Discovery procedures are used:
  1. interrogatories
  2. bill of particulars
  3. depositions
  4. request for admissions
  5. request for production and inspection of documents or things
  6. request for physical or mental examination.	

i) Pretrial motions, e.g., motion for a summary judgment.	
j) Efforts at settlement.	
k) Pretrial conference may be held to crystallize the issues and to encourage settlement or arbitration.	
l) Jury selection—voir dire.	

3. TRIAL STAGE (see Chart 3)

The procedures for civil and criminal trials are relatively similar. Hence they will be discussed together.

The first order of business at the trial is the opening statement by counsel (or by the parties themselves if they are not represented by counsel). Normally, the party that has the burden of proof goes first. This is usually the plaintiff in a civil case and the state or prosecutor in a criminal case. (The burden of proof is the necessity of affirmatively convincing the court of one's version of the facts in a dispute.) In the opening statement, the attorney briefly states the factual issues, the position of his/her client, and how s/he will go about establishing that position.

The party with the burden of proof must then present evidence. At this stage, the evidence must be sufficient to establish a *prima facie case,* which is enough evidence to win if the other side fails to contradict the evidence presented. The attorney tries to establish the prima facie case through demonstrative evidence as well as through testimonial evidence. The latter consists of the testimony or oral statements of witnesses on the stand. Demonstrative evidence is physical evidence addressed directly to the senses without the intervention of testimonial evidence (e.g., a contract, map, photograph, weapon).

While trying to establish a prima facie case through testimonial evidence, the attorney calls witnesses for direct-examination. This attorney asks all the questions of the witness on direct. The other attorney will have the opportunity to cross-examine the witness after the direct-examination is complete.

In order to establish the relevance of certain demonstrative evidence, the attorney will usually lay the foundation for the evidence through questions asked of the witness on direct-examination. For example, suppose the attorney wants to admit into evidence certain business records prepared by the witness on the job. Before submitting the records, the attorney lays the foundation by asking questions such as: on your job, do you prepare records; what kind; do you recognize this document; would you describe it for the court and the circumstances under which you prepared it, etc. The attorney then offers the records into evidence.

The other attorney may object to any question asked of a witness. The judge will then make a ruling on the objections raised. The more common objections made during direct-examination are:

- Being unduly repetitive.
- Asking leading questions (where the answer is stated or strongly implied in the question, e.g., you weren't home at noon, were you? See p. 435.)
- Asking questions calling for a conclusion. (Normally, the witness must state what s/he knows about the facts and not give his/her opinions or conclusions about the facts (p. 450). The exception is the expert witness. A doctor, for example, can, under certain circumstances, be asked to give an opinion, such as, "Was the accused capable of seeing the sign 100 feet away?")
- Impeaching your own witness. (If you call a witness on direct-examination, the strict rule in the past was that you could not impeach, attack, or discredit the witness if s/he surprised you on the stand and said something that hurt your client. This rule has been somewhat relaxed in recent years and is often not strictly enforced.)

The rules change somewhat when an attorney is cross-examining the witness of the other side. Presumably, such a witness is hostile to the attorney conducting the cross-examination. Hence the attorney *is* allowed to ask leading questions as an aid in dealing with this hostility. Clearly, the attorney on cross-examination can impeach the witness, since impeachment is a main purpose of cross-examination. The attorney cannot, however, ask unduly repetitive or irrelevant questions. (Note that at this point, the other side has not yet presented its case through direct-examination of its witnesses nor through the offering of its own physical evidence. All that has happened thus far is the presentation of the case of the party with the burden of proof and the cross-examination of witnesses by the other side.)

There is another rule that often governs cross-examination: the attorney on cross-examination cannot ask questions outside the scope of the subject matter covered on direct-examination. If on direct-examination, for example, the witness is asked questions about an automobile accident, the attorney on the other side cannot raise new subject matters on cross-examination such as questions pertaining to slander or libel. This subject is outside the scope of the automobile accident. If the attorney wants to cover slander or libel (assuming it is relevant to the litigation at all) s/he must do so when s/he presents his/her own case after the other side has rested. Like the rule on impeachment, however, this rule is also not always strictly enforced.

Finally, some courts allow the party who initially directly examined a witness to conduct a brief re-direct-examination after the other side has completed cross-examination. The purpose of re-direct is to give the attorney the chance to rebut what s/he feels the other attorney tried to accomplish on cross-examination (p. 351).

At the close of the plaintiff's case (in civil litigation) or of the state's case (in criminal litigation), the defendant can make a motion to dismiss on the ground that the other side has failed (through its demonstrative and testimonial evidence on direct examination) to establish a prima facie case. It is also called a motion for a directed verdict. If this motion is granted, the trial is over. If it is denied, it is the defendant's turn to put on its own case to establish the facts in the light most favorable to its position. The defendant directly examines his/her own witnesses and the plaintiff subjects them to cross-examination. Defendant introduces demonstrative evidence at strategic moments. S/he then rests his/her case.

Throughout the presentations of cases by the two sides, there frequently are interruptions during which the attorneys make motions and argue the legality of procedural and evidentiary points. If a jury is deciding the case, these arguments are usually held outside their hearing range, either at a bench conference with the judge, or with the jury removed from the room. If no jury is involved in the case, the arguments can be made in the open.

Once the defendant has rested and the legal points have been argued, the judge must instruct or "charge" the jury on the standards it will apply in reaching a verdict. Again, if there is no jury, there is no charge or instructions since the judge decides everything him/herself. If there is a jury, its basic responsibility is to decide the factual issues in dispute under the guidance of the judge's charge. The jury is told, for example, what standard of proof to apply in resolving the factual disputes. In civil cases, the standard of proof is often the "preponderance of the evidence," which generally means that the jury is more convinced of one version, i.e., the existence of a contested fact is more probable than its nonexistence. In some civil cases, the standard is much stronger: "clear and convincing evidence." This standard requires more convincing evidence than the preponderance test. The strictest standard of all is used in criminal cases: "beyond a reasonable doubt." If the jury has *any* reasonable doubt as to *any* of the elements of the crime, the defendant must be found not guilty.

Before or after the jury has been charged, the attorneys make their closing statements in which they summarize their cases, state what they think they proved and what they think the other side failed to prove. Finally, the jurors go off to the jury room to deliberate alone. They occasionally come back into the court to ask the judge to clarify certain points of the instructions to them or to deal with other problems that arise. When they have reached a verdict, they return to the courtroom to have the foreman of the jury announce it to the court.

In a civil case, several kinds of verdicts are possible. A *general verdict* simply states who wins and how much must be paid, if anything. A *general verdict with interrogatories* is the same as a general verdict with the addition of answers that the jury provides to a series of specific factual questions concerning critical aspects of the case. A *special verdict* consists of jury answers to specific factual questions. The judge then concludes who wins and how much must be paid, if anything, based on the answers to the questions in the special verdict.

A *judgment notwithstanding the verdict* is a decision of the judge that is contrary to the verdict of the jury. The judge concludes, in effect, that the verdict was unreasonable. Another option of the judge is to use a *remittitur,* which tells the winning party that a new trial will be granted unless this party agrees to

Source: Justice Assistance News, Vol. 2, No. 1 (Feb. 1981).

lower the damage award reached by the jury. An *additur* calls for a new trial unless there is an agreement to add to the damage award provided by the jury.

In a criminal case, the person convicted is then brought before the judge for sentencing. The judge will often conduct a separate hearing on the sentence. The person's background, the likelihood of his/her committing crimes in the future, his/her degree of repentance, etc., are all taken into consideration in deciding whether to send him/her to prison, grant probation, or impose a fine. The attorneys for both sides take turns arguing for the sentence they are seeking. Usually, new witnesses are not called at this hearing, but letters of recommendation, written reports on family and employment background, and the like are frequently submitted. The technical rules of evidence and procedure that apply during the trial normally do not apply at this hearing.

In a civil case, the plaintiff will usually be asking for money damages and the jury's verdict will state how much should be awarded. In some states, however, there is a separate damage hearing after the jury has found a party liable. This separate damage hearing will be limited to the amount that the losing party should pay the winner. Of course, if the defendant won, s/he will not receive any damages unless s/he has successfully established a counterclaim against the plaintiff.

The final act of the trial is the judgment of the court, which embodies the verdict of the jury and the judge's determination of the rights and responsibilities of the parties resulting therefrom.

CHART 3
STAGES OF LITIGATION: TRIAL

CIVIL AND CRIMINAL
a) Opening Statement of plaintiff (civil case) or of the state (criminal case).
b) Opening Statement of other side.
c) Party with burden of proof presents evidence: 1. Demonstrative evidence introduced 2. Direct-examination of the party's own witnesses 3. Cross-examination of these witnesses by the other side 4. Re-direct examination.
d) Motion to dismiss for failure to establish a prima facie case.
e) Other side presents evidence: 1. Demonstrative evidence introduced 2. Direct-examination of this side's own witnesses 3. Cross-examination of these witnesses by the other side 4. Re-direct examination.
f) More motions.
g) Closing Arguments to jury by counsel.
h) Instructions to jury.
i) Verdict of jury.
j) Judgment of court.

4. APPEAL STAGE (see Chart 4)

Following the trial, an appeal process is available. In some judicial systems (p. 332) there is a two-step appeal or appellate process, first to an intermediate appeals court and then to the highest (or supreme) court in the system. In other judicial systems, only one appeals court is provided.

Before an appeal is taken, the losing party makes a motion to "stay" (suspend) the execution or operation of the judgment pending what happens on appeal. In a criminal case where the defendant is sentenced to prison, this motion asks the court to permit the defendant to remain on bail while s/he appeals the conviction. In a civil case, where the judgment orders a party to do something (e.g., pay money or build a bridge according to the terms of a contract), the motion to stay execution, if granted, would prevent the winning party from forcing this to be done until the appeal process is over.

By statute, a party usually has a limited number of days within which to appeal, e.g., thirty. To start the appeal, a party serves a Notice of Appeal on the other party and files it with the clerk of the appellate court. The party bringing the appeal is the *appellant.* The party against whom the appeal is brought is the *appellee* or *respondent.* It is quite possible that *both* sides are unhappy with aspects of what occurred below. Each side will then bring the appeal on the issues with which it is dissatisfied.

Figure 3. Notice of Appeal.

CIRCUIT COURT FOR THE COUNTY OF . . . .
STATE OF MISSOURI

. . . .
Plaintiff
vs.   No. . . . .
. . . .
Defendant

NOTICE OF APPEAL TO SUPREME COURT
OF MISSOURI

Notice is given that . . . . appeals from the
. . . . entered in this action
(Judgment) (appealable order, etc.)
on the . . . . . . day of . . . . . ., 19 . . .

Jurisdiction of the Supreme Court is based on fact that this appeal involves:

(Check appropriate box)

(   ) The validity of a treaty or statute of the United States.
(   ) The validity of a statute or provision of the Constitution of Missouri.
(   ) The construction of the revenue laws of Missouri.
(   ) The title to any state office in Missouri.
(   ) The punishment imposed is death or imprisonment for life.

. . . .
Attorney for . . . .
Address: . . . .
. . . .

DATED: . . . ., 19 . . . .

An appeal is significantly different from the trial. The case is *not* re-tried on appeal. The purpose of the appeal is limited primarily to questions of law. At the trial, two events occurred: (1) factual disputes were considered and resolved by the judge and jury and (2) legal rulings were made by the judge on these facts and on the conduct of the trial. It is the latter that is the major concern of the appeals court. On appeal, no witnesses are called and no evidence is introduced. The appeals court addresses issues such as:

1. Did the trial court have jurisdiction to try the case?
2. Were the right rules of evidence applied by the judge?
3. Did the judge apply the correct law?

An appeals court will entertain an allegation that the evidence was insufficient to support the verdict, but this does not mean that the case is re-tried on appeal. The court will look at the entire record and disturb the fact findings only if it concludes that the trial court was irrational in its findings or that no substantial evidence exists to support the findings.

The vehicle by which the attorneys raise these objections on appeal is the appellate brief (p. 695). First the appellant files a brief, then the appellee files one, and finally, the appellant may file a reply brief to the appellee's brief.

The appellant's brief summarizes what took place at trial, states what errors the attorney thinks the trial judge made, provides a legal analysis of why they were harmful errors, and states what conclusions the attorney wishes the appeals court to make. By the time the briefs are filed, the entire transcript (i.e., a word-by-word account of what was said on the record during the trial) has been typed and is referred to throughout the brief.

A standard rule in the appeals process is that a party cannot raise legal arguments on appeal that were not raised at trial. Suppose that an attorney introduces a document into evidence and the other attorney makes no objection to its admission during the trial. On appeal, it is improper for the latter to argue for the first time that the document was inadmissible according to the laws of evidence even if it *was* an error for the trial court to have admitted it. The attorney should have raised this objection at the trial. For the appeals court to address this issue for the first time would probably require it to conduct a fact-finding hearing, which it does not want to do. The same is true of new theories or new causes of action against the other party. Suppose that at the trial, "A" is suing "B" for breach of contract. On appeal, "A" cannot claim for the first time that during his/her troubles with "B" over the contract, "B" slandered "A." "A" should have brought this out at trial in the pleadings and in the evidence, or should have brought a separate suit against "B." Hence the general rule is: if you should have raised something at trial and didn't, you are deemed to have waived it for purposes of the appeal.

Once the briefs are in, a time is set for oral argument before the appeals court (which may contain three to nine judges, or more). As the attorneys take turns arguing the case before the judges, the latter often interrupt with questions. The parties to the litigation may be present during oral argument, but do not participate in the proceedings.

Finally, the judges withdraw in private to deliberate on the case and to vote. The majority controls. The judges could make a number of decisions. For example:

- Affirm the lower court's ruling.
- Reverse the lower court's ruling and remand the case (send it back) to the trial court with instructions to award the judgment to the other side.
- Remand the case with other specific instructions, e.g., conduct a new trial, apply a different law to a particular set of facts in dispute.

The appellate court's opinion is often written and published in reporters (p. 525).

This opinion can sometimes consist of three different kinds of opinions:

- The *majority* opinion, which contains the conclusions and the reasoning that govern the case.
- One or more *concurring* opinions that agree with the conclusions of the majority opinion but not with its reasoning.
- One or more *dissenting* opinions that disagree with the conclusions and reasoning of the majority opinion.

What happens after the appellate court reaches its decision? If the state has only one level of appellate courts the case is over in the state. If, however, there are two levels (intermediate and supreme or final), then the case moves to the highest appellate court in the state. Again, appellate briefs are submitted, oral argument takes place, and an opinion is written by the court.

In the federal courts, most trials are conducted in the United States District Courts. Then two appellate levels are available. The first appeal is to the United States Court of Appeals, and the final is to the United States Supreme Court.

Sometimes an appellate court *must* hear an appeal from a dissatisfied party. This is called an appeal of right. At other times, the appellate court has discretion on whether to take the appeal. If the court decides not to hear the appeal, the prior ruling of the court below remains in effect. A *writ of certiorari* is the method by which an appellate court exercises its discretionary power to hear an appeal. The writ orders the lower court to send up a certified copy of the record so that the higher court can determine whether any errors of law occurred in the proceedings below.

CHART 4
STAGES OF LITIGATION: APPEALS

CIVIL AND CRIMINAL
a) Motion to stay execution of judgment pending appeal.
b) Filing of Notice of Appeal with middle appeals court.
c) Filing of Appellant's brief.
d) Filing of Appellee's brief.
e) Filing of Appellant's reply brief.
f) Oral Argument.
g) A decision is rendered.
h) Appeal to highest court, if any, within the judicial system.
i) Briefs filed, oral argument, decision rendered.

For a discussion on the relationship between federal and state courts, see the topic of authority in the research chapter, p. 561.

4. ENFORCEMENT STAGE
(see Chart 5)

In a civil case, one of the greatest fears of the party who wins a damage (money) award is that s/he will not be able to collect. The loser does not take out a checkbook immediately upon hearing the adverse judgment. Collection is often difficult, possibly involving further litigation. The party who owes money, called the judgment debtor, can be very uncooperative. There are a number of options available to the judgment creditor, the party who won the damage award:

- Execution: An execution is a document requiring a sheriff or marshal to seize property of the judgment debtor to be sold at public auction with the money used to satisfy the judgment of the judgment creditor.
- Investigative procedures: The judgment creditor can often force the judgment debtor to disclose his/her income or property. An execution can then be brought against these assets.
- Garnishment: The judgment creditor may be able to force the employer of the judgment debtor to turn over part of the latter's salary until the judgment is satisfied.
- Contempt: In some cases (see below) a judgment debtor may be called before the court and held in contempt for failure to comply with a court order involving the judgment.

If the losing party is ordered to refrain from doing something or to do something (other than pay money to the loser), the contempt sanction is frequently used to obtain compliance. Other methods, in addition, could be employed by the court. For example, a court could require the loser to submit periodic reports to the court detailing his/her progress in complying with the order. Recently a court declared a prison system to be unconstitutional and ordered major improvements in the administration of the system. The correctional administrators who lost the case were required to submit reports to the court on their progress in making these improvements. Also, a court might appoint a special monitor to check on compliance and report back to the court.

When an administrative agency is a party in the litigation and the agency loses, the attorney for the winning side may have difficulty determining whether the machinery of the agency's bureaucracy is conforming to the court order. This may not be so if, for example, an agency is simply ordered to pay the winning party an amount of money. The problem cases are those that order an agency to change or modify long-standing procedures by which it conducts its business. In a tax or social security case, for example, the court may place limitations on the way in which investigators can make home visits on individuals they suspect are violating the law. Such limitations can be difficult to enforce. In an agency with many employees, departments, and subdepartments, it may be a large task to obtain full compliance within the immediate future.

In a criminal case, the court could reach a number of judgments:

- acquittal
- fine paid to court
- restitution to victim
- jail or prison term
- probation.

If the defendant does not pay the fine imposed, or fails to return to the victim of the crime what was illegally taken (i.e., fails to make restitution), the district attorney could bring the defendant back into court and ask that s/he be held in contempt or sentenced to prison. If the individual has been placed on probation (a decision to let the individual remain in the community under certain conditions, e.g., do not leave the state without permission, join a job counseling program, support a spouse), the probation officer will be supervising him/her to ensure that s/he is abiding by the terms of the probation order.

A person sentenced to jail or prison may also have enforcement problems against the state, many of which deal with sentence computation. The judge may order that the person be given a sentence of five years with credit for "time served" while waiting for trial. The state may also have "good time" provisions, by which an inmate has a certain number of days taken off the sentence for every month of good behavior in prison. Correctional personnel may make mistakes in calculating the time that must be served (p. 25). The inmate must exert pressure on the prison to re-do its calculations, or the inmate may file a habeas corpus action in court charging that s/he is being kept in prison longer than the judge's sentence contemplated.

CHART 5
STAGES OF LITIGATION: ENFORCEMENT (COMPLIANCE)

CIVIL	CRIMINAL
a) Execution	a) Contempt
b) Investigative proceedings	b) Re-sentencing
c) Garnishment	c) Revocation of probation
d) Contempt proceedings	d) Sentence computation
e) Periodic reports	• informal pressures on the prison
f) Appointment of monitor	• habeas corpus proceeding
g) Subsequent compliance litigation	
h) Informal pressures on the judgment debtor	
i) Informal pressures on the administrative agency	

Section B. INTRODUCTION TO LITIGATION ASSISTANTSHIP

1. *Litigation can be very complex.*

Generally speaking, the "easy" cases are not litigated. The tough ones find their way into the dispute settlement mechanism that we call litigation. Such cases require attention to a multitude of concerns. What are the facts? What facts are relevant? What facts can be introduced into evidence? Which of these admissible facts will a judge or jury believe? What facts will the other side introduce? Should the case be settled? Have there ever been similar cases litigated? What result did they reach? What law will govern the facts that may be established at trial? Such questions necessitate considerable skill in the design of litigation strategy.

When you are assigned a task by your supervisor, you will often find that the task leads you into other tasks, other questions, other unknowns, other problems that must be dealt with in order to complete the assigned task effectively. To say that the answer to every question has within it the seeds of another question is not to argue that the process of litigation is by definition chaotic. It is to say, however, that the process is very much alive, very much in a state of flux, and very much in need of people who can keep up with, and indeed who can keep one step ahead of, its developments.

2. *Like the incoming lawyer fresh out of law school, the newly hired paralegal may initially have considerable anxiety about litigation.*

It will probably surprise paralegals to discover that law school, by and large, does not train law students to be litigators. Law schools tend to concentrate on the theory of law at the expense of the practical skills that the lawyer will need to represent clients. Prestigious law schools often look with disdain on practice-oriented training. The development of clinical programs, however, in which students handle "real" cases while in school, has helped to change this somewhat. Yet it is still true that law firms must continue to devote substantial resources to skills-training for their newly hired attorneys because law schools have not been *practice* schools. The new lawyer often starts the first job with considerable anxiety. S/he looks for every opportunity to find ways to translate theory into practice. One of the best examples of the frustration comes when the new lawyer makes the first appearance in court. To his/her great dismay, s/he often discovers that a good deal of court procedure is not written down anywhere, or if it is written down it is not easily accessible. Everybody simply assumes that everybody else knows the intimate workings of the operation of the court.

In a very real sense, the paralegal has a potential ally in the new attorney. The paralegal should watch his/her development closely and try to become part of the formal or informal training program that the law firm has set up for him/her. To be sure, the complexity of the initial assignments given the new attorney will probably exceed that of the tasks delegated to paralegals. Nevertheless, there are "chunks" of the new lawyer training that could fit very nicely into the paralegal's own development and training.

3. *Find, study, and at least partially understand a completed case file.*

As soon as possible after you enter the job, you should ask someone to give you a completed case file of a case that was litigated. The file may be anywhere from a half inch to six feet thick—or much more depending on the length and complexity of the case. Normally a file will be organized chronologically *in re-*

verse, with the most recent letter or document from the case on top. Whatever filing arrangement is used (p. 766), you should look at every item in it and try to determine from its cover or first sheet where it fits into the litigation process. Use the five charts presented in section A on the stages of litigation of this chapter as a guideline. Have you picked up a brief? For what court? Have you found an offer of settlement? etc. Whenever you are not sure what a particular item is from its cover, and reading a page or two does not help, you should ask someone in the office.

As each document is identified, write it down on a separate piece of paper with its relevant date beside it. Then go back on a separate sheet of paper and arrange all the items chronologically from beginning to end. The result will be a biography of a case in litigation. If the file that you happen to be studying already has its own itemized biography or index (p. 489), you should ignore it until you have attempted to write your own. This exercise is important because one of the most vital functions a litigation assistant can perform is information retrieval from the files of current or past cases. Your ability to perform this function competently is greatly increased if you can read a file and identify its component parts.

4. Many law offices have their own forms and manuals.

It is quite possible that you will be told, upon starting a new job, to forget everything you have learned about forms and procedures in a particular area of the law because the office has developed its own unique forms and procedures that you must learn to use. There are certain forms that practically everyone in the area uses. Sometimes a court will issue its own forms and require that they be used. You will invariably find, however, that the office has developed its own system of practice forms and procedures intermixed with those that are commonly used or required in the area. It is essential that you learn the system used by your office as soon as possible.

The system may be highly structured with checklists, forms, and instructions placed within a large manual or a series of manuals. On the other hand, the "system" may be scattered throughout the office in bits and pieces (p. 193). There may be a checklist buried in one of the files. Copies of forms may be available but without any clear indication to a newcomer of what the form is used for. No one in the office has taken the time to coordinate the system into a central manual that is kept up to date. The "how-to-do-it's" are all in the minds of office staff, and since the staff is coordinated, the system works. The problem for the newcomer is that you cannot rely on a unified manual because it does not exist. The mandate for the paralegal in this situation is clear: collect as many forms and instructions that do exist, determine if they are still valid and for what purposes, and encourage the staff to centralize the system or systems into manuals. *In the meantime, collect and build your own manual for the repetitive tasks that you perform* (p. 318). You may well find that after a year or so on the job, your manual will become the nucleus of the manuals that should have existed when you first arrived.

Having extolled the virtues of manuals, forms, and centralized procedures in this way, there is a need to remind ourselves of the possible limitations of these tools:

- They can quickly become out of date.
- Certain attorneys in the office may disagree with them and refuse to follow them, or portions of them.
- They can be misleading in the sense that the user is tempted to follow them slavishly rather than adapt them to the needs of a particular problem.

5. *There is a paramount need for the paralegal to "feel" the interconnections among the events in the litigation process.*

You will probably be given the opportunity to make site visits to courtrooms, clerks' offices, and wherever else the stages of litigation take place. These should not, however, be tourist orientations. You should make every effort to make your trip as meaningful as possible. When you watch an office attorney cross-examine an adverse witness at trial, for example, you should read beforehand the deposition of the witness that the attorney may have taken earlier. If you are watching an attorney take a deposition, you should read beforehand any field investigation reports that involve the person being deposed. If you are watching an attorney give oral argument before an appellate court, you should beforehand read the appellate briefs and segments of the trial transcript that the attorney tells you will be relevant to the oral argument. Normally, any single item in the litigation process relates forward and back to other items and events. Your goal should be to sense this interconnectedness as soon and as often as possible.

6. *It is no vice for the litigation assistant to be obsessed by dates and time.*

When did you receive that? What time did you speak to him? When can she be available to testify? When was this written? When do I have to be there? Can it be postponed? If so, for how long? When was the photograph taken? When does this have to be filed? How much time does the statute give us to object? How many days do we have to appeal? Are weekends included in the number of days that we have? When will the lab test be ready? How long would it take if you send it special delivery?

It is almost impossible to overstate the importance of time in the litigation process. So many decisions are based upon when things are due. The clock is a pervasive "third party" in most cases in litigation. You must be aware of this reality and develop the self-discipline to record dates that are or that could be significant. Many offices have devised "tickler" systems that alert the office to due dates and other time requirements. You should learn how the tickler functions. If there is no adequate tickler system in the office, you should learn how to develop one for the cases you are working on.

7. *Learn how to "peek over someone's shoulder" creatively; learn how to observe.*

When you complete your formal education, you will find yourself in the position of graduates of most training: there is a staggering amount still to learn on the job. The formal education is a very useful starting point. It provides an overview, guidelines, and specifics where appropriate. It is absolutely essential that the formal education also prepares you for the *self-training* that will be your responsibility when you are hired (p. 307).

One component of this self-training for the litigation assistant is learning how to watch someone else do something and to translate what you are seeing into the skills that you will need to be an effective litigation assistant. The checklist in chart 6 is designed to assist you in observing creatively. You should use it as a guideline, particularly during the early stages of your employment.

Section C. LITIGATION ASSISTANTSHIP: AGENCY STAGE

Following the initial client interview (p. 385), there is often a need to know more about the agency, if any, involved in the case:

- The functions and structure of the agency.
- The details on the agency's contacts with and decisions concerning the client thus far.

The first concern may not be applicable if the agency is relatively small or if the office has often dealt with the agency before. If not, then there are a number of things that the office may want to know about the agency:

- Who funds it?
- Who runs it, and who are the senior staff members? What powers do they have?
- What are the application procedures? What forms are used?
- What are the revocation or termination procedures? Do they have different kinds of hearings?
- How does the agency make its regulations? Are they published (p. 672)?

You can assist the attorney in obtaining answers to such questions in a number of ways. You can go to the agency or write for informational literature published by the agency. You can call agency personnel with specific questions. You can check with people outside the office and outside the agency who are familiar with the agency. Finally, you can go to the law library and do some legal research on the agency (p. 672).

As for the agency's contacts with and decisions on the client's case thus far, much of this information can be obtained from the client. Information that is usually needed includes: date of first contact, agency personnel working on the client's case, dates of meetings and phone calls, copies of letters, etc. The paralegal may also be asked to contact agency personnel who have dealt with the client to confirm such information.

Field investigation to uncover and verify facts is a critical function that must be undertaken (p. 427). As the attorney tries to resolve the case informally with line and upper-echelon personnel, s/he will want to make specific references to the facts. The same is true in those criminal cases in which there is some contact between the district attorney and the client's attorney before ar-

CHART 6
CHECKLIST FOR EFFECTIVE OBSERVATION

WHAT YOU HAVE SEEN (e.g., a hearing, a deposition, a settlement conference)	WHAT YOU HAVE READ (other than published library material)
a) Describe briefly what you saw.	a) Summarize briefly what you read.
b) What facts are involved in what you saw?	b) What facts are involved in what you read?
c) Name everyone involved or participating in what you saw.	c) Who wrote it? Was it written in-house or by someone else?
d) What stage or stages in the litigation process are involved (agency, pre-trial, trial, appeal, enforcement)?	d) What stage or stages in the litigation process are involved (agency, pre-trial, trial, appeal, enforcement)?
e) Describe how you think it fits into the stage or stages.	e) Describe how you think it fits into the stage or stages.
f) What written documents (already prepared or drafted) were connected with what you saw?	f) Will it be re-written by someone? If so, why? What's wrong with it as now written?
g) Find those documents, read them and determine if what you saw makes any more sense to you.	g) What are the significant dates involved in it?
h) What written documents (not yet prepared) were referred to as documents that had to be prepared?	h) Make a note of everything you don't understand in what you read and ask people in the office to help you understand what you have noted.
i) Why do these documents need to be prepared?	i) Ask someone to direct you to material in the library that provides a legal basis for anything that is contained in the writing you read.
j) Ask whoever is going to prepare these documents to let you see them when they are finished. Read them and determine if what you saw now makes any more sense to you.	
k) Make a note of everything you don't understand about what you saw and ask people in the office to help you understand what you have noted.	
l) Is there a formbook or a manual available that describes any aspect of what you saw? If so, read the relevant sections.	
m) Ask someone to direct you to material in the library that provides a legal basis for some aspect of what you saw.	

rest or indictment. Bringing certain facts (uncovered in field investigation) to the attention of the D.A. may help him/her to decide whether to prosecute or what charges to initiate against the client.

Section D. LITIGATION ASSISTANTSHIP: PRETRIAL STAGE

The litigation assistant plays his/her greatest role at the pre-trial stage after administrative remedies have been exhausted. Most of the tasks involve fact finding, fact analysis, drafting, and legal research.

In addition, the assistant is often asked to file papers in court and serve documents on parties. Numerous pleadings (complaint, summons, affidavits, motions, etc.) must be filed in court and served on the other party.

The main responsibility in court filings is to learn the structure of the courts. The paralegal does not simply walk up to the courtroom door and hand the papers over to an official. S/he must find the appropriate clerk's office. S/he may have to pay a fee, obtain a receipt, and have a number assigned to the case, or see to it that the same number initially assigned to the case is used again for subsequent filings. Simple as these tasks may seem, the civil service structure of court bureaucracies can complicate matters considerably. Often there is no substitute for becoming friendly with a court clerk in order to receive recognition and assistance when needed.

Serving or delivering papers on parties to litigation is a very technical undertaking. The paralegal must take great care in carrying it out. Normally, service must be made in person. If personal service is not possible, the law of the jurisdiction in which the paralegal is working must be consulted to determine when substitute service (e.g., by mail, by publishing a notice in the newspaper) is valid. The person who executes service usually must file an affidavit in court swearing that s/he served the party, and may have to appear in court to give testimony on the execution of service.

There are eight major pre-trial tasks that the litigation assistant can be asked to perform:

1. Data retrieval
2. Digesting and indexing
3. Calendar control and scheduling
4. Organization and coordination of exhibits
5. Drafting interrogatories and answers to interrogatories
6. Drafting pleadings
7. Fact investigation
8. Legal research

The remainder of this section will primarily cover the first six of these tasks. Some of the tasks mentioned at the top of the list will also be discussed in chapter 14 on Law Office Administration (p. 737). Computerization of some of these tasks will be discussed in chapter 13 (p. 707). Fact investigation (p. 427), interviewing (p. 385), and legal research (p. 505) are treated elsewhere in the book.

1. DATA RETRIEVAL

As soon as a lawsuit starts, letters, memoranda, affidavits, and other documents are collected at a rather fast pace. The filing problems presented by this volume of documents can be enormous (p. 766). A usable index system is needed to let everyone know what is in a file. Even with a good index, however, portions of an active file may be scattered throughout the office on the desks of different people working on the case. The data retrieval function involves a confrontation with this document maze.

"Has the defendant filed his counterclaim?" A rather innocent question such as this can sometimes be difficult to answer. Similar questions could also be asked of cases that are no longer active, but that the attorney feels may have a bearing on an active case. Several basic guidelines should be part of the paralegal's standard practice when engaged in any data retrieval assignment:

a. Have a comprehensive knowledge of the office's filing system. Be sure you know who in the office already has this knowledge so that they can be consulted. Is there an index system? Is there a cross-index system? Are there file summaries available?
b. Have a comprehensive knowledge of the five stages of litigation (p. 466) and the most common documents involved in each stage.
c. If possible, find out who wrote the document that contains the data you are trying to retrieve. Ask him/her for leads.
d. Determine whether the data you are seeking may be found in more than one document and, if so, look for each such document.
e. Recognize that data in a document may be contradicted by other data in other documents. To determine the most current status of data, start examining the most recent documents in the file and work back.

The person trying to retrieve data must know how to interpret missing documents as well as the documents that are there. If you know what documents are usually found in a file, you will have a sense for what documents are conspicuously absent. The document may be lost, may be in use by someone in the office, may be on its way to the files, or may be in the process of drafting or redrafting. An understanding of the chronology in which documents are normally prepared can be very helpful in determining whether something is missing. You should review again the documents identified in the five stages of litigation outlined in this chapter, pp. 466–482 and the overview of many of these same documents presented in chapter 6, pp. 364–367. Paradoxically, it takes considerable skill to be able to determine whether something is missing.

2. DIGESTING AND INDEXING

To digest a document is simply to summarize it according to a given organizational principle. The summary, in effect, becomes an index to the document. The complexity of the digest depends entirely on the complexity of the case. Some cases are so involved that only a computer digest/index system will be adequate (p. 718). Some of the basic objectives of digesting include:

- Creating order out of what might be hundreds or thousands of pages of data.
- Providing ready access to selected topics in these pages once the summaries are correlated by subject matter.

- Providing a way of comparing testimony, spotting inconsistencies, and identifying evidentiary holes that need to be filled by further investigation and discovery.
- Assisting the attorney to organize the trial, particularly in designing questions to be used in the direct and cross-examination of witnesses on the stand; such strategy considerations will often go into the attorney's trial brief (p. 493), which you can help prepare.

The method of summarizing data is fairly simple. Suppose, for example, the following material comes from page 65 of the transcript of a deposition of Mr. Smith:

```
LINE
  1.   Q. Could you tell me please exactly how long after the accident
  2.       you first felt the pain in your spine?
  3.   A. Well, it's hard to say precisely because everything happened so
  4.       fast and my head was spinning from. . . .
  5.   Q. Was it an hour, a day, a week?
  6.   A. Oh no, it wasn't that long. I'd say the pain started about ten min-
  7.       utes after the collision.
```

The above transcript testimony could be digested into:

Began feeling pain in spine about 10 min. after collision: page 65, lines 1–7

As you can see, a great deal of space can be saved by eliminating the question and answer format and by focusing directly on the information sought. Such summaries could be placed on small file cards under the heading "Injury" or on summary sheets that are categorized by such headings. In this way, you can collate all statements made by the same witness on a particular topic. You can compare what this same deposition witness said about a particular topic in his/her answers to interrogatories. You can compare what other witnesses have said about the same topic. The possibilities are endless once you have prepared careful, readable summaries.

Before examining some of the major kinds of digesting that are used in a law office, some general guidelines should be kept in mind:

CHART 7
GUIDELINES FOR DIGESTING DISCOVERY DOCUMENTS

a) Obtain clear instructions from your supervisor. What precisely have you been asked to do? Prepare a comprehensive digest? Index the content of documents by specified category or topic? Prepare a chronological index or digest? What have you expressly or by implication been told not to do? It is a good idea to write down the supervisor's instructions.

b) Know the difference between paraphrasing testimony and quoting testimony. To paraphrase is to put the testimony into your own words. To quote is to use the words of the witness even though you may leave out part of what the witness said. Your supervising attorney may not want you to do any paraphrasing. S/he may want to do his/her own paraphrasing. Again, you need to know precisely what the attorney wants.

c) Know the case inside and out. You cannot digest something you do not understand. You must understand the causes of action and the defenses so that you can grasp the meaning of the testimony. Read the client file including interview and investigation reports, pleadings, other discovery documents, etc.

d) The answers given in a deposition often ramble. (The same may be true of some interrogatories.) Given this reality, act on the assumption that the same topic is covered more than one place in the discovery document. Look for this diversity and record it in your summary by pointing out *each* time the same topic is mentioned.

e) Don't expect the answers to be consistent—even from the same witness. Do not consciously or unconsciously try to help the witness by blocking out potential inconsistencies. If on page 45 the witness said she saw a "car" but on page 104 said she saw a "truck," do not blot out the distinction by saying she saw a "motor vehicle," or by failing to mention both. The danger of doing this is more serious than you think, particularly when you are reading hundreds of pages and are getting a little red in the eyes.

f) Always think in terms of categories as you summarize. Place your summaries into categories. The categories may be as broad as the name of a given witness. Other categories include:
   • background information
   • education
   • past employment
   • present employment
   • prior medical history
   • insurance
   • prior claims
   • facts of the accident
   • medical injuries
   • damage to property
   • prior statements made

   Your supervisor will tell you what categories or topics to use in organizing your summaries. If not, use your common sense.

g) Each summary should include the specific document you used (e.g., deposition), the page, and, if possible, the lines on the page that are the basis of the summary.

h) Find out if the law firm has an office manual that gives instructions on digesting. If not, check closed case files for samples of the kind of digesting and indexing that the firm has done in the past. Ask your supervisor if you should use such samples as models.

i) Prepare summaries of your summaries whenever you have an extensive digesting job requiring the examination of numerous documents for numerous topics.

j) Update the summaries. After you finish your digest, more facts may become known such as through further discovery. Supplement your earlier summary reports by adding the new data.

k) Keep a list (or know where to find a list) of every piece of paper in a particular file. Some digesting/indexing assignments will require you to examine everything in the file.

There are two major kinds of summaries:

• Digest by person
• Digest by subject matter

Digest by Person

Here you are asked to focus on a particular witness such as the person questioned in a deposition. Your instructions may be to provide a page-by-page summary of what the witness said. For example:

PAGE

SUMMARY

1. John R. Smith, 12 Main St. Buffalo, NY
   Employed at XYZ Factory as mechanic since Feb. 1, 1980

2. Has known plaintiff for over ten years. Is the plaintiff's supervisor at XYZ.

   Was working on the day of accident. Saw the plank fall on plaintiff.

3. Etc.

You simply go through the entire document and provide a page-by-page summary of everything. Include a table of contents at the beginning of your summary report. For example:

DIGEST OF DEPOSITION

CASE: Jones v. XYZ Factory   OFFICE FILE NUMBER: 86-341
DEPONENT: John R. Smith,   COURT DOCKET NUMBER:
  supervisor of plaintiff   Civ. 2357-1
                         ATTORNEY ON CASE: Linda Stout
DATE OF DEPOSITION: 2/24/86
DATE SUMMARY PREPARED: 5/16/86
SUMMARY PREPARED BY: George Henderson

TABLE OF CONTENTS

TOPIC	PAGES IN DEPOSITION
Background Information	1–4, 9
Smith's Knowledge of Accident	2–3, 5, 7–10
Company Report Filed by Smith	23
Smith's Instructions to Plaintiff Just Before Accident	15–17
Etc.	

Digest by Subject Matter

Here you are asked to focus on a particular topic only. For example:

- Everything the witness has said about a certain exhibit.
- Everything that all the witnesses have said about the condition of the car after the accident.
- Everything that all the witnesses have said about what occurred after 6 P.M. on 5/30/86.

- All statements made to the police after the accident.
- All references to the meeting of 7/23/86.

The subject-matter inquiry can be limited to a particular discovery document, e.g., a deposition, or it can cover a large number of documents:

- The complaint.
- The answer.
- Interrogatory answers.
- Deposition transcript.
- Responses to requests for admission.
- Reports from motion to produce documents or other things.
- Medical examination reports.
- Other investigation reports.
- Etc.

Hence, one digest summary can pull together everything on a particular topic from all of the above sources so that comparisons, correlations, and commentary are facilitated. Such summaries can become a master litigation index by subject matter.

3. CALENDAR CONTROL AND SCHEDULING

Calendar control involves feeding relevant dates into the office tickler system and/or maintaining your own calendar of events, past and to come. Lawyers need constant reminders of due dates, particularly when a lawyer is working on more than one case or more than one lawyer is working on a single case.

Scheduling events is sometimes assigned to the secretaries in the office, although for complex scheduling problems, the paralegal may become involved. Some of the more common events that need scheduling and coordination are as follows:

- Arrange for the taking of a deposition or for an informal interview with a prospective witness.
- Arrange for the arrival of an expert witness.
- Arrange for the client to take a physical examination.
- Send out reminders to clients and witnesses on scheduled events.
- Notify individuals of postponements or cancellations of scheduled events.

4. ORGANIZATION AND COORDINATION OF EXHIBITS

Before an attorney goes to trial, s/he must have all physical evidence and exhibits in order and ready for trial presentation. A trial book or trial brief (p. 695) is often written as part of this preparation. A trial brief is an attorney's set of notes on how to conduct the trial. The brief will cover the opening statement, witnesses to be called and for what purposes, evidence to be introduced and for what purpose, exhibits, etc. Chart 8 presents a number of guidelines for the paralegal in assisting the attorney in this area.

CHART 8
GUIDELINES FOR PREPARING PHYSICAL EVIDENCE
AND EXHIBITS FOR TRIAL

1) Ask the attorney in what order s/he would like each item of evidence or exhibit prepared. Possible arrangements:
   a) Separating those that s/he *might* introduce from those that s/he will *definitely* introduce.
   b) Arranging them chronologically in the order that s/he expects them to be introduced at trial.

2) Prepare a summary sheet for each item containing:
   a) the name of the case it will be used in.
   b) a brief description of what it is.
   c) a brief analysis of what facts the attorney will try to use it to help establish at trial.
   d) the source of the item (who wrote it, where was it obtained, etc.?).

3) Describe the facts the attorney must establish in order to lay the foundation for the item *before* s/he tries to introduce it. Describe the facts needed to show that it is relevant (p. 449). For written evidence, describe the facts needed to show that it is authentic (p. 456).

5. DRAFTING INTERROGATORIES AND REPLIES TO INTERROGATORIES

Considerable skill is required in drafting and replying to interrogatories (p. 347). Each task has an opposite objective: in drafting interrogatories you want to obtain as much information as possible from the other side, while in responding to interrogatories, you usually want to say as little as possible. If, however, the attorney instructs the paralegal to reply with full openness and candor, s/he obviously does so. As a matter of strategy, the attorney may decide to be fully cooperative in order to encourage the other side to take a certain position. Suppose, for example, that the attorney wants to impress the other side with certain facts in order to encourage a settlement. This objective may call for a certain openness in the responses to the interrogatory questions that might not otherwise be used. See charts 9 and 10 for guidelines on drafting and responding to interrogatories.

Of course, the work done by the paralegal in this area will usually be checked by the attorney and by the client who will be ultimately responsible for the answers given.

EXCERPT FROM A SET OF INTERROGATORIES

INJURIES AND DAMAGES

551. *State the name of each person for whom you claim damages for personal injuries*

552. *Describe in detail all injuries and symptoms, whether physical, mental, or emotional, experienced since the occurrence and claimed to have been caused, aggravated, or otherwise contributed to by it*

CHART 9
GUIDELINES ON DRAFTING INTERROGATORIES

a) Obtain general and specific instructions from your supervisor on the questions to be asked in the interrogatories.

b) Read all the documents on the case that have been prepared thus far (e.g., client interview report, field investigation report, complaint, answer).

c) Look at drafts of other interrogatories that have been used in other cases that are similar to your case. Determine whether courts in your area have approved any standard form interrogatories.

d) Recognize the need to adapt other interrogatories to the peculiar needs of your case.

e) Start out with requests for basic data (e.g., name, address, age, occupation, etc.)

f) Try to avoid questions that call for simple yes/no answers unless you also ask questions on the factual basis for such answers.

g) Try to avoid questions that call for an opinion from the respondent unless the opinion might be relevant or provide leads to other facts.

h) Phrase the questions to elicit facts.

i) Know what facts will be necessary to establish your client's case, and ask specific questions focusing on those facts. Know the elements of the course of action and defenses in the case (p. 373). Ask questions specifically designed to uncover facts for each element.

j) As to each fact, ask questions calculated to elicit the respondent's ability to comment on the fact (e.g., how far away was s/he, does s/he wear glasses, etc.).

k) Phrase the fact questions so that the respondent will have to clearly indicate whether s/he is talking from first-hand knowledge or hearsay.

553. *As to each medical practitioner who has examined or treated any of the persons named in your answer to Interrogatory Nr. 551, above, for any of the injuries or symptoms described, state:*
   (a) The name, address, and specialty of each medical practitioner
   (b) The date of each examination or treatment
   (c) The physical, mental, or emotional condition for which each examination or treatment was performed

554. *Has any person named in your answers to Interrogatory Nr. 551, above, been hospitalized since the occurrence? _____ If so, state:*
   (a) The name and location of each hospital in which each was confined
   (b) The dates of each hospitalization
   (c) The conditions treated during each hospitalization
   (d) The nature of the treatment rendered during each hospitalization

555. *Have any diagnostic studies, tests, or procedures been performed since the accident? _____ If so, state:*
   (a) The nature thereof
   (b) The name, address, and occupation of the person performing same
   (c) The place where performed, and, if in a clinic, laboratory, or hospital, the name and address thereof

> (d) *The name and present or last known address of each party now in possession or control of any records prepared in connection with each study, test, or procedure*

556. *Is any person named in your answer to Interrogatory Nr. 551, above, still under the care of any medical practitioner? _____ If so, state:*
>   (a) *The name and address of each practitioner*
>   (b) *The nature of each condition for which care is being rendered*
>   (c) *Which of the conditions are related to the accident*

557. *State as to each item of medical expense attributable to the accident:*
>   (a) *The amount*
>   (b) *The name and address of the person or organization paid or owed therefor*
>   (c) *The date of each item of expense (attach copies of itemized bills, if desired)*

. . . .

CHART 10
GUIDELINES ON RESPONDING TO INTERROGATORIES

a)	Obtain general and specific instructions from your supervisor on drafting the answers.
b)	Check all proposed answers with available documents (e.g., report on client interview, field investigation reports, complaint).
c)	Do not volunteer information beyond the confines of the question unless necessary to clarify a position (e.g., when a simple answer would be damagingly misleading without the clarification).
d)	When an answer to a question is not known, say so.
e)	Preface most answers by saying "to the best of my knowledge" or "as far as I can recall" in order to provide some leeway if the answer later proves to be invalid.
f)	Recognize that the other side will try to use the answers against you. For example, opposing counsel may try to get the client to say something on cross-examination that will contradict the answers given in the interrogatories.
g)	Recognize the kinds of improper questions that do not have to be answered. For example: • clearly irrelevant questions • unduly repetitive or burdensome questions • questions inquiring into the attorney's work product, e.g., questions that ask for the attorney's legal opinion or that ask for copies of legal memoranda. • questions that expressly or impliedly call for a violation of the attorney-client privilege, e.g., "what did your attorney tell you?" (p. 455).

CHART 11
HOW TO AVOID ABUSING A STANDARD FORM

a)	A standard form is an example of the document or instrument that is being drafted, e.g., pleading, contract, or other agreement.
b)	Standard forms are found in a number of places, e.g,. formbooks (p. 543), manuals, practice texts, in some statutory codes, in some court rules.

c)   Most standard forms are written by private attorneys. Occasionally, however, a standard form will be written by the legislature or by the court as the suggested or required format to be used.

d)   Considerable care must be exercised in the use of a standard form. Such forms can be very deceptive in that they appear to require little more than filling in the blanks. The intelligent use of the forms usually requires much more.

e)   The cardinal rule is: *adapt* the form to the particulars of the client's case on which you are working.

f)   Do not be afraid of changing the printed language of the form if you have a good reason for doing so. Whenever you make such a change, bring it to the attention of your supervisor for approval.

g)   You should never use a standard form unless and until you have satisfied yourself that you know the meaning of *every* word and phrase on the form. This includes boilerplate, which is standard language that is often used in the same kind of document. The great temptation of most form users is to ignore what they do not understand because the form has been used so often in the past without any apparent difficulty. Do not give in to this temptation. Find out what everything means by:
  • using a legal dictionary (p. 545);
  • asking your supervisor;
  • asking other knowledgeable people;
  • doing other legal research (p. 505).

h)   You need to know whether the entire form or any part of it has ever been litigated in court. To find this out, you must do some legal research in the area of the law relevant to the form.

i)   Once you have found a form that appears useful, look around for another form that covers the same topic. Analyze the different or alternative forms available. Which one is preferable? Why? The important point is: keep questioning the validity of the form. Be very skeptical about the use of any form.

j)   Do not leave any blank spaces on the form. If a question does not apply, make some notation to indicate this, e.g., "N.A."

k)   If the form was written for another state, be sure that the form is adapted to the law of your state.

l)   Occasionally you may go to an old case file to find a document that might be used as a model for a similar document that you need to draft on a current case. All the above cautions apply equally to the adaptation of documents from closed case files (p. 771).

6. DRAFTING PLEADINGS

The major pleadings in litigation are the complaint, answer, reply, counterclaim, etc. (p. 470). Very often you will use standard forms as the starting point in drafting pleadings. The guidelines in Chart 11 on using standard forms should be closely examined.

On the following pages, we will concentrate on drafting a complaint through an examination of its basic structure. The components of a complaint are illustrated in Figure 4 on p. 498.[4]

---

[4] Adapted from MacDonald, Pick, DeWitt & Volz, *Wisconsin Practice Methods, 2d,* Section 1530, p. 239 (West, 1959).

Figure 4. Structure of a Complaint.

CAPTION

DESIGNATION OF PLEADING

ALLEGATION OF JURISDICTION

BODY

PRAYER FOR RELIEF

SUBSCRIPTION

VERIFICATION

STATE OF _____   COUNTY OF _____
_____COURT
John Doe, Plaintiff
                    v.   Civil Action No. _____
Richard Roe, Defendant

COMPLAINT FOR NEGLIGENCE

Plaintiff alleges that:

1. The jurisdiction of this court is based on section _____, title _____ of the [State] Code.

2. Plaintiff is a plumber, residing at 107 Main Street in the City of _____ _____ County, State of _____.

3. Upon information and belief, defendant is a traveling salesman, residing at 5747 Broadway Street in the City of Chicago, Cook County, Illinois.

4. On or about the second day of January, 1959 an automobile driven by defendant, on Highway 18 in the vicinity of Verona, _____, struck an automobile being driven by the plaintiff on said highway.

5. Defendant was negligent in the operation of said automobile at the aforesaid time and place as to:
   a. Speed,
   b. Lookout,
   c. Management and control.

6. As a result of said negligence of defendant his automobile struck plaintiff's automobile and caused the following damage:
   a. Plaintiff was subjected to great pain and suffering,
   b. Plaintiff necessarily incurred medical and hospital expense,
   c. Plaintiff suffered a loss of income,
   d. Plaintiff's automobile was damaged.

Wherefore plaintiff demands judgment in the amount of ten thousand dollars ($10,000), together with the costs and disbursements of this action.

_____
Plaintiff's Attorney
1 Main Street

_____, _____

STATE of _____
                                                              ss
COUNTY of _____

John Doe, being first duly sworn on oath according to law, deposes and says that he has read the foregoing complaint by him subscribed and that the matters stated therein are true to the best of his knowledge, information and belief.

_____
John Doe

Subscribed and sworn to before me on this _____ day of _____, 19____.

_____
Notary Public

My commission expires:

Caption

The caption is the heading of the pleading. It should contain the name of the court, the name of the parties, and the number assigned by the court.

Designation of the Pleading

The title of the pleading should be clearly stated at the top. In the example in Figure 4, the pleading is a Complaint for Negligence.

Allegation of Jurisdiction

Not all states require a statement of the court's subject-matter jurisdiction—its power or authority to hear this kind of case (p. 469). A complaint filed in federal court, however, will usually contain a statement of the U.S. District Court's jurisdiction.

For venue purposes (p. 343), the complaint may also have to allege the residence of the parties, where the accident or wrong allegedly occurred, etc.

Body

The claims of the plaintiff are presented in the body of the complaint. A claim is a cause of action (p. 343). Every separate cause of action being used by the plaintiff should be stated in a separate "count," e.g., Count I, Count II, or simply as First Cause of Action, Second Cause of Action, etc. The paragraphs should be numbered with each containing a unified theme or point.

With what factual detail must the complaint state the cause of action? There are two main schools of practice on this question.

1. Fact Pleading

There must be a statement of the *ultimate facts* that set forth the cause of action. Every detail that the plaintiff intends to try to prove at trial is *not* pleaded. The complaint must not contain a catalog of the evidence that the plaintiff will eventually introduce at the trail. There is, however, no satisfactory definition of an ultimate fact. Generally, an ultimate fact is one that is essential to the establishment of the elements of the cause of action (p. 373).

The complaint must *not* state conclusions of law, e.g., Jones "assaulted" Smith; Jones "violated section 23 of the state code." The problem, however, is that it is as difficult to define a conclusion of law as it is to define an ultimate fact. Some statements are mixed statements of fact and law, e.g., "Jones 'negligently' drove his car into . . ." As a matter of common sense and practicality, a pleader can use the word "negligence" or "negligently" in the statement of the facts. If the conclusion of law is a convenient way of stating facts, it will be permitted.

The only reliable guide for a pleader is to determine what the prior decisions of the courts in his/her state have concluded are proper and improper statements of fact in a complaint.

2. *Notice Pleading*

Under the federal system and under states that have adopted the lead of the federal courts, the goal of the complaint is say enough to notify or inform the defendant of the nature of the claims against him/her. There is no requirement that ultimate facts be alleged. The plaintiff must simply provide a "short and plain statement of the claim showing the pleader is entitled to relief." The technicalities of pleading facts, conclusions of law, etc., are unimportant in notice pleading.

In a notice pleading state, it is not improper to fail to plead an ultimate fact. The critical point is that the complaint will not be thrown out if it *fails* to plead an ultimate fact or if it *includes* conclusions of law—so long as the complaint gives adequate notice of the nature of the claim.

Notice pleading does not necessarily require a different kind of pleading from fact pleading; notice pleading is simply more liberal or tolerant in what is acceptable.

When the plaintiff lacks personal knowledge of a fact being alleged, the fact should be stated "upon information and belief" as in the third paragraph of Figure 4.

There are times when the law requires specificity in the pleading. For example, allegations of fraud must be stated with particularity. Also, when special damages are required in defamation cases, the facts must be pleaded with some specificity.

Prayer for Relief

In the prayer, the complaint must ask for a specific amount of damages, or other form of relief such as an injunction against a nuisance. In the event that the defendant fails to appear and answer the complaint, a default judgment is entered against the defendant. The relief given the plaintiff in a default judgment cannot exceed what the plaintiff asked for in the prayer for relief.

Subscription

The subscription is the signature of the attorney who prepared the complaint and who represents the plaintiff. If the plaintiff wrote the complaint and is acting as his/her own attorney in the case, the plaintiff signs.

Verification

A verification is an affidavit that is submitted with the pleading. It is signed by a party on whose behalf the pleading was prepared who swears that s/he has read the pleading and that it is true to the best of his/her knowledge, information, and belief. (Not all states require that complaints be verified.)

Section E. LITIGATION ASSISTANTSHIP: TRIAL STAGE

An assistant's role at trial depends, in part, upon the involvement that s/he has had with the case up to trial. If the involvement has been minimal, then s/he may not have much to do to assist the attorney at trial. If, on the other hand, s/he has been working closely with the attorney on the case all along, his/her role at trial could include a number of tasks:

- Monitor all the files, documents, and evidence that the attorney will need to present the case, to plan and to re-plan strategy as outlined in the trial brief (p. 695).
- Do some spot legal research on issues that come up during the trial that require an answer fairly quickly.
- Prepare preliminary drafts of certain motions and other documents that are required during the course of the trial.
- Assure the presence of witnesses and assist the attorney in preparing them for direct-examination, and in anticipating what may be asked of them on cross-examination.
- Take notes on the testimony of certain witnesses (p. 99). The attorney may be able to use these notes in his/her preparation for other segments of the trial. A typed transcript of the testimony may not be available until after the trial.
- Make suggestions to the attorney on what questions to ask a particular witness based upon the assistant's close following of what has happened thus far in the trial, and based upon his/her involvement with the documents and files prepared during the pretrial stage.

In a criminal case in which the defendant is convicted, considerable work will have to be done in making the case for the most favorable sentence possible, which will usually be probation. Judges are normally reluctant to send a person to prison if alternatives to incarceration are available. (This, of course, would not apply to cases in which the judge is mandated to impose a prison term or in which the nature of the crime and the individual's prior criminal background make it unlikely that the judge would consider alternatives to prison.) The judge will be primarily interested in the person's "social history" and prospects for living a "clean" life if granted probation. The paralegal might be sent into the community to track down data such as:

- Are there vocational training programs available and willing to accept the defendant?
- Will his/her old employer take him/her back?
- Can s/he go back to school?
- Will his/her family or other relatives take him/her in?
- Are there school counselors, members of the clergy, or other community leaders who would be willing to take an interest in his/her progress, e.g., will they state that they will take some initiative in inviting him/her into their activities?

The judge will be reluctant to release the person into the streets without assurance that there will be people and programs available to support him/her in addition to the supervision that would be provided by an overworked probation officer. The paralegal can be of great help in identifying these resources (p. 78).

Section F. LITIGATION ASSISTANTSHIP: APPEAL STAGE

One of the key functions served by the paralegal at the appeal stage is data retrieval and fact digesting. After the trial, the attorney who is dissatisfied with the trial judgment plans appeal strategies. The trial may have lasted anywhere from a day to a number of weeks. Throughout the trial the attorney applies two tests to practically everything s/he does:

1. How can I use this effectively to win?
2. How can I turn a setback during the trial into a ground for an appeal?

The second test will require the attorney to go back after the trial and reconstruct, from all the documents and testimony, the data that will support his/her grounds for an appeal. Here the paralegal's data retrieval and fact digesting role can be invaluable.

The attorney may ask the paralegal to go back over the record and do the following:

- Make a list of every time I objected to something during the trial. Include the page number where my objection is found, a brief summary of what my objection was, and the ruling of the judge on my motion.
- Make a list of every time opposing counsel made reference to a particular topic, e.g., the plaintiff's prior involvement in other litigation.
- Make a list of every time the judge asked questions of witnesses.

A great deal of legal research is usually required before the attorney writes the appellate brief (p. 695) for submission to the various appeals courts. The paralegal can be very helpful in a number of areas:

- Research the legislative history of relevant statutes (p. 655).
- Shepardize cases (p. 613) and conduct cite checking (p. 585).
- Read over briefs to cross-check the accuracy of quoted testimony from the typed transcript of the trial.
- Conduct legal research on assigned issues of law.
- Monitor the typing, printing, and filing of briefs.

Section G. LITIGATION ASSISTANTSHIP: ENFORCEMENT/COMPLIANCE STAGE

If a money judgment was awarded to the client, considerable work may be required in collecting it from the judgment debtor. The paralegal can arrange for the sheriff to deliver an execution. The judgment debtor may be ordered by the court to submit to an examination of what his/her assets are. Investigation work will probably be required to determine what assets exist, where they are, and how they might be reached. In some cases, the attorney may petition the court for the contempt order against the judgment debtor for noncompliance (p. 481). The paralegal can help by assembling the factual basis to support this charge and in drafting some of the court papers involved.

In criminal cases, unfortunately, the inmate rarely has the assistance of counsel in ensuring compliance of the prison to the sentence. Very often they are their own lawyers or they act as paralegals for each other in providing the needed assistance on issues such as sentence computation (p. 25).

At probation revocation proceedings, the probationer is usually represented by counsel. A good deal of field investigation work may be required to check the probation officer's charge that the probationer violated the conditions of probation.

THE USE OF COMPUTERS IN LITIGATION

See pp. 707 ff.

11

Legal Research

Section A. INTRODUCTION

This chapter does not cover every aspect of legal research, nor does it treat every conceivable law book that could be found in a law library. Rather, the chapter examines the major components of legal research with the objective of identifying effective starting points.

The strategy used in designing this chapter is as follows:

1. *Introductory* concepts are presented.
2. The *ten major search resources* are presented as the heart of the chapter.
3. These ten search resources are then used to train you to *find* case law, statutes, legislative history, constitutional law, administrative law, local law, court rules, and international law.

A great deal of information is provided in the pages that follow. You should first read the chapter through quickly in order to obtain an overview and to begin seeing where some concepts are covered in more than one place. The second time you read the chapter, you should begin collecting the terminology called for in Assignment 72, on page 512. The best way to avoid becoming overwhelmed is to start feeling comfortable with terminology as soon as possible.

CHAPTER COVERAGE

When you walk into a law library, your first impression is likely to be that of awe. You are confronted with row upon row of books, most of which seem unapproachable; they do not invite browsing. To be able to use the law library, the first responsibility of the legal researcher is to break down any psychological barrier that you may have with respect to the books in it. This is done not only by learning the techniques of research but also by understanding the limitations of the law library: What is the library capable of doing for you and what should you *not* ask it to do?

A major misunderstanding about the law library is that it contains the answer to every legal question. In many instances, as we shall see, legal problems have no definitive answers. The researcher often operates on the basis of "educated guesses" of what the answer is. To be sure, your guess is supported by what you uncover through legal research in the law library. The end product, however, is only the researcher's opinion of what the law is, rather than the absolute answer because no one will know for sure what the "right" or final an-

A STRATEGY FOR STUDYING LEGAL RESEARCH

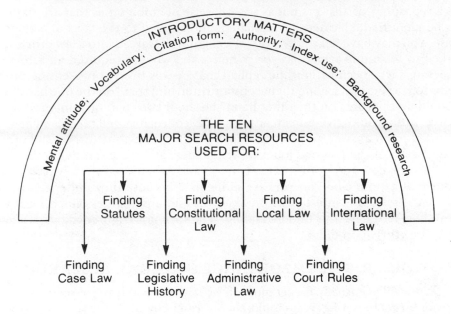

INTRODUCTORY MATTERS

Mental attitude; Vocabulary; Citation form; Authority; Index use; Background research

THE TEN
MAJOR SEARCH RESOURCES
USED FOR:

| Finding Statutes | Finding Constitutional Law | Finding Local Law | Finding International Law |

| Finding Case Law | Finding Legislative History | Finding Administrative Law | Finding Court Rules |

swer is until the matter is litigated in court. If the problem is never litigated, then the "right" answer will be whatever the parties accept among themselves through negotiation or settlement. The researcher will not know what answer carries the day for the client until the negotiation process is over.

Many simple problems, however, can be answered by basic (easy) legal research. If someone wants to know, for example, the name of the government agency in charge of incorporating a business or the maximum number of weeks one can receive unemployment compensation, finding the answer is not difficult if the researcher knows what books to go to and how to use their indexes. Most legal research problems, however, are not this simple.

Perhaps the most healthy way to approach the law library is to view it not as a repository of answers but as a storehouse of ambiguities that are waiting to be identified, clarified, manipulated, and applied to the facts of a client's case. You may have heard the story of a client who walked into a law office and asked to see a one-armed lawyer. When asked why he required an attorney meeting such specifications, he replied that he was tired of presenting problems to lawyers and having them constantly tell him that "on the one hand" he should do this, but "on the other hand" he should do that; he hungered for a lawyer who would give him an answer. This concern is well taken. A client is entitled to an answer, to clear guidance. At the same time (or, on the other hand), part of the lawyer's job is to weigh alternatives constantly, to think of options and counteroptions, of the benefits and liabilities of any one particular course of action. Good lawyers are so inclined because they understand that our legal system is infested with unknowns and ambiguities. Good legal researchers also have this understanding. They are not frightened by ambiguities; they thrive on them.

Section B. THE IMPORTANCE OF LEGAL RESEARCH

You will eventually forget most of the law that you learn in school. If you do not forget most of it, you should! No one can know all of the law at any given time, even in a specialty. Furthermore, the law is always changing. Nothing is more dangerous than someone with out-of-date law. Law cannot be practiced on the basis of the rules learned in school, since those rules may no longer be valid. Thousands of courts, legislatures, and administrative agencies spend considerable time writing new laws and changing or adapting old ones.

The law library and the techniques of legal research are the indispensable tickets of admission to current law. School teaches you to think. *You teach yourself the law through the skill of legal research.* Every time you walk into a law library, you are your own professor. You must accept nothing less than to become an expert on the topic of your research, no matter how narrow the topic. The purpose of the law library is to enable you to become an expert on the current law of your topic. Do not fall into the trap of thinking that you must be an expert in an area of the law in order to research it properly. The reverse is true. A major way for you to become an expert in an area is through what you discover in the law library on your own.

Never be reluctant to undertake legal research on a topic because you know very little about the topic. Knowing very little is often the most healthy starting point for the researcher! Preconceptions about the law can sometimes lead you away from avenues in the library that you should be traveling.

To become an expert through comprehensive legal research does not necessarily mean that you will know everything. Experts are not simply people who know the answers; they also know how to *formulate the questions that remain unanswered even after comprehensive legal research.* An expert is someone who can say:

> This is what the current law says, and these are the questions that the law has not yet resolved.

You cannot, of course, know what is unresolved until you know what is resolved. The law library will tell you both.

Section C. FRUSTRATION AND LEGAL RESEARCH

You are in the position of the king who sadly had to be told that there is no royal road to geometry. If he wanted to learn geometry, he had to struggle through it like everyone else. Legal research is a struggle and will remain so for the rest of your career. The struggle will eventually become manageable and even enjoyable and exciting—but there is no way out of the struggle no matter how many short cuts you learn. The amount of material in a law library is simply too massive for it to be otherwise, and the material is growing every day with new laws, new formats for law books, and new law publishers offering different services that must be mastered. The first step in being able to handle the law library is to accept the fact that the struggle will never go away.

Unfortunately, many cannot handle the pressure that the law library sometimes seems to donate in abundance. Too many lawyers, for example, stay away from the library and practice law "from the hip." Such lawyers need to be sure that they have extensive malpractice insurance!

Legal research will be difficult for you at the beginning, but with experience in the law library, the difficulties will become manageable. The most important advice you can receive is, stick with it. Spend a lot of time in the library. Be inquisitive. Ask a lot of questions of fellow students, teachers, librarians, lawyers, paralegals, legal secretaries, etc. Be constantly on the alert for tips and techniques. Take strange books from the shelf and try to figure out what they contain, what they try to do, how they are used, and how they duplicate or complement other law books that are not strange to you. Do not wait to be taught how to use sets of books that are new to you. Strike out on your own.

The coming of computer technology to legal research (p. 632) is of some help, but computers cannot eliminate your need to learn the basics. The struggle does not disappear if you are lucky enough to study or work where computers are available. Intelligent use of computers requires an understanding of the fundamental techniques of legal research.

At this stage of your career, most of the frustration will center on the question of how to *begin* your legal research of a topic. Once you master this problem, the concern will then become how to *end* your legal research. After having located a great deal of material, you will worry about when to stop. In this chapter, our major focus will be the techniques of beginning. Techniques of stopping are more troublesome for the conscientious researcher. It is not always easy to determine whether you have found everything that you should find. Although guidelines do exist and will be examined, a great deal of experience with legal research is required before you can make the judgment that you have found everything available on a given topic. The important point is, do not be too hard on yourself. The techniques will come with time and practice. You will not learn everything now; you can only begin the learning that must continue throughout your career.

Keep the following "laws" of legal research in mind:

1. *The only books that will be missing from a shelf are those that you need to use immediately.*
2. *The only sets of law books and legal research techniques that are worth learning are those that you will forget about soon after learning them.*
3. *Each time you forget something, relearning it will take half the time it previously took.*
4. *When you have relearned something for the fourth time, you own it.*

At times you will walk away from a set of law books that you have used and wonder what you have just done—even if you obtained an answer from the books. At times you will go back to a set of books that you have used before and draw a blank on what the books are and how to use them again. These occurrences are natural. You will forget and you will forget again. Stay with it. Be willing to relearn. You cannot master a set of books after using them only a few times. Learning legal research is a little like learning to play a musical instrument: A seat is waiting for you in the orchestra, but you must practice. A royal road does not exist.

Section D. FLEXIBILITY IN LEGAL RESEARCH

Researchers have reached an enviable plateau when they understand the following paradox: You sometimes do not know what you are looking for until you find it. Since simple answers are rare, researchers are constantly confronted with frustration and ambiguity. As they pursue avenues and leads, they invariably come upon new avenues and thoughts that never occurred to them initially. An entirely new approach to the problem may be uncovered that radically changes their initial perceptions. They reached this stage not because they consciously sought it out but because they were flexible and open-minded enough to be receptive to new approaches and perceptions. This phenomenon is by no means peculiar to legal research. Take the situation of the woman in need of transportation. She sets herself to the task of determining the most economical way to *buy* a good car. In her search, she stumbles upon the practice of leasing cars. After studying this option, she concludes that leasing is the most sensible resolution of her transportation problem. She did not know what she was looking for—a car *leasing* deal—until she found it. Compare this situation with that of a client who comes into a law office for advice on how to write a will so that a certain amount of money will pass to designated individuals upon death. The lawyer asks you to do some legal research in the area of wills. While in the law library studying the law of wills, you see reference to life insurance policies as a substitute for wills in passing cash to beneficiaries at death. You bring this to the attention of the attorney, who decides that this option is indeed worth pursuing. You did not know what you were looking for—a will substitute—until you found it.

Section E. WRITING TO COMMERCIAL LAW PUBLISHERS

Writing to each of the following law publishers, particularly the ones with an asterisk (*) next to their names, will be well worth the investment in time and postage. Send the same short note to each publisher.

I would appreciate receiving a catalog of the law books you publish as well as any pamphlets you may have available on how to use your books. Thank you.

Most publishers will respond (free of charge) with updated material describing their publications. Have this material sent to your home address. When it arrives, compare it with what you will learn from this course. The material will probably be of most use as a review rather than as introductory reading.

MAJOR COMMERCIAL LAW PUBLISHERS

(The most important are indicated by an asterisk.*)

Anderson Publishing Co.
646 Main St.
Cincinnati, Oh. 45201

*Matthew Bender & Co.
235 East 45th St.
New York, N.Y. 10017

*Bureau of National Affairs (BNA)
1231 25th St. NW
Washington, D.C. 20037

Callaghan & Co.
3201 Old Glenview Rd.
Wilmette, Ill. 60091

Clark Boardman Co.
435 Hudson St.
New York, N.Y. 10014

*Commerce Clearing House
   (CCH)
4025 W. Peterson Ave.
Chicago, Ill. 60646

Congressional Information Service
   (CIS)
4520 East-West Highway
Bethesda, Md. 20814

*Lawyers Co-operative Publishing
   Co.
Rochester, N.Y. 14603
(Also ask for information on
   AUTO-CITE.)

Little, Brown & Co.
Law Division
34 Beacon St.
Boston, Mass. 02106

*Mead Data Central
200 Park Ave.
New York, N.Y. 10166
(Ask for information on the
   LEXIS computer.)

Michie Co.
P.O. Box 7587
Charlottesville, Va. 22906

*Prentice-Hall
Englewood, N.J. 07632

*Shepard's/McGraw-Hill
P.O. Box 1235
Colorado Springs, Colo. 80901

Warren, Gorham & Lamont
210 South St.
Boston, Mass. 02111

*West Publishing Co.
50 W. Kellogg Blvd.
P.O. Box 64526
St. Paul, Minn. 55164
(Also ask for information on the
   WESTLAW computer.)

Wiley Law Publications
P.O. Box 177
627 N. Webster St.
Colorado Springs, Colo. 80901

Section F. THE VOCABULARY OF LEGAL RESEARCH: A CHECKLIST

This section includes a list of 194 words and phrases, most of which are examined in the remainder of the chapter. The page number in parentheses indicates where the item is covered in the text. The list is the vocabulary of legal research. Before you are finished with this text, one of your goals should be to know the meaning or function of everything on the list. You must learn to "talk" the language of legal research as well as "do" legal research.

ASSIGNMENT 72

For each of the words and phrases on page 513, prepare a three-by-five-inch index card on which you include the following information:

- The word or phrase.
- The pages in this text where the word or phrase is discussed (begin with the page number given in parentheses, then add other page numbers as the word or phrase is discussed elsewhere in the text).
- The definition of the word or phrase, or the function of the word or phrase, or the list of the techniques or methods called for by the word or phrase.
- Other information about the word or phrase that you obtain as you use the law library.
- Comments by your instructor in class about any of the words and phrases.

Some words and phrases will call for more than one card. You should strive, however, to keep the information on the cards brief. Place the cards in alphabetical order. The cards will become your own file system on legal research, which you can use as a study guide for the course and as a reference tool as you do legal research in the library. Be sure to add cards for words and phrases that are not on the following list as you come across new words and phrases in class and in your use of the library.

See also Assignment 77, p. 600 for other data that you can add to your cards.

Section G. FINDING LAW LIBRARIES

First things first. Before learning how to do legal research, you must have access to a law library. Since you will rarely be able to find *everything* you need in a single library, a more accurate statement is that you must know how to locate the variety of law libraries that are potentially available to you. It is not uncommon for the precise law book you need to be missing from the shelf of an otherwise comprehensive library. It is not uncommon for even a large library to fail to subscribe to a set of books that you need or to be out of date on a set of books that you must use. Finally, it is not uncommon for you to have such particular legal research needs that you must search for specialized collections of books.

THE VOCABULARY OF LEGAL RESEARCH: A CHECKLIST

(The number in parentheses refers to a page in the text).

1. Act (519)
2. Acts and Resolves (519)
3. Administrative code (520)
4. Advance sheet, reporter (521)
5. Advance sheet, Shepard's (521)
6. ALR, ALR2d, ALR3d, ALR4th, and ALR Fed (521)
7. ALR Blue Book of Supplemental Decisions (524)
8. ALR2 Digest (606)
9. ALR2d Later Case Service (607)
10. American Digest System (536)
11. American Law Institute (550)
12. Am Jur 2d (522)
13. Am Jur Pl & Pr Forms (558)
14. Am Jur Trials (630)
15. Am Jur Proof of Facts (630)
16. Amicus curiae brief (525)
17. Annotated reports (522)
18. Annotation (522)
19. Appellant (478)
20. Appellate brief (695)
21. Appellate court (478)
22. Appellee (478)
23. Atlantic Digest (541)
24. Atlantic 2d (A.2d) (528)
25. Authority, mandatory (561)
26. Authority, persuasive (561)
27. Authority, primary (561)
28. Authority reference in CFR (673)
29. Authority, secondary (561)
30. AUTO-CITE (639)
31. Bill (523)
32. Blue Book (citations) (523)
33. BNA (511)
34. Brief of a case (695)
35. Brief of a statute (653)
36. Brackets in text of unofficial reporter (642)
37. California Reporter (Cal Rptr) (641)
38. Case (516)
39. Casebook (532)
40. Case on point (563)
41. CCH Congressional Index (668)
42. CCH U.S. Supreme Court Bulletin (526)
43. Century Digest (537)
44. Certiorari (cert) (480)
45. Charter (516)
46. CARTWHEEL (591)
47. Citation (570)
48. Citator (533)
49. Cited material (Shepard's) (611)
50. Citing material (Shepard's) (611)
51. Code, Codify (533)
52. Code of Federal Regulations (C.F.R.) (520)
53. Committee reports (659)
54. Common law (377)
55. Concurring opinion (645)
56. Congressional Information Service (CIS) (668)
57. Congressional Record (534)
58. Constitution (516)
59. Corpus Juris Secundum (C.J.S.) (534)
60. Cumulative (535)
61. Cumulative Table of Key Numbers (604)
62. Current Law Index (CLI) (626)
63. Decisions, administrative (516)
64. Decennial Digests (537)
65. Defendant-Plaintiff Table of Cases (in digests) (603)
66. Descriptive Word Index (in digests) (603)

67. Desk Book (court rules) (534)
68. Dictum (645)
69. Digests (for reporters) (535)
70. Docket number (642)
71. Et seq. (621)
72. Executive order (516)
73. Federal Digest (538)
74. Federal Practice Digest 2d (538)
75. Federal Practice Digest 3d (539)
76. Federal Quick Index (606)
77. Federal Supplement (F.Supp.) (527)
78. Federal Register (542)
79. Federal Reporter 2d (527)
80. Federal Rules Decisions (F.R.D.) (526)
81. Formbook (543)
82. General Digest (537)
83. Handbook (544)
84. Headnote (544)
85. Hornbook (544)
86. Index to Legal Periodicals (ILP) (626)
87. Index Medicus (628)
88. Interstate compact (544)
89. Key topic and number (544)
90. Key topic and number, four techniques for finding (603)
91. Law review (546)
92. Lawyers Co-operative Publishing Co. (Lawyers Co-op) (557)
93. Lawyers' Edition (L.Ed.) (reporter) (525)
94. Legal dictionary (545)
95. Legal encyclopedia (545)
96. Legal newspaper (546)
97. Legal periodical literature (625)
98. Legal Resource Index (LRI) (626)
99. Legislative History (656)
100. LEXIS (633, 720)
101. List of CFR Parts Affected (in Federal Register) (673)
102. List of Sections Affected (LSA) (673)
103. Loose-leaf service (547)
104. Majority opinion (645)
105. Martindale-Hubbell Law Directory (548)
106. MEDLINE (628)
107. Memorandum opinion (643)
108. Military Justice Reporter (527)
109. Modern Federal Practice Digest (538)
110. "n" found to the right of citing material in Shepard's (617)
111. National Reporter Blue Book (524)
112. National Reporter System (528)
113. New York Supplement (NYS) (532)
114. Nominative reporters (576)
115. Nonauthority (562)
116. North Eastern 2d (N.E.2d) (529)
117. North Western Digest (542)
118. North Western 2d (N.W.2d) (529)
119. Notes of decisions (650)
120. Official citation (525, 575)
121. Opinion (516)
122. Opinion of the Attorney General (517)
123. Ordinance (516)
124. Pacific 2d (P.2d) (529)
125. Pacific Digest (540)
126. Parallel cite (573)
127. Parallel cites for cases, four techniques for finding (573)
128. Parallel Table of Statutory Authorities and Rules (in CFR) (655)
129. Per curiam (643)
130. Permanent ALR Digest (606)
131. Plaintiff-Defendant Table (table of cases in digests) (603)

132. Pocket part (590)
133. Popular Name Table (654)
134. Practice Manual (543)
135. Private statute or law (516)
136. Public Law (PL) (516, 667)
137. Quick Index (606)
138. Record (550)
139. Regional digest (540)
140. Regulations, administrative (516)
141. Remand (644)
142. Reporter (525)
143. Respondent (641)
144. Restatements (550)
145. Rules of court (534)
146. "s" found to the right of citing material in Shepard's (617)
147. Scope note (603)
148. Series (551)
149. Session Law (618)
150. Shepardize a case, six kinds of data obtained thereby (613)
151. Shepardize a headnote or syllabus number (614)
152. Shepardize a statute, seven kinds of data obtained thereby (618)
153. Slip law (555)
154. Slip opinion (556)
155. South Eastern Digest (542)
156. South Eastern 2d (S.E.2d) (530)
157. Southern Digest (542)
158. Southern 2d (S.2d) (530)
159. South Western 2d (S.W.2d) (530)
160. Star-paging (525)
161. Statute (516)
162. Statutory code (557)
163. Superseded annotation (607)
164. Supplemental annotation (607)
165. Supreme Court Reporter (S.Ct.) (525)
166. Syllabus Number (614)
167. Table of Courts and Circuits (607)
168. Table of Jurisdictions Represented (607)
169. Table of Laws and Regulations Cited in ALR Fed (606)
170. Table 2 in U.S. Code Congressional and Administrative News (559)
171. Table 4 in U.S. Code Congressional and Administrative News (558)
172. Table III in the Tables volume of USC/USCA/USCS (655)
173. Treatise (558)
174. Treaty (517)
175. Total Client-Service Library (557)
176. Trace a key topic and number in West digests (603)
177. Union List of Legislative Histories (668)
178. Unofficial citation (525, 575)
179. U.S. Code (U.S.C.) (557)
180. U.S. Code Annotated (U.S.C.A.) (557)
181. U.S. Code Congressional and Administrative News (558)
182. U.S. Code Service (U.S.C.S.) (557)
183. U.S. Court of Appeals (333, 572)
184. U.S. District Courts (333, 572)
185. U.S. Law Week (USLW) (559)
186. U.S. Reports (U.S.) (525)
187. U.S. Statutes at Large (Stat.) (559)
188. U.S. Supreme Court Digest (L.Ed.) (539)
189. U.S. Supreme Court Digest (West) (539)
190. WESTLAW (632, 720)
191. West Publishing Co. (528)
192. Word Index for ALR (606)
193. Word Index for ALR2d (606)
194. Words and Phrases (545)

The availability of law libraries depends to a large degree on the area in which you live, work, and study. Rural areas will have fewer possibilities than large cities or capitals. Furthermore, some libraries may be open to you only with special permission.

You begin, of course, with the library where you are a student. Find out if it will meet your research needs. Visit the law librarian as soon as possible. Ask this person if there is a list or directory of law libraries or librarians in your city. (Check the latest edition of the *Directory of Law Libraries* published by the American Association of Law Libraries. The *Directory* identifies some of the larger libraries by state and city.) Ask your law librarian which libraries are open to the public and which require special permission for use. Also ask for guidance in obtaining this permission.

The following is a list of possible libraries in your area, with suggestions on how to obtain information about them and whom to contract for help in gaining access. In addition to these suggestions, you should consider asking your own librarian or program director to seek permission for you to use the libraries.

1. Law school libraries
   - Ask students who attend the school if it is open to outsiders.
   - Ask the librarian or the dean of the school if you may use the facilities.
   - Find out if any of the law school libraries in your area are federal depository libraries. These libraries receive free government legal publications in exchange for making them available to the general public. Hence you must be allowed access.
2. State law libraries
   - Ask a lawyer who uses the library for help in gaining access.
   - Ask a local politician's office to help you.
   - Ask the state law librarian for permission.
3. Law libraries in the legislature
   - Ask your legislator for help.
   - Ask the librarian in the legislature's law library.
4. Law libraries of administrative agencies (e.g., worker's compensation agency, human services agency)
   - Ask the director of the agency for permission.
   - Ask staff lawyers or paralegals who work at the agency for help.
   - Ask a local politician's office for help.
   - Ask a staff member of the agency's library.
5. Bar association law libraries
   - Ask a member of the association if you may be his or her guest at the library.
   - Contact the president of the association for help.
   - Ask the association's law librarian.
6. The law libraries of other associations (e.g., insurance companies, real estate agents, unions)
   - Ask a member of the association if he or she will sponsor your use of the library.
   - Contact the president of the association for help.
   - Contact the association's librarian.

7. Public interest law office libraries (e.g., a legal service office, a conservation or environmental law office)
    - Ask a staff lawyer or paralegal for help.
    - Ask the director of the office.
    - Ask the librarian of the office's library.
8. The law office of the attorney general or corporation counsel
    - Ask a staff attorney or paralegal for help.
    - Ask a local politician's office for help.
    - Ask the law librarian there for permission.
    - Ask the attorney general or the corporation counsel for permission.
9. The law library of courts
    - Ask the librarian at the court for permission.
    - Ask a judge for permission.
10. The law library of private law firms
    - Ask a lawyer or paralegal at the firm for help.
    - Ask the firm's librarian.

In short, you will have to use some ingenuity to locate these libraries and gain access to them. Try more than one avenue of entry. Some libraries might be willing to let you use the facilities in exchange for several hours of volunteer work in the library. Do not give up when the first person you contact tells you that the library is for members only. Some students adopt the strategy of walking into any library and acting as if they belong there. Rather than ask for permission, they wait for someone to stop them or to question their right to be there. The theory of this approach is that forgiveness is often easier to obtain than permission. Other students take the wiser course of seeking permission in advance. Yet, even here, some creativity is needed in the way that you ask for permission. The bold question, "Can I use your library?" may be less effective than an approach such as, "Would it be possible for me to use some of your law books for a short period of time for some important research that I must do?"

Section H. A GLOSSARY OF LAW AND LAW BOOKS: INTRODUCTION

You should be familiar with approximately ten categories of law. The purpose of legal research is to find these laws, to check their current validity, and to apply them to the facts of the research problem. Step one is to know the definitions of the categories.

A word of caution in approaching the vocabulary of law and legal research: The same word or phrase can often have a different meaning depending upon the context in which it is used. *Supreme Court,* for example, refers to the *highest* court in our federal judicial system as well as to the *trial* court in New York State; and the word *opinion* often refers both to administrative decisions of agencies and to the judicial decisions of courts. Although standard definitions are generally used, you should be prepared to find variations.

KINDS OF LAW

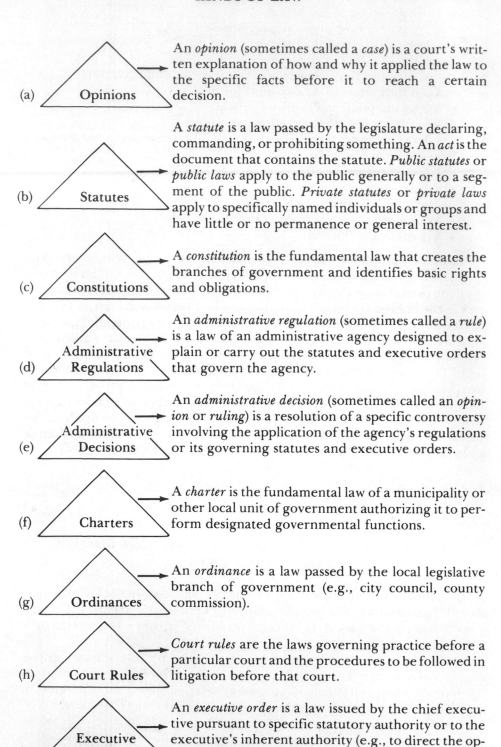

(a) **Opinions**

An *opinion* (sometimes called a *case*) is a court's written explanation of how and why it applied the law to the specific facts before it to reach a certain decision.

(b) **Statutes**

A *statute* is a law passed by the legislature declaring, commanding, or prohibiting something. An *act* is the document that contains the statute. *Public statutes* or *public laws* apply to the public generally or to a segment of the public. *Private statutes* or *private laws* apply to specifically named individuals or groups and have little or no permanence or general interest.

(c) **Constitutions**

A *constitution* is the fundamental law that creates the branches of government and identifies basic rights and obligations.

(d) **Administrative Regulations**

An *administrative regulation* (sometimes called a *rule*) is a law of an administrative agency designed to explain or carry out the statutes and executive orders that govern the agency.

(e) **Administrative Decisions**

An *administrative decision* (sometimes called an *opinion* or *ruling*) is a resolution of a specific controversy involving the application of the agency's regulations or its governing statutes and executive orders.

(f) **Charters**

A *charter* is the fundamental law of a municipality or other local unit of government authorizing it to perform designated governmental functions.

(g) **Ordinances**

An *ordinance* is a law passed by the local legislative branch of government (e.g., city council, county commission).

(h) **Court Rules**

Court rules are the laws governing practice before a particular court and the procedures to be followed in litigation before that court.

(i) **Executive Orders**

An *executive order* is a law issued by the chief executive pursuant to specific statutory authority or to the executive's inherent authority (e.g., to direct the operation of governmental agencies).

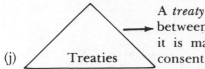

A *treaty* is an international agreement entered into between two or more countries. In the United States it is made by the President with the advice and consent of the Senate.

(j)   Treaties

(The following falls into a separate category. They are advisory and hence are not considered laws in the same sense as the above ten.)

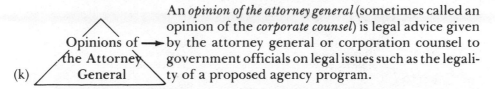

An *opinion of the attorney general* (sometimes called an opinion of the *corporate counsel*) is legal advice given by the attorney general or corporation counsel to government officials on legal issues such as the legality of a proposed agency program.

(k)   Opinions of the Attorney General

Next we begin examining the sets of books in the library that are relevant to the ten categories of laws. For each category, four types of books should be kept in mind:

1. Sets of books that contain the full text of a certain kind of law.
2. Sets of books that can be used to locate that kind of law.
3. Sets of books that can be used to help explain that kind of law.
4. Sets of books that can be used to help determine the current validity of that kind of law.

Some sets of books serve more than one of the above four functions. The following chart presents a catalog of research materials according to the above functions. After the chart, you will find a glossary of descriptions and definitions of the major materials in the chart.

CHART 1

A CATALOG OF RESEARCH MATERIALS				
KIND OF LAW	SETS OF MATERIALS THAT CONTAIN THE FULL TEXT OF THIS KIND OF LAW	SETS OF MATERIALS THAT CAN BE USED TO LOCATE THIS KIND OF LAW	SETS OF MATERIALS THAT CAN BE USED TO HELP EXPLAIN THIS KIND OF LAW	SETS OF MATERIALS THAT CAN BE USED TO HELP DETERMINE THE CURRENT VALIDITY OF THIS KIND OF LAW
(a) Opinions	Reports Reporters ALR, ALR2d, ALR3d, ALR4th, ALR Fed. Legal newspapers Loose-leaf services Slip opinion Advance sheets WESTLAW, LEXIS	Digests Annotations in ALR, ALR2d, ALR3d, ALR4th, ALR Fed. Shepard's Legal periodicals Encyclopedias Treatises Loose-leaf services Words and Phrases	Legal periodicals Encyclopedias Treatises Annotations in ALR, ALR2d, ALR3d, ALR4th, ALR Fed. Loose-leaf services	Shepard's

(b) Statutes	Statutory Code Statutes Statutes at Large Session Laws Laws Compilations Consolidated Laws Slip Law Acts, Acts & Resolves WESTLAW, LEXIS	Index volumes of statutory code Loose-leaf services Footnote references in encyclopedias, legal periodicals, etc.	Legal periodicals Encyclopedias Treatises Annotations in ALR, ALR2d, ALR3d, ALR4th, ALR Fed. Loose-leaf services	Shepard's
(c) Constitutions	Statutory Code Separate volumes containing the constitution	Index volumes of statutory code Loose-leaf services Footnote references in encyclopedias, legal periodicals, etc.	Legal periodicals Encyclopedias Treatises Annotations in ALR, ALR2d, ALR3d, ALR4th, ALR Fed. Loose-leaf services	Shepard's
(d) Administrative Regulations	Administrative Codes Separate volumes or pamphlets containing the regulations of certain agencies Loose-leaf services	Index volumes of the administrative code Loose-leaf services Footnote references in encyclopedias, legal periodicals, etc.	Legal periodicals Treatises Annotations in ALR, ALR2d, ALR3d, ALR4th, ALR Fed. Loose-leaf services	Shepard's (for some agencies only) List of Sections Affected
(e) Administrative Decisions	Separate volumes of decisions of certain agencies Loose-leaf services	Loose-leaf services Index or digest volumes to the decisions Footnote references in other materials	Legal periodicals Treatises Annotations in ALR, ALR2d, ALR3d, ALR4th, ALR Fed. Loose-leaf services	Shepard's (for some agencies only)
(f) Charters	Separate volumes containing the charter Municipal Code State session laws Official journal Legal newspaper	Index volumes to the charter or municipal code Footnote references in other materials	Legal periodicals Treatises Annotations in ALR, ALR2d, ALR3d, ALR4th, ALR Fed.	Shepard's
(g) Ordinances	Municipal Code Official journal Legal newspaper	Index volumes of municipal code Footnote references in other materials	Legal periodicals Treatises Annotations in ALR, ALR2d, ALR3d, ALR4th, ALR Fed.	Shepard's

(h) Court Rules	Separate rules volumes Statutory code Practice manuals	Index to separate rules volumes Index to statutory code Index to practice manuals Footnote references in other materials	Practice manuals Treatises Annotations in ALR, ALR2d, ALR3d, ALR4th, ALR Fed. Encyclopedias Loose-leaf services	Shepard's
(i) Executive Orders	Federal Register Code of Federal Regulations U.S. Code Congressional and Administrative News U.S.C./U.S.C.A./ U.S.C.S. (for some orders only)	Index volumes to the sets of books listed in the second column Footnote references in other materials	Legal periodicals Treatises Annotations in ALR, ALR2d, ALR3d, ALR4th, ALR Fed.	Shepard's Code of Federal Regulations Citations
(j) Treaties	Statutes at Large (up to 1949) United States Treaties and Other International Agreements Department of State Bulletin International Legal Materials United Nations Treaty Series	Index within the volumes listed in second column World Treaty Index Current Treaty Index Footnote references in other materials	Legal periodicals Treatises Annotations in ALR, ALR2d, ALR3d, ALR4th, ALR Fed.	Shepard's
(k) Opinions of the Attorney General	Separate volumes containing these opinions	Digests Index in separate volumes of the opinions Footnote references in other materials		

The following is a glossary of some of the major legal research books and terms, including many used in the above chart:

ACTS; ACTS AND RESOLVES

An act is the official document that contains the statute passed by the legislature. Acts and Resolves is the set of books that contain all the acts of the legislature. They are also sometimes called Session Laws, Statutes, Statutes at Large, Laws, etc. A major characteristic of all of these books is that the statutes in them are printed chronologically as they are passed. They are not classified or organized by subject matter. (See Code p. 533.)

ADMINISTRATIVE CODE

An administrative code is a collection of the regulations of one or more agencies. The regulations in a code are organized by subject matter. Generally, the regulations of state and local administrative agencies are poorly organized and difficult to obtain. Not so for the federal agencies.

Code of Federal Regulations (C.F.R.) containing many of the regulations of federal agencies, e.g., U.S. Department of Agriculture. (See p. 672.)

ADVANCE SHEET

An advance sheet is a pamphlet printed before (in "advance" of) a bound volume, or before a thicker pamphlet, which will consolidate the material in several of the earlier advance sheets. When the bound volume or thicker pamphlet comes out, the advance sheet is thrown away. There are two kinds of advance sheets in the law library: an advance sheet for reporters and one for Shepard's.

Advance sheet for a reporter (here the Supreme Court Reporter). The advance sheet contains the full text of court opinions that will later be printed in a bound Supreme Court Reporter volume.

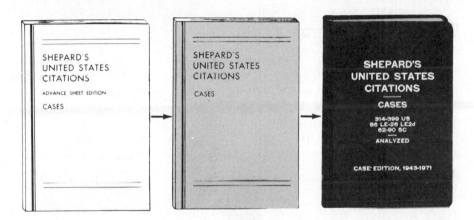

Advance sheet for Shepard's (here United States Citations covering cases of the U.S. Supreme Court). The advance sheet contains the "sheparding" data that will later be printed in thicker pamphlets and eventually in a bound Shepard's volume. (See p. 552.)

ALR, ALR2d, ALR3d, ALR4th, ALR Fed

- ALR: American Law Reports, First Series
- ALR2d: American Law Reports, Second Series
- ALR3d: American Law Reports, Third Series
- ALR4th: American Law Reports, Fourth Series
- ALR Fed: American Law Reports, Federal Series.

These sets of books contain the complete text of *selected* court opinions followed by extensive commentary or research papers on issues within the opinions selected. These research papers are called annotations. The sets of books are therefore called annotated reports. They are published by Lawyers Co-operative Publishing Company. As we shall see later, annotations are excellent case finders (p. 605).

American Law Reports, Third Series

AMERICAN DIGEST SYSTEM

See Digests (p. 535, p. 600).

AMERICAN JURISPRUDENCE 2d (Am.Jur.2d)

Am.Jur.2d is a national legal encyclopedia (published by Lawyers Co-operative Publishing Company) that provides numerous discussions and summaries of almost every area of the law. It is particularly useful (1) as background reading before beginning legal research on a topic and (2) as a case finder because of the extensive footnotes. (Am.Jur.2d is the second edition of Am.Jur. First.) The main competitor of Am.Jur.2d is Corpus Juris Secundum (p. 534).

ANNOTATION

To annotate means to provide critical notes or commentary. An annotated bibliography, for example, is a list of references (citations) plus brief summaries or comments on each entry in the list. (See p. 677.) An "annotated report" is the full text of a court opinion plus notes or commentary on the opinion or on a part of it. The word *annotation* mainly refers to the notes and commentary that follow the opinions found in ALR, ALR2d, ALR3d, ALR4th, and ALR Fed (see p. 605). You are being directed to these sets of books when someone asks you to "find out if there are any annotations on this issue." The phrase *annotated code* or *annotated statutes* is also sometimes used (e.g., Unites States Code Annotated). Annotated codes or statutes are sets of statutes that contain the full text of the statutes plus research references such as summaries of opinions interpreting the statutes (p. 650). The abbreviation for annotation is usually "ann." (e.g., Del. Code Ann).

ATLANTIC DIGEST

See Digests (p. 541).

ATLANTIC REPORTER 2d (A.2d)

See Cases (p. 528).

BALLENTINE'S LAW DICTIONARY

See Legal Dictionary (p. 545).

BILL

A bill is a proposed statute (i.e., one that has not yet been enacted into law). Bills are printed in small booklet or pamphlet form. (Federal bills are also printed in the Congressional Record.)

BLACK'S LAW DICTIONARY

See Legal Dictionary (p. 545).

BLUE BOOK

The phrase *blue book* will usually refer to one of the three following books or sets of books:

1. A Uniform System of Citation
2. ALR Blue Book of Supplemental Decisions
3. National Reporter Blue Book.

A Uniform System of Citation. A small blue pamphlet published by the law reviews of several law schools. The pamphlet covers the "rules" of citation form. It is considered by many to be the bible of citation form (p. 571).

The ALR Blue Book of Supplemental Decisions will enable you to update the annotations found in ALR First Series (p. 607).

National Reporter Blue Book. A set of books published by West that will enable you to find a parallel cite to a court opinion (p. 574).

BRIEF, APPELLATE

An appellate brief is a written document prepared by a party for submission to an appellate court in which arguments are presented on the correctness or incorrectness of what a trial court or lower court of appeals did or failed to do.

IN THE

Supreme Court of the United States

OCTOBER TERM, 1977

No.

JOHN DOE, *et al.*,

Petitioners,

v.

JOHN L. McMILLAN, *et al.*,

Respondents.

**PETITION FOR WRIT OF CERTIORARI
TO THE UNITED STATES COURT OF APPEALS
FOR THE DISTRICT OF COLUMBIA CIRCUIT**

ROBERT S. CATZ
BURTON D. WECHSLER
Urban Law Institute
of the Antioch School of Law
1624 Crescent Place, N.W.
Washington, D.C. 20009
(202) 265-9500

Counsel for Petitioners

Of Counsel:
SUSAN McDUFFIE
MABLE CHU
Washington, D.C.

Amicus curiae means friend of the court. An *amicus curiae* brief is also an appellate brief, but it is prepared and submitted by a nonparty. A court must give permission for the nonparty to submit such a brief.

Locating appellate briefs written on recent cases is often possible. The briefs are found in the clerk's office of the court where they were submitted, in large law school libraries, in court libraries, and in state law libraries. They can provide excellent research leads for cases with similar issues.

The word *brief* is also used in two other senses. First, a trial brief (sometimes called a trial manual or trial book) is a collection of all the documents, arguments, and strategies that an attorney plans to use at trial. It is a blueprint for conducting the trial (p. 695). Second, a brief of a case (court opinion) is your own notes on the case including the key facts of the case, the issues in the case, the reasoning of the court, the disposition, etc. (p. 645).

BULLETIN

A Bulletin is a publication issued on an ongoing or periodic basis (e.g., Internal Revenue Bulletin).

CALIFORNIA REPORTER
(Cal. Rptr.)

See Cases (p. 532).

CASES

The word *case* is often used interchangeably with the word opinion. The full text of cases are found in volumes called reports or reporters. An official reporter is published under the authority of the legislature and is often printed by the government itself. An unofficial reporter is printed by a private publishing company (e.g., West) with or without authority from the legislature. First we examine the reporters containing opinions of the federal courts. Then we will look at the reporters for state courts.

Federal Court Opinions

The opinions of the United States Supreme Court are printed in an official report, United States Reports (abbreviated "U.S."), and in several unofficial reporters: the Supreme Court Reporter published by West Publishing Company (abbreviated "S.Ct.") and United States Supreme Court Reports, Lawyers' Edition, published by Lawyers Co-operative Publishing Company (abbreviated "L.Ed.").

When an opinion is printed in the United States Reports, it will also be printed word-for-word in S.Ct. and in L.Ed., the unofficial reporters—but not necessarily on the same page numbers. Suppose that you are reading an opinion in an unofficial reporter and you want to quote from it. The standard practice is to give the reference or citation to the quote as it appears in the *official* reporter. Suppose, however, that the latter is simply not available in your library. How do you quote a page number in an official reporter when all you have available is an unofficial reporter? The answer is a technique called "star-paging." While you are reading a page in an unofficial reporter, you will find a notation of some kind provided by the printer (e.g., an asterisk, a star, a special indentation) plus a page number, usually in black bold print. The latter is a reference to a page number of the same case in the official reporter. Star paging therefore enables you to determine on what pages the same court language can be found in official and unofficial reporters.

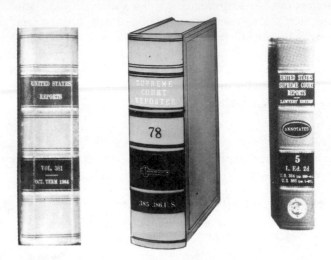

Two loose-leaf services (p. 547) also print the text of all U.S. Supreme Court opinions:

1. United States Law Week (USLW) published by Bureau of National Affairs (BNA).
2. United States Supreme Court Bulletin published by Commerce Clearing House. S.Ct.Bull. (CCH).

We turn now to reporters for the *lower* federal courts. Two major reporters contain the full text of opinions from lower federal courts:

1. Federal Reporter (abbreviated "F.")
   Federal Reporter, Second Series (abbreviated "F.2d")
2. Federal Supplement (abbreviated "F.Supp.")

These are all unofficial reporters published by West.

These two reporters do *not* print every opinion written by the courts that they cover. The courts decide which opinions are sufficiently important to submit to West for publication.

In addition to F., F.2d, and F.Supp., West publishes several specialty or topical reporters that also cover federal courts.

1. Federal Rules Decisions (F.R.D.)
   • Contains opinions of the U.S. District Courts on the Federal Rules of Criminal and Civil Procedure, and also

Federal Reporter, Second Series (F.2d). Currently contains the full text of the opinions written by the United States Courts of Appeals.

Federal Supplement (F.Supp.) Currently *Case* contains the full text of the opinions written by the United States District Courts and the United States Court of International Trade.

* Contains articles, speeches, and conference reports on procedural issues.
2. Military Justice Reporter (M.J.)
   * Contains opinions of the United States Court of Military Appeals and the Courts of Military Review for the Army, Navy-Marine, Air Force, and Coast Guard.
3. Bankruptcy Reporter (Bankr.)
   * Contains opinions of the United States Bankruptcy Courts and of other federal courts.
4. Education Law Reporter
5. Social Security Reporting Service
6. United States Claims Court Reporter.

State Court Opinions

At one time, all states had official reports of their highest state courts. An example of an official state report:

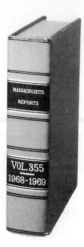

A large number of states, however, have discontinued their official reports. For such states, the unofficial reporters are the main or only source where you can find the opinions of their state courts.

The major publisher of unofficial state reports is West Publishing Company through its National Reporter System. The following seven *regional* reporters in the System contain the opinions written by the courts indicated:

Atlantic Reporter (A.), Atlantic Reporter, Second Series (A.2d). The opinions of the highest state court and some intermediate appellate courts in the following states: Conn., Del., Maine, Md., N.H., N.J., Pa., R.I., Vt., plus the District of Columbia.

North Eastern Reporter (N.E.), North Eastern Reporter, Second Series (N.E.2d). The opinions of the highest state court and some intermediate appellate courts in the following states: Ill., Ind., Mass., N.Y., Ohio.

North Western Reporter (N.W.), North Western Reporter, Second Series (N.W.2d). The opinions of the highest state court and some intermediate appellate courts in the following states: Iowa, Mich., Minn., Nebr., N. Dak., S. Dak., Wis.

Pacific Reporter (P.), Pacific Reporter, Second Series (P.2d). The opinions of the highest state court and some intermediate appellate courts in the following states: Alaska, Ariz., Calif., Colo., Hawaii, Idaho, Kan., Mont., Nev., N. Mex., Okla., Oreg., Utah, Wash., Wyo.

South Eastern Reporter (S.E.), South Eastern Reporter, Second Series (S.E.2d). The opinions of the highest state court and some intermediate appellate courts in the following states: Ga., N.C., S.C., Va., W.Va.

Southern Reporter (S.), Southern Reporter, Second Series (S.2d). The opinions of the highest state court and some intermediate appellate courts in the following states: Ala., Fla., La., Miss.

South Western Reporter (S.W.), South Western Reporter, Second Series (S.W.2d). The opinions of the highest state courts and some intermediate appellate courts in the following states: Ark., Ky., Mo., Tenn., Tex.

These seven regional reporters and the states they cover can be seen on the following map:

**NATIONAL REPORTER
SYSTEM MAP**

If a law office subscribes to a regional reporter covering its own state, the office is also receiving opinions of other states in the same region. These other opinions may be of little practical value to the office. West therefore publishes special state editions for many of the states. These special edition state reporters contain only the opinions of an individual state that are also printed in the regional reporter. For example, you saw above that the opinions of the highest court in Kansas are printed in the Pacific Reporter. A Kansas lawyer who does not want to subscribe to the Pacific Reporter can subscribe to the special edition Kansas reporter, called Kansas Cases.

A volume of **Kansas Cases** (a special edition state reporter) containing all the Kansas opinions printed in Pacific Reporter, 2d.

Finally, West publishes three separate reporters for New York, California, and Illinois:

- New York Supplement.
- California Reporter.
- Illinois Decisions.

Each contains the opinions of the highest court in the state as well as selected opinions of its lower courts.

Major Characteristics of West Reporters

- The reporters contain the full context of court opinions.
- The opinions are arranged in rough chronological order.
- The reporters have advance sheets that come out before the bound volumes (p. 521).
- There are Table of Cases at the beginning of each reporter volume.
- There is a Table of Statutes Construed in many reporters listing the statutes interpreted within an individual reporter volume.
- There is *no* traditional subject-matter index in any individual reporter volume (the main index to the opinions in reporters is the separate set of books called digests, p. 535).
- At the beginning of each opinion there are small-paragraph summaries of the opinion. As we will see later, these are headnotes which are also printed in digests (p. 601).

CASEBOOK

A casebook is a law school textbook. It consists mainly of a collection of edited court opinions and other materials relating to a particular area of the law, e.g., Lockhart, Kamisar, and Choper, *Constitutional Rights and Liberties: Cases and Materials.*

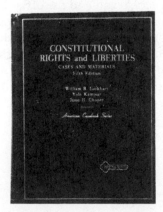

CENTURY DIGEST

See Digests (p. 537).

CITATION

A citation (also called a cite) is a reference to any written material, e.g., a case, statute, law review article, treatise, treaty, annotation, report. The reference tells you how to locate the item, e.g., by volume number, name of book, edition, page number, section number. A *complete* cite gives all the information required by proper citation form (p. 571). A *parallel* cite is an additional reference to the *same* material. If there are two parallel cites to a case, for example, you will be able to find the same case—word for word—in two different reporters (p. 573). The major book on citation form is A Uniform System of Citation (p. 524).

CITATOR

A citator is a book containing lists of cites that serve two functions: first and foremost, to help you assess the current validity of a case, statute, or other law; and secondarily, to provide you with leads to additional laws. Citators often provide other features as well, e.g., they will give you a parallel cite (p. 573). The major citator in legal research is Shepard's. The columns of Shepard's contain nothing but citations that are relevant to whatever you are "shepardizing" (pp. 608, 552).

CODE

A code is a collection of laws or rules classified by subject matter. To codify something means to rearrange it by subject matter. The arrangement of *un*codified material is chronological as it is created; the arrangement of *codified* material is by topic. When statutes are first passed by the legislature, they are placed in uncodified books called Session Laws, Acts and Resolves, Statutes at Large, etc. Most of these statutes are later codified into statutory codes. (See Statutory Code, p. 557.) Administrative regulations are also often codified. (See Administrative Code, p. 520.)

CODE OF FEDERAL REGULATIONS (C.F.R.)

See Administrative Code, pp. 520, 672.

CONGRESSIONAL RECORD

The Congressional Record is an official collection of the day-to-day happenings of Congress. It is one source of legislative history (p. 668) for federal statutes. It also contains many items that are relevant only to the districts of individual legislators.

CORPUS JURIS SECONDUM (C.J.S.)

Corpus Juris Secondum (C.J.S.) is a national legal encyclopedia (published by West) that provides numerous discussions/summaries of almost every area of the law. (C.J.S. is the second edition of Corpus Juris.) It is very useful (a) as background reading before beginning legal research on a topic and (b) as a case finder because of the extensive footnotes. Its competitor is American Jurisprudence 2d (p. 522).

COURT RULES

Court Rules are the procedural rules governing the mechanics of litigation in a court. They are usually printed in separate rules volumes and/or within the statutory code for the jurisdiction. There are also "Desk Copy" rules for the state and federal courts in most states.

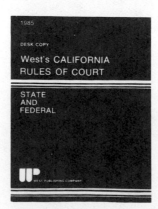

CUMULATIVE

Cumulative means that which consolidates earlier material. A cumulative supplement, for example, is a pamphlet or volume that updates and consolidates all earlier pamphlets or volumes. The earlier material can be thrown away. Similarly, pocket parts (containing supplemental material at the end of a book) are often cumulative. (See p. 590.) When the most recent pocket part comes out, the old one can be thrown away.

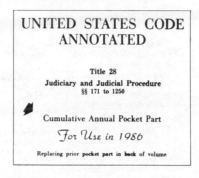

```
        UNITED STATES CODE
             ANNOTATED

                 Title 28
      Judiciary and Judicial Procedure
               §§ 171 to 1250


      Cumulative Annual Pocket Part
          For Use in 1986
      Replacing prior pocket part in back of volume
```

DECENNIAL DIGEST

See Digests (p. 537).

DIGESTS

Our goals in this section are to define digest, to identify the major digests, and to explain the relationship between digests and reporters. Later in the chapter, we will cover the techniques of using digests in research (p. 600).

Digests are volumes containing small-paragraph summaries of court opinions organized by subject matter. Their primary purpose is to serve as case finders. The major publisher of digests is West. Its *key topic and number system* is the organizational principle used to classify the small-paragraph summaries of the opinions in the digests. Every topic and subtopic in the law is assigned a key topic and number by West. For example:

```
 290. Strikes and lockouts.


 984. Sentence on conviction on dif-
          ferent counts.


 406.3(9). Clearly erroneous findings
              of court or jury.
```

Once you find a key topic (and subtopic) plus its key number that is relevant to your research problem, you are given paragraph summaries of cases under that topic and number. For example, the following are cases digested under the topic of "Obscenity" and the subtopics of "Nature and elements of offenses in general" and "Statutory provisions":

> # OBSCENITY
>
> **☞1. Nature and elements of offenses in general.**
>
> **Ill.App. 1973.** Obscenity vel non is not constitutionally protected. People v. Rota, 292 N.E.2d 738.
>
> **Iowa 1973.** Knowledge of obscene material is an essential element in obscenity prosecutions. I.C.A. § 725.5. State v. Lavin, 204 N.W.2d 844.
>
> **☞2. Statutory provisions.**
>
> **D.C.Md. 1972.** Although Maryland motion picture censorship statute did not provide disseminator of motion picture film with an adversary hearing before board of censors on issue of obscenity, disseminator was not constitutionally prejudiced in this regard because the statute requires an adversary judicial determination of obscenity with circuit court for Baltimore City exercising de novo review of the board's finding of obscenity, and with burden of proving that the film is unprotected expression resting on the board. Code Md. 1957, art. 66A, §§ 6(c, d), 19(a); 28 U.S. C.A. § 100. Star v. Preller, 352 F.Supp. 530.

Notice the citations to the cases that follow each paragraph summary, e.g., *People v. Rota* in the first paragraph listed.

There are a few digests that are *not* published by West, e.g., the United States Supreme Court Digest, L.Ed., published by Lawyers Co-operative Publishing Company. (See p. 539.) These digests also contain small-paragraph summaries of court opinions, but since they are not published by West, they are not organized by the key topic system. They use their own organizational principle.

We now turn to an overview of the West digests. Four main kinds can be identified:

- A national digest covering most appellate state and federal courts and some lower state and federal courts.
- Federal digests covering only federal courts.
- Regional digests covering the courts found in the regional reporters.
- Digests of individual courts or states.

National Digest

There is one national digest: the American Digest System published by West. It contains small-paragraph summaries of the court opinions of most appellate state and federal courts and some lower state and federal courts. The American Digest System has three main units: (a) Century Digest, (b) Decennial Digests, and (c) General Digests:

(a) Here is a sample volume from the **Century Digest,** covering summaries of opinions written between 1658 and 1896.

(b) The **Decennial Digests** cover summaries of opinions for ten-year periods starting in 1897. Here is a sample volume from the Ninth Decennial, Part I, covering the period from 1976 to 1981. Part II will cover 1981–1986. (Prior to the Ninth Decennial, all of the Decennial Digests were issued in one part only—covering the entire ten years.)

(c) The **General Digests** cover summaries of opinions since the last Decennial was published. The General Digest volumes are kept on the shelf only until they are eventually consolidated (i.e., cumulated) into the next Decennial Digest unit.

Federal Digests
Covering Only Federal Courts

There are four large digests that cover the main federal courts: the U.S. Supreme Court, the U.S. Courts of Appeal, and the U.S. District Courts. These four digests are distinguished primarily by the years that they cover:

- Federal Digest.
- Modern Federal Practice Digest.
- Federal Practice Digest 2d.
- Federal Practice Digest 3d.

Federal Digest. Contains small-paragraph summaries of federal cases decided through 1939.

Modern Federal Practice Digest. Contains small-paragraph summaries of federal cases decided between 1939 and 1961.

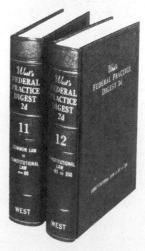

Federal Practice Digest 2d. Contains small-paragraph summaries of federal cases decided from 1961 to 1975.

Federal Practice Digest 3d. Contains small-paragraph summaries of federal cases decided from 1975 to the present.

Finally, West publishes a number of special digests that cover specific federal courts and/or specific topics of federal law:

- West's Bankruptcy Digest.
- West's Military Justice Digest.
- U.S. Court of Claims Digest.

Given the tremendous importance of the U.S. Supreme Court, there are two extensive digests covering only its opinions. These two digests are published by competing companies:

United States Supreme Court Digest. Published by West, containing small-paragraph summaries of every opinion of the U.S. Supreme Court. (Uses the key topic system.)

United States Supreme Court Digest, L.Ed. Published by Lawyers Co-operative Publishing Company, containing small-paragraph summaries of every opinion of the U.S. Supreme Court. (Does not use key topic system.)

Regional Digests

A regional digest contains small-paragraph summaries of those court opinions that are printed in its corresponding regional reporter. The opinions in the Pacific Reporter, for example, are digested in the Pacific Digest:

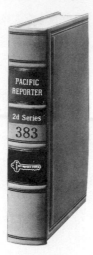 

As we will see in the chart below, not all regional reporters have their own regional digest. There is no regional digest for the North Eastern Reporter and for the South Western Reporter. The other five regional reporters, however, have corresponding regional digests.

Digests of Individual States

A state digest contains small-paragraph summaries of the opinions of the state courts within that state as well as the opinions of the federal courts that are relevant to that state. The following are examples of state digests:

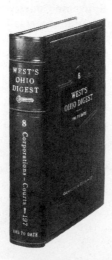 

Now let us summarize. In the following chart, there is a list of reporters, the names of the courts whose full opinions are currently printed in those reporters, and the names of the digests that give small-paragraph summaries of those opinions.

CHART 2

REPORTERS AND DIGESTS: A CHECKLIST		
NAME OF REPORTER	**THE COURTS WHOSE OPINIONS ARE CURRENTLY PRINTED IN FULL IN THIS REPORTER**	**THE DIGESTS THAT CONTAIN SMALL-PARAGRAPH SUMMARIES OF THE OPINIONS IN THIS REPORTER**
United States Reports (U.S.) Supreme Court Reporter (S.Ct.) United States Supreme Court Reports, Lawyers Edition (L.Ed.) United States Law Week (USLW) United States Supreme Court Bulletin (CCH)	United States Supreme Court	American Digest System United States Supreme Court Digest (West) United States Supreme Court Digest, L.Ed. Federal Digest (up to 1939) Modern Federal Practice Digest (1939–1961) Federal Practice Digest, 2d (1961–1975) Federal Practice Digest, 3d (1975–present) Individual state digests (for Supreme Court cases relevant to that state)
Federal Reporter, 2d (F.2d)	United States Courts of Appeal	American Digest System Federal Digest (up to 1939) Modern Federal Practice Digest (1939–1961) Federal Practice Digest, 2d (1961–1975) Federal Practice Digest, 3d (1975–present) Individual state digests (for federal cases relevant to that state)
Federal Supplement (F.Supp.)	United States District Courts United States Court of International Trade	American Digest System Federal Digest (up to 1939) Modern Federal Practice Digest (1939–1961) Federal Practice Digest, 2d (1961–1975) Federal Practice Digest, 3d (1975–present) Individual state digests (for federal cases relevant to that state)
Atlantic Reporter 2d (A.2d)	The highest state court and some intermediate appellate courts in Conn., Del., Maine, Md., N.H., N.J., Pa., R.I., Vt., District of Columbia	American Digest System Atlantic Digest Individual state digests

North Eastern Reporter 2d (N.E.2d)	The highest state court and some intermediate appellate courts in Ill., Ind., Mass., N.Y., Ohio	American Digest System Individual state digests (There is *no* North Eastern Digest)
North Western Reporter 2d (N.W.2d)	The highest state court and some intermediate appellate courts in Iowa, Mich., Minn., Nebr., N. Dak., S. Dak., Wis.	American Digest System North Western Digest Individual state digests
Pacific Reporter, 2d (P.2d)	The highest state court and some intermediate appellate courts in Alaska, Ariz., Calif, Colo., Hawaii, Idaho, Kans., Mont., Nev., N. Mex., Okla, Oreg., Utah, Wash., Wyo.	American Digest System Pacific Digest Individual state digests
South Eastern Reporter, 2d (S.E.2d)	The highest state court and some intermediate appellate courts in Ga., N.C., S.C., Va., W.Va.	American Digest System South Eastern Digest Individual state digests
Southern Reporter, 2d (S.2d)	The highest state court and some intermediate appellate courts in Ala., Fla., La., Miss.	American Digest System Southern Digest Individual state digests
South Western Reporter, 2d (S.W.2d)	The highest state court and some intermediate appellate courts in Ark., Ky., Mo., Tenn., Tex.	American Digest System Individual state digests (There is *no* South Western Digest)

FEDERAL CASES

Federal Cases is the name of the reporter that contains very early opinions of the federal courts (up to 1880) before F., F.2d, and F.Supp. came into existence.

FEDERAL DIGEST

See Digests (p. 538).

FEDERAL PRACTICE DIGEST 2d; FEDERAL PRACTICE DIGEST 3d

See Digests (pp. 538–39).

FEDERAL REGISTER (Fed.Reg.)

The Federal Register is a daily publication of the federal government that prints proposed regulations of the federal administrative agencies; executive orders and other executive documents; news from federal agencies, e.g., announcements calling for applications for federal grants. Many of the proposed regulations that are adopted by the federal agencies are later printed in the Code of Federal Regulations (C.F.R.).

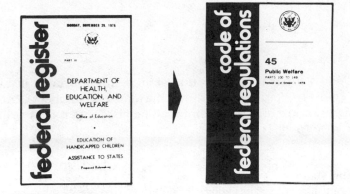

FEDERAL REPORTER

See Cases (p. 527).

FEDERAL RULES DECISIONS (F.R.D.)

See Cases (p. 526).

FEDERAL SUPPLEMENT

See Cases (p. 527).

FORMBOOK

A formbook is a manual written by private individuals (or by a public official writing in a private capacity) giving practical information on how to practice law in a given area. It contains summaries of the law, checklists, sample forms, etc. Formbooks are how-to-do-it texts. They can be single-volume or multi-volume. Other names for a formbook are *treatise, practice manual, handbook,* etc. Examples:

GENERAL DIGEST

See Digests (p. 537).

HANDBOOK

A formbook (see p. 543).

HEADNOTE

A headnote is a summary of a portion of an opinion, printed just before the opinion begins. In West reporters, each headnote is numbered consecutively and is assigned a key topic and number. The headnote is later printed in the digests of West (p. 601).

> **3. Libel and Slander**   ⌐ 28
> Since one may not escape liability for defamation by showing that he was merely repeating defamatory language used by another person, a fortiori he may not escape by falsely attributing to others the ideas to which he gives expression.

Here is the third headnote printed at the beginning of an opinion from a West reporter. It summarizes a portion of the opinion. (If you went to the body of the opinion, you would find the text, which this headnote summarizes, preceded by the same number in brackets—here #3.) West assigns this headnote a key topic and number: Libel and Slander 28. The paragraph will also go into the digests of West, where the researcher will be able to find other case law under this same topic and number.

HORNBOOK

A hornbook is a legal treatise (p. 558) on a topic that is often covered from A to Z with summaries, commentaries, extensive footnote references, etc. Hornbooks differ somewhat from formbooks in that hornbooks are often less practice oriented than formbooks.

INTERSTATE COMPACT

An interstate compact is an agreement between two or more states governing a problem of mutual concern, e.g., the resolution of a boundary dispute. The compact is passed by the legislature of each state and is therefore part of the state statutes. Also, Congress must give its approval to the compact.

KARDEX

Kardex is a file in which the library records incoming publications that are part of serial or ongoing subscriptions. Kardex contains the latest volume and numbers of reporters received in the mail, the most recent Shepard's pamphlets received, etc., If, for example, you are not sure whether certain volumes on the shelf have the latest pocket parts in them, you would ask the library staff to check the Kardex for the most recent material received by the library for those volumes. Not all libraries use Kardex. If a library does not have Kardex files, it has some equivalent system of recording updated subscription material.

LEGAL DICTIONARY

A legal dictionary contains definitions of words and phrases used in the law. Examples of single-volume dictionaries: Black's Law Dictionary (West), Ballentine's Law Dictionary (Lawyers Co-operative Publishing Company), Oran's Law Dictionary (West), Statsky's Legal Thesaurus/Dictionary (West). The major multi-volume legal dictionary is Words and Phrases by West. The definitions in the latter consist of thousands of excerpts from court opinions that have treated the word or phrase. Hence, this set of volumes can also serve as an excellent case finder.

LEGAL ENCYCLOPEDIA

A legal encyclopedia is a multi-volume discussion/summary of almost every legal topic (p. 629). It is valuable (a) as background reading for a research topic that is new to you and (b) as a case finder due to its extensive footnotes. The two competing national encyclopedias are American Jurisprudence 2d (p. 522) published by Lawyers Co-operative, and Corpus Juris Secundum (p. 534) published by West. A number of states have their own encyclopedias covering the law of that state, e.g., Florida Jurisprudence, Michigan Law and Practice (p. 630).

LEGAL NEWSPAPER

A legal newspaper is a local newspaper published (often daily) by a private company that lists court calendars, legal announcements, the full text of some opinions of local courts, new court rules, job announcements, etc. Most large cities have their own legal newspaper. It may be called the daily law journal, the daily law reporter, etc.

LEGAL PERIODICAL

A legal periodical (often called a law review or a law journal) is an ongoing publication of scholarly commentary published by law students of specific law schools. (See p. 626.) There are a few periodicals published by private companies or by bar associations that tend to be more practice oriented (and more expensive). The periodical is first published as small pamphlets, which are later bound by most libraries.

As we will see later (p. 626), the major general indexes to legal periodical literature are:

- Index to Legal Periodicals (ILP).
- Current Law Index (CLI).
- Legal Resource Index (LRI).

In addition, there are special indexes to legal periodical literature on topics such as tax law.

LEGISLATION

Legislation is the process of making statutory law by the legislature. The word legislation also refers to the statutes themselves. (See Acts, p. 519; Statutory Code, p. 557.)

LEXIS

LEXIS is a legal research computer system. (See p. 633, p. 720.)

LOOSE-LEAF SERVICE

Most law books come in one of three forms:

- Pamphlets.
- Bound volumes.
- Loose-leaf.

A loose-leaf text or service is a three-ring (or post) binder containing pages that can easily be inserted or taken out. As new material is written covering the subject matter of the loose-leaf text, it is placed in the binder, often replacing the pages that the new material has changed or otherwise supplemented. Since this kind of updating can sometimes occur as often as once a week, loose-leaf services frequently contain the most current material available at any given time.

There are few areas of the law that are *not* covered by one or more loose-leaf services. Examples of such services include: Employment and Safety and Health Guide; Standard Federal Tax Reporter; United States Law Week; Criminal Law Reporter; Family Law Reporter; Media Law Reporter; Sexual Law Reporter; Environmental Law Reporter; Labor Relations Reporter.

While some loose-leaf services do little more than print the most current cases in its speciality, most have more varied features:

- The full text and/or summaries of court opinions in the area of the specialty.
- The full text and/or summaries of administrative regulations and decisions in the area of the specialty (some of which may not be available elsewhere).
- Summaries of the major statutory provisions of the specialty.
- Practical tips on how to practice in the specialty.

The major publishers of loose-leaf services are Commerce Clearing House (CCH), Bureau of National Affairs (BNA), and Prentice-Hall (PH).

MARTINDALE-HUBBELL LAW DIRECTORY

The Martindale-Hubbell Law Directory is a multi-volume set of books that serves three major functions:

- Gives an alphabetical listing of attorneys and law firms by state and city.
- Gives short summaries of the law of all fifty states (in its separate Digest volume).
- Gives short summaries of the law of many foreign countries (in its separate Digest volume).

MICROFORMS

Microforms are images or photographs that have been reduced in size. Among the material stored on microforms are pages from reporters, codes, treatises, periodicals, etc. Vast amounts of material can be stored in this way, e.g., an entire volume of a thousand-page law book on a single plastic card! Special machines, e.g., reader-printers and fiche readers, magnify the material so that it can be read. Several kinds of microforms are available. (a) *Microfilms* store the material on film reels or cassettes. (b) *Microfiche* stores the material on single sheets of film. (c) *Ultrafiche* is a microfiche with a considerably greater storage capacity.

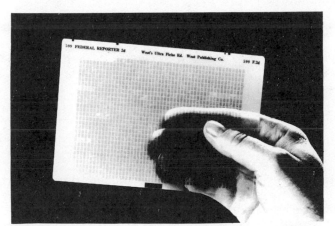

Example of West's ultrafiche containing a volume of the Federal Reporter.

MICROFICHE

See microforms.

MILITARY JUSTICE REPORTER (M.J.)

See Cases (p. 527).

MODERN FEDERAL PRACTICE DIGEST

See Digests (p. 538).

NEW YORK SUPPLEMENT (N.Y.S.)

See Cases (p. 532).

NORTH EASTERN REPORTER 2d (N.E.2d)

See Cases (p. 529).

NORTH WESTERN DIGEST

See Digests (p. 542).

NORTH WESTERN REPORTER 2d (N.W.2d)

See Cases (p. 529).

PACIFIC DIGEST

See Digests (p. 540).

PACIFIC REPORTER 2d (P.2d)

See Cases (p. 529).

PRACTICE MANUAL

See Formbook (p. 543).

RECORD

The record is the official collection of what happened during a particular trial. It includes a word-for-word transcript of what was said, the pleadings, all the exhibits, etc. (See also Congressional Record p. 534.)

REGIONAL DIGEST

See Digests (p. 540).

RESTATEMENTS

Restatements are scholarly *treatises* (see p. 558) published by the American Law Institute (ALI), which attempt to formulate (i.e., restate) the existing law of a given area. Occasionally the Restatements also state what the ALI thinks the law *ought* to be.

Restatement of Agency

Restatement of Conflicts of Law

Restatement of Contracts

Restatement of Foreign
  Relations Law

Restatement of Judgments

Restatement of Property

Restatement of Restitution

Restatement of Security

Restatement of Torts

Restatement of Trusts

While the restatements are not law, since they are written by a private organization (ALI), they are extensively relied upon and cited by courts.

SERIES

An "edition" is a *revision* of an earlier version of a book or set of books. The word "series," on the other hand, refers to a new numbering order for new volumes within the *same* set of books. Reporters, for example, come in series. Federal Reporter, First Series (abbreviated "F."), has 300 volumes. After the last volume was printed, the publisher decided to start a new series of the same set of books—Federal Reporter, Second Series (abbreviated "F.2d"). The first volume of F.2d is volume 1. After a large number of F.2d volumes are printed, we will probably see an F.3d, which will begin again with volume 1. There is no consistent number of volumes that a publisher will print before it decides to start a new series for a given set of books.

SESSION LAW

See Acts; Acts and Resolves, p. 519 and p. 618.

SHEPARD'S

Our goals in this section are to provide a brief overview of Shepard's and shepardizing, and to identify the major sets of Shepard's volumes that exist. Later in the chapter we will learn how to use Shepard's—how to shepardize. (See p. 608.)

```
                 – 327 –        (
                 ICT§2.16      622F2d²¹.
     ₐn89                      492FS³774
                 – 365 –
  – 946 –          Cir. 4       – 485
    Cir. 9       623F2d¹²891      W V:
 ₂3F2d⁴561         Cir. 5      268S₤23(
                 623F2d¹⁰359
  – 953 –        623F2d¹¹359     – 5ᶠ
    Cir. 4       623F2d¹²359       C
 ₍24F2d³510      623F2d¹³359    613P2
                 623F2d¹⁴359
  – 995 –        623F2d¹⁵359     – ₍
    Cir. 7       623F2d¹⁶359       (
491FS⁴970        f623F2d³360     4BR
e491FS¹²972      f623F2d⁷360
                 623F2d¹⁰397     –
  – 1010 –       623F2d¹¹397
    DC           j623F2d403     492ₗ
 412A2d35        f623F2d
                       [¹⁰1088
   3   – 1202 –  f623F2d
         Cir. 2        [¹²1089    ⁄
   –   d490FS⁹1218 f624F2d¹³539
                 f624F2d¹⁰554
  242    – 1209 – f624F2d¹¹55⁄
           Kan   f624F2d¹²5ᶜ
 ₍–    615P2d135  f624F2d¹¹
  5              f624F2⁻
```

Excerpt from a page in a Shepard's volume.

Shepard's Citations are citators (p. 533). To "shepardize" an item means to use the volumes of Shepard's to collect the research references provided for that item. The references differ depending on what you are shepardizing. If, for example, you are shepardizing a case, you will be given the parallel cite (if one exists) for this case; the history of the case, e.g., appeals within the same litigation; other cases that have interpreted or mentioned the case you are shepardizing; legal periodical literature on the case, etc. If you are shepardizing a statute, you may be given the parallel or session law cite for the statute; amendments; repeals or additions to the statute; court opinions that have interpreted the statute; legal periodical literature on the statute, etc.

What can you shepardize? Here is a partial list:

- Court opinions
- Statutes
- Constitutions
- Some administrative regulations
- Some administrative decisions
- Ordinances
- Charters
- Court rules
- Some executive orders
- Some treaties
- Patents, trademarks, copyrights
- Restatements
- Some legal periodical literature

As we shall see later, the items in this list constitute the *cited* material—that which you are shepardizing. When you go to the references to these cited materials in the volumes of Shepard's, you will be given a variety of other references on the cited materials, e.g., cases that have interpreted statutes, amendments to statutes, cases that have overruled prior cases. These other references are called *citing* material. (See p. 611.)

The following is an overview of some of these items that can be shepardized with the sets of Shepard's used to do so:

You want to shepardize an opinion of the United States Supreme Court:

Here is the set of Shepard's you use to shepardize an opinion of the United States Supreme court:

Supreme Court Reporter [the same opinions, of course, are also found in United States Supreme Court Reports (L.Ed.) and in United States Reports (U.S.)].

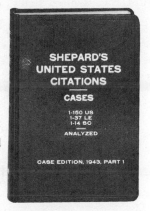

Shepard's United States Citations, Case Edition.

You want to shepardize opinions found in Federal Reporter, 2d:

Here is the set of Shepard's you use to shepardize an F.2d opinion:

Federal Reporter, 2d (F.2d).

Shepard's Federal Citations.

You want to shepardize opinions found in Federal Supplement:

Here is the set of Shepard's you use to shepardize an F.Supp. opinion:

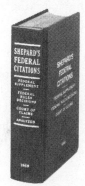

Federal Supplement (F.Supp.).

Shepard's Federal Citations.

You want to shepardize a statute of Congress: a statute found in U.S.C.A. (United States Code Annotated) or in U.S.C.S. (United States Code Service) or in U.S.C. (United States Code):

Here is the set of Shepard's that you use to shepardize a federal statute:

Shepard's United States Citations, Statute Edition.

The same set of Shepard's (United States Citations, Statute Edition) can be used to shepardize: (1) A U.S. constitutional provision, (2) A U.S. treaty, and (3) A federal court rule.

You want to shepardize a regulation of a federal agency found in C.F.R.:

Here is the set of Shepard's that will enable you to shepardize a regulation in C.F.R.:

Regulation in C.F.R.

Shepard's Code of Federal Regulations Citations.

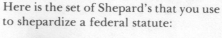

You want to shepardize opinions found within the following regional reporters:

Atlantic Reporter 2d
Pacific Reporter 2d
South Western Reporter 2d
South Eastern Reporter 2d
North Eastern Reporter 2d

Here are the sets of Shepard's that you use to shepardize the opinions in these regional reporters.

You want to shepardize the following:

A Rhode Island court opinion
A Rhode Island statute
A Rhode Island constitutional provision
A New Hampshire court opinion
A New Hampshire statute
A New Hampshire constitutional provision

Here are the sets of Shepard's that you would use.

Every state has its own set of Shepard's similar to Shepard's Rhode Island Citations and Shepard's New Hampshire Citations above. Other sets of Shepard's include the following:

1. Shepard's United States Administrative Citations
   - Enables you to shepardize the administrative decisions of some federal agencies.
2. Shepard's United States Patents and Trademarks Citations
   - Enables you to shepardize patents, trademarks, and copyrights.
3. Shepard's Federal Labor Law Citations
   - Enables you to shepardize administrative decisions of the National Labor Relations Board.
4. Shepard's Restatements of the Law Citations
   - Enables you to shepardize restatements of ALI (p. 550) that have been cited in court opinions.
5. Shepard's Military Justice Citations
   - Enables you to shepardize decisions and rules relating to military law.
6. Shepard's Criminal Justice Citations
   - Enables you to shepardize the American Bar Association's Standards Relating to the Administration of Criminal Justice.
7. Shepard's Code of Professional Responsibility Citations
   - Enables you to shepardize the American Bar Associations code of conduct for lawyers and judges.
8. Shepard's Bankruptcy Citations
9. Shepard's Federal Energy Law Citations
10. Shepard's Uniform Commercial Code Citations
11. Shepard's Partnership Law Citations
12. Shepard's Immigration and Naturalization Citations
13. Shepard's Federal Occupational Safety and Health Citations.

SLIP LAW

A slip law is the form in which laws or acts of legislatures are first printed. They may be printed on several pieces of paper or in pamphlet form, depending upon the length of the act. All slip laws are later printed in volumes that may be called Session Laws, Acts, Statutes at Large, etc. (see Acts; Acts and Resolves p. 519). Finally, if the slip law is a public law or statute (pp. 516, 667) it is also printed in a *statutory code* (p. 557).

```
                    Public Law 87-17
                87th Congress, H. R. 4363
                     April 7, 1961

                        AN ACT                      75 STAT. 41.

To amend Public Law 86-272 relating to State taxation of interstate commerce.

    Be it enacted by the Senate and House of Representatives of the
United States of America in Congress assembled, That section 201 of    Interstate
Public Law 86-272 (73 Stat. 556) is amended to read as follows:        commerce.
    "SEC. 201. The Committee on the Judiciary of the House of Repre-    Taxation
sentatives and the Committee on Finance of the United States Senate,   studies.
acting separately or jointly, or both, or any duly authorized subcom-  15 USC 381
mittees thereof, shall make full and complete studies of all matters   note.
pertaining to the taxation of interstate commerce by the States, terri-
tories, and possessions of the United States, the District of Columbia,
and the Commonwealth of Puerto Rico, or any political or taxing sub-
division of the foregoing."
    Approved April 7, 1961.
```

Example of a slip law.

SLIP OPINION

When a court first announces a decision, it is usually published in what is called a slip opinion or slip decision. It contains a single case in pamphlet form. The slip opinions are later printed in advance sheets for reporters (p. 521), which in turn become bound reporters (p. 525).

SOUTH EASTERN DIGEST

See Digests (p. 542).

SOUTH EASTERN REPORTER 2d (S.E.2d)

See Cases. (p. 530).

SOUTHERN DIGEST

See Digests (p. 542).

SOUTHERN REPORTER 2d (S.2d)

See Cases (p. 530).

SOUTH WESTERN REPORTER 2d (S.W.2d)

See Cases (p. 530).

STATUTES AT LARGE

See Acts; Acts and Resolves (p. 519). *See also* United States Statutes at Large (p. 559).

STATUTORY CODE

A statutory code is a collection of the statutes of the legislature organized by subject matter; e.g., the statutes on murder are in one place, the statutes on probate are together. Statutory codes are often annotated, meaning that there are research references provided along with the full text of the statute, e.g., summaries of cases that have interpreted the statute, information on the legislative history of the statute such as earlier amendments.

Example of a state statutory code.

Shown below are the three major codes of the federal statutes of Congress:

U.S.C.A.—United States Code Annotated (published by West Publishing Company)
U.S.C.S.—United States Code Service (published by Lawyers Co-operative Publishing Company)
U.S.C.—United States Code (published by the U.S. Government Printing Office)

SUPREME COURT REPORTER
(S.Ct.)

See Cases (p. 525).

TOTAL CLIENT-SERVICE LIBRARY

The Total Client-Service Library is the system by which Lawyers Co-operative Publishing Company refers you to many of the law books it publishes. If, for example, you are reading an annotation in ALR, ALR2d, ALR3d, ALR4th, or ALR Fed (p. 605), you may be referred to other Lawyers Co-op books on the same subject matter, e.g., American Jurisprudence 2d, U.S.C.S. (United States Code Service), Federal Procedural Forms L.Ed., Am Jur Pleading and Practice Forms etc.

TOTAL CLIENT-SERVICE LIBRARY* REFERENCES

62 Am Jur 2d, Process §§ 100, 102

1 Federal Procedural Forms L. Ed, Actions in District Court § 1:745

11 Am Jur Pl & Pr Forms (Rev Ed), Federal Practice and Procedure, Form 292; 20 Am Jur Pl & Pr Forms (Rev Ed), Process, Forms 142, 143

USCS, Court Rules, Rules of Civil Procedure for United States District Courts, Rule 4(d)(1)

US L. Ed Digest, Writ and Process § 24

ALR Digests, Writ and Process §§ 12, 20, 22, 23

L. Ed Index to Annos, Age; Discretion; Writ and Process

ALR Quick Index, Age; Constructive or Substituted Service of Process; Discretion; Rules of Civil Procedure

Federal Quick Index, Age; Constructive or Substituted Service of Process; Discretion; Federal Rules of Civil Procedure

---

TREATISE

A treatise (not to be confused with treaty) is any book written by a private individual (or by a public official writing as a private citizen) that provides an overview, summary, and commentary on a topic of law. The treatise will usually attempt to give an extensive treatment of that topic. Hornbooks (p. 544) and formbooks (p. 543) are also treatises.

ULTRAFICHE

See microforms (p. 549).

UNITED STATES CODE (U.S.C.)

See Statutory Code (p. 557).

UNITED STATES CODE ANNOTATED (U.S.C.A.)

See Statutory Code (p. 557).

U.S. CODE CONGRESSIONAL AND ADMINISTRATIVE NEWS (U.S.C.C.A.N.)

U.S.C.C.A.N., published by West, will enable you to

- Obtain leads to the legislative history of federal statutes (primarily through its Table 4).

Table 4

LEGISLATIVE HISTORY

Bill numbers in parentheses ( ) are companion bills reported either in the Senate or the House

Public Law				Report No. 91–		Comm. Reporting		Cong.Rec.Vol. 116 (1970) Dates of Consideration and Passage	
No.91–	Date App.	94 Stat. Page	Bill No.	House	Senate	House	Senate	House	Ser
101	Feb. 3	3	S.J.Res. 131	810	533	FA	FR	Jan. 30	H
102	Feb. 4	4	H.J.Res.	none	647	none	J	Jan. 30	
103					ne	none	none	Feb. 7	
							App	D-	
						App	App		
							J		
							Agr		

- Obtain the complete text of public laws or statutes (pp. 516, 667) of Congress.
- Obtain the complete text of some congressional committee reports (important for legislative history).
- Translate a Statute at Large cite into a U.S.C./U.S.C.A./U.S.C.S. cite (through Table 2).
- Obtain the complete text of some federal agency regulations (duplicating what is found in the Federal Register—F.R., and in the Code of Federal Regulations—C.F.R.).
- Obtain the complete text of executive orders and other executive documents.
- Obtain the complete text of all current United States Statutes at Large (see below).

UNITED STATES CODE SERVICE (U.S.C.S.)

See Statutory Code (p. 557).

UNITED STATES LAW WEEK (USLW)

USLW is a loose-leaf service (p. 547) published by the Bureau of National Affairs (BNA) that prints the full text of every U.S. Supreme Court case on a weekly basis. It also prints other data on cases in the Supreme Court and summarizes important cases from other courts.

UNITED STATES REPORTS (U.S.)

See Cases (p. 525).

UNITED STATES STATUTES AT LARGE

The United States Statutes at Large (abbreviated "Stat.") contains the full text of every public law or statute and every private law or statute of Congress. The

OUTLINE OF LEGAL REFERENCE MATERIALS

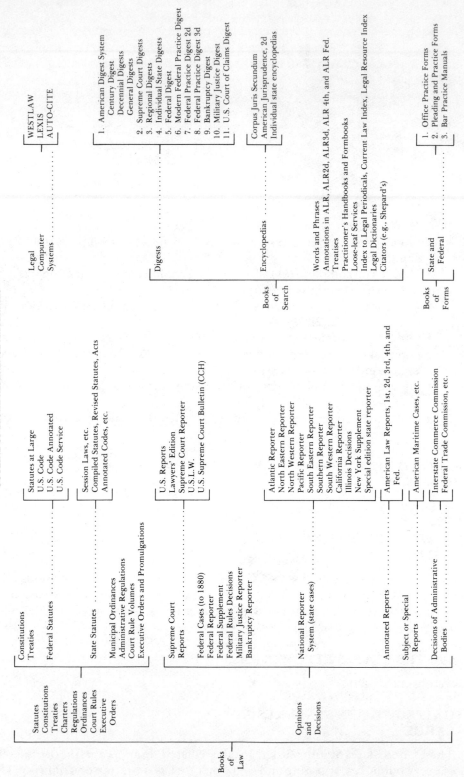

statutes within it are printed chronologically. All current statut
now also printed in U.S. Code Congressional and Administrative
as well as in separate Stat. volumes. (The public laws of gener
later codified and printed in each of the three sets of codified fe
U.S.C., U.S.C.A., U.S.C.S.)

UNITED STATES SUPREME COURT BULLETIN (CCH)

See Cases (p. 526).

UNITED STATES SUPREME COURT DIGEST, L.Ed.

See Digests (p. 539).

UNITED STATES SUPREME COURT DIGEST (WEST)

See Digests (p. 539).

UNITED STATES SUPREME COURT REPORTS, L.Ed.

See Cases (p. 525).

WESTLAW

WESTLAW is a legal research computer system. (See p. 632, p. 720).

Section I. AUTHORITY IN RESEARCH AND WRITING

1. INTRODUCTION

Authority

Authority is anything that a court could rely upon in reaching its conclusion.

Primary and Secondary Authority

Primary authority is any *law* that the court could rely upon in reaching its conclusion. Examples include statutes, regulations, constitutional provisions, executive orders, charters, ordinances, treaties, and other court opinions.

Secondary authority is any *nonlaw* that the court could rely upon in reaching its conclusion. Examples include legal and nonlegal periodical literature, legal and nonlegal encyclopedias, legal and nonlegal dictionaries, legal and nonlegal treatises.

Mandatory Authority and Persuasive Authority

Mandatory authority is whatever the court *must* rely upon in reaching its conclusion. Only primary authority can be mandatory authority, e.g., another court opinion, a statute, a constitutional provision. A court is never required to rely on secondary authority, e.g., a law review article or legal encyclopedia. Secondary authority cannot be mandatory authority.

Persuasive authority is whatever the court relies upon even though it is not required to do so. There are two main kinds of persuasive authority: (a) a prior court opinion that the court is not required to follow but does so because it finds the opinion convincing or persuasive and (b) any secondary authority that the court is not required to follow but does so because it finds the secondary authority convincing or persuasive.

Nonauthority

Nonauthority is (a) any primary or secondary authority that is not "on point" since it does not cover the facts of the client's case, (b) any invalid primary authority, or (c) any book that is solely a finding aid, e.g., Shepard's Citations, digests.

2. MANDATORY AUTHORITY

Courts *must* follow mandatory authority. The two broad categories of mandatory authority are (a) enacted law: a statute, a constitutional provision, a charter, an ordinance, a regulation, a treaty; and (b) other court opinions. Both categories will be considered separately.

a. Enacted Law as Mandatory Authority

Any enacted law is mandatory authority and must be followed if the following two tests are met:

i. The authors of the enacted law (e.g., the legislature that wrote the statute) intended to cover the facts that are currently before the court; and
ii. The application of this enacted law to these facts does not violate some other law that is superior in authority (e.g., the statute does not violate the constitution).

Suppose that Smith is arrested for burglarizing a house. Section 14 of the state code provides, "It shall be a felony to break and enter a dwelling for the purpose of stealing property therein." Section 14 is mandatory authority for the court so long as it is clear that the statute was intended to cover these facts and the statute does not violate a higher law—the constitution. Suppose, however, that Smith was arrested for breaking into a car. Is a car a "dwelling" for purposes of Section 14? Did the legislature intend to include motor vehicles within the meaning of "dwellings?" Would it depend on whether the owner ever slept in the car? These are questions of legislative intent. If the statute was not intended to cover these facts, it is not applicable; it cannot be mandatory authority.

Even if the enacted law was intended to cover the facts before the court, it is not mandatory authority if it violates some higher law. The authors of a regulation, for example, may intend to cover a particular individual's activities, but if this regulation is inconsistent with the statute that the regulation is supposed to be carrying out, the regulation is not mandatory authority; it is invalid. Similarly, a statute may be intended to cover a given set of facts but be invalid because the statute is unconstitutional. For example, a statute that prohibits marriage between the races is clearly intended to prevent whites from marrying blacks, but the statute is not mandatory authority because it is in violation of the constitution.

Federal enacted law can be mandatory authority in state courts. For example, the United States Constitution is superior in authority to all other laws. If a provision of this Constitution applies, it controls over any state law to the contrary. Federal statutes and the regulations of federal agencies are also superior in authority to state laws in those areas entrusted to the federal government by the United States Constitution, e.g., regulation of interstate commerce, patents, bankruptcy, foreign affairs. Federal statutes and regulations in these areas are mandatory authority in state courts.

Can the enacted law of one state ever be mandatory authority in another state? Generally no, with two exceptions involving the principles of conflict of law, and full faith and credit. We will consider these principles next when we examine court opinions as mandatory authority.

b. Court Opinions as Mandatory Authority

When is a court *required* to follow an opinion? Two conditions must be met:

i.   The opinion must be "on point," i.e., it must be analogous; and
ii. The opinion must have been written by a court that is superior to the court currently considering the applicability of the opinion.

For an opinion to be "on point," or analogous, there must be a sufficient similarity (1) between the key facts of the opinion and the facts of the current case and (2) between the rule of law (e.g., statute, common-law principle, p. 377) that was interpreted and applied in the opinion and the rule of law that must be interpreted and applied in the current case.

If the opinion is not on point, if it is not analogous because the similarity listed above does not exist, then the opinion cannot be mandatory authority; it is nonauthority.

The second condition for the existence of mandatory authority requires an examination of the court that wrote the opinion and the court that is currently considering that opinion. In the discussion that follows, you will find frequent references to "judicial systems" that are either the same or different. By judicial system we mean an overall court structure. A state court in one state, for example, is always part of a different judicial system from a state court in another state. Furthermore, federal courts and state courts comprise different judicial systems. If there is a direct line of appeal from one state court to another state court, both courts are part of the same judicial system. Similarly, all federal courts in a direct line of appeal are part of the same judicial system.

Six variations will be briefly examined:

i.   A higher court in the judicial system is considering an opinion written by a lower court in the same judicial system.

   ii. A lower court is considering an opinion written by a higher court in the same judicial system.

  iii. A court is considering an opinion written in the past by the same court, i.e., the court is considering one of its own prior opinions.

  iv. A court in one state is considering an opinion written by a court from another state.

   v. A state court is considering an opinion written by a federal court.

  vi. A federal court is considering an opinion written by a state court.

In each of these six situations a court is attempting to determine whether a prior opinion applies to the facts currently before the court. Assume that each opinion *is* analogous, i.e., that the facts currently before the court are similar to the key facts in the opinion under consideration and that the rules of law (e.g., statute, common-law principle) are also the same or similar.

i. Higher Court Is Considering an Opinion Written by a Lower Court in Same Judicial System. A higher court is never required to follow an opinion written by a lower court in the same judicial system whether or not the opinion is analogous. If the opinion is analogous, it can only be persuasive authority; the higher court can follow it if it so chooses.

ii. Lower Court Is Considering an Opinion Written by a Higher Court in Same Judicial System. A lower or inferior court *must* follow and apply an analogous opinion written by a higher court in the same judicial system. A California trial court or a California middle appeals court, for example, must follow an analogous opinion written by the state California Supreme Court.

iii. A Court Opinion Being Considered by the Same Court That Wrote the Opinion. Does a court have to follow its *own* prior opinions? If, for example, the Florida Supreme Court wrote an opinion in 1970, is that opinion mandatory authority for the Florida Supreme Court in 1986 if the facts before the court in 1986 are similar to the key facts in the 1970 opinion and the rules of the law are similar? No. A court is always free to *overrule* its own prior opinions.

     Suppose that the opinion was written by an intermediate or middle appeals court. Does that same court have to follow this opinion later if the opinion is analogous? No. *Any* court can later overrule itself and reach a result that differs from the holding it reached in the earlier opinion, so long as there is no opinion in existence written by a higher court that is contrary to the result that the middle appeals court now wants to reach.

iv. One State Court Considering an Opinion Written by Another State Court. One state court generally does not have to follow an opinion written by another state court even if the opinion is analogous. An Idaho court, for example, does not have to follow an opinion written by a Massachusetts court.

     There are two main exceptions to the principle that the law of one state is not mandatory authority in another state. The first involves conflicts of law and the second, full faith and credit.

   a. *Conflicts of Law.* Suppose that an accident occurs in New York, but the negligence suit based on this accident is brought in an Ohio state court. Assume that the Ohio court has jurisdiction over the dispute and over the parties. What negligence law does the Ohio court apply: Ohio negligence law or New York negligence law? The negligence law of the two states may differ in significant respects. This is a conflicts-of-law problem. Under the principles of the conflicts of law, a court of one state may be required to apply the law of another state. It may be, for example, that the law to be applied will be the law of the state where the injury occurred or the law of the state that is at the center of the dispute. If this state is deemed to be New York, then the Ohio court will apply New York negligence law. Analogous opinions of New York courts on the New York law of negligence or a New York statute on negligence will be mandatory authority in the Ohio court.

b. *Full Faith and Credit.* The United States Constitution provides that "Full Faith and Credit shall be given in each State to the public Acts, Records, and judicial Proceedings of every other State" (Art. IV, § 1). Suppose that Richards sues Davis for breach of contract in Delaware. Davis wins. Richards cannot go to another state and bring a breach-of-contract suit against Davis in this other state arising out of the same facts. If the Delaware court had proper jurisdiction when it rendered its judgment, the Delaware opinion must be given full faith and credit in every other state. The case cannot be relitigated by the parties. The Delaware opinion is mandatory authority in every other state.

v. and vi. State Court Considering an Opinion Written by a Federal Court and Vice Versa. The general rule is that state courts are the final arbiters of state law, and federal courts are the final arbiters of federal law. Thus, state courts do *not* have to follow opinions written by federal courts *unless* the issue before the state court involves a federal question—one arising out of the United States Constitution or out of a statute of Congress, e.g., does a state statute violate a provision of the United States Constitution? Federal courts do not have to follow state court opinions *unless* the state court was interpreting the meaning of state law.

3. COURT OPINIONS AS PERSUASIVE AUTHORITY

Review the two tests mentioned earlier on when an opinion is mandatory authority: the opinion must be analogous, or on point, *and* it must have been written by a court that is superior to the court currently considering that opinion. If *both* these tests are not met, the opinion is either nonauthority or it might be *persuasive authority.*

Assume that the holding in the *X v. Y* opinion is not analogous to the legal issues currently being considered by a court involved in the *A v. B* litigation. Assume also that within *X v. Y* there is some *dictum* that has relevance or some bearing on the issues before the *A v. B* court. By definition, the dictum cannot be part of the *X v. Y* holding, since dictum is a statement by a judge that was not necessary to resolve the narrow legal issues before the court in *X v. Y* (p. 645). Dictum, therefore, can never be mandatory authority. The *A v. B* court is not *required* to follow the *X v. Y* dictum. This is so whether the two courts involved are part of the same or part of different judicial systems. The *A v. B* court, however, has the discretion of adopting the *X v. Y* dictum, since it does relate to the issues before the *A v. B* court. If the court does adopt it, it has become persuasive authority.

Suppose that you are reading an opinion that *is* analogous, or on point, but that is not mandatory because:

a. It was written by an inferior court and is now being considered by a court within the same judicial system that is superior to the court that wrote the opinion; or
b. It was written by a court from a judicial system that is different from the judicial system where the court considering that opinion sits.

If either of these two situations exists, the court, as we have seen, does *not* have to follow the opinion; it is not mandatory authority. If, however, the opinion is on point, the court would be free to adopt it as persuasive authority.

Sometimes a court will be faced with a variety of on-point opinions from which to choose. If none of them are mandatory authority, they are all potentially persuasive authority. Suppose that these opinions are not consistent with each other; they reach different results. Suppose further that they were written by different states or jurisdictions. How does a court select among them? No clear formula is used. A court might count the number of states that take one position and the number that take another. The "majority rule" or school of thought is sometimes an important factor. A court might also be impressed by the fact that a particular opinion has been frequently cited with approval by other courts. In the final analysis, however, the most significant consideration will be how well reasoned an opinion is. This will determine its persuasiveness. Furthermore, it is human nature for judges to gravitate toward those opinions that are most in tune with their personal philosophies and biases—although preferences on this basis are rarely stated.

4. SECONDARY AUTHORITY AS PERSUASIVE AUTHORITY

Secondary authority is not the law itself. It is *not* written by the legislature, a court, an agency, a city council, etc. Secondary authority can never be mandatory authority; it can only be persuasive. The following chart provides an overview of the major kinds of secondary authority that a court could decide to rely upon in reaching its conclusion:

CHART 3

SUMMARY OF SECONDARY AUTHORITY		
KIND	CONTENTS	EXAMPLES
1. Legal encyclopedia	Summaries of the law, particularly case law, organized by topic	*Corpus Juris Secundum* *American Jurisprudence 2d*
2. Nonlegal encyclopedias	Summaries of many topics on science, the arts, history, etc.	*Encyclopedia Britannica*

3. Legal dictionaries	Definitions of legal terms	*Words and Phrases* *Black's Law Dictionary* *Ballentine's Law Dictionary* Oran's *Law Dictionary* Statsky's *Legal Thesaurus / Dictionary*
4. Nonlegal dictionaries	Definitions of all words in general use	*Webster's Dictionary*
5. Legal periodicals	Pamphlets (later bound) containing articles written on a variety of legal topics	*Harvard Law Review* *American Bar Association Journal*
6. Nonlegal periodicals	Pamphlets on general topics	*Newsweek* *Foreign Affairs*
7. Legal treatises	Summaries of and commentaries on legal topics	*McCormick on Evidence* Johnstone and Hopson, *Lawyers and Their Work* *Restatement of the Law of Torts*
8. Nonlegal treatises	Perspectives on a variety of topics	Samuelson, *Economics*
9. Loose-leaf services	Collections of materials in three-ring binders covering current law in designated areas	*Abortion Law Reporter* *Prison Law Reporter* Commerce Clearing House, *Products Liability Reporter*
10. Formbooks, manuals, practice books	Same as legal treatises with a greater emphasis on the "how-to-do-it" practical dimensions of the law	Dellheim, *Massachusetts Practice* Moore's *Federal Practice* *Am. Jur. Pleading and Practice Forms Annotated*
11. Legal newspapers	Daily or weekly compilations of information relevant to local practice	*Daily Washington Law Reporter*
12. Nonlegal newspapers	General circulation newspapers	*New York Times* *Detroit Free Press*

Some of these secondary authorities quote from the law itself, i.e., they quote primary authority. As a general rule, *you should never use someone else's quotation of the law*. Quote *directly* from the primary authority. Use the secondary authority to bolster your arguments on the interpretation of the primary authority. This is the main function of such secondary authority: to help you persuade a court to adopt a certain interpretation of primary authority. You are on very dangerous ground when you use secondary authority as a substitute for primary authority.

Secondary authority will frequently *paraphrase* primary authority, e.g., a hornbook or legal encyclopedia will summarize the law of a particular state on a topic. You will be *very* tempted to use such summaries in your own legal writing. There are several serious dangers, however, in relying on excerpts containing such summaries. While they can be used and sometimes *should* be used (with proper citation to avoid the charge of plagiarism), the difficulties with using quotes from such excerpts are as follows:

a. The excerpts are secondary authority, and the main goal of your writing is to use primary authority to support your arguments.
b. The excerpts often consist of summaries of court opinions; those opinions should be analyzed before you use them in your writing.
c. The excerpts are often based upon opinions from a variety of jurisdictions, and your legal writing must focus on the law of the jurisdiction in which the client of your office is litigating his or her case.

Too much reliance upon such excerpts represents little more than laziness in legal research. It is sometimes not easy to find and apply the law. If someone else at least appears to have done all the work for you, why not use the secondary authority? Again, the answers to this question are found in the three difficulties mentioned above.

Before covering the *proper* use of secondary authority in your legal writing, the value of secondary authority *as a research tool* should be reemphasized. Often the most valuable parts of these texts are the footnotes. The citations in the footnotes to court opinions (and to other authority) can be invaluable to you as you pursue your search for opinions "on point," i.e., for opinions that are analogous. If the secondary authority has led you to laws that you eventually use in your writing (after proper legal analysis), the secondary authority will have been of tremendous service to you.

Secondary authority can provide another service, independent of whether you use it directly in your writing. You will often be reading court opinions and doing legal research in areas of the law that are new to you. You may need help in trying to make sense of what might appear to be quite formidable and esoteric areas of the law—with or without the inevitable Latin phrases. One approach is to read a chapter in a hornbook, a section in a legal encyclopedia, or material in any other secondary authority in order to:

• Obtain an overview of the law under consideration in the opinion;
• Obtain some of the basic definitions in the area.

Armed with this general understanding, you will be better equipped to resume your research and analysis in the unfamiliar area of law. See p. 597 on doing such background research.

Suppose that you want to *use* a quote from the secondary authority *in your legal writing.* What is the proper *foundation* for the use of secondary authority in legal writing? The following principle governs:

> You must satisfy yourself through independent legal research that the quote from the secondary authority that you want to use does not contradict any law (opinion, statute, constitutional provision, etc.) that exists in the jurisdiction where the client is litigating the case. Stated more simply: There must be no contrary mandatory authority.

Hence you cannot avoid extensive legal research simply by quoting from secondary authority—no matter how tempting the latter appears. Unless you have conducted adequate research and analysis of the relevant *mandatory* authority, you will be unable to establish the necessary foundation to use *secondary* authority.

Many well-written and comprehensively researched legal memoranda and appellate briefs will make very *few* references to secondary authority. Experienced advocates know that judges are suspicious of secondary authority. It is true that some secondary authorities are highly respected (e.g., *Prosser on Torts,* any of the *Restatements* of the American Law Institute). Yet even these must be used with caution. The preoccupation of a court is on primary authority. Before you use secondary authority in your writing, you must be sure that (a) the secondary authority is not used as a substitute for the primary authority, (b) the secondary authority is not unduly repetitive of the primary authority, (c) the secondary authority is helpful to the court in adopting a particular interpretation of primary authority, particularly when there is not a great deal of primary authority on point, (d) you discuss the secondary authority after you have presented the primary authority, and (e) the foundation for the use of secondary authority (see above principle) can be demonstrated if needed.

Suppose that you find a quote from a secondary authority that does not contradict any law within the jurisdiction where the client is litigating the case but that compactly states the law that does exist. The excerpt from the secondary authority in such an example is, in effect, an accurate summary of the law. While you are on much safer ground in using the quote, you should provide some indication in your legal writing that there is such a parallel between the law and the quote. At the very least, you should state in your writing that the quote from the secondary authority is consistent with the law of the jurisdiction and be prepared to back up this statement if it is later challenged or questioned by anyone.

Finally, you may find statements in secondary authority that neither contradict nor summarize the law of your jurisdiction. The issue being discussed in the secondary authority may simply have never arisen in your jurisdiction. Such issues are usually called issues of "first impression." Again, you are on relatively safe ground in using such discussions in your legal writing. In fact, the use of secondary authority is usually *most* effective when it treats issues that have not yet been resolved in your jurisdiction. Courts are often quite receptive to adopting secondary authority as persuasive authority when novel questions or issues are involved.

Section J. CITATION FORM

A citation or cite is a reference to any written material. The cite tells you where you can go in the library to find the cited document.

Are there any consistent rules on citation form? If you pick up different law books and examine the citations of similar material within them, you will notice great variety in citation form. You will find that people abbreviate things differently, they do not include the same order of information in the cite, they use parentheses differently, they use punctuation within the cite differently, they include different amounts of information in the same kind of cite, etc. There does not appear to be any consistency. Yet, in spite of this diversity and confusion, you are often scolded by supervisors for failing to use "proper citation form." What, you may well ask, is "proper"?

Start by checking the court rules (p. 534) of the court that will have jurisdiction over the problem you are researching. There may or may not be citation rules within it. If such rules exist, they must obviously be followed in spite of what any other citation rule book may say. These are, in effect, citation *laws*. The following is an excerpt from Michigan court rules that contain citation rules:

In the Matter of Michigan Uniform System of Citations

On Order of the Court, all courts within the State of Michigan and all reported decisions of this Court and the Michigan Court of Appeals shall adhere to and follow the "Michigan Uniform System of Citations" set forth in the pages attached hereto and made a part hereof, to be effective February 1, 1972.

Statutes.

1.   Michigan statutes.
     (a) Do *not* use the section symbol "§" or "sec." or "section" in citing Compiled Laws, MCLA and MSA
     (b) Public acts: cite year, "PA," and act number, *e.g.,* 1945 PA 87
     (c) Compiled Laws of 1948: cite as 1948 CL
     (d) Michigan Compiled Laws Annotated: cite as MCLA (Do *not* indicate a Cumulative Supplement.)
     (e) Michigan Statutes Annotated: cite as MSA
          (Do *not* use the date of a revised volume or indicate a Cumulative Supplement.)

. . . .

Suppose, however, that there are no official citation laws in the court rules for your court, or that these citation rules do not cover the citation question that you have. In such circumstances, *ask your supervisor what citation form you should use.* You will probably be told, "Use the Blue Book." This is a reference to the Uniform System of Citation we looked at earlier (p. 524). It is a small blue pamphlet (although in earlier editions, white covers were used). The Blue Book is published by a group of law students on the law reviews of their law schools. Caution is needed, however, in using the Blue Book. It is a highly technical and sometimes difficult-to-use pamphlet because it packs so much information in a relatively small space. Primary users of the Blue Book are law schools that wish to have their law reviews typeset by professional printers. The Blue Book sets forth a detailed style for displaying various types of references. Such directions would not apply to the normal kind of memorandum of law that is the product of most research assignments. Also, be aware that many courts do *not* follow the Blue Book even if there are no court rules on citation form for that court. Judges often simply use their own "system" of citation without necessarily being consistent.

GENERAL GUIDELINES ON CITATION FORM

1. Find out if there are citation laws in the court rules.
2. Ask your supervisor if he or she has any special instructions on citation form.
3. Consult the Blue Book.
4. Consult the basic citation rules presented below.
5. Remember that the *functional* purpose of a citation is to enable readers to locate your citation in a library. You must give enough information in the cite to fulfill this purpose. Courtesy to the reader is as important as compliance with the niceties of citation form.
6. Often a private publisher of a book will tell you how to cite the book. ("Cite this book as . . . .") Ignore this instruction! Instead, follow guidelines 1–5 above.
7. When in doubt about whether to include something in a citation after carefully following guidelines 1–5 above, resolve the doubt by including it in the cite.

BASIC CITATION RULES

Use the following citation forms unless General Guidelines 1–3 above tell you otherwise:

I	Citing Opinions
II	Citing Constitutions and Charters
III	Citing Federal Statutes
IV	Citing State Statutes
V	Citing Administrative Regulations
VI	Citing the Documents of Legislative History
VII	Citing Secondary Authority

I. Citing Opinions

The following are the most common kinds of opinions and decisions that you will be citing:

EXAMPLE A: FORMAT OF A CITATION TO AN OPINION OF THE HIGHEST FEDERAL COURT (the United States Supreme Court):

Taglianetti v. United States, 394 U.S. 316, 89 S.Ct. 1099, 22 L.Ed.2d 302 (1969). [As indicated below, there is a disagreement over the proper citation form for this Court. The Blue Book says the correct cite would be: *Taglianetti v. United States,* 394 U.S. 316 (1969).]

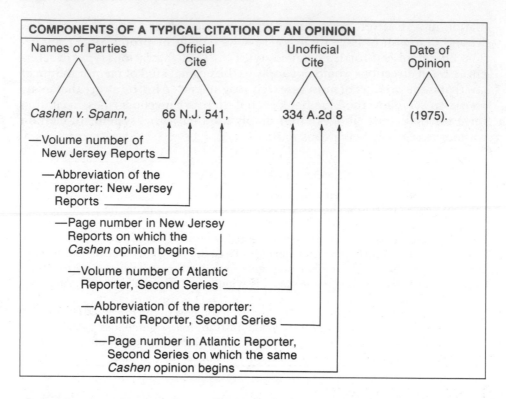

COMPONENTS OF A TYPICAL CITATION OF AN OPINION

Names of Parties   Official Cite   Unofficial Cite   Date of Opinion

Cashen v. Spann,   66 N.J. 541,   334 A.2d 8   (1975).

—Volume number of New Jersey Reports

  —Abbreviation of the reporter: New Jersey Reports

    —Page number in New Jersey Reports on which the *Cashen* opinion begins

      —Volume number of Atlantic Reporter, Second Series

        —Abbreviation of the reporter: Atlantic Reporter, Second Series

          —Page number in Atlantic Reporter, Second Series on which the same *Cashen* opinion begins

EXAMPLE B: FORMAT OF A CITATION TO AN OPINION OF A FEDERAL MIDDLE APPEALS COURT (the United States Court of Appeals, Second Circuit):

Sterling Nat'l Bank and Trust Co. of N.Y. v. Fidelity Mortgage Investors, 510 F.2d 870 (2d Cir. 1975).

EXAMPLE C: FORMAT OF A CITATION TO AN OPINION OF A FEDERAL TRIAL COURT (the United States District Court, Western District in Wisconsin):

Stone v. Schmidt, 398 F.Supp. 768 (W.D.Wisc.1975).

EXAMPLE D: FORMAT OF A CITATION TO AN OPINION OF THE HIGHEST STATE COURT (New Jersey Supreme Court):

Petlin Associates, Inc. v. Township of Dover, 64 N.J.327, 316 A.2d (1974).

EXAMPLE E: FORMAT OF A CITATION TO AN OPINION OF A LOWER STATE COURT (Conn. Superior Court, Appellate Session):

Huckabee v. Stevens, 32 Conn.Supp. 511, 338 A.2d 512 (Conn.Super. Ct., 1975).

EXAMPLE F: FORMAT OF A CITATION TO AN ADMINISTRATIVE DECISION (National Labor Relations Board):

Standard Dry Wall Products, Inc., 91 N.L.R.B. 544 (1950).

**EXAMPLE G: FORMAT OF A CITATION TO AN OPINION OF THE ATTOR-
NEY GENERAL:**

40 Op.Atty.Gen. 423 (1945).

Guidelines:

1. You will note that some of the citations in the above examples have *parallel
   cites* (see Examples A, D, and E) and some do not. Before examining the
   rules of providing parallel cites and the techniques of finding such cites,
   some basics need to be covered.

2. The same opinion can be printed in more than one reporter. A parallel cite
   is a reference to an *additional* reporter where the same opinion (word-for-
   word) can be found. In Example D, the *Petlin* opinion can be found in New
   Jersey Reports (abbreviated "N.J.") and in Atlantic 2d ("A.2d").

3. Do not confuse (a) parallel cite with (b) same case on appeal. Examine the
   following three citations:

   - *Smith v. Jones,* 24 Mass. 101, 19 N.E.2d 370 (1920).
   - *Jones v. Smith,* 26 Mass. 228, 21 N.E.2d 1017 (1922).
   - *Smith v. Jones,* 125 F.2d 177 (2d Cir. 1925).

   Assume that these three opinions involve the same litigation—the same
   parties and the same issues. The case went up on appeal three times: twice
   to the Massachusetts Supreme Judicial Court and once to the United States
   Court of Appeals for the Second Circuit. The first two opinions have parallel cites. For example, the first opinion is printed in both Massachusetts Reports (24 Mass. 101) and in North Eastern Reporter, 2d (19 N.E.2d 370).
   The third opinion has no parallel cite. The second two opinions are references to the "same case on appeal." They are *not* parallel cites to the first
   opinion. While the same litigation is involved, the citations are to three distinct opinions, two of which have parallel cites.

4. There are four main techniques of finding a parallel cite:
   a. Shepardize the case (pp. 552, 613). The first cite in parentheses in
      Shepard's is the parallel cite. If you find no cite in parenthesis, it means
      (a) that no parallel cite exists, (b) that the reporter containing the paral-
      lel cite has not been printed yet, or (c) the parallel cite was given in one
      of the earlier units of Shepard's and not repeated in the unit you are
      examining.

– 717 –	
(439US438)	ʋ،
592F2d²288	e61.
f615F2d¹739	f473ʜ
f615F2d²739	94 A3 18
f615F2d⁵739	94 A3 19ʂ
471FS⁵101	94 A3 211
f476FS¹92	94 A3 24ʿ
477FS961	
ʿ77FS⁴969	
⁷33	

b. National Reporter Blue Book (p. 524). Go to this set of books published by West to try to locate a parallel cite. The National Reporter Blue Book will also tell you which official reporters have been discontinued (p. 528).

c. Top of the caption. Go to the reporter that contains the opinion. At the beginning of the opinion, there is a caption giving the names of the parties, the court, etc. At the top of this caption, see if there is a parallel cite. (This technique does not often work, but it is worth a try.) The following is an excerpt from a caption that does provide a parallel cite:

169 Conn. 677

Application of Verne Freeman SLADE for Admission to the Bar.

Supreme Court of Connecticut.

Dec. 2, 1975.

d. Table of Cases in Digest. Go to every digest (p. 541) that gives small-paragraph summaries of court opinions for the court that wrote the opinion, e.g., the American Digest System. Go to the table of cases in these digests. See if there is a parallel cite for your case. In the following excerpt from a digest table of cases, you find two cites for *Ames v. State Bar*—106 Cal.Rptr. 489 and 506 P.2d 625:

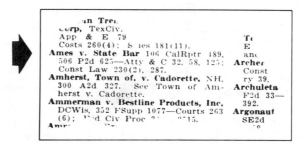

5. When should you provide a parallel cite? The short answer is, whenever one exists. As we shall see, however, there are some exceptions to this guideline.

6. Although an opinion may eventually be printed in more than one reporter, the reporters are rarely, if ever, printed at the same time. An unofficial reporter, for example, may come out a month after the court issues the opinion as a slip opinion (p. 556), whereas the official reporter may take as much as a year to be published. At the time you want to cite a recent opinion, you may have only the unofficial reporter available. Hence, you could not provide a parallel cite.

7. As indicated earlier, loose-leaf services often provide the most current legal material available (p. 547). Some services will send out opinions within a week of their issuance by the court. Generally, however, you do *not* in-

clude the citation to the loose-leaf service *unless* no other citation to the opinion is available at the time.

8. There is some disagreement as to whether parallel cites are needed for opinions of the U.S. Supreme Court. The Blue Book (p. 524) says you should not provide a parallel cite for such opinions if you have the official cite ("U.S.") available, even if the parallel cites in "S.Ct." and "L.Ed." are also available. The better view, however, is to give all three cites when they are available. (See Example A, p. 571.)

9. When parallel cites are to be cited, always place the official cite first before the unofficial cite. (See Examples A, D, and E, pp. 571–72.)

10. There is no parallel cite for Federal Reporter 2d cases (F.2d). (See Example B, p. 572.) Abbreviate the Circuit in parentheses at the end of the cite before the year. 2d Cir. means the opinion was decided by the U.S. Court of Appeals for the Second Circuit. D.C. Cir. would mean the case was decided by the U.S. Court of Appeals for the District of Columbia Circuit. The caption of the opinion will tell you which circuit court wrote the opinion.

11. There is no parallel cite for Federal Supplement cases (F.Supp.). (See Example C, p. 572.) Abbreviate the U.S. District Court in parentheses at the end of the cite before the year. W.D.Wisc. means the opinion was written by the United States District Court, Western District, sitting in Wisconsin. The caption of the opinion will tell you which U.S. District Court wrote the opinion.

12. Note the abbreviation N.J. in Example D, p. 572. Whenever a reporter is abbreviated solely by the initials of a state, you know that the highest state court in that state wrote the opinion. There is no need, therefore, to abbreviate the name of the court in parentheses at the end of the cite before the date. N.J. are the initials for the state of New Jersey. Therefore, you know that the highest state court in New Jersey wrote the *Petlin* case in Example D.

13. In Example E, p. 572, none of the reporters are abbreviated solely by the initials of a state. (The abbreviation for Connecticut is "Conn.", not "Conn.Supp.") You must therefore include the abbreviation of the court that wrote the opinion in parentheses at the end of the cite before the date.

14. Include only the last name of individual parties in litigation. For example, if the parties are listed as "Frank Taylor v. Mary Smith" by the court, your cite should list them as *Taylor v. Smith.*

15. If a party is a business, use the full name of the business, but abbreviate words such as Corporation (Corp.), Incorporated (Inc.), Company (Co.), Limited (Ltd.), and Brothers (Bros.). If, for example, a party is listed by the court as "John J. Dover, Incorporated," your cite would read *John J. Dover, Inc.* (If, however, John J. Dover was a party suing or being sued as an individual rather than as a business, your cite would simply list this party as *Dover.*)

16. When the United States is a party, do not use the abbreviation "U.S."

17. Assume that New York State is a party. Your cite should say "State" (rather than "State of New York" or "New York") *if and only if* the opinion was written by a New York state court. Suppose, however, that New York is a party in a case written by an Ohio court. In such a case, use "New York" (not

"State of New York" or "State") in your cite as the name of this party. This same guideline applies for the words "Commonwealth" and "People." These words are used alone in a cite only if the court that wrote the opinion you are citing is the same state referred to by the words "Commonwealth" and "People." Example: You are citing an opinion of the California Supreme Court, which describes the parties as follows:

People of California v. Gabriel S. Farrell

Your cite of this opinion would be *People v. Farrell.*

18. Underline (or italicize) the names of the parties.

19. Some opinions consolidate more than one litigation. A supreme court, for example, may use one opinion to resolve similar issues raised in several different lower court cases. The opinion written by the supreme court will probably list all the parties from these different lower court cases, e.g., *A v. B; C v. D; E v. F.* When you cite this opinion, include only the *first* set of parties listed by the court—here, *A v. B.* On the other hand, the court may not list all the multiple parties, but may simply say "et al." (and others) after the name of a party. Do not include the phrase "et al." in your cite.

20. Often the court will tell you the litigation status of the parties, e.g., plaintiff, defendant, appellant, appellee. Generally, you should not include this information in your cite.

21. Titles of individual parties (e.g., Administrator, Secretary) should be omitted from your cite. One exception is the Commissioner of Internal Revenue. Cite this party simply as "Commissioner," e.g., *Jackson v. Commissioner.*

22. Include the phrase "in re" (meaning "in the matter of") in your cite, e.g., *In re Jones.*

23. Include the date of the decision at the end of the cite in parentheses. If more than one date is given in the caption of the opinion, include the date the opinion was "decided."

24. Do not include the docket number (p. 642) of the case in the cite.

25. The reporter volumes that contain current opinions are conveniently arranged by volume number. All the volumes of the same set have the same name, e.g., Atlantic Reporter, 2d; New York Reports, etc. There was a time, however, when life was not this simple. Volumes of opinions were identified by the name of the individual person who had responsibility for compiling the opinions written by the judges. These individuals were called reporters. "7 Cush. 1," for example, refers to an opinion found on page 1 of volume 7 of Massachusetts cases when Mr. Cushing was the official reporter. When he ended his employment, Mr. Gray took over, and the cite of an opinion in the volume immediately after "7 Cush." was "1 Gray 1." Simply by looking at the cover of the volume, you *cannot* tell what court's opinions were inside unless you happen to be familiar with the names of these individuals and the courts for which they worked. These volumes are called *nominative reporters* because they are identified by the name of the individual person who compiled the opinions for the court.

26. Assume that all you know are the names of the parties and the name of the court that wrote the opinion. How do you obtain the full cite?

   a. Go to every digest that covers that reporter (p. 541). Check its table of cases.

b. Call the court clerk for the court that wrote the opinion. If it is a recent case, the clerk may be able to send you a copy. Occasionally, the clerk will give you the cite of the case. (It may help if you can tell the clerk the docket number—p. 642—of the case.)

c. Go to the reporter volumes that cover the court that wrote the opinion. Since you do not have a volume number, you cannot go directly to the volume that has the opinion. If, however, you can *approximate* the date of the case, you can check the table of cases in each reporter volume that probably covers that year. You may have to check the table of cases in ten to fifteen volumes before achieving success. The opinions are printed in the reporters in rough chronological order.

When quoting from or referring to specific language in an opinion, you must list both the number of the page on which the opinion begins *and* the number of the page on which the quoted language begins. The latter page number is inserted in the citation immediately following the former, and is set off with a comma. If a parallel cite is included, do the same for the parallel cite. In the following example, the quote is from p. 20 of Maryland Reports ("Md.") and from p. 379 of Atlantic 2d ("A.2d"):

EXAMPLE

"Even though laches may not apply, one must use reasonable promptness when availing himself of judicial protection." *Bridgeton Education Ass'n v. Board of Education,* 147 Md. 17, 20, 334 A.2d 376, 379 (1975).

II. Citing Constitutions and Charters

Constitutions and charters are cited to (a) the abbreviated name of the constitution or charter, (b) the article, and (c) the section to which you are referring.

EXAMPLE

"No Bill of Attainder or ex post facto Law shall be passed." U.S.Const. art. I, § 9, cl. 3.

In citing constitutions and charters, the date of enactment should *not* be given unless the provision you are citing has been amended or repealed.

III. Citing Federal Statutes

1. All federal statutes of Congress are collected in chronological order of passage in the United States Statutes at Large (p. 559). If the statute is of general public interest, it is also printed in *each* of three codes:
   - United States Code (U.S.C.)
   - United States Code Annotated (U.S.C.A.)—West Publishing Co.
   - United States Code Service (U.S.C.S.)—Lawyers Co-operative Publishing Co.

   The preferred citation format is to U.S.C. For example:

   42 U.S.C. § 3412(a) (1970).
   or
   Narcotic Rehabilitation Act of 1966, 42 U.S.C. § 3412(a) (1970).

While it is not necessary to give the popular name of the statute (as in the second version of the above example), citing the popular name when known is often helpful.

2. A new edition of the U.S.C. comes out every six years. The date you use in citing a statute in U.S.C. is the date of the edition you are using unless your statute is found in one of the annual Supplements to the U.S.C., which come out in between editions. If your statute is in a Supplement, you cite the volume and year of this Supplement. Suppose your statute is found in the sixth Supplement published in 1982. Your cite would be as follows:

   29 U.S.C. § 169 (Supp. VI 1982).

The date you use in citing a statute in U.S.C. is not the year the statute was enacted by the legislature. It is the date of the edition of the code or of the Supplement year.

3. Although citation to U.S.C. is preferred, it is not uncommon to find citations to the other two codes: U.S.C.A. and U.S.C.S. (There is never a need, however, to cite more than one of the three codes.) The format is as follows:

   29 U.S.C.A. § 169 (West 1983).
   29 U.S.C.S. § 169 (Law. Co-op. 1982).

In parentheses before the date, include the name of the publisher. Use the year that appears on the title page (p. 588) of the volume or its latest copyright year (p. 588), in this order of preference. If your statute is in one of the annual pocket parts of either of these two codes, include "Supp." and give the year of the pocket part, e.g., (West Supp. 1984).

4. There is one instance in which you *must* cite to the United States Statutes at Large (Stat.) rather than to U.S.C. The rule is as follows: Cite to the statute in Statutes at Large if (a) there is a difference in the language of the statute in Stat. and in the U.S.C. and (b) the statute in U.S.C. is in a title that has *not* been enacted into positive law by Congress.

   It is highly unlikely that you will find a difference in language between Stat. and U.S.C. Yet the conscientious researcher must check this out before relying on any statutory language.

   All the statutes in U.S.C. fall within one of fifty titles, e.g., title 11 on Bankruptcy, title 39 on the Postal Service. If Congress goes through all the statutes in a particular title and formally declares that all of them are valid and accurate, then that title has been enacted into positive law. You can rely exclusively on the language of such statutes even if the language is different from the statute as it originally appeared in Statutes at Large. At the beginning of the first volume of U.S.C., you will be told which titles of the U.S.C. have been enacted into positive law.

5. A Statute at Large cite, when needed, should include (a) the name of the statute if one exists; if one does not exist, include "Act of" and give the full date of enactment—month, day, and year, (b) the Public Law number of the statute or its chapter number, (c) the section of the statute you are citing, (d) the volume number of the Statutes at Large used, (e) the

abbreviation "Stat.," (f) the page number on which your statute is found in the Stat. volume, (g) in parentheses, the year the statute was passed by the legislature. Do not include the year here, however, if you used the "Act of" option referred to above in (a).

EXAMPLE

Narcotic Addict Rehabilitation Act, Pub.L.No. 80-793, § 9, 80 Stat. 1444 (1966).

Note that the year in parentheses at the end of the cite is the year the statute was passed. Guideline 2 above said that you do not use the date of enactment when citing a statute in U.S.C. The rule is otherwise when giving a Stat. cite.

Note the section number (9) of this Public Law in the example. The statute might also have several title numbers. If so, section 9 would be found within one of these titles. Assume, for example, that section 9 is in title III of the Public Law. It is important to remember that these section and title numbers are found in the original *session law* edition of the statute. When this statute is later printed in U.S.C. (assuming it is a public law of general interest), it will *not* go into section 9 of the third title. The U.S.C. has its own title and section number scheme. (For example, title VII, section 9 of the above statute might be found in title 45, section 1075(b) of the U.S.C.) This can be very frustrating for the researcher new to the law. If you are reading a statute in its original session or Public Law form, you cannot find this statute under the same title and section number in U.S.C. You must *translate* the Public Law or Stat. cite into a U.S.C. cite. Phrased another way, you must translate the session law cite into a code cite. Later, we will see that this is done by using one of two tables: Table III in the Tables volume of USC/USCA/USCS; or Table 2 in U.S. Code Congressional and Administrative News. (See p. 655.)

6. Of course, if the statute is a private law or is a public law that is deemed to be of no general public interest, it will not be printed in the U.S.C. It will be found only in Statutes at Large.

7. The Internal Revenue Code is within the U.S.C. Hence, you use guideline 1 above in citing a tax statute. For example:

26 U.S.C. § 1278 (1976).

For such statutes, however, there is *another* option that is considered acceptable:

I.R.C. § 1278 (1976).

8. There is a special format for citing Federal Rules of Civil Procedure, Federal Rules of Criminal Procedure, Federal Rules of Appellate Procedure, and the Federal Rules of Evidence. Examples:

Fed.R.Civ. P. 15
Fed.R.Crim. P. 23
Fed.R.App. P. 3
Fed.R.Evid. 310

IV. Citing State Statutes

1. Like federal statutes, the statutes of the various states are compiled in two kinds of collections: state *codes* (arranged by subject matter) and *session laws* (arranged in chronological order of enactment).
2. Citations to state codes vary from state to state. Below are examples of standard citation formats. Use these as guides unless local court rules dictate otherwise. The year at the end of the cite should be the year that appears on the spine of the code, or the year that appears on the title page (p. 588), or the latest copyright year (p. 588)—in this order of preference.

Alabama:	Ala. Code § 37 (1975)
Alaska:	Alaska Stat. § 1805 (1980)
Arizona:	Ariz. Rev. Stat. Ann. § 73 (1976)
Arkansas:	Ark. Stat. Ann. § 211 (1950)
California:	Cal. Penal Code § 90 (West 1970)
	Cal. Penal Code § 90 (Deering 1970)
Colorado:	Colo. Rev. Stat. § 100 (1960)
Connecticut:	Conn. Gen. Stat. § 95.1 (1976)
	Conn. Gen. Stat. Ann. § 95.1 (West 1976)
Delaware:	Del. Code Ann. tit. 4, § 38 (1980)
Dist. of Col.:	D.C. Code Ann. § 12–402 (1981)
	D.C. Code § 12–402 (Michie 1981)
Florida:	Fla. Stat. § 23 (1970)
	Fla. Stat. Ann. § 23 (West 1970)
Georgia:	Ga. Code § 657 (1980)
	Ga. Code Ann. § 657 (1980)
Hawaii:	Hawaii Rev. Stat. § 888 (1979)
Idaho:	Idaho Code § 45 (1979)
Illinois:	Ill. Rev. Stat. ch. 4, § 53 (1980)
	Ill. Ann. Stat. ch. 4, § 53 (Smith-Hurd 1979)
Indiana:	Ind. Code § 29 (1976)
	Ind. Code Ann. § 29 (Burns 1978)
	Ind. Code Ann. § 29 (West 1977)
Iowa:	Iowa Code § 72.3 (1979)
	Iowa Code Ann. § 72.3 (West 1980)
Kansas:	Kan. Stat. Ann. § 47 (1980)
	Kan. Civ. Proc. Code Ann. § 299 (Vernon 1970)

Kentucky:	Ky. Rev. Stat. § 222 (1979) Ky. Rev. Stat. Ann. § 222 (Baldwin 1980) Ky. Rev. Stat. Ann. § 222 (Bobbs-Merrill 1978)
Louisiana:	La. Rev. Stat. Ann. § 110 (West 1980) La. Code Crim. Proc. Ann. art. 3 (West 1980)
Maine:	Me. Rev. Stat. Ann. tit. 8, § 627 (1969)
Maryland:	Md. Fam. Law Code Ann. § 40 (1980)
Massachusetts:	Mass. Gen. Laws Ann. ch. 10, § 598 (West 1980) Mass. Ann. Laws ch. 10, § 598 (Michie/Law. Co-op. 1979)
Michigan: (see rules on p. 570)	MCLA 2.1 (1980) MSA 2.1 (1981)
Minnesota:	Minn. Stat. § 3678 (1980) Minn. Stat. Ann. § 3678 (West 1979)
Mississippi:	Miss. Code Ann. § 123 (1970)
Missouri:	Mo. Rev. Stat. § 48 (1979) Mo. Ann. Stat. § 48 (Vernon 1981)
Montana:	Mont. Code Ann. § 1.23 (1982)
Nebraska:	Neb. Rev. Stat. § 97 (1979)
Nevada:	Nev. Rev. Stat. § 990 (1969)
New Hampshire:	N.H. Rev. Stat. Ann. § 538 (1980)
New Jersey:	N.J. Rev. Stat. § 50 (1980) N.J. Stat. Ann. § 50 (West 1979)
New Mexico:	N.M. Stat. Ann. § 717 (1979)
New York:	N.Y. Crim. Proc. Law § 150 (McKinney 1979) N.Y. Crim. Proc. Law § 150 (Consol. 1980)
North Carolina:	N.C. Gen. Stat. § 373 (1979)
North Dakota:	N.D. Cent. Code § 241 (1980)
Ohio:	Ohio Rev. Code Ann. § 434.2 (Page 1979) Ohio Rev. Code Ann. § 434.2 (Baldwin 1980)
Oklahoma:	Okla. Stat. tit. 5, § 12 (1982) Okla. Stat. Ann. tit. 5, § 12 (West 1980)
Oregon:	Or. Rev. Stat. § 3636 (1980)
Pennsylvania:	12 Pa. Cons. Stat. § 578.9 (1979) 12 Pa. Cons. Stat. Ann. § 578.9 (Purdon 1980) Pa. Stat. Ann. tit. 12, § 578.9 (Purdon 1979)

Puerto Rico:	P.R. Laws Ann. tit. 25, § 299 (1980)
Rhode Island:	R.I. Gen. Laws § 257 (1981)
South Carolina:	S.C. Code Ann. § 266 (Law. Co-op. 1980)
South Dakota:	S.D. Codified Laws Ann. § 43 (1979)
	S.D. Comp. Laws Ann. § 43 (1980)
Tennessee:	Tenn. Code Ann. § 343 (1980)
Texas:	Tex. Penal Code Ann. § 777 (Vernon 1980)
Utah:	Utah Code Ann. § 1888 (1979)
Vermont:	Vt. Stat. Ann. tit. 3, § 26 (1978)
Virgin Islands:	V.I. Code Ann. tit. 9 (1979)
Virginia:	Va. Code § 345 (1979)
Washington:	Wash. Rev. Code § 2356 (1978)
	Wash. Rev. Code Ann. § 2356 (1980)
West Virginia:	W.Va. Code § 377 (1979)
Wisconsin:	Wis. Stat. § 7 (1980)
	Wis. Stat. Ann. § 7 (West 1979)
Wyoming:	Wyo. Stat. § 5656 (1980)

V. Citing Administrative Regulations

1. Federal administrative regulations are published in the Federal Register (Fed.Reg.). Many of these regulations are later codified by subject matter in the Code of Federal Regulations (C.F.R.).
2. Federal regulations that appear in the Code of Federal Regulations are cited to (a) the title number in which the regulation appears, (b) the abbreviated name of the code, (c) the number of the particular section to which you are referring, and (d) the date of the code edition which you are using.

EXAMPLE

29 C.F.R. § 102.60(a) (1975).

3. Federal Regulations that have not yet been codified into the Code of Federal Regulations are cited to the Federal Register using (a) the volume in which the regulation appears, (b) the abbreviation "Fed. Reg.," (c) the page on which the regulation appears, and (d) the year of the Federal Register you are using.

EXAMPLE

27 Fed. Reg. 2092 (1962).

VI. Citing the Documents of Legislative History

1. The main sources of legislative history (p. 656) are: copies of the bills and amendments introduced, copies of the reports and hearings of congressional committees, the Congressional Record that contains transcripts of floor debates and material submitted from the floor, etc.

2. Bills and amendments are cited by referring to (a) the number assigned to the bill by the House or Senate and (b) the number and session of Congress during which the bill was introduced.

EXAMPLE

H.R. 1746, 92nd Cong., 1st Sess. *and* S. 2515, 92nd Cong., 1st Sess.

3. Reports of congressional committees are cited by reference to (a) the number of the report, (b) the number and session of the Congress during which the report was published, (c) the number of the page to which you are referring, and (d) the year in which the report was published.

EXAMPLE

H.R.Rep. No. 238, 92nd Cong., 1st Sess, 4 (1971) *and* S.Rep. No. 415, 92nd Cong., 1st Sess., 6 (1971).

4. Hearings held by congressional committees are cited by reference to (a) the title of the hearing, (b) the number and session of Congress during which the hearing was held, (c) the number of the page in the published transcript to which you are referring, and (d) the year in which the hearing was held.

EXAMPLE

Hearings on S. 631 before the Subcommittee on Labor of the Committee on Labor and Public Welfare of the United States Senate, 92nd Cong., 1st Sess., 315 (1971).

5. The Congressional Record is issued on a daily basis and later collected into bound volumes. The *bound* volumes may be cited by referring to (a) the number of the volume in which the item appears, (b) the abbreviation "Cong.Rec.," (c) the number of the page on which the item appears, and (d) the year. The *unbound* daily volumes are cited in the same manner except that (a) the page number should be preceded by the letter "H" or "S" in order to indicate whether the item appeared in the House pages or the Senate pages of the volume, (b) the date should include the exact day, month, and year, and (c) the phrase "daily ed." should go before the date.

EXAMPLE

Bound volumes: 103 Cong. Rec. 2889 (1975).
Unbound volumes: 22 Cong. Rec. S2395 (daily ed. Feb. 26, 1976) *and* 132 Cong. Rec. H1385 (daily ed. Feb. 26, 1976).

VII. Citing Secondary Authority

1. Treatises and other books are cited to (a) the number of the volume being referred to (if part of a set), (b) the first initial and full surname of the author, (c) the title of the book, (d) the number of the section and/or page to which you are referring, (e) the edition of the book, if other than the first, and (f) the date of publication. The title of the book should be italicized or underscored.

EXAMPLE

6 M. Belli, *Modern Trials,* § 289 (1963) *and* G. Osborne, *Handbook on the Law of Mortgages* 370 (2d ed. 1970).

2. Law review *articles* are cited by reference to (a) the full surname of the author, (b) the title of the article, (c) the number of the volume in which the article appears, (d) the abbreviated name of the law review, (e) the number of the page on which the article begins, and (f) the date of publication. The title of the article should be italicized or underscored.

EXAMPLE

Catz and Robinson, *Due Process and Creditor's Remedies,* 28 Rutgers L.Rev. 541 (1975).

3. Law review *notes* and *comments* written by law students are cited in essentially the same manner as the law review articles (see #2, above) except that the name of the author is omitted. Use "Note," "Comment," or "Special Project" in place of an author's name

4. Short law review *case notes* are cited in essentially the same manner as law review articles (see #2) except that both the name of the author and the title or heading of the case note are omitted.

5. Legal encyclopedias are cited by reference to (a) the number of the volume, (b) the abbreviated name of the encyclopedia, (c) the subject heading to which you are referring, (d) the number of the section to which you are referring, and (e) the date of publication of the volume you are citing. When referring to a specific point within the section, you should, if possible, refer to the number of the footnote that corresponds to that point. This reference should be inserted in your citation between the section number and the date of publication.

EXAMPLE

83 C.J.S., *Subscriptions* § 3, n. 32 (1953) *and* 77 Am.Jur.2d, *Vendor and Purchaser* § 73 (1975).

6. Restatements of the Law published by the American Law Institute are cited by reference to (a) the title of the Restatement, (b) the edition being referred to (if other than the first edition), (c) the number of the section being referred to, and (d) the date of publication.

EXAMPLE

Restatement (Second) of Agency § 37 (1957).

7. Annotations in ALR, ALR2d, ALR3d, ALR4th, and ALR Fed. are cited by (a) the abbreviation "Annot.," (b) the volume number, (c) the abbreviation of the ALR unit, (d) the page number where the annotation begins, (e) and the date of the volume. Do not include the title or the author of the annotation.

EXAMPLE

Annot., 23 A.L.R.4th 1022 (1984).

ASSIGNMENT 73

There is one or more things wrong with each of the following citations. Describe the errors and gaps in format, e.g., a parallel cite is missing, something is abbreviated incorrectly. You do not have to go to the library to check any of these cites. Simply use the guidelines presented above.

1. Smith v. Jones, 135 Mass. 37, 67 N.E.2d 316, 320 (1954). *opinion* *unlined*
2. *Paul Matthews v. Edward Foley, Inc.,* 779 F.2d 729, (W.D.N.Y., 1979). *unlined*
3. *Jackson v. Jackson,* 219 F.Supp. 1276, 37 N.E.2d 84 (1980). *No parell cite*
4. *Davis v. Tompson, et al,* 336 P.2d 691, 210 N.M. 432 (1976). *official Reports should be first*
5. *Washington Tire Company v. Jones,* 36 N.J.Super. 222, 351 A.2d 541 (1976).
6. *State of New Hampshire v. Atkinson,* 117 N.H. 830, 228 A.2d 222 (N.H.Super., 1978).
7. *Richardson v. U.S.,* 229 U.S. 220 (1975).
8. American Law Institute, *Restatement of Torts* (2d ed 1976).
9. U.S.Const. Art. III (1797).
10. Smith, F., Products Liability (3rd ed. 1985).
11. 42 USC 288 (1970).
12. 17 U.S.C.A. 519 (1970).
13. 40 Fed. Reg. § 277 (1976).

Section K. CITE CHECKING

In a cite-checking assignment you are given a document written by someone else and asked to check the citations provided by the author of the document. The assignment is quite common in law firms, particularly when the document to be checked is an appellate brief (p. 695). Students on law reviews (p. 626) in law school also do extensive cite checking on the work of fellow students and outside authors.

While our focus in this section will be the writing of others, the guidelines discussed below are in large measure equally applicable to your own writing.

GUIDELINES FOR CITE CHECKING

1. The first step is to obtain clear instructions from your supervisor on the scope of the assignment. Should you do a "light check" or a comprehensive

one? Should you focus solely on citation form, or should you determine the accuracy of all cites as measured by the content of the library material relied on by the writer of the document? On citation form, what rules should you use? The Blue Book (p. 524)?

The following guidelines assume that you have been asked to undertake a comprehensive check.

2. Make sure that you have a *copy* of the document on which you can make comments. Avoid using the original.

3. If the pages of the document already have pencil or pen markings made by others (or by the author who made last-minute insertions), use a pencil or pen color that is different from any other markings on the pages. In this way it will be clear to any reader which corrections, notations, or other comments are your own. If you find that you do not have enough room to write in the margins of the pages, use separate sheets of paper.

4. If the document is an appellate brief, be sure that you have in front of you any citation rules that are required by the court where the brief will be submitted (p. 570). If such rules exist, they must be followed. Then determine from your supervisor what citation system should be used for citations that are not governed by court rules, e.g., the Blue Book.

5. Before you begin, try to find a model. By going through the old case files of the office, you may be able to locate a prior document, e.g., an old appellate brief, that you can use as a general guide. Ask your supervisor to direct you to such a document. While it may not cover all the difficulties you will encounter in your own document, you will at least have a general guide approved by your supervisor.

6. Check the citation form of *every* cite in the document. This includes any cites in the body of the text, the footnotes, appendix material, and in the introductory pages of the document, e.g., in the Table of Authorities (p. 697) at the beginning of a brief.

7. For longer documents, you need to develop your own system for ensuring the completeness of your checking. For example, you might want to circle every cite that you have checked and found to be accurate, and place a small box around (or a question mark next to) every cite that is giving you difficulties. You will want to spend more time with the latter, seeking help from colleagues and your supervisor.

8. When you find errors in the form of the citation, make the corrections in the margin of the pages where they are found.

9. For some errors, you will not be able to make the corrections without obtaining additional information, e.g., a missing date or a missing parallel cite. If you can obtain this data by going to the relevant library books, do so. Otherwise, in the margin, make a notation of what is missing or what still needs correction.

10. Consistency in citation format is extremely important. On page 2 of the document, for example, the author may use one citation form, but on page 10 may use a completely different form for the same kind of legal material. You need to point out this inconsistency and make the corrections that are called for.

11. Often your document will quote from legal materials such as cases, statutes, etc. Check the accuracy of these quotations. Go to the material being quoted, find the quote, and check it against the document line by line, word by word, and punctuation mark by punctuation mark. Be scrupulous about the accuracy of quotations.

12. Shepardize anything that can be shepardized, e.g., cases, statutes. Review the list of what can be shepardized presented earlier in the chapter (p. 552). Later in the chapter, we will cover the techniques of shepardizing (p. 608). Examples of what you need to determine through shepardizing:
    - Whether any of the cases cited have been overruled
    - Whether any of the statutes cited have been repealed, amended, or changed in any way

13. Check the accuracy of all "*supra's*" and "*infra's*." The word *supra* means "above" or "earlier." It is a reference to something mentioned earlier in the document. For example, on page 23 of the document, there might be a footnote that says, "See *Smith v. Jones, supra* p. 9." Go to page 9 and verify that *Smith v. Jones* is discussed or mentioned there. *Infra* means "below" or "later" and refers the reader to something that will come later in the document. In the same manner as you checked the *supra's*, determine whether the *infra* references are accurate.

Section L. COMPONENTS OF A LAW BOOK

There are similarities in the structure of many law books. To be sure, some books are totally unique, e.g., Shepard's Citations. In the main, however, there is a pattern to the texts. The following is a list of components that are contained in many:

1. Outside Cover
On the outside cover you will find the title of the book, the author(s) or editor(s), the name of the publisher (usually at the bottom), the edition of the book (if more than one edition has been printed), and the volume number (if the book is part of a series of books). After glancing at the outside cover, the researcher should ask the following questions:

a. Is it a book *containing* law (written primarily by a court, a legislature, or an administrative agency), or is it a book *about* the law (written by a scholar who is commenting on the law)?
b. Is this book still operative? Look at the books on the shelf in the area where you found the book that you are examining. Is there a replacement volume for your book? Is there a later edition of the book? Check your book in the card catalog (p. 599) to see if other editions are mentioned.

2. Publisher's Page
The first few pages of the book often include a page or pages about the publisher. The page may list other law books published by the same company.

3. Title Page
The title page repeats most of the information contained on the outside cover: title, author, editor, publisher. It also contains the date of publication.

4. Copyright Page
The copyright page (often immediately behind the title page) has a copyright mark (©) plus a date or series of dates. The most recent date listed indicates the timeliness of the material in the volume. Given the great flux in the law, it is very important to determine how old the text is. If the book has a pocket part (see item 16 below), it has been updated to the date on the pocket part.

COPYRIGHT © 1974 through 1981 WEST PUBLISHING CO.

COPYRIGHT © 1986
By
WEST PUBLISHING CO.

The dates on this copyright page indicate that the material in the book is current up to 1986, the latest copyright date.

5. Authenticity Page
Books containing statutes and cases often have a page prepared by the secretary of state or the chief judge of the court, indicating that the materials in the book are authentic. These are usually official editions of the material. Of course, a book that does not have such a page is not to be considered fraudulent. Unofficial editions prepared by private publishers have usually achieved great respectability and are used regularly. In some instances, courts and legislatures have adopted the private publisher's edition as the "official" edition for the jurisdiction and so indicate on the authenticity page.

6. Foreword, Preface, or Explanation
Under such headings, the reader will find some basic information about the book, particularly material on how the book was prepared and guidance on how to use it.

7. Summary Table of Contents
On one or two pages, the reader can find the main topics treated in the book.

8. Detailed Table of Contents

The detailed table can be very extensive. The major headings of the summary table of contents are repeated, and detailed subheadings and sub-subheadings are listed. This table can be used as an additional index to the book.

9. Table of Cases

The table of cases lists, alphabetically, every case that is printed or referred to in the text, with the page(s) where the case is found.

10. Summary of Headnotes

If the volume contains unofficial reports of cases, there may be a number of pages with a listing of headnotes (p. 544) that summarize portions of those cases.

11. Table of Statutes

The table of statutes gives the page numbers where every statute is interpreted or referred to in the text.

12. List of Abbreviations

The abbreviation list is critical. A reader who is unfamiliar with law books should check the list immediately. It may be the only place in the book that spells out the abbreviations used in the body of the text. In Shepard's Citations, for example, the following abbreviations are found in the first few pages of bound volumes and in most of the pamphlets covering case citations (a different abbreviation page will be found for statutory citations):

History of Case

a	(affirmed)	Same case affirmed on appeal.
cc	(connected case)	Different case from case cited but arising out of same subject matter or intimately connected therewith.
D	(dismissed)	Appeal from same case dismissed.
m	(modified)	Same case modified on appeal.
r	(reversed)	Same case reversed on appeal.
s	(same case)	Same case as case cited.
S	(superseded)	Substitution for former opinion.
v	(vacated)	Same case vacated.
US cert den		Certiorari denied by U. S. Supreme Court.
US cert dis		Certiorari dismissed by U. S. Supreme Court.
US reh den		Rehearing denied by U. S. Supreme Court.
US reh dis		Rehearing dismissed by U. S. Supreme Court.

Treatment of Case

c	(criticised)	Soundness of decision or reasoning in cited case criticised for reasons given.
d	(distinguished)	Case at bar different either in law or fact from case cited for reasons given.
e	(explained)	Statement of import of decisions in cited case. Not merely a restatement of the facts.
f	(followed)	Cited as controlling.
h	(harmonized)	Apparent inconsistency explained and shown not to exist.
j	(dissenting opinion)	Citation in dissenting opinion.
L	(limited)	Refusal to extend decision of cited case beyond precise issues involved.
o	(overruled)	Ruling in cited case expressly overruled.
p	(parallel)	Citing case substantially alike or on all fours with cited case in its law or facts.
q	(questioned)	Soundness of decision or reasoning in cited case questioned.

13. Statutory History Table

In statutory codes (p. 557), there may be a table that will list every statute cited in the book and indicate whether it has been repealed or whether there is a new section number and title for the statute. The legislature may have changed the entire name of the statutory chapter (e.g., from Prison Law to Correction Law) and renumbered all the sections. Without this table, the researcher can become lost. In the example below, note that former Prison Law sections 10–20 are now found in Correction Law sections 600–610. You may find a citation to a Prison Law section in a book that was published before the state changed to Correction Law sections. When you go to look up the Prison Law section, you will find nothing unless you have a way to translate the section into a Correction Law section. The history table is one way to do it.

TABLE OF PRISON LAW SECTIONS

Showing the distribution of those sections of the former Prison Law in effect prior to the general amendment by L.1929, c. 243, which are contained wholly or in part in the Correction Law, or which have been omitted or repealed.

Prison Law Section	Correction Law Section
1	1
10–20	600–610
21	Repealed
22 L.1919, c. 12	611
22 L.1920, c. 933	612
23–32	613–622
40–50	40–50

14. Body of the Text

The fundamental characteristic of the body of many legal texts is that it is arranged according to divisions, subdivisions, chapters, subchapters, parts, subparts, sections, subsections, etc. Everything is often numbered and subnumbered. Each of these units will usually contain a similar subject matter. You should thumb through the entire book to obtain a feel for the numbering and classification system used by the author or editor. (A major exception to this structure is the reporter (p. 532) in which opinions are printed in rough chronological order rather than by divisions or sections.)

15. Footnotes

Footnotes are very important in law books; researchers place great emphasis on them. Footnotes often give extensive citations to cases and other cross-references.

16. Pocket Parts

A unique and indispensable feature of many law books are the pocket parts. They are small-booklet additions to the text, placed at the very end of the text in a specially devised "pocket" built into the inside of the rear cover. The pocket parts are published after the book is printed and are designed to bring the book up-to-date with the latest developments in the field covered by the book. Of course, pocket parts can also grow out of date. Normally they are replaced every one or two years. On the front cover of the pocket-part booklet, there will be a date telling you what period is covered. Hence the title page (see above) may say that the last edition of the book was published in 1970, but the front page of the pocket part may say "for use during 1986–1987."

Normally the organization of the pocket part exactly parallels the organization of the main text. To find out, for example, if there has been anything new in the area covered by chapter 7, part 2, section 714 of the main text, you go to chapter 7, part 2, section 714 of the pocket part. If nothing is found there, then nothing new has happened. If changes or additions have occurred, they will be found there.

Pocket parts are cumulative (p. 535) in that whenever a pocket part is replaced by another pocket part, everything in the early pocket part is consolidated into the most recent one.

Reporters (p. 525) never have pocket parts. Cases published subsequent to the date of the volume you are examining are always found in slip opinions and advance sheets (p. 521) that are later consolidated into bound volumes.

17. Appendix

The text may include one or more appendixes. Normally, they will include tables, charts, or the entire text of statutes or regulations, portions of which are discussed in the body of the book.

18. Glossary or Dictionary

The book may include a glossary or dictionary that defines a selected number of words used in the body of the book.

19. Bibliography

A brief or extended bibliography of the field covered by the book may be included at the end of each chapter or at the end of the book.

20. Index—Specific

The index is a critical part of the book. Unfortunately, some books either have no index or do a sloppy job of indexing (e.g., some sets of administrative regulations and loose-leaf services fall into this category). The index is arranged alphabetically and should refer the reader either to the page number(s) or the section number(s) where the item is treated in the body of the text.

The specific index is usually at the back of the book. If the book has two or three volumes, the index may be at the end of the last volume.

21. General Index

If there are a large number of volumes, e.g., over twenty, there is often a separate series of volumes called "index," "general index," or "words and phrases." This broader index covers every volume in the series. The specific indexes to the individual volumes are consolidated within the general index.

Section M. THE CARTWHEEL: A TECHNIQUE OF USING INDEXES AND TABLES OF CONTENTS

We now come to one of the most important skills in legal research: the creative use of indexes and tables of contents in law books. If you have mastered this skill, 50 percent of the research battle is won. The CARTWHEEL is a technique designed to assist you in acquiring the skill.

The objective of the CARTWHEEL can be simply stated: to develop the habit of phrasing every word involved in the client's problem *fifteen to twenty different ways!* When you go to the index or table of contents of a law book, you naturally begin looking up the words and phrases that you think should lead you to the relevant material in the book. If you do not find anything relevant to your problem, two conclusions are possible:

1. There is nothing relevant in the law book.
2. You looked up the wrong words in the index and table of contents.

Most of us make the mistake of thinking that the first conclusion is accurate. Nine times out of ten, the second conclusion is the reason why we fail to find material in the law book that is relevant to the client's problem. The solution is to be able to phrase a word in as many different ways and in as many different contexts as possible. Hence, the CARTWHEEL.

In the center of the CARTWHEEL you place major words or phrases (one at a time) that come from the facts of the research problem. Each of these words or phrases is to be CARTWHEELED individually as demonstrated below.

Suppose that your research problem involves a wedding. You CART-WHEEL this word as follows:

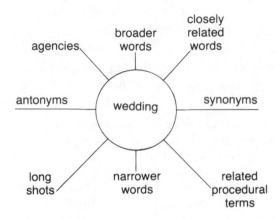

The first step in using the index and table of contents in any law book is to look up the word *wedding* in that index and table. Assuming that you are not successful with this word (either because the word is not in the index and table, or because the page or section references after the word in the index and table do not lead you to relevant material in the body of the book), the next step is to think of as many different phrasings and contexts of the word *wedding* as possible. Here is where the steps of the CARTWHEEL can be useful.

If we were to apply these eighteen steps of the CARTWHEEL to the word *wedding*, here are some of the words and phrases that would be checked in the index and table of contents of *every* law book that you examine.

BROADER WORDS: celebration, ceremony, rite, ritual, formality, festivity, event, etc.

NARROWER WORDS: civil wedding, church wedding, golden wedding, proxy wedding, sham wedding, shotgun marriage, etc.

SYNONYMS: marriage, nuptial, etc.

ANTONYMS: alienation, annulment, divorce, separation, etc.

CLOSELY RELATED WORDS: matrimony, marital, domestic, husband, wife, bride, anniversary, custom, children, blood test, premarital, spouse, relationship, family, home, consummation, cohabitation, sexual relations, betrothal, minister, wedlock, oath, contract, name change, domicile, residence, etc.

CHART 4

THE CARTWHEEL: USING THE INDEX AND TABLE OF CONTENTS OF LAW BOOKS

---

1. Identify all the *major words* from the facts of the client's problem. (Most of these facts can be obtained from the intake memorandum written following the initial interview with the client, p. 385.) Place each word or small set of words in the center of the CARTWHEEL.
2. In the index and table of contents, look up all these words.
3. Identify the *broader* categories of the major words.
4. In the index and table of contents, look up all these broader categories.
5. Identify the *narrower* categories of the major words.
6. In the index and table of contents, look up all these narrower categories.
7. Identify all the *synonyms* of the major words.
8. In the index and table of contents, look up all these synonyms.
9. Identify all the *antonyms* of the major words.
10. In the index and table of contents, look up all these antonyms.
11. Identify all *closely related* words.
12. In the index and table of contents, look up all these closely related words.
13. Identify all *procedural* terms connected with the major words.
14. In the index and table of contents, look up all these procedural terms.
15. Identify all *agencies* and *courts* that might have some connection to the major words.
16. In the index and table of contents, look up all these agencies and courts.
17. Identify all *long shots*.
18. In the index and table of contents, look up all these long shots.

NOTE: The above categories are not mutually exclusive.

PROCEDURAL TERMS: action, suit, statute of limitations, liability, court, complaint, discovery, defense, petition, jurisdiction, trial, appeal, etc.

AGENCIES and COURTS: Bureau of Vital Statistics, county clerk, license bureau, secretary of state, justice of the peace, etc.; trial court, superior court, court of appeals, supreme court, etc.

LONG SHOTS: dowry, common law, single, blood relationship, fraud, religion, license, illegitimate, remarriage, antenuptial, alimony, bigamy, pregnancy, gifts, chastity, community property, impotence, incest, virginity, support, custody, consent, paternity, etc.

There may be some overlapping of the categories; they are not mutually exclusive. Also, it is *not* significant whether you place a word in one category or another so long as the word comes to your mind as you comb through the index and table of contents. The CARTWHEEL is, in effect, *a word association game,* which should become second nature to you with practice. Often you will be led to a section or page containing material that is not directly relevant to your research. Yet this section or page may give you a cross-reference to other material that is relevant. This is one of the reasons why it is useful to check antonyms. Perhaps you might think that some of the word selections in the above categories are a bit farfetched. The problem, however, is that you simply will not know for sure whether a word will be fruitful until you try it. To be imaginative, one must be prepared to take some modest risks.

Indexes and tables of contents are often organized into headings, sub-headings, sub-subheadings and perhaps even sub-sub-subheadings. In the following excerpt from an index, "Burden of proof" is a sub-subheading of "Accidents" and a subheading of "Unavoidable accident or casualty." The latter is a subheading of "Accidents," which is the main heading of the index entry.

```
Accidents
    Opportunity to avoid accident, application of last
        clear chance doctrine, § 137(5), pp. 154–160
    Parents' responsibility, attractive nuisance doc-
        trine, § 63(76)
    Pleading unavoidable accident as defense, § 197
    Precautions against injury from dangerous place,
        agency, etc., §§ 84–89, pp. 1016–1034
    Presumption of negligence from happening, § 220.1,
        pp. 506–512
    Proximate cause of injury, § 115, pp. 1231–1234
    Res ipsa loquitur, accident and defendant's rela-
        tion thereto, §§ 220.10–220.15, pp. 551–578
    Restaurant patron's injuries, liability, § 63(131)
    Storekeeper's liability, § 63(121), p. 892
    Unavoidable accident or casualty, § 21, pp. 647,
        649
        Burden of proof, § 204, p. 450, n. 86; § 209,
            p. 482
        Consistency between general verdict and find-
            ings, § 304, p. 1072, n. 5
```

If you were looking for law on burden of proof, you may be out of luck unless you *first* thought of looking up "accidents" and "unavoidable accident."

Suppose that you identify the following words to check in an index.

minor	sale
explosion	warranty
car	damage

The index may have no separate heading for "minor," but "minor" may be a subheading under "sale." Be sure, therefore, to determine not only if the word has a separate heading, but also *whether it is a subheading under the other words you are checking.* Under each of the above six words, you should be alert to the possibility that the other five words may be subheadings for that word. Hence the process of pursuing these six words in an index (or table of contents) would be as follows (the word in capital letters is checked first and then the five words *under it* are checked to see if any of them are subheadings):

CAR	DAMAGE	EXPLOSION
damage	car	car
explosion	explosion	damage
minor	minor	minor
sale	sale	sale
warranty	warranty	warranty

MINOR	SALE	WARRANTY
car	car	car
damage	damage	damage
explosion	explosion	explosion
sale	minor	minor
warranty	warranty	sale

ASSIGNMENT 74

One way to gain an appreciation for the use of indexes is to write one of your own.

1. Write a comprehensive index of your present job or the last job that you had.
2. Pick one area of the law that you have thus far covered in class or read about. Write your own comprehensive index on what you have learned.
3. Write a comprehensive index of the following statute:

> **§ 132. Amount of force.** The use of force against another for the purpose of effecting the arrest or recapture of the other, or of maintaining the actor's custody of him, is not privileged if the means employed are in excess of those which the actor reasonably believes to be necessary.

ASSIGNMENT 75

CARTWHEEL the following words or phrases:

1. Paralegal
2. Woman
3. Rat bite
4. Rear end collision
5. Monopoly

ASSIGNMENT 76

Examine the index on p. 596 from a legal encyclopedia. It is an excerpt from the heading of Evidence. Death is the subheading of Evidence. What sub-subheadings and/or sub-sub-subheadings of Evidence would you check to try to find material on the following?

1. Introducing a death certificate into evidence.
2. The weight that a court will give to the personal conclusions of a witness.
3. Introducing the last words of a decedent into evidence.
4. A statement by the person who died disclaiming ownership of land around which he or she had placed a fence.

Section N. THE FIRST LEVEL OF LEGAL RESEARCH: BACKGROUND

There are three interrelated levels of researching a problem:

1. Background Research
Background research provides you with a general understanding of the area of law involved in your research problem.

2. Specific Fact Research
Specific fact research provides you with primary and secondary authority that covers the specific facts of your research problem.

3. Validation Research
Validation research provides you with the most up-to-date information on the current validity of all the primary authority you intend to use in your research memorandum on the problem. (See cite checking, p. 585.)

At times all three levels of research will be going on simultaneously. If you are new to legal research, however, it is recommended that you approach your research problem in the above three stages. Our concern in this section is level 1: background research. The other two levels are covered throughout the remainder of the chapter.

Our assumption here is that you are researching a topic that is totally new to you, and/or that you are totally new to *any* field of law. Spend an hour or two (depending on the complexity of the area) doing some reading in law books that will provide you with an overview of the area—a general understanding. This will help you identify the major terminology, the major agencies involved, if any, and some of the major issues. Of course, while doing this background research, you will probably also come up with leads that will be helpful in the second and third levels of research.

All this background research will be in the secondary sources—legal encyclopedias, treatises, legal periodical literature, legal dictionaries, etc. Caution must be exercised in studying these materials. As we have seen, they must never be used as a substitute for mandatory primary authority, which is the objective of your research (p. 561). In your research memorandum, it will be rare for you to quote from a legal dictionary or a legal encyclopedia. Many courts do not consider them to be very persuasive. Treatises and legal periodical literature are considered somewhat more persuasive (depending on the author), but again, even these secondary sources should be infrequently quoted once you have laid the proper foundation for their use (p. 569). Judges want to know what the primary authority is—opinions, statutes, constitutional provisions, regulations, etc. Use the secondary material for the limited purposes of (1) background reading and (2) providing leads to primary authority—particularly through the footnotes in the secondary sources.

CHART 4

TECHNIQUES FOR DOING BACKGROUND RESEARCH ON A TOPIC

1.   *Legal Dictionary* (p. 545)
      Have access to a legal dictionary throughout your research. For example:
         Black's Law Dictionary
         Ballentine's Law Dictionary
         Oran's Law Dictionary
         Statsky's Legal Thesaurus/Dictionary
         Words and Phrases
 Look up the meaning of all important terms that you come across in your research. These dictionaries are starting points only. Eventually you want to find primary authority that defines these terms.

2.   *Legal Encyclopedias* (p. 629)
      Go to the General Index of each of the major national legal encyclopedias:
         American Jurisprudence 2d (p. 522)
         Corpus Juris Secundum (p. 534)
 Also check any encyclopedias that cover only your state. Use the CARTWHEEL to help you use their indexes and tables of contents (p. 591).

3.   *Treatises* (p. 630)   Go to your card catalog. Use the CARTWHEEL to help you locate cards on treatises such as hornbooks, handbooks, formbooks practice manuals, scholarly studies, etc. Many of these books will have KF call numbers. Use the CARTWHEEL to help you use the indexes and tables of contents of these books.
4.   *Annotations* (p. 605)   Go to ALR, ALR2d, ALR3d, ALR4th, and ALR Fed (p. 521). Each of these sets of books has a Quick Index (p. 606). Use the CARTWHEEL to help you use this index to find annotations on your topic.

5.   *Legal Periodical Literature* (p. 546)
      Go to the three major indexes to legal periodical literature (p. 626):
         Index to Legal Periodicals
         Current Law Index
         Legal Resource Index
 Use the CARTWHEEL to help you use these indexes to locate legal periodical literature on your topic.

6. *Agency Reports/Brochures*

    If your research involves an administrative agency, call or write the agency. Find out what brochures, reports, or newsletters the agency has available to the public. Such literature often provides useful background information.

7. *Committee Reports*

    Before statutes are passed, committees of the legislature often write reports that comment on and summarize the legislation. In addition to being good sources of legislative history on the statute (p. 655), the reports are excellent background reading. If practical, contact both houses of the legislature to find out which committees acted on the statute. If the statute is fairly recent, they may be able to send you copies of the committee reports or tell you where to obtain them. Also check the law library of the legislature. The committee reports of many federal statutes are printed in U.S. Code Congressional and Administrative News (p. 558).

8. *Reports/Studies of Special Interest Groups* (p. 61)

    There are special interest groups for almost every area of the law, e.g., unions, bar associations, environment associations, tax associations, insurance company and other business associations. They often have position papers and studies that they could send you. Although one-sided, such literature should not be ignored.

9. *Martindale-Hubbell Law Directory*

    The Digest volume of Martindale-Hubbell (p. 548) provides concise summaries of the law of the fifty states and many foreign countries.

Of course, you will not have time to use all of the above nine techniques on background research. Usually one or two of the techniques will be sufficient for the limited purpose of providing you with an overview and getting you started.

Section O. CHECKLISTS FOR USING THE TEN MAJOR SEARCH RESOURCES

    We have said that the main objective of legal research is to locate mandatory primary authority (p. 561). There are three levels of government—federal, state, and local. An overview of their primary authority is as follows:

FEDERAL LEVEL OF GOVERNMENT	STATE LEVEL OF GOVERNMENT	LOCAL LEVEL OF GOVERNMENT (CITY, COUNTY, ETC.)
U.S. Constitution	State Constitution	Charter
Statutes of Congress	State Statutes	Local Ordinances
Federal Court Opinions	State Court Opinions	Local Court Opinions
Federal Agency Regulations	State Agency Regulations	Local Agency Regulations
Federal Administrative Decisions	State Administrative Decisions	Local Administrative Decisions
Federal Court Rules	State Court Rules	Local Court Rules
Executive Orders of the President	Executive Orders of the Governor	Executive Orders of the Mayor
Opinions of the U.S. Attorney General	Opinions of the State Attorney General	Opinions of the Corporation Counsel
Treaties		

In the remainder of this chapter we examine methods of finding most of the above kinds of primary authority. Throughout our examination, you will be referred back to this section where ten checklists for the major finding tools are presented. These ten finding tools (or search resources) are often useful for locating more than one kind of primary authority. Hence they are presented together here.

Many of the ten search resources are also helpful in doing background research in the secondary sources (p. 566). Indeed, some of the search resources *are* secondary sources themselves. Finally, some of the search resources are helpful in doing the third level of research—validation research, particularly Shepard's. In short, the following ten search resources or finding tools are the foundation of legal research itself:

1. Card catalog
2. Digests
3. Annotations
4. Shepard's
5. Loose-leaf services
6. Indexes to legal periodical literature
7. Legal encyclopedias
8. Treatises
9. Phone and Mail
10. Computers

I. CARD CATALOG

A well-organized card catalog is one of the researcher's best friends. It is often an excellent place to begin your research. Most law libraries use the Library of Congress classification system. Under this system, many law books have KF call numbers. The following is an example of a card from a card catalog:

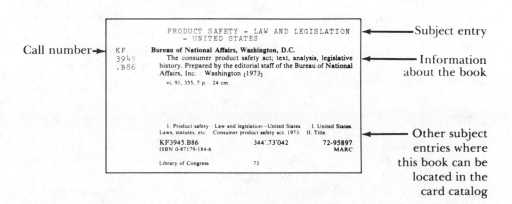

CHECKLIST #1

CHECKLIST FOR USING THE CARD CATALOG
1. Find out if your law library has more than one card catalog. Is there a catalog with entries by subject matter and another with entries by author? Are there different catalogs for different topics or areas of the law?
2. Find out if the library has any descriptive literature on how to use the catalog.
3. Pull out a tray from the catalog at random. Thumb through the cards. Put a paper clip on an example of each kind of card that appears to be organized differently or that contains different kinds of information. Ask a librarian to spend ten minutes with you explaining the features of the cards that you have paper-clipped. (You should not remove the cards from the tray, but it may be possible in some libraries to bring the entire tray to the librarian.)
4. Be sure you understand all the information on the cards that tells you where the books are located in the library. Some books may be on reserve, in special rooms, or in other buildings.
5. Select several cards at random, particularly where the books have different locations. Try to find these books. Ask for help if you cannot locate them.
6. Now try the reverse process. Select three different kinds of books from the shelves of the library at random (not the same books you looked at in #5 above). Take these books to the card catalog and try to find the card for these books in the catalog. Your goal is to become as proficient in the structure and use of the card catalog as possible. Steps #3–6 are designed to help you achieve this goal before you are under the pressure of actual research.
7. Ask the librarian what kinds of research material, if any, are *not* located through the card catalog, e.g., microfilm, ultrafiche, appellate briefs, old exams.
8. Ask the librarian what other lists of law books, if any, are in the library, e.g., lists of legal periodicals, lists of reserve books.
9. Ask the librarian to explain the difference between the library's card catalog and Kardex (the latter is the place where many libraries keep records of current serial publications that come into the library every day). If your library does not use Kardex, ask what it uses instead. (See p. 545.)
10. When using any card catalog, the CARTWHEEL will help you think of words and phrases to check (p. 591).
11. Never antagonize a law librarian! You are going to need all the help you can get!

ASSIGNMENT 77

On page 512 it was suggested that you organize a system of three-by-five-inch index cards for each of the legal research words and phrases listed there. For each card that contains the name of a law book on it, find out where the book or set of books is located in your law library. Obtain this information from the card catalog or other library list and enter it on the index cards.

2. DIGESTS

We have already examined the major digests that exist and the names of reporters whose opinions are summarized (in small paragraphs) in the digests. You should review this material now (p. 541).

Our focus here is on the digests of West, which are organized by the key topic and number system. Lawyers Co-operative Publishing Company also has digests for Supreme Court opinions (p. 539) and for its annotations (p. 605), which are organized differently.

The beauty of the West digests is that once you know how to use one of the digests, you know how to use them all. A good way to begin this understanding is to follow the journey of a court opinion from the time it arrives at West:

JOURNEY OF A STATE COURT OPINION, e.g., CALIFORNIA	JOURNEY OF A FEDERAL COURT OPINION, e.g., A U.S. COURT OF APPEALS
(i) The California Supreme Court sends a copy of its opinion to West Publishing Company in St. Paul.	(i) The U.S. Court of Appeals sends a copy of its opinion to West Publishing Company in St. Paul.
(ii) West editors write brief paragraph headnotes for the opinion. Each headnote summarizes a portion of the opinion.	(ii) West editors write brief paragraph headnotes for the opinion. Each headnote summarizes a portion of the opinion.
(iii) The headnotes go at the beginning of the full text of the opinion in the reporter—here, the Pacific Reporter 2d (P.2d).	(iii) The headnotes go at the beginning of the full text of the opinion in the reporter—here, the Federal Reporter 2d (F.2d).
(iv) The editors assign each headnote a key topic and number, e.g., Criminal Law ☞1064(5).	(iv) The editors assign each headnote a key topic and number, e.g., Appeal and Error ☞ 1216.
(v) This headnote is *also* printed in the appropriate digests of West. The above example will go in the "C" volume of these digests where "Criminal Law" is covered. The headnote will be placed under key number 1064(5) along with summaries of other opinions on the same or similar point of law. In what digests will such headnotes from a recent California opinion be printed? The list follows:	(v) This headnote is *also* printed in the appropriate digests of West. The above example will go in the "A" volume of these digests where "Appeal and Error" is covered. The headnote will be placed under key number 1216 of Appeal and Error along with summaries of other opinions on the same or similar point of law. In what digests will such headnotes from a recent F.2d opinion be printed? The list follows:
(vi) All headnotes go into the American Digest System. First, the headnote goes into General Digest bound volumes. After a ten-year period (in two five-year intervals), all the General Digests are thrown away, with the material in them printed in the next Decennial Digest.	(vi) All headnotes go into the American Digest System. First, the headnote goes into a General Digest bound volume. After a ten-year period (in two five-year intervals), all the General Digests are thrown away, with the material in them printed in the next Decennial Digest.
(vii) All headnotes of Pacific Reporter 2d cases are *also* printed in its regional digest—the Pacific Digest.	(vii) All headnotes of Federal Reporter 2d cases are *also* printed in the most current federal digest—the Federal Practice Digest 3d.
(viii) All headnotes of California cases are *also* printed in the individual state digest—the California Digest.	(viii) If our F.2d case dealt with a particular state, the headnotes of the F.2d case will *also* be printed in the individual state digest of that state.

(ix) Hence, the headnote from the California opinion will be printed:
—at the beginning of the opinion in P.2d.
—in the American Digest System (first the General Digest and then the Decennial Digest).
—in the regional digest—Pacific Digest.
—in the individual state digest—California Digest.

In all the above digests, the headnote will be printed in the "C" volume for Criminal Law under number 1064(5) along with headnotes from other opinions on the same area of the law.

(ix) Hence, the headnote from the opinion of the U.S. Court of Appeals will be printed:
—at the beginning of the opinion in F.2d.
—in the American Digest System (first in the General Digest and then in the Decennial Digest).
—in the Federal Practice Digest 3d.
—in an individual state digest if the F.2d case dealt with a particular state.

In all the above digests, the headnote will be printed in the "A" volume for Appeal and Error under number 1216 along with headnotes from other opinions on the same area of the law.

All state court opinions printed in the reporters of West go through the same process as outlined in the *first* column above, e.g., opinions in A.2d, N.E.2d, N.W.2d, P.2d, S.E.2d, S.2d, S.W.2d. The exception would be step (vii) above for N.E.2d opinions and for S.W.2d opinions. There is no regional digest that covers N.E.2d and S.W.2d (p. 540).

All U.S. District Court opinions printed in Federal Supplement (F.Supp.) go through the same process as opinions of U.S. Courts of Appeal in Federal Reporter 2d (F.2d) as outlined in the *second* column above. All U.S. Supreme Court opinions printed in Supreme Court Reporter (S.Ct.) also go through the same process as outlined in the *second* column above. For Supreme Court cases, however, there is an additional digest where all their headnotes are printed—the U.S. Supreme Court Digest of West (p. 539).

Assume that you are doing research on the right of a citizen to speak in a public park. You find that the digests of West cover this subject under the following key topic and number.

Constitutional Law ⟳211

West publishes about sixty digests—state, federal, and national. You can go to the "C" volume of *any* of these sixty digests, turn to "Constitutional Law" and find number "211" under it. Do you want only Idaho case law? If so, go to Constitutional Law ⟳ 211 in the Idaho Digest. Do you want only case law from the states in the western United States? If so, go to Constitutional Law ⟳211 in the Pacific Digest. Do you want only current federal case law? If so, go to Constitutional Law ⟳ 211 in the Federal Practice Digest 3d. Do you want only U.S. Supreme Court cases? If so, go to Constitutional Law ⟳211 in the U.S. Supreme Court Digest (West).

Do you want the case law of *every* court in the country? If so, trace Constitutional Law ⟳ 211 through the American Digest System:

- Go to Constitutional Law ⟳ 211 in every bound and unbound General Digest.

- Go to Constitutional Law ☞211 in every Decennial Digest.
- Go to Constitutional Law ☞211 (or its equivalent number) in the Century Digest.

To *trace a key topic and number* through the American Digest System means to find out what case law, if any, is summarized under that key topic and number in every unit of the American Digest System. (For the Century Digest, you will need an equivalent number, since there are no key topics and numbers in the Century Digest. See step 8 in the following checklist.)

CHECKLIST #2

CHECKLIST FOR USING THE DIGESTS OF WEST

1. Locate the right digests for your research problem. This is determined by identifying the kind of case you want to find. State? Federal? Both? Review pages 535 ff. on the American Digest System, the five regional digests, the four major federal digests, the two digests for U.S. Supreme Court cases (only one of which is a West digest), the individual state digests, etc. You must know what kind of case law is contained in each of these digests. See the chart on page 541.

2. Find a key topic and number to cover your research problem. There are thousands of topics and subtopics in the digests. How do you find the ones relevant to your research problem? There are four techniques:
   (i) Descriptive Word Index (DWI). Every digest has a DWI. Use the CARTWHEEL (p. 591) to help you locate key topics and numbers in the DWI.
   (ii) Table of Contents. There are approximately four hundred main topics (e.g., Constitutional Law, Criminal Law), which are scattered throughout the volumes of the digest you are using. At the beginning of each main topic you will find a table of contents, which can be anywhere from one to over twenty pages in length. If you can find one of these main topics in the general area of your research, you then use its table of contents to locate specific key numbers. These tables of contents have different names: "Scope Note," "Analysis," or "Subjects Included." Use the CARTWHEEL to help you locate key topics and numbers in them.
   (iii) Headnote in West Reporter. Suppose that you already have an opinion on point. You are reading its full text in a West reporter. Go to the headnotes at the beginning of this opinion. Each headnote has a key topic and number. Use this key topic and number to go to any of the digests to try to find *more* case law on that topic and number.
   (iv) Table of Cases in the Digests. Suppose again that you already have an opinion on point. You are reading its full text in a reporter. Go to the table of cases in the American Digest System and/or in any other digest that covers the reporter. Look up the name of the case in this table of cases. There you will find out what key topics and numbers that case is digested under in the digest. Go to that topic and number in the body of the digest to find that case summarized as well as *other* cases on the same topic and number. (Note: The Table of Cases in some West digests is listed as Plaintiff-Defendant Table *or* as Defendant-Plaintiff Table, depending on which party's name comes first. The Defendant-Plaintiff Table is useful if you happen to know only the name of the defendant or if you want many cases where the same party was sued, e.g., General Motors. Defendant-Plaintiff Tables usually refer you back to the Plaintiff-Defendant Table where the key topics and numbers are listed.)
   The table of cases in the digests might also provide you with a parallel cite to the case, supra p. 574.

3. Assume that while using the Descriptive Word Index (DWI) in any of the digests, you come across a key topic and number that appears to be relevant to

your research problem. When you go to check that topic and number in the body of the digest, however, you might find no case law and the phrase "See Scope Note for Analysis." The DWI has, in effect, led you to nonexistent case law! The editors are telling you that there are no cases digested under this topic and number *at this time.* Go to the table of contents for the main topic you are in (see step #2(ii) above). Check the Scope Note there to see if you can find a more productive key topic and number. Or, go to a different digest to see if you can be more lucky with your original key topic and number.

4. The West editors are adding new key topics and numbers all the time. Hence, you may find topics and numbers in the later digests that are not in the earlier digests.

5. The first key number under most topics and subtopics is often labeled "In General." This is obviously a broad category. Many researchers make the mistake of overlooking it in their quest for more specific topic headings. Go after more specific key numbers, but do not neglect this general one.

6. The West digests obviously duplicate each other in some respects. The American Digest System, for example, contains everything that is in all the other digests. A regional digest will duplicate everything found in the individual state digest covered in that region. (See the chart on page 541.) It is wise, nevertheless, to check more than one digest. Some digests may be more up-to-date than others in your library. You may miss something in one digest that you will catch in another.

7. Be sure you know all the units of the most comprehensive digest—the American Digest System: Century Digest, Decennial Digests, General Digests. (See page 536.) These units are distinguished solely by the period of time covered by each unit. Know what these periods of time are: Century Digest (1658–1896), Decennial Digests (ten-year periods), General Digests (the period since the last Decennial Digest was printed).

8. At the time the Century Digest was printed, West had not invented the key number system. Hence, topics are listed in the Century Digest by *section* numbers rather than by key numbers. Assume that you started your research in the Century Digest. You located a relevant section number and you now want to trace this number through the Decennial Digests and General Digests. To do this you need a corresponding *key* number. There is a parallel table in volume 21 of the First Decennial that will tell you the corresponding *key* topic number for any section number in the Century Digest. Suppose, however, that you started your research in the Decennial Digests or the General Digests. You have a key topic and now want to find out its corresponding section number in the Century Digest. In the First and Second Decennial, there is a "see" reference under the key topic number that will tell you the corresponding section number in the Century Digest.

9. Tricks of the trade are also needed in using the General Digests, which cover the most recent period since the last Decennial Digest was printed. When the current ten-year period is over, all the General Digests will be thrown away. The material in them will be consolidated or cumulated into the next Decennial Digest (which is issued in two parts beginning with the Ninth Decennial). When you go to use the General Digests, there may be twenty to thirty bound volumes and five or six pamphlets on the shelf. To be thorough in tracing a key topic and number in the General Digest, you must check *all* these bound volumes and pamphlets. There is, however, one short cut. Look for the "Cumulative Table of Key Numbers" within some bound and unbound General Digests. This table tells you which General Digests contain anything under the key topic and number you are searching. You do not have to check the other General Digests. There will be more than one such table covering different clusters of General Digest volumes (referred to as "Series"). Find all these tables to use this short cut.

3. ANNOTATIONS

An annotation is a collection of notes or commentary on something. The most extensive annotations are those of the Lawyers Co-operative Publishing Company in the following sets of books:

ALR: American Law Reports, First

ALR2d: American Law Reports, Second

ALR3d: American Law Reports, Third

ALR4th: American Law Reports, Fourth

ALR Fed: American Law Reports, Federal

All five sets are reporters in that they print opinions in full. They are *annotated* reporters in that notes or commentary is provided after each case in the form of an annotation. Unlike West reporters, only a selected number of opinions are printed in these ALR volumes. The editors select opinions raising novel or interesting issues, which then become the basis of an annotation. The following is an example of an annotation found on page 1015, volume 91 of ALR3d (cited as Annot., 91 A.L.R.3d 1015):

One of the joys of legal research is to find an annotation on point. A wealth of information is contained in annotations, e.g., a comprehensive, state-by-state survey of law on an issue. It would not be uncommon for a single annotation to contain hundreds of citations to court opinions. Picture yourself having the capacity to hire your own team of researchers to go out and spend weeks finding just about everything there is on a particular point of law. While none of us are likely to have this luxury, we do have a close equivalent in the form of annotations in the five sets of American Law Reports. They are a goldmine of research references. Since there are hundreds of volumes available to us in these five sets, the chances are very good that we will find an annotation that is on point, i.e., that covers the facts of our research problem.

Most of the references in the annotations are to case law. Their primary service, therefore, is to act as a case finder for us. Because of this, the annotation system of Lawyers Co-operative Publishing Company is the major competitor of the other massive case finders—the digests of West. It is to our advantage that each system claims to do a better job than the other. Their competition has led to a rich source of material at our disposal.

The annotations cover both federal and state law. ALR First, ALR2d, and most of ALR3d cover both state and federal law. The later volumes of ALR3d and all of ALR4th cover mainly state law. ALR Fed covers only federal law. The annotations in these five sets do not follow any particular order. There may be an annotation on burglary, for example, followed by an annotation on defective wheels on baby carriages. The annotations in ALR First and ALR2d are older than the annotations in the other sets, but this is not significant because all of the annotations can be updated.

We turn now to the two major concerns of the researcher:

1. How do you find an annotation on point?
2. How do you update an annotation that you have found?

Fortunately it is much easier to find and update annotations in ALR3d, ALR4th, and ALR Fed than in the earlier ALR First and ALR2d.

(1) Finding an Annotation on Point

The indexing of ALR First and ALR2d are similar. Each set has three index systems:

INDEX SYSTEMS FOR ALR First	INDEX SYSTEMS FOR ALR2d
• Quick Index	• Quick Index
• Word Index to Annotations	• Word Index to Annotations
• Permanent ALR Digest	• ALR2d Digest

Start with the Quick Index for each set. If it is not productive, use the more comprehensive Word Index to Annotations. The digests summarize the annotations in the sets and can be used as an index. They are not as effective, however, as the Quick Index and Word Index.

Next we turn to ALR3d, ALR4th, and ALR Fed. How do you find annotations in them? At present there is only one index system: the Quick Index volumes.

The Federal Quick Index serves as an index not only to annotations to ALR Fed but also to other books by the same publisher, e.g., Am.Jur.2d. In effect, the Federal Quick Index functions as an index to the publisher's Total Client-Service Library (p. 557) for issues of federal law.

Suppose that you are researching a federal law problem involving statutes in U.S.C. (p. 557) and/or regulations in C.F.R. (p. 672). The Quick Index volumes should be used to try to locate annotations on your problem. In *addition,* you should examine a special volume called

ALR Fed Tables of Cases, Laws, Regs

In this volume you will find a very important table:

"Table of Laws and Regulations Cited in ALR Fed"

If you already have the citation to a statute or regulation on point, you can use this table to determine whether any annotations exist on your statute or regulation.

As indicated earlier, some of the annotations in the five sets are very long and comprehensive. How do you find the law of a *particular* state or court within an annotation without having to read the entire annotation? At the beginning of annotations in ALR3d and ALR4th, you will find a "Table of Jurisdictions Represented," which will direct you to specific sections of the annotation that cover the law of your state. At the beginning of annotations in ALR Fed, there is a "Table of Courts and Circuits," which will direct you to specific sections of the annotation dealing with certain federal courts.

TABLE OF JURISDICTIONS REPRESENTED
Consult POCKET PART in this volume for later cases

US: §§ 2[b], 3, 4[a], 5[b], 6[a], 7[a], 10[b]
Ala: §§ 2[b], 4[a], 6[a], 7[a], 8, 10[b]
Cal: §§ 4[a, b], 7[a, b], 10[b], 11
Fla: §§ 5[a]
Ga: §§ 3, 4[b], 5[b], 6[b], 10[a]
Ill: §§ 4[b], 5[a, b], 6[a, b], 10[a]
Ind: §§ 4[a], 5[b], 6[a], 7[a, b], 8, 9, 10[b]
Iowa: §§ 7[a], 8
Ky: §§ 3, 4[a], 5[b]
La: §§ 5[b], 7[a, b]
Me: §§ 5[b], 7[a], 10[b]
Md: §§ 4[b]
Mich: §§ 4[a], 10[b]

Miss: §§ 4[a]
Mo: §§ 4[a], 6[a], 10[b]
NH: §§ 3, 4[b]
NC: §§ 7[a]
Ohio: §§ 4[a, b], 6[a], 7[a, b], 10[b]
Or: §§ 4[a], 10[b]
Pa: §§ 4[a], 7[a], 10[b]
Tenn: §§ 4[a], 5[b], 6[a]
Tex: §§ 4[a], 7[a], 10[b]
Vt: §§ 9
Wash: §§ 6[a], 7[a], 8
Wis: §§ 7[a], 8, 10[b], 11

TABLE OF COURTS AND CIRCUITS
Consult POCKET PART in this volume for later cases and statutory changes

Sup Ct: §§ 2[a], 3[a], 5, b, 14
First Cir: §§ 5[b], 6[b], 15[b], 16[a], 18[a]
Second Cir: §§ 2[b], 3[a, b], 5[a], 12[a], 16[a], 18[a]
Third Cir: §§ 3[a], 5[a], 7, 11[b], 12[b], 13[a], 15[b]
Fourth Cir: §§ 2[b], 3[a], 4[b], 5[a, b], 8, 9, 10[b], 12[a, b], 13[b], 14, 15[a, b], 16[a], 17, 18[a]
Fifth Cir: §§ 3[a], 5[a, b], 8, 10[a], 11[a, b], 13[a], 15[a], 16[b], 18[b]

Sixth Cir: §§ 5[b], 6[b], 10[a, b], 12[a], 13[a], 15[b]
Seventh Cir: §§ 2[a, b], 4[b], 5[b], 10[b], 15[b]
Eighth Cir: §§ 3[a], 4[a, b], 5[a, b], 6[a], 12[a], 13[a], 15[b], 16[a], 17, 19
Ninth Cir: §§ 2[a, b], 3[a], 4[a], 5, a, 6[b], 7, 8, 10[a], 11[a, b], 12[a, b], 13[a, b], 15[a, b], 16[b], 17, 18[a, b]
Tenth Cir: §§ 2[b], 3[a], 5[a, b], 6[a, b], 9, 11[a, b], 12[a], 14, 17, 18[b]
Dist Col Cir: §§ 3[b], 5[b], 6[b], 10[a, b]
Ct Cl: § 16[a]

In addition to these tables, there will usually be other indexes or tables of contents found at the beginning of the annotations.

(2) Updating an Annotation

Let us assume that you have found an annotation in one of the five sets. The annotation is current only up to the date of the particular volume in which the annotation is found. How do you bring the annotation up to date? How do you find more recent law on the topics of the annotation?

The answer is simple for annotations in ALR3d, ALR4th, and ALR Fed: simply check the pocket part (p. 590) of the volume where the original annotation is found. The answer is not so simple for annotations in ALR First and ALR2d.

How to Update an Annotation in ALR First	*How to Update an Annotation in ALR2d*
Check *every* volume of the ALR Blue Book of Supplemental Decisions (p. 524).	Check the specific volume (and its pocket part) of ALR2d Later Case Service that covers the cite of the annotation you want updated.

If the volumes of ALR First and ALR2d had pocket parts (which they do not), there would be no need for the ALR Blue Book of Supplemental Decisions nor for the ALR2d Later Case Service.

Finally, you must check the Annotations History Table. This table will tell you if there is a *supplemental* annotation for the annotation you are examining. A supplemental annotation totally updates an earlier annotation. The table also directs you to *superseded* annotations, which totally replace earlier annotations. To find this Annotation History Table, check the Quick Index volumes for ALR3d, ALR4th, and ALR Fed.

Note on Another Annotated Reporter of Lawyers Co-op. Lawyers Co-op also publishes United States Supreme Court Reports, Lawyers' Edition (abbreviated L.Ed). (See p. 525.) This also is an annotated reporter in that it prints the full text of opinions (those of the U.S. Supreme Court) with annotations on issues following some of these opinions.

CHECKLIST #3

CHECKLIST FOR FINDING AND UPDATING ANNOTATIONS IN ALR, ALR2d, ALR3d, ALR4th, and ALR FED
1. Your goal is to use all five sets to find annotations on your research problem. The annotations are extensive research papers on numerous points of law.
2. Start with all the Quick Index volumes on the shelves for all the sets. (For annotations in ALR First and ALR2d, also consult the Word Index to Annotations.) Use the CARTWHEEL (p. 591) to help you locate annotations in these indexes.
3. If you already have the cite of a federal statute or a federal regulation, find out if there are annotations on it. Check the "Table of Laws and Regulations Cited in ALR Fed." This table is in the separate volume called ALR Fed Tables of Cases, Laws, Regs.
4. Once you have found an annotation, use the tables and/or other indexes at the beginning of the annotation itself to help you locate specific sections of the annotation.
5. Once you have an annotation, you must update it. Updating features differ depending on the set in which the annotation is found: (a) To update annotations in ALR First: —check every volume of the ALR Blue Book of Supplemental Decisions. —check the Annotation History Table (in one of the later Quick Indexes). (b) To update annotations in ALR2d: —check the volume of ALR2d Later Case Service that covers the cite of your annotation. —check the pocket part of this volume of ALR2d Later Case Service. —check the Annotation History Table. (c) To update annotations in ALR3d, ALR4th, and ALR Fed: —check the pocket part of the volume where the annotation is found. —check the Annotation History Table.
6. AUTO-CITE (p. 639) and LEXIS (p. 633) are computer services that also provide access to annotations.

4. SHEPARD'S

There are four great research inventions in the law:

- The key number system of the West digests (p. 544).
- The annotations in ALR, ALR2d, ALR3d, ALR4th, and ALR Fed (p. 605).
- Computers (p. 632, p. 720).
- Shepard's.

Among the functions served by these four systems is case finding; they are all excellent ways of locating case law. In a sense, they duplicate each other for this function.

We now turn to Shepard's and the techniques of *shepardizing*. You should review the material on pages 551–555 covering the kinds of Shepard's volumes that exist, the material on page 573 covering the use of Shepard's as one of the four techniques of finding a parallel cite, and the material on page 573 describing an advance sheet for Shepard's.

Shepard's is a citator (p. 533), which means that its function is to provide you with relevant citations to whatever you are shepardizing. We will examine Shepard's through the following topics:

1. The units of a set of Shepard's.
2. Determining whether you have a complete set of Shepard's ("reading the box").
3. The distinction between "cited material" and "citing material."
4. Abbreviations in Shepard's.
5. Shepardizing a case (court opinion).
6. Shepardizing a statute.
7. Shepardizing a regulation.

We will limit ourselves to shepardizing cases, statutes, and regulations. Knowing how to shepardize these items, however, will go a long way toward equipping you to shepardize other items as well (e.g., constitutions, administrative decisions, charters, rules of court). For a list of what you can shepardize, see p. 552).

1. The Units of a Set of Shepard's

By "set of Shepard's" we mean those volumes of Shepard's that cover a specific reporter, statutory code, administrative code, state, topic area, or whatever else is being shepardized. There are two main units to every set of Shepard's: (a) *bound* red volumes and (b) white, gold, yellow, or red *pamphlet* volumes. The bound volumes and pamphlets are sometimes broken into parts, e.g., Part 1, Part 2. The white pamphlet is the advance sheet (p. 521) that is later thrown away and cumulated (or consolidated) into a larger pamphlet. Eventually all the pamphlets are thrown away and cumulated into bound red volumes. The pamphlets contain the most current shepardizing material.

2. Determining Whether You Have a Complete Set of Shepard's ("Reading the Box")

You should not try to shepardize until you are satisfied that there is a complete set of Shepard's on the shelf in front of you. As we saw above, Shepard's comes in sets, e.g., the set of Shepards for United States statutes, the set for New Mexico laws. You need a complete set in order to shepardize. To determine whether you have a complete set, go through the following four steps:

a. Pick up the advance sheet or the most recently dated pamphlet for that set of Shepard's (the date is on the top of the pamphlet).
b. What month and year is at the top of this advance sheet or other pamphlet? If the month is not the month of today's date or the immediately preceding month, ask the librarian for the date of the most recent pamphlet the li-

brary has received for the set of Shepard's you are using. (The librarian will check the office Kardex, (p. 545), or other system of recording serial or subscription material that the library has received.)

c. Once you are satisfied that the advance sheet or latest pamphlet is the most current the library has, go to the box on its front cover. You must now read this box. It will tell you what constitutes a complete set of Shepard's for the set you are using. Go down the list in the box and make sure that the library has on its shelf everything the box tells you should be there. Use the box as a checklist.

d. The last entry in the box is always the advance sheet or other pamphlet that contains the box you are reading.

Here is the box on the cover of the set of Shepard's that will allow you to shepardize Hawaii cases:

> *What Your Library Should Contain*
> 1983 Bound Volume
> Supplemented with
> Oct. 1984 Cumulative Supplement Vol. 25 No. 3
> *Destroy All Other Issues*

To be complete, there must be a 1983 Bound Volume of Hawaii Shepard's and an October 1984 Cumulative Supplement for Hawaii Shepard's (vol. 25, no. 3). This last entry is the pamphlet on which the above box is located.

We now examine a more complicated box. Below you will find a box from Shepard's Federal Citations.

> *What Your Library Should Contain*
>
> PART 1
> (Covering
> Federal Reporter
> and Federal Cases)
> (3) 1969 Bound Volumes
> (1) 1969–77 Bound Volume
> (1) 1977 Bound Volume
>
> PART 2
> (Covering
> Federal Supplement,
> FRD, Court of Claims)
> (1) 1969 Bound Volume
> (1) 1969–75 Bound Volume
>
> Supplemented with
> July, 1980 Semiannual Supplement Vol. 70 No. 4
> (Parts 1A, 1B and 2)
>
> Oct., 1980 Cumulative Supplement Vol. 70 No. 7
> (Parts 1 and 2)
>
> Dec., 1980 Cumulative Supplement Vol. 70 No. 9
> (Parts 1 and 2)
>
> *Destroy All Other Issues*

This unit of Shepard's comes in two parts: Part 1 for the shepardizing of Federal Reporter cases, and Part 2 for shepardizing Federal Supplement cases. Assume that the present date is December of 1980 and that you have in front of you two cases that you want to shepardize. One case is in F.2d and the other is in F.Supp.:

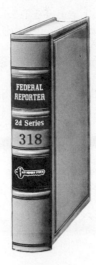

By reading the box, you know that you have a complete set of Shepard's when the following units are on the shelf:

F.2d case
—A 1969 bound volume
—A second 1969 bound volume
—A third 1969 bound volume
—A 1969–1977 bound volume
—A 1977 bound volume
—Part 1A, July, 1980 Semiannual Supplement (vol. 70, no. 4)
—Part 1B, July, 1980 Semiannual Supplement (vol. 70, no. 4)
—Part 1, Oct., 1980 Cumulative Supplement (vol. 70, no. 7)
—Part 1, Dec., 1980 Cumulative Supplement (vol. 70, no. 9)

F.Supp. case
—A 1969 bound volume
—A 1969–1975 bound volume
—Part 2, July, 1980 Semiannual Supplement (vol. 70, no. 4)
—Part 2, Oct., 1980 Cumulative Supplement (vol. 70, no. 7)
—Part 2, Dec., 1980 Cumulative Supplement (vol. 70, no. 9)

If you cannot check off all the items for either column (depending on whether you are shepardizing an F.2d case or an F.Sup. case), then you do not have a complete set of Shepard's with which to proceed.

Finally, some sets of Shepard's cover cases and statutes within the same volumes, while other sets are subdivided into case volumes (called Case Edition) and statute volumes (called Statute Edition). Again, let the box be your guide.

3. The Distinction Between "Cited Material" and "Citing Material"

- Cited Material: whatever you are shepardizing, e.g., a case, statute, regulation.
- Citing Material: whatever mentions or discusses the cited material, e.g., another case, a law review article, an annotation in ALR, ALR2d, ALR3d, ALR4th, ALR Fed, etc.

Suppose you are shepardizing the case found in 75 F.2d 107 (a case that begins on page 107 of volume 75 of Federal Reporter 2d). While reading through the columns of Shepard's, you find the following cite: f56 S.E.2d 46. The *cited* material is 75 F.2d 107. The *citing* material is 56 S.E.2d 46, which followed (f) or agreed with the decision in 75 F.2d 107.

Suppose you are shepardizing a statute: 22 U.S.C. § 55.8 (section 55.8 of title 22 of the United States Code). While reading through the columns of Shepard's, you find the following cite: 309 U.S. 45. The *cited* material is 22 U.S.C. § 55.8. The *citing* material is 309 U.S. 45, which interpreted or mentioned 22 U.S.C. § 55.8.

Shepard's always indicates the cited material by the black bold print along the top of every page of Shepard's and by the black bold print numbers that are the volume or section numbers of the cited material. In the following excerpt, the cited material is 404 P.2d 460. The citing material follows the number **460:**

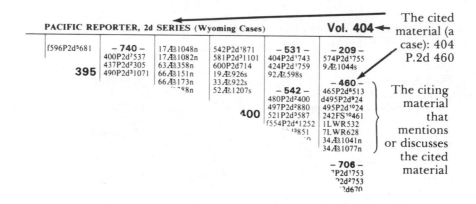

In the following excerpt, the cited material is a statute: Article 2, § 37–31 of the Wyoming Statutes. The citing material is indicated beneath § **37–31.**

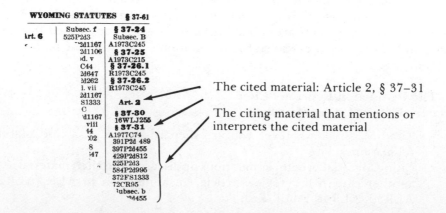

4. Abbreviations in Shepard's

Shepard's packs a tremendous amount of information (the cites) into every one of its pages. Each page contains about eight columns of cites for the cited and the citing materials. For the sake of economy, Shepard's uses many abbreviations that are peculiar to Shepard's. For example:

FS ⟶ means Federal Supplement

A3 ⟶ means American Law Reports 3d

* ⟶ means that a regulation of a particular year was discussed

△⟶ means that a regulation was discussed without mentioning the year of the regulation.

It would be rare for an ordinary researcher to know the meaning of every abbreviation and signal used by Shepard's. *But you must know where to find their meaning.* There are two places to go:

- In the abbreviations tables at the beginning of most of the units of Shepard's (for an example, see p. 589).
- In the preface or explanation pages found at the beginning of most of the units of Shepard's.

Many researchers neglect the latter. Buried within the preface or explanation pages may be an interpretation of an abbreviation or symbol that is not covered in the abbreviation tables.

5. Sheperdizing a Case (Court Opinion)

In order to shepardize a case, you must know the reporter in which the case is printed in full. The Shepard's volumes that enable you to shepardize cases correspond to the reporter volumes for those cases. For example, if the case you want to shepardize is 193 Mass. 364, you go to the set of Shepard's that covers cases in Massachusetts Reports—Shepard's Massachusetts Citations. If the case you want to shepardize is 402 F.2d 1065, you go to the Shepard's set that covers F.2d cases—Shepard's Federal Citations. Almost every reporter has a corresponding Shepard's set, which will enable you to shepardize cases in that reporter (p. 553).

Of course, many cases have parallel cites—the case is found word-for-word in more than one reporter (p. 573). You can shepardize the case through *either* reporter for most cases with parallel cites. Assume you want to shepardize the following case:

Welch v. Swasey, 193 Mass. 364, 79 N.E. 745 (1907)

This case is found in two reporters: Massachusetts Reports and North Eastern Reporter. Hence, you can shepardize the case and obtain the same citing material from two different sets of Shepard's: **Shepard's Massachusetts Citations** and **Shepard's Northeastern Citations.**

To shepardize a case means to obtain the following six kinds of information about the cited case (i.e., the case you are shepardizing):

1. The parallel cite of the case. The first entry in parenthesis is the parallel cite. (See p. 573 on the reasons why you may find no parallel cite here.)
2. The history of the case—all cases that are part of the same litigation, e.g., appeals, reversals (p. 573).
3. Citing cases—other opinions that have mentioned or discussed the cited case, e.g., followed it, distinguished it, or just mentioned it.
4. Citing legal periodical literature—articles or case notes (p. 626) that have analyzed or mentioned the cited case.
5. Citing annotations—annotations in ALR, ALR2d, ALR3d, ALR4th, ALR Fed that have analyzed or mentioned the cited case.
6. Citing opinions of the attorney general—opinions of the attorney general that have analyzed or mentioned the cited case.

The great value of Shepard's as a case finder comes thorough items 3 to 5 above. The citing material in them enables you to locate case law in addition to the cited case. If a citing case mentions or discusses the cited case, the two cases probably deal with similar facts and law. All citing cases, therefore, are potential leads to more case law on point for you. Similarly, a citing law review article or annotation will probably discuss a variety of cases in addition to the discussion of the cited case. Hence, again, you are led to more case law through Shepard's.

Items 2 and 3 above also enable you to do validation research (p. 676). They tell you if the cited case is still good law. Has it been reversed? Has it been discussed with approval by citing cases? Has it been ignored by other courts?

One final point before examining an excerpt from a Shepard's page. Recall that cases in reporters are broken down into headnotes at the beginning of the case (p. 601). These headnotes are written either by the private publisher (such as West) or by the court clerk in official editions of the case. Shepard's calls these headnotes of the case the "syllabus" of the case—small-paragraph summaries of portions of the case found at the beginning of the case.

A case can involve many issues, only a few of which may be relevant to your research problem. The question then arises as to whether it is possible to narrow your shepardizing to those parts of the case that are most relevant to your research problem. Yes. It is possible to shepardize a portion of a case through its headnote or syllabus numbers. In effect, you are shepardizing the headnote! How is this done?

- The editors of Shepard's count the headnotes or syllabus paragraphs of the *cited* case.
- When the editors of Shepard's come across a *citing* case that deals with only one of the headnotes or syllabus paragraphs of the *cited* case, they indicate the number of the headnote or syllabus paragraph as part of the *citing* case in the columns of Shepard's.
- The number is printed as a small raised or elevated number—called a small superior figure—within the reference to the *citing* case.

Be careful. It is easy to become confused. The superior figure refers to the headnote or syllabus number of the *cited* case, not the citing case.

For example, assume again that you are shepardizing Welch v. Swasey, 193 Mass. 364. In the columns of Shepard's you find the following:

f193Mass.⁸476

The *citing* case is 193 Mass. 476. The case follows (agrees with) the *cited* case: Welch v. Swasey, 193 Mass. 364. Note the raised number 8—the superior figure. This 8 refers to the eighth headnote or syllabus of the *cited* case, *Welch v. Swasey.* The *citing* case dealt with that portion of *Welch* that was summarized in the eighth headnote or syllabus of the *Welch* case. Again, do not make the mistake of thinking that the small raised number refers to a headnote or syllabus in the citing case. It refers to a headnote or syllabus number of the *cited* case.

We now look at a specimen page from Shepard's Massachusetts Citations (see p. 616), where we will begin to shepardize Welch v. Swasey, 193 Mass. 364. Read the oval inserts on this specimen page now—before carefully studying the following comments.

Let us assume that in your legal research you have located the case of *Welch v. Swasey,* reported in volume 193 Massachusetts Reports at page 364. This is the cited case that we want to shepardize.

The specimen page contains a reproduction of page 726 in the 1967 Case Edition of Shepard's Massachusetts Citations. Note the number of the volume of reports, "Vol. 193" in the upper left corner of the page.

An examination of the boldface numbers appearing in the third column locates our page number "—**364**—". See the arrow. This is the initial page of our cited case under consideration. Following this page number you will find the citations "(79 NE 745)," "(118 AS 523)," "(23 Lns 1160)," indicating that the same case is also reported in 79 North Eastern Reporter 745, 118 American State Reports 523, and 23 Lawyers Reports Annotated, New Series 1160. These are parallel citations (p. 573). As indicated earlier, abbreviations are explained at the beginning of Shepard's volumes (p. 613).

Next comes the history of the cited case. You will observe that upon appeal to the United States Supreme Court, our cited case was affirmed "a" in 214 United States Reports "US" 91; 53 Lawyers' Edition United States Supreme Court Reports "LE" 923; and 29 Supreme Court Reporter "SC" 567. Also, the cited case has been followed "f" and distinguished "d" in subsequent cases of the Massachusetts and federal courts.

In the citation "f242 Mas⁶34" (see top of next column), the small superior figure "⁶" before the citing page number 34 indicates that the principle of law brought out in the sixth paragraph of the syllabus (i.e., of the headnotes) of 193 Mass. 364 has been followed in 242 Mass. 34.

This case has also been cited in several legal periodicals: Harvard Law Review "HLR," Boston University Law Review "BUR," and Massachusetts Law Quarterly "MQ."

The citations appearing in annotations of the American Law Reports are grouped together after the legal periodical citing references.

By examining this same volume and page number of the cited case in the other units of Shepard's Massachusetts Citations, all citing material for this case will be found.

SPECIMEN PAGE—Shepard's Massachusetts Citations, Case Edition, 1967

Vol. 193

MASSACHUSETTS REPORTS

317Mas^{2}432
326Mas^{2}147
184F^{1}220
216F^{1}507
248F^{2}263
f258F^{1}299
263F^{2}1014
f39F2d540
6BUR234
8BUR151
8BUR210
11BUR142
24MQ(1)2
24MQ(4)9
59AR157n

—324—
(79NE734)
196Mas483
d197Mas
[^{1}178
200Mas^{1}35
206Mas^{2}389
207Mas^{1}501
d216Mas
[^{1}422
216Mas^{2}339
220Mas^{1}30
220Mas^{1}299
273Mas^{2}29
273Mas^{2}476
326Mas^{1}795

—327—
(79NE818)
199Mas^{4}11
202Mas^{4}113
222Mas^{5}261
266Mas^{4}546
292Mas^{4}550
299Mas^{4}3
299Mas^{5}4
321Mas^{5}198
174F8^{4}455

—331—
(79NE749)
194Mas^{1}446
199Mas^{3}411
220Mas^{1}581

—332—
(79NE765)
(7Lns1076)
196Mas^{2}31
199Mas^{2}448
199Mas^{2}475
201Mas^{2}185
203Mas396
204Mas^{2}68
206Mas^{5}388
d207Mas^{3}329
207Mas^{3}448
217Mas^{3}118
220Mas^{3}31
220Mas^{4}32
224Mas^{2}407
241Mas^{4}79
245Mas^{4}121
246Mas^{3}521
260Mas^{1}337
263Mas^{4}218
266Mas^{4}543
267Mas^{3}366
f269Mas^{4}63
270Mas^{4}266
276Mas^{3}384
277Mas^{3}365
279Mas^{4}845

d283Mas^{3}561
284Mas^{4}607
269F^{2}782
297Mas^{3}273
304Mas^{2}642
d314Mas^{2}682
322Mas^{3}219
322Mas^{3}227
328Mas^{3}534
d339Mas^{2}728
343Mas^{3}779
182F^{4}127
252F^{3}516
245F2d^{3}447
50AR1366n

—336—
(79NE771)
242Mas^{1}392
282Mas376
101AR237n

—339—
(79NE733)
197Mas^{1}292
d197Mas

201Mas^{1}157
5.AR815n

—341—
(79NE815)
(118AS516)
(7Lns729)
f194Mas^{5}459
d195Mas
[^{1}318
196Mas^{1}71
201Mas^{4}70
205Mas^{1}3
d205Mas^{2}36
208Mas486
207Mas^{4}1498
d207Mas
[^{2}563
208Mas^{3}447
210Mas^{2}456
212Mas^{2}309
213Mas^{5}329
f213Mas^{2}597
217Mas^{2}421
217Mas^{1}517
223Mas^{4}494
d227Mas
[^{2}115
d229Mas^{3}67
f232Mas^{2}551
d233Mas
[^{2}350
238Mas^{3}231
239Mas^{1}227
239Mas^{1}567
244Mas^{2}452
d245Mas
[^{1}122
d248Mas
[^{2}496
d250Mas
[^{2}245
f206Mas^{7}433
208Mas^{1}622
208Mas^{7}630
219Mas
[^{3}328
264Mas^{2}368
297Mas^{1}195
222Mas
[^{1}1580
303Mas^{1}244
d316Mas^{2}619
225Mas
[^{1}1196
322Mas^{5}294
338Mas^{1}128

341Mas^{1}642
293F^{2}406
324AR1316n
155AR643n
41AR1304n

—351—
(79NE790)
cc222F349
203Mas^{2}130
203Mas^{2}424
241Mas^{2}474
250Mas^{2}314
281Mas^{2}166
343Mas^{1}371
343Mas^{2}723
4BUR30
39BUR494
40BUR228
78AR1040n
45AR119n
45AR143n
45AR183n
45AR250n
46AR160n
46AR191n
46AR219n
46AR265n
46AR385n

—359—
(79NE742)
(9Lns874)
202Mas^{1}495
207Mas^{1}131
209Mas^{1}88
214Mas^{2}541
224Mas^{2}360
245Mas^{3}10
265Mas^{3}412
272Mas^{3}220
295Mas^{2}55
339Mas^{2}250
266F^{2}198
28FS^{2}157
46FS^{1}957
46FS^{2}958
41AR127n
44AR1068n
126AR1095n
126AR1097n

—364—
(79NE745)
(118AS523)
(23Lns1160)
a214US91
a53LE923
a29SC567
f193Mas^{8}476
198Mas
[^{1}1256
200Mas^{1}484
d203Mas^{8}29
203Mas^{1}155
206Mas^{1}432
f206Mas^{4}433
208Mas^{1}622
312Mas^{1}645
323Mas^{1}567
f337Mas^{1}30
339Mas^{1}14
339Mas^{1}16
4AG279
8AG474
3AR1456n
23AR249n
73AR825n
86AR2675n

230Mas^{7}190
234Mas^{2}602
234Mas^{4}604
234Mas^{5}609
241Mas^{1}528
242Mas^{3}32
f242Mas^{6}34
245Mas88
f250Mas^{5}60
250Mas^{8}71
255Mas^{7}171
257Mas^{1}53
264Mas^{1}87
270Mas^{1}524
286Mas^{1}618
286Mas^{2}618
289Mas^{4}185
315Mas^{7}342
323Mas^{1}650
323Mas^{4}650
324Mas^{10}448
328Mas^{1}676
333Mas^{4}778
339Mas208
f41F2d^{1}938
6AG182
6AG440
7AG451
6BUR166
6BUR306
8BUR79
10BUR322
10BUR324
18BUR92
21BUR650
22BUR381
37HLR842
13MQ(6)72
43MQ(3)61
48MQ(4)492
34AR46n
8AR965n
58AR1088n

—378—
(79NE777)
233Mas^{1}253
32AR215n

—383—
(79NE737)

—392—
(79NE739)
(9Lns695)
201Mas^{1}540
237Mas^{2}398

—400—
(79NE774)
203Mas^{1}327
217Mas^{1}32
244Mas^{1}306
250Mas^{1}87
256Mas^{1}153
270Mas^{1}39
284Mas^{1}9
308Mas^{1}405

—402—
(79NE776)
f195Mas^{1}128

303Mas^{1}447
317Mas^{1}566

315Mas^{2}345
319Mas^{2}674
7AG6
42AR1467n

—412—

—419—

219Mas^{1}506
301Mas^{3}327
167F^{1}81
53AR145n

(包含)

280Mas^{1}330
f208Mas^{2}566
210Mas^{1}552
213Mas^{1}294
f236Mas^{1}223
256Mas^{2}56
257Mas^{1}50
262Mas^{1}580
319Mas^{2}314
319Mas^{1}599
326Mas^{1}460
335Mas^{2}700
47ABA602
22AR578n
11AR434n

201Mas^{1}265
f202Mas^{3}10
202Mas^{4}65
204Mas^{2}229
209Mas349

Followed with reference to para-graph six of syllabus

(79NE797)
(7Lns148)
197Mas^{3}396
202Mas^{2}446
205Mas^{3}171
208Mas^{3}157
215Mas^{2}470
216Mas^{3}180
d216Mas214
217Mas^{3}95
223Mas^{1}184
230Mas^{2}391
236Mas^{1}14

Cited by lower federal court

254Mas^{1}189
211Mas^{1}485
d263Mas^{1}75

Cited in Boston University Law Review

327Mas^{3}73
341Mas^{1}699

Cited in Harvard Law Review

Cited in Massachusetts Law Quar-terly

Cited in annotations of Annotated Reports System

46MQ(3)243
48MQ(3)318
171AR369n

—453—
(79NE775)

Same case reported in Northeast-ern Reporter, American State Reports and Lawyers Reports Annotated, New Series

—455—
(79NE770)

Affirmed by United States Su-preme Court

Distinguished with reference to paragraph eight of syllabus

—415—
(79NE821)
f196Mas^{2}551
200Mas^{2}193
200Mas^{2}343
202Mas^{3}224
204Mas^{1}481
205Mas^{2}179
205Mas^{1}370
f212Mas^{3}170
216Mas^{3}498

—444—
(79NE769)
204Mas^{2}354
208Mas^{2}403
224Mas^{1}584
h234Mas^{1}23
d239Mas
[^{1}232
[^{1}213
248Mas^{1}289

—458—
(79NE807)
216Mas^{1}143
216Mas223
222Mas^{5}82
236Mas^{1}347
240Mas^{1}370
262Mas^{1}53

264Mas^{2}100
270Mas^{1}173
312Mas^{1}289
320Mas^{1}626
321Mas^{1}675

212Mas^{2}109
227Mas^{2}51
237Mas^{2}507
274Mas^{2}501
284Mas^{2}506
292Mas^{1}193
300Mas^{2}88
309Mas^{2}531
313Mas^{2}416
337Mas^{2}546
6MQ(2)27
16MQ(5)218

311Mas^{7}370
'03-22EC64
190AR755n
55AR324n

—464—
(79NE784)
295Mas^{8}100
242Mas^{1}534
250Mas^{1}457
250Mas^{1}535
319Mas^{1}308
10BUR39
10BUR168
35AR963n

—470—
(79NE878)
247Mas^{1}203
333Mas^{1}777
344AR49n
8AR965n

—479—
(79NE787)

—482—
(79NE794)
284Mas^{1}521
339Mas^{1}710

—486—
(79NE763)
201Mas158
204Mas337
208Mas510
205Mas^{1}461
221Mas^{1}320
308Mas^{1}545

—488—
(80NE583)
cc191Mas441
cc198Mas580
194Mas573
198Mas^{1}582
276Mas^{1}286

—495—
(79NE738)
198Mas^{1}531
d203Mas^{1}261
204Mas^{1}201
205Mas^{1}274
229Mas144
335Mas^{1}427
345Mas^{1}41

—498—
(79NE796)
194Mas^{3}575
1MQ311

—500—
(79NE781)
201Mas^{2}607
205Mas^{4}328
210Mas280
241Mas^{3}544
254Mas^{2}79
267Mas^{4}101
304AR1164n

—507—
(79NE764)
195Mas^{4}160
196Mas^{1}128
196Mas^{2}486
198Mas^{2}571
200Mas^{2}543
201Mas384
f203Mas^{3}584
206Mas^{4}545
208Mas^{4}118
Continued

For later citations see any subsequent bound supplement or volume, the current issue of the periodically published paper-covered cumulative supplement and any current issue of the advance sheet

CHECKLIST #4a

CHECKLIST FOR SHEPARDIZING A CASE
1. You have a case you want to shepardize. In what reporter is this case found? Go to the set of Shepard's in the library that covers this reporter.
2. If the case you want to shepardize has a parallel cite that you already have, find out if the library has a set of Shepard's for the other reporter volumes in which the case is also found. You may be able to shepardize the case through more than one set of Shepard's. (There are sets of Shepard's for the individual state official reports and for all the reporters of West's unofficial National Reporter System, p. 553.)
3. Go through the four steps to determine whether you have a complete set of Shepard's (p. 609). Read the box.
4. The general rule is that you must check the cite of the case you are sheparding (the cited case) in *every* unit of a set of Shepard's. With experience you will learn, however, that it is possible to bypass some of the units of the set. There may be information on the front cover of one of the Shepard's volumes, for example, that will tell you that the date or volume number of the reporter containing your cited case will not be covered in that Shepard's volume. You can bypass it and move on to other units mentioned in the box.
5. In checking all the units of Shepard's, it is recommended that you work *backward* by examining the most recent Shepard's pamphlets first so that you obtain the latest citing materials first.
6. Suppose that in one of the units of a set of Shepard's, you find nothing listed for the cited case. This could mean one of three things: (a) You are in the wrong set of Shepard's. (b) You are in the right set of Shepard's, but the Shepard's unit you are examining does not cover the particular volume of the reporter that contains your cited case. (See #4 above.) (c) You are in the right set of Shepard's. The silence in Shepard's about your cited case means that since the time of the printing of the last unit of Shepard's for that set, nothing has happened to the case—there is nothing for Shepard's to tell you.
7. Know the six kinds of information that you can obtain when shepardizing a case: parallel cites, history of the cited case, citing cases, citing legal periodical literature, citing annotations, citing opinions of the attorney general.
8. The page number listed for every citing case is the page on which the cited case is mentioned. It is not the page on which the citing case begins.
9. Use the abbreviations tables and the preface pages at the beginning of most units of Shepard's—and use them often.
10. A small "n" to the right of the page number of a citing case (e.g., 23 ALR 198n) means the cited case is mentioned within an annotation (p. 605). A small "s" to the right of the page number of a citing case (e.g., 23 ALR 198s) means the cited case is mentioned in a supplement to or pocket part of the annotation (p. 590).
11. Special care is needed in shepardizing a U.S. Supreme Court opinion in United States Shepard's, Case Edition (p. 553). We have seen that there are three major cites to every opinion of the U.S. Supreme Court: U.S. (official), S.Ct. (West), and L.Ed. (Lawyers Co-op). These are all parallel cites. Guideline #2

above said that cases with parallel cites can often be shepardized through more than one set of Shepard's. There is, however, only one set of Shepard's for U.S. Supreme Court opinions (United States Citations, Case Edition). The question arises as to whether you can shepardize the Supreme Court opinion through any one of the three cites. For older opinions, the answer is no; you must shepardize through the U.S. cite. Today, you can shepardize through any of the three cites. It is recommended, however, that you shepardize *only* through the U.S. cite, since you may pick up some citing material through the U.S. cite that is not available when you shepardize through the S.Ct. or L.Ed. cites.

6. Shepardizing a Statute

You shepardize a statute in order to try to find the following seven kinds of information:

1. A parallel cite of the statute (found in parentheses immediately after the section number of the statute). The parallel cite (if given) is to the *session law* edition of the statute (see discussion below).
2. The history of the statute in the legislature, e.g., amendments, new sections added, sections repealed, renumbered, etc.
3. The history of the statute in the courts, e.g., citing cases that have analyzed or mentioned the statute, declared it constitutional, etc.
4. Citing administrative decisions, e.g., agency decisions that have analyzed or mentioned the statute.
5. Citing legal periodical literature, e.g., law review articles that have analyzed or mentioned the statute.
6. Citing annotations in ALR, ALR2d, ALR3d, ALR4th, ALR Fed that have analyzed or mentioned the statute.
7. Citing opinions of the attorney general that have analyzed or mentioned the statute.

When a statute is passed by the legislature, it comes out as a slip law (p. 555) and then in a form that may be called Session Laws, Laws, Acts, Acts and Resolves (p. 519), Statutes at Large, (p. 559), etc. (For convenience, all the latter items will be referred to below as the session law for the statutes.) Session laws are arranged chronologically by year—the statutes are not arranged by subject matter in the session law volumes. Finally, many but not all of the session laws are also printed in statutory codes (p. 557). The are *codified,* which means that they *are* organized by subject matter rather than chronologically. As indicated earlier, not all session laws are codified. The statute may not be considered of sufficient general interest to be codified (p. 533). If codification has occurred, there will be two cites for the same statute:

Codified Cite	**Session Law Cite**
↓	↓
Ohio Rev. Code Ann. § 45 (1978)	1975 Ohio Laws, C. 508
34 U.S.C. § 18(c) (1970)	87 Stat. 297 (1965)

Notice the totally different numbering system in the codified and session law cites—yet they are the same statutes. Section 45 of the Ohio Revised Code Annotated is found word-for-word in Chapter (C.)508 of the 1975 session laws of

Ohio. And section 18(c) of title 34 of the United States Code is found word-for-word in volume 87 of Statutes at Large (Stat.) on page 297. Notice also the different years for the same statute. The year in the session law cite is the year the legislature passed the statute. The year in the codified cite, however, is usually the year of the codification, which comes later.

Now the question becomes, when do you shepardize a statute through its session law cite and when do you shepardize it through its codified cite?

There are two instances when you *must* shepardize the statute through its session law cite:

- If the statute will never be codified because it is not of general public interest, and,
- If the statute has not yet been codified because it is so recent, although it eventually will be codified.

If the statute has been codified, you must shepardize it through its latest codified cite. How do you find the codified cite of a session law if you have only the session law cite? Go to the current code that will contain your statute. Look for special tables at the beginning or end of the code. For federal statutes in the United States Code, for example, there is a Tables volume in which you will find Table III that will enable you to translate a session law cite into a codified law cite (p. 655).

Shepard's has its own abbreviation system for session laws. Suppose that you are shepardizing Kan.Stat.Ann. § 123 (1973)—a codified cite. Section 123 is the cited statute—what you are shepardizing. In the Shepard's columns for Kansas statutes, you might find:

> **Section 123**
> (1970C6)
> A1972C23
> Rp1975C45

The parallel cite in parentheses is "1970C6," which means the 1970 Session Laws of the state of Kansas, Chapter 6. The mention of a year in Shepard's for statutes usually refers to the sessions laws for that year. (You find the meaning of "C" by checking the abbreviations tables at the beginning of the Shepard's volume.)

Immediately beneath the parentheses in the above example you find two other references to session laws:

A1972C23	In the 1972 Session Laws of Kansas, Chapter 23, there was an amendment to section 123 (which is what "A" means according to Shepard's abbreviation tables)	Rp1975C45	In the 1975 Session Laws of Kansas, Chapter 45, section 123 was repealed in part (which is what "Rp" means according to Shepard's abbreviation tables)

You will note that Shepard's does *not* tell you what the amendment was, nor what was repealed in part. How do you find this out? Two ways. First, you go to the session laws if your library has them. Second, you go to the cited statute (§ 123) in the codified collection of the statutes (here the Kansas Statutes Annotated). At the bottom of the statute in the code, there may be historical or legislative history notes (p. 650), which will summarize amendments, repeals, etc. (Also check this same note for the cited statute in the pocket part of the code volume you are using.)

Other citing material given in Shepard's for a statute (p. 618) is less complicated. For example, there are cites to citing cases, citing law review articles, etc., that follow a very similar pattern to the citing material for cases you are shepardizing.

Assume that you want to shepardize a federal statute—in the United States Code (U.S.C.). As with the shepardizing of every statute, you must shepardize through the most current edition of the code. A new edition of the U.S.C. comes out every six years, e.g., 1970 Edition, 1976 Edition. In between editions, the U.S.C. is supplemented by annual Supplement volumes, e.g., Supplement 1972, Supplement 1973. Shepardize your statute through the latest code edition *and* through any of the Supplement years indicated at the top of the pages used to shepardize a federal statute in Shepard's United States Citations, Statute Edition (p. 554).

Assume that the most current code edition is the 1970 edition and that the latest Supplement year is 1972. You want to shepardize 18 USC § 700 (1970). You trace this cite through all the units of Shepard's United States Citations, Statute Edition. The following is an excerpt containing one column from a page in one of these units:

United States Code, 1970 Edition and Supplement, 1972 TITLE 18 § 700	
Ad82St291	**1**
C302FS1112	**2**
394US604	
22LE592	
89SC1372	
445F2d226	
462F2d96	
479F2d1177	**3**
313FS49	
317FS138	
322FS593	
324FS1278	
343FS165	
41Aℒ3504n	**5**
Subsec. a	
C454F2d972	
C462F2d96	
445F2d226	
479F2d1179	
324FS1278	
Subsec. b	**6**
C462F2d96	
445F2d226	
Subsec. c	
394US598	
22LE588	
89SC1360	
322FS585	

Citations to section "§" 700 of Title 18 of the United States Code, 1970 Edition and the 1972 Supplement are shown in the left margin of this page.

Citations for each cited statutory provision are grouped as follows:

1. amendments, repeals, etc. by acts of Congress;
2. citing cases of the United States Supreme Court and the lower federal courts analyzed as to constitutionality or validity;
3. other citing cases;
4. citing legal periodical literature;
5. citing annotations;
6. citing material for specific subdivisions of the statute.

For the purpose of illustration only, this grouping has been indicated by brackets. It will be noted that as yet there is no citing material in group four.

The first citation shown indicates that section 700 of Title 18 was added "Ad" by an act of Congress printed in 82 United States Statutes at Large "St" at page 291. This section is next shown to have been held constitutional "C" by a lower federal court in a case reported in 302 Federal Supplement "FS" 1112 and to have been cited in several cases before the federal courts and the United States Supreme Court. The section was also cited in an annotation "n" of the American Law Reports, Third Series "Aℒ".

Citing references to specific subdivisions of the section are then shown. Subsection (Subsec) a of section 700, for example, was held constitutional in two lower federal court cases reported in 454 F2d 972 and 462 F2d 96.

CHECKLIST #4b

CHECKLIST FOR SHEPARDIZING A STATUTE
1. Go to the set of Shepard's that will enable you to shepardize your statute. For federal statutes, it is Shepard's United States Citations, Statute Edition. For state statutes, go to the set of Shepard's for your state. This set of Shepard's may cover both state cases and state statutes in the same units or in different case and statute editions of the set.
2. If the statute has been codified, shepardize it through its latest codified cite. If all you have is the session law cite of the statute, translate it into a codified cite by using the tables in the current code, e.g., in Table III of the Tables volume of U.S.C./U.S.C.A./U.S.C.S. (p. 655).
3. If the statute has not been codified, you can shepardize it through its session law cite.
4. Go through the four steps to determine whether you have a complete set of Shepard's (p. 609). Read the box.
5. Check your cite in *every* unit of Shepard's. It is recommended that you work *backwards* by examining the most recent Shepard's pamphlets first so that you obtain the latest citing material first.
6. At the top of a Shepard's page, and in its columns, look for your statute by the name of the code, year, article, chapter, title, section—according to how the statute is identified in its cite. Repeat this for every unit of Shepard's.
7. Know the seven kinds of information you can try to obtain by shepardizing a statute: parallel cite (not always given), history of the statute in the legislature, history of the statute in the courts, citing administrative decisions, citing legal periodical literature, citing annotations, citing opinions of the attorney general.
8. The history of the statute in the legislature will give you the citing material in session law form, e.g., A 1980 C 45. This refers to an amendment (A) printed in the 1980 Laws of the legislature, chapter 45. Another example: A 34 St. 654. This refers to an amendment (A) printed in volume 34, page 654, of the Statutes at Large. If you want to locate these session laws, find out if your library keeps the session laws. Also, check the historical note after the statute in the statutory code (p. 650).
9. Watch for this notation in the columns of Shepard's: "et seq." It means "and following." The citing material may be analyzing more than one statutory section. You should check the citing material beneath an "et seq." notation. Your specific statute may be covered by the discussion in this citing material. Also see if there is additional citing material under your specific statutory section number elsewhere in the columns of Shepard's.
10. Use the abbreviation tables and the preface material at the beginning of most of the units of the set of Shepard's.
11. If your state code has gone through revisions or renumberings, read the early pages in the statutory code and in the Shepard's volumes to try to obtain an explanation of what has happened. This information may be of considerable help to you in interpreting the data provided in the Shepard's units for your state code.

7. Shepardizing a Regulation

You cannot shepardize regulations of state agencies. No sets of Shepard's cover state regulations. Until recently, the same was true of most federal regulations. Today, however, it is possible to shepardize federal regulations in the Code of

Federal Regulations (C.F.R.). This is done through Shepard's Code of Federal Regulations Citations, p. 554. (It will also allow you to shepardize executive orders and reorganization plans.)

The C.F.R. comes out in new edition every year (pp. 520, 672). All the changes that have occurred during the year are incorporated in the new yearly edition. Two kinds of changes can be made:

1. Those changes made *by the agency* itself, e.g., amendments, repeals, renumbering—this is the history of the regulation in the agency.
2. Those changes forced on the agency *by the courts,* e.g., declaring the regulation invalid—this is the history of the regulation in the courts.

Unfortunately, Shepard's will give you only the history of the regulation *in the courts* (plus references to the regulation in legal periodical literature and in annotations). The columns of Shepard's will *not* give you the history of the regulation in the agency. (To obtain the latter, you must check elsewhere, e.g., the "CFR Parts Affected" tables in the Federal Register, the LSA pamphlet, p. 673.) The main value of the Shepard's for C.F.R. is that it will tell you what *the courts* have said about the regulation (plus the periodical and annotation references).

When shepardizing through the Shepard's C.F.R. Citations, the cited material, of course, is the federal regulation—referred to below as the cited regulation. There are two kinds of *citing* material provided by Shepard's:

1. Citing cases, periodicals, and annotations that refer to the cited regulation *by year,* i.e., by C.F.R. edition.
2. Citing cases, periodicals, and annotations that refer to the cited regulation *without* specifying the year or edition of the regulation in the C.F.R.

To indicate the first kind of citing material, Shepard's gives you a small elevated asterisk just before a given year. If, for example, you were shepardizing 12 C.F.R. § 218.111(j), you might find the following:

§ 218.111(j)
420F2d90 *1965

The citing material is a citing case—420 F.2d 90. The small asterisk means that the citing case discussed section 218.111(j), and this case specifically identified the year of this regulation—1965. This year is *not* the year of the citing case. It is the year of the cited regulation. We are not given the year of the citing case.

Now let us examine the second kind of citing material mentioned above. There may be citing material that mentions the regulation, but does *not* tell us the specific year or edition of that regulation. Shepard's uses an elevated triangle in such situations. If, for example, you were shepardizing 12 C.F.R. § 9.18(a)(3), you might find the following:

§ 9.18(a)(3)
274FS628 △1967

The citing material is a citing case—274 F.Supp. 628. The small triangle means that the citing case discussed section 9.18(a)(3) but did not refer to the year or edition of section 9.18(a)(3). The year 1967 is the year of the citing case and not the year of the cited regulation. The citing case in 274 F.Supp. 628 was decided in 1967.

(sample column from Shepards C.F.R. Citations.)

CODE OF FEDERAL REGULATIONS

Shepard's Code of Federal Regulations Citations shows citations to the Code of Federal Regulations and to Presidential Proclamations, Executive Orders, and Reorganization Plans as cited by the United States Supreme Court, by the lower federal courts, and by state courts in cases reported in any unit of the National Reporter System, and in annotations of American Law Reports. In addition, citations appearing in articles in legal periodicals are shown.

If the citing source refers to the date of the cited CFR regulation, the cited year is shown, preceded by the symbol *. If a regulation is cited without a CFR date, the year of the citing reference is shown, preceded by the symbol △.

Citations to each provision of the Code of Federal Regulations are grouped as follows:

1. citing federal cases;
2. citing state cases;
3. citing legal periodical literature;
4. citing annotations.

The 1973 edition of section 53.111 was held unconstitutional in part "Up" by a United States District Court case reported in 453 Federal Supplement "FS" 410. Another United States District Court decision held § 53.111 void or invalid in part "Vp." The United States Court of Appeals in 1977 determined that § 53.111 was valid, "Va."

Section 53.111 has also been cited by the Courts of Massachusetts, New York, and Oregon. A citing legal periodical is shown by the reference 88 Yale Law Journal "YLJ" 277, and a citing annotation "n" is shown by the reference 11 American Law Reports, Federal "ALRF" 1972.

CHECKLIST #4c

CHECKLIST FOR SHEPARDIZING A FEDERAL REGULATION
1. Go to Shepard's Code of Federal Regulations Citations. The regulation you want to shepardize must appear in the C.F.R.
2. Follow the four steps to determine whether you have a complete set of Shepard's for this set. Read the box (p. 609).
3. Shepardize your regulation through every unit of this set of Shepard's.
4. This set of Shepard's will give you two kinds of information: (a) Citing material that analyzes a regulation of a specific year or edition (indicated by an asterisk next to the year) (b) Citing material that analyzes a regulation without referring to the specific year or edition of the regulation (indicated by a triangle next to the year) The citing material includes citing cases, citing legal periodical literature, and citing annotations.

5.	This set of Shepard's does not directly tell you what amendments, revisions, or other changes were made *by the agencies* to the regulations. You are told only what *the courts* have said about the regulations. (To find out what the agencies have done to the regulations, you must check the "CFR Parts Affected" tables in the Federal Register, and the LSA pamphlet. See p. 673.)
6.	Check the abbreviation table and preface at the beginning of most of the Shepard's units.
7.	All regulations in C.F.R. are based on statutes of Congress. You can find out what statutes in U.S.C. are the authority for particular regulations in C.F.R. by checking the "authority" reference under many of the regulations in C.F.R. (See p. 673.) Once you know the statute that is the basis for the regulation, you might want to shepardize that statute for more law in the area. (See Checklist 4b above on shepardizing a statute.)

5. LOOSE-LEAF SERVICES

Loose-leaf services are law books with a three-ring or post-binder structure (p. 547). Additions to these services are made frequently, e.g., monthly or sooner. The main publishers of these services are Bureau of National Affairs (BNA), Commerce Clearing House (CCH), Prentice-Hall (PH), and Matthew Bender (p. 511). They cover numerous broad areas of the law, e.g., criminal law, taxes, corporate law, unions. You should assume that one or more loose-leaf services exist for the topic of your research problem until you prove to yourself otherwise. Benefits provided by the loose-leaf services often include the following:

- Recent court opinions and/or summaries of opinions.
- Relevant legislation—usually explained in some detail.
- Administrative regulations and decisions, and/or summaries of them (some of this material may not be available elsewhere).
- References to relevant studies and reports.
- Practice tips.

In short, the loose-leaf services are extremely valuable. Unfortunately, however, they are sometimes awkward to use. Occasionally, library staff and/or students misfile some of the updating pages, and/or library users of the loose-leaf services misfile pages that they take out for Xeroxing or other photocopying.

There is no standard order to the loose-leaf books. You may find the following, for example:

- Organization by page number, organization by section number, organization by paragraph number, combination of the above.
- Different colored pages to indicate more recent material.
- Indexes at the end of the books, in the middle, at the beginning.
- Summaries, summaries of summaries.
- One volume or multi-volume.
- Bound volumes that accompany the three-ring volumes.
- Transfer binders that contain current material.

You should approach the structure of each loose-leaf service as a small puzzle that is sitting on the shelf waiting for you to unravel.

CHECKLIST #5

CHECKLIST FOR FINDING AND USING LOOSE-LEAF SERVICES
1. Divide your research problem into its major topics, e.g., family law, tax law, anti-trust law, etc. Assume that one or more loose-leaf services exist for these topics until you have demonstrated to yourself otherwise.
2. Find out where the loose-leaf services are located in your library. Are they all together? Are they located in certain subject areas? Does the library have a separate list of them?
3. Check the card catalog. (See Checklist #1, p. 600.) Check subject heading cards for your topics to see if loose-leaf services are mentioned. Check the names of the major publishers of loose-leaf services, e.g., Bureau of National Affairs, Commerce Clearing House, Prentice-Hall, Matthew Bender.
4. Ask librarians if they know of loose-leaf services on the major topics of your research.
5. Call other law libraries in your area (p. 512). Ask the librarians there if they know of loose-leaf services on the major topics of your research. See if they can identify loose-leaf services that you could not identify through your own library.
6. Speak to experts in the area of the law, e.g., professors. (See Checklist #9, p. 631.) Ask them about loose-leaf services.
7. Once you have a loose-leaf service in front of you, you must figure out how to use it: (a) Read any preface or explanation material in the front of the volumes of the loose-leaf service. (b) Ask librarians to give you some help using it. (c) Ask teachers who are experts in the area if they can give you a brief demonstration on its use. (d) Ask a fellow student who is familiar with the service. (e) Read any pamphlets or promotional literature by the publishers on using their loose-leaf services (p. 510). (f) Do the best that you can to struggle through the set on your own. For each loose-leaf service you need to know the following: • What it contains and what it does not contain. • How it is indexed. • How it is supplemented. • What its special features are. • How many volumes or units it has and the interrelationship among them. You obtain this information through techniques (a) to (f) above.
8. In your research memo, you rarely cite a loose-leaf service unless the material you found there does not exist elsewhere. Use the loose-leaf service mainly as background research (p. 595) and as a search tool to find cases, statutes, regulations, etc., i.e., to find primary authority (p. 561).

6. LEGAL PERIODICAL LITERATURE

Legal periodical literature (p. 546) consists of the following:

- Lead articles and comments written by individuals who have extensively researched a topic.
- Case notes that summarize and comment upon recent important court opinions.
- Book reviews.

Most periodicals are published by law students who are "on law review" or "on the law journal" at their law school. There are hundreds of legal periodicals containing a wealth of information for the researcher.

The big question is, how can you locate legal periodical literature on point? What index systems exist for the hundreds of periodicals and the tens of thousands of articles, case notes, comments, and other material in them? There are three major index systems:

- Index to Legal Periodicals (ILP)
- Current Law Index (CLI)
- Legal Resource Index (LRI)

While all three systems are extensive, CLI and LRI are more comprehensive than ILP. Comprehensiveness is determined by the number of periodicals indexed. The benefit of a comprehensive index is that you obtain access to many periodicals. Unfortunately, most law libraries will *not* have all the periodicals mentioned in the index. You may be obtaining cites to periodicals that your library does not have. For such periodicals that you need, you must check other libraries in the area (p. 512).

(1) Features of Index to Legal Periodicals (ILP)

- The ILP first comes out in pamphlets that are later cumulated into bound yearly volumes.
- You must check each ILP pamphlet and each ILP bound volume for whatever years you want.
- ILP regularly adds new periodicals to be indexed.
- Every ILP pamphlet and bound volume has several sections:
    (i) A subject-and-author index
    (ii) A table of cases commented upon
    (iii) A table of statutes commented upon (added recently)
    (iv) A book review index
- There are abbreviations tables at the beginning of every pamphlet and bound volume.
- The "subject" portion of the subject-and-author index is easy to use; you are given full bibliographic references to periodical literature under the subjects relevant to your research topics.
- Beginning in 1983, the "author" portion of the subject-and-author index also has full bibliographic references to periodical literature by that author. Prior to 1983, however, the use of the "author" position was more complex. If you know the name of an author but not the title of his or her article, you look for that author's name in the

subject-and-author index. Under his or her name you will find one or more topics and capital letters in parentheses after the topics. Go to those topics in the subject-and-author index. Under those topics, look for articles beginning with the capital letters you initially found in parentheses until you locate the article by the author you want.

- Toward the end of every ILP pamphlet and bound volume there is a Table of Cases Commented Upon. Suppose that elsewhere in your research you come across an important case, and you now want to know if that case was ever commented upon (i.e., noted) in the legal periodicals. Go to the ILP pamphlet or bound volume that covers the year of the case and check the Table of Cases Commented Upon.
- The Table of Statutes Commented Upon will tell you where you can find periodical literature analyzing certain statutes.
- At the end of every pamphlet and bound ILP volume there is a book review index. If you are looking for a review of a law book you have come across elsewhere in your research, go to the ILP pamphlet or bound volume that covers the year of publication of the book for which you are seeking reviews.

(2) Features of
Current Law Index (CLI)

- The CLI first comes out in pamphlets that are later cumulated into annual issues.
- CLI indexes more periodical literature than ILP.
- CLI regularly adds new periodicals to be indexed.
- Check all current pamphlets and all annual issues for the years you want.
- There are four indexes within each CLI unit:
    (i) A subject index
    (ii) An author-title index
    (iii) A table of cases
    (iv) A table of statutes
- There are abbreviations tables at the beginning of every CLI unit.
- The subject index gives full citations to periodicals under a topic and under an author's name.
- Book reviews are included under the author-title index along with cites to periodical literature by the authors.
- The table of cases is valuable if you already know the name of a case located elsewhere in your research. To find out if that case was commented upon, check the table of cases in the CLI unit that covers the year of the case.
- The table of statutes is equally valuable. If you already have the name of a statute from your other research (e.g., Atomic Energy Act; California Fair Employment Practices Act), look for the name of that statute in the table of statutes for the CLI unit that covers the approximate time the statute was passed.
- The CLI began in 1980; it does not index periodicals prior to this date. The ILP must be used for this period.

**(3) Features of
Legal Resource Index (LRI)**

- LRI comes out in microfilm to be used with a special viewer machine, some of which have coin-operated copiers (see illustration below).
- LRI provides the same material as CLI; they are both published by Information Access Corporation.

Note on Other Index Systems

A number of other index systems exist:

- Jones-Chipman Index to Legal Periodical Literature (covering periodical literature up to 1937 only)
- Index to Federal Tax Articles
- Index to Foreign Legal Periodicals
- Index to Canadian Legal Periodical Literature
- Index Medicus (covers medical periodicals—available in medical libraries)
- Medline (a computer search system for medical periodicals—available in medical libraries).

CHECKLIST #6

CHECKLIST FOR FINDING LEGAL PERIODICAL LITERATURE
1. Use legal periodical literature for background research (p. 595) and for leads to primary authority (p. 561), particularly through the extensive footnotes in legal periodical literature. Scholarly articles can also be cited in your research memo.

2.	There are three major index systems: Index to Legal Periodicals (ILP), Current Law Index (CLI), and Legal Resource Index (LRI).
3.	Use all three of the major index systems in your legal research. The CARTWHEEL will help you locate material in them (p. 591).
4.	Within ILP there are separate indexes. Within CLI and LRI there are also separate indexes. You should become familiar with all these internal index features (pp. 626ff.).
5.	Start with the subject headings index within ILP, CLI, and LRI.
6.	Identify the name and date of every important case that you have found in your research thus far. Go to the table of cases in ILP, in CLI, and in LRI to find out if there is any periodical literature that has commented on that case. (Go to the ILP, CLI, and LRI units that would cover the year the case was decided. To be safe, also check their units for two years after the date of the case.)
7.	If you are researching a statute, find out if there is any periodical literature that has commented on the statute. This is done in two ways: (a) Check the table of statutes in CLI, LRI, and ILP. (b) Break your statute down into its major topics. Check these topics in the subject indexes of ILP, CLI, and LRI to see if any periodical literature has been written on them.
8.	If you have the name of an author who is known for writing on a particular topic, you can also check for literature written by that author under his or her name in ILP, CLI, and LRI.
9.	Ask your librarian if the library has any other indexes to legal periodical literature, particularly in specialty areas of the law.
10.	It is possible to shepardize some legal periodical literature (p. 555). If you want to know whether the periodical article, note, or comment was ever mentioned in a court opinion, go to Shepard's Law Review Citations.

7. LEGAL ENCYCLOPEDIAS

Here our main concern is using the major national encyclopedias: American Jurisprudence 2d (Am.Jur.2d), p. 522, and Corpus Juris Secundum (C.J.S.), p. 534.

CHECKLIST FOR USING LEGAL ENCYCLOPEDIAS

1. Use both Am.Jur.2d and C.J.S. for the following purposes:
   (a) As background research for areas of the law that are new to you
   (b) For leads in their extensive footnotes to primary authority, e.g., cases, statutes, etc.

2. Both legal encyclopedias have multi-volume general indexes at the end of their sets. Use the CARTWHEEL to help you locate material in them (p. 591). In addition to these general indexes, Am.Jur.2d and C.J.S. have a separate index to most of the individual volumes.
3. There is no table of cases in either Am.Jur.2d or C.J.S.
4. There is no table of statutes in C.J.S. In Am.Jur.2d, however, there is a separate volume called Table of Statutes and Rules Cited. Check this table if you have found a relevant statute from your other research that you want to find discussed in Am.Jur.2d.
5. Am.Jur.2d is published by Lawyers Co-op. C.J.S. is published by West. Within these legal encyclopedias, the publishers provide cross-references to other research books that they publish. In Am.Jur.2d, for example, Lawyers Co-op will refer you to annotations in ALR, ALR2d, ALR3d, ALR4th, and ALR Fed. In C.J.S., West will refer you to its key number digests.
6. Find out if your library has a *local* encyclopedia that is limited to the law of your state. Among the states with such encyclopedias are California, Florida, Illinois, Maryland, Michigan, New York, Ohio, Pennsylvania, and Texas.

8. TREATISES

A treatise is any book written by private individuals (or by public officials writing in a private capacity) on a topic of law (p. 558). Falling into the category of treatises are hornbooks, handbooks, formbooks, and practice manuals. Treatises give overview summaries of the law and references to primary authority. There are single-volume treatises such as Prosser on Torts, as well as multivolume treatises such as Am.Jur. Legal Forms, Am.Jur. Proof of Facts, Am.Jur. Pleading and Practice Forms, Am.Jur. Trials, Moore's Federal Practice, Collier on Bankruptcy, etc.

CHECKLIST FOR FINDING AND USING TREATISES
1. Always look for treatises on the topics of your research problem. Assume that three or four such treatises exist and are relevant to your problem until you prove to yourself otherwise.
2. Treatises are useful as background research (p. 595) and as leads to primary authority (p. 561). Scholarly treatises can also be cited in your research memo (p. 569).
3. Many treatises are updated by pocket parts, supplemental volumes, and page inserts if the treatise has a three-ring or post-binding structure.
4. Start your search for treatises in the card catalog. See Checklist #1 on using the catalog (p. 600).
5. Check with experts in the area of law in which you are interested, e.g., teachers, for recommendations on treatises you should examine. See Checklist #9, p. 631.

6.	If your library has open stacks, find the treatise section (e.g., with KF call numbers). Locate the areas where treatises on your topic are shelved. Browse through the shelves in these areas of the stacks to try to find additional treatises. (Some treatises that you need, however, may be on reserve.)
7.	Once you have found a treatise, check that author's name in the Index to Legal Periodicals (ILP), the Current Law Index (CLI), and the Legal Resource Index (LRI) to try to find periodical literature on the same topic by this author. You can also use these indexes to see if there are any book reviews on the treatises. (See Checklist #6 on finding legal periodical literature, p. 628.)

9. PHONE AND MAIL—SPEAK WITH THE EXPERTS

Don't be reluctant to call or write recognized experts on the topics of your research. You can ask for leads to important cases, regulations, treatises, legal periodical literature, leads to other experts, leads to current or recent litigation, etc. Sometimes you can even discuss the facts of your research to obtain their perceptions of your direction. The worst that can happen is that they will ignore your request or simply say no. You will find, however, that many experts are quite willing to help you free of charge, so long as you are respectful and do not give the impression that you want more than a few moments of their time. You do not ask to come over to spend an afternoon!

CHECKLIST #9

CHECKLIST FOR DOING PHONE AND MAIL RESEARCH	
1.	Your goal is to contact someone who is an expert in the area of your research problem. You want to write this person or talk with him or her briefly on the phone. It is usually not wise for you to try to go see the expert (unless he or she is on the faculty of your school).
2.	Do not try to contact an expert until you have first done a substantial amount of research on your own, e.g., you should have already checked the major cases, statutes, regulations, treatises, legal periodical literature, annotations, etc., that are readily available in the library.
3.	Prepare the questions you want to ask the expert. Make them short and to the point. For example, "Do you know of any recent case law on the liability of a municipality for . . . ?" "Could you give me any leads to literature on the doctrine of promissory estoppel as it applies to . . . ?" "Do you know anyone who has done any research on the new EPA regulations whom I could contact?" "Do you know of anyone currently litigating section 307?" Do *not* recite all the facts of the research problem to the expert and say, "What should I do?" If the expert wants more facts from you, let him or her ask you for them. You must create the impression that you want no more than a few moments of the expert's time. If the experts want to give your request more attention, they will let you know.
4.	Introduce yourself as someone doing research on a problem, e.g., as a student. State how you got their name (see guideline below) and then state how grateful you would be if you could ask them a "quick question."
5.	Your introductory comments should state how you came across their name and learned of their expertise, e.g., "I read your law review article on . . . ." "I saw your name as an attorney of record in the case of . . . ." "Mr/Ms _____ told me you were an expert in this area and recommended that I contact you."
6.	Calling is preferable to using the mail, unless calling is impractical because of cost.

7. Where do you find these experts? A number of possibilities exist:
   (a) *Special interest groups and associations*
       Contact lawyers within these groups and associations, e.g., unions, environmental groups, business associations. Ask your librarian for lists of such groups and associations, e.g., the Encyclopedia of Associations, the Directory of Directories.
   (b) *Government agencies*
       Contact the law department of the agencies that have something to do with the topics of your research problem. The CARTWHEEL should help you think of these agencies (p. 591).
   (c) *Specialty libraries*
       Ask your librarian for lists of libraries, e.g., Directory of Special Libraries and Information Centers (p. 514).
   (d) *Law professors*
       Start with your own school. Also, ask your librarian if the library has the AALS Law Teachers Directory, which lists teachers by name and specialty across the country.
   (e) *Attorneys of Record*
       If you have found a recent court opinion on point, the names of the attorneys for the case are printed at the beginning of the opinion (p. 643). Try to obtain the addresses of the attorneys in Martindale-Hubbell Law Directory (p. 548). These attorneys may be willing to send you a copy of appellate briefs on the case. Also try to find out about ongoing litigation in the courts. Often you are permitted to go to the court clerk's office and examine pleadings, appellate briefs, etc., on pending cases. Finally, do not forget to check the closed case files of your own office for prior research that has already been done in the same area as your problem.
   (f) *Authors of legal periodical literature and of treatises*
       Write to the author of a treatise or law review article that is relevant to your research. If you cannot obtain the author's address from the Law Teacher's Directory, Martindale-Hubbell, or other directory, write the author care of the publisher of the treatise or periodical.

10. COMPUTERS (See also pp. 720–725.)

If you have access to any of the legal computers, ask for a demonstration on how to operate the computer from the librarian or from the company that produces the computer. The major legal computers are listed below.

WESTLAW®
by West Publishing Company

WESTLAW stores the full text opinions of the National Reporter System, the headnotes of these opinions, the United States Code, U.S. Supreme Court opinions, U.S. Court of Appeals opinions, U.S. District Court opinions, the Code of Federal Regulations, the Federal Register, and federal administrative decisions. You can Shepardize on WESTLAW; find the most current case history in West's Insta-Cite™; conduct research in specialty areas such as securities, tax, and international law; research compatible data bases in medicine, social sciences, public affairs, etc. Each day more material is added to WESTLAW.

LEXIS® by Mead Data Central

LEXIS stores the full text of the United States Code, federal court opinions, decisions of the Federal Trade Commission, the Securities and Exchange Commission, congressional reports, state court opinions, etc. You can Shepardize on LEXIS; conduct patent searches; locate references to annotations in ALR, ALR2d, ALR3d, ALR4th, and ALR Fed via Auto-Cite citation services; or use the LEXIS service to do fact research in leading daily newspapers, magazines, wire services, and newsletters, as well as research reports from top brokerage and investment banking firms. As with WESTLAW, material is being added to LEXIS regularly.

Courtesy of Mead Data Central

Vast amounts of legal information are stored on computer systems such as WESTLAW and LEXIS.* Users gain access to these computers by using terminals, which are connected to the main computers by various telecommunications networks. For a detailed description of how these computer systems operate, see pp. 720ff.

When legal information in documents is stored on the computers, special programs create a concordance or index, which notes the exact location of every significant word in the documents. Searching is then performed by asking the computer to find documents that contain certain terms appearing within specified proximities to one another. The computer consults the concordance to determine which materials fulfill the search criteria and then makes them available for display (p. 719).

To make effective use of computer-assisted legal research, the researcher must know the legal concepts and vocabulary pertinent to an issue. The research works best in specific fact situations in which certain words are used to describe an event. Computer systems are less suited for searching broad concepts in which the vocabulary is "fuzzy."

A hypothetical example will demonstrate different ways to use a system such as WESTLAW. Assume that the client has injured her spine in an automobile accident caused by a tire blowout. The researcher may wish to find products liability cases involving tire blowouts. On WESTLAW, the user could submit the following question or query to find such cases.

```
product strict /s liability &
  tire /s blowout "blew out"
```

This query asks the computer to find cases in which some form of the word *product* or the word *strict* appears in the same sentence as *liability,* and in which *tire* or *tires* appears in the same sentence as some form of *blowout* or the phrase *blew out.* If this query proves unproductive, the question is refined by trying other phrases or word combinations (p. 719).

The screen in figure 1 shows a recent California case retrieved by this query.

Once the researcher has refined the question or search query to the point that it is retrieving relevant cases, the system can print out a list of case citations, which can be used to find the cases on the shelves of a law library—in reporter volumes. Good researchers adopt this method because it is too expensive to read the complete text of the cases on-line. The screen in figure 2 shows a list of Illinois cases involving products liability and tire blowouts.

A researcher may also want to find information about the range of damages that have been awarded in spinal injury cases. WESTLAW's topics and key

* Adapted from Runde, *Computer Assisted Legal Research,* 10 Facts and Findings 13 (National Association of Legal Assistants, July–August, 1983). Reprinted with permission.

Figure 1

```
                              COPR. (C) WEST 1985 NO CLAIM TO ORIG.
                                                  U.S. GOVT. WORKS
        Citation        Rank (R)  Page (P) Database Mode
        186 Cal.Rptr. 26 R 1 of 8  P 1 of 15   CRP    T
    Arizona FULLER et al., Plaintiffs and Appellants,
                            v.
            SEARS, ROEBUCK & COMPANY et al.,
                  Defendants and Respondents.
                    Civ. A. No. 15235.
            Appellate Department, Superior Court,
                    Los Angeles County.
                     August 10, 1982.
    Action was brought by purchasers of tires from seller to recover for
    personal injuries and property damage arising from automobile
    accident which was allegedly the result of blowout of one of the
    tires. The Municipal Court for the Los Angeles Judicial District of
    Los Angeles County, James P. Natoli, J., entered judgments in favor
    of defendant following granting of defendant's motion for nonsuit,
    and appeal was taken. The Superior Court, Appellate Department,
    Rothman, J., held that purchasers of tires could not recover under
    doctrine of res ipsa loquitur, in that accident was not of a kind
    which ordinarily does not occur in absence of someone's negligence
    and it could not be said that the accident was caused by an agency
    or instrumentality in the defendant's control.
    Affirmed.
```

Figure 2

```
                              COPR. (C) WEST 1985 NO CLAIM TO ORIG.
                                                  U.S. GOVT. WORKS
    CITATIONS LIST
       1.  Ill.App. 2 Dist. 1984.  Nave v. Rainbo Tire Service, Inc., 462
    N.E.2d 620, 123 Ill.App.3d 685, 78 Ill Dec. 501.
       2.  Ill. 1984.  Alsup v. Firestone Tire & Rubber Co.  461 N.E.2d 361
       3.  Ill.App. 1982.  Broussard By and Through Broussard v. Huffman
    Mfg. Co.  438 N.E.2d 1217
       4.  Ill.App. 1981.  Livingston Service Co., Inc. v. Big Wheels, Inc.
    421 N.E.2d 1042
       5.  Ill.App. 1979.  Anderson v. General Grinding Wheel Corp.  393
    N.E.2d 9
       6.  Ill.App. 1975.  Mullen v. General Motors Corp.,  336 N.E.2d 338,
    32 Ill.App.3d 122.
       7.  Ill.App. 1975.  Tweedy v. Wright Ford Sales, Inc.,  334 N.E.2d
    417, 31 Ill.App.3d 72.
```

numbers (p. 544) could be used to find this information. The following search query requires the computer to find cases with headnotes dealing with the issue of damages and involving spinal injuries.

```
topic(damages) /p spine spinal
```

This type of search finds those cases that deal with the issue of damage awards in spinal injury cases. The screen in figure 3 shows a headnote from a pertinent New York case.

Figure 3

```
                                    COPR. (C) WEST 1985 NO CLAIM TO ORIG.
                                                      U.S. GOVT. WORKS.

           436 N.Y.S.2d 251   R 6 of 142   P 8 of 42    NYS   T
    115K132(3)

    DAMAGES
    K. Paralysis and other injuries to brain, spine or nervous system. N.Y.
    1981.
    In strict products liability action, damage award of $2,000,000 for
    quadriplegic injuries to 21-year-old plaintiff was not an abuse of
    discretion.
    Caprara v. Chrysler Corp.
    436 N.Y.S.2d 251, 52 N.Y.2d 114
```

Computer systems also enable users to perform special searches such as finding all cases written by a particular judge or in which a specific law firm or party has appeared.

Once relevant cases have been retrieved, WESTLAW allows the researcher to update or validate them through both Shepard's Citations and a new feature called Insta-Cite. With a single command, the user could switch from the *Caprara* case (see figure 3) to a Shepard's display for that case (see figure 4).

Figure 4

```
CITATIONS TO: 436 NYS2d 251

LIMIT  CD ANALYSIS        HEADNOTE-       CITATION- COMMENTS      WESTLAW#
                          ( 52 NY 2d  114           ) SAME TEXT
                          (417 NE 2d  545           ) SAME TEXT        1
SC     SAME CASE            428 S2d    694                             2
SC     SAME CASE            438 S2d   1029
D      DISTINGUISHED     5  436 S2d    480, 483                        3
J      DISSENTING OPIN      436 S2d    480, 485                        4
                        5  436 S2d    625, 632                         5
                           437 S2d    512, 515                         6
                           438 S2d         361                         7
                        5  442 S2d         148                         8
J      DISSENTING OPIN      442 S2d    453, 461                        9
J      DISSENTING OPIN      446 S2d    438, 441                       10
                           449 S2d    162, 164                        11
                        5  450 S2d    615, 616                        12
                        3  450 S2d    615, 618                        13
                           450 S2d    776, 779                        14
J      DISSENTING OPIN      450 S2d         808                       15

COPYRIGHT 1985 BY SHEPARDS/MCGRAW-HILL
(C) COPYRIGHT WEST PUBLISHING COMPANY 1985
```

The screen in figure 5 shows the *Caprara* case as found on Insta-Cite. Like Shepard's, this feature provides current validation information.

Figure 5

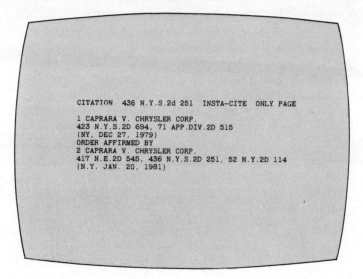

```
CITATION   436 N.Y.S.2d 251   INSTA-CITE   ONLY PAGE

1 CAPRARA V. CHRYSLER CORP.
423 N.Y.S.2D 694, 71 APP.DIV.2D 515
(NY, DEC 27, 1979)
ORDER AFFIRMED BY
2 CAPRARA V. CHRYSLER CORP.
417 N.E.2D 545, 436 N.Y.S.2D 251, 52 N.Y.2D 114
(N.Y. JAN. 20, 1981)
```

WESTLAW also has a file on expert witnesses. In our hypothetical, this file could be used to find experts on tire failures:

Figure 6

```
Citation                          Rank (R)  Page (P)  Database Mode
Hindin, Herbert B.                R 1 of 32 P 1 of 1  FSD       T
SPECIALIZED PROFESSIONAL & TECHNICAL CONSULTANTS
SPECIALIZED PROFESSIONAL & TECHNICAL CONSULTANTS
                          CAUSATION
              ACCIDENT RECONSTRUCTION VEHICULAR
              Tire Defects & Tire Failures
Hindin, Herbert B.
Box 2035
Grass Valley, CA 95945
(916) 273-1005
Specialties Product liability on tires involved in litigation
Federal regulations on tires, retreads & wheels. Affiliation H.B.
Hindin Assoc. (Prin).
END OF DOCUMENT
```

Information on experts and other substantive information about the factual aspects of a case can be found on computer systems that are complementary to WESTLAW. Systems like Dialog, Orbit, BRS, and Dow Jones cover a variety of fields. The user, for example, could consult medical files on Dialog or BRS to find an article on rehabilitation in spinal injury cases:

Figure 7

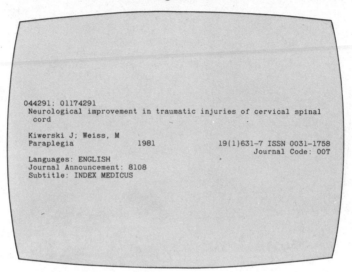

LEXIS works in a similar way with many of the same features (p. 633). Suppose, for example, that you wanted cases in which a juror concealed his or her bias. You would instruct LEXIS to find cases in which the word *bias* appears in proximity to the words *juror* and *conceal* or *concealing:*

Figure 8

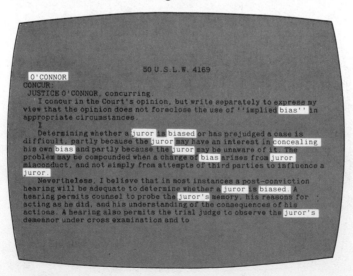

Once you have examined a number of these cases, you can ask the system to display a list of citations of all the cases discovered when LEXIS fulfilled your search request:

Figure 9

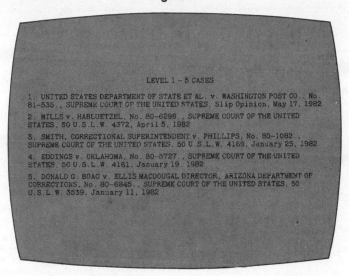

```
LEVEL 1 - 5 CASES

1.  UNITED STATES DEPARTMENT OF STATE ET AL. v. WASHINGTON POST CO., No.
81-535., SUPREME COURT OF THE UNITED STATES, Slip Opinion, May 17, 1982
2.  MILLS v. HABLUETZEL, No. 80-6298., SUPREME COURT OF THE UNITED
STATES, 50 U.S.L.W. 4372, April 5, 1982
3.  SMITH, CORRECTIONAL SUPERINTENDENT v. PHILLIPS, No. 80-1082.,
SUPREME COURT OF THE UNITED STATES. 50 U.S.L.W. 4169, January 25, 1982
4.  EDDINGS v. OKLAHOMA, No. 80-5727., SUPREME COURT OF THE UNITED
STATES. 50 U.S.L.W. 4161, January 19. 1982
5.  DONALD G. BOAG v. ELLIS MACDOUGAL DIRECTOR, ARIZONA DEPARTMENT OF
CORRECTIONS, No. 80-6845., SUPREME COURT OF THE UNITED STATES, 50
U.S.L.W. 3539, January 11, 1982
```

NOTE ON OTHER COMPUTER SYSTEMS

AUTO-CITE by Lawyers Cooperative Publishing Company

AUTO-CITE permits you to check the accuracy of a legal citation and provides parallel cites and cites to other opinions in the same litigation. AUTO-CITE also gives you citations to annotations in ALR, ALR2d, ALR3d, ALR4th, and ALR Fed.

JURIS by the U.S. Department of Justice

JURIS is a computer designed to search case law, federal statutes, internal government files, etc. It is available only to Justice Department employees.

FLITE by the U.S. Department of Defense (Air Force)

FLITE is a computer that enables you to locate federal statutes, some federal court opinions, military law materials, legislative history, etc. It is available only to federal employees.

Section P. READING AND FINDING CASE LAW

In this section we first look at the structure of a court opinion and discuss how it is read. Then we focus on the techniques of finding case law that draws on the material discussed thus far in the chapter.

READING CASE LAW

The following is an opinion printed in full from one of the reporters—the California Reporter. The circled numbers are explained after the opinion.

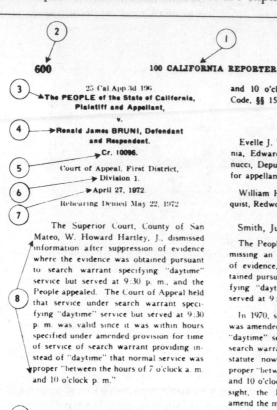

600   100 **CALIFORNIA REPORTER**

25 Cal.App.3d 196

**The PEOPLE of the State of California,
Plaintiff and Appellant,**

v.

**Ronald James BRUNI, Defendant
and Respondent.**

Cr. 10096.

Court of Appeal, First District,
Division 1.

April 27, 1972.

Rehearing Denied May 22, 1972

The Superior Court, County of San Mateo, W. Howard Hartley, J., dismissed information after suppression of evidence where the evidence was obtained pursuant to search warrant specifying "daytime" service but served at 9:30 p. m., and the People appealed. The Court of Appeal held that service under search warrant specifying "daytime" service but served at 9:30 p. m. was valid since it was within hours specified under amended provision for time of service of search warrant providing instead of "daytime" that normal service was proper "between the hours of 7 o'clock a. m. and 10 o'clock p. m."

Judgment reversed and trial court directed to deny motion to suppress the evidence.

1. **Searches and Seizures** ⊂⊃3.8(1)

In light of amendment of provision as to time of service of search warrant providing instead of "daytime" that normal service was proper "between the hours of 7 o'clock a. m. and 10 o'clock p. m.," "daytime" in provision for form for warrant was impliedly amended to provide same period for service as that under the other amended provision. West's Ann.Pen.Code, §§ 4, 7, 1529, 1533; West's Ann.Code Civ. Proc. § 1859.

2. **Searches and Seizures** ⊂⊃3.8(1)

Service under search warrant specifying "daytime" service but served at 9:30 p. m. was valid since it was within hours specified under amended provision for time of service of search warrant providing instead of "daytime" that normal service was proper "between the hours of 7 o'clock a. m.

and 10 o'clock p. m." West's Ann.Pen. Code, §§ 1529, 1533.

Evelle J. Younger, Atty. Gen. of California, Edward P. O'Brien, Robert R. Granucci, Deputy Attys. Gen., San Francisco, for appellant.

William F. DeLucchi, Regalado & Lindquist, Redwood City, for respondent.

Smith, Judge.

The People appeal from a judgment dismissing an Information after suppression of evidence, where the evidence was obtained pursuant to a search warrant specifying "daytime" service, but which was served at 9:30 p. m. at night.

In 1970, section 1533 of the Penal Code was amended to eliminate the provision for "daytime" service for normal service of a search warrant. Instead of "daytime," the statute now specifies normal service as proper "between the hours of 7 o'clock a. m. and 10 o'clock p. m." Apparently by oversight, the Legislature neglected to also amend the mandatory provisions under section 1529 of the Penal Code, which continues to require "daytime" service. An inconsistency exists as to the mandatory requirements of search warrants unless section 1529 of the Penal Code is read as having been amended by implication when section 1533 of the Penal Code was expressly amended. Otherwise, the only warrant an issuing magistrate could authorize, without possibly violating one or the other statute, would be one for unlimited service at any hour of day or night upon a showing of good cause. Nothing suggests that this was the legislative intent.

The provisions of the Penal Code "are to be construed according to the fair import of their terms, with a view to effect its objects and to promote justice." (Pen.Code, § 4.) "In the construction of a statute the intention of the Legislature . . . . is to be pursued, if possible, and when a general and particular provision are inconsistent, the latter is paramount to the former." (Code Civ.Proc., § 1859.)

[1] Under the definition in Section 7 of the Penal Code, daytime is defined as "the

period between sunrise and sunset." This general provision is clearly inconsistent with the particular provision relating to service of search warrants between the hours of 7 o'clock a. m. and 10 o'clock p. m. established under the amendment of section 1533 of the Penal Code. Under the general ⑱ rules of statutory construction, we interpret "daytime" in the particular provisions of section 1529 of the Penal Code as having ⑲ been impliedly amended to provide the same period for service as that under amended section 1533 of the Penal Code.

⑱ ". . . . where the language of a statute is reasonably susceptible of two constructions, one of which in application will render it reasonable, fair and harmonious with its manifest purpose, and another which would be productive of absurd consequences, the former construction will be adopted.' (citation) ; and 'if certain provisions are repugnant, effect should be given to those which best comport with the end to be accomplished and render the statute effective, ⑰ rather than nugatory.'" (Dept. of Motor Vehicles of California v. Indus. Acc. Com. (1939) 14 Cal.2d 189, 195, 93 P.2d 131, 134.)

⑩ⓐ [2] We hold that the People are correct in their assertion that service was valid ⑲ since it was within the hours specified under amended section 1533 of the Penal Code. Any other holding would mean that section 1529 of the Penal Code would now require service at hours determined to be peculiarly abrasive and requiring a higher standard of proof (Tidwell v. Superior Court (1971) 17 ⑰ Cal.App.3d 780, 786–787, 95 Cal.Rptr. 213) without a showing of good cause.

This court has always been scrupulous in demanding a high standard for the admission of evidence pursuant to warrants. Our ruling today does not violate this standard. The integrity of our trial system in large measure depends upon the integrity of the evidence admitted at trial. The case before us deals with the timing of serving a warrant. If the case had involved other ㉑ aspects of the warrant such as its specificity, our result would probably have been different.

The judgment is reversed, and the trial ⑳ court is directed to deny the motion to suppress the evidence.

Jones, Judge (Concurring in result only). ㉒

Thomas, Judge (Dissenting). ㉓

If the California legislature intended to amend section 1529 of the Penal Code, it should have done so expressly. It is not the function of the judiciary to amend the statutes passed by the legislature. The public has a right to rely on the written language of statutes; in fact, we frequently admonish the citizenry if they ignore that language. For the courts to alter the language after the fact not only infringes upon the right of the legislature to be the sole entity under our system that can enact and amend legislation, but also is a signal to the public and to government officials that they can no longer trust the law as validly passed by the legislative branch. Both results are intolerable.

I would affirm the judgment below.

---

① The California Reporter is an unofficial reporter (p. 532) of state opinions in California. The "100" indicates the volume number of the reporter.

② The court opinion begins on page 600. The citation of this case is *People v. Bruni*, 25 Cal.App.3d 196, 100 Cal.Rptr. 600 (1972). The official cite is given at the top of the caption (p. 574) above the word PEOPLE.

③ Normally when the "People" or the state brings an action, it is a criminal case. This is an appellate court decision. Trial court decisions are appealed to the appellate court. The "appellant" is the party bringing the appeal because of dissatisfaction with the ruling or decision of the lower court. California brought the case as the plaintiff and prosecutor in the lower court (Superior Court, County of San Mateo) and is now the appellant in the higher court (Court of Appeal, First District, Division 1).

④ Bruni was the defendant in the lower court since he was being sued or, in this case, charged with a crime. The appeal is taken against him by the People (appellant) because the lower court ruling was favorable to Bruni to the dissatisfaction of the People. The party against whom a case is brought on appeal is called the "respondent." Another word for respondent is "appellee."

⑤ "CR. 10096" means the docket or calendar number of the case. "Cr." stands for "criminal."

⑥ The first step that you should take when reading a case is to make careful note of the name of the court writing the opinion. As soon as possible, you must learn the hierarchy of courts in your state as well as the federal hierarchy (p. 333). In many states, there are three levels of courts: trial level, middle appeal level, and supreme level. (Most cases are appealed from the trial court to the middle appeal level, and then to the supreme level.) Here, we know from the title of the court (Court of Appeal) that it is an appellate court. It is not the supreme court, because in California the highest court is the California Supreme Court.

The name of the court is significant because of "legal authority" (p. 561). If the court is the highest or supreme court of the state, then the case would be applicable throughout the state. A middle appeals court decision, on the other hand, applies only in the area of the state over which it has jurisdiction. When you see that the opinion has been written by a trial or middle appeals court, you are immediately put on notice that you must check to determine whether the case was ever appealed subsequent to the date of the opinion before you. This checking is called shepardizing (p. 614). Even Supreme Court opinions should be shepardized to determine whether anything further has happened to the case.

⑦ When a case is being cited, only the year (here, 1972) is used, not the month or day. April 27, 1972, is the date of the decision. Sometimes, the date of the hearing or rehearing will be given as well as the date of the decision. The latter date is still the critical one for citation purposes.

⑧ Here the editors provide the reader with a summary of what the opinion says. The court did not write this summary; the editors did. It, therefore, is not an official statement of the law. It is merely an aid to the reader. You quickly read this summary to determine whether the opinion covers the areas of law in which you are interested.

⑨ Here continues the unofficial summary, providing the reader with what procedurally must happen as a result of the April 27 opinion.

⑩ These are editor's headnotes (p. 544), which are small-paragraph summaries of portions of the opinion. As we saw earlier, these paragraphs are sometimes referred to as the syllabus (p. 614) of the opinion. When the editors first read the opinion, they decide how many major topics or issues are covered in the opinion. Each of these topics is summarized in a headnote, all of which are then given consecutive numbers, here 1 and 2. These numbers correspond with the bracketed numbers [1] and [2] in the opinion itself. (See ⑩ₐ.) If, for example, you wanted to read the portion of the opinion that was summarized in the second headnote of the opinion, you would go to the text of the opinion that begins with the bracketed [2].

The headnotes also have a topic and a key number, here "Searches and Seizures☞3.8(1)." Each headnote will also be printed in the digest system of the West Publishing Company (p. 600). You can find out what other courts have said about the same or similar points in the paragraph headnotes by going to the digest volumes, looking up the key topic and number of the headnote

(Searches and Seizures ⊕ 3.8(1)), and reading summary paragraphs from other court opinions (p. 601).

⑪ Here are the attorneys that represented the appellant and respondent on appeal. Note that the attorney general's office represented the People. The attorney general or the district attorney's office represents the state in criminal cases.

⑫ The opinion begins with the name of the judge who wrote the opinion, Judge Smith. In this spot you will sometimes find the words "The Court," "Per curium," or "Memorandum Opinion," which simply means that the court decided not to mention the name of any individual judge.

⑬ In reading or briefing a case, make note of the judicial history of the case to date. The lower court dismissed the information (similar to an indictment) against Bruni after certain evidence was suppressed (i.e., declared inadmissible), and the People appealed this dismissal judgment.

If the words "information" or "suppression" are new to you, look them up in a legal dictionary before proceeding. Do this for every strange word.

⑭ It is critical to state the facts of the case accurately. Here the facts are relatively simple: A search warrant that said "daytime" service was served at 9:30 P.M., and evidence was taken pursuant to this search warrant. Defendant objected to the admission of this evidence at trial. In most cases, the facts are not this simple. The facts are sometimes given at the beginning of the opinion, as here, and other times they are scattered throughout the opinion. If you confront the latter situation, you must carefully read the entire case to piece the facts together. The facts are critical because you must assess how analogous or similar the facts of your own problem are to those of the case you are reading (assuming that the issues in the problem are covered in the case at all). If your facts are the same or substantially the same as the key facts of the case, then the law of the case will probably apply to your problem (p. 378). If the facts of your problem are somewhat the same and somewhat different from those of the case, then it is much more debatable whether the case is analogous and therefore whether the law of the case applies.

⑮ The next critical stage of reading a case is to state the issue (or issues) that the court was deciding in the case. This can sometimes be a difficult task, since many opinions are long and complicated. Judges often ramble. The issue in *People v. Bruni* is not difficult to state: Is evidence that was obtained pursuant to a daytime warrant but served at 9:30 P.M. admissible when there is an inconsistency in the statutes as to when service must take place?

The court does not quote extensively from any of the relevant statutes. You should find the full statutes in your library and read them on your own if you think it would aid you in following what the court is saying. If, for example, you want to read the entire version of section 1533 before and after the amendment, you would go to the California statutes, look up the Penal Code and find section 1533. Check the historical note following the statute (p. 650) for references to the 1970 amendment.

According to the court, section 1533 is inconsistent with section 1529. Section 1529 requires a "daytime" service. The legal issue, stated another way, is whether section 1529 was amended by implication. If so, then the 9:30 P.M.

INTRODUCTION TO PARALEGALISM

search was valid (since service would be authorized up to 10:00 P.M.) and the evidence derived therefrom is admissible in court (if otherwise valid).

⑯ The court refers to other statutes to support the conclusion it will reach. Note the interrelationship of the statutory sections. One statute is interpreted by interpreting other statutes. Section 4 of the Penal Code ("Pen.Code") says that the sections of the Penal Code are to be interpreted ("construed") rationally in order to carry out their purpose or objective and promote justice. Section 1859 of the Code of Civil Procedure ("Code Civ.Proc.") says that when there is a general and a particular section that are inconsistent, the latter is preferred.

The sequence of statutory interrelationship in this case is as follows:

1. Section 1529 of the Penal Code says "daytime."
2. Section 7 of the Penal Code defines daytime as sunrise to sunset.
3. Section 1533 of the Penal Code as amended says between 7:00 A.M. and 10:00 P.M.
4. Section 4 of Penal Code and section 1859 of the Code of Civil Procedure provide principles of interpreting statutes that are inconsistent.

⑰ In the same manner, a court will refer to other cases to support its ruling. In this way, the court argues that the other cases are precedent for the case before the court. The court in *People v. Bruni* is saying that *Dept. of Motor Vehicles of California v. Indus. Acc. Com.* and *Tidwell v. Superior Court* are precedents for its own ruling.

⑱ Here is the reasoning of the court to support its ruling. If there is a general statute and a specific statute that are inconsistent, the court will adopt the interpretation that is consistent with the purpose of the statutory scheme. Specific provisions are preferred over general ones. This is what the legislature must have intended. Otherwise the specific amendment to section 1529 would be without effect and the ends of justice would not be promoted.

⑲ The result or holding of the court's deliberation of the issue must then be weeded out of the opinion. In this opinion, as in most, the result is stated in a number of places. The result is that section 1529 was impliedly amended to authorize service up to 10:00 P.M.

⑳ The procedural consequences of the court's resolution of the issue are then usually stated, as here, toward the very end of the opinion. The judgment of the lower court is reversed. The lower court cannot continue to suppress (i.e., declare inadmissible) the evidence seized at the 9:30 P.M. search.

An appeals court could take a number of positions with respect to a lower court's decision, e.g., affirm it: modify it (reverse it only in part); remand the case (send it back to the lower court) with instructions on how to proceed or how to retry the case.

㉑ In theory, a judge must be very precise in defining the issue before the court, and in resolving only that issue. The judge should not say any more than *must* be said in order to decide the case. This theory, however, is sometimes not observed. Judges will go off on tangents, give long dissertations or "speeches" through their opinions. As indicated, this can make your job more difficult; you must wade through all the words to identify (1) the key facts, (2) the precise issues, (3) the precise reasoning, and (4) the precise result.

The worst tangent that a judge can stray into is called *dictum* (p. 565). Dictum is a judge's or court's view of what the law is or might be on facts that are *not* before the court. Judge Smith indicated that the result of the case might be different if the warrant was not specific, e.g., if it did not name the individual to be searched or what the investigator was looking for. This was not the situation in the *Bruni* case; therefore Judge Smith's commentary or speculation is dictum.

(22) On any court there may be several judges. They do not always agree on what should be done in a case. The majority controls. In *Bruni,* Judge Smith wrote the majority opinion. A concurring opinion is one that votes with the majority but adds its own views about the case. In *Bruni,* Judge Jones concurred but specified that he accepted only the result of Judge Smith's opinion. Normally, judges in such situations will write an opinion indicating their own point of view. Judge Jones did not choose to write an opinion. He simply let it be known that he did not necessarily agree with everything Judge Smith said; all he agreed with was the conclusion, i.e., that the warrant was validly served. To reach this result, Judge Jones might have used different reasoning, relied on different cases as precedent, etc.

(23) A dissenting opinion disagrees in part or in full with the result reached by the majority. Dissenting opinions are sometimes heated. Of course, the dissenter's opinion is not controlling. It is often valuable to read, however, in order to determine what the dissenter thinks that the majority decided.

Having studied the *Bruni* case in this way, you should prepare a seven-part *brief:*

1. FACTS: A search warrant that said "daytime" service was served at 9:30 P.M. Evidence was obtained during this search. The People (state) attempted to introduce this evidence at trial. Defendant Bruni objected.

2. JUDICIAL HISTORY: The trial court dismissed the Information against Bruni after refusing to consider the evidence seized pursuant to an improperly served warrant.

3. ISSUE: When section 1533 of the Penal Code was amended to allow service between 7:00 A.M. and 10:00 P.M., did the legislature impliedly also amend section 1529, which continued to require daytime service so that evidence obtained pursuant to a warrant served at 9:30 P.M. can be admitted into evidence?

4. RESULT or HOLDING: Section 1529 was impliedly amended to conform to section 1533. The evidence seized pursuant to the search warrant can be admitted.

5. REASONING: Courts will try to reconcile statutes that are inconsistent. If a general statute is inconsistent with a specific statute, the court will adopt the latter whenever possible to promote justice. The intent and purpose of the statutory scheme is controlling.

6. PROCEDURAL CONSEQUENCES: The trial court's dismissal of the Information is reversed. The trial must resume, and the evidence cannot be excluded on the basis of the time of service.

7. SUBSEQUENT JUDICIAL HISTORY: As of the date of this brief, [here state whether there have been any subsequent decisions in this litigation;

you obtain this information by shepardizing (p. 614) the case you are briefing].

The particular style or format in briefing a case is a matter of personal choice. The important factor is to have all the components of a brief presented. The order or format of the presentation is not significant.

ASSIGNMENT 78

Brief the following opinions:

(a) *Quinn v. Lum & Cronin, Fried, Sekiya & Kekina,* p. 381.
(b) *United States v. Kovel,* p. 894.
(c) *United States v. Cabra,* p. 897.

FINDING CASE LAW

In searching for case law, you will probably find yourself in one or more of the following situations:

- You already have one opinion on point, p. 563 (or close to being on point), and you want to find additional opinions on point.
- You are looking for opinions interpreting a statute, constitution, charter, ordinance, court rule, or regulation that you already have.
- You are starting from point zero. You want to find case law when you do not have a case, statute, or other law to begin with. You may be looking for opinions containing common law (which is judge-made law in the absence of controlling statutory or constitutional law), and you have no such opinions to begin with.

The following search techniques are not necessarily listed in the order in which they should be tried. Your goal is to know how to use all of them. In practice, you can vary the order of using the techniques.

First a reminder about doing the first level of legal research: background research. You should review the checklist for background research presented earlier (p. 597). While doing this research, you will probably come across laws that will be of help to you on the specific facts of your problem (which is the second level of research). If so, you may already have some case law. You now want to find more.

TECHNIQUES FOR FINDING CASE LAW WHEN YOU ALREADY HAVE ONE CASE ON POINT
1. *Shepardize the case that you have.* (See Checklist #4a on shepardizing cases, p. 617.) In the columns of Shepard's, look for cases that have mentioned your case. Such cases will probably cover similar topics.
2. *Go to the West digests.* There are two ways to do this:
(a) Go to the table of cases in all the digests that cover the court that wrote the case you already have, e.g., the table of cases in the American Digest System. The table of cases will tell you what key topics and numbers your case

is digested under in the main volumes of the digest. Find your case digested under those key topics and numbers. Look for other case law under the same key topics and numbers.

(b) Go to the West Reporter (p. 528) that contains the full text of the case you already have. At the beginning of this case in the reporter, find the headnotes and their key topics and numbers. Take the key topics and numbers (that are relevant to your problem) into the digests of West to find more case law.

(See Checklist #2 on using digests, p. 603.)

3. *Find an annotation.* First identify the main topics or issues in the case you already have. Use the Quick Indexes on ALR, ALR2d, ALR3d, ALR4th, and ALR Fed to try to find annotations on the same or similar topics. Once you have such an annotation, you will be given extensive citations to case law. (See Checklist #3 on finding annotations, p. 608.)

4. *Find a discussion of your case in the legal periodicals.* Go to the table of cases in the Index of Legal Periodicals (ILP), the Current Law Index (CLI), and the Legal Resource Index (LRI). There you will be told if your case was analyzed (noted) in the periodicals. If so, the discussion may give you additional case law on the same topic. (See Checklist #6 on finding legal periodical literature, p. 628.)

5. *Go to Words and Phrases.* Identify the major words or phrases that are dealt with in the case you have. Check the definition of those words and phrases in the multi-volume legal dictionary, Words and Phrases (p. 545). By so doing you will be led to other cases defining the same words or phrases.

Now let us assume that you already have a statute and you want case law interpreting that statute. The techniques for doing so are as follows (many of which are the same when seeking case law interpreting constitutions, regulations, etc.):

TECHNIQUES FOR FINDING CASE LAW INTERPRETING A STATUTE

1. *Shepardize the statute that you have.* (See Checklist #4b on shepardizing statutes, p. 621.) In the columns of Shepard's, look for cases that have mentioned your statute.

2. *Examine your statute in the statutory code.* At the end of your statute in the statutory code, there are paragraph summaries of cases (often called Notes of Decisions) that have interpreted your statute. Check these summaries in the bound volume of the code, in the pocket part of this volume, and in any supplemental pamphlets at the end of the code. (See p. 650.) (For federal statutes, the codes to check are U.S.C.A. and U.S.C.S., p. 557. The U.S.C. will not have such case summaries.)

3. *Find an annotation on your statute.* If your statute is a federal statute, check the "Table of Laws and Regulations Cited in ALR Fed" found within a separate volume called ALR Fed Tables of Cases, Laws, Regs. (See Checklist #3, p. 608.) If your statute is a state statute, you must check the various Quick Indexes for the five sets of annotations (p. 606) to see if there are annotations under the topic headings of your statute. The annotations will lead you to more case law on the statute.

4. *Find legal periodical literature on your statute.* There are three ways to do this:
   (a) Shepardize the statute. (See technique 1 above.) Citing material for a statute includes legal periodical literature.
   (b) Check the table of statutes in the Current Law Index (CLI), the Legal Resource Index (LRI), and the Index to Legal Periodicals (ILP), p. 626.
   (c) Go to the subject indexes in ILP, CLI, and LRI and check the topics of your statute.

5. *Go to loose-leaf services on your statute.* Find out if there is a loose-leaf service on the subject matter of your statute. Such services often give extensive cites to cases on the statute. (See Checklist #5 on loose-leaf services, p. 625.)
6. *Go to treatises on your statute.* Most major statutes have treatises on them that contain extensive cites to cases on the statute. (See Checklist #8 on treatises, p. 630.)
7. *Shepardize any cases you found through techniques 1–6 above.* You may be led to additional case law on the statute.

Finally, we assume that you are starting from scratch. You are looking for case law and you do not have a starting case or statute with which to begin. You may be looking for common law and/or for cases interpreting statutes that you have not found yet.

TECHNIQUES FOR FINDING CASE LAW WHEN YOU DO NOT HAVE A CASE OR STATUTE TO BEGIN WITH

1. *Go to the West digests.* CARTWHEEL your research problem (p. 591) to try to find key topics and numbers in the Descriptive Word Indexes (DWI) of the West digests. (See Checklist #2 on using digests of West, p. 603.)
2. *Go to the annotations.* CARTWHEEL your research problem to try to locate annotations through the Quick Indexes of ALR, ALR2d, ALR3d, ALR4th, and ALR Fed. (See Checklist #3 on finding annotations, p. 608).
3. *Treatises.* CARTWHEEL your research problem to try to find treatises in the card catalog. (See Checklist #8 on finding treatises, p. 630.)
4. *Loose-leaf services.* Find out if there are loose-leaf services on the topics of your research. (See Checklist #5 on finding loose-leaf services, p. 625.)
5. *Legal periodical literature.* CARTWHEEL your research problem to try to find legal periodical literature in the subject indexes of ILP, CLI, and LRI. (See Checklist #6 on finding legal periodical literature, p. 628.)
6. *Legal encyclopedias.* Go to the indexes on Am.Jur.2d and C.J.S. CARTWHEEL your research problem to try to find discussions in these legal encyclopedias through their indexes. (See Checklist #7 on using legal encyclopedias, p. 630.)
7. *Computers* (p. 632).
8. *Phone and mail research.* Find an expert. (See Checklist #9 on doing phone and mail research, p. 631.)
9. *Words and Phrases.* Identify all the major words or phrases from the facts of your research problem. Look up these words or phrases in the multi-volume legal dictionary, Words and Phrases (p. 545), which gives case law definitions.
10. *Shepardize.* If techniques 1–9 above lead you to any case law, shepardize what you have found in order to look for more cases. (See Checklist #4a on shepardizing a case, p. 617.)

Section Q. READING AND FINDING STATUTES

READING STATUTES

Here is an example of a statute from a New York statutory code (p. 557). The circled numbers on p. 649 are explained below and on p. 650.

① Here you find the section number of the statute. The mark "§" before "146" means section.

② This is a heading summarization of the contents of the statute. Section 146 covers who can visit state prisons in New York. This summarization was

§ 146.   Persons authorized to visit prisons

The following persons shall be authorized to visit at pleasure all state prisons: The governor and lieutenant-governor, commissioner of general services, secretary of state, comptroller and attorney-general, members of the commission of correction, members of the legislature, judges of the court of appeals, supreme court and county judges, district attorneys and every minister of the gospel having charge of a congregation in the town wherein any such prison is situated. No other person not otherwise authorized by law shall be permitted to enter a state prison except under such regulations as the commissioner of correction shall prescribe. The provisions of this section shall not apply to such portion of a prison in which prisoners under sentence of death are confined.

As amended L.1962, c. 37, § 3, eff. Feb. 20, 1962.

Historical Note

L.1962, c. 37, § 3, eff. Feb. 20, 1962, substituted "commissioner of general services" for "superintendent of standards and purchase".

Derivation. Prior to the general amendment of this chapter by L.1929, c. 243, the subject matter of this section was contained in former Prison Law, § 160; originally derived from R.S., pt. 4, c. 3, tit. 3, § 159, as amended L.1847, c. 460.

Cross References

Promoting prison contraband, see Penal Law, §§ 205.20, 205.25.

Library References

Prisons ⊂⊃13.
Reformatories ⊂⊃7.

C.J.S. Prisons §§ 18, 19.
C.J.S. Reformatories §§ 10, 11.

Notes of Decisions

1. Attorneys

Warden of maximum security prison was justified in requiring that interviews of prisoners by attorney be conducted in presence of guard in room, in view of fact that attorney, who sought to interview 34 inmates in a day and a half, had shown no retainer agreements and had not stated purpose of consultations. Kahn v. La Vallee, 1961, 12 A.D.2d 832, 209 N.Y.S.2d 591.

Supreme court did not have jurisdiction of petition by prisoner to compel prison warden to provide facilities in prison which would not interfere with alleged violation of rights of prisoner to confer in private with his attorney. Mummiani v. La Vallee, 1959, 21 Misc.2d 437, 199 N.Y.S.2d 263, affirmed 12 A.D.2d 832, 209 N.Y.S.2d 591.

Right of prisoners to confer with counsel after conviction is not absolute but is subject to such regulations as commissioner of correction may prescribe, and prisoners were not entitled to confer with their attorney privately within sight, but outside of hearing of a prison guard, when warden insisted on having a guard present in order to insure against any impropriety or infraction of prison rules and regulations during interview. Id.

written by the private publishing company, not by the New York state legislature.

③ Here is the body of the statute written by the legislature.

④ At the end of a statutory section you will often find a reference to session laws (p. 618), using abbreviations such as L. (laws), P.L. (Public Law), Stat. (Statutes at Large), etc. Here you are told that in the Laws (L) of 1962, chapter (c) 37, section 3, this statute was changed or amended. The Laws referred to are the session laws. See the Historical Note ⑥ below for a further treatment of this amendment.

⑤ The amendment to section 146 was effective ("eff.") on February 20, 1962. The amendment may have been passed by the legislature on an earlier date, but the date on which it became the law of New York was February 20, 1962.

⑥ The Historical Note provides the reader with some of the legislative history (p. 655) of section 146. First, the reader is again told that section 146 was amended in 1962. Note that in the second and third lines of the body of the statute, the title "commissioner of general services" is found. The 1962 amendment simply changed the title from "superintendent of standards and purchase" to "commissioner of general services."

⑦ Also, part of the Historical Note is the "Derivation" section. This tells the reader that the topic of section 146 of the Corrections Law was once contained in section 160 of the Prison Law, which dates back to 1847. In 1929 there was another amendment. The Historical Note was written by the private publisher, not by the New York state legislature.

⑧ The "Cross References" refer the reader to other statutes that cover topics similar to section 146.

⑨ The "Library References" refer the reader to other texts that address the subject area of the statute. On the left-hand side, there are two topics, "Prisons" and "Reformatories," each followed by key numbers. The key numbers refer the reader to the digests of West Publishing Company (p. 535). On the right column there is the abbreviation C.J.S. (Corpus Juris Secundum), a legal encyclopedia (p. 534).

⑩ The most important research reference is the "Notes of Decisions." It includes a series of paragraphs that briefly summarize every court decision that has interpreted or applied section 146. Of course, the decisions can only cover cases decided before the book was published. For later decisions, the reader must look to the pocket part (p. 590) of the volume and to any supplemental pamphlets at the end of the code. The first decision that treated section 146 was *Kahn v. La Vallee*. Next is *Mummiani v. La Vallee*. At the end of the final paragraph, you will find "Id.," which means that the paragraph refers to the case cited in the immediately preceding paragraph, the *Mummiani* case.

With this perspective of what an annotated statute looks like, we turn to some general guidelines on understanding statutes.

1. Statutory Codes Are Heavily Stratified

A statutory code can contain anywhere from 5 to 150 volumes. If you are unfamiliar with a particular code, you should examine the first few pages of the first volume. There you will usually find the subject matter arrangement of all the volumes, e.g., "agency," "corrections," "corporations." Different states often have different labels and categorization schemes.

An individual subject matter in a code may be further broken down into titles, parts, articles, or chapters, which are then broken down into sections and subsections. Here is an example of a possible categorization for the state of "X":

> X Code Annotated
> Title 1. Corporate Law
> Chapter 1. Forming a Corporation
> Section 1. Choosing a Corporate Name
> Subsection 1(a). Where to File the Name Application
> Subsection 1(b). Displaying the Name Certificate
> Subsection 1(c). Changing the Corporate Name
> Section 2 . . . .
> Chapter 2 . . . .
> Etc.

Note again, however, that each jurisdiction may adopt its own classification terminology. What is called a chapter in one state may be called a title in another.

You also need to be sensitive to the internal context of a particular statutory section. A section is often a sub-sub-subunit of larger units.

> Example: Examine section 1183 on p. 652. Section 1183 is within Part II of Subchapter II, which is within chapter 12 of title 8.

As indicated earlier, a jurisdiction may completely revise its labeling system (p. 589). What was once "Prison Law," for example, may now fall under the topic heading of "Corrections Law." What was once section 73(b) of "Corporations Law" may now be section 13(f) of the "Business and Professions Law." If such a reordering has occurred, the researcher should be able to find out about it either in a transfer table at the beginning of one of the code volumes or in the Historical Note at the bottom of the section.

2. A Common Sequence of Statutes on Administrative Agencies
Statutes are carried out mainly by administrative agencies. The agency may be a grant-making or service agency (e.g., Social Security Administration) or a regulatory agency (e.g., Federal Power Commission, State Utilities Commission). Statutes that cover agencies are sometimes organized in the following sequence:

a. The agency is created;
b. The major words and phrases used in this cluster of statutes are defined;
c. The agency is given a name;
d. The administrators of the agency are given titles and powers;
e. The budgetary process of the agency is specified;
f. The method by which the public first comes into contact with the agency is established, e.g., how to apply for the benefits or services of the agency;

g. The way in which the agency must act when a citizen complains about the agency's actions is established;

h. The way in which the agency must go about terminating a citizen from its services is established;

i. The way in which a citizen can appeal to a court, if not satisfied with the way the agency handled his or her complaint, is established.

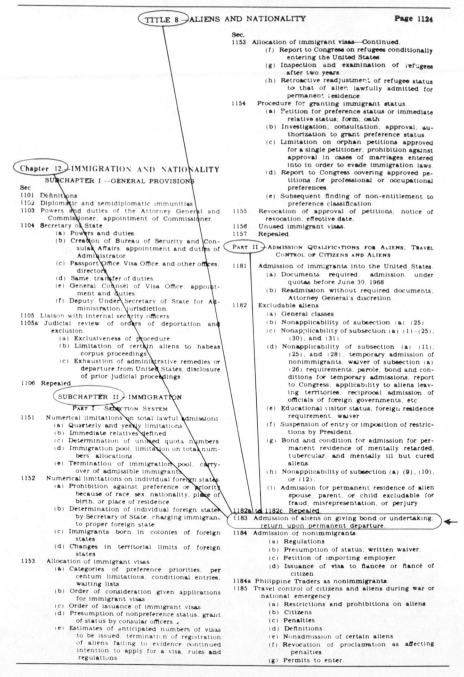

3. All Statutes Must Be Based Upon Some Provision in the Constitution Giving the Legislature the Power to Pass the Statute

Legislatures have no power to legislate without constitutional authorization. The authorization may be the general constitutional provision vesting all legislative powers in the legislature, or, more often, it will be a specific provision such as the authority to raise revenue through issuing bonds.

4. Statutory Language Tends to Be Unclear

Seldom, if ever, is it absolutely clear what a statute means or how it applies to a given set of facts. Because of this, statutory language regularly requires close scrutiny and interpretation.

5. Statutes Are to Be Read Line by Line, Pronoun by Pronoun, Punctuation Mark by Punctuation Mark

Statutes cannot be speed read. They should be read with the same care that you would use if you were translating a foreign language to English. All too often, for example, the careless reader will read "or" when the statute says "and."

Reading statutes is something that you must become familiar with. The style of statutory writing can be very painful. Sentences sometimes appear endless, and there are often so many qualifications and exceptions built into the statute that it appears incomprehensible. Don't despair. The key is perseverance and a willingness to tackle the statute slowly, piece by piece.

6. Check to See if a Statutory Unit Has a Definition Section

At the beginning of a cluster of statutes, look for a definition section. If it exists, the section will define a number of words used in the remaining sections of the unit. Here is an example of such a definition section:

> **§ 31.** **Definitions.**—As used in this article, unless the context shall require otherwise, the following terms shall have the meanings ascribed to them by this section:
>
> 1. "State" shall mean and include any state, territory or possession of the United States and the District of Columbia.
>
> 2. "Court" shall mean the family court of the state of New York; when the context requires, it shall mean and include a court of another state defined in and upon which appropriate jurisdiction has been conferred by a substantially similar reciprocal law.
>
> 3. "Child" includes a step child, foster child, child born out of wedlock or legally adopted child and means a child under twenty-one years of age, and a son or daughter twenty-one years of age or older who is unable to maintain himself or herself and is or is likely to become a public charge.
>
> 4. "Dependent" shall mean and include any person who is entitled to support pursuant to this article.

7. Statutes Should Be Briefed

Briefing a statute simply means outlining it and breaking it down into its elements (p. 373). The following are some of the questions that you should ask yourself in briefing a statute:

  a. What is the citation (the name of the statutory code, volume of the code, number of the section, date of the code edition)? See p. 577.

b. To whom is the statute addressed? (To everybody? To the director of an agency? To citizens who want to do certain things?) Who is the audience of this particular statute?

c. Does the statute make reference to other statutes? (If so, then the statute may be unintelligible without also studying the other statutes.)

d. Is there a condition that will make the statute operative? (Very often the statute will have a "whenever" or a "wherever" clause indicating that whenever a certain set of facts occur, the statute will be applied; without the occurrence of the facts, the statute may not apply.)

e. What or whom does the statute specifically *include* in its provisions?

f. What or whom does the statute specifically *exclude* from its provisions?

g. Is the statute mandatory or discretionary? (Does it say or imply that someone "must" or "shall" do something, or does it say or imply that someone "may" or "can" do something?)

h. Briefly summarize, in your own words, what the statute means to you.

FINDING STATUTORY LAW

TECHNIQUES FOR FINDING STATUTES
1. Go to the statutory code in which you are interested. Some states have more than one statutory code. For federal statutes, there is the United States Code (U.S.C.), the United States Code Annotated (U.S.C.A.), and the United States Code Service (U.S.C.S.). (See p. 557.) Know how to use all available statutory codes that cover the same set of statutes. While they contain the same statutes, the index and research features will differ.
2. Read the explanation or preface pages at the beginning of the first volume of the statutory code. Also read the comparable pages at the beginning of the Shepard's volumes that will enable you to shepardize statutes in that code. These pages can be very helpful in explaining the structure of the code, particularly if there have been new editions, revisions, or renumberings.
3. Most statutory codes have general indexes at the end of the set as well as individual indexes for separate volumes. Use the CARTWHEEL to help you use these indexes (p. 591). Also check any tables of contents that exist. Some statutes have popular names, e.g., the Civil Rights Act of 1964. If you know the popular name of a statute you can find it in the statutory code through the code's popular name table.
4. While reading one statute in the code, you may be given a cross-reference to another statute within the same code. Check out these cross-references.
5. Loose-leaf services. Find out if there is a loose-leaf service on the topics of your research. Such services will give extensive references to applicable statutes. (See Checklist #5 on finding and using loose-leaf services, p. 625.)
6. Treatises. Find out if there are treatises on the topics of your research. Such treatises will often give extensive references to applicable statutes. (See Checklist #8 on finding and using treatises, p. 630.)
7. Legal periodical literature. Consult the Index to Legal Periodicals (ILP), the Current Law Index (CLI), and the Legal Resource Index (LRI). Use the CARTWHEEL to help you locate periodical literature in these indexes on the topics of your research. This literature will often give extensive references to applicable statutes. (See Checklist #6 on finding legal periodical literature, p. 628.)
8. Annotations. Use the Quick Indexes for ALR, ALR2d, ALR3d, ALR4th, and ALR Fed. The CARTWHEEL will help you locate annotations. Annotations

will sometimes refer you to statutes—particularly in ALR Fed for federal statutes. (See Checklist #3 on finding and updating annotations, p. 608.)

9. Legal encyclopedias. Occasionally, legal encyclopedias will give you references to statutes. Use the CARTWHEEL for gaining access to Am.Jur.2d and C.J.S. (See Checklist #7 for using legal encyclopedias, p. 630.)

10. Computers. (See p. 632.)

11. Phone and mail research. Try to find an expert. (See Checklist #9 on doing phone and mail research, p. 631.)

12. For every federal statute that you find, determine whether there are federal regulations on that statute. To find out, check the Parallel Table of Statutory Authorities and Rules (Table 1) in the C.F.R. Index volume.

13. Shepardize any statute that you locate through techniques 1–11 above. (See Checklist #4b on shepardizing a statute, p. 621.)

14. Check the legislative history of important statutes (p. 655).

15. Also update any statute that you find in the statutory code by checking the pocket part of the volume you are using, supplementary pamphlets at the end of the code, bound supplement volumes, etc.

16. Occasionally in your research you will come across a statute that is cited in its session law form (p. 618). To find this statute in the statutory code, you must translate the session law cite into the codified cite. This is done by trying to find transfer tables in the statutory code. For federal statutes, a Statute at Large cite is translated into a U.S.C./U.S.C.A./U.S.C.S. cite by:

    (a) Checking Table III in the Tables volume of U.S.C./U.S.C.A./U.S.C.S. (p. 621).

    (b) Checking Table 2 in U.S. Code Congressional & Administrative News (p. 559).

Some session laws, however, are never printed in the statutory code. Hence there is no codified cite for such statutes. You must go directly to the session laws in the library—if the library has them. (For federal statutes, the session laws are in United States Statutes at Large, p. 559.) It is also possible to shepardize session laws that are not codified, p. 619.

Section R. LEGISLATIVE HISTORY

In this section, we consider four themes:

1. The historical context of a statute
2. Why researchers search for legislative history
3. The controversy over the use of legislative history
4. Finding legislative history

1. THE HISTORICAL CONTEXT OF A STATUTE

Pages 657–658 contain an outline of the steps that a bill goes through before it becomes a statute. The chart assumes that the legislature considering the bill is bicameral, i.e., consists of two houses. The two houses are referred to as the House and the Senate. (In some legislatures the houses may have different names, e.g., the Assembly and the Senate.) Legislatures with only one house are called unicameral. Very few state legislatures are unicameral. Local legislatures, however, such as city councils, are often unicameral.

The process of enactment can involve six major stages:

a. Proposal
b. Initial committee consideration
c. Floor debate
d. Conference committee consideration
e. Floor debate
f. Signature of the chief executive

The legislative history of a statute is what occurs at each of these stages.

a. Proposal

The idea for a statute can come from many sources. The chief executive of the government (e.g., president, governor) may initiate the process by sending the legislature a message in which the reasons for a proposed law are stated. Frequently an administrative agency has made a study of a problem, which is the impetus for the proposal. The agency will usually be the entity with responsibility for administrating the proposal if it is enacted into law.

The bar association may prepare a report to the legislature calling for the new legislation. The legislature or chief executive may have established a special commission to study the need for changes in the law and to propose changes where appropriate. The commission might consist of members of the legislature and outside experts. In some states there are ongoing law revision commissions that frequently make proposals for legislation. In many areas there are councils of government made up of neighboring governments. Such councils often study problems and propose legislative changes. The National Conference of Commissioners on Uniform State Laws is an organization with members from each state. The conference makes proposals to the state legislatures for the enactment of laws where it deems uniformity to be desirable.

Finally, the idea for the legislation may be generated within the legislature itself. An individual legislator can always propose a bill. One or both houses of the legislature may have established an investigating committee to examine a problem and propose legislation where needed.

b. Initial Committee Consideration

The next step is for a member of the legislature to introduce the bill. This introduction is usually accompanied by a statement as to why the bill should be enacted. The bill may be introduced in only one of the houses or in both houses simultaneously by a member of each house. If the latter option is not used, the bill will often be introduced in the other house after it has been considered by the first house. As bills are introduced, they are assigned a consecutive number (e.g., S 250 is the 250th bill introduced in the Senate during the current session; HR 1753 is the 1753rd bill introduced in the House of Representatives during the current session).

Once the bill is introduced, it follows a similar procedure in each house. The bill is sent to the committee with responsibility over the subject matter of the bill, e.g., a bill to change the criminal law might go to the Judiciary Committee. The initial draft of the bill might be considered by this committee and by one of its subcommittees. Hearings are held. Citizens and public officials

The Legislative History of a Statute—How a Bill Becomes a Law

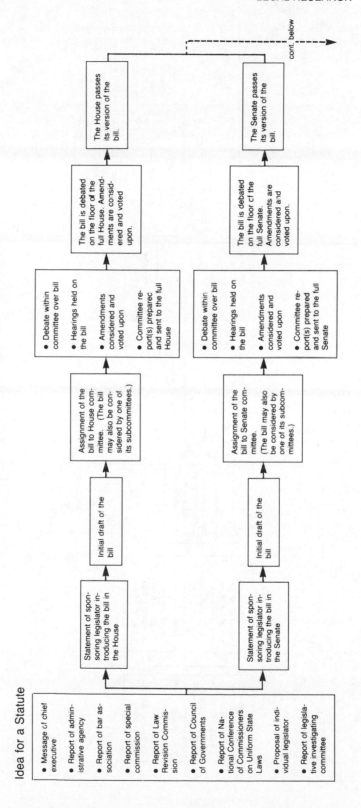

Idea for a Statute

- Message of chief executive
- Report of administrative agency
- Report of bar association
- Report of special commission
- Report of Law Revision Commission
- Report of Council of Governments
- Report of National Conference of Commissioners on Uniform State Laws
- Proposal of individual legislator
- Report of legislative investigating committee

Statement of sponsoring legislator introducing the bill in the House

Initial draft of the bill

Assignment of the bill to House committee. (The bill may also be considered by one of its subcommittees.)

- Debate within committee over bill
- Hearings held on the bill
- Amendments considered and voted upon
- Committee report(s) prepared and sent to the full House

The bill is debated on the floor of the full House. Amendments are considered and voted upon.

The House passes its version of the bill.

Statement of sponsoring legislator introducing the bill in the Senate

Initial draft of the bill

Assignment of the bill to Senate committee. (The bill may also be considered by one of its subcommittees.)

- Debate within committee over bill
- Hearings held on the bill
- Amendments considered and voted upon
- Committee report(s) prepared and sent to the full Senate

The bill is debated on the floor of the full Senate. Amendments are considered and voted upon.

The Senate passes its version of the bill.

cont. below

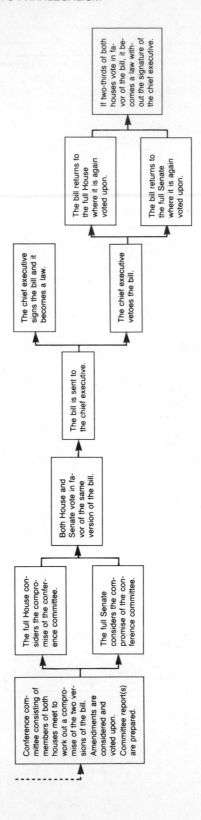

give testimony for or against the bill. In some legislatures this testimony is transcribed so that a word-for-word record is made available. Legislators often propose amendments to the bill, which are voted upon by the committee. The committee then issues a report summarizing why the bill is needed and what its major provisions are. If there is disagreement on the committee, a minority report is often prepared.

c. Floor Debate

The bill with its accompanying report(s) then goes to the floor of the house of which the committee is a part. The bill is debated by the full house. During the debate, which will usually be recorded or transcribed, questions are asked by members as to the meaning of certain provisions in the bill: what is covered and what is not. Amendments are often made from the floor and voted upon.

d. Conference Committee Consideration

Since both houses act independently of each other in considering the bill, it is rare that they will both produce the exact same bill. Inevitably, the amendment process leads to different versions of the proposed law. To resolve these differences, a conference committee is established consisting of key members of both houses, e.g., the chairpersons of the committees that initially considered the bill, the members who first introduced or sponsored the bill. A compromise is attempted in the conference committee. Amendments are considered and a final report of the conference committee is issued. Dissenting members of the committee might prepare a minority report. The majority report summarizes the major terms of the compromise and explains why it should be enacted by each house.

e. Floor Debate

The conference committee compromise then goes back to the floor of each house where more debate, explanations, and amendments are considered. Again, everything is usually recorded or transcribed. If both houses pass the same version of the bill, usually by a majority vote, it goes to the chief executive.

f. Chief Executive

The bill becomes law if the chief executive signs it. When it is signed, the chief executive will sometimes make a statement as to why this action is being taken. If he or she vetoes or refuses to sign the bill, it goes back to the legislature, often with an explanation as to why it is being disapproved. If a designated number of legislators (usually two-thirds) in each house still vote in favor of the bill, it becomes law over the objection of the chief executive.

2. WHY SEARCH FOR LEGISLATIVE HISTORY: ADVOCACY OBJECTIVES

Problem: In 1975 the state legislature enacts the Liquor Control Act, which provides in § 33 that "Liquor shall not be sold on Sunday or on any day on which a local, state, or federal election is being held." The Fairfax Country Club claims that § 33 does not apply to the sale of liquor on Sunday or on election day *by membership clubs;* it applies only to bars that provide service to any customers that come in off the street. The question, therefore, is whether the legislature intended to include membership clubs within the restrictions of § 33. The state liquor board says that it did. The Fairfax Country Club argues that it did not.

In this case, several different kinds of proceedings can occur in which the interpretation of § 33 becomes the main issue. The state licensing agency may hold a hearing on the revocation of the liquor license of the Fairfax Country Club for violating § 33. The result of this hearing may be appealed in court. Or the state may be able to go directly to court to seek an injunction against the club in order to force it to comply with § 33.

The advocates for both sides have the responsibility of marshaling arguments in favor of their respective positions. This will include traditional approaches such as the following:

- Examining the "four corners" of the statute itself (§ 33) to determine the meaning of the words used.
- Examining the preamble or purpose clause of this statute, if any, to help determine the purpose of the statute—what it was trying to accomplish.
- Examining definition sections in the statute, if any, to determine the meaning of words used by the legislature in § 33.
- Examining court opinions that have interpreted § 33, if any.
- Examining administrative regulations that implement § 33, if any.
- Examining administrative decisions that have interpreted § 33, if any.

In addition, both sides will research the legislative history of § 33. An advocate who fails to do so runs the risk of being unprepared. It is true that some courts tend to be antagonistic toward the use of legislative history, for reasons that we examine later. The advocate, however, cannot respond to this antagonism by ignoring legislative history; the antagonism must be handled by presenting the legislative history in such a way that the court cannot ignore it.

An advocate has two objectives while researching the legislative history of a statute:

a. To determine whether the specific facts currently in controversy were ever discussed by the legislature while it was considering the proposed statute, and
b. To determine the broad or narrow purpose that prompted the legislature to enact the proposed statute and to assess whether this purpose sheds any light on the specific facts currently in controversy.

For example, when the legislature was considering § 33, was there any mention of country or membership clubs in the governor's message, in committee reports, in floor debates, etc.? If so, what was said about them? What was said about the purpose of § 33? Why was it enacted? What evil or mischief was it designed to combat? Was the legislature opposed to liquor on moral grounds? Did it want to reduce rowdyism that comes from the overuse of liquor? Did it want to encourage citizens to go to church on Sunday and to vote on election day? Were there complaints made to the legislature about the use of liquor by certain groups in the community? Answers to such questions might be helpful in formulating arguments on the meaning and scope of § 33. The advocate for the Fairfax Country Club will try to demonstrate that the legislature had a narrow objective when it enacted § 33: to prevent neighborhood rowdyism at establishments that serve only liquor. The legislature, therefore, was not trying to regulate the more moderate kind of drinking that normally takes place at membership clubs where food and liquor are often served together. The opponent, on the other hand, will argue that the legislature had a broader purpose in enacting § 33: to decrease the consumption of liquor by all citizens on certain days. The legislature, therefore, did not intend to exclude drinking at a membership club.

3. CONTROVERSY OVER THE USE OF LEGISLATIVE HISTORY

Several interrelated reasons account for the controversy surrounding the use of legislative history as an aid in the interpretation of a statute:

a. Availability and cost
b. Reliability
c. Manipulation
d. Overuse.

a. Availability and Cost

As you can see from the chart on pp. 657–658, a statute can have a great deal of legislative history. Given the vast numbers of statutes in existence, the task of collecting and researching their legislative histories can be enormous. Justice Jackson suggested that this impracticality raises a basic question of fairness:

> Laws are intended for all of our people to live by; and the people go to law offices to learn what their rights under those laws are. [Controversies exist which affect] every little merchant in many States. Aside from a few offices in the larger cities, the materials of legislative history are not available to the lawyer who can afford neither the cost of acquisition, the cost of housing, or the cost of repeatedly examining the whole congressional history. Moreover, if he could, he would not know any way of anticipating what would impress enough members of the Court to be controlling. Schwegmann Bros. v. Calvert Distillers Corp., 341 U.S. 384, 396, 71 S.Ct. 745, 751, 95 L.Ed. 1035 (1951), concurring opinion.

In spite of the increased availability in recent years of the documents of legislative history, they are still generally inaccessible, particularly for state statutes. It is much easier to undertake such research for federal statutes than for state statutes. Yet even for the former, the cost of the research can be substantial. An advocate may have to examine thousands of pages in a variety of books. Few clients can afford this kind of service. Later we explore some of the main books and techniques of researching the legislative history of a statute. Knowing about these books and techniques, however, does not diminish the point made by Justice Jackson. A comprehensive examination of the documents of legislative history can be an expensive and time-consuming task. The records that are needed may not be equally available to everyone.

b. Reliability

Assume that in a particular case there are no problems of availability and cost—you are able to collect and study the entire legislative history of a statute. At this point, another problem arises. How reliable is the history that you are examining? Information from legislative history is reliable to the extent you can establish that:

- The information was considered by the legislature, and
- The information accurately reflects what the legislature ultimately did.

Suppose that Senator Smith sends a letter to a constituent explaining the meaning of a bill and why he or she is supporting it. In a broad sense, this letter is part of the legislative history of the statute that came from the bill, but the letter is totally unreliable. There is no rational way of determining whether the legislature *as a whole* considered the letter and acted in accordance with its contents. The strong likelihood is that neither occurred. Would it make any difference if this letter was also printed in the official record or journal of the legislature while the bill was being considered? Probably not. A great deal is printed during the course of a legislature's consideration of a bill. Much of it is considered junk. According to some commentators, research into legislative history consists in large measure of rummaging through "the ashcans of the legislative process." C. Curtis, *It's Your Law* 52 (1954).

Suppose, however, that this same legislator is speaking to another legislator on the floor of the Senate during a debate on the bill:

> Senator SMITH: *The purpose of this bill is to phase the government out of the business of operating a railroad. It establishes an Interim Management Council, which will run the affairs of the railroad until such time as private capital can take over complete management.*
>
> Senator THOMAS: *Senator, am I correct in understanding that the bill currently before the Senate applies only to those railroad facilities in which the government acquired an interest prior to 1974?*
>
> Senator SMITH: *The senator is indeed correct.*

Here we have an exchange between two legislators during a floor debate on the bill. Presumably there are other legislators listening to this debate, so we are on safer ground in concluding that the legislature considered what they had to say. It would be helpful to know who Senator Smith is. Is he or she the sponsor of the bill or the chairperson of the committee that initially considered it? If so, his or her comments are likely to be given more weight. Courts are more inclined to conclude that the legislature considered what Senator Smith had to say and, if the bill was enacted, that his or her comments accurately reflect what the legislature intended. The views of legislators who did not have such a key role in shepherding the bill through the legislature are usually given less weight. Such views are considered less reliable in deciphering the meaning of the statute.

Yet it must be remembered that this piece of legislative history focuses only on the views of individual legislators. We can *never* be certain that these views accurately record what hundreds of legislators tried to do in passing the bill. This is so even if the individual legislator in question actually wrote the bill. According to an English commentator, Lord Halsbury:

> [I]n construing a statute I believe the worst person to construe it is the person who is responsible for its drafting. He is very much disposed to confuse what he intended to do with the effect of the language which in fact has been employed. At the time he drafted the statute, at all events, he may have been under the impression that he had given full effect to what was intended, but he may be mistaken. . . .
> Hilder v. Dexter, [1902] A.C. 474, 477.

While there is some merit to this skepticism that English courts have toward the use of legislative history, *American* courts have not gone this far. As indicated, our courts do give weight to the statements of legislators who had an important role in passing the bill.

Perhaps the most reliable documents of legislative history are the committee reports that are written after the committee holds hearings on the bill and debates amendments thereto. These reports often have two main components. First, they state the purpose of the bill: what it is trying to accomplish. They will often include discussions of prior law on the subject of the bill (including court opinions). Such discussion is usually provided as background on why the bill is needed. Second, the reports contain a section-by-section summary of the bill. It is sometimes claimed that many legislators do *not* read the technical language of the bill itself. Instead, they rely on the more readable summaries of the bill contained in the committee reports.

Some committees also print transcripts of the testimony of witnesses who appear before the committee on the bill. However, given the diversity of this testimony and the early stage at which it is provided in the legislative process, it is less reliable as an indication of what the legislature intended when it passed the bill.

What about special commission studies, messages of the chief executive, and reports of councils of government and of commissioners on uniform laws? To what extent can their proposals for legislation be relied upon to determine the legislative intent of the bills that are enacted? These proposals, of course, are also made early in the process, and a great deal may happen between the time of proposal and the date of enactment. The reliability of these initiating documents may depend on whether the language of the bill that was enacted is the same as the language of the bill that was proposed by the commission, chief executive, council, etc. If the language is the same or very similar, then the accompanying study, message, or report of these groups is generally accorded great weight in determining legislative intent.

In summary, therefore, the following are considered the most reliable components of legislative history in the interpretation of statutes:

- Committee reports.
- Statements of legislators who sponsored the bill or who chaired committees that favorably considered it.
- Studies, reports, and messages of bodies that initially proposed the bill.

While the use of any legislative history still remains controversial, the above components are most frequently relied upon.

c. Manipulation

Perhaps the most cynical explanation for the reluctance of some courts to use legislative history is the tendency of legislators and legislative staff members to "plant" statements and commentary in the legislative history for the sole reason of influencing later interpretation of the statute:

> But the intentions of some member of the subcommittee staff, buried in a report . . . are not the statute and do not necessarily represent the intentions of Congress. We all know the propensity of people who cannot persuade Congress to include a provision in the statute to insert comments favorable to their position in the legislative history in the hopes of persuading a court later on that what they say is what Congress had in mind. Application of Commonwealth Edison Co. for a Permit for Dresden Unit 3, No. 70–21, Illinois Pollution Control Board, 3/3/71, reported in 5 CCH Atom.En.Rep.Par. 16,613 at 22638. See Murphey, A., *Old Maxims Never Die: The "Plain-Meaning Rule" and Statutory Interpretation in the "Modern" Federal Courts,* 75 Col.L.Rev. 1299, 1312–3, n. 100 (1975).

Under this view, statements and commentary in the legislative history are no more reliable than what someone says on the telephone when he or she knows that there is a wiretap on the phone! Assume that a legislator wants to enact a law that prevents an agency from regulating a particular practice. For various political reasons, the legislator cannot collect enough votes from colleagues to support this provision. Hence the language that is to be voted upon by the legislature is intentionally left vague or general. The legislator then instructs a committee staff member to state in the committee report that the bill is intended to accomplish the specific objective that the legislator had in mind initially. Also, this legislator might conveniently arrange for another legislator to ask a question on the floor during debate on the meaning of the vague or general language in the bill. A response is then made for the record, which is in accord with what the legislator was not able to insert in the bill itself. Such manipulative maneuvers are common enough to cast doubt on the reliability of legislative history in the interpretation of statutes.

d. Overuse

Apart from the problems of availability, reliability, and manipulation, critics charge that legislative history is being overused by advocates and by courts. They are too quick to resort to the "ashcans" of the legislative process and tend to overinterpret what they find. Suppose, for example, that while a bill for a statute is being debated in the legislature, an amendment is considered and *rejected* by the legislature. What conclusions should be drawn on the basis of this rejection? That the legislation did not intend to include the provisions of the amendment in the statute that was enacted? Or, that the amendment was superfluous because the legislature thought that the provisions of the amendment were already included in the original bill? It is arguably self-deceptive to assume that legislative history will automatically yield clarity in the search for meaning.

Another complaint of the critics is that the users of legislative history fail to understand that the documents of this history do not constitute law:

> It is not to be supposed that, in signing a bill the President endorses the whole Congressional Record. Schwegmann Brothers v. Calvert Distillers Corp., 341 U.S. 384, 396, 71 S.Ct. 745, 751, 95 L.Ed. 1035 (1951) (Justice Jackson concurring).

The goal of these critics is to limit the use of legislative history to those circumstances in which the language of the statute is ambiguous. If this is not done, there is a danger that legislative history will be used to alter the intent of the legislature as clearly expressed in the language of the statute. In short, the concern is that the legislative history will be substituted for the statute itself. The entire process is turned on its head, as reflected in the standard joke that a court will examine the language of a statute only if the legislative history of the statute is ambiguous! J. Cory, *The Use of Legislative History in the Interpretation of Statutes,* 32 Can.Bar Rev. 624, 636 (1954).

The problem, however, is that advocates frequently disagree over whether the language of a statute is ambiguous. Law offices spend vast amounts of time and resources trying to demonstrate that statutes are ambiguous. Generally, they have been very successful. It is not surprising, therefore, that the use of legislative history is increasing as courts struggle to interpret and apply statutes to concrete facts before them. The criticism of legislative history has had almost no effect on this increase. As indicated earlier, an advocate who does not appear with an argument based on legislative history is usually considered unprepared.

ASSIGNMENT 79

Mary Franklin is a registered practitioner before the U.S. Patent Office. She is a paralegal who has been registered by and authorized to practice before the Patent Office. She has an office in the state where she meets her clients, renders opinions on patentability, and prepares legal instruments such as applications for letters patent. The state bar association claims that she is illegally practicing law and is seeking an injunction to stop her unless she becomes a member of the bar. In 15 U.S.C. § 31 Congress has provided that the commissioner of patents

> may prescribe regulations governing the conduct of agents, attorneys, or other persons representing applicants or other parties before the Patent Office.

The commissioner has established procedures for the registration of lawyers and nonlawyers to practice before it. The state bar association, however, claims that these procedures are invalid insofar as they authorize practice by nonlawyers, since Congress did not intend such authorization in § 31. Mary (and the Patent Office) disagree with this interpretation of § 31.

    a. What is Mary's argument based on the language of § 31? What is the bar's argument? Is this language ambiguous? Is there a need to resort to the legislative history of § 31?

    b. When § 31 was first introduced in Congress as a bill, it read that the commissioner "may prescribe regulations governing the recognition and conduct of agents, attorneys, and other persons representing applicants or other parties before the Patent Office." This language, however, was amended. The version passed by Congress contained the language quoted at the bottom of p. 665. What arguments can be made on the interpretation of § 31 based on this data of legislative history?

    c. On the floor of the Senate during debate on this provision, the following exchange occurred between Senator Davis and Senator Kline:

> Senator DAVIS: *I would like to ask the distinguished Senator if this bill would allow the Commissioner of Patents to set a maximum limit on the amount of fees that a lawyer can charge clients for services rendered in connection with a case before the Patent Office?*
>
> Senator KLINE: *We examined that question carefully in committee, Senator, and it was our view that any conduct of representatives can be regulated by the Commissioner including the question of fees. I should point out, however, that we did not find much problem with the way in which the bar associations currently handle the question of excessive fees.*

    What arguments can be made on the interpretation of § 31 based on this data of legislative history?

    d. In the report of the Senate committee that recommended the adoption of this law, the following comment is made: "This provision is not intended to authorize persons not members of the bar to practice law." What arguments can be made on the interpretation of § 31 based on this data of legislative history?

4. FINDING LEGISLATIVE HISTORY

In tracing legislative history, you are looking for leads to the documents of this history, e.g., bills, hearing transcripts, proposed amendments, committee reports. Unfortunately, it is often very difficult to trace the legislative history of *state* statutes. The documents are sometimes poorly preserved, if at all. This is not so with *federal* statutes.

TECHNIQUES FOR TRACING THE LEGISLATIVE HISTORY OF STATE STATUTES

1. Examine the historical data beneath the statute in the statutory code (p. 650). Amendments are usually listed there.
2. For an overview of codification information about your state, check the introductory pages in the first volume of the statutory code, or the beginning of the volume where your statute is found, or the beginning of the Shepard's volume that will enable you to shepardize the statutes of that state (p. 621).
3. Ask your librarian if there is a book (usually called a legislative service) that covers your state legislature. If one exists, it will give the bill numbers of statutes, proposed amendments, names of committees that considered the statute, etc. If such a text does not exist for your state, ask the librarian how someone finds the legislative history of a state statute in your state.
4. Contact the committees of both houses of the state legislature that considered the bill. Your local state representative or state senator might be able to help you identify what these committees were. If your statute is not too old, staff members on these committees may be able to give you leads to the legislative history of the statute. Ask if any committee reports were written. Ask about amendments, etc.
5. Ask your librarian (or a local politician) if there is a law revision commission for your state. If so, contact it for leads.
6. Is there a state law library in your area? If so, contact it for leads.
7. Check the law library and drafting office of the state legislature for leads.
8. Cases interpreting the statute sometimes give the legislative history of the statute. To find cases interpreting a statute, check the notes of decisions after the statute in the statutory code (p. 650), shepardize the statute (p. 618), etc. (See also Checklist #4b on shepardizing a statute, p. 621.)
9. You may also find leads to the legislative history of a statute in legal periodical literature on the statute (see Checklist #6, p. 628), in annotations on the statute (see Checklist #3, p. 608), in treatises on the statute (see Checklist #8, p. 630), and in loose-leaf services on the statute (see Checklist #5, p. 625). Phone and mail research might also provide some leads (see Checklist #9, p. 631).

It is easier to trace the legislative history of a *federal* statute, since the documents are more available.

TECHNIQUES FOR TRACING THE LEGISLATIVE HISTORY OF A FEDERAL STATUTE

1. Examine the historical data at the end of the statute in the United States Code (U.S.C.), in the United States Code Annotated (U.S.C.A.), and in the United States Code Service (U.S.C.S.).
2. You will also find the PL number (Public Law number) of the statute at the end of the statute in U.S.C./U.S.C.A./U.S.C.S. This PL number will be important for tracing legislative history. (Note that each amendment to a statute will have its own PL number.)
3. Step one in tracing the legislative history of a federal statute is to find out if the history has already been compiled by someone else. Ask your librarian. The Library of Congress compiles legislative histories. If the statute deals with a particular federal agency, check with the library or law department of that agency in Washington, D.C., or in the regional offices to see if it has compiled the legislative history. Also check with special interest groups or associations

that are directly affected by the statute. They may have compiled the legislative history, which might be available to you. (One question you can ask through phone and mail research is whether the expert knows if anyone has compiled the legislative history of the statute, whom you could contact. See Checklist #9 on doing phone and mail research, p. 631.) Ask your librarian if there is a Union List of Legislative Histories for your area. This list tells you what area libraries have compiled legislative histories on federal statutes.

4. The following texts are useful in tracing the legislative history of federal statutes:
   - U.S. Code Congressional & Administrative News (see table 4 in this set of books)
   - CCH Congressional Index
   - Congressional Information Service (CIS) Annual
   - Information Handling Service (legislative histories on microfiche)
   - Digest of Public General Bills and Resolutions
   - Congressional Record, p. 534 (see Index and the History of Bills and Resolutions for House and Senate)
   - House and Senate Journals
   - Congressional Quarterly
   - Congressional Monitor
   - Monthly Catalog of U.S. Documents
5. Contact both committees of Congress that considered the legislation to ask for leads to legislative history. (They may be able to send you committee reports, hearing transcripts, etc.)
6. Cases interpreting the statute sometimes give the legislative history of the statute. To find cases interpreting the statute, check the notes of decisions after the statute in the U.S.C.A. and in the U.S.C.S. Also, shepardize the statute (see Checklist #4b on shepardizing a statute, p. 621).
7. Find out if there is an annotation on the statute. See the "Table of Laws and Regulations Cited in ALR Fed" in a volume called ALR Fed. Table of Cases, Laws, Regs. (See Checklist #3 on finding and updating annotations, p. 608.)
8. You may also find leads to the legislative history of a statute in legal periodical literature (see Checklist #6, p. 628), in treatises on the statute (see Checklist #8, p. 630), in loose-leaf services on the statute (see Checklist #5, p. 625), and through phone and mail research (see Checklist #9, p. 631).
9. To try to find a discussion of your statute in Am.Jur.2d, a legal encyclopedia, check a separate volume called Table of Statutes and Rules Cited (p. 630).
10. Examine your statute in its session law form in United States Statutes at Large for possible leads (p. 559).

Section S. MONITORING PROPOSED LEGISLATION

Occasionally you will be asked to monitor a bill currently before the legislature that has relevance to the caseload of the law office where you work. To monitor a bill means to determine its current status in the legislature and to keep track of all the forces that are trying to enact, defeat, or modify the bill.

TECHNIQUES FOR MONITORING PROPOSED LEGISLATION

1. Begin with the legislature. Find out what committee in each house of the legislature (often called the Senate and House) is considering the proposed legislation. Also determine whether there are more than two committees considering the entire bill or portions of it.
2. Ask committee staff members to send you copies of the bill in its originally proposed form and in its amended form.

3.   Determine whether the committees considering the proposed legislation have written any reports on it and, if so, whether copies are available.

4.   Determine whether any hearings have been scheduled by the committees on the bill. If so, try to attend. For hearings already conducted, see if they have been transcribed (a word-for-word recording).

5.   Find out the names of people in the legislature who are working on the bill: legislators "pushing" the bill, legislators opposed to it, staff members of the individual legislators working on the bill, staff members of the committees working on the bill. Ask for copies of any position papers or statements.

6.   The local bar association is probably interested in and has taken a position on the bill. Call the association. Find out what committee of the bar is involved with the subject matter of the bill. This committee may have written a report on the position of the bar on the bill. If so, you should try to obtain a copy.

7.   Is there an administrative agency of the government involved with the bill? Do any of these agencies have jurisdiction over the subject matter of the bill? If so, find out who in the agency is working on the bill and whether any written reports of the agency are available. Determine whether the agency has a Legislative Liaison Office.

8.   Who else is lobbying for or against the bill? What organizations are interested in it? Find out if they have taken any written positions.

9.   What precipitated consideration of the bill by the legislature? Was there a court opinion that prompted the legislative action? If so, you should know what the opinion said.

10.   Are any other legislatures in the country contemplating similar legislation? Some of the ways of finding out include the following:

    (a)   Look for legal periodical literature on the subject matter of the bill (see Checklist #6, p. 628).

    (b)   Check loose-leaf services, if any, covering the subject matter of the bill (see Checklist #5, p. 625)—these services often cover proposed legislation in the various legislatures.

    (c)   Check treatises on the area (see Checklist #8, p. 630).

    (d)   Organizations such as bar associations, public interest groups, business associations, etc., often assign staff members to do this kind of state-by-state research on what the legislatures are doing. Such organizations may be willing to share this research with you.

    (e)   Find out if there is a council of state governments in your area. It may have done the same research mentioned in (d) above.

    (f)   Contact an expert for leads to what other legislatures are doing (see Checklist #9, p. 631).

Section T. READING AND FINDING
CONSTITUTIONAL LAW

READING CONSTITUTIONAL LAW

The constitution sets out the fundamental ground rules for the conduct of the government in the geographical area covered by the constitution. It defines the branches of the government, establishes basic rights of citizens, and covers matters that the framers considered important enough (e.g., limitations on the power to tax) to be included in the constitution. The United States Constitution does this for the federal government, and the state constitution does it for the state government. In reading constitutional law, a number of guidelines can be helpful:

1. Thumb Through the Headings of the Constitution or Glance Through the Table of Contents

How is the document organized? What subjects did the framers want covered by the constitution? A quick scanning of the section headings or table of contents is a good way to obtain an overview of the structure of the text.

2. The Critical Sections or Articles Are Those That Establish and Define the Powers of the Legislative, Judicial, and Executive Branches of Government in the Geographic Area Covered by the Constitution

Who passes, interprets, and executes the law? For the United States Constitution, "all legislative Powers granted herein shall be vested in a Congress" (art. I, § 1): "the judicial Power of the United States, shall be vested in one supreme Court, and in such inferior Courts as the Congress may from time to time ordain and establish" (art. III, § 1); and "the executive Power shall be vested in a President of the United States of America" (art. II, § 1). The exact scope of these powers, as enunciated elsewhere in the constitution, has been and continues to be an arena of constant controversy and litigation.

3. The Amendments to the Constitution Change or Add to the Body of the Text

The main vehicle for changing the constitution is the amendment process, which itself is defined in the constitution. Some constitutions, for example, can be amended by a vote of the people in a general election. A condition for most amendments is that they must be approved by one or more sessions of the legislature. Constitutional amendments usually appear at the end of the document.

4. Constitutions Are Written in Very Broad Terms

There are, of course, exceptions to this, particularly with respect to the constitutions of local governments. In the main, however, a common characteristic of constitutional provisions is their broad language. How would you interpret the following section?

> Congress shall make no laws respecting an establishment of religion, or prohibiting the free exercise thereof; or abridging the freedom of speech, or of the press; or of the right of the people to assemble, and to petition the Government for a redress of grievances.

How many words in this provision do you *not* understand? What is an "establishment?" If the school board requires a "moment of silence" at the beginning of each day, is the school board establishing a religion? What does "abridging" mean? If a government official leaks secret documents to the press, and the government tries to sue the press to prevent the publication of the documents, has the "freedom" of the press been abridged? If the people have a right to "assemble," could the government pass a law prohibiting all gatherings of three or more people at any place within one thousand yards of the White House gates? The questions arising from the interpretation of constitutional law are endless; tens of thousands of court opinions exist on questions such as these. The broader the language, the more ambiguous it is, and therefore the greater is the need for interpretation.

5. A Central Question for the Interpreter of Constitutional Law Is, What Meaning Did the Authors Intend?

Common sense dictates that when language is ambiguous, the ambiguity may be resolved in part by attempting to determine what the author of the language intended by it. What was the author's meaning? In what context was the author writing? Does the context shed any light on what was meant? This kind of analysis is fundamental to legal reasoning whether the document is a constitution, a statute, a regulation, or a case. It is particularly difficult to do, however, with most constitutions written over a hundred years ago.

FINDING CONSTITUTIONAL LAW

TECHNIQUES FOR FINDING CONSTITUTIONAL LAW
1. Start with the text of the constitution itself. It is usually found at the beginning of the statutory code of the jurisdiction. (The federal Constitution is in U.S.C./U.S.C.A./U.S.C.S., p. 557.)
2. Use the CARTWHEEL to help you use the general index of the statutory code and the separate index for the constitution itself (p. 591). Also check the table of contents material for the constitution in the statutory code.
3. Following the text of individual constitutional provisions there are often notes of decisions containing summaries of cases interpreting the constitution. Some of these notes can run hundreds of pages. Check the separate index material for these notes.
4. Shepardize the constitutional provision. The set of Shepard's to use is the same set you use for shepardizing a statute (p. 621).
5. Annotations. Find annotations on the constitutional provisions in which you are interested. The CARTWHEEL will help you use the Quick Indexes for the annotations in ALR, ALR2d, ALR3d, ALR4th, and ALR Fed. (See Checklist #3 on finding and updating annotations, p. 608.)
6. Digests. Go to the United States Supreme Court Digest (West) (p. 539). Also use the various digests of West that cover other jurisdictions. (The American Digest System, of course, covers all jurisdictions.) The CARTWHEEL will help you use the Descriptive Word Index (DWI) of a digest to locate key topics and numbers on point. (See Checklist #2 on using West digests, p. 603.) (For cases on the U.S. Constitution, you can also go to the non-West digest—the United States Supreme Court Digest, Lawyers Ed., p. 539.)
7. Treatises. Find treatises on the entire constitution or on the specific portions of the constitution in which you are interested. (See Checklist #8 on finding treatises, p. 630.)
8. Legal periodical literature. Go to the three indexes to legal periodical literature: ILP, CLI, and LRI. Use the CARTWHEEL to help you locate periodical literature on the constitution. (See Checklist #6 on finding legal periodical literature, p. 628.)
9. Loose-leaf services. Find out if there are loose-leaf services on the area of the constitution in which you are interested. (See Checklist #5 on loose-leaf services, p. 625.)
10. Phone and mail research. Contact an expert. (See Checklist #9 on phone and mail research, p. 631.)
11. Words and Phrases. Identify specific words or phrases within the constitutional provision you are examining. Find court definitions of these words or phrases in the multi-volume legal dictionary, Words and Phrases (p. 545).
12. Legal encyclopedias. Use the CARTWHEEEL to help you locate discussions of constitutional law in Am.Jur.2d and in C.J.S. (See Checklist #7 on legal encyclopedias, p. 630.)
13. Shepardize every case you found through the above techniques that interprets the constitution. (See Checklist #4a on shepardizing a case, p. 617.)

14. Ask your librarian how you can trace the constitutional history of a provision of the constitution (i.e., the equivalent of the legislative history of a statute). Many of the above techniques will lead you to material that also discusses constitutional history, particularly cases interpreting the constitution and legal periodical literature on the constitution. There may, however, be additional sources to check. Ask the librarian.

Section U. FINDING ADMINISTRATIVE LAW

A regulation is an official rule of an administrative agency that explains or carries out the statutes and executive orders that govern the agency.

See Section Q above on the organization of statutes (p. 651). Many of the same guidelines apply to regulations. Unfortunately, however, regulations are not as well organized as statutes usually are. There are many agencies writing regulations. Few of them have coherent systems of organizing and distributing the regulations. A major exception is the federal agencies whose regulations are first published in the Federal Register; many are then codified in the Code of Federal Regulations (p. 542).

Normally an agency does not have the power to write regulations unless it has specific statutory authority to do so. An examination of the statute giving the agency this authority can be helpful in understanding the regulations themselves. More broadly, the function of the agency is to carry out the legislative mandates of the statutes; administrators must carry out the law as defined for them in the statutes. Hence, the researcher should be familiar with the statutory foundation of the agency not only to place the regulations in context but also to be constantly conscious of an overriding issue: Is the agency carrying out or violating the intent of the legislature as defined in the statutes?

In theory, the legislature in its statutes sets out the purpose of the agency and defines its overall policies, but leaves to the agency (through its regulations) the task of filling in the specifics of administration. Regulations, therefore, tend to be very detailed.

The other major kind of administrative law is the administrative decision (p. 516), which is a written resolution of controversies brought before the administrative agency. Not many agencies publish their decisions in any systematic order; some agencies do not publish them at all. Regulatory agencies, such as the Federal Communications Commission and state environmental agencies, sometimes do a better job at publishing their decisions than other agencies.

Administrative decisions should be briefed in the same way that court opinions are briefed (p. 695).

TECHNIQUES FOR FINDING ADMINISTRATIVE LAW

1. Start with the agency itself. Call or visit the agency. Many may have regional or district offices near you. Contact the library, the law department, or the public information section. Ask for a list of the publications of the agency, e.g., regulations, decisions, annual reports. Also ask where these materials are located. Find out if you can come to the agency and use the materials. Ask about brochures describing the agency's functions, which can be sent to you.

2. Whenever an agency official is reluctant to let you have access to any publications of the agency, you may have to do separate research to find out whether you are entitled to access, e.g., under the federal Freedom of Information Act and its state equivalents.

3. Many federal administrative regulations are printed in the Code of Federal Regulations (C.F.R.), which are usually first printed in their proposed form in the Federal Register before they are enacted by the agency. The C.F.R. comes out in a new edition every year (p. 622).

   There are three main ways to locate regulations in the C.F.R.:

   (a) The Index volume of the C.F.R. This is a single-volume pamphlet that is reissued every year.

   (b) The Index to the Code of Federal Regulations. This is a new multi-volume publication from the Congressional Information Service. It is a very detailed annual text.

   (c) Loose-leaf services. As indicated earlier, there are numerous loose-leaf services (p. 548) covering many federal agencies and some state agencies. These services usually give extensive references to administrative regulations and decisions. (See Checklist #5, p. 625.)

   Also check the monthly and annual indexes to the Federal Register (p. 542).

   If you find no federal regulations on point in the C.F.R. or in the Federal Register, you should check whether the agency has regulations, rules, bulletins, etc., that are published elsewhere. (See technique 1 above.)

4. Once you have found a federal regulation on point in the C.F.R., do the following:

   (a) Shepardize the regulation. (See Checklist #4c on shepardizing a regulation, p. 623.)

   (b) Find the statutory authority for that regulation. There should be an "authority" reference beneath the specific regulation in the C.F.R. *or* at the beginning of the cluster of regulations of which your regulation is a part. The authority reference will be to a U.S.C. cite, which is the basis of the regulation. Go to the U.S.C./U.S.C.A./U.S.C.S. and read this statute. Make sure the regulation does not contradict, go beyond the scope of, or otherwise violate the statute that the regulation is supposed to implement.

   (c) Find out if the regulation has been *affected* in any way (e.g., changed, added to, renumbered) by subsequent material printed in the Federal Register. This is done by checking your C.F.R. cite in:

   (i) The LSA pamphlet (List of Sections Affected) at the end of the C.F.R. volumes;

   (ii) The lists of "CFR Parts Affected" in the daily Federal Register from the date of the LSA pamphlet to the current date.

   The LSA pamphlet and the "CFR Parts Affected" will tell you what pages of the Federal Register contain material that affects the cite of your regulation in the C.F.R. (You only have to do this in between the date of the C.F.R. edition you are using and the date of the next yearly C.F.R. edition, since anything affecting the regulation during the preceding year will be incorporated in the next edition.)

   (d) Find out if there is an annotation on your regulation by checking the "Table of Laws and Regulations Cited in ALR Federal," which is found in a volume called ALR Fed. Table of Cases, Laws, Regs, p. 606.

5. State administrative agency regulations are much more difficult to find and update. A few states have an administrative code similar to the C.F.R. For most state agencies, you must check with your law library and with the agency itself (see 1 above) on how the regulations are printed, found, and updated.

6. Federal or state administrative decisions are usually printed, if at all, in separate volumes for that agency. Also check loose-leaf services that cover a particular agency. (See Checklist #5, p. 628.)

Section V. FINDING LOCAL LAW

Difficulties sometimes exist in finding local charters, ordinances, etc. There may be a municipal code for your city or county containing such laws. Many charters are also printed in the state's statutory code. Check with your law librarian. Also call city hall, the city council, or the county commissioner's office. Speak with the public information officer or the law department. Ask about the local publications of your city or county. What is printed? Where is it found? How often is it printed? How is it updated?

The following are other items to check:

- Legal periodical literature on local law issues such as zoning, municipal bonds, etc. (see Checklist #6 on legal periodical literature, p. 628).
- The Shepard's volumes for a particular state will enable you to shepardize local charters and ordinances. Use the Index to Ordinances in these volumes as a topical index.
- Case law on charters and ordinances; use the digests (see Checklist #2 on digests, p. 603).
- Annotations on local law in ALR, ALR2d, ALR3d, ALR4th, and ALR Fed (see Checklist #3 on annotations, p. 608).
- Treatises on local law (see Checklist #8 on treatises, p. 630).
- Am.Jur.2d and C.J.S. discussions on local law (see Checklist #7 on legal encyclopedias, p. 630).
- Loose-leaf services cover aspects of local law (see Checklist #5 on loose-leaf services, p. 625).
- Phone and mail research; contact an expert (see Checklist #9 on phone and mail research, p. 631).
- Ordinance Law Annotations (published by Shepard's) summarizes court opinions that have interpreted ordinances.

Section W. FINDING COURT RULES

You must always check the court rules governing practice and procedure before a *particular* court, e.g., how to file a request for an extension of time, the number of days a defendant has to answer a complaint, the format of a complaint or appellate brief.

TECHNIQUES FOR FINDING COURT RULES

Court Rules for State Courts:
- Check your state statutory code for the text of the rules.
- Ask your librarian if there is a publishing service company that produces an updated edition of state court rules.
- Find out if the court itself publishes its own rules.
- Check the desk copy of court rules (p. 534).
- Shepardize court rules in the same set of Shepard's you use to shepardize a statute (p. 618).
- For more case law on the court rules, check the digests for your state (see Checklist #2 on digests, p. 603).
- Check local practice books or formbooks (p. 543, p. 630).
- Check with an expert (see Checklist #9 on phone and mail research, p. 631).

Court Rules for Federal Courts:
- Check the U.S.C./U.S.C.A./U.S.C.S., e.g., title 28, title 18 (appendix).
- Check individual volumes on court rules.
- Check the desk copy of court rules (p. 534).
- Shepardize federal court rules in United States Citations, Statute Edition (p. 554).
- For more case law on court rules, check the digests, e.g., Federal Practice Digest 3d (see Checklist #2 on digests, p. 603).
- Check the Federal Rules Service.
- Check special treatises on the federal rules such as:
    Moore's Federal Practice
    Wright and Miller, Federal Practice and Procedure
    Weinstein and Berger, Weinstein's Evidence
    Federal Procedure Lawyer's Edition
    Federal Procedural Forms, Lawyer's Edition
- Check annotations on the federal rules, e.g., in the "Table of Laws and Regulations Cited in ALR Fed" found in ALR Fed. Table of Cases, Laws, Regs. (see Checklist #3, p. 608).
- Check legal periodical literature on the federal rules (see Checklist #6 on legal periodical literature, p. 628).
- Check Am.Jur.2d and C.J.S. on the federal rules (see Checklist #7 on legal encyclopedias, p. 630).
- Check with an expert (see Checklist #9 on phone and mail research, p. 631).

Section X. FINDING INTERNATIONAL LAW

TECHNIQUES FOR FINDING INTERNATIONAL LAW

1. In general:
    - The yearly U.S. Statutes at Large (p. 559) contain U.S. treaties (p. 517)
    - United States Treaties and other International Acts
    - Treaties and other International Act Series
    - United States Treaties and other International Agreements
    - Blaustein and Flanz, Constitutions of the Countries of the World
    - CCH Tax Treaties
    - Treaties in Force
    - Department of State Bulletin
    - United Nations Treaty Series
    - Catalog of U.N. Publications
    - International Legal Materials
    - Szladits, Bibliography on Foreign and Comparative Law: Books and Articles in English
    - Rohn, World Treaty Index
    - DeLupis, Bibliography of International Law
    - Whiteman's Digest of International Law
    - Schwarzenberger's Manual of International Law

    For other texts summarizing and commenting on treaties and international law generally, see Checklist #8 on treatises, p. 630.
2. Legal periodical literature. There is extensive literature in the periodicals on international law, both in general legal periodicals and in specialty periodicals devoted to international law exclusively. (See Checklist #6, p. 628.)
3. Loose-leaf services such as CCH Tax Treaties mentioned above. (See Checklist #5 on loose-leaf services, p. 625.)
4. American case law on international law. Check the digests. (See Checklist #2 on digests, p. 603.)

5. Case law of foreign countries. Statutory law of other countries. Go to the international law section of a large law library.
6. Annotations on international law. (See Checklist #3 on annotations, p. 608.)
7. Legal encyclopedias. For material on international law in Am.Jur.2d and in C.J.S., see Checklist #7, p. 630.
8. Phone and mail research. (See Checklist #9 on contacting experts, p. 631.)
9. See Restatement (Second) of Foreign Relations Law of the United States.
10. Shepardize all treaties. Go to Shepard's United States Citations, Statute Edition (p. 554).
11. Martindale-Hubbell Law Directory—Digest volume. Contains brief summaries of the law of most countries (p. 548).

Section Y. THE THIRD LEVEL OF RESEARCH (VALIDATION): ENDING YOUR RESEARCH

Earlier, we mentioned the three levels of legal research (p. 595):

1. Background research
2. Specific fact research
3. Validation research

We already examined the steps to take in conducting background research on an area of law that is new to you (p. 597). We also examined the techniques of specific fact research through the checklists (pp. 639ff.) presented above in section P through X of this chapter. If you have done a comprehensive job on the first two stages of research, you may also have completed most of the third stage—validation research.

At the validation stage, you ensure that everything you want to use from your research is still good law. This means making sure that the law is current and has not been affected by any later laws that you have not yet found. A good way to approach validation research is to take the perspective on the other side. Suppose that you have written an appellate brief. It has been filed in court and served on the attorney for the other side. Your brief is handed over to a researcher in the law office of your opponent. That person will do the following:

- Read the full text of all primary authority (p. 561) on which you rely in order to see if you have interpreted the statutes, cases, regulations, etc., properly; to see whether you have taken quotations out of context, etc.
- Shepardize the statutes, cases, regulations, etc., that you cite in order to find out whether the law is still valid (p. 608).
- Read the secondary authority (p. 566) that you cite in order to see whether you have interpreted the treatise, law review article, etc., properly; to see whether you have taken quotations out of context, etc. (p. 587).
- Look for other applicable primary authority that you failed to mention.
- Look for other applicable secondary authority that you failed to mention.

Proper validation research means that you will be able to predict what this other imaginary researcher will find when he or she checks your research through the above steps. In short, at the validation stage of your research you must ask yourself:

- Have I found everything I should have found?
- Is everything I found good law?
- Have I interpreted what I found properly?

The answer to the first two questions should be *no*:

- If you did an incomplete job of CARTWHEELING the indexes and tables of contents of all the sets of books mentioned in the checklists and techniques in this chapter (p. 591).
- If you failed to shepardize cases, statutes, constitutional provisions, court rules, ordinances, treaties, etc., as called for in the above checklists and techniques (p. 608).
- If you failed to take other standard validation steps such as checking the List of Sections Affected material to update a regulation in the C.F.R. (p. 673).

At the outset of your research, the difficulty you face is often phrased as, "Where do I begin?" As you resolve this difficulty, another one emerges: "When do I stop?" Once the research starts flowing, you are sometimes faced with a mountain of material and yet you do not feel comfortable in saying to yourself that you have found everything there is to be found. The only guidance that can be given to you is: be comprehensive in following all the checklists and techniques presented in this chapter. With experience you will begin to acquire a sense of when it is time to stop. But it is rare for you to know this with any certainty. You will always have the suspicion that if you pushed on just a little longer, you would find something new and more on point than what you have come up with to date. Also, there is no way around the reality that comprehensive research requires a substantial amount of time. It takes time to dig. It takes more time to dig comprehensively.

Section Z. ANNOTATED BIBLIOGRAPHY

An annotated bibliography is a report giving a list of library material on a particular topic, with a brief description of how the material relates to the topic. An annotated bibliography on contributory negligence, for example, would list the major cases, statutes, periodical articles, etc., and would explain in a sentence or two what they have to do with contributory negligence. The same would be true of an annotated bibliography on a set of facts that you are researching. If the facts present more than one research issue, you would do an annotated bibliography for each issue, or you would subdivide a single annotated bibliography into sections so that it would be clear to the reader which issue you are covering at any given place in the bibliography. The annotated bibliography is, in effect, a progress report on your research. It will give your supervisor the status of your research. (The following instructions mainly cover the preparation of an annotated bibliography for a topic that requires the application of state and local law. The same instructions, however, would be used when doing the bibliography on a federal topic. The exception would be instruction #9, which calls for local ordinances. For all other instructions below, replace the word *state* with the word *federal* when researching a federal topic.)

INSTRUCTIONS FOR PREPARING AN ANNOTATED BIBLIOGRAPHY

1. CARTWHEEL the topic of your annotated bibliography, p. 591.
2. "Annotated" simply means that you provide some description of everything you list in the bibliography—not a long analysis, just a sentence or two explaining why you included it. If you find no relevant material in any of the following sets of books, specifically say so in your report.
3. Hand in an outline report that will cover what you find on the topic in the sets of books mentioned in the following instructions.
4. Statutes. Go to your state code (p. 557). Make a list of the statutes on the topic. For each statute, give its citation and a brief quotation from it to show that it deals with the topic.
5. Constitutions. Go to your state constitution (usually found within your state code), p. 671. Make a list of the constitutional provisions on the topic. For each provision, give its citation and a brief quotation from it to show that it deals with the topic.
6. Cases. If you found statutes or constitutional provisions on the topic, check to see if there are any cases summarized in the notes of decisions (p. 650) *after* theses statutes or provisions. Select several major cases that deal with the topic. Also go to the digests (pp. 535, 600, and 603). Try to find other major cases that deal with the topic. Select several. For each case you find, give its citation and a brief quote from the opinion to show that it deals with the topic.
7. Key topics and numbers. In instruction #6, you went to the digests. Make a list of the key topics and numbers that you found most productive. (See pp. 544 and 601.)
8. Court rules. Go the the court rules that cover courts in your state (p. 534). Make a list of the court rules, if any, that deal with the topic. For each rule, give its citation and a brief quotation from it to show that it deals with the topic.
9. Ordinances. Go to the ordinances that cover your city or county (p. 674). Make a list of the ordinances, if any, that deal with the topic. For each ordinance, give its citation and a brief quotation from it to show that it deals with the topic.
10. Agency regulations. Are there any agencies that have jurisdiction over any aspect of the topic at the federal, state, or local level? If so, list the agencies. If your library has the regulations of the agencies, make a list of the regulations, if any, that deal with the topic. For each major regulation, give its citation and a brief quote from it to show that it deals with the topic (p. 672).
11. ALR, ALR2d, ALR3d, ALR4th, ALR Fed. Go to these five sets of books (p. 605). Try to find one annotation in *each* set that deals with your topic. Give the citation of the annotations in each set. Flip through the pages of each annotation and try to find the citation of one case from your state court or from a federal court with jurisdiction over your state. Give the citation of the case.
12. Law reviews. Use the Index to Legal Periodicals, the Current Legal Index, and the Legal Resource Index to locate three law review articles that deal with the topic (p. 625). Try to find at least one relevant article in each Index. Give the citation of the articles. Put a check mark next to the citation if your library has the law review in which the article is located.
13. Treatises. Go to your card catalog (p. 599). Find any two treatises (p. 630) that cover your topic. Give the citation of the treatises. Sometimes you may not find entire books on the topic. The topic may be one of many subjects in the trea-

tise. If the card catalog does not give you this information, you may have to examine the treatise itself.

14. Loose-leaf texts. Are there any loose-leaf services on this topic (p. 625)? Check the card catalog and ask the librarian. For each loose-leaf, give its citation and explain how it covers the topic.

15. Words and Phrases. Go to this multi-volume legal dictionary (p. 545). In this dictionary, locate definitions, if any, of the major words and phrases involved in your topic. Limit yourself to definitions from court opinions of your state, if any.

16. Shepardize every case, statute, or constitutional provision you find in order to make sure it is still valid and to locate other material on the topic (p. 608).

17. Other material. If you come across other material not covered in the above instructions, include it in the bibliography as well.

18. When in doubt about whether to include something in the bibliography, include it.

19. There is no prescribed format for the bibliography. One possible outline format you can use is as follows:

   TOPIC: _____

   A. Statutes (Instructions 4 and 16)
   B. Constitutions (Instructions 5 and 16)
   C. Cases (Instructions 6 and 16)
   D. Key topics and numbers (Instruction 7)
   E. Court rules (Instruction 8)
   F. Ordinances (Instruction 9)
   G. Agency regulations (Instruction 10)
   H. ALR, ALR2d, ALR3d, ALR4th, ALR Fed (Instruction 11)
   I. Law reviews (Instruction 12)
   J. Treatises (Instruction 13)
   K. Loose-leaf texts (Instruction 14)
   L. Words and Phrases (Instruction 15)
   M. Other material (Instruction 17)

ASSIGNMENT 80

Prepare an annotated bibliography on the following topics:

a. Common-law marriage
b. Negligence liability of a driver of a car to his or her guest passenger
c. Negligence liability of paralegals
d. Overtime compensation for paralegals
e. Sex discrimination
f. The felony-murder rule
g. Default judgment
h. Worker's compensation for injury on the way to work
i. Fact situation assigned by your instructor

ASSIGNMENTS 81–106

Be sure to include citations that support every position you take in your responses to the problems that follow. In analyzing and researching some of the problems below, you may find it difficult to proceed unless you know more facts about the problem. In such situations, clearly state the missing facts that you need to know. In order to proceed with the analysis and research, you can assume that certain facts exist so long as (a) you state what your factual assumptions are *and* (b) your assumptions are reasonable given the facts that you have.

81. In your state, what entity (e.g., legislature, committee, court, agency) has the authority to prescribe rules and regulations on who can and who cannot practice law?

82. List the kinds (or levels) of courts (local, state, or federal) that sit in your state and identify the powers of each court, i.e., what kinds of cases can each court hear?

83. In your state, define the following words or phrases:

    a. Summons
    b. In personam
    c. Mandamus
    d. Exhaustion of administrative remedies
    e. Judgment
    f. Jurisdiction
    g. Warrant

84. Mary Adams works for a National Welfare Rights Organization chapter in your state. She is a paralegal. An N.W.R.O. member, Mrs. Peterson, has a complaint against a local welfare department branch concerning her welfare check. Mary Adams goes to a Fair Hearing with Mrs. Peterson to represent her. The hearing officer tells Mary that she cannot represent Mrs. Peterson since she (Mary) is not an attorney. Is the hearing officer correct?

85. Using as many statutory codes of different states as are available in your law library (do not go beyond ten different codes, however), find out how old a male and female must be in order to marry without consent of parent or guardian in each of the states.

86. Go to any statutory code that has a pocket part. Starting with the first few pages of the pocket part, identify any three different statutes that have totally repealed *or* partially modified the statute in the body of the bound text. Describe what the modification was. (Note: You may have to compare the new section in the pocket part with the old section in the body of the text in order to be able to describe the change.)

In the following problems, use the state law *of your state* whenever you determine from your research that state law governs the problem.

87. John Jones was sent to a state mental hospital after being declared mentally ill. He has been institutionalized for the last five years. In his own view, he is not now mentally ill. The hospital disagrees. What can John do? What steps might he take to try to get out?

88. Peter Thomas is convicted of petty larceny. At the time for sentencing, his attorney asks the court to grant probation in lieu of a prison term. The judge replies, "Since Mr. Thomas has had three prior felony convictions

(one of which for attempted rape), I could not grant him probation even if I wanted to. I sentence him to a year in prison." On appeal, the attorney argues that the judge was incorrect when he ruled that he had no power to grant probation to a person with three prior convictions. Is the attorney correct?

89. Mrs. Peterson invites a neighbor to her house for dinner. Mrs. Peterson's dog bites the neighbor. Is Mrs. Peterson responsible for the injury?

90. Sam, age fifteen, goes to a used car lot. He signs a purchase agreement on a used car: $500 down and $100 a month for the next ten months. One day after the purchase, Sam allows a friend to drive the car. The friend demolishes the car in an accident. When Sam tells the used car dealer about the accident, he is told that he will still have to make all payments until the purchase price has been paid. Is the dealer right?

91. An elderly woman presented the following facts to you during a legal interview: She and her husband moved into their house in 1946. Next to the house is a vacant lot. She does not know who owns the lot. She planted a small vegetable and flower garden on this lot. She erected a small fence around the garden. She has continued to cultivate this garden for the past twenty-seven years. Neighbors regard this garden as hers. Since her husband's death last fall, men in the neighborhood have been trying to use the garden area as a place to store their old car parts. She is troubled by this. What are her rights?

92. Dorothy Rhodes and John Samualson are the parents of Susan Samualson. (Dorothy married Robert Rhodes after divorcing John Samualson.) Dorothy died in 1967 after separating from her second husband. Susan's father has disappeared.

　　Mr. and Mrs. Ford were neighbors of the Rhodes. Susan lived with them for a long period of time while her mother was having marital difficulties. A court granted the Fords custody and guardianship in 1978. The Social Security Administration sent Susan the Social Security benefits she was entitled to on the death of her mother. In 1979, the Fords formally adopted Susan, but did not inform the Social Security office of this; they did not know that they had to. When the Social Security office learned of the adoption, they terminated the payments for Susan and informed the Fords that the money she had received since the adoption would have to be returned.

　　The Fords want to know what substantive and procedural rights they have.

93. Jane Smith owns a small shoe repair shop. The city sanitation department determines that Jane is a carrier of a typhoid germ. She herself does not have typhoid fever, but others could become infected with the fever by coming in contact with her. The city orders Jane's shop to be closed. She and her husband are not allowed to leave the shop until arrangements can be made to transfer them to a hospital.

a. Can the city quarantine Jane and her husband?
b. If the Smiths enter a hospital quarantine, can they be forced to pay the hospital bill?

    c. Can the Smiths recover loss of profits due to the closing of their business?

94. The Henderson family owns a $40,000 home next door to a small grocery store. The store catches fire. In order for the firefighters to get at the fire from all angles, they decide that they must break through the Henderson home, which is not on fire. Damage to the Henderson home from the activity of the firefighters comes to $4,000. Who pays for this damage?

95. Bill and Mary are married with two children. They are happily married except for one constant quarrel. Bill is upset with Mary because she goes bowling every Friday night. Mary is disturbed with Bill because he plays cards every Tuesday night. To resolve their difficulty, they reach the following agreement: Bill will give up his Tuesday night event if Mary will give up her Friday bowling. On Friday, Mary stays home. On the following Tuesday, however, Bill plays cards. He declares that he wants to continue the card playing. Mary, on the other hand, wants him to live up to his agreement. She brings a suit in court against him, charging breach of contract. (Assume that neither wants a divorce.) What result?

96. After a series of serious accidents in which numerous riders are hurt, a bill is placed before the city council that would require all motorcyclists to wear protective helmets of specified dimensions at all times. Is the bill constitutional?

97. As a measure to enforce a standard of dental care, a bill is proposed that all the drinking water in the state be fluoridated and every citizen be required to visit a dentist at least once a year. Is this bill constitutional?

98. Tom Jones has terminal lung cancer. Modern technology, however, can keep him alive indefinitely. Tom requests that the hospital officials no longer use the technology. He wants to die. What are his rights?

99. Alice Brown is seventeen years old. She is a self-styled hippie. She refuses to take steady work. Alice's parents tell her that they will fully finance a college education for her. She refuses. The parents go to court and ask that their daughter be forced to go to college and avoid ruining her life. What result?

100. In 1942 James Fitzpatrick died, leaving an estate of $50,000. The executor tried to locate the heirs. In 1943 the probate court closed the estate and distributed the money to the heirs that were known at the time. In 1986, an individual claiming to be an heir appears. He wants to go to court to reopen the estate and claim his share of the inheritance. What result?

101. Mary is the sole beneficiary of her father's will. Another sister is intentionally left out of the will by her father. There are no other heirs. Mary murders her father. Who gets his estate?

102. The board of education is alarmed over increasing disturbances in the public schools. A board regulation currently exists that permits school principals to administer corporal punishment to unruly pupils. The superintendent of schools proposes that the board adopt a regulation that would authorize the school nurse, under the direction of the principal, to

administer an oral tranquilizer to disruptive pupils so that they could be rendered "relatively passive" and responsive to school guidance. Discuss the legality of the regulation.

103. The state claims that welfare costs are bringing the finances of the state to the brink of bankruptcy. It is proposed that all children of welfare parents be required to attend vocational classes as part of their regular school curriculum. Discuss the legality of the regulation.

104. The United Kosher Butchers Association is accepted by most of the kosher meat stores as the authoritative certifier that "all the religious requirements have been thoroughly observed." Associated Synagogues, Inc., certifies caterers as authentic carriers of kosher food. Associated Synagogues refuses to certify caterers who buy meat from stores certified by the United Kosher Butchers Association because the latter refuses to submit to supervision by the rabbinical committee of Associated Synagogues. Many caterers then withdraw their patronage from stores supervised by the United Kosher Butchers Association. What legal action, if any, can be taken?

105. The town of Salem has a population of two thousand. A group of avowed homosexuals moves into the area. They begin to run for public offices with some success. The old-time townspeople become very upset. A state law gives courts the power to hospitalize mentally ill individuals. Part of the definition of "mentally ill" is as follows: "He evidences an inclination to sexual depravity such as child molestation, homosexuality, and like perversions." The mayor of Salem files petitions in court to have the homosexuals declared mentally ill and institutionalized. Discuss any law that might apply to these facts.

106. Mary Perry belongs to a religion that believes that medical problems can be resolved through spiritual meditation. Her son Paul is ten years old. One day at school, Paul is rushed to a hospital after collapsing. Mrs. Perry is called at home. When she arrives at the hospital, she is told that Paul will require emergency surgery. She refuses to give her consent. The doctor tells her that if the operation is not performed within the next twenty-four hours, Paul will die. Mrs. Perry responds by saying that "God will cure my son." What legal action, if any, can be taken against her?

REFERENCES

C. Ahearn et al., *Selected Information Sources for the District of Columbia* (1981).

P. Aldrich et al., *A Law Librarian's Introduction to Missouri State Publications* (1980).

M. Aycock et al., *A Law Librarian's Introduction to Virginia State Publication's* (1981).

E. Bander, *Legal Research and Education Abridgement* (1978).

M. Banks, *Using a Law Library* (2d ed. 1974).

R. Beer, *An Annotated Guide to the Legal Literature of Michigan* (1973).

M. Boner, *A Reference Guide to Texas Law and Legal History: Sources and Documentation* (1976).

M. Botsford and R. Matz, *Handbook of Legal Research in Massachusetts* (1982).

R. Brown, *Guide to Florida Legal Research* (1980).

L. Chanin, *Reference Guide to Georgia Legal History and Legal Research* (1980).

M. Cohen and R. Berring, *How to Find the Law* (8th ed. 1983).

R. Danner, *Legal Research in Wisconsin* (1980).

B. Davies, *Research in Illinois Law* (1954).

L. Davis, *An Introduction to Maryland State Publications for the Law Librarian* (1981).

L. Fariss and K. Buckley, *An Introduction to Indiana State Publications for the Law Librarian* (1982).

M. Fink. *Research in California Law* (2d ed. 1964).

H. French, *Research in Florida Law* (2d ed. 1965).

W. Gilmer, *Legal Research, Writing, and Advocacy* (1978).

R. Goehlert, *Congress and Law-Making: Researching the Legislative Process* (1979).

R. Granberg, *Introduction to California Law Finding* (1977).

D. Hanke, *California Law Guide* (2d ed. 1976).

R. Jacobs, et al., *Illinois Legal Research Sourcebook* (1977).

J. Jacobstein & R. Mersky, *Pollack's Fundamentals of Legal Research* (4th ed. 1973).

I. Kavass and B. Christensen, *Guide to North Carolina Legal Research* (1973).

W. Knudson, *Wisconsin Legal Research Guide* (2d ed. 1972).

L. Laska, *Tennessee Legal Research Handbook* (1977).

D. Lloyd, *Finding the Law* (1974).

R. Mills and J. Schultz, *South Carolina Legal Research Methods* (1973).

New Jersey State Law and Legislative Reference Bureau, *Legal Research Guide for the New Jersey State Library* (1957).

A. Poldervaart, *Manual for Effective New Mexico Legal Research* (1955).

M. Price, H. Bittner, and S. Bysiewicz, *Effective Legal Research* (4th ed. 1979).

G. Stromme, *Basic Legal Research Techniques* (4th ed. 1979).

E. Surrency, *Research in Pennsylvania Law* (2d ed. 1965).

University of Washington Law School, *Legal Research Guide* (1980).

K. Wallach, *Louisiana Legal Research Manual* (1972).

C. Wren and J. Wren, *The Legal Research Manual* (1983).

S. Yoak and M. Heinen, *Michigan Legal Documents: An Annotated Legal Bibliography* (1982).

12

Legal Writing

Section A. INTRODUCTION

There are a number of different kinds of writing within a law office:

1. Letters
2. Instruments
3. Pleadings
4. Memorandum of law
5. Appellate brief

1. *Letters*

Many "garden variety" letters are written in a law office every day, e.g., a letter requesting information, a letter requesting payment, a letter notifying someone of the fact that the office represents a particular person or company.

In an "opinion letter," the office writes to its client, explaining the application of the law and advising the client what to do. Such letters try to present technical material in a comprehensible manner. Unlike a brief or memorandum, the opinion letter will not make extensive reference to court opinions or statutes. The client's need is for clear, concise, practical advice.

2. *Instruments*

An instrument is a formal document that gives expression to a legal act or agreement. Examples of instruments are contracts, deeds, wills, leases, bonds, notes, mortgage agreements, etc. Many formbooks (p. 543) provide models for drafting such instruments. Rarely will anyone write an instrument from point zero. The starting point is almost always a standard form or model, which is adapted to the particular facts of the client.

3. *Pleadings*

Pleadings are formal statements of claims and defenses that are exchanged between parties involved in litigation. The major pleadings are the complaint (p. 498), answer, counterclaim, reply to counterclaim, cross claim, and third party complaint. Formbooks are also often used as the starting point in drafting pleadings. Some high-volume litigation firms use computers or word-processing equipment to help prepare repetitive pleadings (p. 715).

Section B. MEMORANDUM OF LAW

A memorandum of law is an analysis of legal authority (p. 561) governing one or more legal issues. It is generally the product of a fairly extensive research effort. There are two kinds of legal memoranda:

a. The *internal* or *interoffice* memorandum
b. The *external* or *adversary* memorandum

The primary feature of an *interoffice* memorandum is its *objectivity*. It must present the strengths *and* weaknesses of the client's case so that the senior members of the office can make intelligent decisions based upon all aspects of the law. The memo will certainly attempt to show how the law can be interpreted in the light most favorable to the client, but it must go beyond this level. The memo also must try to anticipate what the strongest arguments of the *opponent* will be. Such arguments must be presented with precision and honesty. When this is done, the reader of the memo within the office will be in the best position to design *realistic* strategy.

An *external* memorandum, by contrast, is not an objective document at all. It is an *adversary* document that attempts to persuade the reader to adopt a decision favorable to the client. The audience of your external memorandum may be a hearing officer in an administrative agency (if so, it will often be called a hearing memorandum or a "points and authorities memorandum") or a trial court judge (if so, it will often be called a trial memorandum). A trial memorandum is like an appellate brief (p. 695) in that both are advocacy documents directed to a court. An appellate brief, however, is more stylized in format and is not written for an agency or a trial court.

The distinguishing features of the two kinds of memoranda are outlined in the following chart:

CHARACTERISTICS OF INTEROFFICE VERSUS EXTERNAL MEMORANDA OF LAW	
INTEROFFICE MEMORANDUM OF LAW	EXTERNAL MEMORANDUM OF LAW
1. Emphasizes both the strengths and the weaknesses of the client's position on each issue (objective)	1. Emphasizes the strengths but minimizes the weaknesses of the client's position on each issue
2. Emphasizes both the strengths and the weaknesses of the opposing party's probable position on each issue	2. Emphasizes the weaknesses but minimizes the strengths of the opposing party's position on each issue
3. Predicts the court's or the agency's probable decision on each issue.	3. Argues for a favorable decision on each issue
4. Recommends the most favorable strategy for the client to follow	

STRUCTURE OF AN INTEROFFICE MEMO

Not all supervisors agree on the preferred structure of the interoffice memorandum of law. The following are common features of many memos:

1. Heading
2. Statement of the assignment
3. Facts
4. Discussion or analysis
5. Conclusion
6. Recommendations

1. Heading

At the top of the page you state the kind of document you are writing (interoffice memorandum of law). You then list:

- The person to whom the memo is addressed.
- The name of the author of the memo.
- The date the memo was prepared.
- The client's name and opponent.
- The office file number of the case.
- The court docket number if the case has already been filed in court.
- A very brief subject-matter entry (following the notation "RE:") in which you state what the memo is about.

The following sample heading illustrates how this information might be set forth in a heading for a memorandum written on behalf of client Brown, who is suing Miller:

Interoffice Memorandum

TO: Ms. Jane Patterson   RE: Availability of the
FR: John Jackson   contributory negligence
DATE: April 30, 1986   defense to Miller
CASE: Brown v. Miller
OFFICE FILE NUMBER: 86-42
DOCKET NUMBER: CIV. 1-86-307

Note that the subject-matter description in this sample (RE:) briefly indicates the nature of the question that will be treated in the memorandum. This information is needed for at least two reasons. First, the average law office case file will contain a large number of documents, often including several legal memoranda. A heading that at least briefly indicates the nature of the subject of each memorandum makes it much easier to locate the memorandum in the client's file if necessary. Second, it is unlikely that the usefulness of your memorandum will end when the client's case is closed. Some law offices maintain fairly extensive libraries of old office memoranda, which are cataloged and filed by subject matter for reference in future cases. This avoids unnecessary and costly duplication of research time in the event that a similar question arises in a future client's case. The subject-matter heading on your memorandum facilitates the cataloging and filing of your memorandum in such a library.

The inclusion of the date on which the memorandum was completed and submitted is important for similar reasons. While your analysis and conclusions may have been very accurate at the time the memorandum was written, subsequent changes in the law may have occurred by the time the memorandum is next referred to. Upon seeing the date of the memorandum, a reader will know from what date subsequent legal research will be needed.

2. Statement of the Assignment

It is a good idea early in the memo to provide an explicit statement of what your supervisor has asked you to do in the memo.

3. Statement of the Legal Issue(s)

On phrasing issues, see generally p. 371.

Often you must state and discuss certain issues *on the assumption* that the court or agency decides against you on prior issues that you have stated and discussed early in the memorandum. Suppose that the client is a defendant in a negligence action. The first issue may concern the liability of the defendant: was the defendant negligent or not? In the first issue, the defendant will be covering the liability question and will attempt to demonstrate in the discussion or analysis on this issue why the defendant is *not* liable. All the evidence and authority supporting nonliability will be treated in the most effective manner under this issue. At the time that the memorandum is written, there will, of course, be no resolution of the first issue. Hence, you must be prepared for issues that will arise *on the assumption* that you lose on the first issue. For example, all issues concerning damages (how much money must be paid to a plaintiff who has successfully established liability) need to be anticipated and analyzed in the event that the liability issue is lost. The statement of the damage issues in the memorandum should be prefaced by language such as:

> In the event that we lose the first issue, then we must discuss the issue of . . . .

or

> On the assumption that the court finds for [the other party] on the liability issue, the question then becomes whether . . . .

No matter how firmly you believe in your prediction of what a court or agency will do on an issue, be prepared for what will happen in the event that your prediction eventually proves to be erroneous. This must be done in an internal memorandum, in an external memorandum (hearing or trial), *and* in an appellate brief.

4. Statement of the Facts

Your statement of the facts of the client's case is one of the most important components of your memorandum. You should take great pains to see that it is concise, highly accurate, and well organized.

a. Conciseness.   An unduly long fact statement will only frustrate the reader. Try to eliminate any unnecessary facts from the statement. One way of doing this is to carefully review your fact statement *after* you have completed your analysis of the issues. If there are facts in your statement that are not subsequently referred to in your analysis, it may be that those facts are not particularly relevant to your memorandum and can be eliminated in your final draft of the memorandum.

b. Accuracy.   In most instances you will be drafting the memorandum to prepare to go before a court or agency for the first time; there may be no prior proceedings. Hence, there will be no record and no official findings of fact. The temptation will be to indulge in wishful thinking—to ignore adverse facts and to assume that disputed facts will be resolved in favor of the client. Do not give in to this temptation. You must assess the legal consequences of favorable *and* unfavorable facts. If a particular fact is presently unknown, put aside your writing, if possible, and investigate whatever evidence may exist to prove the fact one way or the other. If it is not practical to conduct an investigation at the present time, then you should provide an analysis of what law will apply based upon your most reasonable estimate of what an investigation may uncover. The need for accuracy does not mean that you should fail to state the facts in the light most favorable to the client. It simply means that you must be cautious in doing so, to avoid making false or misleading statements of fact.

c. Organization.   A disorganized statement of facts not only will prevent the reader from understanding the events in question but also will interfere with an understanding of your subsequent analysis. In general, it is best to start with a short one- or two-sentence summary of the nature of the case, followed by a *chronologically* ordered statement of the detailed facts. Occasional variations from strict chronological order can be effective so long as they do not interfere with the flow of the story.

5. Discussion or Analysis

Here you present the law and explain its applicability to the facts, i.e., you try to answer the issues. For memos that require the interpretation of statutes, a suggested organizational structure is as follows:

- State the entire section or subsection of the statute that you will be analyzing. Include only what must be discussed in the memo. If the section or subsection is long, you may want to place it in an appendix to the memo. If you are going to discuss more than one section or subsection, treat them separately in different parts of the memo unless they must be discussed together.
- Break the section or subsection down into its elements (p. 373). List each element separately. You can omit any element or portion of an element that is obviously irrelevant to the case under analysis.
- Briefly tell the reader which elements will be in contention and why. In effect, you are telling the reader why you have phrased the issue(s) the way you did earlier in the memo.
- Go through each element you have identified, one at a time, spending most of your time on the elements that are in contention.
- For the elements not in contention, simply tell the reader why you think there will not be any dispute about them, e.g., you anticipate that both sides probably will agree that the facts clearly support the applicability or nonapplicability of the element.
- For the elements in contention, present your interpretation of each element; discuss court opinions that have interpreted the statute, if any; discuss regulations and administrative decisions that have interpreted the statute, if any; discuss the legislative history of the statute, if available (p. 655); discuss scholarly interpretation of the statute, if any.
- Give opposing viewpoints for the elements in contention. Try to anticipate how the other side will interpret these elements, e.g., what counterarguments will the other side probably make based on its use of court opinions, legislative history, etc.

6. Conclusion

Give your personal opinion on which side has the better arguments. Do not state any new arguments in the conclusion. Simply state your own perspective on the strengths and weaknesses of the arguments you have made above.

7. Recommendations

State any specific recommendations that you feel are appropriate in view of the analysis and conclusion that you have provided, e.g., further facts should be investigated, further research should be undertaken, a letter should be written to the agency involved, the case should be litigated or settled.

8. Appendix

At the end of the memo, include items that you referred to in the memo, e.g., photographs, statistical tables, the full text of statutes.

What follows is an interoffice memorandum of law that conforms with the recommended structure. Assume that the supervisor wants this memorandum within a few hours after it is given to you. You are asked to provide a preliminary analysis of the statute. Hence, at this point there has been no time to do any research on the statute, although you should indicate what research you think will be appropriate.

INTEROFFICE MEMORANDUM OF LAW

TO: Mary Jones, Esq.
FROM: Tim Farrell
DATE: March 13, 1984
CASE: Department of Sanitation v. Jim Donaldson
OFFICE FILE NUMBER: 84-114
DOCKET NUMBER: (none at this time; no action has been filed)
RE: Whether Donaldson has violated §17

A. ASSIGNMENT
    You have asked me to do a preliminary analysis of §17 [23 State Code Ann. §17 (1980)] to assess whether our client, Jim Donaldson, has violated this statute. No research on the statute has been undertaken thus far, but I will indicate where such research might be helpful.

B. LEGAL ISSUE
    When a government employee is asked to rent a car for his agency, but uses the car for personal business before he signs the lease, has this employee violated §17, which prohibits the use of "property leased to the government" for nonofficial purposes?

C. FACTS
    Jim Donaldson is a government employee who works for the State Department of Sanitation. On February 12, 1984, he is asked by his supervisor, Fred Jackson, to rent a car for the agency in order to make an important delivery. At the ABC Car Rental Company, Donaldson is shown several cars available for rental. He asks the manager if he could test drive one of the cars for about 15 minutes before making a decision. The manager agrees. Donaldson then drives the car to his home in the area, picks up a TV, and takes

it to his sister's home. When he returns, he tells the manager that he wants to rent the car for his agency. He signs the lease and takes the car to the agency where it is used for the important delivery. The supervisor, however, finds out about the trip that Donaldson made to his sister with the TV. He is charged with a violation of §17. Since he is a new employee at the agency, he is fearful that he might lose his job.

D. ANALYSIS

Donaldson is charged with violating 23 State Code Ann. §17 (1980), which provides as follows:

§17. Use of Government Property

An employee of any state agency shall not directly or indirectly use government property of any kind, including property leased to the government, for other than officially approved activities.

To establish a violation of this statute, the following must be shown:

(1) An employee of a state agency
(2) (a) directly uses government property of any kind including property leased to the government or
(b) indirectly uses government property of any kind including property leased to the government
(3) for other than officially approved purposes

The main problem in this case will be the second element.

(1) Employee of a state agency

Donaldson works for the State Department of Sanitation, which is clearly a "state agency" under the statute.

(2) Use of property leased to the government

The central issue is whether Donaldson directly used property leased to the government. (The rented car was not owned by the government. Hence it was not "government property." And Donaldson acted "directly" rather than "indirectly" such as by causing someone else to drive the car.) There should be no dispute that when Donaldson drove the car to his sister's, he directly used property. But was it "property leased to the government"?

Donaldson's best argument is that when he made the trip to his sister, he had not yet signed the lease. The car did not become property leased to the government until after he returned from his sister's house. No costs were incurred by the government because of the test drive. Rental payments would not begin until the car was rented through the signing of the lease.

The supervisor, on the other hand, would argue that the statute should not be interpreted narrowly. The overall goal of the legislature in passing §17 was to avoid misuse of government resources. Public employees should not take advantage of their position for private gain. To do so would be a violation of the public trust. This is what Donaldson did. While on the government payroll, he obtained access to a car and used it for a private trip. It is not clear from the facts whether the manager of the ABC Rental Company knew that Donaldson was going to rent the car for a government agency when he received permission to take the test drive. This should be checked. If the manager did know, then the likelihood is that Donaldson used the fact that he was a government employee to obtain the permission. He held himself out as a reliable individual because of the nature of his employment.

The phrase "property leased to the government" should be interpreted broadly to include both the signing of the lease and the necessary steps leading up to the signing. Everyone would agree that Donaldson would have violated the statute if he had made the TV trip moments after he signed the lease. It is illogical to argue that there is no violation if he made the trip moments before he signed the lease. Given the purpose of §17, the legislature could not have intended such a result.

I have not yet checked whether there are any court opinions or agency regulations interpreting §17 on this point. Nor have I researched the legislative history of the statute. All this should be done soon.

(3) Officially Approved Purposes

Nothing in the facts indicates that Donaldson's supervisor, Fred Jackson, gave him any authorization to make the TV trip. Even if Jackson had authorized the trip, it would probably not be "officially" approved since the trip was not for official (i.e., public) business.

E. CONCLUSION

Donaldson has the stronger argument based on the language of the statute. The property simply was not "leased" at the time he made the TV trip. I must admit, however, that the agency has some very good points in its favor. Unlike Donaldson's technical argument, the agency's position is grounded in common sense. Yet on balance, Donaldson's argument should prevail.

F. RECOMMENDATIONS

Some further investigation is needed. We should find out whether the ABC Rental Company manager knew that Donaldson was a government employee at the time he asked for the test drive. In addition, legal research should be undertaken to find out if any court opinions and agency regulations exist on the statute. A check into the legislative history of §17 also is needed.

Finally, I recommend that we send a letter to Donaldson's supervisor, Fred Jackson, explaining our position. I have attached a draft of such a letter for your signature in the event you deem this action appropriate.

There is one matter that I have not addressed in this memo. Donaldson is concerned that he might lose his job over this incident. Assuming for the moment that he did violate §17, it is not at all clear that termination would be an appropriate sanction. The statute is silent on this point. Let me know if you want me to research this issue.

Farrell, Grote, & Schweitzer
Attorneys at Law
724 Central Plaza Place
West Union, Ohio 45693
513-363-7159

March 15, 1984

Frederick Jackson
Field Supervisor
Department of Sanitation
3416 34th St. NW
West Union, Ohio 45693

RE: James Donaldson
84-114

Dear Mr. Jackson:

Our firm represents Mr. James Donaldson. As you know, some question has arisen as to Mr. Donaldson's use of a car prior to the time he was asked to rent it for your agency on February 12, 1984. Our understanding is that he was asked to go to the ABC Car Rental Company in order to rent a car for a certain delivery that was needed at your agency, and that he did so satisfactorily.

Your agency became responsible for the car at the moment Mr. Donaldson signed the lease for the car rental. It is clear that no personal use could be made of the car from that moment. It is also clear that no such personal use occurred. What happened prior to the time the lease was signed is not relevant. The governing statute (§17) is quite explicit. It forbids nonofficial use of property "leased" to the government. Such use did not occur in this case. No one has questioned Mr. Donaldson's performance of his duty once he "leased" the car.

If additional clarification is needed, we would be happy to discuss this matter with you further.

Sincerely,

Mary Jones, Esq.

wps: MJ

ASSIGNMENT 107

The Pepsi Cola Bottling Company is authorized to do business in Florida. It wishes to prevent another company from calling itself the Pepsi Catsup Company because this name violates section 225.25. The Pepsi Catsup Company denies that its name is in violation of this statute. The Secretary of State has the responsibility of enforcing this statute.

> **48 State Code Ann. §225.25 (1979).** The name of a company or corporation shall be such as will distinguish it from any other company or corporation doing business in Florida.

Your supervisor asks you to prepare a preliminary memorandum of law on the applicability of this statute. The office represents the Pepsi Catsup Company. Do no legal research at this time, although you should point out what research might be helpful. After you complete the memo, draft a letter to the Secretary of State giving the position of your office on the applicability of the statute. (You can make up the names and addresses of the people involved as well as any dates that you need.)

Section C. APPELLATE BRIEF

The word *brief* has several meanings.

First, to *brief* a case is to summarize its major components (e.g., key facts, issues, reasoning, disposition, p. 645). Such a brief is your own summary of a particular court opinion for later use.

Second, a *trial brief* is an attorney's set of notes on how to conduct the trial. The notes will be on the opening statement, witnesses, exhibits, direct and cross-examination, closing argument, etc. This trial brief is sometimes called a trial manual or trial book. It is not submitted to the court nor to the other side. A *trial memorandum* on points of law might be submitted, but not the trial brief, which contains counsel's strategy. (This trial memorandum, however, is sometimes referred to as a trial brief. In such instances, the trial brief consists of arguments of law rather than the tactical blueprint for the conduct of the trial.)

Third, the *appellate brief* is the formal written argument to a court of appeals on why a lower court's decision should be affirmed, modified, or reversed. It is submitted to the appellate court and to the other side. The appellate brief is one of the most sophisticated kinds of legal writing in a law office.

The first appellate brief that is usually submitted is the appellant's brief. The appellant is the party initiating the appeal. Then the appellee's brief is filed in response. The appeal is taken against the appellee (sometimes called the respondent). Finally, the appellant is often allowed to submit a reply brief to counter the position taken in the appellee's brief.

Occasionally a court will permit a nonparty to the litigation to submit an appellate brief. This is referred to as an *amicus curiae* (friend of the court) brief (p. 525). The *amicus* brief advises the court on how to resolve the controversies before it.

Not all appellate briefs have the same structure. Court rules often specify what structure or format the brief should take, the print size, number of copies to be submitted, etc. (p. 674). The following are the major components of many appellate briefs.

a. Caption

The caption states the names of the parties, the name of the court, the court file or docket number, and the kind of appellate brief it is. The caption goes on the front cover of the brief (p. 524).

b. The Statement of Jurisdiction

In this section of the brief, there is a short statement explaining the subject-matter jurisdiction of the appellate court (p. 499). For example:

> This Court has jurisdiction under 28 U.S.C. § 1291 (1967).

The jurisdiction statement may point out some of the essential facts that relate to the jurisdiction of the appellate court such as how the case came up on appeal. For example.

> On January 2, 1978, a judgment was entered by the U.S. Court of Appeals for the Second Circuit. The U.S. Supreme Court granted certiorari on February 6, 1978. 400 U.S. 302.

Later in the brief there will be a Statement of the Case in which more detailed jurisdictional material is often included.

c. Table of Contents

The table of contents is an outline of the major components of the brief, including the various *point headings* and subheadings of the argument and the pages in the brief on which each of these components begins. A point heading is a party's conclusion, which it wants the court to adopt for a particular issue. The function of the table of contents is to provide the reader with quick and easy access to each individual portion of the brief. Because the exact wording of the point headings and the pages on which the various components begin will not be known until the brief is completed, the table of contents will, of course, be the last section of the brief to be written. The following excerpt from the respondent's brief illustrates the structure of a table of contents.

	Page
Table of Contents	
Opinions below	1
Jurisdiction	2
Questions presented	2
Constitutional provisions, statutes, and House resolution involved	2
Statement	6
Summary of argument	8

d. Table of Authorities

This Table lists all the cases, statutes, regulations, administrative decisions, constitutional provisions, charter provisions, ordinances, court rules, and secondary authority relied on in the brief. All the cases are listed in alphabetical order, all the statutes are listed in alphabetical and numerical order, etc. The page numbers on which each of these authorities is discussed in the brief are presented so that the Table acts as an index to these authorities.

    Example:

e. Questions Presented

The label used for this part of the brief varies. It may be called "Questions Presented," "Points Relied upon for Reversal," "Points in Error," "Assignments of Error," "Issues Presented," etc. Regardless of the label, its substance is essentially the same: it is a statement of the issue or issues of law that the party wishes the appellate court to consider and decide.

f. Statement of the Case

Here, the dispute is summarized, lower court proceedings to date are summarized, the essential facts of the case are presented, and often jurisdictional data is also included.

Example:

These are actions based upon the Federal Tort Claims Act, 28 U.S.C. §1346(b), initiated by the appellants, Garrett Freightlines, Inc. and Charles R. Thomas in the United States District Court for the District of Idaho. The appellant alleged that appellee's employee, Randall W. Reynolds, while acting within the scope of his employment, negligently caused injury to appellants. The United States denied that the employee was acting within the scope of his employment.

On March 27, 1973, appellant Garrett made a motion for limited summary judgment as to whether Reynolds was acting within the scope of his employment when the collision occurred. The actions of Garrett and Thomas were consolidated by order of the court, and appellee later moved for summary judgment (Tr. 204).

The District Court held that under the authority of dicta in Berrettoni v. United States, 436 F.2d 1372 (9th Cir. 1970), that Reynolds was not within the scope of his employment when the accident occurred and granted appellee's motion for summary judgment. It is from that order and judgment that the injured now appeals.

Staff Sergeant Reynolds was a career soldier in the United States Military and, until November 9, 1970, stationed at Fort Rucker, Alabama. On or about July 30, 1970, official orders directed that Reynolds be reassigned to the Republic of Vietnam. . . .

---

g. Summary of Argument

The major points to be made in the brief are summarized.

h. Argument

Here the attorney explains the legal positions of the client. All the primary and secondary authority relied upon is analyzed.

i. Conclusion

The conclusion states what action the attorney is asking the appellate court to take.

j. Appendixes

The appendixes contain excerpts from statutes, or other primary authority, excerpts from the trial, charts, descriptions of exhibits entered into evidence at the trial, etc.

Section D. SOME WRITING GUIDELINES

1. Forbidden Words

Avoid the following terms altogether:

above (as an adjective)
afore-mentioned
aforesaid
and/or (say "A or B," or say "A or B or both")
before-mentioned
provided that
said (as a substitute for "the," "that," or "those")
same (as a substitute for "it," "he," "her," etc.)
to wit
whatsoever
whensoever
wheresoever

2. Circumlocutions

a. Avoid pairs of words having the same effect:

alter and change
any and all
authorize and empower
by and with
each and all
each and every
final and conclusive
from and after
full and complete
full force and effect
made and entered into
null and void
order and direct
over and above
sole and exclusive
type and kind
unless and until

b. Avoid pairs of words when one word includes the other (use the broader or narrower term as the substance requires):

means and includes

c. Avoid expressions such as:

none whatever
make application, make a determination
shall be considered to be, shall be deemed to be, may be treated as, have the effect of (unless a fiction is intended)

3. Preferred Expressions

Unless there are special reasons to the contrary:

Do Not Say	*Say*
(1) accorded	(1) given
(2) adequate number of	(2) enough
(3) admit of	(3) allow
(4) afforded	(4) given
(5) all of the	(5) all the
(6) a person is prohibited from	(6) a person shall not
(7) approximately	(7) about
(8) at least	(8) not less than (when referring to two or more)
(9) at such time as	(9) when
(10) attains the age of ____	(10) becomes ____ years of age
(11) attempt (as a verb)	(11) try
(12) at the time	(12) when
(13) by means of	(13) by
(14) calculate	(14) compute
(15) category	(15) kind, class, group
(16) cause it to be done	(16) have it done
(17) contiguous to	(17) next to
(18) corporation organized under the laws of Ohio	(18) Ohio corporation
(19) deem	(19) consider
(20) does not operate to	(20) does not
(21) during such time as	(21) while
(22) during the course of	(22) during
(23) endeavor (as a verb)	(23) try
(24) enter into a contract with	(24) to contract with
(25) evince	(25) show
(26) expiration	(26) end
(27) for the duration of	(27) during
(28) for the purpose of holding (or other gerund)	(28) to hold (or comparable infinitive)
(29) for the reason that	(29) because
(30) forthwith	(30) immediately
(31) in accordance with	(31) pursuant to, under
(32) in case	(32) if
(33) in cases in which	(33) when, where (say "whenever" or "wherever" only when you need to emphasize the exhaustive or recurring applicability of a point)
(34) in order to	(34) to
(35) in sections 2023 to 2039 inclusive	(35) in sections 2023 to 2039

(36)	in the case of	(36)	[see (33) above]
(37)	in the event of	(37)	if
(38)	in the event that	(38)	if
(39)	in the interest of	(39)	for
(40)	is able to	(40)	can
(41)	is applicable	(41)	applies
(42)	is authorized to	(42)	may
(43)	is binding upon	(43)	binds
(44)	is directed to	(44)	shall
(45)	is empowered to	(45)	may
(46)	is entitled (in the sense of "has the name")	(46)	is called
(47)	is entitled to	(47)	may
(48)	is hereby authorized and it shall be his or her duty to	(48)	shall
(49)	is hereby authorized to	(49)	shall
(50)	is not prohibited from	(50)	may
(51)	is permitted to	(51)	may
(52)	is required to	(52)	shall
(53)	is unable to	(53)	cannot
(54)	it is directed	(54)	shall
(55)	it is his or her duty to	(55)	shall
(56)	it is the duty of	(56)	shall
(57)	it shall be lawful	(57)	may
(58)	it shall be unlawful for a person to	(58)	a person shall not
(59)	no later than June 30, 1986	(59)	before July 1, 1986
(60)	on or after July 1, 1987	(60)	after June 30, 1987
(61)	on or before June 30, 1985	(61)	before July 1, 1985
(62)	on the part of	(62)	by
(63)	or, in the alternative	(63)	or
(64)	paragraph (5) of subsection (a) of section 2097	(64)	section 2097(a)(5)
(65)	per annum	(65)	a year
(66)	per centum	(66)	percent
(67)	period of time	(67)	use period *or* time
(68)	provision of law	(68)	law
(69)	render (in the sense of give)	(69)	give
(70)	State of Massachusetts	(70)	Massachusetts
(71)	subsequent to	(71)	after
(72)	suffer (in the sense of permit)	(72)	permit
(73)	under the provisions of	(73)	under
(74)	until such time as	(74)	until

4. Action Verbs

Wherever possible, draft your sentences to use action verbs instead of participles, gerunds, and other noun or adjective forms. Action verbs are shorter and more direct.

Do Not Say	*Say*
(1) give consideration to	(1) consider
(2) give recognition to	(2) recognize
(3) have knowledge of	(3) know
(4) have need of	(4) need
(5) in the determination of	(5) to determine
(6) is applicable	(6) applies
(7) is dependent on	(7) depends on
(8) is in attendance at	(8) attends
(9) make an appointment of	(9) appoint
(10) make application	(10) apply
(11) make payment	(11) pay
(12) make provision for	(12) provide for

Compare the following versions of the same sentence:[1]

In neither the motion nor appellant's brief was there any reliance on ORC §2943.39.	Appellant did not rely on ORC §2943.39 in either his motion or his brief.
The testimony of the defendant was contradicted by the fact that he had the receipt showing partial payment.	The receipt showing partial payment contradicted defendant's testimony.
The result obtained from a properly administered breathalyzer test is the percentage by weight of alcohol in a person's blood.	A properly administered breathalyzer test shows the percentage by weight of alcohol in a person's blood.

5. Verbosity

Avoid unnecessary words. Compare the following versions of the same sentence:

He consulted *with* a doctor *in regard* to his injuries.	He consulted a doctor *about* his injuries.
He drove to the left *due to the fact* that the lane was blocked.	He drove to the left *because* the lane was blocked.
This product is used for *hair dyeing purposes.*	This product is used to *dye hair.*
The continuance was requested *in order to obtain the presence of a witness who was not then available.*	The continuance was requested *because a witness was unavailable.*

---

[1] Grey, *Writing A Good Appellate Brief,* 88 Case and Comment *44, 48–50* (No. 6, November–December, 1983). Reprinted by special permission. Copyrighted ©1983 by the Lawyers Co-operative Publishing Co.

Read these sentences, with and without the italicized words.

> The court directed a verdict in favor of defendant *and against the plaintiff.* (Verdicts for defendants usually are against the plaintiff.)

> The car was green *in color.* (This distinguishes it from the car that was green in size.)

> A stipulation by *all of* the parties. (A stipulation by some of the parties is not of much use.)

> A delivery was made every Tuesday *on a regular weekly basis.* (What does *every Tuesday* mean?)

6. Shorter Sentences

Use short sentences. A short precise sentence is more comprehensible and more effective. Read this. What is the writer saying?

> The Appellee contends that there is not reversible error in the trial court's sustaining the Appellant's objections given the immediate corrective instructions of the trial court as well as the weight of the evidence against the Appellant.

Shorter sentences add considerable clarity:

> There is no reversible error. The trial court sustained the objection and immediately cautioned the jury. Considering all the evidence, there is no prejudice to Appellant.

Compare these versions:

> The de-icer spray had admittedly been sprayed on the inside of the windshield. However, without knowing the name of the manufacturer or having an independent analysis made of the de-icer spray, it could not possibly be ascertained what quantity of methanol was in the product and that would be essential to ascertaining what effect, if any, having breathed the chemical would have upon the intoxilizer test.

> The de-icer sprayed on the windshield contained methanol. It was not possible to analyze the product and determine the amount of methanol without knowing the name of the manufacturer. It was not possible to learn what effect, if any, inhaling the methanol would have on the intoxilizer test.

> The defendant, ABC, an Ohio Corporation for profit, is engaged in the subsidized housing business and incident thereto is the owner of six dwelling units containing 46 apartment units housing 100 people. To provide for the culinary and sanitary needs of the occupants the defendant purchases from LeAx approximately 5300 gallons (22 tons) of water per day, and since opening for business in July 1975 has purchased 11,308,000 gallons of water

> The defendant, ABC Corp., owns and operates a 46-unit apartment complex containing 100 residents. Water for the apartments is supplied by LeAx at the rate of 5300 gallons, 22 tons, per day. All waste water from the apartments is treated in defendant's sewage plant and discharged into a drainage ditch that runs across plaintiff's property.

704 INTRODUCTION TO PARALEGALISM

which is all collected following use, placed in a sewage plant, treated, and discharged into a drainage ditch, which in turn discharges onto the plaintiff's property.

This case involves an incident which occurred on November 16, 1978. The plaintiff, Oilcorp, was the owner of a drilling rig which was located in a rural section of Athens County for the purpose of drilling for petroleum. Prior to November 16, 1978, it had been determined that the drilling was completed and it was necessary to move the rig to another location. The defendant was notified of this need and was requested to bring equipment to the drill site for the purpose of moving the drilling rig and associated apparatus from that location to a new location.

The plaintiff, Oilcorp, owned an oil drilling rig located in rural Athens County. It was necessary to move the rig to another location. Oilcorp requested defendant to bring his equipment to the drill site to move the drilling rig.

7. Pronoun Reference

a. Use pronouns only where the nouns to which the pronouns refer are unmistakably clear. The use of pronouns with ambiguous referents can confuse the meaning of a sentence.

b. If the pronoun could refer to more than one person or object in a sentence, repeat the name of the person or object to avoid the ambiguity.

Do Not Say: After the Administrator appoints a Deputy Assistant, he or she shall supervise the . . . . [Who does the supervising? The Administrator or the Deputy? If the latter is intended, then:]

Say: After the Administrator appoints a Deputy Assistant, the Deputy Assistant shall supervise the . . . .

8. And/Or

Do not use "and/or," since the combination of conjunctive ("and") and disjunctive ("or") indicates an alternative. Decide whether "and" or "or" is appropriate for the sentence and use that word alone. Use "or both" when necessary to include items both individually and together.

Violation of any provision of this Act is punishable by a fine of $100 or imprisonment of six months, or both.

9. Sexism in Language

Avoid gender-specific language when the intent is to refer to both sexes. If neutral language is not available, rewrite the sentence to avoid the problem.

	Gender-Specific Language		*Gender-Neutral Alternatives*
(1)	businessman	(1)	executive, member of the business community
(2)	chairman	(2)	chairperson, chair
(3)	draftsman	(3)	drafter
(4)	husband, wife	(4)	spouse
(5)	man	(5)	person, human, humankind
(6)	man-hours	(6)	worker hours
(7)	mankind	(7)	humanity
(8)	manpower	(8)	work force, personnel
(9)	workmen's compensation	(9)	workers' compensation

REFERENCES

F. Cooper, *Writing in Law Practice* (1963).

G. Gopen, *Writing from a Legal Perspective* (1981).

D. Mellinkoff, *Legal Writing: Sense & Nonsense* (1982).

W. Statsky and J. Wernet, *Case Analysis and Fundamentals of Legal Writing* (2d d. 1984).

H. Weihofen, *Legal Writing Style* (2d ed. 1980).

13

Computer Literacy for Paralegals:
An Introduction to the Use
of Computers in a Law Office
by Dale Hobart*

In this chapter we will provide (1) an overview of computers and computer programs and (2) their current applications in law offices. Throughout the chapter we will assume that you are new to the field of computer technology. To be sure that the basics are covered, we will further assume that you have been given the responsibility of purchasing a computer system for your law office. Hence you *need* an effective overview from A to Z.

Section A. INTRODUCTION

One problem for many people is a fear that a computer will embarrass them because it is so smart. Not so. You will soon learn that computers are not very bright. Working with a computer is very much like working with a two-year-old. Unless you use instructions that the two-year-old understands, the child will say no or wander away. Computers will do the same. Unless given instructions that they understand, computers will do nothing or will do the equivalent of wandering out of the room. Furthermore, like a two-year-old who wants to obey, the computer will do exactly what you tell it to do and not necessarily what you intend it to do.

* Director of Legal Assistant Program, Ferris State College; Assistant director of Academic Computing, Ferris State College.

Suppose, for example, that you wanted a two-year-old to throw away the paper cups that are on the kitchen table. You say to the child, "Go into the kitchen and throw the cups that are on the table into the garbage." Later you discover that not only the paper cups were thrown into the trash, but also your good china cups, left on the table after your guests departed the night before. In a similar situation, a computer will do the same thing. If you want the computer to clear out old information on a diskette, an instruction that is too general will destroy the good as well as the bad.

Many of us have been misled about what computers are and what they can do. They are not magic boxes that can perform miracles. At the simplest level, the computer can understand only 1 and 0. All the fantastic feats accomplished by computers are the result of clever people using 1's and 0's to get the computer to do what they want. The vehicle they use is called a *program*.

Even with very good programs, computers can be stubborn. The program and the computer will respond only to words or directions that are in the program's vocabulary, and in most programs today, correct spelling is essential. Unlike a person, most computers cannot recognize a misspelled instruction for what it should be. As computers become more and more powerful, however, the available programs have become increasingly powerful. As a result, some computers *are* able to understand misspelled words and common English. Yet, small computers are still a long way from being able to understand the many word combinations that even our two-year-old can understand.

Section B. TERMINOLOGY

The world of the computer, like the world of the law, has its own language. Initially, this language can be very confusing. Persistence and time, however, will help rectify this problem.

First we begin with some basic definitions:

Hardware: The computer and its physical parts. Hardware is what you take out of the box and plug together when you purchase a computer system. It is any part of the system that can be physically touched.

Figure 1. Typical Computer System.

Backup: A copy of information that a computer uses. The copy is made just in case the original is destroyed.

Command: A word or group of words typed into the computer to tell the computer what to do next.

Data: Information of any type that can be used by computers. The data may consist of numbers, words, or pictures. Data is used by programs to create reports and to make decisions.

Disk Drive (also called a disk): In this chapter, we will use the term *disk drive* (rather than disk) to describe the part of your hardware that is used to store and retrieve programs and information to and from diskettes (see next definition). The disk drive has the capability of placing program information on a diskette. This is often referred to as *writing information to the diskette.* The disk drive also has the capability of "reading" the information from the diskette into the computer. If the information is a program, the program can then be "run" (see definition below) by the computer. Disk drives can be hard or floppy. A *floppy* disk drive is one that can use diskettes. The diskettes can be easily inserted and removed from the disk drive. *Hard* disks have a much greater capacity than diskettes but cannot be removed from the computer.

Figure 2. Floppy Disk Drive.

Diskette: Sometimes these are also called disks, floppy disks, or just floppies. In this chapter, the term *diskette* will be used. A diskette is a flat round piece of plastic that has been covered with the same magnetic substance that is used on a magnetic tape. Information is placed on the diskette in a manner similar to the way music is stored on a cassette. The information can be a program or data to be used by a program. This information can then be read into the computer for the computer to use.

File: A file refers to any information that a computer can use and that is stored or kept as a group. A file can consist of data or a program.

k: A measure of capacity. The letter k often refers to the amount of information that can be kept on your diskette. 100k is not very

Figure 3. Diskettes and Their Storage Boxes.

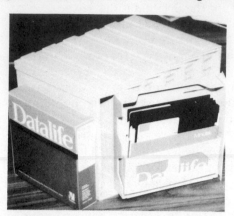

much. 800k or more is a lot. The number of k can also refer to the work area of the computer. The work area is the amount of space available to the computer for keeping programs and information where it can be directly accessed. When microcomputers were new, 64k was considered a great deal of memory (see definitions below). Today, however, even the smallest microcomputers usually have 64k of memory. Many of the newer programs require 256k or more in order to function properly.

Language: A program that allows a computer to understand commands and carry them out. BASIC, COBAL, and PASCAL are common computer languages.

Load: To move a program or information from a disk drive into the computer.

Memory: The area inside a computer that the computer uses for keeping programs that it is using and the data that the programs need.

Microcomputer: A computer that is small enough to fit on a desk. An IBM PC, an Apple IIe, and a Commodore 64 are microcomputers. The term is not clearly defined because the power of small computers has increased dramatically in the past few years.

Monitor: A TV-like device that is part of the hardware of the computer. On the screen the monitor displays whatever you type at the keyboard and displays information from the computer to the user. It can be color or monochrome (black and white, amber, or green).

Operating System: A program that the computer must have in order to do anything. The operating system is in charge of what is displayed on the screen, what is sent to the printer, and all other facets of a computer's operation.

Run: This means to cause a program to be loaded into the computer from a disk drive and to begin to perform its task.

Save: To save something means to cause a program or data that is in the computer memory to be moved or stored on a diskette in the disk drive.

Figure 4. A Monitor Displaying a Directory or Menu.

Software: The programs that make the computer seem so smart. To use a program, you must get it into the computer. This is usually done by transferring the program from a diskette.

There are, of course, many other computer terms—such as bits and bytes. While you must know such terms if you wish to become an expert on how a computer works, they are not necessary in order to use a computer.

Section C. HARDWARE

One of the decisions that must be made when starting to use a computer is which computer to buy. The choices are overwhelming. Many people make the mistake of buying a computer first and then trying to figure out what to do with it. This is not the best approach. If you know what you want to do with a computer, you should *first find the software or programs* that can do the job and *then buy the computer* that will run the programs.

When investigating available programs, you will probably discover that we live in an IBM world. At the present time, most business application programs are designed first for an IBM or "compatible" computer and then are developed for others. There are many computers that are IBM "compatible."

The word *compatible* or compatible computer is used in different senses. At a minimum, the word simply means that the information or data files created on an IBM computer can also be used by another computer. At the other end of the spectrum of compatibility, some non-IBM computers not only will use information or data from an IBM computer but will also run most *programs* designed for an IBM computer. Among the computers that seem to do this best are the Zenith 150 and 160 series.

Once you have selected your software, you are ready to choose your computer. One of the first considerations is how much memory should be purchased for your computer. Most come with a minimum of 64k. This is not enough for business applications today. The next step up is 128k. This is adequate for single-purpose programs but not for sophisticated multipurpose software, which must be run on computers with a memory of 512k or more. For such software, it is advisable to obtain all the memory possible in a particular computer.

The next item of hardware to consider is the disk drive. Disk drives are used to load programs into the computer and to store letters, documents, and other information. There are several combinations of disk drives for a microcomputer but only two that make sense for business applications.

One choice is two floppy drives (a disk drive that uses diskettes to store data). These are disk drives that use removable diskettes that are usually 5¼ inches in diameter. The disk drives should be *dual-sided,* meaning that the disk drive is capable of writing on both sides of the diskette. It should also be able to store information on a diskette in *condensed* mode. This mode is referred to as *double-density.* Therefore a two floppy drive machine should have dual-sided, double-density disk drives. This will often be abbreviated DS DD. Two disk drives are needed to make the use of a computer faster and easier. If only one disk drive is available, the user will often be required to change the diskette in the drive while using the computer. This is time consuming and frustrating.

The other choice for business purposes is a computer with one floppy disk drive and one hard disk drive. A hard disk normally used in a microcomputer can hold nearly twenty-eight times more information than a diskette. This means that most of the programs and data that are used from day to day can be kept on the hard disk, making use of the computer more convenient. In order to change programs on a hard disk system, there is no need to locate and insert a new diskette. All the programs that you normally need can be stored on the hard disk and accessed directly. Unlike a diskette, a hard disk cannot be removed from the machine. Therefore, when a hard disk is full, some of the information or programs on it would have to be removed in order to place additional materials on the hard disk. If finances allow, a hard disk is preferable

Figure 5. A Hard Drive System.

either in the computer itself or externally as part of a network. (A network, as we will see below, is created when several computers are connected together to share printers or hard disk drives.) You will find that it is nearly impossible to have too much disk storage capacity.

A monitor will be needed as part of your system. Some computers come with a monitor built right in; others do not. Illustration 13–6 contains a built-in monitor. For separate monitors, see illustrations 13–1 and 13–4. Monitors often come in two formats: monochrome and color. The monochrome may be either black and white, green, or amber. Most users prefer the green or amber screen monitors. Color is tempting. Unless, however, the computer is going to be used for color graphics or presentations, monochrome is recommended. Even the most expensive color monitors do not produce as clear an image as a good monochrome monitor. In addition, color can be hard on the eyes of the user. This is beginning to change. As computers become more sophisticated, color quality will improve.

A printer is needed to obtain a printed copy of what has been entered into the computer. This printed copy is often referred to as *hard copy*. There are two common choices when selecting a printer: dot matrix and letter quality. When the two types of printers were first introduced, there were definite differences. A dot matrix printer was fast but the quality of the print was poor. A letter-quality printer was slow but the print was excellent. Today the print quality of dot matrix printers has improved and the speed of letter-quality printers has increased. Dot matrix printers remain faster than letter-quality printers and some of the dot matrix printers produce very high quality print. Many offices have at least one printer of both types. Dot matrix is often used for printing drafts of documents while the letter-quality printer is used for the final copy. There is another type of printer that is being developed for micro-computers—a high-speed laser printer that works very much like a copy machine. Its speed is measured in terms of pages per minute, rather than characters per second as traditional printer speeds are normally measured. A character consists of a single letter, punctuation mark, etc. The print quality of a laser printer is outstanding.

The cost of cables should not be neglected when purchasing a computer system. Cables are wires used to connect the computer to the monitor and to the printer. The monochrome monitor will usually come with a cable, but

Figure 6. Built-In Monitor.

Figure 7. An External Modem.

color and graphics monitors need special cables. Printers also need their own cables to connect them to the computer. These cables are not usually included as part of the cost of the printer or of the computer.

All of the above items are necessities for operating the computer. Now let's consider an extra—*a network*. A network will allow you to connect many computers together, enabling them to share (a) information, (b) a hard disk, or (c) printers. For example, a network can make it possible for everyone in a law office to have access to wills, pleadings, or other frequently used documents without each person needing separate copies on individual diskettes. A network can be cost-efficient since it can provide the means for many computers to share some of the more expensive parts of a system.

A *modem* is needed for any law office wishing to use its computer for communications. The modem makes it possible for a computer to send and receive information using regular telephone lines. This can be useful in doing research (p. 632, 720) and sending documents across the country.

Many other hardware options are available. The above list, however, covers the basics and is sufficient to satisfy the needs of most users.

Section D. SOFTWARE

As mentioned earlier, buying software, or at least identifying the software that you want, should be the first step in acquiring a computer. There are four basic types of software available:

1. word processing
2. data base management
3. spreadsheets
4. communications.

The fifth and latest software is a combination of all four. The selection process for software can, therefore, be a complex challenge.

There are two ways of making a rational choice when selecting software. One is to try out the programs *before* you purchase them. This will work best for someone with experience who knows what to look for. Testing software yourself can be very time consuming. If you have neither the background nor the time to develop the needed expertise (months are needed), consult an expert. Generally the expert should *not* be someone connected with the local computer store who has an interest in selling you the software that is in stock.

A person within your office is your best expert. There are a surprising number of people who develop expertise on their own, yet employers and coworkers often have no idea of this ability. For small computers to be successful in an office, at least one person will need to develop a thorough knowledge of computers.

1. WORD PROCESSING SOFTWARE

A word processor is used instead of a typewriter for writing. It makes little sense to use a typewriter for anything other than addressing one envelope or filling in a simple printed form. Any letter, memo, pleading, brief, or other typed material is easier to prepare with word processing. Once you have used a good word processor, you will be very reluctant to sit at a traditional typewriter again. Since large quantities of writing are done in the law office, a word processor can be a great productivity tool.

Many law offices have used *dedicated* word processing for a long time. A dedicated word processor is one that can do only word processing and none of the other functions that a computer can perform. It is not a computer. The capabilities of the dedicated word processor, however, are now available on computers that can do all the word processing and other jobs for less cost than the single-purpose or dedicated word processors of old.

The most elemental difference between a word processor and the familiar manual or electric typewriter becomes apparent when you prepare a document for the first time. Unlike a traditional typist, the computer user does not worry about location on a line and does not listen for a bell in order to decide whether to finish a word. The computer will *automatically* move a word down to the next line when the end of a line is reached. This feature is called *word wrap*. There is no need to pause or slow down. The only time you strike the carriage return key is at the end of a paragraph. When a typing error is made at the computer keyboard, there is no need to reach for the bottle of "white out." Nor is there ever a need to worry about a messy final draft caused by insertions or corrections. With the computer you simply go back and correct the error(s). If you left out a letter or sentence, you can easily insert it. If you typed the wrong letter, type the correct one directly over the wrong one. If there are too many letters, just press the delete key over the excess letters. Furthermore, there is no need to worry about what such changes will do to paragraph alignment. The computer will take care of it. The task of typing becomes infinitely easier. Someone with limited typing skills soon becomes a confident and competent typist.

Easy text entry is just the beginning. Once a document has been put into the computer, it can be used over and over again. Standard paragraphs can be saved, modified, and inserted whenever needed. Documents can be initially designed so that names can be entered once and automatically included in the final output at fifty different locations. Standard documents can be rearranged by moving paragraphs and sentences within the document. Large or small parts of a document may be moved, deleted, or duplicated to create the final document desired.

A helpful feature on many word processors is the spelling checker. After a document has been typed, a spelling program is activated. Different types of spelling programs exist, all of which are based on a large number of words in the program's dictionary. The simpler programs place a mark on any word *not* contained in the program's dictionary. You have probably misspelled such words. The marked words can then be reviewed and corrected as needed. More sophisticated spelling programs not only will mark a word that is not in the program's dictionary but also will present several possible correct spellings of the word. Spelling checkers are great for catching transposed letters that are easily overlooked by a proofreader. Be aware, however, that a spelling checker will not tell you that you used "to" when you should have used "two" or "too." Since all these words are correctly spelled, they will not be marked by the program.

Word processors can print out a document in many formats. You can change formats if you discover that you are not satisfied with the format of your document. A variety of formats or formatting styles can be selected. The type can be *right justified* (similar in appearance to the right margin on the pages of printed books) or have a ragged right edge. Left margins can be set at many different places throughout the document. Pages can be numbered or unnumbered, and the numbering can start with any digit you choose. Some word processors can include footnotes and keep the textual material that has been footnoted on the same page with the footnote even if you later insert a lot of material on this page. Many word processors can place the same heading at the top of each page without your having to retype the heading for all the pages in the document. A few word processors come with the capability of creating indexes for the document. You simply mark the word or phrase that is to be included in the index and run the index part of the program. An index is then created with all the page numbers for the location of the word or phrase.

Word processors format in two ways. The first is the what-you-see-is-what-you-get approach. Using these word processing programs, the document must be put into the desired format *before* it is printed out. The document will be printed exactly as it appeared on the screen the last time you saved it on the diskette. The second type is called a *print-time* formatter. With this type of program, the document is formatted as it is printed. You do not format the materials before they are printed. What you see on your monitor may not be what you get. Most sophisticated word processors can use both types of formatting.

Programs are also available that allow you to include the print commands (p. 709) used by a commercial printing company. There are some printing companies that have the capability of receiving materials over the phone (see communications section, p. 732) that you have prepared for printing. The company prints the materials and ships them to you. This service is relatively inexpensive and can be used for important documents such as appellate briefs.

Probably the most powerful capability of a word processor is called *merge printing*. It allows you to combine several whole files and to place data from one file into specific locations in another.

Merge printing whole files is very useful in creating documents with standard paragraphs. Each paragraph is usually saved in a computer file with its own name. When you wish to include the paragraph in a document, you simply enter the proper code and the name of the file. When you print out the document, the paragraph will be included at the location indicated without the necessity of retyping it.

Merging data from one file into another allows the creation of letters or other documents with appropriate names and addresses included in the finished document at all the proper places. This can be particularly useful in mailing the same document to many people. Code words are used for the placement of each bit of information, e.g., code words for address, for city, for state. The words "name," "address," "city," "state," and "zip" are often used as code words for obvious reasons. Once the code words are created, the address, city, or whatever is represented by the code word will be included in the final document wherever the code word is found.

When selecting a word processing program, the first step is to determine what current tasks could be done better and more efficiently with a word processing program. If the law office uses standard forms or standard language in documents or mass mailings (e.g., billings), a word processor with good merge capabilities will be very helpful.

If you already have word processing capabilities, you may be considering a change in your system. It is critical to determine whether the current system performs all the tasks that you need. If it does, you probably should not change your system. The current system is known by the current users. The retraining necessary for a new system can be very disruptive. Do not buy new software just to have the latest system. When new programs are first sold, they frequently have defects ("bugs"). Some of the defects can be serious. If the new features are not critical to your operation, wait six months. After that time, most of the "bugs" will be found and fixed by the manufacturer. Let someone else be the guinea pig.

Once you have determined what your current needs are, you should consider the future. How much will the law office grow? How will the office change? What is your ideal? Think of your dream system. Even if you cannot afford your dream system today, you should make sure that the system you obtain (both hardware and software) can *grow into* your dream system.

For some users, the computer is like owning a boat. As soon as they have one boat they want a bigger and better model. When the bigger and better one is obtained, however, they often discover that bigger and better is not what they thought it would be. Again, if what you have is doing the job, a new and improved version of the program may not be what you want. Sometimes new features make software more difficult to use with few resulting benefits.

Many magazines review software. Go to the library and find at least three reviews on a software program that you are thinking of purchasing. Read them carefully. Usually you will find a consensus within the reviews.

Often new versions of a program *are* an improvement. The new version can work faster, be more powerful, and is easier to use. These new features will require more memory. Hence, you will need a computer with a memory that can be easily expanded.

Many offices now have *dedicated* word processors. As indicated above, a dedicated word processor is equipment that is designed to perform only word processing. It is not a computer. If the dedicated system is doing the job, switching to a microcomputer will not be a good investment for handling word processing. If there are other good reasons to purchase a microcomputer (e.g., timekeeping, billing, and document control), then obtain it. If an office is not

Figure 8. Examples of Available Computer Magazines.

already equipped with dedicated equipment, it should not be purchased. A computer can do word processing and additional tasks for less money.

2. DATA BASES

A *data base* is software used to store and organize information. The information is entered into the data base in an organized manner so that the computer can extract it, reorganize it, consolidate it, summarize it, and create reports from it. As a business management tool in a law office, a data base is used for timekeeping, calendars, ticklers, billing, and client records. As a case management tool, it can be used for document control in cases that have a large number of documents that must be indexed and cross-referenced. Also, as we shall see, *Westlaw* and *Lexis* are large data bases used for legal research.

Step one is to design the data base. You must decide what information to include in the data base. You also need to determine how much space is required for each piece of information. For example, if you wish to keep last names as part of your data base, you would need to determine how many letters are in the longest name used. Also decide what reports you wish to make with the data.

Information must be entered into the data base. This will usually require someone to sit at a terminal and manually type in the information. If the data base is to contain documents, each document entered will need an ID code, a brief description of the document, and index words for the document. One of the major features of a data base is that it can serve as a large index, thereby allowing rapid retrieval of information.

Once all the data has been entered, the data base can be used to retrieve, compare, or compile information. To use any of these functions, a search of the data base must be made. There are two ways to search a data base: *key word* searches and *full text* searches.

A *key word* search is like looking through the index of a book. The data base program will build an index using information that it is told to use for the index. The computer searches through this index and displays all information associated with the key word. For example, assume that you create a data base to keep the membership list for your national paralegal association, and you instruct the data base program that you wanted an index created that uses the state in the address of members of the association. You could then ask the computer to list all the members from the state of Ohio or from any other state. This type of search can be completed very quickly. The quality of the results of such a search depends upon how well indexed the data base is. If the person who made the list of index words for each document did not do a very good job, the search will not be very productive. Poor indexing will cause either too little or too much information to be reported from the search.

The second way to search a data base is called a *full-text* search. With this type of search, the computer will not "look" in an index but will examine *all* the information stored by the data base program. You might, for example, create a document-control data base that contains a summary of the document including important dates, names, and events. A full-text search would be a search of all the words in the summaries of the documents that were entered in the data base. The computer will look through the summaries and display a list of documents that meet the search criteria. If, for example, the documents that were entered into the data base concerned an automobile accident and you wished to find all the documents that referred to Helen Johnson (who is the chief witness for the opposition), you could make a full-text search of the document summaries and receive a list of all the documents that mentioned Helen Johnson.

To make a search, the computer must be told what to search for and where to search for it. This is called the *search criteria*. Search criteria can become quite complex. Many large data bases allow search criteria that use the words AND, OR, and NOT. A search criteria using such words might be:

GUN AND ROBBERY AND NOT BANK.

This would cause a search of the data base to return a list of documents in which the summary had the words *gun* and *robbery* but excluding any summary that also included the word *bank*. The problem with this type of search is that if the term "holdup" instead of "robbery" were used in the summary of one document, that document would not be found by the search. To find that document, the following search criteria must be used

GUN AND (ROBBERY OR HOLDUP) AND NOT BANK.

The parentheses show that the OR applies only to *robbery* and *holdup*. At the time you phrase your search request, if you did not think of the word *holdup,* an important document will be missed because you did not use the same terms as the person who wrote the summary for the data base.

Most data base programs can perform several simple tasks. Calendar keeping is one of them. A data base would be very efficient in keeping trial and appointment calendars for a law office. Each lawyer would receive a printed calendar of appointments for the day. All office calendars can be kept on one computer so that scheduling can be done without creating time conflicts among the lawyers. There are special programs designed to serve this specific purpose.

Calendaring programs can only do one thing. A *general* data base program, on the other hand, provides general data base capabilities and can be programmed to provide calendars and other data base services. A simple data base, for example, could be used to keep a tickler system (p. 493) for a law office so that files are not neglected. This data base could also be designed to print out a list of all the cases for the office where the statute of limitations is due to expire during the next month.

Name, address, family status, phone numbers, case type, and other pertinent information for all the clients of a law firm can be kept in a data base. This information could be used for mass mailings of informational letters about certain types of cases to those clients. The data base can be used to identify the types of cases handled by different lawyers in the office and the completion time for each type. This information will be very helpful in making management and marketing decisions for the law firm (p. 757).

For more complex tasks, the usefulness of the computer increases. Time-keeping and billing can be made more efficient with a good data base system. There are many data base programs designed specifically to perform time-keeping and billing tasks. These programs can handle multiple rates for attorneys and paralegals for different clients. All office employees must still record their time manually. What the program will do is make the compilation and mailing of billings a much more efficient process.

The data base will also make it possible to analyze which types of cases are more profitable to the law firm and which people are more productive in terms of billed hours. Of course there are other factors that must still be evaluated subjectively. The attorney who brings in new clients for the law firm could very well show up poorly on a billable-hours evaluation. Like all other tools, the numbers produced by a computer must be evaluated in perspective.

Data bases can be very useful for document control, e.g., keeping track of the content and location of 20,000 documents in an antitrust case. Document-control programs were once available only for large computers and were very expensive. Consequently, document control with computers was used only in very large cases. Today, programs have been developed that enable small computers to perform document control functions.

a. WESTLAW/LEXIS
(See also pp. 632–639)

WESTLAW and LEXIS are commercial data bases that are available for anyone who wishes to do (and can pay for) computer-assisted legal research. (For pictures and an overview of WESTLAW and LEXIS, see the chapter on Legal Research, p. 632.) A user agreement with the companies offering WESTLAW or LEXIS must be entered before you will be allowed to conduct legal research using their data bases. The agreement will establish the fees charged for the different services available. The most basic service is a data base search. When figuring the cost of using the service, your telephone bill must also be considered. To use WESTLAW or LEXIS, you must call them with your computer. (See the communications section, p. 732, for more information on this.) If the call is a long distance call, you must pay this fee in addition to your charges from

WESTLAW or LEXIS. This is relatively infrequent, however, because of the availability of local accessing networks.

Both services include data bases of cases, statutes, regulations, and citation checking services. Individual data bases and files may be searched separately or as part of a larger data base or file. For example, you can ask the computer to retrieve all the product liability cases involving hair dryers decided by a particular district court, a particular appellate court, or the United States Supreme Court just by selecting the appropriate data base to run your search. You could also select a data base or file composed of some or all of these individual data bases or files.

Both WESTLAW and LEXIS also allow searches to be made on either the full text of the data base or file, or a subset or portion of a data base or file. In WESTLAW, for example, you could search only a subset (field) of a data base. The fields of a WESTLAW data base are: title, synopsis, topic, court, headnote, citation, digest, judge, and opinion. Each field contains a specific category of information about cases stored in the data base. If you already have some information about the specific case(s) that you are looking for, you can limit your search to the field containing your information. This will speed up your search and therefore save money.

Title.   The title field contains the names of the parties to a case. Use this field to retrieve a case if you know the case name. The computer will quickly retrieve your case and display it so you can either read it on-line or print it out to read at a later time.

Synopsis.   The synopsis field contains an editorially prepared summary of the case. This summary includes the facts presented by the case, the holding of the lower court, the issues on appeal, and the resolution of those issues. The names of majority, concurring, and dissenting judges are also included in the synopsis field. Since general legal terms and concepts are used to describe the issues before the court, this is a good field to run a conceptual search. A conceptual search is helpful for finding cases that fall into a particular legal category or classification such as product liability even if the court never uses the phrase product liability in its opinion.

Topic.   The topic field contains the Key Topic and Key Numbers that West also uses for its digest volumes (p. 535). This field is searched if you already have a Topic and Key Number (p. 544).

Court.   The court field contains the name of the deciding court. You can use this field to limit a search to a specific court's decisions.

Citation.   The citation field can be used to locate a particular case by its citation.

Digest.   The digest field contains the citation, topic, headnote, court, and title information as the full text of the headnotes that appear in West reporters (p. 528). Because the digest paragraphs contain legal terms and concepts, conceptual searches can be used to search for these terms and concepts. A relevant opinion that does not refer to a specific legal concept may still be retrieved because a digest paragraph referred to the concept.

Headnote. The headnote field contains the actual text of the digest paragraph. This field can be used to search for specific fact patterns.

Judge. The judge field allows a search for decisions by a particular judge.

Opinion. The opinion field contains the full text of an opinion of the court. This includes the majority, concurring, and dissenting opinions, the full name of the court, the docket number for the case, the date of the decision, and the attorneys who argued the case.

LEXIS subdivides its files into similar components called segments, e.g., judge, date, name, and citation. Since the company that owns LEXIS does not publish cases in reporter volumes, LEXIS does not have the same synopsis, headnote, topic, or Key Number capabilities of WESTLAW, which is owned by the same company that publishes the National Reporter System (p. 528). However, LEXIS does permit searching different segments of cases.

Once you have determined which fields or segments of a data base or file that you wish to search, it is time to create your *search query.* The query consists of a list of words you wish to search, plus the connectors used with those words. The connectors are the "ANDs" and "ORs" that were mentioned previously in the general data base section (p. 719). The first step in preparing a query is to make a list of terms and phrases that could be included. This list should contain your important words and their synonyms or closely related words.[1] (Cartwheeling will be helpful in compiling this list, p. 591.) For example, assume that your research problem involves obtaining a copyright for a model airplane. Your list could consist of the following words: *airplane, model, toy, copyright.* The words *model* and *toy* would be used because of their close relationship to each other. Whether you are using WESTLAW or LEXIS the query could be phrased as follows:

MODEL OR TOY AND AIRPLANE AND COPYRIGHT.

This search statement tells the computer to find cases that contain the words *model* or *toy* and the words *airplane* and *copyright.* With this search query, any case that contained these words would be found.

Occasionally, searches will lead you to cases containing your search words that do not pertain to your research problem. Some searches find large numbers of these unwanted cases. To limit this possibility, you can change your query and specify that the search words should occur near one another. This is accomplished by using *proximity limiters,* which are connectors that say how

[1] See Stasky, *Legal Thesaurus/Dictionary* (West, 1985).

close to one another the words must be found in a case. WESTLAW and LEXIS accomplish this with different connectors.

WESTLAW uses three proximity specifications:

$$\text{/p, /s, and /n.}$$

The /p connector means in the same paragraph in any order. The /s connector means in the same sentence in any order. The /n connector means that the terms can be separated by up to n words. N can represent any number that is less than 256. There are also +s, +p, and +n connectors. The +s connector means in the same sentence and in the same order. The +p connector means in the same paragraph and in the same order. The +n connector requires that the terms be in order and they can be separated by up to n words. N can represent any number less than 256. The search query:

$$\text{MODEL +s AIRPLANE}$$

would retrieve cases with the word *model* before the word *airplane* in the same sentence. We could also use the proximity connectors to phrase the search as:

$$\text{MODEL TOY /p AIRPLANE /p COPYRIGHT}$$

This query requires all our terms to be found in the same paragraph. Notice that the OR was left out of the query. WESTLAW automatically assumes that you mean OR whenever a query contains words without connectors between them.

The connectors for LEXIS that set proximity are W/n and PRE/n. The n means any number from 1 to 255 that you want to use to indicate how many words may separate the search terms involved. (Unlike WESTLAW, however, LEXIS does not count some words, e.g., *an, the,* as part of the n.) The search:

$$\text{MODEL W/3 AIRPLANE}$$

would find any case in which the terms *model* and *airplane* occurred within three words of one another. This search would find a case that contained the phrase "model designed airplane" or "airplane designer's model." A search that stated

$$\text{MODEL PRE/3 AIRPLANE}$$

would find any case that used the word *model* as any of the three significant words before *airplane*. This search would find any case that contained the phrase "model airplane," "model of an airplane," or "model of other airplanes." It would not find a case with the phrase "airplane model" in it. Notice that the search automatically includes plural forms of the words.

A search on LEXIS that would contain proximity limiters for our problem could now read

$$\text{MODEL OR TOY W/10 AIRPLANE W/50 COPYRIGHT}$$

This tells the computer to find any case that uses the term *model* or *toy* within ten words of *airplane,* and the word *copyright* within fifty words of any of the others.

Suppose that you made the above search and found no cases, or found 1,500 cases! Either situation would call for a revision of your search query. If you found no cases, your search must be expanded. This is usually accomplished by adding ORs to your search in order to include new words or more synonyms for your current words, or by using larger proximity connectors. To revise and expand the search query for our copyright problem, we could try some word alternatives. For example, for *airplane* we might try *plane* or *aircraft*. The search query would now read:

```
MODEL OR TOY W/10 AIRPLANE OR PLANE OR AIRCRAFT
            W/50 COPYRIGHT.
```

Assume that this search uncovers over 1,000 cases. Again, too many to handle. You need to narrow your search further. As the query now stands, the computer will find any case that has *model* or *toy* within ten words of *airplane, plane,* or *aircraft,* and the preceding words within fifty words of copyright. Parentheses can be used to tell the computer to think of *airplane, plane,* and *aircraft* as one word. Even though not required in LEXIS, parentheses can be used to help the researcher visualize the search groupings. Your search query would now read:

```
(MODEL OR TOY) W/10 (AIRPLANE OR PLANE OR
       AIRCRAFT) W/50 COPYRIGHT.
```

This search will also cause the computer to find a case that has the words *model* or *toy* within ten words of *airplane* or *plane* or *aircraft* as long as the word *copyright* is within fifty words of any of the others.

Both WESTLAW and LEXIS have other connectors that can be used. The major connector that has not been mentioned thus far is the AND NOT connector, which is very useful in limiting a search that is turning up too many cases. Assume that your search for information about model airplane copyrights was returning cases dealing with airplane crashes.[2] The AND NOT connector could be used to exclude such cases. A search query using AND NOT would read:

```
(MODEL OR TOY) W/10 (AIRPLANE OR PLANE OR
   AIRCRAFT) W/50 COPYRIGHT AND NOT CRASH
```

This would eliminate any case that contained the term crash.

WESTLAW and LEXIS will display on your monitor the full text of any cases that are found through search queries. You can either start at the beginning of a case or have the computer display the part of the case that contains your search terms (p. 638). The latter feature can be very helpful in determining how to limit your search. By examining your terms in context in a few of the cases, you can discover a common denominator in cases that you wish to exclude or include. You can then formulate a new search query based on that information.

---

[2] In fact, our search for information about model airplane copyrights would *not* lead you to cases dealing with airplane crashes. Our assumption is simply designed to indicate that the AND NOT connector can be used to limit searches.

As indicated, WESTLAW and LEXIS have data bases that allow you to search for federal statutes, federal agency rules, tax cases, etc. (p. 632). Both systems provide more than one citation checking method (p. 585). Other data bases are also available for both systems. A search of any of these data bases uses the same search query structure that is used for searches for cases. A detailed listing of the data bases available can be obtained from WESTLAW and LEXIS (for addresses, see p. 511).

WESTLAW and LEXIS are both excellent research tools. Remember, however, that a computerized search will not replace research in a library (p. 509). There are many associations that are quickly and automatically made by a good researcher in the library that are not as easily made on a computer.

b. Other Commercial Data Bases

WESTLAW and LEXIS are commercial data bases used primarily to find the law, although other search capacities also exist in both systems. A partial list is found on pp. 632–33. There are other data bases that can be used to find almost anything. For example, Dialog, Dow Jones, and Nexus contain a variety of business information and news. There are data bases that contain bibliographic information, and some that contain the full text of the *New York Times* or other periodicals. All these can be accessed by telephone. The two most popular among consumers are Compuserve and The Source.

Other systems that can be called by phone are referred to as bulletin boards. They are often free to the user and are arranged around interest groups. There are bulletin boards for almost every make of computer. They provide information, programs, and assistance for using the computer that they cover. There are bulletin boards for stamp collectors, sailors, astronomy buffs, etc. They can be a good source for very specific information. Bulletin board lists are found in several computer magazines.

3. SPREADSHEET PROGRAMS

Most law offices can clearly see the usefulness of word processing (p. 715) and data base (p. 718) programs. The usefulness of a spreadsheet, however, is a little more difficult to appreciate. A spreadsheet can be used for almost any project that requires the use or manipulation of numbers. It is a good management tool for creating budgets and tracking expenses of a law firm. Most spreadsheet programs have built-in functions that will make intricate calculations such as determining net present value, loan repayment schedules, averages, and many other statistical functions.

A spreadsheet allows you to create large groups of interrelated numbers. Once this is done, changing one of the important numbers will allow you to see what will happen to all the others. A spreadsheet can quickly recalculate the values of all the numbers that are dependent on the one that was changed. For example, with a spreadsheet you can create a program that will calculate the size of payments on a loan based on the amount, length, and interest rate that apply to the loan. If you change the numbers displayed on the screen for the amount, for the length, or for the interest rate of the loan, the spreadsheet will recalculate the payment size.

A spreadsheet consists of a series of boxes called cells. Numbers and other information can be placed directly into the boxes from the keyboard. Once the information is in a box, it can be a source of information to be used for formulas in other boxes. When a box containing a formula is displayed on the screen, the result of the formula will be seen, not the formula itself. If any of the numbers in the boxes used by a formula are changed, the display for the box with the formula will reflect this change. For example, let us assume that we have a small spreadsheet program that has three boxes. (Large, sophisticated spreadsheets have thousands of boxes that can be used.) Each of our three boxes has a name that is used to refer to the information in them. The names of our boxes are A, B, and C.

Figure 9. Three Empty Spreadsheet Boxes.

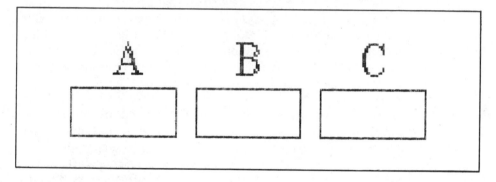

If we placed the number 5 in box A and the number 2 in box B, we could then combine this information in box C by entering the formula A + B into box C.

Figure 10.

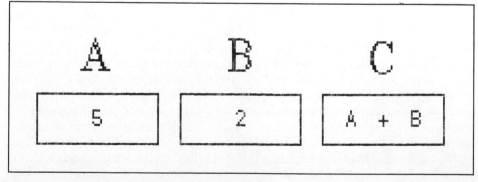

Box C would then display the number 7.

Figure 11.

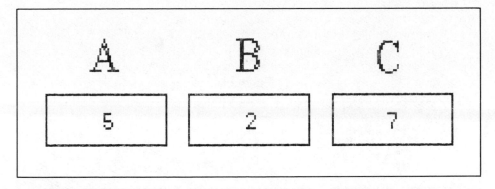

We could change the formula in box C to read (A + B)*2 (the * means *times* on most computers).

Figure 12.

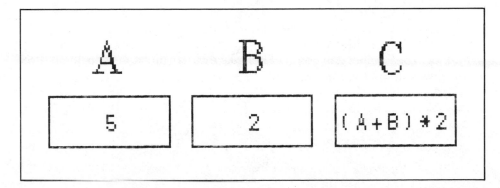

C would now read 14.

Figure 13.

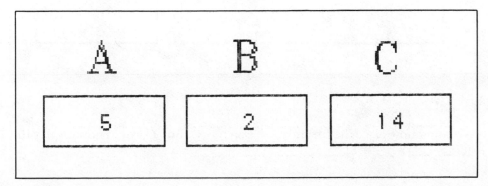

Now if we change the number in box A from 5 to 4, box C would read 12. [(4 + 2) * 2 = 12.]

Figure 14.

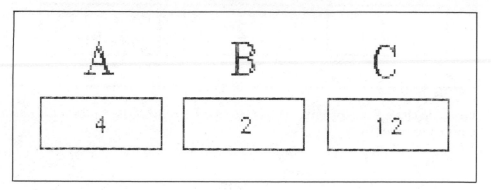

Our small spreadsheet example can be made more complicated. Let's start over. Place the number 2 in box A. Then place the formula A + 2 in box B. Box B will now contain the number 4 [2 + 2 = 4].

Figure 15.

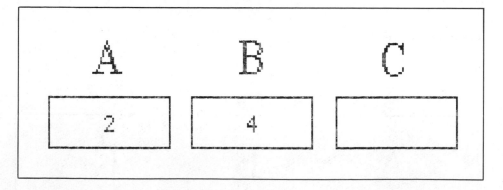

We could now place the formula A * B in box C. Box C would now display the number 8 [2 * 4 = 8].

Figure 16.

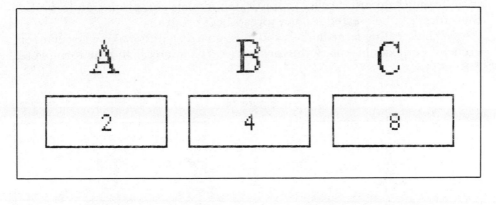

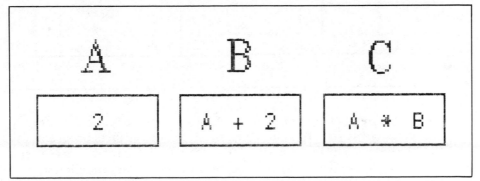

Any time we change the number that is in box A, the numbers displayed in both box B and C will change. If the number 4 is placed in box A, box B will show the number 6 [4 + 2 = 6], and box C will display the number 24. [6 * 4 = 24].

Figure 17.

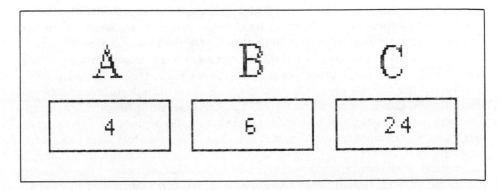

On a large spreadsheet, many cells (boxes) can depend on information from formulas in other cells. Sophisticated models and projection formulas, therefore, can be created using a spreadsheet program.

When creating large models you must guard against making circular references. For example, place the formula (A * C) in box B and the formula (A * B) in box C.

Figure 18.

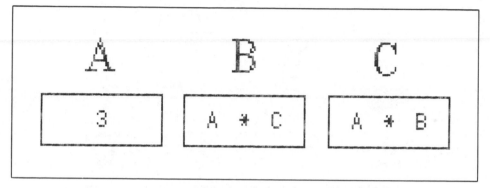

No matter what number is entered in box A, box B looks to box C for information and box C looks to box B for information. Some spreadsheet programs will get stuck on these two formulas and will stop dead. Other spreadsheets will run through the calculations for the two boxes ten or twenty times and then stop.

The capability of a spreadsheet to perform a whole series of calculations based on formulas and numbers makes it possible to do in minutes or seconds what once took accountants days and weeks. The spreadsheet is perfect for doing what users call "what ifs." Suppose you were considering the purchase of a house and wanted to figure out what the monthly payments would be. Three factors determine the size of the payments: the interest rate, the length of the mortgage, and the amount of the loan. Using the proper financial formulas, you could create a spreadsheet that would let you enter an interest rate, the number of years, and the amount that you wished to borrow. In seconds the spreadsheet would display the monthly mortgage payment based on those numbers. You can then play "what if" and change one or more of the numbers to see what happens to the payment level as the interest rate went down, the length of the mortgage increased, or the amount of the loan was greater, etc.

A spreadsheet used as a "what if" device can be very helpful in a law office for working out damage projections and settlement strategies. Once the relationship of the various elements of damages is determined, different interest and inflation assumptions can be tested. You can determine how these assumptions will influence the amount of damages that would be necessary in a particular case. For example, assume you are trying to project lost wages of an injured plaintiff. Interrelated formulas can be created to solve this damage calculation. The first formula would project potential salary over the working life of the person, starting with the current salary and adding increases over time. The increase would be a percent of salary. The formula created can allow

Figure 19. Spreadsheet Mortgage Cost Display.

```
          Real Estate Financial Analysis

                 Assumptions

    House Price:              $35,900.00
    Downpayment:              1,795.00
                             ---------------
    Amount Financed:         $34,105.00
    Interest Rate %:              9.75
    Number of Yrs Financed:     20.00
    Calculated Payment:       $323.49
```

for changing the percent increase so that different increase assumptions can be quickly tested. Another formula can take the results from the salary calculations and determine how many dollars would be needed today to create an amount equal to the future income. Various rates of return can be tested with this formula. Used in a similar manner, a spreadsheet can be productive for estate planning and real estate projections.

Most of the current spreadsheet programs have the capability of creating graphs from the numbers that they produce. They can create line, bar, and pie charts in many different formats. Bar charts can be made to appear three dimensional, or be stacked one above the other. If the computer has a color monitor, the bars representing different items can be in various colors. There are two ways that paper copies of the graphs can be created. The graphs can be printed out with a dot matrix printer. These printers will give you only a black and white representation of the chart. The bars that are displayed in different colors on a monitor will be given different shadings on the printed graph. The other method of obtaining a hard copy of a graph is to use a *plotter*. A plotter is a device that will hold a pen to a piece of paper and draw lines on the paper as instructed by the computer. Most plotters are capable of automatically changing the pen that it uses. This makes it possible for the plotter to draw a graph using different colors. When high-quality graphs are desired, a plotter is a must. The plotter will draw the graph, fill in the colors, and write the labels much more clearly than a dot matrix printer can.

There are many applications for spreadsheets that can be obtained by purchasing a *templet* to perform the needed task. A templet is a set of formulas that has been created by someone else and is sold with instructions on its use. A federal income tax templet, for example, will contain all the lines and forms of a tax return. The templet covers each part of the tax form on which information must be entered, and calculates the taxes based on the information entered. The templet then prints the form as a completed tax return. Templets are available for almost any type of business calculation. There are small bookkeeping programs, purchase-lease comparison programs, linear regression programs, and many others.

Some publishers of spreadsheets claim that bookkeeping and other data base applications can be performed using their programs. This can be done to a limited extent. The bookkeeping and data base systems, however, are limited and awkward, and hence of little practical use in most law offices. Bookkeeping and data base manipulation should be performed on programs designed for that purpose rather than with spreadsheet programs.

4. COMMUNICATIONS

Finally we come to one of the most recent microcomputer developments. Communications software makes it possible to call up WESTLAW or LEXIS in order to do legal research over telephone lines. Such programs also make it possible to call individuals or businesses with the proper equipment and to communicate with their computers. You can send or receive letters, statistical information, programs, or insults! Anything that can be put on paper or into a computer can be sent from one computer to another over telephone lines.

There are two components necessary for successful computer communication that uses the telephone system: a modem and the communications software. A *modem* is a piece of hardware that is plugged into your computer on one end and into your telephone line on the other. The modem controls the transmission of information over telephone lines. The communications software controls the information sent to the modem that is to be sent over telephone lines. When two computers are transmitting information to one another over telephone lines, each one must have a modem and a communications program. The two modems transmit the information that they are told to send by the communications software.

For the modems to be able to do this, they must be "speaking" with the same code and "talking" at the same speed. Most modems sold today use the same code, but they do not all communicate at the same speed. Some can communicate at more than one speed. The speed of transmission is stated in terms of *baud* or the *baud rate*. The most common baud rates used today by modems are 110, 300, 1200, and 2400. 110 baud is very slow. It is an old standard that is not often used anymore. 300 baud is the minimum standard used today; most modems can transmit and receive information at this speed. If large amounts of information are being sent, however, 300 baud is still very slow. The higher the baud rate, the less time it takes to send the same information. 1200 baud is today's high-speed standard. As modem technology improves, 2400 baud modems are becoming available. The only drawback with higher (faster) baud rates is that as the speed goes up so does the error rate. When more information is squeezed into the same space, the equipment used must be more sensitive. Unfortunately sensitive equipment may be less able to distinguish static from the information being sent on the telephone line. Therefore, at higher transmission rates, the information is more likely to become garbled. This problem must be controlled by the communications software.

Not only must modems use the same code, the communications software must speak the same language, which is referred to as the *communications protocol*. Communication software comes with several languages. The most popular are ASCII (askee), XMODEM, and MODEM7. Some communications software can automatically adjust to the language used by the other computer. If one of the computers cannot do this, each must be using the same language at the outset or they will not be able to understand one another.

Most communications software packages allow you to preset the language you are going to use. When a communication link is established for the first time, you should have someone present who understands all the elements of languages for communications. Once a good communications link has been established, most communications software will allow you to save the protocol so that you can use it the next time you wish to establish the same communications link.

Some special communications languages allow you to handle errors in the transmission of information caused by static or other problems on the phone line. One of these is the language called XMODEM. This is really more than a language. Not only does it send or receive the information but also it sends a code that the two computers use to verify that the information sent was received correctly. XMODEM sends the information in small units called *blocks*. The receiver's XMODEM software then checks the code to see if the information was properly received. If it was, the software tells the sender to send the next block of information. If the data was messed up, the software tells the sender to send the last block again. XMODEM is probably the most widely used protocol for transmitting large amounts of data with microcomputers.

When selecting communications hardware, keep in mind the amount of information that you wish to send or receive. The greater the amount of bulk transmission used, the greater the need for high-speed modems. If the greatest use of the communications system is to be for reading or examining materials immediately on screen, 1200 or even 300 baud would be a sufficient communications speed. The higher the speed a modem can use, the more it will cost.

When purchasing software for communications, higher cost does not necessarily mean better software. There are commercial software packages available that are expensive yet difficult to use. You may need a thick instruction manual and a degree in computer science to use them. Other communications packages are available in the public domain, meaning that the programs are available to the public without charge. Some are easy to use and will satisfy 90% of users requiring communications software. Whichever software program you choose, be sure that it is capable of using XMODEM protocol.

Developing the skills necessary for communications can be difficult. Once you have started, however, stopping can be just as hard or harder! It is a fascinating and challenging area of the computer world. A great deal of information is available through bulletin boards (p. 725), e.g., sources of software, user special interest groups, "adult" bulletin boards, and many others. Your phone bill could become very large if you are addicted to calling bulletin boards around the country.

5. COMBINATIONS

We have examined four types of programs: word processing, data base, spreadsheet, and communications. You can now obtain a software package that contains all four types in one program. These are often called *integrated* packages. They are programs that require computers with large amounts of memory. The reason for creating an integrated package is to simplify the process of moving information from one application to another. If, for example, you have information in your data base that you wish to manipulate with a spreadsheet program, the task of moving the information from a format that a data base understands to one that a spreadsheet understands can be monumental or impossible. An integrated package makes it possible. Not all integrated packages, however, move information from one format to another easily.

Two integrated packages have received the most publicity and appear to have a head start in the market place. They are *Symphony* and *Framework*.

Symphony was created by the company that produced Lotus 123, a very popular and powerful spreadsheet program. Since Lotus was the foundation for Symphony, everything in Symphony operates from a spreadsheet. This is an advantage for users who have good spreadsheet experience, especially with Lotus. A Lotus user who wants an integrated package should probably use Symphony. Since the most serious problem with using an integrated package is learning the many commands in the program, if you already know Lotus you do not need to learn a new set of spreadsheet commands to use Symphony. If you are a new user, however, Symphony may not be for you. The command structure for Symphony is not consistent from application to application. Its strong orientation to spreadsheets will make Symphony seem a little awkward to the user whose primary interest is in words.

Framework is more text-oriented or word-oriented than Symphony and is easier to learn for first-time users. Framework has the capability of working with an outline structure that is a good tool for writing and planning. Framework, however, is also very powerful and therefore may take a long time to learn.

Other integrated packages are also available. *Enable,* for example, is a very good integrated program. The beauty of Enable is that the command structure is the same or similar in all of the applications. Enable's spreadsheet looks and acts like Lotus 123. One drawback if you work with large spreadsheets is that Enable's spreadsheet is small compared to Symphony's. Each of Enable's applications is sophisticated enough to be marketed as a separate package. This cannot be said for each part of other integrated programs. Moving graphs and information from one application to another is simple and straightforward.

Another integrated package is the *Smartset.* With this program, each application is in fact a separate stand-alone program designed to be integrated into the others with a controller program. This approach has led to applications that can be purchased and run separately until integration is needed. Then the control program can be purchased to integrate the separate applications packages.

The big question is, "Do you need an integrated package?" If you are not sure, the answer is probably no. If you frequently find yourself wishing that you could put a graph from your spreadsheet into a letter, or wishing that you could easily get your data base information into a spreadsheet, then integrated software is needed.

Section E. THE REAL INVESTMENT: TIME

Thus far we have examined the relative expense of some of the hardware and software options. By far, however, the greatest cost that will be incurred in the adoption of a computer system in a law office is *time*. For the system to be implemented successfully, time must be invested both before and after acquisition of the system. The cost of this time will far exceed the cost of the equipment and software. Considerable time must be spent before the purchase of a system to determine what the law office needs. If this is not carefully done, the system will probably not fulfill the needs of the office. After the system is acquired, time must be spent implementing the system and training all members of the staff to properly use its capabilities. If the time invested before or after installation is not sufficient, the microcomputer system will be a failure.

Another element of cost that is necessary for the successful implementation of a computer system is a guru. The guru is the one who has a knack for figuring out and solving most of the problems of the system. The guru will be a person in the office who has a system at home, or who, when introduced to the training, will learn quickly and want to take the system manuals home to see how the thing "really" works. Encourage this person. Other staff members will need to take over some of the previous duties of the guru. Having someone present in the office who can immediately solve an apparent crisis will save time and minimize frustration.

Other cost factors that must be considered involve "down time" and lost data. *Down time* occurs when the computer breaks. No matter how good, expensive, or reliable your equipment may be, sooner or later it will fail. Many firms have discovered that microcomputers are so inexpensive that they purchase one or more solely to keep in the closet until they are needed to replace the unit that breaks down. This is often less expensive than having to wait a day, a week, a month, or six months for the defective computer to be repaired. The loss of data can be even more expensive. Some data is not replaceable. Other data can be replaced or reconstructed only at great cost. Nothing can compare to the horror of realizing that the diskette that you just erased contained the only copy of the brief that you have been working on for months. Every system should have regular backup procedures. There should be at least one backup copy of all data, and for particularly valuable or difficult-to-reconstruct data, two backup copies are recommended. If possible, a backup copy of important diskettes should be kept at a place other than where the day-to-day or working copies are located. This backup is an added expense, but not nearly as costly as the destruction of the data by fire, magnet, or other calamity.

14

Introduction to
Law Office Administration
and Legal Systems*

For a discussion of law office use of computer technology, see p. 707, p. 735.

Section A. INTRODUCTION

Every organization must have direction. Most professional firms, particularly law offices, tend to forget this basic principle until the office is confronted with a "crisis situation." Lawyers will sometimes respond to the problem by appointing a committee to research and investigate the causes of the problem, and report their conclusions back to other lawyers in the firm. Unfortunately this process does not always lend itself to efficient administration. What is needed is a management plan that anticipates, provides for, and thereby attempts to avoid crisis.

Traditionally lawyers have resisted management principles. A singular characteristic of most organizations is their belief in their own uniqueness. The law office is no exception. When someone suggests the adoption of a pro-

---

* This chapter was co-authored with Robert G. Baylor, Business Manager, Manah, Phelps, Rothenberg and Tunney, Los Angeles, California; BA, University of California, 1956; MBA, Portland State University, 1970.

cedure that has been successfully used in other organizations, the inevitable response of at least one lawyer will be: "It will never work in my office because we are different." If the procedure involves delegation of responsibility, the same lawyer might resist by saying, "If you want something done right, you have to do it yourself." A consequence of this attitude is that many law offices tend to be archaic in the management and operation of their legal and business affairs.

The tide, however, has been turning. More and more lawyers are taking an interest in law office administration. The American Management Association, for example, has been working with the American Bar Association to develop training programs for lawyers. From these developments, there has emerged a greater appreciation of the role of the office manager.

In 1971 an Association of Legal Administrators was established. (See address on p. 853.) The ALA now has over 4,000 members. Its comprehensive job description of the legal administrator, printed below, will give you an overview of this position and of the many facets of the operation of a law office.

LEGAL ADMINISTRATOR: JOB DESCRIPTION
Association of Legal Administrators

1.   General Responsibilities

1.1   Manages on a full-time basis the business functions of a law office.

1.2   Reports to the managing partner or the executive committee.

1.3   Is generally responsible for financial planning, controlling, salary administration, personnel review, purchasing, internal systems, and non-professional personnel supervision.

1.4   Should have a strong voice in making administrative policy as well as in implementing such policy.

1.5   Should be effective at achieving consensus with others who have control over policy decisions.

1.6   Interprets the needs of the law firm and contributes to cost-effectiveness.

1.7   Organizes work, establishes priorities, follows progress, and reports back on problems.

1.8   Anticipates problems and their solutions, as well as planning for the future.

1.9   Has the ability to handle complex problems in management, finance, and human relations.

1.10 Has supervisory and leadership skills.

1.11 Works well with individuals in law firm.

1.12 Has a broad familiarity with firm operations and how legal staff functions interact, including accounting, personnel, and payroll.

1.13 Demonstrates quality and accurate work.

1.14 Delivers prompt service.

1.15 Is available for extra hours when needed.

1.16 Has good interpersonal relations and communications with attorneys and support staff.

1.17 Manages space and equipment effectively.

2.   Financial Planning

2.1   Prepares all financial plans, analyses and presentations.

2.2   Conducts a periodic review of professional and nonprofessional strength and activities compared to projected personnel (and) activities.

2.3   Is responsible for all accounting functions.

2.4   Approves payment of all accounts payable.

2.5   Establishes the procedural aspects of billing verifications and approvals.

2.6 Has responsibility for the layout and information accumulation for management reports.

2.7 Establishes and controls a system of attorney time reporting and operational procedures.

2.8 Reports failures and discrepancies in systems of attorneys' time and expense accounts.

2.9 Prepares analyses of client projects, hours, and costs.

2.10 Reconciles monthly and year-to-date general and administrative expenses.

2.11 Reviews outside counsel activities and fees.

2.12 Supervises the preparation and maintenance of administrative and financial records.

2.13 Reviews and participates in professional and other available salary surveys.

2.14 Manages the office economically and effectively within policy guidelines.

2.15 Maintains controls on delinquent accounts and disbursements to encourage the collection of both.

2.16 Acts as the firm's liaison with its accountants.

2.17 Insures the timely preparation and filing of tax returns, forwarding of withholding and other reporting requirements of all levels of government.

2.18 Administers the firm's pension plan, including computation and payment of contributions and filing of appropriate reports.

2.19 Takes responsibility for maintaining bank relationships.

2.20 Takes responsibility for investment of the firm's liquid assets.

2.21 Assists in tax planning for the firm.

3. Personnel-Staff

3.1 Interviews, screens, and hires applicants for office staff positions.

3.2 Evaluates the performance and contribution of office staff at least annually.

3.3 Counsels employees who are not meeting firm standards and tells them how to improve.

3.4 Takes disciplinary action against employees, including dismissal.

3.5 Is the spokesperson for lawyers in dealing with the support staff.

3.6 Handles all personnel problems on a staff level.

3.7 Maintains up-to-date and comprehensive personnel records on each employee.

3.8 Trains and develops support staff.

3.9 Is responsible for communicating and enforcing firm policies and procedures.

3.10 Regulates work flow within the office and work load of individual staff members.

3.11 Provides a staff which effectively supports the production of legal work.

3.12 Schedules vacations for all staff employees.

3.13 Develops programs for maintenance and improvement of employee morale.

3.14 Arranges for termination of employment of personnel who must leave for personal reasons or because of the inability to perform tasks assigned them.

3.15 Maintains and develops compliance programs for equal employment opportunity.

3.16 Develops individual job descriptions for all staff positions within firm.

3.17 Assists in outplacement of terminating associates, attorneys and paralegals.

3.18 Supervises administrative aspects of rotation of new associate attorneys.

4. Attorneys

4.1 Summer Law Clerk Program.
a. Is a member of recruiting team.
b. Sets up recruiting plan.
c. Coordinates orientation and introduction to all office staff.

4.2 Hiring of Attorneys
a. Schedules appointments.
b. Explains the law firm's policies and procedures.

4.3 Provides attorneys with needed and timely assistance so that they are not burdened by details unrelated to important legal work.

4.4 Assists and implements for attorney management such planning or administrative functions as required.

5. Law Library

5.1 Has responsibility for general supervision of the library.

5.2 Has responsibility for cost estimates of existing and new publications.

5.3 Keeps up-to-date with computerized legal research systems, such as Lexis and Westlaw.

6. Files

6.1 Makes a successful commitment to an effective file retrieval system.

6.2 Sets up, controls, and maintains a filing system for active and inactive files.

6.3 Sets up and controls internal and external routing systems.

6.4 Purchases, leases, or rents equipment as needed.

7. Physical Facilities

7.1 Handles the management and expansion of the law firm's physical facilities.

7.2 Makes recommendations for future needs of the firm.

7.3 Works directly with the architect in drawing layout for use of facilities.

7.4 Works directly with office building facilities personnel regarding maintenance and alterations of office.

7.5 Handles cost projections.

7.6 Is responsible for general appearance of the firm.

7.7 When construction is underway, maintains files and records of construction contracts, progress reports, changes orders and payment schedules, and arranges all physical movements of people, furniture and functions necessary to expedite construction.

8. Office Supplies and Furnishings

8.1 Is responsible for all supply problems, including tasks delegated to others.

8.2 Approves quality and purchase of office supplies.

8.3 Supervises storage and distribution of office supplies.

8.4 Assumes responsibility for purchasing, indexing and distribution of preprinted forms.

8.5 Keeps a current inventory of all furnishings.

9. Mail

9.1 Coordinates the law firm's mail department procedures used in handling both incoming and outgoing mail.

10. Telephone

10.1 Oversees the operation of, and seeks ways to improve, the firm's telephone system.

10.2 Has responsibility for the receptionist and relief switchboard operators.

10.3 Coordinates telephone system changes with involved personnel.

11. Office Manual

11.1 Develops, publishes and constantly updates staff, attorney, law clerk and other office policy and procedure manuals concerning the operation of the firm.

12. Long-Range Planning

12.1 Projects personnel and space growth for future, with projected costs.

12.2 Establishes a solid base for future growth of the firm using systems and procedures which are well documented and will function despite personnel changes.

12.3 Prepares long-range budget projections.

13. Continuing Legal Education (C.L.E.)

13.1 Monitors cost of firm's C.L.E. participation.

13.2 Accumulates and periodically presents materials on future C.L.E. programs.

14. Docket Control

14.1 Sets up a centralized and possibly automated calendar and docket control system.

15. Client and Civic Relations

15.1 Meets and visits with as many of the firm's clients as possible.

15.2 Becomes active in professional, governmental, and community affairs.

15.3 Supervises personnel and procedures employed in telephone answering and client reception, including reception areas and other public/client areas.

15.4 Develops and thereafter updates a firm resume, and provides input for published lists (*e.g.,* Martindale Hubbell p. 123).

15.5 Supervises the preparation and distribution of announcements.

15.6 Assists in implementing public relations (press, government, bar associations and relations with other firms).

15.7 Arranges for client seminars.

15.8 Assists in the preparation of a firm marketing brochure and supervises its distribution.

16. Equipment, Systems and Maintenance of Equipment

16.1 Becomes familiar with new technology, equipment, and systems through regular contact with sales representatives, attending business shows, and subscribing to professional and trade publications.

16.2 Recommends implementation of changes in office systems, or recommends procurement of outside assistance as required.

16.3 With approval of managing partner or executive committee, purchases, leases, or rents necessary equipment, negotiating additional terms and conditions with vendors as required.

16.4 Supervises the operation of, and continuously refines and improves, the firm's systems and procedures, including:
a. Data processing.
b. Automated word processing.
c. Document production (including dictation and typing procedures.
d. Document reproduction.
e. Document retrieval.
f. Conflict of interest systems.
g. Litigation support.
h. Dining and food services.

16.5 Maintains individual equipment expense records for monitoring cost effectiveness and billing verifications.

16.6 Prepares cost studies comparing various equipment alternatives.

16.7 Keeps a current inventory of all equipment.

16.8 Sets up maintenance for all equipment.

16.9 Is responsible for all equipment problems, including tasks delegated to others.

17. Insurance

17. Administers the existing insurance programs for the firm, makes recommendations for changes to modify coverages as appropriate to reduce costs, and analyzes new programs as needed:
a. Accident and h ...th.
b. Casualty, including scheduled contents coverage, if necessary.
c. Professional liability.
d. Bonding.
e. Disability.
f. Computer.
g. Officer's life insurance.
h. Accidental Death and Dismemberment.
i. Worker's Compensation.

18. Storage of Important Documents/Computer Backup Tapes/Diskettes

18.1 Maintains a safety deposit box for all important documents.

18.2 Makes arrangements for all computer backup tapes/diskettes to be stored off premises in a safe place in case of computer failure, fire or any other type of disaster.

19. Meetings

19.1 Partner meetings.
a. Attends all partner meetings.

b. Serves as the secretary and prepares the minutes.
c. Gathers information as requested.
d. Puts together and distributes agendas.

19.2 Firm meetings.
a. Attends all firm meetings.
b. Prepares information for managing partners as requested.

19.3 Sets up and coordinates the firm's retreats.

19.4 Meets with the managing partner weekly or as otherwise needed.

20. Compensation and Profit Distribution

20.1 Keeps adequate records of all aspects of the profit distribution system.

20.2 Continually monitors the system for inequities and makes appropriate recommendations.

Paralegals often report to the legal administrator in addition to individual supervising attorneys. Some large law firms have paralegal managers or supervisors (p. 29) who oversee the recruitment, training, and day-to-day functions of the paralegals. Paralegal supervisors will determine the assignment of paralegals to lawyers, help to decide priorities, e.g., defining when "rush" is "most rush," being sure that everyone is following the common practices and procedures of the firm, and generally overseeing work flow and allocation of work. The supervisor often has the responsibility to help define what functions can be performed by a paralegal who will be supporting an attorney. For example, development of a master information list (a questionnaire used by a paralegal to gather information from a client) will probably be initially developed by the paralegal supervisor for review by an attorney. Such master information lists will then be used as a check-off list by the paralegal in obtaining information for the lawyer.

Section B. TYPES OF PRIVATE LAW OFFICES

Law offices are organized in many different ways. We will look at several law offices at various ends of the complexity scale. Keep in mind that the office descriptions are examples only; they are not intended to describe any particular offices in existence, but rather to explore the range of organizations that exists. We will examine the structure of three law offices from five perspectives:

A. Personnel
B. Type of Practice
C. Governance
D. Finances
E. Equipment and Facilities

LAW OFFICE I

A. Personnel

There are three full-time attorneys, one full-time secretary, and one part-time secretary.

B. Type of Practice

The firm spends most of its time representing plaintiffs in automobile negligence cases, with occasional work in the areas of will drafting and criminal defense. The criminal defense work comes mainly through court assignments.[1]

C. Governance

The three attorneys are equal partners and make all decisions collectively, although one of them makes most of the minor administrative decisions on his/her own, such as overseeing the purchase of supplies by the secretary.

D. Finances

Each attorney individually takes responsibility for fee collecting from the clients with whom s/he is closely working. Since most of the fees are collected on a contingent basis (i.e., the firm takes a percentage of the judgment awarded the plaintiff at trial or obtained through settlement), the attorneys do not keep detailed records of time spent on each case. They do, however, keep records on the expenses they incur in representing a client, e.g., transportation costs, since the client must pay these expenses even if the firm receives no fee due to losing the case.

E. Equipment and Facilities

The firm rents an office on the seventh floor of a downtown office building. They have subdivided the office into five smaller offices, one for each of the three attorneys, one for the full-time secretary (whose office also contains the firm's library and file cabinets), and one for the reception area where the part-time secretary sits. There are two electric and two manual typewriters, an electric calculator, and six file cabinets (four drawers each). The library consists of approximately 125 volumes. There is a complete up-to-date set of the state's statutes, the reported cases of the state's supreme court for the last ten years, and a number of formbooks.

LAW OFFICE II

A. Personnel

The firm was organized in 1936 with seven attorneys. In 1942, it merged with a larger firm, resulting in a firm of twenty-nine attorneys, eleven of whom were partners and eighteen associates. By 1958, there were twenty-nine partners and fifty-three associates. By the end of 1986, there were 224 attorneys in the firm, roughly one-third of whom were partners.

---

[1] In many states, attorneys can place their name on an availability list in criminal court. When defendants are before the court, attorneys are appointed to represent them if they cannot afford to hire their own.

By 1986, the nonlawyer staff amounted to approximately 186:

Office Manager: 1	File Clerks: 8
Bookkeeping: 8	Secretaries/Typists, full-time: 92
Administrative Assistants: 4	Typists, part-time: 17–22
Litigation Assistants: 10	Word Procesing/Computer Staff: 8
Probate Assistants: 8	Reception/Phone: 4
Other Paralegal Staff: 5	Messenger: 4
Library Staff: 4	Xerox Operator: 2
Investigators: 3	Janitorial: 3

B. Type of Practice

Most of the firm's clients are publicly owned commercial corporations, several of which engage in international trade. The second large category of clients involves the firm in trust and estate planning. In addition, the firm does a substantial volume of real estate, anti-trust, tax, and government contract work.

The firm's statement of purpose is as follows:

> The purpose of this firm is to provide the highest possible quality of professional legal services to clients consistent with the principles of good business management. The terms "professional legal services" and "principles of good business management" are not to be viewed as mutually exclusive but rather as complementary terms. The criteria shall be not maximization of profit, but the ethical standards of the practice supported by an efficient and economical system. If such a "corporate mission" is identified and adopted, then all other statements of policy, procedures, operations, and controls, will naturally flow toward this common goal.

C. Governance

There was a time when the firm scoffed at the notion of management principles to govern the operation of the firm. The lawyers considered themselves professionals and not managers. When the firm had about fifty attorneys, they designated one of the partners as managing partner who spent most of his time on personnel, finances, etc. The hope of the partners was that the managing partner would handle all matters of administration with only the major decisions submitted to all the partners for a vote. (Too often the large firm tends to select the managing partner by default since, as indicated, lawyers usually do not want the job and most have little or no business background.) After the firm reached the seventy-five lawyer mark, however, it was clear that the job of administration was too much for one person to handle. Over a period of ten years, a series of major organizational changes were made. The firm was divided into a number of subject-matter departments and a series of committees was established to oversee the conduct of certain phases of the firm's operation (see chart below).

The hierarchical structure of the law firm changes periodically as the various components express a need to use the resources of the firm more effectively. Within the last seven years, the firm has brought in management consultant

FIRM II ORGANIZATION CHART

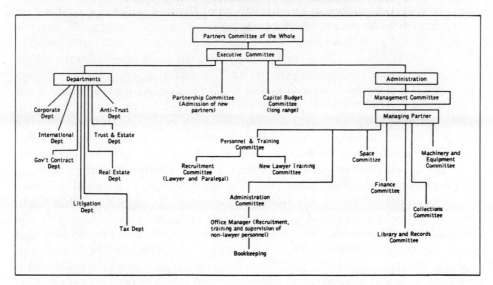

firms to advise it on specific and general problems of administration. The most recent problem addressed by the consultants has been time and billing procedures.

D. Finances

The firm bills its clients mainly on a hour basis. Attorneys and paralegals are instructed to record their time spent on individual cases in blocks of twenty minutes. Although different attorneys bill clients differently based upon the status of the attorney in the firm (senior partner cost per hour is greatest, with junior associate cost per hour the lowest), the average cost per hour to a client is $150.00. Different cost schedules exist for certain kinds of activities, e.g., court appearance, phone consultation.

When the paralegals became an identifiable part of the firm, there was considerable discussion as to how much to charge clients per hour for their time. One proposal was to take one half of the per-hour charge of the young junior associate and assign that figure to the paralegal's time. The matter is still under study due to the problem of trying to distinguish the per-hour costs of more experienced paralegals from those who have been recently hired. Pending a resolution of the problem, the management committee has instructed the bookkeeping division to allocate $45.00 per paralegal hour expended. If an individual has additional skills such as those of a Certified Public Accountant, the firm bills a client $85.00 per hour for this person's time.

E. Equipment and Facilities

The main office of the firm is located in the top four floors of a sixty-story office building in the financial district of the city. In addition, the firm has three branch offices, two in the United States and one in London. Each branch has its own library of about 1,000 volumes. The law library in the main office contains over 20,000 volumes. The firm owns or leases a variety of equipment. Every attorney and paralegal is supplied with a desk model dictation unit, the cost of which is $1,300.00 each. There are also available several portable units for out-of-office use. The firm has implemented integrated systems which allow a division of work among the secretarial staff, e.g., correspondence secretaries to take care of the heavy typing loads and administrative details. Each correspondence secretary is provided with a transcription unit from which s/he can transcribe materials as dictated by the attorney, and additionally s/he is provided with a word processor that allows him/her to do a rough draft of the attorney's dictation for his/her editing and revision. Automatic typewriters allow secretaries to play out recorded material (during which time they can insert any required additions and revisions) at a speed up to 180 words per minute, letter perfect. Every administrative secretary is supplied with a high-quality electric typewriter. All dictation units were purchased from the same manufacturer so as to provide complete interchangeability of equipment and parts whenever necessary. All automatic typewriters, electric typewriters, and word processors were also acquired from one manufacturer so as to enjoy maximum service and maintenance with minimum interruption, to ensure that whenever work product is divided among many typists the finished product will "look the same," and to enjoy the benefits of a common training system and common operating procedure. To further support its system, the firm has high-capacity, high-quality copy machines and offset equipment in a central duplicating room. There are also several small copy machines strategically located throughout the office facilities so that there is a full satellite support system for the central duplicating facility. Anyone can walk up to any of the satellite machines and make a few copies as required. Long runs or high-quality requirements are handled by central duplicating personnel. The firm also owns telecopier devices that allow the transmission of documents across telephone lines, e.g., an 8½ by 11 page of typed materials can be "put in" the transmitter at one end and "printed out" on a special receiving device. Many of the lawyers, paralegals, and administrative secretaries are supplied with adding machines, calculators, or portable electronic calculators. Everyone in the accounting and timekeeping department, of course, has a printing tape calculator. The firm also leases a teletype unit in order to quickly communicate with each one of the offices in the United States and in London. Additionally the firm has purchased (or has had designed) special furniture for much of the sophisticated equipment it uses. For example the automatic typewriters tend to be rather loud when typing automatically at the rate of 180 words per minute so special acoustical treatment had to be provided in areas where automatic equipment is located.

Finally, the firm uses sophisticated computers for its legal research (p. 632) and litigation support (p. 714) needs.

LAW OFFICE III

A. Personnel

The attorneys in this office are salaried employees of a major oil company. In the home office, there are forty-seven attorneys. Nationwide, the company, through its affiliates, employs 112 attorneys, seventeen paralegals, and eighty-two secretaries. The law office is divided into two divisions, general and tax. In the tax division there are sixty accountants working with the attorneys.

B. Type of Practice

The attorneys have only one client, the parent company and its affiliates. The tax division provides company management with advice on the tax implications of certain proposed transactions, e.g., mergers, stock split, foreign business. The general division handles employment contracts, corporate blue sky work, worker's compensation claims, antitrust work, etc. In addition, the division drafts many standardized forms and procedures for use by company employees in the field. When the company is involved in litigation, it usually retains outside counsel since most of the attorneys in the office have not had extensive litigation experience.

C. Governance

A corporate vice-president of the parent company has responsibility for the supervision of the law department. The attorney in charge of the general division is called the general counsel, the attorney in charge of the tax division is called the tax manager. They each have their assistants. For field offices of the company that have their own law department, an attorney is designated as the "head" of that department.

D. Finances

There is no fee collection problem since all activities of the attorneys are paid for out of the corporate treasury.

E. Equipment and Facilities

The law department of the parent company is located on the eleventh floor of the company building. It contains an array of typewriters, dictating equipment, computers, etc. Scattered throughout the subsidiaries are approximately thirty-two offices housing attorneys and their staffs. Each office has a law library geared to the practice needs of the state in which it is located. The tax division of the parent company has a 4,000 volume collection of specialized tax material.

Section C. DEVELOPMENTS IN LAW OFFICE EQUIPMENT

Given the extensive volume of documents in office files and law libraries, and the even greater volume of materials that are being published and will continue to be published by courts, legislatures, and administrative agencies, lawyers have been asking whether the age of automation can lend them any assistance. It has not taken much prompting for the equipment industry to respond. While technology has enticed lawyers with claims of incredible cost efficiency, there are those within the profession who continue to echo the lament of a late nineteenth century attorney who balked at the invention of the typewriter because it demeaned the highly personal relationship that the attorney should have with a client (p. 16). These attorneys, however, are quickly becoming the minority as the proponents of this technology continue to establish their claim that the equipment will not replace the attorney, nor diminish the need to make professional judgments. They are devices that, if intelligently used, will increase the competence of client service. On the range of computer equipment in a law office, see pp. 707ff.

Paralegals will undoubtedly be enlisted to operate this equipment. A word of extreme caution, however, is required for all paralegals who are so assigned. *Whenever possible, the paralegal should know how to complete the task by him/herself without use of the equipment.* This is not to say that s/he should avoid the equipment or use it only as a last resort. It is rather to argue that for intelligent use of the equipment, the paralegal should be able to function without it not only because of the possibility of machine malfunctions, but much more significantly, because of the ever present need to respond to peculiarities in a problem that the machine was not programmed to accommodate. The paralegal should take every opportunity to develop expertise in the operation of the equipment, but at the same time s/he should not let the machine interfere with the development of skills required in the broad range of law practice responsibilities.

1. Automated Legal Research

See p. 632, p. 720.

2. Litigation Support Systems

See p. 714.

3. Automatic Typing of Pleadings and Documents

Very often an attorney will find him/herself preparing essentially the same complaint, interrogatory, will, etc., with minor variations. The costs of typing can be considerable. Automatic typing equipment has been designed to offset these costs, e.g., MT/ST. By feeding certain data into the machine, the document will be typed automatically.

An example of such equipment is Compu-TEXT of LCS Corporation. The company says Compu-TEXT operates in two basic modes:

- text management mode
- transcription mode.

The "text management" mode concerns repetitive typing. Here, prestored paragraphs of texts that are used repetitively in identical or similar form are structured to form different letters or documents. Paragraphs and phrases are input and stored in the computer and later combined into varying combinations to form a required document. Final documents are not limited to the use of only standard statements but nonstandard material can be inserted anywhere within the document. Additional information or new dictation can be inserted when desired.

On instruction, the computer automatically inserts the date. If more than one page is required, the computer will automatically number each page and put a heading on each sheet. Variables can be inserted at any point. The computer will automatically ask the operator for the insert when one or more variables are required within a stored paragraph. Margins are automatically justified no matter how extensively the stored text is altered.

The "transcription" mode concerns daily transcription of letters or unique documents that are not used repetitively but generally require retyping because of revisions or corrections. In the "transcription" mode, the operator has the option of typing the document as an original or draft. Any errors made at this point can be corrected easily by merely backspacing and typing over the incorrect character or word. The typed text is stored in the memory unit of the computer with numbers assigned to each document and each paragraph. In less than a second the computer will retrieve any document or paragraph that needs correcting. A document can go through several revisions with the computer storing the updated version for retrieval at any time.

Section D. TIMEKEEPING

The lawyer as businessperson must employ good management techniques to service his/her clients on a profitable basis. The lawyer providing publicly financed legal services to the poor must also be concerned with management principles in order to provide efficient legal services to as many indigent clients as possible. While our focus in this and subsequent sections will be on the profit-making aspects of practice, it should be remembered that the principles underlying cost analysis are applicable to *any* practice.

The key to increased income for the lawyer is to keep track of and charge for all services rendered. The services provided by a lawyer are measurable in units of time. The lawyer has "time for sale" so it is extremely important to keep track of how time is used since time is one of the basic elements in the creation of a service bill given to a client.

What follows is a series of sample forms that are representative of those used in firms to keep time and billing records.

After the initial client interview, the accounting starting point can be a "New Matter Sheet" such as that shown in figure 1. It is also sometimes referred to as a "New Business Sheet." The "New Matter Sheet" becomes the source document for the creation of all the necessary accounting records involved in the administration of the office on behalf of that client. If the "New Matter Sheet" is wrong, all the records based upon it will be incorrect. An example of the process that flows from the "New Matter Sheet" is presented in figure 2, "Administrative Management Blueprint." The arrows on the chart indicate that it is basically a "downhill flow" system. If a lawyer, paralegal, or secretary tries to initiate a change in the accounting records at some later date (e.g., when they turn in their daily time reports), the change will not be activated throughout the entire system. An additional "New Matter Sheet," often called a "Change Sheet," would have to be entered at the starting point in order for all new or correct information to properly flow throughout the system. At the time the billing attorney opens a "New Matter Sheet," s/he must

Figure 1. New Matter Sheet

(Please type. Please fill in all spaces necessary to set up account correctly. Have account attorney check and initial.) Account Attorney (Billing): _____Date: _____ Other Attorneys Concerned: _____ Client To Be Charged: _____	
Address: _____ _____ Case Name:	**File Information** [ ] Corporate [ ] Tax [ ] General [ ] Litigation [ ] Probate [ ] Labor [ ] Guardianship [ ] Other [ ] Wills _____ Estate Plan _____
Plaintiff	
Defendant Court: _____ Court No.: _____	**Size and Type of File** [ ] Miscellaneous File Folder POUCH: Small [ ] Large [ ] To contain folders:
Bookkeeping Instructions | Timekeeping Instructions Post disbursements to: Post time to: [ ] Existing Sheet [ ] Existing Sheet [ ] New Sheet [ ] New Sheet Other Information: Related files, cross-references, referred by whom, special instructions, etc. _____ _____ _____ _____ _____ _____ _____ _____ _____ _____ _____ Return file to:	[ ] Correspondence [ ] Pleadings [ ] Working Papers [ ] Miscellaneous [ ] Exhibits [ ] Extra Copies [ ] Agreements [ ] Bills [ ] Blue Sky [ ] Client's Papers [ ] Discovery Material [ ] Documents [ ] Evidence material [ ] Memorandum of Law [ ] Minutes of Meeting [ ] Registration Statements [ ] Tax Papers [ ] Corporate [ ] Other _____

Fee arrangement: _____
_____
_____
      File Number: _____
	Billing Attorney's
	   Initials [ ]
	File Room [ ]
	Office Manager [ ]

advise the bookkeeping and timekeeping departments on whether to use the existing ledger page or sheet (for a client already in existence), or open a new page (for a new matter of an old client), or establish a totally new client master page.

This blueprint is typical of the method most firms use to originate and handle the inputs and outputs of information for their administrative system. Once the "New Matter Sheet" has been properly filled out and completed by the originating attorney, it is delivered to a clerical person, normally someone in the file room. This person, using the information from the "New Matter Sheet," will create all the necessary timekeeping records, bookkeeping records, files, and labels, telephone index cards, file room index cards, secretary index cards, etc. The original "New Matter Sheet" is filed in the new client file, with a copy filed in alphabetical order in a master New Matter Book for future reference.

Assuming that the addressograph plate medium is used, the plate itself is placed in a temporary file drawer so that at least once or twice a month a list of all new clients and new matters for old clients can be run off for circulation among all the lawyers in order to (a) advise the lawyers of new office work and (b) determine if there are any conflicts of interest (p. 248) that may have been overlooked. The addressograph plate is a device on which information is "typed." The plate can be used over and over to imprint on folders, files, labels, index cards, etc., information that is generated throughout the "information

Figure 2. Administrative Management Blueprint

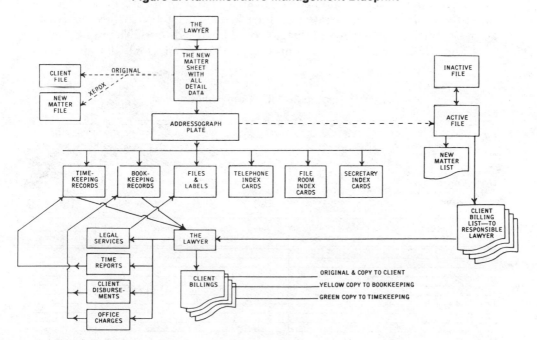

system." After the new work list has been circulated, the addressograph plates are removed from the temporary file and filed in a permanent file drawer in client alphabetical order, per lawyer. For example, lawyer #1 would have all his/her plates filed from A–Z; lawyer #2's plates would be filed in A–Z order; and so on for each lawyer of the firm. This plate filing system now becomes known as an "active file." By maintaining the perpetual inventory of plates for active clients, with only periodic reconciliation with accounting records, the addressograph active file plate drawer can be used to run off a master client billing list on some routine basis (monthly, quarterly, semiannually, or any other time period chosen by the billing attorneys). If the system is a computer-supported system, the list could contain such additional information as the number of chargeable hours invested by each attorney for his/her specific client with the related dollar value of such time invested. The list will then be distributed to the responsible billing lawyer for his/her preliminary review to determine whether or not there are items that s/he wishes to bill. If s/he wishes to bill, s/he normally will ask for further supporting information from the timekeeping and bookkeeping departments to include such things as the breakdown of hours invested by all lawyers, some pro forma billing (the application of guideline rates multiplied by the hours invested per lawyer), a display of the associated diary narratives for each transaction as reported by lawyers from their daily time reports, and all the out-of-pocket disbursements and allocated internal costs to be charged to the client. With that information in hand, the attorney can create his/her legal service billing and disbursement billing for rendering to the client. Again, a computer system can more efficiently produce and develop all the described information in a predetermined format.

This support information comes from a variety of forms. First there is a "Daily Time Sheet," as illustrated in figure 3, on which the attorney records all activities during the day. (A paralegal could be asked to use the same form.)

The "Daily Time Sheet" becomes the journal from which all time entries

Figure 3. Daily Time Sheet

DAILY SERVICE REPORT OF: DATE:

ANS	–Answer	DEPO	–Deposition	K	–Contract	O	–Order	RES –Research
APP	–Appearance or Attending	DIC	–Dictation	L	–Legal	OP	–Opinion	REV –Revision
ARG	–Argue or Argument	DOC	–Document	LT	–Letter to	P	–Preparation	S –Settlement
BR	–Brief	DR	–Drafting	LF	–Letter from	PL	–Plaintiff	TF –Telephone from
COMP	–Complaint	F	–Facts	MT	–Memorandum to	PR	–Praecipe	TT –Telephone to
CW	–Conference–Office	FL	–File	MF	–Memorandum from	PRT	–Pretrial	TR –Trial
CWO	–Conference–Outside Office	H	–Hearing	MOT	–Motion	R	–Reading and Review	TRV –Travel
DEF	–Defendant	INV	–Investigation	NEG	–Negotiation	REL	–Release	W –Witness
DEM	–Demurrer	INT	–Interview					

CLIENT (State billing division or department)	MATTER	DESCRIPTION OF WORK (Use abbreviations above)	TIME	
			Hours	10ths

Figure 4. Time Ticket

DATE	NAME	CLIENT	MATTER	TIME

DESCRIPTION:

Posted: _____

are posted to individual client ledger pages. Law offices normally use tenths of an hour as the common base unit for measurement of time (in increments of six minutes), although a few firms still use one-fourth of an hour as the basic timekeeping unit. The attorney can note his/her investment on the "Daily Time Sheet" each time during the day that s/he completes work on that particular matter. It is sometimes difficult for anyone else to read his/her handwriting, so the secretary will normally type separate time tickets, one such time ticket for each line transaction. See figure 4.

These time tickets are usually perforated or shingled for easy separation so that they can be subsequently sorted into alphabetical order for quick posting to client ledger cards. Several systems can be used in processing these tickets. One may be to retain the individual tickets in an open tray in alphabetical order for eventual retrieval and tabulation for billing; another would use gummed backs for pasting directly onto a client ledger card; or the ticket may be used as the source document for transcribing onto a "Master Ledger Card" (figure 5); or the ticket could be delivered directly to a service bureau (p. 63) for use as the original source document for key punching and entering into a computer system; or the ticket could be key punched directly from the lawyer's daily time sheet and used as an input document for a law firm's in-house computer system.

A "service bureau" is a company that specializes in processing data information. Such a company normally owns or leases computer equipment and sells its services (data processing capabilities) to its customer user. The service bureau will normally receive raw data in the form of accounting vouchers or time tickets. It key punches the information into punch cards and processes the punch cards through its computer equipment in order to develop the necessary reports required by a firm such as an inventory of time, accounting records, and management analyses.

When a lawyer first begins to keep time, there may be parts of the day unaccounted for because the discipline required for timekeeping has not yet been acquired. With practice, however, all parts of every working day will be accounted for. The lawyer should account for a full day. A portion of each lawyer's day will be devoted to nonbillable activities, such as firm administration, continuing legal education, civic activities, and general exposure to the literature. A knowledge of how much time is devoted to these "general office" activities is important for keeping track of how much time is being invested, but the primary emphasis of the timekeeping system should be to identify time spent on chargeable matters. Ultimately, all such information will be useful to the managers of the firm for studies on staff utilization, allocation of invested time between chargeable matters and no-charge matters, dollar return for hours invested, etc.

A paralegal is expected to keep track of time in exactly the same manner as the attorneys report their time. If the firm uses a daily log for purposes of recording time, the paralegal will use the same system. The paralegal's time will be posted to the inventory of time (the client ledger card) in exactly the same manner as the lawyer's time is posted so that at billing time the responsible billing attorney can be appraised of the fact that a paralegal has invested time on behalf of that particular client matter, and the billing attorney can evaluate that investment and price it accordingly.

Section E. BILLING

Once the lawyer has a working timekeeping system, s/he is better able to retrieve relevant information in arriving at a fair legal service bill for a client. Historically, law firms have billed clients only at the conclusion of the matter, or on a once-a-year billing cycle. During the past several years, law firms have recognized that more frequent billings will help resolve their cash-flow problems. Law firms currently employ a variety of billing cycles, e.g., monthly, quarterly, semi-annual, annual, upon completion of the work, or any other basis mutually agreeable with the client.

The billing process is generally activated by lawyer request, but as the use of equipment becomes more popular, the billing process will become "machine activated." Figure 1 (p. 750) suggests that a client billing list can be automatically produced and distributed to the responsible billing lawyer on some routine

Figure 5. Master Ledger Card

DATE	CHARACTER OF SERVICE	LAW-YER NO.	DAILY HOURS	N / C	C O N.	SHEET NO. _____												TOTAL CHARGE HOURS
						TOTAL HOURS WORKED TO DATE BY LAWYER											
						1	2	3	4	5	6	7	8	9	0	

schedule (e.g., monthly). The lawyer can then review that list and determine which client matters s/he wishes to bill, so advise the accounting department, and subsequently receive all the information relevant to activities for that client. The system in figure 1 indicates that timekeeping information and bookkeeping information will be delivered to the lawyer for his/her evaluation and eventual billing. More sophisticated systems have an intervening step, wherein all the information is compiled and tabulated to create a document commonly know as "Prebill Analysis," setting forth a narrative description of the time invested (the time tickets or a synthesized recap thereof), a listing of chargeable time per matter for the client with a price value for such time, subtotals per matter, and a grand total for the legal service bill for that client.

An important tool in a timekeeping-billing system is a table of "time values." Each firm will need to construct its own table that clearly sets forth the hourly billing rate for each lawyer in the firm. A chart such as that illustrated in figure 6 is very helpful in this regard. In a manually oriented system, it is also helpful to set forth the names of the lawyers above the appropriate hourly rate to facilitate clerical computation, i.e., hours invested times the lawyer's hourly rate.

Accurate time records used in conjunction with a value time chart can assist in the creation of a bill and in the development of raw data for evaluation such as determining the number of chargeable hours and the dollar value thereof invested by a particular attorney per client for a month or for the entire year. You can then tabulate that same information for all lawyers in the firm and determine historically how hours have been invested and the subsequent pricing thereof. More important, you will have compiled valuable budgeting and planning data. For example, if the firm expects to generate annual gross income from services rendered by John Smith, Esq., in the amount of $150,000, it becomes clear that if Smith's billing rate is $125 per hour he will have to invest 1200 chargeable hours that year. It then becomes purely a mathematical exercise to develop projections on gross income for the firm, required chargeable hours per attorney, and all the relevant computations that necessarily flow from such basic data.

Once the lawyer has received all the billing information and has evaluated the "Prebill Analysis," if any, the lawyer generally adjusts the final bill either upwards or downwards, depending upon other factors such as the initial agreement with the client on billing, the responsibility assumed by the firm, exposure on the part of the firm (e.g., potential malpractice suit from class action dissidents), results (favorable or unfavorable), expertise required to perform the services, uniqueness of the matter, etc. A straightforward mathematical computation may develop a legal service bill "worth" $12,724 but the attorney may actually tender a bill to the client in the amount of $11,500 or $14,000.

When the attorney decides the appropriate value of a legal service bill, the final bill is typed by the secretary. Large law firms using in-house computer systems (or service bureaus) may elect to mail a computer print-out, but that technique is not yet very popular throughout the profession. The great majority of law firms still hand-create a bill individually typed for transmittal to the client. The style of the bill will fall into one of three identifiable formats: (1) legal services for the period ending _____; (2) legal services rendered on your behalf as follows: (a short prose style narrative description); (3) legal services rendered as follows: (a diary presentation relisting all the transactions as recorded from the lawyer's time sheets).

The format is often custom-tailored in response to the needs of the client, e.g., capital vs. expense chargeability, need to maintain historical information, need to provide complete and accurate reports on the use of lawyer services, or responses to any other idiosyncrasy of the client's needs. Legal fees may be characterized by a client as a capital cost item, subject to "depreciation" or other write-off procedures spread over the life of the contract or some other acceptable term. For example, attorneys fees on the formation and organization of a corporation are normally considered to be organizational costs and become part of "capital" of the corporation. Other legal services may be "expensed" by the client in the year in which the services are rendered and the fee paid, such as general legal services on environmental compliance issues. As a consequence of the accounting characterization of "legal services," a client may need elaborate narrative descriptions for services rendered, or may require a very brief narrative depending upon "capital" or "expense" accountability. Most lawyers feel that the service bill should reflect effort expended by the law firm on behalf of the client. Hence the common tendency is to create a narrative style bill. With the advent of computer use, many very large law firms are working toward sending out monthly bills characterized as "for legal services."

In addition to the value of legal services rendered, it is also very important to recover cash out-of-pocket costs spent by the firm on behalf of the client, such as filing fees, payment to investigators, court reporter costs for depositions, long distance telephone charges, printing copy costs, travel expenses, witness fees, or any other similarly identifiable out-of-pocket items. The common practice is to list these out-of-pocket costs under a "disbursement" caption, just below the legal service fee, with a grand total for the bill being tendered. For example, the legal service bill may have, with appropriate description, a value of $500, with an additional $120.18 for "disbursements,"

Figure 6. Hourly Time x $ Hourly Rate

RATE: TIME:	$20		$25		$30		$35		$40		$45		$50		$55		$60		$65		$70		$75	
0.10 hour	2	00	2	50	3	00	3	50	4	00	4	50	5	00	5	50	6	00	6	50	7	00	7	50
0.20	4	00	5	00	6	00	7	00	8	00	9	00	10	00	11	00	12	00	13	00	14	00	15	00
0.30	6	00	7	50	9	00	10	50	12	00	13	50	15	00	16	50	18	00	19	50	21	00	22	50
0.40	8	00	10	00	12	00	14	00	16	00	18	00	20	00	22	00	24	00	26	00	28	00	30	00
0.50	10	00	12	50	15	00	17	50	20	00	22	50	25	00	27	50	30	00	32	50	35	00	37	50
0.60	12	00	15	00	18	00	21	00	24	00	27	00	30	00	33	00	36	00	39	00	42	00	45	00
0.70	14	00	17	50	21	00	24	50	28	00	31	50	35	00	38	50	42	00	45	50	49	00	52	50
0.80	16	00	20	00	24	00	28	00	32	00	36	00	40	00	44	00	48	00	52	00	56	00	60	00
0.90	18	00	22	50	27	00	31	50	36	00	40	50	45	00	49	50	54	00	58	50	63	00	67	50
1.00 hour	20	00	25	00	30	00	35	00	40	00	45	00	50	00	55	00	60	00	65	00	70	00	75	00
2.00	40	00	50	00	60	00	70	00	80	00	90	00	100	00	110	00	120	00	130	00	140	00	150	00
3.00	60	00	75	00	90	00	105	00	120	00	135	00	150	00	165	00	180	00	195	00	210	00	225	00
4.00	80	00	100	00	120	00	140	00	160	00	180	00	200	00	220	00	240	00	260	00	280	00	300	00
5.00	100	00	125	00	150	00	175	00	200	00	225	00	250	00	275	00	300	00	325	00	350	00	375	00
6.00	120	00	150	00	180	00	210	00	240	00	270	00	300	00	330	00	360	00	390	00	420	00	450	00
7.00	140	00	175	00	210	00	245	00	280	00	315	00	350	00	385	00	420	00	455	00	490	00	525	00
8.00	160	00	200	00	240	00	280	00	320	00	360	00	400	00	440	00	480	00	520	00	560	00	600	00
9.00	180	00	225	00	270	00	315	00	360	00	405	00	450	00	495	00	540	00	585	00	630	00	675	00
10.00 hours	200	00	250	00	300	00	350	00	400	00	450	00	500	00	550	00	600	00	650	00	700	00	750	00

for a total of $620.18. Most firms tend to bill all disbursements simultaneously with legal service billings, but the trend appears to be toward billing disbursements on a separate invoice each month, irrespective of the timing for legal service billing in order to more quickly recover out-of-pocket costs.

Section F. ADMINISTRATIVE REPORTS

There are different types of administrative reports that naturally "fall out" of the timekeeping and billing process. The more common reports used by law firms are:

1. Billable Hours/Delinquent Time Reports
2. Billable Hours Analysis
3. Nonbillable Time Analysis
4. Accounts Receivable Reports
    a. Accounts Receivable Journal
    b. Cash Receipts Journal
    c. Open Invoice Report
    d. Accounts Receivable Aging Report[2]
       billing by client (cumulative for a year)
       billing by attorney (cumulative for a year)
    e. Departmental Profitability Analysis

These reports could be available on a regular schedule such as weekly, monthly, annually, or conceivably they could be produced on request as needed. In any event, the raw data will be available and should be developed and stored in such a fashion as to accommodate easy retrieval, tabulation, and display for the office manager and managing partner, with summary totals being available for presentation to the entire firm. All this historical data: can be compared to the results of the preceding year for the same time period in order to quickly measure "how are we doing this year"; can be compared to the budget, or any other acceptable bench mark; should be used as danger signals to take remedial action where appropriate; can be used as the basis for compensation schedules; can provide the firm with all necessary data for complying with government regulations (e.g., tax laws governing the firm's income); and can be used as a general audit and control device.

A well-thought-out system should give the managers of the law firm effective control and provide additional meaningful data for:

1. Firm Management Reports
    a. Firm activity and work status.
    b. Summary aging of work in progress.

---

[2] An "aging report" is one of the most common reports developed by accountants to provide management with the time outstanding of accounts receivables. For example, an aged accounts receivable will set forth how many of the total receivables are less than 30 days old, how many are 30 to 59 days old, how many are 60 to 90 days old, and how many are more than 90 days old. It is a truism that the older an account receivable is, the less collectable it is. Therefore, management needs to know how old the account is in order to be sure to put the emphasis upon collecting it before it becomes so old that it is worthless.

    c. Summary aging of uncollected bills.
    d. Summary of billings and realizations.
    e. Uncollected bills written off.
    f. Nonlegal staff charges to work in progress.
2. Practice Analysis Reports[3]
    a. Staff utilization.
    b. Lawyer practice experience.
3. Partner Responsibility Reports
    a. Partners' work in progress summary.
    b. Partners' work in progress aging.
    c. Partners' uncollected bills.
    d. Partners' billing and realizations.
4. Work in Progress and Billing Reports
    a. Work in progress ledger—detail.
    b. Work in progress disbursements—detail.
    c. Billing memorandum.
    d. Delinquent diaries.
    e. Client billing history.
5. Special Purpose Reports
    a. Billings by introducing attorney.
    b. Billings by assigned lawyer.
    c. Allocations to prior partnerships.
6. Special Management Reports as Required.

One of the reports that could be generated from the basic timekeeping records is an analysis of how much time is being invested by paralegals in client matters. This analysis is exactly the same kind of analysis that the firm would want for the time invested by lawyers. Sometimes large firms also keep track of time invested by secretaries and other nonlawyers, but generally this is not done. More commonly, firms keep track of lawyer time and paralegal time, distributed to clients and client matters. In addition to tracing the time through to client matters for the purpose of billing, the firm also wants to know the aggregate amount of time invested by everyone charging time into the system (lawyers and paralegals) in order to evaluate profit centers, costs, allocation of work among lawyers and paralegals, etc.

If you have the opportunity to become involved in law office administration, you will undoubtedly inherit an existing system that generally contains many of the items discussed above. As part of your management objectives, you should determine the needs of the firm, and then express those needs in acceptable formats such as timely legal service and disbursement bills, account-

[3] A "practice analysis report" can be very helpful to a firm. It analyzes where the firm is investing its time, how much money it is earning from specific areas of the practice, where its costs lie, and hence how much profit is being earned from the various areas of practice. Specifically, a practice analysis could develop such information for probate practice, litigation practice, general corporate practice, banking practice, anti-trust practice—any of the "specialties" that are identifiable within a firm. Beyond the economic impact, the firm can use these "practice analysis reports" to be sure that everyone is carrying his/her fair share of work.

ing controls, management reports, etc., all of which have critical bench marks for measuring firm productivity and determining future directions.

The American Bar Association has a wealth of material available through their annual law office economic conferences. Other sources include the Andrew J. Cantor economic studies; Price, Waterhouse & Company Law Firm Studies; special economic studies compiled by state bar organizations; information that can be collected from other law firms in the area; standards or guidelines as developed by local business schools and current econometric information in the market place. One objective of the administrative system should be to provide all the necessary administrative and managerial information required to support the firm, with a minimum of lawyer time involvement, for purposes of:

1. Better recordation of all data in the office.
2. Improved office efficiency.
3. Better billing procedures.
4. Stronger client relationships.
5. Complete management information.

We will now examine representative formats for some reports commonly used in law office administration.

WORK SUMMARY

Each attorney in the firm should routinely complete a form such as that illustrated in figure 7, "Work Summary," so that the managing partner of the firm can evaluate the work load of the firm each week. The managing partner should then be able to assign new work or reallocate work to lawyers on the basis of this work summary in conjunction with a review of time utilization reports developed from the timekeeping system.

Paralegals often fill out "Work Summary" sheets, depending on the nature of the work being done. If they are working for many lawyers in one department, the department head will often require a "Work Summary" report in order to keep track of the work they are doing. This would be a current report similar to the "practice analysis report" (see footnote 3, p. 758) except that the latter usually is an analysis of what has gone on over a long time period, whereas the "Work Summary" provides a means to review current status. This device can be an integral part of the firm's ethical obligation to supervise the work of the paralegal (p. 262).

CASH FLOW PROJECTION

Most firms are concerned with cash flow on an ad hoc basis. Many have cash-flow problems but only a few use mathematical methods of determining projected needs. One approach, as suggested by the form in figure 8, is to determine anticipated cash receipts for the time period under consideration by adding to the ending cash balance a certain percentage of new billings (you can anticipate payment within thirty days from approximately 50% of your new billings, with the remaining bills being paid over a sixty-day to one-year period, depending upon the firm's attentiveness to receivable collections), plus the anticipated collection from the more than sixty-day old account receivables, to arrive at "total estimated cash resources" from which you can subtract out-of-pocket costs anticipated for the time period, arriving at a "projected cash balance." You can then quickly determine whether you need to borrow supplemental cash from the bank, or cut overhead, or take whatever remedial action may be necessary.

CHARGEABLE HOUR SCHEDULE

The "chargeable hour schedule" summarizes the actual hours invested by the attorneys on a month-by-month basis (see figure 9). This schedule could be further refined and become more informative by multiplying hours by the attorney's dollar rate, so as to arrive at a total dollar value of the lawyer's investment in the practice each month. This schedule does not analyze what was actually "billed" nor what was actually "collected." There may be three different values for the schedule, the amount billed, and the amount collected. For example, the attorneys of the firm may invest hours (time) valued at certain "guideline rates" for a total dollar value of $1,000 for legal services rendered on behalf of a client for a specific matter. The attorneys may feel that the guideline rate is not the proper economic value of the legal services rendered, so they decide

Figure 7. Work Summary

[ ] Can Handle More Work   * C   (Work Completed Since Last Report)
[ ] Have All the Work I Can Handle   WP (Work in Progress)
[ ] Need Help   IA (Matter Is Inactive)
Report of: Date:

Client	Matter	Description of Work [Designate Specialty Work by Symbol (S)]	Date Assgnd	Partner	Status*

Figure 8. Cash Flow Projection

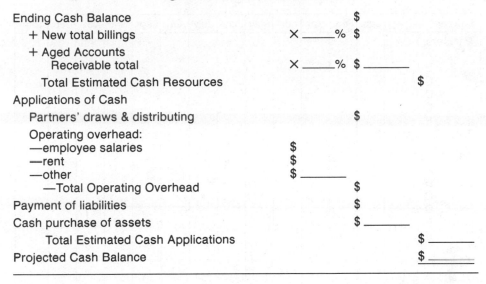

to send a bill to the client in the amount of $500. The client may feel that the fee is too high and decide to pay only $300, and after some compromising with the attorneys, the firm and the client might settle on $400.

Most law firms develop a chargeable hour schedule on the basis of historical information in order to evaluate how lawyers are investing their time throughout the year. It is suggested that this schedule can also be used to develop a budget or anticipatory schedule for the forthcoming year as part of the overall financial budget. A retroactive historical schedule could then be very easily compared to the budget schedule to determine whether the firm on a lawyer-by-lawyer basis is investing an adequate number of hours to support the income expectations of the firm.

AGED ACCOUNTS RECEIVABLE

A list of clients showing the amount due from each client as of a specified date is known as a "schedule of accounts receivable." This schedule can be refined to indicate the number of days outstanding since original billing date, normally into the following categories: 0–29 days old, 30–59 days old, 60–90 days old, and older than 90 days. This now becomes known as the "aged accounts receivable" report.

The schedule in figure 10 is common throughout most businesses. Law firms generally do not develop such a schedule, yet this can be a critical tool in the collection process. It is helpful to provide sufficient space in the right-hand edge of the schedule to indicate any current collection effort or the status of the account on a notation basis. This report should be developed each month so that the managing partner and legal administrator can quickly determine where a special effort may be needed in the collection process, evaluate the status of receivables, and adjust cash-flow predictions in accordance with the status of the receivables. Since most firms are on a cash-basis accounting system,

Figure 9. Chargeable Hour Schedule, 1986

Lawyer	Jan.	Feb.	Mar.	April	May	June	July	Aug.	Sept.	Oct.	Nov.	Dec.	Total
Partners: A B C D E F													
Total Partners													
Associates: A B C D E F													
Total Associates													
TOTAL FIRM													

there may not be an account labeled "accounts receivable" in the formal books or in the chart of accounts. Frequently, copies of service bills are held in a "side file" labeled as "memorandum of receivables" outside of the formal set of books. As a consequence, it is very easy for the firm to lose sight of the substantial investment that may be accumulating in unpaid receivables. National studies reveal that as much as 70% of receivables are older than sixty days, with a substantial portion thereof being frequently older that six months. Law firms tend to neglect the collection of receivables. If you study statistics that are available from the American Bar Association, you will discover that outstanding receivables will average approximately $10,000 per lawyer head, with that number swelling to as high as $25,000 or more per lawyer head in some firms.

Figure 10. Aged Accounts Receivable Billed—Not Yet Collected

Billing Attorney	Client Name	Legal Services	Disbursements	Total Due		Current To 30 Days	31–60 Days	61–90 Days	91–180 Days	More Than 6 Mos. Old
	(Alphabetic listing by client)	$	$	$		$	$	$	$	$
	TOTAL, ALL CLIENTS % Distribution	$ %	$ %	$ 100%		$ %	$ %	$ %	$ %	$ %
	TOTAL RECAP BY BILLING ATTORNEY				% to total					
	(Total by billing lawyer) . . .	$	$	$	% % % %	$	$	$	$	$
	TOTAL ALL LAWYERS				100%					

This means that a firm of ten lawyers could conceivably have outstanding receivables in excess of $250,000. The greatest contribution that a legal administrator can make is to become heavily involved in the billing and collection routine and to do everything possible to speed up the collection process so as to drive down these ratios. No other "business" would tolerate such excesses. The form displayed in figure 10 is subject to considerable alteration depending upon the management style of the firm, but all the basic elements are there.

ANNUAL BUDGET WORKSHEET

One of the most vital tools to the successful management of any business is an annual budget (figure 11). Yet only a handful of law firms use such a tool. Most large law firms use their computers to help achieve budgetary control, but such firms only comprise a very small percentage of the total number of firms in the country.

The annual budget should be one of the very first items to be developed by management. Traditionally law firms have little understanding or control over their financial destiny and, as a consequence, generally tend to react to problems on a "crisis" basis. The use of an annual budget and other such plan-

Figure 11. Annual Budget—Work Sheet

Line Item	Jan.	Feb.	Mar.	April	May	June	July	Aug.	Sept.	Oct.	Nov.	Dec.	Year Total
Income:													
x													
x													
x													
x													
Total Income													
Expenses													
x													
x													
x													
x													
x													
x													
x													
x													
x													
x													
x													
x													
x													
x													
Total Expenses													
Net Income													
Actual Net													
Variance													

ning tools would virtually eliminate or greatly minimize crises throughout the year. Law firms are now tending to become more businesslike in their management style and it is expected that many firms will be adopting and implementing more sophisticated budgetary procedures.

All the above schedules have been presented in a sequence that approximates their potential usefulness to law firms. This is not to suggest that the schedules are in fact ranked in this fashion by firms. As indicated, quite the contrary is often true.

Section G. THE PROCEDURE MANUAL: MAIL, COPYING, AND FILING RULES

Once a firm decides to prepare a procedure manual,[4] the first question is where to begin. Since the manual is not a novel with each chapter flowing inexorably into the next, as long as the index is exhaustive, initially it makes little difference where a particular topic is covered in the manual. Only after the manual has reached thirty or forty sections and its growth has leveled, should parts be moved solely for reasons of style. When that is done, be sure to change the table of contents and index.

INCOMING MAIL

Before touching sophisticated areas, the manual should start with some fairly straightforward routines. One prime candidate is incoming mail. A suggested statement follows:

Mail: Incoming

In addition to the obvious sorting of mail by addressee, the individual responsible for the morning mail should:

1. Date-stamp *everything* with the "Received" stamp. Exceptions are books received on approval or original documents such as deeds that have been mailed to the office for recording or filing elsewhere. It is far better to have stamped in error than not to have stamped at all.
1.1. Whenever possible, place the date stamp at the bottom of an incoming letter or document that is going to be filed. Thus the date will remain visible after filing.
2. When the incoming document will require reference to previous papers, place the appropriate file with it.
3. When the response to the incoming document can be drafted by the person receiving the mail, prepare a draft and place it with the document.

---

[4] Light, T., "The Procedure Manual—Mail, Copying and Filing Rules," 26 *The Practical Lawyer* 71ff. (No. 1, Jan. 1980), Copyright 1980 by the American Law Institute. Reprinted with the permission of *The Practical Lawyer*.

4. Route return receipts for certified mail through the interested individuals in the office. When ultimately returned for filing, the receipts should be stapled to the copies of the documents to which they correspond.

5. File the following documents immediately without circulation:

5.1 Pocket parts or supplements to treatises in the library.

5.2 All CCH (p. 511) and other loose-leaf supplements, except for the covering pages that contain a summary of recent developments in the law. All booklets on varying subjects should be circulated.

5.3 The paperback supplements to the state statutes and the United States Code.

6. For informational purposes, prepare a daily checks and bills received sheet using the format in form 1.

Form 1. Daily Checks and Bills Received
Received on January 6, 1981

Checks

Hammerlee	(title search)	$380.00
Mid-Penn	136.55 C.A.	3,961.43
PNB	164.80 C.A.	724.80
Kalp, Arn	2.25 C.A.	62.25

Bills

Wagners	(clips and rubber stamps)	12.72
Rec'd vol. 97 of *Supreme Court Reporter*		N/C

In conjunction with incoming mail, each attorney should have at his/her desk the following rubber stamp to indicate how the material is to be disseminated to other interested parties:

PHOTOCOPY AND SEND TO: _____

DATE DONE _____ BY _____

The use of this stamp at the bottom of incoming documents, along with a handwritten note to the individuals receiving copies, facilitates quick responses unhampered by dictation, transcription, and revision delays, and also prevents procrastination. Furthermore, forwarding copies is a nearly effortless but effective method for keeping clients informed of activity on their cases.

When the individual receiving the copy is expected to do nothing more than read it, a second stamp should be applied:

FOR INFORMATION ONLY—NO ACTION REQUIRED

COPYING CHARGES

Failure to record legitimate copy charges for later billing to the client can constitute a drain on the firm's financial resources. Copy charges should be recorded as follows:

1. Register on the alphabetical list that is kept on or near the copying machine the client's name, if not already there, and the number of copies.

1.1 It is not necessary to identify the document being copied unless more than twenty-five copies are being made.

1.2 The date of the copying need not be given unless more than twenty-five copies are being recorded.

2. Copies that are not to be charged to any client should be noted as "office" copies or "N/C" copies.

3. On at least a monthly basis, the member of the staff who is responsible for copy charges should post them to the respective client cards.

3.1 All copy charges for a given client during a given month should be accumulated as one entry on the client card, making a separate entry only for a particular document involving an exceptional amount of copying, with twenty-five copies as the minimum.

THE FILING SYSTEM

Rules and Comments

The importance of a good filing system to a firm cannot be overestimated. Lost and misplaced papers are the obvious result of a poor filing system. But the damage can run even deeper. Deadlines can be missed. Hours may be lost in ferreting through files for crucial documents that cannot be found. Appellate briefs can be poorly prepared because files are not in a readily usable form that would allow drafters to gather information and compose in an orderly fashion. Particular tasks are continually overlooked because attorneys, often subconsciously, dread having to search for the information necessary to undertake them or simply do not know how to tell a member of the staff to compile what is needed.

The choice of a particular filing system is not as important as a clear and unambiguous decision. However, a *numerical filing system,* access to which is gained through an *alphabetical card index,* has much to be said in its favor, since it:

- Reduces the misplacement of files. For some reason, individuals are more likely to place files in correct numerical order than in correct alphabetical order, especially when the files carry similar names.
- Permits the grouping of files by subject matter, such as litigation or real estate. Such a system can be useful if, for example, the firm wants to contact all clients for whom wills were prepared within the past five years.
- Makes for easier reference on memoranda, correspondence, and client lists. It is certainly simpler to jot "86.267" on a title abstract sheet than "Stankiewicz: Purchase of Real Estate (1986)."
- Allows cross-referencing within the card index. A purely alphabetical system without a card index would have difficulty handling the industrial development project for a client named Jones who owns New Maker Industries involving a local development agency bearing the acronym SIFT. While someone may think of the project as "Jones: SIFT-New Maker Industries," others may look for the file under "Jones: Industrial

Development Project" or "Jones: New Maker Industries-SIFT" or even "New Maker Industries: SIFT." In the *card* index, any heading may be used, and the file name and cross-reference cards can be employed for each of the other headings.

- Automatically brings old files to the front of the filing system, acting almost as a tickler system.
- Allows the immediate identification of the year of a particular file by the first two digits of the file index, e.g., "86.589."
- Facilitates the differentiation of files that may have confusingly similar designations. "Jones: Personal Injury (1981)" and "Jones: Property Settlement Agreement (1983)" could be next to one another in an alphabetical system and would have the tendency not only to be filed in the wrong alphabetical order but to attract one another's papers. In a *numerical* system, although the index cards would probably be neighbors, the physical separation of the folders in the file cabinet would be more likely to prevent the misplacing of documents among the files.
- Adapts to computerization, when that time comes.
- Eases the handling of closed files. Under an alphabetical system, when the time finally comes to retire a particular file, two choices are available—continue to file alphabetically, or switch to a sequential closed-file numbering system, with files placed one after the other as they are closed regardless of their alphabetical designations. The first choice leads to the situation in which all the files from I through Z have to be moved if H grows rapidly, since nobody anticipated that the Halfpenny National Bank would become the firm's most active client. The second alternative requires an alphabetical card index to allow for the retrieval of particular closed files, which already exists under the numerical system.

Procedure Manual Rules for a Numerical Filing System with an Alphabetical Card Index

Filing: Numerical System.   The categories listed below are arbitrary. Anytime a significant block of cases does not fit within a particular category, a new category will be created. The category number is preceded by the year in which the file was opened. Thus, 87.287 would be a real estate matter opened in 1987.

001–099	Large clients
100–199	Wills and estate planning
200–349	Real estate: purchase and sale
350–399	Estate administration and trusts
400–499	Domestic relations, excluding divorce and custody masterships
500–549	Personal injury, including worker's compensation
600–649	Litigation, excluding personal injury
700–749	Corporations and partnerships
750–799	Financing, bonds, industrial developments, and similar matters

800–849	Tax, excluding estate planning
900–999	Miscellaneous files not appropriate for any other category
1000–	Printed forms, applications, and other miscellaneous documents
1500–	Bar Association and non-client-related matters
2000–2049	Bankruptcy
2100–2149	Divorce and custody masterships and arbitration panels
2200–2299	Criminal matters

These numerical categories will vary widely from office to office according to size and type of practice. Large firms will spread the brackets and employ higher numbers. Avoid the use of letters. The potential for not hearing or not reading like-sounding, like-looking letters properly far exceeds the possible confusion of similar numbers.

Filing: General Principles. Except for the special situations discussed below, a file is opened for each new matter, not each new client. The more files the better. Specific files not only facilitate the retrieval of a particular document, but contribute as well to the proper conceptualization of a given situation as a number of tasks arising out of the same transaction or emanating from the same client. Numerous files also allow the closing of certain files while others remain open—a cumbersome, if not impossible, task when only one or a few larger omnibus files are maintained for each client. The initial responsibility for generating a fresh file lies, in most cases, with the attorney to whom the new matter is presented. S/he sets the following procedures in motion:

1. Either by dictated memorandum, notation on incoming correspondence, transmittal memorandum, or any other means appropriate to the specific situation, the attorney transmits to the member of the staff responsible for filing, the client name, address, and phone number, if not already known, the designation to be given to the file, and the type of case for use with the numerical filing system.
2. Upon receipt of this information, the individual responsible for filing:
2.1 Opens a new folder using the current year's color.[5]
2.2 Immediately binds any available documents into the file. All papers, with rare exceptions, must be bound in the appropriate file. Any documents that, for one reason or another, are not to be bound are attached to the file by a spring binder.
2.3 Ensures that an appropriate "Green Sheets"—inventory control—entry has been made. Malpractice insurance carriers require firms to develop a secondary system of docket control, which is known in some firms as "Green Sheets." The primary control is the individual attorney's tickler system.

---

[5] One possible difficulty with a numerical filing system is the confusion of file 78.325 with file 79.325. The multicolored file folders that are available from stationery suppliers offer a ready solution to this potential problem. If blue folders were used for 1978, red for 1979, and green for 1980, a file is not likely to be misplaced, and if it is in the wrong spot, it will stand out. In order to have the benefit of a fully-integrated system, color-matching index cards should be used for the alphabetical index.

2.4 Opens a new client ledger card, if necessary.

2.5 Assigns a number to the file according to the numerical filing system.

2.6 Generates the following on 3″ × 5″ cards that are of the same color as the current year's folders:

2.6.1 An alphabetical index card with the complete information provided by the person who initiates the file. Include date of death on cards for decedents' estates. Form 2 is a sample alphabetical index card.

2.6.2 A numerical card containing only the file number plus a cross-reference to the client's name and matter description. The numerical card need not carry the full information, since the alphabetical index card will have that. Form 3 is a sample numerical card.

2.6.3 If title work is involved, a third index card for the tax parcel index, indicating on the main card the tax parcel number. Form 4 provides a sample of such a card.

2.6.4 As many cross-reference cards to the main alphabetical card as are necessary. If there is any doubt as to how someone might search for the file, prepare a cross-reference card. There can never be too many cross-references. A sample card is provided by form 5.

FORM 2. A SAMPLE ALPHABETICAL FILE-INDEX CARD

NEW MAKER INDUSTRIES   CF#:
Industrial Park   CF Date:
Fabrictown, Pennsylvania 17000
555-1211

RE: INDUSTRIAL DEVELOPMENT PROJECT
File #: 80.753
Date Opened: January 11, 1980

Tax Parcel 10-164.8

FORM 3. A SAMPLE NUMERICAL FILE-INDEX CARD

File No: 80.7523

NEW MAKER INDUSTRIES

RE: INDUSTRIAL DEVELOPMENT PROJECT

FORM 4. A SAMPLE TAX PARCEL FILE-INDEX CARD

Tax Parcel: 10-164.8

NEW MAKER INDUSTRIES

RE: INDUSTRIAL DEVELOPMENT PROJECT

Date of Certificate of Title:

FORM 5. A SAMPLE CROSS-REFERENCE FILE-INDEX CARD

SIFT: NEW MAKER INDUSTRIES PROJECT

   see "New Maker Industries—Industrial Development Project"

3. For the firm's so-called "large clients," a slight refinement of the general filing system should be employed. Each large client is assigned a number between 001 and 099. For example, the Halfpenny National Bank is client 007. The 001 number is retained for the firm itself. For any given year, the main file number for that client will be constant, e.g., 80.007, for the Halfpenny National Bank for 1980. Each file opened for a large client during the year will bear that number plus an additional number, 80.007.08, and will spawn its own index card. This method gathers all the files for that client in one place, while permitting the maintenance of a plethora of separate, specific files.

3.1 At the beginning of each year, each of last year's large clients will automatically receive a catch-all .01 file to serve as a repository for the inevitable letters and documents that defy or do not deserve categorization. Thus 80.007.01 is the number for the Halfpenny National Bank Correspondence and Miscellany file.

4. As a corollary to the large-client treatment, a similar procedure is followed for a "one-issue" client whose file mushrooms into several subfiles. An example is an automobile accident that has elements of worker's compensation, medical malpractice, and no-fault, as well as four defendants. The main file should be separated into several different folders, each bearing the client's name and a precise description of the offshoots. The number originally assigned to the file is retained, with the new files bearing that number plus .01, .02, and so forth. Unless the case spawns a multitude of matters, it is not necessary to generate new index cards for the separate subfolders. The main index card reference to the original number will suffice. This blossoming-case situation must not be confused with the "one-issue" client who begins to bring other matters and transforms itself into a "large client," necessitating a series of unrelated files that must be separately indexed.

5. In a matter that requires a tabular index—such as an estate or a case in litigation—the index receives the same number as the file to which it is attached, except that the capital letter "I" is appended to the number. For example, 79.006.25I is the index of important noncorrespondence documents in the matter covered by file 79.006.25.

The firm's files are kept in numerical order. Experience has shown that rather than have all of this year's files follow all of last year's files, it is more convenient to have the new year's files for a particular category of the numerical filing system come immediately after the previous year's files for the same group. For example, the 79.200 file would be found after the last file of the 1978 200–349 series, the 80.007 files would be housed directly behind the 79.007 files. To retrieve a file under this system, find the appropriate card in the alphabetical index, obtain the number, and then go to the file cabinets.

Depending on the size of the office, a library-like system for removing files may be necessary in order to prevent the situation where one attorney keeps in his office the file that another attorney needs immediately. Because a checkout system adds an extra layer of administrative effort and expense, it is to be avoided if possible. One way to prevent the problem is to forbid the individual holding of files.

In order to ensure proper filing, all documents must be routed through the individual responsible for filing. In no case should a document be tossed loosely into a file, even if the file is in front of the individual holding the document. In that situation, the loose document and the file should be handed over for binding.

Whenever possible, appropriate file numbers should be noted on documents.

Exceptions.   Certain recurring situations that involve distinct tasks do not require a separate file each time the job is to be done. Rather, these related tasks are bound in a tabular index that has one tab for each task and its several documents. They include:

1. Deed descriptions—always the 200 file for each year.
2. Halfpenny National Bank Mortgage Foreclosure Letters. See checklist maintained with file.
3. Parking Authority Municipal Liens. See checklist maintained with file.

Closed Files

The filing cabinets in the main office contain only files on which work is being done, on which work is likely to be done in the near future, or that are likely to be used for reference in a current matter. Closed file procedures are designed to save active file space as well as allow for easy retrieval of retired information. Theoretically, if the firm's practice is stable, its main filing cabinets should maintain a constant size, while the real accumulation of paper occurs in the closed file storage area.

Anyone may declare a file closed. Such a decision is not crucial or irreversible because the file can be retrieved easily. It is better to close a file than to keep it around. The fewer the active files, the more manageable the filing system.

When a file is to be closed, it is Pendaflexed to the individual responsible for file closings who then:

1. Assigns a CF (closed file) number to the file. This will be the next number for the year, with the first file closed during the calendar year 1980 receiving the number CF 80.001.
2. Indicates on the file's alphabetical index card the CF number.
3. Marks a diagonal slash in the upper left-hand corner of the card. While the diagonal slash on the index card of a closed file may seem trivial, it can save a lot of time should the CF number on the card be overlooked. Most efficient systems are the aggregate of many picayune steps such as this.
4. Writes the CF number on the file label.
5. Places the file in the "upstairs" CF filing drawer. The "upstairs" CF filing drawer contains recently closed files that may be needed. These files are sent "upstairs" for a time, before being relegated to the basement.

The closed files are permanently stored in boxes clearly labeled with the first and last CF file number. To retrieve a closed file, simply check the alphabetical index card, obtain the CF number, and find the file, either in the upstairs CF drawer or in the basement.

15

Informal Advocacy
with Administrative Agencies

Section A. INTRODUCTION

"Advocacy" is the process by which an individual attempts to influence the behavior of others according to pre-determined goals. Advocacy is a basic component of everyday life; we are frequently advocates for ourselves and for others. Note, for example, the advocacy involved, or potentially involved, in the following circumstances:

1. At a supermarket checkout counter, a clerk tells a customer that the price of tomatoes is 49¢ a pound. The customer replies, "But the sign back there said 39¢ a pound." The clerk says, "I'm sorry, but the price is 49¢."
2. A student goes to the teacher to say that a term paper should have been graded "A" rather than "B."
3. A tenant tells the landlord that a $50.00 a month rent increase is ridiculous because the building has been steadily deteriorating.
4. An individual applying for a driver's license is told that he filled out his application incorrectly and that he must wait a week before he will be allowed to fill out another one. The individual feels that his application is not incorrect and that even if it is, he should not have to wait a week to do it over.
5. An employee has been laid off from her job. She calls the unemployment insurance bureau and asks to be sent forms so that she can fill out a claim. The clerk tells her that no forms can be sent through the mail. She asks the

clerk if an exception can be made in her case because she has not been feeling very well and her doctor has told her to stay in bed.

6. A homeowner has been away on a vacation. Upon his return, he finds that his house has been burglarized. When he goes to the police station to report the crime, he asks the desk sergeant why his neighborhood has not been receiving better protection in view of all the burglaries that have been occurring in the area lately. The sergeant replies that there are not enough police available to patrol the neighborhood adequately. The homeowner is not satisfied with this response and asks to see the precinct captain.

The customer, student, tenant, applicant, employee, and homeowner all have complaints. They are complainants. They are not satisfied with a certain product or service. Their natural response is to make an *argument* for better service and in so doing they become advocates for the goals or objectives that they are seeking. Advocacy does not always require courtrooms, judges, and lawyers; all that is needed is a complaint, a complainant, and someone who should be able to act on the complaint.

Sometimes the complaint can be anticipatory in that the individual seeks to influence someone *before* the action is taken. The following examples illustrate this approach:

7. A student makes a request to his high school registrar that the school send his high school transcript to the college to which he will be applying for admission. He hands the secretary in the registrar's office a list of the grades that he has received thus far and asks that the secretary check these grades with the official transcript before sending them to the college. He has friends who asked for transcripts from the school in the past who found that the records sent out were either incomplete or inaccurate. He wants to avoid this problem.

8. A local school board announces that it is considering a revision of its attendance regulations. A parent has some views on what these regulations should be. Before the board enacts any new regulations, the parent takes one or more of the following steps: (a) writes to the board expressing her views, (b) goes to the board office to let her views be known, or (c) attends a regularly scheduled public meeting of the board to look for an opportunity to present her views.

In both these cases, preventive steps are taken in the hope of avoiding an unwanted result.

The distinction between formal and informal advocacy depends primarily on the proceeding or forum (i.e., place) in which the advocacy is taking place, although the distinction is essentially one of degree. Generally speaking, the more the proceeding or forum looks like a court procedure (e.g., a hearing officer present, evidence or testimony taken, written decisions issued) the more formal it is. A government agency's quasi-judicial powers, for example, are often exercised through hearings that have many similarities to courtroom proceedings (p. 465). A quasi-judicial proceeding is one in which the agency is resolving a dispute between a citizen and the agency (e.g., welfare recipient and welfare department) or between two or more citizens under the control of the agency (e.g., two students in the same school or two inmates in the same prison who are having a dispute). If you are representing yourself or someone else at such a hearing, you are engaged in formal advocacy (p. 787).

Our concern in this chapter is *in*formal advocacy that occurs (a) in connection with administrative agencies not involving formal hearings or (b) outside the realm of administrative agencies altogether as in the supermarket case in the first example at the beginning of this chapter. Our primary focus will be the informal advocacy techniques that can be used when confronting employees of *any* organization, e.g., a public agency such as a social security office or a private business such as an insurance company.

Paralegals often have contact with organizations that require the application of informal advocacy techniques. The following list contains several examples of such contacts:

1. Determining the names and addresses of the principal shareholders of a corporation.
2. Gaining access to the records of an agency.
3. Obtaining copies of forms and procedures from the Securities and Exchange Commission relative to the disclosure and reporting requirements of a corporation.
4. Writing to or visiting an agency or company in order to obtain its position on a matter involving a client of the law office.
5. Trying to convince a caseworker or a social worker that the action the agency has taken (or that it proposes to take) is illegal or ill-advised.

A paralegal can meet resistance in any and all of these situations. The basic techniques of informal advocacy should help in handling this resistance.

Section B. THE TECHNIQUES OF INFORMAL ADVOCACY

The following is a summary of nineteen techniques that are sometimes used in trying to obtain action from an agency or from any large organization.

1. *Put your cards on the table.* Be direct and completely above board in telling the agency official what your position is and what you want.
2. *Insist on adequate service.* Point out to the agency official that the purpose of the agency is service and that this principle should guide the official's actions.
3. *Seek the support of third parties.* Before you make your position known, gather the support of individuals or groups within and without the agency so that you can demonstrate that you are not alone.

4. *Be a buddy.* Show the agency official that you are not an enemy, that you respect and like him/her, and that you are aware of how difficult his/her job is.

5. *Find the points of compromise.* Ferret out the negotiable points in the dispute and determine whether you can bargain your way to a favorable result.

6. *Insist on common sense.* Convey the impression to the agency official that common sense dictates the position you are advocating in addition to or in spite of the regulations or technicalities that might be cited against you.

7. *Demonstrate the exception.* Insist on the uniqueness of your client's situation so that the general rule cited by the agency official to deny your client a benefit is shown to be inapplicable.

8. *Uncover the realm of discretion.* Take the position that rules do not exist until they are applied and that in the application of rules, agency officials often have wide discretion in spite of their claim that their hands are tied by the rules.

9. *Ask for authorization.* Insist that the agency official show you the regulation, law, or authority that supports the action taken or proposed by the agency.

10. *Cite the law.* Show the agency official that you know what administrative regulations apply to the case. Also cite statutes and cases when appropriate to demonstrate your point.

11. *Redefine the problem.* If you can't solve a problem, redefine it—so long as you can still achieve what the client seeks, e.g., stop trying to qualify the client for program "Z" if program "Y" will serve the client equally well and the problems of qualifying the client for "Y" are not as great as those encountered in continuing to insist on "Z."

12. *Anger/hostility.* Be completely open about the bad feelings that you have concerning what is being done or proposed.

13. *Preach.* Lecture the civil servant. *Tell* the agency what it should or should not be doing.

14. *Climb the chain of command.* Normally everyone has a boss who can overrule decisions made by those beneath him/her. When you are dissatisfied with the decision or action of an employee, "appeal" or complain "up the chain of command" to the supervisor of the employee, and to the supervisor of the supervisor if needed.

15. *Embarrass the official.* Show the agency official that you do not respect him/her in such a way that the official is made to look silly.

16. *Make clear that you and your office are going to fight this case all the way up.* Make the agency official aware of how important the case is. Point out that you are thinking about taking the case to a formal agency hearing and that your office may go to court if necessary.

17. *Take the role of the tired, battered, helpless citizen.* Do not insist on anything. Play dumb; act exhausted; act in such a way that the agency official will think, "This person needs help;" act as if everyone else has given you the run-around and that you are praying that this official (whom you have not dealt with before) will finally give you a sympathetic ear—and some help.

18. *Do a favor to get a favor.* Be willing to do something (within reason) for the person from whom you are seeking something.

19. *Cite a precedent.* Point out to the agency official (if it is true) that your case is not unusual because the agency has granted what you want to others under the same or under similar circumstances in the past.

Clearly, some of these techniques will be more effective than others. Perhaps some of them should *never* be tried. A great deal would obviously depend upon the circumstances confronting the paralegal at the time. In general how would you assess the nineteen techniques? If you were to list the techniques in the order in which you think that the technique would be effective in *most* situations, what would your order be?

The following outline lists the nineteen techniques in one possible order of effectiveness. The techniques are presented in the context of other considerations that are relevant to the use of the techniques: threshold concerns, evaluation of techniques, adaptation, and recording.

ADVOCACY

I. THRESHOLD CONCERNS
 1. Defining your goals in order of priorities
 2. Deciding when to intervene

II. ADVOCACY TECHNIQUES
 1. Cards on the table
 2. Insist on service
 3. Ask for authorization
 4. Chain of command
 5. Insist on common sense
 6. Act tired, battered, and helpless
 7. Cite a precedent
 8. Find the points of compromise
 9. Uncover the realm of discretion
 10. Demonstrate the exception
 11. Cite the law
 12. Be a buddy
 13. Make clear that the case is important to you
 14. Redefine the problem
 15. Do a favor
 16. Support of third party
 17. Preach
 18. Embarrass
 19. Anger

III. EVALUATE THE TECHNIQUES USED
 1. Are you making yourself clear?
 2. Are you creating more problems than you are solving?
 3. Are you accomplishing your goal?

IV. ADAPTATION
Are you flexible enough to shift your technique?

V. RECORDING
1. Describe what you saw.
2. Describe what you did.

The first threshold concern involves the priority of goals. This concern, of course, would not be applicable if the assignment you are given contains only one goal, e.g., obtain a copy of a certain record at the agency. It may be, however, that the assignment contains a variety of objectives at the outset, or that a single-objective assignment subsequently blossoms into tasks involving more than one goal. Priorities must be set. If you try to do everything, you may end up accomplishing nothing. Every technique of informal advocacy will probably fail if you have unrealistic expectations of what can be accomplished.

The second threshold issue is to decide when to intervene with the advocacy techniques. The decision to intervene involves a strategy judgment of when it would be most appropriate to seek what you are after at the agency. In some situations, a sense of timing will be very important. For example, suppose that you must contact the complaint bureau of a particular agency that is relatively new to you. One approach would be simply to walk up to the complaint bureau and delve right into the matter that brought you there. Another approach would be to try to find out something about the bureau *before* going to it. There may be some literature available on the structure of the agency that will provide you with at least a general idea of what to expect at the bureau. You may be able to talk to attorneys or other paralegals who have had prior contact with the bureau. Suppose you learn that there are two agency employees who rotate their work at the bureau and that one employee has a reputation of being more "cooperative" than the other. You may decide not to go to the bureau until this employee is on duty. In short, you decide to postpone your involvement with, or intervention at, the bureau until the circumstances are most favorable to the objective you are seeking.

Next in the outline is section II where the nineteen techniques are listed. Note that the last three are preaching, causing embarrassment, and becoming angry. These are placed at the bottom of the list on the theory that they are likely to antagonize the agency employee and therefore encourage the latter to set up roadblocks to your objective that might not otherwise be present. Do you agree? Can you think of circumstances when anger, for example, *would* be appropriate? These questions move us to section III of the outline: evaluation of the techniques.

As you use any one of the techniques, you must be simultaneously aware of the *effectiveness* of the technique in light of what you are trying to accomplish. Are you making yourself clear? Are you a catalyst of complication rather than resolution? Are you getting through? Are you pacing yourself properly? Is your insistence on immediate success interfering with building a step-by-step strategy of progress?

One of the major signs of ineffective advocacy is being so involved in the case that you tend to take roadblocks and defeat *personally*. Everyone agrees that objectivity is a good quality and most of us claim to possess this quality most of the time. The unfortunate fact is, however, that *we tend to lose objectivity as friction increases.* We allow our careers and our lifestyles to be threatened when someone says to us, "You can't do that." Of course, we will rarely admit that we can be so threatened. We justify our response by blaming the agency employee for stupidity and/or for being unjust.

Of course, evaluation for the sake of evaluation is worthless. Once you have so disciplined yourself that you are able to identify the techniques you are using and to evaluate the effectiveness of those techniques, you must be flexible enough to *adapt* your techniques and shift from one technique to another in accordance with your sense of what other approaches might be more effective.

Finally, the paralegal usually will have a recording responsibility (part V). Every case you are working on will usually have to be heavily documented in the office files. Your efforts at informal advocacy should be included in those files.

ASSIGNMENT 108

In each role-playing exercise, there are two characters: P (the paralegal) and AE (the agency employee). Students from the class will be assigned each role. As will be indicated, P is seeking something from AE. AE is not cooperative. The objective of AE is to antagonize P (within reason) to the point where P loses objectivity. The objective of P is to refrain from losing his/her objectivity.

> 1. At 4:30 P.M., P goes to Department of Motor Vehicles to apply for a license. AE tells P that the office closes at 5:00 P.M. and the application procedure takes forty-five minutes. AE refuses to let P apply.
> 2. At the post office, P tries to buy $400.00 worth of 22¢ stamps. The AE tells P that no individual customer can buy over $100.00 worth of stamps per day.
> 3. P goes to the bureau of vital statistics and requests a copy of his mother's birth certificate. The AE tells P that no citizen can obtain the birth certificate of another person. P gives the AE a letter from his mother asking the bureau to give P the document. The AE still refuses.

Those members of the class who are not participating in the role-playing exercises should identify and evaluate the techniques of informal advocacy used by P.

We now examine some of the advocacy techniques in the context of the following fact situation:

> You are in your own home or apartment. You receive a letter from the gas company stating that your gas will be shut off in ten days if you do not pay your bill. Your spouse tells you that the bill has already been paid. You call the gas company and when you question the clerk, she says to you, "I'm sorry sir, our records reflect an unpaid bill. You must pay the bill immediately." To try to straighten matters out, you take a trip to the utilities office.

In the dialogue that follows based upon this hypothetical, the complainant is his own advocate. "C" will stand for complainant and "E" will stand for the various company employees.

E: *Can I help you?*
C: *Yes, I want to see someone about my bill.*
E: *I'm sorry, sir, but the customer complaint division closed at 2 P.M. You'll have to come back or call tomorrow.*
C: *Closed! Well, look, I want to see someone about terminating the gas service altogether.*
E: *All right, would you step right over to the desk?*

TECHNIQUE: *If you can't solve a problem, redefine the problem* to manageable proportions if, on balance, it is consistent with your objectives.

The client is taking a risk. He cannot get through to the complaint division so he is going to try to achieve his objective through the termination division. He has substituted one problem (getting through the complaint division) for another problem (getting through the termination division) in the hope of expressing his grievances.

E: *Can I help you?*
C: *Yes, I want to terminate my gas if I can't get this problem straightened out.*
E: *You'll have to go over to the bill complaint division, sir.*
C: *Look, stop sending me somewhere else! Either I get this straightened out or else!*

TECHNIQUE: *Anger/hostility.* Although this is a dangerous tactic to employ, it is a fact of life that some people respond to this kind of pressure.

C: *Aren't you here to serve the public?*

TECHNIQUE: *Insist on adequate service.* Point out to the agency official that the purpose of the organization is service and that this principle should guide its actions.

E: *There are rules and procedures that we all must abide by and . . . .*
C: *Your responsibility is to take care of the public!*

TECHNIQUE: *Preach.* Perhaps the most common way in which people try to change other people is to lecture them, to tell them what they should or should not be doing.

TECHNIQUE: *Embarrass him/her.* Show the agency official that you do not respect him/her in such a way that the official is made to look silly.

At this point, has the complainant lost all objectivity? What risks are being taken? Do you think the complainant is aware of what he is doing? If you asked him if he thinks that he is being effective, what do you think his response would be? Is he more involved with the "justice" of his case than with the effectiveness of his approach?

> C: *I'd like to speak to your supervisor. Who is in charge of this office?*
> E: *Well, Mr. Adams is the unit director. His office is right over there.*
> C: *Fine.*

TECHNIQUE: *Climb the chain of command.* Everyone has a boss who can overrule decisions made by those beneath him/her; when you are dissatisfied with the decision or action of an employee, "appeal" or complain "up the chain of command" to the supervisor of the employee, and to the supervisor of the supervisor if needed.

> E: *Can I help you?*
> C: *I want to speak to Mr. Adams about a complaint. Tell him that it is very important.*
> E: *Just a moment. [She goes into Mr. Adams' office for a few moments and then returns.] You can go in, sir.*
> C: *Mr. Adams?*
> E: *Yes, what can I do for you? I understand you are having a little problem.*
> C: *It's about this bill. I have been talking to person after person in this office without getting any response.*

TECHNIQUE: *Take the role of the tired, battered, helpless citizen.*

> E: *Well, let me see what I can do. I've asked the secretary to get your file. Here it is. The records say that you haven't paid last month's bill. Our policy here is to terminate utility service if payment is delayed thirty days or more.*
> C: *What policy is that? Could I see a copy of this policy and what law it is based on?*

TECHNIQUE: *Ask for authorization.* Insist that the agency show you the regulation, law, or authority that allegedly supports the action it has taken or proposes to take.

What risk is the complainant taking by resorting to this technique? Is the complainant suggesting to Mr. Adams that he does not trust him? How would you have asked for authorization in this situation? Does the request for authorization always have to be made in a hostile manner?

> E: *Well, I'll be glad to show you the brochure.*
> C: *I would like to see it and also the law it is based on. My position, Mr. Adams, is that my wife paid the bill.*

E: *Well our records don't reflect it.*

C: *The cancelled checks have not yet come back from the bank. I would like a Xerox copy of your file on me. Under the law, I am entitled to it.*

TECHNIQUE: *Cite the law.* Show the agency official that you know what administrative regulations apply to the case (and in some instances you also cite statutes and cases to demonstrate your point).

E: *You do have this right, but only if you make the request in writing.*

C: *Let's be reasonable. I'm making the request in person. That should be sufficient.*

TECHNIQUE: *Insist on common sense.* Convey to the agency official the impression that common sense dictates the position you are advocating in addition to or in spite of the regulations or technicalities that might be cited against you.

C: *Surely, your rule calling for a written request can't apply when the person making the request is right in front of you.*

TECHNIQUE: *Interpret the law.* Regulations, statutes, and cases often are susceptible to more than one meaning; identify and argue for the meaning most favorable to the client.

TECHNIQUE: *Demonstrate the exception.* Insist on the uniqueness of your situation so that the general rule cited by the agency official to deny the benefit is shown to be inapplicable.

C: *Don't you have the power to waive this rule in such a case?*

TECHNIQUE: *Uncover the realm of discretion.* Take the position that rules do not exist until they are applied and that in the application of rules, agency officials often have wide discretion in spite of their claim that their hands are tied by the rules.

E: *Well, all right, I'll see if I can't get a copy run off for you while you are here, but it will take a little time and I must point out that it's highly irregular.*

C: *Now, Mr. Adams. I understand that you are a very busy man and that you have responsibilities more demanding than having to listen to people like me all day.*

TECHNIQUE: *Be a buddy.* Show the agency official that you are not his enemy and that you respect and like him and that you are aware of how difficult his job is.

Here the complainant has obviously shifted his tactic; he is no longer antagonistic. Consciously or unconsciously, he has made an evaluation of how successful his techniques have been thus far and has decided on a different course of action. What risk is he running in making this shift?

> C: *All I want is a thirty-day extension of time so that I can collect the proof needed to show you that the bill has been paid.*

TECHNIQUE: *Put your cards on the table.* Be direct and completely above board in telling the agency official what your position is and what you want.

> E: *Well, we seldom give extensions. The situation must be extreme. I don't know. . . .*
> C: *Mr. Adams, suppose we forget my request for a copy of the records for the time being. All I want is thirty days.*

TECHNIQUE: *Find the points of compromise.* Ferret out the negotiable points in the dispute and determine whether you can bargain your way to a favorable result.

> E: *I don't think so.*
> C: *Well, Mr. Adams, it's either that or I'm going to go to court. All I'm asking for is some fair treatment. There's a principle involved and I intend to fight for it.*

TECHNIQUE: *Make clear that you are going to fight this case all the way up.* Make the agency official aware of how important this case is; when you have grounds to back you, point out that you are thinking about taking the case to a formal hearing and, if necessary, to court.

> E: *I'm sorry you feel that way, but we have our rules here. It would be chaos if we broke them every time someone asked for it.*
> C: *Good day, Mr. Adams. [You leave the office, resolved never to come back alone.]*

TECHNIQUE: *Seek the support of third parties.* Gather the support of individuals or groups within or without the agency so that you can demonstrate that you are not alone.

Has the complainant failed? Was he a "bad" advocate? Has he accomplished anything? Should he give up? Do you think he will? If he does not, do you think he has learned (or that he should have learned) enough about the gas company to be able to come back next time better equipped to handle his problem? If he comes back, what approach should he take and whom should he see, e.g., the supervisor of Mr. Adams?

ASSIGNMENT 109

What follows are two exercises for role-playing that will be evaluated through questions that follow the statement of the exercises.

1. A paralegal is asked by his supervisor to file some papers in court that must be filed by 5:00 P.M. that day. At 4:15 P.M. the paralegal takes the papers to the office of the court clerk. The clerk determines that the papers are in order except for the fact that the attorney forgot to sign one of the papers. It would take the paralegal more than an hour to go back to obtain the signature and return to court. The paralegal asks the clerk to accept the *other* papers. The clerk refuses since all the papers are closely interrelated. The paralegal tells the clerk that this happened once before and the clerk (another one) accepted the papers that were properly executed. The clerk refuses.

2. A parent (acting as her own paralegal) asks the principal for a meeting on her child. The child has been selected by the school to be sent to another school. The parent is opposed to this transfer. The principal tells her that she will have to go talk to an official at the City Board of Education about the matter. The parent persists in demanding a meeting with the principal. She wants to know, for example, the position of the principal on the transfer, but the principal wants to avoid controversy and therefore refers her to the City Board.

Evaluation

1. What advocacy technique did the paralegal start out using?
2. On a scale of 10, how effective was this technique? ("10" is very effective; "1" is very ineffective.) Give reasons for your score.
3. When the sequence ended, what advocacy technique was the paralegal using? How would you score this technique?
4. What shifts in technique, if any, did the paralegal make? Score each technique used.
5. On a scale of 10, how effective was the paralegal's overall performance?
6. According to the agency official, what was the problem?
7. According to the paralegal, what was the problem?
8. What, if anything, was standing in the way of communication between them?
9. How could this communication problem have been overcome?
10. Was the paralegal objective, or did the paralegal take anything personally? Explain.
11. Was the agency official taking anything personally? Explain.
12. If the agency official took anything personally, how did the paralegal deal with this?
13. What do you think the paralegal *should* have done about this?
14. Describe the most positive aspects of what you saw the paralegal do.
15. Describe the least effective aspects of what you saw the paralegal do.
16. As specifically as possible, list all the advocacy techniques that you observed the paralegal use that you have not already mentioned in any of the above questions.

17. Re-examine the list of nineteen informal advocacy techniques above, supra p. 777. Do you think that any techniques should be added? If so, how in general would you rate the effectiveness of the techniques that you would add?

16

Formal Advocacy
Before Administrative Agencies

Where paralegals are authorized by law to represent clients at administrative hearings (p. 226), it is one of the great challenges that they enjoy. In this chapter, we will explore some of the skills that are required to perform this task effectively.

The subject matter of a hearing as well as its procedure can range from the very simple to the very complex. Our approach will be to examine closely a particular hearing of relative complexity after identifying the components of procedural due process when a government agency and citizen have a dispute.

Section A. INTRODUCTION TO PROCEDURAL DUE PROCESS

Not every agency uses the word hearing. Not every hearing is conducted alike. Hence a paralegal must be able to determine what a hearing is and what elements of a hearing could or should exist when there is a dispute between an individual and an agency.

> Tom is a civilian employee of the army. One day he receives a call from the assistant manager of his unit who says, "I have finished examining all of the records and it is clear to me that you have been using the agency car for your own personal use. You are fired." As a matter of common sense and fairness, what is wrong with the assistant manager's approach? (Assume that Tom denies the charge.)

Note that in this hypothetical, the assistant manager wanted to end the entire matter right on the phone. What visceral response would you have (if you were Tom) to the action of the assistant manager? Shock? Anger? Some of Tom's responses might be:

1. "I wasn't given a chance to explain myself before I was fired."
2. "I wasn't given a chance to talk to the assistant manager before I was fired."
3. "I wasn't given a chance to be told what records he was talking about."
4. "I wasn't given a chance to talk to the assistant manager's boss before I was fired."

These four responses can be translated into legal language:

1. Someone who is charged with wrongdoing (or who is told that s/he is not entitled to a particular benefit) should be given the opportunity to be *heard*. The *hearing* is the individual's way of presenting his/her version.
2. The individual should be allowed to *appear in person* at the hearing. S/he should be allowed to *confront* and *cross-examine* his/her accuser.
3. The individual should be allowed to *examine the evidence against him/her.*
4. The individual should be allowed to *appeal* the initial decision against him/her.

Note that the individual would be asking for these rights *before* the job is taken away.

Tom could have a number of other responses.

5. "Before he called me to say that I was fired, he should have let me know that I was in trouble."

Here the call, in legal terms, is for adequate *notice.* Before the phone call, and certainly before the actual firing, the employee should have been given notice that there was a grievance or complaint against him so that he could prepare a response.

6. "Since the assistant manager was the one who made the charge, he should not be the one to make the decision."

Legally, this response goes to the issue of *legal bias* and an impartial decision-maker. The basic theory is that the accuser should not be the executioner. If the same person wears both hats, the likelihood is that s/he will lose objectivity. While making the ultimate decision (as executioner), his/her tendency will be to reinforce the decision s/he originally made (as accuser) rather than to approach the final decision with an open mind. In short, the person with both hats is likely to have a bias. In the hypothetical, the assistant manager made the original charge (accuser) of misusing the agency car and he also made the decision to fire (executioner). He appears, therefore, to have a bias.

7. "When and if I am able to confront the assistant manager, I should be able to have someone help me state my case."

Legally, the call here is for the right of *representation:* counsel or counsel-substitute.

8. "When I am able to confront the assistant manager, I should be able to bring with me some of my co-workers who will back up my side of the case."

Legally, the call is for the right to bring *your own witnesses* to the hearing and to *present your own* counter *evidence*.

9. "When the Army finally makes its decision in my case, they should give me their decision in writing with the reasons for their decision."

Legally, this is a call for a *written opinion* or *decision with reasons*.

10. "At my hearing, they should focus only on the charge that they raised and not bring up extraneous facts such as that I am now going through a divorce proceeding."

Legally, the call is for only *relevant evidence* to be considered in making the decision.

Hence the ten elements (presented in a rough chronological order) are as follows:

1. Notice (#5 above)
2. Hearing (#1)
3. Personal appearance at hearing; confrontation and cross-examination of accuser (#2)
4. No legal bias in hearing officer (#6)
5. Representation (#7)
6. Relevance of evidence (#10)
7. Examination of evidence against you (#3)
8. Presenting your own witnesses (#8)
9. Written decision stating reasons (#9)
10. Appeal (#4)

In constitutional law, these elements comprise procedural due process. Of course, every time a government agency has a conflict with a citizen, the agency does not provide all ten elements of procedural due process. The courts have held that the elements required differ from agency to agency depending upon the dispute in question. Lawyers are frequently in litigation over what procedural due process should be in a given agency situation. In a welfare hearing, for example, court decisions have held that all the above ten elements must exist whenever a welfare recipient wishes to challenge a decision of the welfare department to terminate public assistance.

For a number of reasons, the paralegal should have an understanding of procedural due process:

1. To be able to identify what elements are or are not being provided in a particular agency-client conflict.
2. To be able to make at least a common-sense or fairness argument to the agency that the missing elements should be provided.
3. To assist an attorney who decides to litigate the agency's refusal to provide one or more of the elements.

Section B. AN AGENCY PROBLEM

FACT SITUATION

George Temple was born January 1, 1950. His parents, Mr. and Mrs. Sam Temple, live at 435 West 100th Street, New York, New York. He graduated from high school in 1967 and spent six months at Wentworth Technical Institute in Boston before dropping out. He came back to live with his parents in February of 1968. But while in Boston, he began using drugs. He smoked pot regularly and experimented with LSD and heroin. After returning to New York, he got a job with the Thomas TV Repair Shop on April 15, 1968, at 90 South Side Avenue, Queens. The boss, John Adams, fired George on June 1, 1968, because he suspected George of being an addict and of stealing.

On June 30, 1968, George married Ann Fuller. George began using drugs more often. Ann realized that he was not going to be able to support her and their expected child. When the child was born on January 2, 1969, she decided to go to the Amsterdam Welfare Center to apply for public assistance. She did so on January 10, 1969. The caseworker, Brenda Marshall, asked Ann what her husband did for a living. Ann answered that he took odd jobs "off and on" since he was sick. The caseworker asked if he was an addict. Ann was scared and answered "no." The caseworker told her that she would need more information about her husband's employment history and condition before her application could be processed and approved. Ann left the Center confused and frustrated. She never returned.

In the meantime, George was arrested on March 13, 1969, for possession of a dangerous drug in the third degree. He "took a plea" for attempted petty larceny and spent four months at Green Haven prison. When he got out on July 13, 1969, he went to live with his wife at 758 West 85th Street. While George was in prison, Ann worked as a waitress. During this time, her mother-in-law cared for the child. She was laid off from work on August 1, 1969.

George did not want to settle down with a job. He began using drugs again. He wanted to stop but couldn't.

On September 1, 1969, he went to Exodus House, a voluntary drug rehabilitation center in New York City. He stayed only two days since the program, he claimed, demanded too much from him. For example, he would have had to live at Exodus House, which he refused to do. On September 25, 1969, he went to Reality House, another voluntary rehabilitation center at 2065 Amsterdam Avenue. This was not a live-in program; members stayed there from 9 to 5. On October 1, 1969, he left this program because when his urine was tested, it came back positive, meaning that he was still using drugs. He left rather than be confronted with the results of this urine test.

On October 2, 1969, he obtained a job with the ABC Truck Company and worked there part time until February 15, 1970, when he was fired for being late.

On February 16, 1970, he went back to Reality House. He failed to attend every day. On March 1, 1970, he went to the Amsterdam Welfare Center to apply for welfare for himself and his family. The caseworker, Linda Stout, asked him why he could not get a job. He said he was an addict attending Reality House. Linda Stout was skeptical. She demanded verification that he was regularly attending Reality House. George went back to Reality House to speak to his therapist, John Hughey. Mr. Hughey told him that he could not give him a letter stating that he was a member of the program until he began to attend more often.

On March 15, 1970, Linda Stout contacted Brenda Marshall, the caseworker who previously interviewed George's wife on January 10, 1969. Brenda told Linda that Mrs. Temple told her that her husband was *not* an addict.

In the meantime, George still had trouble getting a letter from Reality House stating that he was a full member of the program. On March 17, 1970, Linda Stout called John Hughey at Reality House who told her that George was not coming in every day. On March 18, 1970, she closed George's case, declaring him ineligible for welfare for failure to demonstrate need. She concluded that the welfare regulation that authorized public assistance to addicts attending rehabilitation programs did not apply to George.

Section C. PRELIMINARY CONSIDERATIONS

The first responsibility of the paralegal who has been assigned to this case is to decide when and how to intervene. George comes into the law office and tells you that he wants to fight the decision of the caseworker, Linda Stout. He wants a hearing. Is this an appropriate strategy? What alternatives exist? What about informal advocacy (p. 773)? Would you want to call or visit Linda Stout? Brenda Marshall? Mrs. Temple? John Hughey? Linda Stout's boss? Brenda Marshall's boss? John Hughey's boss? If so, why? Is the time ripe to intervene by asking for a formal hearing?

Suppose that you decide to give informal advocacy a try, but it does not work. The welfare department still refuses to declare George eligible. Therefore, in consultation with your supervisor, you decide to ask for a hearing.

In preparing for a hearing, there are a number of preliminary considerations:

1. *Define your issues.*

What are the issues in George's case? What would you have to show in order to qualify him for welfare? What are the points in doubt? Two questions should come to mind: (1) Is George an addict? (2) Is he a member of a drug rehabilitation center? If you showed that George was an addict, would he be sent to jail or to a hospital? Is this a real danger? How would you find out? Linda Stout demanded verification from George that he was a member of Reality House. Can you identify two reasons she would ask for this? Is she saying that if George is not a member of a drug rehabilitation program, he probably is not an addict? Or is she saying that he cannot obtain welfare unless he is a member of such a program even if he is an addict? Which is the case? How would you find out? What other issues exist? What legal research should be done?

2. *Draft the request for the hearing.*

In welfare cases, the paralegal will often draft the letter to the agency requesting the hearing. The client will sign this letter. The request is extremely important since it can be a major determinant of what the issues at the hearing will be. How broadly or narrowly should the issue be stated? How many issues should be presented? These are problems of strategy that are answered largely in the light of what the paralegal thinks s/he might be able to prove at the hearing.

When a response to the letter of request is received, the client and paralegal will know whether or not a hearing has been granted on the issues requested. If the paralegal is not satisfied with this response, s/he should consult with his/her supervisor on ways to challenge the response before the hearing. If satisfied, then s/he should gear the preparation accordingly.

A careful definition and a thorough understanding of what the issues are can be critical for the following reasons:

a. At the hearing, the other side or the hearing officer may raise matters outside the scope of the issues of the hearing and the paralegal can object based upon the wording of the request for the hearing and the response received to the request.
b. If an office attorney is going to appeal the final decision of the hearing in court, the starting point in preparing for the appeal will often be an analysis of what the issues of the hearing were supposed to be.

3. *Continue efforts to resolve the case through informal advocacy.*

It is almost always preferable to try to solve a problem informally so that the time and expense of formal hearings and court proceedings can be avoided. At the time the paralegal and his/her office decided to request a formal hearing in this case, it was determined that informal advocacy would not be or was not effective. The agency, however, can always change its mind, particularly when it realizes that the client is serious about fighting the case. Throughout the paralegal's preparation of the hearing, s/he will probably be in continued contact with employees of the agency involved in the case. In these contacts s/he may be able to bring new factors to the attention of the agency that may cause it to re-evaluate its position. The result may be a reversal of the agency's decision or the negotiation of a settlement between the agency and the client, eliminating the need for a hearing altogether. The paralegal must be constantly aware of this option.

4. *Familiarize yourself with agency procedures in advance.*

There is no better way to prepare for a hearing than to see one in operation before you conduct your own. You might "tag along" as the assistant of another advocate conducting a hearing. Extensive notes should be taken on procedure and strategy. This will be difficult to do, since the experience will probably be new to you. Give it a try. Later on, organize your notes into an outline covering the procedures used at the hearing as well as the strategy that both sides used.

If the agency has more than one type of hearing, you should determine how many exist and whether you want to ask for more than one type of hearing. Some agencies have pre-hearing conferences during which the advocates for both sides sit down in advance of the hearing to narrow the issues and determine whether a solution can be reached without a formal hearing. When available, this can be a valuable meeting. If the agency does not have pre-hearing conferences as a matter of course, why not ask for one anyway? Besides being a vehicle to attempt a solution, the conference is an excellent way for the paralegal to learn more about the agency's case and hence be better prepared for the hearing if it is held.

5. *Make sure that the client's emergency needs are provided for while waiting for a hearing decision.*

In the case of a welfare recipient, for example, the recipient should not be left destitute while the agency makes a decision following a hearing. Emergency assistance of a temporary nature may be available in the interim. Suppose that the paralegal is representing a client in a worker's compensation case. While the hearing is going on, the paralegal may be of help to this individual in obtaining public assistance or possibly union benefits. To the extent possible, the paralegal should always be alert to a client's total needs and not simply zero in on narrow legal questions. Of course, the paralegal has limited time available and must set priorities on what s/he can do. Very often the paralegal can be of help simply by referring the client to other resources in the community.

6. *Make sure that the client has given you proper authorization to act on his/her behalf.*

The law office may have a standard form for the client to sign authorizing you to represent him/her at the agency proceeding. In addition, you should have the client sign a waiver-of-confidentiality statement authorizing you to examine all documents in possession of the agency that pertain to the case. A similar statement may permit you to gain access to needed doctor or hospital records.

7. *Make a request in writing that the agency send you, in advance, copies of all documents that it intends to rely upon at the hearing.*

Are you curious about what documents the welfare department will be using at the hearing to prove its case against George? Why not ask the department to send you copies of these documents in advance of the hearing? Would this be a fair request? In many situations, the law will back up such a request. (Suppose the agency wanted *you* to send them copies of the documents you will be using? What would you do?)

What documents would you be interested in seeing? Their entire file on George? Their most recent policy statement on addicts? What else?

8. *Find out as much as you can about the witnesses the agency intends to call at the hearing.*

Usually the agency will tell you in advance what witnesses will be called at the hearing to support the agency's position. Often these witnesses will be willing to talk to you before the hearing, particularly if they are agency employees. This is frequently an excellent way to discover more details about the agency's case and how it intends to establish that case at the hearing. Your approach should be casual. Do not say to these witnesses, "What testimony are you going to give at the hearing next week?" Rather, deal with points of information: "I understand that you know George Temple. Could I ask you when you last spoke to him?" Etc.

9. *Make sure that you have completed all necessary field investigation before the hearing.*

What facts do you think need to be checked? What are you unsure of? Are you sure that George is an addict? What is an addict? Someone currently using drugs? What kinds of drugs? How would you find out? Are you also unsure about George's relationship with Reality House? What is a "member"? How many definitions of "member" might exist? Do George, Linda Stout, and John Hughey each define it differently? Would you want to check this out? How often does George go to Reality House? What does "regularly" mean and according to whom? What other items would you want to investigate? Before the hearing, would you want to make a request to the agency that it state its position on George's case in writing? What would you do with such a document? Use *fact particularization* to help you identify factual questions that you need to pursue through investigation and subsequent client interviewing (p. 391).

10. *Study the law governing your case.*

It goes without saying that the paralegal should be thoroughly familiar with the law, particularly the agency regulations that may be applicable to the case. A good deal of legal research may be necessary before the paralegal even requests the hearing. Some aspects of the law governing the case may be unclear due to the ambiguities in the regulations, statutes, or cases. Part of the task of preparation is to identify these ambiguities and to map out a strategy on how to deal with them at the hearing if they arise.

You should bring photocopies of relevant regulations, statutes, or cases with you to the hearing. In addition, you should summarize in your own words the sections of these documents that you feel will be most pertinent to the hearing.

11. *Determine what witnesses you want to call at the hearing and prepare them.*

Who should be present at the hearing to help George make his case? Should George be present? Why? Should John Hughey be present? Why? How about the boss of John Hughey? Do you want George's wife to be present? The tests that you should use in deciding whether to ask a witness to be present are: does the witness have something to say that would help George make his case, and would the witness be able to say it? Someone may have important points to make, but be so frightened at the thought of going to a hearing that s/he is, in effect, not available. Suppose you have a witness whom you want to call, but the person has an acute stuttering problem. How would you handle this?

Tell your witnesses what the hearing is all about to set their mind at ease. They must trust you before they will be willing and valuable participants. Tell them why you want them to come (you do not have to use words such as "witness" and "testimony" if this would frighten them). Get them to role-play part of the proceeding with you. A brief role-playing experience can be very helpful. Explain that the other side may want to ask them some questions after you have introduced them and have asked your own questions. Be sure that your witnesses understand what the issues are. They may try to use the occasion to tirade about everything under the sun. This could be damaging, unless you determine as a matter of strategy that it would be useful to let the witnesses "unload" to some extent.

You must be careful not to place your witnesses in embarrassing situations. The test is: whenever you think that a question that you want to ask might be embarrassing or damaging to your witnesses, check it out with your supervisor before the hearing. What about George's addiction? Can you think of any questions that you could ask that might create difficulties for him?

12. *Assemble all the documentary evidence that you will want to introduce at the hearing and determine how you will lay the foundation for each item of documentary evidence by showing that it is relevant to the issues of the hearing.*

What documents do you want to present at the hearing on behalf of George? Do you want a letter from Exodus House stating that he once attended the program? If so, why? What would it prove? Do you want a letter from Reality House? Saying what? Would you ask them to write down all of the dates that George did attend that program? Would it help or hurt to obtain a letter from ABC Truck company stating that George once worked there? Is it relevant? Suppose that you could arrange a doctor's examination of George. Would you want to use the results of this examination at the hearing? What would it depend upon?

13. *Draft an outline of how you intend to present your case at the hearing.*

The great danger of pre-planning, of course, is that the unexpected almost always happens to "foulup" your preliminary plan. It nevertheless is helpful to have a tentative plan in mind AS LONG AS YOU DO NOT SLAVISHLY TRY TO FOLLOW IT. Flexibility is always the key.

A useful approach is to arrange all the facts according to a chronological history. Every client's story has a beginning, middle, and an end. Your outline should attempt to tell George's story in this way. Simple as this may seem, it is not easy to do. At the hearing, people will raise points out of sequence. These points often have to be dealt with, but if you have prepared your chronology carefully, you at least will have something to come back to after this other point is treated.

Draft a preliminary outline of your strategy in conducting George's hearing. What points do you want to make? What documents or witnesses will you use to help you make these points? Arrange the entire sequence chronologically.

One of the major frustrations you will experience in conducting formal hearings is the confusion that often exists over the precise issue or issues of the hearing. This can arise in a number of ways: (a) the original request for a hearing and/or the response to it was not precise enough; (b) the hearing officer refuses to hear testimony on an issue that you were prepared to argue; (c) your own witness raises an issue that you are not prepared to argue; (d) sub-issues are raised by either side, the relevance of which are dependant on the establishment of other major issues or sub-issues that have not yet been established; (e) you make the dangerous assumption that everyone, including your own witnesses, are focused on the same issue.

Issue control, therefore, is critical. How do you identify the issue in the most favorable light for your client? How do you make sure everyone is on the same wavelength with respect to the issues of the hearing? What do you do when new issues are raised? How do you keep from becoming paralyzed when the issue on which you have based your entire case is taken away from you, not by a failure to prove the issue but by a decision of the hearing officer that the issue is not relevant to the hearing? Again, the answer to these questions is in part found in the seemingly contradictory concept of preplanned flexibility. As you prepare for the hearing, you must do such a thorough job of anticipating the unexpected that you are ready to meet *any* new challenge, even if it is your own witness who poses the challenge.

Suppose that at George's hearing, the welfare department begins by making a major issue of George's poor employment record. They want to prove that he should enter a state vocational training program. What do you do? You should have anticipated this during your preparation, particularly due to the informal contacts that you had with the agency before the hearing. If by some reason this new position of the agency takes you by surprise, or if any other issue comes up that you feel should not be involved, you have a number of options:

a. Argue that the other side is being unfair due to its new position; they should have let you know about it in advance.
b. Argue that the issues at the hearing should conform to the issues defined in the letter granting the hearing in response to your request for one.
c. Ask for a postponement.
d. After you have made your protest and lost, do the best you can with the issues that the hearing officer decides will be discussed.

14. *Make sure that the hearing officer does not have a legal bias.*

The hearing officer should not have been involved in the agency's initial decision against the client which led to the necessity of asking for the hearing.

Normally this will not be a problem since the hearing officer will usually be employed within a separate unit of the agency.

15. *Ask for a postponement of the hearing if it becomes clear after you requested the hearing that you will need more time to prepare.*

Do not be rushed into a hearing unless it is absolutely necessary. Ask for a postponement and be prepared to back up your request with reasons (e.g., you are waiting for a letter to arrive that you want to produce at the hearing).

16. *Make sure that the client and the witnesses know when and where the hearing is to be held.*

Make sure everyone has the address and directions. You may want to bring them there yourself. Send them a reminder note or call them a day or two before the hearing. If they do not appear, be sure to ask for a postponement and try to provide a plausible excuse when you have one.

Section D. HEARSAY, OPINIONS, AND RELEVANCE

Generally, the technical rules of procedure and evidence that are scrupulously followed in court proceedings do not apply to administrative hearings. The standard rule is that hearings are conducted "informally." Nevertheless, the paralegal should have an understanding of some concepts of evidence (p. 448) because they do come up in hearings in spite of the general rule of informality.

As we shall see when we cover direct and cross-examination, two fundamental requirements for the paralegal are: (1) knowing when your witness or a witness for the other side is speaking from first-hand or personal knowledge as opposed to second- or third-hand knowledge (hearsay); (2) knowing when the witness is stating a fact as opposed to an opinion. It is important to know these distinctions not because a hearing officer will exclude hearsay evidence or opinion evidence, but because a paralegal's case is always strengthened when his/her own witness speaks from personal knowledge of facts, and a paralegal will tend to weaken the case of the other side when s/he can point out (through cross-examination) that a witness for the other side is speaking from hearsay or that the witness is relating opinions as opposed to facts. If a paralegal asks his/her witness to state an opinion or conclusion, s/he should be sure that the witness has stated the underlying facts that support the opinion or conclusion before it is expressed.

ASSIGNMENT 110

For each statement made by the witness below, answer the following questions:

1. Is the witness talking from first-hand (personal) knowledge, second-hand, third-hand?

2. Is the witness stating a fact, an opinion, a conclusion?
3. What questions would you ask of the witness so that the same information would come out in a different way?
   a. "My case worker is rude."
   b. "My caseworker called me a liar."
   c. "I am eligible for public assistance."
   d. "My son told me that the caseworker reported me to the supervisor."
   e. "I need welfare."
   f. "My mother can't pay my rent."
   g. "I'm too sick to join the job training program."
   h. "That job does not suit me."
   i. "My husband does not contribute to the support of my family."
   j. "I did report to the job employment agency."
   k. "I was told that no jobs were available."
   l. "You must give me seven days' notice before you terminate me."

———————

Another critical concern of evidence is relevance: only evidence that is relevant to the issues at the hearing should be considered by the hearing officer (p. 449). Something is relevant if it reasonably tends to prove or disprove a matter in dispute. Very often common sense will be the clear guide on whether or not something is relevant. The fact that I am in Chicago is not at all relevant to whether or not it is raining in New York; but the fact that I am in Chicago is relevant to whether or not I *know* if it is raining in New York. In a large number of situations, however, the borderline of relevance and irrelevance is thin. On the question of whether or not George Temple "regularly attends" a drug rehabilitation center, is it relevant that he often plays in baseball games? Is it relevant he has an ulcer? Is it relevant that he is twenty-four years old? Hearing officers will generally lean in the direction of admitting something into evidence if its relevance is at least probable; they are more inclined to let evidence in than to exclude it.

Whenever the hearing officer or the representative of the other side objects to any item of evidence that you plan to introduce, you must be prepared to argue its relevance by explaining how it will contribute to reaching a resolution of the issues. If this approach does not seem to be successful, make a basic "fairness pitch" by asking that you be allowed to present your client's case in the best manner that you can. In effect you are saying, "Don't push me on technicalities; give me some time to show you why this is important. It may not be clear to you now why it is important, but I'll make it clear to you shortly."

Another consideration that bears on the question of whether you will be allowed to produce certain evidence is the extent to which it would be burdensome on the proceeding to allow you to do so. You must be reasonable. You cannot try to introduce 1,000 pages of cancelled receipts and bills, for example, if it is not quite clear that every item is needed to make your case.

Section E. INTRODUCTION TO THE EXAMINATION OF WITNESSES

Before the examination of witnesses begins, you must be sure that you know who everyone is in the hearing room. The hearing officer may ask everyone to state his/her name and connection with the case. If the hearing officer does not, you should ask that this be done.

Another preliminary is the opening statement made by each side. When it is your turn to begin, your opening statement should briefly cover the following:

1. Your understanding of what the issues at the hearing are.
2. A summary of what you are going to establish at the hearing through your witnesses and other evidence.
3. The result(s) the client is seeking from the hearing.

After the opening statements, the next step is usually the examination of witnesses.

You directly examine your own witnesses (e.g., George) and cross-examine the witnesses presented by the other side (e.g., the agency employee, Linda Stout). After you have directly examined your own witnesses, the other side can cross-examine them. After the other side has directly examined their own witnesses, you can cross-examine them. Hence, each side directly examines its own witnesses and cross-examines the witnesses of the other side. When you directly examine a witness, it simply means that you will be the first person to ask questions of that witness.

Normally, one side will present its entire case and then the other side will present its case. The only time you will talk when the other side is presenting its case is when you are cross-examining its witnesses, and vice versa.

After a side has cross-examined a witness, the other side (that originally directly examined the witness) is sometimes allowed to conduct a re-direct examination of the witness in order to cover points raised in the cross-examination.

SEQUENCE:

I. YOU PRESENT YOUR SIDE
   1. You direct-examine your own witnesses.
   2. They cross-examine your witnesses.
   3. You conduct a re-direct examination of your own witnesses to cover points they raised in their cross-examination.

II. THEY PRESENT THEIR SIDE
   1. They direct-examine their own witnesses.
   2. You cross-examine their witnesses.
   3. They conduct a re-direct examination of their own witnesses to cover points you raised in your cross-examination.

This may all sound highly technical. Some hearings are, in fact, conducted this formally. Others are not. You must be prepared to deal with both settings.

To call a witness does not necessarily mean that the person stands in a witness box or is "sworn in." In all probability, everyone will remain in his/her own seat and will not be asked to take an oath. Furthermore, the technical words "direct," "cross," and "re-direct" examination may not be and need not be used. Simpler language can be and often should be used:

DIRECT-EXAMINATION

"Sir (addressed to the hearing officer) I would like to ask (name of witness) a few questions."

CROSS-EXAMINATION

"I would like the opportunity to ask (name of witness) some questions if (name of advocate on the other side) is finished with her own questions."

RE-DIRECT EXAMINATION

"After I asked (name of witness) some questions, Ms. (name of advocate representing the other side) asked some questions of her own, and while I was listening, a few other important and pertinent points occurred to me and I would like to ask a few final questions of (name of witness) if I could."

It does not make any difference what labels are used, so long as you use every opportunity to make your points whenever you are allowed to do so.

Section F. DIRECT-EXAMINATION

Reduced to its simplest level, direct-examination means nothing more than interviewing or talking to someone concerning what s/he knows about a particular event. A direct-examination has three components:

1. *Introduction:* Who is the witness, where does s/he live, where does s/he go to school or work?
2. *Connection to Event:* What relationship does the witness have to the events at issue at the hearing?
3. *Testimony on Event:* What does this witness have to say about the events at issue at the hearing?

GUIDELINES ON CONDUCTING DIRECT-EXAMINATION

1. The witness on direct-examination is *your* witness. You call him/her to give testimony. You are always very cordial to the witness. You never ask anything that might embarrass him/her.
2. You let the witness tell his/her own story in his/her own words. The story should flow naturally from him/her.
3. You ask the witness to speak loudly and clearly. If the witness says something that may not be clear to others, you ask him/her to state it again even though it may have been perfectly clear to *you* what s/he said.
4. You encourage the witness to let you know when s/he does not understand a question.

5. In the introduction of the witness, you let the witness give the basic facts about him/herself. Instead of saying, "This is John Smith of . . . ," you should ask the witness to state his/her name, address, occupation, etc.

6. Before you ask the witness to state what s/he knows about an event, you ask questions to establish his/her relationship or connection to the event. If the witness is a doctor, for example, before you ask if in his/her opinion the client is medically disabled, you should ask if s/he has treated the patient. Before you ask a neighbor whether or not the client earns money as a private babysitter at home, you should ask the witness questions that will establish that s/he is a close neighbor of the client and that s/he often visits the client during the day. By so doing, you will be LAYING THE FOUNDATION FOR THE RELEVANCE OF THE TESTIMONY OF THE WITNESS.

7. It is often helpful to structure your questions to the witness so that s/he will tell his/her story chronologically from beginning to end. Discourage jumping from topic to topic if it is becoming confusing.

8. When the witness is stating things from first-hand knowledge, emphasize the fact that it is first-hand, personal knowledge.

9. When the witness is stating things from second-hand (or hearsay) knowledge, either de-emphasize the fact that it is not first-hand knowledge and/or instruct the witness beforehand to preface his/her statements by saying "to the best of my knowledge."

10. When your witness must state conclusions or opinions, you should structure your questions so that you first bring out all the supporting facts on which the witness has relied in forming the opinions or conclusions.

11. Be aware of the danger of open-ended questions such as, "Tell us what happened." Very often such questions are invitations to ramble on. Confusion can result. The more effective kind of questions are structured to require a brief and concise answer. Use an open-ended question only when you are sure that the witness will be able to handle it.

12. Very often a witness, particularly the client, will have a need to vent his/her feelings. When this happens, s/he often is emotional and raises issues that may not be relevant to the proceeding. You must make a decision when this happens. On the one hand, it is the client's hearing and as a matter of fairness, s/he should have the opportunity to speak his/her mind. It can be very frustrating if questioners keep steering him/her away from what s/he has been waiting a long time to say. On the other hand, you do not want the client to say anything that may be damaging to his/her own case. You must understand the witness psychologically. The best strategy is to determine in advance whether the witness wants to or is inclined to become emotional. If so, then the responsibility of the paralegal is to make the witness aware of the consequences of this occurring at the hearing. In the final analysis, it is the choice of the witness; it is his/her case that is on the line, not yours.

13. You may want to introduce certain documents into evidence after you have asked questions of the witness that will elicit facts that demonstrate the relevance of the document (i.e., you establish a foundation for the documents through your questioning). Once the foundation has been laid,

you introduce the document (i.e., ask the hearing officer to make it part of the record and give a copy to the agency's representative) and then resume your direct-examination of the witness.

14. The hearing officer may interrupt you with questions of his/her own for the witness. S/he, of course, has the right to do so. You may, however, want to politely tell the hearing officer that the subject matter of his/her question will be treated by you in "just a few moments."

15. The advocate for the other side may try to interrupt you with questions. Normally, s/he does *not* have this right. Politely ask the hearing officer if you could finish your own questions before the other side asks any questions on cross-examination.

16. Try to anticipate what the other side will want to question your witness about when it is their turn on cross-examination, and try to cover these points in your own direct-examination.

17. Expect the unexpected. Your witness may say things that you never anticipated. You will have to be flexible enough to deal with whatever comes your way.

ASSIGNMENT 111

Role-play the following situations in class. The instructor will select one student to take the part of the person conducting the direct-examination and someone else to role-play the person being questioned. The latter should make up answers that are generally consistent with the situation stated. (Review the material on fact particularization as a guide to formulating questions, p. 391.)

1. One student conducts a direct-examination (DE) of another student concerning the most frustrating aspect of the latter student's last job.
2. DE of a teenager who just drove up in the family car with a big dent on the side.
3. DE of a pupil who has been charged with fighting.
4. DE of a caseworker who claims that the recipient gave her permission to enter the client's apartment (client denies it).
5. DE of welfare recipient on her claim that she has tried to find suitable work but has been unable to do so.
6. DE of George Temple.

Section G. CROSS-EXAMINATION

Before covering guidelines on cross-examination, you should review the chapter on investigation covering the evaluation of testimonial and physical evidence and the checklist on the validity of physical (tangible) evidence (p. 441). Many of the considerations discussed in the investigation chapter apply to cross-examination at hearings.

GUIDELINES ON CONDUCTING
CROSS-EXAMINATION

1. Be courteous to the witness even though you may be tempted, and indeed baited, into attacking the witness personally.

2. Be sure that it is clear to you who the witness is and what relationship s/he has to the events at issue in the hearing. This may not have been brought out clearly enough while this witness was being direct-examined by the agency representative.

3. If during the direct-examination, this witness said something based on second-hand knowledge (or if it was not clear to you whether it was said from personal or second-hand knowledge), ask about it on cross-examination and be sure that your questions force the witness to admit that no first-hand knowledge exists when that is the case.

4. If during the direct-examination this witness stated conclusions without stating any facts to support the conclusions, ask this witness on cross-examination about these conclusions and the underlying facts that support them according to the witness. Do not use this tactic however (nor the one mentioned in guideline 3 above) if you are absolutely certain that the witness has valid facts to support the conclusions or opinions even though they were not brought out on direct-examination. You do *not* want to give an opposing witness the opportunity to *reinforce* damaging evidence.

5. If it is a fact (or if you are reasonable in suspecting that it is a fact) that the witness has a bias (something personal) against the client, you should try to bring this out on cross-examination. This, of course, will be very difficult and somewhat dangerous to try to do. No one wants to admit that s/he is not being objective (i.e., that s/he has a bias). Probably the best that you will be able to do on cross-examination is to raise some doubts about the objectivity of the testimony of the witness (e.g., by asking questions about any prior hostility that may have existed between the client and the witness) even though you may not be able to conclusively establish a bias.

6. The same point made above about bias against someone applies to bias in favor of a person. A witness can lose objectivity because of partisanship and friendship as well as hostility.

7. If the witness is reading from any papers during cross-examination, politely ask the witness what s/he is reading from and request that you be shown a copy, and, if needed, be given a few moments to read it over before you continue your cross-examination. If the witness is reading from a document that was not sent to you before the hearing (and you requested that the agency send you all records that they were going to rely upon at the hearing), you should object.

8. Sometimes the witness will read from official agency records. These records often refer to statements made by individuals who work for the agency but who are not present at the hearing. The agency representative will try to introduce these records into evidence. It has already been said that you should bring out, through your questioning, the fact that the

witness is not speaking from first-hand knowledge in referring to records of which s/he is not the author. In addition, you should complain that the authors of critically important statements in the records should be present at the hearing as a matter of fairness so that you can confront and cross-examine them. If you are not allowed to do this, you should request that such statements not be allowed to become part of the hearing proceedings.

9. If during cross-examination, the witness raises points that surprise you (and if it was not due to sloppy preparation that you were surprised), you should ask the hearing officer to exclude the matter because of unfair surprise or to postpone the hearing to give you more time to prepare the response of the client to the new point.

10. In courtroom proceedings, it is often the rule that you cannot raise new matters on cross-examination; you can cross-examine a witness only within the scope of the testimony this witness gave on direct-examination. If, for example, the witness testifies only about food stamp eligibility on direct examination, the lawyer conducting the cross-examination cannot ask questions about an invasion of privacy claim since this claim is outside the scope of the direct-examination. This technical rule, however, almost *never* applies to administrative hearings although you should be aware of it since the advocate for the agency may improperly try to apply the technical rule against you while you are cross-examining a witness. You usually do *not* have to limit your questioning on cross-examination to the scope of what was brought out by the other side on direct-examination. Normally, however, it is a good practice not to raise new matters on cross-examination unless you have to. Use direct-examination to make all your major points and use cross-examination as a vehicle to challenge positions of the other side and to buttress the points you have made on direct-examination.

11. On cross-examination you will be questioning witnesses who are normally hostile to your client, although this is not always so. Do not antagonize them unnecessarily. You may find that the witness on cross-examination is willing, either consciously or not, to make statements that are very favorable to your client.

12. As a corollary to the above point, do not be unduly aggressive or defensive. Make your case positively by direct-examination. Do not rely exclusively on establishing your case negatively by trying to show on cross-examination that the witnesses for the other side are fools.

13. Do not help the other side by asking witnesses questions on cross-examination that you know (or reasonably anticipate) will produce damaging statements.

14. You do not have to conduct a cross-examination of a witness if nothing s/he said on direct-examination is unclear to you or to the hearing officer, or if you do not think that you will be able to prompt the witness to contradict him/herself or say anything that would discredit his/her position in any way. In such a case, it would be better to rely solely on what you were able to establish on direct-examination.

15. Remain loose and flexible; anticipate the unexpected.

ASSIGNMENT 112

Role-play the following situations in class. The instructor will select students to play the roles involved. The witness should make up answers that are generally consistent with the situation stated. (Review the material on fact particularization as a guide to formulating questions, p. 391.)

1. On direct-examination, the witness testifies that Mr. Smith was drunk. Conduct a cross-examination of this witness.
2. On direct-examination, the witness (a social worker) testifies that she feels the client is an unfit mother because when she visited the client, the house was dirty, the children were sick, and there was no food in the refrigerator. Conduct a cross-examination of this witness.
3. On direct-examination, the witness (a social worker) testifies that the client should be able to obtain employment for the following reasons: the children are old enough for daycare services, the client is basically healthy in spite of occasional headaches, jobs are available or at least job training programs are available. Conduct a cross-examination of this witness.

Section H. CLOSING THE HEARING AND PREPARING FOR AN APPEAL

At the end of all the questioning and presentation of evidence, ask the hearing officer to let you sum up with your version of what happened. State what you think you proved, state what you think the other side failed to prove. Specifically, state again what result you seek for the client. If you think that the hearing was inconclusive because you were unfairly surprised by what the other side did or because the other side failed to bring individuals to the hearing who are sufficiently acquainted with the case, then:

1. Ask for a decision for the client because of these factors; or
2. At the very least, ask for an adjournment so that the hearing can resume after you have had a chance to study the matter that the other side unfairly surprised you with, or after the other side brings to the hearing individuals who should have been there.

Many hearings are either transcribed or taperecorded by the agency. Every word of the hearing therefore is preserved. Normally, the law office for which you work will be able to purchase a typed copy of the transcript or a copy of the tape. The significance of this, of course, is that the record made at the hearing can become the basis of a court appeal if the client is dissatisfied with the decision of the hearing. You must understand the relationship between what happens at the hearing and a possible subsequent court appeal. To a very large extent, you are responsible for "making a record" for the lawyer to use on appeal.

Lawyers who have litigated cases following administrative hearings should acquaint you with the mechanics of the court appeal process (p. 365, p. 478) and with their version of what a good hearing record should constitute. What kind of information would they like to see in it? What kinds of damaging statements made by clients and witnesses for clients would they like to see omitted or toned down? If possible, you should try to read a copy of an old appellate brief (p. 695) that cites testimony taken at an administrative hearing so that you can see the connection between the hearing and the court action.

In some administrative hearings, an advocate waives any objection that s/he has to what takes place at the hearing *unless s/he specifically objects on the record at the agency hearing* (p. 479). A waiver can mean that the lawyer cannot later raise the point on appeal in court. Whether such a waiver rule applies is a question of local practice.

If it does apply, then you must be familiar with the technique of objecting for the record. When you have an objection to make during the hearing, you should do so simply by saying to the hearing officer, "Sir, I would like to object" and briefly state what you are objecting to and the reasons therefor. It will not be necessary to object constantly to the same point. If the hearing officer decides against you and you object once, it is usually not necessary to object again every time the agency representative brings up what you objected to.

With few exceptions, courts will not allow the client to appeal an issue in court unless the agency involved in the issue has been given the opportunity to resolve the issue within the agency's own hearing structure. This is the doctrine of exhausting administrative remedies (p. 364). For example, at a welfare hearing, a client might claim that s/he failed to receive a check that was due him/her *and* that the caseworker is harassing him/her with unauthorized home visits. At the hearing, if the only issue discussed concerns the check, then the visitation issue cannot be appealed in court since as to this issue the client has not exhausted administrative remedies. Another hearing may have to be brought on the visitation issue before it can be raised in court. You must be aware of this problem as a matter of issue control.

ASSIGNMENT 113

Read each situation. State whether you would raise any objection. If so, state the reasons for your objection. Also, answer any other questions asked in the problem situation.

1. On direct-examination, a witness of the agency representative says that your client "is a liar."
2. On direct-examination, a witness of the agency representative reads from a piece of paper. The paralegal is not sure what the paper is.
3. On direct-examination, a witness of the agency representative says that s/he was told by another caseworker that the client had a secret bank account. On cross-examination of this same witness, what line of questions should the paralegal take?
4. Before the hearing began, the paralegal requested the agency to send him/her all the documents that the agency intended to rely on at the hearing. The agency never did so. Does the paralegal refer to this at the beginning of the hearing?

5. Same as #4 above, except that when the paralegal at the beginning of the hearing mentions that the records were never sent, the agency representative hands him/her forty pages of records.
6. Same as #4 above, except that when the paralegal at the beginning of the hearing mentions that the records were never sent, the agency representative responds by saying that the records are confidential.
7. On direct-examination of a witness of the paralegal, the agency representative keeps interrupting with questions of his/her own.
8. While the agency representative is talking to the hearing officer, s/he uses some legal language that the paralegal does not understand.
9. While talking to the hearing officer, the agency representative hands him/her a document that announces a new regulation of the agency.

ASSIGNMENT 114

Role-play the George Temple hearing in class. As a starting point, use the facts presented on page 790. Participants can make up other facts as they go along so long as they are generally consistent with the facts given on page 790. The instructor will select students to play the parts of the various roles, e.g., hearing officer, paralegal for George, paralegal for the agency, witnesses. The paralegals should review the material on fact particularization as a guide in formulating questions, p. 391. The rest of the class should observe and take notes on how the paralegals conducted themselves. What did they do well? What went wrong and how should it have been handled?

Appendix A

Bibliography

For additional periodical literature, consult the *Legal Resource Index* (p. 628) and the *Current Legal Index* (p. 627). In these indexes, check the following subject headings: "Legal Assistants," "Attorney and Client," "Legal Ethics," "Conflict of Interests (attorneys)," "Unauthorized Practice of Law," "Law Offices," etc. Also consult the *Index to Legal Periodicals* (p. 626). In this index, check the following subjects: "Paraprofessionals," "Legal Ethics," "Attorneys," "Unauthorized Practice of Law," etc.

TABLE OF CONTENTS

The numbers below refer to specific entries in the bibliography.

The numbers below refer to specific entries in the bibliography.

1. *ABA/BNA Lawyers' Manual on Professional Conduct: Bibliography,* R. Peterson, ed. (BNA, 1984).

2. *ABA/BNA Lawyers' Manual on Professional Conduct: Current Reports* (BNA, 1984–_).

3. *Accrediting and Licensing of Paralegals,* 7 Clearinghouse Review 475 (National Clearinghouse for Legal Services, 1973).

4. *Activities of Law Clerks as Illegal Practice of Law,* 13 American Law Reports 3d 1137.

5. *Activities of Massachusetts Bar Association Unauthorized Practice of Law Committee,* 39 Unauthorized Practice News 36 (ABA Standing Committee on Unauthorized Practice of Law, no. 1, Fall–Winter, 1974).

6. Adams, *New Course to Free Lawyers of Routine,* p. 7, St. Louis Post Dispatch (Aug. 28, 1969).

7. Ader, *A Brief Guide to the Training and Development of Paraprofessionals,* 5 Clearinghouse Review 379 (National Clearinghouse for Legal Services, 1971).

8. *Advantages and Methodology of Using Sublegals in the Law,* 6 Suffolk University Law Review 1030 (1972).

9. Akins, *Firm Must Structure Program for Using Paralegals,* 5 Legal Times of Washington 10, col. 1 (July 26, 1982).

10. Alhadeff, *Legal Assistants,* 51 Florida Bar Journal 592 (Nov. 1977).

11. Altman & Weil, *Paralegal Employees, The True Paralegal, Training Paralegals, Status Problems, Maintaining Clerical Morale, Paralegal Assistants,* sections 4.02, 9.07, 9.08, 16.03 (Matthew Bender, 1974).

12. American and Canadian Bar Associations Economics and Management Conference: *Practice Materials and Legal Assistants Check Lists* (ABA, 1972).

13. American Bar Association, Special Committee on Lay Assistants for Lawyers, *Liberating the Lawyer: The Utilization of Legal Assistants by Law Firms in the United States,* Preliminary Draft (1971).

14. American Bar Association, Special Committee on Lay Assistants for Lawyers, *San Francisco Pilot Project: Training for Legal Assistants* (1971).

15. American Bar Association, Special Committee on Lay Assistants for Lawyers, *Status Report* (1969).

16. American Bar Association, Special Committee on Legal Assistants, *Certification of Legal Assistants* (1975).

17. American Bar Association, Special Committee on Legal Assistants, *New Careers in Law II,* R. Yegge & E. Jarmel, eds. (June 1971).

18. American Bar Association, Special Committee on Legal Assistants, *The Paraprofessional in Medicine, Dentistry, and Architecture* (Oct. 1971).

19. American Bar Association, Special Committee on Legal Assistants, *Proposed Curriculum for Training of Law Office Personnel* (April 1971).

20. American Bar Association, Standing Committee on Legal Assistants, *Guidelines and Procedures for the Approval of Legal Assistant Education Programs* (1973).

21. American Bar Association, Standing Committee on Legal Assistants, *Legal Assistant Education: A Compilation of Program Descriptions* (1977).

22. American Bar Association, Standing Committee on Legal Assistants, *Legal Assistant Education and Utilization: A 1978 Status Report* (1978).

23. American Bar Association, Standing Committee on Legal Assistants, *Legal Assistant Update* (1980–__).

24. American Bar Association, Standing Committee on Legal Assistants, *Survey of Non-Degree Legal Assistant Training in the United States* (1976).

25. American Dental Association, *Annual Report on Dental Auxiliary Education 1967/68* (1968).

26. American Dental Association, Council on Dental Education, *Requirements for an Accredited Program in Dental Hygiene Education* (1965).

27. American Institute of Architects, *A Program for Architectural Technicians' Training* (1968).

28. American Law Institute–American Bar Association Committee on Continuing Professional Education, *Legal Assistants for Lawyers* (Oct. 1975).

29. American Paralegal Association, *Code of Ethics for Paralegals* (1969).

30. Amira, *The Legal Assistant As Office Manager,* 4 Facts and Findings 25 (National Association of Legal Assistants, No. 4, January–February, 1985).

31. Amory, *The Legal Assistant,* 9 Trial 45 (Sept./Oct. 1973).

32. *Analysis of Law Staff Functions,* 1 Am Jur Trials, Chapter 4.

33. Anderson, *Formal Training of Legal Assistants,* Law Office Efficiency (American Bar Association, Section on the Economics of Law Office Practice (1972).

34. Anderson & Ruth, *A Comparison of Staff Salaries: 500-Firm Survey also Polls Staff-Attorney Ratios, Hiring Trends,* 6 National Law Journal 15, col. 1 (November 21, 1983).

35. Anderson, *Paraprofessionalism,* 18 The National Association of Legal Secretaries Docket 21 (April–May 1970).

36. *Annotated Model Rules of Professional Conduct* (ABA, 1984).

37. Appleson, *Increase in Paralegals Stirs Ethical Concerns,* 67 American Bar Association Journal 1445 (November, 1981).

38. Arc, *Courses for Paralegal Assistants,* 17 Boston Bar Journal 19 (April 1973).

39. Archibald, *Specialization and the Legal Paraprofessional: Their Impact on the Legal Profession—An Annotated Bibliography, 1962–1972 (California State Law Library, 1973).*

40. *A Report on Paraprofessionals,* Justice Department, Legal Services Division, Attorney General, Province of British Columbia (May 1975).

41. Ashman & Chapin, *Is the Bell Tolling for Nonlawyer Judges?* 59 Judicature 416 (No. 9, April 1976).

42. Association of American Law Schools, *Legal Assistants,* Report of Committee on Legal Assistants (1974). Reprinted from Part One, *Proceedings of the 1974 Annual Meeting of the Association of American Law Schools.*

43. Association of American Law Schools, Committee to Study the Curriculum, *Individual Training for the Public's Profession,* Tentative Draft No. 2, Sept. 1970).

44. *Attorney's Splitting Fees with Other Attorney or Layman as Ground for Disciplinary Proceeding,* 6 American Law Reports 3d 1446.

45. Ault, *Law Office Operations: The Paraprofessional,* Cleveland Bar Journal (July 1969).

46. Avery, *Effective Utilization of Office Staff, Associates and Partners,* Law Office Economics, Proceedings of the Fourth National Conference on Law Office Economics and Management (ABA, 1970).

47. Baer, *A Guide to Training and Employment of Prisoners as Paralegals* (American Bar Association, Prison Legal Services of Michigan, Inc. 1979).

48. Bailey, *Practice by Non-Lawyers Before the United States Patent Office,* 15 Federal Bar Journal 211 (1955).

49. Bailey, Kleeman, & Ring, *Paralegal Functions and Legal Constraints* 9 Clearinghouse Review 851 (National Clearinghouse for Legal Services, No. 12, April 1976).

50. Baker, *Use Nonlawyers,* Law Office Economics and Management (Feb. 1965).

51. Baker, *Benchmarks for Your Practice: Lawyers' Assistants,* Journal of the Missouri Bar (Oct.–Nov. 1976).

52. Baker, "Legal Technicians and Paralegals," *The Changing System of Delivering Legal Services,* 80 Case and Comment 29 (Sept.–Oct. 1975).

53. Bar Association of San Francisco and San Francisco Association of Legal Assistants, *Effective Use of Legal Assistants in Litigation Practice* (June 5, 1980).

54. Bar Association of San Francisco and San Francisco Association of Legal Assistants, *Effective Use of Legal Assistants in Probate Practice* (June 12, 1980).

55. Bar Association of San Francisco and San Francisco Association of Legal Assistants, *How to Manage a Legal Assistants Program* (June 1980).

56. Beard, *Paralegals: The National and State Outlook,* 18 Arkansas Lawyer 189 (October, 1984).

57. Bellow & Kettleson, *Paralegals: The Road Ahead,* National Legal Aid and Defender Association Briefcase 126 (Sept. 1978).

58. Berg, *Annual Survey,* San Francisco Association of Legal Assistants (Dec. 1973).

59. Berkey, *Finding Employment as a Paralegal,* 2 Legal Assistant Today 18, No. 3 (Spring, 1985).

60. Berkey, *New Career Opportunities in the Paralegal Profession* (Arco, 1983).

61. Berkey, *Resumes for Paralegals and Other People with Legal Training* (Arco, 1984).

62. *Bibliography of Legal Articles, Textbooks, and Treatises on Professional Responsibility: 1970–1983* (ABA, 1984).

63. Bigelow, *Help for Lawyers: The Nonlawyer Assistant,* 43 New York State Bar Journal 420 (Oct. 1971). See also 12 Law Office Economics and Management 529 (March, 1972); and 77 Case and Comment 40 (July–Aug. 1972).

64. Bishop & Shelton, "Litigation System Workshop: The Systems Approach to Litigation," *Manual for Lawyers and Legal Assistants: Civil Litigation—Auto Negligence* (Institute of Continuing Education, Ann Arbor, Mich., 1976).

65. Blanchard, *Litigation and Trial Practice for the Legal Paraprofessional,* 2d ed. (West, 1982).

66. Bliss & Cohen, *New Health Professionals* (1977).

67. Bombet, *Working Effectively with a Legal Investigator,* 17 Trial 20(5) (November, 1981).

68. Bookler, *Effective Utilization Is Key to the Paralegal Profession,* 4 Pennsylvania Law Journal Rep. 10, col. 1 (May 11, 1981).

69. Bower, *Can Paralegals Be Profitable?* 54 Florida Bar Journal 223 (March 1980). Reprinted in 59 Michigan Bar Journal 173 (March 1980).

70. Bower, *Paralegals and Profits: Drawing the Bottom Line,* 3 Pennsylvania Law Journal 1 (Jan. 28, 1980).

71. Bowman & Klopf, *New Careers and Roles in the American School: A Study of Auxiliary Personnel in Education* (1967).

72. Boyer, *Use of Paralegals as a Means to Low Cost Legal Services to Middle-Income Persons,* The Legal Intelligencer (Phil. Law Journal, April 1, 1977).

73. Braeman, *Paralegals on the Legal Team: The Use of Legal Specialists in the Government Law Office,* Federal Bar News 103 (May 1980).

74. Brandom, *Comments on Educating the Attorney to Employ, Utilize and Retain Legal Assistants,* 5 Facts and Findings 1 (National Association of Legal Assistants, Jan.–Feb. 1979).

75. Braverman, *Is the Office Manager Worth It?* Illinois Bar Journal (Feb. 1970). See also 12 Law Office Economics and Management 227 (Sept. 1971).

76. Brickman, *Clinical Education and the Legal Paraprofessional,* 7 Council on Legal Education for Professional Responsibility Newsletter 2 (No. 8, Nov. 1974).

77. Brickman, *Expansion of the Lawyering Process through a New Delivery System: The Emergence and State of Legal Paraprofessionalism,* 71 Columbia Law Review 1153 (1971).

78. Brickman, *Legal Delivery Systems: A Bibliography,* 4 University of Toledo Law Review 465 (1973).

79. Brickman, *Legal Paraprofessionalism and Its Implications: A Bibliography,* 24 Vanderbilt Law Review 1213 (Nov. 1971).

80. Brickner, *Law Office Management and Economics (Hiring a Paralegal vs. an Associate),* 25 Res Gestae 161 (March, 1981).

81. Brierly, *The Physician's Assistant: In Legal Limbo?* Physician's Management (Jan. 1971).

82. Brill, *Increasing Efficiency: Utilization of Lay Personnel in Your Office,* Texas Bar Journal 169 (March 1969).

83. Brittain, *Will the Real Legal Assistant Please Stand Up! A Case in Favor of Multi-State Licensing,* 2 Legal Assistant Today 14, No. 3 (Spring, 1985).

84. Brooks, *Do Independent Contractors [Paralegals] Have Special Ethical Considerations?* 10 Facts & Findings 7, No. 3 (National Association of Legal Assistants, November–December, 1982).

85. Brooks, *Neighborhood Social-Legal Program,* 38 Social Service Review 80 (1964).

86. Brooks, *The Paralegal Puzzle,* 15 Law Office Economics and Management 340 (No. 3, Fall, 1974). See also Boston Bar Journal (April 1974).

87. Brooks, *The President's Page,* Boston Bar Journal (April 1974).

88. Brown, *The Authorized Role of the Legal Assistant,* 36 Unauthorized Practice News 9 (1971).

89. Brown, *The Education of Legal Assistants, Technicians and Paraprofessionals,* 22 Journal of Legal Education 94 (1969).

90. Brown, *The Paralegal Profession,* 19 Howard Law Journal 117 (1976).

91. Brown, *Preventive Law and the Legal Assistant,* 24 Vanderbilt Law Review 1181 (Nov. 1971).

92. Brown, *A Suggestion Concerning Pre-Law School Education,* 25 Southern California Law Review 177 (1952).

93. Bruehring, *Setting Standards for Legal Assistants,* 52 Florida Bar Journal 8 (Jan. 1979).

94. Brunner, Hamre & McCaffrey, *The Legal Assistant Handbook* (Bureau of National Affairs, 1982).

95. Bruno, *Paralegal's Litigation Handbook* (1980).

96. Buchanan, *Law Office Economics and Management: Use of Modern Procedures and Paraprofessionals,* 41 Pennsylvania Bar Association Quarterly 408 (1970).

97. Bullough, *The Law and the Expanding Nursing Role,* 2d ed. (1980).

98. Burgess, *Non-Lawyer Seeks Position of Prosecution,* The Washington Post, C1 (June 24, 1975).

99. Burleigh, *Can Disbarred Lawyer Work as a Paralegal?* 130 Chicago Daily Law Bulletin 1, col. 2 (Sept. 28, 1984).

100. Burnham, *As Paralegal Use Grows, Personnel Problems Exist: Similar Work, Lower Pay,* Legal Times of Washington 28 (Aug. 28, 1978).

101. Burnham, *Dental Hygienist in Dental Practice*, 60 Journal of American Dental Association 367 (1960).

102. *Busy Lawyer Needs Assistant*, 2 George Washington Times 13 (No. 5, George Washington University, Dec. 1973).

103. Cain & Fisher, *Paralegals: A Selected Bibliography* (U.S. Dept. of Justice, Nat'l. Criminal Justice Referral Service, Dec. 1978).

104. California State Bar, *Study Continued on Use of Legal Assistants*, Reports 1 (June 1972).

105. Campbell, *Paralegals in the Corporate Setting*, 30 St. Louis Bar Journal 22 (1983).

106. Cantor, *Internal Compensation for Partners, Associates and Clerical Staff*, 1 Law Office Economics and Management 1 (1960–61).

107. Cantor, *Legal Assistant Employment Checklist*, 3 Legal Economics 43 (Spring 1977).

108. Cantor, *A Practical Look at Legal Assistants*, 18 Practical Lawyer 43 (No. 7, 1971). See also 19 The Practical Lawyer 92 (No. 1, 1972).

109. Carlin, *Lawyer's Ethics* (1966).

110. Carlisle, *The Way You Practice Law Will Change*, 44 Florida Bar Journal 26 (1970).

111. Carmichael, *Employment Picture Bright for the Trained Paralegal*, Chicago Tribune (Oct. 16, 1977).

112. Carney, *Make the Most of Your Time: Achieve Efficiency and Flexibility Through the Skillful Use of Paralegals*, 1 Family Advocate 6 (1978).

113. *The Case for Legal Aides*, 26–8 Manpower (June 1969).

114. Cassedy, *The Legal Paraprofessional*, 48 Florida Bar Journal 510 (July 1974).

115. Cavers, *Legal Services in the 21st Century: A Proposal for Creating Law Centers That Will Serve Entire Communities*, Learning and the Law 12 (ABA Section on Legal Education and Admissions to the Bar, Summer 1974).

116. *CCC [Cumberland County College] Recognized as Pioneer in Training Legal Assistants*, Vineland Times Journal 8 (New Jersey, July 16, 1973).

117. Center for Governmental Responsibility, University of Florida, *Paralegals: Legal Assistance by Non-Lawyers*, The Legal Needs of the Poor and Underrepresented Citizens of Florida: An Overview, p. 87.

118. Center for Public Representation, *Meeting Legal Needs Without Lawyers: An Experimental Program in Advocacy Training* (1977).

119. Chadwick, *Progressive Use of Paralegals Is Good Business*, The Retainer Supplement of the Legal Intelligencer (Nov. 8, 1978).

120. Cheatham, *The Legal Paraprofessional: An Introduction*, 24 Vanderbilt Law Review 1077 (1977).

121. Chernowsky, *Through the Looking Glass; As a Paralegal, Is Your Reflection That of a Professional?* Legal Assistant Today 17, No. 3 (Spring, 1984).

122. Chernowsky, *What Makes a Good Paralegal Training Program?* 7 National Paralegal Reporter 1, No. 1 (National Federation of Paralegal Associations, Autumn, 1982).

123. Chicago Association of Paralegal Assistants, Committee on Standards, *The Legal Assistant: A Self-Statement* (May 1, 1974).

124. Chicago Association of Paralegal Assistants, Committee on Standards, *Report on Salary and Benefits of Legal Assistants* (1974).

125. Chicago Bar Foundation, Task Force on Para-Professionals, *Para-Legal Assistants: A Report.*

126. Childers & Jennings, *Paralegal Salary and Job Function Survey of 1980—Arizona,* 21 Law Office Economics and Management 506 (1981).

127. Christensen, *The Unauthorized Practice of Law: Do Good Fences Really Make Good Neighbors—or Even Good Sense?* 1980 American Bar Foundation Research Journal 159.

128. Clark, *Parajudges and the Administration of Justice,* 24 Vanderbilt Law Review 1167 (1971).

129. Cleary, *The New [ABA] Model Rules of Professional Conduct: How Will They Apply to the Legal Assistant,* 10 Facts & Findings 9, No. 4 (National Association of Legal Assistants, January–February, 1984).

130. *CLEPR Hosts Paraprofessional Conferences,* 4 Council on Professional Responsibility Newsletter 12 (March 1972).

131. *Code of Ethics and Professional Responsibility of the Legal Assistants Division of the State Bar of Texas,* 45 Texas Bar Journal 758 (June, 1982).

132. *Code of Professional Responsibility by State* (ABA, Nat'l. Center for Professional Responsibility, 1980).

133. Cohen, *Using Legal Assistants in Estate Planning,* 30 Practical Lawyer 73 (October 15, 1984).

134. Collins & Donnelly, *Paralegal Interviewing: Fact-Gathering and the Human Perspective,* Trainee Handbook (California Rural Legal Assistance, National Senior Citizens Law Center, 1973).

135. *Colorado Bar Association Starts Suit Against Lay Divorce Specialists,* 39 Unauthorized Practice News 87 (No. 2, ABA Standing Committee on Unauthorized Practice of the Law, Spring–Summer, 1975).

136. Commerce Clearing House (CCH), *Nonprofessional Aides,* Poverty Law Reporter, paragraph number 8705.22, pp. 9726 (1972).

137. Commercial Law League of America, Seminar Materials, *A Paralegal Approach to the Practice of Commercial Law* (Nov. 14, 1975).

138. Committee on Continuing Education of the Bar Association of San Francisco, *Report of the Subcommittee on Education and Utilization of Legal Assistants* (June 1968).

139. Committee on Legal Ethics and Professional Responsibility, Pennsylvania Bar Association, *1974 Reports* (Legal Assistants) (April 9, 1975).

140. Comras & Willier, *Consumer Law Training and Practice Materials for Lay Persons* (Boston, National Consumer Law Center, 1971).

141. Cone, *Those Who Stayed and Those Who Left: Case Studies of Legal Assistants,* 4 Legal Assistants Update 1 (1984).

142. *Conflict of Interest: A Trial Lawyer's Guide,* S. Epstein et al (Md., Nat'l. Law Pub., 1984).

143. Conn & Hippler, *Paralegals in the Bush,* 3 UCLA-Alaska Law Review 85 (1973).

144. *The Constitutional Right, if Any, of a Non-Lawyer to Represent Others in the Courts,* 39 Unauthorized Practice News 236 (1975).

145. *Construction and Application of Provision of Federal Patent Act (35 USCS 33) Punishing Unauthorized Representation as Practitioner Before Patent Office,* 13 American Law Reports Fed. 843.

146. *Control of the Unauthorized Practice of Law: Scope of Inherent Judicial Power,* 28 University of Chicago Law Review 162 (1960).

147. Coppleman & Hiestand, *Expanding Legal Services to the Elderly in California through the Use of Paralegals: Findings and Recommendations to the State Legislature,* (California State Legislature, Assembly Rules Committee, 1975).

148. Cooper & Rosenberg, *Legal Service Assistants: Report on Legal Training Phase of a Joint Demonstration Program 1969–1970* (Columbia Law School, 1970).

149. Cornelius, *Career Guide for Paralegals* (Career Blazers, Monarch Press, 1983).

150. Cornelius, *Paralegals Offer Skilled Services to Law Offices,* 183 New York Law Journal 21, col. 1 (March 24, 1980).

151. Cote & Weil, *The First Office Administrator—Painful Failure or Smooth Transition,* Legal Economic News, p. 6 (ABA Standing Committee on Economics of Law Practice, No. 43, Sept. 1973).

152. Council of State Governments, *Occupational Licensing Legislation in the States* (Chicago, 1952).

153. Cowan, *The Legal Service Company: Efficient, Economical Paraprofessionalism by the Piece,* Manual for Managing the Law Office, pp. 1621ff. (Prentice-Hall, 1972).

154. Cowie, *The Legal Paraprofessional in Canada: A Pilot Training Scheme* (Canada, Dalhousie Legal Aid Services, 1972).

155. Cox, *Paralegals to Be Hired for Defender,* 94 Los Angeles Daily Law Journal, p. B1, col. 1 (August 17, 1981).

156. *Criminal and Tort Liability of Unlicensed Healers,* 41 Virginia Law Review 961 (1955).

157. Crump, *What a Legal Assistant Can Do for You,* 44 Texas Bar Journal 739 (July, 1981). See also 22 Law Office Economics and Management 453 (Winter, 1982).

158. Cullen, *On the Right Side of the Law: Paralegals,* 5 Working Woman 73 (June 1980).

159. Cunningham, *The Para-legal and the Lawyer's Library* (Shepard's McGraw-Hill, 1973).

160. Dalton, *The Paralegal's Role in a Wage Garnishment Action,* 22 Law Office Economics and Management 99 (Spring, 1981). See also 55 Florida Bar Journal 49 (January, 1981).

161. DeBenedictis, *Paralegals' Starting Salary Still Low,* 97 Los Angeles Daily Journal 5, col. 1 (April 4, 1984).

162. Deming, *The Paralegal: A New Career* (Elsevier/Nelson Books, 1980).

162a. Department of Justice of Canada, National Legal Aid Research Centre, *Public Sector Paralegalism in Canada Today,* National Workshop on Paralegalism (March 1978).

163. Department of State and Local Bar Services, *Special Issue: Legal Assistants* (ABA, No. 5, Jan. 1975).

164. Derby, *The Unauthorized Practice of Law by Laymen and Lay Associations,* California Law Review 1331 (Aug. 1966).

165. Dickson, *The Bar Behind Bars,* 4 Juris Doctor 33 (No. 11, Dec. 1974).

166. Dodge, *The Evolution of a City Office,* Wisconsin Law Review 180 (1955).

167. *Does a Defendant in a Federal Criminal Case Have a Right to Be Represented by a Disbarred Attorney?* 39 Unauthorized Practice News 100, no. 2 (ABA Standing Committee on Unauthorized Practice of Law (Spring–Summer 1975).

168. Donahue & Kroll, *Survey of Community Legal Workers in Ontario,* 5 Canadian Community Law Journal 1 (Ann., 1981).

169. Douglass, *Legal Assistants Increase Productivity,* 45 Alabama Lawyer 334 (November, 1984).

170. Downs, *Providing the Social Worker with Legal Understanding,* U.S. Dept. of Health, Education, and Welfare Conference Proceedings, the Extension of Legal Services to the Poor (1964).

171. *Drafting of Will or Other Estate-Planning Activities as Illegal Practice of Law,* 22 American Law Reports 3d 1122.

172. *Drafting, or Filling in Blanks in Printed Forms, of Instruments Relating to Land by Real-Estate Agents, Brokers, or Managers as Constituting Practice of Law,* 53 American Law Reports 2d 788.

173. Draper, *Legal Assistants Will Increase Your Income,* 62 Michigan Bar Journal 1083 (December, 1983).

174. Dye & Penner, eds., *Handbook for the Midwestern Conference on Paralegal Education, Developing & Teaching Performance Competencies* (American Association for Paralegal Education, 1985).

175. Dye, *Lawyers' Assistant Occupational Analysis,* Journal of Paralegal Education, Retrospective 1983, p. 189 (American Association for Paralegal Education, 1983).

176. Dye, *Legal Assistant Education—A Guide to Local Paralegal Education Programs,* 38 Journal of the Missouri Bar 111 (March, 1982). See also p. 213 in the April–May issue, 1982.

177. Early, *The Need for Legal Nurses,* 74 Case and Comment 34 (Sept.–Oct. 1969).

178. *Earnings and Benefits of Office Workers, 1966,* 8 Law Office Economics and Management 74 (1967–68).

179. *Earnings and Hours of Office Workers, 1967,* 9 Law Office Economics and Management 323 (1968–69).

180. East Bay Association of Legal Assistants, *Survey 1978* (1978).

181. Eddy, *Professional Negligence* (1955).

182. *The Effective Use of Lay Personnel and Delegation of Work,* Oklahoma Bar Journal (May 17, 1969). See also Oregon State Bar Bulletin (June 1970).

183. Ehrlich, *Paralegal Movement Is Here to Stay, Grow, Prosper,* 4 Legal Times of Washington 14, col. 1 (August 3, 1981).

184. Ehrlich & Manning, *Programs in Law at the University of Hawaii* (Dec. 1970).

185. Eimmermann, *Fundamentals of Paralegalism* (1980).

186. *Elderly Paralegals Aid Boston Project,* 1 Alternatives: Legal Services and the Public 9 (No. 3, ABA Consortium on Legal Services and the Public, Dec. 1974).

187. *Eleven Women Begin On-the-Job Legal Training,* The Atlanta Journal and Constitution, 15-G, col. 1 (Jan. 27, 1974).

188. *The Emergence of Lay Intermediaries Furnishing Legal Services to Individuals,* 1965 Washington University Law Quarterly 313. See also 71 Commercial Law Journal 93 (1966).

189. Emerson, *How to Create an Effective Litigation Management Support System,* Legal Assistant Today 12, No. 2 (Winter, 1984).

190. Emshoff & Davidson, *Training Prison Inmates as Paralegals: An Experimental Project,* 8 Journal of Criminal Justice 27 (January, 1980).

191. Endacott, *Systemization and the Legal Assistant in the Law Office,* 54 Nebraska Law Review 46 (1975).

192. Endleman, *Legal Assistant Utilization in Connecticut Law Firms,* 55 Connecticut Bar Journal 324 (August, 1981).

193. Engel, *The Standardization of Lawyers' Services,* 1977 American Bar Foundation Research 817.

194. Erlandson, *Delegation of Office Duties: Check List for Lawyers,* 2 Law Office Economics and Management 83 (1961–62).

195. Erne, *Use Your Legal Assistants Effectively,* 2 California Lawyer 18 (October, 1982).

196. Eshenroder, *Paralegals Do Legwork for Lawyers,* Ann Arbor News 49 (Dec. 1, 1974).

197. Estes, *Starting and Managing a Long-Term Paralegal Program,* 8 Legal Economics 17(5) (ABA, March–April, 1982).

198. *Ethics and the Rule of Law* by D. Lyons (Cambridge Univ. Press, 1984).

199. Evarts & Peeples, *Mediation and the Legal Assistant,* 2 Legal Assistant Today 28, No. 1 (Fall, 1984).

200. Everett, *Using Legal Assistants in an Initial Interview,* 87 Case & Comment 30 (May–June, 1982). See also 9 Facts & Findings 1, No. 1 (National Association of Legal Assistants, August, 1982).

201. *Expanding Your Law Practice: The Ethical Risks* by H. Hansworth (ABA Section of Economics of Law Practice, 1984).

202. Fairbanks, *Nonlawyers Assistants,* Lawyer's World 14 (Aug.–Sept. 1970).

203. Fairbanks, *Assistants in the Personal Injury Case,* 10 Trial 10 (No. 5, Sept.–Oct. 1974). See also Insurance Law Journal 652 (1974).

204. Fairbanks, *Processing a Personal Injury Case with Legal Assistants,* Legal Economics News 49 (ABA, Section of Economics of Law Practice, Sept. 1974).

205. Farhat, *Legal Assistant Association of Michigan,* 62 Michigan Bar Journal 624 (August, 1983).

206. Feder, *Specialized Use of Legal Assistants: Trial and Litigation Practice,* The Colorado Lawyer 1 (July, 1972).

207. Fellers, *The Economics and Delivery of Legal Services,* 58 Judicature (No. 3, Oct. 1974).

APPENDIX A: BIBLIOGRAPHY   **821**

208. Field, *Legal Assistants: Where Do We Go From Here?* 10 Facts & Findings 17, No. 6 (National Association of Legal Assistants, May–June, 1984).

209. *Film on Lay Assistants,* 11 Law Office Economics and Management 86 (May 1970).

210. *Final Report and Recommendations of the Task Force on Professional Competence* (ABA, 1983).

211. Fins, *Opportunities in Paralegal Careers* (VGM Career Horizons, 1979).

212. *Firms Pay More for Support Services: Breaking a Taboo—Paralegals Pass Lawyers,* National Law Journal, 8 (August 11, 1980).

213. Fischer & Lachmann, eds., *Unauthorized Practice Handbook* (American Bar Foundation, 1972).

214. Fisher, *Legal Assistants Division [of State Bar of Texas],* 45 Texas Bar Journal 271 (March, 1982).

215. Fishman & Pointer, *A Comprehensive Bibliography on New Careers and the Use of Subprofessionals in Human Services,* Procedural Guide for Program Development: Sourcebook for Trainers (U.S. Dept. of Labor, Manpower Administration, Bureau of Work-Training Programs, April, 1968).

216. *Fitting Paralegals into the Corporate Legal Department,* 11 Facts & Findings 24, No. 2 (National Association of Legal Assistants, September–October, 1984).

217. Flood, *Barristers' Clerks: The Law's Middlemen* (England, Manchester University Press, 1983).

218. Florida Bar, *Report of Joint Committee on Legal Assistants to the Board of Governors of the Florida Bar* (Dec. 30, 1974).

219. Fogelson, *How Social Workers Perceive Lawyers,* Social Casework 55 (No. 9, Nov. 1970).

220. Fogg, *Para-legal Aides: Helping Hand or Monkey Wrench for Lawyers?* Chicago Daily News (Aug. 28, 1972).

221. Frank, *Paralegal Burnout: Challenging Work Wanted,* 70 American Bar Association Journal 30 (December, 1984).

222. Frankel, *Experiments in Serving the Indigent,* National Conference on Law and Poverty Proceedings (1965).

223. Fry, *Emerging Work of Paralegals: Florida Legal Services Paralegal Project,* 48 Florida Bar Journal 742 (Dec. 1974).

224. Fry, *The Senior Citizen Paralegal: An Advocate for the Elderly Poor,* Aging, 10–4 (Nos. 231, 232, Jan.–Feb. 1974).

225. Fry, *A Short Review of the Paralegal Movement,* 7 Clearinghouse Review 463 (No. 8, National Clearinghouse for Legal Services, Dec. 1973).

226. Fry & Hoopes, *Paralegal Careers* (Enslow Publishers, 1986).

227. Fuchs, *Legal Assistants: Rediscovered,* Pittsburgh Legal Journal 3 (June 1971).

228. Fuchs, *More Effective Use of Lay Personnel in the Law Office,* 7 Law Notes (Oct. 1970).

229. *Future of Law Assistants,* California Legal Secretary 13 (May 1969).

230. Galec, *Legal Investigator and the Administration of Justice,* 58 Judicature 134 (No. 3, Oct. 1973).

231. Gall, *Practice by Non-Lawyers Before the National Labor Relations Board,* 15 Federal Bar Journal 222 (1955).

232. Gamble, *Developing a Training Program for the Legal Secretary and Paralegal,* 19 Law Notes 7 (ABA, Winter, 1983).

233. Gellhorn, *Qualifications for Practice before Boards and Commissions,* 15 University of Cincinnati Law Review 196 (1941).

234. Genovese, *Paralegals or Paraprofessionals?* 15 Law Office Economics and Management 364 (No. 3, Fall, 1974).

235. Gerald, *Current Status of Paralegals in Law Offices of the United States as Seen by Attorneys-Lawyers, Legal Secretaries, and Paralegals with Implications for Four-Year Colleges and University Curriculums,* Doctoral Dissertation, University of So. Mississippi–Graduate School of Education (August, 1980).

236. Gilhool, *Working Together: Professional and Paraprofessional,* 14 Trial 54 (Feb. 1978).

237. Gilsinan, *Ethical Considerations in the Use of Paralegals in Your Office,* 30 St. Louis Bar Journal 14 (1983).

238. Gilsinan & Pope, *Paralegals: The Making of a Profession,* 30 St. Louis Bar Journal 6 (1983).

239. Ginsbach, *When Prisoners Become "Lawyers,"* Student Lawyer 8 (ABA, Student Lawyer Division, Sept. 1974).

240. Goldfarb, *The Emerging Legion of "Paralegals,"* Washington Post A20 (July 31, 1973).

241. *The Good Lawyer: Lawyers' Roles and Lawyers' Ethics,* D. Luban, ed. (Rowman & Allanheld, 1983).

242. Goode, *The Librarian: From Occupation to Profession,* 31 Librarian Quarterly 306 (1961).

243. Goodman, *Training the Legal Assistant for Litigation Practice in a Large Firm,* 57 New York State Bar Journal 34 (April, 1985).

244. Gorkin, *Burnout . . . There's Lots of Fodder for the Fire if You're a Paralegal,* Legal Assistant Today 22, No. 1 (Fall, 1983).

245. Gottschall, *Training Specialized "Patent Law" and "Trademark and Copyright" Legal Assistants at Montclair State College,* 3 Legal Assistants Update 55 (ABA, 1983).

246. Graham, *Educators Fear Paralawyer Proposal,* New York Times 6 (May 31, 1971).

247. Grant, *Women in the Middle: They're Not Lawyers yet They're More than Secretaries; They're Paralegals,* The Sun Magazine 5, 12 (Baltimore, Feb. 17, 1974).

248. Grapp, *Paralegal's Encyclopedic Dictionary* (Prentice-Hall, 1979).

249. Green, *You've Never Noticed Paralegals?* 6 Juris Doctor 40 (No. 2, Feb. 1976).

250. Gregson, *An Explanation of the Federation's Position on Accreditation,* 7 National Paralegal Reporter 3, No. 3 (National Federation of Paralegal Associations, Spring, 1983).

251. Griner, *The Law Office Business Manager,* 9 Law Office Economics and Management 147 (Aug. 1968).

252. Griner, *Office Manager—Anyone?* Legal Economics News 1 (No. 32, ABA Standing Committee on Economics of Law Practice, Nov. 1971).

253. Groskind, *In One Corner, the Paralegal . . . In the Other, Attorneys-at-Law: Skilled but Upstart Contenders Bid for a Share of a Traditional Area of Turf,* New England Magazine, Boston Globe 38 (Nov. 6, 1977).

254. Grosser, Henry & Kelly, *Nonprofessionals in the Human Services.*

255. Grove, *Estate Work: A Happy Hunting Ground for the Paralegal,* 19 Practical Lawyer 73 (No. 3, 1973).

256. Guinan, *The Developing Role of the Paralegal in Law Firm Administration,* 4 Legal Assistants Update 55 (ABA, 1984).

257. Guinan, *Paralegals in Administration: A Natural Progression?* 6 National Law Journal 14, col. 1 (January 2, 1984).

258. Guinan & Ferguson, *The Changing Role of Paralegals,* 40 Unauthorized Practice News 280 (No. 3, Winter, 1977).

259. Haddon, *Ethical Considerations for Paralegals and Investigators,* 5 The Colorado Lawyer 157 (February, 1976).

260. Haemmel, *Paralegals / Legal Assistants—Five Years of Development and Growth,* 79 Case and Comment 32 (No. 6, Nov.–Dec. 1974).

261. Haemmel, *Paralegal Developments in North Carolina,* 23 The North Carolina Bar 37 (No. 1, 1976).

262. Haemmel, *Paralegals / Legal Assistants: A Report of the Advances of the New Paraprofessional,* 11 American Business Law Journal 103 (Fall, 1973). See also 21 The North Carolina Bar 18 (No. 2, 1974).

263. Haemmel, *Three Paralegal Profiles,* 23 The North Carolina Bar 39 (No. 2, 1976).

264. Hamilton, *A Jailhouse Lawyer's View: Problems Posed by the Jury and Post-Conviction Litigation,* 2 Columbia Survey of Human Rights Law 131 (1969–70).

265. *Handbook on Specialization* (ABA Standing Committee on Specialization, 1983).

265a. *Handling, Preparing, Presenting or Trying Workmen's Compensation Claims or Cases as Practice of Law,* 2 American Law Reports 3d 724.

265b. Hardwick, *Wanted: The Power Paralegal,* 48 Texas Bar Journal 670 (June, 1985).

265c. Harvey, *Paralegal / Legal Assistant Recognition: An Overview of a New Career in Law,* 50 Wisconsin Bar Bulletin 21 (Dec. 1977).

265d. Haskell, *Issues in Paralegalism: Education, Certification, Licensing, Unauthorized Practice,* 15 Georgia Law Review 631 (1981).

265e. Hayden, *Paraprofessionals in a Law Office,* 44 The Hennepin Lawyer 26 (No. 5, Hennepin County Bar Association, Minneapolis, May–June 1976).

265f. Hazard, *The Ombudsman: Quasi-Legal and Legal Representation in Public Assistance Administrations,* Research Contributions of the American Bar Foundation (No. 3, 1969).

266. Hazard, *Para-Professionals in the Private Practice,* Conference on Legal Paraprofessionals, University of Washington (1966).

267. Heath, *Your Future as a Legal Assistant* (Richards Rosen Press, 1982).

268. Hedrick, *Fair Labor Standards Act and Office Administrators,* 7 Law Office Economics and Management (Feb. 1966).

269. Heller & Heller, *Paralegal Practice Handbook* (1979).

270. Hemnes, *Paralegal Profitability Analysis,* 25 Law Office Economics and Management 100 (Summer, 1984).

271. Hennessey, *Develop Legal Technicians,* 7 Law Office Economics and Management 257 (Nov. 1966).

272. Hennessey, *Partnership Agreement for the Firm with Some Lawyer Assistants,* 11 Law Office Economics and Management 571 (1971–72).

273. Hesse, *The Future Role of Legal Assistants,* The Legal Secretary 13 (May 1969).

274. Hesse, *General Practitioners and Legal Assistants: A Position Paper,* 36 Unauthorized Practice News 1 (1971).

275. Hicks & Katz, *The Practice of Law by Laymen and Lay Agencies,* 41 Yale Law Journal 69 (1931).

276. Hildebrandt & Neuhauser, *Legal Assistant Program Development Guide,* Journal of Paralegal Education, Retrospective 1983, p. 35 (American Association for Paralegal Education, 1983).

277. Hill, *The Free-Lance Legal Assistant and Ethics,* 2 Legal Assistant Today 15, No. 2 (Winter, 1985).

278. Hoffman, *Legal Skills Training for the Non-lawyer Advocate in the Public Sector,* 2 Legal Assistant Today 27, No. 1 (Fall, 1984).

279. Holme, *Paralegals and Sublegals: Aids to the Legal Profession,* 46 Denver Law Journal 392 (1969).

280. Horowitz, *Paralegal Education and Academia: Institutional Issues,* 2 Journal of Paralegal Education 1 (1985).

281. *The Hot Market for Paralegal Aides,* Business Week 86 (June 29, 1974).

282. Howard, *Control of Unauthorized Practice Before Administrative Tribunals in Missouri,* 2 Missouri Law Review 313 (1937).

283. *How Lee Turner Came to Organize His Office Along Its Present Lines,* 10 Law Office Economics and Management 99 (Aug. 1969).

284. *How Much Can Legal Assistants Write?* 17 Law Office Economics and Management 397 (Fall, 1976).

285. Huckle, *Strategies for Change: Training for New Careers,* New Careers Project, Seattle University (1969).

286. Hugg & McKay, *Classics Teach Legal Writing,* 2 Journal of Paralegal Education 13 (1985).

287. Hughes, *Employment of Para-legals in Trial Preparation,* 11 Forum 1142 (ABA, Summer, 1976).

288. Hussey, *Paralegals and the Bar: Do Paralegals Belong in the Bar?* Legal Assistant Today 12, No. 1 (Fall, 1983).

289. Hussey, *The Paralegal Profession: Here to Stay,* Legal Assistant Today 18, No. 2 (Winter, 1984).

290. Hussey, *Paralegal Turnover in the Law Firm and How to Minimize It*, 2 Legal Assistant Today 14, No. 1 (Fall, 1984).

291. Illinois State Bar Association, *Report of the Joint Study Committee on Attorney Assistants* (June 21, 1977).

292. Illinois State Bar Association, *Rules Affecting and Discipline of Attorney Assistants* (Nov. 1975).

293. Illinois State Bar Association, *Use of Attorney Assistants in Real Estate Transactions*, 72 Illinois Bar Journal 616 (August, 1984). See also 68 Illinois Bar Journal 391 (February, 1980).

294. *Income Up in Legal & Paralegal Fields*, 24 Law Office Economics and Management 531 (Winter, 1984).

295. *Income Varies Widely in Legal and Paralegal Fields*, 110 New Jersey Law Journal 3, col. 1 (November 25, 1982).

296. Institute for Paralegal Training, *Introduction to Civil Litigation* (1977).

297. Institute for Paralegal Training, *Introduction to Corporate Law* (1978).

298. Institute for Paralegal Training, *Estates and Trusts* (1979).

299. Institute for Paralegal Training, *Real Estate Law* (1978).

300. Institute for Paralegal Training, *This Is a Lawyer's Assistant* (1970).

301. Institute of Legal Executives, *Becoming a Legal Executive* (London, 1970).

302. Institute of Legal Executives, *The Legal Executive* (London, 1970).

303. *Institutions Offering Legal Assistant Education Programs*, 25 Law Office Economics and Management 115 (Summer, 1984).

304. Iowa State Bar Association, *The Role of the Legal Assistant [Paralegal] in Iowa* (1979).

305. Isaacs, *Liability of the Lawyer for Bad Advice*, 24 California Law Review 39 (1935).

306. Israel, *Standards for the Performance of Lawyers and Legal Assistants*, 27 Practical Lawyer 79 (January 15, 1981)

307. Jacob & Sharma, *Justice After Trial: Prisoners' Need for Legal Services in the Criminal-Correctional Process*, 18 University of Kansas Law Review 493, 591, 594 (1970).

308. *Jailhouse Lawyers (Training Jailhouse Paralegals)*, 14 Criminal Justice Newsletter 3 (April 11, 1983).

309. Jameson, *Private Practice Legal Assistants: Still in Need of Definition*, 19 Trial 24(6) (February, 1983).

310. Jarmel & Yegge, eds., *Legal Education Faces a New Problem; New Systems of Delivery of Legal Services* (University of Denver College of Law, 1975).

311. Jarvis, *Lawyers' Clerks*, 2 Law Society of Upper Canada Gazette (March 1968). See also 9 Law Office Economics and Management 359 (Feb. 1969).

312. Jennings, *Paralegals: Intrafirm Problems and Relationships*, 21 Law Office Economics and Management 348 (No. 3, Fall 1980).

313. Jennings & Childers, *Arizona Paralegal Salary and Job Function Survey*, 20 Law Office Economics and Management 519 (1980).

314. Jesperson, *Paralegals: Help or Hindrance?* The Houston Lawyer (March–April 1977).

315. Johnson, *Legal Assistants: Their Place in Your Law Practice,* 51 Oklahoma Bar Journal 2827 (November 29, 1980).

316. Johnson & Holz, *Legal Provisions on Expanded Functions for Dental Hygienists and Assistants: Summarized by State, 1972,* U.S. Dept. of H.E.W., Public Health Service, Health Resources Administration, DHEW Publication No. (HRA) 74–6 (July 1983).

317. Johnstone & Hopson, *Lawyers and Their Work: An Analysis of the Legal Profession in the United States and England* (1969).

318. Jones, *Why Lawyers and Clients Need Trained Legal Assistants,* 15 Law Office Economics and Management 333 (No. 3, Fall 1974).

319. *The Judicial Response to Lawyer Misconduct* (ABA Standing Committee on Professional Discipline, 1984–_).

320. *The Judicial Role in Lawyer Discipline* (ABA Standing Committee on Professional Discipline, 1983).

321. Kacen, *Legal Assistant: New Career in the Making,* Occupational Outlook Quarterly (U.S. Dept. of Labor, Fall 1975).

322. Kadushin, *Games People Play in Supervision,* 13 Social Work 23 (No. 3, July 1968).

323. Kaiser, *Promoting a New Field: The Educator's Role,* 2 Journal of Paralegal Education 1, No. 1 (American Association for Paralegal Education, October, 1984).

324. Kalinowski, *Utilization of Office Staff: Trial and Litigation,* Proceedings of the Fourth National Conference on Law Office Economics (1970).

325. Kall, Kenner, & Holme, *Are Communications with a Paralegal Privileged?* 9 Colorado Lawyer 517 (March 1980).

326. *Kansas City Bar Association and Kansas City Association of Legal Assistants: Resource Manual* (Oct. 1980).

327. Kasic, *Under the Supervision of a Lawyer,* 9 Facts & Findings 7, No. 5 (National Association of Legal Assistants, March–April, 1983).

328. Kaufman, *The Judicial Crisis, Court Delay and the Para-Judge,* 54 Judicature 145 (1970).

329. Kaufman, *The Source and Training of Paraprofessionals,* 12 Law Office Economics and Management 63 (June 1971).

330. Keaton, *Recognition and Opportunity: The Genesis for a Growing Profession [Legal Assistant Division of State Bar of Texas]* 10 Facts & Findings 13, No. 6 (National Association of Legal Assistants, May–June, 1984).

331. Kiernan, *Paralegals' Profession New, But Flourishes Across Nation,* Washington Post C2 (Dec. 2, 1979).

332. Kissim, *Physician's Assistant and Nurse Practitioner Laws: A Study of Health Law Reform,* 24 Kansas Law Review 1 (1975).

333. Klessig, *Utilization of Legal Assistants in the Private Law Firm,* 58 Wisconsin Bar Bulletin 33 (July, 1985).

334. Kotlikoff, *Paralegal's Complaint,* Pennsylvania Gazette (May 1975).

335. Kurlander & Wilson, *The Paralegal's Role in Law Office Efficiency,* 17 Trial 24 (March, 1981).

336. Kurzmand & Gilbert, *Paralegals and Successful Law Practice* (Institute for Business Planning, 1981).

337. Lander, *Legal Assistants: The Experience of the Legal Aid Society of the City and County of St. Louis,* 6 Clearinghouse Review 663 (National Clearinghouse for Legal Services, 1973).

338. Langer, *The Wage and Hour Issue: Exempt vs. Non-Exempt,* 6 National Paralegal Reporter 2, No. 3 (National Federation of Paralegal Associations, Summer, 1982).

339. Langford, *Paraprofessional Power! Case Histories of Legal Assistants and How They Function to Aid Lawyers,* 2 Lawyers' World 30 (Sept.–Oct. 1971).

340. Larbalestrier, *Paralegal Practice and Procedure* (Prentice-Hall, 1977).

341. Larson, *Institutions Offering ABA Approved Legal Assistant Education Programs,* 4 Legal Assistants Update 93 (ABA, 1984).

342. Larson, *Legal Paraprofessionals: Cultivation of a New Field,* 59 American Bar Association Journal 631 (June 1973).

343. Larson & Templeton, *Job Satisfaction of Legal Assistants,* Journal of Paralegal Education, Retrospective 1983, p. 161 (American Association for Paralegal Education, 1983). See also Legal Assistant Update '80.

344. *Law Clerks and the Unauthorized Practice of Law,* 46 Chicago-Kent Law Review 214 (1969).

345. *Lawyers' Professional Liability Update* (ABA Standing Committee on Lawyers' Professional Liability, 1984).

346. Lawyers Committee for Civil Rights Under Law, *Report on the Mississippi Conference on Legal Paraprofessionals,* Office of Economic Opportunity, Office of Legal Services and Dixwell Legal Rights Association (April 1971).

347. *Lay Assistant as Paraprofessional,* 10 Law Office Economics and Management 7 (1969).

348. Lay, *A Trial Lawyer Speaks to the Investigator,* 20 The Practical Lawyer 59 (No. 1, Jan. 1974).

349. *Layman's Assistance to Party in Divorce Proceeding as Unauthorized Practice of Law,* 12 American Law Reports 4th 656.

350. LeClair, McFarland, & Shapiro, *Legal Assistant Programs: A Guide to Effective Program Implementation and Maintenance* (1978).

351. Lee, *Some Comments on the National Paralegal Institute's Memorandum on Credentialing and Licensing Paralegals and Paralegal Training,* 6 Clearinghouse Review 668 (1973).

352. Lee, *The Training of Nonprofessional Personnel,* 6 Nursing Outlook 222 (1958).

353. *Legal Aides for Busy Lawyers,* Business Week 62 (Dec. 26, 1970).

354. Legal Assistant Committee, *Annual Report,* 48 Florida Bar Journal 377 (May 1974).

355. *"Legal Assistant" on Business Card,* 12 Law Office Economics and Management 591 (1972).

356. *Legal Employees' Salaries in New York,* Law Office Economics and Management 74 (May 1966).

357. *Legal Ethics: An Annotated Bibliography and Resource Guide* by Elliston & van Schaick (Rothman, 1984).

358. *Legal Malpractice* by R. Mallen & V. Levit (West, 1977).

359. *Legal Paraprofessionals and Unauthorized Practice,* 8 Harvard Civil Rights and Civil Liberties Law Review 104 (1973).

360. Legal Services Corporation, *Survey of Utilization of Paralegal Education Programs in Legal Service Programs* (Oct. 1976).

361. *The Legal Technician Program in Cumberland County,* 14 New Jersey State Bar Journal (Fall 1970).

362. *Legal Worker Certification Hearing, Guild Statement,* 4 Guild Notes 27 (No. 3, National Lawyers Guild, May 1975).

363. *Legalized Denturism: Consumer Demand, Public Health, and the Legislative Response,* 74 Northwest University Law Review 97 (March, 1979).

364. *Legislative Attempts to Broaden Lay Practice in the Courts and Restrict Lawyers,* 39 Unauthorized Practice News 210 (1975).

365. Lehan, *Ethical Considerations of Employing Paralegals in Florida,* 52 Florida Bar Journal 14 (Jan. 1979).

366. Lehner, *Jailhouse Lawyers: More Prison Inmates Turn to Legal Work for Selves and Others,* The Wall Street Journal 1 (Nov. 20, 1974).

367. Lerner, *Paralegal Paranoia? Do Paraprofessionals Threaten Your Economic Future?* 4 Student Lawyer 8 (1975).

368. Levine, Simon, & Boudreau, *Employment of Para-legal Service by the College Student for the Indigent Defendant: Two Pilot Pre-Law Projects,* 24 Louisiana Bar Journal 41 (July, 1976).

369. Lewis, *The Use of Legal Assistants in the Plaintiff's Personal Injury Case,* 16 Trial 88 (July, 1980).

370. Lickson, *Paralegals May Be Link to Computer Revolution,* 7 Legal Times 25, col. 1 (April 22, 1985).

371. *Life Insurance Company Issues Warning on Do-It-Yourself Law Books,* 39 Unauthorized Practice News 151 (No. 2, ABA Standing Committee on Unauthorized Practice of Law, Spring–Summer 1975).

372. Littleton, *Recruiting and Retaining Paralegals,* 4 Legal Assistants Update 47 (ABA, 1984).

373. Lockwood, *The Role of the Paralegal in the Civil Commitment Process,* 10 Capital University Law Review 721 (Summer, 1981).

374. Los Angeles County Bar Association, *Survey on Training and Employment of Legal Paraprofessionals* (June 15, 1971).

375. Los Angeles Paralegal Association, *Job Hunting Handbook* (1980).

376. Ludvigsen, *Will Paralegals Bring Better Service or Just More Profit?* Student Lawyer (January, 1975).

377. Lundquist, *Law Offfice Employees and the Fair Labor Standards Act,* 6 Law Office Economics and Management 157 (August, 1965).

378. Lupo, *Paraprofessionals . . . Legal Technology Legal Assistants . . . What's in a Name,* 28 Missouri Bar Journal 120 (1972).

379. Lybarger, *Retention of Paralegals in Legal Service Programs: Initial Statement of the Problem,* 11 Clearinghouse Review 858 (1978).

380. Mack, *California Paralegal Handbook* (1977).

381. Maedgen, *Effective Utilization of the Legal Assistant in Litigation,* 44 Texas Bar Journal 989 (September, 1981).

382. *Maine Department of Corrections Adopts New Rules on Visits by Attorneys and Paraprofessionals and on Access of News Media to Correctional Facilities,* 3 Prison Law Reporter 242, No. 8 (August, 1974).

383. Major, *Code of Ethics: Ideals of a Profession? Or Legally Enforceable Law?* 7 National Paralegal Reporter 6, No. 3 (National Federation of Paralegal Associations, Spring, 1983).

384. Malone, *Legal Assistant / Legal Secretary: Friend or Foe?* Legal Assistant Today 19, No. 4 (Summer, 1984).

385. Manikas, *A Paralegal Is Not a Lawyer in a Wheelchair,* Manpower (October, 1975).

386. *Manual For Managing the Law Office,* paragraph 9311: "How to Develop Legal Assistants in Your Office," paragraph 9321: "How to Effectively Train Your Legal Assistants," paragraph 9331: "Take Your Legal Assistant to Trial" (Prentice-Hall, 1980).

387. Manville, *Prisoners' Self-Help Litigation Manual,* Rev. Second Edition (Oceana, 1983).

388. Marbut, "How a Legal Assistant Can Function in a Law Office," *Manual for Managing the Law Office* 9325 (Prentice-Hall, 1980).

389. Marguardt, *Running with the Hares and Chasing the Hounds: The Emerging Dilemma in Paralegal Mobility,* 2 Journal of Paralegal Education 57, No. 1 (American Association for Paralegal Education, October, 1984).

390. Marshall, *The Paralegal Phenomenon: A New Approach,* 9 Pro Bono Report 4 (1973).

391. Massachusetts Bar Association, *Report of the Committee on Paralegals* (1978–79).

392. Mayer, *The Lawyers* (Harper & Row, 1967).

393. McCord, *The American Association for Paralegal Education: A New and Important Voice in the Paralegal Movement,* Legal Assistant Today 22 (Spring, 1984).

394. McCord, *Paralegals: Are You Missing a Good Opportunity?* 44 Kentucky Bench & Bar 24 (April, 1980).

395. McGee, *Lay Advocacy and "Legal Services to Youth:" Summaries on the Use of Paralegal Aides,* 47 Journal of Urban Law 127 (1969).

396. McMenamin, *Dawn of the Age of the Legal Assistant,* 59 American Bar Association Journal 1448 (December, 1973).

397. McMenamin, *Lawyer Associate and Legal Assistant—An Economic Boon,* Oregon State Bar Bulletin 10 (February, 1976).

398. McMenamin, *Legal Assistants,* Oregon State Bar Bulletin 31 (April, 1971). See also 12 Law Office Economics and Management 537 (March, 1972).

399. Melo, *Sexual Harassment in the Work Place: A Flirtation with Liability*, 45 Texas Bar Journal, No. 6 (May, 1982). Reprinted in 9 Facts & Findings 4, No. 1 (National Association of Legal Assistants, 1982).

400. Merzon, *The Status of Legal Assistants in Law Practice: A Cameo Survey*, 10 Facts & Findings 10, No. 1 (National Association of Legal Assistants, July–August, 1983).

401. Merzon, *Survey: Utilization of Legal Assistants*, Michigan Bar Journal 645 (October, 1979).

402. Meyer & Wilson, *Legal Education in the Jailhouse: An Appraisal*, 2 New England Journal on Prison Law 99 (1976).

403. Minnesota Association of Legal Assistants, *Survey Results* (December, 1975).

404. *Minnesota Bar Wins Sweeping Victory Against a Lay Practitioner of Divorce Law*, 39 Unauthorized Practice News 187 (1975).

405. *Model Rules of Professional Conduct and Code of Judicial Conduct* (ABA, 1983–_).

406. Montgomery-Campbell, *The Recruitment and Training of Unadmitted Staff*, Law Society Gazette 242 (1968).

407. Moon, Lashinger & Redic, *Paralegal Malpractice: New Profession, New Responsibility*, 18 Trial 40 (January, 1982). See also 6 National Paralegal Reporter 1, No. 2 (National Federation of Paralegal Associations, Spring, 1982).

408. *More on Divorce Kits*, 39 Unauthorized Practice News 116 (1975).

409. Morrison, *Clerks and Clients: Paraprofessional Roles and Cultural Identities in Indian Litigation*, 9 Law & Society Review 39 (Fall, 1974).

410. Moya, *"Paralegals" Bilked Us: Kansas Charge: Anti-Tax Group Advised How to Beat the IRS*, 2 National Law Journal 5 (February 4, 1980).

411. Moye, *The Law of Business Organizations*, 2d ed. (West, 1982).

412. Muckelstone, *Estate Practice Planning: A Team Approach for Lawyers and Legal Assistants*, 7 Legal Economics 35, No. 6 (November–December, 1981).

413. Mucklestone, *The Legal Assistant in Estate Planning*, 10 Real Property, Probate & Trial Journal 263 (Summer, 1975).

414. Mulligan & Grabert, *Legal Assistants in Probate Administration*, 30 St. Louis Bar Journal 28 (1983).

415. Murry, *Slugging It Out for Justice: Rosemary Furman v. The Florida Bar*, Legal Assistant Today 20, No. 4 (Summer, 1984).

416. Murry, *Team Practice That Works: Putting an End to the Feeling of "Us and Them" in the Law Office*, 2 Legal Assistant Today 28, No. 3 (Spring, 1985).

417. Nassif, *Use of In-House Legal Assistants in Litigation*, 30 St. Louis Bar Journal 36 (1983).

418. National Association of Attorneys General, Committee on the Office of Attorney General, *Use of Paralegal Personnel* (February, 1974).

419. National Association of Legal Assistants, *Manual for Legal Assistants* (West, 1979).

420. National Association of Legal Assistants, *NALA Model Guidelines for Legal Assistants*, 2 Legal Assistant Today 11, No. 2 (Winter, 1985).

421. National Capital Area Paralegal Association, *The Paralegal Job-Hunting Handbook* (1977).

422. National Federation of Paralegal Associations, *The Formation of Paralegal Associations: An Organizational Manual* (1978).

423. National Federation of Paralegal Associations, *The National Directory of Paralegal Training Programs* (1980).

424. National Federation of Paralegal Associations, *1982 Analysis of State Bar Activities in the Paralegal Profession,* 3 Legal Assistants Update 59 (ABA, 1983).

425. National Paralegal Institute, *The Credentialing and Licensing of Paralegals and Paralegal Training,* 6 Clearinghouse Review 664 (1973).

426. National Paralegal Institute, *Introduction to Paralegal Systems,* 9 Clearinghouse Review 534 (1975).

427. National Paralegal Institute, *The Significance of Paralegals in the Legal Service System* (1975).

428. National Paralegal Institute, *Unauthorized Practice of Law by Paralegals,* 9 Clearinghouse Review 21 (1975).

429. *National Reporter on Legal Ethics and Professional Responsibility* (Univ. Publications of America, 1983–_).

430. Nemeth & the American Institute for Paralegal Studies, *Paralegal Handbook: Theory, Practice, and Materials* (Prentice-Hall, 1986).

431. New Hampshire Bar Association, *Guidelines for the Utilization by Lawyers of the Services of Legal Assistants* (1977).

432. New York State Bar Association, Committee on Professional Ethics, *Guidelines for the Utilization by Lawyers of the Service of Legal Assistants* (1976).

433. *NFPA / NALA Focus: Two Perspectives,* 3 Legal Assistants Update 101 (ABA, 1983).

434. Nichols & Kirk, *The Use of Legal Assistants in the Small Law Firm,* Arizona Bar Journal 36 (October, 1978).

435. North Carolina State Bar, *Report of Special Committee on Paralegals* (1980).

436. Norton, *Toward Efficiency; Work Flow Legal Assistant; the Legal Assistant Investigator,* 10 Trial 25 (No. 5, September–October, 1974).

437. *Notre Dame Journal of Law, Ethics & Public Policy* (1984–_).

438. Office of New Careers, U.S. Department of Health, Education and Welfare, *A Summary: Paraprofessional Training in Colleges and Universities* (1970–71).

439. *Office Manager's Name on Letterhead,* Ohio State Bar Association Report, 7 Law Office Economics and Management 450 (February, 1967).

440. Ohio Bar Association, *Report of the Special Committee on Paralegal Training,* 18 Ohio Bar 553 (April, 1975).

441. *On Licensing Accounting Technicians,* Journal of Accountancy 37 (May, 1969).

442. *On the Question of Negligence: The Paraprofessional,* 4 University of Toledo Law Review 553 (1973).

443. *Operations of Collection Agency as Unauthorized Practice of Law,* 27 American Law Reports 3d 1152.

444. Oran, *Law Dictionary for Non-Lawyers* (West, 1978).

445. Oregon State Bar, *Certification Board for Legal Assistants (1978)*.

446. Oregon State Bar, Committee on Continuing Legal Education, Oregon Achievement in Continuing Legal Education, *Probate Manual, Legal Assistants* (1973).

447. Oregon State Bar, Legal Assistants Committee, *Legal Assistant Survey* (1979).

448. Orenstein, *Can a Paralegal Clear More than $15,000 a Year—For You (the Small Firm)*, 4 National Law Journal 14, col. 2 (March 1, 1982).

449. Orenstein, *Delegating Effectively to a Paralegal,* 10 Legal Economics 51 (ABA, January–February, 1984).

450. Orlik, *Ethics for the Legal Assistant* (Scott, Foresman, 1986).

451. Orlik, *The Unauthorized Practice of Law and the Legal Assistant,* 2 Journal of Paralegal Education 120 (1985).

452. Otterbourg, *A Study of the Unauthorized Practice of Law* (1951).

453. Packer & Ehrlich, "Paraprofessionalism: The Emergence of Allied Careers," *New Directions in Legal Education,* 15 (Report for the Carnegie Commission on Higher Education; McGraw-Hill, 1973).

454. Palmer, *Police Paraprofessional: An Alternative to the Police Legal Advisory,* 40 The Police Chief 56, No. 12 (December, 1973).

455. *Paralegal Assistants,* Hearing Before the Subcommittee on Representation of Citizen Interests of the Committee on the Judiciary, U.S. Senate, 93rd Congress, Second Session (July 23, 1974).

456. *Paralegal Code Adopted as Court Rule,* Kentucky Bench and Bar 30 (October, 1979) (Rule 3.700).

457. *Paralegals: A Selective Bibliography* (U.S. Dept. of Justice, Law Enforcement Assistance Administration, National Institute of Law Enforcement and Criminal Justice, 1978).

458. . . .*Paralegals Boost Income for Firms*. . ., 57 Ohio State Bar Association Report 828(5) (July 2, 1984).

459. *Paralegal Fees Recoverable in Antitrust Cases,* 110 New Jersey Law Journal 32, col. 3 (August 26, 1982).

460. *Paramedics and the Medical Manpower Shortage: The Case for Statutory Legitimation,* 60 Georgetown Law Journal 157 (1971).

461. *Paraprofessional Parent-Aides and Disadvantaged Families,* Social Casework (April, 1974).

462. Parness, *The Parajudge: Oiling the Wheels of Justice,* Trial Magazine 54 (March/April 1974).

463. Parrish, *The Legal Secretary and the Lawyer,* 29 The Alabama Lawyer 209 (1968).

464. Pasquesi, *Putting the Paralegal to Work,* 17 Practical Lawyer 29 (October, 1971).

465. Payton, *Law Office Personnel and Legal Ethics,* 48 Florida Bar Journal 747 (December, 1974).

466. Payton, *Use and Function of a Legal Assistant,* 48 Florida Bar Journal 277 (1977).

467. Peeples, *Unionization: Raising the Issue,* 6 National Paralegal Reporter 4, No. 3 (National Federation of Paralegal Associations, Summer, 1982).

468. Pener, *Results of Survey of Legal Assistant Programs,* Journal of Paralegal Education, Retrospective 1983, p. 9 (American Association for Paralegal Education, 1983).

469. Pennsylvania Bar Association, Professional Guidance Committee and Unauthorized Practice of Law Committee, *Report on Use of Paralegals* (1980).

470. Perko, *Paralegals in the Federal Government,* 4 Legal Assistants Update 75 (ABA, 1984).

471. Phelon, *The Legal Technology Program in Cumberland County Three Years Later,* New Jersey State Bar Journal 22, No. 64 (August, 1973).

472. Philadelphia Association of Paralegals, *Report on Salaries and Benefits of Philadelphia Paralegals* (1976).

473. *Physician's Assistant,* 24 Vanderbilt Law Review 1193 (November, 1971).

474. *The Physician's Assistant and the Problem of Statutory Authorization,* 7 University of California Davis Law Review 413 (1974).

475. Piazza, *Fee-Shifting Statutes and Paralegal Services,* 2 Journal of Paralegal Education 141 (1985).

476. Pierce & Wang, *A Review of Educational Programs for Legal Assistants,* 33 Journal of Missouri Bar 432 (October–November, 1977).

477. Pollock, *How Paralegals Pay Off Big,* 5 American Lawyer 7(3) (March, 1983).

478. Polsinelli, *Bar Association Involvement in the Paralegal Profession: Helpful or Harmful?* 6 National Paralegal Reporter 4, No. 2 (National Federation of Paralegal Associations, Spring, 1982).

479. Polsinelli, *Certification Proposed in South Dakota,* 7 National Paralegal Reporter 12, No. 3 (National Federation of Paralegal Associations, Spring, 1983).

480. *Position Paper of the Illinois State Bar Association,* approved by the Board of Governors, May 16, 1984).

481. *A Practical Guide to Preventing Legal Malpractice* by D. Stern & J. Felix-Retzke (Shepard's/McGraw-Hill, 1983).

482. *Practical Issues of Professional Responsibility in the Practice of Law* (Boston, Legal-Medical Studies, Inc., 1984–_).

483. *The Practical Lawyer's Manual on Lawyer-Client Relations* (ALI-ABA Committee on Cont. Prof. Ed., 1983).

484. *Practice by Laymen,* 15 Federal Bar Journal 227 (1955).

485. Practicing Law Institute, *The Lawyer's Assistant 1976: A Workshop for the Law Office Administrator, Paraprofessional, and Secretary, Course Handbook* (1976).

486. Prendergast, *Secretary to Paralegal: A Career Manual and Guide* (Institute for Business Planning, 1984).

487. Prescott, *Legal Paraprofessionals,* 48 Los Angeles Bar Bulletin 132 (1973).

488. Pressly, *Probating Estates Without Legal Counsel: Florida Courts Issue Guidelines,* 39 Unauthorized Practice News 128 (ABA, Spring–Summer, 1975).

489. *Privilege as to Communications between Lay Representative in Judicial or Administrative Proceedings and Client,* 31 American Law Reports 4th 1226.

490. *Procunier v. Martinez . . . Permits Law Students and Legal Paraprofessionals to Assist Prisoners,* 39 Unauthorized Practice News 71 (ABA, Fall–Winter, 1974).

491. *Profiling the Typical Legal Administrator,* 60 American Bar Association Journal 968 (August, 1974).

492. *Progress in Tennessee: The Report of the 1972 Economic Survey of the Bar of Tennessee,* 8 Tennessee Bar Journal 74 (1972). (This report states that the income of lawyers using Paralegals was almost 50% higher than when they were not in use.)

493. Promislo, "The Legal Paraprofessional," *Management Systems for Small and Medium Size Law Firms,* 65 (Practicing Law Institute, 1971).

494. Promislo, *Personnel: Paralegals,* 10 Trial 32, No. 5 (September–October, 1974).

495. *Public Sector Paralegalism in Canada Today,* National Workshop on Paralegalism, Vancouver (Department of Justice of Canada, National Legal Aid Research Centre, 1979).

496. Ragle & Zablock, *Legal Assistants: A New Outlook,* 189 New Jersey Law Journal 4, col. 1 (January 4, 1983).

497. Ranii, *Court Backs Paralegal Fees in Antitrust Case,* 4 National Law Journal 2, col. 3 (August 2, 1982).

498. Rasmussen, *Arsenic and Old Castings—or Why Is She Here and What Does She Do?* 20 Law Office Economics and Management 321 (1979).

499. *Recent Survey of Legal Assistant Training Courses,* 42 Legal Economic News 1 (ABA, Standing Committee on Economics of Law Practice, July, 1983).

500. Reidy, *Court Extends Privilege Rule to Defense's Polygrapher,* 183 New York Law Journal 1, col. 2 (June 2, 1980).

501. Reisner, *Legal Assistants: New Future for the Practice of Law,* 48 Wisconsin Bar Bulletin 7 (August, 1975).

502. *Remedies Available to Combat the Unauthorized Practice of Law,* 62 Columbia Law Review 501 (1962).

503. *Report to the Membership on Legal Assistants,* Oregon State Bar Bulletin (July, 1973).

504. *Representation of Another Before State Public Utilities or Service Commission as Involving Practice of Law,* 13 American Law Reports 3d 812.

505. Reskin, *Paralegals Average $14,400 to Start, Bring Profits to Firm,* 70 American Bar Association Journal 52 (December, 1984).

506. *The Resource: A Pro Bono Manual,* E. Lardent, ed. (ABA, 1983).

507. *Restrictive Licensing of Dental Paraprofessionals,* 83 Yale Law Journal 806 (March, 1974).

508. *Revitalization of the Legal Profession Through Paralegalism,* 30 Baylor Law Review 841 (Fall, 1978).

509. *A Revolution in White—New Approaches in Treating Nurses as Professionals,* 30 Vanderbilt Law Review 839 (1977).

510. Revzin, *More Services Are Performed by Paralegals; Attorneys Have Mixed Feelings about Trend,* Wall Street Journal 38, col. 11 (November 14, 1975).

511. *Right of an Executor to Probate an Estate Without an Attorney,* 39 Unauthorized Practice News 123 (Spring–Summer, 1975).

512. Rivkind, *Paralegal: A Storm Petrel,* 48 Florida Bar Journal 745 (December, 1974).

513. Robinson, *Appearances by Laymen in a Representative Capacity Before Administrative Bodies,* 5 Law and Contemporary Problems 89 (1938).

514. Rocky Mountain Legal Assistants Association, *Employment Handbook for Legal Assistants* (1979).

515. Rocky Mountain Legal Assistants Association, *Salary Questionnaire Analysis* (1976).

516. Rocky Mountain Legal Assistants Association, *The Use of the Legal Assistant* (1975).

517. *The Role of the Nonlawyer in Estate Planning,* 36 Unauthorized Practice News 1 (November, 1971).

518. *Role of Paralegals in Real Estate Transactions,* 68 Illinois Bar Journal 391 (February, 1980).

519. Rollins, *What Is a Legal Assistant?* (definition for purposes of membership in the Legal Assistant Division of the State Bar of Texas), 46 Texas Bar Journal 77 (January, 1983).

520. Ronayne, *Law School Training for Non-Lawyer Judges,* 17 Journal of Legal Education 197 (1964).

521. Rose, *Developing a Pattern for Paralegal Use,* Legal Economics 40 (ABA, Spring, 1977).

522. Ruddy, *Illinois Attorney Assistant Guidelines,* Illinois Bar Journal (November, 1977).

523. Ryan, *Use of Lay Assistants by Larger Law Firms,* Legal Economic News, No. 20 (April, 1969).

524. *Sale of Books or Forms Designed to Enable Laymen to Achieve Legal Results Without Assistance of Lawyer as Unauthorized Practice of Law,* 71 American Law Reports 3d 1000.

525. Sanders, *Volunary Certification for Legal Assistants,* 45 Texas Bar Journal 968 (July, 1982).

526. San Francisco Association of Legal Assistants, *Survey, 1978: A Comprehensive Study of the Status of Legal Assistants in San Francisco* (1978).

527. Sapadin, *A Comparison of the Growth and Development of the Physician Assistant and Legal Assistant,* Journal of Paralegal Education, Retrospective 1983, p. 137 (American Association for Paralegal Education, 1983).

528. Savino, *Prefessionalization of the Paralegal—Quo Vadis?* Public Sector Paralegalism in Canada Today, 55 (Department of Justice of Canada, National Legal Research Centre, 1979).

529. Schrader & Knight, *Task Analysis for Legal Assistant Program* (1977) (Lakeshore Technical Institute, 1290 North Avenue, Cleveland, WS 53015).

530. Schrader, *Legal Assistant Education,* 41 Alabama Lawyer 120 (January, 1980).

531. Schwartz, *Paraprofessionals and Law Librarianship: A Preliminary Perspective,* 66 Law Library Journal 3 (1973).

532. *Selected Checklist of Materials on Paralegals / Legal Assistants,* 33 The Record of the Association of the Bar of the City of New York 91 (January/February, 1978).

533. Selinger, *Functional Division of the American Legal Profession: The Legal Paraprofessional,* 22 Journal of Legal Education 22 (1969).

534. *Services in Connection with Tax Matters as Practice of Law,* 9 American Law Reports 2d 797.

535. Shapiro, *The Recent and Projected Activities of the American Bar Association Standing Committee on Legal Assistants,* 4 Legal Assistants Update 87 (ABA, 1984).

536. Shapiro, *Teamwork in Legal Profession,* 2 Facts and Findings 1, No. 7 (National Association of Legal Assistants, May, 1976).

537. Shayne, *The Paralegal Profession: A Career Guide* (Oceana, 1977).

538. Sheehy, *Attorney-Client Privilege and the Paralegal,* 6 National Paralegal Reporter 1, No. 1 (National Federation of Paralegal Associations, Fall/Winter, 1981).

539. Sheehy, *Attorney-Client Privilege: Expanding or Narrowing?,* 6 National Paralegal Reporter 1, No. 3 (National Federation of Paralegal Associations, Summer, 1982).

540. Shimberg, Esser, & Kruger, *Occupational Licensing: Practices and Policies, A Report of the Educational Testing Service* (Public Affairs Press, 1973).

541. Shipp, *The Recruitment of Minority Students, Faculty and Advisory Board Members,* Journal of Paralegal Education, Retrospective 1983, p. 85 (American Association for Paralegal Education, 1983).

542. *Should the ABA or Anyone Be Involved in Approving or Accrediting Paralegal Training Programs?* Legal Assistant Today 14, No. 3 (Spring, 1984).

543. Shuey, *CBA Legal Assistants' Committee Survey Report,* 9 The Colorado Lawyer 482, No. 3 (March, 1980).

544. Shuman, *Some Observations on the Regulation of Paralegal Activities,* Arizona Bar Journal 44 (May, 1979).

545. Silas, *Legal Assistants Can Join St. Louis Bar,* 10 Bar Leader 26 (January–February, 1985).

546. Silas, *A Risky Stand-in? Paralegals at Realty Closings,* 69 American Bar Association Journal 1812 (December, 1982).

547. Simon, *Paralegals: The Hottest Job Market,* 5 National Law Journal 1, col. 4 (July 4, 1983).

548. Sliters, *Legal Assistant and Lawyer: The Team Approach,* 93 Los Angeles Daily Journal 2 (March 2, 1980).

549. Smith, *Legal Paraprofessionals: Assistants or Assassins,* 47 Florida Bar Journal 649 (1974).

550. Smith, *Physician Extenders: Their Current and Future Role in Medical Care Delivery* (Congressional Budget Office, 1979).

551. Smith, *Law Office Personnel in the Eighties,* 54 Florida Bar Journal 74 (January, 1980).

552. Smith, *Vertical Expansion of the Legal Service Team,* 56 American Bar Association Journal 664 (July, 1970).

553. Sparer, Torkelson, & Weiss, *The Lay Advocate,* 43 University of Detroit Law Journal 493 (1966).

544. Sproul, *Use of Lay Personnel in the Practice of Law: Mid-1965,* 25 Business Lawyer 11 (1969).

555. Sproul, *Training Legal Assistants in Computer Technology,* 3 Legal Assistants Update 23 (ABA, 1983).

556. Stahl & Smith, *Paralegal Services and Awards of Attorney Fees Under Arizona Law,* 20 Arizona Bar Journal 21(6) (October–November, 1984).

557. Stanton, *Paralegal Putdowns,* 4 Student Lawyer 6, No. 3 (November, 1975).

558. State Bar of New Mexico, *Guidelines for the Use of Legal Assistant Services* (1980).

559. Statsky & Wernet, *Case Analysis and Fundamentals of Legal Writing, 2d* (West, 1984).

560. Statsky, *The Education of Legal Paraprofessionals: Myths, Realities, and Opportunities,* 24 Vanderbilt Law Review 1083 (November, 1971).

561. Statsky, *Family Law, 2d ed,* (West, 1984).

562. Statsky, *Inmate Involvement in Prison Legal Services: Roles and Training Options for the Inmate as Paralegal* (ABA, Resource Center on Correctional Law and Legal Services, 1974).

563. Statsky, *The Jailhouse Lawyer,* America Illustrated (United States Information Agency, 1975).

564. Statsky, *Community Courts: Decentralization of Juvenile Jurisprudence,* 3 Capital University Law Review 1 (1974).

565. Statsky & Lang, *The Legal Paraprofessional as Advocate and Assistant: Roles, Training Concepts and Materials,* reprinted in A Compilation of Materials for the Legal Assistant and the Lay Advocate (National Clearinghouse for Legal Services, 1971).

566. Statsky, *Legal Research, Writing, and Analysis: Some Starting Points, 3d ed* (West, 1986).

567. Statsky, *Legal Thesaurus / Dictionary: A Resource for the Writer and Computer Researcher* (West, 1985).

568. Statsky, *Legislative Analysis and Drafting, 2d ed* (West, 1984).

569. Statsky, *Paralegals: A New Career in Law,* 1 Technical Education Reporter 65 (September–October, 1974).

570. Statsky, *Paralegal Advocacy Before Administrative Agencies,* 4 University of Toledo Law Review 439 (1973).

571. Statsky, *Paralegals: Developments in the 1970s,* Conference on Legal Aid: Report and Proceeding, 37 (Canadian Council on Social Development, 1975).

572. Statsky, *Paralegals in the United States,* Public Sector Paralegalism in Canada Today, National Workshop on Paralegalism, Vancouver (Department of Justice of Canada, National Legal Aid Research Centre, 1979).

573. Statsky, *Paraprofessionals: Expanding the Legal Service Delivery Team,* 24 Journal of Legal Education 397 (1972).

574. Statsky, *Teaching Advocacy: Learner-Focused Training for Paralegals, 2d ed* (National Paralegal Institute, 1974).

575. Statsky, *Teaching Corrections Law to Corrections Personnel,* 37 Federal Probation 42 (June, 1973).

576. Statsky, *Techniques for Supervising Paralegals,* 22 Practical Lawyer 81 (June, 1976).

577. Statsky, *The Training of Community Judges: Rehabilitative Adjudication,* 4 Columbia Human Rights Law Review 401 (1972).

578. Stein & Hoff, *Paralegals and Administrative Assistants for Prosecutors* (National District Attorneys Association, November, 1974).

579. Stein, *Paralegals: A Resource for Public Defenders and Correctional Services* (U.S. Government Printing Office, No. 027-000-00399-1; December, 1976).

580. Stein, Hoff, & White, *Paralegal Workers in Criminal Justice Agencies: An Exploratory Study* (Blackstone Associates, September, 1973).

581. Sternin, *Ten Most Frequently Asked Questions About Paralegals,* Legal Economics (Winter, 1978).

582. Sternin, *Your Secretary: Paralegal in Disguise,* 88 Case & Comment 12 (July–August, 1983).

583. Stevenson, *Paraprofessional Worker Eases Job for Professional,* 17 Occupational Outlook, No. 3 (Fall, 1973).

584. Stevenson, *Using Paralegals in the Practice of Law,* 62 Illinois Bar Journal 432 (1974).

585. *Strict Requirements May Stifle England's New Conveyancing Profession,* 59 Law Institute Journal 81 (January–February, 1985).

586. Strong, *Are You Putting It All Together? Rate Your Legal Assistants,* 10 Trial 61, No. 5 (September–October, 1974).

587. Strong, *In-Office Training of Legal Assistants: Why and How,* 79 Case and Comment 38 (March–April, 1974).

588. Strong & Clark, *Law Office Management* (West, 1974).

589. Strong, *Legal Assistants: A Realistic Approach to Their Training and Utilization* (University of Utah, Utah Law Research Institute, 1973).

590. Strong, *Legal Assistant Systems,* 48 Florida Bar Journal 649 (October, 1974).

591. Strong & Henderson, *Legal Assistants: The Systems Approach,* 15 Law Office Economics and Management 344, No. 3 (Fall, 1974).

592. Strong, *The Right/Wrong Way to Use Legal Assistants,* 16 Law Office Economics and Management 1 (1975).

593. Strong, "Small Law Firms", *The Utilization of Legal Assistants by Law Firms in the United States: Liberating the Lawyer* (ABA, June, 1971).

594. Strong, *Use of Legal Assistants; Rating the Management Effectiveness of Your Office,* 21 Practical Lawyer 69, 77, No. 5 (July 15, 1975).

595. *Study of Paralegal Utilization in the California Attorney General's Office,* Management Analysis Section, California Department of Justice (December, 1980).

596. Sullivan & Brooks, *From Partners to Paralegals: Modernizing the Personnel Mix: More Efficient Support Staff Means Firm Can Add More Partners Sooner,* 2 California Lawyer 19(2) (July–August, 1982).

597. *Survey of Lawyer Disciplinary Procedures in the United States* (ABA Center for Professional Responsibility, 1984–_).

598. *Supreme Court Provisional Order No. 18: Guidelines for Use of Legal Assistants,* 31 Rhode Island Bar Journal 19 (April, 1983).

599. Sutton, *The Impact of the Code of Professional Responsibility Upon the Unauthorized Practice of Law,* 47 North Carolina Law Review 633 (1969).

600. Swanson, *Here Come the Independents (Free-Lance Paralegals, That Is),* 8 Virginia Bar Association Journal 9 (Summer, 1982).

601. Swanson, *Legal Assistants: Where Do They Stand?* 7 Virginia Bar Association Journal 8 (Spring, 1981).

602. Symposium, *The Role of the Nonlawyer in Estate Planning,* 36 Unauthorized Practice News (November, 1971).

603. Szuch, *Protecting the Work Product of Paralegals During Discovery,* 3 National Law Journal 30, col. 1 (November 24, 1980).

604. Tapp, *The Increasing Professionalization of Paralegals,* 130 Chicago Daily Law Bulletin 1, col. 2 (May 1, 1984).

605. Teirsky, *Can A Paralegal Pare Down Your Workload?* 23 Decalogue Journal 8 (Summer, 1974).

606. Templeton, *The Free-Lance Legal Assistant: What Is the State of the Art?* 4 Legal Assistants Update 65 (ABA, 1984).

607. Thompson, *Avoiding Legal Malpractice,* 89 Case and Comment 8, No. 6 (November–December, 1984).

608. Tiersten, *As the Law Office Turns (a Day in the Life of the Legal Assistant),* 4 Family Advocate 38 (Summer, 1981).

609. *Title Examination Activities by Lending Institution, Insurance Company, or Title and Abstract Company, as Illegal Practice of Law,* 85 American Law Reports 2d 184.

610. *Tort Liability and the California Health Care Assistant,* 45 Southern California Law Review 767 (1972).

611. *Training an Articled Clerk,* 61 Law Society Gazette 595 (1964).

612. *Training Paralegals in Law Library Skills,* 71 Law Library Journal 658, No. 4 (November, 1978).

613. *The Training and Use of Legal Assistants in Law Office Memos,* 60 American Bar Association Journal 965 (August, 1974).

614. *Training for the Public Profession of the Law: The Report of the Association of American Law Schools Curriculum Study Project,* Proposed Final Draft (February, 1971).

615. *Training of Legal Assistants,* 38 Unauthorized Practice News 158 (1974).

616. Troop, *Paralegals Are Taking the Lead Through Computers,* 2 Legal Assistant Today 21, No. 2 (Winter, 1985).

617. *Trust Company's Acts as Fiduciary as Practice of Law,* 69 American Law Reports 2d 404.

618. Turner, *The Effective Use of Lay Personnel,* 38 Kansas Bar Association Journal 301 (1969).

619. Turner, *Effective Use of Lay Personnel Revisited,* Law Office Economics 115 (1970).

620. Turner, *Legal Assistants Can Save You Time and Money,* in Manual for Managing the Law Office (1971).

621. Turner, *Paralegal Personnel in Law Offices,* 6 Trial 33 (December–January, 1969–1970).

622. Turner, *Systems Management Through Effective Use of Non-Legal Personnel,* 23 For the Defense 29, No. 9 (September, 1981).

623. Tybor, *Paralegals Proliferate—But Problems Pop Up,* 3 National Law Journal 2, col. 3 (February 23, 1981).

624. Ulrich, *Applying Management and Motivation Concepts to Law Offices,* 2 Journal of Paralegal Education 53 (1985).

625. Ulrich, *Legal Assistants and the Organized Bar: Where Do We Go from Here?* 4 Legal Assistants Update 133 (ABA, 1984). See also 24 Law Office Economics and Management 461 (Winter, 1984).

626. Ulrich, *Legal Assistants Can Increase Your Profits,* 69 American Bar Association Journal 1634 (November, 1983).

627. Ulrich, *Long-Term Legal Assistant Job Enrichment,* 4 Legal Assistants Update 37 (ABA, 1984). See also 24 Law Office Economics and Management 366 (Fall, 1983).

628. Ulrich, *Managing an Effective Legal Assistant Program,* Legal Economics 35 (January–February, 1979).

629. Ulrich, *Working with Legal Assistants in Appellate Practice,* 21 Law Office Economics and Management 356 (Fall, 1980).

630. Ulrich & Clarke, *Building Your Law Firm's Legal Assistant Program,* Arizona Bar Journal 20 (October, 1976).

631. Ulrich & Czarnecki, *The Team Approach to Trial Practice—A Case Study,* Law Office Economics and Management 51 (Spring, 1984).

632. Ulrich & Clark, *Working with Legal Assistants: Professional Responsibility,* 67 American Bar Association Journal 992 (August, 1981).

633. Ulrich & Mucklestone, eds., *Working with Legal Assistants* (ABA Section of Economics of Law Practice and Standing Committee on Legal Assistants, 1980).

634. Ulrich & Multhauf, *Law Firm Working Relationships: Developing a Long Term Legal Assistant Program,* 20 Law Office Economics and Management 289 (1979).

635. Ulrich & Tempero, *American Bar Association Associate Membership for Legal Assistants: The Reasons Why,* 10 Facts & Findings 5, No. 4 (National Association of Legal Assistants, January–February, 1984).

636. *The Unauthorized Practice of Law and Pro Se Divorce: An Empirical Analysis,* 86 Yale Law Journal 104 (1976).

637. *The Unauthorized Practice of Law by Lay Organizations Providing the Services of Attorneys,* 72 Harvard Law Review 1334 (1959).

638. *The Unauthorized Practice of Law by Laymen and Lay Associations,* 54 California Law Review 1331 (1966).

639. *An Unrealistic Approach to the Use of Paralegals,* 16 Law Office Economics and Management 19 (1975).

640. *Use of Lay Representatives,* 58 Michigan Law Review 456 (1960).

641. *Use of Paralegals Makes Good Business Sense,* 69 American Bar Association Journal 1626 (November, 1983).

642. *Using Paralegals in the Practice of Law,* 62 Illinois Bar Journal 432 (April, 1974).

643. Vanderbilt Law Review, *A Symposium on Legal Paraprofessionals,* 24 Vanderbilt Law Review 1077 (November, 1977).

644. Vom Baur, *Administrative Agencies and Unauthorized Practice of Law,* 48 American Bar Association Journal 715 (1962).

645. Vom Baur, *Practice Before Administrative Agencies and the Unauthorized Practice of Law,* 15 Federal Bar Journal 103 (1955).

646. Vom Baur, *Standards of Admission to Practice Before Federal Administrative Agencies* (1958). Also printed in *Practice of Laymen Elsewhere in the Government,* 15 Federal Bar Journal 227 (1955).

647. Voorhees, *Paralegals: Should the Bar Employ Them?* 24 Vanderbilt Law Review 1133 (November, 1977).

648. Wade, *Tort Liability of Legal Paraprofessionals and Lawyers Who Utilize Their Services,* 24 Vanderbilt Law Review 1133 (November, 1971).

649. Walker, *In-Office Training for Non-Lawyer Personnel,* 20 Practical Lawyer 79, No. 1 (January, 1974).

650. Watenmaker, *The Impact of the Legal Assistant on the Delivery of Legal Services,* 10 Journal of the Beverly Hills Bar Association 22 (November–December, 1976).

651. Watkins & Logue, *Working with Legal Assistants in Trial Practice,* 7 Legal Economics 12(14) (January–February, 1981).

652. Wells, *The Revitalization of the Legal Profession through Paralegalism,* 30 Baylor Law Review 841 (1978).

653. Wertheim, *Career Paths for Legal Assistants,* 4 Legal Assistants Update 23 (ABA, 1984).

654. Wexler, *The Jailhouse Lawyer as Paraprofessional: Problems and Prospects,* 7 Criminal Law Bulletin 139 (1971).

655. *What Activities of Stock or Securities Broker Constitute Unauthorized Practice of Law,* 34 American Law Reports 3d 1305.

656. *What Amounts to Practice of Law,* 111 American Law Reports 19; 151 American Law Reports 781.

657. White & Stein, *Paraprofessionals in Legal Services Programs: A Feasibility Study,* Report of the National Institute for Justice and Law Enforcement to the Legal Service Program, U.S. Office of Economic Opportunity (December, 1968).

658. Wickham, *Secretary/Legal Assistant—A New Answer to an Old Problem,* The Legal Administrator (March, 1978).

659. Williams, *The Use of Non-Legal Personnel in Law Office,* 16 Practical Lawyer 13 (October, 1960).

660. Williams, *What You Don't Have to Do in Your Law Office. Non-Lawyer Specialization,* 10 Trial 34, No. 5 (September–October, 1974).

661. Winter, *Paralegals Seen Taking Jobs from Associates,* 68 American Bar Association Journal 527 (May, 1982).

662. Wolf, *Lawyers' Assistants, by Any Other Name, Here to Stay,* 33 Missouri Bar Journal 378 (September, 1977).

663. Yarbroff & Matland, *New Careers for the Subprofessional* (National Center for Educational Research and Development, Office of Education, U.S. Department of Health, Education, and Welfare, 1970).

664. Yegge, Moore & Holme, *New Careers in Law: Meeting Present and Prospective Legal Needs* (Denver College of Law, 1969).

665. Yoneyama, *Paralegal Eagles,* 4 District Lawyer 24, No. 4 (Wash. D.C., March–April, 1980).

666. Zella, *California Paralegal's Guide,* 2d ed. (Parker & Son, 1982).

Appendix B

Paralegal Associations

National Association of Legal Assistants (NALA)
1420 S. Utica
Tulsa, OK 74104
918-587-6828

National Federation of Paralegal Associations (NFPA)

Mailing Address
P.O. Box 14103
Ben Franklin Station
Washington, D.C. 20044

Executive Office
P.O. Box 40158
Overland Park, KS 66204
913-381-9302

(Many of the following associations are affiliated *either* with NALA or with NFPA. One asterisk (*) means that the association is affiliated with NALA. Two asterisks (**) mean that the association is affiliated with NFPA. No asterisk means that the association is unaffiliated at the present time. Some of the addresses change yearly with the change of officers. If more than one address is given for an association, you may need to check both.)

ALABAMA

Alabama Association of Legal
  Assistants (*)
c/o Ellen Batt
James R. Sturdivant, Esq.
555 Central Bank Bldg.
Huntsville, AL 35801

Alabama Association of Legal
  Assistants (*)
P.O. Box 55921
Birmingham, AL 35255

Legal Assistant Society of
  Southern Institute (*)
Paralegal Program, Southern
  Institute
2015 Highland Avenue South
Birmingham, AL 35205

ALASKA

Alaska Association of Legal
  Assistants (**)
P.O. Box 101956
Anchorage, AK 99510-1956

Alaska Legal Assistants Association
P.O. Box 1956
Anchorage, AK 99510

Fairbanks Association of Legal
  Assistants (*)
c/o Catherine Davidson
Hughes, Thorsness, et al.
590 University Ave., Suite 200
Fairbanks, AK 99701

Juneau Association of Legal
  Assistants
P.O. Box 786
Douglas, AK 99824

ARIZONA

Arizona Paralegal Association
P.O. Box 13083
Phoenix, AZ 85002

Northern Arizona Paralegal
  Association
Department of Law Enforcement
  & Paralegal Studies
Northern Arizona University
Box 15005
Flagstaff, AZ 86011

Tuscon Association of Legal
  Assistants (*)
c/o Hope Abeyta
1540 W. San Lucas
Tuscon, AZ 85704

Tuscon Association of Legal
  Assistants (*)
P.O. Box 257
Tuscon, AZ 85702

ARKANSAS

Arkansas Association of Legal
  Assistants (*)
c/o Barbara Mills
Mitchell, Williams, et al.
100 Savers Federal Bldg.
Little Rock, AR 72201

CALIFORNIA

American Paralegal Association
P.O. Box 35233
Los Angeles, CA 90035

California Alliance of Paralegal
  Associations
P.O. Box 26383
San Francisco, CA 94126

Central Coast Legal Assistants
  Association
P.O. Box 1582
San Luis Obispo, CA 93406

Channel Cities Legal Assistant
  Association (*)
c/o Elizabeth McGrath
158-E Kingston Ave.
Goleta, CA 93117

East Bay Association of Legal
  Assistants (**)
P.O. Box 424
Oakland, CA 94604

Los Angeles Paralegal
  Association (**)
P.O. Box 241928
Los Angeles, CA 90024

Marin Association of Legal
  Assistants
P.O. Box 2207
San Anselmo, CA 94960

Paralegal Association of Santa
  Clara County (*)
c/o Naomi Sammut
50 Decorah Lane
Campbell, CA 95008

Sacramento Association of Legal
  Assistants (**)
P.O. Box 453
Sacramento, CA 95802

San Diego Association of Legal
  Assistants (**)
P.O. Box 12508
San Diego, CA 92112

San Francisco Association of Legal
Assistants (**)
P.O. Box 26668
San Francisco, CA 94126-6668

San Joaquin Association of Legal
Assistants
P.O. Box 1306
Fresno, CA 93715

Ventura County Association of
Legal Assistants (*)
c/o Delaina E. Finch
Oxnard City Attorney
305 West Third Street
Oxnard, CA 93030

COLORADO

Legal Assistants of Colorado (*)
c/o Joan Ladefoged
2120 Broken Circle Road
Colorado Springs, CO 80915

Rocky Mountain Legal Assistants
Association (**)
P.O. Box 304
Denver, CO 80201

CONNECTICUT

Central Connecticut Association of
Legal Assistants (**)
P.O. Box 3594
Hartford, CT 06103

Connecticut Association of
Paralegals
c/o Nancy Ongley
The Travelers Insurance Company
One Tower Square
Hartford, CT 06604

Connecticut Association of
Paralegals—New Haven
P.O. Box 862
New Haven, CT 06504

Connecticut Paralegal Association
P.O. Box 134
Bridgeport, CT 06604

Legal Assistants of Southeastern
Connecticut
P.O. Box 409
New London, CT 06320

DELAWARE

Delaware Paralegal
Association (**)
P.O. Box 1362
Wilmington, DE 19899

DISTRICT OF COLUMBIA

National Capital Area Paralegal
Association (**)
P.O. Box 19505
Washington, D.C. 20036

FLORIDA

Broward County Paralegal
Association
c/o Leigh M. Williams
Ruden, Barnett, McClosky, et al.
P.O. Box 1900
Ft. Lauderdale, FL 33302

Dade Association of Legal
Assistants (*)
c/o Lori C. Fati
15750 SW 152 Avenue
Miami, FL 33187

Florida Legal Assistants, Inc. (*)
c/o Kathleen J. Hill
Capital Services
345 S. Magnolia Drive
Suite A-23
Tallahassee, FL 32301

Orlando Legal Assistants
Association
c/o Diane Zechar
P.O. Box 20154
Orlando, FL 32814-0154

Pensacola Legal Assistants (*)
c/o Carol Ann Bailey
122 West Gregory St.
Pensacola, FL 32501

Pensacola Legal Assistants (*)
P.O. Box 12308
Pensacola, FL 32581

GEORGIA

Georgia Association of Legal
Assistants (**)
P.O. Box 1802
Atlanta, GA 30301

HAWAII

Hawaii Association of Legal
Assistants
P.O. Box 674
Honolulu, HI 96809

IDAHO

Boise Association of Legal
Assistants (*)
P.O. Box 50
Boise, ID 83728

Boise Association of Legal
Assistants (*)
c/o Tanya Rossum
P.O. Box 1891
Boise, ID 83701

ILLINOIS

Illinois Paralegal Association (**)
P.O. Box 857
Chicago, IL 60690

Peoria Paralegal Association
c/o Sharon Moke
1308 Autumn Lane
Peoria, IL 60604

INDIANA

Indiana Legal Assistants (*)
c/o Kathryn L. Myers
Paralegal Studies
St. Mary-of-the-Woods College
St. Mary-of-the-Woods, IN 47876

Indianapolis Paralegal
Association (**)
P.O. Box 44518
Indianapolis, IN 46204

IOWA

Iowa Legal Assistants
Association (*)
c/o Marlene Smedema
Nymaster Law Firm
10th Floor, Hubbel Bldg.
Des Moines, IA 50309

Iowa Legal Assistants
Association (*)
P.O. Box 335
Des Moines, IA 50302

Paralegals of Iowa, Ltd. (*)
c/o Carla Carter
3324 Kimball Avenue
Waterloo, Iowa 50702

KANSAS

Kansas Association of Legal
Assistants (*)
c/o Nancy Snyder
Pizza Hut, Inc., Legal Dept.
P.O. Box 428
Wichita, KS 67201

Kansas Association of Legal
Assistants (*)
P.O. Box 47031
Wichita, KS 67201

Kansas Legal Assistant
Association (*)
c/o Patricia Armstrong
700 Fourth Financial Center
Wichita, KS 67202

Kansas Legal Assistants Society
c/o Kathleen M. Twitchell, CLA
P.O. Box 1398
Kansas City, KS 66117

Kansas Legal Assistants Society
c/o Julie Widau
P.O. Box 2667
Topeka, KS 66601

KENTUCKY

Kentucky Paralegal Association
P.O. Box 34503
Louisville, KY 40232

Louisville Association of Paralegals
P.O. Box 962
Louisville, KY 40201

LOUISIANA

Baton Rouge Paralegal Association
P.O. Box 3057
Baton Rouge, LA 70821

Lafayette Paralegal Association
c/o Lynn Panoff
P.O. Box 2775
Lafayette, LA 70502

Legal Assistants of Northeast
Louisiana
c/o Mary Ann Greco
P.O. Box 2750
Monroe, LA 71207-2750

New Orleans Paralegal
Association (**)
P.O. Box 30604
New Orleans, LA 70190

Southwest Louisiana Association of
Paralegals
c/o Carol Rochelle
Plauche, Smith & Nieset
P.O. Box 1705
Lake Charles, LA 70602

MAINE

Maine Association of Paralegals
P.O. Box 7554 DTS
Portland, ME 04111

MARYLAND

Baltimore Association of Legal
Assistants
P.O. Box 1653
Baltimore, MD 21203

See also District of Columbia

MASSACHUSETTS

Berkshire Association for
Paralegals & Legal Secretaries
c/o Theresa A. Allmaker
P.O. Box 576
Williamstown, MA 01267

Massachusetts Paralegal
Association (**)
P.O. Box 423
Boston, MA 02102

MICHIGAN

Legal Assistants Association of
Michigan (*)
c/o Randi R. Walters
8342 Norborne
Dearborn Heights, MI 48127

MINNESOTA

Arrowhead Association of Legal
Assistants (*)
c/o Betty Robinet Santa
P.O. Box 221
Duluth, MN 55801

Minnesota Association of Legal
Assistants (**)
P.O. Box 15165
Grain Exchange Bldg.
Minneapolis, MN 55415

St. Cloud Area Legal Services
Association
c/o Mary Yeager
P.O. Box 896
St. Cloud, MN 56302

See also Red River Valley Legal
Assistants under North Dakota

MISSISSIPPI

Mississippi Association of Legal
  Assistants (*)
c/o Lee Myers
P.O. Box 996
Jackson, MS 39205

Society for Paralegal Studies (*)
c/o Ronald G. Marquardt
University of Southern Mississippi
P.O. Box 9267, SS
Hattiesburg, MS 39401

MISSOURI

Kansas City Association of Legal
  Assistants (**)
P.O. Box 13223
Kansas City, MO 64199

St. Joseph Association of Legal
  Assistants
c/o Pat Bailey
510-A Francis
St. Joseph, MO 64501

St. Louis Association of Legal
  Assistants
P.O. Box 8705
St. Louis, MO 63102

Southwestern Missouri Paralegal
  Association
P.O. Box 1624 S.S.S.
Springfield, MO 65805

NEBRASKA

Nebraska Association of Legal
  Assistants (*)
c/o Shirley Stunkel
Badami & Radke
1235 N. St., Suite 402
Lincoln, NB 68508

NEVADA

Nevada Paralegal Association (*)
c/o Susan Gormley
514 So. 3rd St.
Las Vegas, NV 89101

NEW HAMPSHIRE

Paralegal Association of New
  Hampshire
P.O. Box 1087
Nashua, NH 03061

Paralegal Association of New
  Hampshire
c/o Leslye R. Dedopoulos
Wiggin & Nourie
P.O. Box 808
Manchester, NH 03105

NEW JERSEY

Legal Assistants Association of
  New Jersey
c/o Lynn Susan Wurtzberger
Stryker, Tams & Dill
33 Washington St.
Newark, NJ 07102

Legal Assistants Association of
  New Jersey
P.O. Box 142
Caldwell, NJ 07006

New Jersey Legal Assistants
  Association
Central Jersey Paralegal Division
P.O. Box 403
U.S. Highway 130
Dayton, NJ 08810

Paralegal Association of Central
  Jersey
93 Princeton Court
Mercerville, NJ 08619

South Jersey Paralegal
  Association (**)
P.O. Box 132
Lindenwold, NJ 08021

NEW MEXICO

Legal Assistants of New Mexico
P.O. Box 1945
Albuquerque, NM 87103

NEW YORK

Legal Assistants of Broome County
Couglin & Gerhardt—P. Mack
One Marine Midland Plaza
Binghamton, NY 13902

Long Island Paralegal Association,
  Inc. (**)
P.O. Box 40
Carle Place
New York, NY 11514

New York City Paralegal
  Association (*)
FDR Station
P.O. Box 5143
New York, NY 10022

Paralegal Association of Central
  New York (**)
P.O. Box 860
Syracuse, NY 13201

Paralegal Association of
  Rochester (**)
P.O. Box 40567
Rochester, NY 14604

Western New York Paralegal
  Association (**)
P.O. Box 207
Niagara Square Station
Buffalo, NY 14202

NORTH CAROLINA

Cumberland County Paralegal
  Association
P.O. Box 1358
Fayetteville, NC 28302

Metrolina Paralegal Association
c/o Charlene H. Pridgen
Lane and Helms
301 S. McDowell Street
Charlotte, NC 28204

North Carolina Paralegal
  Association (*)
c/o Lee T. Dueto
Allen, Hooten & Hodges

P.O. Drawer 3169
Kinston, NC 28502

North Carolina Paralegal
  Association (*)
P.O. Box 10214
Raleigh, NC 27605

Raleigh-Wake Paralegal
  Association
P.O. Box 10096
Raleigh, NC 27605

Triad Paralegal Association
Drawer U
Greensboro, NC 27402

NORTH DAKOTA

Red River Valley Legal
  Assistants (*)
c/o Margaret Colby
Box 847
Mayville, ND 58257

Western Dakota Association of
  Legal Assistants
c/o Dorthea L. Jorde
P.O. Box 1000
Minot, ND 58702

OHIO

Akron Paralegal Association
c/o Marian K. O'Hear
3361 Boyne
Barberton, OH 44203

Cincinnati Paralegal
  Association (**)
P.O. Box 1515
Cincinnati, OH 45201

Cleveland Association of
  Paralegals (**)
P.O. Box 14011
Cleveland, OH 44114

Greater Dayton Paralegal
  Association
c/o Nancy Martinez-Curtin
Biebel, French & Newman
2500 Kettering Tower
Dayton, OH 45423

Greater Dayton Paralegal
  Association
P.O. Box 515
Mid City Station
Dayton, OH 45402

Legal Assistants of Central
  Ohio (**)
P.O. Box 15182
Columbus, OH 43216

Toledo Association of Legal
  Assistants (*)
c/o William Werynski
Brown, Baker, Schlageter & Craig
711 Adams Street
Toledo, OH 43624

OKLAHOMA

Student Association of Legal
  Assistants of Tulsa Junior
  College (*)
2441 North Harvard, #7
Tulsa, OK 74115

Tulsa Association of Legal
  Assistants (*)
c/o Elizabeth Nellis
Hall, Estill, et al.
4100 BOK Tower
One Williams Center
Tulsa, OK 74172

Tulsa Association of Legal
  Assistants (*)
P.O. Box 1484
Tulsa, OK 74101

OREGON

Oregon Legal Assistants
  Association (**)
P.O. Box 8523
Portland, OR 97207

Willamette Valley Paralegals, Inc.
P.O. Box 1835
Eugene, OR 97440

PENNSYLVANIA

Lancaster Area Paralegal
  Association
c/o Rosemary Merwin
115 East King St.
Lancaster, PA 17602

Pennsylvania Association of
  Paralegals
c/o Janet Brown
Robin Hill, Apt. 1507
Fourth & Preston Avenue
Voorhees, NJ 08043

Pennsylvania Paralegal Association
Central Susquehanna Valley Legal
  Services
142 Market Street
Sunbury, PA 17801

Philadelphia Association of
  Paralegals (**)
P.O. Box 55
Philadelphia, PA 19105

Pittsburgh Paralegal
  Association (**)
P.O. Box 1053
Pittsburgh, PA 15230

Student Legal Assistant
  Association (*)
Central Pennsylvania Business
  School
Campus on College Hill
Summerdale, PA 17093

PUERTO RICO

Puerto Rico Association of Legal
  Assistants
c/o Hedily Schmidt
GPO Box 4225
San Juan, PR 00936

RHODE ISLAND

Rhode Island Paralegal
  Association (**)
P.O. Box 1003
Providence, RI 02903

SOUTH CAROLINA

Carolina Paralegal Association
c/o Anna Chason
7437 Highview Road
Columbia, SC 29204

TENNESSEE

Cleveland State Community
  College Legal Assistant
  Association
P.O. Box 3570
Cleveland, TN 37311

East Tennessee Paralegal
  Association
c/o Lawassa B. Jones
450 Maclellan Bldg.
Chattanooga, TN 37402

Knoxville Association of Legal
  Assistants
c/o Margaret Ailor
P.O. Box 2047
Knoxville, TN 37901

Mid-South Association of Legal
  Assistants (**)
P.O. Box 3646
Memphis, TN 38103

Middle Tennessee Paralegal
  Association
c/o Ruth Foster
810 Bellvue Road #133
Nashville, TN 37221

Tennessee Paralegal
  Association (*)
c/o Collette Jones
Stophel, Cadwell & Heggie
420 Maclellan Building
Chattanooga, TN 37402

Tennessee Valley Association of
  Legal Assistants
c/o Paulie Ailor
P.O. Box 2047
Knoxville, TN 37901

TEXAS

Alamo Area Professional Legal
  Assistants
c/o Kathy Williams
Fulbright & Jaworski
2200 InterFirst Plaza
300 Convent Street
San Antonio, TX 78205

Alamo Area Professional Legal
  Assistants
P.O. Box 524
San Antonio, TX 78292

Capital Area Paralegal Association
P.O. Box 2353
Austin, TX 78768

Dallas Association of Legal
  Assistants (**)
P.O. Box 2938
Dallas, TX 75250

El Paso Association of Legal
  Assistants (*)
c/o Lisa Sprinkle
Law Office of Marshall I. Yaker
P.O. Box 3707
El Paso, TX 79923

Fort Worth Paralegal Association
c/o Pam Lambert
Watson, Ice, McGee & Morgan
1212 Texas American Bank Bldg.
Ft. Worth, TX 76102

Ft. Worth Paralegal Association
P.O. Box 17021
Ft. Worth, TX 76102

Houston Legal Assistants
  Association
c/o Karen Bealmear
Liddell, Sapp, Zivley & Laboon
3400 Texas Commerce Tower
Houston, TX 77002

Houston Legal Assistants
Association
P.O. Box 52241
Houston, TX 77052

Legal Assistants
Association/Permian Basin (*)
c/o Denise Kee Holden
P.O. Box 10683
Midland, TX 79702

Legal Assistants
Association/Permian Basin (*)
c/o Karol McVay
P.O. Box 1540
Midland, TX 79702

Legal Assistants Division of the
State Bar of Texas
P.O. Box 12487
Austin, TX 78711
512-475-1381

Lubbock Area Association of
Legal Assistants
c/o Jeri Bryce
2112 Indiana
Lubbock, TX 79410

Southeast Texas Association of
Legal Assistants (*)
c/o Jeannie Grinnell
CLAS, Inc.
San Jacinto Bldg., Suite 1010
Beaumont, TX 77701

Tarrant County Association of
Legal Assistants
P.O. Box 1161
Hurst, TX 76053

Tyler Area Association of Legal
Assistants
P.O. Box 9003
Tyler, TX 75711

West Texas Association of Legal
Assistants (*)
c/o Becky B. Greenwade
5422 32nd Street
Lubbock, TX 79407

UTAH

Legal Assistants Association of
Utah (*)
P.O. Box 112001
Salt Lake City, UT 84147

Legal Assistants Association of
Utah (*)
c/o Carol D. Elggren
250 Bell Plaza, Suite 1610
P.O. Box 30960
Salt Lake City, UT 84125

VIRGINIA

American Academy of Legal
Assistants
Professional Arts Bldg.
1022 Park Avenue, NE
Norton, VA 24273

Central Virginia Legal Assistants
Association
P.O. Box 1163
Lynchburg, VA 24505

Paralegal Association of Virginia
c/o Lydia M. Person
412 S. Main Street
Emporia, VA 23847

Public Service Paralegal
Association of Virginia
P.O. Box 3922
Norfolk, VA 23214

Richmond Association of Legal
Assistants (*)
c/o Margaret Parker
The Life Insurance Company of
Virginia
6610 West Broad Street
P.O. Box 27601
Richmond, VA 23261

Roanoke Valley Paralegal
Association
c/o Denise King
Bird, Kinder and Huffman
126 Church Ave. SW
Roanoke, VA 24011

Tidewater Association of Legal
  Assistants, Inc. (*)
c/o Tobie Cioccia
Willcox, Savage, et al.
1800 Sovern Center
Norfolk, VA 23510-2197

Virginia Paralegal Association
c/o J. McCord
McGuire, Woods & Battle
Ross Bldg.
Richmond, VA 23219

See also District of Columbia

VIRGIN ISLANDS

Virgin Islands Paralegals (*)
c/o Maudlyn Howard
P.O. Box 10197
St. Thomas, VI 00801

WASHINGTON

Washington Legal Assistants
  Association (**)
P.O. Box 2114
Seattle, WA 98111

See District of Columbia for
Washington, D.C.

WEST VIRGINIA

Legal Assistants of West Virginia
c/o M. Shafer
Jackson & Kelley
P.O. Box 553
Charleston, WV 25322

WISCONSIN

Paralegal Association of Wisconsin
c/o Julie Pollak
Foley & Lardner
777 East Wisconsin Ave.
Milwaukee, WI 53202

OTHER ORGANIZATIONS

American Association for
  Paralegal Education
P.O. Box 40244
Overland Park, KS 66204
913-381-4458

American Bar Association
Standing Committee on Legal
  Assistants
750 N. Lake Shore Drive
Chicago, IL 60611
312-988-5000

Association of Legal
  Administrators
1800 Pickwick Ave.
Glenview, IL 60025-1377

Canadian Association of Legal
  Assistants
Box 30, Toronto-Dominion Centre
Toronto, Ontario, M5K 1C1
Canada

The Institute of Legal Executives
Kempston Manor
Kempston
Bedford
England

Legal Assistant Management
  Association
P.O. Box 40129
Overland Park, KS 66204
913-381-4458

National Association of Enrolled
  Agents
1133 Fifteenth St. N.W.
Washington, D.C. 20003
800-424-4339
202-429-9440

National Association of Enrolled
  Agents
5410 Grosvenor Lane
Bethesda, MD 20814
800-424-4339
301-897-4339

National Indian Paralegal
 Association
c/o Allene Burnette
7524 Major Avenue North
Brooklyn Park, MN 55443

National Legal Assistant
 Conference Center
2444 Wilshire Blvd.
Suite 301
Santa Monica, CA 90403

National Notary Association
23012 Ventura Blvd.
P.O. Box 4625
Woodland Hills, CA 91365-4624

National Paralegal Association
P.O. Box 629
Doylestown, PA 18901

Appendix C

State Bar Associations
Local Bar Associations

ALABAMA

Alabama State Bar
P.O. Box 671
Montgomery, AL 36101
205-269-1515

Birmingham Bar Association
900 Jefferson County Court House
Birmingham, AL 35263
205-251-8006

ALASKA

Alaska Bar Association
P.O. Box 279
Anchorage, AK 99510
907-272-7469

ARIZONA

State Bar of Arizona
234 N. Central
Suite 858
Phoenix, AZ 85004
602-252-4804

Maricopa County Bar Association
3033 N. Central Ave.

No. 604
Phoenix, AZ 85012
602-277-2366

ARKANSAS

Arkansas Bar Association
400 W. Markham
Little Rock, AR 72201
501-375-4605

CALIFORNIA

State Bar of California
555 Franklin St.
San Francisco, CA 94102
415-561-8200

Alameda County Bar Association
405 14th St.
Suite 208
Oakland, CA 94612

Bar Association of San Francisco
220 Bush St.
21st Floor
San Francisco, CA 94102
415-392-3960

Beverly Hills Bar Association
300 S. Beverly Dr.
No. 201
Beverly Hills, CA 90212
213-533-6644

Lawyers Club of Los Angeles
304 S. Broadway
Suite 220
Los Angeles, CA 90013
213-933-8185

Lawyers Club of San Francisco
870 Market St.
No. 1115
San Francisco, CA 94102
415-433-2133

Los Angeles County Bar
  Association
P.O. Box 55020
Los Angeles, CA 90055
213-627-2727

Orange County Bar Association
7291 Irvine Blvd.
Suite 309
Tustin, CA 92680
714-838-9200

San Diego County Bar Association
1434 Fifth Ave.
San Diego, CA 92101
714-231-0781

Santa Clara County Bar
  Association
111 N. Market St.
Suite 712
San Jose, CA 95115
408-288-8840

COLORADO

Colorado Bar Association
250 W. 14th St.
No. 800
Denver, CO 80204
303-629-6873

Denver Bar Association
200 W. 14th Ave.

Suite 800
Denver, CO 80204
303-629-6873

CONNECTICUT

Connecticut Bar Association
15 Lewis St.
Hartford, CT 06103
203-249-9141

DELAWARE

Delaware State Bar Association
820 N. French St.
Wilmington, DE 19801
302-658-5278

DISTRICT OF COLUMBIA

The District of Columbia Bar
1426 H. St. NW
Washington, D.C. 20005
202-638-1500

Bar Association of the District of
  Columbia
1819 H. St. NW
Suite 300
Washington, D.C. 20006
202-223-1480

FLORIDA

The Florida Bar Center
Tallahassee, FL 32301
904-222-5286

Dade County Bar Association
111 N.W. First Ave.
No. 214
Miami, FL 33128
305-379-0641

GEORGIA

State Bar of Georgia
84 Peachtree St.
Atlanta, GA 30303
404-522-6255

Atlanta Bar Association
606 Equitable Bldg.
Atlanta, GA 30303
404-521-0781

HAWAII

Hawaii State Bar
820 Mililani
Honolulu, HI 96813
808-537-1868

IDAHO

Idaho State Bar
P.O. Box 895
Boise, ID 83701
208-342-8958

ILLINOIS

Illinois Bar Center
Springfield, IL 62701
217-525-1760

The Chicago Bar Association
29 S. LaSalle St.
Suite 1040
Chicago, IL 60603

Chicago Council of Lawyers
220 S. State St.
Room 800
Chicago, IL 60604
312-427-0710

INDIANA

Indiana State Bar Association
230 East Ohio St.
Indianapolis, IN 46204
317-639-5465

Indianapolis Bar Association
One Indiana Sq.
Suite 2550
Indianapolis, IN 46204
317-632-8240

IOWA

Iowa State Bar Association
1101 Fleming Bldg.
Des Moines, IA 50309
515-243-3179

KANSAS

Kansas Bar Association
P.O. Box 1037
Topeka, KS 66601
913-234-5696

KENTUCKY

Kentucky Bar Association
West Main at Kentucky River
Frankfort, KY 40601
502-564-3795

Louisville Bar Association
200 S. 5th St.
Louisville, KY 40202
502-583-5314

LOUISIANA

Louisiana State Bar Association
210 O'Keefe Ave.
No. 600
New Orleans, LA 70112
504-566-1600

MAINE

Maine State Bar Association
P.O. Box 788
August, ME 04330
207-622-7523

MARYLAND

Maryland State Bar Association
207 E. Redwood St.
Baltimore, MD 21202
301-685-7878

Bar Association of Baltimore City
627 Courthouse East
Baltimore, MD 21202
301-539-5936

MASSACHUSETTS

Massachusetts Bar Association
One Center Plaza
Boston, MA 02108
617-523-4529

Boston Bar Association
16 Beacon St.
Boston, MA 02108
617-742-0615

MICHIGAN

State Bar of Michigan
306 Townsend St.
Lansing, MI 48933
517-372-9030

Detroit Bar Association
600 Woodward Ave.
Detroit, MI 48226
313-961-6120

Oakland County Bar Association
1200 N. Telegraph Rd.
Pontiac, MI 48053
313-338-2100

MINNESOTA

Minnesota State Bar Association
430 Marquette Ave.
Suite 403
Minneapolis, MN 55402
612-335-1183

Hennepin County Bar Association
430 Marquette Ave.
No. 402
Minneapolis, MN 55402
612-340-0022

MISSISSIPPI

Mississippi State Bar
P.O. Box 2168
Jackson, MS 39205
601-948-4471

MISSOURI

The Missouri Bar
P.O. Box 119
Jefferson City, MO 65102
314-635-4128

Kansas City Bar Association
P.O. Box 26276
Kansas City, MO 64196
816-474-4322

Bar Association of Metropolitan
St. Louis
One Mercantile Center
Suite 3600
St. Louis, MO 63101
314-421-4134

MONTANA

State Bar of Montana
P.O. Box 4669
Helena, MT 59604
406-442-7660

NEBRASKA

Nebraska State Bar Association
206 South 13th St.
Lincoln, NB 68508
402-475-7091

NEVADA

State Bar of Nevada
834 Willow St.
Reno, NV 89501
702-329-4100

NEW HAMPSHIRE

New Hampshire Bar Association
18 Centre St.
Concord, NH 03301
603-224-6942

NEW JERSEY

New Jersey State Bar Association
172 W. State St.
Trenton, NJ 08608
609-394-1101

Essex County Bar Association
24 Commerce St.
Newark, NJ 07102
210-622-6207

NEW MEXICO

State Bar of New Mexico
P.O. Box 25883
Albuquerque, NM 87125
505-842-6132

NEW YORK

New York State Bar Association
One Elk St.
Albany, NY 12207
518-445-1211

Association of the Bar of the City
of New York
42 W. 44th St.
New York, NY 10036
212-840-3550

New York County Lawyers
Association
14 Vesey St.
New York, NY 10007
212-267-6646

NORTH CAROLINA

North Carolina State Bar
P.O. Box 25908
Raleigh, NC 27611
919-828-4620

North Carolina Bar Association
P.O. Box 12806
1025 Wade Ave.
Raleigh, NC 27605
919-828-0561

NORTH DAKOTA

State Bar Association of North
Dakota
P.O. Box 2136
Bismarck, ND 58502
701-255-1404

OHIO

Ohio State Bar Association
33 W. 11th Ave.
Columbus, OH 43201
614-421-2121

The Bar Association of Greater
Cleveland
118 St. Clair Ave.
Cleveland, OH 44114
216-696-3525

Cincinnati Bar Association
26 E. 6th St.
Suite 400
Cincinnati, OH 45202
513-381-8213

Columbus Bar Association
66 S. Third St.
Columbus, OH 43215
614-221-4112

Cuyahoga County Bar Association
850 Euclid Ave.
No. 715
Cleveland, OH 44114
216-621-5112

OKLAHOMA

Oklahoma Bar Association
P.O. Box 53036
Oklahoma City, OK 73152
405-524-2365

Oklahoma County Bar Association
311 N. Harvey
Oklahoma City, OK 73102
405-236-8421

Tulsa County Bar Association
619 S. Main St.
Tulsa, OK 74119
918-584-5243

OREGON

Oregon State Bar
1776 S.W. Madison
Portland, OR 97205
503-224-4280

Multnomah Bar Association
1776 S.W. Madison
Portland, OR 97205
503-222-3275

PENNSYLVANIA

Pennsylvania Bar Association
P.O. Box 186
Harrisburg, PA 17108
717-238-6715

Allegheny County Bar Association
920 City-Cty. Bldg.
Pittsburgh, PA 15219
412-261-0518

Philadelphia Bar Association
1339 Chestnut St.
Philadelphia, PA 19107
215-686-5686

PUERTO RICO

Bar Association of Puerto Rico
Box 1900
San Juan, PR 00903
809-721-3358

RHODE ISLAND

Rhode Island Bar Association
1804 Industrial Bank Building
Providence, RI 02903
401-421-5740

SOUTH CAROLINA

South Carolina Bar Association
P.O. Box 11039

Columbia, SC 29211
803-799-6653

SOUTH DAKOTA

State Bar of South Dakota
222 E. Capitol
Pierre, SD 57501
605-224-7554

TENNESSEE

Tennessee Bar Association
3622 W. End Ave.
Nashville, TN 37205
615-383-7421

TEXAS

State Bar of Texas
P.O. Box 12487
Austin, TX 78711
512-475-4200

Dallas Bar Association
2101 Ross Ave.
Dallas, TX 75201
214-742-4675

Houston Bar Association
707 Travis St.
Suite 1300
Houston, TX 77002
713-222-1441

UTAH

Utah State Bar
425 E. First South
Salt Lake City, UT 84111
801-531-9077

VERMONT

Vermont Bar Association
P.O. Box 100
Montpelier, VT 05602
802-223-2020

VIRGINIA

Virginia State Bar
700 East Main St.
Richmond, VA 23219
804-786-2061

Virginia Bar Association
P.O. Box 1029
Charlottesville, VA 22902
804-977-1396

WASHINGTON

Washington State Bar Association
505 Madison
Seattle, WA 98104
206-622-6054

Seattle-King County Bar
   Association
320 Central Bldg.
Seattle, WA 98104
206-624-9365

WASHINGTON D.C.

See District of Columbia

WEST VIRGINIA

West Virginia State Bar
State Capitol
Charleston, WV 25305
304-346-8414

West Virginia Bar Association
P.O. Box 346
Charleston, WV 25322
304-342-1474

WISCONSIN

State Bar of Wisconsin
P.O. Box 7158
Madison, WI 53707
608-257-3838

Milwaukee Bar Association
610 N. Jackson St.
Milwaukee, WI 53202
414-271-3833

WYOMING

Wyoming State Bar
P.O. Box 109
Cheyenne, WY 82003
307-632-9061

Appendix D

Federal Government
Organization Chart

THE GOVERNMENT OF THE UNITED STATES

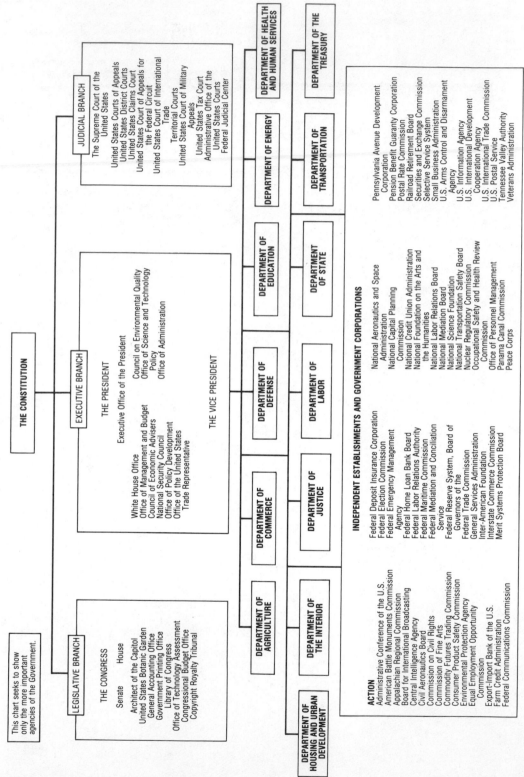

This chart seeks to show only the more important agencies of the Government.

THE CONSTITUTION

LEGISLATIVE BRANCH

THE CONGRESS

Senate   House

Architect of the Capitol
United States Botanic Garden
General Accounting Office
Government Printing Office
Library of Congress
Office of Technology Assessment
Congressional Budget Office
Copyright Royalty Tribunal

EXECUTIVE BRANCH

THE PRESIDENT

Executive Office of the President

White House Office
Office of Management and Budget
Council of Economic Advisers
National Security Council
Office of Policy Development
Office of the United States
Trade Representative

Council on Environmental Quality
Office of Science and Technology Policy
Office of Administration

THE VICE PRESIDENT

JUDICIAL BRANCH

The Supreme Court of the United States
United States Courts of Appeals
United States District Courts
United States Claims Court
United States Court of Appeals for the Federal Circuit
United States Court of International Trade
Territorial Courts
United States Court of Military Appeals
United States Tax Court
Administrative Office of the United States Courts
Federal Judicial Center

DEPARTMENT OF HEALTH AND HUMAN SERVICES

DEPARTMENT OF THE TREASURY

DEPARTMENT OF ENERGY

DEPARTMENT OF TRANSPORTATION

DEPARTMENT OF EDUCATION

DEPARTMENT OF STATE

DEPARTMENT OF DEFENSE

DEPARTMENT OF LABOR

DEPARTMENT OF COMMERCE

DEPARTMENT OF JUSTICE

DEPARTMENT OF AGRICULTURE

DEPARTMENT OF THE INTERIOR

DEPARTMENT OF HOUSING AND URBAN DEVELOPMENT

INDEPENDENT ESTABLISHMENTS AND GOVERNMENT CORPORATIONS

ACTION
Administrative Conference of the U.S.
American Battle Monuments Commission
Appalachian Regional Commission
Board for International Broadcasting
Central Intelligence Agency
Civil Aeronautics Board
Commission on Civil Rights
Commission of Fine Arts
Commodity Futures Trading Commission
Consumer Product Safety Commission
Environmental Protection Agency
Equal Employment Opportunity Commission
Export-Import Bank of the U.S.
Farm Credit Administration
Federal Communications Commission

Federal Deposit Insurance Corporation
Federal Election Commission
Federal Emergency Management Agency
Federal Home Loan Bank Board
Federal Labor Relations Authority
Federal Maritime Commission
Federal Mediation and Conciliation Service
Federal Reserve System, Board of Governors of the
Federal Trade Commission
General Services Administration
Inter-American Foundation
Interstate Commerce Commission
Merit Systems Protection Board

National Aeronautics and Space Administration
National Capital Planning Commission
National Credit Union Administration
National Foundation on the Arts and the Humanities
National Labor Relations Board
National Mediation Board
National Science Foundation
National Transportation Safety Board
Nuclear Regulatory Commission
Occupational Safety and Health Review Commission
Office of Personnel Management
Panama Canal Commission
Peace Corps

Pennsylvania Avenue Development Corporation
Pension Benefit Guaranty Corporation
Postal Rate Commission
Railroad Retirement Board
Securities and Exchange Commission
Selective Service System
Small Business Administration
U.S. Arms Control and Disarmament Agency
U.S. Information Agency
U.S. International Development Cooperation Agency
U.S. International Trade Commission
U.S. Postal Service
Tennessee Valley Authority
Veterans Administration

Source: United States Government Manual 1983–84.

Appendix E

Survey of Nonlawyer
Practice before Federal
Administrative Agencies

STANDING COMMITTEE ON LAWYERS' RESPONSIBILITY FOR
CLIENT PROTECTION AND THE AMERICAN BAR ASSOCIATION
CENTER FOR PROFESSIONAL RESPONSIBILITY

February, 1985

I. BACKGROUND

The American Bar Association Standing Committee on Lawyers' Responsibility for Client Protection disseminated this survey to thirty-three (33) federal administrative agencies in late August, 1984. The survey was intended to provide background information on the experiences of agencies permitting nonlawyer practice (other than for purposes of self-representation). During September and October ninety-seven percent (97%) of the agencies responded either over the phone or by mail following initial contact with their Offices of General Counsel. The ABA Center for Professional Responsibility tabulated the results in October, 1984.

II. BRIEF ANALYSIS AND
CONCLUSIONS

We found that the overwhelming majority of agencies studied permit nonlawyer representation in both adversarial and nonadversarial proceedings. However, most of them seem to encounter lay practice very infrequently (in less than 5% of adjudications), while only a few encounter lay practice as often as lawyer practice. Thus, although universally permitted, lay practice before federal agencies rarely occurs.

Few of the responding agencies comprehensively monitor or control the lay practice that does occur. Only about twenty percent (20%) require nonlawyers to register with the agency before permitting them to practice. Registration procedures may range from simply listing nonlawyers' names to more formalized certifying or licensing procedures which may include testing and character reviews. Proceedings in most of these agencies tend to require highly technical or specialized knowledge. Registration insures that lay representation meets an appropriate level of quality and competence. In at least one agency, registration insures that nonlawyer representatives will charge only nominal fees or no fees at all.

No agencies indicated that they would discipline nonlawyers differently from lawyers, although they clearly have an additional ability to pursue sanctions against lawyers through external disciplinary mechanisms. Only a few agencies indicated any special need for nonlawyer discipline. Most reported they had not encountered any problems with misconduct by nonlawyers or any inability of nonlawyers to meet appropriate ethical standards (though fewer than a third of the agencies studied have actually defined any specific ethical standards). Of those that voiced complaints about nonlawyers' skills in representation, most indicated that the problem they encounter most frequently is nonlawyers' lack of familiarity with procedural rules and tactics. The majority of responses suggest that nonlawyers do not pose any special practice problems, nor do they receive any special disciplinary consideration. Overall, the concern for nonlawyers' competence and ethical conduct seems limited, perhaps because nonlawyer practice is not widespread.

III. METHODOLOGY

Throughout the survey our questions focused on lay representation (other than self-representation) occurring in adjudicatory proceedings. In question 1, in which we asked whether agencies permitted nonlawyer representation, we attempted to distinguish between adversarial and nonadversarial proceedings. Our distinction did not prove particularly informative because all agencies permitting nonlawer practice (97%) allow such practice in both arenas.

Question 2 sought the methods by which agencies control or limit those practicing before them. The responses vary considerably from agency to agency. Questions 3 and 4 requested statistics concerning the frequency of nonlawyer practice. Many of the agencies indicated that statistics were unavailable. These responses also vary considerably. The results of questions 1 through 4 are tabulated in Chart I.

CHART I
REGULATIONS GOVERNING NONLAWYER
REPRESENTATION, FREQUENCY, AND TYPE OF PRACTICE

Agency	Statute/ Regulation Permitting Appearance	Permits Nonlawyer Adversarial Representation	Permits Nonlawyer Nonadversarial Representation	Provisions Limiting or Governing Practice	Frequency of Nonlawyer Representation	Change in Frequency of Nonlawyer Rep. w/in Past 6 Years	Most Common Type(s) of Nonlawyer Representation
Bd. of Immigration Appeals: Immigration and Naturalization Serv.	8 CFR § 292.1-3	Yes	Yes	"Accredited representative"[1] working for "recognized organization"[2] may charge only nominal fees. "Reputable individual"[3] may not charge fees	No statistics available	No statistics available	One time only by family member/friend; charitable, religious or social service organization
Civil Aeronautics Bd.	14 CFR § 300.1-6 14 CFR § 302.11	Yes	Yes	None	Fewer than 6 appearances per yr., less than 1% of appearances[4]	None	Economic consultants for corporations

[1] May become accredited by the Department of Immigration Appeals (D.I.A.) by submitting an application through a recognized organization for review of character and fitness and experience with and knowledge of immigration law. No formal testing requirement or licensing fee.

[2] Typically a religious, charitable or social service organization becomes recognized by submitting an application for approval to the D.I.A. assuring that it will charge only nominal fees and assess no representation charges.

[3] Typically a family member or friend submits declaration that he or she charges no fee, has a preexisting relationship with immigrant-applicant, and appears only on individual basis at request of immigrant-applicant.

[4] Although nonlawyer practice not discouraged, complexity of agency proceedings tends to require specialized legal practice. Typical parties, large corporations or businesses, tend to hire lawyers.

CHART I
REGULATIONS GOVERNING NONLAWYER
REPRESENTATION, FREQUENCY, AND TYPE OF PRACTICE—Continued.

Agency	Statute/ Regulation Permitting Appearance	Permits Nonlawyer Adversarial Representation	Permits Nonlawyer Nonadversarial Representation	Provisions Limiting or Governing Practice	Frequency of Nonlawyer Representation	Change in Frequency of Nonlawyer Rep. w/in Past 6 Years	Most Common Type(s) of Nonlawyer Representation
Comptroller of the Currency	12 CFR § 19.3	Yes[5]	Yes	Nonlawyer may be required to file a power of attorney or show to the satisfaction of the Comptroller the possession of requisite qualifications	None	None	None
Consumer Product Safety Comm'n	16 CFR § 1025.61 et. seq.	Yes	Yes	Filing and approval of proof of qualifications. See 16 CFR § 1025.65	Very infrequent, 2–5% of appearances	None	Non-fee by industry rep., consultant, or private service agency
Dep't of Agric., Agricultural Marketing Serv.	7 CFR § 50.27	Yes	Yes	None	Fewer than 3 appearances per yr., less than 1% of appearances	Decreased,[6] no statistics available	Economist/ accountant providing assistance prior to appearance

[5] Permitted but lay representation rare because of complex proceedings and substantial rights or amounts of money involved.

[6] In agency's early history, economists provided a substantial amount of representation because of the economic nature of agency proceedings. As proceedings became more sophisticated, economists began aiding lawyers rather than assuming primary responsibility for legal representation. Representation by economists is now rare, and lawyers handle the bulk of representation.

CHART I
REGULATIONS GOVERNING NONLAWYER
REPRESENTATION, FREQUENCY, AND TYPE OF PRACTICE—Continued.

Agency	Statute/ Regulation Permitting Appearance	Permits Nonlawyer Adversarial Representation	Permits Nonlawyer Nonadversarial Representation	Provisions Limiting or Governing Practice	Frequency of Nonlawyer Representation	Change in Frequency of Nonlawyer Rep. w/in Past 6 Years	Most Common Type(s) of Nonlawyer Representation
Dep't of Commerce, Office of Secretary	Those of other agencies governing appearances before administrative bodies, e.g., MSPB, 5 CFR Part 1201	Yes	Yes	Reasonable atty's fees for litigated matters set by agency; maximum atty's fees for settlement set at $75./hr.; government pays fees to winning atty.	No statistics available	No statistics available	Non-fee by union reps.
Dep't of Commerce, Patent and Trademark Office	35 U.S.C. §§ 31-33	Yes	Yes	Only registered[7] practitioners permitted to practice	Less than 16% of appearances[8]	None	Repeated practice for a fee by registered agents

[7] Nonlawyers become registered by passing a character and fitness review and an examination. Nonlawyers having served four years in the examining corps of the Patent and Trademark Office (P.T.O.) may waive the exam. *See* 57 CFR § 1.341.

[8] Nonlawyers comprise about 16% of registered practitioners, but not all registered practitioners appear before P.T.O., so that nonlawyers probably appear in less than 16% of patent applications filed with P.T.O.

CHART I
REGULATIONS GOVERNING NONLAWYER
REPRESENTATION, FREQUENCY, AND TYPE OF PRACTICE—Continued.

Agency	Statute/ Regulation Permitting Appearance	Permits Nonlawyer Adversarial Representation	Permits Nonlawyer Nonadversarial Representation	Provisions Limiting or Governing Practice	Frequency of Nonlawyer Representation	Change in Frequency of Nonlawyer Rep. w/in Past 6 Years	Most Common Type(s) of Nonlawyer Representation
Dep't of Health and Human Services, Food and Drug Admin.	21 CFR §§ 12.40, 12.45	Yes	Yes	None	No appearances in recent years	None	None
Dep't of Justice, Drug Enforcement Admin.	21 CFR § 1316.50	Yes	N/A, all proceedings adversarial	None	2 to 3 appearances per yr., 5% of appearances[9]	None	One time only by officer/employee of small family-owned business
Dep't of Justice, Foreign Claims Settlement Comm'n	45 CFR § 500.1-6	No	No[10]	Lawyers' fees set by statute at 10% of claim award and deducted from award	N/A[11]	N/A[11]	Family member providing assistance prior to appearance

[9] Appearances are by the employees or officers of small family-owned businesses, analogous to pro se appearances.

[10] The agency only allows "representation" by bar members. Family members may sometimes assist in preparation of claims or at oral hearings, typically where elderly parent has language barrier problems.

[11] No nonlawyer representation allowed.

CHART I

REGULATIONS GOVERNING NONLAWYER
REPRESENTATION, FREQUENCY, AND TYPE OF PRACTICE—Continued.

Agency	Statute/ Regulation Permitting Appearance	Permits Nonlawyer Adversarial Representation	Permits Nonlawyer Nonadversarial Representation	Provisions Limiting or Governing Practice	Frequency of Nonlawyer Representation	Change in Frequency of Nonlawyer Rep. w/in Past 6 Years	Most Common Type(s) of Nonlawyer Representation
Dep't of Labor, Benefits Review Bd.	20 CFR § 802.201(b) 20 CFR § 802.202	Yes	N/A, all proceedings adversarial	Employer pays fee for successful claimant represented by lawyer; claimant pays fee when represented by nonlawyer; lawyer may acquire lien against award; nonlawyers may not.[12] Professional status is criterion for determining fee.[13]	2–4% of appearances	None	Repeated practice for fee
Dep't of Labor, Employees Compensation Appeals Bd.	20 CFR § 501.11	Yes	N/A, all proceedings adversarial	All fees approved by board	Appear as frequently as lawyers	None	One time only by family member/friend; repeated practice for a fee

[12] These policies may tend to discourage lay representation.

[13] Typically approved rates for nonlawyers are less than half of those attorneys receive.

CHART I
REGULATIONS GOVERNING NONLAWYER
REPRESENTATION, FREQUENCY, AND TYPE OF PRACTICE—Continued.

Agency	Statute/ Regulation Permitting Appearance	Permits Nonlawyer Adversarial Representation	Permits Nonlawyer Nonadversarial Representation	Provisions Limiting or Governing Practice	Frequency of Nonlawyer Representation	Change in Frequency of Nonlawyer Rep. w/in Past 6 Years	Most Common Type(s) of Nonlawyer Representation
Dep't of Labor, National Railroad Adjustment Bd.	45 U.S.C. § 3153	Yes	N/A	Only entities identified in 45 U.S.C. § 151 allowed to practice	Almost 100% of appearances	None	Industry employees
Dep't of Labor, Wage and Appeals Bd.	20 CFR § 725.362(a) 20 CFR § 725.365 20 CFR § 725.366(b)	Yes	N/A	Fees must be reasonably commensurate with services performed[14]; attorney's fee deducted from award; employer pays fee for successful claimant represented by lawyer; claimant prep fee when represented by nonlawyer; lawyer may require lien against award, nonlawyers may not.[15]	3% of appearances; as in 180 case/yr.	Decrease due to investigations by Office of Inspector General into unauthorized receipt of fees	One time only by family member or friend; repeated practice for fee; assistance prior to appearance

[14] *See* 20 CFR § 725.366(b) (black lung) and 20 CFR § 702.132 (longshore).

[15] These policies may tend to discourage lay representation.

CHART I
REGULATIONS GOVERNING NONLAWYER
REPRESENTATION, FREQUENCY, AND TYPE OF PRACTICE—Continued.

Agency	Statute/ Regulation Permitting Appearance	Permits Nonlawyer Adversarial Representation	Permits Nonlawyer Nonadversarial Representation	Provisions Limiting or Governing Practice	Frequency of Nonlawyer Representation	Change in Frequency of Nonlawyer Rep. w/in Past 6 Years	Most Common Type(s) of Nonlawyer Representation
Dep't of Transportation, Maritime Admin.	46 CFR § 201.21	Yes	Yes	Only registered nonlawyers permitted to practice	Very infrequent	None	
Federal Deposit Ins. Corp.	12 CFR § 308.04	Yes	Yes	Only qualified nonlawyers permitted to represent	10 to 20 appearances per yr., 5% of appearances	50% decrease	One time only by family member/friend; nonlawyer assistance prior to appearance
Federal Energy Regulatory Comm'n	18 CFR § 385.2101	Yes	Yes	None	1 or 2 per yr.	None	Engineering firm assisting in technical nonadversarial proceeding
Federal Maritime Comm'n	46 CFR § 502.30	Yes	Yes	Only registered nonlawyers permitted to appear[16]	.5 to 1% of appearances	None	One time only by family member/friend; non-fee by industry rep., consultant or private service agency

[16] Certificates of registration are issued on payment of $13.00 processing fee and completion of application form indicating sufficient educational qualifications and recommendations. There is no testing or formal licensing.

CHART I

REGULATIONS GOVERNING NONLAWYER

REPRESENTATION, FREQUENCY, AND TYPE OF PRACTICE—Continued.

Agency	Statute/Regulation Permitting Appearance	Permits Nonlawyer Adversarial Representation	Permits Nonlawyer Nonadversarial Representation	Provisions Limiting or Governing Practice	Frequency of Nonlawyer Representation	Change in Frequency of Nonlawyer Rep. w/in Past 6 Years	Most Common Type(s) of Nonlawyer Representation
Federal Mine Safety & Health Review Comm'n	29 CFR § 2700.3(b)	Yes, at trial hearings before A.L.J.'s; at appellate reviews before commissioners (A.L.J. = Administrative Law Judge.)	N/A	Nonlawyer may practice only if party, "representative of miners,"[17] or owner, partner, full time officer or employee of party-business entity; otherwise permitted to appear for limited purpose in special proceedings.	5–10% of appearances	None	Non-fee by industry rep., consultant or private service agency
General Accounting Office	31 U.S.C. § 731-732; 4 CFR §§ 11 and 28; GAO Orders 2713.2, 2752.1, and 2777.1	Yes, in adverse actions, grievance proceedings, and discrimination complaints	Yes	Nonlawyers not permitted fees; government pays fees to winning representatives.[18]	Very infrequent	Not aware of any	

[17] *See generally* 30 CFR § 40.1(b).

[18] As provided in discrimination statutes, backpay act, and appeals authorized by law.

CHART I

REGULATIONS GOVERNING NONLAWYER
REPRESENTATION, FREQUENCY, AND TYPE OF PRACTICE—Continued.

Agency	Statute/ Regulation Permitting Appearance	Permits Nonlawyer Adversarial Representation	Permits Nonlawyer Nonadversarial Representation	Provisions Limiting or Governing Practice	Frequency of Nonlawyer Representation	Change in Frequency of Nonlawyer Rep. w/in Past 6 Years	Most Common Type(s) of Nonlawyer Representation
Internal Revenue Serv.	13 CFR Part 10; 31 U.S.C. § 330; Treasury Dept. Circular 230	Yes	Yes	Non-certified public accountant and nonlawyer must become enrolled agent[19] to practice	As frequent as lawyer representation[20]	Increased, no statistics available	Repeated practice for fee by certified public accountant or enrolled agent
Interstate Commerce Comm'n	49 CFR § 1103	Yes	Yes	Fee limitations[21]; only registered nonlawyer permitted to practice,[22] however, self-representation is allowed without registration	1,600 nonlawyers now registered and account for 5% of appearances.[23]	Decreased,[24] no statistics available	Repeated practice for a fee

[19] Nonlawyers and noncertified public accountants become enrolled agents by 1) passing a character and fitness review, and 2) successful completion of special enrollment examination testing on federal taxation and related matters, or 3) former employment with the IRS, provided duties qualify the individual. Lawyers and certified public accountants may practice without enrollment.

[20] Includes representation by certified public accountants as well as enrolled agents.

[21] Practitioners may not overestimate the value of services, accept compensation from party other than client, make contingent fee arrangements or divide fees with laypersons. *See* 49 CFR § 1103.70.

[22] To become registered applicant must 1) meet educational and experience requirements, 2) undergo character and fitness review, 3) pass exam administered by the agency testing knowledge in the field of transportation, and 4) take an oath. *See* 49 CFR § 1103.3.

[23] Figure includes appearances in rulemaking as well as adjudicatory proceedings.

[24] Deregulation has reduced the caseload while proceedings have become more complex, creating a greater need for legal expertise.

CHART I

REGULATIONS GOVERNING NONLAWYER
REPRESENTATION, FREQUENCY, AND TYPE OF PRACTICE—Continued.

Agency	Statute/ Regulation Permitting Appearance	Permits Nonlawyer Adversarial Representation	Permits Nonlawyer Nonadversarial Representation	Provisions Limiting or Governing Practice	Frequency of Nonlawyer Representation	Change in Frequency of Nonlawyer Rep. w/in Past 6 Years	Most Common Type(s) of Nonlawyer Representation
National Credit Union Admin.	12 CFR § 747	Yes	Yes	None	No statistics available	Decreased, no statistics available	Credit union representatives
National Labor Relations Bd.		Yes	Yes	None	Infrequent	None	
National Mediation Bd.	None, agency governed by 29 CFR § 1200 et seq.	N/A, all proceedings adversarial	Yes	None	200 appearances per yr., appear twice as frequently as lawyers	Decreased, no statistics available	Union representatives
National Transportation Safety Bd.	49 CFR § 821 49 CFR § 831 49 CFR § 845	Yes	Yes	In adjudication lawyer representation encouraged; in investigation lawyer participation discouraged because technical expertise required; parties[25] participate in investigations	Very infrequent except at investigatory levels	None	Manufacturers at investigatory levels

[25] "Parties" includes manufacturers, unions, operators and other regulatory agencies.

CHART I

REGULATIONS GOVERNING NONLAWYER
REPRESENTATION, FREQUENCY, AND TYPE OF PRACTICE—Continued.

Agency	Statute/ Regulation Permitting Appearance	Permits Nonlawyer Adversarial Representation	Permits Nonlawyer Nonadversarial Representation	Provisions Limiting or Governing Practice	Frequency of Nonlawyer Representation	Change in Frequency of Nonlawyer Rep. w/in Past 6 Years	Most Common Type(s) of Nonlawyer Representation
Occupational Safety and Health Review Comm'n	29 CFR § 2200.22	Yes	N/A, all proceedings adversarial	Optional simplified procedures to encourage self-representation by small businesses	20% of appearances[26]	20% decrease[27]	Nonlegal employee representing employer; union representative
Small Business Admin.	13 CFR § 121.11 13 CFR § 134.16	Yes	N/A, all proceedings adversarial	None	Less than 1% of appearances[28]	None	

[26] Statistic includes pro se representation.

[27] Nonlawyer practice accounted in 1980 for 40% of the agency's caseload but decreased in 1982–83 to 20%. Decrease may result from increasing complexity in cases causing claimants to seek legal representation.

[28] Figure excludes pro se appearances in size and Standard Industrial Classification (SIC) Appeals. Approximately 50% of size and SIC appeals are conducted pro se by nonlawyers.

CHART I
REGULATIONS GOVERNING NONLAWYER
REPRESENTATION, FREQUENCY, AND TYPE OF PRACTICE—Continued.

Agency	Statute/ Regulation Permitting Appearance	Permits Nonlawyer Adversarial Representation	Permits Nonlawyer Nonadversarial Representation	Provisions Limiting or Governing Practice	Frequency of Nonlawyer Representation	Change in Frequency of Nonlawyer Rep. w/in Past 6 Years	Most Common Type(s) of Nonlawyer Representation
Social Security Admin.	42 USC § 406(a) 29 CFR	Yes, tentatively as part of experiment; generally agency has no adversarial proceedings	Yes	Claimants advised of advantages of representation at hearing level[29]; fees set by agency[30]; attorneys' fees withheld from awards[31]	Appear in 13% of total hearings or in 25–30% of hearings with representation	None, although lawyer representation increased by 56% since 1978[32]	One time only by family member/friend; repeated practice for fee; non-fee rep. by legal services paralegal

[29] When hearing request filed, agency sends a letter to unrepresented claimant describing advantages of representation. Attached to letter is a list of organizations which may provide representation. The list includes lawyer referral services, legal aid groups, law schools, etc.

[30] The agency sets all fees based on criteria listed in 20 CFR § 404.1725(b), including extent and type of services, complexity of case, level of skill and competence required in performing services, time spent, results achieved, level at which representative became involved, and amount requested.

[31] When decision is entered in favor of a claimant represented by a lawyer in a Title II or Black Lung case, normally 25% of the benefits awarded are withheld. After agency has set the fee it forwards fee directly to the lawyer from the amount withheld. If attorney's fees exceed the amount withheld, the lawyer must seek the remainder from the claimant. If the attorney's fees are less than the amount withheld, the claimant receives the remainder. Nonlawyer representatives do not have this withholding benefit.

[32] In fiscal year 1978 lawyers appeared in 32% of hearings; nonlawyers in 12%. In fiscal year 1983 lawyers appeared in 50% of hearings; nonlawyers in 13%. Though the letter discussed in footnote 29 does not exclusively reference lawyers' services, this list may attribute to the increase in lawyer representation. Lawyers also have a high success rate before the agency as well as the advantage of award withholdings to secure fees in Title II and Black Lung cases (see footnote 31).

CHART I

REGULATIONS GOVERNING NONLAWYER
REPRESENTATION, FREQUENCY, AND TYPE OF PRACTICE—Continued.

Agency	Statute/ Regulation Permitting Appearance	Permits Nonlawyer Adversarial Representation	Permits Nonlawyer Nonadversarial Representation	Provisions Limiting or Governing Practice	Frequency of Nonlawyer Representation	Change in Frequency of Nonlawyer Rep. w/in Past 6 Years	Most Common Type(s) of Nonlawyer Representation
U.S. Customs Serv.	None	Yes	Yes	None	5 to 15% of caseload volume	None	Repeated practice for fee by licensed customs brokers and former customs officials
U.S. Environmental Protection Agency	40 CFR § 124 40 CFR § 164.30 40 CFR § 22.10	Yes	N/A	None	No appearances	None	None

Appendix F

Federal Job Information Centers

The Office of Personnel Management (OPM) operates Federal Job Information Centers (FJIC's) in the cities listed below. FJIC's can provide general information on Federal employment, explain how to apply for specific jobs, and supply application materials.

You can get information by mail, by telephone, or by visiting an FJIC. The easiest method, if you want information or application materials for a specific job or occupation and can identify it clearly, usually is to write. All FJIC's operate Monday through Friday (except holidays), but the number of hours each one is open to the public varies from one FJIC to another. Many do not handle walk-in traffic or telephone inquiries for more than four or six hours a day. Because of the large number of people who seek information by telephone, the lines are frequently busy or callers must hold for a time before an information specialist can speak with them. To alleviate this problem, some FJIC's provide recorded telephone messages. These messages give the hours of service for the FJIC, and sometimes provide general job information as well.

OPM provides Federal employment information to State Job Service (State Employment Security) offices and, for college-entry jobs, to college placement offices. In addition, many Federal agencies recruit directly for their own vacancies and provide a variety of information services.

Federal Job Information Centers that also provide information about jobs with city, county, or State governments are identified below with a (•).

Federal Job Information Centers

ALABAMA

Huntsville:
Southerland Building
806 Governors Dr, N.W. 35801
(205) 453-5070

ALASKA

Anchorage:
Federal Bldg. & U.S. Courthouse
701 C St., P.O. Box 22, 99513
(907) 271-5821

ARIZONA

Phoenix:
522 N. Central Ave. 85004
(602) 261-4736

ARKANSAS

Little Rock:
Federal Bldg. Rm. 1319
700 W. Capitol Ave. 72201
(501) 378-5842

CALIFORNIA

Los Angeles:
Linder Bldg.
845 S. Figueroa 90017
(213) 688-3360

Sacramento:
Federal Bldg., 650 Capitol Mall
 95814
(916) 440-3441

San Diego:
880 Front St. 92188
(714) 293-6165

San Francisco:
Federal Bldg., Rm. 1001
450 Golden Ave. 94102
(415) 556-6667

COLORADO

•Denver:
1845 Sherman St., 80203
(303) 837-3506

CONNECTICUT

Hartford:
Federal Bldg., Rm. 717, 450 Main
 St. 06103
(203) 244-3096

DELAWARE

•Wilmington:
Federal Bldg., 844 King St. 19801
(302) 571-6288

DISTRICT OF COLUMBIA

Metro Area:
1900 E Street, N.W., 20415
(202) 737-9616

FLORIDA

•Miami:
330 Biscayne Blvd., Suite 410,
 33131
(305) 350-4725

•Orlando:
80 N. Hughey Ave. 32801
(305) 420-6148

GEORGIA

Atlanta:
Richard B. Russell Federal Bldg.,
75 Spring St. SW, 30303
(404) 221-4315

GUAM

Agana:
238 O'Hara St.
Room 308 96910
344-5242

HAWAII

Honolulu (and Island of Oahu):
Federal Bldg. Room 1310
300 Ala Moana Blvd. 96850
(808) 546-7108

ILLINOIS

Chicago:
Dirksen Bldg. Rm. 1322
219 S. Dearborn St. 60604
(312) 353-5136

INDIANA

Indianapolis:
46 East Ohio Street, Room 123,
 46204
(317) 269-7161 or 7162

IOWA

Des Moines:
210 Walnut St., Rm. 191, 50309
(515) 284-4546

KANSAS

Wichita:
One-Twenty Bldg., Rm. 101,
120 S. Market St. 67202
(316) 267-6311, ext. 106

In Johnson and Wyandott Counties
dial 374-5702

KENTUCKY

Louisville:
Federal Building
600 Federal Pl. 40202
(502) 582-5130

LOUISIANA

New Orleans:
F. Edward Hebert Bldg.,
610 South St., Rm 103 70130
(504) 589-2764

MAINE

Augusta:
Federal Bldg. Rm. 611
Sewall St. & Western Ave. 04330
(207) 622-6171 ext. 269

MARYLAND

Baltimore:
Garmatz Federal Building
101 W. Lombard St. 21201
(301) 962-3822

DC Metro Area:
1900 E St. N.W., 20415
(202) 737-9616

MASSACHUSETTS

Boston:
3 Center Plaza, 02108
(617) 223-2571

MICHIGAN

Detroit:
477 Michigan Ave, Rm. 595,
48226
(313) 226-6950

MINNESOTA

Twin Cities:
Federal Bldg.
Ft. Snelling, Twin Cities, 55111
(612) 725-3355

MISSISSIPPI

Jackson:
100 W. Capitol St. (Suite 335)
39201
(601) 490-4588

MISSOURI

Kansas City:
Federal Bldg., Rm. 129
601 E. 12th St. 64106
(816) 374-5702

St. Louis:
Federal Bldg., Rm. 1712,
1520 Market St., 63103
(314) 425-4285

MONTANA

Helena:
Federal Bldg. & Courthouse
301 S. Park, Rm. 153 59601
(406) 449-5388

NEBRASKA

Omaha:
U.S. Courthouse and Post Office
Bldg.
Rm. 1014, 215 N. 17th St. 68102
(402) 221-3815

NEVADA

•Reno:
Mill & S. Virginia Streets
P.O. Box 3296 89505
(702) 784-5535

NEW HAMPSHIRE

Portsmouth:
Federal Bldg. Rm. 104,
Daniel & Penhallow Streets, 03801
(603) 436-7720 ext. 762

NEW JERSEY

Newark:
Federal Bldg., 970 Broad St.
  07102
(201) 645-3673

In Camden, dial (215) 597-7440

NEW MEXICO

Albuquerque:
Federal Bldg. 421 Gold Ave. SW,
  87102
(505) 766-2557

NEW YORK

Bronx:
590 Grand Concourse, 10451
(212) 292-4666

Buffalo:
111 W. Huron St., Rm. 35, 14202
(716) 846-4001

Jamaica:
90-04 161st St., Rm. 200, 11432
(212) 526-6192

New York City:
Federal Bldg., 26 Federal Plaza,
  10278
(212) 264-0422

Syracuse:
100 S. Clinton St. 13260
(315) 423-5660

NORTH CAROLINA

Raleigh:
Federal Bldg. 310 New Bern Ave.
P.O. Box 25069, 27611
(919) 755-4361

NORTH DAKOTA

Fargo:
Federal Bldg., Rm. 202
657 Second Ave. N. 58102
(701) 237-5771 ext. 363

OHIO

Cleveland:
Federal Bldg., 1240 E. 9th St.,
  44199
(216) 522-4232

Dayton:
Federal Building Lobby
200 W. 2nd St., 45402
(513) 225-2720 and 2854

OKLAHOMA

Oklahoma City:
200 NW Fifth St, 73102
(405) 231-4948

OREGON

Portland:
Federal Bldg., Lobby (North)
1220 SW Third St. 97204
(503) 221-3141

PENNSYLVANIA

•Harrisburg:
Federal Bldg., Rm. 168, 17108
(717) 782-4494

Philadelphia:
Wm. J. Green, Jr. Fed. Bldg.,
600 Arch Street, 19106
(215) 597-7440

Pittsburgh:
Fed. Bldg. 1000 Liberty Ave.,
  15222
(412) 644-2755

PUERTO RICO

San Juan:
Federico Degetau Federal Bldg.
Carlos E. Chardon St.,
Hato Rey, P.R. 00918
(809) 753-4209, ext. 209

RHODE ISLAND

Providence:
Federal & P.O. Bldg., Rm. 310
Kennedy Plaza 02903
(401) 528-4447

SOUTH CAROLINA

Charleston:
Federal Bldg., 334 Meeting St.,
 29403
(803) 724-4328

SOUTH DAKOTA

Rapid City:
Rm. 201, Federal Building
U.S. Court House, 515 9th St.
 57701
(605) 348-2221

TENNESSEE

Memphis:
Federal Bldg., 167 N. Main St.
 38103
(901) 521-3956

TEXAS

Dallas:
Rm. 1C42, 1100 Commerce St.,
 75242
(214) 767-8035

El Paso:
Property Trust Bldg.—Suite N302
2211 E. Missouri Ave. 79903
(915) 543-7425

Houston:
701 San Jacinto St., 77002
(713) 226-5501

San Antonio:
643 E. Durango Blvd., 78205
(512) 229-6600

UTAH

•Salt Lake City:
1234 South Main St., 2nd Floor,
 84101
(801) 524-5744

VERMONT

Burlington:
Federal Bldg., Rm. 614
P.O. Box 489
Elmwood Ave. & Pearl St., 05402
(802) 862-6712

VIRGINIA

Norfolk:
Federal Bldg., Rm. 220,
200 Granby Mall, 23510
(804) 441-3355

D.C. Metro Area:
1900 E Street, N.W. 20415
(202) 737 9616

WASHINGTON

•Seattle:
Federal Bldg., 915 Second Ave.
 98174
(206) 442-4365

WEST VIRGINIA

•Charleston:
Federal Bldg., 500 Quarrier St.
 25301
(304) 343-6181, ext. 226

WISCONSIN

Milwaukee:
Plankinton Bldg., Rm. 205,
161 W. Wisconsin Ave. 53203
(414) 244-3761

WYOMING

Cheyenne:
2120 Capitol Ave., Rm. 304
P.O. Box 967 82001
(307) 778-2220, ext. 2108

Appendix G

Bar Association and Court Opinions on Paralegals

Chicago Bar Association
Real Property Law Committee Recommendations
4/5/83

THE USE OF PARALEGALS IN REAL ESTATE TRANSACTIONS

The paralegal may perform such tasks in connection with a real estate transaction as are assigned by the employing attorney, provided that the tasks are performed under the direction and supervision of, and are reviewed by, the attorney and do not involve the giving of legal advice. The paralegal may attend a closing with the employing attorney. A paralegal may close a real estate transaction, unaccompanied by the employing attorney, only (i) if all documents have been prepared and approved by all parties in advance of the closing, (ii) with prior consent of other counsel, and (iii) with the employing attorney being available for consultation and instructions by telephone. Within the foregoing limitations, the use of a paralegal to close a real estate transaction, unaccompanied by the employing attorney, should be approached with caution, having regard to the skill and experience of the paralegal, the complexity of the transaction and the client-attorney relationship, and bearing in mind that the employing attorney retains ultimate responsibility for the transaction.

Florida Bar Association
Committee on Professional Ethics
Advisory Opinion No. 73-43

. . . .
   2. Whether the employee may attend closings of sales of condominium units to be held in the firm's office but without any attorneys in the firm being present. She will give no legal advice.

. . . .

We answer the second question in the negative. The question itself recognizes that the employee may not give legal advice or perform any acts that would amount to practicing law. The committee, one member dissenting in part, is of the opinion that there is no reason for the employee to attend the closings except to give legal advice and that her presence could be construed as answering unasked questions about the propriety or legality of documents. One committeeman is of the opinion that the employee may properly attend such closings provided she does nothing more than distribute documents for signature.

Below you will find two opinions of the New Jersey Bar Association and one of the New York State Bar Association. Note the differences in the approaches taken by the two bar associations. New Jersey is quite restrictive. New York was also once restrictive, but became considerably less so when the U.S. Supreme Court decided *Bates v. State of Arizona*, 433 U.S. 350 (1977). The *Bates* opinion sent shock waves throughout the legal profession. It struck down laws that prohibited all forms of lawyer advertising. One effect of *Bates* was to cause some bar associations, such as New York, to allow paralegals to have their names printed on law firm stationery. Before *Bates*, this practice was frowned upon as a practice that was contrary to professional dignity and etiquette. It also suggested commercialization and a form of publicity for the firm. Once advertising was permitted after *Bates*, however, the practice was no longer considered unacceptable. Some states, however, such as New Jersey, still adhere to the more conservative position.

New Jersey Bar Association
Supreme Court of New Jersey's Advisory Committee on Professional Ethics,
Opinion 296
(98 N.J.L.J. 105, Feb. 6, 1975)

PARALEGAL EMPLOYEES—IDENTIFICATION WITH LAW FIRMS

Three inquiries have been submitted to this Committee relating to investigators and paralegal employees of a law firm.

Question One
Is it ethically proper for an attorney or firm to permit an investigator-paralegal full-time employee to sign correspondence on the attorney's or firm's letterhead where he identifies himself as a nonlawyer?

A paralegal employee is a lay person employed by an attorney to perform certain law office functions for which legal training and bar admission are not required.

Disciplinary Rule 3–101(A) reads as follows:

"A lawyer shall not aid a non-lawyer in the unauthorized practice of law."

Attorneys should avoid not only unprofessional conduct but also the appearance of such conduct. Our *Opinion* 8, 86 N.J.L.J. 718 (1963) and 9, 86 N.J.L.J. 617 (1963).

If a staff investigator were permitted to sign correspondence on the firm letterhead, such a seemingly innocent practice could foster myriad abuses, not the least of which might be the unauthorized practice of law in violation of *DR*

3–101(A). Such signed correspondence, even accompanied by an identification of the investigatory position of the signatory, might be taken as a representation that the layman is involved in the firm's practice in a manner contrary to *DR* 3–101(A) and *DR* 3-103(A). Given such a possible consequence, it is our conclusion that such practice cannot be sanctioned.

Question Two

May a firm include on its letterhead the name of a full-time investigative employee along with his title as staff investigator?

The American Bar Association, Standing Committee on Professional Ethics, *Informal Opinion* 619 (1962), quoting *Drinker, Legal Ethics* (1953) 228, refused to allow a secretary's name to appear on a lawyer's letterhead stating:

> "A lawyer's letterhead may not carry the name of a client or of a patent agent associate, non-lawyer, notary or engineer or clerk or student or other layman, or give the names of references, or state that a layman's association is associated with him in handling collections. . . ."

Similarly, ABA *Informal Opinion* 845 (1965) held that the inclusion of a name on a letterhead with the designation "office manager" would be improper. Likewise, ABA *Informal Opinion* 1000 (1967), citing both *Informal Opinions* 619 and 845, supra held:

> ". . . that it would be improper to list your salaried investigator on your firm letterhead as 'Staff Investigator' or in any other manner."

Disciplinary Rule 2–102(A)(4) stipulates that an attorney or firm can use no letterhead except one of a prescribed content and dignified form. Additionally *DR* 2–101 inveighs generally against self-laudation, an inescapable effect should we allow the inclusion of a staff investigator's name and title on the letterhead. In ABA *Informal Opinion* 845, supra, it was stated that use of such a letterhead would:

> ". . . impress upon those seeing the letterhead the size, importance and efficiency of the firm. . . ."

Clearly, such a letterhead would have a self-laudatory effect, contravening the spirit of *DR* 2–101 in addition to offending the letter of *DR* 2–102(A)(4), and therefore it cannot be permitted.

Question Three

We are also called upon to consider whether the use by such an investigator-paralegal employee of a business card in the following form would be ethically proper:

> John Doe
> Investigator
> Firm Name & Address Tel. No. 123–4567

We considered this question in our *Opinion* 9, supra, and answered it in the negative. Parenthetically, it might be added, that we maintain this position in full cognizance of the American Bar Association Committee on Professional Ethics, *Informal Opinion* 909 (1966) which saw fit to sanction such cards, though the committee admitted:

". . . It is true, of course, that the card is a physical article and that possibilities of its improper use or effect are far greater than in the case of an oral identification . . . ."

As was stated in *Opinion* 9, supra, of this Committee:

"There are, of course, other ways of identification besides the suggested means, without any possible abuse or misrepresentation."

Therefore, such cards may not be used as they are in possible derogation of the general integrity of the legal profession.

Supreme Court of New Jersey's Advisory Committee on Professional Ethics, Opinion 296 (Supplement) (99 N.J.L.J. 113, Feb. 12, 1976)

PARALEGAL EMPLOYEES—IDENTIFICATION WITH LAW FIRMS

The Professional Economics Committee of the New Jersey State Bar Association and several law firms of this State have petitioned that we reconsider *Opinion* 296, 98 N.J.L.J. 105 (1975), relating to the use of paralegals in law offices.

The original opinion dealt with three inquiries. The petition for reconsideration was limited to Question One.

In response to Questions Two and Three, we had held that the names of nonlawyers may not be included on a firm letterhead and the use of the firm business card identifying a nonlawyer was improper.

For convenience we repeat Question One in full:

"Is it ethically proper for an attorney or firm to permit an investigator-paralegal full-time employee to sign correspondence on the attorney's or firm's letterhead where he identifies himself as a non-lawyer?"

The inquiry as posed called for the approval of the unrestricted right of a paralegal employee to sign correspondence on the attorney's or firm's letterhead.

A hearing was held before this Committee on the petition for review to decide the propriety of our determination and whether it should be modified. The use of paraprofessionals was described as being in a state of development, a development which the petitioners urged as being in the best interests of the public and practicing lawyers.

The American Bar Association has recently concluded extensive hearings concerning the use of paraprofessionals and the subject is still under discussion.

There are two kinds of legal paraprofessionals:

1. Those who assist lawyers on behalf of clients, performing a variety of tasks, such as investigation, drafting, tax return preparation and research, which are performed under the supervision of a lawyer who is completely responsible for that work to a client. See American Bar Association, Committee on Professional Ethics, *Opinion* 316 (1967) and Code of Professional Responsibility *EC* 3–6. These paralegals cannot counsel clients, interpret the law, or represent people in adversary proceedings.

2. Individuals involved in the management of law firms who are not involved in the rendition of legal services, but who assist the partners in the conduct of their practice.

As noted, the original inquiry was unrestricted and made no differentiation between the kinds of paraprofessionals. As to the latter, the ministerial or office-type matters not involving the practice of law, we see no objection to the paralegal's signing such correspondence, since it does not in any way involve the practice of law. As to the former, we believe that routine requests for documents from officials, court stenographers, and the like would not constitute the practice of law and should be permitted.

However, we believe that any interaction with other attorneys, law firms, parties, or agents of parties would tend to aid in the practice of law by laymen. Parenthetically, in the course of the hearings, one of the firms described its use of paraprofessionals in "adjusting" property claims. Whether that would constitute the unauthorized practice of law is a point which we need not decide here, but it is an apt illustration of the difficulty in permitting the unrestricted use of paraprofessional assistance.

It is not the function of this Committee to undertake to designate every particular act or function of lay employees which would constitute the unauthorized practice of law. Whenever any question might reasonably arise, it seems to us that the profession's duty to the public and the recognition of the need to preserve the dignity of the profession suggest that correspondence ought to be signed by the responsible lawyer in the firm. Since the ultimate responsibility must reside with the attorney in the firm, the burden of signing the correspondence ought not to be intolerable.

. . .

In summary, we conclude that *Opinion* 296 should be modified by amending the answer to Question One, to permit the paraprofessional to sign the letter if his identity is clearly stated and under the guidelines noted in this opinion.

We reiterate that a paralegal should never perform services which involve the exercise of the professional judgment of a lawyer, nor should he advise clients with respect to their legal rights, nor should the activities of a paralegal in any way modify or interfere with direct attorney-client relationships or those between an attorney and his opposing attorney.

Our modification of *Opinion* 296 does not extend to Questions Two and Three which are not being amended by this opinion. Accordingly, we would modify our original opinion as follows:

> 1. A lay assistant may sign letterhead stationery of a law firm involving administrative communications not involving the practice of law to ministerial officials, vendors, and others.
> 2. A lay assistant may sign letterhead stationery of the law firm addressed to other administrative personnel, such as court printers, stenographers, court clerks, record custodians, and the like.

New York State Bar Association

New York State Bar Association, Committee on
Professional Ethics, Opinion #500 (12/6/78) (52–78)

Question

May the letterhead of a law firm list certain non-lawyer employees such as registered patent agents and paralegals?

Opinion

Prior to the recent amendment of our Code of Professional Responsibility, DR 2–102(A)(4) rigidly circumscribed the information that could be disclosed on a lawyer's professional letterhead. The former Disciplinary Rule did far more than prohibit the inclusion of untruthful or misleading information. It was intended to set a standard of professional dignity which standard was, in turn, thought to encourage public confidence in both the profession and the administration of justice. See, *e.g.,* former EC 2–9 and EC 2–10.

Under this standard, as well as those of former Canon 27, the listing of all non-lawyer employees on a lawyer's letterhead was prohibited. See, *e.g.,* N.Y. State 261 (1972) (paralegals), N.Y. County 589 (1971) (patent agents), N.Y. City 545 (1940) (non-lawyer patent attorney), N.Y. City 829 (1937) (patent agents), ABA Inf. 1367 (1976) (paralegals), ABA Inf. 845 (1965) (office manager), ABA Inf. 619 (1962) (lawyer's secretary); *cf.,* N.Y. State 85 (1968) and ABA Inf. 571(b) (1962) (involving potentially misleading information concerning lawyers).

The Supreme Court's decision in *Bates* v. *State of Arizona,* 433 U.S. 350 (1977), led to the adoption in this State of major amendments to the Ethical Considerations and Disciplinary Rules under Canon 2. These amendments not only incorporated the court adopted uniform rules governing lawyer advertising and publicity, but included a number of other court authorized liberalizing amendments permitting the free flow of reliable and useful information about lawyers and their services. See, N.Y. State 487 (1978).

The basic impact of these amendments was to bring about a revolutionary shift of emphasis in favor of the dissemination of information "designed to educate the public to an awareness of legal needs and to provide information relevant to the selection of the most appropriate counsel." DR 2–101(D), as amended. Disciplinary Rules which had seemed to interfere with the dissemination of such information primarily for reasons of professional dignity and etiquette were either repealed or substantially modified. In place of the former broad prohibitions on publicity and commercial advertising, the amendments essentially narrowed the ambit of proscription to specified practices which in themselves were thought to be injurious to both the profession and the public. See, amended DR 2–101(A) and (B); see also, amended EC 2–10.

The only explicit references to professional letterheads contained in the amended Code are now set forth in DR 2–102(A)(4) and (D)* Except for the requirements of DR 2–102(D) relating to lawyers not admitted to practice in all jurisdictions listed on a firm's letterhead, the only limitation on information appearing on letterheads is that the information be "in accordance with DR 2–101." The most important of the standards established by amended DR 2–101 are set forth in subdivisions (A), (B) and (D) which now provide:

* As amended, DR 2–102 now provides in relevant part:

A. A lawyer or law firm may use professional cards, professional announcement cards, office signs, letterheads or similar professional notices or devices, provided the same do not violate any statute or court rule, and are in accordance with DR 2–101, including the following:

* * *

4. A letterhead identifying the lawyer by name and as a lawyer, and giving the addresses, telephone numbers, the name of the law firm, associates and any information permitted under DR 2–105. A letterhead of a law firm may also give the names of members and associates, and names and dates relating to deceased and retired members. A lawyer may be designated 'Of Counsel' on a letterhead if there is a continuing relationship with a lawyer or law firm, other than as a partner or associ-

A. A lawyer on behalf of himself or herself or partners or associates, shall not use or disseminate or participate in the preparation or dissemination of any public communication containing statements or claims that are false, deceptive, misleading or cast reflection on the legal profession as a whole.

B. Advertising or other publicity by lawyers, including participation in public functions, shall not contain puffery, self-laudation, claims regarding the quality of the lawyers' legal services, or claims that cannot be measured or verified.

* * *

D. Advertising and publicity shall be designed to educate the public to an awareness of legal needs and to provide information relevant to the selection of the most appropriate counsel. Information other than that specifically authorized in subdivision (C) that is consistent with these purposes may be disseminated providing that it does not violate any other provisions of this rule."

The effect of these amendments is to permit lawyers to include on their letterheads the names of their non-lawyer employees whenever the inclusion of such names would not be deceptive and might reasonably be expected to supply information relevant to the selection of counsel.

While non-lawyer status will no longer preclude the use of a person's name on a firm's letterhead, his name should be accompanied by language that makes clear his non-lawyer status. *Cf.,* DR 2–102(D) (requiring a clear statement concerning the "jurisdictional limitations" of a firm's "members and associates" who appear on its letterhead). Thus, for example, the term "registered patent agent" should be qualified by a designation such as "nonlawyer." Even then, to avoid deception, such persons should only be listed when their non-lawyer status is relevant to the work of the firm. See, DR 2–101(A) and DR 2–102(A).

(Unlike the term "registered patent agent," the term "paralegal," albeit somewhat imprecise, is sufficient without further qualification to make clear the employee's non-lawyer status. Whether use of the term "paralegal" is appropriate to the actual status enjoyed by the employee is another question to be determined under the standards established by DR 2–101(A).)

Our prior opinion in N.Y. State 261, *supra,* is overruled to the extent that the same is inconsistent with the foregoing.

For the reasons stated, and subject to the qualifications hereinabove set forth, the question posed is answered in the affirmative.

ate. A lawyer or law firm may be designated as 'General Counsel' or by similar professional reference on stationery of a client if the lawyer or the firm devotes a substantial amount of professional time in the representation of that client. The letterhead of a law firm may give the names and dates of predecessor firms in a continuing line of succession.

Amended DR 2–102(D) provides:

D. A partnership shall not be formed or continued between or among lawyers licensed in different jurisdictions unless all enumerations of the members and associates of the firm on its letterhead and in other permissible listings makes clear the jurisdictional limitations on those members and associates of the firm not licensed to practice in all jurisdictions; however, the same firm name may be used in each jurisdiction.

United States v. Kovel

United States Court of Appeals, Second Circuit, 1961
296 F.2d 918.

FRIENDLY, Circuit Judge.

This appeal from a sentence for criminal contempt for refusing to answer a question asked in the course of an inquiry by a grand jury raises an important issue as to the application of the attorney-client privilege to a non-lawyer employed by a law firm.

Kovel is a former Internal Revenue agent having accounting skills. Since 1943 he has been employed by Kamerman & Kamerman, a law firm specializing in tax law. A grand jury in the Southern District of New York was investigating alleged Federal income tax violations by Hopps, a client of the law firm; Kovel was subpoenaed to appear on September 6, 1961. The law firm advised the Assistant United States Attorney that since Kovel was an employee under the direct supervision of the partners, Kovel could not disclose any communications by the client or the result of any work done for the client, unless the latter consented; the Assistant answered that the attorney-client privilege did not apply to one who was not an attorney.

On September 7, the grand jury appeared before Judge Cashin. The Assistant United States Attorney informed the judge that Kovel had refused to answer "several questions * * * on the grounds of attorney-client privilege"; he proffered "respectable authority * * * that an accountant, even if he is retained or employed by a firm of attorneys, cannot take the privilege." The judge answered "You don't have to give me any authority on that." A court reporter testified that Kovel, after an initial claim of privilege had admitted receiving a statement of Hopps' assets and liabilities, but that, when asked "what was the purpose of your receiving that," had declined to answer on the ground of privilege "Because the communication was received with a purpose, as stated by the client"; later questions and answers indicated the communication was a letter addressed to Kovel. After verifying that Kovel was not a lawyer, the judge directed him to answer, saying "You have no privilege as such." The reporter then read another question Kovel had refused to answer, "Did you ever discuss with Mr. Hopps or give Mr. Hopps any information with regard to treatment for capital gains purposes of the Atlantic Beverage Corporation sale by him?" The judge again directed Kovel to answer reaffirming "There is no privilege—you are entitled to no privilege, as I understand the law."

Later on September 7, they and Kovel's employer, Jerome Kamerman, now acting as his counsel, appeared again before Judge Cashin. The Assistant told the judge that Kovel had "refused to answer some of the questions which you had directed him to answer." A reporter reread so much of the transcript heretofore summarized as contained the first two refusals. The judge offered Kovel another opportunity to answer, reiterating the view, "There is no privilege to this man at all." Counsel referred to New York Civil Practice Act, § 353, which we quote in the margin.*

Counsel reiterated that an employee "who sits with the client of the law firm * * * occupies the same status * * * as a clerk or stenographer or any other lawyer * * *"; the judge was equally clear that the privilege was never "extended beyond the attorney." The court held [Kovel] in contempt, sentenced him to a year's im-

---

* "An attorney or counselor at law shall not disclose, or be allowed to disclose, a communication, made by his client to him, or his advice given thereon, in the course of his professional employment, nor shall any clerk, stenographer or other person employed by such attorney or counselor * * * disclose, or be allowed to disclose any such communication or advice."

prisonment, ordered immediate commitment and denied bail. Later in the day, the grand jury having indicted, Kovel was released until September 12, at which time, without opposition from the Government, I granted bail pending determination of this appeal.

Here the parties continue to take generally the same positions as below—Kovel, that his status as an employee of a law firm automatically made all communications to him from clients privileged; the Government, that under no circumstances could there be privilege with respect to communications to an accountant. The New York County Lawyers' Association as *amicus curiae* has filed a brief generally supporting appellant's position.

Decision under what circumstances, if any, the attorney-client privilege may include a communication to a nonlawyer by the lawyer's client is the resultant of two conflicting forces. One is the general teaching that "The investigation of truth and the enforcement of testimonial duty demand the restriction, not the expansion, of these privileges," 8 Wigmore, Evidence (McNaughton Rev. 1961), § 2192, p. 73. The other is the more particular lesson "That as, by reason of the complexity and difficulty of our law, litigation can only be properly conducted by professional men, it is absolutely necessary that a man * * * should have recourse to the assistance of professional lawyers, and * * * it is equally necessary * * * that he should be able to place unrestricted and unbounded confidence in the professional agent, and that the communications he so makes to him should be kept secret * * *," Jessel, M.R. in Anderson v. Bank, 2 Ch.D. 644, 649 (1876). Nothing in the policy of the privilege suggests that attorneys, simply by placing accountants, scientists or investigators on their payrolls and maintaining them in their offices, should be able to invest all communications by clients to such persons with a privilege the law has not seen fit to extend when the latter are operating under their own steam. On the other hand, in contrast to the Tudor times when the privilege was first recognized, the complexities of modern existence prevent attorneys from effectively handling clients' affairs without the help of others; few lawyers could now practice without the assistance of secretaries, file clerks, telephone operators, messengers, clerks not yet admitted to the bar, and aides of other sorts. "The assistance of these agents being indispensable to his work and the communications of the client being often necessarily committed to them by the attorney or by the client himself, the privilege must include all the persons who act as the attorney's agents." 8 Wigmore, Evidence, § 2301; Annot., 53 A.L.R. 369 (1928).

Indeed, the Government does not here dispute that the privilege covers communications to non-lawyer employees with "a menial or ministerial responsibility that involves relating communications *to an attorney.*" We cannot regard the privilege as confined to "menial or ministerial" employees. Thus, we can see no significant difference between a case where the attorney sends a client speaking a foreign language to an interpreter to make a literal translation of the client's story; a second where the attorney, himself having some little knowledge of the foreign tongue, has a more knowledgeable non-lawyer employee in the room to help out; a third where someone to perform that same function has been brought along by the client; and a fourth where the attorney, ignorant of the foreign language, sends the client to a non-lawyer proficient in it, with instructions to interview the client on the attorney's behalf and then render his own summary of the situation, perhaps drawing on his own knowledge in the process, so that the attorney can give the client proper legal advice. All four cases meet every element of Wigmore's famous formulation, § 2292, "(1) Where legal advice of any kind is sought (2) from a professional legal advisor in his capacity as such, (3) the communications relating to that purpose, (4) made in confidence (5) by the client, (6) are at his instance permanently protected (7) from disclosure by himself or by the legal advisor, (8) except the protection be waived," . . . § 2301 of Wigmore would clearly recognize the privilege in the first case and the Government goes along to that extent; § 2301 would also recognize the privilege in the second case and § 2301 in the third unless the circumstances negated confidentiality. We find no valid policy reason for a different result in the fourth case, and we do not read Wigmore as thinking there is. Laymen consulting lawyers should not be expected to anticipate niceties perceptible only to judges—and not even to all of them.

This analogy of the client speaking a foreign language is by no means irrelevant to the appeal at hand. Accounting concepts are a foreign language to some lawyers in almost all cases, and to almost all lawyers in some cases. Hence the presence of an accountant, whether hired by the lawyer or by the client, while the client is relating a complicated tax story to the lawyer, ought not destroy the privilege, any more than would that of the linguist in the second or third variations of the foreign language theme discussed above; the presence of the accountant is necessary, or at least highly useful, for the effective consultation between the client and the lawyer which the privilege is designed to permit. By the same token, if the lawyer has directed the client, either in the specific case or generally, to tell his story in the first instance to an accountant engaged by the lawyer, who is then to interpret it so that the lawyer may better give legal advice, communications by the client reasonably related to that purpose ought fall within the privilege; there can be no more virtue in requiring the lawyer to sit by while the client pursues these possibly tedious preliminary conversations with the accountant than in insisting on the lawyer's physical presence while the client dictates a statement to the lawyer's secretary or is interviewed by a clerk not yet admitted to practice. What is vital to the privilege is that the communication be made *in confidence* for the purpose of obtaining *legal* advice *from the lawyer*. If what is sought is not legal advice but only accounting service, or if the advice sought is the accountant's rather than the lawyer's, no privilege exists. We recognize this draws what may seem to some a rather arbitrary line between a case where the client communicates first to his own accountant (no privilege as to such communications, even though he later consults his lawyers on the same matter, Gariepy v. United States, 189 F.2d 459, 463 (6 Cir. 1951)),‡ and others, where the client in the first instance consults a lawyer who retains an accountant as a listening post, or consults the lawyer with his own accountant present. But that is the inevitable consequence of having to reconcile the absence of a privilege for accountants and the effective operation of the privilege of client and lawyer under conditions where the lawyer needs outside help. We realize also that the line we have drawn will not be so easy to apply as the simpler positions urged on us by the parties—the district judges will scarcely be able to leave the decision of such cases to computers; but the distinction has to be made if the privilege is neither to be unduly expanded nor to become a trap.

The judgment is vacated and the cause remanded for further proceedings consistent with this opinion.

---

‡ We do not deal in this opinion with the question under what circumstances, if any, such communications could be deemed privileged on the basis that they were being made to the accountant as the client's agent for the purpose of subsequent communication by the accountant to the lawyer; communications by the client's agent to the attorney are privileged, 8 Wigmore, Evidence, § 2317-1.

UNITED STATES v. CABRA

United States Court of Appeals, Fifth Circuit, 1980.
622 F.2d 182.

AINSWORTH, Circuit Judge:

This appeal raises the novel question whether a district judge can impound notes taken during a criminal trial by a paralegal employed by defense counsel to assist in preparation of the defense. We hold that in this case, the district judge acted improperly in impounding the notes.

Appellants Edwin L. Cabra and Claude "Buddy" Leach were tried in district court on charges of vote buying in connection with the November 7, 1978 general election. After three weeks of trial, appellants were acquitted on all counts. Other charges against Leach alleging illegal receipt of campaign contributions are still pending.

During the trial, the district judge, on his own motion, called a bench conference to ask defense counsel if anyone associated with the defense was taking notes on the proceedings. Defense counsel informed the court that Ms. Mary Jane Marcantel, a paralegal employed by the defense, was taking shorthand notes of portions of the testimony. Counsel stated that the purpose of the note-taking was to assist in the preparation of cross-examination, to provide summaries of testimony, and to aid in the preparation of the defense in anticipated criminal prosecutions in related cases. Ms. Marcantel was not present during the entirety of the trial and thus her notes did not reflect a complete account of the proceedings. The shorthand notes were not verbatim, but merely reflected, as accurately as possible, the substance of the testimony.

After ascertaining the character of the notes, the district judge, over defense counsel's objection, ordered that Ms. Marcantel could continue to take notes but that at the completion of the trial the notes were to be submitted to the court and sealed. After trial, the district judge sent a letter requesting compliance with the order. Appellants moved to vacate the order and filed a memorandum of law supporting their position. The district judge denied the motion, but stayed the order pending this appeal.

The district judge based the order on the court's duty "to insure the orderly process of a case." He stated that since the notes could be considered as an unofficial transcript the validity of the official transcript was at stake. "The court feels that there should only be one official transcript and that such unofficial transcripts should not be allowed. The court by this does not mean that these particular defendants would make any improper use of these notes. Rather this order is required to protect the integrity of the official court reporter's transcript." (R. 1140)

A district judge has the power to issue appropriate orders regulating conduct in the courtroom in order to assure an orderly trial. *See, e.g., United States v. Columbia Broadcasting System, Inc.,* 497 F.2d 102, 104 (5th Cir. 1974); *Seymour v. United States,* 373 F.2d 629 (5th Cir. 1967). *See also United States v. Dinitz,* 538 F.2d 1214, 1223–24 (5th Cir. 1976), *cert. denied,* 429 U.S. 1104, 97 S.Ct. 1133, 51 L.Ed.2d 556 (1977). Often the basis of the power is the need to insure that a defendant obtains a fair trial free from unnecessary disruption. *See United States v. Schiavo,* 504 F.2d 1, 6 (3rd Cir.) *(en banc)* ("The Sixth Amendment imposes a duty on the district courts . . . to take reasonable measures to ensure defendants fair trials, free of prejudice and disruption"), *cert. denied sub. nom. Ditter v. Philadelphia Newspa-*

pers, Inc., 419 U.S. 1096, 95 S.Ct. 690, 42 L.Ed.2d 688 (1974). *See generally Sheppard v. Maxwell,* 384 U.S. 333, 349–51, 86 S.Ct. 1507, 1515–16, 16 L.Ed.2d 600 (1966).

This case is similar to the facts presented in *Columbia Broadcasting System.* There, the district court issued an order prohibiting any sketching of the proceedings. Sketches were made by artists employed by the media for subsequent showing on television news programs. This court, while acknowledging the district court's power to control its proceedings, rejected the order as overly broad. "We are unwilling . . . to condone a sweeping prohibition of in-court sketching when there has been no showing whatsoever that sketching is in any way obtrusive or disruptive." *Columbia Broadcasting System, supra,* 497 F.2d at 107 (footnote omitted). As in *Columbia Broadcasting System,* we cannot understand how Ms. Marcantel's note-taking resulted in any disruption of the courtroom proceedings. There is no evidence that her work had any disturbing or disruptive effect. It appeared that her actions did not differ from the note-taking activities of the press covering the trial or of opposing counsel. Certainly, the note-taking did not interfere with or infringe appellants' rights to a fair trial as the task was performed on their behalf.

The district court placed great weight on the fact that Ms. Marcantel's notes were verbatim. There is no evidence, however, that this was true. Defense counsel stated that the notes were incomplete and that while Ms. Marcantel strived for accuracy, the notes were not always taken in question and answer form. Even assuming that the notes were verbatim, however, we do not believe that the district judge's action was proper. Note-taking at trial is an acknowledged function of paralegals, *see* W.P. Statsky, *Introduction to Paralegalism,* 356 (West 1974). [First edition] A court should not penalize a party on account of the proficiency of its paralegal's performance. The district court's concern for the sanctity of the official transcript is misplaced. While it is the court's responsibility to assure that the official transcript is prepared in accordance with the Court Reporter's Act, 28 U.S.C § 753, *see United States v. Garner,* 581 F.2d 481, 488 (5th Cir. 1978), the Act explicitly states that "[n]o transcripts of the proceedings of the court shall be considered as official except those made from the records taken by the reporter." Moreover, defense counsel stated that they had no intention of relying on the notes as an official summary of the testimony. Thus, the district court was operating under the mistaken assumption that the paralegal's notes challenged the validity of the official transcript.

Since the district court's reasons for impounding the notes were based on unwarranted concerns, the order was an improper exercise of the court's discretionary authority to control courtroom proceedings. Accordingly, the order is reversed.

REVERSED.

Example of Law Firm
Stationery that Prints
Paralegal Names

LAW OFFICES
Melvin M. Belli, Sr.
CABLE "BELEA"

SAN FRANCISCO, CA 94111

(415) 981-1849
THE BELLI BUILDING
722 MONTGOMERY STREET

MELVIN M. BELLI, SR.
MELVIN CAESAR BELLI, JR.
LOU ASHE (1909-1980)
DAVID S. SABIH
RICHARD E. BROWN
PAUL M. MONZIONE
  (ALSO MASSACHUSETTS BAR)
ROBERT A. KIERNAN
  (ALSO IDAHO BAR)
HAROLD BELAN
RENEE B. WASSERMAN
DENNIS R. LODS
DEBORAH BOBEL
STEVEN A. FABBRO
CAROL SHAW

PARALEGALS:
DAMIEN ORSEA
VALERIE J. LAMBERTSON
SHARON M. COHN
RANDY SCARLETT
MICHAEL J. COCORAN

OF COUNSEL
JOHN E. HILL
ALLEN P. WILKINSON
DANIEL A. STENSON
JETTIE P. SELVIG
HERBERT RESNER
FERNANDO CHAVEZ
ARTHUR A. GROZA
MARK SHAW
CHARLES A. DeCUIR, JR.
BETSY W. LEBBOS

CHIEF INVESTIGATOR
STAN HALLMARK

BEVERLY HILLS (LOS ANGELES) CA 90212

(213) 277-3612
THE BELLI BUILDING
9952 SANTA MONICA BOULEVARD

MELVIN M. BELLI, SR.
DAVID S. SABIH
DANIEL W. DUNBAR
HOWARD HIRSCH
ARNOLD W. GROSS
FELIX CAYO
HASKELL SHAPIRO
JOSEPH M. SINDELL
  (OHIO BAR)

OF COUNSEL:
SAM YORTY

PACIFIC GROVE, CA 93950

(408) 649-1849
THE BELLI BUILDING
405 FOREST AVENUE

MELVIN M. BELLI, SR.
DAVID S. SABIH
DONALD H. HUBBARD

SANTA CRUZ, CA 95060

(408) 458-0440
709 MISSION STREET

MELVIN M. BELLI, SR.
DAVID S. SABIH
ROY E. HARPER
RAITH W. BOROFF

STOCKTON, CA 95202

(209) 466-0982
THE BELLI BUILDING
218 NORTH SAN JOAQUIN

MELVIN M. BELLI, SR.
LAURENCE E. DRIVON
STEWART M. TABAK
STEWART M. TABAK
DALE S. BALCAO
DEAN F. COOPER
S. SCOTT VAUGHAN

OF COUNSEL:
LAURENCE DRIVON

SAN DIEGO, CA 92101

(619) 231-4980
317 A611 STREET

MELVIN M. BELLI, SR.
JOHN LEARNARD
JOHN VANARELLI
ANDY ZMURKIEWILE

SACRAMENTO, CA 95814

(916) 448-8800
926 SECOND STREET

MELVIN M. BELLI, SR.
RODNEY J. SHEPHERD
DOUGLAS E. JAFFE

Appendix I

How to Start a Free-lance Paralegal Business

by
Linda Harrington
(see also p. 61)

The best way to get into business is to do it, not talk forever about it. In fact, you may be doing it before you know that you are actually running a business.

The conservative approach to getting into free-lance business it to take work on the side, while you maintain a salaried position. When your side business interferes with your job, then you must decide whether or not the business is enticing enough to promote. If it is not, give up the business, keep the salaried job, and be thankful to have learned a lesson about running a business in an undramatic way.

If the business is satisfying and if you enjoy it, the time has come to devote more time and energy to it. Therefore, you will be resigning your salaried job to tackle a business.

Perhaps you have impressed your current employer enough so that he, she, or it will be your client after you resign.

Preliminary Considerations in Getting Started

What is your area of expertise and is it likely to generate some cash for you if you go free-lance? One of the areas to avoid is claimants' personal injury work where it's contingent, that is, the attorney will get a fee contingent upon success in court. It's been my experience that attorneys will pay you when they get paid on a case. So, if you're working for an attorney who will pay you when that attorney gets paid and that attorney loses the case, then it's likely you won't get paid. I work in probate. Everyone knows that death and taxes are inevitable. That being the case, I find it a very lucrative and interesting area.

An additional aspect of being a free-lance paralegal that's extremely important is whether or not you have a network. A network can be one of two kinds. First, a network of prior employers who respect your skills a lot and will use you when you go free-lance. Second, the network of your peers that's developed through paralegal associations and contacts. Both are equally important; one does not substitute for the other. I found that my activities in the local association have been extremely rewarding to me because they have given me leadership opportunities and the ability to learn current law from the people who work in large law firms and to meet friends who have the same kind of responsibilities I do. For the most part, my job leads have come from people I have previously worked for who are currently my clients.

The other part of the network to explore is the school system. The local paralegal programs can assist you a great deal in establishing a free-lance business. For one thing you can teach there and that provides some of the income that you need when you're first starting a business. The income does come slowly in a new business. Secondarily, if you're teaching, you're meeting people who will one day be your peers and that's expanding your professional network. Third, many paralegal programs have work-study experiences available for the students. The students are placed in offices where they get on-the-job training. I have lots of them come to my office. That keeps my overhead down. I give the student on-the-job training in all aspects of probate and death taxes, and in return, I have people to staff my office. It works to benefit the school, my office, and the students as well. So there are resources, lots of resources, that are available from the local schools.

A high level of expertise is something that I would like to stress. I have seen a lot of people come out of paralegal training programs and not get their dream job. They then decide that they're going to open free-lance business operations, knowing not too much about the practical reality of dealing with attorneys, not to mention the practical reality of working as a paralegal. I would think that you'd need about four or five years' experience in your field before attempting to go free-lance. The first reason, of course, is that you want to have strength in your practice area, and be able to handle some of the problems that you will later encounter as a free-lance paralegal. The second reason is that you have to know about attorneys.

You have to know about their personalities, you have to be able to manage the problems that they often present. My latest line that I tell all my students is that attorneys now have to pass "arrogance" before they are allowed to take the Bar exam, and you have to learn how to deal with this attitude in as cheerful a manner as you possibly can. Dealing with attorneys is just as important an area of expertise to develop as any other aspect of expertise in a practice field. If you're going to go free-lance, you have to handle a situation where hundreds of attorneys call you up, and each one considers him or herself the most important person in the world. You have to deal with that reality.

I think that the most important things I had to learn were to keep a sense of humor and to remember that you have to be compulsive. Some people say that I'm a workaholic; I prefer to state that I work hard. I work very, very hard. The things that most people think are available in free-lance work are independence and free time. The reality is that they don't always exist. If your office does not get the work done, the buck stops with you. You can't blame your staff. The final responsibility rests on your shoulders. If everybody else leaves and the computer breaks down, you must still perform. If you don't get it done, you face the possibility of jeopardizing your entire business operation.

Other Practical Suggestions:

Step 1.   Have business cards printed. The cards should state your name, specialty area, and telephone number.

Have an answering service. A business answering service provides a real, live voice to a caller, not a recording. It is reassuring to a potential customer to hear "a live one" on the line. Limit the service to the hours 9–5 to keep the cost of the service down.

Have "call waiting" installed by the phone company. This feature enables one line to handle several calls at once, by a mere flick of one of the buttons.

Have "call forward" installed by the phone company. This feature enables you to have incoming calls automatically forwarded to the telephone number of your choice. If you are waiting for an important call, but have a visit to make, you can have your call automatically forwarded to your destination.

Step 2.   Systematize your operation immediately. The systems you will need are:

A. Calendar system.
B. Timekeeping system.
C. Billing system.
D. Filing system for both open and closed matters.
E. Procedural manual for your specialty area.

A *calendar system* should include: master calendar, which is easily spotted among clutter; a pocket calendar, which you must carry at all times; and some sort of statute of limitations reminder system. Many companies offer calendar systems at relatively low cost. Some are: Safeguard Business Systems and Lawfax System.

A *timekeeping system* should include: a master time record repository (separate from the case file), time slips, and decision-making on your part concerning standard charges for services and costs. It is easiest to assign a set charge for a particular service, subject to increases for complications or quirks. For example, typical time charges will be incurred for telephone calls. Assign a minimum charge for each call. Each duty should have a minimum charge assigned to it. In this way, your billing will reflect all applicable charges for the particular service involved in the transaction, as well as your research, investigation, and other "write up" expenses. Costs, such as photocopies, should also reflect the time involved to perform the service. Therefore, standard mark-up for costs are advisable. Naturally, these are matters that are internal to the business. Therefore, establish your standards and then keep your mouth shut.

A *billing system* should include: a retainer, which is received when the case work comes in; a statement for services submitted at an advantageous time; and a personal manner; which makes it clear that a bill is an important document to the sender. Set up a system for billing that is realistic. If your clients are most likely to pay on the 30th of the month, send your bills on the 25th. If your clients will not pay the bill until the receipts from the case are received, bill at the end of the work. Billing is as much psychology as anything else. Figure out when the client will want to pay and bill at that time.

A filing system for open cases will include: a repository for case documents, an identification system for file "labels," a spot for the files to be stored, a case matter sheet that generally describes the client, the case, and the work to be done, as well as the billing arrangements between you and the client. Case work can be stored in file folders, in binders, in boxes, and a number of other places. Make sure that all cases are stored in the same fashion and that the case files are easily located.

Closed cases should be stored and retained. A closed file system should be a numerical system. For this type of system, you need: file folders, a rolodex to store the case name and closed file number (retained in alphabetical order by case), and a central register to show the numbers used for previously closed files, so that the number chosen for a closed file will not have been used previously.

A procedural manual will contain: standard correspondence sent for the particular areas of law you specialize in, standard (completed) court forms used in your field, instructions to others concerning processing the documents. A procedural manual can also contain information concerning special and standard requirements of area courts, if your work involves preparing and filing court papers. The latter will assist you to avoid procedural errors and will save time, if it is updated regularly.

Step 3. Fix your goals, make a budget and prepare to stick to them.

Fixing a goal involves knowing why you want to run a business. There are many reasons to want to be in business for yourself. Some are: ego gratification—now you are going to get recognition for how great you've always known you are; free time—now you can set your own hours and go to the the beach whenever you want; money—now you are going to get a piece of the action and can get rich. None of your original goals will be unchanged if you are still in business one year later. Most of the people you work for will never be impressed by your brilliance—you said you could do the work, you did do the work, so what's the big deal? If you are successful, the last thing you will have is free time. Even in the beginning, your clients will want to see you or talk to you when they want to do so, not when you want them to. Most attorneys feel that if you only knew that they wanted to talk to you, you would jump to attention at four in the morning and be grateful for the phone call. All the money you earn will be hard earned. When you finally do earn money, some of it will go to your staff, some to your landlord, some to the IRS, and some to you.

To keep your wits about you, you must budget and you must set limits. How much of what you want do you have to receive in order to stick with it? If you want ego gratification, how many clients have to tell you you are great to make the business worthwhile? If you want free time, how much free time do you have to have to make the business worthwhile? If you want money, how much profit must you make to make the business worthwhile? The "how much" is your minimum. Obviously, the sky is the limit.

If you do not get your minimum, are you willing to quit? If not, do not go into business.

You can generally figure out how you are doing by using the following calculation: Monthly gross × 12 = Year's gross. Do not count on new business to get you by. Count on the status quo as far as income is concerned to figure out how much money you will make by December 31 and budget accordingly. If you need income from the business to pay your personal bills, how much do you need monthly? Does this leave any money to run the business? Of the money that is left, how much will be required for telephone, answering service, supplies, and other fixed expenses? Now how much is left? Use the rest for expansion of your business (equipment purchases, rent, personnel, etc.).

Step 4.   Develop realistic employee relationships.

Once you have done everything you can do to avoid the need of hiring your first employee, and that is not enough to keep pace with your work or to allow you the time off you desire, then it is time to hire help.

Accept what you are—you are the owner of a very small business and cannot offer big-firm benefits, bonuses, or vacations to your prospective employee. Also, you are a person who wishes to protect your business position, so you do not want to hand your business over to a potential competitor. Lastly, you are a person who has certain expectations concerning job performance, productivity, and attendance. You have developed your own ideas about what constitutes a good job in your field.

Do not hire a friend. Being someone's boss does not improve a friendship when you also own the business.

Hire someone trainable. A trainable person is likely to be a recent graduate from a paralegal school. The fact that an applicant has sought education in the field and completed some or all of it is a strong indication that the person has an interest in the field and a desire for practical experience.

Do not hire someone just like you. You are the person who decided to start up the business, who worked (slaved?) to get it going, who knows everything, and who does not want to work so hard now. If you hire someone just like you, you will have two people not wanting to work so hard (you and your employee) or one who wants to start a business and has access to all your clients.

Establish a trial employment first. Whether by hiring a work-study student at minimum wage from a local paralegal program or by hiring an experienced person from some other source, set a review period or termination period for the relationship. Tell your employee what that period is and stick to it.

Be realistic about your employee. Because you are a small business, you cannot compete with larger firms that will offer your employee a better deal after the employee has experience and training. Therefore, accept the fact that the employee will probably move on. Tell the employee that you accept this fact and will assist the person to find a better position after the training has been completed (one to two years, usually). This will motivate the employee to learn as much as possible and to do a good job. This will also avoid you taking personally the job move, which any sensible employee will consider after becoming competent on the job.

Be sure you understand the tax and insurance requirements for your employee. You must have an employer I.D. number, you must withhold taxes and social security and state disability insurance, you must file quarterly reports with the taxing authorities and provide your employee with a W-2 at year end, you must have Worker's Compensation Insurance, and you must contribute as the employer into the unemployment fund and to Social Security. Add 15% to the employee's salary to determine what your employee will cost you for salary and salary-related expenses.

Have your employee work on your premises. This is mandatory during the training period, at bare minimum, so that you can become familiar with the employee's work habits and control work production.

Review the employee's time slips. The time slip review will educate you concerning how long a particular job takes the employee to perform, how many hours during the day the employee devotes to office matters, and how the cases are progressing.

Fire the hopeless. When you know that an employee is not going to work out, do not wait for the realization to come to the employee. It never will. Call the person in to your office, look the person in the eyes, and tell the person how wonderful he/she is and how many fantastic qualities he/she has and how unfortunate it is that the job is so miserable for such a terrific individual and that the job just isn't good enough for such a talented person, *or* call the person in and tell him/her that the employment is not working out and that you wish to ask for his/her resignation, to avoid the stigma to the employee of being fired, *or* call the person in and tell him/her that you can no longer tolerate his/her presence and that he/she is fired. In whatever way you can do it, be sure that it gets done as soon as you have given up hope for improvement. That's your money that your employee is taking home every two weeks. Nothing rankles so much as feeling that you are paying for a mistake again and again.

Reward the hearty. Go out to lunch for a chat and pay the bill. Send the employee home early or give him/her a surprise day off after a hard week. Leave town yourself and let him/her have the office to himself/herself. Give bonuses when a difficult case is completed. Give a raise of one-day off a week. Complement the employee for work well done.

Keep checking. Once the employment situation is favorably resolved and you have a good employee, check up every now and then to be sure that the good qualities are still as good looking presently as they once were.

Accept criticism. Your employee will probably be compelled to express criticism of the systems in your office or, perhaps, your own style. So what? This is how good ideas get born. Think about the recommendations and, if they are good ones, change your office systems. As to the personal failings that may be pointed out, that's why you went off on your own, isn't it, so that you could be yourself?

Conclusion

The worst way to get into business is to assume that there is no way you can fail (90% of all new businesses do fail, the Small Business Administration says), to buy the most expensive equipment, rent the most costly office space, get the most sophisticated telephone system, and generally count on the birds in the bushes before they land in your hand. Hope that you are able to start building your business slowly so that you will have time to learn about building and problem solving. Give it a good try. If it works out and if you like it, keep going. If it works out and you do not like it, or if it does not work out, then give it up and congratulate yourself on having given it a good try-out.

Appendix J

Promoting Paralegals

To order this bumper sticker ("Court a Paralegal"), send $1.00 and a self-addressed, stamped envelope to Southeastern Paralegal Institute, Suite 203, 112 21st Avenue South, Nashville, TN 37203.

State of Iowa

Executive Department

IN THE NAME AND BY THE AUTHORITY OF THE STATE OF IOWA

Proclamation

Whereas,   the legal assistant profession is an expanding element of the legal community, striving to assist in the delivery of quality and affordable legal services to all citizens; and

Whereas,   legal assistants are presently employed with private law firms, corporate legal departments, real estate, banks, insurance, government and public agencies and legal clinics throughout the state of Iowa; and

Whereas,   the Legal Assistants Association encourages and provides continuing legal education opportunities for their members by offering workshops, seminars and a monthly newsletter; and

Whereas,   there should be a day set aside for the recognition of the legal assistant and to acknowledge the services that they provide to the legal community and the people of the state of Iowa:

Now, Therefore, I,   Robert D. Ray, Governor of the State of Iowa, do hereby proclaim August 25, 1982, as

Legal Assistant Day

in Iowa and encourage all Iowans to join in this observance.

In Testimony Whereof, I have hereunto subscribed my name and caused the Great Seal of the State of Iowa to be affixed. Done at Des Moines this 25th day of August in the year of our Lord one thousand nine hundred eighty-two.

Attest

Deputy Secretary

Robert D. Ray
Governor

VICTOR ATIYEH
GOVERNOR

OFFICE OF THE GOVERNOR
STATE CAPITOL
SALEM 97310

April 24, 1984

STATEMENT BY GOVERNOR VIC ATIYEH

The laws of a society are a reflection of its goals and aspirations.
The legal profession plays a crucial role in shaping and understanding
the law as it is practiced today.

Legal Assistants are an increasingly important part of the legal profession. They provide invaluable assistance to attorneys, contributing to
the efficient operation of law firms, corporations, banks and government
agencies. Legal Assistants perform specialized duties under the supervision
of attorneys to provide increased communication and quality legal service
to the client at a considerable savings.

Specialized education and training prepares Legal Assistants to work
in areas such as criminal law, probate, civil litigation, business law and
family law. Other duties they perform include research and investigation,
preparing and filing tax returns, document drafting and analysis, and
participating at hearings and trials.

Legal Assistants are dedicated professionals, and formal recognition
of their contributions to the legal profession and community will allow them
to better serve the people of Oregon and continue to play a progressively
responsible role in the legal field.

Therefore, as Governor, I am pleased to proclaim May 3, 1984, as

"LEGAL ASSISTANTS DAY" in Oregon.

I urge our citizens to be aware of the Legal Assistant profession and
its contribution to quality legal services.

Victor Atiyeh
Governor

State of Connecticut

By His Excellency WILLIAM A. O'NEILL, Governor: an

Official Statement

The laws of a society are a reflection of its goals and aspirations. The legal profession plays a vital role in shaping and understanding the law as it is practiced today.

Legal Assistants are an important part of the legal profession. They provide invaluable assistance to attorneys, contributing to the efficient operation of law firms, corporations, banks, and government agencies. Legal Assistants perform specialized duties under the supervision of attorneys to provide increased communication and quality legal service to the client in a cost efficient manner.

Specialized education and training prepare Legal Assistants to work in diverse areas, including criminal law, probate, civil litigation, real estate, and business and family law. In addition, Legal Assistants perform research and investigation duties, prepare and file tax returns, search titles, draft documents and participate at hearings, trials and closings.

Legal Assistants are dedicated professionals, committed to upholding the highest standards of excellence and integrity within the profession. They fulfill an increasingly progressive and responsible role within the legal profession and work diligently to serve the people of our state.

Therefore, in recognition of the important contributions which Legal Assistants make to the legal community and to improving the quality of life for all our people, I am pleased to designate June 1, 1985 as Legal Assistants Day in Connecticut.

_____
Governor.

STATE OF NEW YORK
EXECUTIVE CHAMBER
MARIO M. CUOMO, GOVERNOR

Press Office
518-474-8418
212-587-2126   FOR RELEASE:

P R O C L A M A T I O N

        The National Federation of Paralegal Associations, a
professional organization of state and local paralegal
associations, was formed in 1974 to foster and promote the
paralegal profession.

        Since its inception NFPA has been committed to increasing
the quality and availability of legal services and strives to
promote the development and implementation of programs that
address the legal needs of the public through the development
of the paralegal profession and the expansion of the paralegal
role in the delivery of legal services.

        It is fitting that all New Yorker's join in saluting the
NFPA in recognition of its ten years of dedicated service to
the paralegal profession and the legal needs of the public.

        NOW, THEREFORE, I, Mario M. Cuomo, Governor of the State
of New York, do hereby proclaim Friday, June 8, 1984, as

                        PARALEGAL DAY

in New York State.

                            G I V E N under my hand and the

                            Privy Seal of the State at the

                            Capitol in the City of Albany

(L.S.)   this seventh day of June in the

                            year one thousand nine hundred

                            and eighty-four.

BY THE GOVERNOR: (Signed) Mario M. Cuomo

      (Signed) Michael J. Del Giudice

      Secretary to the Governor

                            #

Appendix K

Murphy's Laws
for Paralegals

by
Celeste Ciaccia

9 Newsletter 12 (Dallas Association of Legal Assistants,
Sept., 1985). Originally published in Perspectives
of the Paralegal Association of Rochester.

1. The day you wear comfortable, ugly old shoes is the day you are called into the managing partner's office or have to meet with an important client.

2. The day you wear attractive, stylish pumps that pinch your toes, bite your instep and chafe your heels is the day that you have to serve papers at Nick Tahou's and the Eastern School of Music—before 11 a.m. or after 2 p.m.

3. The night when you have a date, theatre tickets, or fifteen dinner guests due at 7:30, is the night you have to stay late.

4. The day your car is in the garage and you carpooled is the day that you receive a 15-hour project that has to be done before you go home.

5. Your mother, your husband, your boyfriend or your bookie always calls when the boss is standing in your office.

6. Clients that work near you never have to sign anything. The number of documents that need to be signed by a client increases in proportion to the number of miles between their home or office and your office.

7. Whatever you lost is what everyone must have immediately.

8. Whatever can't be found was last in the possession of a paralegal.

9. Whatever needs to be hand delivered or picked up is always beyond the messenger's responsibility.

10. The day you have liverwurst and onion for lunch is the day that you have to attend an unscheduled meeting with an important client or another attorney.

11. The volume of Carmody-Wait 2nd that you require to prepare a motion is always missing from the library.

12. Nobody ever asks you about subjects with which you are familiar. If you are an expert on the mating habits of mosquitoes, you will be asked to digest a deposition or prepare research about the malfunction of the farabus and ullie pin connection in Yugoslavian lawnmowers.

Index

Interviewing witnesses, 442
Introduce into evidence, 349
Inventory control, 768
Investigation, 18, 98, 386, 420, 427ff.,
481, 486, 794, 810
Iowa, 52, 529, 542, 580, 810, 846, 857,
882, 908
IRC, 579
IRS, 226
Issue, 348, 371, 372, 645, 688, 791
Issue on appeal, 356, 645, 688
Italicize, 576

Jailhouse Lawyer, 25, 194, 213, 220,
255
Japan, 25
Job hunting notebook, 141
Job interview, 135, 154
Job satisfaction, 159
Jobs. See paralegal employment
Johnson v. Avery, 220
Joint and several liability, 342
Jones-Chipman Index to Legal
Periodical Literature, 628
Journal, House and Senate, 668
Judge field in WESTLAW, 722
Judgment, 354, 477
Judgment collection, 444, 481
Judgment debtor, 481, 503
Judgment, declaratory, 354
Judgment notwithstanding the verdict,
355, 476
Judgment nov, 355
Judgment on the merits, 355
Judicare, 47
Judicial system, 563
Junior Colleges, 27
JURIS, 639
Jurisdiction, 344, 469
Jurisdiction, appellate, 355
Jurisdiction, in rem, 470
Jurisdiction, personal, 469
Jurisdiction, quasi in rem, 470
Jurisdiction, statement of. See statement
of jurisdiction
Jurisdiction, subject matter, 469
Jury, grand, 359, 469
Jury instructions, 353
Jury panel, 349
Jury trial, 344
Justice, Department of, 44, 870
Justice of the Peace, 102, 201, 213
Juvenile delinquency, 68, 213

K, 709
Kansas, 52, 529, 531, 542, 580, 810,
846, 857, 882
Kardex, 545, 600, 610
Kentucky, 5, 38, 53, 214, 255, 530, 542,
581, 810, 847, 857, 883
Key facts, 643
Key topic and number system, 535, 601,
603, 643, 721
Key word search, 718
KF numbers, 599
Kits, divorce, 207

L, 650
Labor, Department of, 44, 871
Labor law, 93, 810
Labor Relations Reporter, 548
Landlord-tenant law, 93
Language, computer, 710, 733
Laser printer, 713
Law clerk, 810
Law Directory, 122, 548, 598, 632
Law Firms, kinds of, 33, 742
Law journal. See legal periodicals
Law, kinds of, 516
Law libraries. See Libraries
Law office administration, 18, 28, 96,
139, 737, 738, 810
Law reviews. See legal periodicals
Law revision commission, 656, 667
Laws, 519
Law school, 483, 514, 547, 632, 810
Law studies, 307, 483
Lawsuit, 335
Law teachers directory, 632
Lawyer ethics, 243
Lawyers. See attorney entries
Lawyer's Co-operative Publishing Co.,
511, 522, 557, 600, 605, 630, 639
Leading questions, 422, 435, 474
L.Ed. See United States Supreme Court
Reports, Lawyer's Edition
Legal administrator, 738
Legal advice, 257, 421
Legal analysis, 174, 177, 371ff., 390, 690
Legal assistant, 4. See also paralegal
entries
Legal Assistant Managers Association,
29, 853
Legal authority, 566, 642, 676
Legal Clerk and Technician Series, 43
Legal dictionary, 545, 567, 597

Send for Information

Please send me information about the Federation.

My Name and Address:

Clip this form and mail to:

Nat'l Federation of
    Paralegal Associations
P.O. Box 14103
Ben Franklin Station
Wash. D.C. 20044

_____

_____

_____

Please send me information about NALA.

My Name and Address:

Clip this form and mail to:

Nat'l Association of
    Legal Assistants
1420 S. Utica
Tulsa, OK 74104

_____

_____

_____

Please send me information about paralegals.

My Name and Address:

Clip this form and mail to:

American Bar Association
Standing Committee on
    Legal Assistants
750 N. Lake Shore Drive
Chicago, Ill. 60611

_____

_____

_____

Please send me information about PLA.

My Name and Address:

Clip this form and mail to:

Professional Legal
    Assistants, Inc.
P.O. Box 31951
Raleigh, NC 27622

_____

_____

_____